THE OXFORD HANDBOOK OF

ISLAM AND POLITICS

THE OXFORD HANDBOOK OF

ISLAM AND POLITICS

Edited by
JOHN L. ESPOSITO
and
EMAD EL-DIN SHAHIN

OXFORD
UNIVERSITY PRESS

OXFORD
UNIVERSITY PRESS

Oxford University Press is a department of the University of Oxford.
It furthers the University's objective of excellence in research, scholarship,
and education by publishing worldwide.

Oxford   New York
Auckland   Cape Town   Dar es Salaam   Hong Kong   Karachi
Kuala Lumpur   Madrid   Melbourne   Mexico City   Nairobi
New Delhi   Shanghai   Taipei   Toronto

With offices in
Argentina   Austria   Brazil   Chile   Czech Republic   France   Greece
Guatemala   Hungary   Italy   Japan   Poland   Portugal   Singapore
South Korea   Switzerland   Thailand   Turkey   Ukraine   Vietnam

Oxford is a registered trademark of Oxford University Press
in the UK and certain other countries.

Published in the United States of America by
Oxford University Press
198 Madison Avenue, New York, NY 10016

© Oxford University Press 2013

First issued as an Oxford University Press paperback, 2016

All rights reserved. No part of this publication may be reproduced, stored in a
retrieval system, or transmitted, in any form or by any means, without the prior
permission in writing of Oxford University Press, or as expressly permitted by law,
by license, or under terms agreed with the appropriate reproduction rights organization.
Inquiries concerning reproduction outside the scope of the above should be sent to the
Rights Department, Oxford University Press, at the address above.

You must not circulate this work in any other form
and you must impose this same condition on any acquirer.

Library of Congress Cataloging-in-Publication Data
The Oxford handbook of Islam and politics / edited by John L. Esposito and Emad El-Din Shahin.
pages cm.
Includes index.
ISBN 978-0-19-539589-1 (hardcover); 978-0-19-063193-2 (paperback)
1. Islam and politics. I. Esposito, John L. II. Shahin, Emad Eldin, 1957–
BP173.7.O945 2013
320.55'7–dc23
2013021154

Contents

Acknowledgments ix
Contributors xi

Introduction 1
JOHN L. ESPOSITO AND EMAD EL-DIN SHAHIN

PART ONE: MAJOR THEMES

1. The Shariʻah 7
   KHALED ABOU EL FADL

2. Salafiya, Modernism, and Revival 27
   ABDULLAH SAEED

3. Islamic Reform between Islamic Law and the Nation-State 42
   SHERMAN A. JACKSON

4. Political Islam and the State 56
   JOHN O. VOLL

5. Islam and Democracy 68
   NADER HASHEMI

6. The Political Economy of Islam and Politics 89
   TAREK MASOUD

7. Political Islam and Gender 112
   MARGOT BADRAN

PART TWO: ISLAMIC IDEOLOGUES, ACTIVISTS, AND INTELLECTUALS

FOUNDERS OR TRAILBLAZERS OF POLITICAL ISLAM

8. Hassan al-Banna — 129
   AHMAD MOUSSALLI

9. Mawlana Mawdudi — 144
   JOSHUA T. WHITE AND NILOUFER SIDDIQUI

REVOLUTIONARY IDEOLOGUES

10. Sayyid Qutb — 159
    SHAHROUGH AKHAVI

11. `Ali Shari`ati — 169
    SHAHROUGH AKHAVI

12. Ayatollah Khomeini — 180
    MOJTABA MAHDAVI

THE "INTELLECTUALS" OF POLITICAL ISLAM

13. Hasan al-Turabi — 203
    PETER WOODWARD

14. Rashid al-Ghannushi — 212
    AZZAM TAMIMI

15. Yusuf al-Qaradawi — 222
    BETTINA GRÄF

16. Mohammad Khatami — 237
    MAHMOUD SADRI AND AHMAD SADRI

17. Abdolkarim Soroush — 246
    BEHROOZ GHAMARI-TABRIZI

PART THREE: ISLAM AND POLITICS AROUND THE WORLD

18. Islam and Politics in North America — 263
    ABDULLAH A. AL-ARIAN

19. Islam and Politics in Europe — 278
    SAM CHERRIBI

20. Islam and Politics in the Middle East — 289
    MOATAZ A. FATTAH

21. Islam and Politics in Central Asia — 307
    SHIREEN HUNTER

22. Islam and Politics in South Asia — 324
    IRFAN AHMAD

23. Islam and Politics in Southeast Asia — 340
    FRED R. VON DER MEHDEN

24. Islam and Politics in North Africa — 352
    AZZEDINE LAYACHI

25. Islam and Politics in Sub-Saharan Africa — 379
    LEONARDO A. VILLALÓN

PART FOUR: THE DYNAMICS OF ISLAM IN POLITICS

POLITICAL ISLAM IN POWER

26. Iran's Islamic Republic — 399
    WILLIAM O. BEEMAN

27. Islam and Power in Saudi Arabia — 411
    NATANA J. DELONG-BAS

28. The AK Party in Turkey — 423
    IBRAHIM KALIN

29. Sudan: The Insecurity of Power and the Revenge of the State — 440
    ABDELWAHAB EL-AFFENDI

30. Islam and the State in Afghanistan 453
    M. Nazif Shahrani

31. The Muslim Brotherhood in Egypt 475
    Tarek Masoud

ISLAMIC MOVEMENTS IN THE POLITICAL PROCESS

32. Hamas in the Palestinian Territories 505
    Beverley Milton-Edwards

33. Hizbullah in Lebanon 516
    Bassel F. Salloukh and Shoghig Mikaelian

34. Islamic Movements in Algeria, Morocco, and Tunisia 532
    Michael J. Willis

35. The Islamic Action Front in Jordan 544
    Shadi Hamid

36. Nahdlatul Ulama in Indonesia 558
    Andrée Feillard

37. Jama`at-i Islami in Pakistan 574
    Kamran Bokhari

38. Islamic Movements in Malaysia 587
    Fred R. von der Mehden

JIHADI POLITICAL ISLAM

39. Al-Jama`a al-Islamiya and the al-Jihad Group in Egypt 603
    Nael Shama

40. Jihadists in Iraq 616
    David Romano

41. Al-Qaida and Its Affiliates 630
    Jason Burke

Index 643

Acknowledgments

We wish to acknowledge the contributions of those whose efforts and support were essential for the production of this volume: our authors, who not only submitted their chapters but then updated them where necessary just prior to publication; OUP senior editor Theodore Calderara, who was with us at every step of the way; and Karin Brown, Mina Rizq, Christina Buchhold, and Khadiga Omar for keeping this project on track.

Contributors

Irfan Ahmad is an anthropologist and a senior lecturer in politics at Monash University.

Shahrough Akhavi is an adjunct professor of political science at Columbia University in New York City.

Abdullah A. Al-Arian is an assistant professor of Middle East history at the School of Foreign Service in Qatar, Georgetown University.

Abdelwahab El-Affendi is a reader in politics at the Centre for the Study of Democracy, University of Westminster and coordinator of the Centre's Democracy and Islam Programme.

Margot Badran is a senior fellow, ACMC, Georgetown and senior scholar at the Woodrow Wilson International Center for Scholars.

William O. Beeman is professor of anthropology at the University of Minnesota.

Kamran Bokhari is a vice president of Middle Eastern and and South Asian Affairs at Stratford. He is also a fellow with the Washington-based Institute for Social Policy and Understanding and a senior consultant to the World Bank.

Jason Burke is a journalist and an author.

Sam (Oussama) Cherribi is a senior lecturer in sociology at Emory University in Atlanta, Georgia, where he also directs the Emory Development Initiative (EDI).

Natana J. DeLong-Bas is a visiting assistant professor of comparative theology at Boston College.

Khaled Abou El Fadl is Omar and Azmeralda Alfi Distinguished Professor of Islamic Law at the UCLA School of Law and Chair of the Islamic Studies Interdepartmental Program at UCLA.

John L. Esposito is a university professor and professor of religion and international affairs and founding director of the Prince Alwaleed Bin Talal Center for Muslim–Christian Understanding in the Walsh School of Foreign Service at Georgetown University.

Moataz A. Fatthah is a professor of political economy and public policy, the American University in Cairo, Cairo University and Central Michigan University.

Andrée Feillard is a senior researcher on Indonesian Islam at the French National Centre for Scientific Research (CNRS).

Behrooz Ghamari-Tabrizi is an associate professor of sociology and history at the University of Illinois.

Bettina Gräf is specialized in Islamic Studies and Political Science and is a postdoctorate research fellow at Zentrum Moderner Orient in Berlin.

Shadi Hamid is a director of research at the Brookings Doha Center and a fellow at the Saban Center for Middle East Policy at the Brookings Institution.

Nader Hashemi is an associate professor and director of the Center for Middle East Studies at the Josef Korbel School of International Affairs, University of Denver.

Shireen Hunter is a visiting professor at the Al Waleed Bin Talal Center for Muslim–Christian Understanding of the Edmond A. Walsh School of Foreign Service of Georgetown University.

Sherman A. Jackson is King Faisal Chair of Islamic Thought and Culture and professor of religion and American studies and ethnicity at the University of Southern California.

Ibrahim Kalin is a senior advisor to the prime minister of Turkey and a fellow at the Prince Alwaleed bin Talal Center for Muslim–Christian Understanding at Georgetown University.

Azzedine Layachi is a professor of political science at St. John's University, New York.

Mojtaba Mahdavi is an associate professor of political science at the University of Alberta.

Tarek Masoud is an associate professor of public policy at Harvard University's John F. Kennedy School of Government.

Shoghig Mikaelian is a PhD candidate at Concordia University.

Beverley Milton-Edwards is a professor of politics at Queen's University Belfast.

Ahmad Moussalli is a professor of political studies at American University of Beirut.

David Romano is Thomas G. Strong Professor of Middle East Politics at Missouri State University.

AhmadSadri is Gorter Professor of Islamic World Studies and a professor of sociology at Lake Forest College.

Mahmoud Sadri is a professor of sociology at the Federation of North Texas Universities.

Abdullah Saeed is Sultan of Oman Professor of Arab and Islamic Studies and director of the National Centre of Excellence for Islamic Studies at the University of Melbourne, Australia.

Bassel F. Salloukh is an associate dean of the School of Arts and Sciences and an associate professor of political science at the Social Sciences Department at Lebanese American University.

Emad El-Din Shahin is a professor of public policy at the School of Global Affairs and Public Policy at the American University in Cairo.

M. Nazif Shahrani is a professor of anthropology, Central Eurasian Studies, and Near Eastern Languages and Cultures at Indiana University, Bloomington.

Nael sp Shama is a political researcher and columnist based in Cairo.

Niloufer Siddiqui is a PhD candidate in political science at Yale University.

Azzam Tamimi is a British Palestinian academic and and author on Islamic political thought and and Islamic movements.

Leonardo A. Villalón is a professor of political science and African studies at the University of Florida.

John O. Voll is a professor of Islamic history and a past associate director of the Prince Alwaleed bin Talal Center for Muslim–Christian Understanding at Georgetown University.

Fred R. von der Mehden is professor emeritus of political science at Rice University.

Joshua T. White is an international affairs fellow with the Council on Foreign Relations.

Michael J. Willis is a university research lecturer and King Mohamed VI fellow in Moroccan and Mediterranean studies at the Faculty of Oriental Studies at the University of Oxford.

Peter Woodward is a professor of politics at the University of Reading.

THE OXFORD HANDBOOK OF
ISLAM AND POLITICS

INTRODUCTION

JOHN L. ESPOSITO AND EMAD EL-DIN SHAHIN

THE interaction of Islam and politics continues to draw the attention of scholars and the concern of policy makers. Under different contexts—the postindependence nation-state, changing ideological maps, globalization, the war against terrorism—Islam and Islamic activists play a visible role. Most recently, the Arab Spring has underlined the significant part Islamists are bound to play in emerging democratic arenas. Islamists have come to power through duly democratic processes and are already shaping the political contours of their respective countries and are eager to have a significant impact on world events. Evidently, the activities of Islamic movements reach beyond politics and cover the social, financial, economic, and educational spheres. Yet it is the relationship between Islam and politics that attracts the greatest attention and concern in both Muslim societies and the international community.

The forces of globalization, neoliberal economics, and democratization have accentuated, not lessened, the significance of religious values as an effective source for identity politics, ameliorating the crushing socioeconomic consequences of restructuring programs and contributing to the role of Islamic movements and Islamists as prominent actors in the political system. Islamists have appealed to Islam in shaping, legitimating, and mobilizing popular support for their diverse political responses and activities.

In recent years, political Islam has manifested itself in two diametrically opposed orientations: an increasing involvement in the democratization process by mainstream movements after the success of pro-democracy popular uprisings in toppling autocratic regimes and a growing inclination toward violence by fringe groups. Political Islam here refers to the attempts of Muslim individuals, groups and movements to reconstruct the political, economic, social and cultural basis of their society along Islamic lines. This process involves different views of the place of Shari`ah in society and the approach to bringing about change. While majorities of Islamic movements have engaged in the democratization process in their respective countries, some have embraced violence and terrorism as an ideological and strategic choice, with devastating consequences for the world and for Islam itself. What are the implications of these strategic choices on the political process in Muslim societies, the prospects of democratization, and regional and international security and stability? Which choice is likely to prevail in Muslim societies? Is political Islam the force of the future in the Muslim world? If so, what are the domestic, regional, and global implications?

Over the past three decades, scholars, government analysts, and terrorism experts have examined the relationship between Islam and politics, resulting in voluminous publications. However, due to the breadth and diversity of political Islam, specialists have tended to limit their analysis to a specific country or focus. Few works have provided a geographically comprehensive, in-depth analysis of the Islam and politics "phenomena." The attacks of September 11, 2001 further increased interest and concern and, as a result, generated a wave of literature on political Islam and global terrorism. Much of the post-9/11 analysis fails to capture the breadth and diversity of Islamic movements as well as their nuanced evolution. This situation underscores the need for a comprehensive, analytical, and in-depth examination of Islam and politics in the post-9/11 era, in an increasingly globalizing world, and in an Arab world transitioning from authoritarianism to democratization.

The Oxford Handbook of Islam and Politics seeks to meet this critical need. Oxford University Press has produced major reference works and books on Islam and the modern Islamic world as well as related books on Middle East politics and history. *The Oxford Handbook of Islam and Politics* makes an important addition, filling a niche in scholarship in an area that enjoys immense academic and policy interest. This handbook addresses several significant questions and issues: What is the current state of Islam and politics? How and why has political Islam been relevant in recent years? What are the repercussions and policy implications of the increased role of Islamic movements? And where is political Islam heading?

Written by prominent scholars and specialists in the field, *The Oxford Handbook of Islam and Politics* is a sourcebook that provides a comprehensive analysis of what we know and where we are in the study of political Islam. It will enable scholars, students, policy makers, and the educated public to appreciate the interaction of Islam and politics and the multiple and diverse roles of Islamic movements, as well as issues of authoritarianism and democratization, religious extremism and terrorism, regionally and globally.

The handbook is organized into four parts. The first part analyzes the contexts and intellectual responses of political Islam. Khaled Abou El Fadl focuses on the issue of the Shari`ah as a central theme and addresses the questions of why and how the Shari`ah is relevant to our present-day life. He also analyzes how Islamists are formulating their views regarding the implementation of divine laws in an increasingly secular society. Abdullah Saeed explores the quest for an Islamic reform and its different orientations (*salafi*, modernist, and revivalist); and Sherman A. Jackson provides a fresh look into the connection between Islamic reform and the nation-state by highlighting the distinction between the application of Islamic law and its application in a homogenizing nation-state. John O. Voll traces the changing ways that the key concepts of *dīn*, *dawla*, and *ummah* reflect the evolution of social and political ideals in the Muslim world and shape the way programs and political visions are articulated. Nader Hashemi assesses the debate on Islam and democracy and seeks to objectively frame an analysis of the relationship between Islam as a religion and democracy as a set of values and a system of government. Tarek Masoud addresses the "political economy" of political Islam and argues that much can be gained from making Islamic political parties the center of our political economy analyses of Islam and politics. Margot Badran examines the consequences political Islam has had for women and gender issues.

The second part focuses on the main ideologues of contemporary political Islam. These are intellectuals-activists whose Islamically informed orientations have given birth to an activist Islam that continues to impact new Islamic movements. They have succeeded in turning faith into a vehicle of social and political change. Ahmad Moussalli, Joshua T. White, and Niloufer Siddiqui discuss the main intellectual frameworks of Hassan al-Banna and Abu al-A`la al-Mawdudi, respectively, as the founders of contemporary political Islam. These revolutionary ideologues strongly believed that Islam presented a viable alternative to capitalism and socialism and, hence, developed a strong critique of the West. They tried to achieve a total break with the existing order and focused on its delegitimization, based on a scathing criticism of authoritarian regimes and the religious establishment. Shahrough Akhavi critically examines the ideological frameworks of the Egyptian Sayyid Qutb and the Iranian Ali Shari`ati; and Mojtaba Mahdavi analyzes the ideas of Ayatollah Khomeini.

The "intellectuals" of political Islam could be credited for their efforts to steer Islamic movements away from the polarizing ideas of Mawdudi and Qutb. They see the West not as an enemy but as an ideological counterweight to Islam and focus on the renewal of religious thought and Islamic jurisprudence, writing prolifically on modernization and Islam, non-Muslims, and women. Peter Woodward focuses on Hassan al-Turabi, Azzam Tamimi on Rashid al-Ghannushi, Bettina Gräf on Yusuf al-Qaradawi, Mahmoud Sadri and Ahmad Sadri on Mohammad Khatami, Behrooz Ghamari-Tabrizi on Abdolkarim Soroush.

The third part provides critical overviews of the interaction of Islam and politics regionally, in North America, Europe, the Middle East, in Central, South, and Southeast Asia as well as North and sub-Saharan Africa. Abdullah A. Al-Arian, Sam Cherribi, Moataz Fattah, Shireen Hunter, Irfan Ahmad, Fred R. von der Mehden, Azzedine Layachi, and Leonardo A. Villalón address the nature, extent, and dynamics of political Islam in these regions across the world, exploring the diverse use of religion by various regimes as well as various reform and opposition movements.

Part four presents an in-depth analysis of the dynamics of political Islam in politics through a wide range of case studies that reveal the diverse manifestations of political Islam or Islamism today, both mainstream and extremist. These cases are divided along three foci: political Islam in power, Islamic movements and the democratization process, and jihadist political Islam. William O. Beeman presents an alternative portrait of the ruling Islamists in Iran by underlining the dynamics of political life that demonstrates the democratic nature of the electoral process and government institutions in the country. Natana J. Delong-Bas focuses on the trajectory of both religious thought and practice as intertwined with politics in Saudi Arabia and on the academic debates surrounding them. Ibrahim Kalin discusses the rise of the AK Party as a center-right political movement with Islamic and national roots and analyzes its political identity and reformist agenda in the context of the state-centered tradition of Turkish politics. Abdelwahab El-Affendi follows the progression of the "National Islamic Front" into power in Sudan as the first modern Islamist group to assume power there and surveys the lessons the military coup of 1989 has produced on the complexity of contemporary Muslim politics. M. Nazif Shahrani focuses on key moments when those in power, including state and substate actors inside Afghanistan as well as international actors, have shaped discourses about Islam and power in modern Afghanistan and the effect these narratives have had in shaping subsequent events. Tarek Masoud closely examines the role of the Muslim Brotherhood in Egypt, anticipating great changes in its structure and orientation toward either more liberalism or conservatism in the wake of the 2011 Egyptian Revolution.

While not in power, other Islamic movements have played key roles in the political process. Beverley Milton-Edwards focuses on Hamas, surveying its foundation and history and ascent to power in the first democratic elections in the Arab world before the Arab Spring. Bassel F. Salloukh and Shoghig Mikaelian look into Hizbollah in Lebanon, tracing its doctrinal, political, and military metamorphoses. They also debate the themes on the party's nature, loyalties, and intentions, and its reconciliation of the domestic with the regional struggle. Michael J. Willis analyzes the Islamic movements in Morocco, Algeria, and Tunisia paying attention to national particularities but also acknowledging significant commonalities. Shadi Hamid examines the Islamic Action Front in Jordan and its interactions with the Hashemite Monarchy. Andrée Feillard examines Nahdlatul Ulama in Indonesia and the major shifts the movement has experienced in the past decade. Kamran Bokhari explores Pakistan's Jamaat-i-Islami's seventy-year pursuit to establish an Islamic state using democracy in a country ruled by the military. Fred R. von der Mehden studies the goals and policies of the United Malay National Organization and probes factors that have influenced the federal government's move toward policies of greater Islamization and control over Islamic affairs.

Jihadist political Islam has had a major impact on regional and global events. Nael Shama looks into the history and development of modern jihadist groups in Egypt and the ideological underpinnings of both the radicalization and the deradicalization phases of the movement. David Romano investigates the Jihadist movement in Iraq both before and after the 2003 American invasion, giving special attention to al-Qaeda in Iraq. Jason Burke explores the various "al-Qaidas" and shows how over time they have interacted, all the while continually evolving in response to both exogenous and endogenous factors.

As this volume demonstrates, since the last half of the twentieth century "political Islam" has increasingly played a significant role across the Muslim world. Understanding its nature, causes, and multiple and diverse manifestations—mainstream and extremist—requires an appreciation of national, regional, and international politics and economic and social conditions. Today, vibrant and effective Islamic political parties and movements across the Muslim Middle East and broader Muslim world play and will continue to play an increasingly important role in the region's democratizing politics.

PART ONE
MAJOR THEMES

CHAPTER 1

THE SHARI'AH

KHALED ABOU EL FADL

Introduction

PART of the unavoidable challenge of providing an adequate account of the Islamic legal tradition is not just its sheer magnitude and expanse but also that the Islamic legal system continues to be the subject of profound political upheavals in the contemporary age and its legacy is highly contested and grossly understudied at the same time. The Islamic legal system consists of legal institutions, determinations, and practices that span a period of over fourteen hundred years arising from a wide variety of cultural and geographic contexts that are as diverse as Arabia, Egypt, Persia, Bukhara, Turkey, Nigeria, Mauritania, Mali, Indonesia, and India. Despite the contextual and historical contingencies that constitute the complex reality of Islamic law, rather paradoxically, the Islamic legal legacy has been the subject of widespread and stubbornly persistent stereotypes and oversimplifications. Whether espoused by Muslim or non-Muslim scholars, highly simplified assumptions about Islamic law, such as the belief that Islamic legal doctrine stopped developing in the fourth/tenth century, the presumed sacredness and immutability of the legal system, and the phenomenon of so-called Qadi justice, are, to a large extent, products of turbulent political histories that contested and transformed Islamic law (or what is commonly referred to as Shari'ah) into a cultural and ideological symbol.

As part of the legacies of colonialism and modernity, Islamic law was then transformed into a symbolic construct of highly contested issues such as legitimacy, authenticity, cultural autonomy, traditionalism, reactionism, and religious oppression. Intellectually, there is a continuing tendency to treat Shari'ah law as if it holds the keys to unlocking the mysteries of the Muslim heart and mind or, alternatively, as if it is entirely irrelevant to the formation and dynamics of Muslim societies. In all cases, however, because of the disproportionately politicized context of the field, Islamic legal studies remains largely undeveloped, and the discipline is plagued by inadequate scholarship, especially in the field of comparative legal studies. It is important to stress the point because, for all the generalizations one often encounters in the secondary literature on Islamic law, the reality is that considering the richness of the legal tradition, our knowledge of the institutions, mechanisms, microdynamics, discourses, and determinations of Islamic law in various places and times is very limited.

The Difference Between Islamic Law and Muslim Law

Much of the secondary literature tends to either lump Islamic law and Muslim law together, especially when dealing with the premodern era, or assume a dogmatic and artificial distinction that is fundamentalist in nature. Not all legal systems or rules followed by Muslims are part of the Islamic legal tradition, but at the same time, the boundaries of Islamic law are far more contested and negotiable than any fundamentalist or essentialist approach may be willing to admit. Part of what makes this issue particularly challenging is that, inescapably, it involves judgments as to the legitimacy and authenticity of what is Islamic and what is not necessarily so. But more critically, the differentiation cannot be intelligibly addressed unless one takes full account of the epistemology and philosophy of Islamic jurisprudence, or the rules of normativity, obligation, and authority, and the processes of inclusion and exclusion in Islamic legal practice and history.

Although Islamic law grew out of the normative teachings of the Prophet Muhammad and his disciples, the first generations of Muslim jurists borrowed and integrated legal practices from several sources, including Persia, Mesopotamia, Egypt and other Roman provinces, Yemen and Arabia, and Jewish law. But at the same time, many existing and actual customary or executive administrative practices prevalent in premodern Muslim societies and polities were not integrated or recognized as being part of, or even consistent with, Islamic law or Islamic normative values. Classical Muslim jurists often denounced a particular set of customary practices, such as the tribal laws disinheriting women, and executive administrative practices, such as tax-farming or excessive taxes known as *mukus*, as inconsistent with Islamic legal principles. Although such legal practices at times constituted part of the universe of rules actually implemented and followed in certain Muslim societies, these practices, even if begrudgingly tolerated as functional necessities, were never endowed with Islamic legitimacy and, thus, were not integrated normatively into the Islamic legal tradition.

Distinguishing Islamic from Muslim law has only become more elusive and challenging in postcolonial modern-day Muslim societies. Most contemporary Muslim countries adopted either the French-based civil law system or some version of the British common law system and limited the application of Islamic law to personal law matters, particularly in the fields of inheritance and family law. In addition, in response to domestic political pressure, several Muslim countries in the 1970s and 1980s attempted to Islamize their legal systems by amending commercial or criminal laws in order to make them more consistent with purported Islamic legal doctrine. The fact remains, however, that the nature of the connection or relationship of any of these purportedly Islamically based or Islamized laws to the Islamic legal tradition remains debatable.

As discussed further below, even in the field of personal law, where the supremacy of Shari'ah law was supposedly never seriously challenged, leave alone the various highly politicized efforts at legal Islamization, Islamic legal doctrine was grafted onto what structurally and institutionally, as well as epistemologically, were legal systems borrowed and transplanted from the West. Practically in every Muslim country, the complex institutional structures and processes of the Islamic legal system, especially in the nineteenth century, were systematically dismantled and replaced not just by Western legal systems but, more importantly, also by the legal cultures of a number of Western colonial powers. Assertions of disembodied Islamic determinations or rules in the modern age, without the contextual legal processes, institutions, and epistemology, and in the absence of the legal cultures that generated these determinations in the first place, meant that the relationship between contemporary manifestations of Islamic law and the classical legal tradition remained, to say the least, debatable.

The Sources of Islamic Law

It is important to distinguish the formal sources of law in the Islamic legal tradition from what are often called the practical sources of law. Formal sources of law are an ideological construct—they are the ultimate foundations invoked by jurists and judges as the basis of legal legitimacy and authority. The practical sources, however, are the actual premises and processes utilized in legal practice in the process of producing positive rules and commandments. In theory, the foundations of all law in Islamic jurisprudence are the following: the Qur'an, the Sunna (the tradition of the Prophet Muhammad and his companions), *qiyas* (analogical or deductive reasoning), and *ijma'* (consensus or the overall agreement of Muslim jurists).

In contrast to mainstream Sunni Islam, Shi'i jurisprudence, as well as a minority of Sunni jurists, recognizes reason (*'aql*) instead of *qiyas* as a foundational source of law. These four are legitimating sources, but the practical sources of law include an array of conceptual tools that greatly expand the venues of the legal determination. For instance, practical sources include presumptions of continuity (*istishab*) and the imperative of following precedents (*taqlid*), legal rationalizations for breaking with precedent and de novo determinations (*ijtihad*), application of customary practices (*'urf* and *'adah*), judgments in equity, equitable relief, and necessity (*istislah, hajah, darurah*, etc.), and in some cases, the pursuit or the protection of public interests or public policies (*masalih mursalah* and *sadd al-thara'i' wa al-mafasid*). These and other practical jurisprudential sources were not employed as legal tropes in a lawless application of so-called Qadi justice. In fact, sophisticated conceptual frameworks were developed to regulate the application of the various jurisprudential tools employed in the process of legal determination. Not only were these conceptual frameworks intended to distinguish legitimate and authoritative uses of legal tools, but, collectively, they also were designed to bolster accountability, predictability, and the principle of rule of law.

Being the ultimate sources of legitimacy, the formal sources of law do not play a solely symbolic role in Islamic jurisprudence. Many legal debates and determinations originated or were derived directly from the textual narrative of the Qur'an and Sunnah. Nevertheless, it would be erroneous to assume, as many fundamentalists tend to do, that Islamic law is a literalist explication or enunciation of the text of the Qur'an and Sunnah. Only very limited portions of the Qur'an can be said to contain specific positive legal commandments or prohibitions. Much of the Qur'anic discourse, however, does have compelling normative connotations that were extensively explored and debated in the classical juristic tradition. Muslim scholars developed an extensive literature on Qur'anic exegesis and legal hermeneutics as well as a body of work (known as *ahkam al-Qur'an*) exploring the ethical and legal implications of the Qur'anic discourse. Moreover, there is a classical tradition of disputations and debates on what is known as the "occasions of revelation" (*asbab al-nuzul*), which deals with the context or circumstances that surrounded the revelation of particular Qur'anic verses or chapters, and on the critical issue of abrogation (*naskh*), or which Qur'anic prescriptions and commandments, if any, were nullified or voided during the time of the Prophet.

Similar issues relating to historical context, abrogation, and hermeneutics are dealt with in the juristic treatment of the legacy of the Prophet and his companions and disciples. However, in contrast to the juristic discourses on the Qur'an, there are extensive classical debates on historicity or authenticity of the hadith (oral traditions attributed to the Prophet) and the Sunnah (historical narratives typically about the Prophet but also his companions). While Muslim jurists agreed that the authenticity of the Qur'an as God's revealed word is beyond any doubt, classical jurists recognized that many of the traditions attributed to the Prophet were apocryphal. In this context, however, Muslim jurists did not just focus on whether a particular report was authentic or a fabrication, but also on the extent or degree of reliability and the attendant legal consequences.

Importantly, Muslim jurists distinguished between the reliability and normativity of traditions. Even if a tradition proved to be authentic, this did not necessarily mean that it was normatively binding because most jurists differentiated between the Prophet's sacred and temporal roles. The Prophet was understood as having performed a variety of roles in his lifetime, including that of the bearer and conveyer of the divine message, a moral and ethical sage and instructor, a political leader, a military commander and soldier, an arbitrator and judge, a husband and a father, and a regular human being and member of society. Not everything the Prophet said or did in these various capacities and roles created normative obligations upon Muslims. The Prophet did not always act as a lawmaker or legislator, and part of the challenge for Muslim jurists was to ascertain when his statements and actions were intended to create a legal obligation or duty (*taklif*), and when they were not meant to have any normative weight. In some cases, Muslims are affirmatively prohibited from imitating the Prophet's conduct because it is believed that in certain situations the Prophet acted in his capacity as God's messenger, a status that cannot be claimed by other human beings.

Other than the normative implications of the Prophet's sacred and temporal roles, a great deal of juristic disputations focused on the practices and opinions of the Prophet's family (*ahl al-bayt*), including his wives and his companions and disciples (*sahabah*). But while Sunni jurists tended to emphasize and exhibit deference to the four caliphs who governed the nascent Islamic state after the death of the Prophet (known in the Sunni tradition as al-Rashidun or the rightly guided), Shi'i jurists heavily relied on the teachings of the infallible imams, all of whom were the descendants of 'Ali, the fourth caliph and the Prophet's cousin, and his wife Fatima, the Prophet's daughter.

It is fair to say that the Qur'an and Sunnah are the two primary and formal sources of legitimacy in Islamic law. Quite aside from the question of whether most of Islamic law is derived from these two sources, the Qur'an and Sunnah play the foundational role in the processes of constructing legal legitimacy. This, however, begs the question as to why instrumentalities of jurisprudence such as analogy or reason and consensus are typically listed among the four formal sources of Islamic law. The response, in part, is that the utilization of the concepts of *qiyas* (or *'aql*) and *ijma'* not just as instrumentalities of law but also as legitimating and foundational origins of law was a necessary legal fiction. The emergence of this legal fiction in the first couple of centuries after the death of the Prophet took place after contentious and, at times, tumultuous jurisprudential debates. Ultimately, these concepts were intended to steer a middle course between unfettered and unrestrained borrowing of local customary laws and practices into Islamic law and, on the other extreme, the tendency toward literalism and overreliance on textualism as the basis of legitimacy in the process of legal development.

The Nature and Purpose of Shari'ah

As an essential point of departure, it is important to underscore that in jurisprudential theory, the ultimate point of Shari'ah is to serve the well-being or achieve the welfare of people (*tahqiq masalih al-'ibad*).[1] The word *Shari'ah*, which many very often erroneously equate with Islamic law, means the Way of God and the pathway of goodness, and the objective of Shari'ah is not necessarily the compliance with the commands of God for their own sake. Such compliance is a means to an end—the serving of the physical and spiritual welfare and well-being of people. Significantly, in Islamic legal theory, God communicates God's Way (the Shari'ah) through what is known as the *dalil* (pl. *adillah*). The *dalil* means the indicator, mark, guide, or evidence, and in Islamic legal theory, it is the fundamental building block of the search for the Divine Will and guidance. The most obvious type of indicator is an authoritative text (sing. *nass Shar'i* or pl. *al-nusus al-Shar'iyyah*),[2] such as the Qur'an, but Muslim jurists also recognized that God's wisdom is manifested through a vast matrix of indicators found in God's physical and metaphysical creation. Hence, other than texts, God's signs or indicators could manifest themselves through reason and rationality (*'aql* and *ra'y*), intuitions (*fitrah*), and human custom and practice (*'urf* and *'adah*). Especially in early Islam, which of these could legitimately be counted as avenues to God's Will and to what extent, were hotly debated issues. Especially with the increasing consolidation of the legal system after the tenth century, both Sunni and Shi'i jurists argued that most indicators are divided into rational proofs (*dalil 'aqli*) and textual proofs (*dalil nassi*). As to rational proofs, jurisprudential theory further differentiated between pure reason and practical or applied reason. Foundational legal principles and legal presumptions, such as the presumption of innocence or the presumption of permissibility (*al-bara'ah al-asliyyah*) and the presumption of continuity (*istishab al-hal*), are derived from pure reason. Interpretive tools, such as *qiyas* and *istihsan*, and hermeneutic categories are all instances of applied or practical reason.

Some Western scholars, such as Joseph Schacht, claimed that the first generations of Muslim jurists initially were not very interested in the text (*nass*) and were much more prone to use custom and reason (*ra'y*).[3] Nevertheless, this view has been adequately refuted, and there remains little doubt about centrality of the text from the very inception of Islamic legal history.[4] It is true that in the first two centuries of Islam, one clearly observes a much greater reliance on custom, practice, and unsystematic reasoning and that both the juristic schools of Medina and Kufah incorporated what they perceived to be the established practice of local Muslims, but both schools also struggled with the role of the text, its authenticity, and its meaning. The critical issue in early Islamic jurisprudence was not the struggle over what role the text ought to play, but, more substantially, it was over the methodologies by which the legal system could differentiate between determinations based on whim or a state of lawlessness (*hukm al-hawa*) and determinations based on legitimate indicators of the Divine Will (*hukm al-Shar'*).

In Islamic jurisprudence, the diversity and complexity of the divine indicators are considered part of the functionality and suitability of Islamic law for all times and places. The fact that the indicators are not typically precise, deterministic, or unidimensional allows jurists to read the indicators in light of the demands of time and place. So, for example, it is often noted that one of the founding fathers of Islamic jurisprudence, al-Shafi'i (d. 204/820) had one set of legal opinions that he thought properly applied in Iraq but changed his positions and rulings when he moved to Egypt to account for the changed circumstances and social differences between the two regions.[5] The same idea is embodied by the Islamic legal maxim "It may not be denied that laws will change with the change of circumstances" (*la yunkar taghayyur al-ahkam bi taghayyur al-zaman wa al-ahwal*).[6]

One of the most important aspects of the epistemological paradigm upon which Islamic jurisprudence was built was the presumption that on most matters, the Divine Will is unattainable, and even if attainable, no person or institution has the authority to claim certitude in realizing this Will. This is why the classical jurists rarely spoke in terms of legal certainties (*yaqin* and *qat'*). Rather, as is apparent in the linguistic practices of the classical juristic culture, Muslim jurists for the most part spoke in terms of probabilities or in terms of the preponderance of evidence and belief (*ghalabat al-zann*). Muslim jurists emphasized that only God possesses perfect knowledge—human knowledge in legal matters is tentative or even speculative; it must rely on the weighing of competing factors and the assertion of judgment based on an assessment of the balance of evidence on any given matter. So, for example, Muslim jurists developed a rigorous field of analytical jurisprudence known as *tarjih*,[7] which dealt with the methodological principles according to which jurists would investigate, assign relative weight, and balance conflicting evidence in order to reach a preponderance of belief about potentially correct determinations.[8]

Contemporary fundamentalist and essentialist orientations imagine Islamic law to be highly deterministic and casuistic, but this is in sharp contrast to the epistemology and institutions of the Islamic legal tradition that supported the existence of multiple equally orthodox and authoritative legal schools of thought, all of which are valid representations of the Divine Will. Indeed, the Islamic legal tradition was founded on a markedly pluralistic, discursive, and exploratory ethos that became the very heart of its distinctive character. According to classical legal reasoning, no one jurist, institution, or juristic tradition may have an exclusive claim over the divine truth, and hence, the state does not have the authority to recognize the orthodoxy of one school of thought to the exclusion of all others.[9] While Shari'ah is divine, *fiqh* (the human understanding of Shari'ah) was recognized to be only potentially so, and it is the distinction between Shari'ah and *fiqh* that fueled and legitimated the practice of legal pluralism in Islamic history.

The Difference Between Shari'ah and *Fiqh*

The conceptual distinction between Shari'ah and *fiqh* was the result of recognizing the limitations of human agency and also a reflection of the Islamic dogma that perfection belongs only to God. While Shari'ah was seen as an abstract ideal, every human effort at understanding or implementing this ideal was considered necessarily imperfect. In theory, Muslim jurists agreed that even if a jurist's determination is ultimately wrong, God will not hold such a jurist liable as long as he exerted due diligence in searching for the right answer.

According to one group of legal theorists, those who are ultimately proven to be wrong will still be rewarded for their due diligence, but those who prove to be right will receive a greater reward. The alternative point of view, however, argued that on all matters of *fiqh* there is no single truth to be revealed by God in the hereafter. All positions held sincerely and reached after due diligence are in God's eyes correct. God rewards people in direct proportion to the exhaustiveness, diligence, and sincerity of their search for the Divine Will—sincerity of conviction, the search, and the process are in themselves the ultimate moral values. It is not that there is no objective truth—rather, according to this view, the truth adheres to the search.

This classical debate had an impact upon the development of various doctrines and institutions in Islamic jurisprudence, the most important of which was negotiating the dynamics between Shari'ah and *fiqh*. In the Islamic legal tradition, there is only one Shari'ah (*Shari'at Allah*) but there are a number of competing schools of thought of *fiqh* (*madhahib fiqhiyyah*). Although all jurists embraced the theological dogma that God's perfection cannot be reproduced or attained by human beings, this did not mean that they considered every aspect of Shari'ah to be entirely unattainable or inaccessible until the hereafter. Some have suggested that Shari'ah contains the foundational or constitutional principles and norms of the legal system. So for instance, Shari'ah imposes a duty (*taklif*) upon Muslims to enjoin goodness and resist wrongfulness. There is little doubt that this duty is a part of Shari'ah, but what it actually means and how or who should implement it are part of *fiqh*. Nevertheless, the exact boundaries between Shari'ah and *fiqh* were often contested and negotiable, and whether there is overlap between the two categories turned out to be challenging and at times ambiguous.

Behind most of the jurisprudential conceptions of Shari'ah was the basic idea that what cumulative generations of Muslims reasonably identified as fundamental to the Islamic religion (for instance, the five pillars of the Islamic faith) ought to be part of the unassailable Shari'ah. As some have contended, this approach might have been important to the field of theology, but in law, Shari'ah could not be limited to inherited or popular ideas. Rather, Shari'ah is comprised of the foundational or constitutional normative values that constitute the grundnorms of the Islamic legal system. For instance, the notion that the Divine Will cannot be represented by a single system of *fiqh* and the celebration of diversity is itself one of those foundational grundnorms. For example, it is firmly established in the Islamic legal tradition that Shari'ah seeks to protect and promote five fundamental values: (1) life, (2) intellect, (3) reputation or dignity, (4) lineage or family, and (5) property. Furthermore, Muslim jurists overwhelmingly held that there are three basic levels of attainment or fulfillment of such values: the necessities, needs, and luxuries.

Under Shari'ah law, legal imperatives increase in proportion to the level demand for the attainment of each value. Thus, when it comes to life, for example, the legal duty to secure a person's survival is a priori to the obligation of guaranteeing human beings any basic needs that are above and beyond what is necessary for survival. Nevertheless, alongside these broad fundamental principles, historically, Muslim jurists developed specific positive commandments that were said to be necessary for the protection of the values mentioned above, such as the laws punishing slander, which were said to be necessary for the protection of reputation or dignity, or the laws punishing fornication, which were said to be necessary for the protection of lineage and family.

I will discuss the *hudud* penalties further below, but for now it is important to emphasize that many of the positive legal determinations purportedly serving the five values were often declared to be a part of Shari'ah, and not just *fiqh*, or were left in a rather ambiguous and contested status between Shari'ah and *fiqh*. Claiming that a positive legal commandment is not a by-product of *fiqh*, but is essentially part of Shari'ah effectively endowed such a commandment with immunity and immutability. The boundaries between Shari'ah and *fiqh* were negotiated in a variety of highly contextually contingent ways in the course of Islamic history, but the dynamics and processes of this history remain grossly understudied.

Purportedly, by the end of tenth century, no fewer than one hundred schools of *fiqh* had emerged, but for a wide variety of reasons most of these schools ultimately failed to survive. Fortunately, however, many of the diverse positions and competing views expounded by extinct schools of thought were documented in huge legal encyclopedias often written by competitors, and in some cases, the actual texts of extinct schools have reached us. The most striking characteristic about the legal schools that dominated the practice of law for more than three centuries after the death of the Prophet is their remarkable diversity, and in fact, one would be hard pressed to find any significant legal issue about which juristic disputations and discourses have not generated a large number of divergent opinions and conflicting determinations. During the age of proliferation, one does notice the incredibly broad expanse of space that came under the legitimate jurisdiction of *fiqh*. Put differently, there did not seem to be many issues in Shari'ah that were off limits for the inquiries of *fiqh*.

Rather, the grand abstract type of questions that were raised when attempting to expound a systematic demarcation of Shari'ah and *fiqh* were handled within the classical *madhahib* through the microtechnicalities of the practice of law. Rather than struggle with the larger abstract conceptual questions, the Shari'ah/*fiqh* balance was negotiated through the microdynamics of legal practice. The broad philosophical issue of theorizing an analytically sound differentiation between the respective provinces of each seems to be a particularly pressing question for Muslim constitutional lawyers in the contemporary age, especially with the challenge of authoritarian religious movements trying to rule in God's name.

Initially, what differentiated one school of law (*madhhab*) from another were methodological disagreements and not necessarily the actual determinations. With the increasing consolidation and institutionalization of schools of thought, each school developed its own distinctive cumulative interpretive culture, structural precedents, and even particular linguistic practices. Importantly, the founders of the schools of *fiqh*, and the early jurists in general, did not intend to generate binding legal precepts. Rather, acting more like law professors and legal scholars, they produced legal opinions and analysis, which became part of the available common law to be adopted by state appointed judges in light of regional customary practices. Legal scholars from the different schools of thought were often far more interested in hypotheticals that illustrated their analytical models and methodologies than in passing judgments on actual disputes. This is why *fiqh* studies did not speak in terms of positive legal duties or prohibitions but analyzed legal issues in terms of five values: (1) neutral or permissible (*mubah/halal*), (2) obligatory (*fard/wajib*), (3) forbidden (*muharram*), (4) recommended (*mandub/mustahab*), and (5) reprehensible or disfavored (*makruh*).

Frequently, jurists wrote in probabilistic terms such as saying "what is more correct in our opinion," referring to the prevailing view within the jurist's school of thought (*al-murajjah 'indana*). The critical point is that the masters of *fiqh* understood that they were not making binding law but issuing opinions of persuasive authority. The difference between *fiqh* and positive law was akin to the distinction between *fatwa* and *hukm*. A *hukm* is a binding and enforceable legal determination, but a *fatwa* (responsa) is a legal opinion on a particular dispute, problem, or novel issue, which by definition, enjoys only persuasive authority. Both *fiqh* and *fatawa* (sing. *fatwa*) become binding law only if adopted as such by a person as a matter of conscience or if adopted as enforceable law by a legitimate authority such as a judge. In other words, *fiqh* and *fatawa* are normative legal proposals that are contingent on essential enabling acts or triggers: the conscientious acceptance of its mandatory authority by a Muslim practitioner or by an official adoption by a proper authority. Failure to appreciate this fundamental point about the construction and structure of the legal views expressed in *fiqh* works has led to a great deal of ill-informed and misguided scholarship about Islamic law.

One of the most entrenched myths about Islamic law is that the legal system ceased to develop or change from the tenth or eleventh centuries because, fearing diversity and fragmentation, the so-called doors of *ijtihad* were declared to be forever closed. According to this claim, Muslim jurists were expected to imitate their predecessors (practice of *taqlid*) without undertaking legal innovations (*ijtihad*). This myth seems to have emerged in the nineteenth century as a simplistic explanation of the purported stagnation of the Islamic legal system and as justification for the legal reforms of the time, which in reality amounted to little more than the importation of European legal systems.[10] More importantly, this myth persisted among contemporary scholars because of the paucity of studies on the microdynamics of Islamic law and because of the failure to properly understand some of the basic historical realities about the development of the Islamic legal system. For example, *taqlid* was not the instrument of legal stagnation; it was an important functional instrument of the rule of law. In general, *taqlid* stabilized the law by requiring continuity in legal application and by creating a legal presumption in favor of precedents unless a heightened burden of evidence is met justifying legal change. Indeed, many of the most important developments in Islamic law were accomplished by jurists centuries after the supposed doors of *ijtihad* were closed.

The essential point about the Islamic legal tradition, and especially the role of *fiqh*, is that the juristic method and the linguistic practices of cumulative communities of legal interpretation became not only the mechanism for legitimacy and authority but also the actual source of law. As a community of guilded specialists with an elaborate system of insignia and rituals, in most cases structured around a system resembling the Inns of Court in England, the jurists played a critical role in upholding the rule of law and in mediating between the masses and rulers.[11] However, the primacy of the juristic method and the organized guilds representing the various schools of law, contrary to some stereotypical claims, did not mean that the application of Islamic law became completely streamlined or simply mechanical and formulaic. Within a single *madhhab*, it was common for various juristic temperaments and philosophical orientations to exist because the established schools of law became the common platforms where conservative or activist jurists had to pursue their legal agendas or objectives. Within a single established school of thought, there could be conservative, traditionalist, rationalist, or equity-oriented trends, but each of these orientations had to negotiate its particular approach within the demands of the juristic method of the *madhhab*. Fundamentally, whether a particular legal orientation emphasized the use of the text, reason, custom, equity, or public interest, these tools had to be justified, channeled, negotiated, and limited by the juristic method.[12] The point is not just that the juristic method became the prevalent mechanism for negotiating the tools and instruments of legal analysis but, even more, that the juristic method became Islamic law itself; it became the mechanism for negotiating the relationship not just between Shari'ah and *fiqh* but also between the realm of God and that of humans, and ultimately, between the sacred and the profane.

THE SACRED AND PROFANE IN ISLAMIC LAW

The relationship between the sacred and profane was negotiated in Islamic law through the ongoing historical dynamics demarcating the boundaries between Shari'ah and *fiqh*. But beyond this, there were several other conceptual categories and functional mechanisms through which sacred and temporal spaces were negotiated in Islamic law. Among these categories was the conceptual differentiation between *'ibadat* (laws dealing with matters of ritual) and *mu'amalat* (laws pertaining to human dealings and intercourses). In theory, all Islamic laws are divided into one of these two categories: *'ibadat* are laws that regulate the relationship between God and humans, and *mu'amalat* are laws that regulate the relationship of humans with one another. As to issues falling under the category of *'ibadat*, there is a legal presumption in favor of literalism and for the rejection of any innovations or novel practices. However, in the case of *mu'amalat* the opposite presumption applies; innovations or creative determinations are favored (*al-asl fi al-'ibadat al-ittiba' wa al-asl fi al-mu'amalat al-ibtida'*).

The rationale behind this categorical division is that when it comes to space occupied exclusively by how people worship the Divine, there is a presumption against deference to human reason, material interests, and discretion. Conversely, in space occupied by what the jurists used to describe as the pragmatics of social interaction, there is a presumption in favor of the rational faculties and practical experiences of human beings. Underscoring the difference between *'ibadat* and *mu'amalat* was the fact not only that the two were identified as distinct and separate fields and specialties of law but also that it was quite possible to specialize and become an authority in one field but not the other (*fiqh al-'ibadat* or *fiqh al-mu'amalat*).

Beyond this clean categorical division, negotiating the extent to which a particular human act or conduct, whether it be public or private, primarily involved *'ibadat* or *mu'amalat* was not a simple and unequivocal issue. For instance, there were lengthy debates as to whether the prohibition of *zina* (fornication or adultery) or consumption of alcoholic substances falls under the category of *'ibadat* or *mu'amalat*, or alternatively, some mixture of both categories. Nevertheless, as in the case of the debates regarding the parameters of Shari'ah and *fiqh*, although in principle there was a philosophical recognition that the spaces occupied by the sacred and profane require different treatments, in reality, it is the juristic method that played the defining role in determining the function of text, precedent, and rational innovation in the treatment of legal questions. Ultimately, it was not the legal presumptions attaching to either category but the institutional and methodological processes of each legal school of thought that most influenced the way issues were analyzed and determined.

Perhaps as a practical result of the epistemology of plural orthodoxy, in Islamic jurisprudence a court's judgment or finding was not equated with or considered the same as God's judgment. At a normative level, a court's judgment could not right a wrong or wrong a right and it could not negate or replace the duties and responsibilities imposed by an individual's conscience. Jurists argued that individuals do have an obligation to obey court decisions as a matter of law and order, but judicial determinations do not reflect or mirror God's judgment. A classic example would be of a litigant who, for instance, follows the Hanafi school of thought and who is forced to submit to the jurisdiction of a Shafi'i court. The Hanafi litigant would have to obey the judgment of the court not because it is correct but because a duly constituted court possesses legitimate positive authority (*sultat al-ilzam*). Not surprisingly, the proper balance between the duty of obedience to the public order and the duty to follow one's conscience, or school of thought, has been the subject of considerable jurisprudential debates.

Because of the reality of pluralist legal orthodoxy, in Islamic jurisprudence it is entirely conceivable even where Shari'ah is the law of the land that an individual legitimately would feel torn between his duties toward the public order and God. The legitimacy of the state and even the law were not absolute—both state and law performed a functional but necessary role. Beyond the fact that the state could not act as a proxy for God, legal determinations could not void the necessary role of personal beliefs or individual conscience because they did not replace the sovereignty of divine judgments.

An out product of the institutions of legal pluralism was the rather fascinating, but little understood, practice of multiple territorially overlapping legal jurisdictions. There were many historical examples of governments establishing as many as four court judicial jurisdictions, each following a different *madhhab*, with a challengingly complex set of conflict of laws rules regulating subject matter and *in personam* jurisdiction. Normally, however, the predominant *madhhab* affiliation of the population of a region would play a determinative role on the *madhhab* followed by a court. Furthermore, frequently there was a senior or chief judge settling issues of adjudicatory law within each *madhhab*. In addition, a common practice was to appoint a supreme chief judge who enjoyed ultimate appellate authority, as far as the positive law was concerned, over all the judicial jurisdictions. Although the research in this field is poorly developed, there is considerable evidence that the supreme chief judge, although personally belonging to a particular *madhhab*, in his official function, sought to resolve conflict among the jurisdictions through synchronistic or conciliatory methodology known as *al-tawfiq bayn al-madhahib* (resolving and balancing between the differences among the schools of legal thought), which was a well-developed jurisprudential field and specialty.

The Rights of God and the Rights of Humans

Perhaps the clearest articulation in Islamic jurisprudence of the distinctive spaces occupied by the sacred and profane is the categorical differentiation between the rights of God (*huquq Allah*) and the rights of humans (*huquq al-'ibad*). Muslim jurists agreed that humans cannot benefit or harm God, and so unlike the rights owed to human beings, the rights of God do not involve any actual interests of God. Depending on the context, the word *huquq* (sing. *haqq*) referred to the province, jurisdiction, boundaries, or limits of God (*hudud Allah*).

Interestingly, *huquq al-'ibad* did not refer to public or common rights but to the material interests and benefits belonging to each human being as an individual. The rights of God do not need a protector or vindicator because God is fully capable of redressing any transgressions committed against God's boundaries or commands. But unlike God, human beings do need an agent empowered to defend them and redress any transgressions committed against their person or properties. Therefore, the state is not simply empowered but obligated to enforce the rights and obligations owed to people and may not legitimately ignore or waive them away. The state was precluded from enforcing the rights of God because the state was not God's representative and God had reserved these rights to God's exclusive jurisdiction and province.

Muslim jurists clearly recognized the exceptionality and exclusivity of the sacred space and even jealously guarded it from the encroachments of the profane. Ironically, however, it is in dealing with the issue of God's clear boundaries and limits that the jurists most famously collapsed the sacred and profane into a single space, at least in theory if not in application. In what is known as the *hudud* penalties, Muslim jurists asserted that there is a category of divinely ordained punishments that apply to violations committed against a class of mixed rights (*huquq mukhtalitah*), which are shared by God and human beings. As a category, mixed rights involve issues where the material interests or well-being of people is involved, but at the same time, there is a discernible Divine Will staking a specific claim for the Divine over these issues. In the case of the divinely ordained *hudud* penalties, for reasons not necessarily known to human beings, God purportedly explicitly determined not only the punishable act and the exact penalty but also the exact process by which the crime is proven and the penalty is carried out.

Although not all the *hudud* crimes were mentioned in the text of Qur'an, a general juristic consensus was said to exist as to the divine origin of the penalties. In the classical tradition, fornication or adultery (*zina*), robbery (*sariqah*), consumption of alcohol, defamation (*qadhf*), and apostasy (*riddah*) were the violations most commonly included within the *hudud*. The real paradox of the *hudud* is that while in contemporary Islam they are often imagined to be the harbinger and flagship of Islamic law, in the classical tradition, the *hudud* penalties were rarely applied precisely because of the space occupied by the Divine in defining and redressing the crime. On the one hand, by categorizing a crime under the *hudud*, the definition of the crime and the appropriate penalty became sanctified and immutable. But, on the other hand, by placing it within the category of *hudud*, the jurists effectively endowed the penalty with a largely symbolic role because the technical requirements and administrative costs of enforcing these sacred penalties were largely prohibitive.

As with all matters involving the rights of God, as far as the state is concerned, it is imperative to tread cautiously lest in trying to uphold the bounds of God, whether through ignorance, arrogance, or incompetence, the state itself ends up committing an infraction against the Divine. Prophet Muhammad's injunction, which was adapted into a legal maxim, commanded that any doubt must serve to suspend the application of the *hudud*. In addition to the presumption of innocence in application to all criminal accusations, Muslim jurists often cited the injunction above in greatly circumscribing the application of the *hudud* penalties through a variety of doctrinal and procedural hurdles. In general, repentance, forgiveness, and doubt acted to prevent the application of the *hudud*. In dealing with the rights of God, it was always better to forgive than to punish; repentance of the defendant acted to suspend the *hudud*, and all doubt had to be construed in favor of vindicating the accused.

As far as the classical jurists were concerned, the *hudud*, like all matters implicating the rights of God, were better left to divine vindication in the hereafter. In most cases, instead of pursuing a *hudud* penalty, the state proved a lesser included crime under a less demanding burden of proof and applied lesser penalties, normally involving imprisonment, some form of corporal punishment, banishment, or a fine. Lesser penalties for non-*hudud* crimes, or lesser included crimes, fell into two categories: *qisas* (talion, or punishment in kind to the offense, e.g., eye for an eye) or *ta'zir* (penalties prescribed by the state for offenses against public interest). *Qisas* was treated as a private recourse and right, where pardon or forgiveness was always preferable, but *ta'zir* were thoroughly profane punitive measures left to the authority and jurisdiction of the state applied to protect the public through deterrence. Classical Muslim jurists enunciated various principles regulating and restricting the powers of the state over *ta'zir* punishments. Fundamentally, however, while *hudud* punishments were greatly circumscribed throughout Islamic history, what and how *ta'zir* punishments were applied greatly varied from one time and place to another.

By circumscribing the enforcement of the rights of the Divine, the classical jurists of Islam constrained the power of the state to act as God's avenger. However, doctrinally the rights of God, as a concept, played an important normative and ethical role in the Shari'ah dynamics taking place within Muslim societies. The rights of God symbolically represented the moral boundaries of appropriate social mores and values in the public space. This does not mean, as some contemporary reformists have claimed, that the rights of God are equivalent to, or substantially the same as, public interests or space. Normatively, the Shari'ah is expected to pervade the private and public spaces by appealing to the private consciences of individuals and to societies as collectivities. But there is one way this could happen and that is through voluntary compliance. For the most part, Islamic jurisprudence invoked the compulsory powers of the state in order to enforce obligations or rights owed to people—not to God. Functionally, Islamic law was thought of not as a means for empowering the state to act on God's behalf, but as setting limits to the powers of the state through the imposition of the rule of law. Therefore, the greater legacy of the Islamic tradition deals with questions involving *mu'amalat* or social intercourses and dealings or the resolution of conflicts arising from competing claims and interests. Questions of social etiquette or proper public manners were not treated in books of jurisprudence, but were relegated to the status of moralistic pamphlets (*kutub al-raqa'iq*) written often by religious preachers or sometimes by qualified jurists for the consumption of the laity.

MODERNITY AND THE DETERIORATION OF ISLAMIC LAW

With the advent of the age of colonialism, the Islamic legal system was consistently replaced by legal systems imported from Western colonial states. The factors contributing to the deterioration and replacement of Islamic law are numerous, but primary among those factors was the pressure exerted by foreign powers for a system of concessions and special jurisdictions that served the economic and political interests of the colonizers and a parasitical native elite that derived and maintained its privileged status from the financial, military, and cultural institutions of colonial powers. Frequently, colonial powers and their dependent native elites found that their economic and commercial interests were not well served by the pluralism and localized indeterminacy of the Islamic legal system. In response, some colonial powers such as Great Britain created hybrid legal institutions such as the Mixed Courts of Egypt and the Anglo-Muhammadan courts of India. Of greater significance, however, was the fact that colonial powers and their native ruling elites found that the organized legal guilds, and the system of religious endowments (*awqaf*) that supported these guilds, leveraged a considerable amount of power that was often used to resist the hegemonic powers of the modern state. Throughout the Muslim world, this led to a protracted process by which colonial powers or, in the postcolonial age, local nationalistic governments consistently undermined the autonomy, and eventually completely controlled, the traditional legal guilds and the network of religious endowments, not only depriving them of any meaningful political role but also deconstructing their very legitimacy in Muslim societies.

Perhaps more destructive to the Islamic legal system was the fact that the institutional replacement of Islamic law was accompanied by a process of cultural transformation that led to the deconstruction of the very epistemological foundations of Islamic jurisprudence. Colonial powers exerted considerable pressures toward greater legal uniformity and determinism, and, in what has been described as a process of cultural invasion, both the ruling elites and intelligentsia of various Muslim societies turned mostly to western and to a much lesser extent to eastern Europe for inspiration and guidance in all fields of the arts and sciences. Increasingly, educational institutions and systems in the Muslim world were fashioned or remodeled along the lines of the educational systems of the major colonial powers. From the beginning of the nineteenth century to this very day, an academic degree from Western schools became a cultural symbol of prestige and privilege. In the legal field, a Western education became a powerful venue for upward professional mobility and social status, and this led to a marked deterioration in the position and authority of classical Muslim jurists as well as in the role of the centuries-old schools of Shari'ah law all over the Muslim world.

The cultural impact of colonialism upon Muslim societies was and continues to be immeasurable. In the nineteenth century, the Western educated intelligentsia played a critical role in the birth of the reform movement that sought to modernize Islamic law. In response to the transplantation of European codes of law into the Muslim world, especially in the 1850s and 1860s, Muslim legal experts, most often trained in Western institutions, sought to reform Islamic law by making it more deterministic, uniform, and predictable. In most cases, this amounted to a process of codification, the most famous of which was the Mejelle (also known as *Majallat al-Ahkam al-'Adliyyah*) completed in 1877. But these efforts at reform meant challenging the epistemological foundations of the Islamic legal system and a radical reinvention of Islamic law from a common law-like system to a system tailored after the civil law, especially the Napoleonic Code of 1804. Very frequently legal reformers unwittingly transformed Islamic law from a system of common laws united by shared communities of legal sources, methodological and analytical tools, technical linguistic practices, and a coherent system of authoritativeness and legitimacy to something that, other than being a compilation of deterministic commands, held little coherence and was strangely at odds with the system of law that had existed for well over a thousand years.

Perhaps among the cultural and intellectual transformations that contributed a great deal to the retreat of Islamic law in the contemporary age was the birth of the myth of the closing of *ijtihad* in the nineteenth century. It appears that this myth was invented by orientalist scholars, many of whom were enlisted in the service of imperial colonial powers and who as part of carrying the "white man's burden" of civilizing backward native cultures sought to convince the native intelligentsia that Islamic law had ceased developing around a thousand years ago. According to the myth of closing the doors of *ijtihad* in the fourth/tenth century, Muslim jurists decided that all the questions of the divine law have been now and forever answered, and therefore, legal innovations or original determinations are not necessary and are no longer permitted. According to the myth, ever since the doors were closed Muslim lawyers have practiced blind imitation or *taqlid*. This unsupported historical claim was frequently exploited in the context of justifying the replacement of Islamic law with transplanted Western law and also in restricting the jurisdiction of Shari'ah courts to the fields of family and personal law. Although orientalist scholars might have invented and exploited this myth, the fact remains that Muslim intellectuals from all over the Muslim world accepted this fiction as a settled historical fact and constructed reform agendas and stratagems on the assumption that the reopening of the proverbial doors of *ijtihad* is a talismanic solution to all the challenges and woes of Islamic law in the modern age.

Both the reform movements emphasizing codification or the practice of *ijtihad* were symptomatic of a more ingrained and obstinate cultural problem. Islamic schools that used to provide training for the judges, lawyers, and law professors no longer attracted the best and brightest students because job opportunities, higher levels of pay, and professional respect and prestige had all migrated to the non-Shari'ah European-styled schools of law. Throughout the second half of the nineteenth century and the first half of the twentieth century, Islamic courts and law were abolished and replaced by transplanted Western legal systems. The lasting impact of these developments was that successive generations of Muslim lawyers were very poorly trained in Islamic law and thus became increasingly alienated and distant from their own native legal tradition. In most parts of the Muslim world, lawyers by virtue of their training gained technical competence in the legal systems of their former colonizers as they grew more disassociated and distant from their own Islamic legal heritage. In short, the process that unfolded all over the Muslim world meant that the most gifted and competent legal minds found Islamic law to be marginal to their professional activity, and those who did attend the few Islamic law schools that remained in the Muslim world, in most cases, were not gifted or talented legal minds. But even worse, having become state-owned and, very often, state-controlled institutions, the surviving Islamic schools of law no longer offered legal curriculums that provided adequate training for lawyers. Therefore, in most Muslim countries training in Shari'ah does not qualify the student to join the lawyers' guild or bar, appear in court, or undertake any of the functions typically reserved for professional lawyers.

The 1970s and 1980s witnessed a highly politicized attempt at reasserting and reviving the role of Islamic law in Muslim societies. The reasons for this revival were many, but they included a long list of economic, political, and cultural grievances, all of which were made more acute by mass frustrations with the authoritarianism, ineffectiveness, and corruption of many of the governments ruling Muslim societies in the postcolonial age. Much of the populist revivalism was met with severe state repression, which usually followed short-lived periods of governmental accommodation or begrudging tolerance. The impact of the confrontations and political violence between dictatorial governments and Islamic movements was the further radicalization of those who offered the ire of the state and survived. Such radicalization led to the articulation of visions of Islamic law that were severely distorted by siege mentalities that, inspired by their own sufferings, challenged the legitimacy of ethical principles and the practicality of insisting on lawful means. Not surprisingly, radicalized movements had no patience, use, or even opportunity to engage the layered discourses of the Islamic jurisprudential tradition.

Alongside the repression, a number of governments in the Muslim world attempted to bolster their legitimacy by engaging in highly symbolic gestures of perceived Islamicity, such as amending state constitutions to add a provision declaring that Shari'ah is the source of all legislation, or by purportedly Islamizing particular provisions in their criminal and commercial codes. Substantively, however, the state-led Islamization initiatives were of very little consequence because they were readily understood to be publicity ploys pursued for their symbolic value and not for any normative commitment in favor of the regeneration of the Islamic legal system. These so-called Islamization campaigns were undertaken to mitigate the political effects of repressing Islamic movements and to persuade the masses that the state is no less committed to Islamic law than its foes. But even in rare cases where governments were genuinely committed to Islamization, or when Islamists did in fact succeed to one extent or another in to coming to power, the results were still pitiful.

The problem remained to be a product of the dual impediments: on the one hand, those who were skilled and gifted lawyers were not rooted in or in command of the Islamic jurisprudential system and, on the other hand, those who qualified as *fuqaha'* in the modern age no longer received the training that would qualify them as lawyers. The irony is that the mythology of closing the doors of *ijtihad* and the popularized belief that reform requires a reopening of the gates was used to make Islamic law more accessible to activists who enjoyed no specialized competence either in Islamic law or in legal reasoning and practice, in general. Reopening the proverbial doors became the means for licensing a chaotic condition where numerous participants under the slogan of practicing *ijtihad* claimed to be authoritative experts of Islamic law. So for instance, many of the leaders of Islamic movements were trained as engineers or computer scientists and many of the most popular and influential voices of reform were never trained in law, let alone Islamic law. Predictably, as the twentieth century came to a close and the twenty-first century began, the field of Islamic law suffered a crippling crisis of authority as Muslims struggled to rediscover the rules and criteria for defining the authoritative in modern Islamic law.

Shari'ah and the Arab Spring

The Islamization campaigns of the 1970s and 1980s in countries such as Pakistan, Sudan, and Nigeria manifested with a heavy emphasis on the application of technical positive rules of law, such as the *hudud* punishments, as symbolic affirmations of identity. The revolutions or protests that swept through the Arab world in 2011–2012 displayed a very different set of dynamics in relation to Shari'ah law. The mass protests in Tunisia, Libya, Egypt, Yemen, Bahrain, and Syria did not call for the imposition of Shari'ah law or ideological Islamic states. The protests placed a far greater emphasis on issues of political liberty and rights of citizenship, such as civil societies, civic rights, rule of law, limited and accountable government, and social and political justice. Nevertheless, Shari'ah played an active normative role through the course of the protests and also in the postrevolution elections held in Libya, Tunisia, and Egypt. Shari'ah norms permeated the revolutions as witnessed in the cries of

"Allahu akbar" ("God is greatest"), the idea of jihad as revolt against despotism, and the reverence afforded to those killed as *shuhada' lillah* (martyrs in the way of God).

Especially with the start of the Egyptian revolution, a considerable number of notable Muslim scholars and jurists asserted that the Shari'ah of Islam not only supports but also mandates rebelling against the corrupt and despotic governments in power. Significantly, a number of Saudi jurists and Wahhabi activists tried to counter the revolutionary zeal by issuing legal proclamations appealing, albeit unsuccessfully, to God-fearing and pious Muslims to refrain from supporting or joining the revolutions. The proclamation claimed that Shari'ah law prohibits demonstrations and also prohibits rebelling against rulers even if such rulers are unjust or despotic.[13]

Partly in response to the Wahhabi position, the prominent Egyptian jurist Yusuf al-Qaradawi spoke out in clear support of the revolutions.[14] Qaradawi appealed to the principles of Shari'ah in arguing that there was a religious and moral obligation upon Muslims to support revolutions against despotism, degradation, and injustice. Importantly, Qaradawi reasserted a position articulated years earlier in which he argued that a proper understanding of Shari'ah would give precedence to a democratic system of governance over any system of government that would implement the technical positive commandments of the Islamic legal tradition regardless of the outcome. According to Qaradawi, democracy or a political system that honors and upholds human dignity is more fundamental to the fulfillment of Shari'ah than the enforcement of a set of positive legal commandments that ultimately might or might not lead to the realization of justice.

One of the most important Shari'ah-related developments since the beginning of the Arab Spring was a proclamation issued by Shaykh al-Azhar Ahmad al-Tayyib on February 16, 2011. The proclamation (known as *Wathiqat al-Azhar*) was issued after extensive meetings and discussions with Egyptian scholars and intellectuals, but it was ultimately adopted as a normative position on the role of Shari'ah in modern democratic Muslim states.[15] *Wathiqat al-Azhar* set forth the following. First, it stated that Shari'ah endorses the principle of majoritarian rule; therefore, whatever legal system is desired by the majority, as long as it upholds the principles of Shari'ah, is also the Islamically mandated and required legal system. Second, it set forth the objectives and principles of Shari'ah, which according to *Wathiqat al-Azhar* are (1) to promote knowledge and *'ilm* (science), (2) to establish justice and equity, and (3) to protect liberty and human dignity. Third, *Wathiqat al-Azhar* asserted that any political system capable of upholding the basic moral values and natural principles of justice, known to and shared by all religions, is as if mandated by Islam. Fourth, the *Wathiqah* affirmed that democracy is a fundamental and basic objective of any Shari'ah-based system because it is the political system most capable of leading to (1) upholding the dignity of all citizens, (2) prohibiting cruel and degrading treatment and torture, and (3) bringing an end to political and economic corruption and despotism.

The proclamation went on to state that the protection of human dignity, the prohibition of cruelty and torture, the elimination of corruption, and the end of despotism are, in turn, basic and fundamental Shari'ah values. Finally, the proclamation affirmed that as an institution, al-Azhar calls for a system of governance that respects the rights of all citizens and that despotism is inherently and fundamentally a breach of Shari'ah. According to the *Wathiqah*, among other things, despotism creates social ills such as cowardice, hypocrisy, social alienation, and a lack of a collective or communal ethos, all of which are fundamentally at odds with Shari'ah.

At the most basic level, *Wathiqat al-Azhar* underscores the reality that the Shari'ah, its role, and its function continue to be dynamically renegotiated by those who consider the Shari'ah to be authoritative and influential in their lives. *Wathiqat al-Azhar* will reverberate through Islamic history, but in what ways and to what end is impossible to say. Since the democratic elections in Egypt, Tunisia, and Libya, in each of these countries, there has been an ongoing active process of negotiations about the role and nature of Shari'ah in relation to constitutional and democratic systems of government. Perhaps these political developments, not just in countries directly impacted by the Arab Spring but also in Malaysia and Indonesia, indicate that although the twentieth century ended with a real crisis in the structures of Shari'ah authority, the twenty-first century might witness the birth of equally dynamic and energetic structures of legitimacy and authoritativeness.

Conclusion

The legal tradition of Islamic law continues to carry considerable normative weight for millions of Muslims around the world and also continues to influence, to one degree or another, the legal systems of a number of countries. The crisis of authority plaguing Islamic law today does not affect its relevance or importance. It does mean that Islamic law is going through a period in which Shari'ah has lost the effective means for regulating the reasonableness of the determinations generated on its behalf or attributed to it. In the contemporary age, many voices speak in the name of Shari'ah and some of these voices are quite unreasonable. However, there are many indications that, as attested by its dynamic historical record, Shari'ah as a normative set of values will reinvent the epistemological instrumentalities for its continued legitimacy and authoritativeness and will in due time find its new reasonable equilibrium in Muslim societies.

Notes

1. Subhi Mahmasani, *Falsafat al-Tashri' fi al-Islam: The Philosophy of Jurisprudence in Islam* (Leiden, the Netherlands: E.J. Brill, 1961), 172–175; Muhammad Abu Zahrah, *Usul al-Fiqh* (Cairo: Dar al-Fikr al-'Arabi, n.d.), 291; Mustafa Zayd, *al-Maslahah fi al-Tashri' al-Islami wa Najm al-Din al-Tufi*, 2nd ed. (Cairo: Dar al-Fikr al-'Arabi, 1964), 22; Yusuf Hamid al-'Alim, *al-Maqasid al-'Ammah li al-Shari'ah al-Islamiyyah* (Herndon, VA: International Institute of Islamic Thought, 1991), 80; Muhammad b. 'Ali b. Muhammad al-Shawkani, *Talab al-'Ilm wa Tabaqat al-Muta'allimin: Adab al-Talab wa Muntaha al-'Arab* (Cairo: Dar al-Arqam, 1981), 145–151.
2. A more historical translation for text would be *matn* or *khitab*.
3. Joseph Schacht, *An Introduction to Islamic Law* (Oxford: Oxford University Press, 1983), 37–48. See also, Patricia Crone and Martin Hinds, *God's Caliph: Religious Authority in the First Centuries of Islam* (Cambridge: Cambridge University Press, 1986), 43–57; Norman Calder, *Studies in Early Muslim Jurisprudence* (Oxford: Clarendon Press, 1993), 198–222.
4. Schacht, *Introduction*, 45–48. See also, Noel J. Coulson, *A History of Islamic Law* (Edinburgh, UK: Edinburgh University Press, 1995), 53–61, who considers al-Shafi'i to have

been the "master architect" of Islamic jurisprudence. For a refutation of this view, see Wael B. Hallaq, *Shari'a: Theory, Practice, Transformations* (Cambridge: Cambridge University Press, 2009), 30–35; idem, "Was al-Shafi'i the Master Architect of Islamic Jurisprudence?" *International Journal of Middle East Studies* 25 (1993): 587–605; Yasin Dutton, *The Origins of Islamic Law: The Qur'an, the Muwatta, and Madinan 'Amal* (Surrey, UK: Curzon Press, 1999), 4–5.

5. Mahmasani, *Falsafat al-Tashri' fi al-Islam*, 59; Badran Abu al-'Aynayn Badran, *Usul al-Fiqh* (Cairo: Dar al-Ma'arif, 1965), 322; Subhi al-Salih, *Ma'alim al-Shari'ah al-Islamiyyah* (Beirut: Dar al-'Ilm li al-Malayin, 1975), 46; Mohammad Hashim Kamali, *Principles of Islamic Jurisprudence*, rev. ed. (Cambridge: Islamic Texts Society, 1991), 285.

6. Mahmasani, *Falsafat al-Tashri' fi al-Islam*, 200–202; Ahmad b. Muhammad al-Zarqa, *Sharh al-Qawa'id al-Fiqhiyyah*, ed. Mustafa Ahmad al-Zarqa, 4th ed. (Damascus: Dar al-Qalam, 1996), 227–229; C. R. Tyser, trans., *The Mejelle: Being an English Translation of Majallah-el-Ahkam-Adliya and a Complete Code on Islamic Civil Law* (Lahore, India: Punjab Educational Press, 1967), 8.

7. In jurisprudential sources this field is known as *'ilm al-tarjih* or *'ilm al-ta'arud wa al-tarjih* or *'ilm al-ta'dil wa al-tarjih*—the field of conflict and preponderance or the field of balance and preponderance.

8. Bernard G. Weiss, *The Search for God's Law: Islamic Jurisprudence in the Writings of Sayf al-Din al-Amidi* (Salt Lake City: University of Utah Press, 1992), 734–738.

9. Jalal al-Din 'Abd al-Rahman b. Abi Bakr al-Suyuti, *Ikhtilaf al-Madhahib*, ed. 'Abd al-Qayyum Muhammad Shafi al-Bastawi (Cairo: Dar al-I'tisam, 1404 A.H.), 22–23; Dutton, *The Origins of Islamic Law*, 29; Crone and Hinds, *God's Caliph*, 86.

10. See Hallaq, *Shari'a: Theory, Practice, Transformations*.

11. John Makdisi, "The Guilds of Law in Medieval Legal History: An Inquiry into the Origins of the Inns of Court," *Cleveland State Law Review* 34 (1985–1986): 3–18.

12. Muhammad Said al-Buti, *Dawabit al-Maslahah fi al-Shari'ah al-Islamiyyah* (Mua'ssasat al-Risalah, n.d.) 178–189; Muhammad Khalid Masud, *Islamic Legal Philosophy: A Study of Abu Ishaq al-Shatibi's Life and Thought* (New Delhi, India: International Islamic Publishers, 1989), 165, 174–175; Wael B. Hallaq, *A History of Islamic Legal Theories: An Introduction to Sunni Usul al-Fiqh* (Cambridge: Cambridge University Press, 1997), 208.

13. The Saudi Grand Mufti, Sheikh Abdul-Aziz al-Sheikh, spoke out against the protests, claiming that they were orchestrated by the "enemies of Islam." *See*, "Saudi Top Cleric Blasts Arab, Egypt Protests-Paper," *Reuters Africa*, February 5, 2011, http://af.reuters.com/article/egyptNews/idAFLDE71403F20110205. Shaykh al-Rajhi, a Saudi jurist, issued a fatwa condemning the protests. *See*, Shaykh Abd al-Aziz Abd Allah al-Rajhi, *Fatwa on the Egyptian Revolution*, February 8, 2011, http://www.dd-sunnah.net/forum/showthread.php?t=98063. *See also*, "Saudi Scholars Forbid Protest Calls," *Al Jazeera*, March 6, 2011, http://english.aljazeera.net/news/middleeast/2011/03/201136154752122275.html.

14. For a brief account of his address, see David D. Kirkpatrick, "After Long Exile, Sunni Cleric Takes Role in Egypt," *New York Times*, February 18, 2011, http://www.nytimes.com/2011/02/19/world/middleeast/19egypt.html.

15. For brief accounts of his speech in English, see "Al-Tayeb: Al-Azhar Supported Revolution," *News Pusher*, February 16, 2011, http://www.newspusher.com/EN/post/1298400531-2/EN-/al-tayeb-al-azhar-supported-revolution.html; "Al Azhar Sheikh Calls for a Speedy Transition to Democracy," *Islamopedia*, February 16, 2011, http://www.islamopediaonline.org/news/al-azhar-grand-sheikh-calls-speedy-transition-democracy.

Further Reading

Abou El Fadl, Khaled. *And God Knows the Soldiers: The Authoritative and Authoritarian in Islamic Discourses* (Lanham, MD: University Press of America, 2001).

Abou El Fadl, Khaled. *Speaking in God's Name: Islamic law, Authority and Women* (Oxford: Oneworld Publications, 2001).

Abou El Fadl, Khaled. *The Great Theft: Wrestling Islam from the Extremists* (San Francisco, CA: HarperSanFrancisco, 2005).

Calder, Norman. *Studies in Early Muslim Jurisprudence* (Oxford: Clarendon Press, 1993).

Crone, Patricia and Martin Hinds. *God's Caliph: Religious Authority in the First Centuries of Islam* (Cambridge: Cambridge University Press, 1986).

Dutton, Yasin. *The Origins of Islamic Law: The Qur'an, the Muwatta', and Madinan 'Amal* (Surrey, UK: Curzon Press, 1999).

Hallaq, Wael B. *A History of Islamic Legal Theories: An Introduction to Sunni Usul al-Fiqh* (Cambridge: Cambridge University Press, 1997).

Hallaq, Wael B. *Shari'a: Theory, Practice, Transformations* (Cambridge: Cambridge University Press, 2009).

Kamali, Mohammad Hashim. *Principles of Islamic Jurisprudence*, rev. ed. (Cambridge: Islamic Texts Society, 1991).

Mahmasani, Subhi. *Falsafat al-Tashri' fi al-Islam: The Philosophy of Jurisprudence in Islam* (Leiden, the Netherlands: E.J. Brill, 1961).

Makdisi, John. "The Guilds of Law in Medieval Legal History: An Inquiry into the Origins of the Inns of Court." *Cleveland State Law Review* 3 (1985–1986): 34.

Masud, Muhammad Khalid. *Islamic Legal Philosophy: A Study of Abu Ishaq al-Shatibi's Life and Thought* (New Delhi, India: International Islamic Publishers, 1989).

Weiss, Bernard G. *The Search for God's Law: Islamic Jurisprudence in the Writings of Sayf al-Din al-Amidi* (Salt Lake City: University of Utah Press, 1992).

CHAPTER 2

SALAFIYA, MODERNISM, AND REVIVAL

ABDULLAH SAEED

THIS essay[1] explores aspects of the project of "reform" associated with the Modernist-Salafiya movement (or Modernist-Salafism), the movement's precursors, the context of its emergence and key figures associated with it, including Jamal al-Din al-Afghani (d. 1897), Muhammad ʿAbduh (d. 1905), and Muhammad Rashid Rida (d. 1935), and aspects of their thought. As its focus is on Modernist-Salafiya in the context of mid-nineteenth- to twentieth-century Islamic modernism, it does not explore other movements that have been described as "Salafi" in contemporary Islamic literature, for instance the Islamist-Salafism of the Muslim Brotherhood (Egypt); the Puritanical-Salafism of the followers of Muhammad b. Abd al-Wahhab (d. 1792); or the Militant-Salafism of Usama Bin Laden (d. 2011), Ayman al-Zawahiri, and their followers. The Modernist-Salafiya movement with which this article is concerned has little to do with these other forms of Salafism and can be distinguished from these trends in terms of their basic outlook, approaches to text and interpretation, and priorities, strategies, and arguments for reform. In fact, it could be argued that using the term "Salafiya" itself is problematic as far as the Modernist-Salafiya movement is concerned. Given these concerns, in this essay, in order to keep a clear distinction between this modernist movement labeled "Salafiya" and other conservative movements labeled "Salafi," I will use the term "Modernist-Salafiya" throughout the essay to refer to the reformist movement, championed by figures such as Afghani, ʿAbduh, and Rida.

Some of the key concerns of the Modernist-Salafiya included the urgent need to reform Islamic thought so that Muslims could meet and respond to modern challenges; the need to give up blind imitation of early scholars, particularly in the legal sphere; flexible interpretation of Islam's primary sources (the Qur'an and Sunnah) so that institutions commensurate with modern conditions could be developed; emphasizing scientific knowledge as a way to catch up with the West; the proposition that revelation does not clash with reason; the need to reform Islamic education by introducing modern disciplines and reforming curricula and methods of teaching; an emphasis on more rights for women; and, more importantly, the return to a simpler Islam,[2] such as that originally practiced by the earliest generations of Muslims (*salaf*).[3] It is from this last emphasis that these otherwise "modernists" came to be labeled "Salafi."

Renewal, Reform, and Ijtihad

The terms *tajdid* (renewal) and *islah* (reform) often arise in modern debates on reform in Islamic thought. Historically, the term *mujaddid* (from *tajdid*) referred to a renewer and was often associated with a scholar who "renovated" belief in and practice of the Sunnah (Traditions) of the Prophet.[4] Opposing *bid`ah* (innovation in religious matters), a renewer supposedly scraped away "innovations" that had accrued with the passing of time, taking Islam back to its first sources: the Qur'an and the Sunnah. In the modern period the term *islah* appears to be more frequently used to refer to renewal and reform.

The idea of renewal and reform has always been part of Islamic tradition. Although Islamic theology does not recognize the rise of prophetic figures after Prophet Muhammad, Muslims accept that at different times and in different parts of the Islamic world renewers and reformers have emerged, challenging the status quo and arguing for change.[5] The issues they dealt with, however, naturally varied according to time, place, and circumstances.

The task of renewal has been generally attributed to those with the skills to perform *ijtihad*: those who could independently derive legal opinions from the Qur'an and the corpus of Traditions of the Prophet. A *mujtahid*—a person able to perform *ijtihad*—can either be an "absolute" *mujtahid*, a title usually reserved for the "founders" of the schools of law (for example, Abu Hanifa, Malik, Shafi'i, and Ahmad b. Hanbal) or an "affiliated" *mujtahid*, a scholar with the ability to derive rulings using the principles and guidance given by an absolute *mujtahid*.[6]

Ijtihad, and who had the ability or authority to undertake it, was a key issue in Muslim reformist thought during the eighteenth and nineteenth centuries. Some scholars argued for absolute *ijtihad*, while others permitted affiliated *ijtihad*. Shah Wali Allah (d. 1762)[7] and Muhammad b. Ali al-Sanusi (d. 1859)[8] belonged to the category of affiliated *mujtahids*. Shah Wali Allah was primarily concerned about the pervasive Hanafi fanaticism that he observed in his community. Instead of condoning this he was more inclusive and argued for a synthesis of all of the schools of law.[9] Al-Sanusi believed that he had the right to exercise *ijtihad* within the Maliki school of law, to which he belonged, with freedom to accommodate the other schools of law. In contrast, Muhammad b. Ali al-Shawkani (d. 1834), the Yemeni Zaydi scholar, felt that he had the right and the knowledge to exercise absolute *ijtihad*. He opposed *taqlid* (blind acceptance of or submission to legal methodology), where a Muslim simply followed the legal rulings of a scholar and/or legal school, rather than personally attempting to understand God's will.[10] For al-Shawkani, believers were equal—through assiduous study any member of the Muslim community could be elevated to the rank of *mujtahid*.[11] In line with this approach, Muhammad Ahmad al-Mahdi (d. 1885) also argued that *taqlid* should be replaced by *ijtihad* and that the Qur'an and Sunnah should be the basis of legal rulings.

Precursors of the Modernist-Salafiya Movement

Although the Modernist-Salafiya movement that emerged during the nineteenth century was a response to the modern context of the time, it relied heavily on some of the key ideas of renewers from the previous two centuries. While responding to very different contexts the movement's forerunners, from places as diverse as India, Arabia, and North Africa, argued against blind imitation (*taqlid*) as well as the fanatical following of the earlier schools of law (*madhhabs*).[12] Among those who had an impact on nineteenth-century Modernist-Salafiya thought, albeit in varying degrees, were Shah Wali Allah, Muhammad b. Abd Al-Wahhab and Muhammad b. Ali al-Sanusi.

In India, the legacy of Ahmad Sirhindi (d. 1624), founder of the Sufi order of Mujaddidi Naqshbandiya, was carried on by Shah Wali Allah. Like Abu Hamid al-Ghazali (d. 1111) before him, Shah Wali Allah was able to draw on vast scholarship and apply key Islamic intellectual and spiritual disciplines, including Sufism, philosophy, law, and *hadith*, to the issues that concerned him.

In legal thought Shah Wali Allah developed a form of critical (and some would say "liberal") thinking that was almost unequalled in his time. He argued that divine laws were often connected to the context of the prophets and their communities to whom those laws were given:

> You should know that the divine laws of the prophets, may peace be upon them, differ due to reasons and beneficial purposes. This is because the religious rituals of God were rituals for intended purposes and the quantities in their legislation take into account the situation and the customs of those on whom they were imposed.[13]

His substantial intellect, which left its mark on figures such as Sayyid Ahmad Khan (d. 1898) and Muhammad Iqbal (d. 1938), can be seen in the *Hujjat Allah al-Balighah (God's Conclusive Argument)*, one of his most widely known works. For many prominent reformers of the modern period Shah Wali Allah was a "modernizer" who responded to the crisis of his time with moderation and a search for the spirit behind the specific injunctions of Islamic traditions.[14] Many important reformers of the modern era, particularly on the Indian subcontinent, were almost direct inheritors of his intellectual legacy.

In Arabia, Muhammad b. Abd al-Wahhab (d. 1792) believed that Islam in much of Arabia had descended into a superstitious folk religion that was very similar to the religion that existed in pre-Islamic times in Hijaz. He felt that this compromised the unity of God (*tawhid*) and therefore sought to purify Islam by focusing on polytheism (*shirk*) and the unity of God and rejecting all forms of innovation (*bid'ah*). In law he followed the Hanbali school and was influenced by key figures such as Ibn Taymiya (d. 1328) and Ibn al-Qayyim (d. 1350). His followers came to be referred to by the pejorative term "Wahhabi," although they themselves used terms such as *muwahhidun* ("unitarians") or followers of the way of the *al-salaf al-salih* (righteous ancestors).[15]

Muhammad b. Abd al-Wahhab's writings, though few, addressed some of the issues that concerned key reformers of the eighteenth century: return to the pristine purity of the Islam of the Qur'an and the Sunnah; rejection of the blind following of earlier scholars; and an emphasis on some form of *ijtihad*.[16] He particularly argued for a return to the methodology of the *salaf* and a literal reading of the Qur'an, as far as the theological question of the names and attributes of God were concerned. Unlike many other reformers, he vehemently rejected popular Sufi practices, such as venerating saints and revering their tombs as shrines, describing such practices as heretical and against Islam.[17]

His main work, the booklet *Kitab al-Tawhid* (Book of the Unity of God), focused on notions of *tawhid* and *shirk*. Based on a literal reading of the Qur'an and those hadith texts he chose to focus on, Ibn Abd al-Wahhab associated *shirk* with matters such as seeking help and intercession from anyone other than God[18] ; what he referred to as "saint worship";

celebrating the birthday of Prophet Muhammad; and sacrificing an animal to any being other than God or on any occasion not clearly spelled out in the hadith. Although he argued for strict adherence to the teachings of *tawhid* and observance of the *Shari'ah,* he did not hesitate to bypass the formulations of the four *madhhabs* when necessary.[19] However, unlike Shah Wali Allah, Ibn Abd al-Wahhab was not keen to consider the impact of time, space, and cultural specifics on the formation of law. Skeptical of philosophy and rational intellectualism, Ibn 'Abd al-Wahhab was prone to stand by the "letter" of the scripture rather than by its "spirit."[20] Thus for him Islamic reform meant a movement back in time, away from the present situation toward the more glorious past, in order to re-experience Islam anew.[21]

The Sanusiya movement, founded by Muhammad b. Ali al-Sanusi (d. 1859), also emerged in the context of concern to regenerate the moral and social fiber of Muslim society, particularly in North Africa.[22] As al-Sanusi looked at Muslim societies around him he realized their degraded state from a religion moral and a sociopolitical point of view. The more he contemplated this state of affairs, the more he realized how important it was for Muslims to return to the pristine purity of the Islam of the Prophet and the *salaf*.[23]

However, al-Sanusi's awareness of the Ottoman administration in North Africa and what he believed to be its unjust rule led to conflict with the authorities. He had to move frequently, not only in search of knowledge but also because of his political views. This led him from Fez to Algeria, Tunisia, Libya, Egypt, and Hijaz. During his travels he came under the influence of various Sufis (mystics) from the Tijaniya, Shadhliya, and Qadiriya orders.[24]

His difficulties with religious and political authorities, however, followed him. In Egypt his teachings aroused the ire of the *ulama* (scholars) of the Azhar seminary and made the political authorities suspicious, given his criticism of their atrocities and injustices. Despite these difficulties he established a series of *zawiyas* (hostels for accommodating members of Sufi orders and their visitors) and attracted numerous disciples.[25] By the time he died in 1859, Muhammad b. Ali al-Sanusi had become so influential that the Ottoman authorities had to give his institutions some form of recognition. His work was continued by his son Muhammad, who eventually became the leader of the Sufi order established by al-Sanusi.[26]

Among the important teachings of the Sanusiya movement was a focus on returning to the Islam of the early Muslims; purification of Islam from various heresies and innovations; and a simpler and purer form of religion and practice.[27] Although they maintained a strong emphasis on the spiritual dimension of Islam (hence Sufism), they rejected Sufi practices such as music, dance, and singing, which some Sufis use to facilitate their spiritual journey toward God. The Sanusiya were also keen to combine Sufism with a following of the law that avoided blind imitation and legalism. Thus, they emphasized a moderate, less fanatical version of Islam and a more liberated understanding of the faith. Their flexibility was demonstrated by the fact that they did not adhere to one particular school of law, just as they did not follow one particular Sufi order. They were eclectic, bringing together a range of approaches and schools.[28]

The Context of the Modernist-salafiya Movement's Emergence

With the coming of the modern era (from the mid-nineteenth century), the tradition of religious renewal and reform continued in a more intensive way than ever before. The era ushered in the military and political confrontation of Western powers with Muslim states where Muslims were defeated militarily, politically, economically, and intellectually. For many Muslim reformers, the West had developed superior intellectual skills to which it owed not only its power but also its economic ascendancy. As the confrontation between the West and the Muslim world was sudden and comprehensive, and as the Muslims faced modernity not gradually and piecemeal but in a highly developed form, they had little time to adjust. The impact of the West (and Western modernity) required a response commensurate with the enormity of this challenge.[29] Thus, modernist movements and thinkers emerged across the Muslim world—from Egypt (where Muhammad ʿAbduh became prominent) to India (where Sayyid Ahmad Khan and Muhammad Iqbal were based) and Ottoman Turkey where Namik Kemal (d. 1888) and Mehmet Akif (d. 1936) lived.

For modernists, reform was a key theme. Figures such as Jamal al-Din al-Afghani (d. 1897) argued that Muslims should have a reform movement to renew Islamic heritage, like those that had arisen in Christian Europe under Martin Luther and others. For many modernists, the advent of modernity demanded a reappraisal of Islamic intellectual traditions, which required giving up the blind imitation of early scholars.[30] They argued for a flexible reinterpretation of Islam and its sources that would help Muslims to develop institutions commensurate with modern conditions. A return to Islam as it was originally practiced would inject into Muslim societies the intellectual dynamism required to catch up with the West. Islam would then gain its proper place in the world. To achieve this, political, legal, and educational institutions had to be reformed.

For many modernists of the nineteenth century the supremacy of Europe/the West had occurred as a result of the West's advances in the fields of modern science and technology. Although they had to be discerning in what they borrowed from the West, Muslims were encouraged to embrace these developments. Reform of Islamic education was another key issue. To modernize "Islam," Ahmad Khan, for example, wanted Indian Muslims to adopt modern ways of learning and knowledge, moving away from the antiquated ways of the *madrasahs* (traditional seminaries). In his view this education system was outmoded and in dire need of change. Modern science was crucial to his educational vision, and much of what he termed his "new *kalam*" (dialectical theology) sought to harmonize the tenets of modern natural sciences and philosophy with the doctrines of Islam.[31]

For some modernists, a study of the new sciences was necessary even to preserve the legacy of medieval Islamic learning.[32] Ahmad Khan was convinced that Indian Muslims would never find a place in the civilized world unless they acquired Western knowledge and developed their society along the lines of Europe:

> I state it unambiguously: if people do not break with *taqlid* and do not seek that light which is gained from the Qur'an and *hadith* and if they are going to prove unable to confront religion with present-day scholarship and science, then Islam will disappear from India.[33]

Modernists also argued that revelation does not necessarily clash with reason. In this respect an effort was made to revive Islam's rationalist philosophical tradition. Even those theses held by the long-discarded rationalist Muʿtazilis came into vogue among some modern scholars. Based on the views of the eighteenth- and nineteenth-century reformers about the *salaf*, modernists also condemned what they saw as deviations and accretions unworthy of the *al-salaf al-salih*.

Jamal al-Din al-Afghani was among a small but influential number of thinkers who defended rationalism and critical thinking while insisting that religion (especially Islam) had an important social function.[34] Afghani emphasized the compatibility of Islam and modernity,[35] stressing that Muslims could benefit from European successes without undermining Islamic values or culture.[36] Indeed, instead of subscribing to the view that rationalism and sciences were Western imports, he argued they were traditional elements of Islamic culture.[37] Afghani defended both empiricism (Western science) and rationalism because he felt that both were necessary to advance Islamic civilization. In his view Western science was needed to bring about the military and material advances that would make the Muslims (particularly in the heartlands of Islam) competitive with Europe. He also believed that wealth and technology were important, in and of themselves, as means to improve oneself and the world. God had also given humankind the gift of reason for this purpose, in his view.[38] However Afghani did not go as far as to accept that civilizational advance required the uncritical assimilation of European models.

Afghani also believed that religion would be the "cause" of material and moral progress in the world because it inculcated and encouraged morals, fostered intellectual development, and (especially in Islam) provided a uniform legal code.[39] Afghani felt that prophetic religion in general and Islam in particular civilized "barbarous" people by teaching them skills such as self-restraint and abstract thought. This not only improved their individual character but also established the conditions necessary for higher capabilities such as justice and wisdom, precursors necessary for society as a whole to advance.[40] In this regard Prophet Mohammed not only introduced a set of eternal truths but also gave birth to a new, progressive Islamic civilization.[41]

Like earlier reformers, Afghani preached a return to the pious ancestors (the *salaf*) but mainly with the broader aim of reviving Muslims' political and military successes from the time of the Prophet and his first successors.[42] According to Weismann, the appeal of Afghani and later Muhammad ʿAbduh lay in their political and rationalist bent rather than in their call for religious reform.[43]

Muhammad ʿAbduh as the Key Figure of the Modernist-Salafiya Movement

Muhammad ʿAbduh (d. 1905) remains perhaps one of the most studied Muslim modernists. He began his career in Egypt, one of the most important intellectual hubs for Muslims at that time.

Despite political difficulties, Egypt encountered Europe earlier than did many other Muslim lands. The modernization program of Muhammad Ali Pasha (Egyptian ruler from 1805 to 1848), with its heavy focus on military and technological know-how, led to Egypt's awareness of the major developments that were taking place in Europe and the degree to which Muslims were being left behind.[44] Without consulting Egypt's religious authorities Muhammad Ali quickly introduced political, economic, and educational institutions into Egypt that soon became an accepted feature of Egyptian life. Spurred on by the incentives of reformist Rifaʿah Rafiʿ al-Tahtawi (d. 1873), Egypt was tempted to borrow indiscriminately from the West, hoping that this would restore to Islam its past glory. At the same time many students were sent to European universities, exposing a small but significant section of the society to the ideals of European thought. These developments led to a duality in Egypt's cultural landscape, between a younger generation who eagerly espoused the ideas of Europe and conservatives who resisted all change.[45] Bridging the gap between these intellectual trends became part of Muhammad `Abduh's vision. As "Westernism" antedated `Abduh's reform (*islah*) project, he was left with little choice but to opt for an inclusive and "pragmatic" approach, open to modern science, among other developments.

Like other reformers of his time `Abduh argued for a return to the "simple" and "pristine" Islam of the Salaf, using *ijtihad* to deal with contemporary problems while referring directly to Islam's primary sources (the Qur'an and Sunnah).[46] According to `Abduh, Islam could be simplified by going back to the time of the Prophet and the earliest Muslims (*salaf*) and purified from the obstacles that had marred its history, allowing a place for reason and modern knowledge. By restoring the simple and pure Islam of the Salaf, `Abduh hoped, in part, to reduce the sectarian differences that had emerged in Egypt. In his view this simplicity of faith was the only way to reduce divisions among Muslims and create a foundation for reform. To promote unity, `Abduh espoused the idea that different schools of thought among Muslims were equally true and acceptable. Addressing debates among Muslims about the attributes of God, `Abduh argued for the recognition of the limitations of human reason and the importance of being humble in our claims to truth.[47]

`Abduh also shunned the theological disputes of earlier generations as irrelevant. In works such as *al-Islam wa al-Nasraniya*, he stressed that religion should be perceived not only as theology but also as civilization. `Abduh did not reject modernity. Instead, he argued that there was no conflict between Islam and modern civilization. In `Abduh's view modernity was not problematic because it was based upon reason. As Islam, too, was based on this notion he could see no conflict. Islam was the religion of *fitrah* (nature), which meant that Islam could not and would not go against nature, natural laws, or the sciences that were emerging based on the study of nature. Any apparent opposition between the two, in `Abduh's mind, was simply because of erroneous interpretations of Islam's primary sources.[48]

One of the most striking aspects of `Abduh's legal thought was in the area of moral law, around which most of his legal deliberations revolved. `Abduh was interested in debates about good and evil and the ability of reason to discern between the two and sought to give reason a higher status in law making than it had been assigned previously among Muslims. One of the questions that earlier Muslim scholars had devoted time to was whether actions in themselves can be judged virtuous or evil and whether, as the Mu'tazilis argued, reason is capable of discovering this difference unaided, for example by revelation. In his attempt to solve this longstanding theological dispute, `Abduh treated the problem of moral law as part of the general question of value, using the term "beautiful" to mean good and the term "ugly" to mean evil.[49] He found that human beings had the essential ability to make this distinction:

> We find essentially, within ourselves the faculty of distinction between what is beautiful and what is ugly.... Tastes may differ—but things *are* either beautiful or ugly.[50]

In `Abduh's view, actions, too, were to be judged according to their consequences. Every action that warded off pain or caused pleasure was, generally speaking, beautiful, while the opposite was ugly. In other words, actions were to be judged by the principle of utility: they were beautiful if beneficial, and ugly if harmful. In this way, as the Mu'tazilis did in the past, 'Abduh maintained that people could use reason to decide whether an action was moral or immoral.

With regards to lawmaking, 'Abduh emphasized not only the indispensability of reason but also the importance of *maslahah* (consideration of public interest). He was also critical of some aspects of Islam's juristic tradition. According to 'Abduh, it was the failure of traditional jurists to appreciate humankind's ability to discern and the practical and liberating qualities of reason that had caused the rigidity of Islamic law. 'Abduh also referred to the difficult language of the classical legal texts and the diversity of opinions that made understanding and applying their rulings a daunting task. In his view law should come from Islam's primary sources, not necessarily from the schools of law. Thus 'Abduh argued that the rulings of the *madhhabs* and their founders were not binding on Muslims as such.[51]

MUHAMMAD RASHID RIDA: TAKING THE MODERNIST-SALAFIYA MOVEMENT TOWARD CONSERVATISM

Muhammad Rashid Rida (d. 1935) has been called the mouthpiece of 'Abduh. While this description shows his reverence for Muhammad 'Abduh and their close relationship, Rida's views were not limited to a reiteration of 'Abduh's. Indeed Rida developed his own distinctive position and legacy during the thirty-year period after 'Abduh's death (1905). Under Rida Islamic reformism took a more conservative turn.[52]

Rida became a devoted disciple of 'Abduh in 1894 and remained as such until his death in 1905. In 1887 he joined 'Abduh in Cairo and in 1898 they published the first edition of their journal, *al-Manar*. This publication remained the primary vehicle for Modernist-Salafiya thought in Egypt, and its contents reflected the broad range of their concerns for Islamic reform: from doctrine and spirituality to the Qur'an and *tafsir* (commentary) and political and legal modernization.[53]

Rida considered the *ulama* one of the major obstacles to the reform of Islamic thought and, by extension, the Muslim world. In the third and fourth volumes of *al-Manar* (1900 to 1902), he cleverly reveals this in a series of articles entitled *Muhawarat al-muslih wa al-muqallid* (literally, "Conversations between the Reformer and the Imitator"). In this work a young Modernist-Salafi intellectually debates with a traditional scholar (*shaykh*) and, buttressing his arguments with a mixture of erudition and earnestness, gradually earns the older man's respect and convinces him of the soundness of his position.[54] Throughout his life Rida criticized the *'ulama*'s aversion to adapting Islam to the new times.[55]

Rida argued that the original conception of legislation in Islam had been obscured by a disease, which he sometimes referred to as congealment (*jumud*) or blind imitation (*taqlid*). In the sphere of law this took the form of slavish obedience to one or another of the four recognized legal schools.[56] Rida recognized the challenge of the modern world and wanted Islam to accept the new civilization so far, and only so far, as it was essential for a recovery of strength.[57] In accepting European civilization, Muslims were only accepting what had once been theirs, for Europe had only progressed because of what they had learned from the Muslims.[58]

Following 'Abduh, Rida believed that the return of Islam to a central position in public life required the restoration and reform of Islamic law. The starting point for him was to develop a modern Islamic legal system. He rejected the authority of medieval law but drew a distinction between different kinds of legal matters when it came to reform. Ritual and worship, on the one hand, were to be regarded as fixed matters, while those related to social laws could be subject to change or adaption by successive generations of Muslims, especially when public welfare required reform.[59] Rida's view of legal reform did not advocate the complete abandonment of the four traditional schools but rather a gradual approximation and amalgamation of them. Like 'Abduh he appealed to the principle of *talfiq* (derivation of rules from material of various schools of Islamic law) but wanted it to be applied more systematically than it had been previously. *Talfiq*, when used in a rational way, was a kind of *ijtihad* and as such legitimate in itself.[60]

Rida also believed that Islamic legal reform required an Islamic government—namely the restoration of the caliphate.[61] He became an ardent defender of the caliphate as the only legitimate form of government for Muslims and wrote a series of articles in *al-Manar* (1922–1923) that would be collected later under the title "The Caliphate or the Supreme Imamate."[62] He contended that the caliphate was superior to Western parliamentary democracy, arguing that *ahl al-hall wa al-'aqd* (those qualified to elect or depose a ruler on behalf of the Muslim community) were like members of parliament but "wiser and more virtuous." Whatever levels of justice Western legislators had arrived at, the Shari'ah had established this first and in a better way.[63]

Rida saw that the process of restoring the caliphate had two stages: first, the establishment of a "caliphate of necessity" to coordinate the efforts of Muslim countries against foreign danger and then, when the time was ripe, the restoration of a genuine caliphate of *ijtihad*.[64] For Rida the dilemma was finding those people who could work together actively to restore the caliphate. He could not find them among the Muslim nations that had been subject to European powers or among the great institutions of learning such as the Azhar in Cairo, Zaytuna in Tunis, or the Deoband seminary in India, nor among the "Westernizers."[65] Rida identified, however, a middle group: the "Islamic progressive party," which in his view had the independence of mind necessary to understand the laws of Islam and the essence of modern civilization at the same time.[66] They would be able to accept the changes that were necessary but relate them to valid principles; in other words, to reconcile change with the preservation of the moral basis of the community.[67] However the realities of the post-WWI period eventually forced Rida to accept political compromises and to shift his reformation to a more assertive conservative position.[68] In this regard his longstanding support for a universal caliphate eventually gave way to a grudging acceptance of an Arab nationalism informed by Islam.[69]

Despite Rida's commitment to Islamic reform and the important role of *al-Manar*, his modernism gave way to an increasing conservatism after WWI. Reacting to the growing influence of Western liberal nationalism and culture in Egyptian life, Rida became more critical of the West. Unlike 'Abduh, Rida had only limited contact with Europeans. Alarmed at what he perceived to be the growing danger of Westernization, he drifted toward a more conservative position.[70] As a supporter of Abd al-Aziz b. al-Saud's revival of the Wahhabi movement in Arabia, Rida emphasized the comprehensiveness and self-sufficiency of normative Islam. In Rida's view the fundamental sources of Islam provided a complete code of life. Thus Muslim reformers need not look to the West for answers but single-mindedly return to the sources of Islam—the Qur'an, Sunnah of the Prophet, and the consensus of the Companions. His increasing conservatism was reflected in his restricted understanding of the term *salaf*. For 'Abduh it was a general reference to the early Islamic centuries, but for

Rida *salaf* was restricted solely to the practice of Prophet Muhammad and the first generation of Muslims.⁷¹

As the forces of secular modernism became more firmly entrenched among Egyptian political elites Rida became increasingly literalist in his understanding of the driving force behind the Salafiya movement. While ʿAbduh had advocated a general spirit of intellectual rejuvenation inspired by the model of the Prophet's early companions, Rida later tended toward a constrained normativity based exclusively on the Qur'an and the Traditions of the Prophet and his companions. In this regard his later orientation was closer to the approach of contemporary groups that go under the banner of Salafism⁷² than to that of ʿAbduh.

In recent times the view that a movement called "Salafiya" should be attributed to the ideas of ʿAbduh and Rida has come under challenge. According to Lauzière, one scholar who challenges this notion:

> Apart from the weight of scholarly tradition, there is little reason to consider al-Afghani and ʿAbduh as self-proclaimed Salafis or proponents of a broad *Salafiya* movement. The fact that both men invoked the pious ancestors, as did many other Muslims before them, does not constitute a sufficient explanation and must not become a red herring. The danger here is to vindicate a problematic narrative of Salafism through *post facto* rationalization, that is, by attributing our own conceptual rationale to past Muslims.⁷³

On the other hand Lauzière also acknowledges that:

> One may posit that they were Salafis because they took the *salaf* as role models for religious, social, and political reform, but such a conceptual declaration has yet to be found in the writings of the reformers. That said, there were individuals within the Islamic modernist network of Muhammad ʿAbduh and Rashid Rida (especially in the urban centers of Iraq and Syria, where Hanbali theology had deeper historical roots) who used the Salafi epithets that had existed since the medieval period.⁷⁴

In his view, Afghani, ʿAbduh, and Rida were a generation and movement of scholars who sought to continue the tradition developed by Ibn Taymiya. They also sought to counter the hegemony of the Ottoman empire and that of the traditional *ulama* whom the empire had fostered. According to Lauzière, ʿAbduh and others were more "tolerant" of theological diversity than their forebears but still followed the "*madhhab al-salaf*."⁷⁵ For him, the belief that Afghani and ʿAbduh spearheaded a movement of Islamic modernism called Salafiya in the late nineteenth century relies more on assumptions than evidence. He argues that contrary to conventional wisdom "and despite numerous attempts to portray these two men as 'Salafis' after the fact, there is still no proof that they ever promoted Salafi epithets, used the substantive Salafiya, or conceptualized a religious orientation of that name."⁷⁶

The Modernist-Salafiya Movement in Other Parts of the Middle East

Despite recent debates about its origins, the Modernist-Salafiya movement with its reformist ideas continued to have influence in various parts of the Middle East and North Africa. In the 1930s, for instance, it concerned itself with criticizing Western ideologies such as secularism and feminism and practices such as the consumption of alcohol and prostitution. The movement spread its influence in wider society through the establishment of free schools,[77] alternatives to the educational institutions provided by the colonial powers, which stressed Arabic language and culture.[78]

In Algeria, Abd al-Hamid b. Badis (d. 1940), a reformer greatly influenced by the ideas of ʿAbduh, became a key figure in the movement. Through his journal *Shihab*, somewhat equivalent to Rida's *al-Manar*, which was published between 1925 and 1939, he had a significant influence on Algerian society. In 1931 he established the Association of Algerian Muslim ʿUlama' (AUMA) to promote his views; however, tensions grew between the worldview of the Modernist-Salafiya and the non-Salafi ʿulama', with the latter accusing the Modernist-Salafiya of Wahhabism. In any case, throughout much of the twentieth century the influence of the Modernist-Salafiya remained strong in Algerian society,[79] and its teachings of reform and return to the pristine purity of early Islam were spread through its schools, press, and mosques. Even in postindependence Algeria its ideas still held sway, largely due to the high level of organization surrounding its activities and the institutions it had established.

In Morocco, while the Salafiya did not enjoy the same sophisticated level of organization of Algeria, the movement still had influence, particularly among society's elite, such as the sultans, ʿulama', and sections of the middle class.[80] It was particularly concerned with eradicating the practice of saint worship from Moroccan Islam and reforming the education system in line with the ideas of ʿAbduh. Among the leading figures of the Modernist-Salafiya in Morocco was Abu Shuʿayb b. Abd al-Rahman al-Dukkali (d. 1937), a friend of Rida known as the Moroccan ʿAbduh, whose eloquence and charisma earned him a wide following.[81]

Concluding Remarks

In the twentieth century two trends of Salafism have emerged: Islamist-Salafism (sometimes referred to as "neo-Salafiya"), represented by the thought of the Muslim Brotherhood of Egypt and Puritanical-Salafism of Wahhabism. While Islamist-Salafism is often discussed in relation to Political Islamism and can be seen, at least to some extent, as an extension of Rida's conservative bent, it should not be confused with the Modernist-Salafiya movement of Afghani, ʿAbduh, and Rida. Movements such as the Muslim Brotherhood, which fall under the banner of Islamist-Salafism, are generally preoccupied with bringing the goals of the Modernist-Salafiya down from an intellectual level to one that can be disseminated among the people by way of *daʿwah*.[82] In many countries the ideas of the Islamist-Salafism have been taken up and converted into political action, resulting in their suppression, to various degrees, and in some cases persecution.

On the other hand Puritanical-Salafis focus on matters that seem to contradict the "oneness of God," such as pilgrimage to the tombs of saints and the appearance of Muslims, including insisting on beards and the veil. They reject any perceived "innovation" in religious matters; are obsessed with "deviant" groups among Muslims who do not follow their way; and have a particular distaste for the *kuffar* (the "infidels"), including interactions with them, their values, and cultural practices as well as traveling to their countries. This usually extends to hatred of the West and its ideologies and trends of thought, such as secularism, modernism, nationalism, and the like. Puritanical-Salafis are also particularly sensitive about people of the opposite sex and encourage segregation, separation, covering, and protection of the "honor" of men. More recently another trend in Salafism has also emerged, known as Miltiant-Salafism (or Jihadi-Salafism).

Salafism, in its varying guises, has been an important trend in Islamic thought for more than a century. It began and developed largely in the context of efforts to revive and renew Islam and Islamic thought during the late nineteenth and twentieth centuries. Faced with the intellectual and economic ascendancy of the West and the onslaught of modernity, the Salafism sought to regenerate Islam by returning to the tradition represented by the "pious forefathers" of the faith. For some reformers, this meant breaking with the tradition of blind imitation and returning anew to Islam's primary sources. For others it meant ridding Islam of the religious innovations that had crept in, returning the religion to its past pristine state. For still others, it meant the total reform and Islamization of the political, legal, and educational institutions of Muslim states.

Salafism has evolved under a number of key reformers, each of whom has brought his own unique insights and vision to the movement in response to the challenges of his national context. Although today the term "Salafi" is at times used synonymously with ultra-conservatism, radicalism, or even militancy, it is only recently that certain Salafi trends (particularly Militant-Salafism) have begun to embrace violence as a means of Islamic revival.

Notes

1. I thank my research assistants Patricia Prentice and Andy Fuller for their generous contributions to research and polishing up of this paper.
2. "Simple" or "simpler" Islam is used in the essay to refer to the Islam as practiced in the first generation of Muslims without the added weight of the intellectual traditions developed from the second century of Islam around areas such as Islamic law, theology, and philosophy.
3. Abdullah Saeed, *Islamic Thought: An Introduction* (Oxon, UK: Routledge, 2006), 134. There are several ideas and points in this essay that rely on the author's *Islamic Thought: An Introduction*, pp. 129–141. See also the references provided there for specific ideas referred to in this essay.
4. Saeed, *Islamic Thought*, 129.
5. Ibid.
6. Ibid.
7. Marcia K. Hermansen, "Translator's Introduction," *The Conclusive Argument from God: Shāh Walī Allāh of Delhi's Hujjat Allāh al-Bāligha*, trans. Marcia K. Hermansen. Islamic Philosophy, Theology, and Science 25 (Leiden: Brill, 1996), xxxi–xxxiii.
8. Knut S. Vikor, *Sufi and Scholar on the Desert Edge: Muhammad b. ʿAli al-Sanusi and His Brotherhood*, Series in Islam and Society in Africa (London: Hurst, 1995), 221–227.
9. Hermansen, "Introduction," xxxi–xxxiii.
10. Bernard Haykel, *Revival and Reform in Islam: The Legacy of Muhammad al-Shawkānī* (Cambridge: Cambridge University Press, 2003), 96, 102.
11. Rudolph Peters, "*Idjtihād* and *Taqlīd* in 18th and 19th Century Islam," *Die Welt Des Islams* 20, nos. 3–4 (1980): 133.
12. Rudolph, "*Idjtihād*," 132–145.

13. Hermansen, *Conclusive Argument*, 263–264.
14. Fazlur Rahman, "Shah Waliyullah and Iqbal: The Philosophers of the Modern Age," *Islamic Studies* 13 (1974): 225–234.
15. Saeed, *Islamic Thought*, 131.
16. Ibid.
17. Ibid.
18. Ibid.
19. Ibid., 132.
20. Ibid.
21. Ibid.
22. Ibid.
23. Ibid.
24. Ibid.
25. Ibid., 133.
26. Ibid., 132.
27. Ibid., 133.
28. Ibid.
29. Ibid., 134.
30. Ibid.
31. Ibid., 136.
32. C. W. Troll, *Sayyid Ahmad Khan: A Reinterpretation of Muslim Theology* (New Delhi: Vikas Publishing House, 1978), 310.
33. Ibid., 128.
34. Margaret Kohn, "Afghani on Empire, Islam, and Civilization," *Political Theory* 37, no. 3 (2009): 398, 401.
35. Ibid., 398, 399.
36. Azzam S. Tamimi, "The Renaissance of Islam," *Daedalus: On Secularism & Religion* 132, no. 3 (2003): 51, 54.
37. Kohn, "Afghani on Empire, Islam, and Civilization," 398, 400.
38. Ibid., 398, 409.
39. Ibid., 398, 410 (citing Afghani, "The Truth about the Neicheri Sect," 169).
40. Ibid., 398, 402.
41. Ibid., 398, 403.
42. I. Weismann, "Between Sufi Reformism and Modernist Rationalism: A Reappraisal of the Origins of the Salafiya from the Damascene Angle," *Die Welt des Islams* 41, no. 2 (2001): 232.
43. Ibid., 232.
44. Saeed, *Islamic Thought*, 137.
45. Albert Hourani, *Arabic Thought in the Liberal Age, 1789–1939* (London: Oxford University Press, 1962), 138.
46. Saeed, *Islamic Thought*, 138.
47. M. Abduh, *Risalat al-tawhid* [*The Theology of Unity*] (Cairo, 1897); trans. I. Musa'ad and K. Cragg, *The Theology of Unity* (London: George Allen & Unwin, 1966), 39.
48. Saeed, *Islamic Thought*, 139.
49. Abduh, *The Theology of Unity*, 66.
50. Ibid., 67.
51. Saeed, *Islamic Thought*, 137–139.

52. John L. Esposito, *Islam and Politics: Contemporary Issues in the Middle East*. 4th ed. (Syracuse: Syracuse University Press, 1998), 64.
53. Ibid., 64.
54. Ana Belen Soage, "Rashid Rida's Legacy," *The Muslim World* 98 (2008): 1, 5. For a study of these Conversations, see Jakob Skovgaard-Petersen, "Portrait of the Intellectual as a Young Man: Rashid Rida's *Muhawarat al-muslih wa-al-muqallid*. (1906)," *Islam and Christian-Muslim Relations* 12, no. 1 (2001): 93–104.
55. Soage, "Rashid Rida's Legacy," 1, 5.
56. Hourani, *Arabic Thought in the Liberal Age*, 235.
57. Ibid., 236 (citing Rida, *al-Khilafa*, 29–30).
58. Ibid., 236.
59. Esposito, *Islam and Politics*, 65.
60. Hourani, *Arabic Thought in the Liberal Age*, 237.
61. Esposito, *Islam and Politics*, 65.
62. Soage, "Rashid Rida's Legacy," 1, 9.
63. Ibid., 1, 10 (citing *al-Manar*, 59, 272).
64. Hourani, *Arabic Thought in the Liberal Age*, 241.
65. Ibid., 242.
66. Ibid., 243 (citing Rida, *al-Khilafa*, 62 p. 104]).
67. Ibid., 243.
68. Esposito, *Islam and Politics*, 65.
69. Ibid., 66.
70. Ibid., 67.
71. Ibid., 67–68.
72. Peter Mandaville, *Global Political Islam* (London: Routledge, 2007), 52.
73. H. Lauzière, "The Construction of Salafiya: Reconsidering Salafism from the Perspective of Conceptual History," *International Journal of Middle East Studies* 42 (2010): 374–375.
74. Ibid., 375.
75. Ibid.
76. Ibid., 384.
77. P. Shinar and W. Ende, "Salafiyya." *Encyclopaedia of Islam, Second Edition*. Edited by P. Bearman, Th. Bianquis, C. E. Bosworth, E. van Donzel, and W. P. Heinrichs (Leiden: Brill, 2010). Brill Online. University of Melbourne. November 8, 2010 http://www.brillonline.nl.ezp.lib.unimelb.edu.au/subscriber/entry?entry=islam_COM-0982.
78. Library of Congress Country Studies Series, "Algeria." http://countrystudies.us/algeria/25.htm, November 8, 2010.
79. Shinar and Ende, "Salafiyya."
80. Ibid.
81. Ibid.
82. Ibid.

References

ʿAbduh, Muhammad. 1897. *Risalat al-tawhid (The Theology of Unity)*. Cairo: trans. I. Musa'ad and K. Cragg. 1966. *The Theology of Unity*. London: George Allen & Unwin.

Esposito, J. L. 1998. *Islam and Politics: Contemporary Issues in the Middle East*. Syracuse: Syracuse University Press.

Haykel, Bernard. 2003. *Revival and Reform in Islam: The Legacy of Muhammad al-Shawkānī.* Cambridge Studies in Islamic Civilization. Cambridge: Cambridge University Press.

Hermansen, Marcia K. 1996. *The Conclusive Argument from God: Shāh Walī Allāh of Delhi's Hujjat Allāh al-Bāligha* (trans. Marcia K. Hermansen). Vol. 25 of Islamic Philosophy, Theology, and Science. Leiden: Brill.

Hourani Albert. 1962. *Arabic Thought in the Liberal Age, 1789–1939.* London: Oxford University Press.

Kohn, M. 2009. "Afghani on Empire, Islam, and Civilization." *Political Theory* 37, no. 3: 398–422.

Knut, V. 1995. *Sufi and Scholar on the Desert Edge: Muhammad b. ʿAli al-Sanusi and His Brotherhood.* Series in Islam and Society in Africa. London: Hurst.

Lauzière, H. 2010. "The Construction of Salafiya: Reconsidering Salafism from the Perspective of Conceptual History." *International Journal of Middle East Studies* 42: 369–389.

Mandaville. P. 2007. *Global Political Islam.* London: Routledge.

Peskes, Esther, and W. Ende. 2010. "Wahhābiyya." *Encyclopaedia of Islam, Second Edition.* Edited by P. Bearman, Th. Bianquis, C. E. Bosworth, E. van Donzel, and W. P. Heinrichs. Leiden: Brill. (online)

Peters, R. 1980. "*Idjtihād and Taqlīd* in 18th and 19th Century Islam." *Die Welt Des Islams* 20, nos. 3–4: 131–145.

Rahman, F. 1974. "Shah Waliyullah and Iqbal: The Philosophers of the Modern Age." *Islamic Studies* 13, no. 4: 7–11.

Saeed, Abdullah. 2006. *Islamic Thought: An Introduction.* Oxon, UK: Routledge.

Scharbrodt, O. 2007. "The Salafiya and Sufism: Muhammad ʿAbduh and his *Risalat al-Waridat* (Treatise on Mystical Inspirations)." *Bulletin of SOAS* 70, no. 1: 89–115.

Shinar, P., and W. Ende. 2010. "Salafiya." *Encyclopaedia of Islam, Second Edition.* Edited by P. Bearman, Th. Bianquis, C. E. Bosworth, E. van Donzel, and W. P. Heinrichs. Leiden: Brill. (online)

Soage, A. B. 2008. "Rashid Rida's Legacy." *The Muslim World* 98: 1–23.

Tamimi, A. S. 2003. "The Renaissance of Islam." *Daedalus: On Secularism & Religion* 132, no. 3: 51–58.

Troll, C. W. 1978. *Sayyid Ahmad Khan: A Reinterpretation of Muslim Theology.* New Delhi: Vikas.

Weismann, I. 2001. "Between Sufi Reformism and Modernist Rationalism: A Reappraisal of the Origins of the Salafiya from the Damascene Angle." *Die Welt des Islams* 41, no. 2: 206–237.

CHAPTER 3

ISLAMIC REFORM BETWEEN ISLAMIC LAW AND THE NATION-STATE

SHERMAN A. JACKSON

In his celebrated 1992 book, *The End of History and the Last Man*, Francis Fukuyama announced that the twentieth century marked the decisive triumph of liberal democracy (along with capitalism) as the incontrovertibly optimal political (and economic) arrangement. Whereas previous ideologies contained fundamental flaws and shortcomings that rendered them temporary modi vivendi, the modern West had at long last arrived at the ultimate form of human government. This terminus ad quem signaled the "end of history" in that it terminated, once and for all, the debate over how human societies should arrange themselves politically. The nation-state, and most optimally liberal democracy, had emerged as the final solution (Fukuyama 1992).

In considering the legacy of twentieth-century Muslim political thought, one wonders if Muslim thinkers and activists, especially in the central lands of Islam, might have effectively preceded Fukuyama to this conclusion and in so doing institutionalized a mode of thinking about, imagining, and analyzing political reality that informs as much as it limits the meaning of Islamic reform as well as the range of its possibilities. To be sure, Muslims continue in significant numbers to contest liberal democracy; and even the notion of democracy itself has produced its share of doubters and naysayers. Still, liberal or illiberal, pro- or anti-democratic, the basic *structure* of the nation-state has emerged as a veritable grundnorm of modern Muslim politics. The basic question now exercising Muslim thinkers and activists is not the propriety of the nation-state as an institution but more simply—and urgently—whether and how the nation-state can or should be made Islamic.[1] This invariably implicates Islamic law, either as the sine qua non of any authentically "Islamic" state or as a flawed, deleterious contagion that threatens to undermine any true, Muslim democracy. On these understandings, the bulk of reformist energy goes either into rendering Shari`ah[2] more adaptable to the norms and dictates of the nation-state, along with its putatively inextricable trappings (viz., democracy, human rights, monopoly over law) or to pointing out its utter incompatibility with the latter. Meanwhile, *no* attention goes to examining the basic structure of the nation-state itself and the extent to which *it* might promote its own set of problems for an Islamic politics, independent of and perhaps only compounded by any commitment to Shari`ah per se. Indeed, the *Western* story of the rise, necessity, and panacean effectiveness of the secular, liberal state appears to have gained acceptance, even among the majority of Muslims, as the *only* relevant story of successful modern political evolution, as a result of which little effort is devoted to exploring ways in which the presumed structural necessities and accoutrements of the modern nation-state might be questioned, modified, and possibly brought into greater conformity with the needs, interests, and aspirations of majority Muslim lands.

In this essay I hope to add another perspective on the question of Islamic reform by highlighting the distinction between the application of Islamic law in general and its application as the basis of a legally monistic, homogenizing nation-state. I shall begin by looking at a fundamental feature of the nation-state that is often overlooked in analyses of and proposals for Islamic reform. From here I will compare this particular feature of the modern nation-state with the basic thrust of the premodern Muslim state, in part to highlight the extent to which the tendency toward legal homogenization among modern Muslims is more indebted to modern than premodern history. I will then look at one of the major problems associated with this tendency to homogenize the law and look at a particular instance of it in modern Egypt. I will end with a comment on secularism as a mode of modern Muslim reform and suggest that, rather than addressing, as it purports to, the problem of religious domination, secularism merely relocates the problem and in so doing fails to solve it.

THE RISE, NATURE, AND UBIQUITY OF THE MODERN NATION-STATE

While precise and universally agreed-upon definitions of the nation-state remain elusive, general accounts of its nature and evolution in sixteenth- to nineteenth-century Europe point to a number of distinctive, if not essential, features (Pierson 1996, 5–34).[3] For our purposes, the most important of these is a particular characteristic that accompanies the nation-state as it comes to full maturity in the twentieth century, when Muslim-majority countries were wresting, incidentally, their independence from their European colonizers and establishing (or inheriting) their own independent modern nation-states.[4] I am speaking here of what anthropologists and sociologists of law commonly refer to as "legal centralism" or "legal monism," according to which all law is and should be state-sponsored law, which is *uniform* and *equally applied* to all citizens across the board, being emphatically *superior* to, if not exclusive of, all other reglementary regimes (Jackson 2006, 158–176, 158–163). At bottom, legal monism might be seen as the cumulative result of the dialectical interaction between the modern state's concern for its territoriality, legitimacy, sovereignty, and monopoly over the legitimate use of violence, as these concerns unfolded in the context of early modern European history.

In response to the so-called Wars of Religion, when the Protestant Reformation divided Europe into endemically warring religious factions, the modern state emerged to marginalize religious prejudice (and loyalty) and secure societal peace and order by monopolizing the means of violence. In effect, this constituted a transfer of ultimate authority and loyalty (and according to some a sense of the holy) from the Church to the state (Cavanaugh 2009,

10). No longer would it be legitimate to kill in the name of religion, only in the name of the state (Cavanaugh 2009, 123–180).[5] But since the state now professed to be neutral and equally the patron of all, all citizens could rest assured that they were equally protected. At the same time, while an infinite plurality of "purely religious" concerns (i.e., deeply held theistic beliefs and ritual practices) might be recognized as falling within the domain of personal or religious freedom, in all matters of a "civil nature" the state would both monopolize and standardize a uniform legal régime and brook no challenge to the absolute and exclusive primacy thereof. Thus, for example, in order to be integrated into the French state in the late eighteenth century, Jews were called upon to give up not their theological "beliefs" but their separate religious laws and judges. For, as stated in the French National Assembly in 1789, to grant Jews citizenship without requiring them to relinquish and renounce their distinctive laws on marriage, divorce, heritage, tutelage, majority, etc. would be like "granting French citizenship to Englishmen and Danes without asking them to cease being Englishmen and Danes" (Szajkowski 1970, 578–579).[6]

By the twentieth century, legal monism would be widely accepted as the sine qua non of almost every nation-state's effective operation.[7] At the same time, bolstered by more fully developed (especially American) notions of equality,[8] legal monism would come to be seen as the most effective means of averting discrimination and effectively relegating some members of society to second-class citizenship. This is clearly reflected, inter alia, in the rise of the hallowed principle of "equality before the law." Yet, despite its theoretical neatness and functional utility, legal monism, along with certain modern constructions of equality and individualism, effectively rules out the possibility of legal pluralism as an acceptable arrangement for accommodating mutually divergent groups within society. Indeed, it seems increasingly difficult to suppress the fact that the modern notion of the "citizen" as an autonomously instantiated individual entails a rather facile ideological pasting over of the reality that modern humans, much like their premodern predecessors, are consciously storied collectives attached to much larger and deeply running narratives that often include sustained commitments to quite particular reglementary regimes and traditions. In sum, the basic theory and presumptions underlying the modern nation-state continue to call upon modern citizens to forfeit substantive aspects of deeply valued regimes and commitments as part of the simple and inevitable price of citizenship. And in this regard, it makes little difference whether the nation-state in question is Islamic, secular, or an attempted hybrid. Nor does it matter whether the regime or commitment to be forfeited was an actual party to the struggle that led to the putative need for the modern state to begin with. This type of forfeiture is simply part and parcel of the basic, fundamental structure of the modern nation-state.[9]

Forfeiture and the Premodern Muslim State

By contrast, the basic structure of premodern "Muslim states" did not require anything near this type or level of forfeiture. In fact, in contradistinction to the "strong state" structure of the modern "Islamic State," which, in its most popular iteration, is essentially a modern nation-state governed by a sociopolitically homogenizing Islamic law, the "weak state"[10] structure of premodern Muslim polities not only assumed legal pluralism, within and without the Muslim community, but openly embraced the reality that the arena for state-sponsored homogenization would be necessarily, if not ideally, limited. Rather than assume or insist, in other words, that Jews, Christians, and other non-Muslims, indeed, even all Muslims, be inducted or assimilated into a single, all-encompassing Muslim sociopolitical identity cum substantive legal order, the Muslim state acquiesced to the opposite reality. Even in the area of criminal law (i.e., outside the sanctum of family law where non-Muslim idiosyncrasy was most manifestly uncontested) Muslim jurists reveal themselves to be not only reconciled with a pluralized public space but also equally at home in a certain antihomogenizing predisposition. For them, neither uncontested Muslim sovereignty nor the full or ideal application of Shari`ah implied the absolute necessity of subjecting all non-Muslims to every aspect of the applied Islamic legal order. Nor did Muslim "political theory" or state sovereignty connote the necessity of non-Muslim forfeiture of any and all commitment to non-Islamic practices and reglementary regimes.

For example, premodern Mâlikî jurists are explicit in their insistence that Islam, that is, one's status as a Muslim, is a formal legal prerequisite (*shart*) for being subject to the Shari`ah-based rules governing adultery/fornication (*zinā*; `Abd al-Wahhâb 2008, 197–198). In other words, non-Muslims were not subject to this rule. The going opinion among Hanifis (with the exception of Abû Yûsuf) was basically identical, while the numerically smaller Shâfi`îs and Hanbalî's dissented. Even the latter schools, however, held opinions on related subjects that underscore the fact that non-Muslims could be exempted from Shari`ah-based rules without this being perceived as either violating any would-be theory of Muslim statecraft or the zealously guarded sovereignty of the Muslim state. For example, the Hanbalî, Ibn Qayyim al-Jawzîyah (d. 751/1350), star pupil of the allegedly puritanical Ibn Taymîya (d. 728/1328) defended the Zoroastrian right to engage in "self-marriage," according to which a man could marry his mother, sister, or daughter, despite what Ibn Qayyim identifies as the morally repugnant nature of this institution.[11] The Shâfi`îs, meanwhile, while extending the rule on *zinā* to non-Muslim "citizens" (*ahl al-dhimmah*), exempt non-Muslim "temporary or permanent residents" (*al-mustāmin*) from its application.[12] Of course, the Shâfi`îs, like all the other schools, exempted non-Muslims from such prescribed punishments (*hadd*/pl. *hudûd*) as those imposed on Muslims for drinking wine.[13]

These views were all proffered and debated in a historical and political context that held out the practical possibility of alternative approaches. Muslims, in other words, at least in practical terms, *could* have opted to pursue much more palpably homogenizing arrangements. In purely theoretical terms, however, beyond the material constraints and allowances of their largely inherited political structure, including the logistical difficulties of extending the effective application of the law over vast geographical areas, it seems that the premodern understanding of Islamic law itself naturally militated against legal monism. Of course, even the resulting legal pluralism could result in any number of "rights," "freedoms," and "exemptions" that modern (and perhaps many premodern) non-Muslims could only experience as discrimination (e.g., "exemption" from military service might be experienced as "exclusion" from such). But even here we should be careful about conclusions that are based solely on modern biases and the largely normalized sociopolitical sensibilities and expectations that evolve out of the normalization of the nation-state. And we should be equally careful about equating modern communities' acquiescence in the face of the many forfeitures they are called upon to make with the total absence of feelings of being discriminated against.

The Wages of Legal Monism in a Majority Muslim Polity: the Case of Copts in Modern Egypt

The point of the foregoing has been simply to underscore the fact that legal pluralism was to the premodern Muslim state what legal monism has become to the modern nation-state. To this we must now add the truism that, in basic structural terms, the modern so-called "Islamic State," at least in its most popular iteration, is far more indebted to the modern nation-state than it is to any premodern Muslim antecedent. This becomes easy to appreciate when we consider that the mere application of Islamic law (tatbîq al- Shari`ah), as *the* recognized regime of a modern Muslim nation-state is commonly deemed to be enough to render a state Islamic. On this filiation, I would like to suggest that some of the anxieties and problems associated with the anticipated rise of so-called Islamic States, most especially (though not exclusively) the treatment of religious minorities, which so exercises Western observers, are at least as much, if not more, a function of the grafted underlying structure of the so-called Islamic State as they are of the substantive content of Islamic law. This is clearly manifested in the fact that modern Muslim states that do *not* apply Islamic law as the exclusive law of the land (and are therefore routinely the target of efforts at Islamization) confront similar if not identical problems. While the tendency has been to assume a causal relationship between these problems and the inalterable nature of Shari`ah as a system divinely legislated rules, a more recent iteration of the problem of religious minorities casts the matter in a palpably different light.

On May 29, 2010, facing a rising tide of petitions from divorced Coptic Christians seeking to contract new marriages, the High Administrative Court in Egypt (*al-Mahkamah al-Idârîyah al-'Ulyâ*) issued orders to the Coptic Church to issue marriage licenses to Coptic divorcees authorizing the latter to remarry. The Court insisted that it was on solid procedural grounds, based on legal provisions unanimously adopted, with Coptic approval, back in 1938. In response to this 2010 order, however, the Coptic Church objected that it was a violation of the principle of religious freedom and of the sovereignty of the Church as the final religious authority for Coptic Christians. The problem, according to Church authorities, was that the Bible (*al-Injîl*) had explicitly stipulated that divorce was on option *only* for aggrieved parties in instances of adultery (*zinâ*).[14] Where there was no adultery or the where the party who had actually committed adultery sought to remarry, the position of the Coptic Church was that this was flatly forbidden.

The decree by the High Administrative Court set off a firestorm. Pope Shanoudah III, leader of the Orthodox Egyptian Coptic Church, protested that the Church would not—indeed, could not—comply with this order. Facing possible charges of contempt, Pope Shanoudah insisted that the 1938 law had been propounded on the basis of teachings that ran counter to the Bible, as a result of which previous Coptic Popes, for example, Pope Macarius III and Pope Kerlos IV, had objected to it.[15] He went on to affirm that marriage (or at least Coptic marriage) was a holy ritual and a fundamentally religious institution in the regulation of which the Coptic Church should and could not be asked to recognize any higher authority.[16] The Coptic laity roundly supported the Pope's position and organized public demonstrations to protest the High Administrative Court's decree.[17] This was joined by highly publicized emergency meetings of the Coptic establishment and even a full quarter page add in the official government daily newspaper, *al-Ahrâm*, part of which read:

> The full membership of the General Confessional Council (*al-Majlis al-Millî al-'Âmm*) fully supports His Holiness Pope Shanoudah III in his recent declarations regarding the obligation to abide by the texts of the Holy Book on the matter of Christian marriage, in accordance with Christian law (*al- Shari`ah al-masîhîyah*). Indeed, the Council deems it entirely unthinkable that any individual would be so bold as to take it upon himself to change the texts of the Holy Book on the basis of any other pretext. Similarly, the General Confessional Council reiterates that no marriage can be considered a Christian marriage unless it is consistent with all the teachings and professions of the Master Messiah, be he glorified. Thus, the Council affirms that the Church considers any marriage that contradicts these teachings to be a civil marriage and not a religious, Christian marriage.[18]

The last line of this declaration entails a critical clarification. Pope Shanoudah III was not denying Coptic Christians the right to seek or obtain subsequent *civil* marriages; in fact, he stated explicitly that those wish to seek and obtain such marriages or divorces are free to do so. This they should do, however, "far away from the Church" and on the understanding that they would not be readmitted to the Church. For the Church, he insisted, "does not recognize civil marriages, and anyone who does not want to be a member of the Church is free not to be (*nahnu lâ na'tarif bi al-zawâj al-madanî wa illî mish 'ayyiz yakun min abnâ' al-kanîsah huwa hurr*)."[19] In sum, Pope Shanoudah was insisting that Coptic Christians were fundamentally defined by their commitment to a religiously based reglementary regime governing marriage and divorce and that they should not be called upon, by dint of their status as citizens of the modern Egyptian state, to forfeit this commitment. By forcing the Church, however, to issue the said marriage licenses, the state was both undermining its religious authority and violating the integrity of the Coptic community as a whole.

But the real significance of all of this, for our purposes at least, emerges when we consider a basic strand of argument adduced by Pope Shanoudah and other Coptic officials in defense of their right to withhold marriage licenses. While certain secular advocates, Muslim and Christian, voiced concerns over what they deemed to be the Church's unwarranted mixing of religion with politics, its threatening the unity and challenging the sovereignty of the Egyptian state and its denying Coptic divorcees the fundamental human right to marry, Pope Shanoudah and Church officials turned to Islam and Shari`ah as their counter. They noted that Islam guaranteed religious minorities the right to preserve their commitment to their own religious law. Indeed, in several pieces published in Egyptian newspapers, Coptic officials went on record invoking what they presented to be a hallowed principle of Islamic law: "When confronted with People of the Book, adjudicate among them on the basis of their own religion (*idhâ atâka ahl al-kitâb fa'hkum baynahum bimâ yadînûn*)."[20] In fact, in one of his weekly sermons, Pope Shanoudah even quoted directly from the Qur'an: "Let the People of the Bible adjudicate according to what God revealed therein. And whoever does not adjudicate in accordance to what God reveals, they are among the corrupt" (5: 47); "Ask the People of Remembrance, if you do not know" (16: 43).[21] Cleary, for the Coptic Church, it was neither Islam nor Shari`ah that were calling upon them to forfeit their commitment to their sacred texts and tradition but the basic, homogenizing structure of the modern Egyptian state. This distinction between the status of the Church under Shari`ah and its status before the decree and authority of the High Administrative Court was thrown into bold relief by a statement by Pope Shanoudah published in the official *al-Ahrâm* newspaper: "We simply ask the judges, if they want to reconcile with the Church, to apply the Islamic Shari`ah (*fa nahnu natlub min al-qudâh an yunaffidhû al-sharî`ah al-islâmîyah idhâ arâdû al-tasâluh ma'a al-kanîsah*)."[22]

It would be wrong, of course, if not disingenuous, to conclude from this clearly tactical approach that Pope Shanoudah III and the Coptic Church were advocating the application of Shari`ah in any general, across-the-board sense, that is, on a par with the Muslim Brotherhood or other such Islamists groups. At the same time, however, it seems abundantly clear that both the Coptic pontiff and the Church recognized an important distinction between the mere application of Shari`ah and applying Shari`ah in the service of the homogenizing, monistic tendencies of a modern nation-state. Applying Shari`ah in the context of the weak state, premodern Muslim model would pose no threat to the Church's authority in general or to the Coptic community's ability to regulate marriage and divorce as it saw fit. Applying Shari`ah, however, as the uniform and supreme law of the land implemented in an undifferentiated, across-the-board fashion would almost invariably call on non-Muslim communities to forfeit numerous and deeply valued aspects of their own, religion-based reglementary régimes.[23] Ultimately, the question in the present case came down not to how the Egyptian state could reconcile Shari`ah with the interests of the Coptic Church and community but to how it could reconcile its own sense of sovereignty and the hegemonic tendencies of its embedded legal monism with Coptic claims to the right to be governed by their own reglementary regime and religious authority regarding marriage and divorce.

Having said all of this, one could ask if the Muslim Brotherhood, for example, or other modern Islamist advocates of an Islamic State would have been any less discomfited by this Coptic claim to judicial exemption than was the secular Egyptian state. After all, an Islamic State is, to all intents and purposes, a nation-state governed by Islamic law. Should the legal monism implied by the nation-state be sublimated into the meaning of "applying Islamic law," this would clearly raise similar difficulties for non-Muslim (and even a number of Muslim) minorities. Here, however, I think it is important to avoid the tendency to compress all calls for an Islamic State into a single, undifferentiated articulation. For rather than a single position on the status and treatment of religious minorities, proponents of the Islamic State demonstrate a range of attitudes and positions. On matters of personal status or family law, they appear more or less accepting of claims of exemption by non-Muslims, especially People of the Book (*Ahl al-Kitāb*). Beyond that, however, attitudes appear to become more nuanced and in some instances even vague.

For example, in his short treatise *Rights of Non-Muslims in Islamic State*, Abu al-A`la Mawdudi, by all accounts one of the major architects and proponents of the modern Islamic State, is unequivocal in granting non-Muslim "citizens" full autonomy in the area of family law:

> All personal matters of the Zimmis are to be decided in accordance with their own Personal Law. The corresponding laws of *Shari`ah* are not to be enforced on them. If anything is prohibited for the Muslims in their personal law but the same is not forbidden to the Zimmis by their religion, they will have the right to use that thing and the courts of the country will decide their cases in the light of *their* Personal Law. (Mawdudi 1961, 15)

Yet, when it comes to criminal sanctions beyond the realm of family law, Mawdudi insisted, with one exception, that "the Penal Laws are the same for the Zimmis and the

Muslims, and both are to be treated alike in this regard. The Zimmis are subject to the same punishment as are the Muslims.... The punishment for adultery is also the same in both cases. In the matter of drinking wine, however, the Zimmis are exempt from punishment" (Mawdudi 1961, 13).

In another articulation, the redoubtable Sayyid Qutb appears a bit more diffident. On the one hand, he cites the standard principle to the effect that the People of the Book "are not to be compelled to follow any rules that do not appear in their religious law (*sharî`atuhum*) and/or are not connected with the public order (*al-niẓām al-`âmm*)."[24] This includes the right to eat pork and drink wine but not to deal in "interest" (*ribā*). It also subjects them to the punishments on theft or adultery.[25] This is all muddled, on the other hand, by what appears to be his limiting these provisions to the early stages of the Prophet's career only to be later superseded by the law of Islam. Thus he writes,

> The binding rule (*qâ`idah*) is to adjudicate in accordance with what God has revealed and nothing else. And they (i.e., Christians) like the Jews will not stand upon anything until they implement the Torah and the Gospels—before Islam—and what has been revealed to them from their Lord—after Islam. All of this is a single Shari`ah by which they are bound. God's final Shari`ah is the operative Shari`ah.[26]

In yet a third articulation, the traditionally trained cleric Shaykh Yûsuf al-Qaradâwî echoes the view of Mawdudi on family matters but partially dissents on the matter of criminal law. He writes:

> As for family relations regarding matters connected to marriage, divorce and the like, they have the choice of applying their own religious laws or seeking adjudication on the basis of our religious law. But they are not to be forced to comply with the religious law of Islam on the grounds that this represents [the state's] standard "Personal Status Regime," as it is called.... As for other matters concerning civil, commercial, administrative and other forms of legislation, their status here is as that regarding any other legislation that may be appropriated from the East or the West based on the consent of the majority. Regarding criminal sanctions, the jurists have established that the prescribed punishments (*al-hudûd*) are not applicable to them except regarding matters that they themselves believe to be illicit, such as theft or adultery/fornication (*zinâ*), not regarding matters that they believe to be licit, such as wine-drinking.[27]

Again, all of these advocates of an Islamic State, with the *possible* exception of Qutb, would recognize non-Muslim claims to exemption in the area of family law. In fact, one gets the sense that this particular feature of the premodern Muslim state is recognized as having been so definitive of a normative Islamic order that no modern arrangement could be deemed truly "Islamic" without it. Beyond the realm of family law, of course, advocates of the modern Islamic State are clearly more homogenizing in orientation. But the antihomogenizing predisposition of the premodern Muslim state suggests that this impetus is more a discontinuation than a continuation of the Muslim past. Indeed, it appears to be far more indebted to the perceived need to accommodate modernity's seemingly seamless introduction of the nation-state structure as the sine qua non of modern politics than it is to any attempt to recapture some presumably normative aspect of classical Islamic statecraft or sovereignty or theory that was somehow tragically lost in the Muslims' early encounter with the hegemonic, modernizing West.

Islamic Reform Between Shari`ah and the Modern State: Secularization or Dehomogenization?

All of this brings us to a consideration of secularization (i.e., removal of Shari`ah from the state apparatus) as a mode of modern Islamic reform. For, while Shari`ah is clearly a central concern for Muslim (as well as non-Muslim, Western) secularists, the modern, not the traditional Muslim, state structure is clearly their point of departure, even if this is not always recognized or openly acknowledged. Unlike any premodern Muslim state, the state that is assumed and contemplated by Muslim secularists has a complete and unassailable monopoly on law and the use of violence; its law is absolutely superior to all other reglementary regimes and is absolutely binding and normative; moreover, its very sovereignty is underwritten by an explicit commitment to legal monism (i.e., there can be only one legal regime uniformly applied across the board). At bottom, the secularization thesis is grounded in the belief that Shari`ah and/or the religious establishment that determines its substance and implementation cannot be effectively reformed to the point that Islamic law could consistently find positive acceptance across the many variegated segments of modern society. As a solution, religious law should simply be separated from the state apparatus, and whatever legal regime ultimately comes to govern society should come as a result of the entire community (i.e., all citizens, Muslim and non-Muslim alike) negotiating its substance via the medium of "civic reason" (an-Na`îm 2008, 7, 29, 97–101).

This is essentially the thesis of Abdullahi an-Na`îm in his latest book, *Islam and the Secular State: Negotiating the Future of Shari`ah*.[28] To be clear, an-Na`îm is not an advocate of European secularism or *laïcité*, wherein the aim is to remove or minimize the influence of religion upon society. He is more an advocate of American-style secularism, where the point is simply to free the state apparatus from the influence of formal religious authority and institutions, leaving society at large free to indulge religious beliefs and sensibilities. And yet, again, his point of departure is clearly the modern legally monistic nation-state. Thus, he allows that, to the extent that individual citizens invoke them in the course and context of their own civic engagement, Shari`ah principles may and should be allowed to serve as a source of public policy and legislation. This, however, should all be "subject to the fundamental constitutional and human rights of all citizens, men and women, Muslims and non-Muslims, *equally and without discrimination*" (an-Na`îm 2008, 28–29).[29] Indeed, he insists, even if the vast majority should hold Shari`ah principles to be binding as a matter of religious conscience, "that cannot be accepted as sufficient reason for their enforcement by the state, because they would then apply to citizens who may not share that belief" (an-Na`îm 2008, 29). In sum, legal monism and the absolute authority of the state's singularly deduced and uniformly applied legal regime is simply an unassailable grundnorm. Shari`ah, for its part, is either incapable of treating all citizens equally or is constituted by substantive laws that would simply result in all citizens being treated equally bad. Secularism, in this context (i.e., separating Shari`ah from the state apparatus) becomes the only viable option because,

> Any and all proposed possibilities of change or development must...begin with the reality that European colonialism and its aftermath have drastically transformed the basis and nature

of political and social organization within and among the territorial states where all Muslims live today. A return to precolonial ideas and systems is simply not an option, and any change and adaptation of the present system can be realized *only* through this local and global postcolonial reality. (an-Na'îm 2008, 31–32)[30]

In other words, the nation-state, including its basic legal monism, is here to stay, and any attempt to improve the political reality of modern humans will have to proceed on the recognition that there are no alternatives to this basic arrangement. Indeed, according to an-Na'îm, it is precisely their inability or unwillingness to recognize or accept this fact that leaves many Muslims laboring under the delusion that there could actually exist in modern times "an Islamic state that can enforce Shari'ah principles as positive law" (an-Na'îm 2008, 32).

Leaving aside the many issues on which one might want to cross-examine Professor an-Na'îm, I would like to return to Pope Shanoudah III and the High Administrative Court of Egypt. Professor an-Na'îm seems to think that the problem of meting out fair treatment to religious minorities is largely solved by secularizing the political order. But Egypt is a secular state,[31] in many ways consistent with Professor an-Na'îm's own normative description thereof: the religious establishment neither dictates the substance nor oversees the implementation of the law, but Shari'ah principles ultimately influence the legal order by way of a certain upward pressure from society at large. And yet, none of this would seem to be of much use to the Coptic Church or community in their quest to preserve the right to restrict marriage licenses as deemed proper. The reason for this, however, has nothing to do with any romantic refusal or inability to recognize or accept the modern state, nor is it in any way connected with Shari'ah per se forming the legal basis of that state.[32] It is, rather, the legal monism that defines Egypt as a *secular* state and the resulting tendency to dictate that Copts be bound by the same rights and restrictions as everyone else in society. Thus, secularization alone would seem to fall short of the needs of the Copts as a religious minority.

We might say the same when it comes to Muslims as a majority. While they all subscribe to the same religious sources (Qur'an, Sunnah, and perhaps precedents upheld in the traditional schools of law), they also subscribe to mutually competing modern and premodern interpretations of these. Ultimately, however, as long as the state is defined by a commitment to legal monism, sizeable groups of Muslims will be called upon to make significant forfeitures of their attachments to these legal regimes and traditions. Secularization, for its part, again, while presumably protecting society from the imposition of any *particular* interpretation of law promulgated by a religious establishment, does nothing to undo the fact that, as long as legal monism remains the norm, *some* single regime will be ultimately—and uniformly—imposed upon the entire populace.

This raises the question, to my mind at least, of whether much of modern Muslim reform has been simply barking up the wrong tree. For neither altering the substance of Islamic law nor separating Shari'ah from the state would seem to solve the fundamental problem of religion-based domination or massive forfeiture. In this context, rather than secularization, Islamic reform might begin with the goal of dehomogenizing modern Muslim states and finding effective ways of reducing the types and degrees of forfeiture imposed upon large and historically constituted groups in society, even as Muslim reformers pay adequate attention to such modern realities as the fact that only highly centralized states can accommodate such massive undertakings as regulating airspace, food and drug integrity, education, highway safety, and a host of others. Indeed, it seems to me, on purely political (i.e., not necessarily religious) grounds, that the secularization thesis is simply inadequate. For no amount of secularization will reduce the type and magnitude of forfeiture demanded by legal monism. And in this context, beyond whatever adjustments Muslims might see fit to make to the actual substance of Islamic law, finding ways to sustain the modern state's capacity to fulfill its many nonlegal functions while reducing the need for legal forfeiture to what is absolutely necessary should be recognized as being among the most pressing goals of any meaningful Islamic reform. This will require, of course, a more critical look at and engagement with the nation-state and its underlying structure. Ultimately, however, if and when Muslim reformers arrive at the point where they can realistically contemplate and effectively pursue the dehomogenization of the nation-state in ways that do not otherwise compromise or undermine its overall efficacy, we might witness not only the end of one history but also perhaps the auspicious beginning of another.[33]

Notes

1. This is actually a reiteration of a point I made back in 1996 in my *Islamic Law and the State: The Constitutional Jurisprudence of Shihâb al-Dîn al-Qarâfî* (Leiden: E. J. Brill, 1996), xiii ff.
2. In this article, I shall limit "Islamic law," or "Shari`ah" to *fiqh*, i.e., the principled deductions of Muslim jurists from the sources of the law and/or established precedents upheld in the schools or madrasahs, ignoring for the moment the equally important and equally legitimate instrument of *siyāsah*, i.e., essentially a "state-owned *maṣlaḥah al-mursalah* (public interest) and *istiḥsān* ('equity')." (See, e.g., F. Vogel, *Islamic Law and Legal System* (Leiden: E. J. Brill, 2000.) While this constitutes an underinclusive (mis)representation of Shari`ah, it is justified in the present context on two considerations: (1) the overwhelming majority of advocates and critics of Shari`ah limit their advocacy and critique to *fiqh*; and (2) even the admission *siyāsah* to the present discussion will change little as long as the state remains committed to legal monism and homogenized regelementary régimes applied uniformly across the board.
3. These include (1) monopoly (or control) of the means of violence; (2) territoriality; (3) sovereignty (i.e., ultimate authority); (4) constitutionality; (5) impersonal power; (6) public bureaucracy; (7) legitimacy; and (8) citizenship.
4. One might note in this context the dates of independence of emerging majority Muslim Middle Eastern and North African states: Syria, 1946; Pakistan, 1947; Libya, 1951; Egypt, 1952; Algeria, 1962; Morocco, 1955; Tunisia, 1956; Sudan, 1956; Iraq, 1958.
5. The alleged role of the "Wars of Religion" in prompting the move to the modern state has been severely challenged by Cavanaugh, where he devotes an entire chapter to "The Creation Myth of the Wars of Religion." Here Cavanaugh speaks of the manipulation of history carried out by proponents of the modern state to serve the crucially felt need to legitimate the secular turn of the modern West and underwrite the absolute necessity and goodness of the modern secular state as a protection from chaos, bigotry, and mortal peril.
6. Of course, the conclusion that this constituted a violation of religious freedom could be averted by the fact that "religion" had now come to be understood as simply "private beliefs." In fact, according to Cavanaugh, this was the whole point of inventing this essentially new understanding of "religion" (i.e., in order to be able to deny public recognition to

religion without this being seen as a violation of religious freedom). As he put it, on this new definition, "Religion is 'inward'; it is essentially about beliefs that cannot be settled publicly to the satisfaction of all by any rational method" (Cavanaugh 2009, 126).

7. Notable exceptions might include, in certain respects at least, Canada, Belgium, South Africa, Singapore, and India.
8. By more fully developed, I am alluding to the fact that while the French, e.g., extolled the value of *equalité*, this did not fully contradict anti-Semitic sentiments. The American delegitimizing of anti-Black racism, on the other hand, seems to have placed the concept of equality on a more absolute footing, no longer susceptible to being surreptitiously deployed and manipulated as a synecdochic "'*âmm yurâdu bihi al-khusûs*," i.e., a general expression intended to have only restricted or qualified application.
9. Indeed, according to Cavanaugh, it was the view of Hobbes that the Behemoth, i.e., civic division and civil unrest grounded in religious differences sponsored and stoked by popes and other religious figures, could only be defeated by obliterating any distinction between temporal and spiritual rule and transferring both coercive power and spiritual authority (i.e., patriotism) to the Leviathan, i.e., "Hobbes's 'mortal god,' the state" (Cavanaugh 2009, 126).
10. By "weak state" I am referring to neither military power nor the ability to exercise requisite control over a populace. Rather, as S. P. Huntington described it, the weak state model is a less centralized model that operates much like a "U," with family and tribe at the upper left extremity and religious, professional, or other public confessions functioning at the upper right, as the highest repositories of commitment, dependence, and sense of belongingness. The state, meanwhile, stands in the valley of the "U" as the very lowest point of commitment, dependence, and sense of belongingness. The modern nation-state by contrast, operates in reverse, i.e., as an inverted "U," where the state functions at the summit as the highest point of commitment, dependence, and sense of belongingness, with family, religious affiliation, etc. operating at the lower extremities (Huntington 2004, 16–17).
11. See his *Ahkâm ahl al-dhimmah*, 3 vols., ed. Y. al-Bakrî and A. A. al-'Arûrî (Beirut: Dâr Ibn Hazm, 1418/1997), 2: 764–769.
12. See, e.g., Shams al-Dîn Muhammad b. Ahmad al-Sharbînî, *al-Iqnâ' fî hall alfâz abî shujâ'*, 2 vols. (Cairo: Matba'at Mustafâ al-Bâbî al-Halabî wa awlâduh, 1359/1940), 2: 179: "*fa kharaja bihi al-musta'man fa innâ lâ nuqîmu 'alayhi al-hadd 'alâ al-mashhûr* (this implies the exemption of temporary and permanent residents; for, according to the going opinion, we do not apply the prescribed punishment (for adultery/fornication) to them)."
13. al-Sharbînî, *al-Iqnâ'*, 2:187.
14. The Church also allowed widowers (*al-Ahrâm*, June 9, 2010, p. 14) to remarry as well as spouses of those who have left the Coptic Church for another religion (*al-Anbâ' al-Dawlîyah*, June 8, 2010, p. 6).
15. *al-Ahrâm*, June 1, 2010, p. 3.
16. *al-Shurûq al-Jadîd*, June 9, 2010, p. 1.
17. *al-Shurûq al-Jadîd*, June 10, 2010, p. 1, p. 3.
18. *al-Ahrâm*, June 8, 2010, p. 9.
19. *al-Shurûq al-Jadîd*, June 9, 2010, p. 1.
20. *al-Dustûr*, June 8, 2010, p. 5; *al-Ahrâm*, June 10, 2010, p. 3 (substituting non-Muslim "citizens" [*ahl al-dhimmah*] for People of the Book [*ahl al-kitāb*]).
21. *al-Anbâ' al-Dawlîyah*, June 8, 2010, p. 6 (where "People of Remembrance" are identified as Christians).

22. *al-Ahrâm*, June 10, 2010, p. 3.
23. In this case, for example, Coptic Christians would essentially be granted the right to no-fault divorce on grounds other than *zinâ*, along with the parallel right to remarry, as is the case in Islamic law.
24. Sayyid Qutb, *Fî zilâl al-qur'ân*, 6 vols. (Cairo: Dâr al-Shurûq, 1417/1996), 2: 894.
25. *Zilâl*, 2: 894.
26. *Zilâl*, 2: 901. But see also the discussion at 2: 893–894, where he appears to limit the aforementioned exemptions to the early stages of the Prophet's career.
27. *al-Aqallîyât al-dînîyah wa al-hall al-islâmî*, 2nd ed. (Cairo: Maktabat Wahbah, 1420/1999), 15–16. In a footnote following his statement on the punishment for adultery/fornication, al-Qaradâwî notes, "Abû Hanîfa held that non-Muslim 'citizens' were only subject to lashes as a punishment for adultery and that they could not be stoned, as Islam (one's status as a Muslim) constituted a legal prerequisite to being rendered eligible for the most exacting sanctions. This is despite the fact that there is much discussion and wide disagreement among the (pre-modern) jurists over the whole question of applying prescribed punishments to non-Muslim 'citizens.'"
28. "This book is an attempt to clarify and support the necessary but difficult mediation of the paradox of institutional separation of Islam and the state, despite the unavoidable connection between Islam and politics in present Islamic societies" (an-Na'îm 2008, 6).
29. Emphasis added.
30. Emphasis added.
31. At least it was at the time this article was written, i.e., before the January 25, 2011, revolution. Whether Egypt will remain a secular state over the coming years remains to be seen.
32. While Shari'ah's forming the basis of a nation-state could lead to problems of forfeiture, my point here is that it is not so much the substance of Shari'ah that raises this problem but the actual dictates of legal monism. In other words, *any* legal regime applied uniformly across the board will raise such problems. In fact, given its explicit allowances to non-Muslims on various issues, Shari'ah would actually seem to raise the least problems.
33. It is interesting that, while an almost preconscious reaction to the notion of legal pluralism in many circles is simply to scoff at it as wildly untenable, just a century ago this is exactly what the West was demanding of and imposing on Muslims in the form of the Ottoman capitulations.

References

'Abd al-Wahhâb, al-Qâdî. 2008. *al-Ishrâf "alâ nukat masâ"il al-khilâf*, ed. A.M.H. Âl Salmân, 4:197–198. Riyadh: Dâr Ibn al-Qayyim.

an-Na'îm, Abdullahi. 2008. *Islam and the Secular State: Negotiating the Future of Shari'ah*. Cambridge, MA: Harvard University Press.

Cavanaugh, William. 2009. *The Myth of Religious Violence*. New York: Oxford University Press.

Fukuyama, Francis. 1992. *The End of History and the Last Man*. New York: The Free Press.

Huntington, Samuel. 2004. *Who Are We?: The Challenges to America's National Identity*. New York: Simon and Schuster.

Jackson, Sherman. 2006. Legal Pluralism between Islam and the Nation-State: Romantic Medievalism or Pragmatic Modernity? *Fordham International Law Journal*. 30.1: 158–176.

Mawdudi, Abul Ala. 1961. *Rights of Non-Muslims in Islamic Law*. Trans. K. Ahmad. Lahore: Islamic Publications. Originally published in K. Ahmad trans., *Islamic Law and Constitution*, 293–321 (Lahore: Islamic Publications, 1960).

Pierson, Christopher. 1996. *The Modern State*. London: Routledge.

Szajkowski, Zosa. 1970. *Jews and the French Revolutions of 1789, 1830 and 1848*. New York: KTAV Publishing.

CHAPTER 4

POLITICAL ISLAM AND THE STATE

JOHN O. VOLL

"Islam is not simply a creed to be preached to the people by pronouncements. It is a comprehensive and manifest path, representing a liberating movement to free all of humanity" (Qutb n.d., 89–90). Sayyid Qutb, the Egyptian Islamist ideologue of the 1960s, affirms a common position among Muslims that Islam is "a complete comprehensive way of life" (Ahmad 1979, 367). For many, this means that in the Islamic tradition, there is no distinction between religion and politics and no separation of church and state. The slogan that Islam is "*dīn* and *dawla*" (religion and state; *dīn wa dawla*) became common among Islamic movements by the middle of the twentieth century. However, for others, Islam as a comprehensive way of life means that Islam is a faith and a community of believers, or *dīn* and *ummah* (community). The changing ways that these key concepts of *dīn*, *dawla*, and *ummah* are defined both reflect the evolution of social and political ideals in the Muslim world and shape the way that programs and political visions are articulated.

During the second half of the twentieth century, issues involved in defining the relationships between religion and state evolved as the nature of modernity itself changed. From the time of World War II until the early decades of the twenty-first century, the transformation of what is called religion from being a traditional obstacle to modernization into the basis for ideologies of postmodern revolutionary challenges to modernity is a significant part of the changing nature of modernity itself.

Islamic discussions about religion and state since World War II reflect the changing nature of global historic conditions. Four broadly defined phases can be identified for purposes of analysis. In the years immediately following World War II, older issues of nationalist opposition to imperialism and of Westernizing-reformist efforts to modernize Muslim societies dominated political and cultural discussions. Then, as most Muslim countries achieved greater independence from European control, a second phase witnessed the articulation of radical ideologies of societal and political transformation, as the new generation of leaders rejected both foreign control and the old-style, socially conservative local political elites. However, by the early 1970s, the programs of both the old-style conservative modernizers and the new radicals became increasingly unpopular.

The third phase, emerging in the 1970s, involved the rise of political opposition articulated in Islamic terms. The first major victory of this new mode was the establishment of the Islamic Republic of Iran in 1979. During the final two decades of the twentieth century, leftist radicalism was replaced by Islamist activism as the major expression of political opposition, creating what came to be called "Political Islam," characterized by calls for the establishment of the Islamic State. The fourth phase began by the end of the century as many began to speak about the "failure of Political Islam." New types of movements and organizations reflecting the processes of globalization and electronic communication became increasingly important.

In each of these four eras, Islamic vocabulary played an important role in providing the terms for the debates. In discussions in the twentieth century, terms such as *dīn*, *dawla*, and *ummah* had central importance. However, these concepts were used in ways that reflect modern understandings and definitions. In this way, asking the basic question, "Is Islam '*dīn* and *dawla*' or '*dīn* and *ummah*?'" can provide an important window through which to view the evolution of Political Islam and the state in contemporary times.

DĪN AND *DAWLA* IN THE ERA OF OLD-STYLE NATIONALISM

In the years immediately following World War II, the major political objective of most Muslim leaders was achieving independence from Western imperialism. Attempts to define and possibly establish an Islamic State were secondary to the efforts to bring an end to foreign domination. By the middle of the twentieth century, the concept of the nation-state shaped the way most educated Muslims thought about politics, making nationalism the most powerful ideology of that time. Even explicitly Islamically oriented organizations, such as the Muslim Brotherhood in Egypt and the *Jamāʿat-i Islāmī* (Islamic Society) in South Asia, operated within the framework of nation-state politics. A revolutionary *jihad* group such as *Darul Islam* in Indonesia defined its *jihad* in terms of the nation-state, proclaiming in 1949 that its "Holy War or Revolution will continue until the Islamic State of Indonesia emerges safe and secure...in all of Indonesia" (Riddell 2001, 265).

Within the framework of the nationalist struggle, there were debates about the nature of the states to be created. By the middle of the century, the concept of Islam as *dīn* and *dawla* had become an important part of the political debates. In a number of countries, the adoption of an Islamic Constitution was actively considered. However, as in the case of the early party platforms of PAS (*Persatuan Islam se Malaya* and, later, *Partai Islam se Malaysia*), the Islamic party in Malaya in the 1950s, these discussions emphasized the nation-state base on which the Islamic political structure was to be built.

The most vigorous disagreements concerned the nature of the modern nation-state itself. Frequently, the affirmation that Islam is *dīn wa dawla* aimed at refuting the claims that states must be secular if they are to be effectively modern. These deliberations took place in the shadow of earlier debates, especially the turmoil caused by a book written in the 1920s by an Egyptian scholar, Ali Abd al-Raziq. He argued that the Prophet Muhammad was a messenger of God and not a king or ruler, that "he did not have a government...[and] did not establish a kingdom, in the political sense of the term" (Kurzman 1998, 29–10; Donohue

2007, 31). Abd al-Raziq placed his analysis squarely in the framework of *dīn* and *dawla* and made his position clear in the title for the third chapter in the part of his book dealing with the caliphate and government in Islam: "Mission not rule, *Dīn* not *Dawla*" (Abd al-Raziq 1925).

The controversy set the terms for much of the subsequent political discussions in the Muslim world. In these debates, by midcentury less attention came to be given to the nature of the caliphate itself. Instead, increasing attention was given to the issue of the secular nature of the modern state and the question of whether or not Islam was a *dawla* as well as a *dīn*. These disputes were highlighted by a book published, again in Egypt, in 1950 by Khalid Muhammad Khalid, *Min hunā nabda'* (From Here We Begin) and an Islamist response by Muhammad al-Ghazali, *Min hunā na'lam* (From Here We Learn). In a later summary of his book, Khalid says, "I asserted that Islam is a *dīn* and not a *dawla*, and that it was not necessary for it to be a *dawla*" (Khalid 1981, 9). In the book, he argued that there is no special religious form of government and that "every government that accomplishes the goal for which governments are established, which is realizing social welfare for the community (*ummah*), is both recognized and blessed by the *dīn*" (Khalid 1969, 157).

In his response, al-Ghazali identified Khalid's work as being in the tradition of Abd al-Raziq and similarly in error. He argued that Islam is not simply a rationalist philosophy that humans can study when they feel like it. "Instead, it is a comprehensive path...for the reconstruction of the affairs of the individual, the society, and the state [*dawla*]," and he argued that "governance is an unavoidable necessity in order for *dīn* to achieve its goals" (al-Ghazali 2005, 10–11, 16, 45).

Most of the participants in the debates in this era about the desirable political system were conceptually within a modern framework. People could talk about "traditional" leaders, but even those rulers spoke in modern frameworks. Muhammad V in Morocco, for example, may have been socially conservative and heir to a traditional sultanate, but he became king of independent Morocco in 1956 with the support of the more secularist nationalists as well as the explicitly religious groups. In this era, viewing Islam as *dīn* and *dawla* did not mean an attempt to restore the caliphate or to construct some distinctive new and clearly Islamic political system. Instead, the major developments involved attempts to add explicitly Islamic dimensions to the modern political systems that had developed in the Muslim world. *Dīn* and *dawla* and *dīn* and *ummah* describe the basic nature of the alternative visions involved in defining the nature of the emerging secular state systems and nationalist movements.

Radical Nationalism: *Dīn* and Revolution

"All divine messages in their very nature are human revolutions whose goals are the nobility and happiness of humanity" (*Al-Mīthāq* 1962, 109). The 1962 National Covenant in Egypt identified true religions as revolutions and, in this way, reflected the significant transition from the old-style nationalist movements for independence toward, in many places, a self-consciously revolutionary nationalism. This new radicalism did not reject religion. Instead, it viewed religion in general terms, seeing it as only a part of the broader revolutionary mission. The new message often, as in the Egyptian Covenant, affirmed that the "eternal spiritual values based on the religions provide guidance for humanity" and that conflict with religion only occurs when reactionaries exploit religion to obstruct progress (*Al-Mīthāq* 1962, 108–109).

Discussion shifted from the old-style debates about secularism in emerging national *dawla*s to debates about the role of religion in the new radical ideologies. This shift involves changing global understandings of modernity itself. Modernity in the age of empires and nationalisms was conceived as the modernity of Western Europe and North America. In that era, reform programs involved replacing premodern institutions and worldviews (usually called traditional) with Western-style modern structures. In political terms, this framework involved validating secularism. However, by the 1960s, it was clear that modernity could take many different forms. The great competition was no longer between traditional and modern but, rather, between conservative and radical visions of modernity. The global competition between capitalist and communist modes of modernity in the Cold War had its parallels in the Muslim world, where virtually no one advocated a return to premodern modes.

In these new debates, all religions, and not just Islam, were seen as contributing to the strength of the nation, when correctly understood. In Indonesia, for example, Sukarno, the leader of the independence movement at the end of World War II, proclaimed the Five Principles (Pantjasila) on which the independent nation-state should be based. The principle of "religion" was stated in inclusive terms rather than identifying the state with Islam: "The principle of Belief in God! Not only should the people of Indonesia have belief in God, but every Indonesian should believe in *his own* particular God.... The whole people should worship his God in the cultural way that is, without 'religious egoism'" (*Lahirnja Pantjasila* 1955, 28). The new revolutionary movements could oppose conservative religious institutions while still expressing faith in "true religion." This type of program does not define a religion-based state, but it also does not define a secular state.

In this era, Islam usually was viewed as being a supportive element within the broader frameworks of radical ideologies of social revolution, although old-style secular nationalists and some conservatives still argued that Islam and nationalism were incompatible. In the emerging views, rather than Islam defining the state, Islam was defined within the ideology of the new state, becoming something like a national religion. Abd al-Rahman al-Bazzaz, an Iraqi pan-Arabist in the 1960s, gave a lecture in 1952 on "Islam and Arab Nationalism" that is widely quoted and represents the basic radical nationalist position. He argued that "although Islam is a universal religion suitable for all peoples..., it is undeniably also a religion that came down first and specifically for the Arabs. In this sense it is their special religion" (Atiyah 1965, 35; al-Bazzaz 1954, 201–218). Although other nationalist movements could not make this specific claim, the general view of non-Arab Muslims in their own nationalist movements was that there was no contradiction between their nationalism and Islam.

In the 1960s, revolution was a central concept in the political discussions within the Muslim world and became part of most major political programs. In this new framework, the old debates about *dīn* and *dawla* were often submerged in discussions of *dīn* and *thawra* (revolution). This development is reflected in the comprehensive discussions from that era and later by Hasan Hanafi, who viewed this as a desired transition "from creed (*al-ʿaqīda*) to revolution" (Hanafi 1987, 1988).

The rhetorical appeal to revolution was so popular that even some leading conservatives presented their programs in the terminology of revolution. The shah of Iran, for example, promulgated a major reform program in 1963–1964. It was presented as "the White Revolution," which the shah hoped was "a deep and fundamental revolution" that would transform Iranian society and was based on a foundation that included the principle of "reliance on spiritual principles and religious beliefs, which in our case is the religion of Islam" (Aryamehr 1967). While other monarchs did not explicitly identify their reform programs as revolutions, they presented their programs in terms of contemporary progressive ideologies. The monarchy in Libya, before it was overthrown in 1969, worked to transform the message of the Sanusiyya Sufi brotherhood, whose leader was also the king, from a distinctive movement of Islamic renewal into "Senoussism," a modern political ideology whose "progressive principles" were said to be best reflected, in one government publication, in a massive public housing scheme (Annane 1968, 139). King Hussein in Jordan and King Faysal, who came to the Saudi throne in 1964, were equally clear in identifying their visions for their countries as progressive and modern.

All of these rulers identified their reformist programs as having a basis in Islam. However, the competition was not between an old-style secularism and visions of an Islamic State, because the radicals also defined their programs as having an Islamic base. Some advocated "Islamic socialism." In Pakistan, for example, Zulfikar Ali Bhutto was a relatively leftist political intellectual who came to oppose the military rule of Ayyub Khan during the 1960s. When he established the Pakistan People's Party (PPP) in 1967, he proclaimed its creed as "Islam is our faith; democracy is our politics; socialism is our economy; all power to the people." This slogan did not mean that the PPP advocated the establishment of an Islamic State but, rather, that Islam was a part of the broader program of social transformation. Within this framework, the older disputes about defining Islam as *dīn wa dawla* were submerged in the conflict between conservative and radical modernizers for whom Islam was basically a rhetorical resource within a broader ideological struggle. Islam as *dīn* and *thawra* was a more visible issue.

The importance of the modern nation-state concept in defining Islamic political visions in this era was emphasized by the establishment of a global Muslim organization in 1969. At a summit convened in Morocco in response to an arsonist's attack on al-Aqsa Mosque in Jerusalem, the assembled Muslim leaders established the Organization of the Islamic Conference (OIC). By the beginning of the twenty-first century, the OIC had a membership of fifty-seven states. The OIC Covenant identifies the objectives: the first is "to enhance and consolidate the bonds of fraternity and solidarity among the Member States"; the second notes the common interests of the member states and states that the OIC will "coordinate and unify" their efforts "in view of the challenges faced by the Islamic world"; and the third identifies the pledge "to respect sovereignty, independence and territorial integrity of each Member State." The emphasis is on the sovereign states that are in what in the Arabic version of the Covenant is *al-'ālim al-Islāmī* or, specifically, "the Islamic world," not the *ummah*. In its vision, the "OIC claims to revive the ideal *ummah* of Islamic history, but it faces the reality of the Muslim world being divided into nation-states" (al-Ahsan 1992, 113).

In this second era, the old disputes about whether or not a modern state could be Islamic shifted to debates about defining the role of religion within the framework of existing modern state systems. In this, Islam was a component part of the political ideologies, whether radical or conservative, and the broader *ummah* tended to be viewed as a network of sovereign states. The concepts and mottos of Islam as *dīn* and *dawla* and *dīn* and *ummah* continued to be important, but in this second era, the meanings were different, reflecting both the visions of Muslims and the changing nature of modernity itself.

THE AGE OF POLITICAL ISLAM: *DĪN* AS *DAWLA*

Already in the 1960s, the beginnings of the next stage in the debates about Islam and politics were being set. When Sayyid Qutb affirmed that Islam is a comprehensive path, he did not use the phrase that Islam is *dīn* and *dawla*. He said that Islam provides a comprehensive path or program, using the word *minhaj*, referring to the Qur'anic verse where God says that for each group there is a revealed law and a program (*shirʿatan wa minhājan*; 5:48). Qutb and others presented their visions in terms of Islam as a faith and a complete program for human life rather than as "religion and state." Qutb directly attacked the concept of Islam as a part of Arab nationalism or of socialist revolution. His explanation for the success of the great revolution in the time of the Prophet spoke of *dīn* and *dawla* but included them as part of the broader "Qur'anic program." The new society was possible "because those who established this religion (*dīn*) in the form of a state (*dawla*), a system and laws, had first established it in their hearts and lives" (Qutb n.d., 34). This shifts the frame of reference from Islam as *dīn* and *dawla* to *dīn* as *dawla* or religion comprehensively understood as the foundation for state, society, and faith.

Qutb provided no specific definition of an Islamic State, but he developed an important rationale for opposition to the contemporary states in the Muslim world. By the 1970s, as the radical and conservative modernizing political leadership in the Muslim world appeared to be ineffective in providing for the welfare of their peoples, this Islamist critique became a rallying cry for opposition movements. Calls for the establishment of Islamic states that would implement the *Sharīʿah* became the key to the rise of what came to be called "Political Islam," with the state being the manifestation of Islam.

Although Islamically identified political movements are important throughout Islamic history, by the late 1970s such movements were taking new forms as politics was embedded in the structures of modern sovereign nation-states. Earlier efforts aimed at modernizing Islam, creating a strong tradition of Islamic modernism. However, the basic effort was now reversed. Political Islam can be understood as the project of "Islamization of modernity," in contrast to the old efforts to modernize Islam.

The new political activism involved two different approaches to the Islamization of the modern state and society. One method was to gain control of the state and have the state implement and enforce the *Sharīʿah*, in effect, affirming that *dīn* is *dawla*. The second approach is the "hearts-and-lives" approach as suggested by Qutb, in which the political system would be transformed "from the bottom up." The result is two different forms of Political Islam during the 1980s and 1990s.

The successful revolution in Iran in 1978–1979 resulted in the establishment of a state that was the public expression of Islam. The revolution's leader, the Ayatollah Khomeini, defined the nature of this centrality clearly: "We have in reality, then, no choice but to destroy those systems of government that are corrupt in themselves.... This is a duty that all Muslims must fulfill, in every one of the Muslim countries, in order to achieve the triumphant political revolution of Islam.... Islamic government may ... be defined as the rule of divine law over men" (Algar 1981, 48, 55). This system was succinctly summarized in an Iranian official broadcast at the time: "Islam is a state; Islam is a government" (BBC/ME Report 1979).

During the 1980s, three rulers who came to power as a result of military coups undertook programs of state implementation of *Shari'ah*. They represented a distinctive form of the affirmation of *dīn* as *dawla*, in which a conservative understanding of the content of *Shari'ah* was imposed through dictatorial means. Opposition to these programs often took the form of an Islamically based advocacy of democracy, arguing that a truly Islamic State would be democratic.

General Zia ul-Haq took control of the government of Pakistan in 1977 and affirmed frequently his commitment to "transform the country's socioeconomic and political structure in accordance with the principles of Islam" (*Dawn* 1977). Over the following decade, until his death in 1988, Zia's state engaged in a major effort of Islamization of law, created a special system of *Shari'ah* courts, and developed his own Islamic form of democracy, labeled *shuracracy*, a system of nonparty "consultation" (*shura*).

In Sudan, Ja'far Numayri, who had ruled Sudan since taking control in a military coup in 1969, announced a major program of Islamization of law and the state in 1983. Significant religiously identified political leaders such as Sadiq al-Mahdi, a great-grandson of the nineteenth-century Sudanese Mahdi and head of the largest political party in the northern Sudan, vigorously opposed this new program as presenting an inaccurate and outdated version of *Shari'ah*. Even his Islamist political ally at the time, Hasan Turabi, had reservations about the actual program. These regulations survived the overthrow of Numayri in 1985, and the following civilian government was unable to make major revisions. In 1989, the civilian government was overthrown in another military coup, led by Umar Hasan al-Bashīr, who worked with Turabi and the National Islamic Front (NIF). Although Turabi had a major role in the new NIF regime, Bashīr's state was in the authoritarian mode, imposing a conservative understanding of *Shari'ah*.

The second mode of Political Islam believed that the Islamization of society is the primary goal and that politics is a major arena in which activism is necessary. Hasan Turabi, along with his association with the state programs in Sudan, was also an internationally known intellectual whose ideas influenced Islamist thought in many areas. In a review of the developments in the 1980s, Turabi emphasized the importance of action in the public political arena: "You don't develop a program by sitting in an ivory tower and writing out an economic program or a social program. You develop it in public life through interaction with public opinion.... This is how political programs are developed" (Lowrie 1993, 17). In this perspective, activists still affirmed that Islam is both *dīn* and *dawla*, but the emphasis shifted to Islam as the comprehensive program (*minhāj*) for state and society. By the early 1990s, "Islam is the solution" (*Islam huwa al-hal*) became a widely used slogan of Islamist opposition movements. This programmatic emphasis defines the vision of an Islamized modernity in the final decades of the twentieth century.

A wide spectrum of movements and organizations developed under the label of "Political Islam" in the 1980s. Some important movements were outside of this grouping—the Tablighi Jama'at, possibly the largest Islamic organization in the world, remained resolutely aloof from direct political involvement as it expanded and globalized its mission. Some organizations were illegal in their home countries but, like the Muslim Brotherhood in Egypt, gained increasing influence though careful participation in electoral politics. Others presented conservatively conceived Islamization programs and had some impact in the political arena. PAS in Malaysia, for example, won majorities in some provincial legislatures.

The prototypical new mode of the 1980s saw efficient organizations developing around charismatic activist intellectuals who articulated programs of renewal and actively participated in politics. This process often involved a reassessment of the medieval heritage and the call for a new understanding of the fundamentals of the *Shariʿah* in ways that changed the meaning of "implementing the *Shariʿah*" from simply applying specific rules framed by medieval scholars to a redefinition of the Islamic legal systems themselves.

Three movements and their leaders, in addition to Turabi in Sudan, are major representatives of this new style of Political Islam. Anwar Ibrahim in Malaysia began as a student activist in the cause of Malay cultural nationalism in the late 1960s. However, in the early 1970s, he helped to establish the Angkatan Belia Islam Malaysia (ABIM) that advocated a progressive and somewhat pluralist understanding of Islam. By the 1980s, Anwar joined the dominant government coalition of Mahathir Mohammad and became an important political force in the country. A second prominent example is Rāshid al-Ghannushi in Tunisia. Following study in Damascus and France, he returned to Tunisia as a secondary school philosophy teacher in the 1960s. He and some other young Tunisians became increasingly dissatisfied with the secular authoritarianism of Bourguiba and viewed progressive Islam as a positive, democratic alternative. Identified as the Islamic Tendency Movement, they soon clashed with security forces. Following the overthrow of Bourguiba in 1987, they reorganized as the Nahdah Party in order to participate in the new electoral politics. The new government of General Ben Ali did not allow the party to compete, and Ghannushi chose to live in political exile. For the next twenty years, Nahdah, even though illegal, remained an important expression of opposition to continued authoritarian rule. When the Ben Ali regime was overthrown in 2011, Nahdah and Ghannushi won the elections and formed a coalition government reflecting the new era of Islamic and Arab politics.

The third movement, in Algeria, illustrates the challenges of the participatory "hearts-and-lives" approach. A key figure in this movement is Abbasi Madani, who began as an active member of the National Liberation Front (FLN) in the 1950s but by the 1980s became an opponent of the secularist ideology and authoritarian rule of the FLN. When the FLN government allowed the formation of new parties, Madani established the Islamic Salvation Front (FIS). FIS won major victories in municipal elections in 1990s and in the first stage of the national elections in 1991 and was in a position to win an absolute majority in the new parliament, until the military intervened in 1992. The FIS platform presented a comprehensive program of Islamic transformation. The emphasis was not simply on Islam and *dīn* and *dawla* but, rather, on presenting a program identified with the affirmation: "Islam: It Is the Solution" (*Islam Huwa al-Hal*).

In the developments in this third era, Islam as *dīn* and *dawla* became Islam as *dawla* in explicitly political Islamist movements. Whether framed in conservative, statist ideologies or in the more progressive programs of activist intellectuals, the debates of the early 1990s were far different from the old-style debates about a secular state in the midcentury. Not only do these differences reflect the changing of modern Muslim thought, but they also are part of the changing global experiences of modernity. Modernity in the 1990s was global and no longer a Western center surrounded by a non-Western periphery.

Globalization and the Return of the *Ummah*

"As Western civilization becomes increasingly worn out and senile, humanity is today searching for a new vision for its future, awaiting a new civilization which is more capable of meeting its material and spiritual needs and wants. Through our Islamic revolution, we have endeavored to create a new system" (Khatami 1998, 66–7). In 1997 Mohammad Khatami, then the newly elected president of the Islamic Republic of Iran, saw the 1990s not simply as a new phase in the processes of Islamizing modernity; he believed that humanity was entering a whole new age of world history in which both Western civilization and the old Muslim civilization were in decline. "Our new civilization [based on the Islamic revolution] is on the verge of emergence." This vision is not a program for transforming the modern nation-state into an Islamic State; it is a vision of global socioreligious transformation in which issues of relations between Islam and the modern state are being displaced by greater emphasis on the *ummah* as the central unit of Muslim identity.

This shift from Political Islam to a more broadly cultural framing of Islamic society and politics is well illustrated by political developments in Malaysia at the beginning of the twenty-first century. The state constitutionally recognized Islam but, reflecting the religious and ethnic diversity of the country, had long maintained a relatively secular (but not antireligious) mode of politics. PAS, as an opposition party since independence, advocated the establishment of a national Islamic State, and Political Islam had emerged in the 1980s with ABIM and Anwar Ibrahim. However, at the beginning of the twenty-first century, Mahathir Mohamad, who had been prime minister since 1981, declared that Malaysia was an Islamic State.

During 2001 and later, debates in Malaysia about what it meant to be an Islamic State reflected the changing concepts in much of the Muslim world, going beyond Islam as *dīn* and *dawla* and *dīn* as *dawla* to viewing Islamic values as the normative foundations for state and community. PAS, for example, repositioned itself as a party of reform reflecting views of "a new generation of technocratic-inclined professionals who were different from the older generation of religious scholars who were the traditional leaders" of the party (Noor 2010). Anwar Ibrahim, who had been removed from his leadership positions in Mahathir's government in 1998 and imprisoned, became the major leader of the pluralist, reformist opposition coalition. Abdullah Badawi, who became prime minister in 2003, proclaimed *Islam hadhari* (civilizational Islam) as central to his party's program in "an effort to bring the *ummah* (the worldwide community comprising all adherents of the Muslim faith) back to the basics of Islam" (Badawi 2006, 3). As in the perspective of Khatami, the discourse had shifted from *dīn* and *dawla* to Islam as civilization and community in a globalized world. A similar transition from older leaders with old-style understandings of an Islamic State to more cosmopolitan businesspeople and technocrats was part of the political victory of the Justice and Development Party (AKP) in Turkey.

Relations between religion and state are conceived in different ways in the contexts of global interactions of civilizations and communities. As the nature of the old-style modern nation-state changes, Islam as *dawla* or *dīn* and *dawla* has less relevance. The older debates about the need to separate religious institutions from the state continue but are often marginalized. The more visible debates involve social issues and the nature of lifestyle, such as secularist opposition to limitations on women's participation in public life, as in Saudi Arabia, or to the imposition of restrictions in general on social life in the public sphere. However, strictly enforced secularism also becomes an issue when governments prohibit religiously identified groups from participating in politics as a way of reducing the ability of opposition parties to compete effectively in elections. Turkey provides possibly the major example of how contemporary political developments have changed the debates about religion and state by setting limits on established secularism, as in the political battle over whether or not women could wear headscarves in government buildings. In addition, although many still identify secularism with atheism, an Islamic secularism is emerging with people such as Abdullahi an-Na`im, who states, "In order to be a Muslim by conviction and free choice...I need a secular state" (an-Na`im 2008, 1).

The shift in emphasis from political debates framed primarily in terms of nation-states and the old-style debates about secularism reflects the interconnection between the changing modernities and changing conceptualizations in the Muslim world. In the twenty-first century, Muslims are increasingly aware of themselves as part of global networks of human interaction. The result of this for Muslims is expressed clearly by an important contemporary Turkish intellectual, Ali Bulaç: "The world has embarked on a new process.... Even though what appears to be on the rise is nationalism, the main decisive and transformative factor is global concepts. The response to something global should be made with global language. That can only be possible if you use the language of the *ummah*" (Bulaç 2010). This shift away from the *dīn wa dawla* vision is emphasized at the beginning of the twenty-first century by Gamal al-Banna, the brother of Hasan al-Banna, the founder of the Muslim Brotherhood. He argues that his brother "coined the phrase 'Al-Islam *dīn wa dawla*'... Hassan al-Banna's ideas could have been applied or accepted in the 1940s, but they cannot be applied or accepted in 2004" (al-Banna 2004). By the beginning of the twenty-first century, the terms of debate had changed significantly.

Conclusion

The political transformations of the Arab Spring in 2011–2012 show that important changes have occurred in Muslim societies. Whatever may be the specific long-terms results of the protests and civil conflicts, the dynamics of social and political action have clearly changed during the decades since World War II. The campaign slogan of Mohammed Morsi, who won the Egyptian presidential election in 2012, reflects the changing world of Muslim political debate. He was the candidate of the party created by the Muslim Brotherhood, which had long used the slogan "Islam is the solution." However, the new campaign platform and slogan was "Renaissance—the will of the people." The emphasis in the Renaissance Project was on pragmatic programs rather than ideological principles.

Similarly, the Islamist parties that were successful in elections in Morocco and Tunisia emphasized issues of social justice and development rather than the old ideological claims. In this vision, Islam provides a moral foundation for both state and society. Old questions such as "Is Islam compatible with democracy?" are irrelevant when people such as Ghannushi argue that in the twenty-first century democracy is inherently part of Islam and to be undemocratic is to be un-Islamic.

People still debate about the relationships between religion and politics, but at the beginning of the twenty-first century it is no longer *dīn wa dawla* in a world of nationalisms and European empires.

References

Abd al-Raziq, Ali. 1925. "*Risala lā Hukm, Dīn lā Dawla*,"*Al-Islām wa Usul al-Hukm*. Cairo: Matbaʿat Misr.
Ahmad, Khurshid, and Zafar Ishaq Ansari. 1979. "Mawlānā Sayyid Abul Aʻlā Mawdūdī: An Introduction to His Vision of Islam and Islamic Revival." In *Islamic Perspectives*, ed. Khurshid Ahmad and Zafar Ishaq Ansari. Leicester: Islamic Foundation, 359–383.
al-Ahsan, Abdullah. 1992/1413. *Ummah or Nation? Identity Crisis in Contemporary Muslim Society*. Leicester: Islamic Foundation. [Official Arabic and English versions of the Covenant, OIC Website at www.oic-oci.org. Accessed May 10, 2013.
Algar, Hamid, trans. 1981. *Islam and Revolution: Writings and Declarations of Imam Khomeini*. Berkeley: Mizan Press.
Annane, Mohammad. 1968. *Libya of Idris el Senoussi*. Beirut: Systeco.
Aryamehr, Mohammed Reza Pahlavi. 1967. *The White Revolution*. Tehran: The Imperial Pahlavi Library. As reprinted in Lenczowski, George, ed. 1970. *The Political Awakening in the Middle East*. Englewood Cliffs: Prentice-Hall.
Atiyah, Edward, trans. 1965. *Al-Bazzaz on Arab Nationalism*. London: Embassy of the Republic of Iraq.
Badawi, Abdullah Ahmad. 2006. *Islam Hadhari*. Selangor, Malaysia: MPH Publishing.
al-Banna, Gamal. 2004. "Where Are We Headed in the Next 25 Years? in Moderate Islamic Thinker, Yasmine Moll." *Egypt Today* 25 (September): 9.
al-Bannā, Jamāl. 2003. *al-Islām dīn wa ummah wa laysa dīnan wa dawlah*. Cairo: Dār al-Fikr al-Islāmī.
al-Bazzaz, Abd al-Rahman, and Sylvia G. Haim. 1954. "Islam and Arab Nationalism." *Die Welt des Islams* n.s.: 3.
BBC/ME report. 1979, February 15. As quoted in Kramer, Martin. 1980. *Political Islam*. London: Sage.
Bulaç, Ali. 2010. "The Tension of the Future." March 23. www.worldbulletin.net. (Accessed April 10, 2010).
Dawn. September 30, 1977. As quoted in Esposito, John L. 1998. *Islam and Politics*. 4th ed. Syracuse: Syracuse University Press.
Donohue, John J., and John L. Esposito, eds. 2007. *Islam in Transition*. 2nd ed. New York: Oxford University Press.
al-Ghazali, Muhammad. 2005. *Min Hunā Naʿlam*. 5th printing. Cairo: Nahda Masr.
Hanafi, Hasan. 1987. *al-Dīn wa al-Thawra, 1952–1981*. Cairo: Maktaba Madbuli.
Hanafi, Hasan. 1988. *Min al-ʿAqīda ilā al-Thawra*. Cairo: Maktaba Madbuli.
Khalid, Khalid Muhammad. 1969. *Min Hunā Nabda'*. 11th printing. Cairo: Anglo-Egyptian Bookstore.
Khalid, Khalid Muhammad. 1981. *al-Dawla fī al-Islām*. Cairo: Dar al-Thabit.
Khatami, Mohammad. 1998. *Islam, Liberty and Development*. Binghamton: Binghamton University Press.
Kurzman, Charles, ed. 1998. *Liberal Islam: A Sourcebook*. New York: Oxford University Press.

Lahirnja Pantjasila: President Soekarno's Speech. 1955. Jakarta: Republic of Indonesia, Ministry of Information. Emphasis in text. Translation of speech delivered June 1, 1945.

Lowrie, Arthur, ed. 1993. *Islam, Democracy, the State, and the West: A Round Table with Dr. Hasan Turabi, May 10, 1992.* Tampa: World & Islamic Studies Enterprise.

an-Na`im, Abdullahi Ahmed. 2008. *Islam and the Secular State.* Cambridge: Harvard University Press.

Nasser, Gamal Abdel, 1962. *Al-Mīthāq, Qaddamahu al-Ra'īs Jamāl Abd al-Nāsir li-l Mu'tamir al-Watanī li-l-Qawā al-Sha`biyyah, 21 Mayū 1962.* Cairo: Maslahah al-Isti'lamat.

Noor, Farish A. 2010. "State, Society and Politics in Malaysia (Week 9): Crisis and Radical Contingency." February 12. Lecture notes posted on www.othermalaysia.org. Accessed April 11, 2010.

Qutb, Sayyid. n.d. *Ma'ālim fī al-Tarīq.* Cairo: Dar al-Sha ruq.

Riddell, Peter G. 2001. Quoted in *Islam and the Malay-Indonesia World.* London: Hurst.

CHAPTER 5

ISLAM AND DEMOCRACY

NADER HASHEMI

The 2011 Arab Spring has placed the issue of Islam and democracy back on top of the international agenda. While these democratic revolts were initially celebrated in the West, the popularity and rise of Islamist parties, with their frequent references to Shari`ah, after the demise of longstanding dictators, has cast a shadow of doubt over the future democratic prospects for the Arab-Islamic world. Has the Arab Spring turned into an Islamist Winter?

Pessimism about compatibility between Islam and democracy is perhaps best captured by the following anecdote. Twenty years ago, Jeane Kirkpatrick, a former American United Nations (UN) ambassador and Republican Party foreign policy advisor, was asked to comment on the topic. She paused for a moment, thought about the question, and then replied: "The Arab world is the only part of the world where I've been shaken in my conviction that if you let the people decide, they will make fundamentally rational decisions" (Sieff 1992).

This sentiment is not new or unique. It is a reflection of a longstanding, widespread, and deep-rooted anxiety in the West about the relationship between Islam and modernity. Such frustration reached new heights and was thrust to the top of the global agenda after September 11, 2001, giving this topic a pressing new urgency.

Writing at this time, Francis Fukuyama articulated a broad intellectual concern when he noted that "there does seem to be something about Islam...that makes Muslim societies particularly resistant to modernity. Of all contemporary cultural systems, the Islamic world has the fewest democracies (Turkey alone qualifies), and contains no countries that have made the transition from Third to First World status in the manner of South Korea or Singapore" (Fukuyama 2001). Similarly, Bernard Lewis has asked:

> There is an agonizing question at the heart of the present debate about democracy in the Islamic world: Is liberal democracy basically compatible with Islam, or is some measure of respect for law, some tolerance of criticism, the most that can be expected from autocratic governments?... Is it possible for the Islamic peoples to evolve a form of government that will be compatible with their own historical, cultural, and religious traditions and yet will bring individual freedom and human rights to the governed as these terms are understood in the free societies of the West? (Lewis 2010, 62)

While questions about the relationship between Islam and democracy are sometimes dismissed as a result of an entrenched Eurocentric and Orientalist view of Islam and Muslim societies, hard empirical facts cannot be easily ignored. In 2001, Freedom House, a respected nongovernmental organization that monitors global democratic development, released a major study on the "Islamic World's Democracy Deficit." The core findings of this report documented an expanding gap at the dawn of the twenty-first century between Muslim-majority countries and the rest of the world in terms of basic levels of freedom and democracy. A non-Muslim country, this report concluded, was three times more likely to be democratic than a Muslim one. The most recent statistics from Freedom House in 2010 show no discernible change in the global Muslim democracy gap (Freedom House 2001, 2010).

During the same time period, the United Nations Development Program (UNDP) confirmed the Freedom House findings in a series of widely discussed reports on Arab human development. The region is at a crossroads, the first report concluded, and is "hampered by three key deficits that can be considered defining features: the freedom deficit; the women's empowerment deficit [and] the human capabilities/knowledge deficit relative to income." Compared to the rest of the world "the Arab countries had the lowest freedom score in the 1990s" and "the Arab region...[had] the lowest value of all regions of the world for voice and accountability" (UNDP 2002, 27–29). In terms of the status of women, the Arab world ranks next to last based on the UN gender empowerment measure (GEM); only sub-Saharan Africa had a lower score.[1]

Empirical evidence and arguments to the contrary, however, can also be cited to challenge this pessimistic picture. Relying on the most recent rankings by Freedom House, more than half of the global Muslim population (about 800 million) is located in countries that are listed as "free" or "partly free."[2] Indonesia, for example, the most populous Muslim country in the world, receives very high scores for human rights and democratic development, a remarkable achievement for a country that recently has undergone a democratic transition. Furthermore, the research firm Gallup published in 2007 the most comprehensive survey of global Muslim opinion based on six years of polling that represented more than 90 percent of the world's Muslim population. It not only found widespread support for democracy but also found that substantial majorities, including the most conservative Muslim societies (73 percent of Saudis, 89 percent of Iranians, 94 percent of Egyptians), believe that men and women should have equal rights and that "substantial majorities in nearly all nations surveyed...say that if drafting a constitution for a new country, they would guarantee freedom of speech, defined as 'allowing all citizens to express their opinion on the political, social, and economic issues of the day'" (Esposito and Mogahed, 2007, 47; 2008). Finally, in his recently published magnum opus, *The Life and Death of Democracy*, the renowned scholar of democracy John Keane locates the origins of democracy not in Greece but in the ancient tribal assemblies of the Middle East. In calling for a rethinking of the roots of democracy he argues that "democracy of the Greek kind had eastern roots and that therefore in a very real sense today's democracies are indebted to the first experiments in self-government by assembly of 'Eastern' peoples traditionally written off as incapable of democracy in any sense. *Ex oriente lux*: the lamp of assembly-based democracy was first lit in the East" (Keane 2009, 113).[3]

How does one begin to make sense of this data and the conflicting interpretations that go with it? To what extent is the theology of Islam a barrier to liberalization and democratization? Are Muslim societies disadvantaged by a set of enduring and exceptional qualities, rooted in their civilizational ethos, that are preventing them from democratizing or are the roots of political authoritarianism and the general absence of democracy to be located elsewhere? This essay seeks to engage with these questions by providing a broad historical overview and assessment of the debate on Islam and democracy. The focus will be on how to objectively frame an analysis of the relationship between Islam and democracy. In the course of doing so, key debates, schools of thought, and arguments that have shaped an understanding of this topic will be surveyed with special attention to historical background and the question of secularism and its discontents in Muslim societies. This chapter will not address the broader theme of the various obstacles to democratization and the persistence of authoritarianism in the Muslim world. Several excellent studies are available that already do this (Salamé 1994; Brynen et al. 1995; Niblock 1998; Hunter and Malik 2005; Posusney and Angrist 2005). Here, the focus is on the scholarly and intellectual debate on the compatibility between Islam and democracy as it emerged during the post-Cold War era.

At the outset two clarifications are in order. It is often stated that democracy is a contested concept and that no universal definition of it exists. While historically this may be true, today the term "democracy" is utilized in intellectual debates at a global level to refer to "liberal democracy." This understanding of democracy now enjoys a broad consensus and consequently will be employed in this essay (Sen 1999). In other words, a political order where legitimate authority is rooted in the consent of the governed based on the institutional guarantees of political freedom as defined by Robert Dahl's concept of "polyarchy" and where basic human rights, as enshrined in the 1948 UN Universal Declaration of Human Rights, are upheld (Dahl 1989, 220–221).

Similarly, the concept of "secularism" is deeply contested and no universal understanding of the terms exists. This is because secularism has multiple histories both within the Western tradition and in non-Western societies. In this essay, references to secularism are to "political secularism," which refers to the separation between religion and state, not to the more robust and popular understandings of secularism that speaks to the philosophical or sociological distancing from religion based on the understanding of secularism as defined by Harvey Cox and Peter Berger (Hashemi 2010, 326–328).

Religion and Democracy: Historical and Theoretical Caveats

Before entering into a discussion about Islam and democracy, a deeper historical and theoretical grasp of the topic is required. The debate on the compatibility between Islam and democracy is rooted in the larger historical conflict between religion and democracy; Islam is not the first religious tradition that has grappled with question of democratic governance (Casanova 2001; Woodberry and Shah 2004; Diamond et al. 2005). Indeed the tension between the two is as old as the study of politics itself. Recall that democratic Athens brought Socrates to trial and sentenced him to death on two accounts: corrupting the minds of the young and *religious* impiety.

In the modern period, all the key thinkers in the Western canon who have shaped our understanding of democracy and liberalism, from Hobbes, Locke, and Rousseau to Hegel,

Mill, and Marx, were deeply concerned about the role of religion in public life. Alexis de Tocqueville, in *Democracy in America* (1835), noted that the "organization and the establishment of democracy in Christendom is the great political problem of our times" (Tocqueville 1990, 325), and some of the most difficult disputes among the founding fathers of the American Republic were over the place of religion in the new democratic order that was emerging (Witte 2005, 21–69).

On a theoretical level and at first glance, religion and democracy speak to two different aspects of the human condition. Religion, especially the Abrahamic faiths, is fundamentally (but not exclusively) concerned with the relationship between human beings and the divine, whereas democracy's core definition is concerned with the secular realm and the regulation of interhuman relationships. When these lines become blurred conflict arises (Straus 1938). On a political level, the tension between religion and democracy is rooted in a debate on the proper location of legitimate political authority. In other words, where does sovereignty ultimately lie; with the people or a smaller subset of them: the clerics, the monarch, the wealthy, the majority religion/ethnicity, or the military? The history of democracy and the broader process of modernization are indelibly intertwined with resolving this question.

The dominant mainstream view, based on the received wisdom of the Enlightenment, is that religion is a problem for democracy and the less we have of it the better. This is, however, a superficial and limited view of the development of democracy. Sociologists from Tocqueville and Durkheim to Robert Bellah and José Casanova have written about the critical role that religion has played in the development and social construction of democracy in civil society. Jean Jacques Rousseau famously noted that "we should not...conclude from this that politics and religion have a common object among us, but that in the beginning stages of nations the one serves as an instrument of the other" (Rousseau 1987, 41). More recently, Jean Bethke Elshtain, in her ruminations on the topic, has noted that "every major social movement in American history (until recent decades, perhaps) has been interlaced with religious language, inspiration, and enthusiasm: the American Revolution itself ("No King but King Jesus" was one of its rallying cries); abolitionism; women's suffrage; many of the social reforms of the Progressive Era; labor organizing; the Social Gospel movement; and the civil rights movement, which was, after all, headed by the Southern Christian Leadership Conference. In the United States, religion has never been an exclusively 'private' matter" (Elshtain 2009, 8).

Finally, Alfred Stepan has drawn attention to various "maps of misreading" in the history of religion-state relations in Europe. He is critical of an ahistorical approach to this topic, which erroneously suggests that the development of democracy requires a hostile and rigid separation between religion and state. A closer reading of the topic reveals that virtually "no Western European democracy now has a rigid or hostile separation of church and state. Indeed, most have arrived at a democratically negotiated freedom of religion from state interference and all of them allow religious groups freedom, not only of private worship, but to organize groups in civil society." It is in the "constant political construction and reconstruction" of what he terms "the twin tolerations"—whereby the institutions of the state and religious authorities learn to respect certain minimum boundaries of freedom of action—that a scholarly understanding of the relationship between religion and democracy must be rooted (Stepan 2001). Recent empirical work on democracy and religion-state separation by Jonathan Fox confirms and reinforces Stepan's theoretical claims. He concluded that the "empirical results strongly indicate that SRAS [separation of religion and state], no matter which operationalization of the concept one uses, is not necessary for a functioning democracy or liberal democracy" (Fox 2007, 19; 2008).

In short, the normative role of religion in any emerging democracy is a source of deep conflict and political tension. No religious or civilizational tradition is born with a pro-democratic orientation. Ideas and new arguments need to be developed and unavoidable contradictions resolved based on a democratic bargain and a negotiated consensus. A large part of the history and struggle for democracy, often ignored in retrospective reflections on the subject, is how to resolve the question of religion's role in the polis. Muslim societies have only recently begun to grapple with this topic on a mass level.

Islam and Democracy: Historical Overview

While modern debates on democracy in the West can be traced back to the seventeenth century, principally to the writings of Baruch Spinoza and John Locke, in the case of Muslim societies, a serious engagement with democracy and Islamic tradition did not begin until the twentieth century. "Historically speaking," according to one prominent scholar, "democratic ideals of free opinion, free speech, free assembly and representative government impressed themselves on the Muslim mind as corollaries to the goals of national independence and unity" (Enayat 1982, 125). On the eve of World War I, most of the Islamic world was either directly or indirectly controlled by European powers, and the primary focus of political debate and energy among Muslims was directed toward ending foreign rule and promoting self-determination.

Normatively, Islam does not mandate or prefer a particular political system. In the Qur'an the idea of mutual consultation (*shura*) is praised and in classical jurisprudential theory governance should be based on a civil contract (*'aqd*) between the ruler and the ruled, while a pledge of support (*bay'a*) from influential members of the community should be obtained. There are also longstanding Islamic juridical concepts of consensus (*ijma'*) and independent interpretive judgment (*ijtihad*) that have political connotations conducive to the social construction of democracy.

Institutionally, the dominant form of political regime for most of Islamic history was the caliphate. Legitimacy was embodied in the ruler who pledged to preserve the legacy of the Prophet Muhammad and the teachings of the Qur'an, to protect the community from outside attack, and to promote spiritual and political unity, worship, education, and the upholding of Islamic law. The legitimacy of the ruler was also enhanced by the support given by Islamic jurists (*fuqaha*), who often played an advisory or consultative role, some of whom were appointed to judicial positions to administer justice. Over time, however, the caliphate system became increasingly dynastic, corrupt, and authoritarian, not unlike the various authoritarian monarchial regimes that dominated the European landscape for over a millennium (Lapidus 2002, 45–66, 215–218; Abou El Fadl 2003).

Constitutionalism preceded a discussion of democracy in Muslim societies. In the late nineteenth and early twentieth centuries, these political experiments (in Tunisia 1861, Egypt 1868, Ottoman Empire 1876, and Iran 1906) sought to limit the authority of rulers, establish the rule of law, and allow elite groups an opportunity to participate in governance.

Coincidentally, the trajectory of democratization in the West proceeded along similar lines. While the Iranian constitutional experience was unique in that it resulted from mass action, the questions, themes, and points of political conflict that emerged from this experience prefigured democratic experiments and debates in other Muslim societies throughout the twentieth century, especially those related to the role of religion in government and the debate on sovereignty, the power of the existing state, the role of elite groups in politics, and the pivotal role played by external powers in shaping internal developments.

In Abdelwahab El-Affendi's scholarly survey of political themes in the Muslim world during the twentieth century, he identifies three categories of Muslim attitudes toward democracy: those who enthusiastically supported it and tried to prove its compatibility with Islam, those who rejected it as alien to Islamic norms, and those who accepted democratic procedures but voiced philosophical objections to aspects of democracy and proposed limits on it to conform with *Islamic* law. It is this last group, which is arguably the largest in number and is most closely identified with mainstream Islamist organizations, whose intellectuals and leaders have extensively written about and wrestled with question of democracy (El-Affendi 2004, 2010).

One point of contention that emerges in their writings is the tension between popular sovereignty and God's sovereignty. As religious believers, God is ultimately sovereign, yet democracy is rooted in the idea of popular sovereignty. How can this apparent contradiction be reconciled? A common approach was to support popular sovereignty but to limit it by a council of religious experts who could ensure the Islamic authenticity of legislation. This is most clearly evident in Iran's clerical-controlled Guardian Council, which oversees and has the right to veto parliamentary bills. Similarly, the 2007 draft party platform of the Egyptian Muslim Brotherhood called for a similar council of religious experts and for similar reasons: fear that left unchecked the masses might pass legislation that violated Islamic values.

Broadly speaking, these mainstream Islamist groups have also supported crucial elements of democracy such as political pluralism and human rights but always within the framework of *Shari`ah*—a key element of their political platforms. Those liberal aspects of democracy that are associated with personal autonomy and freedom of action, belief, and association, as understood in the West today, are not values upheld by these groups. The question of citizenship based on equal rights for all members of society, regardless of religious affiliation, has also been a bone of contention as has the question of full gender equality. Finally, these groups are also explicitly against notions of secularism, a complicated topic that will be explored below (Krämer 1997, 71–82; Esposito and Voll 1996, 21–34; Euben and Zaman 2009, 29–35).

Summarizing the weakness of Muslim writing on democracy in the late twentieth century, Hamid Enayat has noted that what "is blatantly missing from contemporary Muslims writings on democracy...is an adaptation of either the ethical and legal precepts of Islam or the attitudes and institutions of traditional society, to democracy. This is obviously a much more complex and challenging task than the mere reformulation of democratic principles in Islamic idioms. It is because of this neglect that the hopes of evolving a coherent theory of democracy appropriate to an Islamic context have remained largely unfulfilled" (Enayat 1982, 135; Abou El Fadl 2004).

It is important to remember that the early debates on Islam and democracy did not occur in a vacuum. They developed gradually against the backdrop of the struggle against colonialism and the emergence of new states from old empires. The debate was also shaped by and deeply intertwined with the rise of nationalism and the processes of modernization and Westernization. Regional and international events such as Israel-Palestine conflict, the 1979 Iranian Revolution, the demise of the Soviet Union, and ongoing Western intervention in Muslim societies, culminating in the US-led invasions of Iraq and Afghanistan in 2001 and 2003, respectively, have significantly influenced the debate as well. But most significantly, the increasing authoritarianism and despotism of the modern state, which has dominated the political landscape of Muslim societies in recent decades, has most immediately shaped the moral context in which the debate on Islam and democracy has unfolded.

Islam and Democracy: the Establishment View

The intellectual debate on Islam and democracy has been shaped by an "establishment" perspective. This refers to a group of academics who are located at elite universities in the West and whose writings reach a large audience by virtue of their dissemination by mainstream and influential newspapers, intellectual journals, and publishing houses. Also, this group has been most closely associated with advising the US governments on foreign policy toward the Muslim world. Collectively, but for different reasons, they are pessimistic about the prospects for democracy primarily due to problems that they claim are endemic to Islamic history, culture, and theology. The "idea of democracy is quite alien to the mind-set of Islam," noted Elie Kedourie (London School of Economics), because "there is nothing in the political traditions of the Arab world—which are the political traditions of Islam—which might make familiar...the organizing ideas of constitutional or representative government" (Kedourie 1992, 1, 5). A common motif among these writers is that contemporary Muslim societies are shaped by an essential core set of beliefs, rooted in early Islamic and medieval history, which are resistant to change by modern socioeconomic and political forces.

The most prominent member of this group has been the Princeton historian Bernard Lewis. He is not totally dismissive of the prospects of democracy and recognizes that aspects of Islamic tradition may have a democratic potential. In this context, he lists a rich literature in Islamic law on the nature of political power, the strong disapproval of arbitrary rule based on the social contract features of the caliphate system, and the recognition of diversity and political pluralism in Islamic history. On the negative side, however, he notes a long tradition of autocracy that has been strengthened by the rise of the modern state. The absence of the notion of citizenship and the absence of a tradition of elected assemblies are listed as key features of Islamic political history that mitigate the prospects for democracy. Most significantly, however, it is the "absence of a native secularism in Islam" that tips the balance for Lewis (Lewis 1996, 52–63; 2003a, 96–116; 2010, 55–74).

Harvard political scientist Samuel Huntington has addressed this topic as well. In an early work he examined the statistical correlations between various religious traditions and democracy whereby he noted that "significant differences in their receptivity to democracy appear to exist among societies with difference cultural traditions" and that in particular "Islam...has not been hospitable to democracy." His explanation was that "in Islam, no distinction exists between religion and politics or between the spiritual and the secular, and political participation was historically an alien concept." He developed this idea further in a later, more popular book by claiming that "God and Caesar, church and state, spiritual and temporal authority, have been a prevailing dualism in Western culture," in contrast to other civilizations, Islam in particular, that are devoid of this feature. This was all leading to a "clash of civilizations" in the post-Cold War era, he argued. "The underlying problem for the West," Huntington concluded, "is not Islamic fundamentalism. It is Islam" (Huntington 1984, 208; 1996, 70, 217).

Other prominent scholars who subscribe to the "Islamic exceptionalism" thesis and who have been influential in shaping the debate on the topic include Ernest Gellner (University of Cambridge), who wrote of an elective affinity between Islam and Marxism while advancing a sophisticated anthropological thesis that sought to explain why Muslim societies were modernity resistant. The following scholars can also be listed: Fouad Ajami (Johns Hopkins University), Martin Kramer (Harvard University), Patricia Crone (Institute for Advanced Study, Princeton University), and Daniel Pipes (Hoover Institute, Stanford University); (Gellner 1991; Ajami 1998; Kramer 1996; Crone 2005; Pipes 2002).[4] The newly formed Association for the Study of the Middle East and Africa (ASMEA) institutionally represents this school of thought. While over the years they have advanced different arguments, they coalesce around the point that democracy is unlikely to emerge from within Muslim societies based on their own internal traditions and political convictions. This pessimistic reading has sparked the emergence of a rival interpretative school that has a more optimistic outlook on the topic.

ISLAM AND DEMOCRACY: RESPONSES TO THE ESTABLISHMENT

The leading advocates of this school have a more confident and sympathetic reading of Islamic civilization and the prospects for democratic development. Its most prominent members are also senior scholars and public intellectuals who teach at elite universities, but the thrust of their reading of Islamic theology and Islam's political heritage is rooted in an ecumenical, tolerant, and constructively critical approach to the topic.

Professors John Esposito and John Voll (Georgetown University) are two leading scholars from this perspective. They have written that the "Islamic heritage contains both broad concepts of potential positive significance for democratization" as well as "many concepts and traditions that could provide the foundation for concepts of 'constitutional opposition' and limits on arbitrary government power." However, they are careful to note that "none of these...represent an explicitly democratic conceptualization of opposition as understood in the modern era, but they do provide some basis within the heritage on which such formulations can be based." They also have critiqued the negative interpretations of Islam's democratic potential because they are based on "two faulty assumptions...that democracy is possible in one form, and that Islam can be expressed in only one way." Their approach is rooted in a comparative study of religion, history, and politics and a criticism of the mainstream scholarly and media's one-dimensional representations of Islam/Muslims that suggest that Muslim societies and political movements are monolithic and a threat to the West.

A core argument from this group is that violent elements on the fringe of society do not represent or reflect the moderate mainstream (Esposito and Voll 1994, 3; 1996, 51, 42). In their work, they have sought to highlight the diversity of Muslims societies and political movements by focusing on their evolutionary character and the points of commonality between evolving Islamic traditions and the modern demands of politics.

Dale Eickelman and James Piscatori have also written extensively on the relationship between Islam and politics. In a jointly authored book, *Muslim Politics* (1996), they sought to challenge the Islamic exceptionalism thesis by exploring the nature of Muslim political behavior via a focus on the intersection of values, symbols, and political change. "Doctrinal change, like all change," they have written, "is complex and is often tied to rearrangements in political structures." Criticizing the establishment school's claim of Muslim essentialism they have argued that assertions "that credos, beliefs, or traditions are timeless and immemorial should not obscure the fact that they are subject to constant modification and change." In this Islam is no different from any other religious tradition. Their emphasis is on the socioeconomic, political, and historical context that shapes debates on Islam and democracy, and they categorically reject the idea that there is a fossilized Islamic "blueprint" that shapes Muslim attitudes toward democracy today (Eickelman and Piscatori 1996, 16).

A more recent contribution has been advanced by Noah Feldman. Rejecting both an extreme Eurocentric and a Bin Laden interpretation of Islam that emphasizes Islam's alleged pristine and unchanging nature, he argues that both Islam and democracy are "mobile ideas" with sufficient elasticity to develop a synthesis to meet the demands of the modern age and promote political development: "The question is not whether that 'democratic' structure is 'really there' in early Muslim history or classical Islamic political theory; that is an interpretive question for Muslims to address. What matters is that the potential democratic readings of Islamic tradition are possible and that Muslims today are reading their tradition that way" (Feldman 2004, 54). Abdulaziz Sachedina, Khaled Abou El Fadl, Abdelwahab El-Affendi, and Abdou Filali-Ansary have also written extensively, insightfully and optimistically on the topic in ways that challenge the establishment perspective (Sachedina 2001; Abou El Fadl 2004; El-Affendi 2006; Filali-Ansary 2003).

Three Points of Contention in the Islam and Democracy Debate

While the above schools of thought are not monolithic, their members do share common assumptions and advance similar arguments on Islam and democracy thus meriting these broad schools of interpretation. The two schools clash, however, on three issues that have been central to the debate on Islam and democracy: (1) the question of Islamism, (2) the role of Western policy, and (3) the question of liberalism.

The global processes of religious resurgence at the end of the twentieth century have led to the rise of various Islamist movements and religious-based political parties across the Muslim world. In many countries they are the leading voices of opposition and important players in domestic politics with substantial grass roots sympathy and support. The establishment scholars interpret this development as proof that Islam is incompatible with democracy. They view these movements as authoritarian movements at best, totalitarian at worst with a proclivity toward violence, terrorism, and a hidden antidemocratic agenda best captured in the famous statement by Edward Djerejian, the veteran American Middle East ambassador that these Islamists groups believe in "one man, one vote, *one time*" (Djerejian 2008, 17–29). In short, they are viewed as a posing a threat to both the societies in which they operate and to Western interests in the Middle East. The case of the Islamic Republic of Iran and Sudan are frequently cited as proof of this claim (Tibi 2008; Kramer 1996, 265–278; Lewis 2003b, 109–112; Skelly 2009; Berman 2010).

Their critics respond that mainstream Islamism, in contrast to its extreme manifestations, is compatible with democratization over the long term. The Egyptian Muslim Brotherhood and the Ennahda Movement in Tunisia are contrasted with al-Qa`ida and the Taliban with special emphasis on their evolving attitudes toward democracy. Characteristics of these mainstream Islamist groups that are highlighted include their rejection of violence in obtaining political power (in contrast to the regimes that rule over them), their enthusiastic participation in elections (when allowed to do so), and the important social welfare role they play in civil society in meeting the needs of the poor. These groups are viewed as organically connected religious nationalist movements deeply engaged with the problems in their own societies who should not be judged uniformly but contextually, with a sense of history and sensitivity both to the repressive context they inhabit and the variation among and within these groups (Ayoob 2008; Wickham 2002; Esposito 1998; Fuller 2003; Lynch 2010).

Western policy toward the Muslim world, both in the past and in the present, is another point of conflict between these rival camps of interpreters. The establishment school views the history of Western intervention as having a benign influence at worst on political development in Muslim societies. They generally downplay or ignore criticism of the legacy of colonialism while focusing on internal factors that have impeded democratization. Generally, they have been supportive of US policy and Western intervention in the Middle East. This was brought to light during the lead up to the 2003 invasion of Iraq when Bernard Lewis and Fouad Ajami publicly supported the invasion and became key advisors to the Bush administration on US Middle East policy (Shatz 2003; Waldman 2004; Ajami 2006). According to Bernard Lewis, "Either we bring them freedom, or they destroy us" (Lewis 2010, 168).

Critics of this establishment perspective highlight the negative legacy of Western colonialism and imperialism in undermining Muslim political development. They extend their criticism to the modern period with an emphasis on US policy that has supported dictatorial regimes and opposed popular social movements. A key issue that demarcates both schools is the Israel-Palestine conflict. The establishment school strongly supports Israel and its security needs, while their critics are sensitive to the plight of the Palestinians and the destabilizing effects that flow from the nonresolution of this conflict on Islam-West relations and the politics of the Middle East more generally (Ayoob 2005; Nasr 1999).

Finally, there is the question of liberalism. The establishment perspective argues that democratic elections that bring illiberal Islamists to power are a setback for political development. They warn against the "tyranny of the majority" and argue that the goal in the debate on Islam and democracy should be liberty for Muslim societies, along the lines that exist in the West, not mere elections per se. The building of democratic institutions and the development of a political culture that can sustain liberal democracy over time are viewed as necessary preconditions to holding free and fair elections (Clawson 1994; Zakaria 2007, 89–159).

Their critics respond that liberal democracy, along a Western model, is not necessarily a universal aspiration for all societies and that fundamentally Muslims should be allowed to determine their own social and political norms, which may or may not be liberal. They also point out that any discussion of liberalism and its discontents in Muslim societies requires a sense of history. In the post-September 11 euphoria about the superiority of Western values, it is useful to recall that Western history did not begin with human rights, democracy, and free markets but rather that the manifestation of these ideals took centuries to evolve, often by experimentation and setback and with considerable bloodshed, violence, and injustice. These scholars argue that to expect Muslim societies to follow a less acrimonious trajectory of modernization is a judgment that is both historically unfair and analytically distorting (Parekh 1993; Bulliet 1993; Hashemi 2009, 31–66).

The debate on liberalism reintroduces the question of secularism and its relationship to Islam and Muslim societies. It is widely recognized that modern liberal democracies require the existence of a form of political secularism to sustain themselves, yet seemingly most Muslim polities today are characterized by political trends that are deeply antisecular. Skeptics often point to this fact as evidence that the future democratic possibilities look bleak for Muslim societies.

The 2007 comprehensive Gallup survey of global Muslim opinion is relevant here. Notwithstanding the widespread compatibility of values between Western and Muslim societies in terms of support for basic human rights and democracy, the West and Islamic world parted ways on the relationship between religion and state. Muslims overwhelmingly do not believe that greater democracy requires a Western-like separation of church and state (Esposito and Mogahed 2007, 35). Untangling this problem requires an appreciation for history and a sensitivity to the different historical lessons bequeathed to the West and the Islamic world with respect to religion-state relations over the past 500 years.

Secularism and Religion-State Relations Across the Islam-West Divide

The standard explanation as to as why secularism has emerged in the West, but not in Muslim societies, is that profound differences in theology and early religious experience between these civilizations has made all the difference. According to a famous formulation by Bernard Lewis, the "reasons why Muslims developed no secularist movement of their own, and reacted sharply against attempts to introduce one from abroad, will thus be clear from the contrasts between Christian and Muslim history and experience. From the beginning, Christians were taught by both by precept and practice to distinguish between God and Caesar and between the different duties owed to each of the two. Muslims received no such instruction" (Lewis 2003a, 103). Variations of this perspective have been advanced by other scholars over the years highlighting the uniqueness of Islam and its alleged secular-resistant essence (Gellner 1992, 5–22; Huntington 1996, 69–71).

This view has been widely popular for three reasons: it reinforces preexisting biases about Islam and Muslim societies, prominent scholars have given it an academic stamp of approval, and prominent Islamist voices have routinely decried secularism as a concept that is essentially anti-Islamic. While space does not allow for a comprehensive treatment of this topic, a brief alternative reading reveals that while history is important to understanding religion-state relations and the crisis of secularism in the Muslim world, it is not the early seventh century history of Islam that is significant. Rather events in the West and in the Islamic world in the early modern and late modern periods (the seventeenth through twentieth centuries) that have made all the difference. An analysis of the origins of political secularism in the Anglo-American tradition sheds considerable light on this topic (Hashemi 2010, 325–328).

The Origins of Political Secularism in the Anglo-American Tradition: Lessons For the Muslim World

In his widely acclaimed book *The Stillborn God: Religion, Politics and the Modern West*, Mark Lilla observes that historically almost every human civilization based its original understanding of legitimate political authority on the divine nexus between God, man, and the world. A close union between politics and theology, Lilla suggests, is the original condition of all civilizations as they try to make sense of the relationship between religion and politics and the natural order of the world that surrounds them (Lilla 2007). The questions that are germane for this discussion are how did this divine nexus between God, man, and society gradually erode in the case of Latin Christendom, thus leading to political secularism, and what are the comparative lessons today for Muslim societies?

In an authoritative overview of the history of secularism, José Casanova identifies four broad social trends that had secularizing consequences for the West: (1) the rise of modern capitalism; (2) the rise of modern nation-states and nationalism; (3) the scientific revolution; and, most importantly (4) the Protestant Reformation and the Wars of Religion during the sixteenth and seventeenth centuries (Casanova 1994, 11–39). It is this latter development that is central to the rise of political secularism, especially in the Anglo-American tradition, and that is particularly helpful in illuminating the question of religion-state relations in Muslim societies.

Post-Reformation Europe saw the emergence of new debates about religious toleration, not only between Catholics and Protestants but also, critically, among the various Protestant sects. In an age of gross intolerance, most Christian denominations were interested in enforcing religious uniformity on their societies, each of them claiming exclusive knowledge of God's will on earth and warning of the dangers of social disorder and chaos if religious toleration were allowed to flourish. In brief, religious toleration and political stability were thought to be negatively correlated. Uniformity of religious practice in the public sphere and the need for an established state religion were widely believed to be a prerequisite for peace, order, and prosperity. This was the dominant view at the time, right up to the late seventeenth century (Zagorin 2003).

It was left to John Locke to rethink the relationship between toleration and political order. In his famous *A Letter Concerning Toleration* (1685), he rejected his earlier support for the firm union of church and state and posited a new solution to the core political problem that was plaguing Europe. Religious pluralism in the public sphere and political stability were indeed compatible, Locke argued, on the condition that we can "distinguish exactly the business of civil government from that of religion and to settle the just bounds that lie between the one and the other" (Locke 1983, 26). In other words, a soft form of secularism was required. The key interpretive point here is that political secularism emerged in England as the direct result of an existential crisis that was tearing the country apart. This conflict raged for many years and without a solution, Locke believed, Europe would know neither peace, prosperity, nor stability. The colossal size of this crisis cannot be overstated. Without a resolution of this issue, the self-immolation of the West was a very real possibility. Quite literally, the future political stability of the Western world hung in the balance. Political secularism thus emerged in the Anglo-American tradition as the result of a critical crisis of survival. It was intimately and indelibly connected to these transformative events in the early modern period of Europe, or as Charles Taylor has noted, "The origin point of modern Western secularism was the Wars of Religion; or rather, the search in battle-fatigue and horror for a way out of them" (Taylor 1998, 32). In short, the idea of a separation between church and state originated as a political solution out of an existential dilemma. A contrast between this picture and the case of the Muslim world, with respect to the relationship between religious toleration and political order, is most illustrative.

Muslim Toleration and its Political Consequences

Historians are in broad agreement that comparatively speaking, in the premodern era, Muslim societies were more tolerant of religious pluralism than Christendom. The fact that until the mid-twentieth century, for example, the city of Baghdad had a population that was one-third Jewish speaks to this point. It is not claimed here that the Muslim world was a bastion of liberal tolerance as we understand this concept today or that minorities and dissidents were never persecuted; far from it. The claim is simply that Muslim societies and empires at their zenith were historically more tolerant than Christendom during this time period, and consequently they did not face the same all-consuming Wars of Religion and debates over religious toleration and political order that were so central to European political history in the early modern period (Russell 1972).

The key political point that flows from the fact of relative Muslim tolerance (in contrast to centuries of Christian intolerance, especially during the early modern period) is that no burning political questions emerged between state and society where religion was the key, all-consuming and overriding bone of political contention. As a result, no inner political dynamic emerged within the Middle East that would necessitate the development of intellectual or moral arguments in favor of religion-state separation (political secularism) as a way out of an existentialist political dilemma in the same way these arguments developed and were so critical to the rise of secularism in Europe during the seventeenth century.

The primary political problems facing Muslim societies that threatened sociopolitical order were the corruption and nepotism of the royal court, rival dynastic claims, natural famines and disasters, and most importantly, foreign intervention and invasions such as the crusades of the eleventh to thirteenth centuries, the Mongol invasion of 1258 (which sacked the Abbasid caliphate), the Castilian reconquest of the Iberian Peninsula, and increasingly in the modern period growing Russian, French, British, and later American penetration, colonialism, and imperialism (to varying degrees depending on the country, region, and time frame in question; Lapidus 2002; Hodgson 1974). Due to this significantly different historical experience with respect to religious toleration—and this is key to understanding the relationship between Islam and secularism—*Muslim societies never had the need to think about secularism*—in the same way the West did, as there was no existential crisis that resulted from debates on religion-state relations where secularism might be posited as a solution to a pressing political dilemma.

Moreover, as Noah Feldman has recently argued in *The Fall and Rise of the Islamic State*, religion-state relations in the Muslim world were far more stable and amicable than they were in the West. For over a millennium, religion often played a constructive role as an agent of stability and predictability. In contrast to the European experience where religion in the post-Reformation period became a source of deep conflict, in the Muslim world religion and the scholars who interpreted it managed to place restrictions on the personal whims and ambitions of the caliphs and sultans by forcing them to recognize religious limits to their rule in exchange for conferring legitimacy on the state. In short, the rulers were not above the law—as they later became during the twentieth century—but they were often constrained by it, thus limiting autocracy and arbitrary rule. Religion-state relations in the Muslim world have thus bequeathed different historical lessons and memories to the faithful where religion is viewed by large segments of the population not as a natural ally of political tyranny and a cause of conflict but, much more positively, as a possible constraint on political despotism and as a source of stability. According to Feldman, this partly explains why demands for a greater role for religion in politics have a sympathetic hearing in the Muslim world today (where Islamists are not in power). This brings us to the modern period (Feldman 2008).

The Modern Muslim Experience With Secularism

In the past 200 years, the Muslim world's experience with secularism has been largely negative. It is important to appreciate that in Europe secularism was an indigenous and gradual process evolving in conjunction with socioeconomic and political developments while supported by intellectual arguments—and critically by religious groups and leaders—that eventually sunk deep roots within its political culture. By contrast, the Muslim experience has been marked by a perception of secularism as an alien ideology first imposed from the outside by colonial and imperial invaders and then kept alive by local elites who came to power during the postcolonial period. In short, secularism in Europe was largely a bottom-up process that was intimately connected to debates from within civil society, whereas in Muslim societies secularism was largely a top-down process that was driven first by the colonial state and then by the postcolonial state. As a result, secularism in the Muslim world has suffered from weak intellectual roots, and with few exceptions, secularism has never penetrated the mainstream of Muslim societies.

Furthermore, by the end of twentieth century most states in the Muslim world were developmental failures. A pattern of state-society relations unfolded in the postcolonial era that further impugned the reputation of secularism. An autocratic modernizing state, often with critical external support, suffocated civil society, thus forcing oppositional activity into the mosque, inadvertently contributing to the rise of political Islam. A set of top-down, forced modernization, secularization, and Westernization policies by the state—within a short span of time—generated widespread social and psychological alienation and dislocation. Rapid urbanization, changing cultural and socioeconomic relationships, coupled with increasing corruption, economic mismanagement, rising poverty, and income inequality undermined the legitimacy of the state. These developments reflected negatively on secularism because the ruling ideologies of many postcolonial regimes in the Muslim world were openly secular and nationalist (Nasr 2009, 85–115).

Thus, for a generation of Muslims growing up in the postcolonial era, despotism, dictatorship, and human rights abuses came to be associated with secularism. Muslim political activists who experienced oppression at the hands of secular national governments logically concluded that secularism is an ideology of repression. This observation applies not only to Iran (under the Shah) but also to Tunisia, Algeria, Egypt, Syria, Iraq (under Saddam), Yemen, and to a certain extent Turkey in the latter half of the twentieth century. Summarizing this trend, Vali Nasr has noted, "Secularism in the Muslim world never overcame its colonial origins and never lost its association with the postcolonial state's continuous struggle to dominate society. Its fortunes became tied to those of the state: the more the state's ideology came into question, and the more its actions alienated social forces, the more secularism was rejected in favor of indigenous worldviews and social institutions—which were for the most part tied to Islam. As such, the decline of secularism was a reflection of the decline of the postcolonial state in the Muslim world" (Nasr 2003, 69).

Thus, a different set of historical experiences, both in the premodern and modern eras, has produced a situation whereby secularism is today a deeply controversial concept in Muslim societies. There is infinitely more to this story, but with respect to the development of democracy it is interesting to note that in those Muslim societies that have in recent years registered the largest gains for democracy this development have been accompanied by the cultivation of an indigenous and organic form of "Muslim secularism" (Hashemi 2009, 152–169). This suggests that in Muslim societies the process of democratization cannot be separated from the debate on political secularization. The cases of Turkey and Indonesia come to mind and more recently Iran, where the rise of the reformist Green Movement has advanced arguments firmly rooted in Iran's Shiite Islamic and post-1979 revolutionary heritage while simultaneously calling for, as they did in their recently released charter, "maintaining the independence of religious and clerical institutions from the government" (Hashemi and Postel 2011).[5]

These intellectual transformations are closely related to the rise of what Asef Bayat has called the "post-Islamist" turn in Muslim politics. This emerging trend "represents an endeavor to fuse religiosity with rights, faith and freedom, Islam and liberty. It is an attempt to turn the underlying principles of Islamism on its head" by former Islamists themselves "by emphasizing rights instead of duties, plurality instead of a single authoritative voice, historicity rather than fixed scriptures and the future instead of the past. It wants to marry Islam with individual choice and freedom, with democracy and modernity…to achieve what some have termed an 'alternative modernity'" (Bayat 2005, 2007). Politicians such as Recep Tayyip Erdoğan in Turkey, Anwar Ibrahim in Malaysia, and Mir Hossein Mousavi in Iran represent this political trend that has distinct parallels with the rise of Christian democratic parties in Europe. Firmly rooted in a conservative political theology, they have gradually reconciled tradition with modernity, in particular the principles of democracy, human rights, pluralism, and political secularism, and today they represent a very encouraging trend for the promotion and development of democracy in the Muslim world (Nasr 2005; Kalyvas 2003).

Conclusion

The debate on Islam and democracy has generated considerable controversy and acrimony over the years. It has been one of the key political and intellectual debates of the post-Cold War era, rising in importance after the tragic events of September 11, 2001 and then again after the 2011 Arab Spring. One reason it remains of interest is due to its perceived connection to several important issues on the international agenda: the debate on immigration and multiculturalism in Europe, the universality of human rights, Turkey's admission into the Europe Union, the Israel-Palestine conflict, US foreign policy toward Iraq and Afghanistan, and indeed the future political trajectory of the Arab and Islamic world, whose total population now constitutes almost a quarter of humanity.

Objectively examining this topic is difficult because this is not a neutral part of the world to study. When Westerners approach it, they often do so with unexamined cultural baggage rooted in a long and complicated history of Islam-West relations that distorts internal Muslim politics (Hentsch 1992; Sells and Qureshi 2003). Critical thinking on the topic of Islam's compatibility with democracy needs to be aware of these ideological constraints and should keep the following points in mind.

Religion is not a monolithic and unchanging category that speaks with one voice throughout history. It is shaped by changing political and socioeconomic contexts and can be interpreted in a myriad of different ways. One need only think about the multiple uses to which the Bible has been put throughout history: justifying both the divine right of kings and democracy, slavery and abolitionism, misogyny and gender equality, colonialism and third world struggles for self-determination, and Jim Crow laws and the US Civil Rights Movement.

Like other religious traditions whose origins lie in the premodern era and that are scripturally based, Islam is neither more nor less compatible with modern democracy than Christianity or Judaism. Not too long ago it was argued that Catholicism was an obstacle to democracy and that only Protestant majority countries respected popular sovereignty. The key interpretive point here is that religious traditions are a highly complex body of ideas, assumptions, and doctrines that, when interpreted in a modern context 1,500 years later, contain sufficient ambiguity and elasticity to be read in a variety of different ways—both in support of and in opposition to democracy. This is not to suggest that religious doctrine should be completely ignored when discussing democracy in the Middle East but rather that Islamic political thought is not fossilized in some premedieval essence.

Gudrun Krämer has astutely noted that "it is not possible to talk about Islam and democracy in general but only about Muslims living and theorizing under specific historical circumstances." In the debate on Islam and democracy sometimes one encounters arguments that "the Islamic position is" such-and-such regarding democracy, human rights, or pluralism, rejecting alternative formulations. This is misleading because while all religions have basic tenets, the rest is subject to debate and interpretation, particularly the structure of a modern political system and the role of religion within it. The point here is that Muslim societies are diverse and one cleric, group, or political leader cannot justly claim to represent all Muslims. Likewise, internal debates on democracy are vastly different when one moves from Saudi Arabia to Turkey to Iran to Indonesia to Muslims living with the United States. Required in this debate are not generalities but specificities (Krämer 1997, 72).

Asking the right questions is important as well. Graham Fuller has suggested that rather than asking whether Islam is compatible with democracy, the more appropriate question to ask is what do Muslims want? If it is a political system that is rooted in the ideals of liberal democracy and that is simultaneously compatible with their religious heritage then it is up to Muslims themselves to invoke and produce the necessary moral arguments, interpretations, and sacrifices that can bring this vision into reality (Fuller 1999). There is no fait accompli here—only interpretive possibilities and opportunities.

Similarly, Asef Bayat has suggested that "the pertinent question is not whether Islam and democracy are compatible... but rather how and under what conditions Muslims can *make* their religion compatible with desired notions of democracy." He notes that the congruence between Islam and democracy is not a philosophical question but a political one, thus debate on the topic should be less abstract and more rooted in solid empirical analysis of the social conditions that can promote political change (Bayat 2007, 197). The domestic, regional, and international economic and political context is highly relevant here in shaping internal political struggles in Muslim societies.

Sadly, this context for most of the past century has not been conducive to internal struggles for democratization. Most of the postcolonial states of the Muslim world continue to be plagued by problems that affect all developing societies in the global south: poverty, high unemployment, rapid population growth, environmental decay, political corruption, and illegitimate and repressive regimes, some but not all of whom have been supported by the West. The ongoing Israel-Palestine conflict and the wars in Iraq and Afghanistan have further destabilized the Middle East, inadvertently strengthening political authoritarianism throughout the region. Thus, the social conditions for democratization have been far from optimal and Western policy, significantly driven by the vast petroleum resources of the region, have made matters worse.

Finally, a sense of history is needed. The development of democracy is a historical process that is evolutionary and gradual. Democracy, in other words, requires patience. It should be remembered that the United States of America, one of the oldest democracies in the world, maintained the legal institution of slavery for the first ninety years of its republic and that it took another hundred years before African Americans could achieve meaningful levels of civil rights protection and a further forty-three years before the first African-American could be elected president. In the same vein it should be recalled that for the first 150 years of American democracy, women did not have the right to vote. This raises the question of whether the United States can be considered a democracy, given that half its population was legally disenfranchised for most its history.

In Muslim societies, the debate on Islam and democracy is relatively recent and the topic does not emerge as a major theme in its own right before the 1980s. In this sense, the journey is just beginning for Muslims. In contrast to the Western experience with democracy, the Muslim experience—of which there are many—is unfolding in a rapidly different and more complicated domestic, regional, and international context. In the end it should be remembered that one of the most difficult issues for any emerging polity to resolve is the normative role of religion in politics. There are no easy formulas to follow or exact models to emulate. Trial, error, and experimentation are the only ways forward.

Notes

1. All five reports can be accessed at http://www.arab-hdr.org.
2. Figures are based on total Muslim populations of Indonesia, Bangladesh, India, Pakistan, Nigeria, and Turkey.
3. Also see Amartya Sen, *Identity and Violence: The Illusion of Destiny* (New York: W.W. Norton, 2006), 51–55.
4. For a thorough critique of this genre, see Yahya Sadowski, "The New Orientalism and the Democracy Debate," in Joel Beinin and Joe Stork eds., *Political Islam: Essays from Middle East Report* (Berkeley: University of California Press, 1997), 33–51.
5. For the philosophical roots of Muslim secularism in postrevolutionary Iran, see Abdolkarim Soroush, *Reason, Freedom and Democracy in Islam: Essential Writings of Abdolkarim Soroush*, translated and edited with a critical introduction by Ahmad Sadri and Mahmoud Sadri (New York: Oxford University Press, 1999), 54–68.

References

Abou El Fadl, Khaled. 2003. "Islam and State: A Short History." In *Democracy and Islam in the New Afghan Constitution*, ed. Cheryl Bernard and Nina Hachigian, 13–16. Santa Monica: Rand Corporation.

Abou El Fadl, Khaled. 2004. *Islam and the Challenge of Democracy*. Ed. Joshua Cohen and Deborah Chasman. Princeton: Princeton University Press.

Ajami, Fouad. 1998. *Dream Palace of the Arabs: A Generation's Odyssey*. New York: Pantheon.

Ajami, Fouad. 2006. *The Foreigner's Gift: The Americans, the Arabs and the Iraqis in Iraq*. New York: Free Press.

Ayoob, Mohammed. 2005. "The Muslim World's Poor Record of Modernization and Democratization: The Interplay of External and Internal Factors." In *Modernization, Democracy and Islam*, ed. Shireen Hunter and Huma Malik, 186–202. Westport, CT: Praeger, 2005.

Ayoob, Mohammed. 2008. *The Many Face of Political Islam: Religion and Politics in the Muslim World*. Ann Arbor: University of Michigan Press.

Bayat, Asef. 2005. What Is Post-Islamism? *ISIM Review* 16, 5.

Bayat, Asef. 2007. *Making Islam Democratic: Social Movements and the Post-Islamist Turn*. Stanford: Stanford University Press, 2007.

Berman, Paul. 2010. *The Flight of the Intellectuals*. New York: Melville House.

Brynen, Rex, Baghat Korany, and Paul Noble. 1995. *Political Liberalization and Democratization in the Arab World: Theoretical Perspectives*. Boulder, CO: Lynne Rienner, 1995.

Bulliet, Richard. 1993. *Under Siege: Islam and Democracy: Rhetoric, Discourse, and the Future of Hope*. Proceedings of a conference at Columbia University, June 18–19, 1993. New York: The Middle East Institute.

Casanova, José. 1994. *Public Religions in the Modern World*. Chicago: University of Chicago.

Casanova, José. 2001. "Civil Society and Religion: Retrospective Reflections on Catholicism and Prospective Reflections on Islam." *Social Research* 68: 1041–1080.

Clawson, Patrick. 1994. Liberty's the Thing, Not Democracy. *Middle East Quarterly* 1: 12–13.

Crone, Patricia. 2005. *God's Rule: Government and Islam—Six Centuries of Medieval Islamic Political Thought*. New York. Columbia University Press.

Dahl, Robert. 1989. *Democracy and Its Critics*. New Haven: Yale University Press.

Diamond, Larry, Marc Plattner, and Philip Costopoulous. 2005. *World Religions and Democracy*. Baltimore: Johns Hopkins University Press.

Djerejian, Edward. 2008. *Danger and Opportunity: An American Ambassador's Journey through the Middle East*. New York: Threshold Editions.

Eickelman, Dale, and James Piscatori. 1996. *Muslim Politics*. Princeton: Princeton University Press.

El-Affendi, Abdelwahab. 2004. "On the State, Democracy and Pluralism." In *Islamic Thought in the Twentieth Century*, ed. Suha Taji-Farouki and Basheer Nafi, 180–203. New York: I.B. Tauris.

El-Affendi, Abdelwahab. 2006. "Democracy and Its (Muslim) Critics: An Islamic Alternative to Democracy?" In *Islamic Democratic Discourse: Theory, Debates, and Philosophical Perspectives*, ed. Muqtedar Khan, 227–256. Lanham, MD: Lexington Books.

El-Affendi, Abdelwahab. 2010. "The Modern Debate(s) on Islam and Democracy." The Asia Foundation. http://www.ndid.org.my/web/wp-content/uploads/2010/04/The-Modern-Debate-on-Islam-and-DemocracyAbdelwahab-El-Affendi-4.htm (accessed June 15, 2010).

Elshtain, Jean Bethke. 2009. "Religion and Democracy." *Journal of Democracy* 20: 5–17.

Enayat, Hamid. 1982. *Modern Islamic Political Thought*. Austin: University of Texas Press.

Esposito, John. 1998. *Islam and Politics*. 4th edition. Syracuse: Syracuse University Press.

Esposito, John, and Dalia Mogahed. 2007. *Who Speaks for Islam?: What a Billion Muslims Really Think*. New York. Gallup Press.

Esposito, John, and Dalia Mogahed. 2008. "Muslim True/False." *Los Angeles Times*, April 2, A15.

Esposito, John, and John Voll. 1994. "Islam's Democratic Essence." *Middle East Quarterly* 1: 3–11.

Esposito, John, and John Voll. 1996. *Islam and Democracy*. New York: Oxford University Press.

Euben, Roxanne, and Muhammad Qasim Zaman. 2009. *Princeton Readings in Islamist Thought: Texts and Contexts from al-Banna to Bin Laden*. Princeton: Princeton University Press.

Feldman, Noah. 2004. *After Jihad: America and the Struggle for Islamic Democracy*. New York: Farrar, Straus & Giroux.

Feldman, Noah. 2008. *The Fall and Rise of the Islamic State*. Princeton: Princeton University Press.

Filali-Ansary, Abdou. 2003. "Muslims and Democracy." In *Islam and Democracy in the Middle East*, ed. Larry Diamond, Marc Plattner, and Daniel Brumberg, 193–207. Baltimore: Johns Hopkins University Press.

Fox, Jonathan Fox. 2007. "Do Democracies Have Separation of Religion and State?" *Canadian Journal of Political Science* 40: 1–25.

Fox, Jonathan. 2008. *A World Survey of Religion and State*. Cambridge: Cambridge University Press.

Freedom House. 2001. "New Study Reveals Islamic World's Democracy Deficit." December 18. http://www.freedomhouse.org/template.cfm?page=70&release=101 (accessed June 1, 2010).

Freedom House. 2010. "Freedom in the World 2010: Erosion of Freedom Intensifies." http://www.freedomhouse.org/template.cfm?page=505 (accessed June 1, 2010).

Fukuyama, Francis. 2001. "History Is Still Going Our Way." *Wall Street Journal*, October 5, A14.

Fuller, Graham. 1999. "Islam, a Force for Change." *Le Monde Diplomatique*. September, http://mondediplo.com/1999/09/16islam.

Fuller, Graham. 2003. *The Future of Political Islam*. New York: Palgrave.

Gellner, Ernest. 1991. "Islam and Marxism: Some Comparisons." *International Affairs* 67: 1–6.

Gellner, Ernest. 1992. *Postmodernism, Reason and Religion*. New York: Routledge.

Hashemi, Nader. *Islam, Secularism and Liberal Democracy: Toward a Democratic Theory for Muslim Societies*. New York: Oxford University Press, 2009.

Hashemi, Nader. 2010. "The Multiple Histories of Secularism: Muslim Societies in Comparative Perspective." *Journal of Philosophy and Social Criticism* 36: 325–338.

Hashemi, Nader, and Danny Postel. 2011. *The People Reloaded: The Rise of the Green Movement and the Struggle for Iran's Future*. New York: Melville House.

Hentsch, Thierry. 1992. *Imagining the Middle East*. Montreal: Black Rose Books.

Hodgson, Marshall. 1974. *The Venture of Islam*. Vol. 3. Chicago: University of Chicago Press.

Hunter, Shireen, and Huma Malik. 2005. *Modernization, Democracy and Islam*. Westport, CT: Praeger.

Huntington, Samuel. 1984. "Will More Countries Become Democratic?" *Political Science Quarterly* 99: 193–218.

Huntington, Samuel. 1996. *The Clash of Civilizations and the Remaking of the Modern World*. New York: Simon & Schuster.

Keane, John. 2009. *The Life and Death of Democracy*. London: Simon and Schuster.

Kedourie, Elie. 1992. *Democracy and Arab Political Culture*. Washington, DC: Washington Institute for Near East Policy.

Kramer, Martin. 1996. *Arab Awakening and Islamic Revival: The Politics of Ideas in the Middle East*. New Brunswick, NJ: Transaction Publishers.

Krämer, Gudrun. 1997. "Islamist Notions of Democracy." In *Political Islam: Essays from Middle East Report*, ed. Joel Beinin and Joe Stork, 71–82. Berkeley: University of California Press.

Lapidus, Ira. 2002. *A History of Islamic Societies*. 2nd ed. Cambridge: Cambridge University Press.

Lewis, Bernard. 1996. "Islam and Liberal Democracy: A Historical Overview." *Journal of Democracy* 7: 52–63.

Lewis, Bernard Lewis. 2003a. *What Went Wrong?: The Clash Between Islam and Modernity in the Middle East*. New York: Harper Collins.

Lewis, Bernard Lewis. 2003b. *The Crisis of Islam: Holy War and Unholy Terror*. New York: Random House.

Lewis, Bernard. 2010. *Faith and Power: Religion and Politics in the Middle East*. New York: Oxford University Press.

Lilla, Mark. 2007. *The Stillborn God: Religion, Politics and the Modern West*. New York: Knopf.

Locke, John. 1983. *A Letter Concerning Toleration*. Ed. by James Tully. Indianapolis, IN: Hackett.

Lynch, Marc. 2010. "Veiled Truths: The Rise of Political Islam in the West." *Foreign Affairs* 89: 138–147.

Nasr, Vali. 1999. "European Colonialism and the Emergence of Modern Muslim States." In *The Oxford Dictionary of Islam*, ed. John Esposito, 549–599. New York: Oxford University Press.

Nasr, Vali. 2003. "Secularism: Lessons from the Muslim World." *Daedalus* 132: 67–72.

Nasr, Vali. 2005. "The Rise of 'Muslim Democracy.'" *Journal of Democracy* 16: 13–27.

Nasr, Vali. 2009. *Forces of Fortune: The Rise of the New Muslim Middle Class and What It Will Mean for Our World*. New York: Free Press.

Kalyvas, Stathis. 2003. "Unsecular Politics and Religious Mobilization." In *European Christian Democracy*, ed. Thomas Kselman and Joseph Buttigieg, 293–320. Notre Dame: University of Notre Dame Press.

Niblock, Tim. 1998. "Democratization: A Theoretical and Practical Debate." *British Journal of Middle Eastern Studies* 25: 221–233.

Parekh, Bhikhu. 1993. "The Cultural Particularity of Liberal Democracy." In *Prospects for Democracy: North, South, East, West*, ed. David Held, 156–175. Stanford: Stanford University Press, 1993.

Pipes, Daniel. 2002. *In the Path of God: Islam and Political Power*. New Brunswick, NJ: Transaction Publishers.

Posusney, Marsha Pripstein, and Michele Penner Angrist. 2005. *Authoritarianism in the Middle East: Regimes and Resistance*. Boulder, CO: Lynne Rienner.

Russell, Bertrand. 1972. "Reading History as It Is Never Written." In *The Collected Stories of Bertrand Russell*, ed. Barry Feinberg, 290–310. London: George Allen and Unwin.

Rousseau, Jean-Jacques. 1987. *On the Social Contract*, trans. by Donald A. Cress. Indianapolis: Hackett Publishing.

Sachedina, Abdulaziz. 2001. *The Islamic Roots of Democratic Pluralism*. New York: Oxford University Press.

Sadowski, Yahya. 1997. "The New Orientalism and the Democracy Debate." In *Political Islam: Essays from Middle East Report*, ed. Joel Beinin and Joe Stork, 33–51. Berkeley: University of California Press.

Salamé, Ghassan. 1994. *Democracy without Democrats?: The Renewal of Politics in the Muslim World*. New York: I.B. Tauris.

Sells, Michael, and Emran Qureshi. 2003. *The New Crusades: Constructing the Muslim Enemy*. New York: Columbia University Press.

Sen, Amartya. 1999. "Democracy as a Universal Value." *Journal of Democracy* 10: 3–17.

Sen, Amartya. 2006. *Identity and Violence: The Illusion of Destiny*. New York: W.W. Norton.

Shatz, Adam. 2003. "The Native Informant." *The Nation*, April 10: 15–24.

Sieff, Martin. 1992. "New Challenge for the West: Islamic Fundamentalism." *Washington Times*, February 16, A19.

Skelly, John Morrison. 2009. *Political Islam from Muhammad to Ahmadinejad: Defenders, Detractors and Definitions*. Westport, CT: Praeger.

Soroush, Abdolkarim. 1999. *Reason, Freedom and Democracy in Islam: Essential Writings of Abdolkarim Soroush*. Trans. and ed. with a critical introduction by Ahmad Sadri and Mahmoud Sadri. New York: Oxford University Press.

Stepan, Alfred. 2001. *Arguing Comparative Politics*. New York: Oxford University Press.

Straus, Roger. 1938. "The Relation of Religion to Democracy." *Public Opinion Quarterly* 2: 37–38.

Taylor, Charles. 1998. "Modes of Secularism." In *Secularism and Its Critics*, ed. by Rajeev Bhargava, 31–51. New Delhi: Oxford University Press.

Tibi, Bassam. 2008. "Islamist Parties: Why They Can't Be Democratic." *Journal of Democracy* 19: 43–48.

Tocqueville, Alexis de. 1990. *Democracy in America*. Vol. 1, trans. by Henry Reeve. New York: Vintage Books.

United Nations Development Program. 2002. *Arab Development Report 2002: Creating Opportunities for Future Generations*. United Nations: New York.

Waldman, Peter. 2004. "A Historian's Take on Islam Steers U.S. in Terrorism Fight." *Wall Street Journal*, February 3.

Wickham, Carrie. 2002. *Mobilizing Islam: Religion, Activism and Political Change in Egypt*. New York: Columbia University Press.

Witte Jr., John. 2005. *Religion and the American Constitutional Experiment*. 2nd ed. Boulder, CO: Westview Press.

Woodberry, Robert, and Timothy Shah. 2004. "Christianity and Democracy: The Pioneering Protestants." *Journal of Democracy* 15: 47–61.

Zagorin, Perez. 2003. *How the Idea of Religious Toleration Came to the West*. Princeton: Princeton University Press.

Zakaria, Fareed. 2007. *The Future of Freedom: Illiberal Democracy at Home and Abroad*. New York: W.W. Norton.

CHAPTER 6

THE POLITICAL ECONOMY OF ISLAM AND POLITICS

TAREK MASOUD

INTRODUCTION

THE study of political Islam's "political economy" actually embraces two distinct forms of social scientific inquiry. The first focuses on the relationship between the economic conditions prevalent in most modern Muslim societies and either individual attitudes toward religion (Monroe and Kreidie 1997; Blaydes and Linzer 2008) or decisions to join or otherwise support "Islamist" or "Islamic fundamentalist" groups (Ibrahim 1980; Alam 2003; Rosendorff and Sandler 2005). The second form involves interrogating and explaining the economic beliefs of Islamic thinkers and scholars—identifying their positions on such ostensibly economic matters as distributive justice, rights of ownership, and the role of the state in the economy and evaluating their workability in practice (Kuran 1996; Tripp 2006; El-Gamal 2006; Visser 2009).

Neither of these forms of "political economy," however, has been sufficiently attentive to politics or political institutions. For example, treatments of the second kind of Islamic political economy—the analysis of Islamic economic ideas—have generally ignored the economic ideas put forth by Islamic political parties, such as Egypt's Muslim Brotherhood (Jamā`atal-Ikhwānal-Muslimīn), Tunisia's Renaissance Movement Party (ḤizbḤarakah al-Nahda) Jordan's Islamic Action Front (ḤizbJabhat al-`Amal al-Islāmī), and Turkey's Party of Justice and Development (AdaletveKalkinmaPartisi), preferring instead to study the exertions of intellectuals whose connection to real world economic policies is tenuous and distant at best. Similarly, individual-level analyses of the causal role economic factors in generating support for Islamism tend to assume that, to paraphrase Hechter (2004), Islamist ideas simply float down from the ether to take root in minds made receptive by socio-economic conditions, without reference to the exertions of Islamist political parties in generating these ideas or attracting and mobilizing support for them.

This essay argues that much can be gained from making Islamist political parties the center of our political economy analyses of Islam and politics. As the most vibrant and effective political parties across the Muslim Middle East, such parties have come to represent nearly the totality of the phenomenon we call "political Islam," andwill play an important role in the region's democratizing politics. It is vital, therefore, that we attend to what these parties believe about the economic realm, and to the economic and sociological factors that make people more or less likely to support them.

In this essay, I first review the state of our knowledge on the economic roots of support for Islamic parties and politics. I trace the evolution of our understanding of why people support Islamism—from essentialist accounts that locate the Islamism's appeal in the inherent charisma of Islam, to accounts that describe Islamism as a pathological result of the action of social strains on individual cognitive processes, to rationalist accounts that link support for political Islam to the receipt of selective benefits from Islamic parties. I show that all of these accounts offer highly static conceptions of what causes support for Islamist parties, neglecting how changing political institutions can alter dramatically the nature of political Islam's constituencies. I advance an alternative theory that puts at its center how political institutions both constrain and enable the mobilizing activities of Islamist parties, determining which segments of the socioeconomic spectrum they can appeal to, and how likely those segments will be to render their suffrages in return.

Turning to the "second" kind of political economy inquiry, I discuss the economic ideas and policy proposals of Islamic parties, with particular attention to their views on two major challenges facing contemporary Muslim societies: the privatization of large public sectors after decades of state socialism and the alleviation of the increasing inequalities that attend the transformation from command to market economies. I interrogate the extent to which Islamic parties employ economic policy proposals as signals of identity rather than as serious attempts to remedy problems facing their countries, and I investigate the extent to which these parties' economic platforms change with shifts in political incentives and constraints. The essay concludes by raising questions for future research into both strains of inquiry into the political economy of Islam and politics.

2 Socioeconomic Foundations of Islamist Support

A deft encapsulation of the conventional wisdom regarding the sources of popular support for Islamist parties can be found in an old cartoon published in an Egyptian magazine during that country's 1945 parliamentary elections (figure 6.1). In it, we see two candidates—one secular, one Islamist—addressing the same constituency. In the first panel, the irreligious politician lavishes potential voters with a series of eminently practical oaths: "I'll dig irrigation canals and sewers for you. I'll get you more rations. I'll get your sons government jobs." The voters, however, appear unmoved. Turning their backs on him, they grumble, "We have had our fill of such promises." In the second panel is a candidate of the Muslim Brotherhood, the world's oldest Islamic political movement, which contested the elections unsuccessfully that year. "God is our destiny!" he declares, reciting the first item from the Brotherhood's catechism. "The Prophet is our leader! The Qur'an is our constitution! And death in the path of God is our fondest wish!" The voters lean toward him intently, craning their necks, beaming in approval, exclaiming, "How beautiful is such talk!" Presumably the next panel, if there were one, would show the pious politician contentedly counting votes.

FIGURE 6.1: A cartoon representation of the foundations of Islamist support, from the newspaper of the Muslim Brotherhood, January 1945

The cartoon communicates a fully fledged and widely held, if unsubtle, explanation of why citizens support Islamist political parties. It tells us that Islamic political actors win adherents by offering comforting, emotionally satisfying religious rhetoric that is devoid of policy content or plans for concrete action (which are themselves inherently suspect as empty promises). An implication is that by shifting political discourse from talk of sewers, rations, and government jobs to talk of God and His Prophet, Islamist parties induce voters to ignore their material interests, to sublimate economic rationality on the altar of morality and spirituality.[1]

There are numerous hypotheses advanced to explain precisely why Islamic political appeals might possess this kind of advantage. Some have argued that Islamic appeals enjoy an electoral advantage by virtue of their resonance and cultural legitimacy with the average Muslim (Eickelman and Piscatori 1996; Wickham 2003; Singerman 2004). Still others argue that political Islam's appeal is not a function of that creed's special qualities but of the mobilizing power of religion more generally. Laitin (1986, 178) argues that political leaders who deploy religious and cultural symbols will be more likely to engender voter trust. Likewise, Tarrow (1998, 112) tells us that religion is a potent tool for seducing the masses because it is "so reliable a source of emotion" and offers politicians a toolkit of "ready-made symbols, rituals and solidarities." According to Aminzade and Perry(2001, 161), religious politicians are at an advantage because "their followers can be 'moved by the spirit' rather than persuaded by rational arguments."

However, these arguments are unable to explain variation in receptivity to Islamically inflected political appeals. Not all Muslims respond to the Islamist call, and even those who do now may not have in the past (and may not in the future). Moreover, in many of the countries of the Muslim world, there are multiple "Islamic" parties, all of which deploy Islamic rhetoric and symbols, but not all of which are able to capture votes and seats. For example, in Jordan, in addition to the Islamic Action Front (Ḥizb Jabhat al-`Amal al-Islāmī)—the country's most electorally successful political party—we have the ineffectual Islamic Centrist Party (Ḥizb al-Wasaṭ al-Islāmī). In Egypt, in addition to the Muslim Brotherhood are much smaller parties such as the Umma Party, founded in 1983 on a pro-*sharī`a* platform but which nonetheless has not managed to put any sort of stamp on Egyptian political life.[2] Similarly, parliamentary candidates of Egypt's Socialist Labor Party have long campaigned under the Brotherhood's slogan of "Islam Is the Solution" (*al-Islām Huwa al-Ḥal*), but the words worked no magic for them. And though the Muslim Brotherhood and Salafist Nur Parties captured two-thirds of the seats in the country's first post-Mubarak parliamentary elections, the partisans of political Islam performed much more poorly in the country's first genuine presidential election. Muhammad Morsi, the standard bearer of the Muslim Brotherhood, captured only a quarter of the vote (he was elevated to the presidency only after a runoff that saw many non-Islamists rally to his side to defeat his pro-Mubarak opponent.) The shifts in Islamism's electoral fortunes and the poor fortunes of Islamist also-rans demonstrate that, however stirring Islamic rhetoric may be, it alone cannot account for support for Islamist parties.

Other scholars have looked to economic and social factors to explain variation in support for Islamist parties. Drawing on Durkheim's (1951) explanation of suicide, one influential set of accounts of political Islam's appeal argue that it is a function of social strains—such as poverty or rural-urban migration—that cause individuals to seek refuge in the certainties of faith or culture. Ayubi (1980, 495) offers the quintessential Durkheimian narrative of political Islam, which is worth reproducing here in full:

> "Just imagine a recent immigrant from a village or a small town who has to cope with the dismal problems of a city like Cairo (the crowding, the noise, the crumbling, decayed, and moribund infrastructure, etc.), and who would on top of all that suspect that, under all kinds of pressures, his father might not be so correct (financially) and his sister might not be so correct (sexually); is not this the kind of situation that would lead people to search for a simple, strong, and clear-cut formula that would answer their many disturbing questions and provide them with certainty and assurance?"

There are multiple glosses on this basic logic, each identifying a different social phenomenon as the source of the strain—crushing poverty, modernization, urbanization, authoritarianism, to name a few (Roy 1994; Berman 2003; Almond et al. 2003; Wickham 2003). However, as Munson (2001, 493–494) has pointed out, such theories are difficult to adjudicate, dealing as they do with psychological states that cannot be observed directly or tested empirically.

Others have argued that such social phenomena as poverty and urbanization work to the advantage of religious parties not because they put people in religious frames of mind, but because they create social problems that these parties are able to step in and solve. For example, parties such as Egypt's Muslim Brotherhood, Palestine's Ḥamas, and Lebanon's Ḥizb Allāh are thought to earn the poor's allegiance through the provision of material succor at a time when the increasingly cash-strapped (non-oil-rich) states of the Arab world are unable to meet their citizenry's basic needs (Wedeen 2003). Kepel (1985, 2002) tells us that

Egyptian Islamic groups courted impecunious university students by providing (among many other things) free bus service to and from their campuses. Sullivan and Abed-Kotob (1999, 23–24) suggest that "the willingness of Islamist groups, led by the Brotherhood, to step in and help local communities suffering from unemployment, poverty, inflation, and government neglect" is the major source of their "popularity" and "legitimacy." Likewise, Tessler and Nachtwey (1998, 624) attribute Islamist popularity to "the fact that many of these movements carry out an extensive array of welfare and development activities at the grassroots level especially in poorer neighborhoods." Ismail (1998), Rubin (2002), Bayat (2002), Murphy (2002), and Mahmood (2005) all offer similar formulations.

However, these explanations fail for three reasons. First, few studies have been able with any precision to detail the exact nature or extent of the social service operations of Islamist parties or the precise ways in which these may contribute to voter loyalties.[3] The groundbreaking study by Clark (2004) actually found that Islamic social services in Jordan, Egypt, and Yemen were generally divorced from any kind of political activity, far more modest in scope than is generally believed, and geared not to the poor but to affluent individuals who could afford to pay higher prices for better service than available in government hospitals. Further testimony as to the limited role social service provision plays in Islamic party success is offered by a leader of the Lebanese Shiite party, ḤizbAllāh. Asked to describe how his group's vaunted social service organizations contributed to its impressive showing in the 1992 Lebanese parliamentary elections, he said, "The main thing is that these services are not free. [Therefore] they could have played only a minor role in the victory of our candidates" (Kfoury 1997, 141).

Second, the longstanding and popular account of Islamists providing services to the poor and getting votes in return ignored the political dynamics of the authoritarian regimes within which Islamic parties were forced to operate for much of their history. First, several scholars (Wiktorowicz 2000; Wickham 2003) have noted that authoritarian regimes heavily regulate what nongovernmental actors can do, making it difficult for Islamists or anyone else to engage in the sorts of broad, politically motivated service provision that popular accounts ascribed to them. Second, it was particularly difficult for opposition parties under authoritarianism to compete for the votes of the economically disadvantaged. Recent research has demonstrated that authoritarian regimes work to maintain monopolies over the political loyalties of the poor, dispensing patronage to needy constituencies to keep them in the ruling camp (Diaz-Cayeros et al. 2003; Lust-Okar 2006). In two studies of the Egyptian case, Bin-Nafisa and ʿArafat (2005) and Blaydes (2006) describe how wealthy, pro-regime local notables and businessmen deployed their wealth to buy the votes of the poor. Opponents of the state—including Islamists—were unable to match the regime's patronage resources or the blandishments of big businessmen and were thus ill equipped to compete with these actors for the suffrages of poor voters.

Third, and finally, existing economic accounts of political Islam's support base lead us to expect a static relationship between economic factors and the success of Islamist parties. Specifically, arguments that cite political Islam as the outcome of poverty or other forms of economic distress blind us to the dynamism of Islamist parties and the ways in which they shift their political appeals and messaging in response to shifts in the availability of particular political constituencies. In the following section, I outline an alternative theory of Islamist support that takes into account both economic and institutional factors and which is better able to account for change in the socioeconomic makeup of the coalitions underpinning Islamist electoral victories.

2.2 Institutions, economics, and Islamist support

Contrary to existing theories, support for political Islam is not the special province of a particular sliver of the population, but is rather a function of the mobilizing activities of Islamist parties under the constraints posed by the institutional environment. Under authoritarianism, for example, Islamists are faced with a political environment in which poor voters are invariably captured by offers of material goods from the ruling party and its satraps. Therefore, Islamist parties under such conditions were forced to direct their efforts toward more constituencies whose votes they are more likely to be able to secure. Specifically, if the poor are so dependent on the largesse of the regime that they, in the words of Bayat (2007), "cannot afford to be ideological," then Islamists must seek voters who are less likely to need to exchange their votes for material goods. Middle class voters were more likely to enjoy the kind of "positive" or "substantive" freedom (Sen 1985) that could allow them to cast ballots for parties on the basis of those parties' ideas rather than their offers of material goods. Thus, under authoritarianism at least, support for Islamist parties in elections was primarily a middle class phenomenon, and not primarily a phenomenon of the poor and disenfranchised.

However, just as it was a mistake to think of Islamism as somehow appealing uniquely to the poor, it would also be a mistake to think of it as a purely middle class phenomenon. If Islamists were constrained to appeal to the middle classes by the particular electoral dynamics of semi-authoritarianism, we should expect the nature of their political outreach to change as semi-authoritarian elections give way to genuinely democratic ones. After the dissolution of the ruling party and the scattering of the regime's former allies among the business class, poor voters who had previously been captured by offers of state patronage suddenly become available for political mobilization by Islamist parties. We should therefore observe the Muslim Brotherhood shift from appealing to a middle class constituency under authoritarianism to building a cross-class or even largely poor constituency upon the advent of genuinely competitive elections.

In order to test this hypothesis, I analyze the social correlates of Muslim Brotherhood's electoral support in three elections: the penultimate parliamentary election of the Mubarak era, the first post-Mubarak parliamentary election (which took place from November 2011 to January 2012), and the recent presidential election concluded in June 2012. To adumbrate my findings here, the analysis shows that the Muslim Brotherhood appealed mainly to the middle classes during the Mubarak period, but that it shifted to a cross-class strategy during the 2011 parliamentary elections, before moving decisively to the poor and rural during the presidential elections of the summer of 2012.

One of the difficulties with studying elections during the Mubarak era is that election results were often fraudulent, and complete election returns (even with "rigged" data) are unavailable. Therefore, it is impossible to observe correlation between the Muslim Brotherhood's relative vote shares and socioeconomic factors across Egypt's 222 electoral districts (in 2005). Instead, I use the presence or absence of a Muslim Brotherhood candidate in a particular district as a proxy for the group's level of support in a given district.[4] The Brothers opted not to run in a third of the districts in the 2005election—it stands to reason that this was a function of their assessment of their chances of success in those districts. Thus, districts with Muslim Brotherhood candidates are coded as high support districts, districts without MB candidates were coded as ones in which the movement's support base was relatively small.

I conducted a logistic regression, with a dichotomous dependent variable, Muslim Brotherhood mobilization, coded 1 if the Muslim Brotherhood nominated a candidate in the district, 0 otherwise.[5] The main independent variable in this analysis is the district's average socioeconomic status. Since the Egyptian census does not provide straightforward data on income, I employ the adult illiteracy rate as a proxy for income. As Blaydes (2006) has argued, illiterate voters are more likely to have the kind of diminished opportunities that rendered them good targets for ruling party candidates dispensing money and patronage. One difficulty with using this variable as a straightforward proxy for income, however, is its high negative correlation with the rate of urbanization. Nonetheless, the results presented here are suggestive. (I also include a control for district population.)

The analysis reveals that the Muslim Brotherhood was more likely to nominate candidates in more affluent districts (see table 6.1). Specifically, a district with 54 percent illiteracy was approximately 54 percent *less* likely to feature a Muslim Brotherhood candidate than one with only 27 percent illiteracy.[6] The results of the analysis are represented graphically in figure 6.2, which contains two kernel density plots of the simulated probabilities of Muslim Brotherhood nomination—one plot is the distribution of simulated probabilities when illiteracy is constrained to a low value (one standard deviation below the mean) the other is the distribution of simulated probabilities when illiteracy is set at a high value (one standard deviation above the mean). For example, as we can see from figure 6.2, the average probability of observing a Muslim Brotherhood candidacy at a high value of illiteracy is around 0.5, while the probability of observing it at a low value is closer to 0.9.

Thus, as the theory expects, the Muslim Brotherhood focused on the middle classes during the Mubarak era. What about the post-Mubarak era? The theory presented here suggests that the movement should move away from the middle classes in order to capture a much broader constituency of poor voters. Scholarly and journalistic observers of the Brotherhood have noted the movement's expenditure of significant resources, such as election-day handouts of foodstuffs and household necessities, intended to win the votes of the poor in the post-Mubarak era. In order to test whether this is a general pattern, I analyze the relationship between the Muslim Brotherhood's vote share at the governorate level in Egypt's 2011-12 parliamentary election and the average illiteracy rate (figure 6.3). Instead of the negative correlation between illiteracy and Muslim Brotherhood support we observed during the authoritarian period, we essentially observe no correlation in the first elections of the post-authoritarian period, suggesting that the Brotherhood broadened its support base beyond core middle class supporters to include poor voters who would previously have been captured by the old regime. We repeat the analysis for the first round of the presidential election, which took place in May 2012 (figure 6.4). There, we see that the correlation between illiteracy and support for the Muslim Brotherhood's candidate becomes strongly

Table 6.1: Effects of independent variables on probability of Muslim Brotherhood nomination, 2005

Variable	μ	σ	X_{low} $(\mu - \sigma)$	X_{high} $(\mu + \sigma)$	Change in probability of Muslim Brotherhood nomination
% Illiterate	40.54	13.62	26.92	54.17	-53.73 ± 10.36

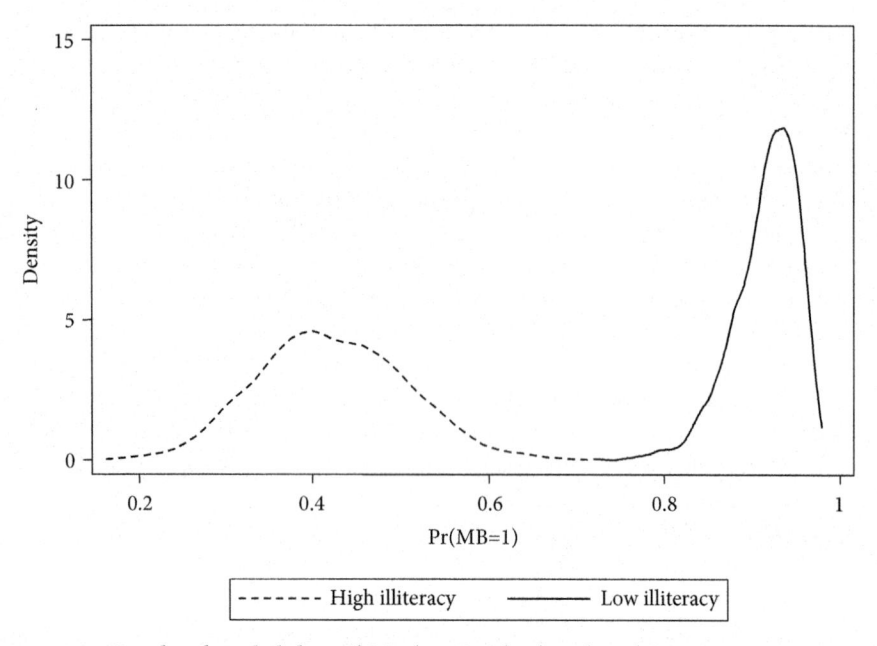

FIGURE 6.2: Simulated probability of Muslim Brotherhood parliamentary nomination at different rates of illiteracy (2005)

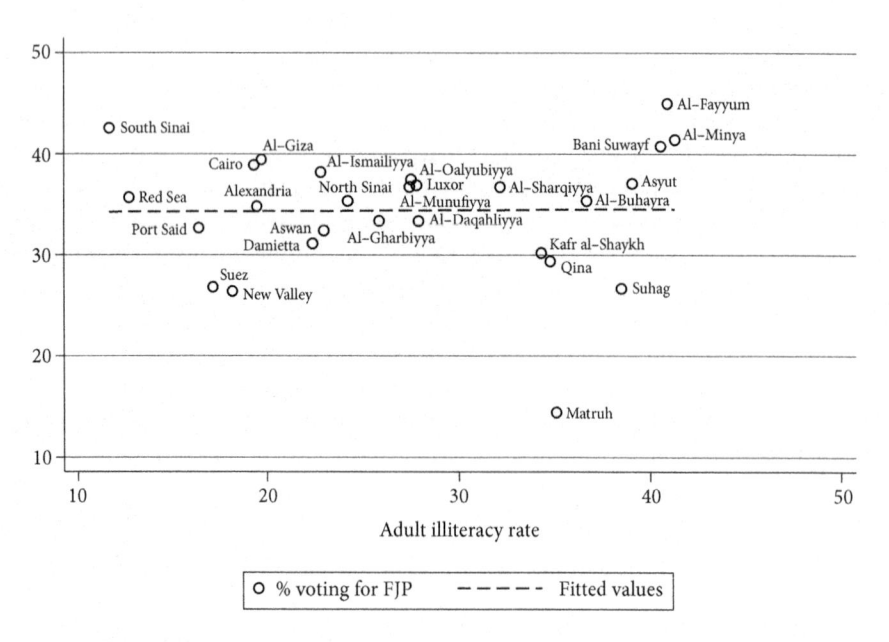

FIGURE 6.3: Voting for FJP versus adult illiteracy, 2011

FIGURE 6.4: Voting for MB presidential candidate Mohammed Morsi versus adult illiteracy, 2012

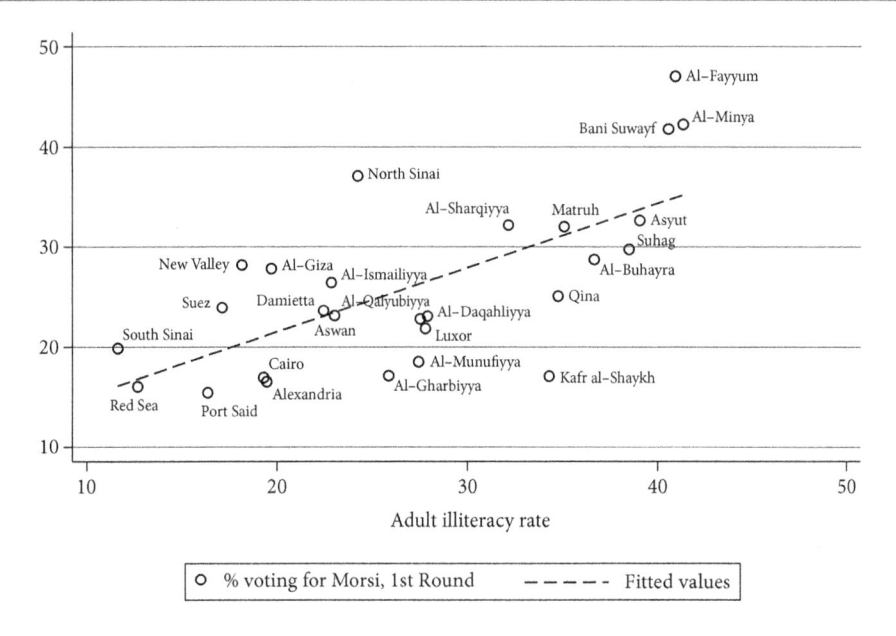

positive, meaning that the Brotherhood earned more votes in places with higher degrees of illiteracy (i.e. more poor and more rural). Though these data are at the governorate level, and thus prone to the limitations attending all attempts at ecological inference, the general narrative suggested by these data is consisted with theory offered here, which is that the support coalition of Islamist parties is not a stable function of enduring socioeconomic processes, but rather is contingent on political institutions and the opportunities these create to reach constituencies across the socioeconomic spectrum.

Therefore, to summarize: In authoritarian contexts, the political mobilization of the poor is largely monopolized by regime-allied elites, forcing Islamists to tend more affluent constituencies. Under genuine democratic competition, however, poor voters are no longer unavailable to Islamist parties, and the support coalition of those parties changes accordingly. The determinants of support for Islamism are thus not simply social and economic, but political.

3 Islamist Parties and Their Economic Platforms

In the previous section, I explored one facet of the political economy of Islamism—the role of economic and social factors in shaping support for Islamic political movements. I have argued that these factors contribute to support for Islamism not through their influence on individual cognitive processes but through political and institutional mechanisms that shape the ability of Islamist parties to appeal across the economic spectrum. In this section, I analyze a second facet of Islamic political economy—the economic ideas that Islamic parties put forward in their attempt to attract votes and win seats. As noted earlier, most scholarship on Islamist economics is inattentive to the platforms of political parties. Instead, they devote the bulk of their attention to the ways in which religious scholars have derived economic precepts from their interpretations of Islam's holy texts. But the political or real-world relevance of such inquiries is limited. If Islamic economics—if such a thing can be said to exist—is ever to be implemented in the world, its main instruments will be the Islamic political parties that are becoming an increasingly entrenched feature of the Muslim political landscape.

One objection to this line of inquiry is that Islamist parties are not serious generators of economic ideas. We often read that Islamist parties generally offer only airy platitudes that fall far short of articulating anything like a comprehensive view of the economy or how it should be managed. For example, the platform of Yemen's Brotherhood-affiliated Iṣlāḥ party for that country's 2001 local elections devotes a scant eight lines to economic policy, most of which are, at best, vague declarations of intention:

- "The best use of the financial resources dedicated to the administrative units and spending them on what they were intended for.
- "Developing plans to achieve the principle of justice in the distribution of service and development projects and combating poverty and unemployment.
- "Taking advantage of all of the available resources that will ensure comprehensive development.
- "Ending the collection of all illegal fees.
- "Conducting studies that will ensure the development of local resources and searching for sources of funding development and service projects.
- "Encouraging local manufactures that can be internationally competitive.
- "Supporting the encouragement of cooperative and consumer and mutual aid associations.
- "Encouraging and developing traditional industries and crafts."[7]

But this is the exception. Even during the authoritarian period, Islamist electoral successes thrust them into legislative arenas where they were called upon to exercise some oversight of government policies. As a result, they were forced to develop detailed critiques of those policies as well as propose alternatives of their own. Moreover, this "mainstreaming" of Islamic parties meant that the political classes long ago began to demand from them a measure of specificity on precisely how they would govern if they managed to win a share of power. For example, Egypt's Muslim Brotherhood, which in 2005 won 20 percent of the seats in that country's parliament, in 2007 released a 130-page program that goes into great detail on issues of economic and political reform.[8] The Brotherhood's 2010 reelection program was similarly detailed, covering everything from national issues such as unemployment insurance and consumer protections to microlevel ones such as allocating the necessary funds to clear the WWIIera minefields that prevent the development of part of the country's northern coastline.[9]

The specificity and granularity of the economic proposals of Islamic parties represents a genuine challenge to the view that "the main purpose of Islamic economics is not to improve economic performance [but] to prevent Muslims from assimilating into the emerging global culture whose core elements have a Western pedigree" (Kuran1996, 438). Though identity concerns do matter to these parties, they do not, by and large, attempt to assert them through the economic realm. For example, the prohibition on interest (*riba*), which in Kuran's view is the "centerpiece of Islamic economics" whose principal role is to serve as a cultural signifier of the Muslim world's fundamental difference from the West, actually figures very little in the platforms of Islamic parties.

Note that in the glib list of economic desiderata put forth by the Yemeni Muslim Brotherhood affiliate, there is no mention at all of Islamic banking. Similarly, the 2007 draft party program of the Muslim Brotherhood mentions the need to replace interest rate mechanisms with other tools of monetary policy but notes that this must be done "gradually" and in such a way that it avoids economic dislocations.[10] The Brothers' 2010 platform devoted even less attention to the matter, repeating only the need to "gradually" replace Western-style banks with Islamic ones. After the January 25 2011 revolution, the party program of the Freedom and Justice Party only mentions interest (riba) twice in more than 90 pages, and only as one item in a long list of generic ills to be combatted, including: "injustice and exploitation, interest (riba) and cheating, bribes and nepotism, monopoly and hoarding, defrauding and devaluing, extravagance and miserliness, fraud, and all other forms of economic corruption."[11] The word does not appear at all in the presidential campaign platform of candidate Muhammad Morsi. Similarly, the Brothers' Jordanian counterparts, in a 2005 document on reform in Jordan, reference interest only obliquely, calling for "ridding the economy at all of its levels and practices from that which contradicts the rulings of the Islamic shari`ah, combating corruption seriously in all its forms, and achieving transparency in preservation of rights and public funds, and encouraging investment."[12] A report of activities circulated by Islamic Action Front (IAF)'s parliamentary block in 2007 goes into great detail regarding the party's economic aims and the work of its parliamentarians in this realm but makes nary a mention of interest.[13]

Identity concerns do figure, however, in these parties' attitudes toward free trade and globalization. Though most Islamic parties make note of the need to attract foreign investment, they are nonetheless wary of further dependence on the West. Thus, while the IAF talks of creating "an investment environment that offers freedom, security, transparency, and administrative amenities that provide the investor with tax exemptions on inputs for production, export, and sales and offers technical and trade support necessary for success," it specifically mentions that the capital it is trying to attract with these policies is "domestic, Arab, and Islamic."[14] Similarly, the Egyptian Muslim Brotherhood criticizes the Egyptian government for orienting its trade and investment policy toward the United States and the European Union, calling instead for "giving priority to cooperation with Islamic, then Arabic, then African, then southern countries," in part because this "keeps the identity of Egypt in its proper context regarding its Arab, Islamic, African, southern, and international obligations and interests."[15]

Nonetheless, we err if we make too much of these "identity" issues in our assessment of Islamic parties' economic policies. After all, the government of Mohammed Morsi is currently trying to conclude a $4.5 billion loan with the International Monetary Fund. Moreover, the primary focus of Islamic parties has long been on local problems and the failures of their governments to solve them. A handbill distributed by a Muslim Brotherhood candidate during Egypt's 2010 parliamentary elections provides a sober illustration of this fact:

"87 billion L.E. budget deficit
"145 billion L.E. trade deficit
"323 billion L.E. foreign debt
"328 billion L.E. smuggled abroad
"863 billion L.E. domestic debt
"22,000 arrested under the emergency law
"6 million stricken with cancer and liver and kidney failure
"7 million unemployed
"9 million unmarried
"31 million illiterate
"34 million under the poverty line
"45 million without sewage"[16]

These are not issues of identity, and the Islamic parties that put these issues in the public consciousness understand that addressing them will require more than inveighing against the West or simple assertions of cultural difference. In this section, I analyze the views of the Egyptian and Jordanian Muslim Brotherhoods toward two major economic challenges facing their countries: the privatization of state-owned enterprises and the redistribution of income. Both have important implications for the welfare of citizens and as such are the subject of much political debate and attention.

3.1 Privatization

One might assume that Islamic parties' orientation toward privatization is a straightforward function of Islamic teachings regarding private property. However, although Sait and Lim (2006, 10) note the existence of "scores of references to land in the Qur'an that provide for and respect property rights," the precise extent of these rights is unclear. For example, SayyidQutb (2000, 134) argued for a highly limited conception of property rights, declaring that "the individual must realize that he is no more than the steward of [his] property, which is fundamentally the possession of society; this must make him accept the restrictions that the system lays upon his liberty, and the bounds that limit his right of disposal." But Qutb's communitarian view is by no means universal. In his study of economic thought in revolutionary Iran, Behdad (1994) has identified three contemporary Islamic views on private property rights, ranging from what he calls a "radical" view that rejects private ownership entirely in favor of a communal model, to a "populist-statist" approach that accepts private ownership but seeks to control it and prevent it from becoming "excessive or monopolistic," to the "conservative laissez faire" view of the "`ulamā'"(including, in his time, Ayatollah Ruhollah Khomeini), who see no contradiction between the precepts of the faith and contemporary liberal conceptions of the free market economy. (See also Utvik 1995 for a discussion of the spectrum of Islamic economic beliefs in 1990s' Egypt.)

Contemporary statements by the Egyptian Muslim Brotherhood all uphold property rights. In a 2005 pamphlet, the movement's general guide, Muḥammad Mahdī 'Ākif, puts forth its belief in "the freedom of economic activity, and the role of the individual in this activity" but notes that private ownership is "conditioned on its fulfillment of its social role," which means that property must not be put to impious uses and must be subject to zakāt.[17] MaḥmūdGhuzlān, a member of the Brotherhood's Guidance Bureau, echoes this view in an essay circulated during the 2005 elections: "We believe in the right to private property and its inviolability, provided it is from Islamicallypermissible sources and activities that violate neither God nor the society."[18] Similarly, the Jordanian Muslim Brotherhood, in its 2005 statement, declared its "affirmation of the inviolability of private property and money," so long as these were not the result of abuses of power.[19]

However, these affirmations of private ownership do not translate into total opposition to state intervention in the economy. In the case of the Egyptian Brothers, for example, the group's views on this issue have oscillated between the populist-statist and laissez-faire positions, in keeping with the wider rhythms of Egyptian politics. In the 1970s, for example, after the Brothers' release from the prisons to which Gamal Abdel Nasser had confined them, the group looked favorably on Anwar Sadat's efforts to pare down the massive public sector that Nasser had built up during his sixteen-year rule (Abed-Kotob 1995, 327). According to Lesch (1995, 231), the Brotherhood's 1987 electoral program featured economic demands that were "congruent with the government's own approach, including the call to decrease the size of the public sector and reinforce the private sector as the backbone of the economy."

In the past twenty years, however, the Brotherhood have moved away from this position, with much of the change occurring in the past ten years, as the Brothers found themselves the principal opposition party in parliament. In their 2007 draft party program, the Brothers joined the already loud chorus of voices against the privatization program (see King 2007, 439–441), arguing that privatization has opened the way for "boundless corruption," allowing regime cronies to obtain state assets at artificially depressed prices. Moreover, the Brothers argued, this has had the effect of draining Egyptian businessmen of initiative and entrepreneurial spirit, since instead of being forced to search for new productive investments, they are handed risk-free ready-made state-owned firms that are already profitable.[20] In the movement's 2010 reelection platform, it takes credit for "stopping the train" of privatization—a reference to the government's decision in June 2010 to postpone indefinitely the sale of Egypt's 149 remaining state-owned companies.[21] Calling privatization "organized looting" and a "disaster for workers and the homeland and its citizens," the Brothers argued instead for better management of state-owned enterprises, declaring that "the sale of public assets is not appropriate for the Egyptian economy at this stage."[22]

This shift in Brotherhood attitudes toward privatization of public sector enterprises appears to have occasioned a shift in attitudes toward the role of the state in the economy more generally. Where Ghuzlān in 2004 could restrict the role of government to the undertaking of "grand projects" that "are vital for the nation, such as military and heavy production," but beyond the ken of individuals due to their unprofitability, the Brotherhood now outlines a more robust role for the state (see table 6.2).[23] The movement's 2007 draft platform advocates an "Islamic system [that] occupies a middle position…between communism, in which the state exerts hegemony over the market, and excessive capitalism that aims at nothing but the realization of material gains by any means available."[24]

Table 6.2: The role of the state in the economy, from the 2007 party platform of the Egyptian Muslim Brotherhood, August 2007, p. 76

1. Managing insurance and pension funds (through a state agency).
2. Managing national investments and reserves of cash and commodities.
3. Breaking monopolies.
4. Providing strategic commodities.
5. Supporting struggling sectors.
6. Supporting disadvantaged citizens.
7. Undertaking strategic and development projects that the private sector avoids.

The Egyptian Brotherhood is not alone in its opposition to increasingly unpopular privatization policies. The Jordanian Muslim Brotherhood in 2005 called for the cessation of that country's privatization program, declaring that it had "not achieved the broad hopes that were cited as justifications for it, but rather contributed to the rising of prices and the consumption of water and electricity and communications, in a manner that has exacerbated the decline of the standard of living."[25] In the IAF's 2007 report on the performance of its deputies in Jordan's Chamber of Deputies, the party notes that its parliamentary bloc refused the government's decision to sell 37 percent of its share in a state-owned phosphate mining company, as part of "a principled rejection of the sale of the country's resources."[26]

As the evolution of the Egyptian Brotherhood's position toward privatization demonstrates, there is no unique "Islamic" orientation to the question of state ownership of the means of production. Indeed, the attitude of the Turkish Justice and Development party toward the question of privatization seems almost diametrically opposed to the one now espoused by its Arab counterparts. Of the 42 billion dollars' worth of Turkish firms privatized from 1985 to 2010, 33.5 billion were generated after the AdaletveKalkınmaPartisi(AKP) took power in 2002.[27] The AKPs aggressive privatization program—which seeks to privatize not only factories and firms but also infrastructure including roads, bridges, and energy generation and distribution facilities—has sparked worker protests and accusations against the AKP that are strikingly similar to the ones that Islamist parties in Arab countries level against their own privatizing regimes.[28]

3.2 Redistribution

Just as we might have been tempted to locate the roots of Islamic party attitudes toward privatization in the teachings of the faith, so too might we attempt to discern the influence of Islamic beliefs on these Islamic parties' attitudes toward wealth redistribution and welfarist policies. For example, it is common knowledge that Islam commands some measure of redistribution through the mechanism of *zakāt*, which demands that all able Muslims surrender 2.5 percent of their annual surplus wealth for the upkeep of the poor. Moreover, the Qur'an and Ḥadith frequently command Muslims to help their less fortunate brethren. At the same time, however, there is evidence that Islam views the existence of income inequality as part of the natural order of things, so long as it does not lead to abuse and exploitation.

For example, in the Qur'an's sixteenth chapter we read, "God has bestowed His gifts of sustenance more freely on some of you than on others: those more favoured are not going to throw back their gifts to those whom their right hands possess, so as to be equal in that respect. Will they then deny the favours of God?"[29]

There is a great deal of scholarship that attempts to link religious beliefs to attitudes toward redistribution. For example, Scheve and Stasavage (2006) find that national rates of religious observance in OECD countries are negatively correlated with rates of social spending and argue that this is because personal piety functions as a form of insurance against "adverse life events," thus obviating the need for state interventions in the form of free health care or unemployment insurance.[30] Davis and Robinson (2006, 168), however, argue the opposite. In a study of personal beliefs in seven Muslim countries, they find that piety is positively correlated with economically progressive attitudes. They argue that this is because the religiously orthodox subscribe to a "moral cosmology" that views all individuals "as subsumed by a larger community of believers and as subject to the timeless laws and greater plan of God." Pepinsky and Welborne (2010), employing survey data from a wider range of Muslim countries, find little support for this hypothesis, arguing instead that more pious Muslims are less likely to favor government efforts to reduce income inequality (although the authors are unable to determine whether this means that religious Muslims believe that the state should not provide the poor with social insurance or guarantees of a basic standard of living).

Given that we are unlikely to be able to attribute Islamic party positions on redistribution to the teachings of the faith or to psychological processes, we would do better to attend to the details of these positions. For although we have seen earlier that Islamic social movements have developed reputations for providing social services to the poor, little attention has been paid to the policies Islamic parties say they would enact in order to alleviate poverty.

The problem of the maldistribution of wealth figures prominently in the discourse of contemporary Islamic parties and is generally seen as a symptom of corrupt and autocratic political systems that allow regimes' cronies to exploit their closeness to power in order to extract personal fortunes. In the most recent report of its parliamentary bloc, Jordan's Islamic Action Front laments the fact that "the economic policies of the last 25 years have clearly favored the wealthy and powerful classes in society and have been biased to the interests of the makers of profits and fortunes at the expense of the poor and those of limited incomes and the middle class."[31] The party complains that "5 percent of the population owns 75 percent of the wealth while suffering has increased for the majority of Jordanians."[32]

The IAF in particular targets the country's regressive sales tax, which they claim currently generates approximately 40 percent of treasury revenues, the majority of which, they say, is paid by poor and middle-class Jordanians. Meanwhile, the party notes that "tax exemptions have been granted to trading firms and banks and financial institutions and the owners of wealth and profits on the pretense of encouraging investment."[33] The party advocates a progressive tax code and notes that during the 2003–2007 parliamentary session, its representatives in the Chamber of Deputies fought to prevent the reduction of taxes on banks and financial institutions and to stop plans to raise taxes on agriculture and industry (which in its view are the only real generators of jobs and national income) and certain types of small businesses.[34]

The Egyptian Muslim Brotherhood adopts a similar stance. In the party's 2007 platform, it declares that the state "must care for the poor, and this requires the redistribution of income."[35] The basis of the Brotherhood program is the Islamic concept of *takāful*, or shared responsibility. In one of the platform's most developed sections, the Brotherhood explains that Islam "guarantees for [the poor] the provision of their basic needs and necessities—homes and nourishment and clothes and health care in sufficient quantities to meet the needs of the ordinary individual."[36] Quoting from the Qur'an's fifth chapter—"and cooperate with one another in charity and piety"[37]—the Brothers declare that *takāful* is "not merely a matter of voluntary charity left to the desires of individuals who can offer it or not depending on their wishes, but rather... a recognized right [for the poor] in the wealth of the rich." Though this right generally refers to *zakāt*, the platform makes clear that "if mandatory zakāt and voluntary charity are not sufficient..., it is incumbent upon the authorities of the state to demand from the wealth of the rich that which will suffice to care for the poor."[38]

The Brotherhood's concern with redistribution is not simply a function of its desire to better the lives of the poor but also emerges out of a belief that stark class differences are inimical to social peace.[39] In the 2010 election platform, the Brotherhood explains how it would go about redistributing wealth, promising to propose amendments to the income tax law to make it more progressive and declaring its intention to fight to raise the minimum wage as well as to specify a wage ceiling in order to "prevent the concentration of wealth in the hands of a few."[40]

The salience of these redistributive issues is in large part a function of the rise over the past thirty years of a new, crony capitalist class of extraordinary wealth at a time when the country's economic fortunes appear, to the average citizen, to be dwindling. Moreover, many of these new rich also occupy key positions within the ruling apparatus—for example, the deputy secretary general of the ruling party is also a steel magnate who controls more than two-thirds of the Egyptian steel market. An illustration of the prevailing view of this new class of businessman is offered by the title of a book on the subject authored by a senior Muslim Brotherhood member from the Nile Delta province of al-Sharqiyya—"Beware the Enemies of Islam: Qarūn's Grandsons"—a reference to a Qur'anic (and biblical) figure of great wealth whom God struck down for his arrogance.[41] According to the Brothers, the "marriage of wealth and power"[42] is one of the principal causes of poverty in Egypt—harnessing the resources and energies of the country to the benefit of a small few. Thus, in the Brotherhood's view, the most important requirement for restoring social justice and ensuring a more equitable distribution of wealth is not the observance of *zakāt* or any other religiously mandated practice but rather to sever the connection between wealth and power, to "purify economic life from all forms of oppression."[43]

4 Conclusion

In this essay, I have argued for bringing politics back into the political economy of Islam, for putting the exertions of political parties and the workings of political institutions at the center of our explanations of public support for political Islam, and for taking Islamist parties seriously as generators of economic ideas. But a more important aim has been to restore rationality to our understanding of these parties—both in terms of why people support them and in terms of how we view them as actors in the political world.

As we have seen, irrationality has always been inextricably intertwined with the study of political Islam. In impoverished countries like Egypt or Jordan, the question of why the poor would vote for or otherwise support a political agenda that does not speak to their core concerns—how much they get to eat and how long they live—has puzzled scholars. Is it a case of false consciousness, of the subordination of "real" material interests to spiritual or moral ones (Frank 2004; Beinin 2005; Ibrahim 1999; El-Guindi 1981)? But, as this essay has shown, we err when we viewIslamist parties as depending on the irrationality of the poor. As we saw, under authoritarianism, the Muslim Brotherhood was forced to appeal not to the poor, but to the middle classes, as the former were captured by offers of patronage. However, with the advent of genuine democratic competition, the Brotherhood has adopted a clientelistic strategy that allows it to gain the votes of the poor. The upshot of this analysis is that the dominant paradigm for explaining support of Islamist parties, which has typically involved identifying how social and economic dynamics generate cognitive changes that make individuals more hospitable to religious appeals is inadequate. Instead, we gain more leverage on the question by examining the ways in which political institutions determine whom Islamist parties are able to reach out to in the first place.

The rationality of Islamist parties extends to their policy proposals. As this essay has shown, they offer their potential constituents more than simply a steady diet of religious rhetoric. They compose detailed economic platforms that are inspired less by the dictates of the holy texts than by the particular economic circumstances and challenges facing their countries. Moreover, these parties demonstrate an ability to shift their positions depending on the political winds—as in Egypt, for example, when the Muslim Brotherhood abandoned its previous support for the *ancien regime's* privatization initiatives. And though these parties hold fast to the prohibition of interest as mandated by the Qur'an, they do not give it pride of place in their agendas, preferring to call for its "gradual" implementation in a manner that minimizes economic disruptions.

Nonetheless, this essay raises new questions. Though it is clear that Islamic economic proposals do not map onto the theoretical writings of Islamic economic thinkers and scholars, we do not yet have an account of the relationship between these two things. How do Islamic parties use the ideas generated by Islamic economists? How are these ideas modified and reframed by the parties before presenting them to voters? And to what extent are these modifications based on differences of principle or political expediency?

Finally, as parties such as Tunisia's al-Nahda and Egypt's Freedom and Justice and Nur parties continue to play a role in governing, we must redouble our efforts to understand them as economic actors and makers of economic policy. Though much attention has been paid to how Islamists would deal with Western interests or the rights of women and religious minorities if elected, their governance of the economy should be of equal or greater concern. Previous studies of Islamists have neglected the economic dimension of their activities, even in places like Iran and Turkey, where they have had experience in governance. Islamist parties in Jordan and Morocco and Indonesia and Malaysia have in recent history been given ministerial responsibility for policy areas that impinge on economic life—from housing to education to agriculture—as well as control of local governments. These limited experiences of Islam in governance offer us a trove of information and data about how Islamists actually manage those pieces of the economy over which they have some control, and yet they have generally not been the subject of sustained scholarly inquiry. The coming generation of scholars on political Islam thus is faced with a tremendous opportunity to fill a significant and important gap in our knowledge about one of the Muslim's world's most important political phenomena.

Notes

1. The fact that the magazine in which the cartoon appeared sixty-five years ago was not that of a secular faction but of the Muslim Brotherhood itself suggests that the illustrator intended to communicate something else entirely.
2. MakramEbeid (1989, 38) wrote of the party that it "is indeed a petty opposition...with hardly any members."
3. An important exception is Cammett and Issar (2010).
4. Details of the construction of the dataset and the sources used can be found in Masoud(2009).
5. In eighteen districts the Muslim Brotherhood nominated two candidates (one for each of the two seats). I coded these districts in the same way as those where the Brothers fielded just one candidate. Ordered probit regressions, in which the dependent variable could take on values of 0, 1, or 2 candidates, yielded substantially the same results as the logits reported here, with insignificant cut points between the categories for one and two candidates.
6. In the interests of conserving space, I do not present detailed logit results here, but they can be found in Masoud (2008). Instead, the probability estimates I present here were generating using King, Tomz, and Wittenberg's (2000) Monte Carlo simulation routines to generate predicted probabilities of observing Muslim Brotherhood nominations at different levels of the key proxies for district socioeconomic status (holding all other variables at their means).
7. Al-birnāmijal-initkhābīlil-tajammu`al-yamanīlil-iṣlāḥlil-intikhābāt al-maḥaliyya[The Electoral Program of the Yemeni Gathering for Reform for the Local Elections], February 2001, pp 12–13.
8. Birnāmijḥizbal-Ikhwānal-Muslimīn, al-iṣdār al-awwal[The Program of the Muslim Brotherhood Party, First Draft], August 25, 2007.
9. Al-birnāmijal-initkhābīlil-Ikhwānal-Muslimīn, intikhābātMajlis al-Sha`b 2010 [The Electoral Platform of the Muslim Brotherhood, 2010 People's Assembly Elections], November 2010.
10. Birnāmijḥizbal-Ikhwānal-Muslimīn, 2007, p 65.
11. BirnamijHizb al-Hurriyawa al-Adalah (Program of the Freedom and Justice Party), November 2011, Page 51
12. Al-Ikhwānal-Muslimīn, ḤizbJabhat al-`Amal al-Islāmī, Ru'yat al-ḥaraka al-Islāmiyyalil-iṣlāḥ fi al-Urdun, 2005, p 36.
13. Al-taqrīr al-idārī li-kutlatnuwwābḤizbJabhat al-`Amal al-Islāmīfimajlis al-nuwwāb al-urdunī al-rābi'`ashr 1424–1428H, 2007.
14. Al-Ikhwānal-Muslimīn, ḤizbJabhat al-`Amal al-Islāmī, Ru'yat al-ḥaraka al-Islāmiyyalil-iṣlāḥ fi al-Urdun, 2005, p 36.
15. Birnāmijḥizbal-Ikhwānal-Muslimīn, 2007, p 70.
16. From a flyer circulated by AḥmadFahmī, Muslim Brotherhood candidate from al-Zaqāzīq in al-Sharqiyya governorate, entitled "Arqāmtataḥadath`anMiṣr 2010"[Numbers That Illustrate Egypt 2010], November 2010.
17. Muḥammad Mahdī `Ākif, Mubādarat al-Ikhwān al-Muslimūnḥawlmabādi' al-iṣlāḥfiMiṣr[The Initiative of the Muslim Brothers on the Principles of Reform in Egypt], Dār al-Manāra, 2004.
18. MaḥmūdGhuzlān,Na`m,al-Islāmhuwaal-ḥal[Yes,IslamIstheSolution],al-Manṣūrah:Dār al-Wafā' lil-nashrwal-tawzī`, 2005, p 12.

19. Ru'yat al-ḥaraka al-Islāmiyyalil-iṣlāḥ fi al-Urdun, 2005, p 35.
20. Birnāmijḥizbal-Ikhwānal-Muslimīn, 2007, pp 73–74.
21. Ashraf Khalil, "Egypt's Privatization Drive Shifts," Wall Street Journal, June 24, 2010.
22. Al-birnāmijal-initkhābīlil-Ikhwānal-Muslimīn, intikhābātMajlis al-Sha`b 2010.
23. Ghuzlān, Na`m, al-Islāmhuwa al-ḥal, 2005, p 26.
24. Birnāmijḥizbal-Ikhwānal-Muslimīn, 2007, p 72.
25. Ru'yat al-ḥaraka al-Islāmiyyalil-iṣlāḥ fi al-Urdun, p 40.
26. Al-taqrīr al-idārī li-kutlatnuwwābḤizbJabhat al-`Amal al-Islāmīfimajlis al-nuwwāb al-urdunī al-rābi``ashr 1424–1428H, 2007, p 28.
27. Source: Republic of Turkey, Privatization Administration, Prime Ministry, 2010. Available at http://www.oib.gov.tr/program/uygulamalar/privatization_in_turkey.htm.
28. See,forexample,"PrivatizationstoGainPace,"HurriyetDailyNews,September9,2009.http://www.hurriyetdailynews.com/n.php?n=privatizations-to-gain-pace-2009-09-09; "Sugar Factories against Foreign Investors," Hurriyet Daily News, November 17, 2009, http://www.hurriyetdailynews.com/n.php?n=sugar-factories-against-foreign-investors-2009-11-17; "Energy Meeting Focuses on Plant Privatization in Turkey," October 18, 2010, http://www.hurriyetdailynews.com/n.php?n=energy-meeting-focuses-on-plant-privatizations-2010-10-18.
29. al-Qur'ān, 16:71.
30. Gill and Lundsgaarde (2004), however, argue that the causal mechanism runs the other way—lower state welfare spending means that citizens must seek recourse to nongovernmental providers of welfare foods, most of which are religious in nature. As a result of their reliance on religious organizations, individuals become more pious.
31. Al-taqrīr al-idārī li-kutlatnuwwābḤizbJabhat al-`Amal al-Islāmīfimajlis al-nuwwāb al-urdunī al-rābi``ashr 1424–1428H, 2007, p 24.
32. Ibid., 24.
33. Ibid., 25.
34. Ibid., 10.
35. Birnāmijḥizbal-Ikhwānal-Muslimīn, 2007, p 76.
36. In a passage that echoes AmartyaSen's (1985) work on well-being and freedom, the Brothers declare that poverty is not simply a function of low income but is rather a comprehensive phenomenon that deprives the individual of his basic capabilities. Ibid., 88.
37. al-Qur'ān, 5:8.
38. Birnāmijḥizbal-Ikhwānal-Muslimīn, 2007, 86.This is a rare admission that merely applying the zakāt may not be sufficient to solve the problem of poverty. The general attitude by Muslim Brotherhood members seems to be that if everyone paid zakāt as is commanded by the faith, poverty would vanish—an echo of the Marxist belief in the superabundance of wealth that communism would generate. See, for example, AmīrBassām l-Najjār, Iḥdharū al-Muḥāribūn al-Jududlil-Islām: AḥfādQarūn (Beware the New Enemies of Islam: The Grandsons of Qarūn), al-Qāhirah: Dāral-Tawzī`wal-nashr al-Islāmiyya, 2005, p 72.
39. Birnāmijḥizbal-Ikhwānal-Muslimīn, 2007, p 84.
40. Al-birnāmijal-initkhābīlil-Ikhwānal-Muslimīn, intikhābātMajlis al-Sha`b 2010.
41. AmīrBassām l-Najjār, Iḥdharū al-Muḥāribūn al-Jududlil-Islām: AḥfādQarūn[Beware the New Enemies of Islam: The Grandsons of Qarūn], al-Qāhirah: Dāral-Tawzī`wal-nashr al-Islāmiyya, 2005.
42. Al-birnāmijal-initkhābīlil-Ikhwānal-Muslimīn, intikhābātMajlis al-Sha`b 2010.
43. Birnāmijḥizbal-Ikhwānal-Muslimīn, 2007, p 61.

References

Abed-Kotob, S. (1995). The Accommodationists Speak: Goals and Strategies of the Muslim Brotherhood of Egypt. *International Journal of Middle EastStudies*, 27(3):321.

Alam, A. (2003). The Sociology and Political Economy of ÂislamicTerrorismâ in Egypt. *Terrorism and Political Violence*, 15(4):114–142.

Almond, G. A., Appleby, R. S., and Sivan, E. (2003).*Strong Religion: TheRise of Fundamentalisms around the World*. University of Chicago Press.

Aminzade, R. R., and Perry, E. J. (2001). The Sacred, Religious, and Secular in Contentious Politics: Blurring Boundaries. In Ronald R. Aminzade, Jack A. Goldstone, D. M. E. J. P. W. H. S. J. S. T. C. T., eds.,*Silenceand Voice in the Study of Contentious Politics*, 155–179. Cambridge University Press.

Ayubi, N. N. M. (1980). The Political Revival of Islam: The Case of Egypt. *International Journal of Middle East Studies*, 12(4):481–499.

Bayat, A. (2002). Activism and Social Development in the Middle East.*International Journal of Middle East Studies*, 34:1–28.

Bayat, A. (2007). Radical Religion and the Habitus of the Dispossessed: Does Islamic Militancy Have an Urban Ecology? *International Journal of Urbanand Regional Research*, 31(3):579.

Behdad, S. (1994). A Disputed Utopia: Islamic Economics in Revolutionary Iran. *Comparative Studies in Society and History*, 36(4):775–813.

Beinin, J. (2005). Political Islam and the New Global Economy: The Political Economy of an Egyptian Social Movement. *The New Centennial Review*, 5(1):111–139.

Berman, S. (2003). Islamism, Revolution, and Civil Society. *Perspectives onPolitics*, 1(2):257–272.

Bin-Nafisa, S., and ʻArafat, A. (2005). *al-Intikhabatwa al-Zaba'iniyyaal-Siyassiya fi-Misr*[Elections and Political Clientelism in Egypt]. Cairo Center for Human Rights Studies.

Blaydes, L. (2006). Who Votes in Authoritarian Elections and Why? Vote Buying, Turnout, and Spoiled Ballots in Contemporary Egypt. University of California, Los Angeles.

Blaydes, L., and Linzer, D. (2008). The Political Economy of Women's Support for Fundamentalist Islam.*World Politics*, 60(4):576–609.

Cammett, M., and Issar, S. (2010). Bricks and Mortar Clientelism: Sectarianism and the Logics of Welfare Allocation in Lebanon. *World Politics*, 62(3):381–421.

Chhibber, P. (1996). State Policy, Rent Seeking, and the Electoral Success of a Religious Party in Algeria.*Journal of Politics*, 58(1):126–148.

Clark, J. A. (2004). Social Movement Theory and Patron-Clientelism: Islamic Social Institutions and the Middle Class in Egypt, Jordan, and Yemen. *Comparative Political Studies*, 37(8):941–968.

Davis, N., and Robinson, R. (2006). The Egalitarian Face of Islamic Orthodoxy: Support for Islamic Law and Economic Justice in Seven Muslim-Majority Nations. *American Sociological Review*, 71(2):167.

Diaz-Cayeros, A., Magaloni, B., and Weingast, B. R. (2003). Tragic Brilliance: Equilibrium Hegemony and Democratization in Mexico. Stanford University Press.

Durkheim, E. (1951).*Suicide, a Study in Sociology*.New York: Free Press.

Ebeid, M. M. (1989).*Egypt under Mubarak*: chapter The Role of the Official Opposition, pages 21–52. Routledge.

Eickelman, D., and Piscatori, J. (1996). *Muslim Politics*. Princeton University Press.

El-Gamal, M. (2006).*Islamic Finance: Law, Economics, and Practice*. Cambridge University Press.

Fahmy, N. (1998). The Performance of the Muslim Brotherhood in the Egyptian Syndicates: An Alternative Formula for Reform? *The Middle EastJournal*, 52(4):551–562.

Frank, T. (2004). *What's the Matter with Kansas? How Conservatives Wonthe Heart of America*. Metropolitan Books.

Gellner, E. (1991). Islam and Marxism: Some Comparisons. *InternationalAffairs*, 67(1):1–6.

Gill, A., and Lundsgaarde, E. (2004). State Welfare Spending and Religiosity. *Rationality and Society*, 16(4):399–436.

Greene, K. F. (2007). *Why Dominant Parties Lose: Mexico's Democratization inComparative Perspective*. Cambridge University Press.

Guindi, F. E. (1981). Veiling Infitah with Muslim Ethic: Egypt's Contemporary Islamic Movement. *Social Problems*, 28(4):465–485.

Hechter, M. C. (2004).From Class to Culture.*American Journal of Sociology*, 110(2):400–445.

Ibrahim, S. E. (1980). Anatomy of Egypt's Militant Islamic Groups: Methodological Note and Preliminary Findings. *International Journal ofMiddle East Studies*, 12(4):423–453.

Ibrahim, S. E. (1999).The Changing Face of Egypt's Islamic Activism. In Marr, P., ed., *Egypt at the Crossroads: Domestic Stability and RegionalRole*. Washington, DC:National Defense University Press.

Ismail, S. (1998). Confronting the Other: Identity, Culture, Politics, and Conservative Islamism in Egypt. *International Journal of Middle EastStudies*, 30(2):199.

Kandil, A. (1998). The Nonprofit Sector in Egypt. In *The Nonprofit Sector inthe Developing World: A Comparative Analysis*, 122. Manchester University Press.

Kepel, G. (1985). *TheProphetandPharaoh:MuslimExtremisminEgypt*.AlSaqiBooks:Distributed by Zed Books, London.

Kepel, G. (2002). *Jihad: The Trail of Political Islam*. Cambridge, MA:Belknap Press of Harvard University Press.

Kfoury, A. (1997). Hizb Allah and the Lebanese State. In Beinin, J., and Stork, J., eds.,*Political Islam: Essays from Middle East Report*. University of California Press.

King, Gary, M. T., and Wittenberg, J. (2000). Making the Most of Statistical Analyses: Improving Interpretation and Presentation. *American Journal ofPolitical Science*, 44(2):347–361.

King, S. (2007). Sustaining Authoritarianism in the Middle East and North Africa. *Political Science Quarterly*, 122(3):433–459.

Kuran, T. (1996).The Discontents of Islamic Economic Morality.*TheAmerican Economic Review*, 86(2):438–442.

Laitin, D. D. (1986). *Hegemony and Culture: Politics and Religious Changeamong the Yoruba*. Chicago:University of Chicago Press.

Lee, C. (1991). Regional Inequalities in Infant Mortality in Britain, 1861–1971: Patterns and Hypotheses. *Population Studies*, 45(1):55–65.

Lesch, A. M. (1995). Domestic Politics and Foreign Policy in Egypt. In Tessler, M., and Garnham, D., eds.,*Democracy, War, and Peace in the MiddleEast*, 223–243. Indiana University Press.

Lia, B. (1998). *The Society of the Muslim Brothers in Egypt: The Rise of anIslamic Mass Movement, 1928-1942*. Reading, England:Ithaca Press.

Lust-Okar, E., and Jamal, A. A. (2002). Rulers and Rules: Reassessing the Influence of Regime Type on Electoral Law Formation. *Comparative PoliticalStudies*, 35(3):337–366.

Lust-Okar, E. (2006). Elections under Authoritarianism: Preliminary Lessons from Jordan. *Democratization*, 13(3):456–471.

Lynch, M. (2007). Young Brothers in Cyberspace.*Middle East Report* (245).

Magaloni, B. (2006). *Voting for Autocracy: Hegemonic Party Survival andIts Demise in Mexico*. Cambridge University Press.

Mahmood, S. (2005). *Politics of Piety: The Islamic Revival and the FeministSubject*. Princeton University Press.

Masoud, T. (2008). *Why Islam Wins: Electoral Ecologies and Economies ofPolitical Islam in Contemporary Egypt*. PhD thesis, Yale University.

Mehanna, O. (2008). Internet and the Egyptian Public Sphere. Presented at the Twelfth General Assembly of the Council for the Development of Social Science Research in Africa.

Mitchell, R. P. (1993). *The Society of the Muslim Brothers*. Oxford University Press, New York.

Monroe, K. R., and Kreidie, L. H. (1997). The Perspective of Islamic Fundamentalists and the Limits of Rational Choice Theory.*PoliticalPsychology*, 18(1):19–43.

Munson, Z. (2001). Islamic Mobilization: Social Movement Theory and the Egyptian Muslim Brotherhood. *Sociological Quarterly*, 42(4):487–510.

Murphy, C. (2002). *Passion for Islam: Shaping the Modern Middle East: TheEgyptian Experience*. Simon & Schuster.

Patel, D. S. (2006). *The Bridge over the River Jordan: Islam, Ethnicity, and Electoral Rule Manipulation*. Stanford University.

Pepinsky, T., and Welborne, B. (2010).Piety and Redistributive Preferences in the Muslim World.*Political Research Quarterly*.

Pripstein-Posusney, M. (1998). Behind the Ballot Box: Electoral Engineering in the Arab World. *Middle East Report*, (209).

Qutb, S. (2000).*Social Justice in Islam*[Adalah al-ijtimaiyah fi al-Islam], 1949; rev. ed., trans. John B. Hardie, 1953; rev. ed., trans, Hamid Algar, 2000.

Rosendorff, B., and Sandler, T. (2005). The Political Economy of Transnational Terrorism.*Journal of Conflict Resolution*, 49(2):171–182.

Roy, O. (1994). *The Failure of Political Islam*.Cambridge, MA:Harvard University Press.

Rubin, B. M. (2002). *Islamic Fundamentalism in Egyptian Politics*.New York:Palgrave Macmillan.

Sait, S., and Lim, H. (2006).*Land, Law and Islam: Property and Human Rightsin the Muslim World*. Zed Books.

Scheve, K., and Stasavage, D. (2006). Religion and Preferences for Social Insurance.*Quarterly Journal of Political Science*, 1:255–286.

Schwedler, J. (1998). A Paradox of Democracy?Islamism Participation in Elections.*Middle East Report*, (209).

Sen, A. (1985). Well-Being, Agency and Freedom: The Dewey Lectures 1984. *The Journal of Philosophy*, 169–221.

Singerman, D. (2004). The Networked World of Islamism Social Movements. In Wiktorowicz, Q., ed., *Islamic Activism: A Social Movement TheoryApproach*. Indiana University Press.

Sullivan, D. J., and Abed-Kotob, S. (1999). *Islam in Contemporary Egypt:Civil Society vs. the State*. Lynne Rienner Publishers.

Tarrow, S. G. (1998).*Power in Movement: Social Movements andContentious Politics*. Cambridge: Cambridge University Press.

Tessler, M., and Nachtwey, J. (1998). Islam and Attitudes toward International conflict: Evidence from Survey Research in the Arab World. *Journal ofConflict Resolution*, 42(5):619–636.

Tripp, C. (2006). *Islam and the Moral Economy: The Challenge of Capitalism*. Cambridge University Press.

Utvik, B. O. (1995). Filling the Vacant Throne of Nasser: The Economic Discourse of Egypt's Islamism Opposition. *Arab Studies Quarterly*, 17(4):29.

Visser, H. (2009).*Islamic Finance: Principles and Practice*. Edward Elgar Publishing.

Wedeen, L. (2003). Beyond the Crusades: Why Huntington, and bin Ladin, Are Wrong. *Middle East Policy*, X(2):56–61.

Wickham, C. R. (2003).*Mobilizing Islam: Religion, Activism, and PoliticalChange in Egypt*. New York:Columbia University Press.

Wiktorowicz, Q. (2000). Civil Society as Social Control: State Power in Jordan. *Comparative Politics*, 33(1):43–61.

Wiktorowicz, Q., ed. (2004).*Islamic Activism: A Social Movement TheoryApproach*. Indiana University Press.

Zureik, E. (1983).The Economics of Dispossession.*Third World Quarterly*, 5(4):775–790.

CHAPTER 7

POLITICAL ISLAM AND GENDER

MARGOT BADRAN

POLITICAL Islam has had profound consequences for women and gender issues that were assiduously promoted as well as unforeseen and undesired. Patriarchal ideology has been at the center of political Islam. In the name of "true Islam" political Islam has promoted the reinvigoration of patriarchal ideology, institutions, and practices that have been eroding since the early decades of the twentieth century. In its drive to gain power and ascendancy, political Islam attempted to reverse the erosion of the hierarchical system of male predominance and control over women and youth and to put a renewed "Islamic" stamp on patriarchal culture. This trajectory toward a reinvigorated patriarchal culture, however, was on a collision course with the social justice that political Islam has claimed to uphold, and it would be a matter of time before the pressures of this contradiction would be made manifest. This happened with great force and clarity during the recent, ongoing, Arab spring, when women and youth—many from within the ranks of political Islam—come forth to challenge the intertwined inequalities and injustices. I start and end with the same question: will the forces of political Islam embrace the necessary admixture of equality along all social axes including gender and social justice and thus an egalitarian understanding and practice of Islam? This essay focuses on political Islam and gender from the 1970s to the present, looking at manifestations of political Islam in Muslim societies in parts of the Middle East and Africa and ending with Islamists' present-day conundrum: will they opt for continuing to uphold a patriarchal version of Islam and therefore render the enjoyment of any meaningful democracy impossible or will they take the leap and resolutely and publicly affirm an egalitarian Islam?

Political Islam needs to be carefully contextualized as its meanings, configurations, and practices shift over time and place. The terms "political Islam" and "Islamism" are used interchangeably as commonly done while acknowledging that Islamism may also be seen as a more capacious category. Ongoing debate over terminology and definitions reflects the dynamism of political Islam or Islamism and the changing environments in which it operates.[1]

When they first appeared around the 1970s, the terms "political Islam" and "Islamism" connoted activist politics directed at eradicating injustice and corruption at the state level by replacing "secular states" with "Islamic states." There was a deliberate indictment of the secular state as ipso facto deviant and "culturally alien" and the concomitant assertion that an Islamic state as "culturally authentic" would embody and translate into practice ideals found wanting in the operation of the secular state. Islamism presented its political project by claiming cultural legitimacy and announcing itself through demonization of "the (secular) other" most vividly in the terrain of women and gender. Women became symbols of (patriarchal) Islamism, its activist adjuncts, and objects of control.

In its bid for political ascendancy, emergent Islamism: (1) redefined and narrowed down "the secular"—which in Islamic modernist thinking included the religious (and the explicit protection of religion)—to signify un-Islamic or anti-Islamic; (2) redefined and narrowed down "the religious," according itself interpretive exclusivity as it foreclosed civic debate of the sort Abdullahi An-Naim[2] advocates whereby citizens can respectfully discuss "secular" and "religious" concerns; (3) constructed a hostile binary of the secular and the religious and built its identity politics around this; and (4) used women and gender to discredit and delegitimize the secular other. In the Islamist reckoning women were either "religious," manifested in their upholding of the (so-called Islamic) patriarchal order, or "secular," expressed in their move toward (allegedly Western) egalitarianism in rights and opportunities for all. Political Islam tout court set up a contest between a patriarchal reading of Islam as culturally indigenous or authentic and an egalitarian understanding of Islam as a manifestation of cultural subversion instigated by the West or by Western-influenced elements from within. Many women went along with Islamism's patriarchal political cum cultural agenda. However, significant numbers did not, and these are increasing.[3]

Viewing women's historical experience and their challenges to Islamist dictates is a telling lens through which to examine political Islam.[4] From the early twentieth century to the 1970s women in diverse parts of the Muslim world had made significant gains in education and in economic, social, and political participation. Inspired by the Islamic modernism of the late nineteenth century exhorting Muslims to engage in *ijtihad* or independent reasoning to reexamine the Qur'an and other religious texts for guidance in dealing with their changing everyday lives, women of the middle and upper strata in Egypt at that time, followed by women elsewhere, began to break through patriarchal constraints imposed on them as religious fiat. They decried the domestic confinement imposed upon women of the middle and upper urban strata pointing out the absence of this in the lives of the Muslim female majority from poor families who needed their labor outside the household.

During the twentieth century women in various Muslim majority countries launched feminist movements, which were often called *secular* feminist movements to indicate their *national* character, that is, the inclusivity of all citizens within the national polity whatever their religious affiliation while at the same time upholding religious freedom and difference. Explicit declarations of Islamic modernist thinking were embedded in Muslim women's secular feminism, most frequently simply called "feminism."[5] This was seen vividly in the pioneering Egyptian feminist movement early last century and in feminist movements in countries of the East Mediterranean and Iraq, which formed the Arab Feminist Union in 1945. Nevertheless, those who privileged patriarchy over equality, both secularists and the religiously identified, discredited women's feminism as a Western cultural intrusion and antithetical to Islam, which were trump cards of delegitimization.

In Egypt in the 1970s and elsewhere in the 1980s, building upon earlier gains, Muslim women in different locations embarked on second wave feminist movements, taking their gender activism into new domains.[6] In the second half of the 1980s and especially in the 1990s, the growing numbers of women—who by then in many Muslim societies had gained access to the highest levels of education, including religious education—began to articulate a discourse of gender equality and social justice grounded in the Qur'an and other religious texts. This equality and justice discourse that spanned the public-private continuum (as opposed to the patriarchal construction of a public-private divide) came to be known as "Islamic feminism." The Iranian anthropologist Ziba Mir-Hosseini has called Islamic feminism the unwanted child of political Islam.[7] As a discourse emerging simultaneously in far-flung parts of the globe, Islamic feminism was also the product of Muslim women's experience as converts and immigrants in the West for whom the conventional patriarchal narrative of Islam was incongruent with their ideas of equality and justice.

In the final third of the twentieth century Islamist movements (initiated and led by men, albeit with women followers) and feminist movements (created and led by women, sometimes joined my men) moved on parallel courses. Women and gender became touchstones of their respectively patriarchal and egalitarian understandings of Islam. *Both* Islamism and feminism were created by Muslims with secular educations employed in the secular professions and institutions. *Both* Islamists and feminists expressed passionate commitment to the pursuit of social justice as the sine quo non of a just state and society. Islamists and feminists, however, disagreed on what social justice necessitated, on the idea of human equality and citizenship or civil equality, and on the role of Islam in the state. As long as Islamists operate within the framework of patriarchy that subordinates women, youth, and any human being on the basis of class, ethnicity, race, or religion, they position themselves in conflict with the principle of human equality to be found in the Qur'an. Feminists, using Islamic language--which they find congruent with the languages of universal human rights and constitutional democracies--demonstrate the necessary link between human equality and social justice. Islamists, referencing the same religion, find it possible to speak of justice without full human equality.

Movements of Political Islam and Women

In examining political Islam and gender it is important to consider experience in specific places. There are commonalities as well as differences in Islamist approaches to women and gender across countries at any given time. There are also contradictory approaches *within* movements and divergent approaches *between* Islamist men and women as well as *among* Islamist women. Common features of political Islam's approach to gender across locations have included (1) calls for women to exit the public arena and retreat to the home as their "proper place" ordained by Islam, (2) a rearticulation of separate roles for the two sexes grounded in biological difference that religion is said to consecrate, and (3) the resumption of the *hijab* as a religious dictate vociferously promoted by Islamist movements and imposed by Islamist states.

Women have been vital to movements of political Islam (as they were previously to anticolonial nationalist movements), particularly in their initial stages as recruiters and providers of services and as social glue. As movement activists women acquired invaluable political and organizational experience in the public arena. Meanwhile, Islamists objected to women's more independent economic roles in the public sphere—which had given women a sense of self-worth and empowerment—calling upon them to quit them for a return to the home as their "religiously" ordained place, as just noted. The contradictory push and pull of Islamists' approaches to women in the public arena vis-à-vis their economic roles, which Islamists eschewed, and their political roles as activist adjuncts within movements of political Islam, which Islamists encouraged, both in the name of Islam, motivated some women who were uncomfortable with these contradictions to explore Islam for themselves. Some women came to challenge inequalities and injustices from within Islamist organizations. Others quit Islamist parties and associations altogether to go their separate way and to form their own entities.

The rest of this section looks at Islamists' impositions in different places and moments concerning women and the ensuing dialectic between imposition and resistance. Themes include the *hijab*, the call for the retreat of women from the public arena to the home, the call for women to enter the public sphere to engage in Islamist political activism, the political collaboration of Islamist and secular women as well as the collaboration of Muslim women and non-Muslim women, and women's use of classical *fiqh* to achieve gender justice. Women both from within Islamist movements and as external actors have impacted political Islam. The following discussion is meant to indicate the dynamism and point to complexities and contradictions. For fuller treatments of experience in particular countries, readers may consult the quickly growing literature on the subject of women and gender and political Islam.

The *hijab*

The Islamist movement that emerged in Egypt in the late 1960s and 1970s and the establishment of the Islamic Republic of Iran in 1979 together inspired the rise of Islamism elsewhere. Islamism set out to recast "the ideal Muslim woman" and to reorder gender relations and the use of public space within a reintensified patriarchal model of Islam using women as the markers of a "return to Islam."

Most immediately striking among Islamism's recuperation of disappearing practices was promoting a "return to the veil" in the guise of a newly invented form of the *hijab* or head cover that could extend variously to more fully cloak the body. The Islamist movement in Egypt initially surfaced on university campuses, where women with their new veils were strikingly visible among the new student activists. The *hijabs* these women took up (the practice of covering the face and hair had disappeared by the mid-twentieth century among the middle and upper classes in the cities) signaled what the new Islamist activists claimed to be a return to correct religious behavior. Importantly, while advertising women's Islamist affiliation, the *hijab* became a symbol of political Islam itself.[8] Islamists labeled women who did not don the *hijab* "secularists," which they used as a pejorative word, branding them as deviant Muslims and women influenced by the West. This catalyzed a polarization of state and society into adversarial "secular" and "religious" camps. At both political and symbolic levels a contest between warring forces was fought over Muslim women's bodies: their dress and comportment and their use of public space. The principle of equal rights of citizens, women and men, and Muslims and non-Muslims that national constitutions guaranteed came under challenge with the ascendancy of political Islam.

Veiling has been viewed in the literature by liberals as both a means of liberation for women and as a constraint. However, when the choice to veil or not to veil is removed or threatened, women are deprived of their free will and disempowered.

Retreat from the public sphere to the private sphere

In Egypt in the 1970s and 1980s the Islamists' call for women to retreat to the home as their religiously ordained place met with swift, outspoken resistance from high-profile Islamist women. Zainab al-Ghazali joined the Egyptian Feminist Union in 1935 and left a year later to form the Muslim Women's Society. After holding off for over a decade, she joined the Muslim Brothers in 1948 bringing her women's group with her, which was renamed the Muslim Sisters. Al-Ghazali retained her public role as a religious leader while simultaneously extolling women's family and domestic roles. Making herself an exception she stood out as an example of a powerful public religious figure who promoted women's Islamic knowledge as a base for claiming their lawful rights. A generation younger, Islamist Safinaz Kazim, a writer, theater critic, and prominent journalist and one of the first young women to take up the *hijab* in the late 1960s as a public sign of her renewed commitment to Islam, adamantly rejected the Islamist call for women to leave their work in the public arena, branding it non-Islamic. From yet a generation younger, Islamist Hiba Rauf, currently a professor of political science at Cairo University, from the late 1980s likewise upheld the right of women to be productive members of society, which she insisted would benefit from their work.[9]

The Islamist states of Iran and Sudan discouraged work for women in the public arena and banned women from continuing to occupy the position of judge. Meanwhile, until early in the twenty-first century, the secular state of Egypt had historically barred women from being judges. The question of women in the public sphere in Iran and Sudan, as elsewhere, was fraught with contradictions. As seen, exigencies could make women's absence in the public workforce impossible to sustain. In Iran during the Iran-Iraq war in the 1980s, for example, women were needed to fill jobs vacated by men. In other places, notably, Saudi Arabia, in order to maintain the gender segregation Islamist regimes encourage women to work in the public sphere in order to fill jobs catering to women, most notably in education and health.

Calling women into the public sphere for Islamist activism

Islamists' association of women with the private sphere, as religiously prescribed, clashed with the economic needs of the majority of families and society. Moreover, Islamist movements for reasons of political expediency violated their own dictum when they enticed women back out of the home into activism in the public arena. Islamist movements understood that women were crucial in expanding their base. If the so-called religiously ordained public-private dichotomy aiming to keep women under control in the domestic sphere could not be upheld, patriarchal structures could be maintained by preserving a gendered hierarchical order within Islamist movements through imposing the authority and control of men over women as a religious mandate. However, as movement activists, women gained new forms of agency and expanded self-confidence as well as acquiring a degree of legitimization in the public sphere through their activist work within Islamist contexts.

Women in Turkey's Refah Party in the 1980s and 1990s, through the separate committees that men encouraged them to set up, honed organizational and political skills as they played critical roles in bringing the party to power.[10] From their positioning within the Refah Party women also influenced Islamist thinking and religious notions more broadly. The political scientist Yeşim Arat notes, "Through their experience we can assess how religion can assume new meanings, threaten or expand boundaries of secular democracy, and re-shape socio-political reality."[11] The building of an egalitarian understanding of Islam from within the female ranks of the Refah Party together with a growing inability to tolerate subordination prompted some women to quit the party. Notably, the lawyer Sibel Eraslan, who had founded and headed the Refah Party's Women's Division in Istanbul, left the party to set up an association of women lawyers to fight for women's rights and social justice marshaling an egalitarian Islamic discourse.

The experience of Palestinian women in Hamas' National Salvation Party, established in 1995 as the political arm of Hamas distinct from its military organization, indicates the influence women activists from within an Islamist party can exert on conservative mainstream ideas of gender. The gender segregation ideology of the Hamas mainstream was less rigid than that of the Refah Party. This can be seen to reflect the Palestinian party's more dire need for women to be integrated into its political work in conditions of occupation. Women held positions in the main bodies of the National Salvation Party and also set up a Women's Action Department in Gaza, where expanding the base has been essential. Women in Gaza have been critical in recruiting support for Hamas. The sociologist Islah Jad observes that women in the National Salvation Party were able to push against Hamas's conservative gender ideology and "stretch their public space." She also astutely observes that "Islamists' search for an alternative to the secular feminist platform ironically brought them into continuous engagement with it."[12] While the antagonism and rivalry between Islamist and secular women that male Islamists encouraged kept women divided, there were bottom lines to what Islamist women could accept. Zones of common interest across the female ideological spectrum sometimes spurred collaboration against the wishes of the Islamist leadership and the mainstream.

Political collaboration between secular and Islamist women

An instance of Islamist and secularist women's collaboration is found in Yemen, where members of the women's division of the Islah Party and secular women, along with some secular men, joined forces in 1997 to fight a regressive new draft family law that reinstated some of the most excessive features of patriarchy concerning marriage and divorce that had been previously eliminated in the family law drafted after unification. The Islamist-secularist women's opposition deployed strong Islamic legal arguments against the new family law as they meanwhile scrambled to engage in joint strategizing to prevent the adoption of the regressive draft family law. Yet, while Islamist and secular women concurred concerning the regressive draft family law, they were not in agreement over the still recently won political rights for women in Yemen. Islahi women, like Islahi men, supported women's suffrage.

The ballot was another tool for Islamists to widen their base. However, Islahi women, unlike secular liberal women and like Islahi men, did not favor women's eligibility to be elected to parliament.[13]

Kuwait has also witnessed cooperation between Islamist and secularist women who joined forces in the final stage of the campaign for political rights. Islamist women supplied cogent religious arguments for women's suffrage, while secular women reiterated constitutional arguments and brought to bear skills sharpened during their decades-long campaigning for women's political rights. Experience in the resistance struggle during the Iraqi occupation of Kuwait from mid-1990 to early 1991 spurred women across the ideological spectrum into a stepped-up push to win full political rights in the country they had played key roles in liberating.[14] Joining forces, Islamist and secular liberal women powerfully defended women's right to vote and successfully defeated the stubborn resistance of Islamists and other conservatives to women's suffrage. Haya al-Mughni foresees that any ongoing collaborative activism of Islamist and secular liberal women could extend other citizens' rights to women, such as the ability of Kuwaiti women to transmit their nationality to their children that Islamist and secular patriarchal forces alike in many Muslim majority countries have fought. Recently progressive forces in some countries have made headway on this front.[15]

Political collaboration across groups in mobilizing *fiqh* in the cause of gender justice

Central to Islamists' political projects has been the issue of sexuality and more specifically women's sexuality and the control of women's bodies. Ironically while Islamists have been able to find ready support through recourse to classical Islamic jurisprudence or *fiqh* in upholding a patriarchal model of the family, in the case of *zina* (sex outside marriage) classical *fiqh* exhibits a resolutely gender egalitarian approach that necessitates examination of both parties in instances of alleged illicit sex. Moreover, so onerous are the consequences of *zina* that the proofs necessary for conviction are virtually impossible to provide. Historically matters of crime and punishment were the purview of Islamic jurists or *fuquha,* but in modern times in Islamist regimes such as Iran, Sudan, and Pakistan, crime and punishment are regulated by state-enacted statutory *hudud* laws. Such Islamic laws of crime and punishment that criminalize *zina* have led to particularly aggressive state-condoned forms of patriarchal oppression. In the real world of patriarchal politics and culture, women and the poor are powerless have been the scapegoats and targets of summary "justice."

In Nigeria at the end of the twentieth century and in the early years of the twenty-first century, governors of several states in the North imposed *hudud* laws in a political power move opportunistically billed as a "return to Shari`ah." Nigerian women activists who had seen the dire results of such moves elsewhere accurately predicted that women would be the first victims. In northern Nigeria when two women among the poor were pronounced guilty of *zina* in Shari`ah courts and sentenced to death by stoning, Muslim women across the secular-religious spectrum, along with non-Muslim women as human rights activists, feminists, and concerned citizens, together with some Muslim male supporters, rallied to the defense of the condemned women. The Nigerian women activists, Muslim religious and secular women, and Christian women provided legal teams that included experts in Islamic jurisprudence to successfully defend the two condemned women. The activist women at the same time engaged in public awareness campaigns bringing to public attention the flaunting of Islamic principles and legal procedures expressed by the convictions.[16]

In Morocco contestations between Islamist and secular liberal women that involved careful appropriations of their respective discourses and activist tools, along with propitious political circumstances, led to the revision in 2004 of the *Mudawwana*, the only explicitly religiously grounded egalitarian family law. The complex choreography of Islamist and secular liberal women's activism and the volatile "larger" political realities of the moment illustrate the dynamism and contradictions among Islamists and their gender politics and how "dogma" can be expediently tweaked. It also demonstrates how secular women did not continue to advance exclusively universalist secular rights arguments but marshaled religious argument as well. As Pruzan-Jorgensen put it, "Members of the liberal women's movement adopted a conscious strategy of challenging their components on their own turf—religion."[17] When the liberals, especially the liberal women's movement, were gaining momentum in the promotion of an egalitarian family law, Islamist women came out full force with their own critique. After the enactment of the revised law Islamist women, notably Nadia Yassine of the Ihsan wa Adl Party, applauded it and claimed it as a victory for themselves. Expedient political activism pushed Islamist women to assert their approval of the egalitarian family that became enshrined in the revised 2004 Mudawanna.

POLITICAL ISLAM AND ISLAMIC FEMINISM

Political Islam in both the form of oppositional movements and Islamist states ignited the rise of Islamic feminism in the older Muslim societies in Africa and Asia.[18] Islamic feminism emerged, in part, as an answer back to patriarchal interpretations and practices of Islam offering in its stead an egalitarian reading of the religion.

In the preceding glimpse into women's experiences within movements of political Islam and inside Islamist states, we have seen how women came to question patriarchal ideas and practices imposed on them in the name of religion. In the 1980s, and increasingly from the 1990s, women in different parts of the global Islamic world began to articulate a discourse of gender equality and social justice that came to be called "Islamic feminism." If Islamic feminism was the unexpected and undesired child of political Islam it was also the unanticipated offspring of secular feminism in Muslim societies. As noted, Muslim secular feminism included an Islamic modernist strand that enabled early feminists to make headway in ending women's domestic seclusion and gaining access to new forms of education, new employment, and political rights (although in some countries more recently women would gain their political rights through combined secular and Islamic feminist campaigning). Meanwhile, secular states as part of their modernizing schemes provided new opportunities for women in the public arena. The ideas, rights, and practices that feminists and states opened up to women exposed them to egalitarian notions while their new educational opportunities extending to the highest levels in all fields, including the religious sciences, equipped women to embark on their own investigations of Islam, rather than remaining reliant upon male interpretations.

When movements of political Islam, starting in the final third of the twentieth century, began to roll back the gains women had acquired, especially in the area of work, women balked, including highly accomplished women fervently committed to Islam, as we have seen. Women increasingly objected to being forced to choose between their religion and their (lawful) rights. Ironically by blatantly *imposing* patriarchal ideas and practices political Islam played a major role in *exposing* patriarchy's inequities and clash with Islamic principles of equality and justice. Accordingly political Islam provoked the disconnecting of patriarchy from Islam or, as Asma Barlas put it, "unreading patriarchal interpretations of Islam."[19] Political Islam's imposition of patriarchal controls on women pushed many to fight back and find an Islam of their own.

Among the earliest sites of the emergent discourse of Islamic feminism in the late 1980s and 1990s in the old Muslim societies in Africa and Asia were Egypt, Iran, Malaysia, Morocco, South Africa, and Turkey.[20] Islamic feminism appeared in the form of a discourse that articulated an egalitarian reading of Islam. Succinctly put, Islamic feminism that "derives its understanding and mandate from the Qur'an, seeks rights and justice for women and for men in the totality of their existence."[21] There have been many elaborations of the discourse of Islamic feminism in the quarter of a century since it first appeared. There have also been intensifying efforts to translate Islamic feminism's discourse of gender equality and social justice into practice through collective organizing and everyday activism.[22]

Gender and a New Islamism?

Islamism, like other dynamic political and cultural phenomena, arises in particular contexts and its thinking, policies, and practices undergo modification. Islamist movements and regimes today are not those of yesterday. Islamist regimes, such as Iran, have been subjected to mounting pressures to honor the right of citizens and deliver justice, as seen in the Green Movement of 2010. Islamist movements, as noted, have had to reposition and to renegotiate over the many decades since the 1970s. By 2011 following national uprisings in some countries, most notably Tunisia and Egypt, Islamist groupings previously proscribed as oppositional and accordingly suppressed have been welcomed to the collective table of democratic activism and cease to be resistance movements but rather are becoming part of the building of new democratic states.

Egypt offers a tantalizing look at the implications of turbulent transformation. The Islamist movement that emerged there in the 1970s in opposition to corrupt states promoted a solution in the form of replacing the secular state with an Islamic state. In time as the movement of political Islam, and especially in its radical forms, was contained, the Islamist mainstream epitomized by the Muslim Brothers, who focused attention on service provision among the needy throughout the country, at the same time reinforced conservative "Islamic" patriarchal culture. As a staunch opponent of injustices emanating from the state including economic injustices and lack of service provision and through its ability to connect with the majority throughout Egypt, the Muslim Brothers acquired a wide following.

Now that the Muslim Brothers for the first time have been allowed to form political parties it is not to be expected that the majority will change their patriarchal cultural politics and thus risk diminishing their conservative countrywide base. Yet there is a fundamental problem of ideology and ethics they will have to face. How can the Islamists continue to uphold a patriarchal model of Islam that negates the fundamental equality of all human beings and citizens integral to the democracy and justice they have been calling for all these years? Islamic feminism, with its stringent articulation of an egalitarian Islam, has been in existence for a quarter of a century, and its outreach has steadily increased while its arguments have been sharpened and made widely accessible over the years. Egalitarian Islam has made inroads but the continuing battle will be uphill in the short run as patriarchal proclivities, dressed in Islamic rhetoric, are hard to dispel.

How will the Islamists manage the contradiction between their long and assiduous demands for justice and democracy—and neither can be achieved without equality—with their patriarchal model of Islam? The clash between patriarchal inequalities that Islamists uphold in the name of religion and egalitarianism that is integral to democracy is a contraction they will ultimately have to resolve. Meanwhile, the Islamists' unruly child, Islamic feminism, is raising the decibel level of its cry for an egalitarian Islam. The nemesis of the Muslim Brothers' patriarchal politics is Muslim women and the Muslim Brothers' own youth, who were at the heart of the recent massive youth-instigated uprising and who together with women and others clamoring for equality and justice have remained on the revolutionary ramparts. Youth and women are publically challenging this hegemonic patriarchal order imposed in the name of Islam that subordinates both as unequals at the bottom of the pyramid. Perhaps Islamism can score a victory through claiming its offspring that upholds an egalitarian Islam[23]

Notes

1. See "Islamism" with three subheadings—"Concepts and Debates," by William E. Shepherd; "Sources," by Francois Burgat, updated by James Piscatori; and "Nature of Islamist Movements," by Armando Salvatore—in the *Oxford Encyclopedia of the Islamic World*, online, accessed May 1, 2011. For further discussion, see also Salwa Ismail, *Rethinking Islamist Politics: Culture, the State and Islamism* (London: I. B. Taurus, 2006) and Ziba Mir-Hosseini, "Beyond 'Islam' vs. 'Feminism,' " *IDS Bulletin*, "Gender, Rights and Religion at the Crossroads," 42, no. 1:67–77, see p 71.
2. Abdullahi An-Naim, *Islam and the Secular State: Negotiating the Future of the Shari`a* (Cambridge: Harvard University Press, 2008).
3. On feminism and Islamism in Egypt in the 1980s and 1990s, see Azza M. Karam, *Women, Islamisms, and the State: Contemporary Feminisms in Egypt* (New York: St. Martin's Press, 1998). Karam atypically uses the term "Islamist feminist," which most find an oxymoron, as Islamists (whatever their gender) have accepted a patriarchal model of Islam that feminists reject. For a longer historical overview, see Margot Badran, "Competing Agenda: Feminists, Islam, and the State in Nineteenth- and Twentieth-Century Egypt," in M. Badran, *Feminism in Islam: Secular and Religious Convergences* (Oxford: Oneword, 2009).
4. See Valentine M. Moghadam, *Modernizing Women: Gender and Social Change in the Middle East* (Boulder: Lynne Rienner, 1993).
5. On the pioneering and widely influential Egyptian feminist movement, see Margot Badran, *Feminists, Islam, and Nation: Gender and the Making of Modern Egypt* (Princeton: Princeton University Press, 1995).

6. See Margot Badran, Chapter 5 "Independent Women: More Than a Century of Feminism in Egypt," in *Feminism in Islam*, 116–140; Parvin Paidar, *Women and the Political Process in Twentieth Century Iran* (Cambridge: Cambridge University Press, 1995); Yeşim Arat, "Women's Movements of the 1980s in Turkey: Radical Outcome of Liberal Kemalism?" in Fatma M. Goçek and Shiva Balaghi, eds., *Reconstructing Gender in the Middle East: Tradition, Identity, and Power, 100–112* (New York: Columbia University Press, 1994); and Julie M. Peteet, *Gender in Crisis: Women and the Palestinian Resistance Movement* (New York: Columbia University Press, 1991).

7. While Islamic feminism can be seen as the child of political Islam, where this new discourse surfaced in Africa and Asia in the West, Islamic feminist discourse was generated from within convert and immigrant communities responding to their own challenges in living Islam in new environments. See Margot Badran, "Feminism and Conversion: Comparing British, Dutch, and South African Stories," in Karin van Nieuwkerk, ed., *Women Embracing Islam: Gender and Conversion in the West* (Austin: University of Texas Press, 2006), 192–232.

8. On the rise of a renewed practice of veiling in Egypt, see Fadwa El Guindi, "Veiling Infitah with Muslim Ethic: Egypt's Contemporary Islamic Movement," *Social Problems* 28, no. 4 (1981): 465–485 and her later, more comprehensive treatment in *Veil: Modesty, Privacy and Resistance* (Oxford: Berg, 2000). See also Arlene Elowe Macleod, *Accommodating Protest: Working Women, the New Veiling, and Change in Cairo* (New York: Columbia University Press, 1991); and Sherifa Zuhur, *Revealing Reveiling: Islamic Gender Ideology in Contemporary Egypt* (Albany: State University of New York Press, 1992).

9. See Badran, "Competing Agenda" and "Gender Activism: Feminists and Islamists in Egypt," in *Feminism in Islam*, 141–168. On Al-Ghazali, see Miriam Cooke, *Women Claim Islam: Creating Islamic Feminism through Literature* (London: Routledge, 2001).

10. See Nilüfer Göle, *The Forbidden Modern: Civilization and Veiling* (Ann Arbor: University of Michigan Press, 1996).

11. Yeşim Arat, *Rethinking Islam and Liberal Democracy: Islamist Women in Turkish Politics* (Albany: State University of New York Press, 2005).

12. "Islamist Women of Hamas: Between Feminism and Nationalism," *Revue des Mondes Musulmans et de la Méditerranée*, special issue on *Féminismes islamiques*, 128 (2010–12): 183–208.

13. Margot Badran, "Unifying Women: Feminist Pasts and Presents in Yemen," in Badran, *Feminism in Islam*, 253–278. See also Janine Clark, *Islam, Charity, and Activism: Middle-Class Networks and Social Activism in Egypt, Jordan, and Yemen* (Bloomington: Indiana University Press, 2004); and Gillian Schwedler, *Faith in Moderation: Islamist Parties in Jordan and Yemen* (Cambridge: Cambridge University Press, 2006).

14. See Margot Badran, "Gender, Islam, and the State: Kuwaiti Women in Struggle, Pre-Invasion to Postliberation," Yvonne Haddad and John Esposito, eds., *Islam, Gender, and Social Change* (Oxford: Oxford University Press, 1998).

15. Haya al-Mughni, "The Rise of Islamic Feminism in Kuwait," *Revue des Mondes Musulmans et de la Méditerranée*, special issue on *Féminismes islamiques*, 128 (2010–2012): 167–182.

16. Ayesha Imam, "Fighting the Political (Ab)Use of Religion in Nigeria: BAOBAB for Women's Human Rights, Allies, and Others," in Ayesha Imam, Jenny Morgan, and Nira Yuval-Davis, eds., *Fundamentalism: Warning Signs, Law, Media, and Resistances* on WLUML website (www.wluml.org) and Margot Badran, "Shari`a Activism in Nigeria in the Era of *Hudud*," in Badran, *Feminism in Islam*, 279–299.

17. Julie E. Pruzan-Jørgensen, "Islam, Gender, and Democracy in Morocco: The Making of the Mudawanna Reform," Margot Badran, ed., *Gender and Islam in Africa: Rights, Sexuality, and Law* (Washington and Stanford: Woodrow Wilson Press and Stanford University Press, 2011), 233–263; and Souad Eddouada, "Women and the Politics of Reform in Morocco," in *Middle East Program Occasional Paper Series*, Fall 2010: 15–17.
18. In the West and especially North America, Islamic feminism surfaced from among the communities of women converts and immigrants needing in their newfound situations to work out what Islam means for themselves. Since Islamism is a global phenomenon, its effects have also been felt in certain ways by Muslim women in the West.
19. This is the subtitle of her book *Believing Women in Islam: Unreading Patriarchal Interpretations of the Qur'an* (Austin: University of Texas Press, 2002), which is considered one of the foundational texts of Islamic feminism although Barlas does not use this term herself.
20. Among the earliest to observe the new phenomenon of Islamic feminism are Ziba Mir-Hosseini, "Stretching the Limits: A Feminist Reading of the Shari`a in Post-Khomeni Iran," in Mai Yamani, ed., *Feminism and Islam: Legal and Literary Perspectives* (New York: New York University Press, 1996), 285–320; Afsaneh Najmabadi, "Feminism in an Islamic Republic: Years of Hardship, Years of Growth," in Yvonne Haddad and John Esposito, eds. *Islam, Gender, and Social Change* (New York: Oxford University Press, 1998), 59–84; Badran, "Toward Islamic Feminisms," 215–241; "Islamic Feminism: What's in a Name?" 242–252; and "Islamic Feminism on the Move," 323–339 in *Feminism in Islam*.
21. Margot Badran, "Islamic Feminism: What's in a Name?" in Badran, *Feminism in Islam*, 242.
22. The term "Islamic feminism" has come to be used so loosely that it is often emptied of gender equality and social justice as its core principles.
23. This essay was completed before the parliamentary and presidential elections occurred that brought Islamists to power in Tunisia, Egypt, and elsewhere. In Egypt, for example, there are indications that Islamists as well as staunchly patriarchal secularists will push hard to enact retrogressive gender legislation and policies. Yet, women, of both secular and religious inclination, are assiduously fighting to preserve the rights they have gained and to extend further their rights and the reach of social justice for all citizens through the promotion of egalitarian laws and insistence on the everyday practice of justice grounded in secular constitutions, human rights discourse, and religious principles. *This* is the new essay.

PART TWO

ISLAMIC IDEOLOGUES, ACTIVISTS, AND INTELLECTUALS

*Founders or Trailblazers of
Political Islam*

CHAPTER 8

HASSAN AL-BANNA*

AHMAD MOUSSALLI

This essay focuses on Hasan al-Banna's religious and political discourse, which still provides substantive ideological foundations for the Muslim Brotherhood in Egypt and elsewhere as well as for many other Islamist movements throughout the Islamic world. This discourse is discussed under three central and general principles that constitute the essence of political Islam: first, Islam and politics; second, the Islamic state and the *Shari`ah*; and third, democracy and *shūrā*. An assessment of al-Banna's views on these matters follows in the conclusion.

The agreement of most Islamists over these issues at a theoretical level does not mean that an agreement over a practical discourse or praxis is reached. On the contrary, a spectrum of discourses has spread. For instance, the discourses of Sayyid Qutb, Abu al-A`la al-Mawdudi, and Ayatollah Khomeini are more radical than those of al-Banna, Hasan al-Turabi, and Rashid al-Ghannushi. The first three discourses have no notion of gradual change or possible compromise and emphasize the need to overthrow secular governments as a nonnegotiable religious duty. They hold tightly and uncompromisingly to both divine governance and universal paganism. However, al-Banna's discourse is more open and less particular about a forceful overthrow of un-Islamic regimes.[1] In fact, his discourse shows readiness to compromise, both practically and theoretically, and relegates ultimate earthly authority to the community. Social agreement is in itself an embodiment of divine will. If a community is not willing to adopt an Islamic state, then its imposition does not reflect the nature of Islam. The focus is here on discussing al-Banna's discourse, which is elaborated under three main principles. But we start first with a brief of his life.

The Beginnings

Hasan al-Banna was born in October 1906, in al-Buhayra, one of Egypt's northern Nile delta provinces, to a religious father. He was educated first at a traditional Islamic Kuttab

---

* This is a collection of Friday sermons published in *Al-Ikhwan al-Muslimun* newspaper

(religious school) and, then at the age of twelve, joined a primary school. During the early part of his life, al-Banna became involved with Sufism and continued that association for most of his life. At the age of fourteen, he joined a primary teachers' school and two years later enrolled in *Dar al-'Ulum* College from which he graduated as a teacher.[2]

In Cairo, during his student years, al-Banna joined religious societies involved in Islamic education. However, he soon realized that this type of religious activity was inadequate to bring the Islamic faith back to its status in the public life of Egypt. He felt that more activism was needed, so he organized students from al-Azhar University and *Dar al-'Ulum* and started to preach in mosques and popular meeting places. During this period, al-Banna came to be influenced by the writings of Muhammad 'Abduh, Rashid Rida, and Ahmad Taymur Pasha (Brynjar 1998; Moussalli 1999).

When he graduated in 1927, he was appointed as a teacher of Arabic in a primary school in al-Isma'iliya, a new small town with a semi-European character. It hosted the headquarters of the Suez Canal Company and a sizable foreign community. In Isma'iliya, al-Banna started to preach his ideas to poor Muslim workers, small merchants, and civil servants. He kept warning his audience against the liberal lifestyle of the Europeans in the town and the dangers of emulating it, thus cultivating strong feelings of fear and anxiety in them.

In March 1928, he founded the Muslim Brotherhood or, actually, Brethren. In the first four years of its existence, al-Banna's primary goal was to recruit membership, establishing branches along the eastern and western edge of the delta. The quick and remarkable spread of the Brethren engendered governmental resistance, especially during the cabinet of Isma'il Sidqi Pasha.

In 1932–1933, al-Banna was transferred to Cairo, and his group merged with the Society for Islamic Culture, forming the first branch of the Muslim Brothers, which then became the headquarters of the society. During this period, the number of branches went from 1,500 to 2,000; most of which ran schools, clinics, and other welfare institutions. Not only that, but branches in Sudan, Syria, and Iraq were established, and the society's publications were distributed throughout Islamic countries.

At the beginning of his political career, al-Banna did not have an elaborate program and his message focused on the centrality of Islam. Gradually, he developed the notion of Islam as a religion that embraces all aspects of human life and conduct. He declared that the objective of the Muslim Brotherhood was to create a new generation capable of understanding the essence of Islam and of acting in accordance. He believed that Islam was the solution to the problem of Egypt and the Islamic world. However, following World War II, al-Banna assumed a greater political role. He started to call for the replacement of secular institutions by Islamic-oriented ones and asked for major reforms. However, al-Banna did not advocate violent political action as the means toward achieving political goals.

In fact, several members of his organization and he ran for parliamentary elections more than once and lost. For al-Banna accepted the legitimacy of the Egyptian regime and tried to work from within the system. His condemnation of Egyptian parties was not based on rejecting the idea of multiparty systems but more on the rejection of corruption and manipulation. This is why the Egyptian Brethren today have been able to theoretically introduce the legitimacy of pluralism, human rights, and democracy as respectively *ikhtilaf* (difference of opinion), *al-huquq al-Shari'ah* (legal rights), and *shūrā* (consultation).

By the end of World War II, al-Banna had become an acknowledged political figure, and the Muslim Brethren emerged as a strong force presenting itself as a political alternative.

As was the case with other parties, the society established a military wing, which assassinated a number of its adversaries. The Brethren reached its apogee during the Arab-Israel War (1948), in which the Muslim Brothers participated through their paramilitary organs. However, the expansion of the society, its growing influence, and its development of a strong military force brought it into a clash with the government. In February 1949, al-Banna was assassinated by police agents. Today, his ideology still informs most of the moderate Islamic movements across the entire Islamic world, and his movement is still the leading ideological power behind the expansion of Islamism.

THE DISCOURSE: THREE PRINCIPLES

The Islamic state and *Shari`ah*

The Muslim Brotherhood in Egypt focused more on the political aspect of Islam as the cornerstone in promoting a modern Islamic revival. It called for the urgent need of establishing an Islamic state as the first step in implementing the *Shari`ah*. While the Brotherhood centered its intellectual reinterpretation on going back to the fundamentals, they selectively accepted major Western political concepts such as constitutional rule and democracy as necessary tools for overhauling the doctrine of an Islamic state. However, the Brotherhood's extremely antagonistic dealing with the Egyptian government of Gamal Abd al-Nasser led some Brothers to rally under the leadership of Sayyid Qutb. While Qutb upheld the need for establishing an Islamic state, he rejected any openness to the West or others. He made the existence of an Islamic state an essential part of creed. It represented to him and his followers the communal submission to God on the basis of *Shari`ah*. It became, as well, the representation of political and legal abidance to the *Shari`ah* that was the basis of both legal rules and the constitution. The absence of *Shari`ah* would remove any shred of legitimacy that the state may enjoy and bring it into *jahiliyya*. On yet another level, Ayatollah al-Khumayni restricted further his concept of a legitimate Islamic government. Although *Shari`ah* was the basis of government, it was only through the rule of the jurist that its existence was legally actualized.

Within the Islamic world today, the demands of the mainstream Islamist movements in Algeria, Tunisia, Jordan, and Egypt follow mostly al-Banna's discourse. However, radical Sunni movements follow mostly the discourse of Sayyid Qutb, and Shiite political movements follow that of al-Khumayni.

A prerequisite for understanding the demand of the majority of Islamists requires an in-depth study of al-Banna's doctrine of Islamic state. However, this cannot be even entertained—although people, including scholars, do so anyway—without an analysis of al-Banna's political discourse. Again, this in turn requires an understanding of al-Banna's philosophy of life as well as his religious discourse, which are derived from the basic sources of the Qur'an and the *sunnah* and the historical role of religion in the life of Muslims. He not only was concerned with political rule but also believed that the impurity of politics resulted from the unethical exercise of power as well as from mishandling multilayered social, economic, and educational crises. A mere change of government did not seem to be what was required or desired for the revival of the ethical spirit of the community. The state was an agency that organized people's affairs and transcended such a description to be morally involved in protecting creed and religion's supremacy so that a human regeneration was affected and humankind's lifestyle was amended in accordance with the spirit of religion. The state's function, though limited, must help the people to live a virtuous life by, for example, redirecting the course of education toward God. A view of life that was accepted by the people became the conditioning ground for establishing the desired state. The legitimate exercise of authority or the withdrawal of legitimacy depended then on the same conditions, and, once the Islamic state was established, the state could not nullify the original contract between the people and the ruler.

Of course, reestablishing the Islamic caliphate has been generally entertained by al-Banna and most Islamic movements as the highest political institution. As was the case historically, it is still viewed as the cornerstone for theoretical political discourses on government and politics. It represents politically the highest goal for Islamic movements and constitutes the symbol of Islamic unity and power. Because it brings together religion and politics, its field of study is not restricted to jurisprudence but includes also theology and the science of the principles of religion (*usul al-din*).

In the history of Islam, great theoreticians, such as al-Mawardi in *Al-Ahkam al-Sultaniyya*, Ibn Taymiyya in *Al-Siyasa al-Shari'ah*, Abu Yusuf in *Kitab al-Kharaj*, al-Ghazali in *Al-Iqtisad fi al-I'tiqad*, Ibn Jama'a in *Tahrir al-Ahkam*, and Ibn Khaldun in the *Muqaddima*, started tying the caliphate's functions and qualifications to political and economic development. In this sense, it must therefore shoulder the responsibility of tuning the community with the ups and downs of history and represent the realities of a given age. However, when it was al-Banna's turn to discuss the caliphate, it had then already been abolished by Ataturk. Thus, the symbol of Islamic unity in al-Banna's eyes was gone, and this was why the existence of the caliphate was to him a nostalgic affinity with glory and power as well as the supremacy of Islam. Because the caliphate was a historical event, its regeneration required an awesome task. For it represented nothing less than the unification of Muslims again in an international state, the achievement of which was a task whose difficulties al-Banna knew. For its revival must be preceded by a total program of reforming the Muslims of his day and must include issues such as preparations of complete educational, social, and economic cooperation between Muslim peoples; the formation of alliances and conferences among these peoples; and finally, founding a league of nations responsible for the caliph's choice (al-Banna 1984b, 70–71). Such issues, however, were not much easier than establishing the caliphate itself and this was why an alternative institution was called for that seemed more practical and achievable. As an indispensable step for establishing the caliphate the concept of an Islamic state became as important, both theoretically and practically, as the caliphate itself.

The Muslim Brotherhood, according to al-Banna, believes that the caliphate is the symbol of Islamic unity and the sign of commitment to Islam. It is a rite that the Muslims must be concerned about achieving. It is the caliph who is in charge of applying numerous divine legal commands. Al-Banna shows the importance of the caliphate by describing a major event surrounding the Prophet's death. This event is that the Muslims discussed and resolved the issue of political succession even before the Prophet's burial. But, because the caliphate does not exist anymore, al-Banna calls for some rethinking about the issue of political rule, since it is the center of political contract between the people and their unifying agency. This is why the Muslim Brotherhood makes the revival of Islam dependent on establishing an Islamic system of government. However, the flourishing of Islam cannot take place without spreading the Qur'an and its language as well as achieving a comprehensive political unity among Muslims. At the same time, a modern Islamic government to al-Banna can take many forms, with new military, economic, and political organizations (al-Banna 1984, 70–71; 1984a, 95–96).

The scriptural Qur'anic references to political rule constitute the legitimacy of Islamic rule and its function: the spiritual, political, and economic well-being and defense of the community. Furthermore, its function is extended worldwide, especially since geographical limitations are not, in al-Banna's view, applicable to the Islamic call and therefore to the state that universalizes that call. Therefore, the well-being of humankind as a concern of the Islamic call makes the role of the Islamic state moral and universal (al-Banna, 194?).[3] In turn, the universality of the call (the message is fine but the call is more general) makes the existence of a universal caliphate a necessity, since it is the institution that transcends localities, borders, and the like. However, and for the time being, al-Banna looks at the geographic Islamic entity, or the state, as more pivotal for instituting the Islamic system. Practically speaking, it is more possible to achieve the Islamic state than the caliphate (al-Banna n.d., 63, 72, 347; *Minbar*).

To al-Banna, an Islamic state is the essential first step for achieving the good Islamic society. Without the state, the society would rather find many difficulties in voluntarily organizing itself on an Islamic basis. For the nature of many basic Islamic doctrines requires an organizing agency of the first rate. Within modern geographic realities, that agency is the Islamic state (al-Banna n.d., 317).

To al-Banna, it is only the state that can function as both an executive agency that remedies all problems and an institution that develops Islamic laws suitable for this age. His perception of Islam as "as a complete system regulating all aspects of life and including a system of social norms, government, legislation, law, and education" cannot be realized without the state. Furthermore, because a great substance of reform is of political nature, the state must be involved as well. Al-Banna finds that mere religiosity without solid commitment to political, social, and economic activism is useless to the community of Muslims (al-Banna 1984b, 53–5; n.d., 101, 104).

More importantly, not committing to political Islam is *jahiliyya* to al-Banna. He subordinates the legitimacy of the state to fulfilling basic Islamic goals. Because these goals include a commitment to apply the Islamic law and the spread of the Islamic call, religious commitment is linked to political legitimacy. Thus, the call to Islam is a moral and religious duty that must be carried out privately by the community and officially by the Islamic government. But it is the government that must carry out the broader essentials of the Islamic call, that is, addressing the general moral or spiritual atmosphere within the *ummah* and curbing moral and political degeneration and atheistic orientations (al-Banna 1974, 15–17). In this sense, the government becomes the executive arm of the virtuous society, and, by trust, it performs the society's moral, religious, and political objectives. Only through following such an attitude does an Islamic government receive legitimate recognition from Hasan al-Banna (al-Banna 1984, 55). Thus, an Islamic government could not be conceptually and functionally compartmentalized, that is, to function at one time as a secular agency, at another, as religious. By following the demands of a virtuous society, the state does not produce conflicting claims but becomes the popular guiding social executive power in charge of executing just laws. Only through such a role could the necessary conditions for the legitimacy of government be fulfilled (*Minbar*, 24–45).

This conclusion about the state's function and attitude is entertained by al-Banna because he builds his political discourse on a reinterpretation of the doctrine of God's *rububiyya* (lordship) and *hakimiyya* (sovereignty). God's universal *rububiyya* makes Islamic revelation the basic text in matters relating to both politics and political philosophy. To him, the history of Islam shows testimonies to Muslims' subordination of politics to religion; for instance, all political expansions were made in the name of Islam (al-Banna n.d., 36–37, 317). And insofar as Muslims did that, they were victorious, but when they disassociated politics from true religion and lost their religious zeal, they became losers. Consequently, Islam lost the role it had played throughout history (al-Banna 1984b, 56).

In line with al-Ghazali's thought, al-Banna still does not give the government the upper hand in all domains of life but views it as only an appendix to the *Shari'ah* and constrained by it. The government cannot then change the *Shari'ah* under the guise of its development. It can, however, rework its principles in accordance with the changing needs and demands of society. The government's policies should not, therefore, neglect the general and guiding principles of the *Shari'ah*.

For instance, universal principles as the necessity of Islamic unity cannot forever be replaced by narrow bonds of patriotism and nationalism, though the two can be used to strengthen the universal principle. For such an act of replacement distorts the true spirit of the Qur'anic discourse, which aims at unity, not disunity. To al-Banna, denying God's *uluhiyya* (divinity) over this life and the concomitant disavowal of universal unity lead simply to unbelief (al-Banna 1984a, 317; n.d., 347). Therefore, al-Banna believes that a major function of the Islamic state is not to yield to those ideologies and philosophies that disrupt the unity of humankind and the Muslims in particular. In fact, the state must counterattack the political and philosophical endeavors to limit the scope of Islam through imposing humanly developed systems over God's system. If the Islamic state yields to such an act, it would be solidifying *jahiliyya* and contributing to the disunity of humankind, and thus breaking the postulates of the *Shari'ah* (al-Banna 1984a, 317; n.d., 54).

Islam and Politics

Al-Banna links his political discourse to developing a religiously derived Qu'ranic discourse that includes both creed and action. The testimony that there is "no god but God" is to al-Banna a call to establish divine governance on earth. The perfection of a Muslim's creed must lead him to act on behalf of society (al-Banna, 178–179).[4] Furthermore, Islam's comprehensiveness makes it fit for human *fitra* (innate constitution) and capable of influencing not only the majority of people but elites as well. Because Islam to al-Banna provides the worldliest just principles and the straightest of divine legal codes, it uplifts the human soul and sanctifies universal brotherhood. It also gives practical ways to achieve all of this in people's daily life, social living, education, and political aspirations. It is also on these bases that Islam sets its state and establishes its universal call to humankind. For while Islam asks humans to satisfy themselves spiritually and materially, it provides them with regulations that prevent extreme behaviors and arrive at balanced fulfillment. Such a balance is important to al-Banna because humans do not live in isolation but are members of a community. The community has, however, its "collective reason," which differs from the individual's. Thus, diverse Islamic regulations satisfy different needs: the economic, for material well-being; the political, for unity, justice, and freedom; and the social, for equality. To al-Banna, all these regulations are only fractions of the authentic Islamic method. Only this method can lead humankind to remove itself from its miserable existence (al-Banna 1974, 65–66).

Al-Banna adds that what distinguishes Islam from most other religions is its concern with not only worship but also a social system. To al-Banna, Islam is thus composed of creed, worship, and governance and is a collective and state religion. Muslims must then derive their general principles from it. Islam as a social system deals with all social phenomena, and as such the Qur'an and the *sunnah* must represent the highest fundamental authority and point of reference. But their interpretations must be conducted through analogical deduction and consensus. In brief, to al-Banna, Islam is concerned with all aspects of life and postulates precise methods, fundamentals, and foundations for humankind. It is simply a general code for all races, peoples, and nations (al-Banna 1974, 66–67, 38–39).

Activism is to al-Banna the sign of good belief, and political action should be in line with Islamic teachings. In fact, separating Islam from politics is not Islamic. Theoretically, Islam is more comprehensive than politics and absorbs it. Individual perfection requires politicizing Islam. In this sense, Islam is a complete active religion that must relate to all aspects of life. For instance, al-Banna believes that one of the main religious objectives is to provide society with laws of organization. From al-Banna's perspective, Islam must act as a regulator of behavior of both Muslim communities and all human societies. Its general goals are designed to fit all societies, and this can be done through reinterpretations of texts to suit different times and ages (al-Banna 1984a, 157–159, 119–121; 1974, 71–83).

Islam, then, aims at setting up a good nation with a message of unity and sacrifice. It also aims at establishing a just Islamic government without tyranny or authoritarianism and in the service of the people. A government like this helps in establishing a virtuous society (al-Banna 1969, 112–115). The function of Islam is based on four foundations: first, pure creed that brings humans closer to God; second, correct worship and good religious deeds such as praying and fasting that add meaning to life; third, unity, which completes the faith and reduces the tension between sects and political tendencies; and fourth, just legislation and good laws that are derived from the Qur'an and the *sunnah* (al-Banna 1969, 192–194; 1970, 23–29).

As for other revealed religions, al-Banna argues that Islam is the last of them and their complete manifestation. Islam does not negate their ethics and ways of worship and life because it contains most of the teachings of other religions. What constitutes good religion is good behavior toward the self, the other, the community, and God, and not necessarily better argumentations (al-Banna 1970, 62).

Creed to al-Banna is the soul's tranquil acceptance of a notion without any doubt. Thus, in matters of belief no force can have its way on people's heart. Furthermore, because the source of Islamic creed is God's divine text and the Prophet's *sunnah*, it is not opposed to but supported by reason. The Qur'anic discourse speaks of reason as the source of responsibility and makes its existence a requirement for applying the *Shari`ah*. The Qur'anic discourse exhorts also the human being to think, search, and contemplate and asks its opponents to produce their evidence. Thus, Islam does not call for limiting the function of reason but makes it the instrument of knowledge by providing it with a framework to prevent its aimlessness (al-Banna 1984a, 379–381). God's essence, to al-Banna, is beyond the comprehension of human reason. Being limited in time and space, reason precludes its understanding of the essences of things. This does not mean that Islam is against the freedom of thought or the search for truth. To al-Banna, it is a warning to the human being against falling into falsehood and total dependence on reason. It cannot provide everlasting truths but rather partial interpretations that depend on human conditions and the power of an individual's reason. A Muslim must still exert his reason, but such an action cannot constitute a categorical understanding. To al-Banna, when humans disagree they must always fall back to the basic religious texts that are the ultimate source of justification. Because the metaphysical realm is beyond human understanding, the Qur'anic discourse gives humans few basic metaphysical ideas (al-Banna 1984a, 357–359, 382–390).

Thus, the role of religion to al-Banna is not to set forth a detailed discourse on metaphysics but to aim at specific existential outcomes. It aims at, first, the revival of conscious awareness of the self's powers; second, cultivation of virtues to uplift the self; third, sacrifice in quest of truth and guidance toward God; fourth, removal of humans from ephemeral material happiness and providing ways for achieving real happiness; fifth, making God the ultimate goal of the soul; sixth, making religion the source of unity and the resolution of conflicts; seventh, the encouragement of sacrifice for humankind's sake; and eighth, making Islam the focus of development of individuals, societies, nations, and the world (al-Banna 1984a, 71–73).

The issues of renaissance, knowledge, and the good society require, according to al-Banna, establishing an Islamic state. Otherwise, religion becomes separated from politics, and politics become outside the realm of religion. The Islamic state cannot be established except by a general religious message, or else its attainment becomes unattractive. The separation of religion from politics is now in practice and has made politics equivalent to corruption. Furthermore, al-Banna argues that when a Muslim community is ruled by laws other than its own, a clash is bound to erupt between it and the ruling power, thus posing difficulties for believers to accept a secular ruler. Furthermore, most Egyptian laws, which are derivatives of European ones, are contrary to the divine law and shed doubts on the integrity of Islam in the modern world. The laws of a nation should not contradict its system of beliefs, especially that the divine law is not opposed to modernity or change (al-Banna 1984a, 317; 1970, 37–45).

Democracy and *Shūrā*

The *shūrā*'s assimilation of, and not subordination to, democracy is an example of not yielding to other philosophies and systems. The modern *shūrā* as advocated by al-Banna and others postulates the necessity of people's involvement not only in political matters but also in all issues concerning the community. *Shūrā* denies the legitimacy of authoritarian rule or political monopoly over the community and makes the community the source of executive power. Al-Banna argues that the ruler, regardless of his social or religious position, must not single-handedly regulate state affairs: in the final analysis, he must resort and yield to people's choices (al-Banna 1974, 99–100). Further, employing *shūrā* makes the ruler sensitive to, or at least accommodating of, popular demands. From an Islamic point of view, the supremacy of God's law must be maintained in all aspects: political, social, economic, and personal. Current laws are, however, against people's consciousness (al-Banna 1970, 37–39). The authority of Islamic law over society and people is grounded, according to al-Banna, in the following verses (al-Banna 1970, 40–41):[5]

> And this (He commands): Judge thou between them by what God hath revealed, and follow not their vain desires, but beware of them lest they beguile thee from any of that (teaching) which God hath sent down to thee. And if they turn away, be assured that for some of their crimes it is God's purpose to punish them. And truly most men are rebellious. (V: 49)
>
> But no, by thy Lord, they can have no (real) Faith, until they make thee judge in all disputes between them, and find in their souls no resistance against thy decisions, but accept them with the fullest conviction. (IV: 65)

These verses not only indicate the supremacy of Islamic law but also provide most Islalmists, starting with Hasan al-Banna, with textual references to political *hakimiyya* as the major political doctrine of Islamist ideologies. These verses are now interpreted by the Islamists in general and the radicals in particular to indicate the non-Islamicity of contemporary states. For nonadherence to this political *hakimiyya* has been viewed by the radicals as *kufr* (disbelief) and *shirk* (polytheism). However, the possibility of such a charge has arisen because the Islamists have removed these verses from their social and political contexts and have universalized their use metahistorically to include every age and every country. While decontextualizing many verses may be liberating such as is the case concerning verses related to knowledge and *shūrā*, yet at times this process may lead to the opposite, that is, to hardening and narrowing the meaning of the verses within a specific context. Harsh contexts pave the way for harsh interpretations, while favorable conditions lead to accommodating interpretations.

The disavowal of any legitimate theoretical possibility of legislation and political action without proper grounding in the comprehensive flexible and total Islamic legislation leads al-Banna to ground the appropriateness of actions in correct doctrines. This is why he calls for the derivation of all civil, criminal, commercial, and international affairs from Islamic law. To al-Banna, it is Islamically self-defeating to ground laws for Muslims in non-Islamic laws that deal with foreign cultural particularities, not to mention their possible contradiction to Islam. This becomes more acute since Islamic law, along with its eternal and comprehensive principles, has not precluded the possibilities of individual and collective reformulations (al-Banna 1970, 40–45). In fact, when Islam was the dominant ideology in the life of the government and the people, the history of Islam shows that the development of Islamic law was comprehensive and flexible (al-Banna 1984a, 61–62).

Because of the flexible nature of Islamic law, al-Banna argues that its development does not lead to reactionary thinking. He adds that the nature of Islam cannot be reactionary since Islamic law itself allows progressive individual and collective adaptations to meet the needs of changing living conditions (al-Banna 1984a, 165). While Islam postulates specific eternal doctrines and ordinances, this does not mean that everything considered Islamic is divine and, thus, not subject to change. Every philosophy or ideology includes basic unchanging doctrines, but this does not make it reactionary. In this sense, al-Banna feels that labeling Islam in this way exemplifies ignorance of the nature of both divine law and Islamic jurisprudence (al-Banna 1974, 95). Focusing only on a juristic fraction of Islamic law and neglecting the overall organizing religious roots lead to misinterpreting Islam. The truth of the matter is to understand Islam, one has to see the multiple functions of Islam as a religious, social, and political system. It includes codes of worship and behavior. Religious beliefs constitute only one part of the Islamic system, and Islam regulates both religion, in the narrow sense, and life, in a general sense. True Muslims to al-Banna could not but subject all aspects of their life to Islam (al-Banna n.d., 304).

In order to get over the problem of the priority of implementing the Islamic law over establishing the Islamic government or vice versa, al-Banna specifies no particular method for implementing the law. What is important is its implementation, whether carried out by a secular or religious government. Al-Banna posits no problem with Western-style constitutional rule because it maintains, in accordance with Islam, personal freedom; upholds *shūrā*; postulates people's authority over government; specifies the responsibilities and accountability of rulers before their people; and delineates the responsibilities of the executive, the legislative, and the judiciary. Constitutional rule to al-Banna is thus harmonious with the *Shari'ah* (al-Banna 1984b, 56–58; n.d., 355–357).

However, al-Banna's adoption of constitutional rule is not a matter of exact copying of a particular Western constitution. The concept is Islamized through a process of philosophical reformulation on religious grounds and is applied through objective institutions. Thus, when al-Banna criticized Egypt's experimentation with constitutional rule, he was calling for its reorientation toward Islamic law and was condemning its failure to perform objectively in the Egyptian political life (al-Banna 1984b, 58–60).

On the theoretical level, al-Banna grounds constitutional rule in *shūrā* by claiming that the former is the closest form of government to the nature of Islamic politics. More importantly, al-Banna finds textual justifications for adopting constitutional rule as *shūrā* and grounds its necessity in a Qur'anic text: "and consult them in affairs (of moment). Then, when thou hast taken a decision, put thy trust in God…" (III: 159). Such a derivation is possible to al-Banna because this Qur'anic revelation is interpreted as "the basic principle of rule of government and exercise of authority." The Qur'anic power is employed by al-Banna to highlight the power of the community in making and unmaking of political systems, governments, forms of government, and political behavior. It provides the community with further powers vis-a-vis the state that must act in conformity with the ambitions and needs of people.

Because to al-Banna the Islamic government represents the central organ of an Islamic system of government, it derives its legitimacy to exercise power from the people. The responsibility of the government is twofold: religious before God and political before the people. Furthermore, it is morally and politically responsible for the community's unity and therefore must be responsive and defer to communal preferences and wishes. The ruler's power over and responsibility before his people derives from the fact that Islam views the setting up of governments as a social contract between the ruler and the ruled so that the interests of the latter are taken care of. The ruler's reward and punishment must hinge on people's opinions. People enjoy moral supremacy over the ruler in matters of general and particular concerns. Therefore, a legitimate ruler or government must always refer to consultation with the community and yield to its will. Political forms may change from time to time and from one locality to another, but the basic rules of Islam must always be adhered to (al-Banna 1984b, 318–319).

While the role of reason is not denied in political matters, it is employed more at the theoretical level to extract political rights and duties. Equality among human beings is postulated by the Qur'an. That this equality means equal political rights and duties is only a rational derivation. Again, this means that no individual or group can claim privileged positions, whether political or religious. Al-Banna does not refer equality to any natural quality such as reason but refers it to Qur'anic texts as a means to prove the necessity of people's rule within divine *hakimiyya* (al-Banna 1984a, 160–161; 1974, 99; Qur'an V: 48–50).

Another reason for al-Banna's democratization of *shūrā* is related to his ability to distinguish divine *hakimiyya* from human *hakimiyya*. The first one can never be properly represented; consequently no individual, group, or institution can properly claim to represent a specific mandate or a divine right to rule. However, the legitimacy of representing human *hakimmiya* must be sought in fulfilling and adhering to Qur'anic instructions (or, in al-Banna's words, "the Islamic constitution") and on the proper conditions for carrying out *shūrā*. This theoretical principle, applying the Islamic constitution, defines to the *ummah* at large the kind of *nizam* (system) to be upheld. However, the practical principles that lead to applying *shūrā* make the *ummah* the sole legitimate *sulta* (authority) for government. Al-Banna converts *al-amr bi-l-ma'ruf wa-l-nahi 'an al-munkar* (enjoining the good and forbidding evil) from an ethical concept into a formulation of public, legal, and political right to watch over the government. Moreover, the ruler is made accountable not only to God but to the *ummah* as well. By believing that the exercise of authority requires the continuous ratification and approval of the *ummah*, governance is transformed into nothing more than a contract between the ruled and the ruler. In this sense, Muslim politics is democratized (al-Banna 1984a, 317–318; n.d., 63, 332–337).

Two central doctrines are needed however for legitimacy, namely, justice and equality. They are to al-Banna the philosophical and religious guidelines that both the ruler and the ruled must adhere to and take into consideration while legislating or exercising power (*Minbar*, 78–9; al-Ikhwan 1979, 9). *Tawhīd* then manifests itself politically and morally in equity and justice (*Minbar*, 79, 136; al-Ikhwan 1979, 9).

Furthermore, al-Banna argues that a more apparent manifestation of *tawhīd* is political unity. It centers on the Qur'an and its language under one central government. This unity does not exclude however the existence of the *ummah* in many states, if *tawhīd* constitutes the ideological framework and if *Shari'ah* is the law of the land (al-Banna 1984a, 95–96, 317). That many legitimate Islamic states can co-exist is to al-Banna possible under the practical orientations of modern Islamic thought and due to the conditions of modern existence. Al-Banna stands, however, against any ideological religious disunity and internal division, which he equates with *kufr* (unbelief). From this perspective, ideologically based multiparty politics and opposed political fundamentals cannot be justified. Hence, once ideological unity becomes the basis of multiparty politics, policy differences and programs are acceptable. Al-Banna does not accept the notion that parties represent opposed doctrinal views, since all parties must adhere to *tawhīd* and *wahda* (unity; al-Banna 1984a, 165–167).

More specifically, political partisanship to al-Banna does not function properly in Egypt since it is exploited by foreign powers to interfere in the affairs of Egypt, and the Egyptians have suffered regardless of the party that is ruling. Before a party system can function properly, Egypt must be delivered from the occupiers, the British. Furthermore, Egyptian parties are not real parties but reflect personal ambitions and foreign affiliations. Their role has exhorted itself. As an example he mentions the *Wafd* party, which started by demanding independence only to splinter later on into the party of free constitutionalists. The *Itihad* party was the result of a deal between many parties and the king (al-Banna 1984a, 166–167). Notwithstanding this, the rejection of this kind of party politics does not lead al-Banna to impose a ban on multiparty politics or to restrict the freedom of expression. The freedom of expression must aim at showing the truth that both the majority and the minority must adhere to it (al-Banna 1984a, 167–169). To him, political opposition finds justification only when political authorities neither adhere to nor apply the rules of Islam. The Muslim Brothers, according to al-Banna, are neither advocates of revolution nor believers in its utility. In fact, their belief in the capacity of Qur'anic principles to stand against any ideological creed allows the *ummah* through either the process of Arabization or Islamization of political doctrines, like multiparty politics, to transcend any danger to its social and political unity (al-Banna 1984b, 53; 1984a, 96–97, 161–162).

On the international level, the legitimacy of any world power must stem, to al-Banna, from its adherence to Islam. But such a situation cannot be brought about except by an Islamic state that positions itself as a guide to other nations (al-Banna 1984a, 162–163). Islam has postulated the superiority of Islamic sovereignty and the necessity of power building so that the just nation should hold power. Al-Banna grounds this view in the Qur'anic injunction that calls on Muslims to enjoin what is right and to forbid what is evil (al-Banna 1984a, 163).[6]

In order to bring out the full context of this call, al-Banna hastens to provide an *aya* (verse) that guarantees the rights of non-Muslims and quells their fears about an Islamic state or an international Islamic order: "God forbids you not, with regard to those who fight you not for (your) Faith nor drive you out of your homes, from dealing kindly and justly with them: For God loveth those who are just" (LX: 8). In fact, al-Banna believes in the duty of the governing authority to liberate and guide other nations into Islam: "We, the Muslims, are neither communists nor democrats nor anything similar to what they claim; we are, by God's grace, Muslims, which is our road to salvation from Western colonialism" (al-Banna 1984a, 304–307; n.d., 53).

Conclusion

Al-Banna's political discourse is grounded in his view of metaphysical *tawhīd* and its political articulation, divine *hakimiyya*. While al-Banna could have theoretically stressed not compromising and denial of the other, he did not—an act that was taken up later by others. Al-Banna opened during his time the theoretical possibility of harmonizing Western political thought with the Islamic. Unlike al-Mawdudi and Sayyid Qutb, who radicalized the doctrine of *hakimiyya*, he transformed it into a human act. To him the divine governance might at times co-exist with the worldly *jāhilīyya*. "No governance (*hukm*) except God's" becomes to al-Banna a linchpin that could be employed by the people to claim certain rights and powers that have been historically denied to the Muslims by their rulers. Governance is an all-comprehensive doctrine that could be used morally, legally, politically, and internationally. Because its power is originally textual and its exercise is basically communal, it has become a powerful tool used by most Islamists to evaluate political rules on scriptural bases. But the reality of the matter is that they were judging political governments in terms of the actual exercise of power. Whenever *hakimiyya* is mentioned nowadays, it means this kind of rule based on scriptural Qur'anic precepts extracted from their social, economic, political, and historical contexts. This is why all Islamists, whether radical or not, advocate the fulfillment of God's order, the minimum of which is replacing existing governments with Islamic ones. But it does not mean by necessity closing up on oneself and rejecting any dealing with the community. In fact, al-Banna dealt openly with and tried to practically influence Egyptian politics.

Although divine governance has become to al-Banna an absolute political doctrine, so has the doctrine of *shūrā*. In fact, the good realization of the former becomes dependent on the good exercise of the latter. What al-Banna's development of *shūrā* has done is to absorb democracy within Islamic political thought and, consequently, to take the initiative from its secular advocates. It has also provided legitimate religious means toward the control of government since legitimacy is linked to popular approval. By denying any contradiction between democracy and constitutional rule with *shūrā* and divine law, al-Banna became capable of postulating their correspondence. This view has become a part of his and the Islamists' nonhistorical discourses that transform Islam into a system capable of absorbing what is best in philosophy, politics, economics, science, and history without the need to deny the validity of Islam. On the contrary, this shows to the Islamists the true nonhistorical and metaphysical power of the Islamic revelation as an eternal message capable of meeting the needs that arise from development.

Shūrā has become to al-Banna and almost all of the Islamist movements the source of legitimation of any authority, while the continuation of legitimacy hinges on the application of the *Shari'ah* and the approval of the people. While great political thinkers such as al-Mawardi, al-Ghazali, and Ibn Taymiyya have justified the seizure of power if the ruler, the sultan, or the prince upheld nominally the superiority of *Shari'ah*, one wonders what prevents contemporary Islamic movements from seizing power in the name of Islam! If people do not want an Islamic state and if an Islamic movement succeeds in setting up an Islamic state, could such a state be legitimate from an Islamist point of view? In other words, if the ultimate organizing principle is *shūrā*, then the Islamists should accept a secular government if chosen by people; but if the ultimate government stands on its own then there is no need to postulate *shūrā* as being the ultimate organizing principle. One could get around this theoretical difficulty only when the people are devout Muslims and employ *shūrā*. The historical experience of Muslims shows that by giving the state the power to employ and to execute *Shari'ah* in the name of the *ummah* more substantial doctrines of *Shari'ah* were overlooked in favor of a political interpretation of Islam. What is needed seems more than just an overhauling of doctrines that might ultimately be used by political authority.

Notes

1. Numerous studies have attempted to focus on his political arguments. Older references include al-Husayni 1956; Heyworth-Dunne 1950; Harris; Adams 1968; Mitchell 1964. Ishaq Musa al-Husayni, Moslem Brethren (Beirut: Khayat's College Book, 1956); James Heyworth-Dunne, Religious and Political Trends in Modern Egypt (Washington, D.C., 1950); Christina Harris, Nationalism and Revolution in Egypt; Charles Adams, *Islam and Modernism in Egypt* (New York: Russell and Russell, 1968); Richard Mitchell, *The Society of the Muslim Brothers* (London: Oxford University Press, 1964). Recent references to him occur throughout the literature on modern Islamic thought and fundamentalism; see, for instance, Marsot 1–9; Lapidus 1983, 23–29; Taheri 1987, 37–49; Munson, 29–37; Warburg,

4–9, 24–27, 46–47; GommaGomaa 143–147; and Carre, 262–280; Hussain, 117–121, 174–177; Mortimer, 250–257; Hiro, 60–69. Ira Lapidus, *Contemporary Islamic Movements in Historical Perspective, Policy Papers in International Affairs*, 18 (Berkeley and Los Angeles: University of California Press, 1983), pp. 23–29; Amir Taheri, *The Holy Terror: The Inside Story of Islamic Terrorism* (Johannesburg: Hutchinson, 1987), pp. 37–49.

2. For biographical information see Shaikh 1981; Muru Qarqar 1980; al-Sa'id 1980; Shaikh 1981. See also Harris 1964, chaps. IV–V by M. N. Shaikh (Karachi: International Islamic Publishers, 1981); Muhammad Muru Qarqar, *Dawr al-Haraka al-Islamiyya fi Tasfiyat al-Iqta'* (Kuwait: Dar al-Buhuth al-Iqlimiyya, 1980); Rif'at al-Sa'id, Hasan al-Banna, *Mu'assis Harakat al-Ikhwan al-Muslimin* (Beirut: Dar al-Tali'a, 1980); M. N. Shaikh, *Hasan al-Banna Shahid: A Brief Life Sketch* (Karachi: International Islamic Publishers, 1981). See also Christina Harris, *Nationalism and Revolution in Egypt* (The Hague: Mouton, 1964), chs. IV–V.
3. Hassan al-Banna, *Nazarat fi Islah al-Nafs* (Cairo: Matba'at al-I'tisam, 1969), 194.
4. Ibid., 178–179.
5. See also *Sura* V: 44, 45, 47 where the Qur'an describes those who do not rule by what God has revealed as unbelievers, unjust and infidel.
6. See the verses III: 110, II: 143, LXIII: 8, and VIII: 60.

References

Adams, Charles. 1968. *Islam and Modernism in Egypt*. New York: Russell and Russell.
al-Banna, Hasan. 1969. *Nazarat fi Islah wa-l-Mujtama'*. Cairo: Maktabat al-I'tisam.
al-Banna, Hasan. 1970. *Din wa Siyasa*. Beirut: Maktabat Huttin.
al-Banna, Hasan. 1972. *Kalimat Khalida*. Beirut.
al-Banna, Hasan. 1974. *Al-Imam al-Shahid Yatahaddath*. Beirut: Dar al-Qalam.
al-Banna, Hasan. 1978. *Minbar al-Jum'a*. Alexandria: Dar al-Da'wa. (hereafter cited as *Minbar*).
al-Banna, Hasan. 1984a. *Majmu'at Ras'il al-Shahid Hasan al-Banna*. 4th ed. Beirut: al-Mu'assasa al-Islamiyya.
al-Banna, Hasan. 1984b. *Rasa'il al-Imam al-Shahid Hasan al-Banna*. Beirut: Dar al-Qur'an al-Karim.
al-Banna, Hasan. n.d. *Majmu'at Rasa'il al-Imam al-Shahid, Hasan al-Banna*. Beirut: Dar al-Qalam.
al-Banna, Hasan. 1969. *Nazarat fi Islah al-Nafs*. Cairo: Matba'at al-I'tisam.
al-Banna, Hasan. 1971. *Al-Salam fi al-Islam*. 2nd ed. Beirut: Manshurat al-'Asr al-Hadith. 1979. *Al-Da'wa*, no. 7.
al-Sa'id, Rif'at, and Hasan al-Banna. 1980. *Mu'assis Harakat al-Ikhwan al-Muslimin*. Beirut: Dar al-Tali'a.
Brynjar, Liya. 1998. *The Society of Muslim Brothers in Egypt: The Rise of an Islamic Mass Movement, 1928–1942*. Reading, UK: Ithaca Press.
Carre, Oliver. 1983. "The Impact of the Egyptian Muslim Brotherhood's Political Islam since the 1950s." In *Islam, Nationalism and Radicalism in Egypt and Sudan*, ed. Gabriel Warburg and Uri Kumpferschmidt. New York: Praeger; 262–280.
Gomma, Gomaa Ahmed. 1983. "Islamic Fundamentalism in Egypt during the 1930s and 1970s: Comparative Notes." In *Islam, Nationalism and Radicalism*, ed. Warburg and Kumpferschmidt. ed. Gabriel Warburg and Uri Kumpferschmidt. New York: Praeger; 140–150.

Harris, Christina. 1964. *Nationalism and Revolution in Egypt*. The Hague: Mouton.
Heyworth-Dunne, James. 1950. *Religious and Political Trends in Modern Egypt*. Washington, DC.
Hiro, Dilip. 1989. *The Rise of Islamic Fundamentalism*. New York: Routledge.
Hussain, Asaf. 1984. *Political Perspectives*. New York: St. Martin's Press.
Lapidus, Ira. 1983. *Contemporary Islamic Movements in Historical Perspective*. Policy Papers in International Affairs, 18. Berkeley: University of California Press.
Marsot, Afaf Lutfi al-Sayyid. 1984. *Protest Movements and Religious Undercurrents in Egypt, Past and Present*. Washington, DC: Georgetown University.
Mitchell, Richard. 1964. *The Society of the Muslim Brothers*. London: Oxford University Press.
Mortimer, Edward. 1982. *Faith and Power*. London: Faber and Faber.
Moussalli, Ahmad. 1999. *Moderate and Radical Islamic Fundamentalism: The Quest for Modernity, Legitimacy, and the Islamic State*. Gainesville: University Press of Florida.
Munson, Henry. 1988. *Islam and Revolution*. New Haven: Yale University Press.
Musa al-Husayni, Ishaq. 1956. *Moslem Brethren*. Beirut: Khayat's College Book.
Qarqar, Muhammad Muru. 1980. *Dawr al-Haraka al-Islamiyya fi Tasfiyat al-Iqta'*. Kuwait: Dar al-Buhuth al-Iqlimiyya.
Shaikh, M. N. 1981. *Hasan al-Banna Shahid: A Brief Life Sketch*. Karachi: International Islamic Publishers.
Shaikh, M. N, trans. 1981. *Memoirs of Hasan al-Banna Shahid*. Karachi: International Islamic Publishers.
Taheri, Amir. 1987. *The Holy Terror: The Inside Story of Islamic Terrorism*. Johannesburg: Hutchinson.
Warburg, Gabriel. 1983. "Introduction." In *Islam, Nationalism and Radicalism in Egypt and Sudan*, ed. Warburg and Kumpferschmidt. New York: Praeger; 4–9, 24–27, 46–47.

CHAPTER 9

MAWLANA MAWDUDI

JOSHUA T. WHITE AND NILOUFER SIDDIQUI

Mawlana Sayyid Abu Al-`ala Mawdudi stands as one of the leading Islamic figures of the twentieth century. His political and religious vision of Islam and the Islamic state have gained widespread currency within his adoptive country of Pakistan, as well as in the broader Middle East, North Africa, and throughout Central, South, and Southeast Asia. Mawdudi's expansive influence is due in large part to his dual role as a scholar and an advocate. Not only a political theorist, he was also a well-known translator and commentator of the Qur'an; a best-selling author; a frequently jailed political activist; and the founder of South Asia's leading Islamic party, the Jama`at-i Islami.

Born in 1903 to a religious family in Hyderabad Deccan, India, Mawdudi began his career as a journalist, ascending in his early twenties to the editorship of *al-Jamiah*, the newspaper of India's leading Muslim clerical organization. He went on to assume the editorship of *Tarjuman al-Qur'an* (Interpreter of the *Qur'an*), which he used as a platform from which to advocate for a systematic and uniquely Islamic way of life and against the influences of the West, which he believed had captivated the Muslims of India. Mawdudi's emphasis became increasingly political following the landmark Indian elections in 1937 and the growing agitation against British rule by Hindu and Muslim leaders. He remained pointedly opposed to the political visions of both the Indian National Congress and the Muslim League, declaring that Muslims had little in common with the Hindus of India, while at the same time decrying the Muslim League's nationalist vision as an un-Islamic substitute for true religious devotion. In 1941 he founded the Jama`at-i Islami, a party he would lead for the next three decades (Nasr 1994).[1] Although Mawdudi rejected the League's "two nation" theory and opposed the formation of Pakistan, following the partition of 1947 he quickly became the leading advocate for the Islamization of the Pakistani state, thrusting his party into debates over the nature of the constitution and participating actively in electoral politics until his death in 1979.

Mawlana Mawdudi's ideas were deeply grounded in the historical context in which he wrote. First the dismantling of the Mughal empire in 1857 and then the formal abolishment of the Ottoman caliphate after World War I fueled feelings of powerlessness among the Muslims of India. Stripped of the formal symbols of their political rule, Muslims viewed themselves as doubly isolated, first as colonial subjects of the British and second as a subservient class to the increasingly confident and politically aware Hindu majority. At the same time, new ideologies were gaining currency, imported from Europe and from other anticolonial movements. The early successes of communism and fascism appeared to demonstrate the power of mobilizing small, ideological cadres for social and political revolution. It was in this milieu that Mawdudi's ideas found a warm reception. By borrowing aspects of the `ulamas traditionalism, joining them with the social mobilization theories of the modernist narrative, and appealing all the while to the sense of profound political disenfranchisement felt by the Muslims of the subcontinent, Mawdudi delivered a message that spoke to his age and provided a template for those engaged in constitutional experimentation in a newly established Pakistani state.

Inasmuch as Mawdudi's worldview was a product of his times, his ideas and impact have far transcended the South Asian context of the early twentieth century.[2] Countless scholars and ideologues have drawn on Mawdudi's writings on subjects as diverse as Islamic economics, war, gender roles, the Islamic state, and international relations. Indeed, his ideas have widely shaped the discourse of modern political Islam, often contributing concepts and vocabulary that today are so ubiquitous as to seem ordinary and unremarkable.

In the discussion that follows, we highlight four particular areas in which Mawdudi's ideas have shaped Islamic discourse in Pakistan and the wider Muslim world[3] : first, his expansive vision of Islam as a worldview but also as a complete way of life for which the Qur'an and Sunnah provide an infallible guide; second, his compelling (if overly abstract) rationale for an Islamic state, led by righteous rulers and tasked with the goal of purifying society; third, his efforts to describe the prerequisites for political participation by non-Muslims in a modern Islamic polity; and finally, his simple (if simplistic) framing of the relationship between Islam and the West as a choice between religious submission and utter godlessness. Mawdudi's contribution on each of these subjects varied. But in each case, both his writings and his political activities served to shape the contours of modern Islamic discourse and frame the ways in which debates on religion and politics have been conducted by scholars and activists alike.

Islam as a Way of Life

One of Mawdudi's most fundamental contributions to public discourse about religion was his championing of the idea that Islam constitutes a *nizam-i zindagi*—a complete system of life that is simultaneously an ideology, a civilization, and a legal-political order. Much of his teachings revolved around this seemingly elementary concept.

Islam, for Mawdudi, was not merely a collection of disconnected rituals, rites, and practices. Nor was it an abstract set of identities and allegiances. It was, instead, a totalizing ideology that allowed no distinction between the public and private spheres and was structured as "an all-embracing social order where nothing is superfluous, and nothing is lacking" (Maududi 2005, 52). Analyzing the Qur'anic use of the Arabic word *din* (commonly translated as "religion"), Mawdudi declared that it referred broadly to "law, code, the Shari`ah, method, and system of thought and a praxis by which humans live their collective existence" (Mawdudi 2006, 157).

This systemic view of Islam can be understood, in part, as a natural response to the social and political milieu of the day; the early twentieth century had seen the promulgation of numerous conflicting ideologies and metanarratives. If Islam were to compete vigorously with alternative worldviews, it needed to frame its agenda in a similar vein. Thus Mawdudi insisted that Muslims constituted "an ideological society," that is, a social enterprise based upon a contract between man and God. Once members of this society, Muslims could not adopt any other way of life without becoming un-Islamic.

Mawdudi made tangible his view of the "ideological society" by invoking the authority of the Shari'ah. In essence, he claimed that the Shari'ah, based on the Qur'an and Sunnah, contains directives that are necessary and sufficient to "fulfil the needs of human society in every age and in every country," and in every possible sphere: religious, personal, moral, familial, social, economic, judicial, international, etc (Maududi 2005, 58). Moreover, he insisted that one had to accept or reject this "system of life" in its entirety; there could be no half-measures.

If this vision of an expansive Shari'ah sounds banal to modern ears, it must be remembered that, in the context of the early twentieth century, it was anything but ordinary. Muslim intellectuals at the time were grappling with the political powerlessness of their communities, while simultaneously being confronted with new ideologies and the solidification of the modern state system—a system from which they were largely excluded. Mawdudi's claim that the Shari'ah spoke clearly to every aspect of social and political life not only stretched the traditional scope of Islamic law, which historically had restricted itself to personal and family matters rather than affairs of state, but also appealed to an Islamic community that was yearning for a broader political profile.[4]

The impact of Mawdudi's insistence on Islam as a *nizam-i zindagi* has been widespread. It has, in one sense, allowed Islamic political thinkers to drive a wedge between "true believers" and *kafir*, the infidels. Mawdudi's analysis left no room for individuals or societies to accept certain tenants of Islam while rejecting others; he regularly mocked those who privatized Islamic law and adopted their own interpretations of its scope. Challenging the applicability of the Shari'ah over any area of life was thus framed as a denial of true Islam.

Mawdudi's logic has thus been used to justify the relentless expansion of the scope of the Islamic reform agenda. Not only did it provide, as described below, an integral part of Mawdudi's rationale for the Islamic state, but it also afforded a basic conceptual template for religious parties such as the Jama'at-i Islami and others who have pursued the systematic Islamization of legal and economic sectors. In Pakistan, for example, the gradual acceptance of Mawdudi's expansive rhetoric led to the establishment of independent Shari'ah courts and Shari'ah review mechanisms within the existing civil courts—developments that have become almost impossible to challenge without appearing to reject Islam itself. Many of Mawdudi's disciples, most notably Khurshid Ahmad, undertook efforts to extend Shari'ah to the finance sector with "Islamic banking." Although this movement largely failed in its efforts to change the fundamental structures of finance, it has nonetheless legitimized the notion that the Shari'ah is naturally applicable to every field of human endeavor.

Few intellectuals, particularly in Pakistan, have bothered to challenge Mawdudi's totalizing rhetoric of the *nizam-i zindagi*. Some, most prominently Javed Ahmed Ghamidi, have argued that Mawdudi gave too much weight to the legal-political aspects of Islam at the expense of its philosophical and ethical dimensions and inexplicably judged the narrowly scoped Shari'ah to be a sourcebook for every possible sphere of life. Such criticisms, powerful as they may be, have nonetheless failed to seriously diminish the impact of Mawdudi's discourse. Even critics from traditions that opposed him have frequently mimicked his language; witness the Barelvi `ulamas advocacy for *nizam-i mustafa* (system of the Prophet) and the Deobandis' regular use of *nifaz-i* Shari`ah (enforcement of the Shari`ah). Muslims around the world have been shaped by Mawdudi's insistence that Islam cannot be confined to the sphere of personal devotion, or even community life, but must by necessity spill over into law and statecraft. This insistence was guided by his radical belief that *din* "actually means the same thing as state and government" and that a life of Islamic devotion is inadequate absent a drive for political influence (Mawdudi 2008, 295).

THE ISLAMIC STATE

Mawdudi's political theology culminated in a simple imperative: Islam, he argued, craves a state, led by the righteous, for the purpose of establishing a social and political order consistent with the Qur'an and Sunnah.[5] Adopting a deeply state-centric perspective, he insisted that Islam necessitated the acquisition of political power and the creation of ideologically pure states through which to realize an all-encompassing Islamic way of life. This vision sat at the heart of Mawdudi's writings and his creation of the Jama`at-i Islami as a vehicle for political transformation.

Mawdudi's privileging of political power and the state must be understood, nonetheless, as the culmination and not the origin of his political theology. His argument began instead with the idea of *hakimiyyah*, or sovereignty. For Mawdudi, sovereignty represented the fundamental link between the creator and His creation. As he reminded his readers again and again, God is the ultimate sovereign. A life of true submission begins with this stark recognition. Moreover, since God is fully sovereign, man cannot be. At best, he can—and is called to—exercise *khilafat*, or vice regency, over the created world and over his fellowman. It was through the lens of sovereignty that Mawdudi critiqued the modern world and Muslim leaders of his era. Both, he insisted, had ignored God's sovereignty in place of their own and in doing so had committed *kufr*, or infidelity. It was for this reason that much of the world remained in *jahiliyyah*, the ignorance that characterized the pre-Islamic era.

In the face of this endemic infidelity, Mawdudi provided a simple and appealing prescription. Both in his political writings and in his widely read *Tahfim al-Qur'an*, he built his argument not from the top down—the need for an Islamic state—but from the bottom up—the need for the submitted Muslim to channel his devotions into a broader revolutionary agenda in the cause of righteousness.

Since, in Mawdudi's vision, Islam is a complete way of life and organic whole, every Islamic practice from prayer, to fasting, to almsgiving, to pilgrimage must prepare Muslims for the ultimate devotion, which is *jihad*. Mawdudi's writings on *jihad* are voluminous and complex and evolved over the course of his lifetime. On the whole, though, he was less concerned with defining *jihad* as a form of "just war" theory for Muslims (and was, indeed, often dismissive of the distinction between defensive and offensive *jihads*) than he was in defining it as a gradual social and political revolution whereby devout Muslims gain political power for the purposes of establishing an Islamic order.

Thus by connecting a foundational insight about sovereignty with a particular definition of *jihad*, Mawdudi made the necessity of an Islamic state, as an expression of the *hukumat-i ilahiyah*—the divine government—appear almost self-evident. His conclusion rested on two arguments. First, he advanced, in remarkably facile terms, an elite-oriented view that "corrupt rule is the root of all the evils you find in the world" (Mawdudi 2008, 286). And second, he read the Qur'an—in interpretations that have widely been contested by his both contemporaries and later scholars—to say that the believers must therefore possess state power to enjoin the good and forbid the evil.[6] True Islam, at its root, could not be fully practiced without "the coercive powers and authority of the state" (Maududi 2005, 56).

Although Mawdudi was disparaging of Western democracy as an expression of the false sovereignty of the collective, he believed that the Qur'an favored consultative decision making. Joined with his concept of *khilafat*, he proposed what he dubbed an Islamic democracy, or "theo-democracy," which would elect righteous leaders as God's vice-regents on earth (Maududi 2005, 139). Muslims were therefore to join Islamic parties that held to this vision and aspired to state leadership, stand for elections, and agitate for Islamic constitutional language that properly framed the philosophical and legal bases of the state.[7]

Mawdudi's overall line of argument—from sovereignty, to *jihad*, and finally to the Islamic state—proved to be innovative and influential. While his rhetoric of *hakimiyyah* has not been picked up as a common feature of everyday Islamic political language, the very idea of the compulsion for an Islamic state, constitution, and Shari'ah is now so widespread among many Muslims as to seem prosaic. In Pakistan, for example, even relatively liberal parties blithely accept the premise that Muslims ought to live in an Islamic state whose laws, by constitutional design, must accord with the Qur'an and Sunnah and that seeking such a state constitutes a religious obligation. (This assumption about Islam's fundamental objectives, ironically enough, has also been adopted by many commentators in the West.) While Mawdudi by no means invented his notion of the Islamic state from whole cloth—he drew heavily on Islamic history, and particularly historical interpretations of the Medinan state—he did play a major role in reframing for the modern age the idea that political power ought to be the central aspiration of the Islamic community.

Second, Mawdudi gave great currency to the idea that rule by the righteous constitutes a fundamental solution to vice. He argued passionately that if only one could make the state good, people would become good as well.[8] This "outside-in" view of social and personal transformation—deeply at odds with both much of the revivalist Islamic thinking of the nineteenth century and traditional Christian theological narratives—provided a theological basis for Islamic political advocacy in a number of spheres. It influenced Ayatollah Khomeini and his fellow Iranian revolutionaries in 1979. And it continues to shape the development of Islamic legal systems throughout the world, in which calls for powerful religious judges, police, and administrators often clash with Western conceptions of the rule of law that expressly limit the powers of any one government functionary.

Third, it is arguable that the very concept of religious-political parties has its modern origin in Mawdudi's advocacy and his logic of social transformation. It was he who brought together a robust view of the Islamic state with the belief that democratic processes are not a priori un-Islamic. The idea of an Islamic democracy, led by a political party that forms the vanguard of a gradual revolution, found a natural constituency among the middle classes and has become a commonplace feature of political Islam. While scholars in countries from Egypt to Indonesia to Turkey continue to question the extent to which Islamic political parties are truly invested in the democratic process and committed to respecting constitutional bounds, it is notable that these parties are increasingly an accepted part of the global political landscape.

Lastly, Mawdudi's reintroduction and adaptation of the concept of *jahiliyyah* for the modern age has markedly shaped the discourse of many Islamic movements, including some of the most radical organizations. Drawing on Taqi al-Din Ahmad ibn Taymiyyah (1263–1328), Mawdudi critiqued leaders and societies that were ostensibly Muslim, calling them to account for their infidelity. Although he was careful to say that Muslims who do not live according to the sovereignty of God are not *kafir* as such (with the exception of the Ahmadis, against whom he agitated intensely), others who later drew upon his ideas were not so generous.[9] Sayyid Qutb, influenced by Mawdudi, took this logic further, condemning much of the Muslim world as *jahiliyyah*.[10] Similarly, al-Qaeda and modern Taliban groups in Afghanistan and Pakistan have regularly targeted the state and its institutions for being insufficiently Islamic. This theological turn—the willingness to declare other Muslims as *kafir*—did not begin or end with Mawdudi. But it was given succor by his powerful political theology and will likely play out for a long time to come as Muslims grapple with the definition of a "true" Muslim and that of a "pure" Islamic state.

THE ROLE OF NON-MUSLIMS

One of Mawdudi's most significant legacies was the reintroduction into the modern world—and into modern language—of an idealized vision of the Islamic community. This vision demanded, in turn, an ideologically homogenous and exclusive state in which participation by non-Muslims in public life must be circumscribed so that true religious leadership could thrive. While the Qur'an itself, and generations of Muslim jurists after it, had taken up the question of minority rights in Islam, Mawdudi adapted this tradition and applied it to Pakistan—the first ideological religious state of the modern era.

He began with the premise that religious minorities were bound to be treated better under an Islamic system than under a Western pluralistic system. By comparing the most egregious examples of majority domination in Western countries with that of an idealized Islamic state that gave minorities limited but guaranteed rights, he concluded that Islam was more beneficent. While he did indeed grant that non-Muslims should be protected insofar as their basic rights, given equality in the criminal and civil law, and guaranteed that their personal (i.e., family) law would "remain immune from state interference," he also outlined a number of restrictions (Maududi 2005, 274).

Non-Muslims in the Muslim state would be categorized, in classical terms, as *dhimmis*, a protected class; would be restricted from holding high political office; would have to pay the *jizyah* poll tax; would face restrictions on public religious practice in "purely Muslim habitations"; could serve in parliament only so long as they accepted the Qur'an and Sunnah as the chief source of public law; and would be forbidden from practices deemed detrimental to the public interest. In addition, following many Muslim jurists before him, Mawdudi affirmed that conversion from Islam to any other faith amounted to apostasy and was punishable as a capital crime. His view, in short, was that the participation of non-Muslims should not interfere with the compulsions of a true *hukumat-i ilahiyah*; it was, he wrote, "not fair for the minorities to ask us to throw our ideology overboard and introduce laws that are against our convictions merely for the sake of appeasing them" (Maududi 2005, 69).

By themselves, these were not radically new ideas. But Mawdudi did not view them as simply ideas; he sought to integrate them in practice into the architecture of a modern Islamic state. He successfully advocated for constitutional provisions in Pakistan that sought to guarantee Muslim leadership in key posts and declare that no law could contravene the Qur'an or Sunnah. These actions, at least within Pakistan, had an ideational impact that far outstripped their practical legal significance. They propagated the idea that minority religious groups were less than full citizens of the state and that their communities were to be, at best, self-replacing but not permitted to grow by expansion or conversion. They also had the effect of framing laws ostensibly derived from the Qur'an and Sunnah as virtually unimpeachable. As a result it has become almost impossible to challenge laws on blasphemy or apostasy in Muslim countries around the world, even if those laws are of questionable theological merit.

Mawdudi's pernicious impact on religious minority rights was also a function of his political activism. Beginning in the early 1950s, he emerged as one of the most outspoken voices denouncing the Ahmadi sect (the followers of the prophet Mirza Ghulam Ahmad, also known as the Qadianis) as a "constant menace," claiming that they amounted to a fifth column within Pakistan and demanding that they be declared non-Muslims (Maududi 2006, 18). His writings against the Ahmadis contributed indirectly to riots in 1953 against the sect in Punjab province, and it was due to his efforts and those of the Jama'at over the subsequent two decades that the Ahmadis were eventually disenfranchised of their full rights in 1974 and declared non-Muslims.[11]

Modernity and the West

Mawdudi's writings demonstrate a preoccupation with Western civilization and with those Muslims who seek to emulate the West. The centuries-long political and intellectual decline of the Islamic world, he believed, induced two different responses among Muslims, neither of which could provide a sustainable answer to the problems of the *ummah*, Islam's global community. The first response, conservatism, would inevitably fail because it relies on the rigid and unrealistic ways of the orthodox `ulama` who, "still living in the eighteenth century," refuse to adapt religious practice in the face of new problems and challenges.[12] The second response, modernism, would fail because it represents a departure from Islam rather than a genuine attempt to respect it and reform it. Of the two, Mawdudi saw modernism as clearly the greater evil.

By equating modernity with the West and deeming the West irreconcilable with true Muslim devotion, Mawdudi left no room for modernity within the ambit of Islam; Islam and the West, he wrote, "are like two boats sailing in totally opposite directions. Any attempt to sail in both the boats at a time shall split the adventurer into two pieces" (Maududi 2006, 13–14). What modern, educated Muslims paraded as rationalism, he argued, was little more than a thinly veiled attempt at disguising their own confusion: "their minds have embraced apostasy while their hearts are anchored in Islam" (Mawdudi 2004, 59). Modernity, in other words, subjected Muslims to a form of demeaning servitude.

Closely linked in Mawdudi's thinking to the dangers of modernity were those of secularism, which he viewed as a false, irrational, Western paradigm that violated the basic tenants of *hakimiyyah*. If God was all-sovereign, he reasoned, why would one allow him space in the private sphere of life while excluding him from the public domain? Along with denying the true sovereignty of God, secularism also exposed a state to class- or ethnic-based internal schisms. Without a public faith, the community would be riven by competing identities. This dark view of secularism as God denying and politically risky has gained remarkable traction among Muslims in South Asia, in part because of Mawdudi's success in promulgating his translation of secularism in Urdu as *ladiniyat*, literally, "godlessness." This translation has become so widely accepted in Pakistan that discussion of secularism is almost by definition precluded; who, after all, could possibly favor godlessness?

Mawdudi applied the same stark dichotomy of modernity and religiosity to his analysis of gender norms. He held a number of so-called conservative attitudes regarding women—for example, that segregation of the sexes is essential for men to successfully carry out their jobs without distraction.[13] Going beyond traditional arguments, however, he accused those who oppose *purdah* of adopting a Western worldview and suggested that they were outside of the legitimate Islamic tradition. Citing the West's "moral decrepitude" as the "logical consequence" of the emancipation movement that began in the nineteenth century, he lamented that women had become the "victim[s] of a vicious process of de-womanization" masquerading as a movement for women's empowerment (Mawdudi 2004, 58, 29). By framing legitimate differences of interpretation—in this case, on issues of gender—as examples of the Muslim elite's "mental servitude" to the West, Mawdudi positioned himself and the Jama`at-i Islami as the legitimate guardians of Islamic tradition and sought to discredit those who saw a via media between tradition and modernity.

In his writings and speeches, Mawdudi consistently railed against modern liberalism, impugning its values by making use of his own religious concepts and vocabulary. Even as he did so, however, he and his acolytes often pursued a parallel approach, trying to co-opt the rhetorical categories of the West. They did this, to some extent, by defining their *hukumat-i ilahiyah* as an idealized form of democracy. And they did it with respect to human rights discourse as well, framing Islam as the true fulfillment of ideals—such as women's rights, rational thought, and progressive social policy—which were poorly realized in the West. The precise definitions of these terms are, of course, hotly contested. But their continued use by the Jama`at-i Islami and other Islamic movements represents, in many respects, a striking picture of Mawdudi's complicated but enduring relationship with the rhetoric of modern politics. His ability to critique the West, while at the very same time embracing a great many aspects of modernity—human rights rhetoric, the idea of the ideological nation-state, party-based political mobilization, new media, etc.—helped to establish a template for modern Islamic activism. In this sense, Mawdudi can be seen as a precursor of those groups—from responsible Islamic political parties to extremist organizations like al-Qaeda—which today posit a "clash of civilizations" yet go about their activism borrowing liberally from both the political concepts and technologies of the West.

Conclusion

Throughout his lifetime and in the years since his death, Mawdudi has come under withering criticism. One easy target has been his purported lack of ideological consistency. Although Jama`at-i Islami cadres are quick to portray Mawdudi's ideology as internally consistent and essentially unchanging, his views on the political imperatives of Islam were in fact evolutionary, as his polemical early writings gave way to more practical and applied discussions of state power. Believing that the Jama'at had a chance to succeed under Pakistan's new constitutional framework, for example, he shifted gears in the late 1950s to become more accommodating of the democratic process.[14] Contravening his early writings on women in politics, he supported on grounds of political expediency Fatima Jinnah's bid for the presidency in 1965. And he gradually backed away from his emphasis on the centrality of a powerful executive, highlighting instead the values of a strong and accountable parliament.[15]

Critics have also challenged the religious foundations of Mawdudi's political ideology. Here the most trenchant criticisms have come from two of his former followers and members of the Jama'at-i Islami, Wahiduddin Khan and Javed Ahmed Ghamidi, both of whom disputed Mawdudi's core vision of *hakimiyyah* and argued that he fundamentally misread verses in the Qur'an pertaining to political power.[16] Other scholars have questioned the ease with which Mawdudi reconciled his vision of the "pure" Islamic state with democratic norms, contending that his theories left little room for true democratic dissent and placed unrealistic weight on the character of leaders.[17] On a host of other issues he has received criticism from Muslims and non-Muslims alike, most notably on account of his willingness to so harshly criticize other Muslims, his writings on religious minorities and women, his simplistic views of the West, and his inability to recognize his debts to modernity.

As these debates attest, Mawdudi's legacy remains very much disputed. On the one hand, his activism plainly failed to bring about the Islamic revolution that he desired. The Jama'at-i Islami is today an influential but niche player in the politics of South Asia, and neither the party nor other disciples of Mawdudi have succeeded in restructuring the basis of the modern state. On the other hand, Mawdudi has been quite successful in shaping the discourse of Islamic politics. His acolytes see this success as the fruit of his careful restoration of a long-lost "pure" Islam. His critics, particularly in the years since September 11, 2001, have framed it in more sinister terms, drawing an intellectual genealogy from his ideas, to the writings of Sayyid Qutb, and finally to the violent *takfirist* ideology of al-Qaeda.

Neither reading of Mawdudi's legacy captures his most lasting effect on Islamic political discourse, which was to convince middle classes throughout South Asia and the broader Islamic world that Islam is and ought to be an all-encompassing life system and that advocacy for an Islamic state constitutes a fundamentally religious obligation. These ideas gained currency well beyond the scholarly or activist fringes, and they did so because Mawdudi provided Muslims with a political and religious vision that resonated with their sense of disenfranchisement vis-à-vis the West. To the extent that his ideas continue to have currency, it is due in no small part to that enduring malaise.

Mawdudi's ideological contributions have made him a towering figure in modern Islamic thought. Less appreciated, but perhaps no less significant, has been his concurrent role in shifting the locus of debate on Islam and politics away from the *'ulama'* and toward a new generation of ideologues and activists. For all of his emphasis on law and political power, Mawdudi himself devoted remarkably little attention to traditional Islamic jurisprudence and instead privileged innovative readings of the Qur'an that most clerics considered to be unmoored from Islamic tradition. By doing so, and by channeling his energies into the formation of a technocratic, disciplined, middle-class Islamic party, Mawdudi contributed to the gradual marginalization of the *'ulama'* within

Pakistan and created space for other nonclerical voices who declared themselves equally competent to interpret Islam for the modern age. This model of middle-class activism did not go unnoticed and has been emulated widely throughout the Muslim world. And as it has spread, coming into dialogue and confrontation with existing state systems in places as diverse as North Africa, Western Europe, and Southeast Asia, it has continued to do so largely on Mawdudi's own terms—silently borrowing from him a rich lexicon, a simple and compelling ideology of the state, and a religious vision wedded to the pursuit of political power.

Notes

1. For the history of Mawdudi's leadership of the Jama`at, see Nasr 1994.
2. Scholars continue to debate the degree to which Mawdudi's ideology should be situated in the particular interwar, communal context of the subcontinent. Vali Nasr's definitive biography of Mawdudi has sometimes been criticized on this count for overly contextualizing his ideas and downplaying their wider role in Islamic political discourse.
3. The discussion that follows draws upon the authors' interviews with a number of scholars and contemporaries of Mawdudi, conducted in July 2009 in Pakistan, including Mumtaz Ahmad, Zafar Ishaq Ansari, Javed Ahmed Ghamidi, Rafi-ud-Din Hashmi, Muhammad Ibrahim, Khalid Masud, Salman Raja, Khalid Rehman, and Chaudhry Aslam Salimi.
4. On Mawdudi's move beyond the traditional scope of Islamic law see, e.g., Adams 1966, 395.
5. This phrase, "Islam craves a state," has been attributed to Javid Iqbal.
6. Mawdudi drew particularly from Qur'an 4:59, arguing that the command to obey "those invested with authority among you" constitutes "the cornerstone of the entire religious, social and political structure of Islam and the very first clause of the constitution of an Islamic state" (Mawdudi 2006, 171).
7. For more on the ways in which Mawdudi "presented as true democracy what the West regarded as theocracy," see Nasr 1996, 88.
8. See Mawdudi 2008, 285ff; and Maududi 1970.
9. For Mawdudi's views on this subject see, e.g., Mawdudi 2008, 58, 130–131.
10. For comparisons between the ideologies of Mawdudi and Qutb, see Sivan 1990.
11. For a report on Mawdudi's role in the 1953 riots and debates within Pakistan over the nature of Islamic politics, see Munir and Kayani 1954. For a cogent and sharply written Ahmadi critique of Mawdudi and his views of minority religious groups, see Ahmad 1989.
12. Maududi 1992, 42. Mawdudi was condemned frequently by traditionalist `ulama', who were suspicious of his lack of formal theological training, his pointed criticism of several of the companions of the Prophet, and his willingness to question the authority of the hadith as a reliable guide for Islamic practice.
13. See, e.g., Maudoodi 1998.
14. See, e.g., Adams 1966, 378; Nasr 1996, 73ff.
15. Mumtaz Ahmad has suggested that this shift was due in part to Mawdudi's own treatment at the hands of various regimes in Pakistan (Ahmad 1991, 489).
16. For more on Khan's criticisms, see Omar, "Islam and the Other." More recently, American Muslim scholars such as Muqtedar Khan and Khaled Abou El Fadl have also challenged Mawdudi's concept of hakimiyyah.
17. See, e.g., Adams 1983, 118ff.

References

Abbott, Freeland. 1968. *Islam and Pakistan*. Ithaca, NY: Cornell University Press.
Adams, Charles J. 1966. "The Ideology of Mawlana Mawdudi." In *South Asian Politics and Religion*, ed. Donald Eugene Smith, 71–397. Princeton, NJ: Princeton University Press.
Adams, Charles J. 1983. "Mawdudi and the Islamic State." In *Voices of Resurgent Islam*, ed. John L. Esposito, 99–133. New York: Oxford University Press.
Ahmad, Hazrat Mirza Tahir. 1989. *Murder in the Name of Allah*. Trans. Syed Barakat Ahmad. Cambridge, UK: Lutterworth Press.
Ahmad, Irfan. 2009. Genealogy of the Islamic State: Reflections on Maududi's Political Thought and Islamism. *Journal of the Royal Anthropological Institute* 15, no. s1: S145–S162.
Ahmad, Khurshid, and Zafar Ishaq Ansari. 1979. *Mawlānā Mawdūdī: An Introduction to His Life and Thought*. Leicester, UK: Islamic Foundation.
Ahmad, Mumtaz. 1991. "Islamic Fundamentalism in South Asia: The Jama'at-i Islami and the Tablighi Jama'at of South Asia." In *Fundamentalisms Observed*, ed. Martin E. Marty and R. Scott Appleby, 457–530. Chicago: University of Chicago Press.
Ahmad, Sayed Riaz. 1976. *Maulana Maududi and the Islamic State*. Lahore: People's Publishing House.
Binder, Leonard. 1961. *Religion and Politics in Pakistan*. Berkeley: University of California Press.
Hasan, Masudul. 1984. *Sayyid Abul A'la Maududi and His Thought*. 2 vols. Lahore: Islamic Publications.
Hassan, M. Kamal. 2003. The Influence of Mawdudi's Thought on Muslims in Southeast Asia: A Brief Survey. *The Muslim World* 93, no. 3–4: 429–464.
Maudoodi, Syed Abul A'la. 1998. *Purdah and the Status of Woman in Islam*. Trans. al-Ash'ari. 16th ed. Lahore: Islamic Publications, 1998.
Maudūdī, Abūl A'la.. 1970. "The Moral Foundations of the Islamic Movement." In *Muslim Self-Statement in India and Pakistan 1857–1968*, ed. Aziz Ahmad and Gustave E. Von Grunebaum, trans. Charles J. Adams, 158–166. Wiesbaden: Otto Harrassowitz.
Maududi, Sayyid Abul A'la. 2005. *Islamic Law and Constitution*. Trans. Khurshid Ahmad. 13th ed. Lahore: Islamic Publications.
Maududi, Sayyid Abul A'la. 2006. *The Qadiani Problem*. 4th ed. Lahore: Islamic Publications.
Maududi, Syed Abul A'la. 1992. *West Versus Islam*. Trans. S. Waqar Ahmad Gardezi and Abdul Waheed Khan. 2nd ed. Lahore: Islamic Publications.
Mawdudi, Sayyid Abul A'la. 1995. *Jihad in Islam*. Ed. Huda Khattab, Trans. Khurshid Ahmad. Birmingham, UK: UKIM Dawah Centre.
Mawdudi, Sayyid Abul A'la. 2004. *Islam and the Secular Mind*. Ed. and trans. Tarik Jan. Markfield, UK: Islamic Foundation.
Mawdudi, Sayyid Abul A'la. 2006. *Four Key Concepts of the Qur'ān*. Ed. and trans. Tarik Jan. Leicestershire, UK: Islamic Foundation.
Mawdudi, Sayyid Abul A'la. 2006. *Towards Understanding the Qur'ān: Abridged Version of Tahfim al-Qur'ān*. Ed. Zafar Ishaq Ansari. Leicester, UK: Islamic Foundation.
Mawdudi, Sayyid Abul A'la. 2008. *Let Us Be Muslims*. Ed. Khurram Murad. Leicestershire, UK: Islamic Foundation.
Munir, M., and M. R. Kayani. 1954. *Report of the Court of Inquiry Constituted Under Punjab Act II of 1954 to Enquire Into the Punjab Disturbances of 1953*. Lahore: Superintendent, Government Printing, Punjab.

Nasr, Seyyed Vali Reza. 1994. *The Vanguard of the Islamic Revolution: The Jama'at-i Islami of Pakistan*. Berkeley: University of California Press.

Nasr, Seyyed Vali Reza. 1996. *Mawdudi and the Making of Islamic Revivalism*. Oxford: Oxford University Press.

Omar, Irfan A. 1999. Islam and the Other: The Ideal Vision of Mawlana Wahiduddin Khan. *Journal of Ecumenical Studies* 36, no. 3/4: 423–438.

Osman, Fathi. 2003. Mawdudi's Contribution to the Development of Modern Islamic Thinking in the Arabic-Speaking World. *The Muslim World* 93, no. 3–4: 465–485.

Sivan, Emmanuel. 1990. *Radical Islam: Medieval Theology and Modern Politics*. Enlarged edition. New Haven: Yale University Press.

Revolutionary Ideologues

CHAPTER 10

SAYYID QUTB

SHAHROUGH AKHAVI

Introduction

Sayyid Qutb's name has achieved near iconic status in the realm of what has come to be called "political Islam" (*al-islam al-siyasi*). He never viewed himself as a leader of this movement[1] but simply as a passionate missionary urging people to recognize Islam as a total system of life. "Political Islam"—a phrase also captured by the expression, "Islamism," from the French, *Islamisme*—stresses the full and immediate application of Islamic law in all areas of human existence. Qutb's worry was that Muslims had forgotten the essentials of their faith and in a facile manner increasingly tended to relegate their religion to the private sphere. Doing so was, in his opinion, not only absurd—because Islam was indivisible—but a mortal existential threat, since it undermined the necessary and sufficient vehicle for the well-being of Muslims. Given its integral nature, he felt, it was essential to remind believers of the ultimate validity of Islam as "religion and the world" (*din wa dunya*). Any other understanding was tantamount to the destruction of the faith and therefore the believers.

Qutb did not in principle advocate violence to bring about the immediate application of Islamic law to all arenas of life. However, he did ultimately conclude that if the state resorted to violence against the advocates of *din wa dunya*, then it was legitimate for Islamists also to resort to violence to protect the true religion.

Sayyid Qutb, or, in full, Ibrahim Husayn Shadhili Sayyid Qutb, was born in the largest village of Asyut Province, Musha, into a relatively well-known family of peasants whose fortunes had declined. He was frail in health and not very prepossessing in mien, with large, droopy eyes and stooped shoulders. Though personally a pious youth, Qutb did not attend religious schools but instead matriculated and graduated from public school and then the Dar al-'Ulum in Cairo (a teachers' training school established in 1871 with a Western-style curriculum). Upon his graduation in 1933 with a BA in education, Qutb was employed by the Ministry of Education as a schoolteacher. He was attracted to literature and wrote various works of poetry, short stories, and literary criticism, including an autobiography. These writings were secular and contained little hint of his future turn to Islamism. The one exception was a book he published on artistic imagery in the Qur'an, which was published in 1945, prior to his turn to Islamism. Also, it may be noted that he considered himself a protégé of the conservative author 'Abbas al-'Aqqad (d. 1964) and advocated in newspaper columns on behalf of `Aqqad's literary works, which were significantly informed by Islamic themes.

Qutb also had been a member of the nationalist party, the Wafd, but he became disillusioned with what he saw as the opportunistic behavior of its politicians. He abandoned his membership in the Wafd and renounced the party system in 1945, believing that the nationalism of Sa`d Zaghlul, the Wafd's founder, had been unable to resolve Egypt's accumulating problems. In other words, Qutb, as so many Egyptians, gravitated to nationalism but eventually abandoned it in favor of Islamism.

Ultimately, he became so convinced of the moral bankruptcy of the ruling elites and the scandalous economic, political, and social disparities between the wealthy and the poor that he had to take some action in protest. He had as early as his village days become sympathetic to the cause of the *tarahil*, or seasonal workers on the land, because of their desperate economic conditions. Why he began to drift toward Islamism in the late 1940s rather than earlier is not certain. However, we know that when he and some like-minded individuals founded a short-lived magazine entitled *al-Fikr al-Jadid*, which published articles on Islam and Egyptian society from January to April 1948, he had finally and unequivocally turned his back on his literary career and secular perspectives. The magazine was eventually closed down by the government, which considered it to be subversive. He would have lost his job in the Ministry of Education, but apparently someone put in a good word for him, and so instead he was sent to America in September 1948 to learn about its educational system as well as to study for an advanced degree. He actually attended Columbia University Teacher's College for a while and also Colorado State College (currently the University of Northern Colorado) in Greeley.

This trip proved an epiphany for him. Already repelled by the exploitation of Egypt's poor by the wealthy landowners and their allies in the state apparatus, he found in America confirmation of his mounting hostility to capitalism, or at least to that version of capitalism that insisted on the unfettered operation of the market. In addition, he was revolted by the racial discrimination he found in this country and outraged by the unquestioning support for Zionism and the state of Israel in American public opinion and public policy. In America when the founder of the Muslim Brotherhood, Hasan al-Banna, was assassinated by the Egyptian government, he was embittered by the approval he saw in the American reaction to this event.

Even before leaving for America, Qutb had basically completed the draft of his first "religious" work, *Social Justice in Islam*, which was published in 1949. With this work, Qutb turned his back on his previous life as a secular writer and bureaucrat and launched a career that, little did he suspect, would make him an international figure for whom even the Pope would intercede. Upon his return to Egypt in 1951, he promptly joined the Muslim Brotherhood and eventually became director of its propaganda office. One source quotes him as saying, "I was born in 1951" (Kepel 2003, 41).

After the military coup of July 1952 that overthrew the pro-British monarchy, all political organizations were abolished, but the new rulers exempted the Muslim Brotherhood (technically, not an organization but rather a social movement whose support from the masses the new regime feared) from this proscription. Qutb in particular attended early sessions of the Revolutionary Command Council (RCC) and served as the Brotherhood's liaison with the junta leaders. He chaired a major conference in Cairo in August 1952 on the theme of Islam as an emancipating religion and was praised by both Nasser and General Naguib (the nominal leader of the junta) for a job well done.

But Qutb became disillusioned when the regime rejected the Brotherhood's demand for the application of *sharī'ah* throughout society. He was arrested in January 1954 for supporting this cause and served a three-month sentence. The Brotherhood strongly criticized the deal, announced in June 1954, between the government and the British for their withdrawal from Egypt, an agreement that permitted them to reintroduce troops into the Canal Zone over the next seven years should they determine the security situation required it. With this criticism, the die was cast. Matters stood at this pass when, as a result of an incident (to this day it is uncertain whether it was actual or staged) in October 1954 involving an assassination attempt against Nasser, he was caught up in the sweep of arrests that drove the Brotherhood underground, where it stayed until the early 1970s.

He was subjected to a show trial that found him guilty of charges and sentenced to twenty-five years of hard labor. During both his detention and then his incarceration after this trial, he was subjected to atrocious torture. Due to his frail health, he was transferred to the prison hospital, where conditions were somewhat better. It is there that he wrote most of the works for which he has become famous. Released in late 1964, due to the intercession of then President 'Abd al-Salam 'Arif of Iraq, he was rearrested for the publication of his book *Milestones*—no doubt the work for which he is best known and which was immediately placed on the blacklist. Ironically, President Nasser is said to have ordered its removal from censorship, but when it went through several printings, demonstrating its public appeal, it was replaced on that list, and he was arrested again. Though, as in 1954, the government cast its arrest net widely, Qutb was unquestionably its most notable victim. He was again subjected to torture, tried in a kangaroo court in August 1965, found guilty, and sentenced to death. Although international efforts arose to save his life, including by the Vatican, he was executed a year later, thus becoming a martyr and symbol of Islamist resistance.

Social Thought

Qutb's writings contain a strong strain of didacticism, perhaps revealing the influence of his earlier turn in teaching. It is also driven by passionate commitment to the "true faith." At the same time, he never tires of speaking about Islam as a "practical" or "realistic" (*waqi'i*) faith. This leads some scholars, such as Leonard Binder, to consider him as a "non-scripturalist fundamentalist" (Binder 1988, 170). By this, he means that Qutb was perfectly willing to infuse his teachings with "modern" concepts, such as social justice and egalitarianism, something scripturalists avoid because of their conviction that the sacred texts "speak for themselves" and have no need for modern analytical constructs. As to "fundamentalist," this refers to the desire to renew Islam by reverting to its roots, meanwhile eliminating reprehensible accretions that have distorted it.

Yet scripturalism does seem apposite when considering the thought of Sayyid Qutb, because the modern concepts that he deploys are basically reifications whose roots are embedded in the holy scriptures. Thus, even if Qutb stresses that Islam is a practical religion and has reference to such modernist terminology as "mutual responsibility" (*al-takaful al-ijtima'i*), he is nevertheless eviscerating that terminology of any secular meaning and merely materializing it in the purely divine discursive formations of the holy texts. It is as though he is saying to himself, "I live at a time that privileges certain expressions, such as freedom, equality, and justice. It is imperative to address these. But I will reject their anthropocentric roots. Instead, I will materialize them in the holy texts as a way of showing how wrong it is for people to regulate their lives not by those texts but by human constructions. Such constructions by their very nature cause human beings to deviate from God's path and must be defeated." What we have, here, is professions of the practicality of Islam and, in fact, ahistorical attempts to anchor that practicality in Islamic scriptures.

The subtext for all of Qutb's works consisted of his conviction that human beings cannot understand truth by unique recourse to unconstrained rational endeavor; still less, he believed, could they understand it by empirical inquiry. This does not mean he opposed rational discourse. But as is the case with many pious thinkers, the discursive logic that he upheld was one that was at the outset premised upon divine axioms that restricted the scope of inquiry within the bounds of transcendental faith. Accordingly, he totally rejected philosophical inquiry, because in his view it began from premises that could lead the thinker into serious error and, indeed, defiance of God.

Qutb, then, believes that reason is a valuable asset, but it has its limits. In his worldview, God endowed human beings with reason as a gift of His grace. Without reason, human beings cannot carry out their functions as the vice-gerants of God on earth. Qutb notes that several verses of the Qur'an refer to human beings as God's vicar or deputy on earth (Qur'an 6:165, 27:62, 35:39). God's motive in endowing the individual with reason was so that he could be a faithful follower of His commands and also a loyal steward of the earth's resources, made available to mankind and womankind to enjoy in moderation. But, he believes that Western thinkers have taken this gift and shorn it of its carefully constructed restrictions. The result is licentious and wanton application of reason without any moral guidelines. Any exercise of human reason without awareness of the limitations that confine it is nothing less than arrogance, sure to lead its users astray.

The following passage makes Qutb's points:

> Human thought is...a great and valuable tool that grasps the features...of [the Islamic conception]. But thought is not the only thing....A hallmark of this conception...is that it responds to human existence in its entirety. That which [human thought] does not comprehend of [the Islamic conception] is the understanding of essence and truth, the understanding of causality, a situation to which it is possible to [i.e., one must] surrender calmly. (Qutb 1962, 52–53)

These ideas drive Qutb to reject all philosophy, whether ancient Greek, medieval Islamic, or contemporary analytical. Outstanding figures in the Muslim philosophical tradition, such as Ibn Rushd (d. 1198) are denounced for their efforts to reconcile revelation and reason. The ground for doing so is Qutb's belief that their systems of thought are embedded in Platonic and Aristotelian philosophy, both of them alien to Islamic thought because they are purely human constructions. Such constructions, he insisted, amount to word play, or as he puts it, "mere abstract knowledge that traffics with minds." He even accuses Muslim theologians (*mutakallimun*) for edging over into the domain of philosophy. Seeking to decode the nature of God, they depend on Aristotelian logic, he claims, and he sees that logic as reducible to mentalism. And he does not spare the towering figure of Islamic modernism, the former Grand Mufti of Egypt, Muhammad ʿAbduh (d. 1905) for his efforts to reconcile revelation with reason (Qutb 1962, 8–10).

It is true that Qutb clearly *was* offering a different choice to the Muslims of the 1950s and 1960s as well as to those of the decades after his death. Once Qutb came on the scene, Muslims no longer had to choose either to support the unreconstructed clergy, the guardians of a tradition that had for centuries been in decline, or to embrace foreign ways, thereby undermining their own religious heritage. For pious Egyptians hoping to steer a course between stultifying emulation of tradition and arrant embrace of "Western" culture, Qutb seemed to offer something new. On this point, it is worth emphasizing that Qutb was to a great degree working out his own personal understandings of what it means to be a Muslim in modern society. He did not, seemingly, view himself as a leader who was impelled to promote his views in the public arena or even among those who sympathized with his orientation. Of course, he hoped that those who read his works would be won over. But he was at the same time trying to resolve issues affecting his own identity and so he was involved in a very personal journey. Thus, the fact that later activists embraced his substantive ideas concerning the relationship between faith and politics is less an outcome of his own conceits and more the result of such historical conjunctures as the Arab defeat in the June War of 1967, the poor performance of the Egyptian economy, and the parasitic quality of elite political rule and the bureaucratic administration of society.

As he was feeling his way toward a new synthesis of faith and human action, Qutb came across the writings of the Indian Muslim scholar, Abu al-A'la al-Mawdudi (Maudoodi; d. 1979). They had been translated into Arabic, and Qutb was struck by the way Mawdudi crystallized understandings of Islam that were to a significant degree still inchoate in his own mind.

One may examine Qutb's thought by reference to certain concepts that were central to his writings. These include

- God's unicity (*tawhid*)
- God's sovereignty (*hakimiyyat Allah*)
- praxis (*al-waqi'iyyah*)
- the Islamic way (*al-minhaj al-islami*)
- divine immanence (*al-kaynunah al-rabbaniya*)
- living in a state of ignorance of God commands (*al-jahiliyyah*)
- religious call (*al-da'wah*)
- exertion for God's sake (*al-jihad*)
- organic dynamic concrescence (*al-tajammu' al-haraki al-'udwi*)
- consultation (*shura*)
- mutual responsibility (*al-takaful al-ijtima'i*)
- social justice (*al-'adalah al-ijtima'iyyah*).

Qutb borrowed from Mawdudi the two critical notions that positive law cannot be the basis for human well-being and prosperity and that any system that rested upon human beings' subservience to other human beings was bound to fail. Put another way, only God's law could vouchsafe the well-being of the human race, and submission to God alone was the path to human happiness. Both of these principles were, in Mawdudi's and Qutb's views, a violation of the foundational principle in Islam of God's unicity.

The moment these two principles are asserted, however, they beg certain questions. God has already stopped legislating, and some of his commands are difficult to construe. Indeed, the Qur'an itself declares this to be so (3:7). Turning to experts for their meaning does not solve the problem, because this raises these experts into positions of superiority, in violation of the principle that human beings must not be made subordinate to other human beings. Furthermore, there is the problem of situations for which God's legislation has no answer because those situations have arisen as a consequence of the interplay of historical forces and pressures since the end of the revelation. If it is rejoindered that nevertheless human beings, by following the rulings of the religious experts—the 'ulama'—on what constitutes God's law, will be walking on the righteous path, this again ignores that these religious experts are being placed in a position of superordination over others. Qutb might answer that these experts can be counted upon simply to interpret the law. But this is an idealistic assumption that may not bear any relationship to reality. In other words, it is one thing to maintain God's unicity (with its corollary that God must not be associated with others, the cardinal sin (*shirk*) in the Islamic tradition. But it is quite another to hold that only God should rule, since it will always be human beings, prone to error, who will decide how to operationalize this proposition. Qutb, who did not have a very favorable view of the 'ulama' in any case, seems unaware of this contradiction in his enthusiasm to declare that God alone is master.

Another paradox in Qutb's thought is that his theistic (as opposed to deistic) position on God as sovereign and ruler is not easily reconciled with his perspective that Islam is a practical religion. What he means by its practicality, one supposes, is that Islam is a system that is equipped to deal with the hard realities of daily life and, one supposes, that it, as it were, bids the believers to utilize its assets to that end. One would imagine that if this were the case, then Qutb's unit of analysis would be human beings acting toward practical ends. But in fact Qutb's thought is thoroughly suffused with reifications. It is not Muslims who act in his worldview. Instead, he holds that "Islam" believes, "Islam" maintains, "Islam" establishes, "Islam" generates—in a word, that "Islam" is the actor. Human agency is assumed somehow to operate, but in fact, his theory cannot accommodate human agency. Accordingly, whenever he writes about the quotidian problems human beings face as a consequence of their religion being a practical religion, he is forced simply to assert in ad hoc fashion that they act. We never see Qutb problematizing human action. It is within the bounds of his theory, elided. Accordingly, if we follow him we must just assume that it somehow happens. Meanwhile, what is directing all the traffic, as it were, is a reified "Islam."[2]

Such, then, was the "Islamic way" (*minhaj islami*) in Qutb's writing. Taking his cue from Mawdudi, he invoked the classic scripturalist concept of *jahiliyyah*. This word originally referred to the historical era prior to the rise of Islam, a period known as the age of ignorance because people were deprived of the enlightenment provided by Islam. Its antonym, of course, was divine immanence (*al-kaynunah al-rabbaniyyah*). As utilized by Mawdudi and Qutb, however, it referred to the wanton or perhaps unwitting disobedience of modern-day Muslims (not to mention non-Muslims) of God's commands. Under this scenario, it was imperative to call the people (*da'wah*) back to Islam, just as the Prophet had originally called them away from their pagan practices to the new faith.

One of the ways this call would succeed was to remind the people of the admonitions of sacred scripture. Qutb utilized as a vehicle of persuasion innovative interpretations of key Qur'anic verses (5:44, 45, 47; 12:47, 60) containing the warning that those who do not "rule" according to God's revelation are apostates (the traditional rendering of the infinitive in these verses by Qur'anic commentators was "judge," not "rule"). With this innovative rendering, Qutb was sanctioning the anathematizing of contemporary Muslim rulers who were ruling according to secular models of authority. It was imperative to act against such rulers, in his view, invoking the classic principle of exertion for the sake of God (*jihad*).

In adopting this position, Qutb incurred the opposition of Hasan al-Hudaybi (d. 1977), who had become the Supreme Guide of the Muslim Brotherhood after the murder of its founder, Hasan al-Banna, in 1949. Apparently the Nasserist regime, which had earlier allowed Qutb to attend some sessions of the RCC, gave him an opportunity to distance himself from the Brotherhood at the time of the alleged assassination attempt against Nasser in October 1954. But Qutb refused, in effecting siding with Hudaybi. But after the publication of *Milestones* Hudaybi upbraided Qutb for his heretical interpretation of the Qur'anic versions discussed in the previous paragraph. Defiant, Qutb rejoindered:

> Islam is servitude to God alone and assigning divine characteristics to Him, the foremost of which is sovereignty (al-hakimiyyah).... "And those who do not rule according to what God has revealed are unbelievers." What we have said about Islam is not a heretical innovation that we have thought up. (Qutb 1983, 12)[3]

Fifteen years after his execution, Islamists motivated by the need to restore to its rightful place the "forgotten precept" (that is, *jihad*) assassinated Egyptian President Anwar Sadat in the belief that he was not ruling according to God's revelation.

Altogether, Sayyid Qutb embraced organic conceptions of Islamic society, conceptions that dovetail with his ahistorical ideas of change. Rather than examining concrete junctures of Islamic history and inspecting the instances of conflict and cooperation among specific social forces and groups at specific junctures in time, Qutb preferred to paint his canvas with broad brushstrokes, identifying Islam as a quiddity that unfolds dynamically and rhythmically, according to a pattern of movement (*harakah*), vitality (*hayawiyyah*), evolution (*tatawwur*), and growth (*nama'*). Islam, in his opinion, is an organism, and it is characterized by the central trait of all organisms—a whole with interdependent parts. This whole he labeled an "organic, dynamic concrescence" (*tajammu' haraki 'udwi*; Qutb 1964, 37). It appears that this whole is the *ummah*, or community of believers. The individuals who comprise this community are, as in classic organic theories, parts of the whole, but that whole is greater than the sum of the individual parts.

To make sure we understand the organicism of this outlook, Qutb cites Leopold Weiss, an Austrian convert to Islam who adopted the name Muhammad Asad. The latter wrote, "History tells us that all human cultures and civilizations are organic bodies resembling living creatures that pass through all the organic stages of life..." (Qutb 1962, 102). But, aware of the full implications of such a statement, Qutb quickly adds, "Of course, we could never say that, like other civilizations, [Islam] is subject to the passage of time and limited by the organic laws of life" (Qutb 1962, 103). Qutb appears to want to have things both ways. Islam is at bottom a residuum that he calls an organic dynamic concrescence governed by the usual patterns of organisms, but he then wants to limit these patterns to those of growth only. Presumably, its predilection for continued growth is a function of mechanisms of renewal that are immanent in it, such as *tajdid* (renewal). But if this is the case, the operation of this *tajdid* is left unexamined. A disembodied "Islam" is said to be in some mysterious manner subject to this renewal. Qutb, that is, is again reaffirming that it is not specific actors or social groups living at concrete junctures of historical time who act as agents of that renewal. They are merely the bystander beneficiaries of developments that seem to occur over their heads, beyond their reach, and clear of any actual engagement on their part.

Conclusions

Sayyid Qutb's influence on later generations would likely have remained somewhat marginal had not events on the ground transpired in the way they did. Of all these events, the critical ones were Israel's victory in the Six Day War of June 1967, the death of President Nasser in 1970, and the accession of Anwar Sadat (whose narrow base of support forced him to turn to the Muslim Brotherhood). These events drove certain activist-minded Muslims who came after him to utilize Qutb's ideas to vindicate their demand for the immediate application of *sharī'ah* in all areas of life. In 1971 the state responded to a degree to these demands by offering to the people in a plebiscite a draft of a new constitution that stated in its Article Two that "Islam is the state religion" and in an amendment in 1980 added that "Islamic law is the principal source of legislation." The previous "provisional" constitutions of 1956 and 1964 made no such references to Islam.

However, Qutb certainly would not have accepted these 1971 and 1980 changes in the country's constitution as sufficient warrants for his objective of an exclusively integral Islamic system, since in practice they have been interpreted in ways that permit non-Islamic sources of law to figure prominently, even to enjoy priority. Thus, the notion that "Islamic law is the principal source of legislation" has been operationalized by an interpretation that non-Islamic sources of law are acceptable, even preferable, as long as they do not directly contravene the *sharī'ah*. Ruling elites could always define the *sharī'ah* so elastically as to distort it beyond all recognition. Qutb would have totally rejected this kind of interpretation as legerdemain, a recipe bound to perpetuate the supremacy of manmade law and hence a guarantee of the continuing triumph of *jahiliyyah*.

For this reason, Qutb's ideas continue to carry currency. In Egypt, where the official religious establishment is under state authority, the regime has managed to obtain rulings from the '*ulama*' that depict Qutb as a puritanical extremist in the tradition of Islam's original "puritans"—the Khawarij. But this hardly puts the matter to rest, as many Muslims regard the judgments and rulings of the official religious establishment in Egypt with a great degree of cynicism. Even non-violence-prone Islamists have been influenced by Qutb's ideas in important ways. More worrying to ruling circles in Muslim-majority (or even Muslim-minority) countries is the continuing influence of Qutb's ideas on violence-prone groups, such as some elements of the FIS in Algeria and of the Taliban in Afghanistan.

It is, at the time of this writing, unclear whether the star of Sayyid Qutb is waxing or waning. But one thing seems certain: that influence will mainly exert itself in circles where emotional commitment trumps analytical argumentation. For Sayyid Qutb's logical and empirical persuasiveness is less at issue for an assessment of his enduring impact than is the passion that drove his understandings about the real world, the practical world, and the implications of those understandings for Islamic praxis.

NOTES

1. Indeed, the expression did not exist in his lifetime, even though the tendency associated with it that characterized a movement demanding immediate application of Islamic law in all areas of life certainly did.
2. We must, however, not lose sight of the fact that Qutb wrote most of his "Islamist" works while he was in the prison hospital, conditions that were—to say the least—far more conducive to writing with emotion and passion than with analytical clarity.
3. The first edition of this work was published in 1949, obviously at a time when Qutb had not engaged in his commentary on the Qur'an. Later editions of this work, however, came to include material that was new, including this riposte against Hudaybi's criticisms, which came after Qutb had come to a new understanding of the verses mentioned, now frequently glossed under the rubric of the *hakimiyyah* verses.

REFERENCE

Abu-Rabi`, Ibrahim. 1991. Discourse, Power, and Ideology in Modern Islamic Revivalist Thought: Sayyid Qutb. *The Muslim World* 81:3–4.

Abu-Rabi`, Ibrahim. 1996. *Intellectual Origins of Islamic Resurgence in the Modern Arab World.* Albany: State University of New York Press.

Akhavi, Shahrough. 1994. Sayyid Qutb: The Poverty of Philosophy and the Vindication of Islamic Tradition. In *Cultural Transitions in the Middle East*, ed. Serif Mardin, 130–152. Leiden: E. J. Bill.

Akhavi, Shahrough. 1997. The Dialectic in Contemporary Egyptian Social Thought: The Scripturalist and Modernist Discourses of Sayyid Qutb and Hasan Hanafi. *International Journal of Middle East Studies* 29: 377–401.

Akhavi, Shahrough. 2009. *The Middle East: The Politics of the Sacred and Secular.* London: Zed Books.

Binder, Leonard. 1988. *Islamic Liberalism.* Chicago: University of Chicago Press.

Diyab, Muhammad Hafiz. 1987. *Sayyid Qutb: al-Khitab wa al-Idiyulujiya.* Cairo: Dar al-Thaqafah al-Jadidah.

Euben, Roxanne. 1999. *Enemy in the Mirror: Islamic Fundamentalism and the Limits of Modern Rationalism.* Princeton: Princeton University Press.

Haddad, Yvonne Y. 1982. *Contemporary Islam and the Challenge of History.* Albany: State University of New York Press.

Haddad, Yvonne Y. 1983. The Qur'anic Justification for an Islamic Revolution: The View of Sayyid Qutb. *The Middle East Journal* 37:14–29.

Haddad, Yvonne Y. 1983. Sayyid Qutb: Ideologue of Islamic Revival. In *Voices of Resurgent Islam*, ed. John Esposito, 67–98. New York: Oxford University Press.

Kepel, Gilles. 2003. *Muslim Extremism in Egypt.* 2nd ed. Berkeley: University of California Press.

Khatab, Sayed. 2002. Hakimiyyah and Jahiliyyah in the Thought of Sayyid Qutb. *Middle Eastern Studies* 38: 145–178.

Khatab, Sayed. 2008 *The Political Thought of Sayyid Qutb: The Theory of Jahiliyyah.* London: Routledge.

Lee, Robert D. 1997. *Overcoming Tradition and Modernity: The Search for Islamic Authenticity.* Boulder: Westview, 83–116.

Moussalli, Ahmad S. 1990. Sayyid Qutb: the Ideologist of Islamic Fundamentalism. *Al-Abhath* 38: 42–73.

Moussalli, Ahmad S_.1993. *Radical Islamic Fundamentalism: The Ideological and Political Discourse of Sayyid Qutb*. Syracuse: Syracuse University Press.

Musallam, Adnan. 1993. Sayyid Qutb and Social Justice, 1945–1948. *Journal of Islamic Studies* 4: 52–70.

Musallam, Adnan. 2005. *From Secularism to Jihad: Sayyid Qutb and the Foundations of Islamic Radicalism*. New York: Praeger.

Muruwwah, Husayn. 1978. *Al-Naza`at al-Maddiyyah fi al-Falsafah al-`Arabiyyah al-Islamiyyah*. Beirut: Dar al-Farabi.

Qutb, Sayyid. 1949. *Al-`Adalah al-Ijtima`iyyah fi al-Islam*. Cairo: Dar al-Kitab al-`Arabi.

Qutb, Sayyid. 1951. *Al-Salam al-`Alami wa al-Islam*. Cairo: Dar al-Kitab al-`Arabi.

Qutb, Sayyid. 1951. *Ma`rakah al-Islam wa al-Ra'smaliyyah*. Cairo: Dar al-Kitab al-`Arabi.

Qutb, Sayyid. 1952–1957. *Fi al-Zilal al-Qur'an*. Cairo: Dar Ihya' al-Kutub al-`Arabiyyah.

Qutb, Sayyid. 1953. *Dirasat Islamiyyah*. Cairo: Maktabah Lajnat al-Shabab al-Muslim.

Qutb, Sayyid. 1962. *Khasa'is al-Tasawwur al-Islami wa Muqawwimatuhu*. Cairo: Dar Ihya' al-Kutub al-Islamiyyah.

Qutb, Sayyid. 1964. *Ma`alim fi al-Tariq*. Cairo: Maktabah Wahbah.

Qutb, Sayyid. n.d. *Al-Mustaqbal li Hadha al-Din*. Cairo: Maktabah Wahbah.

Qutb, Sayyid. n.d. *Hadha al-Din*. Cairo: Dar al-Qalam.

Qutb, Sayyid. 1983. *Al-'Adalah Al-Ijtima'iyyah fi al-Islam*. 9th edition. Cairo: Al-Shuruq, 1983.

Shehadeh, Lamia Rustum. 2000. Women in the Discourse of Sayyid Qutb. *Arab Studies Quarterly* 90: 45–55.

Shepard, William E. 1989. Islam as a System in the Later Writings of Sayyid Qutb. *Middle Eastern Studies* 25: 31–50.

Shepard, William E. 1996. *Sayyid Qutb and Islamic Activism: A Translation and Critical Analysis of Social Justice in Islam*. Leiden: E. J. Brill.

Shepard, William E. 1997. The Myth of Progress in the Writings of Sayyid Qutb (Egyptian Writer and Activist). *Religion* 27: 255–256.

Shepard, William E. 2003. Sayyid Qutb's Doctrine of *Jahiliyya*. *International Journal of Middle East Studies* 35: 521–545.

Sivan, Emmanuel. 1985. *Radical Islam*. New Haven: Yale University Press.

CHAPTER 11

`ALI SHARI`ATI

SHAHROUGH AKHAVI

Introduction

`Ali Shari`ati (1933–1977), an Iranian political activist and intellectual, emerged into the public eye in his own country around 1967, a mere decade before his death in mysterious circumstances in a suburb of London. His father, Muhammad Taqi Shari`ati, was an independent-minded cleric in Mazinan, a town located in western Khurasan province, who encouraged his son to read avidly. Muhammad Taqi's library of works in the religious sciences served as nourishment for the young Shari`ati's inquisitive and restless mind. Additionally, the father had established a Center for the Propagation of Islamic Verities. The distinctive orientation of the Center was to reform Shi`ism and thus to make it more relevant to the conditions of the time, as opposed to remaining restricted to the narrower confines of ritual and pedagogy in the seminary and mosque. As a sign of his commitment to religious reformation, the father did not wear a turban—a symbol of those to whom the son was later to refer as the "hide-bound" clergy (`ulama'-yi qishri`). Reform and social activism were to remain critical elements in Shari`ati's own thinking and action, but putting himself so explicitly in the public eye could not have been easy for him. For, although he became a famous public figure as a result of his tremendously popular lectures in the Husayniyyah-yi Irshad in northern Tehran and his invited presentations at many universities throughout the country, he in fact was very much of a loner who craved solitude.

Shari`ati and his father both had been supporters of the nationalist prime minister, Muhammad Musaddiq, whose overthrow in a royalist coup d'etat engineered by the British, the Americans, and Iranian royalists in August 1953 marked their turn to oppositional activity against the Shah. They were both arrested and briefly imprisoned after the coup. The two were associated with the movement known as the God-Worshipping Socialists, and the son's idol was Abu Dharr al-Ghifari (d. 652), an early Muslim and companion of the Prophet who had distinguished himself for his piety, inclination toward justice, and unflinching support for the Prophet's cousin and son-in-law, `Ali ibn Abi Talib (d. 661), the founder of Shi`ite Islam.

In 1959, Shari`ati was awarded a government stipend to pursue higher education at the Sorbonne in Paris. He was initially active in the anti-Shah Iranian Student Confederation in Europe during his years of study in Paris in the years 1959–1963. But he apparently later became disillusioned with what he believed was the penchant within this organization for endless discussion and aversion to action. Though he was not a trained philosopher or social theorist, this did not deter him from writing works in these areas after his return to Iran in 1964.

In the French university system at the time, one could pursue the *doctorat d'etat*, a rigorous course of study culminating in a dissertation requiring basic research, or a *doctorat d'universite* (sometimes also referred to as *doctorat de troisieme cycle*), whose requirements were more modest and required a minimum amount of basic research and analysis. It was the latter track that Shari'ati was in, although, since French practice seemed to be to assign all foreign students to that track, it may be that Shari'ati had had no chance to opt for the more rigorous course of studies. At any rate, his supervisor, a philologist by the name of Gilbert Lazard, recalled that Shari'ati had shown a basic knowledge of the French language but otherwise was an average student.

Despite his attitude as a young lad in his father's library who revered learning as an end in itself, Shari'ati's formal work at the Sorbonne was driven by an apparently instrumental perspective—he wanted to get the degree as soon as possible so that he could qualify as a university professor in Iran. For his dissertation, he was not able to come up with a developed research question, much less a methodology of research. So Lazard recommended that he edit for corrections in the original text and translate into French an obscure manuscript in Paris's National Library by an equally obscure fourteenth-century writer, Safi al-Din Abu Bakr 'Abdullah ibn 'Umar al-Balkhi, a work called *Faza'il-i Balkh* [The Moral Excellences of (the City of) Balkh]. This manuscript was itself a Persian translation of an Arabic work. To the editorial emendations and the translation into French, Shari'ati added a nine-page introduction. This thesis was submitted in 1963 and awarded a "pass," the lowest category possible for earning the degree (Rahnema 1998, 117–118).

By contrast, in his informal studies in Paris, Shari'ati was greatly influenced by the orientalist Louis Massignon, the sociologist Georges Gurvitch, the historian Jacques Berque, and the philosopher Jean Paul Sartre. The extent to which these major figures esteemed Shari'ati's intellectual prowess is uncertain, but he did interact with them and regarded their impact upon him as enormous. It is ironic that the Christian Massignon crystallized in Shari'ati his own Muslim faith; the Marxist Gurvitch reinforced Shari'ati's devotion to what he believed was Shi'ism's extraordinary commitment to social justice; the agnostic Berque "taught me [Shari'ati] what religion was" (Rahnema 1998, 126); and the atheist Sartre buttressed Shari'ati's notions that Islam was a liberation theology that stressed the human being's responsibility for his or her actions in the world.

One source on Shari'ati somewhat hyperbolically asserts that "he wished to change, not interpret, lead, not argue, move, not convince, achieve, not rationalize" (Dabashi 1993, 104). I say hyperbolic because this characterization obscures Shari'ati's very real desire to interpret or, perhaps one should say, reinterpret, the Islamic verities; and he was a passionate polemicist for whom argument was highly important; he did seek to win over through persuasion; and he was not averse to rationalization—as can be seen by his determined effort to marry social thought with religious verities.

But it is true that Shari'ati was not a systematic thinker and scholar. He was in too much of a hurry for that. Accordingly, critiques of his writings that try to explore the ontological, epistemological, and the philosophically historical aspects of his thought may, at a certain level, be incomplete. For Shari'ati, a word can be made into an entire conceptual and analytical construct without having to embark on any disciplined, discursive, organized intellectual process for rendering this transformation.

According to Rahnema, Shari`ati learned this "truth" from the French orientalist historian Jacques Berque. Berque apparently impressed upon his students the notion of *degrée* [*sic*, i.e., *degré*] *de signification* (degree of signification). As Shari`ati understood it, this expression

> meant that even though words had a unique and eternal meaning, their purpose and intent was subject to change within a given margin during different periods and under different circumstances. Words could thus be transformed from passive means for idle chatter and tools of stupefaction into instruments for socio-political change... [Shari`ati] took each commonly used term in the vocabulary of every Muslim and reinterpreted it until gentle lullabies became electric currents. Words and concepts resonating with resignation, fatalism and self-pity in the historical memory of Iranian Shi`i were suddenly transformed into forceful and dynamic concepts for action. (Rahnema 1998, 126)

We are, here, in the realm of ideology, rather than social theory. If Shari`ati could impregnate a word with a dynamic meant to mobilize large numbers of people, especially the younger generation, into action, then we should pay more attention to the ideological, rather than the purely intellectual, dimension of his efforts. By ideology, I mean a set of beliefs about politics and society that are utilized as metaphorical weapons to advance ideal and material interests in public arenas. Seen in this light, one can understand more clearly the testimonials of two major leaders of the Iranian revolution about Shari`ati: Ayatullah Mahmud Taliqani (d. 1979) and Ayatullah Muhammad Bihishti (d. 1981). According to Taliqani, "Shari`ati created a new *maktab* (doctrine). It was he who drew the youth of Iran into the revolutionary movement." And in Bihishti's assessment, "The works of Shari`ati were essential for the revolution. Those of Imam Khomeini were not exactly suitable for winning over the younger generation" (Abrahamian 1989, 105).

It is in this context that in Sharia`ati's hands Islam became transformed into a revolutionary world ideology. In saying this, I do not for one moment mean to imply that Shari`ati was an opportunist when it came to matters of faith. Quite the contrary, he was deeply pious. However, the measure of his piety was not to be found in the ritualistic aspects of the faith, enacted under the aegis of the mainstream clergy. Instead, it inhered in the manner in which one could work one's faith into service on behalf of social justice and liberation. The paradox lies in the fact that he was such an intensely private person, and yet he saw it his duty to be a voice for public causes, for the people—*al-nas*—one of his favorite expressions.

Shari`ati considered himself an "enlightened intellectual" (*rawshanfikr*) for whom the critical task was to deconstruct existing forms of Islamic knowledge and reconstitute the latter as socially relevant knowledge. "Islamology" is the nearest expression to the Persian word, *islamshinasi*. When he used the word, everyone knew that by it he did not mean knowledge of Islamic dogma, doctrine, and ritual. Rather, the meaning was knowledge of the ideological relevance of Islamic thought and its materialization in action to promote what he held to be the eternal objective of the faith: the achievement of true liberation and social justice.

Despite the fact that Shari`ati is more appropriately seen as an ideologist rather than a social theorist, it is hard to completely separate the two. Earlier, I defined ideology as a system of beliefs that one uses as metaphorical weapons to advance interests in public arenas. If this can be accepted, then social theory (defined here as systematic application of propositions from a variety of disciplines to generate knowledge about society) is the foundation for ideological discourses. In Shari'ati's case, the relevant social theory frameworks come from Marxist political economy and sociology, existential philosophy, liberation theology, and the sociology of religion.

One will not find a systematically integrated worldview in Shari'ati's oral and written discourse. His work is highly eclectic and lacks disciplined articulation and coherence. But the widespread support given to Shari'ati's thought by the younger generation is largely due, one supposes, to his vindication of equality and justice, values that this generation champions above many others. The following themes emerge from a study of Shari'ati's thinking: (1) history as a dialectical process, (2) the individual as a responsible actor who has the obligation to seek truth on his own and act to uphold it, (3) Shi'ism's true mission as the liberation of the human being, (4) the *ulama*'s claimed monopoly in regard to the interpretation and enunciation of the law as a certain recipe for injustice, and (5) contemporary international relations as a system that secures the domination of interventionist great powers pursuing their interests.

History as a Dialectical Process

Let us take these motifs in the order that they have been listed. Shari'ati accepted the Marxist paradigm of social change, although he added his own ad hoc notions to it. In Marx's view, social change occurs as a consequence of contradictions and class conflict—not as a result of harmonious and consensual accommodations among groups in society. Shari'ati simply accepts this perspective without really problematizing and critiquing it, other than to fault it for leaving religion out of the picture. Doubtless the influence of the European left shaped his thinking in this area. While, as far as can be established, Shari'ati did not read the primary sources of Marxian thought, including Marx himself, Bernstein, Lenin, Trotsky, Lukacs, and Gramsci, he was introduced to Marxism by Georges Gurvitch's lectures at the Sorbonne, Sartre's existential philosophy, and, perhaps, Frantz Fanon's writings on the third world. Because he did not have the background, we can imagine Shari'ati listening to Gurvitch's lectures and focusing his mind on certain concepts and arguments that the latter made that seemed relevant for Shari'ati's own understanding of the contemporary world. Accordingly, he did not acquire an integral understanding of Marxist thought.

This led him to validate the Marxist view that change is dialectical, based on conflicts and contradictions. One of his favorite terms was *jabr-i tarikh*—historical determinism—(though this was not Marx's own phrase). But when it came to applying this framework to social change in a "genuine" Shi'i community, he simply elided its application in ad hoc fashion and thus implied that because the community was a "true" Shi'i community, historical laws that applied in all other circumstances did not apply for pious Shi'ites. The implication is that if people in a community believe they are living the lives that the Shi'i imams[1] enjoined upon them to live, the objective situation did not really matter in their case, since God, as it were, would absolve them of the universal pattern that change must occur dialectically and through conflict. In short, to apply the conflict paradigm for Shi'is seemed, to

Shari`ati, to preempt God's role in guiding people to the truth by ensuring that they abided by the noble religious injunctions.

Liberated by his "Shi`i exceptionalism" thesis (if this expression may be permitted), Shari`ati is thus free to call upon all well-intentioned believers to rally to the standard of Imam Husayn b. `Ali (d. 680), the younger son of Shi`ism's founder, Imam `Ali b. Abi Talib (d. 661). Husayn is the central figure in classical Shi`ism's doctrine of martyrdom. That doctrine emphasizes this figure's sufferings on behalf of his faith and of those who espouse it. But Shari`ati goes far beyond this more limited characterization to convert Husayn into a *revolutionary*, whose paradigmatic act against Sunni impious tyranny centuries ago is dramatically relevant for contemporary politics.

THE INDIVIDUAL AS A RESPONSIBLE ACTOR

Historical determinism and the individual as a responsible actor seem to be two contending themes. On the one hand, we have a structuralist approach, according to which the causes of change lie in dynamics within macroentities, such as classes, states, and markets—all of which structuralists generally see as operating in some impersonal manner. On the other hand, we have an agency approach, according to which the causes of change reside in microlevel voluntary actions by individuals who, when faced with an actual situation, decide to throw the weight of their actions on this side or that side of an issue.

Shari`ati does not have the inclination to think about these antinomies. Nor would it serve his purpose to do so, which is to reach a broad audience and persuade its members to mobilize their energies to achieve freedom and justice. The principle that human beings are ultimately responsible for their actions and the corollary that they are free to choose among alternatives can be found in the thought of some earlier Muslim thinkers. Yet, Shari`ati seems to raise them not in the context of *their* thought but rather through his understanding of French existential notions, which he combines with his own private reconstruction of the motivations of Shi`ism's iconic figures, Imam `Ali and Imam Husayn. His message is that these imams devoted themselves to the masses, and one measure of this devotion was to urge that Shi`ites commit themselves wholeheartedly to the principles of responsibility and choice. Going one step beyond this, Shari`ati appeared to be arguing that if Shi`ites did not make this commitment, they would be betraying these leaders, a deeply wounding charge, of course, given the persistent belief among Shi`ites that they (that is, their ancestors) had betrayed them through abandonment.

SHI`ISM'S TRUE MISSION AS THE LIBERATION OF THE HUMAN BEING

Related to the above discussion is Shari`ati's navigation between the overt meanings of Islamic scripture and their latent, esoteric meanings. Feeling an affinity for the Muslim mystic Mansur al-Hallaj (d. 922), Shari`ati reasoned that exoteric and esoteric truths within the same message of the faith contend with one another in dialectical fashion. This dynamic process, he argued, was essential to maintain the resilience of Islamic thought, which, in their absence, would become stagnant, even sterile (Rahnema 1998, 135–137). He suggested that the clergy cherished the study of law to the detriment of the study of inherent meanings of symbols. He fully realized that his position would (and did) generate hostility from the `ulama' but convinced himself that such opposition would not matter once the broader masses freed themselves of the clergy's influence.

In this context, what mattered in Shi`i thought was not expert advice on the rituals of the faith (which he believed was the traditional preserve of the `ulama') but how the imams of Shi`ism exemplified struggle on behalf of both moral and revolutionary virtues. Shari`ati did not deny the seemliness of ritualistic obedience to the laws of Islam, and so the clergy had an important role to play in society. But he noted that their monopoly of interpretation of the faith had led to its stultification at best and the destruction of the revolutionary imperative at worst. Here, a paradox emerges. Shari`ati was never tired of upholding the cause of the masses (*al-nas*), which seems to be his unit of analysis and generator of change. But esoteric verities are often impervious to the efforts of common folks to understand. This necessitates that "enlightened thinkers" (*rawshanfikr/rawshanfikran*) take the leading role. Shari`ati seems to take it on faith that these enlightened thinkers will always see matters in the light of what best suits the ideal and material interests of the masses. Yet, what ensures that the former will act in ways to uphold the rights and interests of the latter? Another way of putting matters is that in spite of the democratic ethos of parts of Shari`ati's thought, an elitism may be found.

Of course, it is not surprising that a tension of this sort exists, since one could say much the same thing about many bodies of thought, including liberal or social democratic thought themselves. So the fact that Shari`ati wants the individual to think for himself or herself as a responsible actor who is free to make choices but also wants enlightened intellectuals to show the way does not cause his project to fall to the ground. But in eliding the process by which enlightened intellectuals, having led the way, then also facilitate the masses' actions on their own behalf, finally eventuating in Shi`ism's ultimate goal of liberation of the human being, Shari`ati seems to be begging the question of how this process unfolds.

The `Ulama`'s Role and Injustice

Shari`ati had problems with the `ulama' for a number of reasons. The first was that his father was critical of them as a group because of their insularity and pedantry. To the degree that he was influenced by his father's teachings, Shari`ati himself adopted similar views. Note that his father had refused to wear the turban, as though by doffing this symbol he was freeing himself from constraints restricting the breadth of vision and depth of reformist thought of the traditional clerical sodality. Shari`ati never had it in mind to become a professional man of religion, although this did not prevent him from forming associations with them, such as Ayatullah Murtada Mutahhari (d. 1979). And, in the midst of campaigns by the clergy to deny him any credibility as a religious spokesman, Shari`ati expressed his appreciation for the fact that no clergyman had ever signed his name to a protocol, capitulatory agreement, or treaty that alienated a part of Iranian territory or resources to foreign powers or businessmen.

Yet, he blamed the *'ulama'* for two shortcomings: (1) they failed to make themselves relevant to the faithful—and especially to the younger generation—by wrapping themselves in a cocoon of scholasticism and casuistry; and (2) they unjustifiably tried to monopolize understandings of the faith and thus flaunted their elitism within a tradition that, to him, rested on egalitarian foundations. Shari`ati is not the only thinker whose efforts to vindicate the alleged egalitarianism of Shi`ism have foundered on the shoals of an inherently elitist juristic theory of rule. Following the Iranian revolution of 1978-1979, a number of *mujtahids* have blithely argued that Shi`ism rests on the foundations of popular sovereignty, forgetting that its juristic theory of authority identifies the imams as the repositories of divine knowledge; and specially trained jurists as their deputies (Akhavi 1996). It is hard to see how these formulations lay the basis for the liberation of believers. They may do so, but these writers have failed to show how. Shari`ati believes that all believers have the right to engage in *ijtihad*—the utilization of independent judgment to adduce a legal ruling. This position directly conflicts with the *'ulama'*'s unique control over this process. They have ridiculed his argument as ignorant, but their opposition tells us more about their fear of losing power than it does about the state of Shari`ati's knowledge of religious principles.

Yet, Shari`ati cannot simply assert Shi`ism's "natural" tendency to emancipate the human being. He needs to argue this in a sustained analytical process in which the connections are clear between creedal beliefs and human freedom. It is as though at the very point where he needs to substantiate his points he urges his listeners and his readers to "take it on faith" that Shi`ism does causally generate the liberation of humankind.

Clearly his impassioned pleas that Imam Husayn was the revolutionary model for all historical eras disturbed the Shi`i jurists and theologians, for whom that revered figure was the central figure in the faith's soteriological message. Shari`ati did not deny this traditional view of Imam Husayn. But he added to it the perspective of Imam Husayn as a charismatic political prototype of a modern political leader who devotes his efforts to recruiting members into a social movement and mobilizing resources on behalf of a political cause in the hurly burly of the contemporary political process. To the *'ulama'*, Shari`ati was debasing a revered religious icon by rendering him a political demagogue—by which I mean a popular leader espousing the cause of the masses, the hoi polloi—a category greatly distrusted by them. For Shari`ati, however, the *'ulama'*'s refusal to adapt to the world of mass politics was a guarantee of the continued exploitation of Shi`ite believers by powerful elites who benefited either by the clergy's political quietism or outright connivance. In either case, the outcome was injustice. To remedy this injustice necessitated that the *'ulama'* either become substantively and meaningfully politically engaged behind the masses or abandon the field to those who can place religious ideals in the service of the people.

INTERNATIONAL RELATIONS AS A SYSTEM OF DOMINATION BY THE GREAT POWERS

Shari`ati's understanding of international relations was significantly influenced by the writings of third world anticolonial writers, in particular Frantz Fanon (d. 1963) and Fanon's fellow Martiniquean Aimé Césaire (d. 2008) and Che Guevara (d. 1967) as well as his interactions with writers for the Algerian newspaper published in Paris, *al-Mujahid* (*el-Moujahed*). Marxists among his contacts at the university and outside academia were also touchstones in the development of his worldview. In summary, Shari`ati accepted the Leninist and the neo-Marxist perspectives on world politics and the international economic system. But, as often happened, he lent to these leftist perspectives his own understanding of the role of religion as a liberating force. He could readily invoke examples of religiously based resistance movements that opposed colonialism and imperialism, including the Sufi-based movements in North Africa in the nineteenth and twentieth centuries, the Sudan in the 1880s–1890s, the Arab world from the 1870s to the 1950s, and Iran from the 1890s to the 1960s. Behind his rejection of the assumption by socialist and Marxist theorists that the sole product of religious allegiance was false consciousness lay his counterassumption that cultural (in this case, religious) authenticity was a—perhaps *the*—sine qua non of the successful revolutionary struggle of third world colonized peoples against their colonial and imperialist masters.[2]

As indicated in the previous sections, Shari`ati upheld the values of social justice, while holding that those values could not be ultimately vindicated without anticolonial revolutions on the international stage. Because of his idealized understanding of Islam (both Sunni and Shi`i, incidentally), it was axiomatic for him that the achievement of a genuinely just society was indicated by a fully integrated system of ideas and actions. In Islamic thought, going back to the earliest period of Islamic history, the discourse of the Prophet and the relators of the traditions (*ruwwat*), who were the precursors of the clergy, contained references to *tawhid*. This word, which translates as "unicity," originally referred to God's place in human understanding. It meant classically that God is one, and that He has no associates or compeers. But in later discourse, a system of *tawhid* referred not just to God's place in human understanding but also the ideal society, which was fully integrated around the principle of God's unicity and characterized by the noble values of exemplary levels of morality, fraternity, cooperation, and justice. These ideals could not be achieved in a society divided by class cleavages, and Shari`ati, showing the influence of Marxism upon him, was convinced that such distinctions would eventually be replaced by a fully egalitarian society. But the causal mechanism of this dynamic, that is, the transition from an inegalitarian to a fully egalitarian society, was elided in his thought.

I do not know whether Shari`ati was influenced by the thought of Antonio Gramsci, but it would not be surprising that he had heard about him from like-minded intellectuals with whom he associated in his Paris years. Gramsci's determined insistence that culture is exceptionally important for the successful construction of redoubtable revolutionary movements would have found powerful resonance in his own thinking. For in Gramsci's view such movements required the creation of "hegemonic blocs" that, over a long period of time, would incorporate intellectuals, nationalists, and members of the lower classes and integrate their thought and their action. Such blocs, he felt, were alone able to undertake breakthrough revolutions against ruling class systems on the way to the construction of the ideal, classless society. No amount of leadership (Gramsci has Lenin in mind here) can lead people to make revolution if these people are told that their traditional values are a hindrance to the achievement of that end and hence must be abandoned. On the other hand, Shari`ati closely followed the Leninist line that imperialism was "the highest stage of capitalism." This included Lenin's prescription for ending capitalist domination at the international level, that is, move against capitalism's entrenched positions in the colonies and semicolonies.

Conclusions

During his years in Paris, Shari'ati established himself as a strong critic of the Pahlavi state in Iran. Thus, upon his return to Iran in 1964, he was arrested at the Bazargan border crossing point. The government had concluded that he was a dangerous individual, an "Islamic Marxist." He was eventually released and tried to get a teaching job in the capital, but he had been blacklisted. Thus, he had to return to his native province and actually taught secondary school for a while. He did eventually find his way back to Tehran and, starting around 1967 until 1972, established a powerful reputation, especially among younger Iranians, as the indefatigable champion of the masses. In 1972, the government eventually closed down the institution where he was lecturing, the Husayniyyah-yi Irshad (literally, "place of guidance," after the model of Imam Husayn), arrested Shari'ati, and incarcerated him. He was released in 1975 and immediately sought permission to leave for Europe. The government tried to compromise his reputation by expurgating passages from a text called *Islam, the Human Being, and Marxism* in a bid to undermine his reputation by making it seem that he agreed with regime positions on Marxism.

Eventually, in 1977, he succeeded in gaining permission to leave, but his wife and son were not allowed to accompany him. Shortly after arriving in England, he died under mysterious circumstances. His followers suspected foul play by the Iranian intelligence services, but a British inquiry ruled he died of a heart attack. Speculation arose (and continued to the present day) about an alleged deal that he made with the Iranian authorities as the price for getting out of jail and eventually getting permission to leave for Europe. The broad outlines of this alleged deal are that he agreed to tone down his rhetoric and write material that would be subject to censorship prior to publication. Shari'ati was strongly opposed to both the traditional clergy, many of whom supported Ayatollah Ruhollah Khomeini or at least criticized the Shah's domestic policies, and the orthodox communists (Stalinists) of the Communist Party of Iran. The regime, so goes this line of thinking, felt it could use him against these two parties, while carefully undermining his popularity among his ardent youthful supporters.

In the end, Shari'ati was a tragic figure, though on a certain level this may have suited his temperament. He cherished his solitude and viewed it as a metaphor for heroic struggle. While never comparing himself to his early heroes in Islamic history (at least, not publicly), he nonetheless saw his task to be similar to theirs: to speak truth to power and to spread the message of justice, equality, and freedom. He was, it would seem, the nonpareil example of the true believer who had convinced himself that he had a special duty to perform. This duty was to sound the call to people to wake up and commit themselves to act against all those human failings that had made it possible for power holders to exercise their dominion over them and to unite to recapture the highest ideals with which human beings are capable of endowing their lives.

Notes

1. The Imams are the leaders of the Shi`ite community. Twelver Shi`ites, who are politically the most influential of the Shi`ites in the world today, believe that they have been led by twelve Imams. The Prophet's paternal cousin and son-in-law, `Ali ibn Abi Talib, was the first Imam. His two sons, Hasan and Husayn, by his wife, Fatima, were the second and third imams. Later imams were descendants of these three. Imams were considered the proofs of God's existence and paragons of learning, inerrancy, and justice. Only the Imam is entitled to rule the Shi`i community. But the persecution of the Shi`a by the Sunnis led to the doctrinal mandate that they must disguise their true religious beliefs, lest all of their number be rounded up and the entire community massacred. Were that to have happened, in Shi`i beliefs, it would have spelled the end of the religious injunctions. The twelfth imam, then a young boy, disappeared on God's command, for fear that his murder by the Sunnis would have extinguished the line of the imams. The Hidden Imam's return is expected, but until that day, Shi`ites must be cautious and were instructed to be politically quietist. This belief began to change beginning in 1970 when Ayatullah Khomeini declared the need for the Shi`a to emerge into the light of day and take matters into their own hands by establishing a government led by a supreme jurisconsult.
2. Abrahamian notes that Shari`ati specifically challenged Fanon on the latter's relegation of religious values to a secondary plane. See Abrahamian 1982, 25.

References

Abrahamian, Ervand. "Shariati: The Ideologue of the Iranian Revolution," *MERIP Reports* (January 1982): 25–28.

Abrahamian, Ervand. 1989. *Radical Islam: The Iranian Mojahedin*. London: I.B. Tauris.

Akhavi, Shahrough. 1980. *Religion and Politics in Contemporary Iran: Clergy-State Relations in the Pahlavi Period*. Albany: SUNY Press. 143–158.

Abrahamian, Ervand. 1983. Shari`ati's Social Thought. In *Religion and Politics in Iran*, ed. Nikki Keddie, 125–144. New Haven: Yale University Press.

Abrahamian, Ervand. 1988. Islam, Politics and Society in the Thought of Ayatullah Khomeini, Ayatullah Taliqani and Ali Shariati. *Middle Eastern Studies* 24: 404–431.

Abrahamian, Ervand. 1996. Contending Discourses in Shi`ite Law on the Doctrine of *Wilayat al-Faqih*. *Iranian Studies* 29(3–4, Summer/Autumn): 229–268.

Algar, Hamid, ed. and trans. 1979. *On The Sociology of Islam*. Berkeley: Mizan Press.

Bayat-Philipp, Mangol. Shi`ism in Contemporary Iranian Politics: The Case of Ali Shari`ati. In *Towards a Modern Iran*, ed. Elie Kedourie and Sylvia Haim, 155–168. London: Frank Cass.

Dabashi, Hamid. 1993. *The Theology of Discontent*. New York: New York University Press. 102–146.

Keddie, Nikki. 1981. *Roots of Revolution*. New Haven: Yale University Press. 215–230.

Rahnema, Ali. 1998. *An Islamic Utopian: A Political Biography of Ali Shari`ati*. London: I. B. Tauris.

Sachedina, Abdulaziz. 1983. Ali Shariati: Ideologue of the Iranian Revolution. In *Voices of Resurgent Islam*, ed. John Esposito, 191–214. New York: Oxford University Press.

Shari`ati, `Ali. 1347/1968. *Ravish-i Shinakht-i Islam* [Method for Knowing Islam]. Tehran: Husayniyyah-yi Irshad.

Shari`ati, `Ali. 1349/1970. *Kavir* [Kavir]. Tehran: Husayniyyah-yi Irshad.
Shari`ati, `Ali. 1350/1971. *Fatimah Fatimah Ast* [Fatimah Is Fatimah]. Tehran: Husayniyyah-yi Irshad.
Shari`ati, `Ali. 1350/1971. *Hajj* [Pilgrimage to Mecca]. Tehran: Husayniyyah-yi Irshad.
Shari`ati, `Ali. 1350/1971. *Intizar: Mazhab-i I`tiraz* [Waiting (for the Imam's Return): The Religion of Protest]. Tehran: Husayniyyah-yi Irshad.
Shari`ati, `Ali. 1971. *Shahadat* [Martyrdom]. Tehran: Husayniyyah-yi Irshad.
Shari`ati, `Ali. 1350/1971. *Tashayyu`-i `Alavi va Tashayyu`-i Safavi* [Ali's Shi`ism and the Shi`ism of the Safavids]. Tehran: Husayniyyah-yi Irshad.
Shari`ati, `Ali. n.d. *Az Kuja Aghaz Kunim?* [Whence Shall We Begin?]. Tehran: Husayniyyah-yi Irshad.
Shari`ati, `Ali. n.d. *Bazgasht bih Khishtan Bazgasht bih Kudum Khish?* [Return to Self, but to Which Self?]. Tehran: Husayniyyah-yi Irshad.
Shari`ati, `Ali. n.d. *Chih Bayad Kard* [What Is to Be Done?]. Tehran: Husayniyyah-yi Irshad.
Shari`ati, `Ali. n.d. *Islamshinasi* [The Sociology of Islam]. Tehran: Husayniyyah-yi Irshad.
Shari`ati, `Ali. n.d. *Ummat va Imamat* [Ummah (The Islamic Community) and Imamate (Leadership and Rule of the Imams)]. Tehran: Husayniyyah-yi Irshad.

CHAPTER 12

AYATOLLAH KHOMEINI

MOJTABA MAHDAVI

Government can only be legitimate when it accepts the rule of God, and the rule of God means the implementation of the *sharī'ah*.

Ayatollah Khomeini

If we say that the government (*hokumat*) and guardianship (*velayat*) is today the task of the *fuqaha* (religious jurists), we do not mean that the *faqih* (jurist) should be the Shah, the minister, the soldier or even the dustman.

Ayatollah Khomeini

The government is empowered to unilaterally revoke any *sharī'ah* agreement that it has conducted with people when those agreements are contrary to the interests of the country or of Islam.

Ayatollah Khomeini

Introduction

THIS essay aims to contextualize the life and legacy of Ayatollah Khomeini (1902–1989). It suggests that the politics, perspective, and personality of Ayatollah Khomeini, Khomeinism, have been central in the making of Iran's postrevolutionary state. Ayatollah Khomeini's thinking, however, was almost half a century in the making: his thinking evolved over five distinct stages, beginning with political quietism and concluding with political absolutism. The essay is divided into three parts. First, it examines Ayatollah Khomeini's first and second stages of life. While the first and second stages of his politicointellectual journey—quietism and constitutionalism—did not directly contribute to Iranian politics, they remain significant in understanding Khomeinism. In the second section, we will examine the making of Khomeinism, that is the third, fourth, and fifth stages of his politicointellectual journey—Khomeini as the radical revolutionary, the *vali-ye faqih*, and the absolute *vali-ye faqih*. In the third section, we will problematize Khomeini's controversial legacy by examining Khomeinism after Khomeini. Ayatollah Khomeini's death did not put an end to Khomeinism; his contentious legacy is still alive and dominates current Iranian politics. The controversy over the presidential election in June 2009 captures the ambiguity and complexity of his legacy. The conclusion sheds some light on the conditions and possibility of post-Khomeinism.

I. Ayatollah Khomeini: From Quietism to Constitutionalism

Khomeini the quietist (1920s–1940s)

Ruhollah Khomeini, born into a clerical merchant family in Khomein in southwestern Iran, achieved prominence among the students of Ayatollah Abd al Karim Haeri (d. 1936) and received the degree of *itjihad* (independent judgment in legal matters) in 1936.[1] He was only thirty-three when he became known as the *marja-e taqlid*, meaning the source of emulation. Khomeini as a *marja-e taqlid* and a teacher did not restrict himself to the conventional teachings and habits of the *madraseh* (the seminary). By the 1940s Khomeini became a master synthesizer: in Qom's Feyziyeh Seminary he offered an unconventional curriculum, brought together the study of mysticism (`irfan`), philosophy (*falsafeh*), ethics (*akhlāq*), and Islamic law (*sharī`ah*). Not only was he practicing how to combine *irfan* and politics, but he also was insisting on reconciling two opposing schools in clerical thought: `irfan` and *sharī`ah*. Khomeini was "one of the few to have reached the stature of a leading jurisprudent, the highest level of theoretical mysticism and also to have become a highly-regarded teacher of Islamic philosophy. He was unique in being at the same time a leading practitioner of militant Islam."[2]

The young Khomeini's attitude to politics, however, was congruent with the long established apolitical tradition of the clerical institution. Political quietism and social conservatism best represent the dominant tradition of clerical Shiism. In this tradition the clergy remained apolitical and deferred to the monarchy. According to the traditional understanding of the doctrine of the Imamat, the leadership of the community rests solely with the imam. The last/twelfth imam gone into hiding/occultation (260/874) is the sole legitimate leader of the community, and it is believed he shall eventually return to establish the rule of Islam.[3] In the meantime, the community of believers ruled by illegitimate authority remains apolitical. The `ulema` (clerics) guide the community in religious matters and are responsible for the protection of the faith. Although a few clerics were politically active after the establishment of the Safavid dynasty, the clerical establishment remained largely apolitical, meaning it never proposed an alternative polity to the ruling authorities. Political quietism in the Shiite tradition, writes Hamid Enayat, resembles the pragmatic logic of "Sunni realism," meaning that the "supreme value in politics [is]...not justice but security—a state of mind which sets a high premium on the ability to rule and maintain 'law and order' rather than on piety."[4]

Nonetheless, because the authority of the Hidden imam is passed to the `ulema`, the argument goes, they exclusively understand and interpret the *sharī`ah* law. This suggests that "while power might lie with the temporal body, authority would naturally devolve onto the jurists." The Qajar dynasty (1794–1925) recognized this authority, but the Pahlavi monarchs (1925–1979) did not; this eventually caused tensions in state-clergy relations under the Pahlavi dynasty.[5]

After the death of Ayatollah Haeri in 1936, Ayatollah Mohamad Hossein Buroujerdi (d. 1961) became the supreme religious authority in Iran. Khomeini remained a quietist cleric so long as Ayatollah Buroujerdi, an important religious authority and a strong advocate of clerical quietism, was alive. The young Khomeini, although frustrated by Reza Shah's secular reforms, remained quietist, relying on the Shiite practice of *taqīyah*, or dissimulation, which permits people to deny their faith in order to continue its practice.[6] In 1941, the Allies replaced Reza Shah due to his pro-German stance with son, Mohamad Reza, as the new shah. The young shah welcomed religious activities in order to contain the supporters of the communist Tudeh Party connected the Soviet Union. The clerical establishment welcomed the new regime's policy, as it would strengthen its clerical institutions. The young Ayatollah was not an exception; he welcomed the change and remained quietist.

Khomeini the constitutionalist (1940s–1971)

Khomeini's transition from quietism to constitutionalism was prompted by the fear of secularism undermining the traditional role of the `ulema` in society. As a political activist Khomeini's first public statement came in a book published in 1945. The book titled *Kashf al-Asrar* (The Discovery of Secrets) was essentially a detailed, systematic critique of an antireligious tract, but it also contained passages that were critical of the antireligious policy of the Pahlavi monarch. In this small polemical book Khomeini attacked secularism, Reza Shah's anticlerical policies, and a group of clergy who had offended the clerical establishment.[7] The book became the first statement of Khomeini's view on both constitutionalism and the Islamic state. "Government," Khomeini argued, "can only be legitimate when it accepts the rule of God, and the rule of God means the implementation of the *sharī`ah*."[8] But Khomeini did not challenge the institution of monarchy and remained a constitutionalist. He sought a supervisory (*nezarat*) role for the `ulema`. This was in accord with Article 2 of the 1906 Constitution, as suggested by Shaykh Fazlollah Nouri, providing for a clerical committee to supervise laws passed by the *majles* (parliament). If on rare occasions the `ulema` criticized the regime, writes Abrahamian, "it was because they opposed specific monarchs, not the 'whole foundation of monarchy.'"[9] Khomeini the constitutionalist was not an exception; he did not oppose the institution of monarchy.

In *Kashf al-Asrar* the form of government was not Khomeini's main concern as long as the *sharī`ah* law was enforced. Khomeini described the legal procedures and the constitutional arrangement in line of his constitutionalist approach to politics. He argued that

> if we say that the government (*hokumat*) and guardianship (*velayat*) is today the task of the *fuqaha* (religious jurists), we do not mean that the *faqih* (jurist) should be the Shah, the minister, the soldier or even the dustman. Rather, we mean that a *majles* that is...[run] according to European laws...is not appropriate for a state...whose laws are Holy....But if this *majles* is made up of believing *mojtahids* who know the divine laws and...if they elect a righteous sultan who will not deviate from the divine laws...or if the *majles* is under the supervision of the believing *fuqaha*, then this arrangement will not conflict with the divine law.[10]

Khomeini was clearly absent from politics in the years 1951–1953; he was unfriendly to the nationalist movement led by Mohammad Mosaddeq in the 1950s.[11] Khomeini was disappointed with the politics of quietism and was inspired by Islamist militants' idea of Islamic universalism but remained politically inactive and never publicly criticized Ayatollah Buroujerdi's policies.[12] It appears in retrospect that he understood that he had to establish "his credentials as a prominent religious leader before moving on to the political arena in order to both strengthen his standing within the religious establishment and widen his power base in general."[13]

Khomeini's real entry into politics came in 1962–1963 after the inauguration of the shah's reforms known as the "White Revolution." Ayatollah Buroujerdi's death in 1961 opened the space for Khomeini's involvement in politics and also left the religious institution with no single successor. Given the presence of older ayatollahs, Khomeini was a junior candidate for Buroujerdi's position. However, he seized the moment and published a collection of rulings on matters of religious practice (*resaley-e tozihol masael*), and with this book he made himself available to be recognized as the *marja-e taghlid*. The shah regime's difficulties with the White Revolution gave him the opportunity to emerge as a leading clerical opponent. Khomeini attacked the new electoral law enfranchising women as an un-Islamic law and the referendum endorsing the White Revolution as an *unconstitutional* procedure.[14] In response the shah sent paratroopers to attack Feyziyeh Madreseh, the religious seminary where Khomeini taught. The school was ransacked, Khomeini himself was arrested, and some students died. For Khomeini, this event showed the regime's hostility toward Islam and the clerical establishment. Khomeini was released from prison in 1964 and soon denounced the shah's tyrannical regime as being subordinate to US interests in Iran. When legal immunity was granted by the shah to American personnel for offences committed on Iranian territory, Khomeini furiously condemned this policy as humiliating to Muslims in their own country. In his words, "If someone runs over a dog belonging to an American, he will be prosecuted.... But if an American cook runs over the shah, the head of the state, no one will have the right to interfere with him. Why? Because they wanted a loan and America demanded this in return."[15] Khomeini was again arrested in 1964 and sent into exile in Turkey and then to Najaf, Iraq's most important Shiite shrine city. While in exile Khomeini "established himself as a major presence in Najaf."[16] Despite his physical absence from Iran, he maintained his influence among some Muslim political organizations inside Iran.

In *Kashf al-Asrar* Khomeini had argued in 1945 that the clergy should provide legal and moral guidance and not become politically involved. In return, the clergy expected respect for the *sharī'ah* and the clerical establishment. Khomeini's view as a constitutionalist remained unchanged until the 1970s despite the events of 1963.

II. The Making of Khomeinism: The Triumph of a Revolutionary Ayatollah

Although prerevolutionary Iran never experienced a homogeneous Islamist political culture, Khomeinism dominated revolutionary Iran. Khomeinism was built upon a political and pragmatic reinterpretation of religious scripture that evolved into revolutionary populism.[17] Khomeinism is neither traditionalism nor fundamentalism; it symbolizes neither a premodern movement nor a postmodern phenomenon. It is not traditionalism, since Ayatollah Khomeini departed radically from the Shiite tradition of political quietism in the face of sociopolitical injustice. It is not fundamentalism, as the term "fundamentalism" derived from American Protestantism and implies the literal interpretation of scriptural texts.

Similarly, in spite of its critique of modernity, Khomeinism is not a postmodern phenomenon. Khomeinism explicitly associated itself with intellectual absolutism, insisting on the absolute representation of the Truth. Central to Khomeinism is its antihermeneutic claim, insisting that the *core* meaning of the Qur'an is absolutely clear and not open to interpretation. Postmodernity is largely antifoundational, while like other versions of Islamism, Khomeinism insists on some absolute a priori foundation as the basis of its ideology. Finally, it makes little sense to characterize Khomeinism as antimodern or even premodern, given its profound engagement with the modern world such as its ability to equip itself with modern technologies of organization, surveillance, warfare, and propaganda. Khomeinism refashioned and institutionalized a modern theocracy: the "whole constitutional structure of the Islamic Republic was modeled less on the early caliphate than on de Gaulle's Fifth Republic."[18] Ayatollah Khomeini's ideologized account of the tradition offered the country hope of relief from the ill effects of absolutism and imperialism and led to the formation of a nationwide populist revolutionary coalition. His political critique of the shah's absolutism and Western imperialism was more renowned than his theory of the *velayat-e faqih* (guardianship of jurist).

Khomeini the revolutionary (1971–1979)

In the early 1970s, "Khomeini was the first Shiite jurist to open the discussion *(fath-e bab)* of 'Islamic government' in a work of jurisprudence."[19] The theory of Islamic government was a departure point from constitutionalism. Khomeini began to change his position by suggesting that the whole institution of monarchy was illegitimate and that Muslims should be ruled by an Islamic government. He stated, "The Islamic government is constitutional in the sense that the rulers are bound by a collection of conditions defined by the Qur'an and the traditions of the Prophet.... In this system of government sovereignty originates in God, and law is the word of God."[20] He developed, through a series of lectures delivered in Najaf in the early 1970s, the novel idea that a just, knowledgeable, and faithful *faqih*, in the absence of the twelfth Shiite imam, was obliged to exercise both religious and political power. "The ruler," Khomeini argued "must have two characteristics: knowledge of the law and justice. He must have knowledge of the law because Islamic government is the rule of law and not the arbitrary rule of persons. In this sense only the *faqih* can be the righteous ruler."[21]

Khomeini's theory of the *velayat-e faqih* was a radical departure from the dominant traditional trends in Shiism.[22] The theory challenged the conventional Shiite doctrine of *Imamat*, which states that the legitimate leadership of the Muslim community belongs to the Prophet and his twelve successors or imams. Khomeini proposed the novel idea that "our duty to preserve Islam" by establishing an Islamic government "is one of the most important obligations incumbent upon us; it is more necessary even than prayer and fasting."[23] He suggested the task of creating an Islamic government that can be justified on the basis of the "secondary ordinances" *(ahkam-e sanaviye)*, where the "primary ordinances" that is the *sharī'ah* laws are silent or not explicit.[24]

Ayatollah Khomeini established his doctrine of *velayat-e faqih* on two traditional and rational grounds.[25] The government is an essential component of Islam because the Prophet created an Islamic state. Moreover, the *sharī'ah* law cannot be fully implemented without an Islamic state; Islamic government is the only legitimate tool to put the Islamic rules into practice. Muslims cannot live under un-Islamic rule, and the implementation of *sharī'ah* law cannot be stopped during the Great Occultation: "Did God limit the validity of His laws to two hundred years? Was everything pertaining to Islam meant to be abandoned after the Lesser Occultation?"[26] The just *vali-ye faqih* is the only qualified ruler to undertake this task after the Prophet and the imams.

Khomeini initially stated, "Whatever is in [constitutional] accord with the law of Islam we shall accept and whatever is opposed to Islam, even if it is the constitution, we shall oppose."[27] He then increasingly came to believe that Islam was under greater threat from colonialism, "and thus shifted his emphasis from the constitution to Islam."[28] He argued that the Pahlavi regime was bent on destroying Islam because only Islam and the '*ulema*' can prevent the onslaught of colonialism.[29] Khomeini eventually rejected constitutionalism and monarchy: "Islam is fundamentally opposed to the whole notion of monarchy," he argued, because it is one of the most shameful "reactionary manifestations."[30]

Why and how did the constitutionalist Khomeini become a revolutionary? Why did it happen in the 1970s? Ayatollah Khomeini remained in close contact with Iran during his exile years and was deeply influenced by the waves of new ideas and radical trends in Iran. He, for example, read Al-e Ahmad's (1923–1969) pamphlet, *Gharbzadegi* (Westoxification), given his frequent use of the term in the late 1970s.[31] Moreover, Iranians outside the country also played a part in transforming Khomeini's views. In November 1973, Khomeini urged the Iranians to rise against the aggression of the Zionist regime while the shah was considered a friend of Israel. He attacked the shah for creating the Rastakhiz Party and opposed replacing Iran's Islamic calendar with that of the Achaemenid, known as the *Shahanshahi* calendar. He also condemned the shah's celebration of the 2,500-year anniversary of the Iranian monarchy, given the painful reality of Iranian society. By the 1970s, Khomeini was transformed into a populist and revolutionary Ayatollah with an ability to communicate with different groups of people.

The sociopolitical events of the late 1970s pushed Khomeini to become the leader of "the unthinkable revolution."[32] "Acting under another of its erroneous assumptions," the shah's regime requested that the Iraqi government expel Khomeini "in the hope of depriving him of his base of operations and robbing the Revolution of its leadership." [33] Khomeini went to France, which proved beneficial, as communication with Iran was easier from France because Khomeini's declarations were telephoned directly to Iran. His popular speech was articulated in the popular idioms and therefore united Iran's urban middle class and lower class under his charismatic leadership.

The shah was ultimately forced to leave Iran for the last time on January 16, 1979 and within two weeks Khomeini returned to Iran. On February 1 Khomeini received a tumultuous welcome in Tehran. Within ten days the old regime collapsed, and Khomeini established a new regime called the Islamic Republic of Iran. Ayatollah Khomeini spent the last two parts of his life under a polity he created. He successfully transformed the last monarchy into Iran's first republic. However, the republic he founded transformed Khomeini the revolutionary into Khomeini the *vali-ye faqih* (1979–1987) and eventually Khomeini the absolute *vali-ye faqih* (1987–1989).

Khomeini the *vali-ye faqih* (1979–1987)

In the absence of a common enemy, social and political differences in the aftermath of the revolution became more visible. There was division among the Islamists, nationalists of secular thinking, and various groups on the secular left. Each group held different opinions on the future of postrevolutionary politics. For Khomeini, the leader of the revolution, the future could only be an Islamic republic, but its nature remained undefined. Khomeini wanted to place the theory of *velayat-e faqih* as the leading idea of the revolution, merging clericalism and republicanism. Hence, both concepts were redefined. First, the Shiite "jurist law" was "transformed into the law of the state."[34] In his theory of *velayat-e faqih*, Khomeini redefined the role of clergy, suggesting that "in Islam there is no distinction between temporal and religious power. He rejected the prevalent notion that the jurists' task should be limited to understanding and interpreting the *sharī'ah*. They are not mere collectors of traditions; rather it is also part of their duty to implement the law."[35] In fact, the role of the imam, he suggested, "should be represented by a *faqih*, as the sole holder of legitimate authority."[36] In other words, Khomeini's definition of politics was an individual's conformity to the *sharī'ah*. For Khomeini, the structure of authority was divine and the state was instrumental in the implementation of the *sharī'ah*. Second, Khomeini also redefined the concept of republicanism in accordance with clerical rule. The people's participation in politics, or republicanism, resembled for Khomeini the traditional Islamic concept of *bay'a*, meaning the vote of allegiance to authority.[37]

Ayatollah "Khomeini was not setting up government in a vacuum but was taking over an existing one which had undergone considerable modernization in the course of the twentieth century."[38] To incorporate the theory of the *velayat-e faqih* into state institutions required time and experience. In appointing Mehdi Bazargan, a liberal Muslim, to head the interim government Khomeini was seeking time and experience for the clergy to eventually lead the new regime and consolidate Khomeinism.[39] In Paris Khomeini said "the '*ulema*' themselves will not hold power in the government" but instead "exercise supervision over those who govern and give them guidance."[40] But by the end of 1979, Iran had a quasitheocratic constitution, and by the summer of 1981 Khomeini's theory was in practice.[41] Ayatollah "Khomeini's personal role in the gradual transformation of the clergy into a 'clerical regency'—as Bazargan using the French term, called the new theocracy—was significant."[42] Khomeini as the *vali-ye faqih* wanted the clergy in the office of the president: the first clerical president and the Islamic Republic's third president was Ali Khamenei, then secretary general of the Islamic Republican Party and the future successor of Ayatollah Khomeini.

"Yet the results," as Brumberg put it, "were far from the theocracy that Ayatollah Khomeini had zealously proclaimed. Instead of producing a coherent constitutional map, the clerics blended several different ones, thus institutionalizing a new political order based on contending visions of authority," ranging from orthodox to pragmatist to democratic visions.[43] Khomeini's traditional and charismatic authorities were institutionalized in the constitution. The office of the *velayat-e faqih* and Khomeini as the *vali-ye faqih* brought together traditional, charismatic, and legal authorities in the making of the Islamic Republic. This was a "dissonant institutionalization,"[44] which caused many contradictions in the state of Khomeinism and much tension in the Khomeinist state.

The Iran-Iraq war provided Ayatollah Khomeini with a historic opportunity to consolidate his vision of the revolution. The unintended consequences of the eight-year war, the longest war in post-World War II,[45] were to change the state-society relationships and contribute to the reenchantment of the Iranian society. "If Iranians had entered the war as obedient subjects, they emerged from it with a keener sense of their own relationship to the state."[46] The legacy of the war was contradictory: it ironically strengthened both the state and the society, which both emerged with their self-confidence enhanced. To use Charles Tilly words, the war was instrumental in "state making," meaning "eliminating and neutralizing" the state's internal political rivals and enemies.[47] And yet the war changed relations between the state and society, as it simultaneously created a mass society with its demands unfulfilled. More importantly, the Khomeinist state was facing a growing tension between conservative elites or traditional right and revolutionary elites. By 1987, it became "too clear that the regime's emphasis on Islam, war, revolutionary discourse, and the persona of Khomeini were insufficient for governing Iran."[48] The crisis in the economy, the frustration and alienation in society, and the systematic deadlock and ideological factionalism in politics alarmed the regime, pushing the state to take some initiatives for change. "Perhaps more than anyone it was Khomeini who had woken up to this reality: the engine for change was Khomeini himself."[49] The change was aimed at the consolidation of the Islamic Republic. The institutionalization of the *velayat-e faqih* and rationalization of power, however, did not contribute to democratization but instead enhanced the power of the *vali-ye faqih* and made Khomeini more or less into an absolute (*motlaqeh*) *vali-ye faqih*.

Khomeini the absolute *vali-ye faqih* (1987–1989)

Three significant issues exemplified the transformation of Ayatollah Khomeini into the absolute *vali-ye faqih*. In all three issues, Khomeini was concerned about the future of the state he created.

The absolute rule of the state over religion

The elimination of so-called enemies of the *velayat-e faqih* brought to the fore divisions within the Khomeinist camp. These revolved "around the soul of the state," that is, "the characteristics of the government of *velayat-e faqih*" and "its Islamicity."[50] The first faction, the conservative or traditional right, backed by the *bazaari* merchants and the orthodox clergy, held a conservative position on the nature of the Islamic state and "wanted strict implementation of *sharī'ah* in the socio-cultural spheres."[51] The second faction, the revolutionary elites, by contrast "supported state-sponsored redistributive and egalitarian policies."[52] They also believed that primary Islamic ordinances (*ahkam-e awaliye*), derived from two Islamic sources of the Qur'an and the Tradition of the Prophet (the *Sunna*) were insufficient, and therefore Muslims living in modern times needed to issue secondary ordinances (*ahkam-e sanaviyeh*).[53] Ayatollah Khomeini trusted both factions. He appointed the six jurist members of the Guardian Council, the legislative body with veto power over the *majles*' bills, from the conservatives. At the same time he strongly supported the statist-revolutionary bills in the *majles* and the revolutionary plans provided by then Prime Minister Mir-Hossein Musavi (1980–1989). In the struggle between the two Khomeinist camps, "Khomeini shrewdly pursued his unique policy of 'dual containment.'"[54]

Khomeini's charisma was the backbone of his policy of "two-handed way," hiding the constitutional contradictions in the institutional setting of the Islamic Republic. By 1987, however, Khomeini's policy of "dual containment" was no longer effective, given the ever-increasing disagreements over economic, sociocultural, and military policies between the two factions. From December 1987 until his death in June 1989, Khomeini issued various decrees to clarify his sociopolitical positions and sided with the revolutionary camp.[55]

In December 1987, after continuous tensions between the conservative Guardian Council and the revolutionary *majles* over the tax bill and the labor law, Khomeini intervened and authorized the government to introduce bills essential to the interests of the state. In his speech he insisted, "The state can by using this power, replace those fundamental...Islamic systems, by any kind of social, economic, labor...commercial, urban affairs, agricultural, or other system, and can make the services...that are the monopoly of the state...into an instrument for the implementation of general and comprehensive politics."[56] When then President Ali Khamenei interpreted Khomeini's argument, suggesting that "the executive branch...should have a permanent presence in society...within the limits of Islamic laws and Islamic principles,"[57] Khomeini harshly responded by blaming Khamenei for misrepresenting his argument and his ruling. In January 1988 he made it clear that

> The state that is a part of the absolute vice-regency of the Prophet of God is one of the primary injunctions of Islam and has priority over all other secondary injunctions, even prayers, fasting and *haj*.... The government is empowered to unilaterally revoke any *sharia* agreement that it has conducted with people when those agreements are contrary to the interests of the country or of Islam.[58]

Khomeini as the absolute *vali-ye faqih* came to the view that all aspects of Islam were subordinate to the interests of the Islamic state. "From now on religion would serve the Islamic state rather than vice versa."[59] For Khomeini, as Brumberg put it, "the *faqih* was not merely the interpreter of the law, but in some sense the *vehicle* of law itself."[60] Khomeini, indeed, "implied that the vice regent of God had the authority to *create* both divine and secondary injunctions."[61] Even though "Khomeini in theory granted new and unparalleled powers to the *faqih*, he at the same time drastically undermined the religiousness of the regime and bolstered its populist-republican dimension."[62] Khomeini provided the state "with the authority not only to intervene in the economy but the right to use its discretion to suspend even the pillars of Islam."[63]

Ayatollah Khomeini's statement was bold but certainly not new. "Khomeini had long believed in the utilitarian tasks of government and had used the term *interests* in the context as far back as 1941."[64] This time, however, he clearly "broke from the historical position of the religious establishment in Iran with regard to state ordinances."[65] The statement was extremely significant, because "Khomeini emerged as a primary routinizer of his own charisma."[66] Khomeini as the absolute *vali-ye faqih* "by design or default" lay the foundation for greater tensions over his legacy and, indeed, over "the very nature and role of the state." The revolutionary Khomeinists sought to institutionalize "Khomeini's charisma in the *majlis* and government," while the conservative Khomeinists "tried to rescue the idea of charismatic rule by defending the investment of all authority in the *person* of the *faqih*."[67] Khomeini's exceptional statement in 1988, in sum, seemed to point toward an institutionalization of the absolute *velayat-e faqih*—a pragmatic rationalization, if not secularization, of the political order and the subjection of Islamic rulings to the interests of the Islamist rulers.

The "poisonous chalice" of the peace

After accepting the ceasefire in the Iran-Iraq war, reported Khomeini's son, "he could no longer walk.... He never again spoke in public... and he fell ill and was taken to the hospital."[68] By 1988 Khomeini realized the war was no longer in the interests of the state and was undermining the very survival of the republic. Despite his fiery talks against imperialism and the infidel enemy, as the founding father of the republic Khomeini had no choice but, to use his own phrase, to drink from "the poisonous chalice" and save the state: "How unhappy I am because I have survived and have drunk the poisonous chalice of accepting the resolution.... At this juncture I regard it to be in the interest of the revolution and of the system."[69]

Ayatollah Khomeini accepted the ceasefire in the summer of 1988 and died in the summer of 1989. During this period Khomeini expressed his "absolute" authority in three specific events. First, following the end of the war, the People's Mojahedin Organization, the opposition group based in Iraq, launched a military attack against Iran. The regime response was harsh: the Mojahedin's forces were massacred on the battlefronts and several thousand jailed political opponents were executed in the prisons.[70] Second, Khomeini's *fatwa* against Salman Rushdie's novel *Satanic Verses* created much tension between Iran and the West. Third, after a decision by the Assembly of the Experts in 1985 it was expected that Khomeini's loyal student, Ayatollah Hossein-Ali Montazeri, would succeed him. Montazeri was the only high-ranking cleric who supported Khomeini's theory of *velayat-e faqih* and contributed in theory and practice to the institutionalization of the *velayat-e faqih*. However, Montazeri frequently criticized the violation of human rights by the regime. He challenged the regime's new reign of terror in the summer and autumn of 1988. Disappointed with Montazeri's reactions, Khomeini asked him to resign and ordered the Assembly of the Experts to meet and make a decision on the future leadership of the republic. The purge of the only Ayatollah loyal to the doctrine of the *velayat-e faqih* set the stage for the revision and the redefinition of Khomeini's doctrine of the *velayat-e faqih*.

The succession: the rationalization of the velayat-e faqih?

There was one last work for Ayatollah Khomeini to fulfill before he died in June 1989: his succession. With Montazeri's dismissal, Khomeini needed to find a successor. The 1979 constitution was explicit in the theological qualifications of the *vali-ye faqih*, indicating in addition to all personal and political qualifications, only one among the grand ayatollahs as the prominent *marji`a*, or the source of imitation, could hold the office. The problem was that none among the grand ayatollahs was sympathetic to Khomeini's theory of *velayat-e faqih*. Moreover, the leading grand ayatollahs lacked the personal charisma or high political qualifications required for the office. However, there were a number of middle-ranking clerics who accepted Khomeini's theory and held the necessary political requirements. The pragmatic solution was to revise the constitution to save the Khomeinist state.

The 1989 constitution was a departure from the 1979 constitution. It expanded the power of the *faqih* by transferring the president's task of coordinating the three branches of government to the office of the *velayat-e faqih*. It made it explicit that the *vali-ye faqih* holds "absolute" power by adding the phrase *motlaqeh* to Articles 107–110, defining his absolute authority. The 1989 constitution, under Article 110, listed the expanded authority of the *vali-ye faqih*.[71] More importantly, Article 109 of the amended constitution separated the position of the *marji'a* from that of the *faqih*, setting the stage for the selection of a new *vali-ye faqih* who could be a middle-ranking cleric. As specified in Article 109, the *vali-ye faqih* no longer needed to hold the religious qualification of the *marja-e taqlid*, or source of religious emulation. Khomeini's theory of the *velayat-e faqih* "received a blow, as it effectively, in the long run, separated the position of the 'leader' from the institution of *marja'iyat*, subordinating the latter to the state."[72]

Paradoxically, Khomeini's priority respecting the interests of the state led him to revive his own theory of the *velayat-e faqih* by reducing the theological qualifications needed and separating the position of the *marji'a* from that of the *faqih*. This surprisingly was the separation of religion from politics! The rationalization of the office of the *velayat-e faqih*, however, did not lead to the ascendancy of democratic authority in the republic. Rather, it was a boost toward greater institutionalization of political absolutism.

On 3 June 1989 Khomeini died. The elected Assembly of the Experts appointed Ali Khamenei as the new leader of the Islamic Republic. Khomeini died; Khomeinism, however, survived and became routinized. The routinization of charisma and the succession brought some significant changes to the fate and future of the Khomeinist state. First, the religious power shifted from the institution of the *velayat-e faqih* to the religious seminaries, and yet the political authority of the *vali-ye faqih* remained over and above the religious authority of the *marja-e taqlid*. Second, power was concentrated, not in the hands of a *vali-ye faqih* but in the office of the *velayat-e faqih*. Third, the routinization of charisma transferred power, not to the people but to the more authoritarian conservative faction of the state.

III. Khomeinism after Khomeini: Multiple Faces of Khomeinism

Ayatollah Khomeini was "a unique product of unique historical circumstances" and thus "irreplaceable." It was Ayatollah "Khomeini who made the institution of the *velayat-e faqih* powerful, not the other way around."[73] Khomeini's charisma was not transferable to a successor. His successor, Ali Khamenei, who was designated by the ruling clergy, had neither religious credentials nor a charismatic personality, in Max Weber's terms, to be "awakened" or "tested." Thus, unlike Khomeini, who depended on his own charismatic authority, Khamenei was dependent on his conservative peers. Ali Khamenei's "lack of an independent base of support was the critical factor in his selection as the *faqih*; he did not seem threatening to the rival factions. Aware of his shortcomings, Khamenei in the early stage of his rule stayed above factions."[74] And yet, because he lacked the character required for mediating between the rival factions and balancing their power, he became closer to the conservatives with whom he shared attitudes and was indebted to their support.

The first republic (1979–1989) of the Khomeinist state was essentially a "one-man show" dictated by Ayatollah Khomeini.[75] Nonetheless, in the post-Khomeini era, with no charisma in politics, no war, and growing domestic opposition, disagreements over sociopolitical issues divided the Khomeinist forces. The post-Khomeini state went through four different political periods: the second republic (1989–1997), the third republic (1997–2005), the fourth republic (2005–2013), and the fifth republic (2013). Each republic presented a different face of Khomeinism.

The second republic (1989–1997), under President Hashemi Rafsanjani, routinized the revolutionary charisma and institutionalized the office of the *velayat-e faqih*. The neoliberal policy of reconstruction (*sazandegi*) weakened the social base of the regime, escalated elite factionalism, and forced the regime to open up public space and allow a limited degree of sociopolitical liberalization. The politics of *sazandegi*, neoliberal Khomeinism, prioritized economic development over political development; it resembled a conservative revolution or, to use Barrington Moore's analytical concept, a "revolution from above."[76] The policy was far from a success because Iran in the mid-1990s was experiencing a growing socioideological disenchantment. Civil society managed to challenge the repressive intentions of the state. For conservatives, the harsh truth to accept was a growing gap between their sociocultural values and those of the youth, the postrevolutionary generation. The state had failed to create the man/women or the society Ayatollah Khomeini had envisioned. The youth were socioculturally disenchanted, politically disappointed, and economically dissatisfied.

Religious and secular intelligentsia posed serious intellectual challenges to the ideological foundations of Khomeinism. Abdolkarim Soroush challenged authoritarian religious thinking: clerics, like other "professional groups," hold a corporate identity, "a collective identity and shared interest," and thus possess no divine authority.[77] The rule of the *vali-ye faqih*, Mojtahed Shabestari argued, is not divine and thus has to be subjected to democratic procedures. Ayatollah Montazeri came with a more accountable interpretation of the *velayat-e faqih*, suggesting that *velayat-e faqih* "does not mean that the leader is free to do whatever he wants without accountability."[78] The *vali-ye faqih* "we envisaged in the constitution has his duties and responsibilities clearly defined. His main responsibility is to *supervise*."[79] For Mohsen Kadivar, the "central question that the clergy faces today is whether it can preserve its independence...in the face of an Islamic state, since it does not want to fall victim to the fate of the Marxist parties of the former communist states."[80] He boldly argued that such a political version of the *velayat-e faqih* existed neither in the Qur'an, nor in the Prophet's, nor in the Shiite imam's traditions.[81]

By the late 1990s the intensity of Iran's factional politics was a fact, providing much opportunity for the unexpected victory of the reformist presidential candidate, Mohammad Khatami, on May 23, 1997. Khatami became the candidate for change and received the people's protest vote, making him a "Cinderella candidate"[82] and eventually an "accidental president"[83] of the Islamic Republic. The reformist republic stood on three intellectual pillars: Islamic constitutionalism, promoting civil society, and Islamic democracy. All three intellectual pillars were bound to the lasting legacy of Khomeinism, which created a limited and inchoate subjectivity never independent of the *vali-ye faqih*. The fall of the reformist republic (1997–2005) symbolized in part the crisis of *Khomeinism with a human face*.

The 2005 presidential election marked a new era in the Khomeinist state—an era of "neoconservative Khomeinism," which was consolidated in the June 2009 disputed presidential election. The president of Iran's fourth republic (2005–present), Mahmoud Ahmadinejad, was a product of the state-security apparatus, the office of the *velayat-e faqih*, and Iran's neoconservatives: a group of young members of Islamic Revolutionary Guards Corps cultivated in the postwar period. They attempted to revive the social base of the regime among the urban and rural poor, which has been eroded in the post-Khomeini era. The president of the fourth republic spoke about distributive social justice; promised to fight Iran's new class of mafia-like rentiers, the clerical noble-sons (*aghazadeh-ha*); and assured the poor they will bring the "oil money to their table." The irony is that neoconservative Khomeinists were blessed by the state's rents and shadow economy run by the revolutionary foundations controlled by the office of the *velayat-e faqih*.⁸⁴ Their populist slogans were instrumental in serving their pragmatist purpose, that is, to replace the old oligarchy with a new one and to establish a populist, centralized state backed by the lower classes and sponsored by petro dollars.

It is widely believed that with the rise of Iran's neoconservatives to power the Islamic Republic's social base might shift from the coalition of the *mullah*-merchant to that of the revolutionary security and military forces. For the first time, a Khomeinist (ex)military man and not a Khomeinist *mullah* is the president of the republic. The conservatives, in spite of their internal conflicts, gained complete control of the republic, and the absolute rule of the *vali-ye faqih* Khamenei seemed at hand. However, for the first time in the Islamic Republic, the public and the reformist elites have openly challenged the authority and legitimacy of the *vali-ye faqih* in the popular democratic Green Movement. In the presidential elections on 14 June 2013, Hassan Rouhani, a moderate and pragmatist conservative, was elected as the seventh president of the Islamic Republic of Iran. His four-year term, which started on 3 August 2013, brought to an end Iran's fourth republic (Ahmadinejad's presidency) and began Iran's fifth republic. (2013).

In addition to the nonideological, spontaneous, civic, and nonviolent characteristics of Iran's Green Movement, the movement is distinctive for its pluralism; it includes reformist Khomeinists and secular and Muslim post-Khomeinists. Many of the reformist Khomeinists, who accompanied Khomeini on his return to Iran, are now in open revolt. The process of "de-Khomeinization," they believe, has damaged Khomeini's legacy; today Khomeini's Islamic Republic is neither Islamic nor a republic.⁸⁵ The reformist Khomeinists seek a peaceful transformation within the Khomeinist system, while the political spectrum of the Green Movement is both broader and more radical than the reformist discourse. In addition to the quest for free elections and civil rights, it seems Khomeini's legacy of the absolute *velayat-e faqih* is no longer acceptable to the public. Three decades after the practice of Khomeini's ideology, his legacy is contested: for the reformist Khomeinists, "de-Khomeinization" captures the core of the crisis. For others, the nation has gradually moved toward a new era: "post-Khomeinism."

CONCLUSION: TOWARD POST-KHOMEINISM?

In his book *Kitab al 'Asfar'* (Book of Journeys) the mystic-philosopher Molla Sadra discussed the "four journeys" of purification leading to a state of perfection. Khomeini was fascinated by this notion. He saw this (new) Platonic path of perfection as the path of the Prophet. In drawing upon Molla Sadra's "four journeys," Khomeini discussed this path of perfection in his lectures. The first journey is "from mankind to God" in which man leaves "the domain of human limitations" and purges his soul of all earthly desires. The second journey comes "with God in God"; this means man submerges himself in the oceans of secrets and mysteries to acquaint himself with the beauty of God. The third journey is from God to the people, when man returns to the people but is no longer separate from God, as he can now see His omnipotent essence. And the fourth journey is from people to people, in which man has acquired Godly attributes with which he can begin to guide and help others to reach God.⁸⁶

In this final stage the prophethood and the perfect man is realized; the perfect man is the imam and he is obliged to establish the *velayat* (guardianship) on earth, guiding the people and establishing an Islamic society. Ayatollah Khomeini's view of the absolute *velayat-e faqih* derives from his lifelong immersion in mysticism and (Platonic) philosophy, which rendered the absolute Truth, God's words, transparent to him. Such a mystic politician is an absolute *political* sovereign capable of overruling the *sharī'ah*. He does not implement or interpret the *sharī'ah*; he enjoys a full political agency/authority to act on behalf of the interest of the state. The interest and survival of the state/statesmen—*faqih*, not the *fiqh*—is the guiding principle of the Islamic state he envisioned. The events in postpresidential elections of June 2009 is a case in point where the doctrine of the absolute *velayat-e faqih* turns the Islamic Republic into a clerical leviathan accountable to itself, neither to God, nor people, nor human ethics.

Ayatollah Khomeini was a "master synthesizer." His life was full of contradiction. His thinking evolved over five distinct stages and his ideology was almost half a century in the making. Khomeini's transition from quietism to activism was prompted by the fear of secularism undermining the traditional role of the *ulama* in society. In the beginning, the form of state was not Khomeini's main concern as long as the sharia law was enforced. At the end, however, his theory of the absolute *velayat-e faqih* empowered the *vali-ye faqih* to unilaterally revoke *sharia* when it is contrary to the interests of the Islamic state.

Khomeini's most significant political legacy is the postrevolutionary Iranian regime, which can be divided into five Khomeinist republics, the nature of which has been "institutionally dissonant."[87] The state he created combined the theory of *velayat-e faqih* with republican institutions. The Khomeinist state is a mishmash of totalitarianism, authoritarianism, and (semi) democracy, while each republic presents a distinctive face of Khomeinism.[88] The first republic was essentially a "one-man show" dictated by Khomeini's populist and semitotalitarian politics. The absence of Khomeini's charisma in the second republic undermined the totalitarian character of the state, pushing the regime toward a limited degree of pluralism, while the crisis of legitimacy made the political system more authoritarian. The third republic aimed at refreshing the spirit of Iran's quest for democracy. However, the republic failed because it was bound by the institutional and intellectual legacy of Khomeini. The fall of the reformist republic was the failure of *Khomeinism with a human face*. The fourth republic was a product of the state-security apparatus, the office of the *velayat-e faqih*, and the extremist faction of Iran's conservatives, or *neoconservative Khomeinism*. The pragmatist president of the fifth republic challenged domestic and foreign policies of Ahmadinejd and has promised to pull Iran back from the brink of the negative economic growth, political repression, and international sanctions. It remains to be seen whether he is competent to accomplish this.

After three decades, Khomeini's legacy, the Islamic Republic of Iran, both is and is not what he envisioned. His legacy has been challenged at once by "de-Khomeinization" and "post-Khomeinism." For the reformist Khomeinists, "de-Khomeinization" was the official policy of the fourth republic.[89] Ayatollah Khomeini, it is argued, valued people's vote, recognized the *majlis* as the forefront of political affairs, encouraged open *itjihad* in religious thinking, and discouraged the involvement of the Revolutionary Guards in politics. While there is some truth to this argument, it can be argued that Ayatollah Khomeini himself started the process of "de-Khomeinization" after he transformed his doctrine of *velayat-e faqih* into the absolute *velayat-e faqih*. Ayatollah Khomeini was, in fact, the first and last *vali-ye faqih* he envisioned!

More importantly, the rise of the Green Movement suggests that Iran has gradually entered into a new era of "post-Khomeinism," thanks to the crisis of an *Islamic state* and the practice of Khomeini's doctrine of *velayat-e faqih*. If Ayatollah Khomeini's theory of *velayat-e faqih* was a radical departure from the traditional Shi'a political thought, his political legacy has actually contributed to another paradigm shift in the current debates over the possibility and conditions of "post-Islamism" in general and "post-Khomeinism" in particular. According to Asef Bayat, post-Islamism "represents both a *condition* and a *project*." It refers to a *condition* where Islamism, here Khomeinism, "becomes compelled, both by its own internal contradictions and by societal pressure, to reinvent itself." It is also a *project*, "a conscious attempt to conceptualize and strategize the rationale and modalities of transcending Islamism in social, political, and intellectual domains."[90] There is a continuity and change in Islamism and post-Islamism. Similar to Islamism, post-Islamism advocates the participation of religion in the public sphere. Contrary to Islamism, it rejects the concept of "Islamic state"; state is a secular entity no matter who the statesman is. Post-Islamism, post-Khomeinism in the Iranian context is a combination of "Islam *ism*" and "Islam *wasm*"!

Notes

* Another version of this essay appeared in one section of the following journal article: Mojtaba Mahdavi, "One Bed and Two Dreams? Contentious Public Religion in the Discourses of Ayatollah Khomeini and Ali Shariati," *Studies in Religion* (2013; DOI: 10.1177/0008429813496102).
1. Hamed Algar, *Islam and Revolution: Writings and Declarations of Imam Khomeini* (Berkeley: Mizan Press, 1981), 14.
2. Baqer Moin, *Khomeini: Life of the Ayatollah, London* (New York: I.B. Tauris Publishers, 1999), 46–47.
3. The occultation of the last imam had two phases: the shorter phase and the complete occultation. During the first phase (874–941) four special deputies (*nuvvab-e khaas*) were in direct contact with the imam. After the death of the last deputy, the *ulama* have claimed to be the general deputies (*nuvvab-e aam*) of the imam.
4. Hamid Enayat, *Modern Islamic Political Thought* (Austin: University of Texas Press, 1982), 11.
5. Ali M. Ansari, *Modern Iran since 1921: The Pahlavis and After* (London: Pearson Education, 2003), 225.
6. Moein, *Khomeini: The Life of Ayatollah*, 56.
7. The book's real target was "the 'renegade' clergymen who in Khomeini's eyes had 'actively collaborated with him'." Indeed, it was a direct response to an attack on the clerical establishment in a pamphlet called *Asrar-e Hezar Saleh* (Secrets of a Thousand Years) written by Hakamizadeh, the editor of *Homayon*. Hakamizadeh and his colleagues including Ahmad Kasravi were strongly disappointed with the religious establishment and its reactionary approach. See Baqer Moein, *Khomeini: The Life of Ayatollah*, 60–61.
8. Khomeini, *Kashf al-Asrar*, (Tehran: Nashr-e Safar, 1941), 291
9. Khomeini. *Kashf al-Asrar*, pp. 185–188, 226, quoted in Ervand Abrahamian, *Khomeinism: Essays on the Islamic Republic of Iran* (Berkeley and London: 1993), p. 20
10. Khomeini, *Kashf al-Asrar*, p. 185, quoted in Daniel Brumberg, *Reinventing Khomeini: The Struggle for Reform in Iran: The Struggle for Reform in Iran* (Chicago: The University of Chicago Press, 2001), p. 58.

11. The politics of quietism often benefited the shah. Ayatollah Buroujerdi, for example, congratulated the shah when he was brought back to power in 1953. Although, ayatollah Seyyed Abolqasem Kashani (1882–1962), Mojtaba Navab Safavi and his militant group, *Fadaiyan-e Islam*, believed in "political activism, Islamic universalism, anti-colonialism, and populism," they soon withdrew their support from Mossadeq. Khomeini "was a frequent visitor to Kashani's home." Moreover, when Navab Safavi was arrested Khomeini asked the authorities not to harm him. See Moein, *Khomeini: The Life of Ayatollah*, 66.
12. According to Khomeini after he succeeded to overthrow the shah, Mosaddeq's "main mistake was not to have got rid of the Shah when he was strong and the Shah was weak." Khomeini, *Sahifeh-ye Nur*, 3:36, quoted in Moein, *Khomeini: The Life of Ayatollah*, 66.
13. Moein, *Khomeini: The Life of Ayatollah*, 68
14. Abrahamian, *Khomeinism*, 10
15. Algar, *Islam and Revolution: Writings and Declarations of Imam Khomeini*, 181.
16. Ibid., 18.
17. Abrahamian, *Khomeinism*, 13–17.
18. Abrahamian, *Khomeinism*, 15.
19. Said Amir Arjomand, "Authority in Shiism and Constitutional Development in the Islamic Republic of Iran," in Rainer Brunner and Werner Ende, eds., *The Twelver Shia in the Modern Times: Religious Culture and Political History* (Brill: Tuta Pallace, 2001), 301.
20. Khomeini, "Islamic Government," in Hamed Algar, *Islam and Revolution*, 55.
21. Ibid.
22. Although Khomeini's interpretation of the theory of the *velayat-e faqih* was new, the concept was not new to the Shiite tradition. For an insightful discussion, see Farhang Rajaee, *Khomeini on Man, the State and International Politics* (Lanham: University Press of America, 1983).
23. Algar, *Islam and Revolution: Writings and Declarations of Imam Khomeini*, 75.
24. Ibid., 124.
25. Sami Zubaida, *Islam, the People and the State: Political Ideas and Movements in the Middle East* (London: I.B. Tauris, 2009), 16–17.
26. Algar, 42.
27. Huzeh-e Elmiyeh, *Zendeginameh-e Imam Khomeini* [A Biography of Imam Khomeini] (Tehran, n.d.), 95.
28. Hossein Bashiriyeh, *State and Revolution in Iran, 1962–1982* (Kent, UK: Croom Helm, 1984), 59–60.
29. Ayatollah Khomeini, *Khomeini va Jonbesh: Majmueh-ye Nameha va Sokhanraniha* [A Collection of Khomeini's Letters and Speeches] (Tehran: n.p. 1352), 58–60, 68–69.
30. Ruhollah Khomeini, "October 31, 1971, The Incompatibility of Monarchy with Islam," in Algar, 202.
31. Roy Mottahedeh, *The Mantle of the Prophet: Learning and Power in Modern Iran* (London; Chatto & Windus, 1986.), 303. Moreover, waves of radical Islam reached Khomeini via young militant clerics influenced by Iran's People's Mojahedin Organization. Iranian student associations in Europe and North America, impressed by Shariati's ideas, pushed Khomeini toward radicalism.
32. Charles Kurzman, *The Unthinkable Revolution in Iran* (Cambridge: Harvard University Press, 2004).
33. In 1977, Khomeini's elder son, Mostafa, died suddenly in Najaf, likely assassinated by the shah's Security Police, SAVAK. Khomeini "bore this blow stoically," as he termed the tragedy "a divine blessing in disguise." The memorial ceremonies for Khomeini's son

in Iran became a starting point for renewed uprising by the theological seminaries and members of the Iranian religious society. The shah's regime took revenge, publishing an insulting article in the daily *Ettela'at* by attacking Khomeini as an agent of foreign powers. In reaction, the people in Qom displayed anger and frustration. This was the first of a series of revolutionary demonstrations that spread across the country. Hamed Algar, *Islam and Revolution: Writings and Declarations of Imam Khomeini*, 19–20.

34. Said Amir Arjomand, "Authority in Shiism and Constitutional Development in the Islamic Republic of Iran," 302.
35. Ayatollah, Khomeini, *Velayat-e Faqih, Hokomat-e Islami* [The Rule of the Jurisprudent, Islamic Government] (Tehran: n.p. 1357), 28, 39–40, 77–79, quoted in Bashiriyeh, *State and Revolution in Iran*, 62–63.
36. Ibid.
37. According to one view, for Khomeini, the *vali-ye faqih* derives his *popularity* from people but his *legitimacy* is divine. Another interpretation suggests that both popularity and legitimacy of the *vali-ye faqih* derive from people, not God.
38. Arjomand, "Authority in Shiism and Constitutional Development in the Islamic Republic of Iran," 302.
39. Bazargan reluctantly accepted Khomeini's offer, hoping "he would be able to influence the new regime from within." See H. E. Chehabi, "The Provisional Government and the Transition from Monarchy to Islamic Republic in Iran," in Yossi Shain and Juan J. Linz, eds., *Between States: Interim Governments and Democratic Transitions* (New York: Cambridge University Press, 1995), 135.
40. Asghar Schirazi, *The Constitution of Iran: Politics and the State in the Islamic Republic*, John O'Kane, trans. (London: I.B. Tauris Publishers, 1997), 24.
41. After the fall of Bazargan's government in late 1979 and the dismissal of President Banisadr in 1981, the short "spring of freedom" was replaced by a long season of fear and frustration. The regime shut down all political parties and arrested, executed, or jailed the opposition. According to Abrahamian, the figures for the execution of the opposition were 600 by September, 1,700 by October, and 2,500 by December 1981; see Ervand Abrahamian, *Radical Islam: The Iranian Mojahedin* (London: I.B. Tauris Publishers, 1989), 220.
42. Quoted in Moin, *Khomeini: Life of the Ayatollah*, 247.
43. Brumberg, *Reinventing Khomeini: The Struggle for Reform in Iran*, 105.
44. Ibid., 100.
45. Dilip Hiro, *The Longest War: The Iran-Iraq Military Conflict* (New York: Rutledge Chapman and Hall, 1991).
46. Ansari, *Modern Iran since 1921: The Pahlavis and After*, 239.
47. Tilly, "War Making and State Making as Organized Crime," 181.
48. Mehdi Moslem, *Factional Politics in Post-Khomeini Iran* (Syracuse: Syracuse University Press, 2002), 72.
49. Ibid.
50. Ibid., 47.
51. The conservative Khomeinists have been supported by the Society of Combatant Clergy (*Jame'eh Rouhaniyat-e Mobarez*) and the Allied Islamic Society (*Jamiyat-e Mo'talefeh-ye Islami*).
52. The revolutionary Khomeinists have been supported by the Mojahedin of the Islamic Revolution Organization (*Sazman-e Mojahdin-e Enghelab-e Islami*) and the Society of Combatant Clerics (*Maj'ma-e Rouhaniyon-e Mobarez*). The central committee of the Islamic Republican Party, until its dissolution in 1986, was more inclined to the revolutionary Khomeinists and less to the conservatives.

53. Moslem, *Factional Politics in Post-Khomeini Iran*, 48–49.
54. Ibid., 65.
55. Khomeini also created a new institution; the Expediency Council (*Majma'e Tashkhis-e Maslehat-e Nezam*), an institutional mediator between the two Khomeinist camps in the Majles and the Guardian Council, paving the way for further institutionalization of the *velayat-e faqih*.
56. Khomeini, "Khomeini Ruling on State Powers Report," broadcast December 23, 1978, FBIS-NES-87, quoted in Brumberg, *Reinventing Khomeini*, 135.
57. "Khamene'i Delivers Friday Prayer Sermons," broadcast on Tehran Domestic-Service January 1, 1988, FBIS-NES-88-001, January 4, 1988, quoted in Brumberg, *Reinventing Khomeini*, 135.
58. *Ettela'at*, January 9, 1988, quoted in Moslem, *Factional Politics in Post-Khomeini Iran*, 74.
59. Moin, *Khomeini: Life of the Ayatollah*, 260.
60. Brumberg, *Reinventing Khomeini: The Struggle for Reform in Iran*, 135.
61. Ibid., 136.
62. Moslem, *Factional Politics in Post-Khomeini Iran*, 74.
63. Ibid.
64. Brumberg, *Reinventing Khomeini: The Struggle for Reform in Iran*, 136.
65. Moslem, *Factional Politics in Post-Khomeini Iran*, 74.
66. Brumberg, *Reinventing Khomeini: The Struggle for Reform in Iran*, 140.
67. Brumberg, *Reinventing Khomeini: The Struggle for Reform in Iran*, 136–137.
68. Ahmad Khomeini, *Yadegar-e Imam*, 6:468, quoted in Moin, *Khomeini: Life of the Ayatollah*, 270.
69. "Khomeini Message on *Hajj*, Resolution 598," broadcast July 20, 1988, FBIS-NES-88-140, July 21, 1988, quoted in Brumberg, *Reinventing Khomeini: The Struggle for Reform in Iran*, 142.
70. For an insightful account of this event, see Ervand Abrahamian, *Tortured Confessions: Prisons and Public Recantations in Modern Iran* (Berkeley: University of California Press, 1999).
71. The *vali-ye faqih* was given authority to delineate general policies and supervise the execution of decisions; to devise national referenda; to hold the supreme command of the armed forces; to declare war; to appoint, dismiss, and accept the resignation of the six jurists of the Guardian Council, the chief justice, the head of the national radio and television, the chief commanders of the Revolutionary Guard and of the armed forces. Moreover, Article 110 of the new constitution vested constitutional authority in the Expediency Council. In addition to its original task of acting as mediator between the *majlis* and the Guardian Council, the Expediency Council was elevated to a consultative body for the *vali-ye faqih*.
72. Moin, *Khomeini: Life of the Ayatollah*, 294.
73. Milani, *The Making of Iran's Islamic Revolution*, 225.
74. Milani, *The Making of Iran's Islamic Revolution*, 224.
75. Moslem, *Factional Politics in Post-Khomeini Iran*, 143.
76. See Barrington Moore, Jr., *Social Origins of Dictatorship and Democracy: Lord and Peasant in the Making of the Modern World* (London: Penguin Press, 1966).
77. See Soroush, "*Horriyyat va Rohaniyyat*" [Liberty and Clergy]," *Kiyan* 24, April–May 1995, 2-11, quoted in Brumberg, *Reinventing Khomeini*, 205.
78. "Montazeri on State's Road to Destruction," London *Keyhan*, October 10, 1994, EBIS-NES-94-231, October 10, 1994, quoted in Brumberg, *Reinventing Khomeini*, 215.
79. "Montazeri's Speech in Keyhan," December 4, 1997, available at http://eurasianews.com/iran/montadres.html, quoted in Brumberg, *Reinventing Khomeini*, 238.

80. Eric Rouleau, "La Republique Islamique d'Iran Confrontee a la Societe Civile," *Le Monde Diplomatique*, June 1995, available at http/www.mondediplomatique.fr/1995/06/rouleau/1542.html, quoted in Brumberg, *Reinventing Khomeini*, 238.
81. See Mohsen Kadivar, *Andisheh-ye Siyasi dar Islam* [Political Thought in Islam], vols. 1–2 (Tehran: Nay Publications, 1998).
82. Mohsen M. Milani, "Reform and Resistance in the Islamic Republic of Iran," in Esposito and Ramazani, eds., *Iran at the Crossroads*, 29.
83. Shaul Bakhash, "Iran's Remarkable Election," in Larry Diamond, Marc F. Plattner, and D. Brumberg, eds., *Islam and Democracy in the Middle East* (Baltimore: Johns Hopkins University Press, 2003), 119.
84. Ahmadinejad's colleagues such as Sadeq Mahsouli, minister of social welfare, and Mohammad Reza Rahimi, vice-president, among others, are members of the new oligarchy. The former is a billionaire real estate broker and the latter is another billionaire benefiting from exclusive political rents.
85. After the June 2009 events, Ayatollah Montazeri denounced *vali-ye faqih* Khamenei without mentioning his name. He explicitly argued, "This regime is neither Islamic nor a republic; it is a mere dictatorship. This is no longer the 'rule of the qualified faqih'; rather, it is the 'rule of the generals.'" Rasool Nafisi, "Where Is the Islamic Republic of Iran Heading?" *InsideIran*, September 23, 2009, available at http://www.insideiran.org/clerics/where-is-the-islamic-republic-of-iran-heading.
86. Moin, *Khomeini: Life of the Ayatollah*, 49–50.
87. Brumberg, *Reinventing Khomeini: The Struggle for Reform in Iran* (Chicago: University of Chicago Press, 2001), chapter 5.
88. See Chehabi, "The Political Regime of the Islamic Republic of Iran in Comparative Perspective," 48–70.
89. "Mir Hossein Mousavi's Interview with Kalameh," *Khordad88*, June 2, 2010, available at http://khordaad88.com/?p=1623#more-1623.
90. Asef Bayat, *Islam and Democracy: What Is the Real Question?* (Leiden: Amsterdam University Press, 2007), 18–19.

References

Abrahamian, Ervand. *Radical Islam: The Iranian Mojahedin*. London: I.B. Tauris Publishers, 1989.
Abrahamian, Ervand. *Khomeinism: Essays on the Islamic Republic of Iran*. Berkeley: University of California Press, 1993.
Algar, Hamed. *Islam and Revolution: Writings and Declarations of Imam Khomeini*. Berkeley: Mizan Press, 1981.
Amir Arjomand
, Said. "Authority in Shiism and Constitutional Development in the Islamic Republic of Iran." In R. Brunner and W. Ende, eds., *The Twelver Shia in the Modern Times: Religious Culture and Political History*. Brill: Tuta Pallace, 2001.
Ansari, Ali M. *Modern Iran since 1921: The Pahlavis and After*. London: Pearson Education, 2003.
Bakhash
, Shaul. "Iran's Remarkable Election." In L. Diamond, M. F. Plattner, and D. Brumberg eds., *Islam and Democracy in the Middle East*. Baltimore: The Johns Hopkins University Press, 2003.
Bashiriyeh, Hossein. *The State and Revolution in Iran, 1962–1982*. Kent, UK: Croom Helm, 1984.

Bayat, Asef. *Islam and Democracy: What Is the Real Question?* Leiden: Amsterdam University Press, 2007.

Brumberg, Daniel. *Reinventing Khomeini: The Struggle for Reform in Iran*. Chicago: University of Chicago Press, 2001.

Chehabi, H. E. "The Provisional Government and the Transition from Monarchy to Islamic Republic in Iran." In Y. Shain and J. Linz, eds., *Between States: Interim Governments and Democratic Transitions*. New York: Cambridge University Press, 1995.

Chehabi, H. E. "The Political Regime of the Islamic Republic of Iran in Comparative Perspective." *Government and Opposition* 36, no.1 (2000): 48–70.

Enayat, Hamid. *Modern Islamic Political Thought*. Austin: University of Texas Press, 1982, 11.

Huzeh-e Elmiyeh. *Zendeginameh-e Imam Khomeini* [A Biography of Imam Khomeini]. Tehran: n.p., n.d, 95.

Kadivar, Mohsen. *Andisheh-ye Siyasi dar Islam* [Political Thought in Islam]. Vols. 1–2. Tehran: Nay Publications, 1998.

Khomeini, R. *Kashf al-Asrar*. Tehran: Nashr-e Safar, 1941.

Khomeini, R. *Khomeini va Jonbesh: Majmueh-ye Nameha va Sokhanraniha* [A Collection of Khomeini's Letters and Speeches]. Tehran: n.p. 1352/1974.

Milani, Mohsen M. *The Making of Iran's Islamic Revolution: From Monarchy to Islamic Republic*. Boulder: Westview Press, 1994.

Milani, Mohsen M. "Reform and Resistance in the Islamic Republic of Iran." In John L. Esposito and R. K. Ramazani, eds., *Iran at the Crossroads*. New York: Palgrave, 2001.

Moin, Bager. *Khomeini: Life of the Ayatollah*, London. New York: I.B. Tauris Publishers, 1999.

Montazeri, H. "Montazeri's Speech in Keyhan." December 4, 1997. Available at http://eurasianews.com/iran/montadres.html (July 12, 2006)

Mousavi, Mir Hossein. "Mousavi's interview with Kalameh," *Khordad88*, June 2, 2010. Available at http://khordaad88.com/?p=1623#more-1623 (January 21, 2013)

Moslem, Mehdi. *Factional Politics in Post-Khomeini Iran*. Syracuse: Syracuse University Press, 2002.

Mottahedeh, Roy. *The Mantle of the Prophet: Learning and Power in Modern Iran*. London: Chatto & Windus, 1986.

Schirazi, Ashar. *The Constitution of Iran: Politics and the State in the Islamic Republic*. John O'Kane, trans. London: I.B. Tauris Publishers, 1997.

Soroush, Abdolkarim. "*Horriyyat va Rohaniyyat*" [Liberty and Clergy]." *Kiyan* 24, April–May 1995, 2–11.

Zubaida, Sumi. *Islam, the People and the State: Political Ideas and Movements in the Middle East*. London: I.B. Tauris, 2009.

The "Intellectuals" of Political Islam

CHAPTER 13

HASAN AL-TURABI

PETER WOODWARD

Introduction

Hasan al-Turabi has been one of the most controversial figures in the Muslim world in the past half century. To his followers in Sudan he has been ideologically inspiring and a charismatic leader in national politics, while his political opponents have been known to regard him as fundamentally unprincipled. Outside Sudan younger educated Muslims have often found his writings imaginative and innovative, while to conservatives in the field of Islamic thought he has been seen to border on the heretical. Beyond the Muslim world he has been seen as an active supporter of terrorist movements, yet one who has also endeavored from time to time to engage with the non-Muslim world. If there is common ground in these differing judgments it is probably that he is clever, is pragmatic, and cultivates being enigmatic. Trying to assess Turabi as an ideologist only adds to this view. His writings are nowhere brought together into a coherent whole, rather both they and his speeches and interviews on various themes have emerged in a piecemeal manner down the years, often resulting in ambiguity as to where the consistent core of his thinking really lies. This ambiguity is heightened by what often appears to be a deliberate lack of precision in both his conceptual and practical positions. In applying his ideology through his political engagement, his record is similarly varied, leading his critics to see opportunism as often as principle in the positions he has adopted, with regard to both his ascent toward power and the way in which he exercised it following his coup in Sudan of 1989, the first time an Islamist regime had been established in the Arab and sunni world.

Background

Turabi was born in 1932 and grew up in a small village in central Sudan, where his father was a *qadi*, administering the limited areas of Islamic law in what was in effect a British imperial administration (though legally the Anglo-Egyptian condominium in the Sudan), where civil law was essentially secular and largely founded on importing codes then applicable in India. `Abdalla al-Turabi ensured that his son Hasan had a rigorous education in all aspects of Islam alongside his secular studies in the state schools, and some see here a "traditional" background that was to survive Hasan al-Turabi's education in European-style institutions, which culminated in law degrees from the universities of Khartoum, London, and the Sorbonne.

However, if the British rulers were introducing secularizing trends, political mobilization in northern Sudan rested on building its major parties around sectarian Muslim identities that grew specifically from the nineteenth century, while having much older roots. Sufism had a long history in Sudan, including Turabi's illustrious forebear Hamad al-Turabi, which provided fertile soil for Mohammed Osman al-Mirghani, who arrived in Sudan in 1817, shortly before the invasion of Mohammed Ali's troops from Egypt that was to do much to define the country territorially over the next sixty years. Al-Mirghani established the *Khatmiyya tariqa*, which was to spread widely while accepting the new rulers. In the twentieth century *Khatmiyya* connections with Egypt were to survive, especially as political parties emerged after World War II with the Mirghani family becoming patrons of the National Unionist Party (NUP), which was also supported by Egypt, still hoping to achieve "The Unity of the Nile Valley." The NUP's great rival was the *Ummah* Party associated with the Mahdist movement. Mohammed Ahmed al-Mahdi had started the revolt that led to the overthrow of Turco-Egyptian rule (the *Turkiyya* as it was often known in Sudan) in 1885 and the establishment by his successor, the Khalifa Abdullahi, of an Islamic state that was to survive until the Anglo-Egyptian reconquest of 1898. In the following century al-Mahdi's heirs were to make a surprising comeback and after World War II created the *Ummah* Party. With their respective followings in the largely rural northern Sudan, the NUP and *Ummah* dominated both the nationalist era leading to independence in 1956 and the liberal democratic eras thereafter. Even during the long years of military rule from 1958–1964 and 1969–1985 the two parties remained active in various ways. While the sectarian-based parties dominated, the postcolonial state still showed the influence of imperialism's secularizing tendencies—as Turabi put it, "The disestablishment of the '*shari'ah*' and the imposition on Muslim societies of positive western laws"—especially in the attitudes of the Western-educated officials often known as the *effendiyya* (Turabi 1992, 6). Many of these retained their links to the major parties, often through family traditions, but others joined the small but significant Sudan Communist Party (SCP).

These developments provided the context within which Turabi was to evolve his own very distinctive Islamic ideology starting with his rejection of much of Sudan's experience. For him Sudan's history had been one in which Islam had been used in politics, rather than political life having been specifically based upon Islam. The Sufism that had been so dominant in Sudan was insufficiently political in essence; indeed its otherworldly spirituality in practice took Muslims away from the creation of an Islamic state and made them too accommodating of the secularizing processes that the imperial and postimperial state was imposing in the name of modernity. In addition the saintly leaders of the Sufi orders created and occupied a space between man and God, discouraging the individual's quest to actively pursue his or her direct experience of God and the living of a Godly life. Mahdism, which had a long tradition in Sudan preceding the late nineteenth-century movement (Hamad al-Turabi had twice proclaimed himself the Mahdi), was seen by Hasan al-Turabi as a form of revivalism. It rested on the vision of the decay of Islam and sought to return to a better age. It was thus backward looking, failing to engage with the issues of modernity, specifically Islamic modernity, which had come to lie at the core of Turabi's quest. He was also critical of the "official" clerical classes seeking to define Islam and widely influential in the Muslim world, where, far too often in his view, the state passed on its responsibilities with regard to the building of Islamic society. At the same time the clerics claimed a large measure of control through knowledge and interpretation of the Qur'an, rather than encouraging Islamic society as a whole in self-discovery of the true meaning of life, which involves adaptation in order to embrace and build Islamic modernity. All Muslims not only can but also should engage in the search for their own understanding of their religion and then implement it in their lives.

It is his stripping away of the above accretions of Islamic life that led to Turabi being regarded as a "fundamentalist," but he is not somebody who seeks a return to a golden age founded on strict enactment of Qur'anic verses and the *Sunnah* so much as looking forward and building afresh in the spirit of Islam applied to the modern age. Largely for that reason he has been seen as loosely connected to the ancient texts, which he rarely quotes, but rather as an interpreter who uses the style of the great texts on which Islam was founded to express what for him is the essence of the religion. The differentiation between original texts and interpretation today for him would lie in the totally changed circumstances of the contemporary world in which the building of Islamic modernity has to take place. Understandably his criticisms of so many of the existing manifestations of Islam have brought charges of apostasy from some, while also acting as an inspiration to others. Turabi believes that the search for modernity has even led some Muslims in the recent past away from the roots of their religion toward secularist ideologies such as nationalism and socialism in various forms, and these have had to be challenged by a new Islamic modernity, a line of thought that has given him another set of "modernist" critics.

IDEOLOGY

Turabi has in effect given himself a tabula rasa, and for his followers his inspiration has lain in having cleared away so many of the accretions of the past and then laid out a new feast. At its core is his conception of Islam, which lies in *ibtila'*, life's challenge to Muslims laid down by God. The modern world is a God-made world, one in which He has created a series of new challenges for Muslims, and it is through their responses to these that their faith is really put to the test. If they fail to rise to these challenges Islam will indeed degenerate in the face of globalizing secularism. But if they respond and rise to the challenge set by God they can shape a new world truly glorifying Him. In the state of the Muslim world today that means the need for *ibtila'* to be met by the recognition of the need for *tajdid*, renewal. But how is the meaning of *tajdid* to be appreciated having thrown off the accretions of centuries? It is here that *ijtihad*, the interpretation of Islamic law based on first principles, is so central and leads directly to the state, which Turabi believes has responsibility for that interpretation through the introduction and enforcement of the *Shari'ah*.

The state then is central to Turabi's understanding of the implementation of Islam, and the notion of an Islamic state is not the conjoining of two concepts but the pursuit and implementation of one, since Islam is inseparable from statehood, which lies at the center of the building of an Islamic society. In all this the Muslim world has fallen short, and Turabi is seen as a central figure in providing the theological basis for criticizing the existing states of the Muslim world whatever their particular character. The fault in this lies not only in Islam, as previously indicated, but also in Western imperialism, which has first divided the Muslim world, leaving a divided state structure that serves its interests rather than those of indigenous societies, and then co-opted Muslim rulers as local allies more on its terms than theirs, including false ideologies of modernity. The way ahead is toward a new *tawhid,* unification, of the *ummah,* the Muslim world, based upon an interpretation of first principles for the world of today and tomorrow, thus bringing together God, the ultimate sovereign, the rightly constituted Islamic state, and the society of believers.

It is Turabi's interpretation of these principles in public life that is seen as a major cause of the interest in him, especially his reputation for holding liberal and democratic views. Indeed it is the apparent marriage of Islam and democracy that has made him so attractive to the wider Muslim world in which this has become such an often raised subject. However for Turabi this is once more not a joining together of two concepts since it is God who is sovereign, and not the people as normally understood in Western views of democracy, and God's word has come down in the Qur'an and the *hadith,* so that there is an immediate circumscription of the nature of democracy. That is provided by the *Shari`ah,* which is God's law and as such not simply a manmade legal code, though as noted it is required that it be interpreted, codified, and implemented by the state.

> An Islamic form of government is essentially a form of representative democracy. But this statement requires the following qualification. First an Islamic republic is not strictly speaking a direct government of and by the people; it is a government of the *shari`ah.* But, in a substantial sense, it is a popular government since the *shari`ah* represents the conviction of the people, and therefore, their direct will. (Turabi 1983, 244)

With the *Shari`ah* in that framework he chooses not to use the word "democracy," a word usually associated with Western traditions, but rather to speak of *shura,* consultation, a long established concept in the Muslim world. *Shura* acknowledges that ultimate sovereignty rests with God while wishing the believers to participate in arriving at *ijma`,* consensus, with regard to the decisions pertaining to their society within the framework provided by the *Shari`ah.* This is popular government in the sense that it represents the theologically correct view of the people and thus amounts to a common or general will. *Shura* also implies an equality of all the citizens in the process of arriving at *ijma.* It also appears to imply that Turabi envisages a situation where *shura* is not associated with multiparty politics with all its competitive implications so much as an exchange of views among the believers as *ijma* is sought and, with God's guidance, is eventually achieved. What has been fresh is the implied character of constitutionalism apparently associated with *Shari`ah* in Turabi's mind, which often appears to reflect practices associated with the West rather than those of the Muslim world: these include divisions of power, federalism, and an attractive range of freedoms, all of which were given considerable prominence in the campaign of the Muslim Brotherhood (which Turabi had led since 1964) under the banner of the National Islamic Front (NIF) in the multiparty elections of 1986. However, such constitutional aspects are only loosely presented rather than being spelled out clearly, for he sees himself expressing general principles while leaving it to others in formal government positions (which he chose not to hold after the coup of 1989) to handle the details: power without responsibility in the eyes of his critics.

Turabi's approach to democracy, which appeared to be that of liberalism in an Islamic context, led to criticisms of him for a series of steps that seemed opportunistic, though it is possible to argue that there is an underlying consistency. The first occasion was his agreement to national reconciliation with President Nimeiri in 1978. Turabi had been imprisoned by the military ruler who had seized power in 1969 and the Muslim Brotherhood had proved bitter opponents of the regime: yet from Turabi's perspective Nimeiri's turn to reconciliation opened a door of opportunity. He became attorney general, while the movement was to undertake a period of entryism into many areas of the state, the full extent of which was not to become apparent for several years. In 1983 Nimeiri introduced *Shari'ah*, and though it was not specifically the work of the Muslim Brotherhood it was regarded by the movement as a step in the right direction. Following Nimeiri's downfall in 1985, the Brotherhood returned to the liberal democratic path, fighting the 1986 elections as the NIF and obtaining 18 percent of the vote. It was in and out of subsequent coalition governments until itself staging a coup in 1989, an obviously undemocratic move. However it can be argued that Nimeiri's *Shari'ah* was under threat. Civil war in southern Sudan, which had reopened in 1983 after ten years of peace, was intensifying and after much maneuvering it appeared that peace might be negotiated, though only at the price of suspending *Shari'ah*, a measure demanded by the predominantly non-Muslim south. That would be a major setback for Turabi and his followers and it was judged better to seize power than to risk a setback on the path to the Islamic state they sought.

Once in power Turabi's approach could also be seen in his effort to push his Islamic democracy agenda. Following the introduction of revised *Shari'ah* he became the leading promoter of moves toward a non-multi-party national assembly. Later, having become leader of the assembly, he sought in 1999 to challenge President Omar al-Beshir and his military-security colleagues in the name of progressing from military to "democratic" government. However, Beshir responded by suspending the Assembly and ousting Turabi. The latter then formed his own party, the Popular Congress Party (PCP), and with the promise of liberal democratic elections in 2009 (which was contained in the Comprehensive Peace Agreement of 2005 between the rulers of north and south Sudan), Turabi returned to the campaigning mode he had used in the 1986 elections. To his critics this long record put opportunism above principle, while to his defenders he had responded to the changing context while consistently pursuing his path toward his vision of an Islamic democracy, showing the flexibility he had always argued Muslims are required to do.

That Turabi's approach to democracy is ultimately theological based on *Shari'ah* is also reflected in his apparent liberalism. He is noted for the way in which he has called for greater openness within Muslim societies, which some have seen as a call for "civil society": but this is less civil society as understood in Western liberal societies—groups operating independently of the state—than organizations committed to expressing aspects of Muslim society within the framework provided by the *Shari'ah*. It thus involves encouraging the development of a truer Muslim society, which at one time Turabi appeared to think should precede the establishment of an Islamic state. "An Islamic state evolves from an Islamic society" was his view before his 1989 coup (Turabi 1983, 241). Indeed from national reconciliation in 1977 the Muslim Brotherhood had been building up its own activities in civil society. Part of this was with regard to Islamic charitable activities. The growing charities were intended to challenge the influence of Western nongovernmental organizations (NGOs) and assist in the growth of the Islamic movement as a whole. In addition the universities and the small business sector were targeted by the movement as it expanded its membership. In this it was helped by fund raising among the many Sudanese working in the Gulf and Saudi Arabia and by the Islamic banking movement, which grew rapidly in Sudan and elsewhere with capital from the oil-rich states.

However, just as context produced his change with regard to democracy in 1989, so the relationship between civil society and the state had to be turned upside down. The work of the 1980s was incomplete, and the state was now required to embark upon a program of intensified reshaping of society. Non-Islamic NGOs, especially Sudanese "secular" NGOs, were faced by harassment and worse, which resulted in a number of leading Sudanese being persecuted or leaving the country. Meanwhile the state embarked on "the civilizational project" as it was known. It involved a whole range of activities intended to create the true Muslim society but had limited success. De Waal has written of the project's limitations with regard to certain rural areas, while Simone, a researcher brought in by the regime itself, was to describe its lack of progress even in the capital (de Waal 2004, 89–99; Simone 1994). Turabi's critics complained that the attempt to create Islamic society from above contributed to the most repressive actions by the state in Sudan since it became independent in 1956 and reports by many bodies, including the United Nations, have supported this view.

This process of building Islamic society was closely linked to human rights; another area where the potential for paradox in Turabi's thought is often discussed. He has been a defender of human rights, especially in areas such as freedom of thought and freedom of religion, but again in an Islamic context. Contemporary human rights are too often associated with the Enlightenment and depicted therefore as manmade, whereas in Turabi's view man himself is the work of God and under his supreme law, *Shari'ah*. Indeed he has even argued that modern human rights theory is in reality itself derived historically from earlier Islamic thought. Apart from criticism of his argument stretching legal and political history, the reality of human rights following his 1989 coup included practices that even Turabi himself was forced to concede were un-Islamic.

One subject in which Turabi's apparent liberal interpretation of human rights is frequently brought up is that of women, a subject on which he first came to prominence in 1973. In his view women have been held back in Muslim societies, but less by anything specifically included in Islam than by the theological and social developments since that time. Thus in all areas of life, including education in particular, women are to have equal rights with men and are to be regarded as active members of the community rather than confined in domestic incarceration. As well as the practice of patriarchy in some Muslim societies, the principle of avoiding situations that permit un-Islamic relations between the sexes has been exaggerated: instead greater active incorporation of women in all areas of life is to be encouraged. However, women too are part of the Muslim society that is governed by *Shari'ah*, and there are thus standards to which they have to conform while offering personal freedoms from sometimes stifling customary constraints found in parts of the Muslim world. As a result the Muslim Brotherhood fostered women's activities under its aegis, and they became in time a growing and prominent part of the movement. Nevertheless there were women who were less amenable to the "Islamic call" as represented by the Brotherhood and more influenced by the "modern forces," as more secularist movements were often known, and they too had to be challenged. The result was that after 1989 many "uncooperative" women lost their jobs, while in areas such as dress and informal economic activities others were harshly treated for much of the following decade.

Another noted area of Turabi's apparently liberal approach lies in his views on art, which appear to bring out his breadth and his opposition to materialism. While the Muslim world has long appreciated poetry and calligraphy, its approach to the visual arts was too restrictive in his view. The reason, he has argued, has lain in undue influence on avoiding the creation of religious idols or art forms that could be construed as undermining Islam's moral code. However this has been taken to extremes by some clerics in particular and instead Turabi believes that the arts, and the media generally, have a greater part to play in society though once again within a clear Islamic context in which a fusion is reestablished. But instead of a liberation of the arts in Sudan after 1989 many of the practices of the generally easygoing northern Sudanese society, such as music and traditional dancing, were cracked down on for a decade before there was a general easing of the restrictions. How far this easing with regard to civil society as a whole reflected a view amongst the Islamists that their transformation had been achieved and how far it grew from the split in which Turabi was involved and subsequent pragmatism by the military rulers remains a matter of debate.

Turabi's attitude to non-Muslims within an Islamic state is also open to interpretation. On the one hand he put the need for Islamists to construct a specifically Islamic state at the center of his thought, but on the other he sought to present his thought as open with regard to other faiths. The issue arose especially in respect to *jihad*. Turabi has been keen to emphasize that *jihad* is a comprehensive term denoting effort for the Islamic cause and did not simply imply the exercise of armed force. It was a particularly sensitive issue in a context in which successive Sudan governments had been waging a war since 1983 in the predominantly non-Muslim south, where there was a significant Christian community. Whatever was expressed ideologically, in practice the government forces were encouraged to believe that they were engaged in *jihad* in the south and in other areas such as the Nuba Mountains, while soldiers killed in action were heralded in the media as martyrs. It appeared increasingly that few non-Muslims believed that there was the absence of discrimination against them that Turabi claimed should exist; though after his ousting in 1999 he did return to this point, including saying that the conflict was not after all a *jihad*.

Turabi's emphasis on the centrality of the Islamic state in protecting truly Muslim societies gave rise to consideration of his ideas on international politics. Here it becomes apparent that the distinction is fundamentally between those states that are Islamic and should bind together as such and the rest of the world. But first, beyond the Islamic state properly constituted, one must return to his vision of the Muslim world as a whole being in need of *tajdid*, renewal, following centuries of degeneration and division. Again there is a need to return to first principles, and they are far from the Westphalian model so dominant in the contemporary international system. Indeed he believes that there has been a "failure of the territorial national state model," which imperialism had endeavored to impose and construct upon the Muslim world (Turabi 1992, 7). In talking of the Muslim world Turabi is aware that there are complex multiple identities and that these all have their part to play in the reality of the modern world. People have understandable reasons for identifying themselves from family through a series of other layers, including what may be the imposed contemporary state system to *Dar al-Islam*, the Muslim commonwealth, where "Final loyalty must be rendered."

> The Islamic community of believers is unitary and integrated, but it is a structured association with complex bonds and balances that gives coherence and equilibrium, assuring therein the embodiment of the Islamic values of freedom, unity and justice among men. (Turabi 1992, 2)

The end of the Cold War, he argued, gave particular opportunity for the renewal of the *ummah* to take place. One factor was the growth of modern Islamic movements across the Muslim world giving rise to a new awareness of what should and could be achieved. This had been aided by the growth of new forms of mass communication that had penetrated Muslim societies as much as any others around the world. The collapse of the "socialist" world constructed by the Soviet Union removed what had been an alluring and sometimes supportive power for some in the Muslim world. Other major events included the Iranian Revolution in 1979, which had shown that power could be taken from the West's collaborators; and in particular the Gulf War in which predominantly Western troops had deployed on a vast scale in the center of the Muslim world. This had encouraged a new mood that "threatens to wipe out liberal nationalist and socialist tendencies and [will] proceed to take its international course" (Turabi 1992, 7).

How was this to be achieved? True there had been an international organization in existence since the 1960s, the Organization of the Islamic Conference (OIC), but this had been inadequate in Turabi's view. It was supported by states that had had close relations with the Western world and thus it was, "politically impotent and totally unrepresentative of the true spirit of community that animates the Muslim people" (Turabi 1992, 8). Following the coup of 1989 Turabi himself set up and led a new organization, based in Khartoum, called the Popular Arabic and Islamic Conference (PAIC). It invited a heterogeneous range of representatives from groups including Hizbollah, Islamic Jihad, Hamas, and the Palestine Liberation Organization as well as various veterans from the *mujahadin* campaign in Afghanistan against the USSR, including Osama Bin Laden, who lived in Sudan from 1991 until 1996. All were dubbed "brothers in Islam" and seen as part of Turabi's vision of a united *jihad* by the Muslim world in all its diverse parts, even including sunni and shi'a, which contributed to his somewhat ambiguous view of Iran. While the PAIC made a significant contribution, the Muslim world as a whole was looking for a new beacon to set an example of a true Islamic state, with the clear implication that this was what Turabi was inspiring and guiding into being in Sudan itself.

The final vision was of the reestablishment of the Muslim caliphate, but not the same as that which had ended following the collapse of the Ottoman Empire after World War I. The caliphate would in future be less a central political authority than a symbolic leadership of Muslim communities. These would exist under *sharī'ah* as decentralized and democratic but recognizing their ultimate unity as fellow Muslims. "There is no standardization of language or cultural forms as long as an essential minimum of Arabic is assured everywhere and that social life-styles observe the common standards of the *Shari'ah*" (Turabi 1992, 3). As for the non-Muslim world, one finds once more a degree of ambiguity. Clearly Muslim minorities living in predominantly non-Muslim societies were to be supported in whatever ways were necessary and encouraged to keep and develop their faith. Non-Muslims in Muslim countries were to be accorded their rights since freedom of religion was recognized in Turabi's writings, though that did not detract from Muslims engaging in proselytism. A similar attitude was shown toward non-Muslim countries. Turabi both believed in struggling for the Islamic cause and at the same time encouraged interfaith dialogue, especially with leaders of Christian denominations.

The element of struggle for Islam also gave rise to questions about his understanding of *jihad*. While, as mentioned, he saw *jihad* as an effort for Islam broadly understood, he did not rule out violence on behalf of the cause. This became particularly clear in 1995, when

Egyptian Islamists received assistance from Sudan in seeking to assassinate President Hosni Mubarak in Addis Ababa. Turabi described the would-be assassins as "messengers of the Islamic faith" (Collins 2008, 216). However he did also say that justifiable acts of violence in the name of promoting Islam should seek to avoid killing civilians as far as possible.

Conclusion

If Turabi had confined himself to being a theorist his thought would have attracted interest and perhaps served as an inspiration for some. But he has been an ideologist in the fullest sense of the word, turning his ideas into programs of action in Sudan and beyond, which have themselves excited widespread discussion and often critical judgment. He himself has blamed many of the shortcomings in practice on those carrying them out rather than the underlying ideas and intentions themselves and, after his removal from power in 1999, on the military in particular; yet it can be argued that they are based in his thought itself. Many of his fellow believers, while accepting the ultimate sovereignty of God, are of the view that there have been inherent dangers in the vagueness and lack of textual reference in Turabi's writings. Since the state, and the Shari'ah for which it is responsible, is so central it requires tighter definition and clearer constitutional arrangements with adequate legal and political accountability. This in turn will help to clarify the relationship between society and the state that appeared in effect to be reversed in Turabi's thinking by his coup of 1989. This, and much else that has flowed directly or indirectly from his thoughts and actions, leads his Muslim critics to argue that the source of authority is less God as revealed in the texts than Turabi himself as he interprets God's purpose.

References

Al-Turabi, Hasan. 1983. The Islamic State. In *Voices of Resurgent Islam*, ed. John L. Esposito. Oxford University Press, 241–251.
Al-Turabi, Hasan. 1992. "Islam as a Pan-National Movement and Nation States: An Islamic Doctrine on Human Association." Nationhood Lecture presented at the Royal Society of Arts, April 27, London.
Burr, J. M., and Robert O. Collins. 2003. *Revolutionary Sudan: Hasan al-Turabi and the Islamist State, 1989–2000*. Leiden: Brill.
Collins, Robert O. 2008. *A History of Modern Sudan*. Cambridge: Cambridge University Press.
De Waal, Alex, ed. 2004. *Islamism and Its Enemies in the Horn of Africa*. London: Hurst.
El-Affendi, Abdelwahab. 1991. *Turabi's Revolution: Islam and Power in Sudan*. London: Grey Seal.
Gallab, Abdullahi A. 2008. *The First Islamist Republic: Development and Disintegration of Islamism in the Sudan*. Burlington: Ashgate.
Hamdi, Mohamed Elhachmi. 1998. *The Making of an Islamic Political Leader: Conversations with Hasan al-Turabi*. Boulder: Westview.
Ibrahim, Abdullahi Ali. 2008. *Manichaean Delirium: Decolonizing the Judiciary and Islamic Renewal in the Sudan, 1898–1985*. Leiden: Brill.
Simone, T. Abdou Maliqalim. 1994. *In Whose Image?: Political Islam and Urban Practices in Sudan*. Chicago: Chicago University Press.

CHAPTER 14

RASHID AL-GHANNUSHI

AZZAM TAMIMI

Rashid Ghannushi was born on June 22, 1941 in southeastern Tunisia. The youngest of ten brothers and sisters, he grew up in a traditional and observing Muslim community. Within his large extended family, he was particularly impressed by his maternal uncle, Al-Bashir, a staunch supporter of Arabism and a great admirer of its leader President Nassir of Egypt and a member of the Bourguiba-led national liberation movement against the French occupation authorities.

Developing an interest in modern Western literature, in his teens Ghannushi read Arabic translations of Tolstoy's *War and Peace*, Gorky's (1868–1936) *Mother*, and Dostoyevsky's *Crime and Punishment*. He also read some of the works of Irish writer Bernard Shaw (1856–1950), French author Victor Hugo (1802–1885), and American novelist Ernest Millar (1899–1961). The Arab novelists he read included Najib Mahfuz, Yusuf As-Siba`i, Muhammad Abd Al-Halim Abdullah, and Colin Suhail.

When aged eighteen, Ghannushi left the village in 1959 for the capital in pursuit of education at the ancient Arabic-medium A-Zaytouna Institute. The three years he spent in the city exposed him to the identity crisis the conflict between modernity and tradition had created in his country.

In his final high school year, Ghannushi studied philosophy and became passionately fond of arguing about theoretical issues. Yet, the years he spent studying at this historic Islamic institution did not quench his thirst for knowledge nor answer his many questions. Worse still, the Institute's curriculum failed to secure him with confidence about his Islamic faith. Outside the classroom the public sphere was dominated by a Western lifestyle and little within it related to Islam. The students' community of this supposedly religious institution had every reason to be alienated from religion.

Influenced by his maternal uncle, Ghannushi grew up as a Nassirist, a supporter and believer in the pan-Arabism of President Nassir who ruled Egypt between 1952 and 1970. His love and admiration for the Arab *Mashriq* and his displeasure with the situation in Tunisia prompted him to seek refuge in Egypt in pursuit of further education. In 1964, he enrolled with the Faculty of Agriculture at Cairo University. But no less than three months later he was forced to quit because the regimes in Cairo and Tunis decided to reconcile their differences. The presence of anti-Bourguiba students in Egypt was no longer welcome.

Ghannushi thought of escaping to Albania but was advised by a fellow student to go instead to Syria. Once there, he enrolled for a BA in philosophy at Damascus University, where he studied from 1964 to 1968.

While still a student, Ghannushi took time off in 1965 to embark on a seven-month tour of Europe. He traveled by road from Syria to Turkey then on to Bulgaria, Yugoslavia, Germany, France, Belgium, and the Netherlands, earning his living by taking up whatever menial job was available to him.

Intellectually, Ghannushi remained loyal to Nassirism up to the second year of his stay in Damascus. During that period, he underwent a transition from a romantic Arabist to a committed ideologue of Arab nationalism as propagated by Sati` Al-Husri (1879–1968), whose writings were the Arabists' main source of inspiration. Yet, he soon started having misgivings. The foundations of the nationalist ideology crumbled more and more as he progressed in the study of philosophy and as he took a more active part in the intellectual debates of the students' community in Damascus. Soon, his Arab nationalism readings were substituted by Islamic ones. During the last two years of his study in Damascus, he read Muhammad Iqbal, Abu al-`Ala al-Mawdudi, Sayyid Qutb, Muhammad Qutb, Hasan al-Banna, Mustafa al-Siba`i, Malik Bennabi, and Abu al-Hasan al-Nadwi in addition to more traditional writing in various Islamic disciplines.

Searching for a camp that could accommodate both his Arabism and Islamic faith, Ghannushi joined a group of Syrian nationalist students who, after spending hundreds of hours debating the Arab situation and the means of bringing about an Arab renaissance, started having their doubts about the nationalist discourse. In their company, he moved from one Islamic study circle to another, acquainting himself with Islam and Islamic movements. He met with members the *Ikhwan* (the Muslim Brotherhood), with a group of followers of Shaykh Nassir al-Din al-Albani and with some elements of Hizb alTahrir al-Islami (the Islamic Liberation Party). In addition, he made the acquaintance of a number of scholars who were active in Damascus at the time, such as Shaykh Habannaka, Shaykh Adib al-Salih, Shaykh Sa'id Ramadan al-Buti, Shaykh Wahba al-Zuhayli, and Jawdat Sa`id, whom he thought was a very distinguished and impressive personality.

The divorce with nationalism led Ghannushi to the rediscovery of Islam. The night of June 15, 1966 was a turning point and a landmark in his life; that was the night he embraced what he called the true Islam, Islam as revealed and not as shaped or distorted by history and tradition. That night he felt he was reborn with the determination to review and reflect on all that which he had previously conceived.

Following his graduation from Damascus University in the summer of 1968, Ghannushi left Syria for France to pursue his postgraduate studies in philosophy at the Sorbonne. He had not been back to Tunisia since he left it in 1964. France seemed the right place to go. For, should he hope to be recognized in Tunisia upon his return home, he needed to have acquired an academic qualification from France.

Most of the Tunisian students in Paris at the time were communists or Arab nationalists. As a committed Islamist by then, it would have been unthinkable, let alone comfortable, for him to associate with any of these. Soon a small nucleus of Islamist Tunisian students took shape. In addition to Ghannushi, the group included Ahmida Enneifer and Ahmed Manai. In the meantime, Ghannushi frequented a circle at the local mosque belonging to Tablighi Jama`at, a branch of the Indian-based apolitical movement founded in 1926 by the Sufi scholar Mawlana Muhammad Ilyas (1885–1944). The rule within the *Tabligh* group was such that new recruits were expected to make a four-month pilgrimage to Pakistan, and in the case of a "cultured" recruit like Ghannushi it would have been seven months, where he would have undergone initiation and would have been fully indoctrinated. He would have gone there had it not been for an unexpected turn of events.

Upon the completion of his first year of study in Paris, Ghannushi was summoned home to see his mother, whom he was told was rather sick. He traveled home by land via Spain in the company of his elder brother, who was dispatched on a rescue mission to fetch young Ghannushi and deliver him from the "claws" of extreme religiosity.

On the way back home, Ghannushi had an opportunity to stop by at the grand mosque in Cordoba that had been turned into a museum. There, he wrested a guard who endeavored to prevent him from praying at the mosque. Then, transiting in Algiers, he met Algerian Islamic thinker Malik Bennabi for the first time.

Instead of returning to Paris to resume his studies, Ghannushi decided to stay at home. The country was in better shape than he expected. It was not family pressure that succeeded in holding him back but what he believed were promising signs of Islamic revival. A study circle he accidentally came across in one of the mosques convinced him that his country needed him.

Working as a high school philosophy teacher, he joined others in founding *al-Jama'a al-Islamiya* (the Islamic Group). The group used as a platform the government-sponsored Qur'anic Preservation Society (QPS). For a number of years henceforth, he and other founding members of *al-Jama'a*, Shaykh Abdelfattah Moro, al-Fadhil Al-Baladi, Salih bin Abdullah, and Ahmida Enneifer, traveled regularly to Algeria to attend Malik Bennabi's annual Islamic Thought Seminar. This was the period, from 1970 to 1972, that saw Ghannushi's gradual conversion from Qutb's school of thought to that of Bennabi, whose critique of Qutb was the first in a series of experiences that shook his confidence in the thought of al-Mashriq (Arab East).

Ghannushi first drew Tunisian public attention when an article by him entitled "Barnamij al-Falsafah wa Jil al-Daya'" (The Philosophy Curriculum and the Generation of Loss) was published in a leading Tunisian daily newspaper. Sharply criticizing the education system in Tunisia, the article rejected the notion that Western ideas were absolutes accepting them only as possible, albeit partial, explanations of human conduct and of human history. At the same time, he started reading the Qur'an with a new insight. He discovered that, in the Qur'anic discourse, the economy was an essential dimension. He began to realize that a comprehensive reading of Islam would lead one to conclude that economic, political, sexual, and social factors had already been sufficiently emphasized in the Qur'an, and therefore denying the effect such factors have on people's lives, as he used to do, was a mistake.

Upon his return to Tunisia from France, Ghannushi conceived a thought acquired through reading the writings of *Ikhwan* leaders and ideologues including Hasan al-Banna, Sayyid Qutb, Abdel-Qadir 'Awdah, Muhammad al-Ghazali, and Yusuf al-Qaradawi as well as the writings of Mawdudi. Yet, until the Tunisian government outlawed *al-Jama'a al-Islamiya* in 1973, the group emulated the method of the *Tabligh Jamaat*. The banning of the group prompted him to question the utility of the open activity of the *Tabligh*, which might have worked more successfully in an open environment such as that of India or Pakistan or of Western Europe, where basic freedoms are guaranteed. From then on, *al-Jama'a* was compelled to adopt an *Ikhwan* style of dual, clandestine/public, activism.

Working locally, it did not take Ghannushi long to reconnect with what he discovered to be a Tunisian Islamic legacy treasured by the country's most prestigious institute, al-Zaytouna, whose scholars played a significant role in the modernization endeavor that preceded the colonial era. Ghannushi deemed it essential for him and his group to be perceived as the rightful inheritors of the nineteenth-century Tunisian reform effort of Khayr al-Din al-Tunsi (1810–1899), prime minister and author of a book entitled *Aqwam al-Masalik fi Ma'rifat Ahwal al-Mamalik* (The Surest Path to Learning the Conditions of States).

As part of his mission to reconnect with the Tunisian Islamic legacy, Ghannushi returned to al-Zaytouna in search of his roots, studying the writings of Tunisian Islamic thinkers, which together with those of Bennabi constituted what he called the *Magharibi* Islamic heritage.

By the mid-seventies, Ghannushi's Islamic movement acquired a Tunisian characteristic that, according to him, was the product of the interaction of three main components: (1) *al-tadayun al-taqlidi al-Tunisi* (the traditional Tunisian religiosity), which is composed of three elements: the *Maliki* school of jurisprudence, the *ash'ariyah* doctrine of theology, and Sufism; (2) the *salafi* religiosity, of the type he embraced initially following the example of the *Mashariqi* Islamic thought; and (3) *al-tadayun al-'aqlani* (rational religiosity).

In the second half of the seventies, Ghannushi and his group started interacting and communicating with other political and intellectual groups within Tunisia, including the nationalists and the leftists. This coincided with arrival in Tunisia of some of the writings of former members of the *Ikhwan* in Egypt such as Fathi Osman. These writings, which were critical of the *Ikhwan*, prompted a revival of what Ghannushi called *al-turath al-islami al-'aqlani* (the Islamic heritage of rationality) as expressed by the *Mu'tazilah* school of thought.

The strategy of *'aqlana* soon led to a split. Some of Ghannushi's colleagues wanted to pursue it further while others were apprehensive that it might eventually lead to undermining the sacredness of revelation itself by emphasizing reason at the expense of the text. The rationalists, known later as *al-yasar al-islami* (the Islamic left), wanted also to restore recognition and respect for Western culture.

The rationalists' critique of the *Ikhwan* targeted in particular the thought of Sayyid Qutb, whose theory of *jahiliyah* (barbarity) called for *mufasalah* (alienation and departure) from blasphemous society by the community of believers, which he considered to be the *ummah*.

Ghannushi did not entirely disagree with the rationalists' critique of Qutb. Nor did he disagree with them on the need to restore respect for the reformist school of the nineteenth and early twentieth centuries. However, he did not condone their skeptical attitude toward the sacred text, nor did he accept the extension of their critique to the entire *Ikhwan-Salafi* school. Above all, he disliked their suggestion that the *al-burguibiyah* (Bourguibism, referring to the reforms introduced by President Bourguiba) was an extension of the Tunisian reformist school of Khayr al-Din and al-Tahir al-Haddad.

From the mid-seventies to the early eighties Ghannushi's thought and the development of his movement's political standing were influenced by a series of major developments. Locally, there was the liberal democratic current that emerged in Tunisia in the second half of the seventies followed by the 1978 violent confrontation between the trade unions and the government. Regionally, there was the Iranian Revolution and the sociopolitical thought of the Islamic movement in Sudan under the leadership of Hasan al-Turabi.

The communication with the Tunisian democrats coincided with demands for *muhasaba* (accountability) and *ma'sasah* (institutionalization) by some members of al-Jama'a al-Islamiya. These demands prompted the convening of a general conference in 1979, the year of the Khomeini-led Iranian Revolution, henceforth referred to as *al-mu'tamar at-ta'sisi* (the Founding Conference). In addition to adopting a constitution, the conference elected for the first time the top leadership of the movement, which consisted of a *shura* council, an executive bureau, and a president. Ghannushi was the first president.

As democracy was rapidly becoming a primary issue for political opposition trends within Tunisia, including his own, Ghannushi felt the need to revive the democratic thought of nineteenth-century Islamic reformers that had been obscured by the proliferation across the Arab region of the antidemocracy thought, primarily as expressed in the writings of Sayyid Qutb.

The Khomeini-led Islamic Revolution had a considerable impact on Ghannushi and his Tunisian Islamic movement. One important intellectual contribution of the Iranian Revolution was its presentation of the conflict between the poor and the rich as a conflict between the oppressor and the oppressed. The Iranian Revolution seemed to shake what had remained of the foundations of *Mashariqi* thought. Ghannushi was particularly impressed with what he believed was Khomeini's success in uniting behind him all political trends within Iran by mobilizing the oppressed in the name of Islam. Ghannushi's enthusiasm for the Iranian Revolution led him to regard Khomeini a *mujaddid* (a renewer). He believed that three such persons existed in the twentieth century: al-Banna in Egypt, Mawdudi in India, and Khomeini in Iran.

A visit to Sudan in 1979 acquainted Ghannushi with a different model of Islamic activism. The most striking aspect of this model was the liberal attitude toward women. In the Sudanese model women participated fully in the political and social programs of the Islamic movement. In contrast, the Tunisian Islamists had been influenced by *Mashariqi* thought, which was highly critical of the status of women in the West and warned against the dangers posed to family life by liberal attitudes.

Back in Tunisia in 1980, Ghannushi delivered a speech in which he strongly criticized his movement's previous position on women and called for a review in favor of affirming the principle of equality between the sexes. He called for the immediate lifting of any restrictions by members of his group on the education of women and stressed the need for training and developing Islamic women leaders. His remarks reflected a radical change of position, especially as he stressed that the innocent mixing of men and women was not prohibited and that polygamy was not an Islamic duty.

Until about 1984, Ghannushi strongly opposed the Tunisian Personal Status Code and denounced the law prohibiting polygamy. Yet, in 1988, encouraged by Ben Ali's announcement upon assuming power that he would democratize the regime, Ghannushi announced that his movement accepted the Personal Status Code.

Earlier in 1981, Bourguiba Prime Minister Mohamed Mzali announced that his government would allow the formation of political parties in prelude to calling for parliamentary elections. In response, Ghannushi, who a year earlier took the precautionary measure of dissolving al-Jama'a, announced the formation of the of the Mouvement de la Tendence Islamique (MTI). The MTI manifesto expressed the movement's commitment to democratic process, including pluralism and the sharing and alternation of power, and stated that the democratic process should exclude no one, not even communists, and affirmed that the electoral process was the source of legitimacy.

On July 17, 1981, the leaders of MTI and five hundred of its members were arrested. Imprisoned from 1981 to 1984, Ghannushi later said he felt his incarceration was a break he used for contemplation and reflection. In prison, he memorized the Holy Qur'an and studied a number of classical works in different Islamic sciences. He read Ibn Taymiyah, Abu Hamid al-Ghazali, Ibn Rushd, Ibn Hazm, al-Zamakhshari, al-Qarafi, Ibn 'Ashur, and a number of more contemporary authors including the Iraqi Shiite philosopher Baqir As-Sadr.

In 1983 he started working on the draft of a treatise, which he entitled *al-Mujtama' al-Tunisi: Tahlil Hadari* (Tunisian Society: A Civilizational Analysis), with the purpose of reflecting on the path of the movement and the situation of society so as to reinforce positive elements and avoid negative ones, to clarify the image of the aspired civilizational alternative and to determine the short-term objectives and the means of accomplishing them. In addition, he undertook a number of projects, one of which was to study a translation of a book on women by Roger Garaudy, which inspired him—together with his recent experience in Sudan—to write a treatise on women rights and on the status of women inside the Islamic movement. One other important project he undertook while in custody was the translation of a booklet authored by Malik Bennabi entitled *all-Islam wa al-Dimuqratiyah* (Islam and Democracy), which inspired him to begin working on his most important book, *al-Hurriyat al-'Amma fi al-Dawla al-Islamiya* (Public Liberties in the Islamic State).

While in prison, he wrote a piece about the centrality of the Palestinian issue and another one about the relations with Iran in which he criticized the Iranians for the first time since their revolution. This was in response to what was communicated to him of an attack launched in an Iranian Revolutionary Guards' bulletin against a number of Islamic movements in the Arab world, including the Muslim Brotherhood of Egypt and the MTI of Tunisia, accusing them of being counterrevolutionaries and lackeys of the West.

Following his release from prison, and in response to what he perceived as a concentrated endeavor to undermine the guarantees that Islam provided to safeguard public and individual liberties and to protect the rights of political and religious minorities and the rights of women, Ghannushi set out to defend Islam and refute all those allegations made against its social and political systems. As he embarked on this mission he discovered that so much distortion had also been made about the nature of the Western civilization itself and most importantly about the concept of democracy. He felt obliged to remove himself from the tide of everyday life and devote it to the task of finishing what he had started in prison, working on his public liberties book. But no sooner had he finished working on the manuscript than he was once again arrested and held in detention.

In August 1987, Ghannushi and eighty-nine other MTI leading members were brought to trial before the State Security Court, accused of inciting violence and seeking to change the nature of the state. Ghannushi's death sentence was commuted to life imprisonment with labor but Bourguiba ordered a retrial insisting on a death sentence. However, on November 7, 1987, Bourguiba was toppled in a bloodless coup and the new president, Zine El Abidine Ben Ali, ordered the release of Ghannushi and his comrades.

The initial period of President Ben Ali's era saw a commitment to the creation of a multiparty system. In an attempt to gain recognition under a new law, Ghannushi, in December 1988, changed the name of his organization from of the MTI to Harakat al-Nahdah (The Renaissance Movement, written in English as Ennahda), dropping the reference to Islam from its title.

Still not officially licensed despite having lodged an application, Ennahda members ran as independents competing for 129 of the 141 available parliamentary seats in the elections of April 1989. Ennahda-backed independents emerged as the largest opposition force, winning 14.5 percent of the national vote and as much as 30 percent in some urban centers, including Tunis, the capital. On June 6, 1989 Ennahda's application for the status of a political party was rejected, leaving its supporters liable to prosecution on grounds of membership in an illegal organization, an offence punishable by up to five years' imprisonment. Despite Ennahda's impressive showing at the polls, none of its candidates were returned to parliament. In fact, all seats in parliament were awarded to candidates from the ruling Rassemblement Constitutionel Démocratique (RCD) party.

The elections, which were supposed to mark the beginning of a new era of national reconciliation, triggered a government campaign aimed at the complete uprooting of the Tunisian Islamic movement.

In May 1989 Ghannushi fled the country ending up in London, where he has remained ever since. Ghannushi seemed to take the entire organization into exile with him. His departure was to be followed by a series of measures by the regime of President Ben Ali aimed at discrediting and crushing Ennahda once and for all. In January 1991, Ghannushi's deputy Abd al-Fattah Mourou fell victim to a government-sponsored defamation campaign that brought an end to his career. In February of that same year, an arson attack on the ruling party's offices in the Bab Souika district, allegedly carried out by members of the movement, was seized upon by the government as proof of the violent and antidemocratic nature of Ennahda.

Having felt responsible for what had happened to the movement, Ghannushi preferred to leave the task of pursuing the political struggle to somebody else while dedicating his life in exile to further scholarship and to the completion of unfinished writings. But Ennahda members insisted there was a much greater benefit for the movement in his dedicating a greater part of his time and effort to the leadership of the movement. His exiled comrades believed that in view of the tough circumstances experienced by their movement and their country, Ghannushi was obliged to remain in the field where he was most needed.

It was in his exile in London that Ghannushi finally had the opportunity to return to his book and finish it. Published by the renowned Centre of Arab Unity Studies in Beirut in 1993, al-Hurriyat al-'Amma fi al—Dawla al-Islamiya (Public Liberties in the Islamic State) is an important reference in contemporary Islamic political thought, especially on the discussions within the house of Islamism on issues such as civil liberties, democracy, and the aspired to system of good governance.

In his book, Ghannushi defines the ideal system of governance as one that recognizes and protects the dignity of man and provides guarantees for stemming despotism and creating the right climate for the blossoming of man's potential. It is the system in which the political, economic, and cultural gaps between the "ruled" and the "ruler" diminish until they disappear altogether.

While admiring the achievements of liberal democracy, Ghannushi is sharply critical of its philosophies underpinning a worldview that according to him drives a wedge between the soul and the body and is therefore incapable of balancing man's different needs. He believes that an Islamic model of democracy may arise out of a marriage between liberal democratic tools and procedures on the one hand and the Islamic code of ethics and values on the other, thus averting some of the negative features of liberal democracy and its many broken promises. He laments, however, that the emergence of this model in the Muslim world is hindered by a number of obstacles. Ghannushi's ideas about the obstacles impeding democratization in the Arab world, and particularly in the North African region, are subsequent to the publication of his public liberties book and may be the outcome of contemplating the failure of the democratic processes in both Algeria and Tunisia.

The late nineties saw Ghannushi write, in Arabic, about some of these obstacles for the first time. Undoubtedly, his first ten years of exile in London gave much food for thought, having had the opportunity to discuss these ideas with a good number of other Arab exiles as well as with Western thinkers whom he met individually or at workshops and conferences.

He came to the conclusion that the enforced secularization of Arab societies, which began during colonial days, as well as the erosion of traditional institutions, which equaled modern-day civil society institutions, are the main obstacles hindering democratization. Furthermore, foreign powers, which constitute the New World Order, and local elites that share interests with these powers would not want to see genuine democratization in this part of the world simply because they believe it would harm their mutual interests.

While Ghannushi is critical of secularism as a whole, he does distinguish between Western secularism and the secularism that evolved, and is being advocated, in the Arab and Muslim countries. While the evolution of secularism in the West was associated with the need by reformists, especially during the Renaissance, to free their societies from the constraints imposed on them by the Church, secularism in the Arab and Muslim societies was imported by the colonial authorities and imposed by autocracies that took shape in the postcolonial era. Rather than bring about democratization, the Arab version of secularism of which Ghannushi is critical has given rise to some of the most despotic and corrupt regimes in modern history.

Ghannushi's more recent book *Muqarabat fi al-'Almaniyya wa al-Mujtama' al-Madani* (Approaches to Secularism and Civil Society) has documented his ideas on secularism and civil society. These ideas were developed through a series of encounters and exchanges with academics and thinkers he met during his stay in London including John Keane, John Esposito, Ernest Gillner, John Voll, Luis Cantori, Abd al-Wahhab al-Messiri, Fahmi Huwaidi, Muhammad Salim Al-'Awwa, and Tariq al-Bishri.

Ghannushi has argued strongly against the monopoly of the concept of civil society by Arab secularists who deny such a status to Islamic institutions in Arab societies. As far as he is concerned all nongovernmental organizations (NGOs) qualify for the category of civil society whether they are secular or religious. Ghannushi is unprecedented within Islamic intellectual circles in his theory that civil society is an Islamic concept and that religion consolidates civil society whereas secularism, especially the model imported to the Muslim world under the guise of modernization, weakens it.

Among contemporary Islamic thinkers and activists, Rashid Ghannushi is distinguished by his daring and innovative endeavors to introduce new dimensions in contemporary Islamic thought. The impact of his ideological and intellectual standing has extended well beyond the frontiers of Tunisia. His contribution to modern Islamic thought lies in his comprehension of both traditional Islamic literature and modern Western theories and in his strong belief in the compatibility of Islam with Western thought in matters concerning the system of government, human rights, and civil liberties.

Unlike other Islamic thinkers who espouse the democratic cause, Ghannushi is both a thinker and a leader of an Islamic movement. Perhaps this is one reason he has acquired acceptability within many Islamic circles at the global level. However, this may in some other respect be a source of vulnerability. His position as leader of the main opposition party in his country requires him to take certain political factors into consideration, and this in turn is bound to give an impression of an inconsistency in his discourse. As a political leader he has been, on more than an occasion, compelled to make compromises, the most notable of which was his decision to remove the reference to Islam from the name of his movement in order to qualify for registering as a legal political party and reversing the movement's position vis-à-vis the Tunisian Personal Status Code to which he was previously vehemently opposed.

Undoubtedly, Ghannushi's dual role as a political activist and a political thinker imposes a limitation on his mission as thinker engaged in the project of Islamic revival. On certain occasions Ghannushi speaks more as a politician while on others speaks more as a thinker employing a discourse that corresponds to the level and nature of his audience. Sometimes it is too sophisticated for an average Muslim to relate to. Sometimes it is more of political analysis than of philosophical argumentation. On occasions it may even be too populist.

Being a political leader can be a liability in addition to being a heavy burden. The events that led to his exile and the banning of his movement have cost Ghannushi some popularity among his own followers. Yet, he never hesitated to take the blame for his movement's failures, an attitude that is rare among Arab opposition leaders. He regretted trusting President Ben Ali, who upon coming to power promised to start a new democratic era of freedom and power sharing that turned to be a despotic era of oppression and persecution. While some disgruntled and former members of the movement charge that Ghannushi was not qualified as political leader, he continued to be democratically elected as leader of Ennahda.

As a thinker and political leader, Ghannushi's primary concern has been to see the restoration of just and good governance to his own country Tunisia as well as Muslim lands. He has advocated democracy as the best means of achieving this objective, arguing within Islamic circles that the difficulty to extrude, completely, democratic procedures and mechanisms from their liberal philosophical packaging should not be an excuse for Muslims to deprive themselves of the opportunity to get rid of the authoritarian regimes that burdened them and hampered their progress for many decades.

In pursuit of political reform Ghannushi has followed the footsteps of nineteenth- and twentieth-century reformists such as Rifa'a al-Tahtawi (1801–1873), Khayr al-Din al-Tunsi (1810–1899), Jamal al-Din al-Afghani (1838–1897), Muhammad 'Abduh (1849–1905), Abd al-Rahman al-Kawakibi (1849–1903), Muhammad Rashid Rida (1865–1935), al-Tahir al-Haddad (1899–1935), Muhammad Iqbal (1877–1938), and Malik Bennabi (1905–1973), building on their achievements and learning from their experiences. Like most of these reformers, he has tried to assimilate specific Western concepts and ideas, incorporating them into the Islamic discourse on reform and revival. His objective, like theirs, has been the accomplishment of an Islamic renaissance that is founded in Islamic values and capable of benefiting, at the same time, from the positive aspects of Western modernity.

While a firm believer that Divine Revelation for Muslims is the ultimate frame of reference, Ghannushi sees in Western modernity positive aspects that are not only of great benefit but may also be indispensable for a modern Islamic revival.

Ghannushi remains a very important and influential Islamic thinker whose contribution to Islamic political thought will undoubtedly be remembered by future generations and reflected upon by posterity just as he himself used to reflect upon the contributions of great men such as al-Tunisi, Afghani, Iqbal, and Bennabi.

Ghannushi's Published Books in Chronological Order

Tariquna Ila al-Hadara, al-Ma`rifa Publications, Tunis, 1975.
Al-Hraka al-Islamiya wa al-Tahdith, Dar al-Jeel, Beirut, 1980.
Maqalat [Articles], a collection of Ghannushi's articles, Dar al-Karawan, Paris, 1984.
Huquq al-Muwatanah, Huquq Ghayr al-Muslim fi-Mujtama' al-Islami, The International Institute of Islamic Thought, Virginia, 1993. (First published in Tunisia in 1989.)
Al-Qadar `Inda Ibn Taymiyah, Halq al-Wadi, Tunis, 1989.
The Right to Nationality Status of Non-Muslim Citizens in a Muslim Nation. Translated by M. A. al-Iryan, Islamic Foundation of America, 1990.
Min al-Fikr al-Islami fiTunis [From the Islamic Thought], Dar- al-Qalam, Kuwait, 1992 (two volumes).
Al-Mar'ah al-Muslimah fi Tunis Bayna Tawjihat al-Qur'an wa Waqi' al-Mujtama` al-Tunisi, Dar al-Qalam, Kuwait, 1993.
*Al-Hurriyat al-`Amma fi al-Dawla Al-Islamiyya* [Public Liberties in the Islamic State], Markaz Dirasat al-Wihda al-`Arabiyah, Beirut, 1993.
Al-Mabadi al-Asasiya li al-Dimuqratiya wa-Usul al-Hukm al-Islami [The Basic Principles of Democracy and the Fundamentals of Islamic Governance], Al-Furqan Publications, Casablanca, 1994.
Muqarabat fi al-`Ilmaniyyah` wa al-Mujtama` al-Madani [Approaches to Secularism and Civil Society], Maghreb Center for Researches & Translation, London, 1999.
Al-Harakah al-Islamiyyah wa Mas'alat al-Taghyir [The Islamic Movement and the Question of Change], Maghreb Center for Researches & Translation, London, 2000.

Other English Bibliography

F. Burgat and W. Dowell, *The Islamic Movement in North Africa*, Austin, TX: University of Texas Press, 1993.
J. Davis, *Between Jihad and Salaam: Profiles in Islam*, New York: St. Martin's Press, 1997.
M. Dunn, "The Al-Nahda Movement in Tunisia: From Renaissance to Revolution," in *Islamism and Secularism in North Africa*, ed. John Rudy, London: Macmillan, 1994.
A. El-Affendi, "The Long March Forward," in *The Inquiry*, October 1987.
K. Elgindy, "The Rhetoric of Rachid Ghannouchi," *Arab Studies Journal*, Spring 1995.
M. Hamdi, *An Analysis of the History and Discourse of the Tunisian Islamic Movement al-Nahda—A Case Study of the Politicization of Islam*, Ph.D. dissertation, School of Oriental and African Studies, University of London, July 1996.
E. Hermassi, "The Islamicist Movement and November 7" in *Tunisia: The Political Economy of Reform*, ed. I. William Zartman, Lynne Rienner, London, 1991.
N. Hicks, *Promise Unfulfiled: Human Rights in Tunisia Since 1987*, The Lawyers Committee for Human Rights, New York, October 1993.
L. Jones, "Portrait of Rachid al-Ghannouchi" *Middle East Report*, July–August 1988.
D. Magnuson, "Islamic Reform in Contemporary Tunisia: Unity and Diversity" in *Tunisia: the Political Economy of Reform*, ed. I. William Zartman, Lynne Rienner, London, 1991.
A. Zghal, "The New Strategy of the Movement of the Islamic Way: Manipulation or Expression of Political Culture?" in *Tunisa: the Political Economy of Reform*, ed. I. William Zartman, London: Lynne Rienner, 1991.

CHAPTER 15

YUSUF AL-QARADAWI

BETTINA GRÄF

Egyptian Scholar and Activist

The Egyptian-born Yusuf al-Qaradawi is one of the most popular and at the same time highly controversial religious scholars in today's Sunni Islam. He was born in 1926 in the village of Saft al-Turab in the Nile Delta into a rural family of modest means.[1] His father died when he was two years old. He was then raised in his mother's family, who were fruit merchants. He received his primary education in a Qur'anic school (*kuttab*) and memorized the Qur'an at the age of ten. In 1939 he entered an Azhari school in Tanta, a commercial and industrial center in the Egyptian province Gharbiyya, and subsequently went to study at Azhar University in Cairo in 1949. Al-Qaradawi first enrolled in the Faculty of Theology (*usul al-din*) and later transferred to the Arab Language Faculty. He graduated in 1953 as the top student in his class.

Al-Qaradawi got involved in politics at an early age. He was in his teens when he became an admirer of Hasan al-Banna, the founder of the Egyptian Muslim Brothers, after listening to his speeches during the 1940s. In 1942–1943 al-Qaradawi became a member of the Brothers himself. Founded in 1928, the Muslim Brothers advocated an Islamic set of rules in all spheres of life and fought against the appropriation of Egypt by the British colonialists. In the years preceding the Egyptian revolution of 1952 al-Qaradawi took part in student strikes and demonstrations against the British protectoral power. He traveled to Upper Egypt, Syria, Jordan, and Palestine on behalf of the Brothers. In addition he became committed to the modernization of al-Azhar, advocating, among other things, the introduction of English into the curriculum and the admission of female students. During those days, he received the unfailing support of his mentor, the Muslim Brother and Azhar scholar Muhammad al-Ghazali (1909–1996).[2]

Al-Qaradawi was arrested after Hasan al-Banna's assassination in 1949. In 1954, under the Nasser administration, he was twice interned in the military prison of Cairo, along with thousands of fellow Muslim Brothers; and the Brothers were again banned, this time for good, although they continued to exist. Following his release from prison in 1956, al-Qaradawi resumed his studies but not his involvement with the Muslim Brothers. He was officially banned from preaching and teaching in public. Part-time employment at the Ministry of Awqaf and giving private lessons enabled him to make his living.

Before entering al-Azhar in 1957 to undertake further studies, he spent one year at the Department of Arabic Language and Literature at the Arab League's Institute of Higher Studies. For a short period in 1957 he was even allowed to preach at the Zamalek mosque. He passed the qualifying examination at al-Azahr's Faculty of *Usul al-Din* and decided to specialize in Qur'an exegesis and *Hadith*. A year later he started working in the Department of Culture at al-Azhar University. Departmental director Muhammad al-Bahy and the grand imam (Shaykh al-Azhar), reformist scholar Mahmud Shaltut, both encouraged al-Qaradawi to compose his first and most influential book to date, *The Lawful and the Prohibited in Islam*, which was published in 1960. Shortly afterward, in 1961, al-Qaradawi applied for a position at one of al-Azhar's institutes abroad. He left Egypt and went to Qatar, where he was sent to direct a newly established institute of religious studies in Doha. He taught the son of the emir in Ramadan, Shaykh Khalifa b. Hamad Al Thani, who would later become the emir of Qatar (1972–1995). When the Egyptian authorities refused to extend al-Qaradawi's stay in Qatar, the emir offered him a permanent position and a Qatari passport.[3]

Qatar has been an important location for al-Qaradawi in many respects. First, this is where he lived for nearly two-thirds of his life and where his children were born and went to school (although they later left Qatar and went to study in Europe and the United States).[4] Second, upon arriving in Doha he immediately began to preach and give religious instruction during Ramadan. He was also instrumental in shaping the religious education system in Doha, which used to be part of the same Wahhabi and Hanbali branch of Islam as neighboring Saudi Arabia. Third, with the help of his Qatari passport he was able to cross national borders without difficulties.[5] Fourth, he had the means and resources to invite fellow colleagues to Qatar and often played a key role in organizing meetings for scholars and activists, including Muslim Brothers from Egypt and beyond.[6] In comparison to Egypt, Qatar was a safe haven where one could meet and work without interference.

However, al-Qaradawi has never lost contact with Egypt. Ever since Anwar al-Sadat succeeded Nasser as president of the country in 1970, al-Qaradawi has been travelling to his home country regularly. In 1973 the Azhar University awarded him his doctoral degree for his thesis on almsgiving in Islam (*zakat*). In the same year he became director of the Department of Islamic Studies at the newly founded College of Education at Qatar University. This was transformed into the Shari`ah Faculty in 1977–1978, and he served as dean there for many years. He founded the Centre for Sunna and Sira Studies in 1980 as part of Qatar University. Most of his employees there later went to work for the newly established Internet portal IslamOnline.net.

Since the 1970s he has traveled widely throughout the Arab world, as well as to Europe, the United States, Canada, Australia, and Asia, including Japan. He has been invited to conferences to deliver lectures and give interviews. Since the first Islamic banks and investment companies were established in the early 1970s, he has served as consultant or as a member of the board of advisers.[7] He is an associate of major Islamic institutions such as the Board of Trustees of the International Islamic University in Islamabad (created in 1980), the Union des Organisations Islamiques de France (UOIF, founded in 1983), and the Oxford Centre for Islamic Studies (founded in 1985). He is also a member of the Islamic Fiqh Academy of the Muslim World League (founded in Mecca in 1962) and the Organization of the Islamic Conference (since 2011 the Organization of Islamic Cooperation, founded in Rabat in 1969).

After al-Qaradawi retired, he spent the academic year 1990/1991 in Algeria as chairman of the Higher Institutes of Islamic Studies. He never returned to al-Azhar nor did he go back to the Muslim Brothers although he was asked to become their supreme leader (*al-murshid al-ʿamm*) twice, the last time in 2002 after the death of Mustafa Mashhur. However, at the age of eighty-four he returned to lead the prayer at Tahrir Square in Cairo in February 2011 one week after Hosni Mubarak was swept away by the Egyptian revolution.

Books and Subjects

To date Yusuf al-Qaradawi has written over 100 books—mostly paperback—and many journal articles. He addresses at least three different groups: scholars of Islamic jurisprudence, activists seeking the reform of contemporary society, and a wider public that goes beyond the circles of intellectuals and activists. He is involved in debates about Islamic jurisprudence (*fiqh*) and its conflicted relationship with social reality (*fiqh al-waqiʿ*), Islamic reformist thinking since the nineteenth century, and the so-called Islamic Awakening (*al-sahwa al-islamiyya*), which has evolved since the 1970s.[8] His main concerns are the economy in Islam, the role of women in society, education and the bringing up of children, art and entertainment, colonialism, the issue of Palestine, secularism, and minorities. This last addresses both the life of non-Muslims in Muslim societies and that of Muslims in non-Muslim societies (*fiqh al-aqalliyyat*).[9] In his published work he has dealt with notions of *tajdid* (renewal), *al-hall al-islami* (the Islamic solution), and *taysir* (ease), as well as the newly coined concepts of *wasatiyya* (moderation or the middle way) and *shumuliyya* (comprehensiveness).[10]

Besides *The Lawful and the Prohibited in Islam* (1960),[11] al-Qaradawi's best-known books include *The Islamic Awakening between Rejection and Extremism* (1982),[12] *Creative Legal Reasoning in the Present between Discipline and Detachment* (1994),[13] *Secular Extremism in Confrontation with Islam. The Examples of Turkey and Tunisia* (2001),[14] *Study in Maqasid al-Shariʿa. Between Universal Intentions and Specific Texts* (2006).[15] Only *The Lawful and the Prohibited in Islam* and *The Islamic Awakening between Rejection and Extremism* are translated into English.[16] His dissertation *Fiqh al-Zakat* on alms in contemporary Islam, which does not address as wide a readership as his other books, was published in two volumes in 1971. Al-Qaradawi also writes poetry. But although he was raised in an environment where Sufi practices were usual, he was never attracted by Sufism or Sufis.[17]

His books are mostly composed as parts of various series, such as the Series toward an *Intellectual Unity for the Activists of Islam*,[18] which is a commentary on Hasan al-Banna's "Twenty Principles,"[19] or the one on *Ease in Islamic Jurisprudence for the Contemporary Muslim in the Light of Qurʾan and Sunna*,[20] which brings together al-Qaradawi's books on contemporary Islamic religious practice. Another popular publication is the Series for the *Guidance of the Awakening*[21].

Al-Qaradawi's writings have developed over time and he has revised his opinion on certain topics, for example on the participation of women in social and political life,[22] on democracy and political pluralism,[23] and on the concept of *wasatiyya*.[24] These changes are best illustrated in his fatwa collections, which are his only hardcover publications.[25] They have been published so far in four volumes by the publishing house Dar al-Qalam in Kuwait (1979, 1993, 2003, and 2009) with many reprints, including those by other publishers.

Al-Qaradawi's self-definition as a scholar and activist as well as details of his life and thoughts can be found in his memoirs, *Son of the Village and the Kuttab: Characteristics of the Trajectory*, four volumes of which have been published so far.[26]

CALL FOR THE COLLECTIVE AWAKENING OF ARAB–ISLAMIC IDENTITY

Yusuf al-Qaradawi is considered to be intellectually independent of the major Islamic institutions, which in the last century mainly served national interests, as is the case with al-Azhar in Egypt.[27] His work takes up the ideas of the early twentieth-century Islamic reformers. In contrast to those scholars, however, al-Qaradawi does not base his thoughts on the adaptation of Islam to modern requirements. His goal is to develop Islamic answers to the questions of the era. What lies behind this is the notion of an Islamization of modernity and the attempt to give the modern age an Islamic face. Since the 1970s he has applied himself to the so-called Islamic Awakening project (*al-sahwa al-islamiyya*). As a consequence of a new religiosity among the population after Nasser's socialist experiment failed, including the—in the eyes of many—disastrous defeat in the Six Day War in 1967 (*naksa*), Islamic scholars and intellectuals began to push for Islamic renewal in both Egypt and other societies. Al-Qaradawi is regarded to this day as one of the leading minds of a transnational network of Islamic intellectuals pursuing similar goals in their respective nation-states. What they have in common beyond an interest in national affairs is a moral allegiance to the Islamic community (*umma*).[28] Just like al-Qaradawi, most of these intellectuals are close to the Muslim Brothers but without necessarily being organized into Islamic factions. These scholars and intellectuals communicate beyond national borders, for example, via journals, such as *al-Muslim al-Mu'asir*, *al-Umma*, *al-Ijtihad*, or *al-Manar al-Jadid*.

INSTITUTIONAL NETWORKING

Another way for those scholars and activists to communicate is via the International Union for Muslim Scholars (IUMS), founded in Dublin in 2004 with Yusuf al-Qaradawi as chairman. The intellectual Muhammad Salim al-'Awwa, the attorney for the Egyptian Wasat Party, became the secretary-general, with the former Mauritanian justice minister 'Abdallah Bayn Bihi, the Shiite cleric Ayatollah Muhammad 'Ali al-Taskhiri, and the Ibadite Shaykh Ahmad al-Khalili as his deputies. The union established its own website in Arabic, which puts out news as well as publishing studies and pronouncements.[29] IUMS describes itself as a nongovernmental body, whose objective is to establish a global Islamic authority (*al-marji'iyya al-islamiyya al-'alamiyya*). The main characteristics of IUMS are that it is Islamic (i.e., it represents all Islamic schools and groupings), global, people oriented, independent (i.e., it is not connected to governments or political parties), scientific (referring to *'ilm*, i.e., a union of *'ulama'*), missionary, and moderate. The union's basic principle is to apply a middle way for the Islamic community of the middle (*al-minhaj al-wasat li al-umma al-wasat*). The main points in the IUMS's founding declaration, which specifies the work of the union, are first the opposition to undemocratic ruling principles in Islamic countries and second the enforcement of equal legal and legislative rights for men and women.

In 1997, drawing on the American model, Yusuf al-Qaradawi, together with other scholars and intellectuals, founded the European Council for Fatwa and Research (ECFR, www.e-cfr.org), a body he also chairs, although he does not speak any European languages.[30] The questions of European Muslims, sent in by electronic or conventional mail, confront the scholars with the realities of life in Europe. The answers are for the most part pragmatic, mainly due to the fact that European legislation does not allow the fatwa council unlimited leeway. The ECFR scholars argue, for example, that Muslim girls in France should go to school without having to wear a headscarf, as the main concern there is their education. In spite of that, the headscarf ban imposed by the French government has been fiercely criticized.

The *fatawa* issued by the ECFR support the idea of making Muslims in Europe proper citizens. Participation in non-Muslim cultural practices may be allowed, but cultural assimilation is by and large rejected. The scholars' reasoning is based upon what is called the law for minorities (*fiqh al-aqalliyyat*).[31] According to al-Qaradawi there are several principles of legal decision making in the European context, the two most important being the understanding of the reality of daily life (*fiqh al-waqi'*) and the task of making life easy for Muslims and not difficult and full of interdictions (*fiqh al-taysir*). The favored method is called collective reasoning (*ijtihad jama'i*), because no single person may judge the complex social and political changes at work.

Two other recently established institutions connected to this transnational network of Muslim scholars and intellectuals around al-Qaradawi are the Wasatiyya Center in Kuwait, founded in 2006, and the recently founded Al-Qaradawi Center for Islamic Moderation and Renewal in Doha, which is part of the Qatar Foundation.[32]

ELECTRONIC NETWORKING

Yusuf al-Qaradawi is involved in print as well as electronic media production in the name of Islam, even though he lacks the technical skills to produce it himself. He has had a weekly program on Qatar TV since the launch of terrestrial television in Qatar in 1970, in which he answers letters sent in by viewers from the Gulf.[33] Since its inception, Qatar TV has consistently televised his Friday prayer at 'Umar b. al-Khattab Mosque in Doha. Since 1993 it has also broadcast via satellite and reaches a larger audience beyond the Gulf countries. A worldwide audience of millions has seen him on television since 1996 in the program *Shari'a and Life*–shown weekly on satellite channel Al Jazeera since 1996–during which he explains his interpretation of Islamic normativity in layman's terms.[34] In 1997 he was one of the first scholars to launch his own website in the Arabic language, Qaradawi.net. The Internet portal IslamOnline.net, which was founded in Doha and used to be the largest of its kind until it was split up in 2010, was also established with al-Qaradawi's support.[35] It has been online since 1999 in Arabic and English. The body behind the website is the Al-Balagh Cultural Society, which was established in 1997 on the initiative of the Qatari Maryam Hasan al-Hajari, a Information Technology (IT) student from the University of Qatar, and the Qatari Hamid al-Ansari, a religious scholar from the Shari`ah Faculty of the University of Qatar. In the beginning the project was supported and financed by the University of Qatar; later it was supported by donations and the merchandising of its own products. Its headquarters and IT development unit used to be based in Doha, while most of the content has been produced in its Cairo offices.[36] On its homepage al-Qaradawi wrote in missionary style: "It is our duty to acquaint all people in this world with our religion until they understand it, become interested in it, seek it and convert to it."

His extensive exposure in various types of media, which also includes numerous videos on YouTube, has assisted the fast and wide dissemination of his texts and *fatawa*. And it is in no small part due to this that he is the subject of controversial discussion. Web logs, or blogs, which first appeared around 2003, give an impression of how al-Qaradawi's arguments are received around the world. Here one can find both vehement adversaries and fervent supporters.[37]

Reception

A lot of Muslim intellectuals hold him in high esteem for his ideas on the reform of Islamic jurisprudence. A voluminous Festschrift was given to him on the occasion of his seventieth birthday in 1996.[38] The authors are admirers of al-Qaradawi and most of them are themselves scholars, intellectuals, and activists, like the Egyptian jurist Tariq al-Bishri, the Tunisian philosopher Rashid al-Ghannushi, the Egyptian political scientist Hiba Ra'uf 'Izzat, and the Morrocan jurist Ahmad al-Raysuni. From this book one gets a picture of al-Qaradawi drawn by more than sixty friends and followers on various topics, ranging from portraits of al-Qaradawi as scholar (*'alim*), legal interpreter (*mujtahid*), jurist (*faqih*), or preacher (*da'i*) to texts on his jurisprudential methodologies, his commitment to Islamic banking, Islamic internationalism, or on the issue of Palestine.[39] This admiration is echoed by intellectuals in Europe and America. Tariq Ramadan, for example, quotes Yusuf al-Qaradawi extensively.[40]

In the political field, the scholar occupies, to some degree, the role of a diplomat or ambassador in the dialogue between European politicians and so-called moderate Islamists. Both Ken Livingstone, London's former mayor, and French foreign minister Michel Barnier expressed their thanks in letters to al-Qaradawi as a result of his explicit condemnation of hostage takings and attacks by radicals in 2005.[41] Recently, Efraim Halevy, former head of Mossad, the Israeli secret service, even asked Prime Minister Benjamin Netanyahu to negotiate with al-Qaradawi.[42]

The general public, including many Muslims in Europe, revere him as a scholar who does not shy away from contemporary questions. Due to his unmistakable opposition to neoliberal politics he has also become a conciliatory figure for many nonactivist Muslims. But he has many opponents too. These include, on the one hand, people with a left-wing and/or secular orientation who are concerned about the authority of the clerics and Islam in general becoming too pronounced.[43] On the other hand, al-Qaradawi is criticized by Salafi-oriented authors, in whose eyes he is too permissive.[44] From time to time his fatwas also cause tensions with the religious establishments in Egypt or Saudi Arabia, as was the case when he declared his approval of Palestinian suicide attacks[45] or recently when he called for the killing of Mu'ammar al-Ghaddafi in February 2011 via Al Jazeera.

Among academic researchers he is viewed as a reformer of Islamic jurisprudence and one of the leading figures in the Islamic movement.[46] He is also referred to as being at the forefront of a group of "superstar" religious scholars and a spokesperson of contemporary global Islamic discourse.[47] Some label him as an advocate of liberal Islam[48] but this notion is refuted by others: he may be regarded as moderate in comparison to radicals but this is by no means tantamount to his being a liberal.[49]

RENEWAL OF ISLAMIC JURISPRUDENCE (*TAJDID AL-FIQH*)

Al-Qaradawi defines the renewal of *fiqh* as one of the cornerstones of his method.[50] The emphasis on renewal was also a prominent part of wider intellectual debates about the relationship between tradition (*taqlid*), authenticity (*asala*), and contemporary Islam (*al-islam al-mu'asir*) in the last quarter of the twentieth century. These debates are closely related to the discussions about reform (*islah*) that took place at the end of the nineteenth century and the beginning of the twentieth century in the Arab regions and in Asia.

Supported by the readings of legal expert 'Abd al-Razzaq al-Sanhuri (1895–1971), al-Qaradawi distinguishes his approach from the notions of positive law upheld by Western societies, be they socialist or liberal capitalist. He is interested in the subject because of his conviction that a modern interpretation of *shari'a* is not possible without a profound knowledge of its foundational texts and traditions of interpretation.[51] Proper renewal (*al-tajdid al-haqq*) means a development from within (*tanmiyat al-fiqh al-islami min dakhilihi*).[52] However, it is, according to him, a basic principle that there should be no renewal of those parts of *fiqh* that are regarded as fixed (*thawabit*). This includes all rules that are clearly written in the Qur'an, for example, the five pillars of Islam or the laws governing inheritance and marriage. It includes further matters that *shari'a* provides clear rulings on, such as the prohibition of alcohol, pork, and usury.

All other parts of *shari'a*, which are considered flexible (*al-muruna*), that is, which do not explicitly contain positive rulings or interdictions, can and should be interpreted with regard to the relevant contemporary questions. Based on this he suggests a program of renewal for *fiqh* in seven steps. He calls for:

1. the systematization of the principles of Islamic jurisprudence (*tanzir al-fiqh al-islami*).
2. the undertaking of comparative studies (*al-dirasat al-muqarana*).
3. the creative interpretation of the sources (*ijtihad*). Here he suggests a reassessment of the different classical methods of consensus (*ijma'*), analogical reasoning (*qiyas*), courteous action (*istihsan*), and consideration of the public good (*istislah*).[53] Furthermore *ijtihad* should be accomplished collectively (*ijtihad jama'i*).[54]
4. the codification of *fiqh* (*taqnin al-fiqh*).
5. the compilation of an updated encyclopedia of *fiqh* (*al-mawsu' al-fiqhiyya al-'asriyya*).

6. the production of scientific editions of legal literature (*ikhraj 'ilmi l-kutub al-fiqh*).
7. the publication of the old handwritten manuscripts (*nashr al-makhtutat al-fiqhiyya*).

Al-Qaradawi lays strong emphasis on the significance of the classical legal texts. This is due to the fact that legal and religious scholars have been under attack from intellectuals and activists since the 1950s.[55] He is convinced that in order to reform society a reinvigoration of their position and their methods is needed.[56]

MODERATION

Yusuf al-Qaradawi describes his doctrine as the school of the middle way (*wasatiyya*).[57] Based on the phrase "*ummatan wasatan*" from the Qur'an 2/143 ("a justly balanced community" or "a community of the middle" according to different translators), al-Qaradawi argues in favor of an even-handed approach in the implementation of Islamic jurisprudence by legal scholars. The term *wasatiyya* is given various similar descriptions in al-Qaradawi's texts: it is not merely a characteristic of *fiqh* but the nature of Islam, the soul of Islam, one of the general qualities of Islam, the strongest course within the Islamic awakening movement, al-Qaradawi's method and the outstanding characteristic of the Islamic community. First, on the functional level, *wasatiyya* represents a dissociation from both too rigid (i.e., literal) and too free (i.e., oriented to the public interest) interpretations of *fiqh*.[58] Second, in the political field, it stands for the introduction of Islam as a social system that presents an alternative to liberal capitalist and socialist systems. Third, within the realm of Egyptian politics (and Arab politics as a whole), it implies a dissociation from both secular and militant Islamic tendencies and seems to offer a way out of political crisis. Fourth, in the religious sphere, it serves to give Islam a special status when compared to other religions (especially Judaism and Christianity). And fifth, it functions as a counterbalance to terms like radical Islam.

USE OF VIOLENCE AS POLITICAL MEANS

Al-Qaradawi rejects violence as a means of changing society, except when it comes to defending the "most sacred things of Islam." In his opinion, one of these things is Palestine. In the context of the second Intifada in 2001 he expressly endorsed suicide attacks carried out by Palestinians.[59] However, he does not term these as such, since suicide is forbidden in the Qur'an, but refers to them rather as acts of martyrdom. In his view, Palestinians had no other option than to use their bodies as deadly weapons in order to preserve unhindered access to their sacred sites and to demand a just division of the country.[60] Moreover, even though women and children were among the victims of suicide bombings in Israel, he defended these acts, arguing that Israeli society is a society of soldiers. Since everyone could potentially be drafted for military service, there are no civilians in Israel according to al-Qaradawi. This proclamation led the US authorities to revoke al-Qaradawi's entry visa to the United States and deny him entry into the country pending further notice.

Other suicide attacks with an Islamic identification have been condemned by al-Qaradawi, including the attacks of 9/11 and the ones in Madrid in 2004, as well as the suicide missions in Iraq, London, Mumbai, Sharm el-Sheikh, and Turkey in the following years. Following the London bombings he reaffirmed that civilians (a term which, in his words, along with women, children, and the elderly, also covers journalists and aid organization workers) should under no circumstances be involved in armed conflicts.[61]

Gender Relations

In his writings, al-Qaradawi advocates living according to Islam with the aim of introducing a contemporary Islam into everyday life. Since the 1990s al-Qaradawi has been speaking out in favor of legal equivalence for men and women, based on the Qur'an 9:71.[62] Here, the appeal is directed at both sexes, in the belief that men and women are allies, consult with and protect one another, observe the prayers, give *zakat*, and obey God. Accordingly, he concludes, every verse in the Qur'an applies equally to both women and men, except in passages where one of the two genders is specifically addressed. Measured against the standards of liberal democracies, this interpretation can scarcely be considered emancipated, especially in light of the fact that on important issues, such as inheritance laws, men and women are clearly treated unequally.

However, as a legal reformer, al-Qaradawi sees it as his duty to interpret the existing texts of the Qur'an and Sunna, rather than to invent completely new rules. As long as he is acting within the framework of Islamic jurisprudence, he consciously binds himself to certain principles, as in the case of gender equality. Yet, what he offers is the development of a flexible Islamic doctrine that is oriented to the lives of Muslims. This means that scholars, and he insists that it should be scholars, along with knowing the Qur'an and its legal interpretations, must also study modern life, for example by seeking a dialogue with the general public instead of treating its members as ignorant and infidels, as radical interpreters do.[63] As he wrote in the periodical *al-Manar al-Jadid* in 1998, "The doctrine must be adapted when the time, the place and the circumstances of the people change."[64]

Democracy and Pluralism

In the late 1980s, Yusuf al-Qaradawi as well as other activists and intellectuals started to concern themselves with terms such as democracy, the constitution, and party pluralism.[65] Rather than strictly rejecting these terms, they are taken up, adapted, and equated with legal structures and forms of government existing in the Islamic tradition, thus constructing an Islamic form of democracy.[66] Al-Qaradawi sees, for example, the parliament as the legitimate arena for legislation and as an effective means of controlling rulers, an opinion that puts him in opposition to Qutb or Mawdudi who were against a legislative assembly.[67] Islamic scholars nevertheless occupy a central position in al-Qaradawi's envisioned system, as they control those in power, while also offering their advice to the population.

This issue is of vital importance to him, yet it also reveals the challenges to his democratic models, for if the guardians of religious books can decide on what is allowed or prohibited in a society, the freedoms of thought, opinion, and religion are possibly at risk, even when he is proposing a position in the middle (*wasati*).[68]

His commitment to democracy may therefore turn out to be less robust than his rhetoric sometimes suggests. A telling example of this is his view on pluralism (*ikhtilaf*). He distinguishes between two types of disagreement, the one offering alternatives and the other constituting opposition or contradiction. This latter form is forbidden, which means that, in al-Qaradawi's view, disagreement is only possible between otherwise like-minded people and is not meant as a contest between people with different worldviews as in the idealized liberal understanding of democracy.

Conclusion

In many respects, Yusuf al-Qaradawi is a key figure in helping us to understand contemporary Islamic discourse. Born in the mid-1920s, he acts as a link between the early publicists and reformers of Islamic thinking at the beginning of the twentieth century and today's Sunni Islamic intellectuals and activists.

At the beginning of his career al-Qaradawi was, like many of his contemporaries, involved in the anticolonial struggle against the British in the Arab regions. Since the official end of colonialism he has grappled with other adversaries: Salafism and secularism. Subscribing to the notion of *wasatiyya* he has occupied a position between these two poles; he neither advocates literal interpretations of the holy sources as Salafis do nor does he authorize the neglect of religion (*din*) in the course of modernization. The Gulf region and Europe play an important role in this regard, because each represents for al-Qaradawi one side of the two extremes that he struggles with. Another struggle al-Qaradawi undertakes is against the instrumentalization of Islam by different nation-states and he also writes in condemnation of the religious extremism in Egypt and elsewhere.

Al-Qaradawi thinks of the renewal of Islamic jurisprudence (*tajdid al-fiqh*) as the best means available to confront all these different challenges. Several principles of legal decision making are relevant in this context, the two most important being the understanding of the local reality of daily life (*fiqh al-waqi'*) and the task of making life easy for Muslims and not difficult and full of interdictions (*yusr la 'usr*). In addition, he pleads for close cooperation between the different denominations of Islam.

Al-Qaradawi sees himself as independent from the institutions of any nation-state and from political parties although one can doubt his independency from the state of Qatar due to his manifold entanglements with its ruling family. Nevertheless he does not use only the exclusive forms of scholarly communication, such as giving sermons in the mosque, issuing fatwas face-to-face and teaching, but also various kinds of mass media for the dissemination of his message and for networking. Al-Qaradawi is one of the scholars who publicly brought Islamic legal discourse into focus. He is always openly involved in discussions and uses global electronic mediascapes, although he and his assistants sometimes underestimate their peculiar dynamics, as for example during the second Intifada when he legitimized Palestinian suicide attacks in various media.

Al-Qaradawi is a co-founder of different independent organizations that are distinct because of their translocal and global orientation. He seems to have understood at an early stage that belonging to Islam under modern conditions can only be defined by faith and not by territory. His mission therefore is to strengthen the de-territorialized global Islamic community. Meanwhile he has become his own best role model for the kind of position scholars should hold in today's society: as teacher, preacher, counselor, monitor, and admonisher.

Notes

1. For an excellent account of al-Qaradawi's life (based on his memoirs *Ibn al-qarya wa-l-kuttab*, 2002, 2004, 2006), see Gudrun Krämer 2006, 184–200. Further information can be found in Wenzel-Teuber 2005, 35–47 and Gräf and Skovgaard-Petersen 2009, 1–12.
2. Muhammad al-Ghazali was expelled from the Muslim Brothers in 1953; see Krämer 2006, 196 and al-Qaradawi 2000.
3. al-Qaradawi, 2004, 172f.
4. In 1958 al-Qaradawi was married; he has seven children by his first wife.
5. al-Qaradawi, 2004, 271.
6. al-Ansari, 2001, 401–438.
7. Cf. Krämer 2006, 191 and Tammam 2009, 67. See also Mariani 2003.
8. Cf. Salvatore 1997 and Zaman 2004 and 2006.
9. Cf. Caeiro 2010.
10. For commentary on the term *taysir* see Krämer 2006 and Gräf 2010; for *tajdid* and *wasatiyya* Baker 2003; for *shumuliyya* al-Qaradawi 1991 and al-Khateeb 2009b.
11. *al-Halal wa-l-haram fi l-islam*, 1960.
12. *al-Sahwa al-islamiyya bayna l-jumud wa-l-tatarruf*, 1982.
13. *al-Ijtihad al-mu'asir bayna l-indibat wa-l-infirat*, 1994.
14. *al-Tatarruf al-'ilmani fi mawajahat al-islam. numudhaj Turkiya wa-Tunis*, 2001. See also Masud 2005 and Larrson 2010.
15. *Dirasa fi fiqh maqasid al-shari'a. bayna l-maqasid al-kulliyya wa-l-nusus al-juz'iyya*, 2006.
16. *The Lawful and the Prohibited in Islam* has been translated into many languages.
17. Though he was inspired by Muhammad al-Ghazali's book *Ihya' 'ulum al-din*, cf. Krämer 2006, 185.
18. *Silsilat nahwa wahda fikriyya li-'amaliyyin li-l-islam*.
19. Cf. Zaman 2004, 134. Euben and Zaman calls it an "extraordinary series of books.... In its focus not on the Islamic foundational texts but rather on the work of an Islamist founding father, there are no parallels to this work in Islamist literature." Euben and Zaman 2009, 224 Fn 1.
20. *Silsilat taysir al-fiqh li-l-muslim al-mu'asir fi daw' al-qur'an wa-l-sunna*.
21. *Silsilat rasa'il tarshid al-sahwa*; see also Gräf 2010.
22. See Stowasser 2001 and 2009.
23. Cf. Euben and Zaman 2009.
24. Cf. Gräf 2009.
25. *Min hady al-islam. fatawa mu'asira* (From Guidance for Islam. Contemporary Fatwas), 1979, 1993, 2003, and 2009.
26. *Ibn al-qarya wa-l-kuttab. malamih sira wa-masira*, 2002, 2004, 2006, and 2012.
27. Cf. Salvatore 1997 and Skovgaard-Petersen 2009.

28. Cf. Nafi 2004, al-Khateeb 2009a, and Euben and Zaman, who state that allegiance to the Islamic community has since 1924 been defined not by territory but by faith; Euben and Zaman 2009, 54.
29. http://www.iumsonline.net/ar, cf. Gräf 2005.
30. Cf. Caeiro 2010.
31. See al-Qaradawi 2001; for an analysis and translation into German, see Schlabach 2009.
32. Qatar Foundation is a large organization that was founded in 1995 in Doha as an NGO by the wife of the Emir of Qatar. It has established branch campuses of eight international universities at its Education City. Qatar Foundation's general tendency for international exercise of influence became visible to a wider public when it announced the shirt sponsorship deal over five years with FC Barcelona in 2010, http://news.bbc.co.uk/sport2/hi/football/europe/9276343.stm, accessed May 13, 2013.
33. Cf. al-Qaradawi 2006, 240.
34. Cf. Galal 2009.
35. Cf. Gräf 2010.
36. Today the Cairo part has its own site called OnIslam.net; cf. Abdel-Fadil 2010.
37. See, for example, http://en.wordpress.com/tag/yusuf-al-qaradawi.
38. It was published as a book in 2003 by the publishing house *Dar al-Salam* in Cairo: *Yusuf al-Qaradawi. kalimat fi takrimihi wa-buhuth fi fikrihi wa-fiqhihi muhdat ilayhi bi-munasabat bulughihi as-sab'in*.
39. See also Talima 2001.
40. Cf. Ramadan 2004. See also Larsson 2010.
41. Cf. Greater London Authority 2005.
42. According to news printed in *al-Yawm al-Sabi'* newspaper after al-Qaradawi preached at Tahrir Square on February 24, 2011, available at: http://www.youm7.com/News.asp?NewsID=357624. See also the commentary by editor-in-chief of *Asharq Alawsat* Tariq Alhomayed, published on February 26, 2011: http://www.asharq-e.com/news.asp?section=2&id=24305.
43. In 2005 'Abd al-Razzaq 'Id published a critical monograph on al-Qaradawi, in which he tried to make sense of his arguments from his own secular perspective. In doing so, he aligned himself with the French intellectual and specialist in Islamic studies Muhammad Arkoun; cf. Gräf 2009; see also Helfont 2009.
44. As early as 1976 Salih al-Fawzan, a well-known author from Saudi Arabia, wrote a commentary on al-Qaradawi's first and most famous publication from 1960. Al-Fawzan does not agree with al-Qaradawi's details and comments and offers his own more severe interpretations. Two other, more recent publications by authors who can be described as Salafi are in line with this argumentation, Sulayman Ibn Salih al-Harashi 1999 and Ibrahim 'Abduh al-Shafrawi 2001.
45. Euben and Zaman talks about al-Qaradawi's "significant ambiguities." Euben and Zaman 2009, 227. Cf. also Hamzah 2005 and Gräf 2010.
46. Cf. Salvatore 1997 and Nafi 2004.
47. Cf. Mandaville 2007 and Zayid 2007.
48. Kurzmann 1998.
49. Krämer 2006. Zaman speaks of a general hostility of '*ulama*' to liberal conceptions of civil society; cf. Zaman 2004, 131, see also Hallaq 2012.
50. Al-Qaradawi 1986. Cf. Baker 2003, Wenzel-Teuber 2005, and Gräf 2010.
51. Cf. Zaman 2004.
52. Cf. Gräf 2010, based on al-Qaradawi 1973 and 1986.

53. Cf. Zaman's discussion of the controversial notion of the common good (*maslaha*) in al-Qaradawi's writings; Zaman 2004, 134f.
54. Cf. also Nafi 2004.
55. Cf. Krämer 1999, 274 and Zaman 2004, 129.
56. See also Zaman 2002.
57. Cf. Gräf 2009.
58. Cf. also Zaman 2004, 136 and 145.
59. Euben and Zaman 2009, 227.
60. In al-Qaradawi's words the new weapons of "those deemed weak," a Qur'anic expression; cf. Euben and Zaman 2009, 227.
61. Al-Qaradawi, Bombing Innocents: IAMS's Statement: http://web.archive.org/web/20050729032302/http://www.islamonline.net/English/In_Depth/ViolenceCauses-Alternatives/Articles/topic08/2005/07/01.shtml, accessed January 4, 2012.
62. Cf. Stowasser 2001, 2009 and Roald 2001.
63. Al-Qaradawi's severe criticism of Sayyid Qutb's latest texts can be placed in this context, cf. al-Qaradawi 1994.
64. Al-Qaradawi 1998, 6.
65. Al-Qaradawi has never outlined a state theory but sees his "al-Islam wa-l-dimuqratiyya," in *Min hady al-islam. fatawa muʿasira* [From Guidance for Islam. Contemporary Fatwas], vol. 2, 1993, 636–651, *Min fiqh al-dawla fi l-islam* [The Understanding of State in Islam] 1997, and *al-Din wa-l-dawla* [Religion and State] 2006; see Zaman 2004 and Euben and Zaman 2009.
66. Cf. Krämer 1999 and Euben and Zaman 2009.
67. Cf. Euben and Zaman 2009, 226f.
68. See Krämer's article on al-Qaradawi and apostasy, 2006.

References

Abdel-Fadil, Mona. 2011. "The Islam-Online Crisis: A Battle of Wasatiyya vs. Salafi Ideologies?" *Online Journal of the Virtual Middle East*, available at: http://www.cyberorient.net/article.do?articleId=6239. Accessed May 13, 2013.

al-Ansari, Muhammad b. ʿAbdallah. 2001. *Fadilat al-shaykh ʿAbdallah al-Ansari. Waqiʿa wa-l-taʾrikh*. Doha.

Baker, Raymond William. 2003. *Islam without Fear: Egypt and the New Islamists*, Cambridge MA: Harvard University Press.

Caeiro, Alexandre. 2010. "The Power of European Fatwas: The Minority Fiqh Project and the Making of an Islamic Counterpublic" *International Journal of Middle East Studies* 42, no. 3: 435–449.

Euben, Roxanne L., and Zaman, Muhammad Q., eds. 2009. *Princeton Readings in Islamist Thought: Texts and Contexts from al-Banna to Bin Laden*. Princeton: Princeton University Press.

al-Fawzan, Salih Ibn-Fawzan Ibn-ʿAbdallah. 1976. *al-Iʿlam bi-naqd kitab al-halal wa-l-haram*, Jamiʿat al-Imam Muhammad Ibn-Saʿud al-Islamiyya. Riad: al-Matabiʿ al-Ahliyya li-l-Uffsit.

Galal, Ehab. 2009. "Yusuf al-Qaradawi and the New Islamic TV." In Gräf, Bettina and Jakob Skovgaard-Petersen, eds., *The Global Mufti. The Phenomenon of Yusuf al-Qaradawi*, London: Hurst, 149–180.

Gräf, Bettina. 2005. "In Search of a Global Islamic Authority." *ISIM Review* 15: 47.

Gräf, Bettina, and Jacob Skovgaard-Petersen, eds. 2009. *The Global Mufti. The Phenomenon of Yusuf al-Qaradawi*. London: Hurst.

Gräf, Bettina. 2010. *Medien-Fatwas@Yusuf al-Qaradawi: Die Popularisierung des islamischen Rechts*. Berlin: Klaus Schwarz Verlag.

Greater London Authority (ed.). 2005. *Why the Mayor of London Will Maintain Dialogues with All of London's Faiths and Communities. A Reply to the Dossier against the Mayor's Meeting with Dr Yusuf al-Qaradawi*. London.

Hallaq, Wael B. 2012. *The Impossible State: Islam, Politics, and Modernity's Moral Predicament*, New York: Columbia University Press.

Hamzah, Dyala. 2005. "Is There an Arab Public Sphere? The Palestine Intifada, a Saudi Fatwa and the Egyptian Press." In Salvatore, Armando, and Mark Le Vine, eds., *Religion, Social Practice, and Contested Hegemonies. Reconstructing the Public Sphere in Muslim Majority Socities*, 181–206. New York: Palgrave.

al-Harashi, Sulayman Ibn-Salih. 1999. *al-Qaradawi fi l-mizan*. Riad: Dar al-Jawab.

Helfont, Samuel. 2009. *Yusuf al-Qaradawi: Islam and Modernity*. Tel Aviv: Moshe Dayan Center, Tel Aviv University.

'Id, 'Abd al-Razzaq. 2005. *Sadanat hayakil al-wahm, naqd al-'aql al-fiqhi: Yusuf al-Qaradawi bayna l-tasamuh wa-l-irhab*. Beirut: Dar al-Tali'a.

al-Khateeb, Motaz. 2009a. *Yusuf al-Qaradawi faqih al-sahwa al-islamiyya: sira fikriyya tahliliyya*. Beirut: Markaz al-Hidara li-Tanmiyyat al-Fikr al-Islami.

al-Khateeb, Motaz. 2009b. "Yusuf al-Qaradawi as an Authoritative Reference." In Gräf, Bettina, and Jakob Skovgaard-Petersen, eds., *The Global Mufti. The Phenomenon of Yusuf al-Qaradawi*, 85–108. London: Hurst.

Krämer, Gudrun. 1999. *Gottes Staat als Republik. Reflexionen zeitgenössischer Muslime zu Islam, Menschenrechten und Demokratie*. Baden-Baden: Nomos.

Krämer, Gudrun. 2006. "Drawing Boundaries. Yusuf al-Qaradawi on Apostasy." In Sabine Schmidtke, ed., *Speaking for Islam. Religious Authorities in Muslim Societies*, 181–217. Leiden: Brill.

Kurzman, Charles. 1998. *Liberal Islam. A Sourcebook*, 196–204. New York: Oxford University Press.

Larrson, Gören. 2010. "Yusuf al-Qaradawi and Tariq Ramadan on Secularisation: Differences and Similarities." In Marranci, Gabriele, ed., *Muslim Societies and the Challenge of Secularization. An Interdisciplinary Approach*, 47–64. Heidelberg: Springer.

Mandaville, Peter. 2007. *Global Political Islam*. New York: Routledge.

Mariani, Ermete. 2003. "Youssef al-Qaradawi: pouvoir médiatique, économique et symbolique." In Mermier, Franck. éd., *Mondialisation et nouveaux médias dans l'espace arabe*, 35–45. Lyon: Maisonneuve et Larose.

Masud, Khalid M. 2005. "The Construction and Deconstruction of Secularism as an Ideology in Contemporary Muslim Thought." *Asian Journal of Social Science* 33, no. 3: 363–383.

Nafi, Basheer M. 2004. "Fatwa and War: On the Allegiance of the American Muslim Soldiers in the Aftermath of September 11." *Islamic Law and Society* 11, no. 1: 78–116.

al-Qaradawi, Yusuf. 1971. *Fiqh al-zakat. dirasa muqarana li-ahkamiha wa-falsafatiha fi dhaw' al-qur'an wa-s-sunna*. Beirut: Mu'assasat al-Risala.

al-Qaradawi, Yusuf. 1973. *Shari'at al-islam saliha li-l-tatbiq fi kull al-zaman wa-l-makan*. Cairo: Dar al-Sahwa.

al-Qaradawi, Yusuf. 1986. *al-Fiqh al-islami bayna l-asala wa-l-tajdid*. Cairo: Maktaba Wahba.

al-Qaradawi, Yusuf. 1991. *Shumul al-islam*. Cairo: Maktaba Wahba.

al-Qaradawi, Yusuf. 1994. *al-Ijtihad al-muʿasir bayna l-indibat wa-l-infirat*. Beirut: Amman.
al-Qaradawi, Yusuf. 1998. "Fiqh al-waqiʿ wa-taghayyur al-fatwa." *al-Manar al-Jadid* 3: 6–15.
al-Qaradawi, Yusuf. 2000. *Shaykh Muhammad al-Ghazali kama ʿaraftuhu. rihlat nisf al-qarn*. Cairo: Dar al-Shuruq.
al-Qaradawi, Yusuf. 2001. *Fi fiqh al-aqalliyyat al-muslima. hayat al-muslimin wasat al-mujtamaʿat al-ukhra*. Cairo: Dar al-Shuruq.
al-Qaradawi, Yusuf. 2002, 2004, 2006. *Ibn al-qarya wa-l-kuttab. malamih sira wa-masira*. Cairo: Dar al-Shuruq.
Ramadan, Tariq. 2004. *Western Muslims and the Future of Islam*. Oxford: Oxford University Press.
Roald, Anne-Sofie. 2001. *Women in Islam. The Western Experience*. London: Routledge.
Salvatore, Armando. 1997. *Islam and the Political Discourse of Modernity*. Berkshire: Ithaca Press.
Schlabach, Jörg. 2009. *Scharia im Westen: Muslime unter nicht-islamischer Herrschaft und die Entwicklung eines muslimischen Minderheitenrechts für Europa*. Berlin: Lit-Verlag.
Skovgaard-Petersen, Jakob. 2009. "Yusuf al-Qaradawi and al-Azhar." In Gräf, Bettina, and Jakob Skovgaard-Petersen, eds., *The Global Mufti. The Phenomenon of Yusuf al-Qaradawi*, 27–54. London: Hurst.
Stowasser, Barbara Freyer. 2001. "'Old Shaykhs, Young Women', and the Internet: The Rewriting of Women's Political Rights in Islam." *The Muslim World* 91: 99–119.
Stowasser, Barbara Freyer. 2009. "Qaradawi On Women." In Gräf, Bettina, and Jakob Skovgaard-Petersen, eds., *The Global Mufti. The Phenomenon of Yusuf al-Qaradawi*, 181–212. London: Hurst.
Talima, ʿIsam. 2001. *Yusuf al-Qaradawi: faqih al-duʿat wa-daʿiyat al-fuqaha'*. Damascus: Dar al-Qalam.
Tammam, Husam. 2009. "Yusuf al-Qaradawi and the Muslim Brothers. The Nature of a Special Relationship." In Gräf, Bettina, and Jakob Skovgaard-Petersen, eds., *Global Mufti. The Phenomenon of Yusuf al-Qaradawi*, 55–84. London: Hurst.
Wenzel-Teuber, Wendelin. 2005. *Islamische Ethik und moderne Gesellschaft im Islamismus von Yusuf al-Qaradawi*. Hamburg: Verlag Dr. Kovac.
2003. *Yusuf al-Qaradawi. kalimat fi takrimihi wa-buhuth fi fikrihi wa-fiqhihi muhdat ilayhi bi-munasabat bulughihi as-sabʿin*. Cairo: Dar al-Salam.
Zayid, Ahmad. 2007. *Suwar min al-khitab al-dini al-muʿasir*. Cairo: Maktabat al-Usra.
Zaman, Muhammad Q. 2002. *The Ulama in Contemporary Islam. Custodians of Change*. Princeton: Princeton University Press.
Zaman, Muhammad Q. 2004. "The Ulama of Contemporary Islam and their Conception of the Common Good." In Salvatore, Armando, and Dale Eickelman, eds., *Public Islam and the Common Good*, 129–156. Leiden: Brill.
Zaman, Muhammad Q. 2006. "Consensus and Religious Authority in Modern Islam: The Discourse of the 'Ulama." In Krämer, Gudrun, and Sabine Schmidtke, eds., *Speaking for Islam: Religious Authorities in Muslim Societies*, 153–180. Leiden: Brill.

CHAPTER 16

MOHAMMAD KHATAMI

MAHMOUD SADRI AND AHMAD SADRI

Biographical Sketch

Seyed mohammad khatami was born October 14, 1943 to a notable clerical family in the central town of Ardakan in Yazd province and grew up with two brothers and four sisters. The designation "Seyed" signifies that his family is descended from the Prophet of Islam, which, in the Shi`a tradition, confers the black color to his turban. Mohammad Khatami's father, Rouhollah Khatami was an erudite and trusted local cleric who founded a seminary in Ardakan and served as the "imam of Friday prayer," the highest clerical position in town, immediately after the Islamic revolution of 1979. Mohammad completed his primary and secondary education in local schools while completing the introductory courses in religious studies in his father's seminary in town. In 1961 he entered the Qum seminary and in two stints over the course of a decade reached the highest level of studies, *Dars e Kharej* (postgraduate seminars for elite students preparing to become Muslim jurists), at which time he was both an advanced seminarian and a lecturer. In 1970 he entered the University of Isfahan and graduated with a BA in philosophy and later obtained an MA in education from the University of Tehran. While in Isfahan, Mr. Khatami met and collaborated on scholarly and political projects and in the context of the Islamic Student Association with Ahmad Khomeini and Mohammad Montazeri, sons of two of Iran's foremost clerical dissidents: Ayatollah Khomeini and Ayatollah Montazeri. These connections helped place Khatami in the leadership ranks during the first years of the Islamic revolution. Mr. Khatami was later affiliated with "Tarbiat Modarres" University as a lecturer. His chosen field of study at this time was political philosophy. In these years he published a book on the Islamic political philosopher, Al Farabi. In 1974, Mohammad Khatami married Zohreh Sadeghi, a niece of the legendary leader of the Lebanese Shi`a community, Imam Mousa Sadr. They have two daughters and a son together.[1]

The Revolutionary Years

Given his intellectual and spiritual upbringing and his training both in the seminary and in modern educational institutions, one would have expected Khatami to emerge as a reform-minded cleric and a professor of humanities had the revolution not happened. Even with all his preoccupations, Khatami has managed to teach a number of courses in Iranian universities and to publish twenty-one books, by the last count, during the past three decades. This oeuvre includes, of course, several compendiums of his speeches and articles but there are volumes, also, on political philosophy, democracy and dictatorship, dialogue of civilizations, and civil society. Four of his books are available in English.[2]

One year before the revolution, Khatami briefly replaced Mr. Beheshti, an astute cleric at the helm of Iran's impending revolution, as the director of Islamic Center in Hamburg, allowing Beheshti to return to Iran and pursue his revolutionary agenda as a trusted lieutenant of Ayatollah Khomeini. Upon his return to Iran, Mr. Khatami won a seat in Iran's first postrevolutionary parliament as a representative of his region, Ardakan and Meybod, from 1980 to 1982. During this period, Khatami was also appointed as the head of Iran's semiofficial popular daily, *Keyhan,* by Ayatollah Khomeini.

Mr. Khatami's first prominent governmental position came in 1982, when he was appointed the minister of culture and Islamic guidance by Prime Minister Mirhossein Mousavi. At the same time, he was given major responsibilities in Iran's war effort against Iraq, as the head of the joint command of the armed forces and the director of Iran's War Propaganda Headquarters. Khatami's reputation and immaculate record of service within the ranks of Iran's revolutionary elites led to a second ministerial appointment in the government of President Ali Akbar Hashemi Rafsanjani in 1989. This was the post that Khatami resigned in 1992 to protest his frustrated attempts to grant the printed media greater freedoms. Khatami did not leave stealthily. In addition to a detailed and strongly worded letter of resignation in which he assailed the organized opposition of the "regressive and reactionary" elements against his reforms, he orchestrated a highly visible and well attended public appreciation/farewell event in Tehran's opera house ("Talar e Vahdat"), in which representatives of politicians, artists, university professors, clergy, students, and politicians praised him for his intellectual integrity and liberal temperament.[3] The next five years mark a hiatus in Khatami's career during which he held the posts of advisor to President Rafsanjani and director of the National Library. He was also a member of Iran's High Council of Cultural Revolution, which was charged with revising the curriculum of Iran's institutions of high learning. At this time it appeared that Khatami's political career was winding down. His new position at the margins of the Tehran's political scene was a virtual retirement job.

Khatami's Rise as the Political Face of the Reform Movement

In retrospect, Khatami's resignation from his ministerial position over his liberal convictions helped him emerge as the presidential candidate for the nascent reform movement that took Iran's 1997 presidential elections by storm. To the surprise of everyone, including the reformist leaders, Khatami handily won the election by a landslide of a little under 70 percent majority, trouncing, most notably, the establishment's favorite candidate, Ali Akbar Nategh Nouri, to become the Islamic Republic's fifth president. He acknowledged the collective effervescence that brought him to power in his inaugural speech on August 4, 1997 by describing it as an "epic of historical proportions." The presence of women, intellectuals, and the youth who had been absent on the scene ever since the heady days of the 1979 revolution helped immortalize not only Khatami's triumph but also the birth of the "reform movement" that came to be known as "the May 23 Movement" (*Jonbesh e Dovvom e Khordad*) the day of Khatami's 1997 electoral victory. It is noteworthy that Khatami at the moment of his victory was only the political face of the Iranian reform, an intellectual and political movement that had been in gestation for a decade.[4] The intellectual pedigree of reform dates back to the disappointing end of the Iran-Iraq war (1988) when a battle-hardened and formerly idealistic segment of the Iranian revolutionary cadre elite cut itself off its ideological and Islamist moorings and came together in a government sponsored think tank[5] and an independent monthly journal (*Kian*) to form the nucleolus of the religious and political aggiornamento of the Islamic Republic. Others, such as a majority of the formerly radical "students supporting the Line of Imam" (Daneshjouan e Khatt e Emam was the organization behind the taking of the American hostages that led to an international crisis lasting from late 1979 to early 1981), who had become disenchanted with the country's autocratic leadership, also joined this nucleus. Mr. Khatami's connection to this core group was tenuous and tangential.

At this time, Khatami was a mildly liberal and thoughtful politician with excellent connections and a respectable revolutionary dossier at the margins of both the intellectual and political scenes in Tehran. The reason he found himself in a position to run as the candidate of reform was his clerical garb, his personal connections, and his revolutionary credentials. And the reason such qualities mattered had more to do with the political system of the Islamic Republic than either the predilections of Khatami or the preferences of the reformists. The byzantine political system of the Islamic Republic makes election to high office dependent on the approval of the Guardian Council,[6] a right-wing body that is invested with the right to vet candidates[7] for elective office under articles amended to the Iranian constitution in 1995. The reform movement and indeed any party hoping to slate a candidate for presidency cannot afford to ignore the wishes of the Guardian Council—which has not been shy about imposing its partisan wishes by disqualifying up to 99 percent of the candidates, even when they appear to have current elected offices, established Islamic profiles, and revolutionary credentials.[8]

It is in this context that Mohammad Khatami, his scholarly nature, and nonconfrontational style notwithstanding, became indispensable for the reform movement. While Khatami was a reluctant candidate in his first term, it would not be an exaggeration to state that he was forced by the above circumstances to run for his first term of presidency as well as for his second term (2001) and his brief candidacy for a third term in the presidential elections (2009). The reformers begged, cajoled, and pressed Khatami to run not because he was the best-qualified or the most willing candidate but because they feared that anyone else would have been unceremoniously disqualified. Those who have, during the course of the past decade, underlined the shortcomings of Khatami as a political leader (including the authors of this essay) do so with the knowledge that the prime mover of Khatami's political career was not his personal ambitions or political goals but the flawed democracy of the

Islamic Republic that prevents natural representatives of political parties from running for elected office.[9]

By the end of Khatami's first presidential term it was evident that he was neither able to fight the intransigence of entrenched right-wing theocrats[10] nor willing to deliver on the promise of democratization of Iran that was the ultimate objective of the reform platform. But the reformers like Saeed Hajjarian who had no other horse in the presidential race, found themselves begging Khatami to run again.[11]

At this time Khatami's sins were mostly those of omission. Most gave him the benefit of the doubt. His inaction was generously construed as wanting to pick his fights. After all he had shown some courage in confronting the state-sponsored serial murderers of dissidents at the outset of his presidency. Khatami's persistence led to the arrest of four highly placed officials in the Ministry of Information caught for the murder of fifteen Iranian intellectuals, artists, and political figures and the plot to murder many more. The reformist constituency remained hopeful that maybe, just maybe, he would use his second term to good use. Based on his popularity, necessities of the political structure, and wishful thinking, Khatami won his second term by a clear majority. But he did so without giving a single campaign promise. He had not pledged to act more in keeping with the wishes of the reform movement or to stand up to the right wing. The Guardian Council had already disqualified and eliminated Khatami's reformist challengers, offering him the leadership of the reformist constituency on a silver platter. In other words the right-wing Guardian Council usurped the functions of "primaries" in the Iranian elections.

That is not to say that Khatami was even eager to run. He appeared to have burnt out. He had fought, in his first run, a defensive and losing battle against the sustained sabotage of the right wing that by Khatami's own count had fomented a crisis for every nine days of his presidency. He was visibly reluctant to go through another grueling term. But the bizarre political system (through the agency of right-wing opponents and reformist friends) "forced him" to accept the candidacy for the highest elected office of the land. It is little wonder then that in the wake of his easy victory in 2001 Khatami's sins of omission turned into sins of commission. He had not asked for the office and he had no appetite to fight the legal and extralegal conspiracies of the right wing at the risk of triggering more crises and bloodshed.

President Khatami had won his second presidential term amid widespread dissatisfaction and disaffection with his administration's inability to achieve a modicum of success in realizing the reform movement's objectives: liberalizing the civic sphere, greater transparency, and a tangible responsibility for the unelected block of the Iranian regime. To add to the domestic opposition to Khatami's ideals and policies, the price of oil plummeted during this period causing economic hardships beyond his control. The discontent of the 2001 election was marked by lower voter participation and, more indirectly, by an abundance of popular jokes (that reportedly Mr. Khatami himself enjoyed) about his "do-nothing" and "perpetually smiling" profile. Signs of exhaustion were written all over Khatami's second-term leadership. Shortly after being elected he dismissed the plight of the unjustly imprisoned journalists, quipping, "How do we know they have not violated the law?" Then he proceeded to choose a more right-wing cabinet than he had in his first term in office—despite the fact that in 2001 he had a sympathetic parliament (the sixth parliament dominated by reformists) on his side and was no longer beholden to right-wing power brokers such as Rafsanjani.

This preemptive surrender angered many of his supporters. Shortly after this period Khatami was bitterly criticized by reform-minded intellectuals (including Abdolkarim

Soroush, Said Hajjarian, and Mohsen Kadivar) for lacking the courage of his convictions, for his crippling legalism and conservatism, and for missing "golden opportunities" to advance the cause of reform as a president. Some among the reform-minded critics of Khatami (e.g., Mohsen Kadivar and Abbas Abdi) had from the very beginning prophesied that Mr. Khatami, despite all his irrefutable virtues, would not be suitable for presidency. They now had proof.[12] At this point some reformers even started to talk about slating the former "reconstruction president," Ali Akbar Hashemi Rafsanjani as the reform candidate. But he had been savaged by some of the reform publications (for malfeasance and political oppression) at the outset of the reform reign and it would have taken the reformers a paradigm shift to contemplate such a change in course. In short, reformers had little choice but to support Khatami for a second term despite the evidence of his first term and hope against hope that he would somehow change into a real, hardball politician.

Abdolkarim Soroush, the quintessential reform ideologue and theoretician, argued that Khatami's convictions themselves suffered from lack of inner coherence and clarity. He claimed, in the manner of a true intellectual, that it was the inner inconsistencies of Khatami's ideas that led to his notorious indecisiveness.[13] He had failed to stop the brutal, vigilante takeover of the dormitories of the University of Tehran (summer of 1999) and the judiciary's subsequent mass closure of ninety reformist newspapers. Later in his second term (2003) Khatami first started a bold gambit in the form of "twin bills" to expand presidential powers and to enact media freedom, but he was forced to withdraw these proposals under mounting pressure from the right wing. On occasions like this Khatami was reduced to dithering silence as he watched the right wing pick off (assassinate, imprison, defame, and fire) his close associates and allies (student activists, journalists, and parliamentarians) and stymie or roll back reform legislation.

By the end of his second term the disappointment of Khatami's followers was palpable. It was true that he had accepted the job somewhat reluctantly and that the right-wing pressure was enormous. But based on his popular mandate he could have engaged in symbolic action. His critics asked, When his right-wing rivals shut down the reformist press and brutalized the protesting students could he have not gone on a political fast? When the hanging judges of the right-wing judiciary imprisoned his lieutenants and other reformists, could he have not gone to visit them in prison? Was there no alternative between supine passivity and enticement of violence? Had Khatami ignored the beckoning of Fortuna for the path of safety, mediocrity, and appeasement? Had he wasted a unique historical opportunity to transform Iran's decrepit political system? These questions may never be fully answered even in carefully drawn historical counterfactuals. Social scientists who were observing the Iranian scene at the time of transition from Khatami to Ahmadinejad went from depicting the closing of an Iranian equivalent of the French Revolution's "Thermidor" period to adumbrating an Iranian version of the Chinese Revolution's experience of "return of the radicals."[14]

Nevertheless, today, despite the great disappointments of Khatami's two terms of presidency, he remains enormously popular (both at home and abroad) for his decency, civility, and liberality. Actually, it could be said that his international reception dwarfs his domestic popularity. Mohsen Kadivar relates that as a domestic critic of Mr. Khatami he was pleasantly surprised by the level of support Khatami enjoyed abroad and among the educated classes.[15] In 2001 the United Nations designated the year as the "Year of the Dialogue among Civilizations" to support Khatami's doctrine to counter Samuel Huntington's theory of "Clash among Civilizations." He remains popular for his proposal on the international scene, and several other initiatives have followed in the footsteps of his original proposition.

Khatami in the Post-Khatami Era

In 2005 Khatami was constitutionally barred from running for a third term and since the vetting agencies of the regime had disqualified three of the most capable reform candidates, including Khatami's younger brother, an MD and the secretary general of Iran's "participation front" from running, the compromise reform candidate, Dr. Mostafa Mo'in, a lackluster former minister of higher education was defeated by the establishment's candidate, Mr. Ahmadinejad. The fact that reformers had achieved little under Khatami was a factor in the defeat of the reform platform at this time. Also the political backlash of the United States' twin invasions of Afghanistan (for which the Khatami government had acted as a virtual ally but received no rewards but a place on the Axis of Evil from the Bush administration) and Iraq explains the appeal of Ahmadinejad's hardline foreign policy. Khatami's soft approach had won him acceptability, but it had not brought home the "beef" on issues ranging from obtaining a civilian fleet for Iranian airlines to the peaceful use of nuclear energy, and Ahmadinejad knew how to exploit these sensitive nationalist issues.

During the first Ahmadinejad term Khatami returned to his cultural and intellectual activities. However, institutions that pursued his agenda such as "Center for the Dialogue of Civilizations" and "The Rain Foundation" faced dwindling state support and mounting harassments. The election of 2009 marked another watershed in Khatami's role in Iranian politics. He was persuaded by an enormous public campaign waged by artists and intellectuals to stand for a third term of presidency against Ahmadinejad (February 2009). Khatami initially accepted the nomination under pressure but withdrew later in favor of his colleague Mirhossein Mousavi. Such a development does not surprise those who have followed his career.

The charges of fraud in the election of June 2009 that brought Ahmadinejad to power and the ensuing tragic and bloody suppression of the protest rallies led to the birth of the "Green Movement." Within a month after the disputed election and the widespread incarceration and torture of the reformist politicians and intellectuals, Khatami publically denounced the show trials and extraction of forced confessions. He publicly called for a referendum on the legitimacy of the Ahmadinejad's government. Among the arrested were Mr. Khatami's brother, Mohammad Reza Khatami, the embattled leader of "Islamic Iran's Participation Front," his chief of staff, several deputy ministers of his administration, and other close and prominent colleagues and collaborators such as Mostafa Tajzadeh, Mohsen Aminzadeh, and Said Hajjarian. Khatami continued to appear in prestigious international forums as the World Economic Forum in Davos, Switzerland even after these events. In 2006 alone he had fifteen international addresses. Eventually the government revoked his passport and prevented him from flying to Japan on a lecture tour. Later, they blocked his website as well. This, too, is bound to boost his profile as a beloved and popular, though embattled and besieged, dissident in Iran. These days, as Mr. Ahmadinejad's two-term presidency is coming to a disgraceful end with international isolation, economic sanctions, threats of invasion, a precipitous decline in the value of Iranian currency (to one-third of what it was before he took over), and his fall from grace even among the right-wing circles, people cannot help waxing nostalgic about the halcyon days when their Smiling Seyed managed the affairs of Iran in a turbulent world.[16]

In his "Politics as a Vocation" The German sociologist Max Weber describes a good politician as one who is idealistic without being dogmatic, uses power to achieve political goals rather than basking in the glory of the office, and ultimately lives "for" rather than "off" politics.[17] On this scale Khatami can be counted as an excellent politician. But one must also factor in the time, the place, and the political matrix. In normal times Khatami might never have chosen "politics as his vocation." When Khatami did find himself at the helm of Iranian presidency he discharged his duties honorably. What he failed at was not the job he was elected for but a higher mission: to lead the reform movement's thrust to democratize the Islamic Republic. He could have helped the revolution molt out of its hardened exoskeleton and take wing in a new century. Khatami could have been a contender, possibly the greatest leader Iran has had since the days of Cyrus. But, like President Carter before him, Mohammad Khatami has become Iran's best ex-president.

KHATAMI'S DISTINCTIVE DISCOURSE

Lest our account of the intricate contingencies surrounding President Khatami's political life leave the reader with the impression that he is simply a creature of the ebbs and flows of Iran's postrevolutionary realpolitik, we must emphasize that Khatami's discourse on cultural openness, human rights, political participation, and civic liberties has left an indelible mark, not only on Iranian political culture but on the entire Islamic world. This effect is not due to the originality of Khatami's ideas. On the contrary, he treads on the path paved by Iranian and Islamic reformers of the nineteenth and twentieth centuries, who were, in their turn, indebted to the eighteenth- and nineteenth-century European liberal tradition.[18] Rather, what is remarkable in Khatami's discourse is that it is the first time in Islamic history that a committed Muslim, indeed, a clergyman, and a political leader, the fifth president of the Islamic Republic of Iran, proposes these decidedly modern and liberal ideas—and means them. These are ideas that we in the Islamic world have come to expect from idealist academics and exiled intellectuals.

Khatami's pragmatic political agenda is present, in embryonic form, in his letter of resignation from the ministry of culture in 1992. It is endowed, with not only ideals and ideas concerning meaning of Islam and nature of man but with an acute awareness of the nature of entrenched opposition to it and the political groundwork needed to overcome it. Khatami elaborates on this thesis in the ensuing decades. The same ideas are in full bloom and expressed triumphantly in his first-term inaugural speech on August 4, 1997 at the Islamic Consultative Assembly (Majles)

> The legitimacy of the government stems from the people's vote. And a powerful government, elected by the people, is representative, participatory, and accountable. The Islamic government is the servant of the people and not their master, and it is accountable to the nation under all circumstances. The people must believe that they have the right to determine their own destiny and that the power of the state is bound by limits and constraints set by law. State authority cannot be attained through coercion and dictatorship.[19]

Again, what is stunning about these proclamations is not the content but the position of the speaker and the forum in which it is delivered. Khatami's sustained belief in the compatibility of Islam, democracy, and modernity and his natural tendency toward civility and respect has thus engendered nothing short of a cognitive shift in the Iranian political discourse. Even those Iranian politicians who disagree with him find themselves borrowing his rhetoric of human rights and liberties. The only exception to this rule is the kind that proves the rule. His greatest detractors are the rank and file extremists and xenophobic fundamentalists who find the very ideas of democratic right to self-determination, natural liberties, and freedom of conscience as noxious and deleterious to Islam.[20] Thus, Khatami has acquired the right kind of friends and enemies to ensure him a place in the history and political philosophy of modern Iran and Islam.

Notes

1. Seyed Mohammad Khatami, Iran Chamber Society. Accessed October 10, 2010. http://www.iranchamber.com/history/mkhatami/mohammad_khatami.php.
   Profile: Mohammad Khatami, BBC, 2001, 2003, Accessed October 5, 2010.
   http://news.bbc.co.uk/2/hi/middle_east/1373476.stm. http://news.bbc.co.uk/2/hi/middle_east/3027382.stm.
   Encyclopedia Britannica, "Mohammad Khatami," Accessed October 10, 2010.
   http://www.britannica.com/EBchecked/topic/316504/Mohammad-Khatami.
   Wikipedia, "Ahmad Khatami," Accessed October 10, 2010.
   http://en.wikipedia.org/wiki/Mohammad_Khatami.
   Robert Worth, *New York Times*, July 20, 2009. http://topics.nytimes.com/top/reference/timestopics/people/k/mohammad_khatami/index.html.
   Mohammad Khatami, Mehran Kamrava, "Mohammad Khatami," in *Iran Today, An Encyclopedia of Life in the Islamic Republic*, vol. I: A–K.
2. حیاتنامه، سندگینا مهسید محمد خاتمی, Accessed October 01, 2010.
   http://www.hayatname.blogfa.com/post-103.aspx.
   Mohammad Khatami's official website, Accessed September 8, 2010.
   http://www.khatami.ir.
3. Mohsen Kadivar, 1380، دغدغههایحکومتدینی، نشرنی,
   On Khatami's letter of resignation, see Wikisourse.org. Accessed November 4, 2010. http://fa.wikisource.org/wiki/%D9%86%D8%A7%D9%85%D9%87_%D8%A7%D8%B3%D8%AA%D8%B9%D9%81%D8%A7%DB%8C_%D9%85%D8%AD%D9%85%D8%AF_%D8%AE%D8%A7%D8%AA%D9%85%DB%8C_%D8%A7%D8%B2_%D9%88%D8%B2%D8%A7%D8%B1%D8%AA_%D8%A7%D8%B1%D8%B4%D8%A7%D8%AF.
4. Mahmoud Sadri and Ahmad Sadri, "Three Faces of Violence: Cognitive, Expressive, and Traditionalist Discourses of Discontent in Contemporary Iran," in *Iran Faces the New Century* (Routledge, 2007), London. For the reference to Khatami's 1997 inaugural speech, see Mohammad Khatami, *Islam, Liberty and Development* (Binhamton University, 1998), 136.
5. Center for Strategic Studies under the Institution of Presidency, Tehran.
6. "Guardian Council of the Constitution" is a sort of supreme court composed of six Shiite jurists directly appointed by the supreme leader and six legal experts appointed by the head of the judiciary. The head of judiciary is himself appointed by the supreme leader. So, the

supreme leader appoints half of the members of this body by direct writ and the other half are appointed by his appointee.

7. "Nezarat-e Esteswabi."
8. The most notorious of vetting of this body to date is the disqualification of the senior revolutionary cleric, the former, two-term president and the head of the "Expediency Council" Akbar Hashemi Rafsanjani in the presidential elections of 2013.
9. Ahmad Sadri, *Khatami's Swan Song.* http://www.drsoroush.com/English/Interviews/E-INT-HomaTV.html.
10. Under the leadership of Ayatollah Ali Khamenie, the Supreme Leader of the Islamic Republic of Iran.
11. Zhila BaniYaghub, *Hajjarian's Criticisms of Khatami.* http://www.zhila.org/spip.php?article147.
12. Mohsen Kadivar, *Interview with Mahmoud Sadri*, October 3, 2010, unpublished manuscript.
13. Abdolkarim Soroush. تذبذبعملیخاتمیریشهدرتذبذبفکرپایشاندارد. http://www.drsoroush.com/Persian/News_Archive/F-NWS-13830903-Gooyanews.htm. نامهعبدالکریمسزوشبهمحمدخاتمی. http://autnews3.blogspot.com/2008/04/blog-post_5875.html. Abdolkarim Soroush, *Interview with Daryoush Sajjadi.* http://www.drsoroush.com/English/Interviews/E-INT-HomaTV.html.
14. Mathew C. Wells, Thermidor in the Islamic Republic of Iran, *British Journal of Middle Eastern Studies*, 26, no. 1 (May 1999): 27–39; Jack A. Goldstone, The Return of the Radicals, in *Iran, Project Syndicate, A World of Ideas.* http://www.project-syndicate.org/commentary/goldstone1/English. Date accessed, September 28, 2007.
15. Mohsen Kadivar, *Interview with Mahmoud Sadri*, October 3, 2010, unpublished manuscript.
16. It was this enduring popularity that led to the campaign to slate Mr. Khatami as the reformist candidate in the presidential elections of June 2013. Entirely in character, he resisted the pressure and backed Akbar Hashemi Rafsanjani for the position.
17. Max Weber, "Politics as a Vocation" in *From Max Weber*, ed. Hans H. Gerth and C. Wright Mills (Oxford University Press, 1946), 77–128.
18. MahmoudSadri, "Liberalism, Islamic," in *Iran Today: An Encyclopedia of Life in the Islamic Republic*, ed., Kamrava and Dorraj, Westport, Connecticut 300–307.
19. MohammadKhatami, "Covenant with the Nation," Presidential inaugural speech at the Islamic Consultative Assembly (Majles), in *Islam, Liberty and Development* (IGCS, Binghamton University, 1998), Binghamton, N.Y 150–151.
20. For a recent example, see Tebyan.com. Accessed, November 7, 2010 http://www.tebyan.net/Weblog/SAEIDAN/post.aspx?PostID=102923.

CHAPTER 17

ABDOLKARIM SOROUSH

BEHROOZ GHAMARI-TABRIZI

INTRODUCTION

IF Ali Shari'ati was the intellectual par excellence of the Islamic revolution, Abdolkarim Soroush represents one of the most significant postrevolutionary intellectual attempts to end that revolutionary fervor. A prolific writer, Soroush has made important contributions to the advancement of Islamic theology and political philosophy. There are three distinct periods in the development of his thought: (1) critique of Marxism and its influence on Islamist political ideology, (2) epistemological critique of Islamist truth claims, and (3) hermeneutical approach to the Divine text and Prophetic tradition. Whereas during the first period he contributed to the consolidation of postrevolutionary state power, he emerged as one of the most vociferous critics of Islamism, particularly after the death of Ayatollah Khomeini in 1989, during the second and third periods.

CRITIQUE OF MARXISM AND ITS INFLUENCE ON ISLAMIST POLITICAL IDEOLOGY

Abdolkarim Soroush was born in Tehran in 1945 into a lower-middle-class Muslim family. He was named Hossein,[1] for his birth fell on *Āshura*, the day commemorating the martyrdom of Hossein, the third Shi'te imam. After earning a degree in pharmacology from Tehran University, he went to London in 1972 to pursue his studies in chemistry. Although he finished a Master's degree in chemistry, soon thereafter, he concentrated his academic work on the philosophy of science. As a devout Muslim, he remained aloof to the political activism of Iranian students in Europe, which was primarily informed by Marxist ideologies. At the time, Marxian political and philosophical ideas had even penetrated militant Muslim groups, the most influential of which was the Organization of People's Mujahedin (OPM). Despite his reservations about political militancy, he participated in Muslim Youth Association meetings in the United Kingdom.

During his association with the Muslim student movement in the United Kingdom, Soroush emerged as a popular speaker and later as a prolific writer. Like other Muslim intellectuals of his period, such as Morteza Motahhari and Ali Shari'ati, he considered Marxism to be the main intellectual threat that had estranged Iranian intellectuals from their own religion and culture. Unlike Shari'ati, who articulated an Islamic liberation theology, an Islam of *telos,* Soroush engaged Marxism outside its emancipatory politics. He focused on the logical inconsistencies of its philosophy and what he perceived as the totalitarian implications of the materialist conception of history. Shari'ati's indisputable success in attracting the younger generation of Iranian intellectuals to his Islamist ideology afforded Soroush an eager audience who at the time remained oblivious to the fundamental distinctions between competing hermeneutics of Islam.

The result of Soroush's early preoccupation with the critique of Marxism was a series of books in each of which he chastised the "illusive ideology of liberation" from a neopositivist standpoint sheathed in Mulla Sadra's philosophical realism.[2] In the introduction of his treatise on Mulla Sadra's thesis of "(Trans) Substantial Motion" (*harkat-e johari*), he lamented that contemporary generations of Muslims were gradually losing the courage to think independently, to be innovative and original. He declared that they had grown "inept" and "hopeless"; they had become "timid and reluctant to consider positions on which foreigners have not inscribed their stamp of approval. Intellectual independence, the courage to think creatively, and *ijtihad* are the most urgent responsibilities that face Muslims today" (Soroush 1982, 9). The time had come, he declared in the same introduction, "to emit the fragrance of our culture and offer it to those seekers who trust the aroma of a scent and are not bewitched by the promotional squawking of the scent seller" (Soroush 1982, 10).

The publication of his treatise on Mulla Sadra marked a defining moment in Soroush's intellectual and political life. First, by introducing Mulla Sadra to a new generation, he dismissed the orientalist fallacy of the continuous decline of post-Peripatetic Islamic philosophy. He showed that more than three hundred years after the Golden Age of the Islamic Renaissance, in the early seventeenth century, Mulla Sadra brought together the rationalist philosophy of Ibn Sina (*Masha'*), the Illuminationism (*Ishrāq*) of Shahab al-Din Suhrawardi, and the Gnostic teachings of Ibn 'Arabi to create a metaphilosophy (*al-hikma al-muta'āliya*) through which he offered new resolutions to the centuries-old predicament of existence, reality, essence, and their relation to God.

Moreover, Soroush addressed these questions within the frame of Shi'ite theology, with significant stress laid on its principle of imamate and the imperative of *ijtihad*. Soroush concluded his short but meticulously argued treatise by proposing that:

> For the first time, the doctrine of substantial motion introduced two fundamental elements to Islamic thought: first, the historicity of existence; second the concomitant internal tumult and restlessness and external calm and tranquility of the phenomenon.... Rather than being a thing, the world is an unremitting process of becoming.... The inner transformation recreates the phenomenon anew in every given moment.... God manifests his presence in the perpetual demise and birth of the universe. (Soroush 1982, 65)

Second, and more importantly, by regarding Mulla Sadra as the philosopher par excellence of Shi'ite theology, Soroush established himself as part of a philosophical tradition whose main contemporary proponent was Ayatollah Khomeini. Whether Soroush shared Khomeini's political interpretation of Mulla Sadra or not, the publication of *The Restless Universe* brought the philosophical virtuosity of the young Soroush to the attention of the revolution's father. It has been said that with the encouragement of Morteza Motahhari, whose commentary on Mulla Sadra had influenced Soroush, Ayatollah Khomeini read the book and marveled at the erudition of its young author (Quchani 2004, 50).

During the two years that followed the publication of his first major treatise, from 1978 to 1980, Soroush published numerous essays and books, most of which were based on his lectures in the United Kingdom. In these publications, he demonstrated more clearly the extent to which Anglo-Saxon analytical philosophy and the postpositivism of Karl Popper had permeated his Islamic philosophical worldview.[3] He found himself at home with the nonrevolutionary, elitist core of the British political tradition, as well as its liberal anti-Marxian propensities. Even at the height of the revolutionary movement in Iran, Soroush remained committed to his philosophical endeavors and academic rumination. If Ali Shari`ati's political discourse combined with his passionate oratory could inspire thousands of otherwise Marxist young Iranians to join the revolution, in a world apart, with his soft-spoken words and monotonous delivery, Soroush saw himself, and was accepted by the postrevolutionary regime, as the messenger of persuasion.

With its anti-imperialist agenda and focus on social justice, the new regime situated itself as an alternative to Marxist-inspired national liberation movements. To justify this position, the Islamic Republic launched a two-pronged assault on Marxism: first, by hampering the activities of communist groups through a campaign of intimidation and suppression and, second, by positioning itself as a more authentic and legitimate anti-imperialist force. For the first part of their mission they organized *hezbollahi* mob groups, club-wielding thugs mobilized by the Revolutionary Guards. For the second front they relied on the emerging Muslim intellectuals such as Abdolkarim Soroush.

Soroush's philosophical investigations of Mulla Sadra, combined with his knowledge of history and philosophy of science, situated him as an authoritative intellectual. However, the revolutionary events of 1978 and the establishment of the Islamic Republic deterred him from his scholarly path, forcing him to leave the quiet of his mystical love of philosophy for the boorish world of strident ideology. Like many contemporary Muslim intellectuals, he believed that the construction of a vigorous and engaging Islamic philosophy and an alternative discourse of social change would eventually weaken the ideological attraction of Marxism in Iran. Whereas earlier Muslim critics of Marxism advanced their discourse within the context of a struggle against a common enemy, the monarchy and imperialism, Soroush's critique coincided with the strategy of the new regime to consolidate its power by eliminating its Marxist-Leninist and liberal opposition.

Soroush castigated Marxism, a la Popper, for advancing an irrefutable ideological view of history and society wrapped in pseudoscientific claims. Such an ideological conviction, Soroush reiterated, would inevitably render Marxism a deterministic totalitarian ideology (Soroush 1979a, 13). He argued that Marxists invented the idea of scientific philosophy or scientific socialism in order to justify their teleological view of history. "In [Marxists'] minds," he scolded, "there is no distinction between scientific truth claims and what is right or legitimate" (Soroush 1979d, 15).

In contrast to his nuanced treatment of Mulla Sadra, his engagement with Marxism was polemical and narrow in scope. Whereas, in the former, he pursued genuine philosophical investigations, in the case of Marxism, his argument was primarily shaped by political considerations and the state of the Iranian communist movement. Rather than a serious engagement, his critique was mostly shaped by a vulgar interpretation in which Stalinism appeared to be the only logical political manifestation of Marxist philosophy. Marxism seemed to be an uninterrupted continuum from Marx's ideas, communist utopia to Stalinist totalitarianism, operated as a *satanic ideology*.[4] Soroush called this ideology a "masked dogmatism"[5] that wrapped itself in the colorful sentiments of emancipation and freedom.

He wrote that the proponents of the satanic ideology divide societies into two groups: conscious, deliberate actors and unwitting masses. They "consider people to be entrapped in the claws of mysterious elements of history and condemn their rationality to the manipulation of their subconscious or class-based motivations" (Soroush 1980, 27). The bearers of dogmatic ideology bestow upon themselves mysterious powers, afforded to them by history, which enable them to lead the masses to their "true destiny." *Satanic ideology* (Marxism) draws its seductive powers, he warned, from "opening the arms at the expense of closing the mind, unleashing passion by imprisoning Reason." *Satanic ideology* substitutes the "clash of bodies," for "the encounters of minds." Masked dogmatism "would usher in the worship of power," it would "cast its opponents out of the scene and would legitimize itself based only on the power it holds" (Soroush 1980, 71).

The publication of Soroush's attacks on Marxism and its Islamist sympathizers, that is, the Organization of the People's Mujahedin, coincided with the postrevolutionary regime's *la Terreur* and state-building project. One of these efforts for the consolidation of power was the Cultural Revolution of 1980, the purpose of which was to cleanse the university of the undesirable students and faculty. In May 1980, in a well-planned project, *hezbollahi* mob groups, guided by the factions in the ruling Islamic Republic Party, ransacked the universities around the country and demanded their indefinite closing. During the skirmishes scores of students were killed or injured.

On June 12, 1980, after the bloody attacks of the earlier month, Ayatollah Khomeini issued a decree announcing the formation of the Cultural Revolution Council (CRC). He appointed a seven-member committee, the most junior member of which was Soroush, to carry out a systematic project to Islamize and reopen the universities. Admitting the failure of its initial phase, Khomeini reiterated that "no effective measures have been taken for the realization of the cultural revolution." He asked his appointees to draw up a new plan for the "restructuring of higher education based on Islamic culture" (Khomeini 1994, 177).

If the Cultural Revolution shut the doors of the universities, it opened a door through which Abdolkarim Soroush entered the postrevolutionary political landscape. Although he served in the CRC for less than three years, his short tenure continues to be controversial, especially among Iranian expatriate intellectuals. He was an anomaly in the CRC, having neither a significant history of political activism nor an affiliation with any of the factions in power. Despite his obscurity at the time, soon Soroush lent significant weight and legitimacy to the CRC and thereby emerged as an influential intellectual of the new republic. Since his resignation in 1983, he has maintained that his role in the Council was to reopen the universities and has consistently distanced himself from its bloody inauguration and political context.

Nevertheless, it is well documented that Soroush rejoiced at the disgrace and impeachment of his intellectual rival President Bani Sadr and the arrest and execution of members of the Mujahedin and communist groups. He justified the reign of terror as Divine Will, which brought love and kindness to those who assented and agony to those who resisted. "I need to emphasize," he pointed out after more than one year of state-sponsored nightly executions,

> That God has consecrated the emergence and the establishment of the Islamic Republic. This divine blessing has descended upon us like the coming of springtime to an arid land and it

is the duty of all peoples of this country to be content and grateful for the blooming of this spring. Like a tree, they ought to submit themselves to this breeze and wear the green garment of appreciation. Otherwise, God forbid, they will suffer retributions if they show no gratitude towards God's benevolence. (Soroush 1983, 5)

The Orwellian description that Soroush advanced in 1982 of the Islamic regime as a gentle, life-giving breeze could not be more in contradiction to the emerging totalitarian tendencies of the Iranian political apparatus. The young philosopher who condemned Marxism for its dogmatic core and Hegelian philosophy for its historicist negation of freedom found himself exulting in the disappearance of his philosophical rivals, through execution or exile. "We are pleased now," he exclaimed, "that the pain of having such an undesired president is over.... Like a healthy body that excretes its putrid parts, people have egested him" (Soroush 1983, 6–8).

Soroush's early intellectual project focused on demystifying Marxism. He criticized Marxism as a determinist, totalitarian ideology and, more importantly, advanced a vehement critique of the Muslims who had succumbed to the temptations of its emancipatory discourse. But during the late 1970s and early 1980s, Soroush remained oblivious to the fact that such a critique politically situated him on the side of the ruling factions whose measured encroachment into the state power would soon threaten the conditions of his own intellectual livelihood.

Epistemological Critique of the Islamist Truth Claims

From early 1988, a group of Muslim intellectuals began to write for and congregate around the editorial board of *Kayhān-e Farhangi,* a monthly journal of cultural and literary criticism, published by the daily newspaper *Kayhān.* From May 1988 to March 1990, in a four-part essay in *Kayhān-e Farhangi,* entitled "The Theoretical Contraction and Expansion of the Shari'ah," Soroush laid out the foundation of a theoretical, political, and social engagement with the emerging totalitarianism. While he framed his argument as a matter of the epistemological problems of religious knowledge, his readers had no trouble reading the implications of his thesis. With these short essays, Soroush inaugurated an intellectual movement the main premise of which was to salvage Islam from its *officially* sanctioned straitjacket. His daring words proved to be one of most important theoretical foundations of political reform in postrevolutionary Iran. He knew that his ideas could not remain limited to the pages of a journal of social criticism. He therefore congregated in the early 1990s with a number of key political, academic, and intellectual figures and journalists in a group known as the "Wednesday night circle."[6]

Soroush did not advocate a political platform. He left the issues of politics and policies out of these meetings. Rather he intended to develop a community in which a "thousand flowers could bloom." The Muslim students, whose credentials included invading the American Embassy in Tehran, had reentered the political scene bearing postgraduate degrees in the humanities and social sciences from British universities. Soroush had left an important mark on their education abroad. With an invitation from the Islamic Student Association of the United Kingdom, for six months in the mid-1990s, he delivered a series of lectures and held seminars on his theological position in seventeen British towns and cities (Jala'ipour 1999, 45). His formal and informal students emerged as the new voice of Islamism, ready to leave behind their Jacobin past and embark on the project of crafting an Islamic-democratic public sphere.

After Ayatollah Khomeini's death in June 1989, the Soroushians gradually lost their prominence at *Kayhān-e Farhangi*; the journal no longer welcomed their contributions. Soroush's circle therefore launched its own monthly journal called *Kiyān*. Although Soroush did not hold any official position at the paper, from the publication of its first issue it was conspicuously clear that the journal would express the views of these dissident intellectuals. *Kiyān*, which ran for more than ten years from 1991 until its closure by the order of Tehran's chief prosecutor in 2001, became one of the most contentious venues in which dissident Muslim, and at times secular, intellectuals could address their critics. Although it was not the only opposition journal permitted to circulate in these years, it occupied a distinct position among elite literary-political journals.

Ten years after the Cultural Revolution, a majority of those who were involved in its implementation now voiced their opposition to its totalitarian implications. Soroush, who stumbled onto the revolutionary scene and became the reluctant spokesperson for the CRC, was best situated to lead this movement—a movement of those who shared both the culpabilities of the past and the hope for the future.

The combination of his antitotalitarianism and his unwanted role in a totalitarian project to Islamize higher education pushed Soroush into a contradiction. This sociopolitical location contributed to the formation of his project, the central feature of which was rescuing the religion of Islam from its dominant ideological articulations. Soroush advanced his critique of ideological Islam vis-à-vis two tendencies in Iranian politics, both of which he chastised for their reductionist conceptions of Islam. The first, put forward by Ali Shari`ati, demoted Islam into a mere liberation theology and operated as the ideological frame of the Iranian revolution. The second, promoted by the ruling clerical *nomenklatura* with privileged access to its meaning, transformed Islam into a state ideology.

In a series of talks and articles, which were collected in the book *Farbeh-tar az eideolozhi* (Loftier Than Ideology), Soroush called into question Shari`ati's notion of Islam as ideology. Although formally composed as a critique of his philosophy, Soroush's underlying theme was his rejection of the ideological society established by the Islamic Republic. Rejecting Shari`ati's theory of permanent revolution, Soroush argued that although useful as a weapon to fight oppression, Islam as ideology and its prescribed establishment of an ideological society was a plague that must be eradicated in order to constitute a free religious society. Whereas Shari`ati defined ideology as a revolutionary rearticulation of culture, Soroush regarded it as an exclusionary truth claim, which not only distorts the reality of religion but also facilitates the establishment of totalitarianism (Soroush 1994, 135–154).

Soroush proposed that claiming the *Truth* has always been a part of all Islamic revivalist movements. These movements, he wrote, shared three basic elements. First, they campaigned against folk religious practices and rituals. Associated with *Wahhabism* and some trends of *Salafiyyah* movements, their aim was to create a homogenous and universal conception of Islam through strict and a literal reading of the Qur'an and the *Hadīth*. Second, they emphasized the hitherto neglected dimensions of Islam, especially in the realm of *fiqh* (jurisprudence). They offered alternative genealogies of Islamic praxis, as for example in the case of Shari`ati, the Islam of Abu Dharr replaced the Islam of Ibn Sina, an Islam of the political vanguard supplanted the Islam of the ʿālim (scholar). And finally, they appropriated selective Qur'anic verses that would justify the validity of their sociopolitical as well as scientific ideas. Many proponents of Islamic revival, for example, fallaciously locate the root of liberal democracy and electoral politics in the Islamic notion of *shura* or *ijmāʿ* (consultation; Soroush 1987, 368).

Whereas all Islamic revivalist movements had to separate what was permanently sacred from what was situational and changing in the Islamic text, Soroush distinguished religion as intended by God from humanity's mundane knowledge of it. "What remains constant is religion [itself] and what changes is religious knowledge" (Soroush 1995, 52). Humanity could not fathom God's true intentions. Therefore, those who ordain their ideology as the Divine commandment laid the foundation for totalitarianism. All possible interpretations of religion, both the so-called permanent and its historically contingent parts, are mundane and informed by sociocultural particularities. In effect, Soroush argued that *any* claim to the *Truth* of Islam transforms religion into an ideology—a falsified world picture.

Iranian predecessors of Soroush, Shariʿati and Motahhari, had already emphasized the social, cultural, and historical contingencies of religious knowledge. Shariʿati developed the idea in his sociology of Islam, and Motahhari in his critique of *qeshriyyat* (fanaticism). For example, Shariʿati wrote, "*Tawhid* descends from the sky and becomes earthly and enters into particular social relations in the context of which its meaning is constructed" (Shariʿati 1981, 140). Or in another place, Shariʿati retorted to a critic, "I shall emphasize that I am a sociologist of religion and I understand *tawhid* historically. I am not concerned with the Truth of the Book, or with the correct comprehension of the Qur'an, Muhammad or Ali. For me, the important matter is the social and historical *tawhid*, it has always been the most important issue" (Shariʿati 1981, 215).

Similarly, on the problem of the cultural and historical contingency of religious knowledge Motahhari argued, "If one compares *fatwas* of different *fuqahā* and at the same time considers their personal lives and states of mind, it becomes clear that the intellectual presuppositions of a *faqih* and his knowledge of the external world inform his *fatwas*. That is why the *fatwa* of an Arab has an Arab flavor and the *fatwa* of an ʿAjam [non-Arab, Persian] has an ʿAjam flavor" (Motahhari 1962 and 1978, 101). Motahhari often compared the Qur'an to nature, a phenomenon that becomes increasingly comprehensible with the passage of time (Motahhari 1988, 147–152). In contrast to the revivalists who considered pristine renditions of Islam to be more authentic than contemporary interpretations, Motahhari believed that "*future* generations will have a better grasp and a deeper appreciation of the Divine text" (Motahhari 1985, 134).

But neither Shariʿati nor Motahhari developed an epistemological pluralism in which, as Soroush intended, *all* truth claims become contingent. Soroush did not question the certainty of faith but highlighted its *ineffability*. In this light, he rejected the revivalist (reformist or revolutionary) distinction between eternal and ephemeral, text and context. These dichotomies presupposed the responsibility of the reformist to appropriate religion as intended by God in a modern formulation.

In contrast to revivalists' Islamic ideology, which interprets the finality of Islam as a sign of its exhaustive rigidity, Soroush contended that Islam's finality signifies its indeterminate fluidity. The finality of Islam means that every generation experiences revelation *anew*. "Thus," he remarks, "revelation incessantly permeates us, in the same way that it hailed the

Arabs [during the time of the Prophet], as if the Prophet were chosen today. The secret of the finality of Islam lies in the perpetuity of the revelation" (Soroush 1994, 78). Accordingly, he reenvisioned the sharī'ah from a preconceived dogma into a continuously renewed and contested text.

By abandoning Islam as ideology, Soroush seeks to reclaim the enigma of religion. Rather than being a manifesto for action, he proposes that the *sharī'ah* is silent; it is given voice by its exponents. It is like history, which is given voice by the historian, or nature, the laws of which are constructed by the scientist. The *sharī'ah* does not put forward immutable answers to predicaments of all historical moments. That is not to suggest, he asserts, "the silence of the *sharī'ah* empties it of any meaning. Rather, its silence impedes any particular group from claiming access to its essence whereby they would prohibit and condemn competing understandings of religion" (Soroush 1995, 34). One should not regard the *sharī'ah* as an a priori knowledge. Religiosity demands an incessantly renewed exegesis. Accordingly, one cannot presuppose any particular meaning of the *sharī'ah* and then consider changes in its interpretation to be problematic (Soroush 1995, 186).

Various movements, Soroush observes, to make religion contemporary were based on a fallacy: one cannot *make* religion contemporary; any comprehension of religion is already shaped by contemporary concerns. "The modernity of religious knowledge is a description rather than a prescription" (Soroush 1995, 487). Human cognition is contingent on time and place. We comprehend only what religion *is* rather than what it *ought to* be. In other words, one grasps the social-temporal existence of religion, not its Divine-absolute essence (Soroush 1994, 199–231).

Soroush considers the religious text to be *hungry for* rather than *impregnated with* meaning. He believes that meaning is given to religion rather than extracted from it. "In every era," he writes, "the 'ulama' interpolate new questions and devise new responses from the *sharī'ah*.... The *totality* of these questions and answers define the contemporaneous religious knowledge" (Soroush 1995, 442). He argued that the mistaken identification of religion with the knowledge of it emanates from either "fiqhi positivism or popular idealism." For the positivist, the real is the tangible, thus objectively comprehensible through its transmission by senses. In contrast, the idealist regards existential reality as the reflection of a priori ideas lodged in the mind. Thus Soroush refers to "*fiqhi* positivism" as a doctrine that highlights the primacy of jurisprudence (*fiqh*) in religion and equates jurisprudential knowledge of religion with religion itself (Soroush 1995, 342–344). It is only in the idealist's perception that subjectivity and existence were identical and inseparable. "The minimum condition for a realist epistemology is the distinction between the object and the knowledge of it. Therefore, our understanding of the *sharī'ah*, even if we consider it flawless, is distinct from the *sharī'ah* itself" (Soroush 1995, 341).

The official responses to Soroush's theological interventions were uncompromising. In December 1991, the Central Office of the Honorable Leader's Representatives in the Universities warned "the spread of thoughts which consider religion to be a dependent variable of other human sciences is dangerous and negates the legitimacy of the Islamic state" (cited in Soroush 1995, 501). On September 9, 1995, in an editorial in Tehran's state-run paper *Ettelā'āt*, the supreme leader, Ayatollah Khamenei, also cautioned Soroush not to criticize clergy's privileged social position and their interpretive authority. In the words of then Iranian minister of foreign affairs, Ali Akbar Velayati, the "Dr. Soroush issue" was a matter of "threat to our national harmony" and "Iranian national independence." After mob groups attacked Soroush during a lecture in Isfahan, Velayati warned him to cease "dragging [issues of religious authority] into the daily newspapers" (1995).

A vast array of government officials and seminarians uniformly attacked Soroush for calling foundational religious texts historically contingent and equally open to multiple interpretations. Two influential ayatollahs, Mesbah Yazdi (Yazdi 1999) and Naser Makarem Shirazi (Shirazi 1991), both outspoken critics of Ali Shari`ati, warned their disciples and state officials of the perils of Soroush's "relativization of religious knowledge" and especially dangerous attempt to emasculate the interpretive authority of the clergy in religious matters.

During the 1990s, Soroush's theory of contraction and expansion became the conceptual framework for debating the religious justification of the Islamic Republic. From the floor of the parliament to editorial pages, from seminary quarters to street corners in Tehran, friends and foes clashed over the question of the contingencies of religious knowledge. The former speaker of the *majlis*, Ali Akbar Nateq Nuri, called for an end to competing interpretations of Islam and warned that they will weaken Muslims' faith in their religion. In a speech delivered to the Revolutionary Guards, he warned his audience that "the enemies of the revolution are exploiting naive people with these complicated theories to undermine their faith in order to defeat the revolution.... We need, to utilize new technologies of communication such as the internet to generate certainty in defending the principles of Islam and the revolution" (*Asr-e Azadegan*, September 18, 1999, No. 7, p. 3). A day later, in one of his repeated attacks on pluralism, Ayatollah Mesbah Yazdi began his Friday prayer sermon with the declaration that "We need to shut the mouth of anybody who claims that he has a new interpretation of Islam.... The consequence of uttering words against the absolutes of Islam is nothing but burning in hell, we will throw these fashionable ideas into the dustbin of history.... We should cut out the tongue of those who speak of multiple interpretations of the Qur'an" (*Asr-e Azadegan*, September 18, 1999, No. 7, p. 2).

The significance of Soroush's intervention in the postrevolutionary period was that he expanded the exegetical authority to actors outside seminaries. As the many attacks on his person and his ideas demonstrate, what was at stake was the authority to produce religious knowledge, which Soroush expanded to civil actors without clerical religious training. The most influential authorities in the clerical establishment viewed Soroush's ideas as a political intervention, which, if realized, would lead inevitably to the secularization of the Islamic Republic. They were not wrong.

By the end of 1996 it became apparent that the Soroush's public presence would be tolerated by neither his clerical detractors nor the vigilante guardians of the "blood of the martyrs." Even after the election of his friend and ally Mohammad Khatami to the presidency in May 1997, he remained as the main target of the "pressure groups." The failure of his friends in power to engender a safe, sustainable public sphere forced Soroush to head off for a fellowship at Harvard in 2000. For the first time, Harvard fellowship, and thereafter Princeton and the Wissenschaftskolleg in Berlin offered Soroush the possibility of situating himself within a global network of Muslim intellectuals. Before his departure for Cambridge, he published two of his most controversial books. Not only did the pressure fail to deter him from criticizing the orthodoxies of the Shi`ite clerical hierarchy, but also he continued to advance a radical religious pluralism that scandalized even some of those who had politically and theologically invested in his project.

Hermeneutics and Religious Pluralism

Through his epistemological critique, Soroush concluded that (1) God revealed religion so it could enter the domains of human culture and subjectivity within which it is comprehended and observed. The moment religion enters human subjectivity inevitably it becomes particular, and historically-culturally specific. (2) Religious knowledge corresponds to other mundane forms of knowledge. It is related to and inspired by *non*-religious knowledge production. (3) Religious knowledge is also historically progressive. Its advancement depends on the evolution of scientific understanding of the physical world and ever-expanding notions of rights and mutual obligations in society such as civil liberties or the rights of women, and so on.

In his earlier work, Soroush defined the epistemological contingencies of religious knowledge in an ambiguous relation with the historical and cultural contingencies of the Divine text. Whereas he initially approached problems in attaining religious knowledge with logical and systematic reasoning, later he became increasingly concerned with religious hermeneutics. Whereas he originally understood the diversity of religious knowledge as a reflection of historical progression, in his hermeneutics, he underscored regional, ethnic, and linguistic differences in exegesis of the sacred texts. Whereas earlier he put forward epistemological questions about the limits and truthfulness of knowledge claims, later, in two important books, *Straight Paths* (1998) and *Expansion of the Prophetic Experience* (1999), he emphasizes the reflexivity and plurality of human understanding.

The political context of his earlier work forced him to promote a suprahistorical conception of reason against the onslaught of basic institutions of civil society. This is evident in his openly political writings in *Siyāsat-Nāmeh* (Political Letters), where he defines the goal of democracy as the establishment of procedures that guaranteed the free engagement of rational experts (Soroush 2000). He believed that public deliberation of the meaning and social implications of religion should take place in a secure arena for the exercise of public reason, as in John Rawls (1993), and within a public sphere that allows undistorted communication and deliberative politics, as in Jürgen Habermas (1996).

While his detractors continued their assault on paper and pavement, with the publication of *Straight Paths,* Soroush took a significantly greater step away from doctrinal renditions of Islam. As Said Amir Arjomand observes, in *Straight Paths,* which conspicuously pluralizes the key Qur'anic phrase, "Soroush totally disregarded legalistic Islam and drew heavily on the tradition of Gnostic mysticism (*'irfān*), especially in the poetry of his favorite Rumi (d. 1273), to establish the principle of religious pluralism" (Arjomand 2002, 723). Soroush had always referenced Rumi in his argument for plurality of paths to *Truth*; this time he radicalized his rendition of Rumi to establish the plurality of *Truth* itself. "From the standpoint of Rumi," Soroush asserts, "the problem is not that some people have failed to find the Truth, [and] thus remained misguided and deprived. Rather, people's bewilderment results from the multiplicity of truths and the diversity in their manifestation. We are in awe of and attracted to different constituents of this divine diversity" (Soroush 1998, 27).

In Iran, Soroush's ecumenicalism came on the heels of controversies over his promotion of tolerance for diverse interpretations of Islam. Soroush weds these two projects, in his most radical book, *The Expansion of Prophetic Experience.* Walking on the razor's edge between heresy and faith, he ponders the moment when the earthly Prophet encountered the Divine. Soroush regards the Prophet's life and character as absolutely central to the revelation of the Qur'an. "Rather than a mere book or a collection of narratives," he contends, "Islam represents a historical movement; it is the embodiment of a historical mission. Islam is the historical expansion of a *gradually realized* Prophetic experience. Pivotal to its meaning is the Prophet's persona.... The Qur'anic revelation was woven around the Prophet's life circumstances; it revolved around his internal and external life experiences" (Soroush 1999, 19).

By linking revelation to the biography of the Prophet, not only does he bring to light the historicity of the Qur'an and the contingencies of its verses, but he also he draws distinctions between Islam, Christianity, and Judaism without interrogating their inherent Truth. That is to say, by emphasizing the constitutive significance of the Prophet's life circumstances in shaping the Qur'anic text, he transfers the debate over theological incongruities of Abrahamic religions to the realm of history. Soroush's assertion on the significance of the Prophet's life in shaping the message of the Qur'an revives two foundational debates from the formative decades of Islam. The first concerned the indeterminacy and rationality of human action, and the second the eternity (*qadim*) of the Holy Text.

Reason and Religion

Since the emergence of the earliest Islamic schools theology, rationalist philosophers thought that God's Justice (*'adl*) required believers to be responsible for their own actions. In order to accept the principle that a just God rewards salutary deeds and punishes the sinful, one must possess the freedom to determine one's own destiny. The rationalists considered it a violation of the principle of justice if God held people accountable for actions over which they had no power. Reason, the rationalist philosophers believed, was a constitutive faculty of humanity; its realization in action necessitated the recognition that life was essentially indeterminate. An important corollary of this principle was the link between Divine revelation and the actions of the Prophet. The Qur'an could have been different had the Prophet made different decisions in his social and political career. Soroush writes,

> A person would come and ask the Prophet a question, someone brought an accusation against his wife, one would ignite the flames of war, the Jews or Christians made particular decisions, many accused the Prophet of lunacy...they buried their sons and daughters alive, all these are reflected in the Qur'an and in the Prophet's words. Had the Prophet lived longer and faced more predicaments, those incidents would also have been reflected in the Qur'an. So, that is the meaning of the assertion that there could have been more written in the Qur'an. If Ayesha had not been accused of having an affair with another man, would the early verses of the *Sura Nur* have descended? If the war of *Ahzāb* had not occurred, would the *Sura al-Ahzāb* have been revealed? If there had been no Abu Lahab in Hijaz and he and his wife had not behaved with animus towards the Prophet, would the *Sura Abu Lahab* have appeared? These were all unnecessary events the occurrence of which did not have any historical significance. Now that they have indeed occurred, their mark is left in the Qur'an. (Soroush 1999, 20)

He argues that all religions are composed of two categories, *'arazi*, the contingent or accidental, and *zāti*, the substantial or essential. Accordingly, while they differ in their contingencies, all religions in their essence promote the same principles. "Religion," he reiterates, "does not have an Aristotelian nature, it only expresses God's *intentions*. These intentions define the essence of religion" (Soroush 1999, 80, emphasis added). Religious languages, the cultural and historical contexts of their revelations, particular juridical assertions, concrete teachings of everyday life, the wars they launch, and the peace treaties they forge are nonessential and contingent.

THE ETERNITY OF THE QUR'AN

Muslim theologians who rejected the idea of indeterminacy and subscribed to the determinist doctrine of predestination (*Jabriyya*) argued that the principle of eternity of the Qur'an exposed the fallacy of the hermeneutics of the Divine text. They rejected the rationalists' idea that God created (*Hadīth*) the Qur'an in relation to the Prophetic experience of Muhammad. Rather they argued that the Qur'an was eternal (*qadim*) and was revealed in its entirety in one instant to the Prophet. These theologians insisted that the Divine revelations speak eternal Truth without essential relation to the Prophet's biography or character. Not only did they argue that the Qur'an was uncreated and eternal, but more orthodox schools also went further to advocate that since speech was a Divine attribute, the verses in the Qur'an were spoken words of God.

Reviving an old debate, Soroush now stresses that the Prophet did not hear the *words* of God but had an inner experience of divinity, kindled by God, the meaning of which he was able to divulge to his contemporaries in words comprehensible to them. The language of Arabic, its cultural norms, economic and political doctrines, symbols of beauty, and all the other particulars in the Qur'an have nothing to do with the unattainable eternal Truth.

Soroush's detractors did not misjudge the political implications of his theses of religious pluralism. If the word of God, *Kalām Allah,* was not to be understood literally as Divine words but speechless mystic intuits known only to the Prophet, then no leader may justify his political authority as the exclusive and uncontested expression of the Divine Will. That would be tantamount politically to totalitarianism and religiously to blasphemy. "A politically sanctioned official rendition of Islam," Soroush declares, "is thus null and void" (Soroush 1999, 134).

CONCLUSION

Soroush has inaugurated one of the most important intellectual movements in contemporary Iran. He began his journey with an ideology critique first of Marxism and later of Islamism of pre- and postrevolutionary Iran. His hermeneutics and pluralist approach to Islam encouraged a new generation of intellectuals to moderate the Jacobin impulse of the postrevolutionary regime. They interpreted Soroush as calling for struggle for participatory democracy through the recognition of competing interpretations of Islam. For this generation, revolutionary Islamism, with its exclusivist truth claims, provided the ideological justification for totalitarianism. Rather than being an epistemological or cognitive matter, they understood hermeneutical Islam to be a deeply political issue.

Soroush advances his Islamic hermeneutics in response to theocratic tendencies in the Islamic Republic. Through this Islamic hermeneutics, unlike the ideological Islam of his predecessors, Soroush intends to *de*-politicize Islam and to reinvigorate its enigmatic core. For Soroush, political Islam is as an inescapable ground for totalitarianism. Although Soroush does not deny the public significance of religion in the promotion of a just society, this significance, he insists, needs to be exercised outside the sphere of state power.

Notes

1. His real name is Hossein Haj-Faraj-Dabagh, but he has always been known by his penname, Abdolkarim Soroush.
2. Mulla Sadra was a seventeenth-century Persian Gnostic philosopher. Many contemporary Muslim philosophers believe that he was one of the greatest exponents of metaphysical doctrines in Islam. Henry Corbin compared Mulla Sadra to a combination of St. Thomas Aquinas and Jakob Boehme within the Islamic context. According to S. H. Nasr, "Mulla Sadra's *Spiritual Journeys* [*al-asfar*] is the most monumental work of Islamic philosophy, in which rational arguments, illuminations received from spiritual realization and the tenets of revelation are harmonized in a whole which marks in a sense the summit of a thousand years of intellectual activity in the Islamic world" (Nasr 1992, 335–336). While the great ayatollahs and other teachers at the Shi'ite seminaries were generally experts in *fiqh*, Allameh Tabataba'i, revived Shi`i philosophical traditions, especially Mulla Sadra's illuminationist rationalism in the Qom seminary. Ayatollah Khomeini was another exponent of Gnostic philosophical traditions at Qom, where, in addition to Mulla Sadra, he also taught Ibn Arabi's Sufism.
3. Included in these publications were Soroush 1979a, 1979b, 1979c, 1979d, 1980.
4. *Satanic Ideology* was the title of book published in 1980. It contained a series of talks and articles against the perils of Marxism, which he delivered soon after the triumph of the revolution.
5. "Masked Dogmatism" was the title of the talk Soroush delivered in 1979 at the School of Economics at Tehran University, which was later published as a short monograph. *Satanic Ideology* was an expanded version of the same monograph.
6. Among them were influential figures of the reform movement such as Reza Tehrani, Mashallah Shamsolva`ezin, Morteza Mardiha, Majid Mohammadi, Mostafa Tajzadeh, Hamid Reza Jala'ipour, Mohsen Sazgara, Akbar Ganji, Ahmad Borqani, Mohammad Abtahi, Said Hajjarian, and even Mohammad Khatami, who later was elected as the president in 1997.

References

Habermas, Jürgen. 1996. *Between Facts and Norms: Contribution to a Discourse Theory of Law and Democracy*. Cambridge, MA: MIT Press.

Jala'ipour, Hamid-Reza. 1999. *Pas az dovvom-e Khordād* [After the Second of Khordad)]. Tehran: Kavir.

Khomeini, Ayatollah Ruhollah. 1994. *Sahifeh-ye Nur: Majmu`e-ye rahnemudha-ye Imam Khomeini* [The Collected Declarations of Imam Khomeini]). Vol. 12. Tehran: The Organization of the Islamic Revolution's Cultural Documents.
Motahhari, Morteza. 1962. *Bahsi darbāre-ye marja`iyyat va rohaniyyat* [A Treatise on the Source of Imitation and the Clergy]. Tehran.
Motahhari, Morteza. 1978. *Motahhari's Dah goftār* [Ten Discourses]. Tehran: Hekmat.
Motahhari, Morteza. 1988. *Khātamiyat* [Finality]. Tehran: Sadra.
Motahhari, Morteza. 1985. *Shesh maqāleh* [Six Essays]. Tehran: Sadra.
Nasr, Seyyed Hossein. 1992. *Science and Civilization in Islam*. New York: Barnes & Noble Books.
Quchani, Mohammad. 2004. "Qabz va bast-e perātik-e Soroush" [The Practical Expansion and Constriction of Soroush]. *Sharq* (New Year Special Edition) 1383, pp. 50–51.
Rawls, John. 1993. *Political Liberalism*. New York: Columbia University Press.
Said, Amir Arjomand. 2002. Reform Movement in Contemporary Iran. *International Journal of Middle East Studies* 34: 4, pp. 719–734.
Shari'ati, Ali. 1981. *Islamshenāsi* [Islamology]. Vol. 1. Tehran: Entesharat-e Shari'ati.
Shirazi, Naser Makarem. 1991 *Javānān va moshkelāt-e fekri* [Youth and Problems of Mind]. Qom: Khorram.
Soroush, Abdolkarim. 1979a. *Tazād-e diālektiki* [Dialectical Contradiction]. Tehran: Serat.
Soroush, Abdolkarim. 1979b. *Danish va arzesh* [Knowledge and Value]. Tehran: Yaran.
Soroush, Abdolkarim. 1979c. *Falsafeh-ye tārikh* [Philosophy of History]. Tehran: Payam-e Azadi.
Soroush, Abdolkarim. 1979d. *`Elm chist? Falsafeh chist?* [What Is Science? What Is Philosophy?]. Tehran: Serat.
Soroush, Abdolkarim. 1980. *Eideolozhi-ye shaytani* [The Satanic Ideology]. Tehran: Serat.
Soroush, Abdolkarim. 1982. *Nahād-e nā-ārām-e jahān* [The Restless Nature of the Universe]. Tehran: Qalam.
Soroush, Abdolkarim. 1983. *Bani Sadr, Sāzmān-e Mojāhedin va Hegelism* [Bani Sadr, the Mojahedin, and Hegelianism]. Rome: Centro Culturale Islamic Europeo.
Soroush, Abdolkarim. 1987. *Tafarroj-e son': Goftārhā-ei dar Akhlāq va san'at va elm-e ensāni* [Essays on Human Sciences, Ethics, and Technology]. Tehran: Serat.
Soroush, Abdolkarim. 1994. *Farbeh-tar az eideolozhi* [Loftier Than Ideology]. Tehran: Serat.
Soroush, Abdolkarim. 1995. *Qabz va bast-e teorik-e shari`at* [The Theoretical Contraction and Expansion of the Shari`ah]. Tehran: Serat.
Soroush, Abdolkarim. 1998. *Serāt-hā-ye mostaqim* [Straight Paths]. Tehran: Serat, 27.
Soroush, Abdolkarim. 1999. *Bast-e tajrobeh-ye nabavi* [The Expansion of Prophetic Experience]. Tehran: Serat.
Soroush, Abdolkarim. 2000. *Siyāsat-Nāmeh* [Political Letters]. Vols. 1–2. Tehran: Serat.
Velayati, Ali Akbar. December 26, 1995. *Kayhan*, editorial. (Cited in Human Rights Watch Report, *Iran: Power Versus Choice*, March 1996, vol. 8–1 E). Available at: http://hrw.org/reports/1996/Iran.htm. Accessed 20 May 2013.
Yazdi, Mohammad Taqi Mesbah. 1999. *Tahājom-e farhangi* [Cultural Assault]. Qom: Imam Khomeini Teaching and Research Institute.

PART III

ISLAM AND POLITICS AROUND THE WORLD

CHAPTER 18

ISLAM AND POLITICS IN NORTH AMERICA

ABDULLAH A. AL-ARIAN

Over the past half century, the presence of an Islamic community in North America has been treated as a recent phenomenon in the continent's rich history, exhibited through the lives of mid-twentieth-century Muslim converts such as Malcolm X and Muhammad Ali. In the years leading up to the attacks of September 11, 2001, the focus on Muslims in North America shifted to the recent immigrant community, viewed through the lens of the security challenges posed by a perceived impending confrontation between the Western and Islamic worlds. In both cases, Islam has been presented as an alien faith that is largely out of step with mainstream American culture and traditional values. The following discussion will attempt to shed light on Islam's historical legacy in North America, demonstrating its contributions to the complex mosaic of American life. With a proper understanding of the historical context of Islam's presence in this region of the Western hemisphere, one is better able to explain the recent developments in the Muslim community, including the maturation of its identity and its establishment of prominent political institutions. In light of the Muslim community's recent attempts to secure its civil rights and carve out a place within the broader American public square, these efforts have all the hallmarks of prior struggles, whether by indigenous or immigrant communities, making the story of Muslims in this continent a distinctly American experience.

Historical Background

Recent scholarship on Islam in America has attempted to dispel the traditional notion that dates Islam's emergence on the continent to the Black Nationalist movements of the 1930s. In fact, this literature provides a compelling portrait of a Muslim presence in North America from the dawn of the Columbian era.[1] The Age of Exploration, which began with Christopher Columbus's voyage to the New World in 1492, coincided with the end of Islamic rule in Spain after nearly eight centuries that featured the rise of one of the most advanced multicultural civilizations in history, known as *convivencia*. The era in world history that began with European discovery of the Americas cannot be separated from the key developments taking place within the Old World, namely, the establishment of a Christian empire on the ruins of an Islamic one. The legacy of Islamic Spain appears throughout the expedition by Columbus, who relied on Morisco ship owners, African navigators, and Muslim technology to reach the Americas.

In the centuries that followed, as the trajectory of global power continued to tilt in favor of European kingdoms, often at the expense of Islamic dynasties, Muslims who came to America were brought as slaves from West Africa to serve in the rapidly expanding colonial outposts. There are no reliable estimates on the percentage of African slaves in the Americas who were Muslim in background—much of this research is still in its infancy— but a number of historical accounts have been brought to light. In recent years, an attempt has been made to popularize the experiences of Muslim slaves through books and films devoted to the lives of Ayuba Suleiman Diallo, an eighteenth-century slave whose remarkable journey allowed him to eventually return to his home along the Gambia River in West Africa, or ʿAbd al-Rahman Ibrahima Sora, an African prince enslaved in the Americas during the early nineteenth century and freed only after the intervention of President John Quincy Adams. In these cases, the Muslim slaves were highly educated, reading and writing in Arabic and exhibiting a strong Islamic identity with knowledge of the Qur'an and the Hadith. In some instances, they ensured that their families continued to practice the religion, even under the most austere circumstances.

In contrast to these exceptional stories, however, the great majority of Muslim slaves in the American colonies suffered the same hardships and indignities as non-Muslim slaves, with almost no avenues to attain their freedom. Most were forced to repress their Islamic identities, and those who continued to practice their faith did so in secret, severely restricting their ability to pass it on to their descendants. It is no surprise then, that in the homogeneous cultural and political climate of colonial America, little remained of the West African slaves' Islamic character in the generations that followed. It was not until the twentieth century, during the early days of the civil rights movement, that some African Americans made a concerted effort to rediscover their Muslim heritage, finding in it a source of empowerment.

In addition to the population of African slaves, a subtle yet ever present undercurrent of Islamic culture developed throughout the course of early American history. In 2006, when the first American Muslim elected to the US Congress chose to take his oath of office on a Qur'an once owned by Thomas Jefferson, many Americans were surprised to learn that one of their founding fathers had kept a copy of Islam's holy book in his private library. Indeed, some of America's most enduring literary figures, including Edgar Allan Poe and Herman Melville, claim Islamic texts among their influences. In some cases, this curiosity was piqued by Americans embarking on a spiritual quest outside of their dominant religious culture. Such was the experience of Alexander Russell Webb, a journalist and diplomat who became one of the most prominent American converts to Islam before the turn of the century. Recent scholarship has focused on Webb as a foundational figure in the development of a distinctly American Islam.[2] Following his travels abroad and interaction with Muslims in Asia, Webb returned to the United States to establish one of the earliest Muslim institutions in the country. Through his organization and publications, Webb attempted to attract other Americans to Islam, citing the common values and aspirations shared by his cultural background and his new faith.

In the first half of the twentieth century, Islam's presence in America spread at a far more rapid pace, and along several parallel tracks. These divisions represent the background and makeup of these communities, commonly depicted as an indigenous versus immigrant divide. Rising immigration from the Arab territories under Ottoman rule was a sign of the great empire's state of permanent decline. Mostly uneducated and unskilled laborers, Christians as well as Muslims came to North America in search of a new life. They settled mainly in the Midwestern United States, in newly industrialized cities such as Michigan City, Indiana; Detroit, Michigan; and Cedar Rapids, Iowa, home to one of the oldest mosques in America. Further west, immigrants from South Asia began to seek new opportunities in the expanding economy of California. These trends continued steadily until the National Origins Act severely restricted immigration from nonwhite countries for four decades beginning in 1925. Though this era saw the establishment of some of the earliest lasting institutions of the American Muslim community, these mosques and Islamic centers were usually the exception. This wave of Muslim immigration is marked by a far greater tendency toward assimilation into the broader American society, as seen in the number of families in the community who changed their names and ceased religious observances, especially among second-and third-generation immigrants. In both instances, the contributions of this community to its adopted homeland remained constant, with a number of immigrant Muslims serving alongside fellow citizens in the US military during World War II.

The African American experience with Islam in the first half of the twentieth century was vastly different from that of the immigrant community. Continuing to suffer the effects of institutionalized discrimination and inequality decades after the abolition of slavery, African Americans were not granted the same economic opportunities, and therefore did not harbor the same visions of the American dream as many immigrants did. Instead, the African American population engaged in a civil rights struggle and in some prominent circles within that movement, Islam played a significant role as a political, cultural, and spiritual force. Early encounters with Islam in the African American community involved conversion to the faith through particular organizations, such as the Moorish Science Temple or the Nation of Islam. Due to fundamental doctrinal differences, these movements were regarded as conflicting with traditional Islam, but served as an important stepping-stone for many African American converts to mainstream Sunni Islam. Under the leadership of Elijah Muhammad, the Nation of Islam established a number of important institutions addressing the community's needs, including schools, cultural centers, and social service organizations. It also focused on the political demands of the growing African American Muslim community, by creating external avenues for change, rather than encouraging direct political participation. Though by no means the first, Malcolm X (later, El-Hajj Malik El-Shabazz) was one of the most prominent figures to make the transition from an exclusively African American Muslim group to mainstream Islam. El-Shabazz continued to be a powerful voice for African American rights in the context of the larger Black Nationalist movement, but began to integrate traditional Islamic principles, such as universal equality, in his message. His departure from the Nation of Islam and embrace of traditional Islam in the mid-1960s signaled an important transition in the history of Islam in America.

The Modern Community and Early Institutions

Offering a tribute at the funeral of El-Hajj Malik El-Shabazz in February 1965 was Omar Osman, a Muslim college student of Sudanese background. The tragedy of El-Shabazz's assassination brought together the two constituencies of the American Muslim community, with its indigenous and immigrant components, ushering in a new era of Islam in America, one that featured increased fluidity and interaction among communities and greater appreciation of their cultural diversity. Later that same year, the administration of Lyndon Johnson repealed longstanding immigration quotas, paving the way for increased migration to the United States from countries with large Muslim populations. Perhaps more significantly, this wave of immigration featured a qualitatively different profile than that of previous eras. Whether in the indigenous or immigrant communities, the contemporary American Muslim identity is largely the product of the significant developments that began in the late 1960s.

Hailing mainly from the Middle East and South Asia, the Muslim immigrants to America after 1965 were naturally a reflection of the recent changes in their societies. On the heels of the development policies in such countries as Egypt and Pakistan, they were more highly educated, often in technical fields such as engineering and medicine, and came to pursue advanced degrees in the United States or start their own businesses. Unlike earlier Muslim communities, these immigrants became independently wealthy at a rapid pace and were integrated into a growing American middle class. On a cultural level, they held more firmly to their Islamic identity, embodying the recent religious revival across the Islamic world, as represented by such groups as the Muslim Brotherhood and *Jamāʿat-i Islāmī*. The institutions developed during this period signified the growing international character of the American Muslim community, witnessed by the close linkages maintained between local mosques and student groups in the United States and Canada and their counterparts in the Muslim world. It was not uncommon, for instance, for a prominent Islamist figure, such as the Sudanese intellectual Hasan al-Turabi or Egyptian scholar Yusuf al-Qaradawi, to embark on speaking tours across North American universities and Islamic centers.

The Muslim Students Association (MSA), originally established in 1963 to provide local religious services on American campuses, expanded greatly to meet the growing needs of a community that desired to extend its activities beyond fulfilling basic ritual requirements. By the mid-1970s, the MSA had an established national headquarters and was holding regular meetings to address the community's urgent political concerns, such as the recent Soviet invasion of Afghanistan, the fallout from the Islamic revolution in Iran, or the continuing Israeli occupation of Palestine. In later years, the community's great emphasis on international affairs would face internal and external critiques. However, in its time, this activism signaled the first major collective action on the part of the American Muslim community as a coherent political constituency, and signaled a recognition of the growing role the United States was playing in deciding the fate of fellow Muslims around the globe. Early American Muslim political activism generally consisted of keeping community members informed of important developments overseas, using the pulpits of mosques and a burgeoning Islamic press as their main tools, while establishing charitable organizations to provide support to those suffering from various forms of oppression throughout the Muslim world.

The decade that followed witnessed an important development in the state of the community of recent immigrants. Having settled in North America and enjoyed a considerable degree of professional success, the community set out to form permanent institutions commensurate with its established presence in American life. Out of the MSA, an organization serving the needs of students as they pursued their education, came the Islamic Society of North America (ISNA), a national umbrella organization that includes mosques, community centers, professional associations, educational institutions, and family support groups. In addition, ISNA maintains the North American Islamic Trust (NAIT), an institution that provides financial backing for Islamic projects throughout the United States and Canada. This period featured a boom in the number of mosques and Islamic centers and a significant transition from the use of commercial properties and private homes to freestanding structures built for the sole purpose of serving the community's religious and social needs. Another feature of this period was the founding of Islamic educational institutions across the country. Over two hundred full-time Islamic schools educate thousands of Muslim children, yet another sign that the immigrant community abandoned the "myth of return," that is, the conception of America as a temporary economic haven on the road back to one's homeland. Instead, the community began to invest in the future of its American-born children and the cultivation of an Islamic identity in harmony with American values.

For the African American Muslim community, the 1970s and 1980s was a period of great transformation as well. Following the death of his father, Imam Warith Deen Muhammad inherited the leadership of the Nation of Islam. Through his education in traditional Islamic studies, Muhammad led the majority of his community into mainstream Sunni Islam and welcomed many new converts into the fold. Until his death in 2008, W. D. Muhammad's nationwide network of mosques and Sister Clara Muhammad schools made him one of the most prominent Muslim leaders in the United States. He is consistently recognized for his role in bridging the gap between the Islam of the Black Nationalist movement and a mainstream African American Islamic identity that seeks to carve out its place within the larger American cultural landscape.

CIVIL RIGHTS AND ELECTIONS: THE EMERGENCE OF AMERICAN MUSLIM POLITICS

American Muslims had explored the possibility of entering the public domain as a political constituency for many years. As early as 1983, a visionary community leader named Mohammad T. Mehdi founded the National Council on Islamic Affairs in New York as an effort to encourage Muslims to participate in American politics. Among Mehdi's many accomplishments was the successful campaign to place the crescent and star, Islamic cultural symbols, side by side with Christian and Jewish symbols in official decorations at the White House and the World Trade Center.[3] Internally, however, the broader community had yet to embrace the idea of political participation for a number of reasons, including the lack of institutional support and civic education, and questions as to the religious permissibility of participating in a non-Muslim political system. Moreover, the urgency for engagement in the political process was not yet apparent in the 1980s, as the community's priorities lay in the dual tasks of developing internal institutions and assisting struggles abroad. Early in the next decade, however, all of these challenges would be overcome at a lightening pace.

Just as the Cold War had drawn to a close, the United States led a coalition of nations into the Persian Gulf to force Iraq's withdrawal from Kuwait. It was the first large-scale American military action in the Middle East and signaled the beginning of a significant presence in the region that has solidified over the course of two decades. In the aftermath of the Gulf War, American thinkers and pundits contemplated impending challenges to the nascent unipolar system dominated by US power, the "new world order," as described by George H. W. Bush. Noted scholars such as Bernard Lewis and Samuel Huntington advanced the notion that the world of Islam, stretching from Morocco to Indonesia and comprising over 1 billion people, constituted the key threat to the post-Cold War global order. Raising the specter of "Islam's bloody borders," Huntington predicted a "clash of civilizations" between Islam and the West, laying the foundation for an intellectual project that would gain much currency in American policy-making circles in the ensuing years.[4] Seemingly for the first time since it became organized as a national religious constituency, the American Muslim community was forced to confront a rising challenge that pitted its layered identities against one another.

Whatever internal divisions had existed within the American Muslim community regarding the permissibility of participating in the political process had all but disappeared by the mid-1990s. The dominant view that emerged from that debate argued that engagement of the political system was the most effective means of defending the community's rights, advancing its interests, and claiming its place within the broader American political landscape, thereby dispelling the notion that American Muslims stood on the frontlines of an impending battle between the Western and Islamic worlds.

During the early years of this period, the community met with a considerable degree of success. American Muslim leaders established several national political organizations with varying points of emphasis, from promoting civic education in local communities, to monitoring media coverage and legislation concerning Muslims, to outright lobbying of lawmakers. Unlike older organizations such as ISNA that focused mainly on religious and cultural issues within the community, these institutions maintained an outward orientation with a decidedly political emphasis. The American Muslim Alliance (AMA) established nearly one hundred local chapters around the United States to provide civic education and promote an electoral strategy that ranged from local to national elections. The Council on American-Islamic Relations (CAIR) became a prominent fixture in local and national media to provide balance in the coverage on issues of concern to the American Muslim community, and also worked to defend the rights of Muslims in cases of work discrimination or hate crimes.

The American Muslim Council (AMC), based out of the nation's capital, took on the lobbying efforts necessary to bring about real change in the community's most pressing issue areas. Its leaders established strong relationships with top officials in both political parties and AMC was well on its way to building a permanent presence in the Washington corridors. Founded in California, the Muslim Public Affairs Council (MPAC) offers its research and policy papers to political leaders, members of the media, and the entertainment industry in the hopes of bringing about more accurate representation of Muslims in the spheres of policy and popular culture. Another organization, the Muslim American Society (MAS), was established out of the activism of the 1980s and traces its roots to the Islamic movement in the Arab world, whose influence was instrumental in the development of the early American Muslim organizations. Active within a large number of mosques across the country and at the national level, MAS provides charitable support as well as social activism within the community. The Council for Good Government (CGG), the political arm of W. D. Muhammad's organization, also made important strides during this period. In 1992, Muhammad became the first Muslim to offer the opening prayers before a session of the US Senate.[5]

Though modest, the gains made by the early American Muslim political organizations were considerable given the community's prior status as a virtually nonexistent force in politics. Many policymakers were intrigued by the rise of a new political constituency, which, if able to harness its high level of education and vast resources, could form a valuable electoral bloc. Some politicians sought to cultivate a strong working relationship with American Muslims in the hopes of providing Washington with a fresh perspective on many of the crucial issues facing the country. Among their successes, American Muslim organizations raised awareness within the Clinton administration of the plight of Bosnian Muslims in the former Yugoslavia and the victims of hate crimes at home. They also educated policymakers on Islam, resulting in annual holiday greetings addressed to the community and Ramadan *iftars* at the White House. In 2001, the United States Postal Service issued a postage stamp commemorating the Islamic Eid holidays.[6]

On the critical issues, however, it became clear that American Muslim leaders lacked the experience and the political clout to bring about real change. In spite of their calls for the United States to take a more evenhanded approach to the Peace Process in the Middle East, American foreign policy in the region continued much in the same direction. The organizations faced critics from within the community and from the society at large. Internally, the community was frustrated with the lack of coordination among the various political organizations, especially the perception of divisions along ethnic and cultural lines. The community's detractors in the political and media spheres charged that its political activism represented foreign interests that were in conflict with US policy. These critics frequently used the backgrounds and past affiliations of many Muslim leaders as proof of their dual loyalties. In the mid-1990s, a new challenge would swiftly shift the landscape of American Muslim political activism, bringing home many of the concerns that had been simmering in the background for some time.

The secret evidence civil rights crisis was the product of the rising concern over terrorist attacks in the United States. In the ongoing discourse regarding a violent confrontation between the Western and Islamic worlds, minority Muslim communities in Europe, Canada, and the United States became a focal point for national security policy. Out of the ashes of the 1995 Oklahoma City bombing, an attack perpetrated by domestic terrorists, Congress passed antiterrorism legislation that focused primarily on the perceived terrorist threat from immigrant communities. Beginning in 1996, federal authorities initiated legal proceedings against a number of individuals, detaining them indefinitely without charges and on the basis of classified information that they could neither see nor confront in court. In all, thirty secret evidence cases were brought in communities around the country. Nearly every case targeted a Muslim immigrant, usually one who had resided in the United States for years with established family and community ties.[7]

In its early stages, the effort to combat the use of secret evidence occurred primarily at the local level, where communities rallied around a particular case, devising strategies to challenge the detention in the judicial, legislative, and public spheres. American Muslim leaders sought to raise awareness of the secret evidence cases in their local communities, relying on the news media to investigate the new policy and provide a human face to the story by profiling the victims and their families. Realizing that the community could not wage this civil rights battle alone, American Muslim groups enlisted the help of other organizations, ranging from conservative religious groups to civil liberties organizations. Together, these ad hoc coalitions convened informational lectures, held mass protests, and met with public officials to request an investigation into the use of secret evidence by the Department of Justice and propose a legislative remedy for the problem. They also employed top immigration and constitutional attorneys to challenge the cases in court. The struggle against secret evidence centered on two overarching themes: the constitutional concerns arising from the government's tactics and the singling out of a minority community toward whom these abuses were directed.

It was not long before the struggle to end the use of secret evidence and free those detained by it across the country became a national campaign. Nearly all major American Muslim political organizations prioritized the civil rights crisis facing the community, joining with nearly twenty prominent religious and civil liberties groups in what came to be known as the National Coalition to Protect Political Freedom (NCPPF). The new organization took the three-pronged local strategy to the national level, building on the momentum to educate the public and policy makers on the issue. Two dozen newspapers, including the *New York Times* and *Washington Post*, published editorials decrying the use of secret evidence. In the House of Representatives, a bill to ban its use in court proceedings was sponsored by several congressional allies of the American Muslim community. By 1999, the legislation had received over 130 co-sponsors, representing both political parties. In the House Judiciary Committee, a hearing on the issue was held, featuring the testimony of a constitutional law expert and victims of secret evidence. The bill passed a committee vote by a count of 28–2, paving the way for a vote on the House floor. For its part, the Clinton administration had responded to concerns over its practices by pledging to review all future secret evidence cases at the level of the attorney general, effectively suspending the practice, as no new cases were brought following the announcement.[8] Indeed, by early 2000, it appeared as though the American Muslim community had finally come of age as a political constituency. In the first major test to the community's aspirations in the public square, its institutions successfully transformed a civil rights crisis affecting a segment of their community into a national issue that deserved the attention of policy makers in Washington. As the challenges mounted during the course of this battle, it became clear to American Muslim leaders that in order to earn a seat at the decision-making table, first the civil rights struggle had to be won.

Although it had gained considerable momentum, passage of the congressional bill to end the use of secret evidence was interrupted by the 2000 elections. The American Muslim leadership understood that in order to carry its recent gains forward into the next administration, it must engage in the electoral process. Prior attempts to establish an American Muslim voting bloc had largely ended in failure. As recently as 1996, the national leadership could not agree on the main issue areas affecting the community, often prioritizing foreign affairs at the expense of domestic issues, or vice versa. Furthermore, as a young and unproven community, American Muslims did not generate much enthusiasm from the presidential campaigns, receiving virtually no attention from Bill Clinton, while Bob Dole's campaign addressed American Muslim leaders as heads of a foreign lobby.[9]

The scene four years later stood in stark contrast to that of the previous election cycle. With the anticipation of one of the closest presidential races in nearly half a century, and the sudden emergence of an active and organized Muslim community in the United States, the campaigns hoped to elicit the support of this new constituency. The leaders of the American Muslim political organizations came together to harness the electoral power of their community, composed of 6 million citizens, according to their own accounts. The American Muslim Political Coordination Council (AMPCC), an umbrella group comprising all the major political organizations, explored the possibility of demonstrating the community's growth and unity by endorsing a presidential candidate and encouraging all American Muslims to cast their ballots in his favor. The immediate goals for the election were clear-cut: develop an internal consensus on the most pressing issues, engage the candidates on those issues, and ultimately endorse the one who appears most responsive to the community's concerns.

The issue of secret evidence, especially within the larger context of civil rights abuses, took on the status of top priority within the American Muslim community. After all, it had been the issue that mobilized the community into political action and galvanized a nationwide lobbying effort. Another focal point of AMPCC member groups was greater inclusion in the political process. President Clinton had made some moves in this regard, including the appointment of Muslims to various government posts, but these were viewed as largely symbolic gestures. Though continuing to be important, foreign policy issues such as the faltering Palestinian-Israeli peace process or the debilitating sanctions on Iraq were relegated to secondary status for the first time in the community's short history of political activism. The American Muslim community had come to the realization that the foundation for these larger issues would be built upon successes in smaller areas; in other words, the fight for civil rights would place the community on the path toward political empowerment.

With only a few weeks remaining until the 2000 election, the AMPCC made its decision to endorse the Republican candidate George W. Bush for president. The combination of the community's interaction with the candidates during the campaign and a close examination of their respective platforms established Bush as the favorite over Al Gore, then the vice-president and Democratic candidate. Whether as a result of taking American Muslim votes for granted (as they had traditionally voted for Democrats), or out of a desire to avoid confronting the community over the Clinton administration's dismal civil rights record, Gore remained inaccessible to the American Muslim community during the duration of the campaign, repeatedly canceling scheduled events or sending low-level representatives in his place. Bush, on the other hand, not only met with American Muslims but also went out of his way to speak with them during his campaign stops. In early October, when Bush stood before the nation during the second presidential debate and declared secret evidence to be a form of racial profiling, and then proceeded to endorse the legislation to end the practice, many American Muslims believed they had found a candidate who understood their concerns. For his part, Gore could only muster a similar statement in response the following day. As a member of the administration responsible for the secret evidence phenomenon, however, American Muslim leaders expected him to take a more forceful stance and possibly take immediate measures to roll back the abuses in the justice system.

The American Muslim community could not have chosen a more critical election in which to make its presence felt as an electoral bloc. When the smoke settled weeks after the election, Bush had won by the narrowest of margins. Across the nation, various exit polls indicated that the American Muslim vote for Bush ranged from 70 to 80 percent. Florida, the state whose twenty-five electoral college votes determined the outcome of the election, was home to one of the nation's most prominent secret evidence cases and an active Muslim community that voted heavily in favor of the Republican candidate, by a margin of 3 to 1.[10] Even within the African American Muslim community, whose leaders refused to join the AMPCC's endorsement, the rate of those who voted for Bush was twice as high as it was among African Americans generally (18 percent to 9 percent). Some Republican leaders were quick to acknowledge the difference made by the Muslim community's participation and an effort was made to continue the dialogue with the incoming administration. American Muslims running for office also experienced unprecedented success, with 153 elected that November to positions at the state and local levels.[11]

For the first half of 2001, the American Muslim community had reached the height of its political empowerment. The last of the secret evidence victims was freed in December 2000, following a victory in court and an unsuccessful eleventh hour attempt by government officials to block his release by appealing to the attorney general. The new administration was hopeful of establishing a strong working relationship with the American Muslim leadership, inviting representatives of all the major organizations to several high level meetings in Washington. A member of the community, Suheil Khan, was appointed to the White House Office of Public Liaison to assist in coordinating activities with American Muslims. Along with Christian and Jewish groups, Muslim organizations were called upon to participate in the Bush administration's Faith-Based and Community Initiative, a government program designed to provide funds to religious groups who offer social services in their local communities. Finally, the Secret Evidence Repeal Act was reintroduced in the new session of Congress and by late summer had regained its momentum.[12] An announcement from the White House supporting its passage was scheduled for September 11, 2001. As fate would have it, the morning's events would drastically alter the political landscape in the United States and reconfigure the place of the American Muslim community within it.[13]

9/11 AND ITS AFTERMATH

In the American Muslim community's quest for political empowerment, there is no question that the September 11 attacks undid years of dedicated efforts. The domestic fallout from the worst terrorist attack on American soil initially served as a reality check to the recent advancements made by the community's political organizations. The successes in the areas of secret evidence and the bloc vote were placed in their proper perspective once the stakes became much higher. Although political leaders from the president on down made strong public statements against painting all Muslims with the brush of extremism, the toxic atmosphere and the dangerous combination of fear and hysteria in the weeks and months after the attacks made association with the community a dangerous prospect for most public figures. Additionally, in the course of its struggle for political empowerment, the American Muslim leadership had engendered a powerful opposition movement intent on maintaining the status quo and those forces were now mobilized to roll back the modest gains the community had achieved in the public sphere.

With reports of anti-Muslim hate crimes on the rise, CAIR and other organizations were flooded with requests by community members to provide legal assistance and help educate local law enforcement officials to dispel myths about American Muslims. More troubling was the possibility that, in addition to criminal acts targeting Muslims, political leaders would advocate policies with major implications for the civil rights of this religious minority. American Muslim groups had recently made considerable progress in shifting public perception of the community from the prism of the national security to that of civil liberties. In the immediate aftermath of 9/11, however, the pendulum swung swiftly in favor of policies that viewed the American Muslim community as a potential threat to US security. The Patriot Act was passed in Congress to anchor the domestic side of the set of policies that made up the "War on Terror." In one of the first major blows to the American Muslim community after 9/11, the legislation did away with the civil rights restored by the end of secret evidence and brought about a new wave of abuses, many of them far more serious than anything witnessed in the previous decade. Thousands of Muslims were detained without charge and many more were questioned by federal agents regarding their religious and political beliefs and associations. Even more troubling to some was the systematic targeting of American Muslim leaders and institutions, resulting in a number of high profile politically charged arrests and prosecutions.

In the shadow of US military action in Afghanistan and Iraq, the American Muslim community stood on a knife's edge, forced to prove its loyalty to the country, while also wishing to exercise its right to condemn abuses in the War on Terror to which Muslims around the world were subjected. The diverse coalitions that proved so essential to the success of the community's activism in the 1990s no longer played an important part in defending the rights of the vulnerable minority, as self-preservation became the order of the day. For its part, the mainstream media helped stoke the flames of suspicion and fear toward American Muslim groups. This appeared to be part of a downward trend, as a Columbia University study of news coverage during the first anniversary of the September 11 attacks concluded that it was "less contextual, less balanced, and more negative and critical of Muslims and Arabs in the United States than in the immediate post-9/11 period."[14] Politically, the community's national organizations were incapable of making the same impact during the 2004 presidential election as they had in 2000. Both political parties made virtually no attempts to reach out to American Muslims and resisted opportunities to meet with community leaders. Moreover, the community's overwhelming support for Democratic candidate John Kerry was not enough to turn the tide against Bush's reelection, diminishing the importance of the electoral bloc built up in the previous election.

As the decade drew to a close, the American Muslim community reached a critical juncture in its history. Its civil rights were under threat of the excesses of the War on Terror, its institutions were under siege and ill equipped to deal with the challenges of post-9/11 America, and it was nearly powerless in the face of the increased perception that the United States was at war with Islam. Nonetheless, out of the adversity of this period came a number of bright spots that should not be overlooked. American Muslims used the opportunity of the US wars to demonstrate the community's loyalty to its country. A fatwa issued by Islamic scholars affirmed the permissibility of American Muslims to serve in the military, even as it went into war in Afghanistan, a Muslim country.[15] Additionally, the 9/11 tragedy brought about an unprecedented level of interest in Islam across the United States, providing the Muslim minority with the challenge to break through the facile stereotypes and act as ambassadors of their community to the society at large. In the face of a burgeoning Islamophobia, campaigns to educate Americans about Islam and Muslims took off in the years after 9/11. The mainstream media, in spite of its frequent negative coverage, also took a greater interest in the community and actually gave positive portrayals of American Muslims in the days after September 11. There was a discernible shift from topical to thematic coverage that included profiles of the community. For the first time in history, publications such as the *New York Times* appointed reporters to an "American Muslim beat" and featured occasional contributions by writers from the community.

Internally, the American Muslim leadership eventually resumed its efforts to unite various elements of the community and close the divisions in its ranks. A broader coalition was built under the banner of the American Muslim Taskforce on Civil Rights and Elections (AMT) that included more organizations than previous umbrella groups. Though it traditionally shied away from participation in political activities, ISNA joined in these efforts. In 2002, its annual convention was held in Washington for the first time in its forty-year history, symbolizing the influential role that the nation's capital played in the lives of American Muslims. Four years later, Keith Ellison became the first community member elected to the US Congress. In 2008, he was joined by Andre Carson, the second Muslim in the House of Representatives. The election of American Muslims to national office was an important milestone for the community, especially in light of the many challenges it faced during the height of the Bush administration's War on Terror. In addition to the political victories, the American Muslim community also celebrated a number of legal victories. In spite of the numerous court cases that ended with tragic results for the community in the climate of fear that had even gripped the nation's judiciary, several attempts to dismantle charities, think tanks, and other essential institutions ended in failure for federal authorities, who faced frequent accusations of targeting the community for political reasons. Discrimination lawsuits, such as the famous "flying imams" case of 2006, which, three years later, ended in victory for the plaintiffs, sought to demonstrate the consequences for the mistreatment of religious minorities.

Ultimately, the American Muslim community demonstrated its resilience in the face of immense pressures that emerged in the wake of 9/11. In spite of nearly eight years of alienation, its leaders resisted the initial urge to retreat to the margins of society, instead maintaining a keen determination to build upon the accomplishments of prior eras and overcome the challenges of the day. It is in that spirit that the community enthusiastically embraced the message of Barack Obama, the 2008 Democratic presidential candidate who ran on a platform of change. Though the stigma of candidates associating with the American Muslim community was still high during that and successive elections, precluding any engagement on the level of that seen in the 2000 campaign, the community's leaders as well as the rank and file were energetic in their campaigning on behalf of a candidate they believed would signal a real break from the climate of fear and suspicion that had marked the American Muslim experience in the post-9/11 era.

Although engagement with the broader Muslim world was declared to be a priority of the Obama administration, the American Muslim community remained in relative isolation from the national political dialogue. Obama did appoint several American Muslims to his administration, including the US representative to the Organization of the Islamic Conference (OIC), but beyond such token gestures, the civil rights issues afflicting leaders and institutions within the community continued unabated throughout Obama's first term and even after his re-election in 2013. When American Muslims did gain prominence on the national level, it was usually only in the context of a major crisis such as the controversy over the Park 51 Islamic center in New York in 2010 or in the aftermath of the Boston bombings in 2012.

FUTURE OUTLOOK

In looking toward the future of Islam's presence in America, a wider perspective and a proper historical context is not only useful but also essential. The American Muslim community has come a long way from the days of West African slaves yearning to return home or factory workers in turn-of-the-century Detroit pressured to adopt Anglicized names to avoid discrimination. The contemporary American Muslim community has come to terms with its identity and has found an accommodation between its religious obligations and the commitment to its nation. The evolution of a distinct American Muslim identity has been part and parcel of the community's projects to develop a *fiqh* for living as a religious minority and leading the latest struggle for civil rights.

As the community sheds the old ethnic and cultural divisions that have marked its institutions in past eras, new organizations have emerged that reflect the changing profile of the American Muslim community. Based in Chicago, the Inner City Muslim Action Network (IMAN) brings together youth of various backgrounds to assist development projects in their local community. American Muslims for Palestine (AMP) has torn down the old activist model on an issue of central importance to the community in favor of an approach that is more inclusive and in keeping with American traditions of political activism. Organizations such as the American Muslim Civic Leadership Institute (AMCLI) and the Muslim Public Service Network (MPSN) focus on training the younger generation of leaders and provide them with the opportunities and experiences they need to build on prior efforts to bring Muslims into the American public square.

While organizations such as these are a natural extension of the traditional political groups that fall under the AMT umbrella, they are also a signal that the future divisions in the community will not be along ethnic lines, but rather along generational ones. Discouraged by the failures of the older generation, the more highly educated, culturally and politically savvy generation of American Muslim youth has signaled its desire to break with the past and develop a new institutional culture in the community, free from the baggage of their elders. For their part, the established community leaders desire continuity in leadership and for the younger generation to embrace the rich legacy of American Muslim institution building.

Externally, the American Muslim community is likely to continue establishing partnerships with other faith communities and progressive groups. Building upon the experience from the campaign to end secret evidence and the antiwar coalition in the years after 9/11, American Muslim organizations have attempted to broaden their involvement to issues that affect all Americans, such as health care, job creation, and public safety. Members of the community will also continue to raise their political aspirations, not only developing important relationships with policy makers but also seeking to include more American Muslims in public office. In light of its experience with the bloc vote in 2000, the community has since matured enough to recognize the pitfalls of its electoral strategy and hopes to employ a more deliberate and judicious process in endorsing candidates. In time, the fulfillment of this community's political goals will see to it that American Muslims are considered in the same category as other minority groups who have overcome challenges to their status by embarking on a struggle for their rights, and in the process established themselves as part of the American social fabric.

Notes

1. Examples of these works include Abd-Allah 2006; Dirks 2006; Curtis 2009.
2. Abd-Allah, Umar F. 2006. *A Muslim in Victorian America: The Life of Alexander Russell Webb*. New York: Oxford University Press.
3. Haddad, Yvonne. 2004. *Not Quite American? The Shaping of Arab and Muslim Identity in the United States*. Texas: Baylor University Press.
4. Lewis, Bernard. 1990. The Roots of Muslim Rage. *The Atlantic Monthly*. September; Samuel P. Huntington. 1993. The Clash of Civilizations? *Foreign Affairs*. Summer. Vol. 72, No. 3. pp. 22–49.
5. Muhammad, W. D. In Curtis IV, Edward E., ed. 2008. *The Columbia Sourcebook of Muslims in the United States*. New York: Columbia University Press.
6. Goodstein, Laurie. 2001. U.S. Muslims Push Stamp as Symbol of Acceptance. *New York Times*. U.S. Politics section.
7. Dempsey, James X., and David Cole. 1999. *Terrorism & the Constitution*. Los Angeles, CA: First Amendment Foundation.
8. Al-Arian, Abdullah. 2003. *Soul Survival: The Road to American Muslim Political Empowerment*. MSc Dissertation. London School of Economics.
9. Ali, Tahir. 2004. *The Muslim Vote: Counts and Recounts*. Lima, OH: Wyndham Hall Press.
10. Al-Arian.
11. Interview with Agha Saeed, American Muslim Alliance, October 2001.
12. The bill was introduced as H.R. 1266 on March 28, 2001. The Library of Congress: Thomas. http://thomas.loc.gov/cgi-bin/bdquery/z?d107:h.r.01266 (accessed June 14, 2010).
13. Clines, Francis X. 2001. Muslim Leader Presses Agenda of Understanding. *New York Times*. October 3. U.S. Politics section.
14. Nacos, Brigitte L., and Oscar Torres Reyna. 2007. *Fueling Our Fears*. Lanham, MD: Rowman and Littlefield Publishers.
15. Goodstein, Laurie. 2001. Muslim Scholars Back Fight against Terrorists. *New York Times*. October 12. U.S. Politics section. Full text of this fatwa at: http://www.unc.edu/%7Ekurzman/Qaradawi_et_al.htm (accessed June 14, 2010).

References

Abd-Allah, Umar F. 2006. *A Muslim in Victorian America: The Life of Alexander Russell Webb*. New York: Oxford University Press.
Ali, Tahir. 2004. *The Muslim Vote: Counts and Recounts*. Lima, OH: Wyndham Hall Press.
Bukhari, Zahid H., Sulayman S. Nyang, Mumtaz Ahmad, and John L. Esposito, eds. 2004. *Muslims' Place in the American Public Square*. Berkeley: AltaMira Press.

Curtis IV, Edward E., ed. 2008. *The Columbia Sourcebook of Muslims in the United States*. New York: Columbia University Press.

Curtis IV, Edward E. 2009. *Muslims in America: A Short History*. New York: Oxford University Press.

Dempsey, James X., and David Cole. 1999. *Terrorism & the Constitution*. Los Angeles: Beltsville: First Amendment Foundation.

Dirks, Jerald F. 2006. *Muslims in American History: A Forgotten Legacy*. Beltsville: Amana Publications.

Findley, Paul. 2001. *Silent No More: Confronting America's False Images of Islam*. MD: Amana Publications.

Gerges, Fawaz. 1999. *America and Political Islam*. New York: Cambridge University Press.

Haddad, Yvonne, and Adair T. Lummis. 1987. *Islamic Values in the United States*. New York: Oxford Press.

Haddad, Yvonne Y., Farid Senzai, and Jane I. Smith, eds. 2009. *Educating the Muslims of America*. New York: Oxford University Press.

Jackson, Sherman A. 2005. *Islam and the Black American*. New York: Oxford University Press.

McCloud, Amina Beverly. 2006. *Transnational Muslims in American Society*. Gainesville: University Press of Florida.

Nacos, Brigitte L., and Oscar Torres-Reyna. 2007. *Fueling Our Fears*. Lanham: New York: Rowman and Littlefield Publishers.

Nyang, Sulayman S. 1999. *Islam in the United States of America*. IL: ABC International Group.

Smith, Jane I. 1999. *Islam in America*. New York: Columbia University Press.

CHAPTER 19

ISLAM AND POLITICS IN EUROPE

SAM CHERRIBI

Introduction

The relationship between Islam and European politics at the dawn of the twenty-first century is anything but normal. It is characterized by electric tension in the public sphere. News media outlets, manifestos of political parties, and the discourse of politicians at all levels of European governance show that Islam dominates the political agenda. Despite the official separation between religion and politics in Europe, there is a growing obsession of the political elite and the media with Islam. The continuous and growing claims of Muslims as citizens and their case for more inclusion make Europe's traditionally secular public space and its ironclad separation of church and state highly polarizing, not only for the lay public but for European politics as well. These patterns of polarization all over Europe originated at the local level and have progressed to the national level.

In a long-term historical perspective, these patterns are the products of three factors that have inflamed the contentious relationship between Islam and Europe. First, the process of EU enlargement, as part of a rapidly globalizing world, has resulted in an increased social insecurity and fear of loss of national identity. Second, the emergence of Islam as a top security issue has linked the Muslims of Europe to the rise of global militant political Islam and terrorism. Third, the increased religious and ethnic diversity in Europe has led Europeans to discover their inability and inexperience in dealing with "new religious pluralism," a common and fairly comfortable condition in the United States, where there is greater tolerance for religion in the public sphere. These three factors allow us to frame how European policies affect the life of ordinary Muslims, communities, organizations, and the perceptions of Islam in European societies (Berger 2007). European policies at the supranational level toward Islam are still apolitical and at the discretion of those who are in charge at the EU commission (who are themselves not elected but appointed), since the various national contexts are eminently important in electing politicians and articulating and implementing political priorities.

Islam, Europe, and the Politics of Identity

Many writers, pundits, journalists, and politicians have asked the question: What is Europe? For some, Europe refers to a geographical entity and a civilization with a common religion: Christianity. To others, Europe is projected as an idea, combining secular values with diverse countries, ethnicities, and languages.

Since 2004, twelve countries have joined the European Union: Cyprus, Malta, the Czech Republic, Estonia, Hungary, Latvia, Lithuania, Poland, Slovakia and Slovenia, Romania, and Bulgaria, while others still knock at the door, including Serbia, Ukraine, and Georgia. Since 1991 and the dissolution of the Soviet Union, Armenia, Azerbaijan, and Georgia have failed to reconnect with Europe despite appeals to do so. Complicating the picture is the fear of Turkey becoming part of the European Union, something it has been attempting for more than forty years. Europe is a success story because it achieved peace and stability through the use of a common currency and by establishing a Court of Justice of the European Communities (ECJ). Beginning in 1999, this single currency helped the emergence of a singular European economy, which is the largest in the world. Europe, however, still struggles with many issues: the European flag does not rally people like the national flag of the individual countries, it has a presidency that rotates every six months, and, as a result, just recently inaugurated a president who was not elected. Also, national interests are still more important than plural European interests and lastly, words like "transparency," "unity," and "cooperation" hide national interests and are just "Euro-prose" as noted by former Euro-commissioner Frits Bolkestein (Bolkestein 2004). In short, the lack of a shared political European identity and agenda weakens Europe.

The European commission's unelected presidents, the French Jacques Delors, the Italian Romano Prodi, and the Portuguese Jose Manuel Baroso have understood the importance of religious expression in the European public space and sought to codify it in policy. In1992, Delors saw the need to give Europe a soul by creating the Forward Studies Unit (FSU), which he brought to active fruition during his long tenure at the helm of the European Union. In 1999, Prodi continued this theme through the "Group of Policy Advisors" (GOPA). In 2004, Baroso did the same by creating the Bureau of European Policy Advisors (BEPA). All these initiatives tried to include advisors from different religious groups including Islam. Some Muslims were invited to participate along with those of other religious affiliations; however, the problem of representation has never been solved (Silvestri 2009; Massignon n.d.).

Islam and Europe: Two Ideological Constructs

In the previous paragraphs, I mentioned the ambiguities surrounding the term "Europe." Islam refers to a religion with varying traditions and orientations, a religion, which spans a variety of countries, ethnicities, cultures, and languages. In Spain, Islam is a minority religion whereas in Eastern Europe, it is quite the opposite. Europe is now home to transplanted guest workers from the Mediterranean region (from Morocco, Algeria, Tunisia, and Turkey) and from South Asia (India and Pakistan). Very often, little attention is paid to the ordinary Muslims living in Europe, even as their experiences and ideologies give meaning to the construction of Islam as practice, religion, and political force (Waardenburg 2004). After the 1960s and the 1970s, a dominant theme of research and politics dealt with the problems of migration, housing, and health but also with family reunification, education, and women's issues. Islam as a political force was not taken into account. From the 1980s to the 1990s, the height of visibility of Muslim immigrants sparked interest in Islam in Europe: European governments and political parties were more interested in the political organization of Muslims and their associations (Waardenburg 2004). Presenting them as a problem provided a political platform and consequently the media was supported in framing Islam as incompatible with Europe.

Both Europe and Islam through the centuries have had many encounters of Islamization and Christianization: Greek philosophy translated into Arabic, Andalusia's Muslim rulers, and the crusades. In colonial times, some European countries, such as France and Great Britain, dominated the lands of Islam. The Netherlands, meanwhile, reigned over the largest Islamic country in the world: Indonesia.

The politics of past controversies around Europe and Islam reduced the two to historical, cultural, social, but mainly ideological constructs because of the political and ideological escalation on both sides. Keep in mind that "politics" refers to activities, practices, and strategies dealing with the act of governance and the quest for political influence and consider that both Europe and Islam have been victims of terrorist attacks in the name of Islam. The backlash against ordinary Muslims of Europe is unprecedented. As the presence of Islam grows with the third and fourth generations of Muslims born on European soil, Islam is increasingly becoming a permanent player and part of the political outlook of Europe's past, present, and future.

"Muslim" Politicians and the Importance of National Political Context

If the 1960s and 1970s were characterized by a silence of the guest workers in the public sphere, the 1980s were a catalyst for articulating more identity claims through cemeteries, mosques, schools, and so on. In the 1980s political leaders in some Northern European countries, like the Netherlands and Scandinavia, went to mosques and religious organizations of Muslim migrants to campaign and recruit people for their political parties. But some Islamic countries showed their objection to involving these Muslims in the political affairs of their countries. Muslims welcomed the municipal right to vote granted to noncitizens in the Netherlands, Sweden, and Ireland.

The growing visibility of Muslims in urban areas triggered a new kind of politics: far right, focused on the mishaps of little criminality and the problems of migration in general. The media, even mainstream media outlets, joined this chorus of disenchantment. The Muslims who joined political parties at the municipal level, national level in some countries, and some few on the pan-European level have had to carefully strike a balance between the pros and cons of Islam. Recently some Muslim members of the party of President Sarkozy in France felt discriminated against and warned the party not to push them toward communitarianism and ethnic and religious allegiance. Many far right parties, such as the National Front in France, Partij voor de Vrijheid (Party for Freedom) in the Netherlands, and the Liga Nord in Italy, campaigned on an anti-European Union and anti-Islam ticket, making a plea for national identity.

Alain Juppé, former prime minister of France, showed his disagreement with the national debate about the *French* identity by saying, "Let's be honest, this is all about Islam and Muslims." The mayor of Bordeaux echoed that on his blog, saying, "The question 'what does it mean to be French?' does not really arise. We know the answer.... Add to this that secularism was the French identity."

In the Netherlands, the *kopvoddentax*, constructed by the PVV (Wilders wil "kopvoddentaks") is doing well in the polls (Trouw 2009). It is a means for mobilizing the insecurities of a country that has had two political murders since 2000. The quick enlargement of the European Union and the lack of a cohesive political identity or a tangible European interest make Europe unclear about its relation to emerging new religious identities. Clearly, the religious question in Europe remains unsolved since some countries, like Poland, are highly religious, or, like France, highly secular. Dutch sociologist Abram de Swaan explains that the lack of pan-European media outlets, such as an all-Europe television channel or newspaper, makes it impossible to have a European public sphere with European topics (de Swaan 2007). In addition to the euro as a source of unity, the identification of Islam as a threat has also served to galvanize Europe. It is a fear that knows no borders within the continent. The ban on minarets in Switzerland sits comfortably alongside the ban on the burka in the Netherlands.

Since the birth of the European Union, Europe's former North African colonies have assumed responsibility for their independence. At the time, it seemed that these two cultures had decided—painfully and in some cases violently—to pursue divergent paths, but soon it would become apparent that their fates were inextricably entwined and utterly interdependent. The idea that the Islamic crescent, which stretches across North Africa from Morocco into the Middle East, could keep its distance from Europe separated from it only by the Mediterranean—and by only nine miles of the Mediterranean at the Strait of Gibraltar—is a notion that has never withstood the test of time. In 1683, the Ottoman Empire's forces trudged all the way to Vienna before being forced back. Now, once again, Europe feels it is under a sort of Islamic siege, but this time the siege is primarily social and political, and, most significantly, a siege of Europe's own making. This siege has ramifications not only for Europe but also for the entire West according to far right parties that have been experiencing an exceptional growth as Islam-as-threat has grown in the public mind. Far right parties, such as France's Front National, Italy's Fiamma Tricolore, Sweden's National Democrats, Hungary's Jobbik, Belgium's Walloon National Front, the British National Party (BNP), Faustri's Freedom Party (FPO), and the Netherlands Freedom Party (PVV), saw success in the June 2009 elections for the European Parliament (EP). More than 40 seats out of 736 went to anti-Muslim parties, despite the fact that Article 13 of the Amsterdam Treaty on the European Union prohibits racism and Islamophobia.

More than fifty years since its inception, the European Union now anticipates expanding beyond its current membership of twenty-seven countries to include Turkey with its 83 million majority-Muslim population, but that possible inclusion is the source of much tension in the European Union. Like Turkish delight, the Turkish dilemma is sticky for Europeans. Once welcomed in theory as a strong buffer state between Europe and the East, it is now viewed as an enclave of Muslims, and that is not something that Europe, seeking an identity of its own and increasingly afraid that its identity is being Muslimized, can accept. Ironically, Europe, viewed for so long by Americans as a much older, more sophisticated society, now finds itself awkwardly young—both in terms of its status as the European Union, and in terms of its burgeoning young Muslim population, two factors that are undermining its sense of self and raising the specter of long-feared "Eurabia."

THE DISINTEGRATION OF EASTERN EUROPE: A MUSLIM TRAGEDY

If Islam has been part of Eastern European countries for centuries and has been invisible during the Soviet era, it exploded with the fall of the Berlin Wall and became a source of public contention and political polarization. However, Western Europe, after its colonial experience in Indonesia, India, the Middle East, and North Africa, severed its ties with Islam after the decolonization. Islam started to become an issue again in Western Europe in the 1980s when family reunification of migrant workers became more visible and the weight of numbers in big cities started to matter. These produced pressures on health care, the educational system, and housing, and so on. The openness of some Western European nations to multiculturalism and diversity experienced a backlash with the rise of political Islam and terrorism.

The fall of the Iron Curtain in 1989 made it possible for many Eastern European countries to join the European Union. Some of these, like Yugoslavia and Albania, constituted the biggest historic challenge to the stability of Europe since World War II. In that same year, 1989, Slobodan Milosevic was elected president of Yugoslavia and the country soon faced an accelerated ethnic disintegration centered on Kosovo and its Muslim population. This crisis manifested itself in the lack of a unified European defense identity able to settle conflicts in the neighboring former communist countries. Europeans could not do it alone, so the Americans and North Atlantic Treaty Organization were called upon to stop Milosevic's ethnic cleansing in the Balkans. That eventually led to air strikes in Serbia and Kosovo in March 1999 and thus revealed continued tensions within Europe itself aggravated by hundreds of thousands of refugees—most of them Muslim—fleeing to neighboring countries in the European Union.

The Yugoslav crisis brought with it political turmoil for Europe as a whole and for the Netherlands in particular. In the midst of the Yugoslavian debacle, the massacre of at least 6,000 Muslim men and boys while under the protection of a Dutch-United Nations peacekeeping force at the Muslim enclave of Srebrenica in July 1995 is now seen as a national conscience-crippling experience second only to the betrayal of the Jews who sought refuge in Holland in the Second World War in terms of its long-term psychic impact.

The murkiness surrounding the atrocities committed at Srebrenica was an early sign of a deepening identity crisis and the end of a number of old certainties about the future. The Dutch government asked the Netherlands Institute for War Documentation (NIOD) in 1996 to set up independent research into the events that took place before, during, and after the fall of the enclave. When the NIOD report was finally released on April 10, 2002, after being postponed for more than a year, Dutch Prime Minister Kok announced six days later, on April 16, 2002, that his government would bear full responsibility for the massacre and he and his cabinet subsequently offered their resignations.

The aftershocks of Srebrenica still continue today, though the trauma has now been overshadowed entirely by the fear of Islamic terror in the Netherlands. No one asked if perhaps an Islamic threat were needed to numb the shame of what had happened at Srebrenica, but the threat, needed or not, had already presented itself in the events in New York on September 11, 2001, seemingly absolving many Dutch citizens of something they would rather not think about anyway.

In the Netherlands, national parliamentary elections were held just weeks after the resignation of Kok and his cabinet, on May 15, 2002, which ushered in the new outsider party, the Lijst Pim Fortuyn (LPF) with twenty-six seats, making it the second largest party in the parliament, despite the assassination of its leader by a Dutch animal rights activist just a week before the election. Fully 79 percent of voters cast their ballots, nearly 6 percent more than had voted in the previous national election in 1998.

The Srebrenica investigation findings and Dutch frustration about the challenges to the Dutch educational, health, and welfare system posed by Muslim migrants, which were often the subject of negative stories in the press, was the background against which public discontent deepened in the country as Pim Fortuyn and his new political party LPF moved ahead in the polls, preaching populist politics based on ethnic distinction and exclusion. The patterns of ethnicization of Islam and Muslims, as in the Balkans, though without the physical violence, were duplicated in many European countries without, it seems, any awareness that ethnic distinction was being used in almost the same way that it had been used politically by the Serbs. Europeans were oblivious to the fact that the construction of Islam as a race would have long-term, inescapable, and broad disintegrational effects.

The break-up of Yugoslavia and the ensuing civil war in the mid-1990s had dispersed thousands of Bosnian Muslim political refugees across Europe (as well as to the United States, Canada, and Australia). Those who had been relocated to Western European countries were sent back to Bosnia when the war ended despite their often successful integration—they had learned the local language and sent their children to local schools—and despite some protests from concerned European citizens.

THE RISE OF SINGLE-ISSUE PARTIES

Political parties all over Europe are experiencing a decline in their traditional constituencies. The taken-for-granted identification with the party as a vehicle for political action is past tense. The ideological lines are becoming more fluid and there is more support for issues than for parties (Eik and Franklin 1996). The rise of many parties like LPF (Livable Netherlands), Party for Freedom (PVV), and the Animal Rights Party started as one-issue parties.

Illegal immigration in Europe soon became the top issue among all European leaders, particularly at the European Summit in Seville in June 2002. At the summit, prime ministers from all over Europe agreed that immigration was such a major problem that it could no longer be addressed effectively at the national level and had to be dealt with by the European Union. At the same time, within the discussion of immigration, the alleged lack of integration of legal immigrants, especially Muslim migrants from North Africa and Turkey, and the ways in which they lived in Europe became an increasingly important issue frequently featured in the media. Consequently, Europe in the 1990s and the early twenty-first century saw an emphasis on populist appeals and the growth of support for populist political parties with strong anti-immigrant policies, including Filip de Winter's Vlaams Belang in Belgium, Jorg Haider in Austria, Pia Kjaersgaard's Danish People's Party (DPP) in Denmark, the Republican Party (REP), the German People's Union (DVU), and the National Democratic Party (NPD) in Germany with no dominant leader, Jean-Marie Le Pen's Front National in France, Makis Voridis's Hellenic Front in Greece, Umberto Bossi's Northern League, and National Alliance in Italy, and Pim Fortuyn's LPF in the Netherlands.

Politicians often take their cues from the media and shape public policy accordingly. The increase in public support for far right parties cannot be seen in isolation from the demographic changes in Europe's major cities over the past two decades and the subsequent media coverage of those changes. A recent comparative study of neopopulism in its variety of forms in societies around the world shows how the media are instrumental in the rise and fall of populist parties and leaders. Some researchers have found that there is a connection between support for the far right and one's daily news diet. In particular, there seems to be a correlation with one item on the menu: crime news, a topic easily sensationalized and often linked to the poor and uneducated—a population in Europe that is usually mostly Muslim. In Austria, for example, scholars have established a link between the type of newspaper one reads exclusively and support for far right-wing populists such as Jorg Haider (Mazzoleni 2003).

The Backlash against the Muslim Political Elite

The backlash against Islam and Muslims takes place very often in local politics and then becomes a national, even pan-European event. Not only has the construction of new mosques in Germany, France, Italy, and the Netherlands triggered controversies vis-à-vis Islam but everything related to Islam (rightly or wrongly) has been subject to polarization: "Honor" killing, discrimination against women, prayers in public, movies, the Koran, sermons, imams, the burka, the veil, the headscarf, minarets, and so forth. Coexistence with Islam is a political impasse. The fear of "neo-Islamic- fundamentalism" poses questions about the limits of religious practice.

Local politics are more complicated than we think. In areas with Muslim majorities like West Amsterdam two Muslims fought for the leadership of the county governance, both from the same party. Competition between Muslim candidates is as intense as in any politics. There are Muslim candidates who are pro-gay, pro-euthanasia and others who are anti-Islam or totally pro-Islam (Muslim political voices that are pro-*Shari'ah* are mainly located in England and not in continental Europe).

The polarization in politics has made it more difficult for Muslim politicians to ensure continuity in their constituencies. And in addition to the media drumbeat, with the rise of political Islam there are many attempts to create Islamic parties like the Islamic Party in Great Britain, Le Party des Musulman de France, the Islamistische Partij in Belgium, and die

Islamitische Partij Deutschland. In Eastern Europe, and particularly in Greece where many ethnic parties exist, religion became, after the Balkan war, a mobilizing force.

Europe's Disenchantment with "New" Religious Pluralism

The emergence of more religious claims within the public sphere, engaging politics and society in advanced secular societies, is not typically Islamic, but can be seen in all faiths including Abrahamic traditions. In the book *New Religious Pluralism* edited by Thomas Banchoff, a number of scholars argue that religion in general is increasing as a social and political force. Examples of this around the world include the "under God" clause of the American Pledge of Allegiance and the proliferation of displays of the Ten Commandments, the ban on headscarves and other religious symbols in schools in France, blasphemy laws in the United Kingdom, and the ban on minarets in Switzerland. This religious diversity has serious political implications such as declaring a state of crisis for models of integration.

The lack of understanding of the new religious expression of religious groups in the public sphere has led to the politics of disenchantment against the second religion of Europe: Islam. In the 1980s and 1990s, many European governments like that of France, the Netherlands, Belgium, and Germany tried to find ways to organize Muslim representation. These attempts were not always successful but had the benefit of being a good learning experience for both governments and Muslim groups. Governments understood the difficulty in one representative body for all Muslims because of their diversity. Likewise, Muslim groups understood the logic of governments. However, the plethora of policies that varies from one country to another according to the political contexts of different European countries is reflected in the epicenter of the European Union in Brussels. As the highest level of European governance, the EU commission is concerned with finding established and formal ways to interact with Muslim groups seeking representatives for the Muslims in Europe. Muslims themselves are becoming more active in Brussels and actively seek a voice to be heard. Many Muslim groups are inspired by the ways Catholics and Protestants are organized in lobbying the European commission and the parliament.

With 9/11, the Madrid and London bombings, and the killing of the Dutch filmmaker Theo van Gogh by a young Dutchman of Moroccan descent, Europe woke up to a forgotten dimension of migrants who came to Europe as guest workers: their religion and spiritual well-being.

After the killing of Van Gogh, a Dutch writer of Moroccan descent described how he could not enter a café without being looked at as someone who might be hiding a weapon under his belt. The methodical drumbeat of the media and politicians against Muslims beginning in the aftermath of September 11, 2001 had succeeded in placing Muslim citizens of Europe in the role of an internal threat like that constructed by the media and politicians in America against Japanese Americans during World War II (Cherribi 2013). The result is that "Muslims" have to publicly express their disgust for radicals and their love, affection, and gratitude for the country in which they live in a way not required of others. Despite the fact that the majority of second- and third-generation Muslims have been born and raised in Europe, their loyalty and European identity are constantly subject to doubt. One leader of the guest workers' emancipation in the Netherlands, a Muslim immigrant himself, said, "I refuse to be Islamized" (Cherribi 52:2013). Allowing freedom of expression of religious identity, or the lack of a religious identity, is a privilege of advanced democracies because their foundational tenet of the separation of church and state is intended to provide a shield from manipulation by the religious community, a circumstance that does not exist in most Islamic countries.

When we consider the values of Islam and the values of European societies, the greatest differences can be found in themes of sexual liberalization. With few exceptions, divorce is so socially accepted that it is a nonissue in most European countries, abortion is legal, prostitution is tolerated or state regulated, and individuals are not to be discriminated against on the basis of their sexual orientation. Public attitudes toward gays and lesbians have become much more "liberalized" in Europe as well as in the United States over the past decade. The European Charter of Human Rights and European states' constitutions include protection of religious freedom and nondiscrimination on the basis of gender, race, ethnicity, and sexual orientation. In the context of a discussion about such value conflicts in European societies, it is worth noting that as recently as 1994 the Dutch Parliament passed a constitutional amendment to specifically protect the rights of "minorities" regardless of their religious affiliation including their "ethnic" and "sexual" rights, and implying the freedom not to practice a religion as part of the freedom of religion. However, the Dutch amendment has not been emulated elsewhere in Europe.

Apart from a few recent studies in which immigrant populations in Europe are described in general terms or with reference to particular examples, and primarily in country-based chapters, there is little in the way of research on the different generations of Muslims in European countries. Are younger Muslims in Europe remaining "unchanged" from their traditional parents in terms of sexual mores and values, as Inglehart and Norris suggest? Are they rejecting their parents' values outright and opting for the norms in the countries in which they live? Or are they creating a new set of values and norms? Inglehart and Norris say little about the contribution of Islamic religious leadership to the maintenance of traditional values in Muslim societies, although it is certainly part of the reason young people in Muslim countries today are as traditional in many ways as their parents and grandparents.

Nostalgia for a Forgotten Homeland

Since the 1950s, European countries have allowed or even encouraged immigration from Muslim countries to suit their individual purposes. The United Kingdom opened its doors to Asian Muslims from its former colonized states in India and Pakistan while France brought guest workers from freshly decolonized Algeria, Morocco, and Tunisia; and the Netherlands, though it had no colonial ties to Turkey or Morocco, brought in guest workers from those countries to fill lower-level, menial jobs.

As Europe's establishment became increasingly uneasy regarding what it perceived as the misplaced loyalties of immigrant communities, the status of the mosques was elevated within migrant communities. For the first generation of Muslims, the mosque was seen as a relocated part of their country of origin, the place to heal the *ghorba*, the burning nostalgia of exile. For members of the second and third generations it has become the place where they speak their language of origin, where they read the Qur'an, where they first encounter their own cultural traditions, and where they first experience civic and social engagement.

The most recent generation of Muslims in Europe sees the mosque as a symbol of their own alienated identity. They associate the mosque with distant lands of minarets and *souks*. These lands are not their own, they are their grandfathers', and like the shadowy, foreign countries of all immigrant progenitors, they have become mythologized. These countries—Algeria, Morocco, Tunisia, Turkey, Egypt, Lebanon, India, Pakistan—have become idealized, a place where life, though impoverished, appears across the distance of a generation to have been morally more cohesive and less confusing. With this vision of an Islamic "Promised Land"—a realm defined by ideology rather than actual geographic boundaries— a new leadership fed by this myth and alienation within the European society has emerged even as the original immigrants have aged and died. The result is new social and religious configuration intent upon acquiring and asserting political power, not dissimilar in style to that of the African American religious leaders who birthed the American civil rights movement. This admiration of the American Civil Rights movement will define the religious makeup of new Muslim leadership in Europe because it, like the African American model, relies heavily upon the personalities and devotion of its leaders.

Despite the anti-Islam political agenda driven by the far right and its amalgam with terrorism, Muslims in Europe are challenging, but also adapting and interacting with, the secular political culture. In many ways, Muslims are engaging in the democratic process (Berger 2007). Either by becoming members of established political parties or by creating their own religious institutions and even political parties, Muslims are engaging in the governing processes. Engaged members of established political parties have shown loyalty to citizens and professionals ranging from the many members of city councils and ministers to national and European parliamentarians. A recent survey of the newer generation of Muslims born and raised in Europe does not see being European, and respecting Europe's secular culture, as contradicting the fact of being devout Muslims. Secular Muslims and devout Muslims equally feel as if they are capable of convincing others of their tolerant and benign nature, despite persistent images of fanaticism in the popular media.

The most successful experience is on the local level in the Netherlands, the United Kingdom, and Belgium, where many Muslims have been elected to municipalities and have become aldermen or even mayors. At the national level, the Netherlands and the United Kingdom remain the most promising examples in including Muslims in the political arena; they are members of parties all along the full political spectrum from Christian Democrats to the communists parties and Greens (and even in the far right party LPF in the Netherlands). France has had the first Muslim national minister of justice, Rachida Dati.

At the European Union level, a new arena for potential Muslim parties is emerging, but ironically, the majority of Muslims in Europe would not vote for an Islamic party even if they send their children to Islamic schools, buy *halāl* food, and wear headscarves. This has to do with the fact that there is still no political tradition within Muslim communities to be mobilized on the basis of religion and ethnicity. In the future, it is likely the new generation of Muslims who experience more segregation and exclusion would opt for an Islamic party just like the Christian Democrats not because of religious reasons but because of problems with issues of identification.

REFERENCES

Arkoun, Mohammed. 2007. *Histoire de L'Islam et des Musulmans en France, du Moyen age nos jours*. Paris: Albin Michel.
Berger, Peter L. 2007. Pluralism, Protestantization, and the Voluntary Principle. In *Democracy and the New Religious Pluralism*, ed. Thomas Banchoff, 203–222. New York: Oxford University Press.
Bolkestein, Frits. 2004. *The Limits of Europe*. Tielt: Lannoo Publishers.
Byrnes, Timothy A., and Peter Katzenstein. 2006. *Religion in an Expanding Europe*. Cambridge: Cambridge University Press.
Cherribi, Sam. 2007. Politician's Perceptions of the "Muslim Problem": The Dutch Example in European Context. In *Democracy and New Religious Pluralism*, ed. Thomas Banchoff, 113–132. New York: Oxford University Press.
Cherribi, Sam. [2010] 2013. *In the House of War: Dutch Islam Observed*. London: Oxford University Press.
de Swaan, Abraam. 2007. The European Void: The Democratic Deficit as a Cultural Deficiency. In *The European Union and the Public Sphere: A Communicative Space in the Making?*, ed. John Fossum and Philip Schlesinger, 135–153. New York: Routledge.
Eik, Cees and Mark Franklin. 1996. *Choosing Europe? The European electorate and national politics in the face of the Union*. Ann Arbor, MI: University of Michigan Press.
Emerson, Michel. 2009. *Ethno-Religious Conflict in Europe: Typology of Radicalization in Europe's Muslim Communities*. Brussels: Centre for European Policy Studies.
Hervieu-Leger, Daniele. 2007. Islam and the Republic: The French Case. In *Democracy and the New Religious Pluralism*, ed. Thomas Banchoff, 203–222. New York: Oxford University Press.
Klausen, Jytte. 2005. *The Islamic Challenge: Politics and Religion in Western Europe*. Oxford, England and New York, USA Oxford University Press.
Lechner, Frank. 2008. *The Netherlands: Globalization and National Identity*. New York: Routledge.
Marechal, Brigitte, Stephano Alievi, Felice Dassetto, and Jorgen Nielson. 2003. *Muslims in the Enlarged Europe: Religion and Society*. Leiden: Brill.
Massignon, Berengere. 2007. Islam in the European Commission's System of Regulation of Religion. In *Islam in Europe: Diversity, Identity and Influence*, ed. Aziz Al-Alzmeh and Effie Fokas, 125–182. Cambridge: Cambridge University Press.
Mazzoleni, Gianpietro, Julianne Stewart, and Bruce Horsfield. 2003. *The Media and NeoPopulism: A Contemporary Comparative Analysis*. Westport, CT: Praeger.
Semetko, Holli A., and Patti M. Valkenburg. 2000. Framing European Politics: A Content Analysis of Press and Television News. *Journal of Communications* 50: 93–109.
Silvestri, Sara. 2009. Islam and Religion in the EU Political System. *West European Politics* 32, no. 6: 1212–1239.
Trouw. Newspaper "Wilders wil 'kopvoddentaks.'" http://www.trouw.nl/nieuws/politiek/article2865224.ece/Wilders_wil__kopvoddentax_.html (accessed September 16, 2009).
Waardenburg, Jacques. 2004. Diversity and Unity of Islam in Europe: Some Reflections. In *Muslims in Europe, From the Margin to the Center*, ed. Jamal Malik. Munster: Lit Verlag.
Watts, Duncan. 2008. *The European Union*. Edinburgh: Edinburgh University Press.

CHAPTER 20

ISLAM AND POLITICS IN THE MIDDLE EAST

MOATAZ A. FATTAH

This article is set to provide a panoramic view of the landscape of Islam and politics in the Middle East. To be more specific, this article is an attempt to answer the following questions: Who speaks for Islam? And how do they situate politics in their Islamic discourse? As the reader will see that these questions have no simple answers yet, eight different agendas have developed in Muslim societies of the Middle East to account for these two questions.

The reader of this article will encounter several conclusions. First, having several agendas and discourses is not that new to the complexity of the Muslim history. There has always been different *fiqhi madhabs* (jurisprudential schools), philosophical schools, Sufi orders, Shi`a formations, military rulers, and bureaucrats who have existed, and often contested, parallel to the caliphate institution (Esposito 2005; Lapidus 2002; Lewis 2001).

Second, this article demonstrates how different influential opinion leaders, politicians, parties, and Islamic formations adopt different and possibly contradictory discourses that might eventually serve similar agendas without formal or documented coordination. Here one should note the power of the unintended consequences of one's choices and discourses. For instance, there are five groups, as we will see, of Muslims and non-Muslims who all adopt, to different degrees, an agenda of apolitical Islam though their discourses emanate from categorically contradicting interests and assumptions.

Third, the dynamics of these agendas suggest that Islam is very present in the public and political debates in Middle Eastern countries. Some accounts state without qualification that "Muslims are addicted to religion. Thus any attempt to reform Muslims' affairs will fail unless it starts from Islam or at least not to ignore it" (Omara 1998, 28). Thus, it is no wonder that Islamists appear to be the main winners of the so-called Arab Spring (Berman 2013). The real debates, as we will see, are where to locate Islam in modern societies and polities. Should it be limited to the personal lives of its followers? Can it expand from the "personal" to the "public" sphere? How can (or should) it be limited to these two spheres without delving into the political/legislative sphere?

Fourth, though, historically, the `ulama` "were the purveyors of Islam, the guardians of its tradition, the depository of ancestral wisdom, and the moral tutors of the population" (Marsot 1972, 149), this is not the case anymore. *`Ulama'*, with official degrees in *shari`ah* are just one group of opinion leaders, albeit so different in their political opinions and positions, and definitely they are now in the minority among so many other producers of political discourse in the name of Islam.

Fifth, these agendas are widespread among Middle Eastern countries. There is no state that is fully dominated by one agenda. There is always vibrant competition and even cutthroat conflict among some of them. Each agenda is challenged by others, which is a positive sign that *ijtihad* is a continuous endeavor and the dialectical process of qualifying positions and reacting differently to common challenges is underway. Yet, there is another negative aspect of this diversity that it reflects plurality more than it reflects tolerant pluralism. Following the analysis of some Arab scholars, there is some type of inter- and intraideological civil war not only between Islamists and secularist but even inside each camp (al-Azmeh 1992; Bishri 1996). We will note in this article that this is not entirely true; warring discourses might, without explicit coordination, end up endorsing common agendas following the famous Arab saying: "My brother and I are against our cousin; and my cousin and I are against strangers." The details will follow.

1. The Apolitical Muslimhood Agenda

There is, first, the ritualistic apolitical agenda. This agenda, surprisingly, is adopted by five different discourses that emanate from formations that are highly critical of each other. This agenda limits Islam to the personal domain, depriving it, thereby, of any role as far as legislation and political action is concerned. In other words, Islam according to this agenda should have no impact on the allocation of resources decisions made by the state. Questions of who gets what, when, where, why, and how should be made solely on nonreligious grounds. This is the model of an "Islam" that is locked up in mosques and whose role is limited to matters of faith, ethics, and rituals. This agenda is endorsed by (1) secular Muslims, whether autocrats or pluralists; (2) non-Muslims; (3) a group of modern preachers who do not want to get involved in political affairs; (4) Sufis; and (5) apolitical Salafis.

Religious minorities in the Middle East, for self-serving purposes, advocate secularism and total separation between religion and states and preach full citizenship à la liberal secular models of the United States and Canada, where there is no official religion of the state, or the British and Spanish models, where the official religion has only minimal symbolic relevance. Most Egyptian Copts, Israeli Arabs, Lebanese Christians, Moroccan Jews, Saudi Shi`a, and Iranian Sunnis have been endorsing a secular agenda emphasizing full citizenship irrespective of religious affiliation at the constitutional, legal, and popular levels.

Secular Muslims (headed by a group of intellectuals, leftists, and liberal political parties) along with non-Muslims perceive Islam as a personal relationship between God and his servants. This is the point on which they utterly disagree with Islamists (Baghdadi 1999; Mernissi 1992). This group of secular intellectuals and politicians (Muslims and non-Muslims) are highly influenced by nonreligious education obtained outside the Muslim world or from translated materials.

This agenda typically starts from two compatible assumptions. The first is that religion, and for that matter Islam, does not offer a concrete guide for governance. Holy texts do not tell Muslims much about how to run their political systems. Holy texts are sources of `aqida (creed) and ethics but not politics and economics. Even when they discuss political and economic issues, they emphasize broad principles such as justice, equality, and so forth.

Secularists refuse the Islamists' argument that Islam has an answer to all questions: "Islam is the Solution." They argue that the Prophet told Muslims that they were encouraged to brush their teeth before prayer. Yet he did not tell them how to select his political successor (al-Sa`eed 2001).

The silence of *shari`ah* regarding many political issues is a sign that Allah wants the human intellect to function and flourish without textual constraints.

The other assumption is that Muslims need to follow the paths of the most advanced societies in order to outdo them. This is exactly what the West did by learning from ancient Muslims and others. The Islamists' slogans about the peculiar and idiosyncratic nature of Muslims have been obstacles rather than catalysts for development and modernization. Secularists, in particular, argue that interaction with and learning from other civilizations is a human necessity, yet it will never succeed until Muslims are emancipated from the hold of "holy" interpretations and traditions that are assumed to come as a package with the holy texts (Arkoun 1994). Actually, they lament, Muslims imprison themselves in the *turath* (old books of the past) whether they are useful or not, while the world around them advances in all fields.

This agenda is reflected in the platforms of most secular Arab parties ranging from the Socialist Union for Popular Forces and Nationalist Party of Istiqlal in Morocco to the Algerian Party for Democracy and Socialism, the Free Egyptians Party, the Republican People's Party and Nationalist Movement Party in Turkey, along with socialist and liberal parties and candidates in Jordan, Kuwait, and Bahrain. It is reflected as well in the debates about the postrevolution constitutions in Egypt, Libya, and Tunisia.

Interestingly, there are other groups of Muslims who advocate the same agenda though they are very critical of each other: Sufis, apoliticized Salafis, and modern televangelist preachers. They focus on creed, rituals, and ethics to create a pious Muslim personality as a step toward a pious society. But, unlike the Muslim Brotherhood and postrevolution politicized Salafis in Egypt and Tunisia, for instance, they do not extend their discourse to mention the goal of creating a Muslim "state." They all avoid the politicization of their discourses. However, one can argue that their apolitical discourse is by itself politicized since it serves the status quo by diverting peoples' attention from the political plights of their societies. One can even argue that they represent a modern manifestation of Marx's depiction of religion as an opium of the masses. Despite the large gulf between them in style and sharp criticisms that they mount against each other, they all try to stay away from direct confrontations with the state. They do not propose themselves as alternatives to the ruling elites; rather they work within the area left to them by autocratic rulers. Modern televangelist preachers have at least one element that distinguishes them from the Sufis and apolitical Salafis. This element is the modern preachers' emphasis on social activism of leading a life of faith and fun, helping the poor, serving society without challenging authority, and gain Islamic knowledge without going to the extreme of being an Islamist with a political agenda (Haenni 2005). In comparison with the patronizing manner of a typical Azhari shaykh or Saudi imam, the amiable and compassionate modern preachers appear "...to be true democrats. For those who had learned to look for shortcuts to knowledge and were trained to be docile learners... [these preachers] are superior sources of wisdom" (Bayat 2007, 154).

As for the Sufis and dervishes and other mystic and ascetic orders, they are generally apolitical and focus on internal *jihad* and usually give oath of allegiance (*bay'ah*) to the ruling power. Estimations vary of how many Sufis are there. Some scholars estimate that there are more Sufis than Islamists in most Muslim countries (Hoffman 1995).

Heads of Sufi orders in Egypt claim that they have around 15 million affiliates. Others, such as the World Christian Database, estimate the total number of Sufis at 237 million in the whole Muslim world. One cannot verify that number given the fact that Sufis are scattered and not centrally organized (Allen 2009).

However, one knows for sure that they exist and are usually supported by autocratic states given the fact that they are the most complacent group with the status quo and least interested in delving into the world of opposition politics (Heck 2007).

The apolitical Salafis are one branch of "Salafism"—a term that typically refers to a number of different flavors of beliefs, most notably, politicized conservatives like the Wahhabi *shaykhs* in Saudi Arabia or Kuwait's Islamist Salafi movement, radical Islamists (or jihadists) such as al-Qaeda, reformers like Muhammad 'Abduh and Jamal al-Din Al-Afghani, and the apolitical preachers and groups such as Said Nursi's faith-based movements in Turkey (Nurcus), supporters of Mohamed's Sunna (Ansar al-Sunna al-Muhammdiyya) in Egypt and several Arab countries, and Tablighi Jama'at in several Arab countries. Popular apolitical Salafi movements identify a lack of spirituality and decline in personal religious observance as the root cause of the Muslim world's problems, and claim that Muslim identity cannot be successfully revived until these deficiencies are addressed. Interestingly, several groups that were typically antidemocracy and antirebellion against autocratic rulers seized the Arab Spring to form political parties and to deal with democracy as a legit form of government as long as it functions under the constraints of Islamic *shari'ah*.

These apolitical Salafi groups, such as Wahabi *'ulama'* in Saudi Arabia, mount sharp criticisms on Sufis and modern televangelist preachers as heretics, heterodox, and innovators. They are critical as well of violent jihadists such as al-Qaeda Islamists' competition in elections and jihadists' propagation of *takfir* against Muslims have been subject to different waves of criticisms from these apolitical Salafis. Typically Middle Eastern countries tolerate the freedom of expression and association for these groups as long as they do not get beyond their purely spiritual and ritual agendas, and when they talk politics, it is in the direction endorsed by the ruling elites.

However, one cannot understand the political impact of this agenda, without understanding how it is instrumentalized by the statist seculareligious agendas, especially before the Arab Spring.

2. Statist Seculareligious Agenda

Islam is too important as a source of political legitimacy to be ignored by autocrats and too deeply rooted in the hearts and minds of Muslims to be categorically eliminated from the public sphere.

That is why most Middle Eastern ruling elites have adopted an agenda that has been labeled "seculareligious" (Bayat 2007). These elites adopt positions, discourses, and laws with roots in both religious and secular values. Religious symbols and justifications are important techniques for the ruling elites to maintain moral mastery over society and secure political legitimacy but not to the extent that Islam by itself becomes a political constraint on the pragmatic agenda of the ruling elites. That is why they have to act *as if* they were the true representatives of Islam, even if they do not abide by its teachings in their personal lives or political decisions. These rulers concurrently wage raids against political Islam while taking every opportunity to publicly display themselves as the guardian of religious values and morality and supportive of the apolitical Islamic agenda. The regime of Bashar Al-Assad in Syria started to use Islamic symbols in their war against the rebels whom they started to call *kofar*, or infidels.

The secularreligious agenda has a common tendency to include in the constitution an article that states that Islam is the official religion of the state and that Islamic *shari'ah* is a/ the (main) source of legislation. Out of the twenty-five countries under investigation in this article, twelve countries declare Islam as the official religion without having such institutional review or control over legal and judicial processes.[1]

Another seven countries officially claim that law making and judicial processes are under the review and control of an Islamic body of scholars and courts.[2] Egypt's 2012 constitution includes an article that enables state's bodies to consult Al-Azhar on issues related to Islamic *shari'ah*.

Only Lebanon, Syria, and Turkey among the Middle Eastern countries, as defined in this article, are the countries that adopt the French *Laïcité* with no religious control over law making and judiciary, nor an official religion (Kuru 2009).

Tunisia throughout its history since independent in 1956 till 2011 provides us with a good example of a secularreligious structure of power where the state fully controls and dominates the Islamic establishment. Habib Bourguiba (1957–1987) claimed that his program of development and progress was more important than observing the ritual of fasting Ramadan. That is why in 1960, he asked the grand mufti of Tunisia (Shaykh abdel-Aziz Gheit) to issue a fatwa for all Tunisians to break their fast during the days of Ramadan. When the mufti refused, Bourguiba fired him and the position remained vacant for two years, singling a message that Muslims can live without official spokesmen of Allah's will. Despite this disguise to Islamic intelligentsia, Bourguiba and his successor did not give away Islam as a source of legitimacy. In the constitution, adopted June 1, 1959, Article 1 declared Islam the state religion, and Article 38 that the religion of the president must be Muslim. Ben Ali, the Tunisian president ousted in the revolution of 2011, used in his inauguration speech (after the November 7, 1987 coup) clear Islamic expressions ushering "reconciliation between Tunisia and its Arab and Islamic identity." Thus, Tunisian TV started airing the calls of prayer since then. Even when the regime cracked down on Islamists in the early 1990s, this was done with the full support of the official Islamic establishment as a mechanism to protect Islam from the misleading frenzy minority that is misusing and misrepresenting Islam (Burgat and Dowell 1993).

Thus, Islam, in this secularreligious agenda, is not only a set of symbolic articles placed in constitutions, laws, and expressions whose main aim is to provide the ruling regime with a religious façade but also a technique to empower the ruling elites against their enemies. Here the ruling elite seeks to benefit from the legitimacy conferred by Islam, but without really abiding by the restrictions of its *shari'ah*. Abd Al-Nasser openly declared his respect for Al-Azhar. In the meantime, he got rid of some of Al-Azhar scholars and even greatly undermined the institution's independence under the pretext that the institution was dominated by obscurantist *shaykhs* who opposed his socialist policies of nationalization and confiscation of private properties. Similar to that is Sadat's assertion in the second article of the constitution that the Islamic *shari'ah* is the principal source of legislation, to sell his proposal to remove the term limits of the president. Intermittently, secularelligious rulers resort to Islamic symbols and rhetoric to garner support. Saddam Hussein wrote Allah Akbar on the flag to boost the morale of his soldiers and people during Desert Storm and Qadafi declared *jihad* on Switzerland and issued a fatwa that any Muslim in any part of the world who works with Switzerland is an apostate, is against Muhammad, God, and the Koran.[3] Most Muslims know that Saddam and Gaddafi had no clout from a religious perspective. Yet, at least for their own peoples, the use of Islamic rhetoric is an important source of legitimacy that they cannot ignore.

This agenda and the previous one are strategically linked to each other. For this secularelligious agenda to pay off, three tactics should be used that use the services of the previous agenda:

1. Control of '*ulama*': After independence of most Middle Eastern states, the '*ulama*'s dependence on the state was intensified since most states nationalized *al-awqaf* (endowments), abolished religious court, and restructured religious education. Thus, most '*ulama*' have become salaried state technocrats. Imams of mosques either have become appointed by the state or have to get the approval of the ministries of religious affairs to give sermons and preach. Moreover, the states issued their own official Islamic magazines and newspapers. '*Ulama*' who traditionally constituted a distinct status have become, despite internal differentiation (according to seniority and economic status), more preoccupied with their shared common interests in income security and social and spiritual legitimacy. Official '*ulama*' have come under sharp criticisms from Islamic activists for being henchmen of the ruling elite and thus Islamists curtail the '*ulama*'s'' control over religious discourse.
2. Supporting or at least leaving room for the apolitical discourses of "Muslimhood" adopted by Sufis, apolitical Salafis, and modern preachers who control hundreds of mosques and scores of schools, welfare associations, independent satellite channels, and their own websites. These discourses become complementary to the discourse adopted by state-appointed '*ulama*'.
3. Series of wars (some of maneuver and others of position using Gramscian terms) against political Islamists who produce antiregime political discourses on Islamic grounds as the reader will note when we discuss the partisan Islamist agenda.

The reaction to the secularelligious agenda has come in different formats. Some are militant and others are nonviolent.

3. The Radical Militant Islamist Agenda

A radical militant agenda launched its violent attacks in forms of waves to completely alter, even to destruct the political status quo—because they consider it anti- or un-Islamic. This group of violent Islamists has many names in public discourses, including fundamentalists, terrorists, and Salafi-*jihadi* groups. This agenda, regardless of the label attached to it, is adopted by some formations that have based their ideologies on their own interpretations of three concepts: *takfir* (declaring unbeliever, or *kafir* [pl. *kuffār*], an individual or a group previously considered Muslim), *hisba* (to claim control of observance of Islamic principles), and *jihad* (understood by them to mean using violence to force Muslims to abide by Islamic *shari`ah*). These radical formations share, more or less, a very radical interpretation of the previous three concepts giving themselves the right to declare their opponents non-Muslims, and believe that they can act as *muhtasib*, which entitles them to punish those who do not abide by Islam's teachings, and they do that under the banner of *jihad* against the enemies of Islam who might be any Muslim who does not accept their interpretation of *shari`ah* or even non-Muslims who happen to live in Muslim societies. Though they share the previous aspects, they act at different levels: local, regional, and global.

Table 20.1 demonstrates an operational typology with some illustrative examples of different Islamist groups. The main distinction in this table is between nonviolent Islamists who believe in incremental evolutionary change and others who preach and practice radical revolutionary ruptures against their respective regimes, societies, and others.

Islamists working on the local scale do not extend their goals or operations beyond the state they belong to. They might have sympathizers or funders abroad, but they are basically limited to the radical change within their own states. Some examples include the Islamic Salvation Front of Algeria, al-Jama`a Islamiya of Egypt before their recent revisions, and Somalis Union of Islamic Courts, to name a few.

Likewise, regional Islamists are limited to their own regions yet with systematic alliance with other state actors within their regions against common enemies. Hamas and Hizbollah have been operating with full support from Syria and Iran against Israel but never went beyond it. Taliban associates who have never fought the North Atlantic Trade Organization troops beyond Afghanistan and western Pakistan are another case in hand. These two types of groups, local and regional, have been called "religious nationalists" who operate within national and regional boundaries and have local, rather than global or cosmic, objectives. These are different from the transnational *Jihadi* networks such as al-Qaeda that have universal agendas (Gerges 2009).

Table 20.1 Operational Typology of Islamic Formations with Political Agendas

	Violent	Nonviolent
Global	Al-Qaeda and its supporting groups, such as Jama`at al-Tawhid wal-Jihad (al-Qaeda in Iraq)	Al-Tahrir Party, Muslim Brotherhood*
Regional	Hezbollah (Lebanon, Syria, Iran), Hamas (Gaza, Syria and Iran), Taliban (Afghanistan and Pakistan)	Salafi and Shi`a movements in the Arab Gulf area
Local	Islamic Salvation Front (Algeria), al-Jama`a Islamiya (Egypt), Somalis Union of Islamic Courts, Al-Mahdi Army in Iraq	Yemeni Congregation for Reform, AKP (Turkey), Party of Justice and Development (Morocco), Islamic Constitutional Movement (Kuwait)

*Some allegations and reports have accused Muslim Brotherhood of Egypt to be sponsoring violence after ousting president Mohamed Moursi from office in Egypt on July 3rd, 2013.

A second important difference between al-Qaeda and other violent Islamists is that al-Qaeda members do not perceive themselves as citizens of separate Muslim countries; rather they are the vanguards of the *ummah* as a whole. That is why they largely flourish in failed states within a power vacuum. Afghanistan's descent into a civil war following the withdrawal of Soviet troops was a good opportunity for the formation of Taliban-al-Qaeda nexus (Ayoob 2008, 147). The Taliban's agenda was primarily domestic, aiming at "purifying" Afghan society, yet al-Qaeda's Arab leaders had their own version of creative chaos.

A third important difference between al-Qaeda and other violent Islamist formations is that al-Qaeda is not a centralized or structured movement; rather it is more of a franchise. Gilles Kepel has pointed out: "Al-Qaeda ... [is] less a military base of operations than a data base that connected *jihad*ists all over the world via the Internet ... [US politicians] gave it a vivid, reductionist name—al-Qaeda—but this served only to reify the network's fluidity, thereby masking its true source of strength" (Kepel 2004, 37). Al-Qaeda, as such, has a very limited political impact as an alternative for any of the regimes in the Muslim world unless it is linked and supported by local partners. That is when it cannot be described as a political alternative to the status quo; rather it is just an element of destabilization.

However, the link between the local, regional, and global groups should not be obscured. The Egyptian Islamic jihad was disillusioned because of their inability to overthrow the Egyptian secularreligious autocratic regime at home (till the 2011 revolution) and thus decided to make common cause with transnational groups to target the "far enemy"—the West in general and the United States in particular. These groups in support of al-Qaeda see the "far enemy" as the principal supporters of un- or anti-Islamic repressive regimes at home, the "near enemy." Therefore, they believe that hitting the United States or the West would undermine support in America and Europe for authoritarian pro-Western regimes in the Arab/Muslim world, leading to the collapse of these regimes (Ayoob 2008; Esposito 2005).

However, a deradicalization process took place in several Middle Eastern countries in the past decade. This deradicalization took the shape of "a radical group or individual reverses behavior and ideology to abandon and de-legitimize the use of violence to achieve political goals" (Ashour 2009, 12). Militant Islamist groups in Egypt, Algeria, Saudi Arabia, Iraq, Libya, Yemen, and Jordan have gone through revisionist endeavors based on reinterpreting their attitudes toward the concepts of *takfir*, *hisba*, and *jihad* to be less violent and more in agreement with most classical interpretations that limit the right to declare *takfir* to well-versed *'ulama'*, and to limit the *hisba* to some type of verbal act of enjoining the good and forbidding the evil and violent *jihad* to be a decision that should be made only by the legitimate authority of the Muslim state.

The most important cases of deradicalization were the in Egypt's al-Jama`a al-Islamiya and Al-Jihad group. Al-Jama`a al-Islamiya declared a unilateral ceasefire in July 1997 that evolved into a comprehensive deradicalization process in 2002. This particular group cooperated with the al-Jihad group in the assassination of President Anwar al-Sadat in 1981. The leaders of al-Jama`a al-Islamiya wrote around twenty-five volumes condemning their radical violent approach, criticizing al-Qaeda's claim of monopoly on Islam, refusing the idea of clash of civilizations, calling for peaceful coexistence between Muslims and non-Muslims on the land of Islam, giving oaths of allegiance to whoever acts as the president of Egypt, declaring repentance, and asking Muslims to forgive them for the violent course of action they had taken. These revisionist writings do not mean that they gave up Islamism but rather that they are self-transformed into nonviolent Islamists.

Another equally influential group went through the same revisionist process of deradicalization, namely the Egyptian *jihad* group that has been the early habitat for Ayman al-Zawahri, Mustafa Abu al-Yazid, the al-Qaeda commander in Afghanistan, and Yusuf al-Dardri, the al-Qaeda commander in Iraq.

The revision was mainly championed by the former leader of al-Jihad and one of the mentors of al-Qaeda, Dr. Sayyid Imam al-Sharif (also known as Dr. Fadl). In two books, Dr. Fadl, mounted a sever attack on al-Qaeda's leaders, describing them as ignorant, arrogant, seeking personal gains,... and acting against Islamic teachings.[4] Al-Zawahri defended his ideology based on rational and religious grounds by writing a book entitled *al-Tabra'a* (The Vindication). *Jihad*'s deradicalization process, however, has not been fully successful since numerous factions within the group came up with their own counterarguments.

The Saudi government launched a program of *munasaha* (advising) to complement the efforts of other `ulama` who were not affiliated with the state. This effort paid off in the deradicalization of individuals who have been affiliated with al-Qaeda. In Algeria, similar deradicalizing transformations occurred between 1997 and 2009. As was the case in Egypt, the self-declared armed wing of the Islamic Salvation Front (FIS), known as the Islamic Salvation Army (AIS), declared a unilateral ceasefire in October 1997. The demilitarization process included almost all militant Islamists except for the so-called al-Qaeda in the Islamic Maghreb. Unlike the Egyptian groups, however, the Saudi and Algerian militant Islamists did not produce any literature to constitute a new ideology.

Likewise, in Libya, the Fighting Islamic Group, former ally of al-Qaeda, initiated a deradicalization process in 2006–2007. Its commanders in Afghanistan refused to accept the process then. Yet, with the death of Abu Layth in 2008, the process has been reactivated. On September 1, 2009, on the occasion of Muammar Qadhafi's fortieth year in power, a militant Islamist prisoner issued a public apology to the colonel, declaring that the group will abandon political violence and dismantle its secret units.

Iraq has witnessed the disarming of Jama`at Ansar al-Sunnah (or Group of the Followers of Sunnah) that has been fighting the US-led occupation and the elected government led by Nouri al-Maliki. The leaders of Sunni tribes in Anbar gave up their support to this group and started to fight them back after they stroke a deal with the US commanders and the al-Maliki government.

In Yemen, the Houthis declared that they were trying to reverse the political, economic, and religious marginalization of the Zaydi Shi`a community. Yet, the raids from the Saudi troops and Yemeni army forced them to back down, most likely temporarily.

Failure to achieve their goals, selective incentives, government raids, interaction with moderate Islamists, and the political ramifications of the Arab Spring propelled radical Islamists to reexamine their ideologies, revise their strategies, and moderate their tactics. That is why several of these repressive regimes claimed victory and garnered popular support given what they call their capacity to "repress, deter and de-radicalize the misguided groups" as stated by King Abdullah of Saudi Arabia before the Shoura Council on April 14, 2007.

There is some evidence that there is domino effect for the deradicalization process. Deradicalized groups often interact with violent ones and in some cases the former influences the latter, as demonstrated in the militant groups in Egypt, Algeria, Saudi Arabia, Libya, and others (Ashour 2009).

There is no guarantee that this process of deradicalization is sustainable. Reverse radicalization, either for these same groups and individuals or others, is still a possibility given the perpetuation of political repression, ban of these organizations by autocratic regimes, lack of addressing the grievances of Muslims at large, and the support they might get from other regional actors.

4. Armed Resistance the Islamist Agenda

This agenda is adopted by resistance and liberation formations that turn to Islam as their principal instrument for mobilization when secular parties and groups fail to achieve their nationalist goals, be they ending foreign occupation or gaining independence from existing parent states (Ayoob 2008; Esposito 1999). The foremost examples of this phenomenon are Hezbollah in Lebanon and Hamas in the Gaza strip yet there are other examples in Iraq (e.g., the al-Mahdi army under the leadership of Muqtada al-Sadr) and Somalia (e.g., the Union of Islamic Courts). Six characteristics shape this agenda.

First, groups endorsing this agenda emerge because of the failure of other secular groups to achieve the nationalist objectives of liberation and independence. Both Hizbollah and Hamas were born as a result of the Israeli occupation of the Gaza Strip and the West bank and its invasion of Lebanon in 1982. The same goes for al-Sadr's army in Iraq, which emerged only after 2003.

Second, the violence that these groups have engaged in is context specific and principally in the nature of national resistance to foreign occupation. What distinguishes both Hamas and the Lebanese Hezbollah from al-Qaeda and other global Islamist violent organizations is that the former groups' violence is restricted territorially and directed toward specific targets that they consider to be obstructing their goals of achieving national independence or freeing occupied territory. Al-Qaeda and its supporting groups have no respect for national borders or identities. Hamas and Hezbollah work within the parameters of the state system even if they defy the legitimacy of their national opponents.

Third, there is a tendency among these groups not to give up their arms even when they choose to join the national government. All of them continue to be ambivalent regarding their roles in their respective polities, refusing to surrender arms, because they see them as an essential component of their popularity among their constituencies.

Fourth, these groups tend to straddle the violent and nonviolent worlds by having a political wing and a military wing. They field candidates in elections and even gain the majority, such as Hamas's wining the majority in the 2006 elections and al-Sadr's movement, which was key to the efforts of forming the new Iraqi government, winning 39 seats in the 325-seat parliament of the 2010 elections; that is up 10 seats from their previous standing.

These groups have social wings besides their political and military wings. Part of their electoral gains can be attributed to their vast network of social services that cater to the needs of the most underprivileged and vulnerable sections of their societies. However, each has accumulated popularity because of their success in driving Israeli troops from most of southern Lebanon, the Gaza strip and the promised US withdraw from Iraq.

Fifth, Hamas and Hizbollah are foes by proxy to the United States, since they feel the United States is waging a war by proxy against them through their closest ally in the region: Israel. The more the United States associates itself with Israel's policies, the more it is perceived as an enemy on its own merit.

Sixth, having an armed wing is another distinction between Islamists with a liberation agenda and other Islamists with partisan agendas, as we will see in the coming pages.

This resistance and liberation Islamist agenda is driven almost equally by nationalist considerations and religious ones, although they are still Islamists who use Islamic symbols to legitimize their behavior and mobilize their respective constituencies.

5. The Partisan Islamist Agenda

There is, fifth, a group of Islamists who work as a part of a trend toward moderation and constitutionalism, not violence and extremism. These formations adopt a party-like Islamic platform as an alternative from among others available for electors to choose. This agenda is endorsed by those seeking to win a parliamentary majority where elections are possible. A part of this discourse involves the formulation of a party program that addresses economic, social, and political aspects and offers better solutions to problems that existing parties already suggest solutions for.

Different Middle Eastern regimes have handled the proposed partisan agenda of Islamists differently in the past decade. Five models can be monitored.

First, partial inclusion and partial exclusion of Islamists: The Egyptian case under Mubarak represented this model par excellence. In this model there is a degree of partial assimilation and a degree of partial elimination without clear lines for what is or is not acceptable on the part of Islamists (Bayat 2007; Norton 2005, 157). Practically, the Brotherhood in Egypt was allowed somewhat free participation in national, syndicate, and students' elections, yet, under the condition that they do not win a majority of votes. Otherwise, election results get manipulated or the candidates of the Brotherhood get administratively excluded or even arrested. One can think of it as freedom of participation but no freedom after participation. The Muslim Brotherhood's credible performance in the 2005 elections indicated that the free and fair elections in Egypt will give more power to Islamists (Rubin 2007; Shahin 2010).

Second, legal assimilation and political neutralization: This model is best represented by the monarchic models of Jordan, Morocco, Kuwait, and Bahrain in addition to the examples of Algeria, Sudan, and Yemen. In this model, Islamists exist legally but no matter how they do in elections, the monarch or president has the ultimate say on the allocation of resources and deciding who gets what, when, where, why, and how. The Islamic Action Front in Jordan, the Movement of Society for Peace in Algeria, the Justice and Development Party in Morocco, the National Islamic Front in Sudan, and the Yemeni Congregation for Reform are all legally assimilated but politically tamed. Thus, they have to work under the iron ceiling determined by their oppressive regimes. In other words, Islamists can oppose (if they are the minority) or administer and manage (if they are the majority) but cannot rule and govern the affairs of their societies.

Third, autocratic exclusion of Islamists: This is the model of elimination of Islamists through legal, political, and police coercion as witnessed in the cases of Tunisia, Syria, and Libya before the Arab Spring. In these three cases, there was no space, legally or politically, for a group of people who might call themselves Islamists. A political Islamist in these countries used to be either in jail, exile, or the grave. This was particularly true for all the leaders of the Tunisian Renaissance Party, the Syrian Muslim Brotherhood, and the Libyan Islamic group before the Arab Spring.

Fourth, the secular democratic assimilation: In this model, which is solely adopted by Turkey, all political formations are assimilated and included in the political sphere as long as they abide by the rules of a secular and democratic state. These powers are carefully monitored by the Supreme Court and the National Security Council that is dedicated to the protection of supraconstitutional rules, that is, rules that no one can agree to break and that no one can seek to change or amend. In an example of how institutions create the culture conducive to them, the Justice and Development Party (AKP) in Turkey has repackaged its platform in a conservative democratic party emphasizing "Muslimhood," similar to the Christian Democrats in Western Europe, while giving up any radical exclusivist Islamist agenda.

Fifth, postrevolution regimes: The overthrow of five authoritarian regimes in the Arab world gave democracy a chance to bloom but at the same time it has also created opportunities for a wide spectrum of Islamist parties to raise demands for applying Islamic *shari'ah*. Though many of the protest movements associated with the Arab Spring in Tunisia, Egypt, Libya, and Yemen appeared to be largely secular in nature, Islamist parties have been winning most elections across the region, causing unease and uncertainty both domestically and abroad. In Egypt, there are roughly twenty-one new parties that have been formed claiming to endorse Islamic principles. Tunisia, Libya, and Yemen are taking the same path. Indeed, there is more space for procedural democracy to expand, yet it is not clear if this kind of democracy would be liberal enough to meet the minimum requirements of consolidated democracy (Recknagel 2013). One cannot fully predict where these countries are heading, but certainly they are not similar to the cases of Saudi Arabia, Iran, or Sudan, where an Islamist political agenda is fully in control.

6. The Ruling Islamic Agenda

In the name of Islam, three regimes in particular have reached power and continue to control it. Saudi Arabia, Iran, and Sudan are the three states within this region that have three traits in common: (1) they officially declare themselves as Islamic states and always make reference to Islam as their frame of reference in domestic and international affairs; (2) they officially apply Islamic *shari'ah* in personal and penal laws, besides an institutionalized review of their legal and judicial processes; and (3) their ruling elites have based their legitimacy since their inception on applying Islamic discourse. This is true by looking at the discourses of the leaders of these regimes during the unifying war in Saudi Arabia in the early 1930s, the mass revolution in Iran in 1979, and the coup d'état in the Sudan in 1989. In the three cases, the ruling elites have turned Islam from one of many cultural characteristics of societies into the defining element of their identities, institutions, and policies. These regimes work to have full monopoly over the political use of Islam, like other secularelegious countries, yet they seem to be more successful in Iran and Saudi Arabia than they are in Sudan.

Iran is a unique case since there is no other modern example where the *'ulama'* have themselves taken control of a state. The Islamic Republic of Iran is a case of unifying political power with official religious control of Shi'a clerics as it is embodied in Iran's Assembly of Experts. The Assembly of Experts is comparable to the Vatican's College of Cardinals. It is made up of eighty-six elected clerics whose chief responsibilities are the election of the supreme leader and ensuring the compatibility of official acts with Islam. The preamble to the Iranian constitution says that the Islamic Republic reflects the hopes of Iran's "Muslim people" in an assertion that the previous regimes have ignored the Islamic nature of the Iranian people. This new identity has been reflected clearly in the regime's ideology and state institutions.

Saudi Arabia provides another pattern where the family of al-Saud (possessing political power) and the family of Ibn Abd al-Wahab (possessing religious legitimacy) coalesced to form a state following the traditional pattern that first appeared with the Umayyad dynasty. To achieve primacy, Abdel-Aziz al-Saud formed an alliance with Shaykh Abd al-Wahhab and used religion to offset tribal affiliation and social segmentation. To consolidate the Saud's overall hereditary control, Abd al-Aziz and his sons after him formed strong marriage alliances with the Sudairi, Ibn Jelawi, and Shammar tribes, among others.

Unlike the two other examples of the ruling Islamic agenda, the Saud family rarely needed to resort to modern procedures of elected bodies. Domestically, the *'ulama'* have been the main supporting constituency for the Saud family. Practically, if the *umara* (princes) and *'ulama'* agree, then there is little room for generalized dissent. This has guaranteed the kingdom's stability for the past seventy-five years, although it is stability without democracy. That is why, in Saudi Arabia, the word "democracy" has no tradition of being officially used, misused, or abused. Even the Westernized intellectual elite that looks to Europe and the United States as models of liberal democracy does not think of achieving many liberal reforms in the near future, mainly because of the illiberal Wahhabi religious establishment that holds up its generally nonpluralistic interpretation of Islam as a guide (Korany and Fattah 2008).

Likewise, except for the short transitional period of 1953–1957 during which the Sudan had implemented secular and liberal laws, every single constitution had a clear reference to Islam as the official religion and *shari'ah* serving as the sole or primary source of legislation with clear reference to the rights of non-Muslims to practice their religions freely.

Since the three major currents of the Ansar (led by the al-Mahdi family), Khatmiyyah (led by the al-Mirghani family), and the Muslim Brotherhood, which comprise the major forces on the contemporary Sudanese political scene, are religiously based, Sudan's political history has been colored by Islam, and the implementation of Islamic laws is, therefore, a main component of the Muslim Sudanese portion of the population (roughly 70 percent; Hassan and Ray 2009). Following the same path, the current regime, that launched its coup d'état in 1989, has been actively engaging in a process of Islamizing the political and public spheres in the Sudan. In line with the commitment of al-Bashir's regime to Islamic path, the enforcement of *hudud* law was resumed in December 1990 after its suspension following the overthrow of the Numayri's regime in April 1985.

The architect of the 1989 coup d'état, Hassan al-Turabi (who later became a major opposition figure), described the mission of the regime as follows: "It is to Islamise public life—civil, business, police, military, economy and culture in all dimensions. When I say 'Islamise' I mean not only in forms, according to Islamic *Shari'ah*, but also attitude and disposition… Madinah is our model" (Al-Turabi 1993, 9).

However, this assertion of the Islamist identity has been one of the major causes of the two civil wars (1955–1972 and 1983–2005) that have caused the deaths of around 2 million civilians due to the desire of the southern Sudanese to secede. Unfortunately, the three examples of an "Islamic governance" are not of any appeal to harbingers of democracy and liberalism and have ranged from theocracy to fake democracy.

7. Lobbying Islamic Agenda

This agenda is adopted by organized groups as well as spontaneous movements pursuing short-term microgoals. One finds it manifested, for example, in demonstrations demanding the prohibition of a certain novel or book that is considered anti-Islamic; objecting to opening up a store that sells alcoholic beverages; and protesting governments' decision or permission to allow interests on loans and bank deposits, show inappropriate movies and music on national television, invite singers (usually known for dressing in revealing clothes), and organize beauty pageants.

Additionally, the lobbying techniques (such as demonstrations) might be used as a show of support for the Palestinians, Iraqis, or Lebanese especially during times of bloody tensions.

In most cases, the proponents of Islamism and Muslimhood explicitly or implicitly find themselves in coalition to achieve these microgoals. In Algeria, for instance, in March 2010, a temporary coalition was formed by Islamists, conservative Muslims, and official `ulama` around the grand mufti who accused Louisa Hanoun of being an "enemy of Islam," calling upon her to repent and stay away from issues that she is ignorant about upon her objection to the perpetuation of applying the capital punishment. Hanoun is a veteran, left wing Trotskyite and leader of the country's Worker's Party and an important secularist figure in Algeria.

In some cases, the interests and attitudes of university students and official `ulama` converges with the view of the Islamist formations and results in the adoption of a pressing discourse into a specific direction. However, this pressing role is not considered an ideal option by any of the parties involved. For the Islamists it is just a "minimum," for the secularists it stimulates fears about the "theocracy" ghost, and for the state it signifies pressure that it needs to address, either through coercion or through dialogue.

Typically this agenda works well if there are supporters of the cause on the part of the ruling elite. Islamists in Bahrain failed to prevent a female Lebanese singer from entertaining her audience in 2003 despite condemnations and violent protests against the police. Yet, with the support of some members of the ruling family, in coalition with Islamists (Shi`a and Sunni) and the official religious establishment, the parliament passed a law forbidding a private company from organizing a similar musical festival in 2008.

However, it looks as if they were minor successes on the part of Islamists, yet they are important indicators of their success in the Islamization of Muslim *societies* and failure to Islamize several Muslim *states*. This Islamization takes the format of influencing policies in the direction of increasing the communal activity (*da`wa*) within the existing order with the aim of changing it peacefully and gradually. Islamic resurgence (or *al-sahwa*) manifested both on the individual level (religious rituals and accessories) and on the collective level (proliferation of new mosques, religious charitable associations, and religious satellite channels).

Ruling elites in most seculareligious states left some space for this lobbying agenda as long as they are noninfluential regarding macrosovereign decisions of governance (such as relations with the West and Israel). That is why the lobbyist agenda does not openly challenge the powerful institutions of the presidency or the monarch.

However, this Islamization of society has not yet produced Islamization of the state apparatus because of the glass ceiling imposed by the police (Diamond et al. 2003). In almost all Muslim states with seculareligious agendas, an active Islamist cannot join the army, police, minister of foreign affairs, or any position that might empower the Islamist agenda in these pivotal power centers of the state.

8. Ecumenical Islamic Agenda

This survey would not be comprehensive without discussing the intellectual agenda of a group of `ulama', thinkers and intellectuals who theorize an ecumenical foundational agenda that appreciates the diversity of Muslims' agendas and regards Islam as a frame of reference over and above political conflicts of any type; analogically comparable to liberalism that constitutes the foundational framework for the political life in Western regimes. Under this overarching umbrella, diversity exists and should continue to exist as long as it acknowledges the authentic and indisputable (*qat`ai al-dalala* and *qat`ai al-thubout*) verses of the Qur'an and sayings of the Prophet.

They regard these holy texts to be a frame of reference comparable to the American Declaration of Independence or the British Magna Carta, so these texts should constitute jus cogens out of which no one can contract.

To give their discourse more coherence and organize their efforts, some of the champions of this agenda founded the International Union of Muslim Scholars (IUMS), headed by Shaykh Yusuf al-Qaradawi. It has members from almost all Muslim countries. Grand Ayatollah Shaykh Muhammad Ali Al-Taskhiri (Iran), Shaykh Taha Jabir al-Alwani (Iraq), Dr. Haytham Al-Khayyat (Syria), Ahmad Al-Raysouni (Morocco), Shaykh Salman Al-`Udah (Saudi Arabia), Isam al-Din Al-Bashir (Sudan), `Abd Al-Wahhab Al-Daylami (Yemen), and Selim al-`Awwa (Egypt) are among its leaders.

They argue that the *ummah* has been divided in so many directions without a compass or a roadmap. This agenda wants to emphasize the common grounds of all Muslim and Islamist agendas. That is why they accept all the nonsecular agendas (except for the militant radical ones) and are even ready to accept dialogue with secularists and non-Muslims.

They act as the champions of *wasatiya* (moderation) and against the seeds of sedition between Sunnis and Shiites and extremism against non-Muslims. The World Forum for Proximity of Islamic Schools of Thought in Iran is a manifestation of this agenda.

Having a common agenda does not mean that there are no internal debates regarding some issues. Dr. Yusuf Al-Qaradawi raised the issue of Shiite proselytizing in some Sunni countries, especially Egypt in 2008. However, Ayatollah Muhammad Ali At-Taskhiri rejected the issue as nothing but baseless rumors. Though it was a tough test for the IUMS, they managed to focus their attention on the common aspects of all Muslims such as the situation in Palestine. The IUMS Statement on Zionist Plots against Al-Aqsa Mosque and the Palestinian Issue is a very tough call upon all Muslims, rulers, and ruled, and even upon people of conscious among non-Muslims to save the Muslim and Christian holy shrines from the hands of Israeli occupying troops.

They think that all Islamists and religious Muslims are partners in a grand project of restoring the Islamic civilization (al-Qaradawi 2000). Modern preachers focus on ethics and rituals; Salafis are important yet they fight heterodox ideas and praxis; and armed resistance movements are the natural reaction to occupation. Their support as well goes to the partisan and lobbying agendas as peaceful expression of political demands. Yet, they unequivocally condemn the radical militant groups and they actually do not shy away from calling them terrorists. They are supportive of the rights of the ruled to choose their own rulers in free fair periodic multicandidate elections that they may or may not use the word "democracy" to describe it (al-Qaradawi 2001).

The proponents of this agenda play the role of the *ummah*'s conscience through issuing statements and giving sermons in mosques and media outlets. Yet, their real influence comes from their impact on other political players on the ground.

Conclusion

People of this part of the world have always been fascinated with "unity." The Qur'an says: "This is your *ummah*, one *ummah*, and I am your God…" However, this article has demonstrated that Muslims are very remote from unity at this point in their history.

Islam that united Muslims in the past has become an arena for political competition among Muslims nowadays. A fuzzy set of multiple (and even conflicting) agendas have been created on the ground. Each agenda creates its own logic, rhetoric, narrative, and constituents. This plurality is more political than it is religious. In other words, Islam is rarely the sole source of any of these agendas. It is usually used, misused, or abused by various groups of Muslims. Understanding these mixed and multifaceted phenomena is an indispensable step to fully comprehend who speaks for Islam in the Middle East and how different forces situate politics in their Islamic agendas.

Notes

1. States with symbolic reference to Islam in their constitutions and basic laws are Algeria, Djibouti, Egypt, Iraq, Jordan, Kuwait, Libya, Morocco, Qatar, Somalia, Tunisia, and United Arab Emirates.
2. States with Islamic review of laws are Bahrain, Iran, Mauritania, Oman, Saudi Arabia, Sudan, and Yemen.
3. http://news.bbc.co.uk/2/hi/africa/8537925.stm.
4. Kamal Habib, Another Wave of Jihadist Adjustment: Internal Debates of the Movement, *Arab Insights*, 2, no. 6, (Winter 2009), pp. 21–25. Jarret Brachman, Al Qaeda's Dissident, *Foreign Policy*, December 2009), pp. 19–20.

References

al-Azmeh, Aziz. 1992. *Al-'Almaniya min manzour mukhtalif* [Secularism from a Different Perspective]. Beirut: Markaz Dirasat al-Wehda al-Arabiya.

al-Qaradawi, Yusuf. 2000. *Ummatuna Bayna Qarnayen* [Our Nation between Two Centuries]. Cairo: Dar al-Shorouq.

al-Qaradawi, Yusuf. 2001. *Min Fiqh al-Dawla Fi al-Islam* [On the Jurisprudence of the Islamic State]. Cairo: Dar al-Shorouq.

al-Sa`eed, Rif`at. 2001. *Al-'alamnya Bayna al-Islam wa al-Taa'slum* [Secularism between Islam and Fake Islamization]. Kitab Al-Ahali; Cairo: Al-Tagamu` Party in Egypt.

Al-Turabi, Hasan. 1993. "Challenging Times but Medina Is Our Model." *Impact International*, 23, pp. 3–4.

Allen, John L. 2009. *The Future Church: How Ten Trends Are Revolutionizing the Catholic Church*. New York: Doubleday. pp. viii, 469.

Arkoun, Mohamed. 1994. *Rethinking Islam: Common Questions, Uncommon Answers*. Ed. and trans. Robert D. Lee. Boulder: Westview.

Ashour, Omar. 2009. *The De-radicalization of Jihadists: Transforming Armed Islamist Movements*.Contemporary Terrorism Studies. London: Routledge. pp. xv, 205.

Ayoob, Mohammed. 2008. *The Many Faces of Political Islam: Religion and Politics in the Muslim World*. Ann Arbor: University of Michigan Press. pp. xii, 213.

Baghdadi, Ahmad. 1999. *Tajdid al-Fikr al-Dini [Renovation of the Religious Thought]*. Damascus: al-Mada Publishing Company.

Bayat, Asef. 2007. *Making Islam Democratic: Social Movements and the Post-Islamist Turn*. Stanford Studies in Middle Eastern and Islamic Societies and Cultures. Stanford, CA: Stanford University Press. pp. xxi, 291.

Berman, Sheri. 2013. "The Promise of the Arab Spring." *Foreign Affairs*, January/February, pp. 22–28.

Bishri, Tariq. 1996. *Al-Hiwar al-Islami al-'Almani* [The Secular–Islamic Dialogue]. Cairo: Dar al-Shuruq. pp. 95.

Burgat, François, and Dowell, William. 1993. *The Islamic Movement in North Africa*. Middle East Monograph Series. Austin: Center for Middle Eastern Studies, University of Texas at Austin. pp. xi, 310.

Diamond, Larry Jay, Plattner, Marc F., and Brumberg, Daniel. 2003. *Islam and Democracy in the Middle East*. A Journal of Democracy Book. Baltimore: Johns Hopkins University Press. pp. xxvi, 322.

Esposito, John L. 1999. "'Clash of Civilizations'? Contemporary Images of Islam in the West," in Gema Martin Munoz, ed., *Islam, Modernism and the West: Cultural and Political Relations at the End of the Millennium*. New York: I.B. Taurist Publisher.

Esposito, John L. 2005. *Islam: The Straight Path*. Rev. 3rd ed. New York: Oxford University Press. pp. xvi, 304.

Gerges, Fawaz A. 2009. *The Far Enemy: Why Jihad Went Global*. 2nd ed. Cambridge: Cambridge University Press. pp. xiii, 386.

Haenni, Patrick. 2005. *L'islam de Marché: L'autre Révolution Conservatrice*. La république des idées. Paris: Seuil. pp. 108.

Hassan, Salah M., and Ray, Carina E. 2009. *Darfur and the Crisis of Governance in Sudan: A Critical Reader*. Ithaca: Cornell University Press. pp. 528.

Heck, Paul L. 2007. *Sufism and Politics: the Power of Spirituality*. Princeton: Markus Wiener Publishers, pp. 197.

Hoffman, Valerie J. 1995. *Sufism, Mystics and Saints in Modern Egypt*. Columbia, SC: University of South Carolina Press.

Kepel, Gilles. 2004. *The War for Muslim Minds: Islam and the West*. Cambridge, MA: Belknap Press of Harvard University Press. pp. 327.

Korany, Bahgat, and Fattah, Moataz. 2008. 'Irreconcilable Role-Partners?: Saudi Foreign Policy between the *'ulama'* and the US', in Ali E. Dessouki and Bahgat Korany, eds., *The Foreign Policies of the Arab States: The Challenge of Change*. Colorado: Westview Press.

Kuru, Ahmet T. 2009. *Secularism and State Policies toward Religion: the United States, France, and Turkey*. Cambridge: Cambridge University Press. pp xvii, 313.

Lapidus, Ira M. 2002. *A History of Islamic Societies*. 2nd ed. Cambridge: Cambridge University Press. pp. xxx, 970.

Lewis, Bernard. 2001. *The Multiple Identities of the Middle East*. New York: Schocken Books.

Marsot, Afaf Lutfi al-Sayyid. 1972. "The *'ulama'* of Cairo in the Eighteenth and Nineteenth Century," in Nikki Keddi, ed., *Scholars, Saints, and Sufis*. Berkeley: University of California Press.

Mernissi, Fatima. 1992. *Islam and Democracy: Fear of the Modern World*. Reading, MA: Addison-Wesley, 195.

Norton, Augustus Richard. 2005. "Thwarted Politics: The Case of Egypt's Hizb al-Wasat," in Robert W. Hefner, ed., *Remaking Muslim Politics: Pluralism, Contestation, Democratization*. Princeton, NJ: Princeton University Press, xii, 358.

Omara, Mohamed. 1998. *Hal al-Islam Hoa al-Hal?* [Is Islam the Solution?] Cairo: Dar al-Shorouq.

Recknagel, Charles. 2013. "What Happened to the Arab Spring?" *The Atlantic*, January 2013, pp. 13–14.

Rubin, Barry M. 2007. *Political Islam: Critical Concepts in Islamic Studies*. New York: Routledge.

Shahin, Emad El-Din. 2010. "Democratic Transformations in Egypt: Controlled Reforms...Frustrated Hopes," in Nathan J. Brown and Emad El-Din Shahin, eds., *The Struggle over Democracy in the Middle East: Regional Politics and External Policies*. New York: Routledge, xi, 201.

CHAPTER 21

ISLAM AND POLITICS IN CENTRAL ASIA

SHIREEN HUNTER

Introduction

The vitality of Islam in Central Asia and the Caucasus and its emergence in the last two decades as a potent social and political force after a century and a half of Russian and Soviet rule and subjection to policies aimed at its elimination came as a surprise to many observers and analysts.[1] However, for those familiar with these regions' Islamic history, including Islam's central role in their cultural, social, and political life, Islam's emergence and vitality in the post-Soviet era appear quite natural. This phenomenon becomes even more understandable if seen in light of the growing profile of Islam as a sociocultural and political force in the neighboring regions of Iran, Afghanistan, and Pakistan.

Factors behind Islam's Vitality

Many factors account for both Islam's resilience and staying power in Central Asia and the Caucasus, despite being actively undermined, and its current political relevance. The first factor is its deep historic roots. Most of Central Asia and the Caucasus were Islamized during the first centuries of Islam. Parts of Central Asia, notably Bukhara and Marv, became important centers of Islamic learning and Central Asians of both Turkic and Iranian stock such as Abu Nasr al-Farabi (c.872–c.950), Abu Ali Ibn Sina (Avicenna; 980–1037) and Muhammad Ibn Musa al-Khwarazmi (c.780–c.850), among others, greatly contributed to the development of Islamic civilization. A second factor is Islam's central place as an identity marker for the peoples of these regions. Islam's central role as the ethical, moral, legal, and cultural framework for collective life is the third factor. Until the Russian/Soviet control, in Central Asian political entities such as the Emirate of Bukhara and the Khanat of Khiva and Khokand, educational and legal systems were based on Islam. These institutions were severely undermined during the Russian/Soviet rule. Nevertheless part of their legacy managed to survive underground.

Fourth, the inconsistent character of tsarist and Soviet treatment of Islam is an important factor. This inconsistency allowed for periods of relative tolerance of Islam, which enabled it to retain some aspects of its traditional role. Certain requirements of the Soviet Union's foreign policy as early as the 1930s led the Soviet regime to periodically allow a degree of freedom in the practice of Islam and encourage a certain level of contact between Soviet Muslims and the rest of the Islamic world. For example, in the 1940s, Stalin tried to prevent Soviet Muslims from turning to Germany, which enjoyed a degree of sympathy among its Muslims by loosening some of the restrictions on Muslims' practice of their faith. The USSR also used Muslims as ambassadors to Arab states, especially under Khrushchev (Dawisha and D'encausse 1983, 166).

The fifth factor is Islam's role as an instrument of resistance against Russian/Soviet domination and Russification/Sovietization. Throughout the tsarist period in Central Asia and the Caucasus Islam was a main force behind the indigenous peoples' resistance to the advancing Russian armies and periodic revolts against the imperial administration. This pattern of resistance and Islam's role in it continued under the Soviet rule, albeit in a less overtly confrontational manner. Rather often secret practice of Islamic traditions, including those more cultural than religious, contributed to the preservation of the Central Asian and Caucasian Muslims' identity and traditions.[2]

The sixth factor is the failure of the USSR to deliver on its economic and political promises. The final factor is the paradoxes of Russia's nationalities policies that failed to engender a strong ethnic or civic nationalism in the Muslim-inhabited regions and hence further enhancing Islam's role as individual and collective identity marker.

Although Islam retained its hold on the peoples and societies of Central Asia and the Caucasus, the long Russian and Soviet rules and their anti-Islam policies had significantly adverse consequences for Central Asian and Caucasian Islam. The negative legacy of these policies and the consequences that have flown from them are responsible for some of the sociopolitical and religiocultural problems faced by these regions today, including problems posed by a degree of Islam's radicalization.

Islam in Central Asia and the Caucasus under the Russian and Soviet Rule

The Russian treatment of Muslims in Central Asia and in the Caucasus differed somewhat under the tsars. In the South Caucasus, or to be precise in what is now the Republic of Azerbaijan, Russia did not interfere with the local practice of Islam. The North Caucasus was not completely conquered until 1865, largely because of the resistance of such Muslim leaders as Shaykh (Imam) Mansur and Shaykh Shamil. During a period from 1785–1791, Shaykh Mansur Ushurma succeeded in uniting diverse North Caucasian groups through an elaborate network of Naqshbandi Sufi brotherhoods in resistance to the Russians. However, he was captured in 1793. After a lull of thirty years the Chechens resumed their fight against Russia, this time under the leadership of Shaykh Shamil who fought the Russians from 1825 to 1852. Shaykh Shamil's resistance, which after the Prophet's wars was named the Gazawat, has left a legacy that greatly contributed to later Chechen rebellions under the Soviets and to the post-Soviet events in Chechnya, Dagestan, and other parts of the North Caucasus.[3]

In Central Asia, the extent and magnitude of anti-Islam policies partly depended on the character and inclination of Russian officials. In general, however, Islam suffered under the tsarist rule as the number of mosques and religious schools declined as did the quality of Islamic learning. However, the tsarist regime did not pursue an aggressive policy of religious proselytizing in Central Asia and the Caucasus.

Before victory over the tsar, the Bolsheviks tried to attract the empire's Muslims by promising them freedom to pursue their religion, as reflected in the famous appeal of Lenin and Stalin to the Muslims of the east. This *Appeal to All Laboring Muslims of Russia and the East* said: "Muslims of Russia, Tatars of the Volga and Crimea, Kyrgyz and parts of Siberia and Turkmen, Turks and Tatars of Trans-Caucasia, Chechen and mountain peoples of Caucasus, all of you whose mosques and prayer houses have been trampled upon by tsars and oppressors of Russia; *your beliefs and usages, your national and cultural institutions are forever free*" (cited in Pipes 1997, 155, emphasis added).

This appeal had certain success and rallied many Muslims to the Bolsheviks' cause. The so-called *Shari`ah* squadrons, the militia of Zaki Validi Togan (1890–1970) in Bashkortostan, and the Chechen Red Army under the leadership of Aslanbek Shapirov, which served in the Red Army, and the fact that 70 percent of General Mikhail Frunze's Turkestan Red Army was made of Muslim soldiers reflects the success of Bolshevik propaganda (Salahetdinov 2001).

The Bolsheviks' other Muslim allies were the Muslim National Communists, whose leader was Mirsaid Sultan-Galiev (1880–1939), as well as some segments of the *Jadid* movement (Zenkovsky 1960, 189). All these Muslims joined the Bolsheviks because of their bad memories of tsarist conquest and hoped that the Bolsheviks would grant them more freedom.

The approach of Russia's Muslims toward the Bolsheviks reflects an old pattern of behavior on their part, namely that Russian Muslims always have sided with reformist elements in Russia. From 1905 to 1907, when hopes for political reforms in Russia had risen, Russia's Muslims joined the liberal group called the Kadets.[4]

However, not all of Russia's Muslims believed the Bolsheviks' propaganda. Moreover, the Bolsheviks' promise of freedom for Muslims had the paradoxical effect of reviving and intensifying Muslims' old aspirations for political freedom and independence. Thus, Muslims of the South Caucasus declared the formation of the Republic of Azerbaijan in 1918, and several autonomist movements were formed in Central Asia, such as the Alash Orda (the nation of Alash; Alash is the mythical ancestor of Kazakh people), which declared the autonomy of the Kazakh people in 1917 and the Ittifaq al Muslimin (the Union of Muslims), which declared the autonomy of the Muslims of Turkestan in November 1917 (Haghayeghi 1995, 17). Meanwhile, the Crimean Tatars elected a constituent assembly that adopted a constitution for the region, assumed legislative authority over the internal affairs of the Crimean Tatars, and appointed a military commander to oversee all Tatar military units in the Crimea and ministers for foreign affairs and war (Pipes 1997, 79–81). In the Volga-Ural regions Tatars and Bashkir formed the Idel-Ural Republic.

Because of the expressions of desire for independence on the part of Russian Muslims, in practice, the Bolshevik forces, notwithstanding their promises, treated Muslims more harshly than other minorities, especially in Central Asia. Thus the Tashkent Soviet formed by the local supporters of the Bolsheviks dismantled Muslim organizations, including mosques, and embarked on atheistic propaganda and profaned mosques. This behavior contributed to the outbreak of the Basmachi revolt in 1918, which continued with diminishing degrees of intensity until the mid-1930s (Broxup 1983, 57–83).

The Bolsheviks' attitude toward the Muslims hardened even further once they succeeded in defeating their opponents and consolidating their hold on power. Consequently, the new Soviet regime in a reversal of earlier policies proceeded to dismantle Muslim political organizations formed after the October Revolution.

Moreover, the USSR's nationality policies developed by Joseph Stalin were based on the principle of dividing the Muslims and other ethnic groups and leaving substantial ethnic and religious minorities in the newly formed republics. This policy was against Muslims' desire for greater consolidation of Muslim-inhabited areas into large political units. For example, in 1918, many of Russia's Muslims, especially those with pan-Turkist tendencies, had wanted to create three large Muslim political units (Hunter 2004, 27).

Russia's policy of Muslims' fragmentation along ethnic lines was complemented by its policy of cultural fragmentation by, among other things, developing dialects of a single language into full-blown separate languages. This policy of ethnic, cultural, and territorial fragmentation has been primarily responsible for the ethnic, sectarian, and border disputes and cultural competition that has plagued the Muslim-inhabited parts of the post-Soviet space.

THE USSR'S ANTIRELIGIOUS POLICIES: IMPACT ON ISLAM AND MUSLIMS OF CENTRAL ASIA AND THE CAUCASUS

The USSR's strategy against Islam, which began to be implemented in 1924, was based on the following principles:

1. The eradication of Muslim judicial and educational institutions;
2. The elimination of the clerical establishment's financial independence by dismantling the *waqf*; and
3. Anti-Islam propaganda.

Of course, all religions were anathema to the Bolsheviks and to the Communist ideology, but Islam was especially targeted because it was viewed as particularly reactionary and backward.[5] This view of Islam and Muslims predated the advent of the Bolsheviks to power and is the reason many of the Bolsheviks' tactics against Islam resemble those of the tsarist era.[6]

Another reason for the Soviet authorities harshness toward Islam was what they saw as Islam's all-embracing nature and its pivotal role in the Muslims' individual and collective identities. This aspect of Islam was seen as threatening to the Bolsheviks' project of building a new socialist society and a new Soviet Man (*sovestskii Chelovek* or *Homo sovieticus*). *Homo islamicus* had to be eradicated in order to make room for *Homo sovieticus*.

As a result of this policy the number of functioning mosques in Russia/Soviet Union had dropped from 26,000 during the tsarist times to 1,312 and the number of clergy from 45,000 to 8,000 (Hunter 2004, 28–9). These numbers were further reduced in the following decades. In 1979, there were only 300 registered mosques and the number of clergy had sharply declined (Hunter 2004, 34).

The Second World War affected Soviet Muslims' fate in a contradictory fashion. On the one hand, the defection of a large number of Muslim Soviet soldiers to Germany brought Stalin's wrath on them. On the other hand, it forced Stalin to make some concessions to Muslims such as creating the Muslim Spiritual Boards in order to regulate Muslims' religious affairs and allowing the resumption of instruction at the Mir Arab Madrassa in Bukhara.

The Soviet Unions' policies toward Islam and Muslims had several highly negative consequences for Muslim-inhabited regions of the Soviet empire including the following: the deterioration of Islamic learning and quality of Islamic clergy; the undermining of these regions' mostly *Hanafi* traditions and the growing influence of nonindigenous Islamic traditions, as people from Central Asia and the Caucasus went to other parts of the Islamic world to get religious education; and the erosion of the credibility and, hence, influence of the official clergy among the people because of their perception of them as mere government officials and part of the corrupt Soviet bureaucracy.[7] Since the 1970s, and increasingly in the 1980s, this phenomenon has led to the peoples' gravitation toward unofficial figures educated in the Arab World and often with radical tendencies.

Meanwhile, folk Islam, which is deeply mixed with local traditions, continued to flourish, aided by the fact that the paradoxical nature of Soviet nationalities policy failed to foster a strong sense of nationalism and statehood (Hunter 2004, 34). Moreover, in these regions, there had always been a close link between a sense of nationalism and Islam as reflected in the following comment by the antireligious Dagestani writer S. Muslimov writing in 1983: "It is well known that religious revivals are tightly linked to nationalistic trends. The nationalistic revivals often take on a religious appearance, whereas religious revivals are propagandized under the flag of defense of national traditions" (Muslimov 1983, 38–39).

THE IMPACT OF OUTSIDE DEVELOPMENTS ON SOVIET MUSLIMS: THE IRANIAN REVOLUTION AND THE SOVIET-AFGHAN WAR

Developments in the neighboring countries of the Soviet Union's Muslim-inhabited regions significantly impacted the evolution of Soviet Muslims. In particular, they led to their greater politicization. One such development was the Iranian revolution, but the most influential factor was the Soviet invasion of Afghanistan and the ensuing Soviet-Afghan war. Four consequences of the Afghan war were particularly significant in Islam's revival and its politicization in the USSR. First, the war introduced Central Asian members of the Soviet army to their fellow Muslims in Afghanistan. Some found fighting against other Muslims difficult, thus leading the Soviets to refrain from sending Central Asian soldiers to Afghanistan.

Second, the war galvanized both the West and the Muslim World against the Soviet Union and led to an all-out propaganda campaign against the USSR through a variety of radio programs aimed at Soviet Muslims from stations based in Muslim and Western countries. Even the Islamic Republic of Iran, despite its anti-Western ideology, in its broadcasts to the Soviet Union's Muslim-inhabited areas took a consistently anti-Communist line, and its leaders condemned Soviet policies toward Islam in Central Asia and the Caucasus (Bennigsen 1982). These broadcasts had an important impact on the perceptions of the Soviet Muslims, the extent of which can be judged by the intensity of Soviet responses. In 1980, the head of Azerbaijan's KGB general Zia Yusuf Zade denounced "…the harmful influence of imperialist propaganda on certain representatives of our [Azerbaijani] intelligentsia and youth" (Dzhabarov 1985).

Third, the war led to the establishment of direct contacts between Afghan Mujāhidīn and their Pakistani and Saudi supporters and the Central Asian Muslims. Hundreds of illegal students in Central Asia and elsewhere in the USSR went to study in religious schools and train in the military camps set up by Pakistan's General Zia ul Haq with the financial assistance from Saudi Arabia and Western support. In these camps they learned about Islamic movements, their ideology, and their tactics. P. I. Dzhabarov characterized what was taught in these camps as "Western anti-Communist reactionary Islamic clericalism" and accused Pakistan's Jama'at-i Islami, Turkey's Society for Struggle against Communism, and the Muslim Brotherhood of being involved in these activities. Fourth, the Soviet Union's withdrawal from Afghanistan shattered the perception of its invincibility and enhanced Islam's image as an effective instrument of resistance and liberation.

Islam, Nationalism, and Transnationalism in Central Asia and the Caucasus on the Eve of Soviet Collapse

The outpouring of nationalist and Islamic sentiments in Central Asia and the Caucasus during the period of Perestroika and Glasnost starkly exposed the failure of the Soviet Union's policy of creating a *Homo sovieticus* and eliminating religious and ethnonationalist feelings.

When independence was thrust upon Central Asian and South Caucasian republics a need emerged to find a new framework for social and political organization and a new basis of state legitimacy. In this context, Islam, nationalism, and transnationalism emerged as the main competitors to fill the ideological vacuum left by the Soviet demise as reflected in the names and agenda of various political parties that had emerged during Perestroika.

During the period of Perestroika a number of Islamically oriented political groups emerged in Central Asia and the Caucasus including the following: the Alash Party (named after Alash the mythical ancestor of the Kazakhs) in Kazakhstan, which also had pan-Turkist tendencies; the Edolat Party (Justice Party) in Uzbekistan; and the Islamic Rebirth Party, which was initially conceived as extending to all Muslim-inhabited regions of the USSR. The founding conference of the Islamic Rebirth Party was held in Astrakhan in June 1990 and its first leader was a native of Dagestan. However, the party soon splintered and its center of gravity shifted to Central Asia, especially to Tajikistan and Uzbekistan (Hunter 1996).

In Azerbaijan in the South Caucasus the following were the most significant of Islamically oriented political parties: the Party of Islam (Islam Partiyasi), a Shi'a party whose leader was Hadji Hadji Agha; the Muslim Brethren (Islam Ghardaslari); and Union of Young Muslims (Javan Islam Chilarin Birliki; Hunter 1994, 78–79). In the postindependence period most of these parties either disappeared or refashioned themselves under different names. Other Islam-based political groups and parties also emerged, most of which were forced underground.

THE CONSOLIDATION OF SECULAR AUTHORITARIANISM: ISLAM'S RADICALIZATION

The demise of the USSR did not result either in the democratization of Central Asia's politics or in the dismantling of the Soviet era bureaucracy and nomenclature, with few exceptions and for brief periods, such as the presidency of Abul Fazl Elcibey in Azerbaijan (1992–1993).

Consequently, the political trend in Central Asia and Azerbaijan has been toward the establishment of authoritarian rule under the so-called presidents for life and with a growing tendency toward dynastic presidencies. Notably, in Azerbaijan, Heidar Aliev's son, Ilham, assumed presidency after his father's death, and it is widely speculated that the daughters of Uzbekistan's Karimov and Kazakhstan's Nazarbaev have presidential ambitions.

The result of this development has been the closure of the democratic and parliamentary road for political engagement for independent political parties, including those that are Islamically oriented. Indeed, the latter have fared worse than others, as they have been banned.

The inability to pursue their goals through legal and legitimate channels has led these parties either to resort to violence—as was the case in Tajikistan with the IRP (Islamic Rebirth Party), which led to a long and highly destructive and debilitating civil war from 1992 to 1997[8] —or to transform into radical movements engaged in terrorist acts—as happened with the Edolat Party, which became subsumed under the Islamic Movement of Uzbekistan (IMU).

The Edolat Party and its leader Tahir Yoldash were particularly bitter against Islam Karimov, Uzbekistan's Soviet era leader who sought and won election to the presidency against the nationalist Muhammad Salih. Their bitterness was due to the fact that Karimov used them in his 1992 campaign against Salih by promising him and his supporters to establish an Islamic state. According to an article in Ferghana.ru, dated October 15, 2007, during a meeting on December 12, 1991 organized by Yoldash and his supporters in which demands were made that Uzbekistan be declared an Islamic state, Islam its official religion, and elections be postponed so that Muslims could field their own candidates, Karimov promised he would implement all their demands once elected president. Because of this promise the Namangan region voted for Karimov. One year later, all of Tahir Yoldash's supporters were behind bars and he himself had fled to Tajikistan, where he became involved in the civil war on the side of the Islamic opposition.[9] There is none.

Interestingly, during the first years of his presidency Karimov tried to use Islamic symbols to enhance his government's legitimacy. For instance, during his inauguration he swore on a Qur'an. He also performed the *Umra Hajj* pilgrimage during a visit to Saudi Arabia in 1992. However, he soon embarked on a policy of suppressing all Islamic groups, including nonpolitical groups, and bringing the entire Islamic establishment of the country under governmental control.

Pushed out of Uzbekistan by Karimov in 1996, Yoldash, together with another founder of the Edolat Party, Jumma Namangi, and the remnants of another Islamically oriented group, Islom Lashkeri, formed the IMU (Baran 2006, 25–27). IMU established close connections with the Taliban and Al-Qaeda, and between 1999 and 2001 it was responsible for a number of terrorist attacks in Uzbekistan and Kirghizstan.[10]

After the US invasion of Afghanistan the IMU moved to Pakistan, where it got into conflict with the Taliban. Reportedly, Jumma Namangani was killed as a result of US air strikes, but so far his death has not been confirmed.[11] In Tajikistan, the IRP is legal but powerless.

The radicalization of Central Asia's Islamic movements has also been abetted by the region's economic problems, notably unemployment, especially among the youth, and poverty. In fact, there appears to be a clear correlation between the economic situation and Islamic militancy. Thus the Ferghana valley, which comprises parts of Uzbekistan, Kirghizstan, and Tajikistan and is one of Central Asia's poorest regions, has most of the region's Islamists. It is also in this region that new movements such as the Hizb al-Tahrir have developed roots by attracting the followers of the region's indigenous, but now banned, Islamic groups as well as new recruits.[12]

In addition to economic problems, government repression, pressure on nonpolitical Muslims, and a general disregard for human rights enhance the appeal of more radical interpretation of Islam. The Andijan revolt in 2005 and the way the Uzbek government dealt with it best exemplify the combined result of economic problems and repression.[13]

Until the last few years Kazakhstan had denied the existence of any radical Islamic groups except in the country's southern parts, which are inhabited by ethnic Uzbek. However, recent evidence has emerged of the development of radical groups among ethnic Kazakhs, some of which reportedly have links with Al-Qaeda. One such organization, which reportedly was discovered and dismantled, was the Jamā'at of the Central Asian Mujahedin. Reportedly the group included four female members trained as suicide bombers. Another group is the "*Takfirchilar*, in other words *Takfiris*. They are also known as *Hizb ul Takfir*. This group reflects the influence of Salafi, the Takfiris of Pakistan, and Afghanistan (Azizian 2005). Among recent groups also with alleged links to Al-Qaeda is the Jaish ul Khalifa, which was involved in terrorist acts in 2012. In general Islamic radicalism has been spreading in Kazakhstan. For example, it is no longer limited to the southern part of the country, which borders Uzbekistan and has spread to the western parts of the country (see Jacob Zenn, "Salafists Challenge Kazakh Future," *Asia Times*, September 19, 2012).

In Azerbaijan, meanwhile, the interaction between Islam and politics has become more complex. The fact that the majority of the Azerbaijanis are Twelver Shi'as, coupled with the Republic's historical and cultural ties with Iran, which goes back to pre-Islamic times, and political differences between the Republic's leadership and Iran has meant that the government has had a more hostile attitude toward Shi'ism.

As part of its policy of countering Iran's influence, at one point during the second Chechen war (1999–2000),[14] the government of Heidar Aliev encouraged the spread of Salafi Sunni Islam in Azerbaijan. Other influences came through Turkey, especially the Nourjou (Followers of Said Nursi) and its offshoot, the Gullen movement (Cornell 2006). The result has been growing sectarian tensions in Azerbaijan, which according to one Azerbaijani professor has even affected universities where Shi'as and Salafi students do not talk to each other.[15]

However, as the number of Salafis grew in Azerbaijan, and in 2006 were estimated between 7,000 and 15,000, the government began to curb their activities (Cornell 2006). Thus the Abu Bakr mosque in Baku where the Salafis congregate was closed for a period in 2001. So far the Salafis have concentrated on religious proselytization and staying out of politics. According to some non-Salafi sources, two factors, namely the country's economic and political problems notably, high youth unemployment and corruption plus the availability of resources probably coming from the Persian Gulf region, help the Salafis to attract disadvantaged and disaffected youth (Cornell 2006).

The Abu Bakr mosque has also been accused of recruiting fighters for Iraq, Chechnya, and Afghanistan. In 2006, it was revealed that one of the Guantanamo prisoners was an ethnic Azeri by the name of Polad Safarov. Reportedly, he worked as translator for Bin Laden and was recruited through the Abu Bakr mosque. The mosques' Imam Gamet Suleimanov denied having ever met Safarov (Day.az 2005).

The Azerbaijani government has tried to promote the Gullen movement in the Sunni-inhabited regions of the north as a counterweight to the Salafis, but so far without much success. The Salafis have an extremist wing, which calls itself the Jeyshullah (Army of God). It has been engaged in terrorist acts, including against the followers of Hare Krishna, and was suspected of wanting to bomb the American embassy in Baku. The leaders of the group were imprisoned in 2000 (BBC 2005).

The Azerbaijani government's treatment of Shi`a activists has been much harsher. For example, unlike the Abu Bakr mosque, which was reopened and its imam remained free, the Shi`a Jummă mosque was closed in 2003 and its Imam Ilgar Ibrahimoghlu was tried and condemned to five years in prison. Part of this harsher treatment has to do with factors noted above and partly because Ibrahimoghlu became involved in politics, including during the 2003 presidential elections. His combining of religious discourse with that of human rights is also viewed as more threatening. In fact, the charge against him was that he had mixed religion and politics and thus had endangered the country's secular political system. Ibrahimoghlu has studied in Iran and in Poland where he became acquainted with Polish resistance during Soviet times. Earlier, he was compared to Muqtada Al Sadr of Iraq, but now he is a human rights activist and has created an organization called the Center for Protection of Religious Freedoms.

Another controversy erupted in 2009–2010 when the Azerbaijani government tried to demolish the Fatima Al Zahra Shi`a mosque. However, it had to back down in the face of strong Shi`a opposition. Key Iranian clerics, notably Ayatullah Safi Golpayegani, also intervened. He wrote a letter to the president of Azerbaijan admonishing him that he should protect the Shi`a faith and not undermine it.

Interestingly, the upshot of the government's anti-Shi`a policies has been a revival of Shi`ism and its influence has been referred to as the "Shi`a Renaissance" by the Azerbaijani professor Altoy Gayushov ("Islamic Revival in Azerbaijan").

The other Shi`a political group is the Islamic Party of Azerbaijan, not to be confused with the Party of Islam, which was formed during Perestroika. The party was formed in the mid-1990s. In 1995–1996 it suffered a crackdown reportedly because it wanted to acquire paramilitary forces (Rotar 2000). When riots broke out in 2003 in the village of Nardaran, which was the party's power base, its chairman Haci Ali Akram Aliev was arrested and the party's registration was revoked. The party has tried to register again and has staged protests but no avail. The IPA (Islamic Party of Azerbaijan) has leftist leanings as well and is part of a coalition of leftist parties. Neither the supporters of Ibrahimoghlu, nor the IPA have been accused of involvement in terrorist acts. Haci Ali Akram died in 2012.

In Azerbaijan, the question of Islamic veiling has also become very controversial, reflecting a growing secular-religious divide in the country. There have been a number of protests against banning the Hijab in Azerbaijan, which often also have political undertones.

Islam, Politics, and Conflict in the North Caucasus

The dynamics set in motion by Gorbachev's reforms and the competition, which ensued within the Soviet Union's top leadership between first Gorbachev and the hardliners led by Ligachev and later between Gorbachev and Yeltsin, also deeply affected developments within those Muslim-inhabited regions of the USSR, such as Tatarstan Bashkortostan and in the North Caucasus (Hunter 2004).

In both of these regions, Islam experienced a significant revival as did ethnic nationalism and pro-independence movements. The pro-independence movements were greatly encouraged by Yeltsin's statement to the Soviet minorities to get as much sovereignty as they could handle.

However, after the Soviet demise, Yeltsin resumed power and he set upon reining in the independence-seeking republics. In the case of Tatarstan, this goal was achieved through negotiations. However in Chechnya Moscow's efforts led to a bloody war, first from 1994 to 1996 and then from 1998 to 2000.

The Chechen War and the Politicization and Radicalization of Islam in the North Caucasus

The Chechen conflict was the outcome of a complex set of factors including the following: power struggles and rivalries in the Kremlin; personal animosity between Boris Yeltsin and Dzhokar Dudaev, the Chechen leader and hence Yeltsin's unwillingness to reach a negotiated settlement with Chechnya as it had with Tatarstan; tribal rivalries in Chechnya; and regional and international competition over pipeline routes.

Initially, Islam played little or no role in the start of the Chechen war (Isayev 2007). For instance, Dudaev was not a particularly observant Muslim. Rather he was a product of the Soviet system and as a fighter pilot had participated in the carpet bombing of Afghanistan, a fact that Russia used to undermine his Islamic credentials once he discovered Islam as a useful instrument in his quest for power and Chechen independence (Praslov 1995, 5). Moreover, during his first year in office, he ruled out the establishment of an Islamic state in Chechnya. In an interview in August 1992 he told the *Literaturnaya Gazeta*, "Where any religion prevails either the Spanish inquisition or Islamic fundamentalism [will] emerge" (Malashenko 1995, 46). For this reason, the 1992 constitution of the self-declared Chechen Republic stated that "religious organization are separate from state organs, administer their affairs autonomously, and operate independently from state organs" (Chechen constitution, 35).

It was first the Russian intrigues and then the war that led to the flow of foreign fighters to Chechnya, including the so-called Afghan Arabs, namely the veterans of the Soviet-Afghan war, and figures such as the Saudi-born Samir Abdullah Al Suweilam, known as Emir Khattab, that finally led Dudaev and even more so leaders who came after him to resort to Islam both as an instrument of legitimation of power and as a way to foster opposition to

Russia. Later Islam became a tool in the power struggles of various Chechen leaders who engaged in a race to prove which one was more Islamic.[16]

Consequently, in August 1994, the National Congress of the Chechen People gave Dudaev the authority to declare an Islamic uprising in the tradition of the Gazavat of Imam Shamil the legendary Chechen leader, and in September 1994, Dudaev declared Chechnya an Islamic state (Interfax News Agency 1994). He also created an Islamic Battalion to counter the activities of opposition forces supported by Moscow and indicted that he wanted to apply the *Shari'ah* (Dunlops 1998, 149).

After the Russian campaign began in full, the Chechen public's identification with Islam became stronger. When after Dudaev's assassination in April 1996 Zelimkhan Yanderbaev became Chechnya's acting president, he declared that he would "take the lead in a war, in a 'jihad' of the Chechen people in the name of Allah and in the name of the freedom of the Chechen people" (Hirst 1996). The end of the first round of the Russo-Chechen war in 1996 did not stop the increasing use of Islam for political purposes. Thus shortly after the signing of the Kasavyurt agreement in August 1996, Yanderbaev abolished secular courts, created a supreme *Shari'ah* court, and implemented a criminal code for Chechnya based on the *Shari'ah*, which included the death punishment for apostasy (Akaev 1999; Human Rights Watch 1997).

Maskadov, who became president in January 1997, went even further and renamed Chechnya the Islamic Republic of Ichkeria (Walker 1998). The only country to recognize it was Afghanistan under the Taliban.

Since the end of the intense period of the Chechen war in 2003 and the relative stabilization of the Republic under the presidency of Ramazan Kadyrov, the son of Chechnya's former Imam Ahkmed Kadyrov, the use of Islam as an instrument of political legitimation has continued.[17] In 2009, Kadyrov imposed strict Islamic law as part of its strategy of combating the influence of extremist Muslims and gaining legitimacy for his arbitrary rule. He has also resurrected local traditions, which have nothing to do with Islam, such as honor killing (Berry 2009).

Between the period of the end of the first Chechen war and the start of the second, militant Islamic groups with a very strict interpretation of Islam and with links to Afghanistan and Pakistan gained influence in Chechnya and in the neighboring Dagestan (Hunter 2004). In fact, it was their activities that provoked the second Chechen war.

Contagion Effect of Chechnya: Dagestan

In view of the close ties between the peoples of Dagestan and Chechnya the contagion effect of Chechnya was first felt in Dagestan, where Arab missionaries and fighters who had come to Chechnya crossed over into Dagestan. This led to the emergence of a number of extremist groups, some of which engaged in terror attacks on Russian targets. For example in November 1996 in Kaspisk in Dagestan, a bomb destroyed a building housing Russian border guards. Then in April 1997, a bomb exploded in the railway station in Russia's Krasnodar Krai and two bombs in May 1997 in the railway station in Pyatigorsk in the Stavropol Krai.

The activities of the Islamists went beyond terrorist acts, and in summer 1998 had led to the creation of miniature Islamic states known as "autonomous *Shari'ah* territory" in the villages of Karamakhi, Shabanmakhi, and Kadar. In addition, Chechens who had always had always considered Dagestan as part of Chechnya and nurtured the hope of uniting Chechnya and Dagestan and possibly the rest of the North Caucasus within an Islamic state set out to prepare the groundwork for it. In August 1997, the first deputy prime minister of Chechnya, Movladi Ugodov, organized a meeting of more than thirty representatives of Muslims of the North Caucasus in order to found the Nation of Islam along the lines of earlier efforts dating back to the period immediately following the falloff of the tsarist regime to create a political entity made of all the so-called mountain peoples of the North Caucasus.

However, differences that emerged between those loyal to Dagestan's traditional Islam highly influenced by Sufism and the new followers of Salafi Islam resulting in fighting, division, and rivalries among Muslim leaders of Chechnya and between them and Dagestanis prevented the success of these plans.

In the summer of 1999, large-scale warfare erupted in the North Caucasus when several thousand Muslim militants together with volunteers from Central Asia, Arab countries, and others crossed into Dagestan with the stated objective of liberating Dagestan from Russian rule and establishing an Islamic state. The Chechen President Aslan Maskhadov condemned this incursion, but Chechen commander Shamil Basaev and Khattab assumed the leadership of the invading forces. This attempt by Muslim militants to push Russia out of the North Caucasus was a main reason for the second Russian war. However, it must be added that some sources have claimed that plans for a second war on Chechnya were prepared by Russia by March 1999 well before the Dagestan incursions (Felshtinsky 2008, 105). Dagestan's extreme poverty, ethnic, tribal, and sectarian divisions, plus the region's massive corruption contributed to the success of extremist ideas and groups (International Crisis Group 2008).

The Chechen conflict also deeply affected the Republic of Ingushetia through the influx of Chechen refugees. At their peak the number of Chechen refugees in Ingushetia was 240,000. Influx of refugees also brought with it militants who flourished in Ingushetia, which had since the 1990s experienced a degree of Islamization (Kantysheva 2007). Some of these militants created military wings such as the Ingush Regiment, whose members were disarmed by Russian forces in 1999 (Jamestown Foundation 1999).

However, it was Ingushetia's extreme poverty, massive corruption, and harsh treatment of its people by its president, Murat Zyazikov, that led to the growth of radical Islamic cells known as *Jama'at*, which finally resulted in full-scale civil war in 2007. The Russian overreaction to activities of a group of Islamists imported from Chechnya, including a massive security operation in July 2007, contributed to the worsening of the crisis.

The assassination of a major opposition figure, Magomad Yevloyev, further intensified the conflict. Finally in October 2008, Dmitry Medvedev dismissed Zyazikov. The new president, Yunus Bek Yevkurov, is said to try to rule with a softer hand (Pan 2009). However, the fighting with Islamist groups continued in 2009, and reportedly between January and March 2009 led to fifty people, including twenty-seven rebels, eighteen policemen, and two civilians, being killed. On June 10, the deputy chief justice of the Ingush Supreme Court Aza Gazgireeve was killed, and on June 13 former Deputy Prime Minister Bashir Aushev was wounded (BBC 2009; AP 2009). Then in August 2009 the police department in Nazran was attacked. In general it is agreed that Ingushetia has replaced Chechnya as the main trouble spot in the North Caucasus (Eckel 2009).

The Chechen conflict and the general revival of Islam have also spread to Kabardino-Balkaria, Adygeya, and Karachaevo-Cherkessia (Matveeva 1999; East-West Institute 2001). The *Jama'at* movement has been particularly active in Kabardino-Balkaria. Some of them such as the Yarmuk Jama'at have been engaged in violent actions (McGregor, 2006). Russia's efforts to reign in these groups, including the closing of mosques in Kabardino-Balkaria, especially after the school siege and massacre in Beslan in the neighboring Republic of North Ossetia in 2004 (Borovnikov 2005), finally led to the so-called Nalchik uprising when in October 2005, 200 militants targeted security forces in the Republic. After that the government closed down many mosques and has, according to some sources, targeted not only armed militants but also observant Muslims charging them of subscribing to what it calls Wahhabism (Fagan 2008). However, these actions do not seem to have eradicated extremist groups, and in January 2008 it was reported that militants had killed the director of the region's antiorganized crime directorate Colonel Anatoly Kyarov (Radio Free Europe Radio/Liberty 2009).

The causes of the growth of extremism and violence related to it, in addition to the contagion effect of the Chechen conflict, are strikingly similar to those in other North Caucasian republics, namely, poverty, unemployment, ethnic divisions, and rampant corruption. According to one report, "The economy of the entire North Caucasus is based on black market industries and theft from the Federal government." Moreover, "the local government elite [are] interested in self-enrichment and for ordinary people there is nothing" (Finn 2005). However, the desire for independence from Russia, especially in the absence of any economic benefits, should also be factored in as inspiration for violent acts.

The upsurge in Chechen-inspired violence against Russian targets in 2010, especially the devastating attack on the Moscow underground by the so-called Black Widows (women who have lost husbands or close relatives as a result of Chechen conflict) in March 2010, reflected the fragility of the country's Russian-imposed calm ("Russian Security Services Hunt 21-Strong 'Black Widow'cell," TIMESONLINE, March 30, 2010).

Violence in the North Caucasus continued unabated throughout 2012. In Dagestan sectarian differences, notably between the Salafis and the Sufis have even increased the risk of civil war (see "UPDATE1-Islamic Cleric Warns of Civil War In Russia's Dagestan" *Reuters*, August 29, 2012).

This same has been true of other North Caucus republics, notably Kabardino-Balkaria and Ingushetia (see "Russia Police Launch Deadly Raid in Kabardino-Balkaria," BBC News-Europe, September 20, 2012).

Observers expect more violence in the region as the 2014 winter Olympics, which will be hold in Sochi, is approaching. However, the event might encourage the development of other resorts in the region, which could tackle some of area's poverty and unemployment issues and possibly help reduce militancy and violence (see "Russia Boosts Ski Resort Security after Attacks," BBC News-Europe, February 21, 2011).

Conclusions

Given Islam's deep roots in Central Asia and the Caucasus, its central role as an identity marker both at individual and collective levels, and its traditional role as the basic ethical and legal framework for collective life in Central Asia and the Caucasus, its emergence and a degree of its politicization after the Soviet collapse were inevitable.

However, Islam's radicalization, which has occurred to varying degrees, was not inevitable and has directly resulted from the evolution of Central Asia's and the Caucasus's governments and polities in an authoritarian direction, economic degradation, corruption, and repression of even peaceful practice of Islam.

In addition, regional and international developments, most importantly the Afghan civil war and growth of extremist Islamist groups in Pakistan and Afghanistan, have further helped radicalize Islam in Central Asia and the Caucasus.

Moreover, Central Asia and the Caucasus is paying a price for the Russian/Soviet practice of undermining these regions' traditional and more moderate Islam, which has created an opportunity for more strict and/or radical interpretations of Islam and their proponents from the Arab World and South Asia to find their way into these regions. This, too, has given a radical tinge to the interaction of Islam and politics in Central Asia and the Caucasus.

Notes

1. Some parts of Central Asia and the Caucasus did not come under Russian control until the 1860s. In the Caucasus the present-day republic of Azerbaijan was conquered by 1828 after Iran's defeat in the second round of the Russo-Iranian wars (1824–1822). The conquest of Chechnya, Dagestan, and the neighboring areas was not completed until the late 1860s. Some parts of Central Asia such Turkmenistan came under Russian control also later in the nineteenth century.
2. Sufi brotherhoods were very important in Islam's preservation. See Bennigsen and Wimbush 1985 and Bennigsen and Broxup 1983.
3. For an account of the Chechen resistance to Russia's advance, see Broxup 1992.
4. For a brief summary of Muslim political activism under the tsars, see Hunter 2004, 16–22.
5. For a list of Islam's flaws, according to the Bolsheviks, see Hunter 2004, 29.
6. Alexander Pushkin's characterization of the Muslim holy book the Qur'an as "a collection of new lies and old stories" sums up the Russian view of Islam. Cited in Karam 1999, 31.
7. Since the time of Catherine the Great, Russia has tried to bring Muslim religious organizations under state control. See Hunter 2004, 9–10. For recent times, see Hunter 2004, 102–120.
8. The Tajik Civil war, however, had many complex reason behind it, including the unwillingness of the Communist era Khojandi Uzbek economic and political elite to share power plus Uzbek and Russian manipulation. See Gretsky 1995.
9. "Tahir Yoldash: US Fiasco Is Nearing. Look Us up in Washington" 2007.
10. Among attacks attributed to the IMU was the abduction of a Japanese geologist in 1999 in Kyrgyzstan and the 2002–2003 bombings in Bishkek and Osh.
11. "Notes on Jumma Namangani" 2001.

12. Reportedly in 2005 there were at least 2000 to 3000 HT members in Kyrgyzstan. See Azizian 2005 and Kasmali 2000.
13. For background to the Andijan events, see Raman 2005 and on the Akramia movement that was involved in the events, see Rotar 2005.
14. The year 200 marks the end of the active phase of full-scale warfare. The insurgency continued well into 2005 and is still alive, albeit in a diminished way.
15. Conversation with the Azeri professor visiting Georgetown University.
16. One such race was between Aslan Maskadov, who became Chechnya's president in January 1997, and Shamil ` Basaev, who broke away from him.
17. It is hard to establish the exact date of the end of the Chechen war. However, the passing of a new constitution in April 2003 that granted Chechnya a significant degree of autonomy is a reasonable date. However, it must be added that insurgent groups are still active in the republic.

References

Akaev, Vahid. 1999. Religious and Political Conflict in the Chechen Republic of Ichkeria. In *Political Islam and Conflicts in Russia and Central Asia*, ed. Lena Jonson and Murad Esenov. Luela, Sweden: Center for Social and Political Studies. Available at: http://www.ca-c.org/dataeng/m_akaev.shtml.

Avtorkhanov, Abdurakhman, and Marie Broxup, eds. 1992. *The North Caucasus Barrier: Russian Advance towards the Muslim World*. New York: St. Martin's Press.

Azizian, Rouben. 2005. Islamic Radicalism in Kazakhstan and Kyrgyzstan: Implications for the Global War on Terror. *CSRS discussion paper* 5, no. 56 (September 2005).

Baran, S. Zeyno, Fredrick Starr, and Svante E. Cornell. 2006. Islamic Radicalism in Central Asia and the Caucasus: Implication for the EU Silk Road Paper. Central Asia and Caucasus Institute. Available at: www.silroadstudies.org.

Bennigsen, Alexandre. 1982. Soviet Islam since the Invasion of Afghanistan. *Central Asian Survey* 1: 2.

Bennigsen, Alexandre, and Marie Broxup. 1983. *The Islamic Threat to the Soviet State*. New York: St. Martin's Press.

Bennigsen, Alexandre, and S. Enders Wimbush. 1985. *Mystics and Commissars: Sufism in the Soviet Union*. Berkeley: University of California Press.

Berry, Lynn. 2009. Chechen Leader Imposes Strict Islamic Code. *New York Times*, March 2.

Borovnikov, Vladimir. 2005. The Beslan Massacre. *ISIM Review* 15.

Broxup, Marie. 1983. The Basmachi. *Central Asian Survey* 2: 57–83.

Chechen Constitution, Article IV. 1992. In Paul Henze. 1995. *Islam in the North Caucasus: The Example of Chechnya*. Santa Monica, CA: RAND.

Cornell, Svante E. 2006. The Politicization of Islam in Azerbaijan. *Silk Road Paper*. Washington, D.C.; Central Asia—Caucasus Institute. Available at: www.silroadstudies.org.

Dawisha, Karen, and Helene Carrere D'Encausse. 1983. Islam in the Foreign Policy of the Soviet Union. In *Islam in Foreign Policy*, ed. Added Dawisha. Cambridge: Cambridge University Press.

Day.az. 2005. Interview with the chair of Azerbaijan's State committee for Religious Affairs, Rafiq Aliev. Available at: http://www.Day.az.

Dunlop, John. 1998. *Russia Confronts Chechnya: The Roots of a Separatist Conflict*. Cambridge: Cambridge University Press.

Dzhabarov, I. B. 1985. Religious Propaganda Aimed at Muslims in USSR: Ideological Subversion. *Soviet Uzbekistani*.

Eckel, Mike. 2009. Ingushetia Is Latest Kremlin Trouble Spot. *Associated Press*, October 4. Available at: http://www.sfgate.com/cgi-bin/article.cgi?f=c/a/2009/10/04/MNRG19TFIE.DTL&type=p.

Fagan, Geraldine. 2008. Russia: Detained and Tortured for Faith, Kabardino-Balkaria Muslims Claim. *The Muslim News*, August 18. Available at: http://www.muslimnews.co.uk/news/news.php?article=14722.

Felshtinsky, Yuri, and Vladimir Pribylovsky. 2008. *The Age of Assassins: The Rise and Rise of Vladimir Putin*. London: Gibson Square Books. Sergei Stepashin's interview with the Russian minister of interior.

Finn, Peter. 2005. Crackdown Provoked Shootout in Russia. *Washington Post*, October 15.

Gretsky, Sergei. 1995. Civil War in Tajikistan: Causes, Developments and Prospects for Peace. In *Central Asia: Conflict, Resolutions and Change*, ed. Roald Z. Sagdev and Susan Eisenhower. Washington, DC.

Haghayeghi, Mehrdad. 1995. *Islam and Politics in Central Asia*. New York: St. Martin's Press.

Hirst, David. 1996. Chechen Leader Pledges Holy War. *The Guardian*, April 16.

Hunter, Shireen T. 1994. *The Trans-Caucasus in Transition: Nation—Building and Conflict*. Washington, DC: Center for Strategic and International Studies.

Hunter, Shireen T. 1996. *Central Asia Since Independence*. Westport, CT: Praeger.

Hunter, Shireen T. 2004. *Islam in Russia: The Politics of Identity and Security*. Armonk, NY: M.E. Sharpe.

Isayev, Ruslan. 2007. The Role of Religion in the Chechen Conflict. *Prague Watchdog*, May 27. Available at: http://www.watchdogcz/?show=000000-000015-000006-000017&lang=1.

Kantysheva, Saida. 2007. Islam in the Life of Ingush People Today. *Prague Watchdog*, December 20. Available at: http://www.watchdog.cz/?show=000000-000015-000006-000026&lang=1.

Karam, Patrick. 1999. La Russie et l'Islam: entre alliance et rejet. *Les Cahier de l'Orient* 41.

Kasmali, Gulnara. 2000. Will Fighting Return To Batken, Kyrgyzstan This Spring. Central Asia—Caucasus Institute, *Analyst*, March 15. Available at: http://www.cacianalyst.org/?q=node/533.

Malashenko, Alexei. 1995. Does Islamic Fundamentalism Exist in Russia. In *Muslim Eurasia: Conflicting Legacies*, ed. Yaakov Roi. London: Frank Cass.

Matveeva, Anna. 1999. *The North Caucasus: Russia's Fragile Borderland*. London: Royal Institute of International Affairs.

McGregor, Andrew. The Movement in Kabardino-Balkaria. *Terrorism Monitor* 3: 7.

Muslimov, S. 1983. In Search of Persuasiveness—Some Pressing Problems of Atheistic Propaganda [in Russian]. *Sovetskiy Dagestan* 6: 38–39.

Pan, Phillip P. The Softer Hand. *Washington Post*, November 12.

Pipes, Richard. 1997. *The Formation of the Soviet Union: Communism and Nationalism, 1917–1923*. Cambridge, MA: Harvard University Press.

Praslov, Alexander. 1995. Contazvedka e Chechne [Counterintelligence in Chechnya]. *Argumenty i Fakty* 5.

Raman, B. 2005. The Andijan Uprising: The Background. South Asia Analysis Group, Paper no. 1380, May 14. Available at: http://www.southasiaanalysis.org/%5Cpaper1380.html.

Rotar, Igor. 2000. Islamic Fundamentalism in Azerbaijan: Myth or Reality. *Jamestown Prism* 6.

Rotar, Igor. 2005. Uzbekistan: What Is Known about Akramia and the Uprising. Oslo, Norway, *Forum 18 News Service*, June 16, 2005. Available at: http://www.forum18.org/Archive.php?article_id=586.

Salahetdinov, Muhammed. 2001. Unification under the State Roof. *Nezavisimaya Gazeta* 74.

Walker, Edward. 1998. Islam in Chechnya. *Contemporary Caucasus Newsletter*. University of California at Berkeley, Issue 9.

Zenkovsky, Serge A. 1960. *Pan-Turkism and Islam in Russia*. Cambridge, MA: Harvard University Press.

1994. Detailsof Mobilization Edict. Interfax News Agency's *Daily News Bulletin*. Moscow, August 11.

1997. *Civil and Political Rights in Post-War Chechnya*. Human Rights Watch.

1999. Muslim Extremists Suspected in Vladikavkaz Blast. *Jamestown Foundation Monitor* 5: 58 (March 24).

2001. Islamic Groups Active in Adygeya: East-West Institute. *Russian Regional Report* 6: 37.

2001. Notes on Jumma Namangani. November 19. Available at: http://www.spongobongo.com/em/em9873.htm.

2005. Azeri God's Army Cult Members to Stand Trial for Murder. *BBC Monitoring Central Asia*, July 25.

2007. Tahir Yoldash: US Fiasco Is Nearing. Look Us up in Washington. *Ferghna.ru*, October 15. Available at: http://enews.ferghana.ru/article.php?=id2167.

2008. Russia's Dagestan: Conflict Causes. *Europe Report*, 192, International Crisis Group, June 3.

2009. Attack on Russian Regional Leader. *BBC News*, June 12. Available at: http://news.bbc.co.uk/1/hi/world/europe/8112109.stm.

2009. Another Killing in Region Bordering Chechnya. *Associated Press (New York Times)*, June 10. Available at: http://www.nytimes.com/2009/06/14/world/Europe/14ingushetia.html?_=1&ref=world.

2009. Four Years after Nalchik, How Strong Is insurgency in Kabardino—Balkaria. *Radio Free Europe Radio/Liberty (RFE/RL)*, October 13. Available at: http://www.rferl.org/articleprintview/1850860.html.

CHAPTER 22

ISLAM AND POLITICS IN SOUTH ASIA

IRFAN AHMAD

The Argument

JULY 2010: The Bangladesh government led by Mrs. Sheikha Hasina of the Awami League (AL), considered a "secular" party, ordered libraries and mosques to remove from their shelves books written by Abu al-A'la Mawdudi (1903–1979), founder of South Asia's Jama'at-e Islami (hereafter Jamaat). Justifying the ban, a government official remarked that Mawdudi's books promoted "militancy and terrorism" (BBC 2010).

September 2007: The Conservative Party leaders from London's Tower Hamlets took to the streets demanding that the Whitechapel Idea Store not stock books written by Islamic authors. According to BBC (2007) Phil Briscoe, the local councilor said that "although *Mein Kampf* by...Hitler might be available in libraries for educational purposes, some books by Islamic thinkers were too offensive to have a place in libraries." He further explained that "some of the books have been written by convicted...terrorists and in those cases those books are not suitable to be...in a public library." The libraries of Tower Hamlets had become a hot topic in the media after a think tank, the Centre for Social Cohesion, reported that they stored books by authors like Mawdudi and Egypt's Qutb.

Clearly, both in Bangladesh and the United Kingdom there were local factors behind the ban on books by authors like Mawdudi. However, at work were also supralocal factors in these two global sites. Behind the ban on Mawdudi's books, apparently more dangerous than *Mein Kampf*, is a larger premise: a liberal, geostrategic understanding of Islam. Central to this understanding is the notion that religion in general and Islam in particular is a storehouse of illiberalism, extremism, and intolerance. Qutb's borrowing from Mawdudi's (Shepard 2003) and Berman's (2003) christening in the *New York Times* of Qutb as "The philosopher of Islamic terror" further exemplifies such a framework. Integral to this framework is the reigning assumption that for Islam to become "moderate" and "secular" it must be liberalized and reformed. Holding that Muslims are outside of modernity, Rushdie (2005) advised them that "a new Reformation will bring your faith into the modern era."

Based on an analysis of the changing trajectory of Jama'at-e Islami in Bangladesh, India, and Pakistan, I critically examine Breman's and Rushdies's line of thought also manifest in dominant academic writings. Demonstrating the folly, even poverty, of such a framework, I aim to offer a nuanced (and possibly a fresh) understanding of Islamism[1] in south Asia. Central to my argument is that we begin to study the transformative moments in Islamism for it marks a shift from discourse to the profoundness of praxis. Here I am persuaded by Trouillot's (1995, 89) observation that the Haitian revolution "thought itself out politically and philosophically as it was taking place," in a context where "discourse always lagged behind practice." Critical to this is the process of transformation. Since it is a process, Islamism is not a frozen entity immutably locked into a dead end. In showing this dynamism, my aim is to destabilize the premise that while liberalism is open to self-examination, thinkers like Mawdudi and their followers are not. My contention is to the contrary. It seems that Muslims and Islamists such as Ghannoushi (1998) have reexamined many of their assumptions; it is liberals like the French secularist (see Bowen 2007), notably the philosopher Blandine Kriegel (Foucault's associate, advisor to Jacques Chirac, and the chair of the High Integration Council), and Indian academics like Zoya Hasan who are obstinate on not reexamining theirs. This obstinacy has only been accentuated with the ascendance of the post-9/11 paradigm I have called "securitization" of Islam (Ahmad 2009, 6). "Alarmed" at the recent initiative (2010) by Indian Jamaat to participate in democracy, Zoya Hasan described it as "unfortunate and uncalled for." The electoral participation of a "Muslim party [Jamaat]," she warned, "will trigger polarization" and derail "progress" and "growth" (*Times of India* 2010). Javed Anand, a fellow liberal and secularist, was more explicit: "They [Jamaat] want to weaken the political culture from within by first being part of it.... The Jamaat too will launch into its true mission once it gets a firm political foothold in India" (*Times of India* 2010, 6; see also Anand 2012). This paranoia resembles the West's where commentators justified the denial of Islamists' participation in democracy saying Islamists believed in "one man, one vote, one time" (Esposito 1994, 21).

I am also critical of the dominant post-9/11 framework, which often links south Asia's Jamaat with terrorism. Before 9/11, most writings on Jamaat referred to it as "antiprogressive," "antisecular," "conservative," "militant," "fundamentalist" (e.g., see Agwani 1986; Ahmed 1994; Bahadur 1977; Hasan 1997); post-9/11 these terms either stand mostly replaced or subsumed under "terrorism." In discussing radicalization in the Middle East, Juergensmeyer (2003, 84, 261n53) suggests how Mawdudi's thought contributed to terrorism. He, however, does not dwell on the complexity of Mawdudi's thoughts and transformation of his politics and how Jamaat in south Asia underwent change. If Juergensmeyer's position is reflective of the post-9/11 *global discourse* on terrorism, Ganguly's (2006, 5) is the *Indian version* informed by the geopolitics of south Asia. Despite denial by Jamaat of its any ties with militant organizations and categorical condemnation of terrorism (Bangladesh Jama`at-e Islami 2012; Kabir 2006, 190ff.), Ganguly directly links the 2005 Bangladesh bomb blasts to Jamaat and its student wing, Islami Chhatra Shibir (ICS), arguing how Bangladesh, in cahoots with Pakistan's Inter Service Intelligence (ISI), is set to harm India through terror. Indeed there is a striking resonance between a position such as Ganguly's and *The Washington Post's*, which, in 2006, called Bangladesh "a new regional hub of terrorist operations that reach into India and Southeast Asia." To Karlekar (2005, 264), Bangladesh is on the path of Talibanization led by Jamaat; hence the title of his book: *Bangladesh: The Next Afghanistan?*[2]

Against this dominant post-9/11 framework of securitization of Islam, I argue that political Islam as represented by Jamaat in south Asia is neither monolithic nor static. My main contention is that Jamaat has significantly transformed itself in India, Bangladesh, and Pakistan and thereby become an important participant in politics of the respective nation-states. However, an understanding of Jamaat in south Asia will remain skewed as long as we continue to see it through the mere lenses of the nation-states because globalization entails transcending the (neo)relist premise of the nation-state as the ultimate unit of analysis.[3]

This essay is divided into three sections. In the first, I historically situate the formation of Jamaat and its ideology as formulated by Mawdudi in colonial India. In the second section I discuss Jamaat's monumental transformation in postcolonial India. Continuing this theme of transformation, I discuss how Jamaat also changed in Pakistan and Bangladesh. For reasons of space, my discussion of Jamaat in three different countries will be purposively brief. I will conclude with some general observations on the modality and nature of Islamist politics in south Asia, especially on its ideological templates.

Formation and Ideology of Jama`at-e Islami

The founder of Jama`at-e Islami, Mawdudi, did not have a fully fledge traditional Islamic education. Till the age of nine, he received his education in Urdu, Persian, Arabic, *fiqh*, law, and *hadith* through private tutors.[4] At eleven he went to a madrasa, but studied there only briefly. Largely self-taught, Mawdudi was well versed in the history and theology of Islam as well as modern social sciences, including Marxist literature. In his diagnosis of Muslims' decline, he held that Muslims lagged behind Europe because the latter produced philosophers such as Fichte, Hegel, Comte, Adam Smith, Malthus, Rousseau, Voltaire, Goethe, Herder, and so on. He admired the Turkish writer Halide Edip (a judgment he later revised), who visited India in the mid-1930s. His call to Muslims was to master modern sciences. Not only were his thoughts influenced by modern sciences, to some *ulema*, Mawdudi's appearance was also modern. Until 1936 he remained clean shaven. In 1938, when Manzoor Nomani, a Deoband theologian, first met Mawdudi in Delhi he was "jolted" to see an Islamic figure with too short a beard. He was also aghast at his "Western (*angrezī*) hair" (Ahmad 2009, 54). A year before he founded Jamaat, he wrote:

> In the age of *jāhiliyat* I have read a lot on ancient and modern philosophy, science, history, economics, politics, etc. I have digested a whole library. But when I read the Qur'an with open eyes then I realized, by God, that whatever I had read was insignificant. Now I got the root of knowledge. Kant, Hegel, Fichte, Marx, and all other great philosophers of the world now appear to me as kids. (Ahmad 2009, 53)

Mawdudi initially supported the Indian National Congress (formed in 1885; hereafter the Congress) and published biographies of Mohandas Gandhi and Madanmohan Malaviya, a Hindu nationalist leader. He edited *Muslim*, the Urdu organ of the Jamiatul-Ulema-e-Hind, an organization of *ulema* (Islamic theologians) allied to the Congress. During the late 1930s, however, Mawdudi felt disillusioned with Congress's nationalism, which, he held, was far from secular as it favored Hindus against Muslims.

The turning point in Mawdudi's career was the elections of 1937 and the subsequent formation of provincial ministries by the Congress. He equated the policy of the ministries (1937–1939) with heralding a "Hindu raj." He criticized the ministries for marginalizing Muslims and for gradually making them Hinduized. Another reason for his distrust of nationalism stemmed from the dismemberment of the Ottoman Empire by Western powers along nationalist lines.

After his turn to Islamism, Mawdudi began to interpret Islam unconventionally. He held that Allah sent his prophets to establish a state. Human history, he held, was the history of a contest between Islam and *jāhiliyat*, the period of ignorance before the Prophet Muhammad. For Mawdudi, *jāhiliyat* was a system with many forms. Politically, it expressed itself in human sovereignty. In 1941, Mawdudi founded Jamaat for the "establishment of an Islamic state (*ḥukumat-e-ilāhiya*)." Since the Muslim League, the party fighting for Pakistan, did not have as its goal the establishment of a *sharia*-based state, he described future Pakistan as "infidel state of Muslims." Secular democracy, to Mawdudi, was *haram* for it replaced divine sovereignty with human sovereignty. To Mawdudi, Muslims should boycott what he called *jāhiliyat, ṭāghūti niẓām*—an anti-Islamic polity.[5] The Jamaat's constitution obligated its members to boycott the following:

- Assemblies that legislate secular as opposed to sharia laws;
- An army that kills "in the path of non-God";
- Secular judiciary; also banks based on interest;
- Teaching or studying in colleges or universities, including Muslim ones, that serve *jāhiliyat*; Mawdudi called them "slaughterhouse[s]"; and
- Services and jobs in the antigodly system (Mawdudi 1942, 178–182).

Such a call to its members as the above, however, did not mean that Jamaat nursed no relations with non-Muslims. It sometimes invited non-Muslims to its open sessions. The Hindu leader Gandhi, for instance, took part in its regional meeting in Patna, the capital of Bihar, in April 1947 and appreciated Jamaat. Three months after this meeting, India was partitioned in August 1947. With Partition, Jamaat was divided into Jamaate-Islami Hind (India) and Jama`at-e Islami Pakistan. Mawdudi himself chose Pakistan. Jamaat was a tiny organization with a rather limited influence among educated people. In undivided India of 1947, its members numbered less than 1,000 (Ahmad 2009, 63).

THE TRANSFORMATION OF JAMA`AT-E ISLAMI ACROSS SOUTH ASIA

With this admittedly synoptic historical account of Jamaat's formation, in this section I describe important turning points in Jamaat's transformation across south Asia. Central to this descriptive analysis is my argument of how in each nation-state Jamaat gradually came to join the very mainstream (regarded as largely "un-Islamic") that its constitution of 1941 sought to replace with its own Islamic system (*niẓām*). I begin with Indian Jamaat. Next I will discuss the transformation of Jamaat in Pakistan and Bangladesh.

India

After India's Partition, Jamaat continued to stick to its earlier position. In 1951–1952, India held the first parliamentary elections in which non-Jamaat Muslims participated, but Jamaat did not. Abullais Islahi Nadwi, the first *amīr* (president) of Jamaat in independent India, justified the boycott of elections along Mawdudi's lines. "In whatever form you participate in elections," he wrote, "you are flouting the commandments and guidance of sharia" (Nadwi 1951, 63). However, before the third elections in 1962, a debate began in Jamaat's *markazī majlis-e-shura* (the central consultative council, hereafter *shura*). It centered on the (il)legitimacy of democracy and secularism. In July 1961, *shura* set up a committee to determine whether elections could be used for pursuing *iqāmat-e-dīn* (establishment of religion). The Qur'anic phrase *iqāmat-e-dīn* was the new objective Jamaat had inserted into its constitution after Partition to replace its earlier mission of *ḥukumat-e-ilāhiya*—a change also incorporated in the constitution of Pakistani (and Bangladeshi) Jamaat. The committee concluded that Jamaat could compete in elections to make the Indian constitution Islamic. The *shura* accepted the recommendation and went on to pass two separate resolutions that had no reference to *iqāmat-e-dīn* but to the legitimacy of participating in the elections, both as voters and candidates. It did not lift the ban on voting for the 1962 elections. In 1967, however, *shura* approved some criteria under which members could vote. The most important criterion was that the candidate "must believe in the *kalima* [i.e., he must be a Muslim]" and regard legislation against Allah as *haram*.

Debate continued with many in *shura* favoring a lifting of the ban on voting. The issue, however, remained in limbo until emergency imposed by Mrs. Indira Gandhi in 1975. When the emergency was lifted and elections announced, Jamaat ended its ban, disregarding its earlier criteria (e.g., the candidate must be a Muslim), and participated actively. The foremost criterion now was that the candidate must favor the "restoration of democracy," because Mrs. Gandhi had banned most parties, including Jamaat. The debate further continued until 1985 when *shura* permanently lifted the ban against voting. Since 1985, participation in and defense of democracy and secularism by Jamaat only intensified.

Another significant development since 1985 took place in April 2011 when Jamaat backed the formation of a political platform aiming to contest elections, the Welfare Party of India (WPI). Mujtaba Farooque and Qasim Rasool Ilyas—well-known leaders of Jamaat—are president and secretary, respectively, of WPI. WPI will work "not only for Muslim causes," Farooque said, "but will try to deliver justice to…every section of India…" (Beyondheadlines 2011a). WPI's objectives (Beyondheadlines 2011b) are as follows:

- "Party will aim at the establishment of a welfare state. Party believes that sufficient nutritious food, decent clothing, proper shelter, essential healthcare, and elementary education are among the fundamental human rights…"
- "…women should get full growth and development opportunities with full protection to their femininity."
- "Party envisages a society where all cultures have full opportunities to thrive…in…India, all cultural entities should get fullest opportunities, resources, and powers to protect and promote their cultural values and identities."

Five of WPI's sixteen national leaders were non-Muslims—Christian and Hindu—as well as women (*Indian Express* 2011). How WPI will fare in elections is yet to be seen. However, what is less uncertain is that formation of WPI by Jamaat marked yet another watershed. So significant was it that some critics suggested if WPI's aim was "the establishment of a welfare state" there was no need for it for this objective was already enlisted in India's constitution and espoused by a plethora of parties. One such critic (Sayyid 2011) hoped that by forming WPI, Jamaat would not get derailed from its goal of *iqāmat-e-dīn* and that it would maintain a balance. Another critic (on other side of ideological divide) disapproved of WPI, saying that though its aims were noncommunitarian, one of its leaders spoke of establishing *nizām-e-muṣṭafā*, Prophetic Order (TwoCircles.Net 2011).

How and why did Jamaat undergo such a monumental change? Clearly, democracy played a key role. This factor distinguished Indian Islamists from their counterparts in the Middle East, where neither nonauthoritarian secularism nor democracy is well established.[6] It was manifest in the Muslim public's disavowal of Jamaat, which also played itself out in the realm of democratic politics. Critical to this disavowal is what I call an "ideological dissonance" between Jamaat's agenda and political subjectivity of Muslim public. Before I might get misunderstood, let me clarify that I do not take democracy as external to Islam. Contra many Muslims (including the Deoband ulema), Mawdudi regarded, as a matter of contingency, *a specific form of democracy* as external to Islam (see Conclusion).

Democracy not only acted upon Jamaat externally but did so internally as well. The whole debate was conducted on the principle of majority votes. This democratic basis of decision making became so crucial that even the Islamic creed, the *kalima*, from which, according to Mawdudi, the voting ban had been derived, was put to vote, and clinched by a majority vote. The debate took place within two fora—*shura*, and *majlis-e-numāindegān*. While *shura* existed in Mawdudi's time, the *majlis* did not. However, the role of *shura* significantly changed in postcolonial India. Mawdudi, as the Jamaat's *amīr* had been the sole decision maker. The task of the *shura* whose members he himself nominated had been to advise the *amīr*. With Jamaat's democratization, *shura* members began to be elected, and the *amīr* had to accept decisions made democratically by *shura*. The formation of *majlis* was a new development. It is like the Jamaat Parliament elected directly by its members who, on occasions, are required to vote.

During its transformation, Jamaat indeed became more democratic than other political formations. None of the Indian parties ever practice democracy internally as the leaders in the party are *not elected*; they are *selected* or *nominated* along multiple ascriptive grids: family, caste, region, religion, and so on. In contrast, Jamaat practiced democracy internally but opposed democracy (elections) externally. Jamaat's initial opposition to democracy was *not intrinsic* but *contingent* as its subsequent transformation shows.

Pakistan

In line with his opposition to future Pakistan as an "infidel state of Muslims," until 1949 Mawdudi regarded it as a sign of *jāhiliyat*, because it based itself on popular sovereignty.[7] In 1948 the western Punjab government mandated its employees to pledge an oath to the state. Mawdudi forbade his party members to do so until the state became Islamic. In March 1949 Pakistan's Constituent Assembly passed the Objectives Resolution acknowledging God's sovereignty. Only then did Mawdudi (2003) no longer regard contesting elections or joining the Pakistani army as *haram* (Nasr 1994, 121–124, 246n40; Nasr 1996, 42; Niazi 1973, 106–13). Mawdudi justified many changes in his position by grounding them in the so-called Islamic orientation of the Pakistani state and its constitution.

Soon after Pakistan's formation Mawdudi was jailed because he had dubbed Pakistan's covert support (1948) to insurgents in Kashmir while upholding a ceasefire with India un-Islamic and reeking of "hypocrisy." The government accused Mawdudi and Jamaat of sedition. Released in 1950, Mawdudi activated his party, which, in 1951, took part in provincial elections but with little impact. This failure, *inter alia*, led to fights in Jamaat with many leaders leaving the party. The 1953–1954 anti-Ahmadi mobilization aimed at pressuring the government to declare Ahmadis as "non-Muslims" brought Mawdudi to prominence. Mawdudi himself did not play a role in that mobilization; he wrote a pamphlet on Ahmadis. However, with the crackdown on anti-Ahmadis activists a military tribunal charged Mawdudi with "sedition" and served him a death sentence (later annulled).

With the installation of military rule in 1958 by the Sandhurst-trained General Ayub Khan, the government became harsher toward Jamaat. Khan's developmentalist and modernizing regime (1958–1969) viewed figures like Mawdudi at best as nuisance. Jamaat's offices were closed, its publications curbed, and its leaders monitored. Mawdudi himself was jailed in 1964 and again in 1967. So opposed was he to the regime that Mawdudi backed a woman, Fatimah Jinnah, against Khan for the presidency of Pakistan. The result, however, went against Mawdudi's wish. Mawdudi's support to Fatimah Jinnah contradicted his earlier position according to which Islam did not allow a woman to lead the government. Yet, it is important to note that Mawdudi was perhaps the first South Asian thinker to open his party's membership to women on the basis of the Qur'an and *hadith*. Jamaat's constitution even urged women to "disobey the commands of their husbands and guardians if such commands were sins against Allah." In Pakistan, Jamaat women now contest elections. In India Jamaat's *shura* discussed in 1999 women's absence in leadership (in 2000, of 4,776 members, 303 were women). It proposed that Jamaat's president be empowered to nominate women to assume leadership roles (Ahmad 2008; Nasr 1996).

The outcome of Pakistan's national elections of 1970 was not favorable to Mawdudi either: only four of his party members won. In the war of 1971, Mawdudi's sympathy lay with the army as he did not support Bangladesh's independence. Following the breakup of Pakistan, Mawdudi battled against Zulfikar Ali Bhutto's (d. 1979) socialist populism, including his land reforms. As an alternative, Mawdudi intensified the movement for the installation of *niẓā m-e muṣṭafā*. So effective did the slogan of *niẓā m-e muṣṭafā* become that, after the 1977 military coup, General Zia-ul-Haq (d. 1988) made it the cornerstone of his regime. Mawdudi died in 1979; more than a million people participated in his funeral (Nasr 1996).

In Pakistan's national elections of 1988, 1990, 1993, Jamaat won seven, eight, and three seats, respectively (Nasr 1994, 208, 213; Gardezi 1994, 111). It boycotted the 1997 elections. Electorally, student wings of Jamaat on college campuses have performed better than the parent party. In Pakistan and Bangladesh, Jamaat's student wings exercise considerable influence and are known to have resorted to violence. Compared to mainstream parties, Jamaat activists, however, are often seen, even by their nemesis, as less corrupt and more dedicated to their cause. Seeking to transform itself into a popular party, in the 1990 elections Pakistani Jamaat used the repertoire of mass mobilization: posters, billboards, sloganeering, mass rallies, processions, film songs, and by some accounts, even dancing to the tune of popular numbers. It also floated an allied organization, Pāsbān, whose membership was open to a broad range of Muslims, including those who did not stick to *sharia*. The 1990 elections demonstrated that Jamaat was no longer the party for the few pious Muslims averse to using the modern repertoire of politics. In early 1940s, claiming that Jamaat's structure and workings were "exactly like those of the party Muhammad had established," Mawdudi had described processions, flags, sloganeering, resolutions, addresses, and so on as poison (Ahmad 2009, 72; Moten 2003).

Under Qazi Hussain Ahmed's leadership (1987–2009), Jamaat underwent many changes. To broaden its reach, Jamaat began to speak to lower strata hit hard by liberalization of economy. When General Musharraf's military regime intensified privatization of higher education, Jamaat opposed it. Ahmed invited even leftists to jointly resist globalization. Contra Mawdudi, Ahmed attacked feudalism and advocated the interests of the dispossessed. During her post-9/11 fieldwork, Iqtidar (2011b) observed how under liberalization there was a shift in Jamaat from a preoccupation with the state to the society/market. Led by Ahmed, Jamaat became a strident critic of West-led war on terror terming Pakistan's role therein as a surrender of its sovereignty (Iqtidar 2011a, 57–58, 90–94; *Outlook* 2002). Supporting the bill aimed at fusing the two posts of president and army chief, in Pakistan's Senate, a pro-Musharraf senator argued that Musharraf's bid for fusion was true to the teachings of the Qur'an and practices of caliphs. Along with other parties, Jamaat decried that move with opposition shouting "no-no, shame-shame" (BBC 2004). Among others, the basis of Jamaat's opposition to Musharraf's regime was its antidemocratic foundation. In the 2002 elections, which took place in the shadow of the war on terror and the invasion of Afghanistan, Jamaat participated as a key partner of the coalition of six religion-based parties, Muttaheda Majlis-e-Amal (MMA). MMA scored notable victory forming government in two out of four provinces: the Northwest Frontier Province, which borders Afghanistan and Baluchistan. MMA won 62 of the 342 seats in the National Assembly (International Crisis Group 2003; Iqtidar 2011a, 164n8). Jamaat boycotted the 2008 elections, arguing that under the military regime they would be far from fair.

Like India's, the case of Pakistan's Jamaat shows that democratic processes make Islamists more democratic/moderate. Over the decades, Pakistani Jamaat's "commitment to the electoral politics" has only increased and it is by now an important participant in the mainstream politics. That some associated with Jamaat later turned cold toward democracy and advocated violence—consider Hafiz Mohammad Saeed, founder of Jamaat-ud-Dawa (Iqtidar 2011, 4–5)—does not mean the dilution of Jamaat's won commitment to democracy and mainstream politics. Individuals influenced by Jamaat adopted a variety of positions, including what some Westerners might call "moderate" and "liberal." An apt example is the group of scholars-activists led by Javed Ahmad Ghamidi, a former Jamaat member and a known intellectual of Pakistan (see Masud 2007; Amin 2010).

Bangladesh

Pakistan consisted of two territorially separate wings—West and East. In 1947, East Pakistan had just one Jamaat member.[8] The West Pakistan Jamaat sent Rafi Ahmad Indori to East Pakistan to build Jamaat; under his leadership a committee of four members was formed in 1948. In 1951, Abdu Rahim of Barisal was made East Pakistan's *amīr*. By 1954,

Jamaat had thirty-eight members (Rahim 2001, 237). Jamaat expanded when, in 1955, Ghulam Azam (b. 1922), a college lecturer with degrees in Islamic studies and political science, joined Jamaat. A student leader, Azam was twice elected as secretary of the prestigious Dhaka University Student Union (DUSU; 1947–1949). He was an early leader of the Bangla language movement. Against the imposition of Urdu, protests broke out in East Pakistan. As DUSU's secretary, Azam submitted a memorandum to Prime Minister Liaqat Khan demanding that Bangla should also be recognized as an official language.

While lecturing (1950–1955) at Carmichael College, Rangpur he joined Tablighi Jamaat and later Tamaddun Majlish. Azam then began reading Mawdudi's books. Fascinated with his "scientific approach to politics," Azam learned Urdu to read wider Islamic literature. He gained Jamaat's membership in jail; in 1952 and 1955 he was jailed for criticizing the government. To work for Jamaat, he resigned his lectureship position. In February 1956, Mawdudi took a forty-day trip to East Pakistan. In his speech in Dhaka, he advocated recognizing Bangla as an official language and criticized the biases East Pakistan faced under the federal government. Azam accompanied Mawdudi during his trip. In 1957, Azam was elected as secretary—a post he held until 1967 when he became Jamaat's *amīr* (Husain and Siddiquee 2004, 386; Rahim 2001, 239; Bangladesh Jama`at-e Islami 2001). During Ayub Khan's rule (1958–1969), Jamaat in East Pakistan too faced the government's ire. In 1963, Azam was imprisoned. Under repression, Jamaat continued its services like establishing schools and clinics and giving funds to the poor. In 1969 Jamaat's membership had risen to 425; associates constituting 40,000. Of 425 members, 40 were full-time workers and most of its leaders had a modern, not madrasa, education (Banu 1994, 86).

Against Ayub Khan's regime, with the AL, National Awami Party, and others, Jamaat joined coalitions like the Combined Opposition Parties (1964–1965), the Pakistan Democratic Movement (1966–1968), and the Democratic Action Committee. However, to the intensified movement for linguistic-regional autonomy in East Pakistan Jamaat stressed that only a return to Islam would keep the country united. Meanwhile, Khan resigned in March 1969. Yahya Khan, a military general reputed for heavy drinking, assumed power and promised elections in 1970. In the 1970 elections, led by Sheikh Mujiburrahman, AL scored a clinching victory in provincial (East Pakistan) and national assemblies over Pakistan People's Party (PPP), and Jamaat which won just four seats. Democratically speaking, AL was destined to form a government at the federal level. However, neither Yahyah Khan nor PPP allowed it on the pretext that it would lead to Pakistan's breakup. Jamaat urged Yahya Khan not to discriminate against Mujiburrahman and allow him to form a government. As Khan rejected its demand, Jamaat accused the general of unadulterated biases against AL and undemocratic favor to PPP (Kabir 2006, 64–66; Nasr 1994, ch. 7).

With the undemocratic denial to AL to form a government, the protests in East Pakistan intensified. The Pakistani military intervened to crush Bengali nationalists, after which Jamaat stopped working as an intermediary between AL and Yahya Khan and sided with the latter. Ghulam Azam, as Jamaat *amīr*, supported the army against the "enemies of Islam" (Nasr 1994, 168–169). During the war ensuing between the army and Mukti Bahini (freedom fighter), the army killed more than 2.5 million people (Ahmad 2012c).[9] With India's military intervention against Pakistan, in 1971, Bangladesh was born. The new state adopted the four-pronged ideology of Bengali nationalism, socialism, secularism, and democracy (Hashmi 2004, 45). In 1972, the state banned Jamaat (and other religion-based parties) thereby aggravating its credibility crisis. In 1973 Azam's citizenship was cancelled for his "collaboration" with Pakistan. In fact Azam's controversial citizenship became part of Jamaat's subsequent history. When Bangladesh was declared as a state, Azam was in Pakistan from where he went to the United Kingdom and returned to Bangladesh in 1978 holding his Pakistani passport. On return, he applied for citizenship, which was granted in 1994 (Moniruzzaman 2009, 90). Earlier, in 1991, Azam's citizenship had become a major issue after Jamaat elected him as its *amīr*. While the liberal-secular section formed a people's court and served him the death sentence for his alleged role in the 1971 war, AL and its allies unleashed violence against Jamaat (Banu 1994, 82; Moniruzzaman 2009, 90). In 2012, the Bangladesh government led by AL again imprisoned him (and others) after the International Crimes Tribunal (ICT) dismissed his bail plea (bdnews24.com 2012).

With the assassination of Bangladesh's founder, Mujiburrahman in 1975—he had turned authoritarian and installed one-party rule—there began the military rule of Ziaurrahman (1975–1981), who legalized parties like Jamaat, substituted secularism in the Preamble with "absolute trust and faith in the Almighty Allah," and, in 1978, formed Bangladesh Nationalist Party (BNP). In 1981, Ziaurrahman was killed. From 1982 to 1990, General Hussain Ershad ruled the country. Faced with a legitimacy crisis, in 1988 he made Islam the official religion (Riaz 2010, 47–49). Most "secularist" accounts depict Jamaat as a supporter of the army; rarely is it recognized that Jamaat opposed Ershad's military regime to institutionalize democratic processes. So hostile was Ershad to Jamaat that, in 1988, he vowed to "eliminate" Jamaat. After Ershad's open call for violence four Jamaat activists were killed (Ahmad, Mumtaz 1991, 503). However, in 1990, Ershad's regime fell because, among other reasons, with en-block resignation of Jamaat's ten members from Parliament, the popular protests against the regime had heightened (Ahmad, Irfan 1991; Rahim 2001, 250).

After Ershad's fall, in the 1990 elections, Jamaat garnered 12 percent of the total votes and won eighteen seats (Parliament comprises 300 members) and backed the formation of BNP government led by Khaleda Zia, wife of Ziaurrahman. However, soon Jamaat sided with BNP's archrival, AL (Kabir 2006, 16–17). The ties between Jamaat and AL thus grew strong. In the 1996 elections Jamaat suffered a loss, winning only three seats. Sheikh Hasina of AL formed the government. After the elections, Jamaat, however, supported BNP. In October 2001 elections that took place in the shadow of war on terror, as a constituent of the alliance headed by BNP, Jamaat won seventeen seats and for the first time two of its members became ministers under Khaleda Zia's leadership. Contrary to the popular view that Jamaat promoted terrorism, the BNP-JI government banned four militant outfits and arrested and put on trial several of their leaders. In the subsequent elections, held in December 2008, Jamaat performed abysmally, as it won only two seats; AL scored a landslide victory to form the government. Jamaat's defeat notwithstanding, it received 3.16 million of the votes (Riaz 2010, 56, 61).

In Lieu of a Conclusion: Some Observations

As the publications on Islam boomed after 9/11, the description of Islamic fundamentalism, even Islam, as innately violent, antisecular, antimodern, a nemesis of democracy, and Manichean/dualistic intensified (Antoun 2010; Appleby 2002; Benjamin and Simon 2002;

Juergensmeyer 2003; Mazarr 2007; Philips 2006). Scholars presented different timelines of the "radical Islam." While some (e.g., Cook 2005, 209) traced the 9/11 attacks back to the early seventh century when the Prophet Muhammad began to receive revelations, others (e.g., Wiktorowicz 2005) traced their antecedents to the writings of the fourteenth-century theologian Ibn Taymiyah. Scholars also presented a list of figures fundamental to radical Islam; virtually all such lists included, among others, Hasan al-Banna, Qutb, Osama Bin Laden, and yes Mawdudi (Appleby 2002, 506 ff.; Hansen 2009, 16; Lincoln 2003, 16).

I disavow such a line of argumentation on two counts. First, it is a selective secularist account of fundamentalism (see Casanova 2009; Van der Veer 2008); in itself it is dualistic even as it sees dualism only in its other, the fundamentalists. Dualism is indeed important to modern politics as articulated by Schmitt (2006) in his notion of politics as drawing a boundary between foe and friend and also manifest in post-9/11 "liberal" politics that saw Muslims as good and bad, moderate and fundamentalist/terrorist (Mamdani 2002; Ali 2002). Manichean worldview is equally central to "New Atheism," itself precipitated, inter alia, by Muslims' presence in the West (Prothero 2010, 322ff). Thus in Bangladesh's secularist history of independence there are only two types of people—freedom fighters and collaborators. The "secular" Awami League that led the independence movement obviously regards itself as freedom fighter and considers Jamaat, sometimes many who disagree with AL, as collaborator. Second, theoretically it is unproductive to posit secular as obverse of fundamentalist; they are not neatly separate. The secular constitutes the religious (fundamentalist) in such a way that it is difficult to distinguish one from the other (Euben 1999). As Asad (2003, 2006) rightly observes, even as secularism is premised on the separation of religion from the state, it is the state that regulates and determines what is religious. From the perspective I maintain, the recurring citation of Mawdudi that he held a depersonalized and totalizing view of religion does not add much because such language is not exclusive to fundamentalists; secularists speak similarly. To the French secularists during the 1970s and later, "*True laïcité, based on the scientific spirit and democracy, provides a complete critical knowledge of reality and encompasses all aspects of human life and activity*" (Roy 2007, 107, italics mine).

An important secularist critique of Mawdudi has been his notion of "theodemocracy," often posited as antithetical to democracy. Theodemocracy, I suggest, is not the obverse of democracy. On the contrary, a certain type of democracy fashions theodemocracy. Let me explain this as most academics also hurriedly quote Mawdudi to prove fundamentalists' (also Muslims') intolerance to democracy. What they do not ask is why Mawdudi coined the term theodemocracy. Initially, Mawdudi championed democracy. It was the majoritarian democracy of the Congress, especially the anti-Muslim practice of the 1937 Congress ministries, which drove him to theodemocracy. In 1938, he wrote:

> The real issue is not if the political system...should proceed along the path of democracy because no sane person can disagree with the spirit of democracy...The spirit of democracy and this specific notion of democracy based on the principle of a single community should not be conflated....It is assumed that because of a shared geography...we Hindus, Muslims, Untouchables, Sikhs, Christians are a single community and thus the grammar of democracy should be such that the state should be run by the wish of the majority community. Based on this ideology, the constitution has been framed....Such a situation has made Hindu nationalism and Indian nationalism coterminous. In contrast to Hindus, our condition is such that under this [democratic] system our community aspirations remain unfulfilled; rather they are...killed because we are in a minority (Ahmad 2011, 466).

This long quotation demonstrates that "fundamentalists" like Mawdudi have not been averse to democracy as such, but to a *specific kind of* democracy. It is this Islamic-modernist impulse that made Mawdudi recast his view. He came to hold that the state "should not be enforcer of the sharia but the implementer of the will of the people" (Nasr 2006, 107). Clearly, such a notion of democracy will not be the replica of Western democracy for the simple reason that democracy has no singular origin or form (Ahmad 2011; Esposito and Voll 1996). The trajectory of Jamaat in India, Bangladesh, and Pakistan I analyzed here shows the democratizing dynamic and impulse Jamaat is at once promoter and product of. Against the view that "Islamic fundamentalists" do not engage in "the quotidian political struggle" and valorize "self-sacrificing acts of true believers willing to risk everything to vanquish *jahiliyya* society once and for all" (Appleby 2002, 511), Mawdudi, his followers, and Jamaat across south Asia, as this essay demonstrates, are keenly engaged in the quotidian political struggle of and for democracy. Whether or not and to what degree Islamists such as Jamaat activists will continue to act as vital agents of democratization and change depends not only on their own sweat desire but, more importantly, also on the (re)alignments of forces in the global, regional, and national field in which Islamists are one among several actors and by no means the dominant ones.

Notes

1. By Islamism I mean a distinct socio-political movement which regards Islam as a comprehensive system of life and foregrounds the pursuit of an Islamic state as its principal aim (Ahmad 2009: 4–8). Islamism, therefore, should not be squarely conflated with Islam as a discursive tradition (Asad 2009).
2. Hashmi's (2004, 62–66) and Kabir's (2006, 208–210) works are rare sober analyses of this issue. Against the sensationalist accounts, such as those of Datta (2007), Ganguly, and others who uncritically take journalistic sources and intelligence/police reports as "truth," Hashmi interrogates the accuracy of such sources to suggest how "terrorism" in Bangladesh might have been manufactured by forces such as the Awami League, among others, by planting stories in magazines such as *Far Eastern Economic Review* so as to position her party as a friend of the United States in the post-9/11 global scenario.
3. For more on this, see Ahmad (2010).
4. In transliterating non-English words, I largely follow the *Annual of Urdu Studies* guideline 2007, also available on the journal's website. However, I write "Jamaat" because Jamaat in India, Bangladesh, and Pakistan write it in English like this.
5. For a succinct account of Mawdudi's life and thought, see Ahmad (2012b); for a different and detailed account, see Nasr (1996) and Ahmad (2009).
6. On the absence of democracy in the Middle East, see Ahmad (2012a).
7. Many Pakistanis still hold that Jamaat opposed Pakistan's creation; see Rashid (2001).
8. Bangladesh's Jamaat has not received much attention in the English-medium academic literature. With the exception of chapter-/article-length works of Ahmad (1991), Ahmed (1994), Banu (1994), Rahim (2001), Husain and Siddiquee (2004), Huq (2008), and Shehabuddin (2008a, also see 2008b), Kabir's (2006) is perhaps the first comprehensive study of Jamaat.
9. According to the Bangladesh government, 15,000 Urdu-speaking Biharis were killed by Bengalis. Other accounts put the figure between 70,000 and 100,000; see Ahmad (2012c).

References

Agwani, Mohammad Shafiq. 1986. *Islamic Fundamentalism in India*. Chandigarh: Twenty-First Century Indian Society.
Ahmad, Irfan. 1991. "Bangladesh aur Jamhūriat." *The Sadā-e-'ām*. Patna. Edit Page. January 30.
Ahmad, Irfan. 2008. "Cracks in the 'Mightiest Fortress': Jama`at-e Islami's Changing Discourse on Women." *Modern Asian Studies* 42(2&3): 549–575.
Ahmad, Irfan. 2009. *Islamism and Democracy in India: The Transformation of Jama`at-e Islami*. Princeton: Princeton University Press.
Ahmad, Irfan. 2010. "Is There an Ethics of Terrorism? Islam, Globalisation, Militancy." *South Asia* 33(3): 487–498.
Ahmad, Irfan. 2011. "Democracy and Islam." *Philosophy and Social Criticism* 37(4): 459–470.
Ahmad, Irfan. 2012a. "How the West De-democratised the Middle East." *Al-Jazeera*. March 30. http://www.aljazeera.com/indepth/opinion/2012/03/201232710543250236. Accessed May 21, 2013.
Ahmad, Irfan. 2012b. "Mawdudi, Abul Ala: 1903–1979." In G. Böwering et al., eds. *The Princeton Encyclopedia of Islamic Political Thought*, 112–115. Princeton: Princeton University Press.
Ahmad, Irfan. 2012c. "Modernity and Its Outcast: The Why and How of India's Partition." *South Asia*. 35(3): 477–494.
Ahmad, Mumtaz. 1991. "Islamic Fundamentalism in South Asia: The Jama`at-e Islami and Tablighi Jamaat of South Asia." In Martin Marty and Scott Appleby, eds., *Fundamentalisms Observed*, 457–530. Chicago: University of Chicago Press.
Ahmed, Rafiuddin. 1994. "Redefining Muslim Identity in South Asia: The Transformation of the Jamaat-I-Islami." In Martin Marty and Scott Appleby, eds. *Accounting for Fundamentalisms: The Dynamic Character of Movement*, 669–705. Chicago: University of Chicago Press.
Ali, Tariq. 2002. *The Clash of Fundamentalisms*. London: Verso.
Amin, Husnul. 2010. *From Islamism to Post-Islamism: A Study of a New Intellectual Discourse on Islam and Modernity in Pakistan*. Unpublished PhD Thesis. Erasmus University.
Anand, Javed. 2012. "Jamaat in Hindustan." http://www.viewpointonline.net/jamaat-in-india. Accessed October 4, 2012.
Antoun, Richard. 2010. "Fundamentalism." In Bryan Turner, ed., *The New Blackwell Companion to the Sociology of Religion*, 519–536. London: Wiley-Blackwell.
Appleby, Scott. 2002. "History in the Fundamentalist Imagination." *The Journal of American History* 89(2): 498–511.
Asad, Talal. 2003. *Formations of the Secular: Christianity, Islam, Modernity*. Stanford: Stanford University Press.
Asad, Talal. 2006. "Trying to Understand French Secularism." In Hent de Vries, ed., *Political Theologies*, 494–526. New York: Fordham University Press.
Asad, Talal. 2009. "The Idea of an Anthropology of Islam." *Qui Parle* 17(2): 1–30.
Bahadur, Kalim. 1977. *The Jama`at-e Islami of Pakistan*. Delhi: Chetna.
Bangladesh Jama`at-e Islami. 2001. "Prof. Ghulam Azam." http://www.Jama`at-e Islami.org/jib/Overview/azam.htm. Accessed May 25, 2001.
Bangladesh Jama`at-e Islami. 2012. "Policies: Introduction." http://www.Jama`at-e Islami.org/en/details.php?artid=MTQ4. Accessed April 11, 2012.
Banu, Razia Akter. 1994. "Jama`at-e Islami in Bangladesh." In Hussin Mutalib and Taj Hashmi, eds., *Islam, Muslims, and the Modern State*, 80–99. London: Macmillan.
Benjamin, Daniel, and Steve Simon. 2002. *The Age of Sacred Terror*. New York: Random House.

Berman, Paul. 2003. "The Philosopher of Islamic Terror." *The New York Times*, March 23.

Beyondheadlines. 2011a. "JIH Political Party: A Journey from 'Politics of Dependence to Politics of Self Reliance.'" http://beyondheadlines.in/2011/04/jih-political-party-a-journey-from-politics-of-dependence-to-politics-of-self-reliance. Accessed January 21, 2012.

Beyondheadlines. 2011b. "Concept Note of Jamaat 'supported' Welfare Party." http://beyondheadlines.in/2011/04/concept-not-of-jamaat%E2%80%99s-welfare-party. Accessed January 21, 2012.

Bowen, John R. 2007. *Why the French Don't Like Headscarves*. Princeton: Princeton University Press.

BBC. 2004. "Vardī aur Qur'an kī barābrī par hangāmā." http://www.bbc.co.uk/urdu/pakistan/story/2004/10/printable/041029_senate_row_rza.sAccessed July 11, 2004.

BBC. 2007. "Tories Complain about Radical Books." http://www.bbc.co.uk/london/content/articles/2007/09/18/towerhamlets_tory_protest_video_feature. Accessed November 9, 2010.

BBC. 2010. "Bangladesh Bans Books Written by Radical Islamic Author." http://www.bbc.co.uk/news/world-south-asia-10661454. Accessed November 9, 2010.

Bdnews24.com. 2012. "Ghulam Azam Lands in Jail." http://bdnews24.com/details.php?id=215760&cid=3. Accessed April 20, 2012.

Casanova, Jose. 2009. "The Religious Situation in Europe." In Hans Joas et al. eds., *Secularization and the World Religions*, 206–227. Liverpool: Liverpool University Press.

Cook, David. 2005. *Understanding Jihad*. Berkeley: University of California Press.

Datta, Sreeradha. 2007. "Islamic Militancy in Bangladesh." *South Asia*. 30(1): 145–170.

Euben, Roxanne L. 1999. *Enemy in the Mirror: Islamic Fundamentalism and the Limits of Modern Rationalism*. Princeton: Princeton University Press.

Esposito, John. 1994. "Political Islam: Beyond the Green Menace." *Current History* 93: 19–24.

Esposito, John L., and John O. Voll. 1996. *Islam and Democracy*. New York: Oxford University Press.

Ganguly, Sumit. 2006. *The Rise of Islamist Militancy in Bangladesh*. Washington, DC: United Institute of Peace. Special Report. 171.

Gardezi, Hassan. 1994. "Politics of Religion in Pakistan's Elections: An Assessment." *South Asia Bulletin* 14(1): 110–113.

Ghannouchi, Rashid. 1998. "Participation in a Non-Islamic Government." In Charles Kurzman. ed., *Liberal Islam: A Sourcebook*, 89–95. Oxford: Oxford University Press.

Hansen, Stig Jarle. 2009. "Asia and the Middle East: Borders at the Centre of Islam?" In Stig Jarle Hansen et al. eds., *The Borders of Islam*, 15–22. New Delhi: Foundation Books.

Harrison, Selig S. 2006. *The Washington Post*. "A New Hub for Terrorism?" http://www.washingtonpost.com/wp-dyn/content/article/2006/08/01/AR2006080101118. Accessed April 11, 2012.

Hashmi, Taj. 2004. "Islamic Resurgence in Bangladesh." In Satu Limaye at el., eds., *Religious Radicalism and Security in South Asia*. 35–72. Honolulu: Asia Pacific Centre for Security Studies.

Hasan, Mushirul. 1997. *The Legacy of a Divided Nation: Indian Muslims since Independence*. London: Hurst.

Husain, Ishtiaq, and Noore Siddiquee. 2004. "Islam in Bangladesh Politics: The Role of Ghulam Azam of Jama`at-e Islami." *Inter-Asia Cultural Studies* 5(3): 384–399.

Huq, Maimuna. 2008. "Reading the Qur'an in Bangladesh: The Politics of 'Belief' among Islamist Women." *Modern Asian Studies* 42(2&3): 457–488.

The Indian Express. 2011. "Jamaat Launches Party, Christian Priest Is Vice-President." http://www.indianexpress.com/news/jamaat-launches-party-christian-priest-is-vicepresident/778016. Accessed April 22, 2011.

International Crisis Group. 2003. *Pakistan: The Mullahs and the Military.* Brussels: ICG, Asia Report, 49.

Iqtidar, Humeira. 2011a. *Secularizing Islamists? Jama`at-e Islami and Jamaat-ud-Dawa in Urban Pakistan.* Chicago: Chicago University Press.

Iqtidar, Humeira. 2011b. "Secularism beyond the State: The 'State' and the 'Market' in Islamist Imagination." *Modern Asian Studies* 45(3): 535–564.

Juergensmeyer, Mark. 2003. *Terror in the Mind of God: The Global Rise of Religious Violence.* 3rd ed. Berkeley: University of California Press.

Kabir, Bhuian Md Monoar. 2006. *Politics and Development of Jama`at-e Islami Bangladesh.* Delhi: South Asian Publishers.

Karlekar, Hiranmay. 2005. *Bangladesh: The Next Afghanistan?* New Delhi: Sage.

Lincoln, Bruce. 2003. *Holy Terrors: Thinking about Religion after September 11.* Chicago: Chicago University Press.

Mamdani, Mahmood. 2002. "Good Muslim, Bad Muslim: A Political Perspective on Culture and Terrorism." *American Anthropologist* 104(3): 766–775.

Mawdudi, Abul Ala. 1942. *Musalmān aur maujūda seyāsī kashmakash.* Vol. 3. Pathankot: Daftar risāla Tarjumānul Qur'an.

Mawdudi, Abul Ala. 2003. *Taḥrīk-e-Islamī kā āinda lāha-e-'amal.* Lahore: Islamic Publications.

Mazarr, Michael J. 2007. *Unmodern Men in the Modern World: Radical Islam, Terrorism and the War on Modernity.* Cambridge: Cambridge University Press.

Masud, Muhammad Khalid. 2007. "Rethinking Sharia: Javed Ahmad Ghamidi on Hudūd." *Die Welt des Islams* 47(3–4): 356–375.

Moniruzzaman, M. 2009. "Party Politics and Political Violence in Bangladesh: Issues, Manifestation and Consequences." *South Asian Survey* 16(1): 81–99.

Moten, Abdul Rashid. 2003. "Maududi and the Transformation of Jama`at-e Islami in Pakistan." *The Muslim World* 93(July–October): 391–413.

Nadwi, Abul Lais Islahi. 1951. *Masala-e-intikhābāt aur musalmānān-e-hind.* Vol. 1. Rampur: maktaba Jama`at-e Islami hind.

Nasr, Syed Vali Reza. 1994. *The Vanguard of Islamic Revolution: The Jama`at-e Islami of Pakistan.* Berkeley: University of California Press.

Nasr, Syed Vali Reza. 1996. *Maududi and the Making of Islamic Revivalism.* New York: Oxford University Press.

Nasr, Syed Vali Reza. 2006. "Maududi and the Jama`at-e Islami." In Ali Rehnema, ed., *Pioneers of Islamic Revival,* 98–124. Updated edition. London: Zed Books.

Niazi, Kausar. 1973. *Jam`āt-e-islamī avāmī 'adālat meñ.* Lahore: qaumi kutubkhana.

Outlook. 2002. "'We Will Continue to Oppose the One-Man Dictatorship': Qazi Hussain Ahmed." http://www.outlookindia.com/article.aspx?217713. Accessed November 3, 2002.

Philips, Melanie. 2006. *Londonistan: How Britain Is Creating a Terror State Within.* London: Gibson Square.

Prothero, Stephen. 2010. *God Is Not One.* New York: Harper One.

Rahim, Enayetur. 2001. "Bengali Muslims and Islamic Fundamentalism: The Jama`at-e Islami in Bangladesh." In Rafiduddin Ahmed, ed., *Understanding the Bengal Muslims,* 236–261. Delhi: Oxford University Press.

Rashid, Amber. 2001. "Opinion: Questions for the Jamaat." *The News International.* London. February 8. p. 10.

Riaz, Ali. 2010. "The Politics of Islamization in Bangladesh." In Ali Riaz, ed., *Religion and Politics in South Asia*, 45–70. London: Routledge.

Roy, Oliver. 2007. *Secularism Confronts Islam*. Translated by George Holoch. New York: Columbia University Press.

Rushdie, Salman. 2005. "Muslims Unite! A New Reformation Will Bring Your Faith into the Modern Era." http://www.timesonline.co.uk/article/0,,1072-1729998,00.html. Accessed on 8/19/2005.

Sayyid, Qasim. 2011. "Taḥrīk-e-Islamī fikrī dorāhe per." *Rāshtriyā sahārā*. Delhi. April 21. Edit Page.

Schmitt, Carl. 2006. *The Concept of the Political*. Translated with an Introduction by George Schwab. Chicago: University of Chicago Press.

Shehabuddin, Elora. 2008a. *Reshaping the Holy: Democracy, Development and Muslim Women in Bangladesh*. New York: Columbia University Press.

Shehabuddin, Elora. 2008b. "Jamaat-i-Islami in Bangladesh: Women, Democracy and the Transformation of Islamist Politics." *Modern Asian Studies* 42(2&3): 577–603.

Shepard, William E. 2003. "Sayyid Qutb's Doctrine of jihad." *International Journal of Middle East Studies* 35: 521–545.

Trouillot, Michel-Rolph. 1995. *Silencing the Past: Power and Production of History*. Boston: Beacon Press.

TwoCircles.Net. 2011. "Why Jamaat-backed Welfare Party Received Cold Response?" http://twocircles.net/2011apr21/why_jamaatbacked_welfare_party_received_cold_response. Accessed April 22, 2011.

Van der Veer, Peter. 2008. "The Religious Origins of Democracy." In Gabriel Motzkin et al., eds., *Religion and Democracy in Contemporary Europe*, 75–81. London: Alliance.

Wajihuddin, Mohammed. 2010. *The Times of India*. "It Will Only Trigger Further Polarisation." Delhi, August 24. p. 6.

Wiktorowicz, Quintan. 2005. "A Genealogy of Radical Islam." *Studies in Conflict and Terrorism* 28(2): 75–97.

CHAPTER 23

ISLAM AND POLITICS IN SOUTHEAST ASIA

FRED R. VON DER MEHDEN

INTRODUCTION

THE complex interaction between Islam and politics in Southeast Asia needs to be interpreted within the historic and cultural milieu of the heterogeneous societies of the region. This interplay takes place within two different environments. Indonesia, Malaysia, and Brunei Darussalam are majority Muslim states. Indonesia's Muslims comprise 86 percent of the population, and Malaysia is a multireligious, multiethnic country with 60 percent Muslims.[1] The second environment is composed of Muslim minorities primarily in southern Thailand, the southern Philippines, the Arakan in Burma-Myanmar, and Singapore. With the exception of Singapore, significant numbers of these minorities have sought autonomy or separation. There are also Muslim minorities who have generally worked with the majority political systems and have been more integrated into the dominant society. These include Thai Muslims outside the more separatist southern provinces and Burmese Muslims in areas other than the Arakan prior to the establishment of military rule in 1962. Singapore's Muslims have the right to participate fully in the political system and have religious courts with limited jurisdiction. All of them are 10 percent or less of their respective national populations, with the exception of Singapore, with 13 percent. This study analyzes both cases of Muslim majority states and where Muslims are in the minority. However, prior to a more detailed analysis of politics and Islam in the individual Muslim societies, it is useful to address the wide range of common, although not universal, factors that have tended to frame Islam and politics in the Muslim world of Southeast Asia.

1. Throughout the region there has been a strong co-identity of Islam and ethnicity. Muslims in most of these societies define themselves in religious-ethnic terms. In preindependence Indonesia, nationalists emphasized the divide between Dutch Christians and Indonesian Muslims. Numerous studies have found that many Muslim communities in Indonesia have difficulty in distinguishing between their Islamic and ethnic identities. In Malaysia the co-identity of Malay and Muslim has dominated politics since before independence. The vast majority of Malays are

also Muslims and most Muslims are Malays, blurring understanding of causality. Both the dominant party in the country's multiethnic and multireligious ruling coalition and its chief Islamic rival must be seen as both Malay and Islamic parties. This interaction of ethnicity and Islam is most obvious in Muslim minority states where these minorities differentiate themselves from the majority society by both religion and ethnicity. This co-identity of religion and ethnicity further separates these Muslim communities from the dominant societies.

2. Unlike the Middle East, there traditionally has been a high level of syncretism among Muslims in Southeast Asia. This reflects the influence of animism and other pre-Islamic beliefs and cultures. This is not unique to Islam but is also to be found in Christian and Buddhist societies. A significant number of Muslims in the region, particularly in Indonesia, have traditionally reflected this pre-Islamic and particularly Hindu foundation. Differing views on the acceptance of "non-Islamic" elements often have divided Indonesian society and politics. Twentieth-century political parties reflected these differing interpretations while several of Indonesia's presidents have supported the more syncretic belief patterns. In Southeast Asia, Hindu influences have also played an important role in molding the institutions and activities of traditional rulers.

3. Radical interpretations of Islam have not succeeded in gaining significant electoral support in Muslim-dominated states. In Indonesia, radical parties have had almost no representation in the elected national parliaments of 1956 or after the return to democracy in 1999. In Malaysia, the ruling Muslim party has rejected radical interpretations and has attempted to eliminate "deviant" Islam. Its Muslim rival promotes a more conservative agenda and supports a stricter implementation of the *sharī'ah*, but both accept political pluralism. In Thailand, Singapore, and the Philippines, where Muslim minorities have elected members of the national legislature, they have tended to be moderate.

4. Although electorally weak, radical Islamic groups have been involved in violent activities in the name of Islam in every Muslim majority and minority country. Muslim separatist movements have clashed with authorities, including the Moros in the Philippines, Malay-Muslims in southern Thailand, and the Arakanese in Burma. At first, many of these groups did not espouse radical Islamic ideology, but recent years have seen an increasing influence of Salafi and radical foreign religious and political interpretations. Domestically, both Indonesia and Malaysia have faced a number of violent Muslim groups, particularly in the past decade. There has also been the rise of cross-national radical Islamic organizations with ties to the Middle East, most notably Jeemah Islamiyh, which has been active throughout Southeast Asia. The strength of international and domestic groups has weakened over the past few years but is still capable of isolated acts of violence.

5. Southeast Asian Islam has been deeply influenced by Islamic ideology and state action from outside the region. At the intellectual and religious level, Modernist interpretations of Islam came to the region at the turn of the twentieth century. After World War II, a range of Islamist writers from the Middle East and South Asia have been translated into indigenous languages and have become part of the religious and political dialogue. Radical interpretations of Islam and Salafi-Wahabbi ideas from Saudi Arabia have been influential among disaffected Muslims in the region.

Muslims in Southeast Asia also have been affected by events such as the Iranian Revolution, the Israeli-Arab conflict, and the Afghan and Iraq wars.

Muslim governments in the Middle East have also attempted to influence Muslims in the region. Funds have been given for Islamic education and other social activities, particularly from Saudi Arabia. International groups, such as the Organization of the Islamic Conference, have passed resolutions regarding problems of Muslim minorities in the region, and individual states have provided training and funds to minority separatists, especially in the Philippines.

6. The Islamic resurgence has influenced both the public face and actions of Muslims in Southeast Asia. There have been changes in dress and a greater observance of Islamic rituals such as prayer and fasting. The region has also experienced an increase in Islamic publications and organizations. Muslim youth have displayed a growing interest in their religion and its relationship to political action, and there has been a significant growth in Islamic educational institutions at all levels. At the local and national levels political leaders have employed more Islamic symbols and language. Internationally, Muslims in Southeast Asia have become more aware of and involved in the wider Islamic world.

Islam and Politics in Muslim Majority States

Majority status does not coincide with religious or political unity and Muslims in Malaysia and Indonesia have been politically fragmented and have not displayed a common Islamic agenda. This section analyzes the interaction of Islam and politics in the two largest Muslim majority states in the region, Indonesia and Malaysia. Three areas will be considered: the role of national leadership, the role of Islamic political parties, and religious issues in the political arena.

The role of national leadership

There have been significant differences between Indonesia and Malaysia in terms of the role of government leadership and Islamic-oriented parties in determining national religious policies. In Indonesia the relationship of Islam to politics has varied since the end of World War II and the achievement of independence. Yet, in spite of having the highest percentage of Muslims of any country in the region, a broad-based Islamic agenda has never been implemented. When the initial debate took place in 1945 over the role of Islam and the state, Muslim organizations were unable to successfully achieve their goals of a state based upon the *sharī'ah* and the requirement that the president of the republic be a Muslim. The only reference to religion was that "the Indonesia state is founded on belief in God." Both President Sukarno (1945–1967) and President Suharto (1967–1999) based their rhetoric upon a more secular and syncretic ideology called the *pancasila* (five principles). Over time, Muslim organizations have differed in their willingness to accept the *pancasila*, although many Muslims have been discomforted by its interpretation of belief in God as also recognizing the legitimacy of religions other than Islam.

Both Sukarno and Suharto sought to restrict the influence of political Islam. After democratic election in 1955 when Islamic parties received more than 40 percent of the vote, the influence of Islam at the national level was short lived. Sukarno declared "guided democracy" in 1959, emasculating the parliamentary system, and sought to establish his power base upon secular parties. Although in his last years Suharto attempted to appear more pious, he saw the role of Islam to be a more private matter and not part of the political dialogue. This view of "Islam yes, but Islamic politics no" was also fostered by some within the Indonesian intellectual community. Islamic activists, severely limited in their national political activities, turned to the mosques and madrasahs as the centers of their opposition to the Suharto regime.

The return of democracy in 1999 brought a vigorous movement toward political pluralism. While the retention of the *pancasila* was not at issue, the new democratic system brought the reentrance of Islam into Indonesian politics. However, Islamic politics were highly fragmented and the series of presidents after the fall of Suharto displayed ambivalence toward a political role for Islam. None of the four presidents that followed attempted to formulate a comprehensive Islamic agenda, although there was support for limited Islamic policies. An obvious exception to Indonesia's more secular-minded presidents was Abdur Rahman Wahib. His father was a well-known *ulama* and Wahid had been head of the mass organization Nahdlatul Ulama. A political and religious pluralist, his presidency failed from combination of weak parliamentary support, governmental style, unpopular policies, and personal illness. All of Indonesia's presidents have found it necessary to deal with violent Islamic groups, but at no time since independence has Islam played a dominant role in Indonesian national politics.

The Malaysian constitution states that Islam is the official religion of the country, and the Malay Sultans have traditionally been the protectors and authority in Islamic matters. However, in the first decades after independence in 1957, Malaysian national governments generally maintained secular policies and emphasized the need to reinforce Malay rights rather than promoting an Islamic agenda. They still attempted to portray themselves as protectors of Islam and as illustrated by the statement in 1959 of then deputy prime minister and later prime minister and "Father of Development," Abdul Tun Razak, that "we have done all we could within our power to maintain the Islamic religion" (*Straits Times*, March 24, 1959). Their administrations did see a proliferation of state-built mosques and the beginnings of the Islamization of the bureaucracy, and at the state level *sharī'ah* laws were reinforced and penalties for noncompliance were increased.

This pattern changed significantly after Mohammad Mahathir became prime minister in 1981. He initially followed his predecessors in accentuating the need to develop Malay economic and social standards. However, prior to the 1982 national elections, he began to develop an Islamic agenda, exemplified by his recruitment of Anwar Ibrahim, leader of the main student *dakwah* movement, ABIM (Islamic Youth League of Malaysia). For the next two decades, until his retirement in 2003, Mahathir sustained a policy of Islamization of Malaysia. His efforts led to the formation of Islamic banking, the establishment of the International Islamic University of Malaysia, the expansion of federal authority in religious affairs that were previously the domain of the states, the formation the Department of Islamic Development in Malaysia to promote the faith and confront un-Islamic activities, attacks upon "deviant Islam," requiring an examination "religious knowledge" for Muslim students, and greater attention to supporting international Islamic policies. This became a concerted effort to bureaucratize the religious establishment and to define the limits and goals of Muslims in Malaysia.

Mahathir's successors have maintained the same Islamic framework but have attempted to give their own emphases. Thus, Prime Minister Abdullah Badawi, who followed Mahathir, promoted "Islam *hadhari*" (civilizational Islam), which tried to meld development and Islam, much like many before him. He also described Islam *hadhari* as supporting a "tolerant, inclusive, moderate, and modern" Islam.

The role of political parties

There have been significant differences in the role of Islamic political parties in Indonesia and Malaysia. In Indonesia, from independence until Sukarno launched "guided democracy," Islamic parties did play an important part in governing in national and provincial governments. Islamic political strength was in evidence in the only free elections held during the Sukarno-Suharto era in 1955. However, the elections also showed the continuance of prewar divisions between more traditional and more Modernist oriented political parties. The two major Muslim parties each obtained approximately 20 percent of the vote for the national parliament. However, there was limited effort within parliament to assert an Islamic agenda. This was largely due to a fragmented parliament that made promulgating controversial legislation difficult, a lack of unity within Muslim parties on a common Islamic agenda and Sukarno's more secular position backed by communist and nationalist parties. These factors hindered the promotion of any significant Islamic political or religious aspirations. Under President Suharto's "new order" political parties were severely limited in their ability to affect policy. All organizations, including religious parties, were required to support the *pancasila*. Islamic political parties were forced to join the PPP (United Development Party), which was prohibited from running on an expressly religious platform. Islamic political power was also weakened by the withdrawal from politics of many Muslims, including the Nahdlatul Ulama, who became frustrated with the limitations put on Islamic political action.

The return of democracy after Suharto's fall from power in 1998 again underscored divisions within the Islamic political community and continued their inability to establish an electoral majority. In spite of 87 percent of Indonesians being Muslim, this has not translated into electoral support. National elections for parliament (People's Representative Assembly or Dewan Perwakilan Rakyat) showed a continuing but declining minority role of Islamic parties, dropping from 38 percent in 1999 to 32 percent in 2004 to 24 percent in 2009. Lack of electoral support arose from a multitude of local and national issues, but significant blame can be put upon Islamic political parties for their lack of agreement on an Islamic agenda and other issues, the personality orientation of Muslim party leadership, and, more recently, charges of corruption.

In stark contrast to Indonesia, Muslims in Malaysia have played the dominant role in determining national and Islamic policies. The Malay-Muslim United Malay National Organization (UMNO) has been the principal party in the multiethnic ruling Barisan Nasional (National Front). Since independence every prime minister, deputy prime minister, and home minister has been a member of UMNO. The dilemma for the party leadership has been how to maintain the multiethnic and multireligious coalition and at the same time appeal to the Malay-Muslim aspirations of its constituents. Malay and Islamic politics have been defined by UMNO and its chief rival the Malay-Muslim Party, Partai Islam (PAS). Historically, UMNO and PAS have each declared themselves to be the best protector of Malay and Muslim interests. However there have also been religious policy differences both within UMNO and between the two parties. PAS and more conservative local UMNO representatives have supported a more aggressive Islamic agenda and questioned decisions made to meet the needs of non-Muslims in the coalition. Both parties have employed religious appeals and have developed political backing from local Islamic leaders.

Indonesia and Malaysia show significantly different political contexts. Attitudes toward Islam between the political leaders in the two countries were markedly different until the return to democracy in Indonesia. Indonesian presidents until the end of the twentieth century reflected secular tendencies and suspicion of political Islam. No president has promoted an extensive Islamic agenda, although there has been support for more limited proposals. In contrast, Malaysian prime ministers prior to Mahathir did not press an Islamic agenda, but recognized their Malay-Muslim constituency and were prepared to buttress their needs. While Sukarno and Suharto supported development as a secular goal, in Malaysia development was interpreted as a means of improving the conditions among Malay-Muslims and allowing them to compete with non-Muslims. There has never been a national leader in Indonesia who implemented an Islamic agenda similar to the policies of Mahathir.

The role of Islamic parties in Malaysia has also been fundamentally different from Indonesia. Islamic parties were marginalized under Sukarno and Suharto and have remained a fragmented minority in this century. In Malaysia, religious policies have been framed by the UMNO-PAS rivalry and internal divisions within these parties.

Islamic political issues

There have been three major interacting long-term points of contention among the plethora of religious issues that have become part of the political dialogue of Indonesia and Malaysia: the establishment of an Islamic state, the role of the *sharī'ah*, and religious and political pluralism. On all of these issues public opinion has not always been reflected in public policy. Polls have shown agreement to issues in the abstract, but a lack of consensus on details. Thus, the idea of an Islamic state and implementation of the *sharī'ah* are widely supported by Muslims in Indonesia and Malaysia, but there is not agreement on their meaning.

In Indonesia, there have been significant differences regarding the establishment of an Islamic state between parties and leaders at the national level and the views of nongovernmental Islamist elements. The establishment of an Islamic state has been rejected by all of Indonesia's presidents, the leaders of the country's major Muslim political parties, and the two mass Muslim organizations Nahdlatul Ulama and the Muhammadiyah. Individual members of these organizations have championed an Islamic state in various guises. Polls have shown that, while there has been a general consensus on public support for an increased role of Islam in the state, there has not been demand for a system similar to Iran.

The most forceful proponents for an Islamic state based upon the *shari'ah* have been from traditional Muslim leaders and more radical Islamic organizations. The most prominent of Islamic *'ulama'* groups has been the Majelis Ulama Indonesia (MUI), which has long called for the establishment of an Islamic state and expansion of the role of the *shari'ah* at the state level. Since independence, various radical Islamic groups have demanded an Islamic state. In the 1940s and 1950s, Dar ul Islam fought the government and rejected the country's secular state. Its ideas remain influential among Islamists. In the 1970s and 1980s a small group, Kommando Jihad, had a similar agenda. It has variously been interpreted as an outgrowth of Dar ul Islam and a product of Indonesian state intelligence. In recent years a number of violent and nonviolent groups have proclaimed the necessity of an Islamic state. These have included *Laskar Jihad*, now disbanded, which carried out attacks against Christians in East Indonesia; Jemaah Islamiyah, which seeks a regionwide Islamic state; and the Majelis Mujahadin Indonesia (MMI), an umbrella organization connected to Jemaah Islamiyah.

Malaysia's constitution states that Islam is the official religion, but the issue of the establishment or existence of an Islamic state has only recently become a major matter of contention. In the first decades after independence, the leadership of the major Malay-Muslim Party, UMNO, rejected the idea of an Islamic state, although more conservative party members have supported it. UMNO's major rival, PAS, has backed the formation of an Islamic state since its formation in 1951, although it has often muted its position to attract non-Muslims. Prime Minister Mahathir initially rejected the idea, in part due to the multi-religious composition of his coalition. However, he later asserted that Malaysia is an Islamic state in that it has met all the necessary religious criteria. This has been defined as a political, not constitutional interpretation and it is asserted that this does not mean the diminishment of the rights of non-Muslims. However, non-Muslims remain skeptical and PAS views it as politically motivated. Mahathir's successor, Abdullah Badawi, stated in 2007 that Malaysia was neither secular nor theocratic, but a parliamentary democracy. Prior to becoming prime minister, Badawi's successor, Tun Razak Najib, increased tensions by defining Malaysia as an Islamic state and not a secular one. However, as prime minister, he has proclaimed Islam in Malaysia to be moderate and modern. While it remains a contentious issue, the vast majority of Malaysian Muslims support an Islamic state, although not like Iran.

The second issue relates to the implementation of the *shari'ah*. The Muslim public has shown wide agreement on the importance of the *shari'ah* in both Indonesia and Malaysia. However, there have been differences on details including what should be the role of the state, what parts of *shari'ah* should be promulgated, and what the effect of its implementation would be on non-Muslims.

The Indonesian public has not been as supportive of the expansion of the *shari'ah* as the Malaysians. However, local and provincial governments have been the most active official entities reinforcing elements of Islamic law. There have been regulations regarding the observance of Ramadan, dress, liquor, tithing, and other religious practices by Muslims. However, they have often not been complied with or enforced and the national government has rarely interfered with these local rules. At the national level there has been a reluctance to expand the official role of the *shari'ah*. However, in order to end its conflict with the strongly Islamic province of Aceh it allowed the implementation of *shari'ah* law, courts, and punishments in the province. This and other efforts to expand the role of the *shari'ah* and "morality legislation" have pitted more conservative Muslims against those with more liberal interpretations.

In Malaysia issues regarding the *sharī'ah* have had political relevance involving differences between PAS and the national government. PAS has asserted that the full *sharī'ah* should be enforced, not just in private matters, and was necessary to the establishment of an Islamic state. The promotion of its interpretation of the expansion of the *sharī'ah* has also been part of the PAS effort to prove itself more Islamic than UMNO. PAS has attempted to enact *hudud* laws and punishments in states under its control and has passed legislation against liquor, gambling, and other "non-Islamic" practices. Non-Islamic groups fear that *hudud* laws would be expanded to cover them, although PAS has stated that only Muslims would be affected. *Hudud* legislation was rejected by the UMNO-led national government as unconstitutional. However, given popular and support for expanding the role of the *sharī'ah* positive statements by Islamic leaders, and the views of some of its own members, UMNO has been publicly ambiguous about expanding *sharī'ah* law.

The third interlocking issue has been religious pluralism. Both the Malaysian and Indonesian governments and all major political parties support freedom of religion. However, this must be viewed against legal restrictions and conservative and radical rejections of religious and political pluralism. In Malaysia, limitations on religious pluralism have usually come from state religious courts and the federal government rather than from religious activists. Non-Muslims are forbidden to proselytize Muslims and apostasy has been effectively blocked by state religious courts. Other religions cannot advertise services or follow other practices that could lead to the conversion of Muslims. The importation of Christian books that use Islamic interpretations of words and Malay translations of the Bible and other Christian literature that might influence Muslims have been targeted. Accusations have been made against local authorities for making difficult the building of non-Muslim places of worship there. In Indonesia, limitations on religious pluralism have come from activists and local religious courts and secular authorities, with limited input from the national government. Thus, conversion is legal, but there have been numerous attacks upon Christians by local groups and Islamic courts have opposed conversion, although without the legal authority found in Malaysia.

Both Indonesia and Malaysia have sought to contain "deviant Islam," although the latter has been more active. This allows the government to define the meaning of Islam and is employed to maintain religious purity, for national security and to contain the political opposition. Thus, UMNO leadership defined as deviant the efforts of PAS to implement *hudud* laws. Government and Islamic organizations in Malaysia have named scores of groups guilty of deviancy including Shi'as. The government has closed many of these alleged deviant groups and members have been punished by fines and imprisonment. In Indonesia local authorities also have fined and imprisoned members of "deviant" groups, frequently on charges of blasphemy or defamation of Islam. However, the national government has been more flexible than its Malaysian counterpart. Thus, the Ahmadiyah is banned in Malaysia, but allowed to exist in Indonesia with restrictions, in spite of political and religious pressure.

A significant difference between the two countries is that Malaysian controls on religious pluralism have centered upon institutionalized local and national laws, although there have been isolated violent incidents in both countries. In Indonesia, there has been far more attacks from nongovernmental activists and conservative religious groups. In the latter, there have been numerous occasions of mob violence against Christian institutions, organizations considered to be un-Islamic such as the Ahmadiyah, and shops and individuals allegedly guilty of breaking

Islamic law or practicing immoral behavior. Major conservative religious groups have also criticized religious pluralism. The `ulama'-based MUI has issued fatwas against the Ahmadiyah, secularism, and religious pluralism, although these fatwas do not have the force of law.

Muslim Minority Communities

The political role played by Islamic minorities can be divided into three patterns: (1) where the minority is completely excluded from power (Myanmar-Burma); (2) where there is a significant separatist or autonomy movements, although the community now has a greater right to participate in national and local government (Muslims in southern Philippines and southern Thailand); and (3) in Muslim communities rejecting separation or autonomy and prepared to participate in the political system (Thai Muslims outside the Muslim-Malays in the far south and Muslims in Singapore). However, there are important common factors among these minority groups including co-identity of religion and ethnicity, economic and social inequality, perceived government repression, and new religious currents.

Ethnicity and religion

Every minority group in the region reflects the co-identity of religion and ethnicity different from the dominant society. This combination can reinforce a sense of alienation and foster political tensions. No Muslim minority in Southeast Asia has been so consistently excluded from national government involvement as in Burma-Myanmar, although Muslims from central Burma did hold political leadership during Burma's democratic era. Muslims in Burma are largely the descendants of immigrants from South Asia and can be divided between the more integrated group that settled into core areas of Burma and those from the Arakan in southwest Burma. The former's origins, religion, and economic power have fostered anti-Muslim antagonism since colonial times. They have been considered *kala* (foreigner) by many Burmese. The Muslim Arakanese originally came into the area in the nineteenth and early twentieth centuries when Burma was still a province of India. Their Bengali background and differences in language and religion have made them distinct from the Burmese Buddhist majority. The desire of some Arakanese for autonomy, separation, or even annexation to Bangladesh has further reinforced official views that they are not loyal. The military regime has defined them as noncitizens because their decedents did not live in Burma before 1824 when colonial power was initially established and has implemented policies limiting their economic development, housing, travel, and education opportunities.

Thailand and the Philippines provide examples of Muslims who generally differ from the majority in their ethnicity, but have gained increasing political power and religious autonomy in the past several decades. Muslims in Thailand can be divided into two groups. Thai Muslims speak Thai and have generally been integrated politically and socially, but remain loyal to their faith. They are multiethnic and include Malays, immigrants, and Thai converts. The second and largest Muslim group is composed of Malay-speaking Muslims who have attempted to maintain their religious and ethnic identity, leading to significant support for autonomy or separation. The difference between the two communities can be explained in large part by history and geography. The majority of Thai Muslims have been part of the traditional boundaries of the kingdom in close proximity with the Buddhist state and society. The most southern provinces, where the Malay-speaking Muslims reside, only became part of the kingdom in 1906. Until the latter half of the twentieth century they were isolated from the rest of the country by poor roads and communications with Malaysia easier to reach than Bangkok. Within this context, they have retained their Malay-Muslim heritage and rejected the political role and religious and social cosmology of the dominant Buddhist state and society.

The Muslims in the southern Philippines, called the *bangsa moro*, are not an ethnic group in the traditional sense, but are composed of some ten ethnic groups that view themselves as a common social and religious culture endangered by an encroaching Christian society, government, and economic power.

Economic and social inequality

Reinforcing this ethnoreligious identity have been the perception and reality of economic inequality. In the case of southern Thailand, it was largely neglected by Thai authorities until the 1960s. An absence of a reliable road network meant that the economy languished. Even after significant government development programs were implemented, more than one third of Malay-Muslims in the southernmost provinces lived under the poverty level and had comparatively low levels of education, although a significant percentage of Buddhists in the area are also poor. Unlike the Philippines, the area has not experienced the large immigration of outsiders.

In the southern Philippines two Muslim provinces ranked seventy-third and seventy-sixth in development out of the republic's seventy-seven provinces. Where, in the past, agricultural land had belonged to the local Muslim population majority ownership became increasingly held by Christian immigrants and large corporations, often with the backing of the national government. Manila under the Spanish, American, and independent republic have sought to encourage the immigration of the Christian population from high-density areas to the south. In recent decades, large agribusiness interests in the area displayed considerable influence in national politics. The *bangsa moro* are now only 20 percent or less of the population in the southern island of Mindanao and issues of land have fired separatist movements and reinforced their ethnoreligious identity.

Perceived government repression

Two major criticisms of government actions have related to assimilation policies and what are perceived to be questionable efforts to contain separatist movements. Thai policy until the last decades of the past century was to assimilate non-Buddhists into the Thai nation. This has led to efforts to press for acceptance of the Thai language, Buddhism, and loyalty to the king. The provincial and district bureaucracy in the south was composed almost entirely of Thais, usually with limited knowledge of the population. Malay-Muslims have seen this assimilation policy as an attack on their religion and customs. They do not want to be integrated into the Thai state, which is intimately entwined in Buddhist cosmology. Malay-Muslims have interpreted police and military action against separatist organizations as an effort to enforce Thai hegemony and weaken aspirations to maintain their own culture.

From the beginning of the Spanish colonial era through the American and Filipino administration, efforts have been made to assimilate the southern Muslims into the nation.

The Spanish reasoning was religious and political; it wanted to convert the entire archipelago to Catholicism and to weaken Islamic power by force and dilute it by bringing Christians into the area. The American and Filipino governments sought to alleviate population pressure, particularly in Luzon and the Visayas, and fostered movement to the south.

This continuing discontent has led to the formation of separatist organizations in both countries and armed conflict remains a serious problem. However, in both cases there have been divisions between groups based upon strategic goals, methods of opposition, and ideology. Differences have centered upon disagreement over what form of autonomy or separation is acceptable, the role of Islam, and willingness to participate in armed conflict. This is best illustrated by separatist organizations in the southern Philippines. Three groups have vied for leadership of the movement. The first major separatist group was the nationalist Moro National Liberation Front (MNLF), a primarily secular group that no longer engages in armed conflict and has worked with the government with the goal of achieving semiautonomy. The largest organization is the Moro Islamic Liberation Front (MILF), which broke from the MNLF. It presents a more Islamic-oriented program and has long called for complete separation and independence. It has more recently shown a willingness to discuss major political and religious autonomy. Finally, the small Abu Sayyaf Group is a faction-ridden, violent group, involved in mass killings, bombing, and kidnapping. It has articulated uncompromising demands for separation, radical Islamic ideals, and Salafi-Wahabbi influences and has demanded the expulsion of all Christians from parts of the southern provinces. Many observers have described it as a criminal organization.

Southern Thailand also displays a factionalized separatist movement, although there is general agreement on the need to protect Islam and the Malay people. Over time groups have ceased to exist, become fragmented, or changed their focus. Differences have existed over tactics, interpretations of Islamic doctrine, and willingness to work with the Thai government. Today almost all favor the necessity of violence as means to confront what is seen as Thai government repression. As a result of this violence and Thai domestic politics, Bangkok has also changed policies over time from forced assimilation to defining the separatist movement, as a criminal plot that could only be defeated by military means, to conciliation.

The governments of Thailand and the Philippines have recognized the religious and development issues facing their Muslim minorities and there have been political and economic reforms and concessions toward greater religious autonomy. However, government policies have not been consistent and separatist groups demand more autonomy, or independence in some cases, and continue to employ violent tactics.

Conclusion

While this essay has presented many similarities in the forces behind the interaction between Islam and politics in Southeast Asia, this is an evolving process with significant differences at the national and local levels. It needs to be underscored that we are dealing within both national and subnational contexts and within differing political environments. Islam plays a significant social and political role throughout the region, but there are important variations both between and within Muslim majority and minority communities. This relationship is further complicated by the interrelationship between religion and ethnicity and the impact of other secular factors. There also exist variations between rhetoric and practice. Thus, there is popular support for an increased role for Islam in the public sector, but little consensus as to how it is to be implemented.

NOTES

1. Brunei is a small sultanate in which the sultan is both the ruler and the prime minister, and there are no parties or competitive elections. Brunei is not considered in this analysis. The Cham Muslims of Cambodia, with 1–2 percent of the population, are also not included.

REFERENCES

Abuza, Zachary. 2003. *Militant Islam in Southeast Asia: Crucible of Terror*. Boulder: Lynne Riener.
Barton, Greg. 2004. *Indonesia's Struggle: Jemaah Islamiyah and the Soul of Islam*. Sydney: University of New South Wales Press.
Chalk, P. 2001. Separatism in Southeast Asia: The Islamic Factor in Southern Thailand, Mindanao and Aceh. *Studies in Conflict and Terrorism* 24: 241–269.
Che Man, W. K. 1990. *Muslim Separatism: The Moros of Southern Philippines and the Malays of Southern Thailand*. New York: Oxford University Press.
Feith, H. 2007. *The Decline in Constitutional Democracy in Indonesia*. Singapore: Equinox Press.
Hefner, Robert. 2000. *Civil Islam: Muslims and Democratization in Indonesia*. Princeton, NJ: Princeton University Press.
Liow, Joseph. 2009. *Piety and Politics: Islamism in Contemporary Malaysia*. New York: Oxford University Press.
McKennan, Thomas. 1998. *Muslim Rebels and Rulers: Everyday Politics and Armed Separatism in the Southern Philippines*. Berkeley: University of California Press.
Means, Gordon. 2009. *Political Islam in Southeast Asia*. Boulder: Lynne Riener.
Milne, R. S., and Mauzy, Diane. 1999. *Malaysian Politics under Mahathir*. London: Routledge.
Nasr, Vali. 2001. *Islamic Leviathan: Islam and the Making of State Power*. New York: Oxford University Press.
Schwarz, Adam. 2002. *A Nation in Waiting: Indonesia's Search for Stability*. Leonards, Australia: Allen & Unwin.
Sidel, John. 2006. *Riots, Pogroms, Jihad: Religious Violence in Indonesia*. Ithaca: Cornell University Press.
Yegar, Moshe. 2002. *Between Integration and Secession: The Muslim Communities in Southern Thailand, Southern Philippines and Western Burma/Myanmar*. Lanham, MD: Lexington Books.

CHAPTER 24

ISLAM AND POLITICS IN NORTH AFRICA

AZZEDINE LAYACHI

Since the seventh century, when the Maghreb (North Africa west of Egypt) was Islamized by the invading Muslim forces coming from the east, Islam has played a direct and profound role in the social and political dynamics of the region. Except for the colonial period, during the past thirteen centuries, Islam has served many functions, including an identity base, a unifying factor in the face of internal conflict and external challenges, an instrument of political legitimation for the ruling authorities, and an inspiration for revolutionary fervor among the masses. Writing in 1964, Carl Brown acknowledged that "it still remains true that Islam remains one of the important indices for understanding developments in North Africa" (Brown 1964, 63). This observation continues to be valid today. It was well confirmed by the fact that, following the popular upheavals of 2011 in the Middle East and North Africa region, religious parties took the leadership reins in Tunisia, Egypt, and Morocco.

This essay examines the political dimension of Islam in the Maghreb region (Algeria, Libya, Morocco, and Tunisia) with a focus on the postindependence era; this is done by tackling several issues, including the role of Islam in national identity and its relationship to the nation-state; the reformist and the revolutionary tendencies inspired by Islam in the region; the interaction between the state and Islam; and the various manifestations of Islam in national political dynamics. These issues are tackled along five chronological sequences: (1) Islam in the nationalist struggle for independence, (2) the postindependence "nationalization" of religion, (3) the rise of grassroots Islam, (4) post-Islamism and the ascendency of Sufism following a bitter confrontation between the state and radical Islamism,[1] and (5) the rise to power of moderate Islamism through the ballot box in the wake of what was termed the "Arab Spring."

Political Islam has stimulated plenty of scholarly writing and journalistic accounts in the past three decades due its ascendency as a phenomenon that seemed to undermine domestic and international orders. In the countries where it appeared as a relatively new, but potent, force to be reckoned with, and in a region where it seemed to threaten the interests of regional as well as extraregional states, political Islam commended attention and stimulated concern and reaction. The way it manifested itself and the manner in which it was understood and dealt with were going to have a direct impact on its own evolution and even transformation. This has been the case of most of the predominantly Muslim countries and regions—Asia and the subregions of the Middle East and North Africa.

In the Maghreb region, political Islam manifested itself in a variety of ways and was tackled differently by state policies and actions. Regardless of the particular convolutions that the interactions between the state and political Islam went through—some violent and others not—in the end, two types of situations have developed across the key states of the region: in Algeria and Morocco, Political Islam has entered mainstream politics through what have been termed by many analysts as a moderation of Islamism or "post-Islamism," on one hand, and successful state co-optation strategies, on the other. In Tunisia and Libya, the initial utterances of grassroots political movements animated by a religious ideology were crushed by the state early enough to avoid a protracted confrontation. This reaction left room for neither the moderation of Islamism nor its co-optation by the state. However, the overthrow in 2011 of Zine al-`Abidin Ben `Ali and Muammar al-Qaddafi, the autocratic leaders of Tunisia and Libya, allowed political Islam to openly return to the political scene and legally and freely compete for election.

In the first two cases, the moderation-integration of grassroots political Islam coincided with a general, albeit limited, opening of the political system, while in the second two cases, the exclusion and repression of all expressions of political Islam coincided with a closing of all venues of political opposition to all forces, be they religious or secular. This might partly explain why political Islam came back with a vengeance after the overthrow of the authoritarian leaders. In Libya, it instantly became a major force in the early post-Qaddafi era, and in Tunisia, it became the main political force in the institutions of transition from the Ben Ali era.

The way political Islam appeared in the postcolonial Maghrebi states, how it manifested itself in recent decades, and how it and its relationship with the state evolved have all been affected by several factors, including,

1. the role and place of Islam in the national liberation movement
2. the relationship that developed between religion and the state in the first decades of independence from colonialism (French in Algeria, Morocco, and Tunisia, and Italian in Libya)
3. the place and role of religious militancy in each country
4. the nature and outcome of the confrontation between the state and grassroots political Islam
5. the extent of doctrinal and political adaptation of both the state and grassroots political Islam to changing domestic and international conditions

These factors are explored below according to the chronological sequencing indicated above.

ISLAM AND NATIONALISM IN THE MAGHREB

In their struggle against French colonialism, Algerian, Moroccan, and Tunisian nationalisms based their calls for resistance to the colonizer and for the establishment of independent nation-states for their respective societies both on secular tenets of nationalism and on Islam. The secular elements included the usual tenets such as the homeland (*watan*), the common history, and its associated myths, the unique culture, and the unifying language. To these elements, which served to distinguish the colonized from the colonizer, was added Islam as a key religious and cultural factor of unity among the indigenous populations as well as a powerful instrument of distinction from the religion and culture of the colonizer.

French colonialism in all three countries stimulated thus nationalist movements, which "activated 'political' Islam as they sought roots in Islamic as well as national identities. Political Islam in turn shaped the nationalist movements against the French presence" in the three Maghrebi countries (Henry 2007, 87).

In Algeria, for example, the words of Shaykh Abdelhamid Ben Badis (1889–1940), a founder of the Association of ʿUlama' (Muslim scholars), which became a nationalist creed, were "Algeria is my country, Arabic is my language and Islam is my religion." Even though Ben Badis's work through the Association of ʿUlama' focused more on religious, cultural, and linguistic revival or affirmation and did not per se call for independence, his motto was successfully used by the secular nationalists, starting with Messali Hadj (1898–1974), whose nationalist association Etoile Nord-Africaine (North African Star) called for the full independence of Algeria. "The *Etoile* rejected assimilation and demanded Algeria's self-determination. Messali's brand of nationalism took over all the major symbols and values of the 'glorious' Arab-Islamic past: 'The Muslim Algerian people have a glorious historic past, a religion and a language totally different from those of France….'" (Stora 1991, 74).

A similar evolution was experienced in Morocco and Tunisia, where the nationalist movements began with an accommodating attitude toward the colonizer but with an affirmation of the unique indigenous identity. However, the harsh and unaccommodating colonial rule pushed these movements toward an uncompromising demand for independence, which was undergirded by both a strong Islamic identity as well as secular nationalist values.

The way the French rulers handled both the nationalist movements and the religious orders of the colonized societies was going to affect the postindependence relationship between state and religion. In Algeria, which was a settlement colony annexed to France, the French rulers destroyed much of the religious structures, institutions, and schools, while preserving them in Morocco and Tunisia—possibly as a result of lessons learned in Algeria and also as a strategy aimed to weaken the secular nationalists in Tunisia and the monarch in Morocco. In Libya, the Sanusi religious order was also not much affected by the relatively brief Italian colonization. In spite of the fact that the Italians closed its lodges, arrested its shaykhs, and confiscated its *habous* land (i.e., those belonging to the mosque) because it actively resisted colonialism, the Sanusiya survived and established a monarchy at independence in 1951.

The religious tendencies in the Maghreb included conservative and modernist Salafi currents,[2] which permeated the nationalist movements, as well as Sufi orders and their respective *zawiyate* (shrines or schools). In Morocco, ʿAllal al-Fasi, a Salafist, founded the nationalist Istiqlal party and led its struggle against colonialism. In the Maghreb, particularly in Algeria, Morocco, and Tunisia, Salafism "corresponded to the patriotic expectations of the peoples who rejected colonial domination" (Addi 2009, 341). Again, in the Moroccan case, "The energy of religious fervor was rationalized, disciplined, mobilized to support the sultan in the struggle for independence" (Addi 2009, 339). The same can be said about the support extended to the secular nationalist movements in Algeria and Tunisia, which were led respectively by the National Liberation Front and the Neo-Destour Party. However, beyond the national unity it incited, Salafism, which inspired the ideological foundation of Islamism, was going to adopt a radical and even revolutionary attitude in the postcolonial Maghreb as it questioned the political, economic, and moral orders of the newly independent states. As will be discussed later, the Salafi tendency took both a peaceful track of Da`awa and protest and a track of violent action for redemption and revolution.

Postindependence "Official Islam" and Its Limits

In the first decade of independence, a common pattern in the relationship between Islam and the state developed in Algeria, Morocco, Tunisia, and Libya. That pattern was the active attempt by the state (and the monarchy in the case of Morocco) to control religion and religious forces by a variety of means. It was probably understood from the start that the reformist fervor of the Salafiya could prove to be a challenge in the early stages of building a secular and modern state. That process began in 1956 in Morocco and Tunisia and in 1962 in Algeria. In Libya it began in 1951 and was, paradoxically, started by the leader of the Sanusi order, who had just accidentally turned king—the process continued after the overthrow of the Sanusi monarchy by Mu`ammar al-Qaddafi in 1969.

The reformist tendencies that had existed during the colonial era but were muted by the need to close ranks in the struggle against a common occupier, oppressor, and non-Muslim enemy resurfaced after independence, as all political and religious tendencies wanted to affect the determination of the developmental path the state was about to in engage in. After the initial independence euphoria and sometimes confusion, as was the case in Algeria, the leaders of the newly independent states moved to not only reign in the Salafi reformist tendencies but also to establish a hegemonic control over the religious sphere through the oversight of the mosques and Friday sermons, the co-optation of the `ulama', the repression of the radical challengers, and the development of an official religious discourse that became the expression of what is termed "official Islam." This process is examined below in the four countries' cases.

Libya: Taming Islamism with Islamic reforms and repression

In Libya, where the Sanusi religious order itself inherited the command over the country, there was a somewhat reverse process whereby, "upon ascending to power, King Idris attempted to secularize the political system, rein in radical traditionalism, and bring about change. In the process, he relegated the Sanusiya order—and with it, religion—to a secondary position" (El-Kikhia 1997, 28). When he came to power in 1969, Qaddafi did not want to take on the religious establishment for fear of loss of popular support, avoiding, thereby, the mistake of his predecessor. However, once his power consolidated, he progressively established control over the religious sphere by openly taking on the traditional `ulama' and by "creating his own type of Islam which he viewed as more progressive and in line with the spirit of the nationalist era" (El-Kikhia 1997, 41). The Libyan leader wanted thus to start with a clean slate in which nationalism and a particular version of Islam were combined to form the ideological core of the Revolution. In his article "Qadhafi's Libya and the Prospect of Islamic Succession," Ray Takeyh indicated,

> During the first few years of the revolution, the regime went beyond rhetorical gestures and initiated substantive Islamic reforms. Qadhafi often spoke in mosques and consulted the clerics regarding public-policy initiatives. The Ulama were given prominent positions in the legal and educational spheres and oversaw the National Guidance Council, designed to reform Libya's legal system along Islamic lines. (Takeyh 2000, pp. 155–156)

In this process, al-Qaddafi pushed for a pan-Arabism and a socialist revolution that were "Islamed." He also introduced some *Shari`ah* law and made alcohol and prostitution illegal (Joffe 1995, 146). In other words, he skillfully pushed aside the old Sanusiyya order and used his relatively liberal version of Islam to build his legitimacy and to implement his socialist vision for Libya.

However, in the 1970s, and in spite of these efforts, al-Qaddafi was unable to prevent political Islam from rising. He faced challenges from the Libyan Muslim Brotherhood (Ikhwan), which he managed to dismantle easily, especially since they were not allowed to form charitable organizations, professional guilds, and student associations as they had done in Egypt. However, in the following two decades, two radical Islamist groups tried to organize a rebellion against his regime. They were the Harakat Al-Jihad (the Jihad Movement, in the early 1980s) and the al-Jama`a al-Libiya al-Islamiya al-Muqatila (Libyan Islamic Fighting Group [LIFG], in the mid-1990s). They too failed in their attempt to destabilize the regime.

The irony was that al-Qaddafi was finally overthrown by a popular rebellion that was not led by the Islamists. In fact, the 2011 popular upheaval was essentially secular without any specific agenda beyond overthrowing the existing regime. Several Islamists groups of different tendencies did finally form and join the rebellion, but when they tried to claim leadership (through the ballot box) after al-Qaddafi was killed, they failed.

Algeria: The socialist revolution challenged

After independence in 1962, the governing elite in Algeria understood well the potential political power of Islam, but they did not want the political order to be based on it or heavily inspired by it. They intended to build a secular system without dismissing the importance of Islam in national life and identity. In 1964, one of the key ideological and political documents of the National Liberation Front (FLN), the Algiers Charter, reinforced the socialist and secular orientation of Algeria. Even though the state was not set to impose its dominance over the religious sphere, it became clear later that the governing leadership would have to exercise some control over religion so as not to allow it to emerge as a political force that could be potentially destabilizing. In order to limit the dissension of the religious factions, the regime attempted to reassure it by declaring that Algeria's socialism would have the "color" of Islam (i.e., "Islamic socialism"), by introducing mandatory religious courses in public schools and by making Friday the weekly day of rest instead of Sunday (Frégosi 1995, 104). There developed also an "official Islam," which monopolized control over the places of worship and public religious discourse in the country.

In much of the 1960s and 1970s, the conservative religious elite, which would later inspire the Islamist movement, expressed at that time a merely moral reaction to the strong leftist tendency that permeated the bulk of the national leadership elite. The religious dissenters accused the government of drawing inspiration not from the Islamic faith but rather from foreign theories and models (e.g., historical materialism of the Marxists and European socialism). Religious conservatism permeated the Association of Algerian Muslim 'Ulama' and was articulated by important religious figures such as Abdelatif Soltani, Bachir Ibrahimi, Ahmed Sahnoun, Mesbah Houidek, and Omar Larbaoui. In 1963, Hachemi Tidjani, general secretary of the Algiers Faculté, created al-Qiyam al-Islamiya (the Islamic Values), an association for the defense of Islamic ideals and culture. Before it was banned,[3] this association had attracted several people who would later become instrumental in transforming this movement for cultural and moral regeneration into a political one. Among the most prominent was Abbasi Madani, who later became leader of the Islamic Salvation Front (FIS).

During the rule of President Houari Boumediene, who had come to power through a military coup in June 1965, the conservative religious elite continued to demand an increase in the overt role of religion in both society and government. It also continued to criticize attempts to link socialism with Islam (Burgat 1988, 45) and denounced the negative moral impact of modernization, which included such things as alcohol distribution, coed education, and women's adoption of Western dress codes. The limited—mainly verbal—opposition of this period became more politically assertive within a few years.

As a response to this mounting religious challenge, the state increased its control over the religious sphere while remaining steadfast on the socialist course. The regime began to repress its religious opponents while at the same time making use of religion in support of both regime and socialism. The use and consolidation of official Islam aimed at lending legitimacy to a regime that had come to power by force. This official Islam manifested itself in a tight supervision of the mosques and of all religious education and institutions, the creation of centers of Islamic learning, and in symbolic acts and events, such as televising weekly the president's attendance of the Friday prayer in the mosque.

In a change of strategy, the religious elite, especially the conservative 'ulama', sought a compromise with the regime and decided to lend support to Boumediene with the hope that such support would help them temper the socialist orientation by way of controlling at least the spheres of culture and education. Due to his need for legitimacy and for support for the socialist revolution, Boumediene responded to the demands and allowed the ministries of culture and information, education, and religious education and affairs to be headed by members of the religious elite, such as Ahmed Taleb Ibrahimi and Mouloud Kassim. By accepting this compromise, Boumediene had hoped to use the religious elite to relay his revolutionary messages and to mobilize popular support behind them. To placate the religious elite, the regime also pushed for a formal and symbolic connection between Islam and the state, without necessarily undermining the inherently secular nature of the system of government and its policies. As a result, the 1976 constitution and national charter (political, economic, ideological, and cultural blueprint) merely reiterated the institutional importance of Islam but without giving it a central role. While declaring Islam to be the religion of the state, the charter confirmed the unshakable commitment to socialism when it stated, "The Muslim people will realize little by little that it is by reinforcing the struggle against imperialism and by committing themselves resolutely in the path of socialism, that they will best respond to the imperatives of their faith, and make action coincide with the principles."[4]

Unsatisfied by these formal concessions and seeking more tangible deeds from the government, the religious conservatives demanded more measures to help deal with the challenges to the faith by rapid modernization and increasing exposure to outside influences. However, the association al-Qiyam al-Islamiya, which expressed these demands, was suspended by the government in 1966 after it sent a letter to Egyptian President Gamal Abdel Nasser to protest against the execution of the Islamist ideologue Sayyid Qutb. Four years later, it was officially banned after its discourse turned more political. Its members, however, increased their *Da'wa* activities and their open opposition to socialism. Unable to attack the regime's social policies, which enjoyed wide support among the masses, they courted people opposed to socialism, such as big merchants and big landowners who stood to lose from state policies. Unable to quiet them, even after an initial crackdown, the government made yet another set of concessions to them, including dismantlement of vineyards, adoption of Arabic as the sole language of education,[5] promotion of religious education in schools, banning of alcohol in some cities, closing all restaurants during the month of Ramadan, prohibition of raising pigs, substitution of Friday instead of Sunday as the weekly day of rest, and reintroduction in 1973 of the recourse to Islamic laws as a secondary source available to civil court judges, and enactment later (in 1984) of a conservative family law code (Frégosi 1995, 106).

Toward the end of the 1970s, Boumediene seemed to have succeeded in establishing a delicate balance between the needs of advancing the socialist project with the help of the left and winning the acquiescence of the religious elite. However, this worked as long as the state was able to respond to the basic needs of society. Once the distributive function of the state started failing by the end of the 1970s and early 1980s, that balance collapsed and the religious sentiment started changing into a powerful political movement seeking a radical change, even by way of violence. This change was also affected by important external factors such as the Iranian Revolution.

The mounting economic crisis that affected negatively the state's distributive function was caused by external constraints due mainly to a high dependency on income from hydrocarbons only, and internal factors such as the failing development strategy itself, an inefficient bureaucracy, rising inflation, growing income inequalities, weak agricultural performance, and urban migration. These economic difficulties helped the development of a militant form of political Islam that proved later to be very violent and highly destabilizing.

At that point, the Islamist claims were no longer limited to the cultural and social spheres; the religious opposition attacked also, and directly, the nature of the political system and its policies, as well as a panoply of phenomena, including corruption, nepotism, injustice, pronounced socioeconomic inequality, and authoritarianism.

As indicated above, important concessions were made by the government to the Islamists, but Islam was not allowed to affect the fundamental structure or policies of the regime. Religion was used only as an instrumental "official Islam" for political purposes. Political freedom was severely curtailed under the banners of socialism, nationalism, unity, and conformity for the sake of the good of the whole society and there were no legal venues for the venting of dissenting opinions. As will be discussed later, this political strategy failed to inhibit the birth and development of a highly politicized grassroots Islam, which was going to constitute a serious challenge to the state and society by the end of the 1980.

Morocco: Salafiya and the "Commander of the Faithful"

The unity fomented by the struggle for independence between the monarchy, the religious leaders, and the secular nationalists came under stress right after independence. The monarch, Mohamed V, who, like his predecessors, claimed religious legitimacy was aware of the potential challenge of reformist Salafiya, which was partly embedded in the nationalist party Istiqlal, the left, represented by the National Union of Popular Forces (UNFP) party, and the military. The king worked then on weakening the Istiqlal party, which was mostly popular in the urban centers, and neutralizing the religious leaders through manipulation and control over the religious sphere (Zeghal 2005, 55). After Mohamed V died in 1961, his son, Hassan II, continued on the same course using political manipulation, control, and the co-optation of the leaders of the nationalist and *salafiya* tendencies, which, by the same token, he would play against the left, which he feared the most in the 1960s and 1970s.

While some religious leaders questioned the religious authority and autocratic methods of the monarch, there was no visible core group behind them capable of mobilizing the masses for political action until the 1980s, when political Islam gained momentum at a time when both the military (after the failed coup attempts of 1971 and 1972) and the left were totally neutralized by the king.

Morocco's Islamist movement was the last to enter the political arena en masse in North Africa. This was due to several reasons, including a tight control of the religious sphere and its symbols by a monarch who claimed to be *amir almu'minin* (Commander of the Faithful, based on a claim of *shorfa* lineage, that is, a descendent of Prophet Mohamed), and the use by King Hassan II of a wide-scale repression of all opposition, both religious and secular, during his reign from 1961 to 1999.

Besides repressing the groups that could not be controlled, King Hassan also tried to monopolize the religious sphere by establishing a whole system of expression of "official Islam" through the promotion of nonpolitical religious organizations, such as *Da`wa* associations—which he also used against the secular left—and the reactivation and control of the Council of `Ulama'. The monarch also promoted traditional religious structures and measures inspired by religion such as the enactment of a conservative Code of Personal Status (*Mudawana*), the creation of Qur'anic schools, and the imposition of prayer in school.

Contrary to his expectations, however, a rising Islamist movement took advantage of this invigorated religious life and developed as a moral, political, and social force. It included several organizations, but the most popular one was that of the al-`Adl wa al- Ihsan of the late Abdeslam Yassin, the schoolteacher who directly challenged the monarch in an open letter in 1974. Yassin's organization increased its appeal by way of social and charitable actions, by taking up the demands and grievances of students, and by denouncing the corrupt elements among the governing elite.

> By assisting the sick, the widowed and the unemployed, they have gained followers in the shanty towns in Tangier, Rabat and Casablanca. Their charities run blood banks and help people organize funerals. [On Aid al-Adha,] they offer lamb or mutton to the poor. [They also] have been steadily reaching into the educational system, enlisting high school teachers and university students [and have recruited urban professionals]. (Simons 1998)

By the time of King Hassan's death, `Adl wa al-Ihsan was a full-fledged Islamist movement that rejected the monarchical order and the legitimacy of the king. However, it was a movement that rejected the use of violence but also resisted being co-opted. Its shunned participation in a political system whose rules are already set in favor of the existing ruling system.

Tunisia: Modernization, demise of the left and the rise of Political Islam

In Tunisia, where the 2011 upheavals in the Arab world began, Islam played an important role in the struggle for Tunisia's independence just as in the rest of the Maghreb. The traditional Qur'anic schools established in the early 1900s helped the nationalist cause, but their role and place in the postindependence political and cultural dynamics was purposefully curtailed by the state, which was placed on a Western-style modernization trajectory. The nonthreatening elements of Tunisia's Salafi tendency were used in the context of nation and state building by Tunisia's first president, Habib Bourguiba.

According to Elbaki Hermassi, after independence, three ideological tendencies informally competed for deciding the course of the new state: the religious, the revolutionary Marxist, and the modern liberal tendencies (Hermassi 1972). It was the last tendency that ended up controlling the country, headed by President Bourguiba, who engaged Tunisia in a Western-style modernization process.

President Bourguiba followed a two-track policy, which, on one hand tried to contain the religious current while advancing social policies deemed clashing with prevailing religious interpretations, and on the other hand used religion as instrument of legitimacy and control, just as was done elsewhere in the Maghreb and other parts of the Arab world. After having promulgated in 1957 a personal status code containing the most liberal laws on gender equality in the region, he tried to preempt the resistance of the conservative religious current in the country. Among the various actions undertaken to limit the role of the traditional religious current—which seemed quite passive at that time—and to prevent it from becoming an obstacle to Bourguiba's modernization plan for Tunisia, the Zaytouna Mosque-University, a traditional center of Islamic learning and scholarship, was denied autonomy by its integration into the University of Tunis in 1960. Bourguiba also tried to institute an "official Islam" by way of rhetoric and action. He created a "Directorate of Religious Affairs," which would later become the Ministry of Religious Affairs, to help direct religious norms and actions from above. The state took control of public *habus* land and of the financial management of mosques and religious schools. The *Shari'ah* courts were abolished and replaced by a single-state judicial system (Perkins 1986, 111). Moreover, Bourguiba proclaimed himself *mufti* (one who issues *fetwas* and interprets Islam) and regularly praised the Islamic heritage of his people. However, his forceful modernization policies irked the then almost dormant religious reformist current in Tunisia, especially when he called on people not to fast during Ramadan because it hurt productivity and, according to him, breaking the fast was permitted in Islam during Jihad, that is, the Jihad for development. A faction of this religious current became politicized by the 1970s in response to the state's control of the religious sphere, to what was perceived as Bourguiba's Westernization of Tunisia, and to the rise of the left.

In the end, Bourguiba was not able to contain the incipient political Islam. On the contrary, when he was faced with an increasingly bold challenge from the left, he allowed the Islamist movement to come out in public and he indirectly supported its open activism, hoping that it would counterbalance the left. In the 1960s, the leftist group Afaq (Perspectives or Horizon) clashed several times with the government and the conflict culminated in the prohibition of the Communist Party in 1963. In the late 1970s, the clash was with the main labor union, the General Union of Tunisian Workers (UGTT) over economic and social policies. After violent clashes in the late 1970s, the labor movement was also tamed, which left the political arena wide open for the Islamist tendency to make headways as a popular movement seeking radical change in Tunisia.

Just as in Algeria, the Tunisian religious movement, which was initially concerned with cultural, social, and religious issues, inched its way into the political arena, expressing opposition to the left and later to the increasingly authoritarian state under Bourguiba. Also, just as in Algeria and Morocco, the regime used the religious current to face off the leftist challenge, and there too, the strategy backfired. By the early 1980s, "[the] Tunisian single-party regime...[which] had successfully mobilized Islam for the purposes of nation-building went furthest in reforms that upend the religious establishment" (Henry 2007, 87).

By the time Bourguiba was overthrown in 1987 by his interior minister, Zine al-'Abidin Ben 'Ali, the Islamist movement was at its highest level of political mobilization under the leadership of Rashid Ghannushi, who had founded in 1979 the Movement of the Islamic Tendency (Mouvement de la Tendance Islamique [MIT]), later renamed al-Nahdah (Renaissance) party. As will be discussed later, the religious movement, which was essentially reformist and seeking change by peaceful means, stimulated a wide repression of all political opposition and ended up being eliminated by the mid-1990s. However, after President Ben Ali was overthrown in February 2011, al-Nahdah was quickly legalized as a political party and it became the most powerful contender in the political arena.

Grassroots Islam Confronts the State

By the mid-1980s, all four Maghrebi countries were facing an Islamist challenge of varying degree and form. The causes of the rise of the Islamist movement as a challenge to the Maghrebi states were various and complex. Including and beyond the factors discussed above, it is important to mention the following internal factors and conditions:

1. worsening socioeconomic conditions for a vast number of people, especially in Algeria, Morocco, and Tunisia
2. the marked decline of the secular opposition due to repression and manipulation—the most challenging opposition figures were jailed, pushed into foreign exile, or eliminated
3. weak or absent ideological sign posts in the midst of a search of identity markers in a context of a waning nationalist and socialist ideologies and a perceived encroachment of Western culture and behaviors
4. weak or controlled independent civic and professional associations and student organizations and unions
5. weak representative institutions (the legislature in Morocco, Algeria, and Tunisia had no power of its own)

6. lack of independence of the judiciary branch, which often sided with government claims against dissidents
   7. strict control of the media by the state

A consequential ideological and institutional vacuum was easily filled by religious slogans and networks that offered a radically different social and political project. With the combination of calls for democratization and religious revival, the Islamists pushed for the widening of the arena of political participation by making more people involved. Members of the governing elites inadvertently played a facilitating role by manipulating religious groups and symbols hoping that that would dampen the religious opposition and increase their own legitimacy. They often used the Islamist sentiment against the secular left and vice versa. That was the case of Presidents Boumediene and Bendjedid in Algeria and Bourguiba Tunisia and King Hassan of Morocco. The next sections will tackle the confrontation that took place between each Maghrebi state and the Islamists and will highlight the state reaction patterns and how they affected the outcome.

Algeria

Massive youth riots in October 1988, which were harshly repressed, brought about a fast-paced series of events with a profound impact on Algeria's political landscape. The following year, sweeping political reforms ended the one-party rule of the FLN and allowed the birth of opposition parties, independent associations, and printing presses. Among the most active new political formations was the al-Jabha al-Islamiya li al-Inqadh (Islamic Front of Salvation, or FIS), which wished to establish an Islamic republic governed by *Shari'ah*. In June 1990, the FIS made a strong showing in Algeria's first free municipal elections, which emboldened it to demand early presidential elections and electoral reform, and prompted it to organize acts of civil disobedience, and to call for a general strike and mutiny of the armed forces. In June 1991, the military cracked down on Islamist sit-ins, arrested thousands of Islamists, including the two leaders of the FIS, and imposed a regime of martial law. In December 1991, in the first balloting of the first multiparty parliamentary elections the FIS won overwhelmingly. However, on January 1992, right before the second balloting (run-offs) took place, the army intervened and cancelled the electoral process. It also forced President Chadli Bendjedid—who was appointed president after Boumediene died in late 1978—to resign and replaced him with a collective ruling body named the High State Council. In response, the FIS militants and other Islamist groups went underground and escalated violent attacks against the state. The government declared a state of emergency, banned the FIS, and a large-scale crackdown against the Islamists ensued.

From that time and until the late 1990s, the armed conflict between the military and the various Islamist groups claimed the lives of around 200,000 people. New armed organizations sprang up, including the al-Jama'at al-Islamiya al-Musallaha (Armed Islamic Groups [GIA]). This group became notorious for a brutality directed against state security services, civilians, journalists, intellectuals, and foreigners. However, its own indiscriminate violence, infiltration by Algeria's secret services, and state counterinsurgency actions, led to its demise. It eventually disappeared and was replaced by a new group known as the al-Jama'a al-Salafiya li-al-Da'wa wa al-Qital (Salafist Group for Preaching and Combat [GSPC]), which, in turn, assimilated itself in 2006 into the al-Qa'ida network and took the name of al-Qa'ida in the Land of the Islamic Maghreb. Since then, this group has mounted some spectacular violent attacks in the country against both state and foreign interests, including an attack against US oil workers and a United Nations building. It is today the most important radical Islamist group that is still active in Algeria and in the whole region of North Africa and the Sahel region (Chad, Mali, Niger, and Mauritania).

In the midst of the terrible violence of the 1990s, important political developments allowed a nonviolent political Islam to enter the political arena as a set of legal and legitimate political parties, starting with the first multiparty presidential election in 1995 and multiparty parliamentary elections in 1997. However, after an initial respectable result at the polls, Islamist parties—mainly, Harakat Mujtama' al-Silm (Movement of Society for Peace [MSP])—started declining.

The Islamist rebellion failed to achieve its objectives and its crude violence has negatively affected the standing of the religious movement among the population. In the 2002 parliamentary elections, there was a decline in support for the Islamist parties, which was due partly to the general irrelevance of opposition parties and to internal conflicts within the MSP, a moderate Islamist party (formerly known as Hamas) and within Harakat al-Nahda al-Islamiya (Movement for Islamic Renaissance [MRI], also known as Ennahda), also a moderate party. The MSP lost thirty-one of its sixty-nine seats and Ennahda kept only one of its thirty-four seats. However, a new party—a breakaway from the latter—Harakat al-Islah al-Watani (Movement for National Reform [MRN], known as Islah) obtained forty-three seats. Overall, the number of seats controlled by the Islamists declined from 103 to 82.

In the November 2005 partial local elections in 143 local municipalities, the Islamists obtained seven seats only, and in the May 17, 2007 parliamentary elections, the number of seats they controlled went down from 82 to 60; the pro-government FLN and the National Democratic Rally (RND)[6] parties had also lost forty-nine of the combined 246 they held—due to FLN losses—but they remained the two dominant formations. Between 2002 and 2007, the process had come full circle with the FLN—which has the highest number of seats—back in control and supportive of President Bouteflika. In the 2012 parliamentary elections, the Islamist lost more seats in spite of the "Green Alliance" they formed and the regional context of that time—Tunisia was already governed by al-Nahda, Morocco's dominant party was the Islamist Party of Justice and Development (PJD), which obtained a majority of seats in the 2011 elections and took over the office the prime minister, and in Egypt, the Muslim Brothers became the most powerful political formation in the post-Mubarak transition institutions.

The 2012 Algerian parliamentary elections were preceded by a high hope of the Islamist formations making up the Green Alliance (MSP, Islah, and Ennahda) that they would follow in the footsteps of their fellow Islamist parties in Egypt, Tunisia, and Morocco. However, the ruling regime had managed to not only dodge the "Arab Spring" altogether, but it also pushed the Islamist parties into an almost irrelevant status. Together, the pro-government FLN and RND parties won 276 seats (out of 462), while the Green Alliance received forty-nine seats only. The newly created Islamist party, the Front for Justice and Development (also known as Adala/FJD) won only 7 seats. These results constituted a major setback for the Islamist parties, but, most importantly, the whole electoral process was received by the majority of people with unprecedented indifference (the real voter participation rate was probably

20 percent to 30 percent, the lowest ever). The government managed to dodge the winds of revolt in the region by lifting a nineteen-year-old state of emergency, promising political reforms, and pumping huge amounts of money into social and economic sectors, including infrastructure works, salary increases across the board, support for microcredit programs, and paid internships for the youth. The government has managed to buy off social discontent for now thanks to substantial windfall gains from hydrocarbon exports, but the strategy may not work forever. In this context, all opposition parties proved to be entirely irrelevant and powerless, including the Islamist ones.

In spite of the setback they experienced over the years since they were legalized, the religious parties continued to take advantage of their political inclusion to affect state policies and actions. The aim of political Islam may be that, once fully entrenched in the political institutions and processes, its militants will then work on implementing their vision for Algeria. As will be discussed later, these parties that have penetrated the state's fortress may have entered what some have called the "post-Islamist" era and, instead of struggling to bring down the secular state, they embarked on a two-track strategy: Islamizing society from below while, at the same time, trying to Islamize public institutions and policies from the top. They may have succeeded in the first track but have not fared well in the second.

Morocco

In Morocco, the monarchy managed to strike a delicate balance between the secular left and the religious forces by way of a constantly shifting game of repression and tolerance of one at a time, or both at once. Numerous Islamist organizations (more than twenty) were established, many of which with the approval of the state. However, most of them remain focused on charitable works in poor neighborhoods and recruit in schools and workplaces. By the late 1990s, some of them began gradually entering the political sphere, armed with a societal and political project that was very different from that of the traditional, secular opposition.

In the last two years of his life, King Hassan II enacted important institutional changes, allowed the opposition to form a government, and permitted, for the first time, a token Islamist representation in parliament, although not through a party of their own.[7] In 1998, the first openly Islamist PJD was admitted as a legal formation.

These changes came as a result of several factors, including strong domestic and international pressures for political liberalization, fears instilled by the violent Islamist rebellion in Algeria, and the need to co-opt the leftist opposition in preparation for the succession of Hassan's son to the throne. Such opposition may have become a serious problem to an inexperienced king if it remained on the outside. King Hassan's last-minute strategy of relative political inclusion worked. It neutralized the left by allowing it to lead the government and made it, thus, share the blame for people's economic hardship. However, one the most important challenges that the new king, Mohamed VI, had to worry about after taking over was the Islamist movement.

The Islamists sought to establish a faith-based social, economic, political, and cultural order but were divided on how to accomplish that. In the 2000s, the two main contenders to Islamist leadership have been the PJD and the unrecognized movement of al-`Adl wa al-Ihsan. Both reject political violence as a means. The first one is inspired by the Muslim Brotherhood and Wahhabi Salafism, recognizes the legitimacy of the monarch and his title of Commander of the Faithful, and accepts to work within the existing system in pursuit of change. The second one, whose leader combines both Sufism and Salafism, refuses to participate in the political process as long as the political order remains dominated by a king whose religious legitimacy is questioned. In spite of not being a legal party, al-`Adl wa al-Ihsan remains the most popular Islamist movement in Morocco. It attracts the sympathy of young and disaffected urban dwellers and has supporters among the poor, school and university students, and educated urban professionals in major cities.

In a stark contrast to his father, the new, young, and popular monarch began his rule with a competition with the Islamists in their traditional works of charity and fight against poverty and injustice—he became known as "the king of the poor." This partly explains why the Islamists (other than al-`Adl wa al-Ihsan) have, in recent years, sought to adapt to the changed circumstances. The discourse of groups like the PJD started focusing less on social, economic, and religious issues and more on the political institutions and processes they seek to change. However, not being able to make a dent in this area, they seem to have resigned themselves to working within the existing rules and to limiting their ambition to placing themselves in the existing system in way that can allow them to have some impact on public policy. In 2011 they succeeded in fulfilling that ambition by winning the most seats in parliament (107 out of 395) in the elections of November 25, which followed a constitutional reform a few months earlier that changed some of the institutional rules without undermining the preeminence of the monarch. In the end, the monarchy, under the new king, remains in control and in charge of the political institutions and their agendas. It managed to upstage the Islamists in their natural field of social works while at the same time relaxing somewhat the general political environment. Mohamed VI also made use of the divisive tactic of his father by agreeing to the legalization of two new Islamist parties, the Renaissance and Virtue Party (PRV), a breakaway movement from the PJD, and the Civilized Alternative Party.

Within the last decade, the Moroccan Islamists increased their pressure for change. They took advantage of the social and economic crisis and of the weakness of the leftist opposition and have tried to lead social protests. The bulk of the Islamist movement has used peaceful means to advance its goals, but a small number of violent radical groups have emerged and some of them have even conducted violent actions in recent years. These violent factions are often referred to as *jihadi Salafism*, which dates back to the early 1990s when an attack in Marrakesh hotel killed two Spanish tourists. These factions include organizations such as *al-Takfir wa al-Hijra* (Excommunication and Exile), Jamâ`at al-Sirat al-Mustaqîm (the Group of the True Path), al-`Jamâ`a al-Salafiya (the Salafi Group), and Ahl al-Sunna wa al-`Jamâ`a (People of the Sunna and of the Community).

On May 14, 2003, 45 people were killed and around 100 were injured by five suicide bomb attacks in Casablanca. The perpetrators were all Moroccans, and many of them were from the slums of Casablanca. The event constituted a real shock to the country and it was immediately feared that the tolerated Islamist parties and movements would be repressed and banned as a reprisal for the attack. However, even though in the aftermath of the attack thousands of Islamists were rounded up for questioning and many were jailed, tried, and given prison or death sentences, the PJD and other Islamist parties and organizations were not banned, but their public image was tarnished by the violence even though they were not directly responsible for it or condoned it.

Another effect of the May 2003 attack was the adoption of a new antiterrorism law that substantially curtails the freedom of expression and gives the state more power to pursue and persecute suspected radicals. This situation made Aboubakr Jamai, editor in chief of the Moroccan newsweekly *Le Journal Hebdomadaire*, to observe that "…the Moroccan government seems to have made the decision to restrict liberty in the name of security, perhaps in imitation of the United States after the September 11 attacks.… But these moves are a mistake. To fight terrorism, Morocco needs more democracy, not less" (Jamai 2003).

Years after this shocking event, the legal Islamist tendency (PJD) and the tolerated one (al-'Adl wa al-Ihsan) remained highly vibrant and active, each according to its own strategy, means, and limitations. However, both thrive in a highly restrictive political environment. The PJD has accepted the preeminence of the monarchy and seemed to limit its action to issues of social justice and development as well as some institutional reform, without questioning, though, the supremacy of the king's political and religious authority, even after taking over parliament and the office of the prime minister. As for al-'Adl wa al-Ihsan, it stands firm on not partaking in a system whose rules are set by the monarch and in the interest of the monarchy, but its social action and its political message remain very attractive for a large portion of the urban population that is increasingly disillusioned by the political establishment and by the powerlessness of representative institutions. This disillusionment is one of the reasons many have in the 1990s and 2000s rediscovered an alternative path, Sufism. In fact, Sufism has become so popular by the end of the first decade of the twenty-first century, that it is praised and espoused by all, including the monarch himself, the leader of al-'Adl wa al-Ihsan, and even the PJD leader, Benkirane, whose early political schooling was in Sufism. The significance of this development in Morocco, as well as in Algeria, is discussed below.

Tunisia

In a context of serious economic difficulties and unabating social unrest, interior minister Zine al-'Abidin Ben 'Ali overthrew President Bourguiba in November 1987. Seeking to swiftly reduce tensions and reconcile the government with most opposition groups, the new leader released hundreds of political prisoners, courted the exiled opposition, and promised political liberalization. The relative political liberalization that ensued allowed the Islamists to quickly turn into a visible and powerful political force after almost a decade of open challenge to President Bourguiba's rule. The Destourian Socialist Party was renamed the Democratic Constitutional Rally (RCD), and other political parties were recognized, except for the Islamist ones.

In the first free parliamentary elections of April 1989, the RCD won most seats in parliament and the Islamists, competing as independents, obtained 13 percent of all votes (even 30 percent in parts of the capital's outskirts). Realizing that the Islamists had become the second political force in country (the secular left had obtained only 3 percent of the vote), President Ben Ali tried to dampen their effect by making some concessions to them and by emphasizing his own religious background. However, after Algeria recognized in the same year several religious parties, Tunisia's Islamists increased their demand for a legal status. The ensuing tension culminated in an attack in May 1991 on the RCD office in Tunis, which killed one person. The state's reaction was swift and an all-out war against the Islamists began. Hundreds of Islamist militants were arrested and many fled the country.

From then on, except for a few tolerated small groups, all open political opposition was repressed and maintained under tight control. Fearing a contagion from the bloody war that was happening in neighboring Algeria in the 1990s, many people in Tunisia seemed to prefer this state of affairs rather than see an all-out Islamist rebellion take hold of their country. The RCD and the security services tightened their grip on the state and society as Tunisia regained stability and engaged in a comprehensive—and most successful in the region—structural adjustment program sponsored by the International Monetary Fund and the World Bank.

Because of tight security controls, an underground Islamist movement was not able to develop as happened in Algeria after the repression of 1992. However, there were a few violent acts attributed either to a homegrown neo-Salafi movement or to al-Qa`ida, such as the bomb attack in April 2002 against a synagogue in Djerba, which killed nineteen people and two shoot-outs between Islamist forces and the police in December 2006 and January 2007. It was suspected also that these actions may have been tied to Algeria's GSPC, which changed into al-Qa`ida in the Islamic Maghreb in 2006.

"Post-Islamism" and the Resurgence of Sufism and Political Islam

The preceding discussion on the rise and evolution of political Islam showed that both exclusion and inclusion have been pursued by different Maghrebi states. Exclusion was favored in Libya and Tunisia, while the inclusion of an accommodating Islamism happened in Algeria and Morocco. This might partly explain why the winds of the "Arab Spring" had moderate effects in Morocco and Algeria while in Tunisia and Libya they resulted in the overthrow of the incumbent regimes.

In Libya, the al-Sanusiya movement, which had inherited the newly independent state, found itself in the awkward position of pushing for a secular outlook for the state. As a result, it ended up antagonizing not only its own ranks and file and constituency but also the truly secular forces in the country. After the Sanusi monarch was overthrown in 1969, no other religious movement was allowed to organize and mobilize people for social and political action. In Tunisia, once the postindependence Islamist movement started making political claims and challenging the ruling elite, it was plainly stopped in its tracks, repressed, and outlawed. For these two countries, the Islamist opposition that manifested itself before 2011 was either in exile or deep underground. In both cases, this opposition was weak and constrained by domestic and international security conditions. It was, however, fully unleashed by popular upheavals of 2011. Once the political system opened up, the Islamist formations were by far the best organized in the new Tunisian political landscape and acquired a substantial presence in Libya's new political scene.

In Algeria and Morocco, after an initial rejection of grassroots political Islam, the two states opted for a strategy of accommodation and inclusion of the least threatening movements, with the hope that such a move would inhibit and even end the radical and violent urges of Islamism. In the particular case of Algeria, political Islam seems to have been tamed for now by strong state repression of its radical fringe and a successful strategy that induced and co-opted its moderate wing (MSP, Nahda, and Islah) to participate in electoral politics. It is safe to say that this policy succeeded in ending the mass rebellion led by the Islamists and in controlling political Islam by incorporating in the political process its nonviolent and less threatening expressions.

Beyond this divergence in the strategic responses of the four states, political Islam in North Africa exhibited the shared patterns discussed above. For one, Salafism, the ancestor of today's Islamism, was widely present in the national liberation struggle, and played a key role in it. That Salafism had two strands: one modern reformist and another conservative. Another commonality was that after independence, the Salafi current attempted to push for reforms while criticizing the postindependence state elite for its secularism and its embrace of Western values. A third common pattern was the fact that, up to the 1970s, most religious currents limited their focus to the religious, cultural, and social spheres. Their shift to political concerns thereafter occurred as a result of domestic factors (economic crisis, state manipulation and repression of opposition forces, injustice, rising Western cultural influence, and the hegemony of secular elites) and international events, mainly the successful overthrow of Iran's authoritarian monarchy by a popular movement led by a religious figure, Ayatollah Khomeini. Another common feature was that, almost immediately after independence, the state leaders used Islam in their own favor and in the plans they had for their respective societies.

By the late 1990s, an important change happened in several countries of the region in the relationship between political Islam on one hand and the state and society on the other. At the same time, a transformation also happened in the Islamist movement itself after its failed confrontation with the states. These changes have been noted by academics and practitioners who saw them both as a plain defeat and an end of uncompromising militant Islamism and as a tactical adaptation to new domestic and international realities.

Several scholars and practitioners of politics have wondered in the past two decades about the future of political Islam and about the best strategy to deal with it, especially its violent expression. Three alternatives seem to have been explored and practiced in North Africa as well as the Middle East:

1. the total exclusion of Islamism from the political arena, as happened in Tunisia, Libya, and Syria
2. neither inclusion nor exclusion of the Islamists, but tolerating their activities as long as they do not forcefully challenge the existing system, as in the case of Egypt's Muslim Brothers
3. the inclusion of nonviolent "moderate" Islamists who agree to work within the existing systems of governance, as has happened in Algeria and Morocco, Jordan, and the special case of Lebanon

As discussed above, in the North African experience three different state responses to Islamism were tried with varying results. In the cases of Algeria and Morocco there was a gradual shift from the first or second alternatives to the third one. In the cases of Libya and Tunisia, the first alternative was the only one pursued until the incumbent regimes were overthrown in 2011. After that, Political Islam became either central in Tunisia or only part of the governing institutions in Libya. The end result of this shift has been that political Islam is now part and parcel of the political landscape of these four countries. Two questions are prompted by this evolution: (a) how did this shift occur, and (b) how did it affect political Islam itself and the overall political dynamics in the these countries?

Post-Islamism in the Maghreb

In the debate of the last decade over the evolution of grassroots political Islam and of the states' response to it, the buzzword in academic parlance became "post-Islamism." This notion generated a lot of writing and acquired several meanings. In a 2005 article titled "What Is Post-Islamism," sociologist Asef Bayat averred,

> The particular way in which [post-Islamism] has been employed seems to have caused more confusion than clarity. For some (e.g., Gilles Kepel), post-lslamism describes the departure of Islamists from the *jihadi* and *Safafi* doctrines, while for others (such as Olivier Roy) it is perceived in terms of the "privatization" of Islamization (as opposed to Islamization of the state), where emphasis is placed on changes in how and where Islamization is carried out, rather than its content. Often used descriptively, post-Islamism has been presented and primarily perceived—including in my own work on Iran—as an empirical rather than an analytical category, representing a "particular era," or an "historical end." (Bayat 2005, 5)

It can be said that two meanings of post-Islamism have stood out so far, each being both empirical/descriptive and analytical. They are:

1. Prior to the "Arab Spring," post-Islamism referred to a political environment without the rebellious and challenging grassroots political Islam and to a return (or almost) to the pre-Islamism political order. Proponents of this definition pointed to what happened after militant Islamism ceased to exist as a significant sociopolitical phenomenon following its defeat in the confrontation with the state in the 1970s to 1990s period.
2. Post-Islamism is the tactical and discursive adaptation of grassroots political Islam whereby Islamism seeks accommodation with the existing political system, which it no longer wants to destroy. Proponents of this definition explain that this transformation happened after Islamism failed to achieve its key aims (overthrowing the existing regimes and establishing an Islamic state ruled by *Shari`ah* laws) and could not win in the frontal confrontation with both state and society.

Before the events of 2011, the first definition seemed to apply to the cases of Libya and Tunisia, where grassroots political Islam was almost entirely eradicated. However, in the wake of the "Arab Spring" an almost sudden and powerful resurgence of political Islam pointed to an almost totally new and unexpected direction: political Islam, which was in a dormant mode during the autocratic rules of Ben Ali and al-Qaddafi, is now at the forefront in Tunisia, Morocco, and Libya, but with less revolutionary fervor than in the previous decades.

Before and after the 2011 events, the second definition seemed to reflect more the situation in Algeria and Morocco. In these cases, and without a revolutionary mass rebellion similar to those of Libya and Tunisia, the state accommodated a "domesticated" brand of Islamism, while Islamism itself (or at least a big part of it) changed into an accommodating force that is willing to play by the existing rules.

In the final analysis, post-Islamism may include elements of the two definitions, but the second one appears to have acquired more credence as reflected in relevant scholarly writings such as those of Gilles Keppel, Oliver Roy, and Asef Bayat. For Bayat, post-Islamism is a conscious effort of "transcending Islamism in social, political, and intellectual domains... it represents an endeavor to fuse religiosity and rights, faith and freedom, Islam and liberty. It is an attempt to turn the underlying principles of Islamism on its head by emphasizing rights instead of duties, plurality in place of a singular authoritative voice, historicity rather than fixed scriptures, and the future instead of the past" (Bayat 2005, 5).

In the Maghreb, these post-Islamist trends and characteristics are apparent in the Justice and Development Party (Morocco), the Movement of Society of Peace and Islah (Algeria), al-Nahda (Tunisia), and the Justice and Construction Party (Libya). The PJD, al-Nahda, MSP, and Islah accepted to work with and within the existing political system, are not calling for the establishment of an Islamic state, and seem to leave their religious agenda and endeavors out of, and independently from, the political sphere. Al-Nahda was not even allowed to exist during the rule of Ben Ali in Tunisia, but when the political system opened up in 2011, it wanted a full change of regime. Since it dominates today Tunisia's transition institutions, it is working hard to fully dismantle the old regime and to establish a new one that it promises will adhere to the fundamentals of liberal democracy.

According to what Oliver Roy called the secularization of the public space in which religious actions develop (Roy 1999b, 13), after the totalitarian and dogmatic attitude was abandoned, the religious movements of Tunisia, Algeria, and Morocco have learned to live with limited religious-political ambitions and among a multitude of contenders for leadership in *Da'wa* actions and religious rituals. As for Libya, the Muslim Brotherhood's party, the Justice and Construction Party, seems for now to exhibit the same post-Islamist characteristics. However, the situation in Libya at the time of this writing was still unclear and murky, which did not allow for a firm determination of the nature of all Islamist forces in place.

In Morocco, post-Islamism may be seen in the fact that the PJD does not question the religious authority of the monarch and does not condemn Sufism as traditional Salafism used to do. In Algeria, Morocco, as well as Tunisia, in this "post-Islamist era," the Islamist parties have come to accept the "individualization of religious practices or their exercise inside closed communal spaces (brotherhoods)" (Roy 1999a). This has manifested itself in the resurgence of Sufist orders in which membership is on an individual basis rather than group solidarity or shared ideology. Beyond the resurgence of the Sufi brotherhood, many other developments seem to have taken away from the Islamists the monopoly over religiosity and social action. There has been a multiplication of independent *Da'wa* groups and of religious festivities often led by independent preachers. This may partly explain why, when political Islam seemed in relative decline before 2011, there was a growing "Islamization" of society.

The Sufi resurgence and the integration of Political Islam

As already stated above, Sufism has an old presence in the Maghreb. The main North African Sufi orders were born between the sixteenth and early twentieth centuries. Each is distinguished by a specific doctrine, organization (*Zawiya*), and rituals. In most cases, they stayed out of the political sphere and focused on spirituality and worship rituals. However, in some periods, circumstances have made them play a political role.

There are today many Sufi orders, such as the Boutchichiya, Tijaniya, Qadiriya, `Isawiya, Jazuliya, Shadhiliya, Darqawiya, Taybiya, Rahmaniya, `Alawiya, and Sanussiya. Each order gave birth to several *zawiyate* (schools) and many were linked by an ancestral spiritual leaders and/or saint.

Sufism has been the object of severe attacks by traditional Salafists, neo-Salafists, and grassroots Islamism. The reasons for these attacks are numerous, including the worshiping of saints and shrines, and passivity in the face of societal and political problems rather than reformist activism. During the colonial era in Algeria, Morocco, and Tunisia, "Islamic reformism spearheaded a consistent, and in each case amazingly successful, campaign against the Sufi brotherhoods. It was essentially a two-pronged attack: the brotherhoods were accused of introducing blameworthy innovations (*bid`a*) into Islam, and also of co-operating with the imperial power" (Brown 1964, 60).

In Morocco, "Salafi reformism coexisted with Sufi religious orders...under the overall supervision of the Alawi dynasty, which had played on both traditions since its emergence from maraboutic origins in 1666" (Henry 2007, 88). In 2002, King Mohamed VI appointed a young Sufi scholar (Ahmed Taoufiq from the Boutchichiya order) as Minister of Islamic Affairs and Habous. This move seemed to reflect both the acknowledgment of Sufism as a national heritage and the will to move official Islam away from doctrinal stiffness and toward some moderation (Pruzan-Jørgensen 2010). Also, in the case of Morocco, Salafi reformism did not entirely reject some aspects of Sufism and many Salafi leaders had some schooling in one Zawiya or another. The monarchy itself is said to have been established on a Sufi foundation. Sultan Sulayman (1760–1822) was a disciple of the Nasiriya *tariqa* (spiritual way) and welcomed the Tijaniya *tariqa* when it moved from Algeria to Fes in 1789 (Zeghal 2005, 43). A few years ago, King Mohammed VI celebrated the *Mawlid al-Nabawi* (birthday of Prophet Muhammad) in the shrine of Sidi al-Hadi Ben `Aissa in Meknes.

Today, Sufi orders know a vibrant life in Morocco partly encouraged by the monarchy as a way to combat political Islam and extremism, and also because some leaders of Salafi movements have themselves been more than keen to Sufism, including Abdesalam Yassin, the spiritual leader of `Adl wa al-Ihsan, which symbolizes the intertwining of political and social activism with spirituality, ethics, mysticism, and spiritual guidance. It is important to note, though, that spirituality and mysticism have been part of Yassin's discourse and practice since 1970s.

> By connecting mystical elements to Islamism, Abd al-Salam Yasin could aspire to transcend [the] hegemonic Salafi epistemology and reach out for the Sufi sensibilities of Moroccan masses.... While the re-appropriation of mystical elements certainly corresponded to his personal religious beliefs, it also allowed him to lay the foundations for a more comprehensive, uniting, and mobilizing approach to Islamism in Morocco. (Lauziere 2005, 244)

In Algeria, Sufism has also had a long history and similar characteristics. It was opposed by the Salafists and neo-Salafists and grassroots Islamism for the same reasons noted above. Also, the secular nationalists despised it for its pro-colonial attitude. Sufism experienced a deep decline after Algeria's independence from France as the governments' efforts to establish an "official Islam" had to cater to the reformist Salafist trend that dominated the Council of `Ulama'. As a result, the activities of Sufi orders diminished drastically, up until the 1980s when their resurgence started after the state leadership began facing the challenge of radical Salafism.

Nowadays, Sufism is thriving again in Algeria not only because of the state's change of heart toward it, but also because many people have been attracted to it lately in search of guidance and identity in times of turmoil and uncertainty—especially after the dark decade of the 1990s. As the government's approach changed, it became common for the president himself to visit a Sufi shrine and its spiritual leader, especially in times of crisis or during an electoral campaign. In 1991, the National Association of the Zawyas was created with the blessing of the state and in 2005, state radio and television stations were created just for Sufism with the hope that they would help move people away from radical Islamism and toward a religious practice that focuses on contemplation—rather than violence—*dhikr* (invocation), social action, and the betterment of oneself and society by peaceful means.

> To give the Sufi "zaouias" a more central role in society, they are encouraged to arrange marriages, help take care of orphans, teach the Quran and distribute charitable donations. Followers of Sufism focus on the rituals of "Dhikr" or "Hadra"—"invocation" or "remembrance"—which feature sermons, reciting the Quran, praising the Prophet Mohammed, requests for intercession and rhythmic invocations of Allah. (Al Arabiya 2009)

Furthermore, Sufism has been presented as the expression of Algerian identity because it was an indigenous religious tradition, as opposed to the Islamism inspired by the Middle East, that is, Wahhabism and neo-Salafism.

In Libya, the dominant Sufi order is that of Sanusiya, sanusi, which goes back to the 1840s. Exceptionally for a Sufi order in the region, this one inherited the rule over Libya from the colonizer, but that did not last, as discussed above. The Sanusiya, sanusi's activities were drastically curtailed by al-Qaddafi, who put forth his own version of Salafism. However, the order survived and was a source of opposition, albeit very restrained by the regime. In the wake of the fall of the regime of al-Qaddafi, Sufism, and more particularly Sufi shrines and mosques, became the target of destructive attacks by what were believed to be hardline Salafists who believe that the popular practice of visits to shrines and mosques with graves of saints to be un-Islamic. "One of Libya's highest-profile cultural clashes since the toppling of Colonel Qaddafi has been between followers of the mystical Sufi tradition and ultraconservative Salafis, who have formed a number of armed brigades. They reject as idolatrous many Sufi religious rituals" (Reuter 2012). In August 2012, several Sufi places were either vandalized or destroyed by armed groups.[8]

In Tunisia, Sufism has also a very long history. The Shadhiliya order, which gave birth to many other orders, was established in Tunis by Sidi Abu al-Hassan al-Shaddili. After his death in 1258, the Shadhiliya, which stressed the intellectual basis of Sufism, flourished in North Africa, from Egypt to Morocco.

Another important order in Tunisia is the Madaniya order,[9] whose founder, Muhammad ibn Khalifa al-Madani, is said to have been the disciple of Ahmad al-Alawi, the spiritual leader of the Darqawi order in Algeria, itself an offshoot of the Shadhiliya order. He created a Zawiya in 1920 in the Tunisian town of Ksibet al-Mediouni. Because of his support for colonial France and opposition to the neo-Destour party and to its political agenda, President Bourguiba imposed restrictions on his activities and caused his self-imposed seclusion and downfall.

The Sufi orders in Tunisia experienced the same fate as those in Algeria after independence, that is, their activities were drastically curtailed and their lands and buildings turned into state property. Many Sufis are said to have migrated out of the country after that.

Although the Sufi community is small in Tunisia today, its mystic tradition still permeates social and religious life, but that remains mostly limited to belief in spirits and visits to saint shrines and tombs for healing and guidance. Unlike the rulers of Algeria and Morocco, the Tunisian government has not felt the need to revitalize Sufism as a means to redirect the Islamist sentiment mostly because radical Islamism was crushed in the early 1990s.

As the above discussion indicates, Sufism is indeed gaining popularity in Algeria and Morocco, but not necessarily as a substitute for the political Islam these two countries have known in the past three decades. Rather, Sufism seems to serve as a complement, just as it has been reflected in the doctrine and actions of Abdeslam Yassin. However, the recent increase in the number of people attracted to it could also be an indication of dissatisfaction with both violent and nonviolent political Islam. The massive move away from violent political Islam—especially in Algeria—was caused by its failure to attain its aims, its horrible consequences on society and state repression. The relative disillusionment with nonviolent political Islam may have been caused also by its inability to deliver on its promises, even after Islamist parties joined parliaments and governments. Beyond these possible reasons, the attraction toward Sufism is also often personal whereby people find in it solace, guidance, and spiritual support in dealing with changing and challenging social and economic conditions.

One of the major consequences on the popular upheavals in the region against autocratic rulers was the rise to power of Islamist groups wherever none was previously allowed to reach that point or even to exist. This pertains to the cases of Tunisia, Egypt, and Libya.

In the Maghreb region, the most stunning rise to power was that of the previously banned al-Nahda party. Even though the Islamist tendency had nothing to do with the popular upheaval that began in December 2010 in the city of Sidi Bouzid, where a fruit stand vendor immolated himself, it, however, enjoyed fully the benefits of liberation from authoritarianism. Right after the fall of Ben Ali, Rachid Ghanouchi, the exiled leader of al-Nahda, led his newly legalized party to victory in the first free parliamentary elections. The party won 40 percent of the transition parliament seats and agreed to lead a coalition government that included seculars (the liberal Congress for the Republic and the left-of-center Ettakatol Party). Even though the party promised to live up to the democratic promises of the "Jasmine Revolution," many Tunisians fear that under an Islamist government, there will be a reversal in liberty and secular laws. Some of these fears were not necessarily inspired by al-Nahda itself but by a small but very active and vocal Salafist and international Islamist party, Hizb al-Tahrir (the Liberation Party), which was not allowed to become legal and partake in the elections due to its radical platform. Hizb al-Tahrir is an ultraconservative Islamist movement that advocates, among many other things, the establishment of the *khilafa* (caliphate).

In Libya, after the fall of al-Qaddafi—and even during the rebellion—Islamist groups of all kinds proliferated to a great extent. They range today from those espousing a pseudoliberal attitude to armed ultraconservative radicals. In the first free parliamentary elections on July 7, 2012, the Justice and Construction Party (Hizb al-A'dala wa al-Bina), which was created a few months earlier, won only 17 of 200 contested seats. Another Islamist group, the National Front Party (Hizb al-Jabha al-Wataniya), successor to the National Front for the Salvation of Libya that was a resistance movement against al-Gaddafi, won 3 seats only. The biggest winner in this election was the National Forces Alliance.[10] This pro-liberal democracy formation was led by Mahmoud Jibril, a US-educated political scientist. While

Libya is in the slow and convoluted process of creating adequate governing institutions, real power seems to reside in the streets, in the hands of armed groups, many of them of Islamist leaning. The latter seem, for now, more powerful than the transition officials and parliament members. It is feared that it is they who may determine the course Libya will follow in the coming years. Due to the historical circumstances of Libya before 2011, it was not possible then for nonviolent, pro-democracy Islamist parties to form and even maintain a latent life while the autocrat leader was in power. Therefore, if political Islam in Libya is to reach the post-Islamist stage, it may have to first go through the pains of building credibility, constituency, and power.

In the Moroccan case, where a movement of protest started in February 2011 calling for political and economic reforms, the Islamist party PJD, which managed to win the most seats in parliament, may owe its victory to four factors:

1. the very distinct nature of the PJD in contrast with the traditional secular opposition, especially, in the discursive area, organization, and leadership by example
2. the general dissatisfaction with the secular, leftist, opposition, which had its chance at running the government under the watchful eye of the king and failed to deliver on much of the promises it made when it was in the opposition
3. the social and economic conditions from which a great number of Moroccan suffer
4. the tailwinds of the "Arab Spring"

If the PJD is conceived as the illustration per se of the transformation of political Islam in Morocco from a radical, antiestablishment, and antimonarchical opposition to a regular political force that accepts to work from within the existing system, then the transition to post-Islamism can be said to have been accomplished. However, if the PJD is considered as only one element of the Islamist tendency in Morocco, then one has to account for the resistance of the remaining Islamist forces to following the same path the party of Benkirane followed.

Conclusion

Political Islam in North Africa, just as in the Middle East, came about as a response to internal and external conditions, challenges, and uncertainties. As shown in this essay, its expression was varied and so was its impact. In Libya and Tunisia, the independent expression of political Islam was repressed until the autocratic rule of Ben Ali and al-Qaddafi finally ended in 2011. After that, political Islam reclaimed its central place in the political landscape of the two countries—in Tunisia through the ballot box and in Libya through the control of the means of violence in a country that still lacks a powerful central authority. Before 2011, it was in Morocco and Algeria that political Islam found its freest expression, albeit within the constraints of the two systems. In these two countries, political Islam entered mainstream politics and may never retreat from it, unless another era of troubles would call for the eradication of all political expressions of religion, something that does not seem likely in the near or far future. The popular postulate that sees Islam as *din wa dawla* (religion and state) still serves as the backbone of the drive of political Islam for not only a perennial presence in the Maghrebi political systems but also for the realization of its self-prescribed comprehensive changes using a variety of means, be they reformed Islamism, that is, "post-Islamism," Sufism, or both.

The problem with the integration of political Islam in Morocco and Algeria today is that it may remain limited to a co-optation aiming to weaken the power of nonviolent religious parties and movements and to lessen the appeal of the violent groups. Since the Islamists have become in the past three decades very popular relays of social, economic, and political grievances, their integration in a system they no longer oppose, may create the ideological and representational vacuum that existed in the late 1970s and 1980s due to the decline of the secular left. This tendency is already visible in Algeria and Morocco, where there is an increasing loss of interest in the Islamist parties in parliament. These parties have become too embroiled in politics at the top at the expense of the interests of the constituencies. They have, in a way, become neutralized by a system with powerless representative institutions and by their own need to conform in order to remain relatively relevant in political systems where power to affect major public policy issues lie elsewhere. The 2011 constitutional amendments introduced by the Moroccan monarchy and approved by popular referendum did not change much in the institutional balance of power but gave some leeway to the PJD to affect public policy. In fact, its own political legitimacy—and that of Morocco's nonviolent political Islam in general—rests on delivering on key promises.

The street riots that developed spontaneously throughout Algeria and Tunisia in January 2011 reflected, in the first case, the failure of political Islam to take on the grievances of society, and, in the second case, the failure of systems that inhibited for too long both religious and secular voices of dissent. In an era of "post-Islamism" and resurgent Sufism, the question now is whether the Islamist parties that have made it to the top offices of political authority (Tunisia and Morocco) will succeed in living up to the high expectations placed in them, for if they, too, fail, as happened in Egypt in 2013, one wonders about who is going to take on those grievances and push, in a sustained way, for a meaningful and peaceful change in the Maghreb.

Notes

1. Islamism refers here to militant mobilization for political change, using Islam as both inspiration and instrument. The Islamists generally belong to the *Salafiya* tendency. While the bulk of the Islamists are nonviolent, some have been extremists who do not hesitate to use violence to reach their main aim, the establishment of an Islamist state. Radical Islamists have also been referred to as neo-Salafists to distinguish them from the dominant, nonviolent, strand of Salafism.
2. Salafism is generally understood as a Muslim current that calls for the strict reading of the scripture (Qur'an), following the model of *al-salaf al-salih* (righteous or pious ancestors), and the return to pristine Islam. One of the targets of its call for the return to the path of the righteous ancestors was Sufism due to its veneration of saints and indulgence in sacred rituals.
3. For more information on this, see Mohammed Harbi, *L'Islamisme dans tous ses états* (Algiers: Rahma Editions, 1991), 133.
4. *National Charter* (Algiers: Popular Printing Press of the Army, 1976), 22.
5. The Arabization of the school curriculum was instrumental in the development of the Islamist movement later. Because of a lack of enough Algerian teachers to staff the schools,

the government resorted to Middle Eastern teachers—mainly Egyptians—many of whom were linked to the Muslim Brothers. Furthermore, the Arabization process attracted many Algerian Islamists who used the schools to deliver their message and exert a strong influence on students.
6. The National Democratic Rally (RND) was created in 1995 to support incumbent president Liamine Zeroual in his bid for another term. It is headed by Prime Minister Ahmed Ouyahia.
7. Nine Islamists were elected to parliament in 1997 as members of a legal party, the Constitutional and Democratic Popular Movement (MPCD). In 1998, the MPCD changed its name to Party of Justice and Development (PJD) and thus became the first officially recognized Islamist party. The PJD managed in the 2007 parliamentary elections to garner a respectable place in parliament, outperforming the tradition leftist opposition represented by the Union of Socialist Forces (USFP). It became thus the second party in parliament, right behind Istiqlal. In 2011, it became the first.
8. It was reported that the destruction affected the Islamic Center of Sheik Abdus Salam al-Asmar in Zlitan, the mosque of Sidi Sha`ab in Tripoli, and the shrine of Sidi Ahmed Zaroug in Misurata. Similar attacks against Sufi shrines took place in the same month in Mali. The perpetrators were armed Islamist groups that were said to have benefitted from large smuggling of weapons from Libya during and after the popular rebellion.
9. For more on the Madaniyya *tariqa*, see its official website at http://www.madaniyya.com.
10. The NFA is made up of 58 political organizations, 236 NGOs, and close to 300 independents.

References

Addi, Lahouari, 2009. "Islam Re-Observed: Sanctity, Salafism and Islamism." *Journal of North African Studies* 12, nos. 3/4: 331–345.

Al Arabiya News Channel, 2009. "Algeria Fights Insurgency with Sufism." July 8. Available at: http://www.alarabiya.net/articles/2009/07/08/78165.html. Accessed June 7, 2010

Asef Bayat, 2005. "What-Is-Post-Islamism?" *ISIM Review*, 16, Autumn. Available at: http://www.nuansa.nl/uploads/ee/3c/ee3c13c38afebf47c6a68ed360afed5f/What-is-post-islamism.pdf. Accessed April 2, 2010.

Brown, Leon Carl, 1964. "The Islamic Reformist Movement in North Africa." *The Journal of Modern African Studies* 2, no. 1: 55–63.

Burgat, François, 1988. "L'Algérie: de la laicité islamique à l'islamisme." *Maghreb/Machrek* 121.

El-Kikhia, Mansour O., 1997. *Libya's Qaddafi: The Politics of Contradiction.* Gainesville, FL: University Press of Florida.

Frégosi, François, 1995. "Les rapports entre l'Islam et l'état en Algérie et en Tunisie: de leur revalorisation à leur contestation." *Annuaire de l'Afrique du Nord* 34: 103–123.

Henry, Clement M., 2007. "The Dialectics of Political Islam in North Africa." *Middle East Policy*, XIV (winter): 4.

Hermassi, Elbaki, 1972. *Leadership and National Development in North Africa: A Comparative Study.* Berkeley: University of California Press.

Jamai, Aboubakr, 2003. "Morocco's Choice: Openness or Terror." *New York Times*, Op. Ed., May 31. Available at: www.nytimes.com. Accessed June 5, 2003.

Joffe, George, 1995. "Qadhafi's Islam in Local Historical Perspective," in Dirk Vandewalle, ed., *Qadhafi's Libya 1969 to 1994.* New York: St Martin's Press, 139–156.

Lauziere, Henry, 2005. "Post-Islamism and the Religious Discourse of Abd al-Salam Yasin." *International Journal of Middle East Studies* 32 (May): 2.
Pruzan-Jørgensen, Julie E., 2010. "The Islamist Movement in Morocco: Main Actors and Regime Responses." *Diis Report* 2010: 5. Copenhagen: Danish Institute for International Studies.
Reuter, "Libyan Islamists Raze Sufi Sites in Bold Attacks." *New York Times*, August 25, 2012. Available at: www.nytimes.com. Accessed August 25, 2012.
Roy, Olivier, 1999a. "Pourquoi le 'post-islamisme'?" *Revue du Monde Musulman et de la Méditerranée*, nos. 85–86: 9–10. Available at: http://www.persee.fr/web/revues/home/prescript/article/remmm_0997-1327_1999_num_85_1_2633. Accessed December 29, 2010.
Olivier Roy, 1999b. "Le post-islamisme." *Revue du monde musulman et de la Méditerranée*, nos. 85–86: 11–30. Available at: http://www.persee.fr/web/revues/home/prescript/article/remmm_0997-1327_1999_num_85_1_2634. Accessed December 29, 2010.
Simons, Marlise, 1998. "Morocco Finds Fundamentalism Benign but Scary." *New York Times*, April 9.
Stora, Benjamin, 1991. *La gangrène et l'oubli, la mémoire de la guerre d'Algérie*. Paris: La Découverte.
Takeyh, Ray, 2000. "Qadhafi's Libya and the Prospect of Islamic Succession." *Middle East Policy*, vol. VII, no. 2. Available at: http://www.cfr.org/world/qadhafis-libya-prospect-islamic-succession/p7437. Accessed March 7, 2006.
Zeghal, Malika, 2005. *Les Islamistes marocain: le defi à la monarchie*. Paris: La Decouverte.

Bibliography

Allani, Alaya, 2009. "The Islamists in Tunisia between Confrontation and Participation: 1980–2008." *Journal of North African Studies* 14, no. 2: 257–272.
Brown, Jack, "Algeria's Midwinter Uproar." *Middle East Research and Information Project* (MERIP), January 20, 2011. Available at: http://www.merip.org/mero/mero012011. Accessed February 10, 2011.
Burgat, Francois, 1997. *The Islamic Movement in North Africa*. Center for Middle Eastern Studies, Austin: University of Texas Press.
Green, Arnold H., 1976. "Political Attitudes and Activities of the Ulama in the Liberal Age: Tunisia as an Exceptional." *International Journal of Middle East Studies* 7, no. 2: 209–241.
Kepel, Gilles, 2000. *Jihad: expansion et déclin de l'islamisme*. Paris: Gallimard.
Kirkpatrick, David D., 2012. "Libya Officials Seem Helpless as Sufi Shrines Are Vandalized." *New York Times*, August 28.
Lowe, Christian, and Lamine Chikhi, 2012. "Algeria Ruling Party Snubs Arab Spring to Win Election." *Reuters*, May 11.
Heisler, Ryan, 2009. "The Secrets and History of the Madaniyya Sufi of Ksibet al-Mediouni, Tunisia." *ISP Collection*. Paper 655. Available at: http://digitalcollections.sit.edu/isp_collection/655. Accessed January 5, 2011.
Khemissi, Hamidi, Ricardo René Larémont, and Taybi Taj Eddine, 2012. "Sufism, Salafism and State Policy towards Religion in Algeria: A Survey of Algerian Youth." *The Journal of North African Studies* 17, no. 3: 553.
Layachi, Azzedine, 2011. "Meanwhile in the Maghreb: Have Algeria and Morocco Avoided North Africa's Unrest?" *Foreign Affairs*, March 31. Available at: www.foreignaffairs.com. Accessed July 30, 2012.

Layachi, Azzedine, 2011. "Algeria's Rebellion by Installments." *Middle East Research and Information Project* (MERIP), March 12. Available at: http://www.merip.org/mero/mero031211. Accessed July 30, 2012

Lee, Robert D., 2008. "Tunisian Intellectuals: Responses to Islamism." *Journal of North African Studies* 13, no. 2: 157–173.

Magnuson, Douglas K., 1991. "Islamic Reform in Contemporary Tunisia: Unity and Diversity." In I. William Zartman, ed. *Tunisia: The Political Economy of Reform*, 169–192. Boulder, CO: Lynne Rienner.

Perkins, Kenneth J., 1986. *Tunisia: Crossroads of the Islamic and European Worlds*. Boulder, CO: Westview Press.

Silverstein, Paul, "Weighing Morocco's New Constitution." *MERIP*, July 5, 2011. Available at: http://www.merip.org/mero/mero070511. Accessed July 27, 2011.

Schwedler, Jillian, 2004. "Is Moderation a Myth? Islamist Parties in Comparative Perspective." Paper prepared for the "Roots of Radicalism" conference at Yale University, May 7–9.

Zghal, Abdelkader, 1991. "The New Strategy of the Movement of the Islamic Way: Manipulation or Expression of Political Culture?" In I. William Zartman, ed., *Tunisia: The Political Economy of Reform*, 205–217. Boulder, CO: Lynne Rienner.

CHAPTER 25

ISLAM AND POLITICS IN SUB-SAHARAN AFRICA

LEONARDO A. VILLALÓN

The Setting: The Muslim Mosaic South of the Sahara

RELIABLE numbers are hard to come by, but a good guess might place the Muslim population of sub-Saharan Africa somewhere in the range of 30–40 percent.[1] As Table 25.1 below indicates, fully thirty-two of the forty-eight countries in the region have significant Muslim populations, ranging widely from 10 to 100 percent, and another ten have smaller but often important Muslim communities.[2]

Geographically, the regions of concentrated Muslim presence reflect the early historical expansion of the religion on the continent (Robinson 2004; Levtzion and Pouwells 2000). Stretching south across the Sahara, the vast savannah zone known as the Sahel is overwhelmingly Muslim until it reaches the forest belt of west and central Africa. Moving south from Egypt through the Nile valley, and across from the Arabian Peninsula, the Horn of Africa represents a second major zone of Muslim importance. And via contact with seafaring traders in the Indian Ocean, Islam came to dominate in what is now known as the Swahili coast, stretching as far south as Mozambique, and touching the island of Madagascar. From these areas, the religion spread gradually over the centuries, moving south and west into more tropical zones, following commerce and migration. This expansion continues today through various means; there are, for example, intriguing indications that Islam is drawing converts in zones of recent turmoil, including Rwanda following the 1994 genocide, and the eastern regions of the Democratic Republic of Congo.

Islam on the continent has been overwhelmingly Sunni, with the *Maliki* legal school dominating throughout the northwestern regions of the continent, and the *Shafi'i* school in the east.[3] Across the continent, Sufi forms of Islam have been key in the spread of the religion, and central to much of religious and social life—although there has been significant variation in what this has meant in practice (Brenner 2000; Piga 2006). Generally the expansion of Islam in Africa was accomplished with a high degree of adaptation to local cultures and societies. Thus Robinson (2004) writes of simultaneous processes of "Islamization of Africa" and of "Africanization of

Table 25.1 Sub-Saharan African Countries by Estimated Muslim Populations

Predominantly Muslim countries (10) 85–100 percent Muslim	Comoros, Djibouti, Gambia, Guinea-Conakry, Mali, Mauritania, Niger, Senegal, Somalia, Sudan
Religiously divided countries (9) 30–70 percent Muslim	Burkina Faso, Chad, Côte d'Ivoire, Eritrea, Ethiopia, Guinea-Bissau, Nigeria, Sierra Leone, Tanzania
Significant Muslim minorities (13) 10–20 percent Muslim	Benin, Cameroon, Central African Republic, Ghana, Kenya, Liberia, Madagascar, Malawi, Mauritius, Mozambique, South Sudan, Togo, Uganda
Small Muslim minorities (10) 1–10 percent Muslim	Botswana, Burundi, Democratic Republic of Congo, Gabon,* Lesotho, Republic of Congo (Brazzaville), Rwanda, Sao Tome and Principe, South Africa, Zambia

Source: author's compilation from diverse sources and estimates.
*Primarily noncitizen residents, mostly West Africans.

Islam." This fact, however, has also fed long internal debates on religious practice and persistent efforts at reform. Thus in West Africa themes of the reformist jihads of the eighteenth and nineteenth century are echoed in the critiques of Sufi practices by contemporary reformists, variously known locally as "Wahhabis," "Salafis," or simply "Sunnites" (Loimeier 1997, 2003; Sani Umar 1993; Miles 2007). Some scholars have labeled this dynamic tension a struggle between "African Islam" and "Islam in Africa" (Westerlund and Rosander 1997).

The rapid European conquest of Africa in the late nineteenth century drew colonial boundaries with little regard to social realities, and within less than a century these were to be inherited as the permanent borders of independent states. The result was a set of countries with a highly varied mosaic of languages, ethnicities, and religions. Consequently, Muslims in sub-Saharan Africa today live in strikingly different political and demographic contexts, resulting in very diverse patterns of religious roles in African political life.

The parameters of the role of Islam in politics in any given country south of the Sahara are thus shaped by several broad characteristics. These would include demographics (the relative size of the Muslim population); the nature of the state (including both the colonial legacy and the subsequent historical transformation in the postcolonial period); and the religious landscape (as shaped by both dominant domestic religious actors and increasingly transnational religious influences). Given the sheer number of countries and their diversity, I cannot in what follows describe the specific dynamics of individual cases. I will, instead, describe some broad African patterns that result from variations in these characteristics, with references to some key cases.

THE ARENA: POSTCOLONIAL STATES AND MUSLIM SOCIETIES

The drawing of the colonial map over the broad zones of historical Muslim presence has meant that contemporary Muslims in Africa find themselves in very diverse demographic situations, with important consequences for the patterns of religion and politics. At the risk of excessive simplification, we can identify some central dynamics in different contexts.

In the countries of clear and strong Muslim dominance, debates about religion and politics have tended to center on the question "What impact—if any—should the fact that we are overwhelmingly Muslim have on our political system?" that is, "Does the fact of being a Muslim country mean that the political system should reflect Islam, and if so how?" This has been most notably the case in the francophone countries of the Sahel.[4] In those countries, with the exception of Mauritania, which is effectively 100 percent Muslim and was set up as an "Islamic Republic" at independence, the presence of Christian minorities has meant that the dominant answer to that question has historically incorporated a version of secularism, reinforced by a consistent discourse insisting on recognizing religious pluralism.

In the countries we might label demographically "divided," where Muslims may represent between 30 and 70 percent of the populations, the major political dynamics of religion tend to center on the competition for relative access to power for the different religious communities. Given the demographic uncertainties that characterize the continent, much debate actually focuses on competing claims concerning the actual size of religious communities. In countries such as Ethiopia or Tanzania, for example, there are widely varying claims of the relative importance of the Muslim population.

There are also significant variations in terms of whether such religious divisions become politically salient, a fact that points to the centrality of politics—and not religion per se—in defining these relations. Thus in the divided country of Sudan before partition in 2011, as well as in neighboring Chad, for example, much of postindependence history has been a conflict over Muslim control of the state. In a somewhat different pattern, Nigeria (by far the largest country on the continent with an estimated population of some 160 million) has also been marked by a rivalry between the Muslim north and primarily non-Muslim south. In most other divided cases, however, the most striking dynamic has been the relatively peaceful nature of interreligious relations and their relative lack of importance as political cleavages (Sanneh 1997). This is the case in such diverse countries as Ethiopia and Eritrea in the Horn of Africa, or Burkina Faso and Sierra Leone in West Africa. It merits noting, however, that contact and rivalry as both major world religions seek to expand, primarily at the expense of historical African religious traditions, as well as the new liberalized political contexts (which we shall discuss below), seem to be producing increased tensions in various places (Becker 2008).

In the large number of countries with Muslim minorities of various sizes, to the extent that religion has had any significant political impact at all, it has been primarily focused on efforts to ensure minority religious rights, often via the pursuit of specific legal or constitutional provisions granting Muslims autonomy in such areas as family law. This is the case in a number of countries with significant Muslim minorities, such as Kenya, Uganda, or Benin, as well as in the case of the very small Muslim community of South Africa (Hashim 2005; Twaddle 2003; Brégand 2007; Tayob 1999).

Beyond the demographic issue, the most important factor shaping the political role of Islam in Africa has been the state context. It is thus useful to consider briefly the nature and trajectory of African states as these have defined the possibilities for religion to assume a political role. With very few and only partial exceptions, African countries today are the direct heirs to a colonial legacy.[5] In addition, their accession to independence was largely driven by transformations in the international system, and that international context has continued to shape the possibilities for African statehood.

The young leaders of African independence movements in the late 1950s and early 1960s came overwhelmingly from the small elite who had received a European education, and they espoused nationalist ideologies centered on the colonial territories. Given the realities of African social pluralism and the strong centripetal forces that marked countries from the moment of independence, they placed strong emphases on policies of "nation-building," and had little tolerance for movements based on ethnic or religious identities. Islam, therefore, was most often fairly marginal to the independence movements. Thus with the exception of Mauritania noted above, set up as an "Islamic Republic" by the French but intended only to reflect a cultural reality and not a political agenda, secular states were the norm everywhere.

There was also, of course, variation, and the distinction between the French and the British colonies remains highly salient in Muslim Africa. However imperfectly applied, the French policy of "assimilation" produced a political elite deeply rooted in a French education, and strongly committed to French notions of *laïcité*, or secularism, with an enduring impact on understandings of constitutionalism and politics more broadly. By contrast, British "indirect rule" and the reinforcement of local authorities and chiefs, and in Muslim zones such as northern Nigeria a careful policy of shielding religion from outside influence, produced a much greater willingness to accommodate religious demands in law and politics.

Strikingly, however, across the continent the optimistic moment of independence and the promise of liberation through popular democratic systems was swept aside very quickly by the emergence of authoritarian regimes of various sorts. This phenomenon, reinforced by the Cold War context and the search by the superpowers for proxy regimes, resulted in military, single-party, or personalized patrimonial political systems in virtually every country. With very limited exceptions, the period from the mid-/late 1960s to 1990 was a time of authoritarian rule in Africa.[6]

The impact of this authoritarian landscape on the possibility for a political role for religion was mediated by dual impulses on the part of the state. On the one hand, the core imperative for African regimes was to maintain control, and hence they had little tolerance for alternative sources of authority, and allowed little space for religious action in the political sphere. On the other hand, there was the constant temptation to attempt to capture or claim religious forces in an effort to legitimize and lend support to regimes with little credibility. This second logic increased in importance in the late 1970s and 1980s, as economic crises and declining legitimacy in the face of the unfilled promises of independence put regimes on the defensive. An extreme example of this dynamic is that of Sudan under the military autocrat Jaafar Nimeiri, where the imposition of *Shariʿah* in 1983, in a deeply divided country, can be understood as a desperate (and ultimately unsuccessful) effort to legitimize the regime in the eyes of the Muslim majority at the expense of the large non-Muslim population.

A common response to these two contradictory impulses was the effort by states to create inclusive and official Muslim organizations that could be domesticated by state sponsorship while also, it was hoped, buying sympathy by such a demonstration of state solicitude toward Muslims. Thus in both Muslim majority and minority contexts, and in both francophone and anglophone countries, such structures were created in the 1970s; the Malian Association for the Unity and Progress of Islam (AMUPI), or the Islamic Association of Niger (AIN) in the Francophone Sahel, and the Supreme Council of Tanzanian Muslims (BAKWATA) or the Supreme Council of Kenyan Muslims (SUPKEM) in East Africa, are key examples (Constantin 1995; Villalón 2010). The important case of Senegal, it merits noting, was long considered exceptional precisely for having found a sociopolitical balance to these competing impulses via a system of symbiotic relations built on the strong collaboration of

Sufi leaders with an officially secular and quasidemocratic state—a system that was largely inherited from the colonial period (Villalón 1995).

The "precarious balance" between state and society in Africa that some political scientists described in the 1980s was to become even more fragile and difficult with deteriorating social and economic conditions on the continent (Rothchild and Chazan 1988). In Muslim Africa, social change in the late 1970s and 1980s was to lead to a seeming "revival" or "resurgence" of religion, first in private life, but quickly taking on implications for public and political life (Brenner 1993; Masquelier 2009). Under the influence of the Iranian revolution, with the increased presence and resources of the Arab Gulf states and Saudi Arabia, and other means of greater contact with the broader Muslim world (Hunwick 1997), we began to see some cases of increased Muslim political activity. These both fed on and contributed to increasing internal debates about Islam, translated in many cases as increased tensions between Sufis and reformists. Thus such movements as the Nigerian "Izala" (Jama`t Izalat al Bid`a wa Iqamat as Sunna; Society for Removal of Innovation and Reestablishment of the Sunna, founded in 1978), perhaps the largest reformist movement in Africa, were born in this context (Sani Umar 1993; Kane 2003).

The political, economic, and social situation of Africa was, almost universally, to continue to decline throughout the 1980s, and by the end of the decade persistent African crises had resulted in the extreme fragility of political systems across the continent. Facilitated by the international transformations marked by the collapse of the east bloc and the end of the Cold War, the examples of popular uprisings in a few countries quickly spread, and as the "third wave" of demands for democratization swept the continent, the political contexts of Africa were profoundly transformed, with equally profound consequences for the potential political role of Islam.

Transformation: Islam in the Public Sphere in the Era of Liberalized Politics

In the early 1990s, then, African states found themselves at a critical juncture, facing the need to reconfigure political systems that were no longer functional, with the looming threat of disorder and collapse as the alternative (Villalón and Huxtable 1998). In sharp contrast with much of the Muslim world—and most strikingly with the Arab states—the vast majority of sub-Saharan countries embraced "democratization" as the way forward. Given the weakened situation of many states on the continent, and hence their inability to control social forces that were unleashed in the process, there were quickly significant variations in the consequences of this democratic turn on the continent. In the most tragic of cases we saw situations of complete state failure or collapse; the 100 percent Muslim country of Somalia represents the most important of those for our purposes. But in many others we have seen a real liberalization of politics, even if full and substantive democracy has proven an elusive goal for many. It merits emphasizing, in any case, that virtually everywhere on the African continent, regimes in the 1990s and the 2000s were far more liberal than those in most of the Arab world, resulting in a very different set of dynamics for Islam and politics. Most notably Senegal, as well as Mali from 1992 until the tragic collapse of the regime in March 2012, presented rare examples of functioning Muslim democracies.[7]

Islam and politics, of course, influence each other, and it is thus important to consider not only how religion has shaped politics, but also how these transformations in the African political landscape have affected religion. Once again, there is much variety in terms of what liberalization or democratization has meant for the political role of Islam, but also some broad similarities. In a major break from the period of authoritarian and corporatist regimes, the era of liberalization produced a veritable boom in voluntary social associations on the continent. These include the many associations that have been celebrated as part of "civil society," and they have also included many and varied religious associations. The flourishing of what we might call a "religious civil society" in many cases thus led naturally to a heightened political role for Islam (Cruise O'Brien 2003; Holder 2009). This religious assertion has been often interpreted (both domestically and by outside observers) as a "backlash" or challenge to liberalization, but I would argue that in fact the increased political role for Islam should be seen as the logical (and often even healthy) consequence of liberalization. The paradox of democratization is that it empowers groups to speak and make their case, even if they wish to challenge much of what others claim to support in the name of democracy. The challenge of democratization is not to suppress such differences, but to find procedures for reconciling them.

Thus in various African cases this has led to some very important and fundamental debates about the meaning of democracy in a given religious context. In ways analogous to debates on legalizing gay marriage in the United States or parts of Europe, the fundamental debate has been about whether "democracy" demands a specific answer to such issues, or whether it prescribes that the answer should depend on what most citizens would like. This discussion leads naturally to a questioning of the relationship between democracy and secularism, and the appropriate boundaries for religion in a constitutional order (An-Naim 2006). The debates about these issues have been intense in various places, and religious actors have at times been vociferously involved. What we have not seen, however, is any serious effort by Muslim (or other) religious actors in Africa to impose an answer to this question by capturing the state.

In addition to these core debates, political liberalization in Muslim Africa has produced several other effects. Breaking the monopoly of official state Islamic organizations, for example, has in some real senses resulted in a "democratization" of religion, with new claimants to religious legitimacy emerging to challenge established authorities. In virtually every Muslim community on the continent, then, the decades since the 1990s have been marked by increased and often intense disputes about who has the authority to speak in the name of Islam. In many cases this has taken the form of increased tensions between reformers (Salafists, Wahhabis, and others) and practitioners of the historical popular practices of religion, often Sufi in form or inspiration. In cases as diverse as Niger, Ethiopia, and Mozambique, these dynamics have been largely promoted by merchant communities and new economic elites (Meunier 1997; Østebø 2009; Bonate 2009). These religious debates themselves are shaped by local contexts, however, and thus transnational movements such as Salafism are themselves often "localized" in the process (Østebø 2008).

The new possibilities for claiming religious authority has also had the effect of empowering new social categories. Most significantly, perhaps, the liberalized contexts have given new voice to women, and Muslim women's movements of varying religious and political positions have emerged as significant actors in diverse settings (Alidou 2005; Augis 2005; Badran 2011). Given the increased social prestige associated with "modern" religious knowledge, particularly in settings where strong elite commitment to secularism had previously devalued religious training, people whose education had been primarily Arabic based (referred to as *arabisants* in the francophone countries) found themselves increasingly recognized and called on to comment on public affairs. This phenomenon is having in turn a significant impact on education, and there has been in many countries a significant expansion in religious as well as Arabic language education in both state and private schooling (Brenner 2001; Galilou 2002; Villalón 2012).

These general dynamics have varied significantly in different contexts, and the specific pattern of such transformations in any given case has shaped the resulting politicization of Islam in that country. Although we cannot do justice to the full range of such situations, it may be instructive to comment on a few important cases.

In the overwhelmingly (90 percent plus) Muslim countries of the Francophone Sahel—namely Mali, Niger, and Senegal—the democratic turn was very much led by a secular elite, with a conception of democracy rooted in the European experience and incorporating French notions of *laïcité*, prescribing a particularly strict distancing of the religious from the political (Villalón 2010). For religious groups the French term had strongly negative connotations, and in all three countries they thus initiated challenges to using it in the new constitutions. In Niger, in fact, it was ultimately replaced in the constitution by a statement about the "nonconfessional nature" of the state, although the term *laïc* remains in common usage to describe it. Gradually, however, the debate moved from whether there should be *un état laic* to what *laïcité* actually means. Almost universally, political actors have distanced themselves from secularism in the French mode to adopt something closer to an American understanding of secularism: freedom to freely practice religion includes the need for the state to make space for religious practice.

Liberalization in the Sahel also produced a rapid proliferation of new religious voices. In Mali and Niger the collapse of the old single official Muslim associations mentioned above led to veritable explosion of new associations, and a somewhat analogous process resulted from the declining authority of Sufi elites in Senegal. Brief efforts at founding religious parties by some Muslim groups were quickly aborted, but almost immediately religious voices began to protest that the "democratic" systems being proposed did not reflect the Muslim majority's views, and some began to question whether democracy was even desirable. In each country there were early clashes between religious and secular actors, some on symbolic issues (beauty pageants and the like), but others on more substantial ones—most centrally family law. Strikingly, however, the fact that democratization gave religious actors a voice they had not previously had was not lost on them, and they quickly moved from protests that democracy was not compatible with Islam to arguing instead that democracy in Muslim societies should reflect Muslim values and interests. In the cases of Mali and Niger this shift was particularly apparent in the debates about family law (Villalón 1996; Soares 2009). In both cases, French-inspired "family codes" that civil society activists insisted were central to democratization processes were stalled as religious groups argued—in the name of democracy—that family law should be publicly debated and reflect popular will.

In the process, the democratic debate moved from what seemed a two-sided struggle between "secular" and "Islamic" actors to a much more fluid and open debate about what the content of democracy should be in a Muslim society. And this included an internal debate among Muslims about what—in fact—was the "correct" position of Islam on any given issue. Should polygamy be banned? Is the death penalty acceptable or required? These and similar questions became not just subjects for contention between secularist and religious groups, but also internal debates within Muslim society. Democracy facilitated these debates, and hence was largely embraced by Muslim actors in these countries. Unsurprisingly, then, opinion polls have found that African Muslims are no less—and frequently more—supportive of democracy than non-Muslim Africans (Bratton 2003).

In many religiously divided countries, liberalization has produced intensified debates about the communal rights of Muslims, often inscribed in constitutional issues. Such dynamics have been particularly pronounced in Kenya and Tanzania, home to the most significant populations of Swahili-speaking Muslims, important minorities in each (although there are occasional Muslim claims to be a majority in Tanzania).

Muslims probably represent approximately 10 percent of the population of Kenya. At independence in 1963, there were provisions for special legal status for Muslims in the constitution, inherited from special colonial provisions that had been made and maintained as part of a deal with the Sultan of Zanzibar. In the single-party period that was to last through the 1980s, however, there were various state efforts to remove those provisions and to standardize family law across the country and much of Muslim politics were an effort to resist this. Thus the 1972 "succession act" eliminated special status for Muslim inheritance, and became a major point of contention, though it was never fully implemented.

As elsewhere, the 1990s saw a tense sociopolitical climate rocked by prodemocracy activism in Kenya. In this context, SUPKEM, which had been the sole officially recognized Muslim association since 1979, along with many other new Muslim civil society groups, were increasingly politicized, and agitated in defense of the interests of Kenya's Muslim minority (Oded 2000). In particular, Muslim groups were active participants in the ongoing debates on a new constitution for Kenya over the course of the 2000s. When a first draft was released in 2002, it in fact provided for Muslim *Kadhi* courts to deal with personal law issues. The ensuing controversy furthered an open politicization of Muslim-Christian tensions (Hashim 2005). The issue remained a point of contention in the subsequent rocky history of Kenya's efforts at democratization, marked by the rejection of the draft constitution in the referendum of 2005, and by an unprecedented wave of violence after the strongly contested elections in 2007. In the complex politics of building a coalition in support of the constitution, the Kadhi courts were ultimately included in the version approved in 2010, but the issue remains highly controversial. Among the many political tensions that mark Kenya are religious politics centered on Muslim efforts to maintain their special status and Christian efforts to resist this. It is clear that liberalization has brought these issues to the forefront, and that democratization must meet the challenge of balancing these competing claims.

In the United Republic of Tanzania, similar debates concerning the role of *Kadhi* courts for Muslims have centered on whether they should be instituted on the divided mainland, paralleling those that exist on 99 percent Muslim Zanzibar. It has also paralleled Kenya in an ongoing debate on family law and special constitutional provisions for religious communities (Hashim 2005). This has been complicated by—and contributed to—rising tensions between Muslims and non-Muslims, in part due to competing claims about who constitutes the majority.

Despite the fact that the successor to Tanzania's founding father president, Julius Nyerere, was the Muslim Ali Mwinyi (president from 1985 to 1995), Muslims in the country have expressed a growing sense of marginalization (Mbogoni 2004; Loimeier 2007). In February 1998, an unprecedented incident in which four Muslims were killed by state police sparked increasing tensions. Further complicating the situation is the fact that liberalization in the 1990s sparked a proliferation of religious voices even within the Muslim community, and resulted in rising tensions as BAKWATA—closely tied to the ruling single party until 1994—was challenged by Islamic reformist groups.

Religious tensions have thus been one complication of the democratic process in both countries, but they have by no means defined that effort. The challenge for both is to find means of balancing the concerns of separate religious communities while constructing a system that could be characterized as democratic. And they are by no means unique in Africa; there are similar challenges in defining legal and constitutional provisions for Muslim communities in the context of liberalization in various other countries, including Burkina, Benin, Ghana, and the unique and particularly interesting case of South Africa.

Perhaps the most interesting, and certainly among the more important, African experiments with political Islam in liberalized contexts are presented by twelve Muslim majority states in the northern region of the Federal Republic of Nigeria. These may represent the most significant case in the world of *Shari'ah* adoption as part of a process of electoral democratization. Nigeria, Africa's most populous country, has a federal political system, constructed out of a long history of ethnoregional tensions, the seeds of which were sown in different British colonial policies and the incomplete merger of the north and south prior to independence. The tensions that marked the country at birth gradually took on a more religious coloration starting in the 1970s. In the late 1980s and early 1990s, the military ruler Ibrahim Babangida, maneuvering to stay in power, took a number of steps that politicized religion further, such as joining the Organization of the Islamic Conference (OIC) in 1986.

Following a failed effort at transition to democracy, a particularly repressive military regime under General Sani Abacha was to rule from 1993 to 1998, leaving little room for religious organizations in politics. Unsurprisingly, however, the return to civilian rule and holding of democratic elections in 1999 reopened possibilities for religious political mobilization. Seizing the opportunity, the candidate for governor in the state of Zamfara campaigned on the promise of adopting *Shari'ah* law, and quickly did so once elected. Other states promptly followed suit, and by 2002 twelve northern states (of Nigeria's thirty-six) had adopted *Shari'ah* law, with broad popular support. While the constitutionality of these actions at the federal level was challenged, the federal government had no effective power to challenge these moves.

The governments of *Shari'ah* states quickly undertook a series of symbolic actions intended to moralize society, such as bans on alcohol, gambling, and prostitution. They also adopted a number of criminal penalties based on Islamic, *hudud*, punishments. Quickly, two very high profile cases of young women sentenced to death by stoning for adultery provoked a major outcry, in Nigeria and abroad. Following intense debates, however, both of these sentences were eventually overturned by *Shari'ah* courts of appeal, on Islamic grounds. Reflecting this, what most significantly marked the first decade of *Shari'ah* in these states is the fact that rather than a mechanical imposition of established law, the process has rather provoked significant internal debate about the meaning of *Shari'ah*, a process that has had the effect of moderating application of stricter penalties (Ostien et al. 2005). These states thus represent an unexpected situation: the centrality of *Shari'ah* in the establishment of some measure of democracy.

We should be careful, of course, not to romanticize this experience; the *Shari'ah* and democratic experiment has coexisted with the continued periodic appearance of stridently radical Islamist movements in northern Nigeria, leading to occasional bouts of intense violence, and provoking in turn ferocious governmental retaliation. Much media coverage as well as scholarly attention understandably focuses on these episodes, the most significant of which have involved the so-called Boko Haram movement. But contextualizing the violent movements also allows us to note the more interesting face of the *Shari'ah* experiment, as an open political debate about what should be the legitimate government for Muslims situated within a broadly chaotic political environment at the national level.

As these cases demonstrate, Islamic political involvement within the liberalized contexts of post-Cold War Africa show interesting variation, and most importantly a wide range of possibilities for politics in Africa's Muslim societies, with potentially instructive lessons for the rest of the Muslim world.

Political Islam and Weakened States in the Age of Terror

The age of terror started in Africa before the events of September 11, 2001 in the United States; it began specifically with the simultaneous bombings of the US embassies in Kenya and Tanzania on August 7, 1998. These attacks left over 300 people dead, the vast majority Kenyans. For our purposes here, what was most striking is that these attacks were carried out by outsiders, and gained no popular sympathy in either country. As implied in my discussions of those countries above, these events also had relatively little domestic impact on Islam and politics. Despite this, however, they set the stage for what was to be an intense and growing anxiety in the West, and among some African elites, about the potential danger of "radicalization" of African political Islam. Many of the dynamics I have discussed above as phenomena linked to liberalization—religious discourse in the public sphere, increased demands for Islamic education, opposition to Western-inspired family law, and such—have been read as symptoms of this looming danger (Lyman and Morrison 2004; Rotberg 2005).

Two major zones of concern have been identified in this respect: the countries of the Horn of Africa and Sahelian (or more specifically Saharan) West Africa (International Crisis Group 2005). Northern Nigeria, although part of the Sahel, is also sometimes singled out for its unique dynamics. Elsewhere in the Sahel the concern was fueled by various violent kidnappings and killings, mostly in the open Sahara, and carried out by groups apparently affiliated with or inspired by the Algerian GSPC (Salafist Group for Preaching and Combat), reconfigured as Al- Qa'ida in the Maghreb (AQIM) in 2006, although certainly shaped by highly local concerns. These events placed significant pressure on governments in the region, and resulted in several major US-led initiatives to attempt to contain or defeat *jihadi* Islam in the region. While this complex situation remained difficult to sort out, the most striking fact has been the almost complete lack of support for such Islamist activities among local populations, among the materially poorest people on earth. Despite massive military efforts, however, it has proven extremely difficult to eliminate all such groups in the vast and largely ungoverned spaces of the region. Such *jihadi* activities thus seem likely to remain a thorn in the side of governments across the region, but also seem unlikely in themselves to be able to mount major offensives against states.

This precarious situation was abruptly disrupted by forces unleashed by the fall of the Qaddafi regime in Libya. The flow of arms and returning fighters who had been recruited from the Sahel to fight in Qaddafi's army, as well as refugees and returning migrant workers, placed extraordinary pressures on Sahelian countries in late 2011 and early 2012. In the particularly fragile situation of Mali the initial impact was to spark a new rebellion among the ethnic Tuareg population of the northern regions, feeding on historical grievances, but importantly with no religious agenda or motivation. In a complicated and still unclear sequence of events, government mishandling of this uprising provoked a military mutiny, which in turn ended in the overthrow of the government, abruptly ending Mali's twenty-year period as a much-lauded democracy in Muslim West Africa.

Most dramatically following the coup, both the Malian military and the Tuareg separatist movement quickly lost control of the northern half of the country, including the historical and important cities of Timbuktu and Gao. In their place, the region was quickly and opportunistically occupied by a shifting assortment of militant *jihadi* groups, including AQIM, an affiliated Tuareg-led group that took the name of the Ansar Ad-Dine, and eventually a new group calling itself the Movement for Unity and Jihad in West Africa (MUJWA). Terrorized local populations have shown no support for these small but well-armed movements, which seem to be drawing both resources and fighters from outside the region. Political paralysis in the Malian capital of Bamako, however, and the ambivalence of outside actors to intervene in a fragile political situation and an extraordinarily inhospitable vast desert region, have produced a stalemate whose ultimate resolution is far from clear.

An equally difficult and ambiguous situation has been presented by political Islamic movements in the Horn of Africa. Islamism as a political ideology has long been present across the region, perhaps more than elsewhere in sub-Saharan Africa, and its various ideological strains are genealogically linked to Egyptian and Sudanese Islamist movements (de Waal 2004). In the two divided countries of Ethiopia and Eritrea, countries that have in addition experienced significant strife and violence, what is most striking is the fact that despite deep political divisions Islam has not been politicized as a major force in either country, and in neither would the Muslim-Christian cleavage be considered a major force in national politics.

And finally, Somalia. What might appear in some accounts as the site of Africa's most politicized Islamic society, may on closer look appear as one of its least significant in terms of our analysis of Islam and politics—despite the deep and damning tragedy that it represents for the world community. Somalia's state, the most heavily armed and one of the most highly involved in Cold War rivalries for most of its independent history, collapsed into anarchy as the support structure for Africa's authoritarian regimes crumbled in the early 1990s. Two decades, a full generation, later, there is still no functioning state. Appearing in significant measure only in the second decade of this tragic picture of human suffering, political Islam in Somalia has been much more an epiphenomenal product of this history than a key factor in explaining the situation (Menkhaus 2004). Indeed, the one hope for Somalia in the mid-2000s was the de facto Islamic government known as the "Islamic Courts Union" (ICU), which effectively ruled much of the country until pushed out by Ethiopian troops, with US support, in late 2006. The ICU appears to have gained some significant legitimacy for the stability that it was able to impose, and its breakup following the Ethiopian invasion spawned a more radical set of smaller *jihadi* groups, "pirates," and other seeming threats to the international community. In this context it is extremely difficult to predict the fate of political Islam in the region, but it is also unimaginable that a stable government could be constructed without explicitly building on a religious identity and the legitimacy it would confer.

In the highly politicized global context of Islam in the age of terror, we see wide variations in the role of Islam in its multiple sub-Saharan contexts. The fate of individual states in Africa has clearly been central to setting the parameters for Islam's political role. And Muslim societies on the continent have demonstrated a capacity for innovation and significant experimentation with political models. Unfortunately Africa has been largely neglected in much of the voluminous recent literature on Islam and politics, and there is much that we still do not know about dynamics on the continent. But it is also clear that Africa presents important possibilities that need to be considered if we are to fully describe the multifaceted political roles of Islam in the modern world.

Notes

1. Very few countries have carried out reliable censuses in Africa, and even in those few that have done so the political sensitivity of relative demographic importance means that the question of religion is usually not asked, or the results not released.
2. The partition of Sudan in July 2011 left the remaining north of that historically *divided* country as a new Muslim majority state (Sudan) and produced the new Muslim minority state of South Sudan. No reliable figures are available for the religious demography of either country, and questions of citizenship on both sides will no doubt long complicate efforts to count. Various informed sources suggest, however, that the resident Muslim population of South Sudan currently comprises a significant minority, perhaps in the range of 10 percent.
3. Very small Shi`a populations in some places are either primarily of non-African origin, or of relatively recent vintage as politically motivated movements.
4. Following the Africanist convention, "francophone" refers to the former French colonies where French has been maintained as the official language, although it is never spoken by the majority.
5. The commonly cited exceptions, namely Liberia and Ethiopia, were nevertheless heavily shaped by the broader colonial experience of the continent, both in terms of boundaries and by external influences on the elaboration of the state apparatus.
6. The rare exceptions that were presented at the time as indicators of the possibilities for democracy in Africa included the small island republic of Mauritius, and the cases of Senegal and Botswana, both stable and civilian regimes, but whose "democracy" was marked by significant limitations—namely the persistent hold on power of the parties that had led them to independence.
7. An ongoing research project on Muslim democracies, led by Mirjam Künkler at Princeton University, used various political datasets to identify only five democracies in predominantly Muslim countries in 2010: Turkey, Indonesia, and Albania, in addition to the two African cases named here. It merits noting that the collapse of the democratic system in Mali in 2012 was unrelated to religious issues, but rather attributable largely to a weakened state structure unable to withstand strong pressures resulting from the consequences of the collapse of the Qaddafi regime in Libya.

References

Alidou, Ousseina. 2005. *Engaging Modernity: Muslim Women and the Politics of Agency in Post-Colonial Niger.* Madison: University of Wisconsin Press.

An-Naim, Abdullahi Ahmed. 2006. *African Constitutionalism and the role of Islam.* Philadelphia: University of Pennsylvania Press.

Augis, Erin. 2005. Dakar's Sunnite Women: The Politics of Person. In *L'Islam politique au sud du Sahara: Identités, discours et enjeux*, ed. Muriel Gomez-Perez, 309-326. Paris: Karthala.

Badran, Margot, ed. *Gender and Islam in Africa: Right, Sexuality, and Law.* Washington D.C.: Woodrow Wilson Center Press, and Stanford UP, 2011.

Becker, Felicitas. 2008. *Becoming Muslim in Mainland Tanzania, 1890-2000.* Oxford: Oxford University Press.

Bonate, Liazaat J. K. 2009. Transformations de l'Islam à Penda au Mozambique. In *L'économie morale et les mutations de l'Islam en Afrique sub-saharienne*, eds. Jean-Louis Triaud and Leonardo A. Villalón. *Afrique Contemporaine* (Paris), no. 231: 61-76.

Bratton, Michael. 2003. Briefing: Islam, Democracy and Public Opinion in Africa. *African Affairs* 102: 493-501.

Brégand, Denise. 2007. Muslim Reformists and the State in Benin. In *Islam and Muslim Politics in Africa*, eds. Benjamin F. Soares and René Otayek, 121-136. New York: Palgrave Macmillan.

Brenner, Louis, ed. 1993. *Muslim Identity and Social Change in Sub-Saharan Africa.* Bloomington: Indiana University Press.

Brenner, Louis. 2000. Sufism in Africa. In *African Spirituality*, ed. Jacob K. Olupona. New York: The Crossroad Publishing Company: 324-349.

Brenner, Louis. 2001. *Controlling Knowledge: Religion, Power and Schooling in a West African Muslim Society.* Bloomington: Indiana University Press.

Centre d'Etude d'Afrique Noire. *L'Afrique politique 2002: Islams d'Afrique, entre le local et le globale.* Paris: Karthala.

Constantin, François. 1995. Muslims and Politics: Attempts to Create Muslim National Organizations in Tanzania, Uganda and Kenya. In *Religion & Politics in East Africa: The Period since Independence*, eds. Holger Bernt Hansen and Michael Twaddle, 19-31. London: James Currey.

Cruise O'Brien, Donal. 2003. *Symbolic Confrontations: Muslims Imagining the State in Africa.* London: Hurst and Company.

De Waal, Alex, ed. 2004. *Islamism and Its Enemies in the Horn of Africa.* Bloomington: Indiana University Press.

Galilou, Abdoulaye. 2002. The Graduates of Islamic Universities in Benin: A Modern Elite Seeking Social, Religious and Political Recognition. In *Islam in Africa*, eds. Thomas Bierschenk and Georg Stauth, 129-146. Yearbook of the Sociology of Islam 4. Berlin: Lit Verlag.

Gomez-Perez, Muriel, ed. 2005. *L'Islam politique au sud du Sahara: Identités, discours et enjeux.* Paris: Karthala.

Hanretta, Sean. 2005. Muslim Histories, African Societies; the Venture of Islamic Studies in Africa. *Journal of African History* 46: 479-491.

Hashim, Abdulkadir. 2005. Muslim Personal Law in Kenya and Tanzania: Tradition and Innovation. *Journal of Muslim Minority Affairs* 25(3): 449-460.

Holder, Gilles, ed. 2009. *L'Islam, nouvel espace public en Afrique.* Paris: Karthala.

Hunwick, John. 1997. Sub-Saharan Africa and the Wider World of Islam: Historical and Contemporary Perspectives. In *African Islam and Islam in Africa: Encounters between Sufis and Islamists*, eds. David Westerlund and Eva Evers Rosander. London: Hurst & Company: 28–54.

International Crisis Group. Islamist Terrorism in the Sahel: Fact or Fiction? Africa Report No. 92, March 31, 2005. Available at: http://www.crisisgroup.org/home/index.cfm?id=3347&l=1 (accessed February 20, 2010).

Kane, Ousmane, and Jean-Louis Triaud, eds. 1998. *Islam et islamismes au sud du Sahara*. Paris: Karthala.

Kane, Ousmane. 2003. *Muslim Modernity in Postcolonial Nigeria: A Study of the Society for the Removal of Innovation and Reinstatement of tradition*. Leiden: Brill.

Levtzion, Nehemia, and Randall L. Pouwells, eds. 2000. *The History of Islam in Africa*. Athens: Ohio University Press.

Loimeier, Roman. 1997. *Islamic Reform and Political Change in Northern Nigeria*. Evanston: Northwestern University Press.

Loimeier, Roman. 2003. Patterns and Peculiarities of Islamic Reform in Africa. *Journal of Religion in Africa* 33(3): 237–262.

Loimeier, Roman. 2007. Perceptions of Marginalization: Muslims in Contemporary Tanzania. In *Islam and Muslim Politics in Africa*, eds. Benjamin Soares and René Otayek, 137–156. New York: Palgrave Macmillan.

Lyman, Princeton N., and J. Stephen Morrison. 2004. The Terrorist Threat in Africa. *Foreign Affairs* 83(1): 75–86.

Masquelier, Adeline. 2009. *Women and Islamic Revival in a West African Town*. Bloomington: Indiana University Press.

Mbogoni, Lawrence E. Y. 2004. *The Cross versus the Crescent: Religion and Politics in Tanzania from the 1880s to the 1990s*. Dar es Salaam: Mkuki na Nyota Publishers.

Menkhaus, Kenneth J. 2004. *Somalia: State Collapse and the Threat of Terrorism*. Adelphi Paper 364, International Institute for Strategic Studies. Oxford: Oxford University Press.

Meunier, Olivier. 1997. *Dynamique de l'Enseignement Islamique au Niger: Le cas de la ville de Maradi*. Paris: L'Harmattan.

Miles, William F. S., ed. 2007. *Political Islam in West Africa: State-Society Relations Transformed*. Boulder: Lynne Rienner Publishers.

Oded, Arye. 2000. *Islam and Politics in Kenya*. Boulder: Lynne Rienner Publishers.

Østebø, Terje. 2008. Localising Salafism: Religious Change among Oromo Muslims in Bale, Ethiopia. PhD diss., Stockholm University.

Østebø, Terje. 2009. Une économie salafie de la prière dans la region du Balé en Éthiopie. In *L'économie morale et les mutations de l'Islam en Afrique sub-Saharienne*, eds. Jean-Louis Triaud and Leonardo A. Villalón. *Afrique Contemporaine* (Paris), No. 231: 45–60.

Ostien, Philip, Jamila M. Nasir, and Franz Kogelmann, eds. 2005. *Comparative Perspectives on shari'ah in Nigeria*. Ibadan: Spectrum Books, Ltd.

Otayek, René, ed. 1993. *Le radicalisme Islamique au sud du Sahara: Da'wa, arabisation et critique de l'Occident*. Paris: Karthala.

Paden, John N. 2005. *Muslim Civic Cultures and Conflict Resolution: The Challenge of Democratic Federalism in Nigeria*. Washington: Brookings Institution Press.

Piga, Adriana. 2006. *Les voies du soufisme au sud du Sahara: Parcours historiques et anthropologiques*. Paris: Karthala.

Robinson, David. 2004. *Muslim Societies in African History*. Cambridge: Cambridge University Press.

Rotberg, Robert I., ed. 2005. *Battling Terrorism in the Horn of Africa*. Washington: Brookings Institution Press.

Rothchild, Donald, and Naomi Chazan. 1988. *The Precarious Balance: State and Society in Africa*. Boulder: Westview Press.

Sani Umar, Muhammad. 1993. Changing Islamic Identity in Nigeria from the 1960s to the 1980s: From Sufism to anti-Sufism. In *Muslim Identity and Social Change in Sub-Saharan Africa*, ed. Louis Brenner. Bloomington: Indiana University Press: 154–178.

Sanneh, Lamin. 1997. *The Crown and the Turban: Muslims and West African Pluralism*. Boulder: Westview Press.

Soares, Benjamin F. 2005. Islam in Mali in the Neoliberal Era. *African Affairs* 105(418): 77–95.

Soares, Benjamin F., and René Otayek, eds. 2007. *Islam and Muslim Politics in Africa*. New York: Palgrave Macmillan.

Soares, Benjamin F. 2009. The Attempt to Reform Family Law in Mali. *Die Welt des Islams* 49: 398–428.

Tayob, Abdulkader. 1999. *Islam in South Africa: Mosques, Imams, and Sermons*. Gainesville: University Press of Florida.

Triaud, Jean-Louis, and Leonardo A. Villalón, eds. 2009. L'économie morale et les mutations de l'Islam en Afrique sub-Saharienne. Special issue of the journal. *Afrique Contemporaine* (Paris), No. 231.

Twaddle, Michael. 2003. The Bible, the Qur'an and Political Competition in Uganda. In *Scriptural Politics: The Bible and the Koran as Political Models in the Middle East and Africa*, ed. Niels Kastfelt, 139–154. London: Hurst.

Villalón, Leonardo A. 1995. *Islamic Society and State Power in Senegal: Disciples and Citizens in Fatick*. Cambridge: Cambridge University Press.

Villalón, Leonardo A. 1996. The Moral and the Political in African Democratization: The *Code de la Famille* in Niger's Troubled Transition. *Democratization* 3(2): 41–68.

Villalón, Leonardo A., and Phillip A. Huxtable, eds. 1998. *The African State at a Critical Juncture: Between Disintegration and Reconfiguration*. Boulder: Lynne Rienner Publishers.

Villalón, Leonardo A. 2010. From Argument to Negotiation: Constructing Democracies in Muslim West Africa. *Comparative Politics* 42(4): 375–393.

Villalón, Leonardo A. 2012. Rethinking Education in the Sahel: Democracy, Religious Change, and the Politics of reform. In *Governing Africa's Changing Societies: Dynamics of Reform*, ed. Ellen Lust and Stephen Ndegwa, 177–201. Boulder: Lynne Rienner Publishers.

Westerlund, David, and Eva Evers Rosander, eds. 1997. *African Islam and Islam in Africa: Encounters between Sufis and Islamists*. London: Hurst and Company/Athens: Ohio University Press.

PART IV

THE DYNAMICS OF ISLAM IN POLITICS

Political Islam in Power

CHAPTER 26

IRAN'S ISLAMIC REPUBLIC

WILLIAM O. BEEMAN

WASHINGTON politicians and the press have cultivated, among Americans, the impression that Iran is a "theocracy" with no democratic institutions. Ignorance grew during the Bush administration as the conflict in Iraq escalated, and the administration continuously looked to blame Iran for US failures. Larry Diamond, a scholar at the Hoover Institution who advised the Coalition Provisional Authority in Iraq (CPA), told the Inter Press Service that the Mahdi Army of young cleric Muqtada al-Sadr, and other Shi`a militias (which, at the moment are giving Coalition forces a very hard time in Iraq) were being armed and financed by Iran with the aim of imposing "another Iranian-style theocracy."[1] Diamond's comments were reiterated by another Coalition provisional authority advisor, Michael Rubin.[2] The story was echoed by influential *New York Times* conservative columnists William Safire and David Brooks, further compounding the misinformation[3] and continued to be a running theme in the US press on into the Obama administration, particularly in the *New York Times* as reflected in the reporting of Michael R. Gordon. The claim is simply untrue. No official body in Iran is supporting al-Sadr and the idea that al-Sadr could ever dream of imposing an "Iranian-style theocracy" is absurd. Nevertheless, the impression that Iran has nothing even resembling democratic institutions makes the neoconservative claims more believable to many Americans, who know nothing of Iran and who are fearful of Islamic attacks on Western culture.

The very appellation "theocracy" is in itself misleading and shows a poor understanding of the governmental structure that was set up following the Iranian Revolution of 1978–1979. Moreover, contrary to neoconservative implications, the original government of the Islamic Republic of Iran was not "imposed" by anyone. It was established through an electoral process following the Iranian Revolution. Iranians may regret having ratified the constitution they did, but they follow its provisions assiduously. Every election in Iran in the last twenty years has been free, and has followed the prescribed electoral process to the letter. The problems that have arisen in the country are related to the fact that half of the institutions in the Iranian government are unelected, and these institutions have veto power over the elected institutions. Furthermore, the army and the judiciary are both controlled by these unelected bodies. However, this would not be a problem, except for the fact that those occupying positions in these unelected bodies are by and large the most conservative religionists in Iran. Therefore, problems with government in Iran stem not from the system of government, but rather from the political bent of those that occupy positions of power in the government.

An accurate picture of Iranian electoral institutions helps in assessing both their strengths and weaknesses, and puts aside the notion that Iran is some kind of theocratic dictatorship. Consequently, I present here a sketch of the Iranian electoral procedure, the main governmental institutional bodies in Iran, and some of the underlying dynamics of political life in Iran today.

Theocracy and Legitimacy

The Iranian form of government is unique. Although it is intrinsically bound up with Shi`a religious philosophy, to merely label it a "theocracy" is to miss both the characteristics that set it apart from other governmental institutions, and the characteristics that make it unlikely to be adopted anywhere else in the world.

Shi`a Islam differs from Sunni Islam in a number of historical and philosophical ways. One important difference is that Sunni Islam is organized into legal "schools." Shi`ism is dependent on individual personalities—*marja-e-taqlid*. There is no formal clergy in Islam. Anyone (male or female) can study theology, and technically any Muslim can lead prayer or offer religious opinions.[4] The Shi`a system is based on consensus. When a person is known for his or her knowledge and wisdom, they are a *faqih*, or "jurisprudent." A very prominent faqih is known as a *Mujtahid*, or "practitioner of exegesis." Such people are trusted to interpret Islamic law. When such a person, due to his (or her) superior leadership qualities and knowledge becomes a focal point for a following, and prominent religious persons endorse the views of that Mujtahid, the Mujtahid becomes a Marja`-e-Taqlid. Technically, a Marja`-e-Taqlid is a "Grand Ayatollah" in common parlance.[5]

Ithna-Ashara Shi`ism, or "Twelver" Shi`ism, is the dominant doctrine in Iran. Its name derives from adherents' belief in twelve Imams, who were leaders of the faithful and direct descendants of the Prophet Mohammad. The twelfth Imam, Mohammad al-Mahdi, disappeared in infancy. He is said to be in "occultation" until the end of the world. The Mahdi and his predecessors are believed to possess the "true" esoteric knowledge of religious law through a far more extensive set of pronouncements from God known only to them. Therefore, the line of imams terminating with the Mahdi is the only legitimate line of rulers. In the meantime, adherents to the Twelver Shi`a doctrine are technically without a present leader.

For more than three centuries since Shi`ism became the state religion in Iran, the question of legitimacy of rule in the face of the absent Imam has been a matter of serious political contention. Two basic theories of governance emerged. The first theory espoused secular rule with "advice" from religious officials to guarantee. The second theory advocated rule by the wisest and most revered jurisprudent (*faqih*). For most of the nineteenth and twentieth centuries the first theory prevailed; however, the desire for religious rule never died. Iran's 1909 Constitutional Revolution highlighted this with two major religious leaders, Sheikh Fazlollah Nuri, defending religious rule, and Ayatollah Mohammad Na'ini, defending the incipient constitution and secular rule. The secular constitutionalists won and Sheikh Nuri was executed.[6] The secular view has prevailed in public and theological opinion down to the present.

Grand Ayatollah Ruhollah Khomeini, who at the time of the Iranian Revolution was the Marja`-e-Taqlid with the largest number of followers in the Twelver Shi`a world, favored the second theory—spiritual rule. He introduced a new doctrine institutionalizing the authority of the *faqih* in the absence of the Mahdi: the Velayat-e-Faqih or "Regency of the Jurisprudent." Ayatollah Khomeini's doctrine was rejected by every other Grand Ayatollah at the time, and continues to be opposed today. Traditionally, since the Shi`a spiritual leaders had eschewed temporal power, and many felt that Khomeini's innovation was heretical. Nevertheless, his charisma and leadership skills were sufficient to convince the Iranian electorate to ratify a constitution granting the unelected spiritual leader power over all aspects of government.

The presidential election of 2009 in which the reelection of President Ahmadinejad was severely challenged by oppositionists was mistakenly characterized by Western commentators as "democracy" versus "theological dictatorship." In fact the controversy at base, while not rejecting the basic idea of the Islamic Republic, involved a continuation of the spiritual versus secular authority conflict that had been raging for centuries. The oppositionists were seen as a threat to the Velayat-e Faqih and Ayatollah Khomeini's successor, Ayatollah Ali Khamene'i, and were brutally repressed. Since Ayatollah Khamene'i has no obvious successor, the controversy is likely to continue indefinitely.

Iranian Governmental Structures

Once the spiritual leader was in place, other governmental institutions flowed from this office. Initially, the spiritual leader was intended to be a remote figure, intervening to resolve questions of government and national leadership only when other means failed. As the early years of the Islamic Republic devolved into internal factionalism between moderate and conservative factions, Khomeini found himself having to intervene more and more. Over time, the institutions of the Iranian state came to be distributed according to the schema indicated on the chart below:

As shown in the chart, the spiritual leader controls directly or indirectly almost every aspect of government. However, the spiritual leader is, himself, chosen by an Assembly of Experts, who are elected by the people.

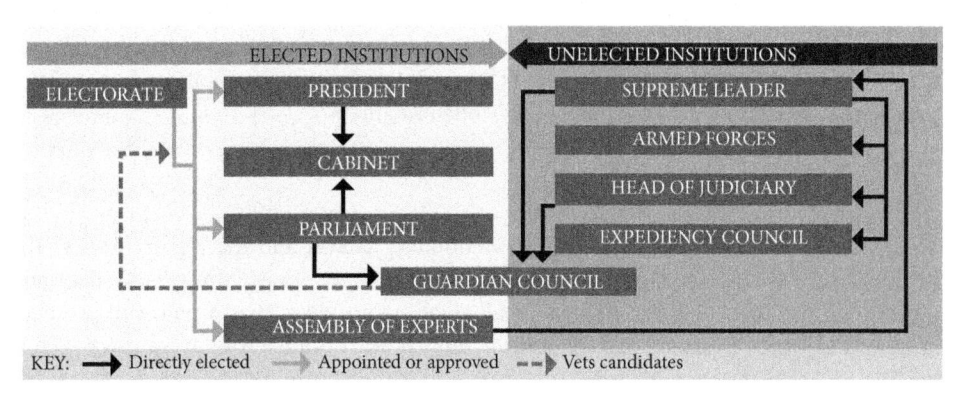

Basic Iranian Governmental Structure—Elected and Unelected Institutions

The electorate

Voting rates are typically high in Iran. In the parliamentary elections of 2000, around 70 percent of voters cast ballots. In the presidential election of 2001, voter participation was nearly 80 percent. In the 2004 parliamentary elections, the rate fell to just above 50 percent despite a call on the part of reformers to boycott the elections. Participation in Tehran was around 30 percent, showing both the effect of the urban dwellers' disaffection and that rural voters continued to vote at high rates.

Of a total population of about 65 million, more than 46 million people are eligible to vote and some 8 million of these were born after the 1979 revolution, and women and young people increasingly make up the majority of voters. The gap between male and female literacy has narrowed among the younger generation. Women now make up an estimated 60 percent of students enrolling in higher education, although the number of women working remains well below the number of men. Women have had the vote since 1963, and there are currently thirteen female members of the parliament. Youth and women were the main bloc of voters who brought reformist Mohammad Khatami the presidency in 1997, and through their support, Advocates of reform have also come to dominate the parliament. However, Reformists have not had it all their own way in elections. Conservative candidates made a comeback—aided by low voter turnout in local council elections in March 2003. This was a harbinger of the February 2004 elections, where conservatives won decisively.

Unelected bodies

Spiritual leader

The role of the spiritual leader (frequently referred to as the supreme leader in the Western press) in the constitution is based on the ideas of Ayatollah Khomeini. The spiritual leader, currently Ayatollah Ali Khamene'i, appoints the head of the judiciary, six of the members of the powerful Guardian Council, the commanders of all the armed forces, Friday prayer leaders, and the head of radio and television. He also confirms the election of the president. The spiritual leader is chosen by the clerics who make up the Assembly of Experts. Tensions between the office of the leader and the office of the president have often been the source of political instability. These tensions increased since the election of President Mohammed Khatami—a reflection of the deeper tensions between religious rule and the democratic aspirations of most Iranians. The election of President Mahmud Ahmadinejad seemingly relaxed these tensions, but in fact President Ahmadinejad's political ambitions have continued to prove troublesome to the office of Ayatollah Khamene'i.

Armed forces

The armed forces are made up of the Revolutionary Guard and the regular forces. The Revolutionary Guard was formed after the revolution to protect the new leaders and institutions and to fight those opposing the revolution; today it has a powerful presence in other institutions, and controls volunteer militias with branches in every town. While the two bodies were once separate, the army under the control of the president, and the Revolutionary Guard under the control of the spiritual leader, during the administration of

President Hashemi Rafasanjani, both bodies were placed under a joint general command under the direction of the spiritual leader. Today, all leading army and Revolutionary Guard commanders are appointed by the spiritual leader and are answerable only to him.[7]

The paramilitary Basij Force grew as a voluntary force during the Iran-Iraq War from 1980 to 1988. These forces were organized under the aegis of the Revolutionary Guard and continue to be attached to them in formal organizational terms. In fact the Basij members have tended to be largely unregulated. They have taken it on themselves to enforce public "morality" through violent action and to serve as an informal strike force against oppositionists to the government. They also were active in the presidential elections of 2005 and 2009 in "getting out the vote," sometimes in a coercive manner.

Head of judiciary

The Iranian judiciary has never been independent of political influence. Until early in the twentieth century it was controlled by the clergy, and after the revolution the Spiritual Court revoked all previous laws that were deemed un-Islamic. New laws based on Shari'ah law—derived from Islamic texts and teachings—were introduced soon after.

The judiciary defines legal policy and ensures that the laws of the Islamic Republic are enforced. It also nominates the six lay members of the Guardian Council (see below). The head of the judiciary is appointed by, and reports to, the spiritual leader. As in the United States, different judges interpret the law according to their own judgments. In recent years, the hardliners have used the judicial system to undermine reforms by imprisoning reformist personalities and journalists and closing down reformist papers.

Expediency council

The council is an advisory body for the leader with ultimate adjudicative power in disputes over legislation between the parliament and the Guardian Council. The spiritual leader appoints its members, who are prominent religious, social, and political figures. Its present chairman, former President Hashemi Rafsanjani, has turned it into an influential strategic planning and policymaking body. Because it "mediates," it has allowed Hashemi Rafsanjani to actually initiate policy, since he can provide some guarantee that they will pass. As an example of its work, the Guardian Council demanded in June of 2003 that the Majles rewrite certain provisions of its newly passed election law. The Majles refused, and the bill was referred to the Expediency Council. In effect, the Expediency Council then had the power to shape the bill as it saw fit.[8]

Elected bodies

Assembly of experts

The responsibilities of the Assembly of Experts are to appoint the spiritual leader, monitor his performance, and remove him if he is deemed incapable of fulfilling his duties. The assembly usually holds two sessions a year. Direct elections for the eighty-six members of the current assembly were last held in 2009. Only clerics can join the assembly and candidates for election are vetted by the Guardian Council. The assembly is dominated by conservatives.

President

The president is elected for four years and can serve no more than two consecutive terms. While most nations in the Middle East have continually elected leaders "for life," Iran, by contrast, has adhered strictly to presidential term limits. Nevertheless, former presidents have frequently been "recycled" into other leadership positions—the foremost being former President Ali Akbar Hashemi Rafsanjani, who is deputy leader of the Assembly of Experts, and head of the Expediency Council, and Ayatollah Ali Khamene'i, now the nation's spiritual leader. The constitution describes the president as the second-highest ranking official in the country. He is head of the executive branch of power and is responsible for ensuring the constitution is implemented. Presidential powers are limited by the members of unelected bodies in Iran's power structure, most of whom are clerics, and by the authority of the spiritual leader. It is the spiritual leader, not the president, who controls the armed forces and makes decisions on security, defense, and major foreign policy issues.

Mohammad Khatami was elected president in May 1997 with nearly 70 percent of the vote and reelected in June 2001 with over 77 percent. The Guardian Council has frustrated most of his reforms, particularly in the areas of presidential power and electoral supervision, since they have veto power over all legislation. His failure to carry out reforms largely resulted in disaffection on the part of the voters in the parliamentary elections of 2004.

Mahmud Ahmadinejad was elected president in 2005 and reelected in a publically contested election in 2009. President Ahmadinejad is the first nonclerical president of the nation since the Revolution of 1978–1979. His administration is dominated by secular functionaries, which now outnumber clerics in the government by considerable numbers. President Ahmadinejad is often seen in the West as conservative, due in part to disparaging remarks he has made about the state of Israel. However, he has attempted small liberalizations in government, some of which have succeeded, and others that have been flatly quashed by the Guardian Council or other conservative officials.

Parliament

The 296 members of the Majles, or parliament, are elected by popular vote every four years. The parliament has the power to introduce and pass laws, as well as to summon and impeach ministers or the president. However, all Majles bills have to be approved by the conservative Guardian Council. In February 2000, the sixth Majles was elected in free and fair elections. It was the first in which Reformists gained a majority. However, the election of the seventh Majles 2004 did result in a predominantly conservative parliament. The eighth Majles, elected in 2008, was more conservative still, expressing significant opposition to many of the policies of President Ahmadinejad.

Council of ministers

The Council of Ministers, as the Iranian presidential cabinet is called, are chosen by the president and approved by parliament, which can also impeach them. The spiritual leader is closely involved in defense, security, and foreign policy, and so his office also holds influence in decision making. Ministers responsible for cultural and social issues are heavily monitored by conservatives watching for any sign of deviation from their strict Islamic line. For example, during the past four years, the judiciary would close newspapers, and the ministry of culture would turn around and relicense them under a new name. This game kept up for some time to the frustration of the conservatives. The cabinet is chaired by the president or first vice-president, who is responsible for cabinet affairs. It is assumed that under the new, more conservative Majles, these practices will stop.

Jointly appointed body
Guardian Council

The Guardian Council is the most influential political body in Iran. It is controlled by conservatives and consists of six theologians appointed by the spiritual leader and six jurists nominated by the judiciary and approved by parliament, thus creating a deep conservative bias under the present governmental structures. Members are elected for six years on a phased basis, so that half the membership changes every three years.

The Guardian Council has virtual veto power over every electoral candidate, and every piece of legislation that passes parliament to make sure they conform to the constitution and Islamic law. It is this feature of government more than any other that has caused frustration throughout Iran. Reformists have tried to restrict the council's veto power without success. When they disqualified nearly a third of all candidates who had presented themselves for parliamentary elections in 2004, they faced boycotts and resignations from sitting Majles members. This did not faze them. Only when spiritual leader Khamene'i called them in and pleaded with them to relax their hardline did they allow a few hundred candidates back on the ballot. Even so, as a result of their disqualifications, the elections were virtually rigged in favor of the conservatives.

THE ELECTIONS

Over 6,000 people presented themselves for election to parliament in 2004. They were affiliated with dozens of parties, large and small. Despite the many parties, they are divided into conservative and reform camps. In response to the elimination of most of their candidates by the Guardian Council, the Militant Clerics' Society—the principal reform group, of which President Khatami is a member—called for a boycott of the election, and withdrew its own candidates. Seven smaller reform parties could not mount enough candidates to contest the election. Of the 290 seats, approximately 130 were completely uncontested, resulting in a conservative victory. In some cases, however, there were so many candidates that runoffs were authorized.

A great deal was made of voter participation in this election. Since the last parliamentary election and the last presidential election had high voter turnouts (over 70 percent), it was thought that a low turnout would discredit the government. Turnout in rural areas and smaller towns and cities was heavy, whereas the residents of Tehran and other urban areas stayed away in large numbers. In Tehran, only 30 percent of the population voted, but the overall vote was around 50 percent. A number of races were not decided for some time. In districts where no candidate received more than 25 percent of the vote, runoff elections were held.

Although the presidential election of 2005 was relatively calm, as was the parliamentary election of 2008, the trend toward greater conservatism was quite pronounced. In the presidential election of 2009, President Ahmadinejad was reelected over his rival, Mir-Hossein Mousavi. The election was viewed by many as the first openly corrupt election since the beginning of the Islamic Republic. It is likely that no one will ever know the true outcome. The government demonstrated that President Ahmadinejad has strong support, but they announced his victory mere hours after the polls had closed, raising suspicions of fraud. Demonstrations by the "Green Movement" in opposition to the election outcome continued for many months resulting in attacks by the Basij and other military and police forces. However, President Ahmadinejad remained in office.

The reasons for the conservative victory are complex. It is an undisputed fact that despite boycotts, a new parliament was elected in both 2004 and 2008, and with voter participation higher than is typical in the United States. Of course, the Guardian Council's role in eliminating many reform candidates ahead of time had a great deal to do with the reduced turnout and the overwhelming conservative victories. However, this does not completely explain why conservatives won so decisively after President Khatami's presidency.

Many voters who associated themselves with the reform movement were already displeased with the reform candidates for failing to make good on their promise to change things for the better, and were, as a result, philosophical about the takeover of the conservatives. Indeed, the Reformists main failure has been their inability to connect with the average Iranian, the very ones who gave them 70 percent support in the 2000 elections. Moreover, the reformers, with their great progressive political ideas also espouse neoliberal economic reforms such as making public schools self-supporting with "registration" fees and eliminating subsidies on food and fuel and government services. They also failed to mobilize the popular support into any kind of effective political parties. These are the attribute that hurt them in terms of popularity.[9] Many Iranians simply want a better life for themselves and their families and feel that, perhaps with the parliament no longer expending its energy on internal political struggle, Iran will face better economic times. This is partly reflected in the emergence of one apparently conservative group that emerged in 2003, calling themselves the "Coalition of Builders of Islamic Iran." They were technocrats with a conservative social view, but who rejected "violence and force" to enforce Islamic regulations. Their spokesman, Gholam-Ali Hadad-Adel, declared that improving the economy was the country's top priority. This group also had a large number of veterans from the Iran-Iraq War who felt that they had not been sufficiently rewarded with political and economic success after their war service.

Despite the heavy hand of the Guardian Council, which many Americans might view as a nondemocratic feature of the Iranian elections, the actual voting process up until 2009 seems to have been both free and fair. Typically, rigged elections return astonishingly high percentage figures in favor of current rulers. In Iran, although this time the conservatives won, they by no means took 100 percent of the Majles seats. The example of Tehran in 2004 is instructive. Despite widespread boycotts of the eighty-three seats, forty-three were won by conservatives, twenty-one by Reformists, and seventeen were undecided and will go to runoff elections because no one obtained the requisite twenty-five of the votes, and the other two seats were won by independents whose political views were not known.

Reform?

What do elections mean in Iran? With so many checks against "non-Islamic" legislation and candidates, this is difficult to assess. A few guesses might be made, however. It is clear that reform cannot be turned back. Conservatives have been forced to relax their former draconian regulation of public morality. Women must still adopt modest dress in public, but there are few squads of revolutionary guards throwing women in prison for showing too much hair, or breaking up wedding parties for playing popular music.[10] Iran is some distance from the broad range of freedom in public behavior that was prevalent under the shah, but it is far from being as conservative as in the 1980s. It is important to remember, particularly with regard to public dress and conduct of females, to cite one "index" of conservatism, that a large proportion of the population always adopted modest dress, even under the shah.

The conservative government favors, and will continue to develop, Iran's nuclear power capacity. As worrisome as this is, Iran is nowhere near making a bomb, despite American fears to the contrary.[11] Moreover there is absolutely no proof that a nuclear weapons program exists. This is not to say that Iran might never be tempted to create atomic weapons. In their "neighborhood" there are other states, such as Pakistan and India, with nuclear weapons. Iranians often note with a rueful cynicism that Americans tend to deal differently, and more respectfully, with nations that do have an atomic bomb.

Some other activities of Iranian conservatives have atrophied by themselves. One is the relationship between Iran and Hezbollah in Lebanon. Whereas Iran was instrumental in founding Hezbollah, today it has no effective influence or control over the organization, which has become a political party in its own nation with an agenda far removed from Iran's interests. Iran's relationship with Hezbollah has been one of the chief causes of hostility on the part of the United States,[12] but US critics of Iran are woefully out of date in assessing Iran's influence. The same is true of Iran's relationship with Hamas, which despite some material support, is largely ideological. The idea that either organization could be commandeered by Iran to do Tehran's bidding is a fantasy.

The Coalition of Builders of Islamic Iran and similar conservative groups represent a vanguard of nonclerical social conservative technocrats concentrating on industry and economy. They seem to be promulgating a kind of "China" model for Iran—promising consumer goods and improved living conditions, but eschewing relaxation of social processes. Their orientation is decidedly pragmatic, and their view may significantly shift the focus of the conservatives to more international concerns. It may not be too optimistic to look for a thaw in relations with the United States as these pragmatists begin to exercise power.

The passing of Ayatollah Khamene'i in a few years will be a watershed for Iran. As mentioned above, no successor has been found for him, and the Khomeinist line he represents may die with him. Iran will continue to have conservative and liberal factions, but it is at this point that the form of government itself may change.

The driving source for this change will likely be women and youth. Today, 60 percent of university students in Iran are women. Literacy for women under the age of twenty-five nearly equals that of men. Women are represented in every profession, and there is a higher percentage of women in the Majles than in the US Congress. Seventy-five percent of the entire Iranian population is under twenty-five. They never saw the shah or Khomeini, and have no personal knowledge of the revolution.

The elderly clerics will undoubtedly be supplanted as they pass from the scene. The next generation will be the one to effect change. They are the best educated Iranian population in history, and they have access to computers, satellite dishes, and every device of modern information technology. As a result, they are also exceptionally well informed about their own lives and about international affairs. They will come into political office sooner rather than later, and when they do, the reforms being clamored for will take place. The American neoconservative desire to destroy the current government will not bring about reform; it will set it back by unleashing social unrest. Iranians themselves have no desire for internal conflict. For the time being, they are able to work with their flawed governmental structures despite the undercurrent of social unrest that will bring reform in time. Now, they make up about 40 percent of the voting population. By the next parliamentary election, they will be the majority, and then the world will see something very interesting happen in Iran.

Perhaps the most foolish idea circulated in Washington in the past few years is the notion that the United States could somehow engineer the "overthrow" of the Iranian government and the "establishment of a democracy" there. This idea has been promulgated incessantly in conservative think tanks, such as the American Enterprise Institute.[13] As one can see, although the government of the Islamic Republic has structural flaws that allow a group with a dominant ideology to gain a stranglehold over many areas of government, the system continues to work; albeit with a lot of creaks and groans. Iran is not a dictatorship like Iraq, and it is unclear whom the United States would "overthrow" if it wanted to foment revolution in Iran. Removing the spiritual leader would do nothing at all. One would have to destroy several of the interlocking governmental bodies to have any effect. By that time, the population would be in revolt against the usurpers.

Moreover, there are no good candidates for a replacement government. The public is disaffected with the Reformists, whom they believe betrayed them, or at least proved feckless. There is a small body of monarchists clamoring for the return of the son of the deposed shah, also named Reza Pahlavi, who is now living in the United States. However, he has no real support inside Iran. The Mujaheddin-e Khalq have the support of some elements in Washington, since they were the source of information that tipped Washington off to Iranian nuclear power developments, but this group, which was supported and sheltered by Saddam Hussein, is openly hated in Iran. They would have no chance of ruling.

The Iranian population now also seems to have no stomach for revolution, as seen in the inability of the public to sustain the protests following the 2009 election. They hover between apathy and vague hopes that the future will improve. Evolutionary change, therefore, seems to be the most plausible course. In many ways, the Iranian elections were quite normal. Having had several years to change things in Iran and failed, the Reformists were voted out of office. The same thing would have happened in the United States. The last elections were the first that cast doubt on the Iranian governmental system. Nevertheless, the Guardian Council notwithstanding, the electoral process is certain to be a lively, active, and moderately effective institution for the expression of Iran's public political will.

NOTES

1. Jim Lobe, "IRAQ: Neo-Cons See Iran behind Shiite Uprising," *Inter Press Service*, April 9, 2004.
2. Michael Rubin, "Sadr Signs," *National Review Online*, April 7, 2004. Available at: http://www.nationalreview.com/comment/rubin200404060834.asp.
3. William Safire, "Two Front Insurgency," *The New York Times*, April 7, 2004, 19(A); David Brooks, "Take a Deep Breath," *The New York Times*, April 10, 2004, 15(A).
4. I do not want to give the impression that there is no formal training in Shi`a Islam. There is a formal clergy based on status attained in real seminaries where the religious training is more rigorous than in most Protestant Christian seminaries in the United States. A *mujtahid* is one who has passed all the requirements in the study of Islamic theology, philosophy, ethics, and law and received an *ejazeh-e ijtehad*, or right to interpret law, from senior *mujtahids* upon the recommendation of his or her principal mentor. This is the religious equivalent of a secular PhD. Still, lack of these credentials does not prevent anyone from leading prayer, setting themselves up as a religious leader, or wearing religious garb.
5. Juan Ricardo Cole, *Sacred Space and Holy War: The Politics, Culture and History of Shi`ite Islam*. (London: I.B. Tauris, 2002); Yitzhak Nakash, *The Shi`is of Iraq* (Princeton, Princeton University Press, 2004).
6. Cf. Azar Tabari, "Shi`i Clergy in Iranian Politics." In Nikki R. Keddie, ed., *Religion and Politics in Iran*. New Haven: Yale University Press, 57–59.
7. Eric Hoogland, editor of *Critique* magazine writes in a personal communication: "The military in Iran is NOT under the control of the conservatives, even though top commanders are appointed by the faqih. If it were, the conservatives long ago would have used if to stage a coup against the reformists. The military is divided ideologically; it is a conscript army/revolutionary guards/basij militia, with career officers who are very much divided in their political views/loyalties. This diversity of views among the security forces is, I believe, a main guarantor of Iran's democratic process, which is still in a developing and fragile state."
8. "Iran Parliament Forwards Bill on Press Law to Expediency Council," *Payvand Iran News*, June 23, 2003. Available at: http://www.payvand.com/news/03/jun/1129.html. Accessed June 3, 2003.
9. Thanks to Eric Hoogland for contributions to these firsthand observations (personal communication).
10. Hoogland writes: "It has been many years since any woman was arrested or even fined for showing too much hair in public; if this were happening, then half the women or more would be arrested, as even in small towns and villages many women wear headscarves well back of the forehead; and women in movies and TV shows of the past few years also reveal much head hair, which indicates how much the society has relaxed on this issue in the past few years. When I was in Iran in December 2003 and February 2004, chadors were worn by only about 20 percent of women in Tehran, less in Shiraz. The preferred garment in public is the headscarf and ankle-length coat, although younger women wear a tunic-like cover that is mid-thigh length over tight-fitting pants" (personal communication). See also William O. Beeman, "Lifting the Islamic Women's Veil," *Pacific News Service*, February 27, 2001. Available at: http://news.pacificnews.org/news/view_article.html?article_id=28989d9744ad6346f57372e490d760e6 for similar views. Accessed February 27, 2001.

11. William O. Beeman and Thomas Stauffer, "Is Iran Building Nukes? An Analysis (Parts 1 and 2)," *Pacific News Service 2003*. Available at: <http://www.blogger.com/blogger.g?blogID=10089650#editor/target=post;postID=110547375826877824; onPublishedMenu=overview;-onClosedMenu=overview;postNum=4;src=postname>, and <http://www.blogger.com/blogger.g?blogID=10089650#editor/target=post;postID=110547371257192650;onPublishedMenu=overview;onClosedMenu=overview;postNum=5;src=postname>. Accessed June 27, 2003. William O. Beeman, "Shi`ites and the New Culture in Iraq," *Strategic Insights* 3, no. 5 (2004). Available at: http://www.ccc.nps.navy.mil/si.
12. William O. Beeman, "Iran and the United States—Postmodern Culture Conflict in Action," *Anthropological Quarterly* 76, no.4 (2003): 671–691. See also Beeman, William O., *The "Great Satan" vs. the "Mad Mullahs": How the United States and Iran Demonize Each Other*. Chicago: University of Chicago Press, 2008.
13. Michael Ledeen, The Future of Iran. *National Review Online*, July 9, 2003. Available at: http://www.nationalreview.com/ledeen/ledeen070903.asp; Accessed July 9, 2003. Michael Ledeen, "The Iranian Hand: Regime Change in Tehran Is Necessary for Peace in Iraq." *The Wall Street Journal*, April 16, 2004. Available at: http://www.opinionjournal.com/editorial/feature.html?id=110004959. Accessed April 16, 2004.

CHAPTER 27

ISLAM AND POWER IN SAUDI ARABIA

NATANA J. DELONG-BAS

INTRODUCTION

WORKS on Saudi Arabia generally begin with the assertion that Islam and politics have been intertwined in Saudi Arabia since an alliance was formed between religious revivalist and reformer Muhammad ibn ʿAbd al-Wahhab and tribal leader Muhammad ibn Saud in 1744 CE. This alliance established a working relationship between religion and politics in which the imam was responsible for religious and, in many cases, social and legal matters, and providing religious advice to the state, and the amir was responsible for providing political and military leadership, while following the religious advice of the imam.

This symbiotic relationship, initially formed between two individuals, evolved and became institutionalized at varying levels of relative power and influence through the current third Saudi dynasty and the official religious establishment in which the Al al-Shaykh family, as descendants of Ibn ʿAbd al-Wahhab, play prominent roles. Many Saudis today refer to the king as imam, demonstrating the conflation of these two previously separate roles and the evolution of this relationship over time due to both political necessity and the fluidity of the boundaries between religion and politics in Saudi Arabia. This article focuses both on the trajectory of religious thought and practice as intertwined with politics in Saudi Arabia and on the academic debates surrounding them.

THE NATURE AND DEVELOPMENT OF WAHHABISM

The nature of "Wahhabism," the religious revival and reform movement founded by Ibn ʿAbd al-Wahhab, has long been a source of contention among scholars. The earliest comprehensive Western analyses of the religious movement (Philby 1928; Rentz 2005) focused on the central doctrine of *tawhid* (absolute monotheism) in Ibn ʿAbd al-Wahhab's writings and the impact this had on state formation, arguing that religion and state worked together to found an empire based on Unitarian thought. According to this thesis, Wahhabism from its inception necessarily focused on the political dimensions of the religious message.

This thesis has been carried forward in the contemporary era by scholars who claim that three important religious concepts were outlined by Wahhabi scholars and subsequently used for state expansion, namely migration (*hijra*), excommunication (*takfir*), and militant and religiously motivated and legitimated warfare (jihad). All of these are posited to have contributed to the consolidation of the political realm via political centralization and domination, despite Wahhabism's purported claim to represent "authentic" Sunni tradition. This claim to authenticity has been challenged by some scholars who note that Wahhabism itself has remained anchored in a single geographic region and has been propagated by people with clear regional genealogical connections, resulting in the Wahhabi Islamization of Saudi authoritarianism, rather than the Islamization of society (Al-Rasheed 2007).

However, an alternative analysis of Ibn ʿAbd al-Wahhab's writings from a theological, rather than political, perspective has found that various concepts associated today with Wahhabism were not necessarily present at its foundation. Although the central roles of *tawhid* and *shirk* (associationism) as the foundation of religious thought and practice are present in the writings of the founder, an expansive role for jihad is not. In Ibn ʿAbd al-Wahhab's own writings, jihad played a limited role, largely following the classical parameters of limitations on military engagement and prohibition of attacks on civilians and abject destruction of property. Otherwise stated, the *takfiri* ideology (practice of declaring anyone who disagrees with you as an unbeliever who is to be fought via militant jihad) for which the Wahhabis became noted historically was not present in the foundational writings of the reform movement, suggesting that state formation and jihadist expansionism were not the central vision of the movement's founder. Had jihad been a critical aspect of the original movement, one would expect to find immediate territorial conquests as the state expanded. However, in some cases, it took many years to add towns to Saudi territory because Ibn ʿAbd al-Wahhab insisted on genuine conversion to his religious reform movement as a gradual process requiring education and dialogue, rather than immediately and by the sword (Cook 1989; DeLong-Bas 2008).

Wahhabism and Violence

Although it is posited by some scholars that Wahhabism is a static tradition with violence at its heart in the form of *takfiri* ideology (Algar 2002; Abou El Fadl 2005), others (DeLong-Bas 2008) have noted change and even mutation over time, dating from 1773 when Ibn ʿAbd al-Wahhab withdrew from public life due to disagreement with Ibn Saud's son and successor, Abdulaziz, about Abdulaziz's desire to expand the role of jihad to religiously justify activities related to state consolidation and material and territorial conquest.

Saudi-Wahhabi power reached its height between 1792 and 1814—after Ibn ʿAbd al-Wahhab's death in 1791/2. By this time, Wahhabism had become a tool of not only state expansionism, largely due to the heavy incorporation of the writings of the medieval scholar, Ibn Taymiyya, into Wahhabi ideology by Ibn ʿAbd al-Wahhab's descendants, but also homogenization of religious thought and practice within Saudi territory throughout the nineteenth century (Commins 2005). This trend is argued by some scholars to have had both religious and political dimensions as the ultimate outcome was the Najdization of the country's culture and religion, negating other important intellectual and cultural traditions, particularly from the more cosmopolitan Hijaz region in which pluralism within Islam had long been practiced because of the cross-pollination of religious thought and practice produced by the mixing of pilgrims from many locations in the Hajj and important study circles in Mecca and Medina (Yamani 2004). Consequently, some scholars are working to reintroduce counternarratives to the Saudi national story in order to show the impact of Wahhabization on other regions and interpretations of Islam (Al-Rasheed and Vitalis 2004).

Many scholars who have argued that *takfiri* ideology is the hallmark of Wahhabism have done so based on historical developments that occurred after Ibn ʿAbd al-Wahhab's death, particularly citing the Wahhabi massacre of the Shiʿi inhabitants of Karbala and Najaf in 1802/3 and the often bitter conquests of the Hijaz in the early nineteenth century, as evidence of Wahhabism's lack of tolerance for alternative interpretations of Islam (Algar 2002). This lack of tolerance is posited to have continued in a direct line from the eighteenth century through the present, resulting in a portrayal of Wahhabism as a monolithic, retrograde, ultraconservative, and, ultimately, jihadist school of thought seeking to eliminate any alternative religious thought or practice, particularly Shiʿism and Sufism, versus more progressive, contemporary, and, ultimately, Westernized, thinking that seeks to embrace religious pluralism and contemporary realities (Abou El Fadl 2005). This approach suggests a direct, linear, and static progression from the time of Ibn ʿAbd al-Wahhab through the participation of fifteen Saudis in the terrorist attacks of 9/11. The result has been extreme polarization of the debates about the nature of religion in Saudi Arabia post-9/11.

Although such direct, linear progression makes for a neat and simple analysis, it fails to recognize the changes and even mutations that occurred in Wahhabi thought from the late eighteenth century through the present, including the pluralism that exists within Saudi religious thought today, in favor of highlighting only the most extreme and ultraconservative cases as normative and representative of an entire tradition spanning more than 250 years. They also fail to look more broadly at the use of religion and religious language and symbolism by parties with varying, and sometimes opposing, agendas, such as for calling for reform of the judiciary, religious establishment, and government (DeLong-Bas forthcoming), using Islam as the language of opposition to the state (Fandy 1999; Teitelbaum 2000), and working to institutionalize inclusion of the kingdom's Shiʿi population within official structures and to expand public space for Shiʿi religious observances (Ibrahim 2006). They further suggest that the only organic processes in Saudi religious development are necessarily relegated to ultraconservatism and fear of the modern era, thereby necessitating foreign intervention into Saudi affairs in order to promote reform and progressive thought. Finally, they fail to distinguish between Wahhabism in its purely religious form, as found in contemporary Qatar, versus Wahhabism as carried into the political dimension through the Saudi national project, which raises the question of whether the political manifestations are responsible for the tendency of some toward violence and extremism, rather than the religious interpretation itself (DeLong-Bas forthcoming).

Who Speaks for Wahhabism—One Voice or Many Voices?

Debates by both scholars and Saudis continue over whom one is talking about when one refers to "Wahhabis." Does Wahhabism exist only within the state or does it also necessarily serve to critique and provide advice to the state in accordance with the original alliance? Does the nature of the relationship between the state and religion change and, if so, how does one predict in which direction that change will occur? Ultimately, who, if anyone, speaks for Wahhabism—the religious establishment, the Grand Mufti, the Council of Senior `Ulama', shaykhs who are outside of the religious establishment, or the opposition? Some also debate whether Wahhabism itself is no longer a useful category for analysis because of the multiplicity of voices and relationships represented within this vague construct and because Saudis themselves do not use the term in self-reference, preferring to refer to themselves as Muslims, *Muwahhidun*, or, more commonly today, *Salafis*.

Scholars who assert that Wahhabism is represented only within the state portray it as the institutionalized, subjugated interpretation of religion that is subservient to political authority (Al-Rasheed 2007). Others include in their definition of Wahhabism those who critique and provide advice to the state because this was the function that religious leaders were intended to fulfill according to the terms of the original Saudi-Wahhabi alliance and because those offering such critiques and advice often do it with deliberate reference to this tradition (DeLong-Bas forthcoming). At the heart of the debate are the questions of how much relative influence the religious and political establishments have on each other, how much relative dependence therefore exists between the two, and how much impact either one has on the Saudi public.

Some scholars argue, for example, that the Saudi state from the beginning equated obedience to God with obedience to the ruler, thereby creating a state of consenting subjects who have transferred their presumed religious obedience to God to purported obedience to the *umara'* (rulers) and `ulama' (religious scholars), placing both rulers and scholars in positions of unquestioned authority parallel to that of God. According to this construct, anyone who resists the state is being disobedient to religion in the process, thus rendering such a person subject to jihad as holy war inflicted by the state upon its subjects. Jihad is necessary to keep the gates of *ijtihad* (independent reasoning, or a variety of legal opinions) closed in favor of a single, authoritative voice, namely, the state, in order to maintain public security and stability. Within this construct, the jihadist phenomenon becomes the logical outcome of the state's policies, establishing jihadism as the only possible voice of political opposition (Al-Rasheed 2007).

Notwithstanding that such an approach violates not only the central concept of *tawhid* that lies at the heart of Ibn `Abd al-Wahhab's writings by placing the state in God's position, but also Ibn `Abd al-Wahhab's support for *ijtihad* as apparent in his citation of multiple legal schools of thought, none of which is given more authority than any other, it is also important to note that the assumption of abject obedience on the part of the Saudi public is perhaps overstated. Simply because the religious establishment speaks and asserts a particular position does not necessarily mean that the public will accept, support, and follow it. At the same time, movement toward greater inclusiveness of a multiplicity of voices has occurred most significantly since King Abdullah's accession in 2005, as exemplified by the foundation of the National Dialogues to encourage public discussion of major issues facing Saudi Arabia and the March 2009 shake-up of the government that included the sacking of some senior ultraconservative Wahhabi *'ulama'* known for their support of *takfiri* ideology in favor of diversifying the Council of Senior 'Ulama' to include representatives from multiple schools of Islamic law present within the kingdom, not just the Hanbali school (DeLong-Bas forthcoming).

Furthermore, with respect to jihadism, it is clear from the writings and speeches of jihadis themselves that their opposition is not strictly or even necessarily primarily political, but, rather, stems from youth questioning of the religious establishment's credibility and leadership due to its failure to actively follow its own teachings through to their logical conclusion. One particularly famous case that became a matter of public debate was the martyrdom video of the self-proclaimed al-Qa'ida of the Arabian Peninsula operative, Sultan al-'Utaybi, posted posthumously on the internet in 2007. In this video, al-'Utaybi details his frustration in trying to persuade the religious establishment to take action commensurate with its declared teachings, particularly where instances of *shirk* are concerned. Al-'Utaybi's interactions with senior scholar, Shaykh Saleh al-Fawzan, member of both the Permanent Committee of Ifta' and the Council of Senior 'Ulama', demonstrate the *'ulama'*'s willingness to declare certain behaviors unacceptable in theory, but reflect their impotence to do anything to actively condemn them in practice. It was precisely because al-Fawzan refused to declare *takfir* upon those engaging in grave visitations and purported idol worship in his own voice with jihad against them as the prescribed outcome that al-'Utaybi joined the jihadist movement where he felt that the actions upheld the teachings. For some youth, therefore, the attraction of the jihadist movement is the direct result of the religious establishment's failure to uphold its own teachings rather than a political statement of opposition to the authority of the monarchy (DeLong-Bas forthcoming).

WAHHABISM—INFLUENTIAL OR NOT IN SAUDI SOCIETY?

In terms of relative influence, it is clear that the religious establishment wields power over certain aspects of government, such as the Ministry of Islamic Affairs and the Judiciary. It is assumed by most members of the public that these voices, including that of the Grand Mufti, as well as those that support them, such as the so-called Madkhali *shaykh*s, speak in the name of both the state and the religious establishment. However, this does not mean that the public necessarily listens to them or finds them credible precisely because it is known that they follow the establishment line and are perceived to be tools of the state. In some cases, the voices opposing them gain more credibility simply because they represent the opposition. Multiple voices of opposition via religious reference have become overtly public since the early 1990s with a variety of proposed alternatives to the state-supported religious agenda ranging from calls for peaceful reforms to more militant and, ultimately, revolutionary programs (Fandy 1999; Hegghammer 2010).

The central question debated by scholars is how dependent the state is on the religious establishment or to what degree the state is able to influence the impact and development of the religious establishment, even to the point of controlling it. The reality is that both trends have existed historically and that much of contemporary Saudi history is marked by the swinging of the pendulum of relative influence from one extreme to the other, with the state sometimes asserting greater levels of power and authority and the religious establishment sometimes acquiring greater power and influence over the state. It is important to note that many of the developments in Saudi religious thought and practice involve organic processes, rather than simply responses to external influences or issues.

For example, the era of King Faisal (r. 1963–1975) is typically portrayed as an era of modernization and development, during which much of the kingdom's infrastructure was built, including schools for both boys and girls. Much of this modernization was initially opposed by the religious establishment. However, King Faisal and then Grand Mufti, Muhammad ibn Ibrahim Al al-Shaykh, joined together to provide religious justification and support for the kingdom's progress, focusing on the development of the nation and the role of citizens, both male and female, in making a constructive contribution to society. This demonstrates the capacity of the religious establishment to both oppose and support the monarchy simultaneously, a theme that recurs throughout the twentieth century. It also suggests the importance of recognizing a multiplicity of voices within the religious establishment.

Similar tensions between the state and the religious establishment over the country's future can be seen in a change made following the Grand Mufti's death in 1969—the 1971 formation of the Council of Senior 'Ulama'. Some have argued that this marked a progression away from individual authority by replacing the individual voice of the Grand Mufti with the collective voices of a Council of Senior advisors engaged in collective debate and decision making with respect to religious affairs, noting that the position of Grand Mufti was not filled again until 1993 when the power of the *sahwah* (awakening) *shaykhs*, who were outside of the religious establishment, had risen to the point where the state perceived a need to reassert a very powerful, state-controlled, and singular voice for Islam in the person of senior scholar Abdulaziz bin Baz, the first non-Al al-Shaykh to hold the position of Grand Mufti (DeLong-Bas forthcoming). Others have argued that the establishment of the Council was ultimately designed to weaken the religious establishment altogether by institutionalizing Wahhabism, thus placing it in a position of dependence on the state and altering the original symbiotic relationship by giving the state greater control over religious affairs (Al-Rasheed 2007).

Although it is clear that the state retained some control over the religious establishment through the 1970s, a crisis point was reached in 1979 with the seizure of the Grand Mosque in Mecca by armed and militant religious extremists (Trofimov 2007). In exchange for its legitimation of the contentious recovery of the Grand Mosque, which required both foreign advisors and fighting within the sacred precinct, the state was forced to concede power back to the religious establishment. This was seen most visibly through public demonstrations of piety and religiosity, including attention to public adherence to prayer rituals, more literal and rigid interpretations of Islamic law, and, especially, concentrated attention to women as the culture bearers, resulting in restrictions on their access to public space, requiring them to fully veil in public and the exertion of greater state and patriarchal control over them at the expense of their own ability to engage in personal decision making, all of which was at odds with the prior approach during the King Faisal era of expanding public space and visibility for women through access to public education and employment. All of this would appear to be evidence of the rising power of the religious establishment throughout the 1980s, rather than a lack of it (DeLong-Bas forthcoming).

At the same time, religious scholars themselves were divided over the appropriate relationship between religion and the state. Those who were part of the religious establishment owed their jobs to the state and were expected to support it in order to retain their positions. In opposition stood the *sahwah* (awakening) scholars who rose to visible prominence in the early 1990s following Saddam Hussein's invasion of Kuwait and King Fahd's subsequent "invitation" to US-led Western forces to protect the kingdom and restore Kuwaiti sovereignty, as legitimated by Grand Mufti bin Baz. The *sahwah shaykhs* charged that the religious establishment was failing in its duty to provide religious advice and counsel to the monarchy and instead was simply rubber-stamping whatever policies and plans the king presented. Highlighting the fissure between establishment and antiestablishment religious voices, these *shaykhs* presented petitions and letters offering "advice" to the king that they expected him to follow in keeping with Wahhabi tradition. When this did not happen, some responded by openly calling first for reform and ultimately, as in the case of Usama Bin Laden, for revolution (Fandy 1999).

In some cases, the monarchy responded by imprisoning those who challenged the authority of both the monarchy and the religious establishment. However, after the 9/11 attacks against the United States in which Saudis played a major role and, more importantly, the 2003 and 2004 series of terrorist attacks on Saudi soil, the monarchy recognized the need at least to engage these oppositional voices (DeLong-Bas forthcoming), if not co-opt them altogether (Al-Rasheed 2007). The result was mixed. On the one hand, the *sahwah shaykhs* who joined forces with the religious establishment were perceived by some to have sold out to the state, losing some of their credibility in the process. On the other hand, the credentials of the religious establishment were bolstered by the addition of these voices into the state apparatus. Although some have criticized the *sahwis* for purportedly giving up politics in favor of addressing social issues, thus ceding much of their influence, others have noted the potentially longer term outcome of mutual influence between the two groups, seeing in events since King Abdullah's accession to the throne in 2005 evidence of movement within the religious establishment, including within the judiciary and the legal system, toward greater openness, willingness to reform, and, perhaps most importantly, shifting away from *takfiri* ideology, all of which are traceable to these changes within the religious establishment, whatever the impetus that brought those changes there. Within this reform movement, perhaps the greatest battleground between the state and the religious establishment has been the status of women.

WAHHABISM AND WOMEN—POLITICS, RELIGION, OR CULTURE?

The status of women in Saudi Arabia has long been considered a reflection of Saudi religious thought and practice, in which veiling and the politics of patriarchal protection, as exemplified by the ban on women driving and the requirement of a male guardian's approval for every decision related to women, are understood to be religiously mandated. Certainly the religious establishment made its position clear through the 1980s and 1990s by issuing many *fatawa* (religiously based legal opinions) addressing matters related to women and gender, including dress, access to public space, subservience to male guardians, and other limitations based on biological differences between men and women, such as childbearing and menstruation. Many, particularly in the West, have concluded as a result that Wahhabism is the culprit in limiting women, thereby suggesting that "liberating" Saudi women is not so much a matter of politics as it is of liberating Saudi Arabia in general from Wahhabi influence over both state and society, particularly because of its literalist and legalistic interpretation of Islamic law (Abou El Fadl 2005).

Because the issues are so contentious, attention to historical accuracy and the foundational period of Wahhabism are particularly instructive. Ibn ʿAbd al-Wahhab himself worked to create significant public space for women in his movement, asserting their right to literacy, to education in both the Qur'an and hadith so as to be able to think and interpret for themselves, as well as to evaluate any given scholar's interpretations, to expand and support the grounds for women to initiate divorce, to protection from male violence, whether in the form of rape, forced marriage, or domestic abuse, to inherit according to Islamic law, and to own property and engage in business, including with men (DeLong-Bas 2008). Perhaps the most powerful evidence of his support for these rights for women comes from the biographical dictionaries of prominent women from his lifetime through the early nineteenth century, including his female descendants, and their work in supporting his movement and advancing literacy and access to books (al-Harbi 2008). This foundational period provides a solid religious basis for contemporary reforms.

Although the details have yet to be written, the broad scholarly assumption has been that the status of women followed the same trajectory as the status of religion throughout the nineteenth century in which a single authoritative interpretation based in Najd was enforced on the rest of the country. Historical accounts of women's work and status in Saudi Arabia indicate differences between regions, with Najd being one of the most conservative areas by the twentieth century, particularly after 1979. Some scholars attribute the expanding limitations on women's access to public space to the often forcible spread of Najdi culture to the rest of the kingdom, including the purported "revival" of polygamy and the insistence on full veiling in public, which were specific to Najd (Yamani 2004; Yamani 2008).

Others note the tendency to reduce women to literal subjects of Islamic law who needed to be controlled by males as a reflection of the state's control over society. Although this is typically portrayed by the state as a matter of protecting women from the violence of society, it is viewed by some as yet another example of the violence inflicted by the state on the Saudi family by placing the state in a higher position of authority over a woman's autonomy than her male family members. At stake is both the woman's and the family's honor, both of which these scholars believe are violated, rather than protected, by the state, as the state is essentially emasculating men religiously, tribally and as men by taking control over their women. By assuming the role of decision-maker, the state not only relegates women to the position of perpetual legal minor, but also increases its own legitimacy and power (Al-Rasheed 2007).

At the same time, there are others who note that many Saudi women look to the state for protection from ultraconservative clerics who seek to expand limitations on women's access to public space, particularly employment, due to fear that women will become financially independent and, therefore, a threat to family and social stability. At heart is the question of whether women are subjects, objects, or agents within their families and society and whether rights and limitations are a matter of religion, politics, or culture (DeLong-Bas forthcoming).

Some scholars point to evidence of change over time as the most effective means of evaluating the role of religion in determining women's rights. It is generally agreed that adherence to ritual correctness and the letter of Islamic law in favor of men is the hallmark of twentieth-century interpretation through the era of Grand Mufti bin Baz (d. 1999). For example, in the case of a woman married to a drug addict asking for permission to divorce her husband, the recommendation during the bin Baz era was for the woman to pray about the situation and leave it to God to change the man's heart. If God chose to change the woman's situation, she should be grateful; if not, then she should look forward to reward in the afterlife. However, after bin Baz's death, a much more practical approach to such problems was suggested by the Permanent Committee of Ifta', based on the principle of the preservation of human life outweighing the importance of ritual correctness—a principle originally asserted by Ibn 'Abd al-Wahhab. Thus, the ruling on the case of the woman married to the drug addict changed to one of considering the potential harm to the woman and children in continuing to live with a drug addict, whether due to violence or disease, and concluding that the right of the woman and her children to safety and security was a higher priority than the preservation of the marriage. In other words, a noticeable shift away from ritual correctness and following the letter of the law to consideration of the spirit of the law is quite tangible, at least in *fatawa*. Much work remains to be done in terms of assuring that the court decisions reflect a similar consideration of circumstances and protection of human life and well-being, all of which remain at the heart of contemporary judicial reforms (DeLong-Bas forthcoming).

At the same time, attention should also be given to the state's use of religion to justify expanding public space for women, particularly in business, medicine, and education. Women's education and training in medicine was initially tied to their important roles in the family as mothers who were raising the next generation of children. Literate and educated women were posited as better mothers, particularly because of their important role in teaching children about religion at an early age. Similarly, medical training for women was justified on religious grounds as a matter of preserving female modesty and gender segregation.

Business has also provided important public space for women as the Prophet Muhammad's first wife, Khadija, was a businesswoman and Muhammad himself always supported the right of women to engage in business and commercial matters. Thus, although women were not permitted to contest or vote in elections for the municipal councils in 2005, which were political positions, women were permitted to contest and vote in elections to the boards of directors for the chambers of commerce in the major cities in Saudi Arabia. Some even won election, while others were later appointed to the boards by the state. Ways have also been found around religiously mandated gender segregation through the use of modern technology, such as the telephone, e-mail, and internet chatting, to enable men and women to work productively together and to collaborate while respecting the norms of physical gender segregation.

Wahhabism and the Impact of the Global Communications Era

It would be difficult to overestimate the impact of the global communications era on Saudi society in general and with respect to religious transformation in particular. The dual arrival of the internet and satellite television access during the 1990s, particularly the introduction of *Al-Jazeera* in 1996, marked the end of state control over the media, including in religious matters. No longer bound by state interpretations of religion, the population has discovered a variety of alternative and often competing voices, some of whom enjoy state approval and others of whom do not. Although some have charged that such a process demonstrates the importance of outside voices being projected into the kingdom in order to promote change (Abou El Fadl 2005), others have noted that many of the voices being projected today are Saudi and that Saudis have always maintained the capacity to decide for themselves to whom to listen, even if it has come at the cost of imprisonment.

The terrain for listening to a multiplicity of voices was laid back in the 1960s with the spread of mass education that enabled people to find their own answers through reading rather than relying on the *`ulama`* as transmitters of religious knowledge. This process continued through the 1970s with movement away from the singularly authoritative voice of the Grand Mufti to the inclusion of multiple voices on the Council of Senior `Ulama' and then into the late 1980s and early 1990s through the oppositional voices of the *sahwah shaykhs*, all of which marks the arrival of global communications as a stage in the ongoing development of religious thought and practice in the kingdom, rather than as a complete revolution. The ultimate impact is that neither the state nor the religious establishment has a monopoly on religious discourse within the kingdom today (DeLong-Bas forthcoming).

Some scholars have focused on the potential political impact of unmediated space in Saudi Arabia, noting that the capacity for Saudis to debate history, theology, and politics necessarily undermines authoritarianism in multiple spheres, opening the door to breaking free of the state-sponsored narratives of exclusion, subservience, and obedience and requiring the state to reform how it looks at its constituents (Al-Rasheed 2009). At the same time, challenges remain for turning opposition to authoritarianism into effective action. The ability of Saudis to assemble for political purposes, to hold peaceful rallies or demonstrations, or to engage in acts of civil disobedience remains hampered by both the government and by fear of jihadism. Even the submission of petitions of reform couched in religiously appropriate language can result in state perceptions of disobedience on the part of the signatories, although it is interesting to note that the response of the state is not always uniform. For example, petitions submitted between 2000 and 2004 to senior members of the royal family, many of which are similar to petitions for reform introduced during the 1960s, are reported to have received responsive support from then-Crown Prince Abdullah while meeting with rejection and jail sentences from former Crown Princes Sultan (d. 2011) and Naif (d. 2012). The dual war that ensued against both jihadis and reformists, both of which were accused of causing chaos and discord, highlights the ongoing reality of the contested nature of the relationship between religion and the state, as well as between the state and its people.

Wahhabism and Reform—From Within, From Without, or Simply Impossible?

The nature of the relationship between religion and the state remains a contested topic among both Saudis and scholars. Due to security concerns, much attention has been given to violence and extremism, both within Saudi Arabia (Hegghammer 2010) and abroad as exported by Saudis and incorporated into transnational movements, whether ideologically or financially (Mandaville 2007; Abou El Fadl 2005). These studies are important as case studies, but it should be recognized that they do not represent the fullness of religious debate within the kingdom.

In the end, the main question that both policymakers and academics debate is whether Wahhabism is capable of reforming itself or whether the entire religious approach is beyond the capacity to reform. Some scholars believe that reform is already occurring, much of it from the top-down and demonstrating the role of the royal family in pushing an agenda of reform through the religious establishment, such as the co-educational King Abdullah University for Science and Technology (KAUST) that opened in 2009 with the full support of the king and the prompt sacking of a senior cleric who opposed it on religious grounds, while others point to senior royal family members, such as former Crown Prince Naif (d. 2012), who continued to assert a conservative interpretation of religion, particularly with respect to the state's role in protecting women's status and role in the home as her religiously assigned ideal role. In some cases, reforms have been in progress for decades, such as the shift from a single voice of authority to collective debate and decision making in religious and legal opinions, while others, such as women's right to drive, make only incremental, periodic progress, often set back more by outside interference than by internal dynamics.

The ultimate point is that one should not look simply at 9/11 to understand the political and religious dynamics of Saudi Arabia. Although 9/11 certainly accelerated or gave a jumpstart to some processes of reform, many of these debates had already been underway and had internal, organic developments that are neither directed nor driven by the West, particularly the United States.

References

Abou El Fadl, Khaled. 2005. *The Great Theft: Wrestling Islam from the Extremists*. New York: Harper San Francisco.
Algar, Hamid. 2002. *Wahhabism: A Critical Essay*. Oneonta, NY: Islamic Publications International.
Arebi, Saddeka. 1994. *Women and Words in Saudi Arabia: The Politics of Literary Discourse*. New York: Columbia University Press.
Ayoob, Mohammed, and Hasan Kosebalaban, eds. 2009. *Religion and Politics in Saudi Arabia: Wahhabism and the State*. Boulder, CO: Lynne Rienner Publishers.
Commins, David. 2005. *The Wahhabi Mission and Saudi Arabia*. London: I.B. Tauris.
Cook, Michael. 1989. The Expansion of the First Saudi State: The Case of Washm. In *The Islamic World from Classical to Modern Times: Essays in Honor of Bernard Lewis*, ed. C. E. Bosworth, Charles Issawi, Roger Savory, and A. L. Udovitch. Princeton: Darwin Press, pp. 661–699.

DeLong-Bas, Natana J. 2008. *Wahhabi Islam: From Revival and Reform to Global Jihad*, rev. ed. New York: Oxford University Press.

DeLong-Bas, Natana J. forthcoming. *Jihad for Islam: The Struggle for the Future of Saudi Arabia*. New York: Oxford University Press.

Doumato, Eleanor. 2000. *Getting God's Ear: Women, Islam, and Healing in Saudi Arabia and the Gulf*. New York: Columbia University Press.

Fandy, Mamoun. 1999. *Saudi Arabia and the Politics of Dissent*. New York: Palgrave.

al-Harbi, Dalal Mukhlid. 2008. *Prominent Women from Central Arabia*. Reading, UK: Ithaca Press.

Hegghammer, Thomas. 2010 Jihad *in Saudi Arabia: Violence and Pan-Islamism since 1979*. New York: Cambridge University Press.

Ibrahim, Fouad. 2006. *The Shi`is of Saudi Arabia*. London: Saqi Books.

Mandaville, Peter. 2007. *Global Political Islam*. London: Routledge.

Menoret, Pascal. 2005. *The Saudi Enigma: A History*. London: Zed Books.

Peskes, Esther. 1993. *Muhammad b. Abdalwahhab (1703–1792) im Widerstreit. Untersuchungen zuz Rekonstruktion der Fruhgeschichte der Wahhabiya*. Beirut: Steiner.

Philby, Harry St. John. 1928. *Arabia of the Wahhabis*. London: Constable & Co.

Al-Rasheed, Madawi, and Robert Vitalis, eds. 2004. *Counter-Narratives: History, Contemporary Society and Politics in Saudi Arabia and Yemen*. New York: Palgrave MacMillan.

Al-Rasheed, Madawi. 2007. *Contesting the Saudi State: Islamic Voices from a New Generation*. New York: Cambridge University Press.

Al-Rasheed, Madawi., ed. 2009. *Kingdom without Borders: Saudi Arabia's Political, Religious and Media Frontiers*. New York: Columbia University Press.

Rentz, George Snavely. 2005. *The Birth of the Islamic Reform Movement in Saudi Arabia: Muhammad ibn Abd al-Wahhab (1703/4–1792) and the Beginnings of the Unitarian Empire in Arabia*. London: Arabian Publishing. [This dissertation was originally copyrighted in 1948.]

Teitelbaum, Joshua. 2000. *Holier Than Thou: Saudi Arabia's Islamic Opposition*. Washington, DC: The Washington Institute for Near East Policy, Policy Papers No. 52.

Trofimov, Yaroslav. 2007. *The Siege of Mecca: The Forgotten Uprising in Islam's Holiest Shrine and the Birth of Al Qaeda*. New York: Doubleday, 2007.

Yamani, Maha A. Z. 2008. *Polygamy and Law in Contemporary Saudi Arabia*. Reading, UK: Ithaca Press.

Yamani, Mai. 2004. *Cradle of Islam: The Hijaz and the Quest for an Arabian Identity*. London: I.B. Tauris.

CHAPTER 28

THE AK PARTY IN TURKEY

IBRAHIM KALIN

> I assure you I do not aim at singularity. I give you opinions which have been accepted amongst us, from very early times to this moment, with a continued and general approbation, and which indeed are worked into my mind that I am unable to distinguish what I have learned from others from the results of my own meditation.[1]

THE rise of the Justice and Development Party (Adalet ve Kalkınma Partisi; mentioned hereafter as the AK Party) into prominence in Turkish society and politics is the result of a complex set of circumstances. The AK Party's political outlook, performance in government, electoral base, and successive victories at the ballot box require a proper understanding of Turkish culture and politics at the turn of the second millennium. Major changes in Turkey's surrounding region and the international system since the end of the Cold War have opened up new possibilities for Turkey to assert itself as a major regional power and global player in its foreign policy. Coming to power after a series of economic crises and political stalemate in the late 1990s, the AK Party has been a catalyst of social change and set in motion a new period of reform in Turkish politics. The AK Party's dominance, however, has also been ensured by its ability to be a conduit of change demanded by the Turkish public in general as well as the European Union (EU) criteria. While redefining the main parameters of Turkish politics, the successive AK Party governments since 2002 have made use of the enduring elements of Turkish culture and society, thus treading a carefully crafted path between tradition and change. Acting with a cosmopolitan spirit, the AK Party leaders have embraced both national values and global trends and sought to create a synthesis—a synthesis that suggests new modes of relation between tradition and modernity on the one hand and Islam and the political order on the other.

The AK Party's reformist agenda, while gaining support from its electoral base and the outside world, has brought it into confrontation with the prominent elements of the Turkish establishment including the military, judiciary, media, and pro-status quo business circles. Major divisions have arisen over such critical issues as the 1982 constitution written by the military generals of the 1980 military coup, civil rights and liberties, freedom of religion including the headscarf ban at Turkish universities, the Kurdish issue, demands of the Alevi community, non-Muslim minorities, and civilian-military relations. The AK Party has also faced resistance from the old foreign policy circles that criticize the AK Party for allegedly moving Turkey away from its traditional Western vocation and placing it within a more Eastern and Islamic-looking axis. In addition to the opposition of legal political parties, the AK Party governments have survived several coup attempts in 2003 and 2004, the alleged perpetrators of which have been tried in the Ergenekon and Balyoz cases.

Under the dynamic and bold leadership of Recep Tayyip Erdogan, the successive AK Party governments have had a twofold performance. On the one hand, they have dealt with issues of "high politics" such as democratization, minority rights, secularism, and civilian-military relations and broken many taboos in the country's recent history. On the other hand, they have implemented effective policies to fix the economy, establish a sound financial system, increase trade and foreign direct investment, and inject a new energy into foreign policy—areas in which they have been extremely successful. Steady economic growth, despite the ill effects of the global financial crisis of 2007, has been the backbone of the AK Party's reformist politics and assertive foreign policy. These policies have redefined center-periphery relations in Turkey and created new social and economic opportunities for the disfranchised segments of Turkish society.

In this period of deep social change, massive political realignment, and economic growth, Recep Tayyip Erdogan has been a trailblazer with his charismatic personality, bold political moves, and impressive performance to garner support from among the wide spectrum of Turkish society. Whether confronting the generals, big businesses, media bosses, or Israel, Erdogan has become a powerful voice of the periphery and the marginalized and challenged the establishment in both domestic and international politics. Erdogan has not shied away from taking political risks sometimes at his own peril but has managed to survive several major crises such as the coup attempts of 2003 and 2004 and the closure case against his own party in 2008. Successive electoral victories and increasing popularity have emboldened Erdogan in implementing his reformist agenda and reshaping the main contours of Turkish politics. These elements have brought Erdogan regional and international fame as a regional and global leader watched closely by different constituencies from Europe and the United States to the Balkans and the Middle East. In many ways, Erdogan's personal story, about which he remains rather shy, has become the story of Turkey and the surrounding region in the first decade of the twenty-first century.[2]

In what follows, I will discuss the rise of the AK Party as a center-right political movement with Islamic and national roots and analyze its political identity and reformist agenda in the context of the state-centered tradition of Turkish politics. I shall discuss the AK Party's self-perception as a party of "conservative democracy" within the context of the new dynamics of Turkish politics in the twenty-first century. This will be followed by an evaluation of the AK Party's performance in government since it took office in 2002 and its efforts to strike a balance between politics of identity and politics of services. Finally, I shall look at the AK Party's foreign policy and its struggle to overcome oppositional identities in the new global system with multiple centers and emerging powers.

The AK Party's Political Identity: "Conservative Democracy"

The AK Party's political ideology formulated as "conservative democracy" has emerged in response to the rigid ideological divisions of Turkish politics in the twentieth century. Taking elements from both the right and the left of the political spectrum, the AK Party founders have sought to create a political identity wide enough to embrace different segments of Turkish society from the religious and conservative to the urban and the liberal. They have also embraced the new opportunities of globalization and sought to reconcile them with the traditional Islamic and national values of Turkey. This critical attitude has added an important dimension of cosmopolitanism to the AK Party's brand of Islam and political conservatism and enabled it to look East and West at the same time.[3] Overcoming the fears and threat perceptions of the Cold War era has been one of the hallmarks of the AK Party's political identity and self-perception. Speaking in 2003, Erdogan articulated this point as follows:

> One observes that, like in the case of socialism, liberalism, and conservatism, all political movements are going through a substantive process of interaction with each other. We now witness not a differentiation and polarization of ideologies with sharp and bold lines of division between them, but the formation of new political courses accompanying the pervasiveness of different ideologies. We have before us, therefore, a more colored and multidimensional picture rather than a sharp black-and-white image.[4]

An important component of this "substantive process of interaction" has been the desire to overcome such oppositional identities as religious versus democratic, Islamic versus Western, conservative versus liberal, urban versus rural, and patriotic versus globalist. Such binary oppositions have shaped Turkish culture and politics during the Cold War but can no longer explain the multifaceted realities of the twenty-first century. The new generation of Turkish policy makers, which include many of the AK Party's founders and key players, witnessed the rapid transformation of Turkish culture and politics under Turgut Ozal in the late 1980s and early 1990s. The Ozal years were a period of struggle to integrate Turkey into the global political system after the end of the Cold War, when many policy makers feared that Turkey would lose its strategic significance and relevance for the Western alliance. Acting with a globalist outlook but conservative base, Ozal sought to reform the Turkish political system by opening Turkey up to the new forces of globalization.

The AK Party's political roots, however, go back not to Ozal but to Necmettin Erbakan, the founder of the National Outlook Movement (Milli Gorus). Both Erdogan and Abdullah Gul, Turkey's current president and a close friend of Erdogan, as well as other founders of the AK Party such as Bulent Arinc have entered politics under Erbakan in the 1970s. Until the founding of the AK Party in 2001, they have defended the core political ideas of Milli Gorus regarding Turkey's EU membership, cultural policies, and relations with the Muslim world. But after Erdogan and Gul parted their ways with Erbakan and his Virtue Party in the early 2000 and founded the AK Party, they have adopted a radically different perspective and redefined their political ideology. While the AK Party leadership has been accused by its detractors as a continuation of Milli Gorus and thus maintaining its core Islamist stance, the AK Party has forged a new political identity based on cosmopolitan values, conservative politics, liberal economic policies, and a globalist and pro-active foreign policy.[5]

As the AK Party has positioned itself as a center-right conservative party, it has distinguished itself from the Islamist political parties in the Muslim world. In contrast to Islamist movements that aim to establish a Shari`ah state, the AK Party embraces pluralism and democracy and supports the Anglo-American definition of secularism, which keeps the state at an equal distance to all faiths and religions. This notion of secularism does not establish religion as a source of legislation; instead, it focuses on freedom of religion and the protection of religion from political manipulation. Thus Erdogan separates religion as a source of moral and social values from religion as a basis of state legislation. Articulating this point in 2004, Erdogan said,

> While attaching importance to religion as a social value, we do not think it is right to conduct politics through religion, to attempt to transform government ideologically by using religion, or to resort to organizational activities based on religious symbols. To make religion an instrument of politics and to adopt exclusive approaches to politics in the name of religion harms not only political pluralism but also religion itself. Religion is a sacred and collective value.[6]

Erdogan reiterated this view of secularism in his visit to Egypt in September 2011 in the aftermath of the fall of Hosni Mubarak, causing a lively debate among Egyptian Islamists.

Militant Secularism and Democratization

In order to fully appreciate the AK Party's fine-tuning of secularism, it would be useful to compare and contrast it with the aggressive and militant versions of Turkish secularism. The aggressive Turkish secularists see secularism not simply as a separation of religious and state affairs but as a comprehensive worldview and complete lifestyle. Following the nineteenth-century concepts of rationalism, positivism, scientism, and individualism, the militant secularists see religion and tradition as an absolute other of secularism, modernity, development, and progress and seek to use state power to impose a secularist worldview in the name of modernization. The oppressive nature of Turkish secularism has thus resulted in the curbing of basic religious rights for both the Muslim majority and non-Muslim minorities in Turkey. Not only aggressively antireligious and antitradition programs of social engineering have been turned into a rigid state ideology but also such issues as the banning of headscarves in schools, and universities and public offices have become a deeply divisive issue between secularist-Kamalist elites and mainstream Turkish society. The AK Party's struggle to soften the rigid versions of secularism has been a constant theme of its rule since 2002.

A typical example of the kind of rigid and militant secularism is the 1998 decision of the Constitutional Court of Turkey to ban the Welfare Party (Refah Partisi) of which Prime Minister Erdogan and President Abdullah Gul were members. Deciding to close down the ruling Welfare Party at the height of the infamous February 28 process when the Erbakan government was forced out of office by a "postmodern coup," the Constitutional Court decision stated that secularism is not simply a separation of religion and politics but "separation of religion and worldly affairs.... It means separation of social life, education, family, economics, law, manners, dress code, etc. from religion... It is Turkey's philosophy of life."[7] The Court decision further stated,

> The Turkish Revolution acquired its meaning through secularism. Secularism has separated religiosity and scientific mentality; it accelerated the march toward civilization by preventing the replacement of science by religion. Indeed, [the meaning] of secularism cannot be limited to the separation of religion and the affairs of the state. It is a milieu of civilization, freedom, and modernity, whose dimensions are larger and whose field is broader. It is Turkey's modernization philosophy, its method of living humanly. It is the ideal of the humanity.[8]

This rigid and ideological definition of secularism has created much division and tension between old Republican elites and ordinary citizens. Implementing top-down state secularism as a tool to manage and shape society, the secularist establishment has sought to create a worldview and lifestyle out of a narrow and antireligious definition of secularism.[9] The militant Turkish secularists who have grown to be deeply anti-AK Party see secularism as more essential than democracy for the Republic. They also see the curbing of civil liberties and religious freedom as indispensable for maintaining the secular character of the modern Turkish Republic. Much of the battle over the question of secularism and religion in recent years has raged around this narrow and rigid notion of secularism and the AK Party's struggle to replace "laicism" with an Anglo-American notion of state secularity.[10]

This struggle has been a part of the story of Turkish modernization. The top-down, Jacobean model of Turkish modernization has collided with the moderate and conservative modernity of the ordinary Turkish people. This has created a deep tension between the elites and the people. According to Şerif Mardin, the top-down analyses of Turkish modernization are marred by their simplistic binaries of religion versus secularism (laicism), tradition versus modernity, empire versus nation, reason versus science, progressive enlightenment versus dogmatism, and so forth. Mardin sees this reductionism as a function of the Kamalist ideology of nation building in the early decades of the twentieth century. But he also links it to the "recent attempts to define a Turkish authenticity" as a replay of secular nationalism and radical scientism à la Comte.[11] Attempting to replace Muslim communitarianism with a secular nation-state identity, the founders of the Republic had hoped to change the "superstructure" of Turkish society and create a new "central value system."[12] But they have largely failed in this risky endeavor and instead created artificial and costly divisions across Turkish society.

A New Axis of Center-Periphery Relations

As a result of the process of estrangement and alienation, the center-periphery relations have been a constant theme of social tension and political friction in Turkey. Since coming to power in 2002, the AK Party policies have sought to redefine these relations, allowing more space for the traditionally marginalized members of the periphery. The idea of being a voice for the silent majority and bringing the periphery to the center has been a powerful source of social and political mobilization for the AK Party. Since the AK Party itself comes from the political and economic periphery, it has been able to project itself as an antiestablishment and reformist political movement. Every major confrontation between the AK Party and the establishment has strengthened the AK Party's electoral base and garnered support from liberal writers, columnists, and opinion leaders. This struggle has led to the redefinition of political center in Turkey.[13]

While rejecting militant secularism, the AK Party accepts secularism as the separation of religion and politics, on the one hand, and as the protection of religious belief, on the other. But it also supports the idea of giving more freedom and visibility to religious (and other) identities in the public sphere. The AK Party officials see religious freedom including the freedom of wearing headscarf in universities as part of the larger context of civil liberties and freedoms. It is important to note that the defenders of the right of wearing the headscarf at public institutions oppose the ban on the basis of civil liberties and human rights rather than on the basis of a strictly religious argument. This approach is also adopted by the AK Party, which sees religious freedom as part of the larger framework of human rights. This outlook has been part of the AK Party's political identity and is embraced by the Turkish public, thus giving it a clearly cosmopolitan and globalist outlook in the fiercely patriotic context of Turkish society.

Coming from a political periphery that has long been disenfranchised and disempowered by the state elites, the AK Party leaders emphasize society over the state. They reject secularism as a project of social engineering and instead defend allowing the society in general to develop its own civic identity. Given the largely religious and conservative nature of Turkish society, an organic and free flourishing of the public and civic sphere means that the society at large will maintain its traditional-religious values while embracing such values as democracy, human rights, transparency, accountability, and good governance—values that undergird any civic and democratic regime. Speaking to this point, Erdogan says that "all efforts that impose or order certain principles and aim at a homogeneous society, or are based on social engineering are obstacles to a healthy democratic system.... Our identity as conservative democrats makes us oppose all kinds of social and political engineering."[14] Having suffered from the failed projects of radical social engineering during the single-party rule of the Republican Party (1923–1950), most Turks reject state-imposed policies as creating a deep sense of alienation between the state and the people. One of Erdogan's political virtues has been to fill this gap through social policies based on the traditional values and civic networks of the fairly diverse Turkish society. Erdogan sees not the state but the "people," as he often says, as the ultimate source of political legitimacy. He notes that "the most effective source to make societies more prosperous, open, and democratic, and thus render regimes stronger and more peaceful, can be found within those societies themselves."[15] While critics label this as a form of naïve populism and idealistic nativism, the AK Party's multidimensional and complex identity allows for an inclusive cosmopolitan perspective and political program.

ISLAM AND THE REDEFINITION OF POLITICAL CENTER

The AK Party's first major political manifesto *Conservative Democracy* (2002) written by Prime Minister Erdogan's political advisor Yalçın Akdoğan, currently a member in the

Parliament, and Erdogan's various statements make it clear that the AK Party does not aim to establish a Shari`ah state and thus cannot be called an "Islamist political party." The AK Party's founding leaders hail from a political tradition that has clear affinities with such Islamic movements as the Muslim Brotherhood in the Arab world and the Jama`at-i Islami of the subcontinent of India. There are also causes such as the Palestinian struggle against the Israeli occupation, Afghan war against the Soviets, or the Chechen wars of independence in the 1990s with which the AK Party supporters have identified. But such ideational sympathies and political affinities should not be generalized to assume direct or organic links between the AK Party and the worldwide network of political Islamic movements and organizations. As a ruling political party, the AK Party has developed relations with various political parties and organizations from Greece and Germany to Malaysia and Pakistan.

The AK Party traces its conservatism to the traditional beliefs and practices of the Turkish people as a majority-Muslim society. Erdogan sees Turkey's traditional values and customs as an asset to sustain a fully functioning and pluralistic democracy in such a diverse and multicultural society as Turkey. For instance, in addressing the Kurdish issue[16], Erdogan has appealed to Islam as a unifying bond between Turks, Kurds, Arabs, Circassians, Bosnians, and other ethnic groups. He does not see any contradiction between conservatism and universalism. As he puts it:

> Universal values that are embodied in the concept of democracy and supported by principles such as human rights, rule of law, good governance are the product of the collected wisdom derived from different civilizations. Historically, Judaism, Christianity, and Islam have all played a central role in forming this collective wisdom.[17]

This globalist outlook plays an important role in the AK Party's cosmopolitan political identity and government performance. The process of overcoming oppositional identities and rigid dichotomies, which began with Turgut Ozal after the fall of the Berlin Wall, has reached a new level of maturity under Erdogan. He himself has come to symbolize the ability to manage the multilayered texture of Turkish society with its Muslim, non-Muslim, Turkish and non-Turkish elements. The AK Party's wide appeal with the large parts of Turkish voters stems from its flexible, inclusive, and multilayered political identity. This approach has led to a healthy criticism of the rigid forms of aggressive secularism that have been the hallmark of Turkish modernization since the founding of the Turkish Republic in 1923. Erdogan has articulated this point as follows:

> A significant part of the Turkish society desires to adopt a concept of modernity that does not reject tradition, a belief of universalism that accepts localism, an understanding of rationalism that does not disregard the spiritual meaning of life, and a choice for change that is not fundamentalist. The concept of conservative democracy is, in fact, and answers to this desire of the Turkish people.[18]

Since the AK Party does not incorporate religion into its political program, comparisons with Christian democrat parties in Europe have their limits. The open references to (Christian) religious and moral values in such political parties as the Christian Democratic Union (CDU-CSU) in Germany, the Popular Republican Movement (Mouvement républicain populaire [MRP]) in France, and the Christian Democracy Party (Democrazia Cristiana [DC]) in Italy are not found in the AK Party's political proclamations and election campaigns. In contrast to the Christian democrats of Europe, religion is more subdued in the case of the AK Party, presented as an important source of moral principles and social values of Turkish society rather than a source of legislation or political action. In fact, the AK Party officials have generally avoided comparisons with European Christian democrat parties for domestic political reasons and because of the substantial differences between the experiences of conservative parties in Turkey and Christian political organizations in Europe. Speaking shortly after the November 2002 victory of his party, Erdogan said that "some people may think differently. They may look towards such bodies as the Christian democratic parties in Europe. That is their view and their reality. We do not share it."[19]

In forging a new political identity, the AK Party has sought to reconcile several trends. This identity can be described as conservative in its understanding of history, tradition, and family values, liberal in its economic policies, advocate of social justice in regards to social policies, and Republican and democratic in its notion of representative democracy. While some critics describe this as incoherent and contradictory, the AK Party has managed to maintain its multilayered political identity, and its electoral base seems to be supportive of this inclusive approach. In many ways, this is now a fact of what is described as multiple modernities.[20]

Politics as Good Governance

The AK Party's performance as a ruling party has been a key component of its dominance in Turkish politics since 2002. Maintaining a careful balance between issues of identity and service, the AK Party has outpaced its rivals in successive local and national elections. Several factors have ensured this success for the AK Party. First of all, most Turkish voters, like elsewhere, evaluate a government on its performance in handling the economy and providing services. Coming to power after the disastrous economic crises of 1999 and 2001, the AK Party as a single-party government has performed remarkably well in the economic field, turning Turkey into a major economic power. In 2010, Turkey became the sixth largest economy in Europe and the seventeenth largest in the world, gaining a respectable seat in the G-20. The AK Party's economic team designed one of the most successful economic programs in recent history and brought about an exponential growth in the Turkish gross domestic product (GDP) to the point of parting ways with the International Monetary Fund (IMF) program without an economic or political crisis. Thanks to political stability and a sound financial system, foreign direct investment (FDI) has flown into Turkey despite the global financial crisis of 2007 and 2008. Successive AK Party governments have been largely successful in keeping inflation and unemployment under manageable levels.[21]

Second, Erdogan's background as the mayor of Istanbul has played an important role in delivering services to big cities as well as remote areas of the country. An impressive number of service programs have been designed and implemented to close the gap between urban centers and rural areas while big metropolitan cities have maintained their competitive edge in economic growth and social mobility. The visible success of the AK Party municipalities has given Prime Minister Erdogan a major footing in all corners of the country. The AK Party's socioeconomic policies and programs have maintained a fairly reasonable balance between liberal, free-market policies and the notion of social justice and equal distribution. Providing low-cost social services including free healthcare coverage through green cards for the needy, supplying primary school students with free textbooks, giving monthly stipends for families with children in school, and similar projects have helped low-income families move up the socioeconomic scale. A major housing project undertaken by TOKI, the housing agency under the direct supervision of Prime Minister Erdogan, has built close to half a million apartments for low-income families across the country. All of these policies have paid off in terms of economic and social justice as well as electoral victories for the AK Party.

The balance between identity issues on the one hand, and services and good governance on the other is thus a distinguishing characteristic of the AK Party's political identity. This is reflected in the two words of the Party's official name: justice (*adalet*) and development (*kalkınma*). While "justice" refers to issues concerning identity, equal representation, democracy, civil liberties, human rights, and religious freedom, "development" denotes Turkey's aspirations to become an affluent society and a prosperous country. Widening economic opportunities have opened up new opportunity spaces for new social agents and set in motion new modes of social mobility. This has taken place both horizontally and vertically. While the newly emerging socioeconomic agents have moved more freely and in larger numbers from rural to urban areas, those in the big cities have also moved up in the large scale of social and economic opportunities. For instance, the famous "Anatolian Tigers," composed of medium-size businesses from the central regions and cities of Anatolia, have taken up new opportunities at the national, regional, and global level. Like the other new actors of Turkish modernization, they have embraced globalization in a way that does not negate their religious identities and traditional customs. While the Anatolian Tigers precede the AK Party, they have pushed the social and economic agenda of the Anatolian periphery to the political center.

In regards to social and economic policies, the AK Party has displayed a combination of idealism and pragmatism. Erdogan has refused to follow populist economic policies but also stood up against the IMF's and the World Bank's rigid programs for Turkey. By diversifying the manufacturing sector, inviting foreign investment, keeping a close tap on the banking system, and increasing trade with neighboring countries, the AK Party governments have implemented largely successful economic policies and gained the support and confidence of Turkish voters. Good governance, disciplined work, and self-confidence have undergirded these policies, silencing many of the AK Party's rivals and critics.

JUDICIAL REFORMS AND CIVILIAN-MILITARY RELATIONS

Introducing judicial reforms to democratize the Turkish judiciary and redefining the military under democratic control has been one of the most pressing challenges that the AK Party governments have faced. The Turkish military has not been shy about interfering with civilian politics as evidenced by the four coups and interventions in 1960, 1971, 1980, and 1997. The military generals have justified these interventions on the basis of their narrow definition of the security of the Republic and the very specific notion of secularism discussed above.[22] The 1982 constitution assigns to the military the mission of protecting the Turkish Republic and its core values against "internal and external threats." Combined with the traditional respect of the Turkish people for the military, army generals have been open about assuming a political and ideological role for the protection of the secular Republic and acted both openly and discretely against what they considered to be threats to the state. Most political parties and governments, fearful of the army's power and influence, have acquiesced.[23]

As part of its reformist agenda, the AK Party has come, especially in its early years, into confrontation with the powerful Turkish military that suspects the AK Party and its core leadership of maintaining a hidden Islamist agenda and engaging in political "dissimulation" (*takiyye*). Given the fact that the army generals had forced the Erbakan government out of power in 1997 through a "postmodern coup"[24] and that the AK Party itself has survived several coup attempts in its early tenure in government, the civilian-military relations has been part of the AK Party's political thinking on democracy and democratic control.[25] The AK Party has largely succeeded in redefining the matrix of civilian-military relations to set limits to the military's involvement in politics and to bring the army under democratic control. Erdogan's careful handling of the sensitive issue of civilian-military relations has aimed at keeping the powerful Turkish Armed Forces out of politics and changing Turkey's national security concept while at the same time strengthening the army's military capabilities and professional organization. The politically influential National Security Council, traditionally a platform for the military to dictate its views upon civilian governments, has been turned into an advisory body with a civilian secretary general. In addition to the army, the powers and responsibilities of police forces have been redefined and a "zero-tolerance to torture policy" has been successfully implemented. These measures have been supported by the Turkish public and hailed as one of the most important steps toward the normalization of Turkish democracy. In tandem with Turkey's new security outlook, most state institutions have abandoned their old threat perceptions going back to the Cold War period and adopted a more sophisticated and nuanced understanding of the global political order in the first decade of the twenty-first century.[26]

In regards to judicial reforms and the new constitution, various antidemocratic and tutelary laws have either been changed or abolished. For instance, state security courts with extra powers have been abolished. The 1982 constitution drafted by the military generals who carried out the 1980 coup have been amended with the most substantial changes coming on September 12, 2010 where the Constitutional Court and the judicial bodies have been restructured. In 2007, the AK Party had attempted to draft a new constitution but failed to garner the support of opposition parties. After the September 12, 2010 referendum, the AK Party has again raised the issue of the new constitution but achieving a national consensus with all the political parties on the right and the left, nongovernmental organizations (NGOs), and human rights organizations seems as difficult as before. The new constitution is likely to remain a contentious political issue.[27]

These democratic reforms have been introduced in tandem with Turkey's EU membership goal—a goal that the AK Party governments have taken to heart especially between 2003 and 2007. While the EU regulations and the Copenhagen Criteria have been an important driving force behind the reforms, the demand for more transparency, accountability, and civilian rule has also provided a suitable political environment for the government to carry on with its reforms. The AK Party acted on this political capital and secured the support of liberal intellectuals and academics. But it also mobilized its conservative and traditionally anti-Western base in support of the EU and sought to redefine Turkey's relationship with Western culture and civilization based on universal values, equality, and fairness. This has been one of the most dramatic and unforeseen changes in the recent history of Turkish culture: traditionally anti-Western and anti-European segments of Turkish society have changed their view in favor of joining the EU as a full member whereas the pro-Western secularist establishment has turned against the EU because of its suspicion that EU reforms provide a cover for the AK Party's hidden Islamist agenda.[28]

While critics express concern over the AK Party's loss of enthusiasm for the EU, the domestic agenda of democratization has not lost its steam. The bumpy period since 2005 when Turkey began official negotiations for full membership in the EU has sharpened the general sense that Turkey needs EU reforms not only for the sake of membership but also because of the higher standards of democracy, good governance, transparency, accountability, and human rights that the Copenhagen Criteria stipulate. It should be noted, however, that the once highly enthusiastic Turkish public has become rather frustrated and fatigued about Turkey joining the EU because of the opposition of several key EU members including France and Germany to Turkey's full membership.

The AK Party and Foreign Policy: Turkey Rediscovers the World

Foreign policy is one of the areas in which the AK Party has introduced a new paradigm and changed the strategic thinking of Turkish policy makers. Acting with a mixture of idealism, realism, and pragmatism, the AK Party governments have redefined Turkey's foreign policy priorities and begun to embrace Turkey's traditional hinterland extending from the Balkans to the Middle East. Ever since the traumatic loss of the Ottoman Empire, Turkish policy makers have seldom appealed to anything like the American doctrine of "manifest destiny" as the guiding principle of an interventionist and expansionist foreign policy.[29] Turkish foreign policy during much of the early Republican period has revolved around Ataturk's famous phrase "peace at home, peace in the world," which meant developing good relations with big powers but maintaining a minimum engagement with adjacent neighbors. The Eurocentric thrust of Turkish modernization and its ideological preferences have kept Turkey away from playing a significant role in the Middle East and the larger Muslim world for much of the twentieth century. The geopolitical realities of the twenty-first century, however, are urging Turkey to reclaim its place in the geopolitical areas over much of which the Ottoman Empire had ruled for four centuries.

In its new foreign policy outlook, Turkey is responding to the fundamental changes taking place in the international system and its immediate neighborhood. The current international order is functioning without a center or with multiple centers, which amounts more or less to the same thing. The center(s) of the world are up for grabs, and there are no guaranteed winners on the horizon. The talk about a "post-American world" is increasingly turning into a debate about a post-imperial America, on the one hand, and the "Rise of the Rest," on the other.[30] It remains to be seen how the survival instincts of American power will play out in world politics. Yet it is clear that it is no longer possible to manage the world system from a solely American, European, or Russian point of view. Big contenders such as China and India and emerging powers such as Turkey and Brazil are changing the way international order functions and regional issues are addressed. By becoming an economic powerhouse and a major diplomatic force, Turkey has transformed itself into a regional power and a global actor with ties in both the East and the West.

As a member of the North Atlantic Treaty Organization (NATO) and candidate for the EU, Turkey has maintained a high-level strategic partnership with Europe and the United States. Despite the opposition of France and Germany to Turkey's EU membership, Turkey has good bilateral relations with most European countries and close to half of its foreign trade is still with Europe. The United States-Turkish relations have maintained their significance and momentum under the AK Party rule despite Turkey's refusal to support the US invasion of Iraq in 2003. In his visit to Turkey in April 2009, his first to any country as US president, Barack Obama used the phrase "model partnership" to describe the broad spectrum of United States-Turkish relations from Iraq and Afghanistan to Lebanon and the Balkans. The concept of model partnership, however, has been tested on several occasions involving the Iranian nuclear program and Turkish-Israeli relations after the Gaza war of 2008.[31]

While maintaining good relations with the West, the AK Party has also strengthened Turkey's relationship with its Middle Eastern and Muslim neighbors. The policy of normalization and engagement with neighbors has led to a heavy diplomatic traffic, lifting of visas, the establishment of "high-level strategic councils," increased trade and tourism, and numerous mediation efforts by Turkey. Turkey's engagement policy with Syria has ushered in a new period of political and economic relations though things have taken a dramatic turn after the Asad regime's brutal crackdown on the opposition forces in Syria after the Arab revolutions of Tunisia, Libya, and Egypt. Erdogan has openly supported the Arab revolutions and stood by the legitimate demands of the people of Syria for political reform. This has led to serious tensions between Turkey and Syria especially since the end of 2011. The civil war in Syria has also created divisions between Turkey and the outside supporters of the Baath regime in Syria, i.e., Iran and Russia.

Turkey's refusal to take part in the US invasion of Iraq has not prevented it from playing an active role in the postinvasion Iraqi politics and regional diplomacy. Turkey has been involved in Lebanon and Palestine, where good relations with all political parties and factions have been maintained. Turkey's relations with Iran have increased especially in regards to trade as Iran has become Turkey's second largest gas provider after Russia. Turkey has sought to improve relations with all of its neighbors including Greece, Bulgaria, Georgia, and Armenia. The AK Party governments have succeeded in creating a new sense of confidence with Greece, Turkey's traditional rival in the Aegean Sea, and started a process of increased relationship between the two countries. In 2009, Turkey signed a protocol with Armenia to normalize relations but the Nagorno-Karabakh issue and the Armenian claims to genocide have stalled the process.

This policy of looking East and West at the same time has become a hallmark of the AK Party's foreign policy vision. An important application of this new outlook is the Alliance of Civilizations Initiative co-sponsored by Prime Minister Erdogan and his Spanish counterpart Zapatero under the UN secretary general. Erdogan has opposed Huntington's clash of civilizations analysis and proposed the alliance of civilizations as an alternative platform to bring diverse cultures and societies closer to one another. Reflecting a strong sense of cosmopolitanism, the Alliance of Civilizations Initiative has appealed in particular to Muslim and Western societies to overcome their historical differences and reject calls for clash and confrontation.

While Erdogan's strong political leadership has introduced a new paradigm, Ahmet Davutoğlu, Erdogan's chief foreign policy advisor from 2003 to 2009 and the minister of foreign affairs since 2009, is the main figure to articulate and execute Turkey's new foreign policy. As a rising scholar of international relations, Davutoğlu had already developed the concept of "strategic depth" in his hefty book *Stratejik Derinlik: Türkiye'nin Uluslararası Konumu* (Strategic Depth: Turkey's International Position), where he argued for a new geopolitical outlook for Turkey in the twenty-first century. "Strategic depth" defines the value of a nation on the basis of its geostrategic location in the complex web of international relations. History and geography, the two invariables of a country, can be an asset or burden depending on how one makes use of them. Turkey is perfectly situated across the different geopolitical and civilizational fault lines that unite the Euro-Asian landmass with the Middle East and North Africa. A good part of the current world politics on energy and security, for instance, is shaped in Turkey's immediate neighborhood and adjacent regions. Turkey's geostrategic position, Davutoğlu further argued, is reinforced by its historical and cultural ties to the main lands of the Ottoman Empire, pushing Turkey to a natural position of regional leadership.[32] Also implicit in Davutoğlu's argument was a shift from the classical model of the nation-state to the new civilizational framework of analysis that includes a new understanding of globalization and regional cooperation.

While the detractors of the AK Party and its new internationalist outlook used such labels as Islamist, neo-Ottomanist, and anti-Western to discredit Turkey's new foreign policy, the AK Party officials have defined it as a process of normalization and regional cooperation. According to Davutoğlu, the new Turkish foreign policy is based on five principles that position Turkey as a "center-country" in its region. They include a balance between security and democracy, "zero-problem policy with neighbors," developing relations with neighboring regions and beyond, "multidimensional foreign policy," and "rhythmic diplomacy."[33] Over the years, these principles, underlying much of the AK Party's foreign policy portfolio, have matured and yielded important gains for both Turkey and its allies.

In a world of multiple economic powerhouses and emerging regional actors, new forms of geopolitical alliances and regional partnerships have already begun to emerge. Turkey's geoeconomic and geocultural position allows it to have multidimensional relations with a diverse network of states, societies, and communities.[34] This is reflected in Turkey's increased relations with its Arab and Muslim neighbors as well as in its ability to project itself as a newly emerging soft power. For the Arab world and beyond, for instance, Turkey's soft power is increasingly becoming a point of interest among politicians, policy makers, academics, journalists, NGOs, and businessmen.[35] The interest of the Arab world in Turkey's EU membership process is another area in which Turkey's multidimensional geopolitical position has overcome the traditional East-West divisions.[36]

Turkey's new foreign policy outlook is a result of the newly emerging geopolitical imagination and the tectonic changes in the global and regional order since the end of the Cold War. This new geographic imagery is seen in the public statements of Turkish officials and their reflections on the future of the region. The Turkish President Abdullah Gul's following statement sums up this perspective in a vivid language:

> The Middle East, with its natural and human resources and historical, cultural, and economic background, has been the cradle of civilizations. The people of this region have been the guardians of the spiritual values that we all share and have also been the producers and

distributors of material richness. Science, literature, and art were at their peak in the Middle East for centuries. The region has thus made fundamental contributions to the advancement of human civilization, and the peoples of this region lived together in peace and harmony during the Ottoman centuries. We are indeed a direct witness to the fact that the peoples of this vital area can live and prosper in peace. The Middle East and its peoples do not deserve the cycle of violence and desperation in which they have been living for a long time. I am convinced that peace, progress, and prosperity can again reign in this region.[37]

Conclusion

Combining a mixture of traditional Islamic, national, and cosmopolitan values, the AK Party has transformed the main parameters of Turkish culture and politics in the first decade of the twenty-first century. The AK Party policies have been marked by a desire to reconcile differences and overcome binary oppositions. Whether we talk about Islam and democracy, religion and secularism, national unity and pluralism, security and freedom, Europe and the Middle East, or economic development and ethical norms, the AK Party leaders have sought to craft a multilayered and flexible political identity to move Turkey beyond oppositional identities and create a new set of values. The AK Party's Islamic credentials and patriotic leanings have not prevented it from developing strong cosmopolitan and globalist approaches and policies. Key to the AK Party's success has been its ability to dovetail domestic transformation with global trends in its national politics and foreign policy. The policy of reconciling differences and overcoming oppositional identities is likely to continue under the AK Party.

By keeping a balance of identity issues and providing services to the people, the AK Party has been a voice of change in the post-Cold War period. But it has also been an instigator of change and taken many bold steps to challenge the status quo fiercely defended by the Turkish establishment. The AK Party's reformist political agenda has made Turkey more secure and democratic and redefined the center-periphery relations to allow more space for the new agents of globalization. These new agents include urban and rural actors, religious and conservative entrepreneurs, national and cosmopolitan figures, and local NGOs and institutions with increasing international ties. The AK Party has played a key role in bringing these new actors to the fore and thus diversified the Turkish public sphere in a way that no other political movement has ever done. But it is also this diverse and dynamic public that pushes the AK Party further to implement an agenda of change and reform.

As Turkey continues to become a more democratic and open society, previously suppressed identities such as religious-Islamic, Kurdish, Alevi, or Armenian become more visible and freely expressed. Contrary to the fears of the secular nationalists, the increasing visibility of these identities has not made Turkish society weak or vulnerable. By allowing different identities to express themselves and by empowering the individual and the society against the state, the AK Party governments have sought to close the gap between the state and the public—a gap that has created a deep sense of alienation and disenfranchisement for much of the Republican history. The AK Party's strong electoral base has led to the emergence of a new notion of political legitimacy without disrupting the state. Furthermore, Turkey under the AK Party has become more self-confident and buoyant in its self-perception and the view of the world. This newfound confidence has invited numerous economic and political opportunities for the fairly diverse members of Turkish society, and turned Turkey into an economic powerhouse and a major political force in the region. As Turkey marches towards the first centennial of the Turkish Republic in 2023, it is likely to continue to shed its old fears and recreate itself as regional actor and global player.

Notes

1. Edmund Burke, Reflections on the Revolution in France, 147.
2. For an analysis of Erdogan's profile, see Metin Heper and Sule Toktas, "Islam, Modernity, and Democracy in Contemporary Turkey: The Case of Recep Tayyip Erdogan," *The Muslim World* 93, no. 2 (April 2003): 157–185. For his biography until he became prime minister, see Huseyin Besli and Omer Ozsoy, *Tayyip Erdogan* (Istanbul: Meydan Yayinlari, 2010).
3. Islamic actors with a cosmopolitan outlook include groups outside the AK Party, such as the Gulen movement, the so-called Anatolian Tigers, and their major business association MUSIAD and independent intellectuals. For an evaluation of these actors, see Yildiz Atasoy, *Turkey, Islamists and Democracy: Transition and Globalization in a Muslim State* (London: I. B. Tauris, 2005), 146–176. See also Hakan Yavuz's more comprehensive survey in his *Islamic Political Identity in Turkey* (Oxford: Oxford University Press, 2003).
4. Quoted in Hakan Yavuz, ed., *The Emergence of a New Turkey* (Salt Lake City: University of Utah Press, 2006), 334.
5. For an assessment of the National View Movement (Milli Gorus), see Ahmet Yıldız, "Politico-Religious Discourse of Political Islam in Turkey: The Parties of National Outlook," *The Muslim World* 93 (April 2003): 187–209.
6. Quoted in Yavuz, *The Emergence of a New Turkey*, 336.
7. Quoted in Ergun Ozbudun and William Hale, *Islamism, Democracy and Liberalism in Turkey: The Case of the AKP* (London: Routledge, 2010), 22.
8. Anayasa Mahkemesi, *Kararlar Dergisi* [Constitutional Court Reports], vol. 25, pp 147–148, quoted in Ozbudun and Hale, *Islamism, Democracy and Liberalism in Turkey*, p 166.
9. For a comparison and contrast of two types of secularism called "passive" and "assertive," see Ahmet T. Kuru, "Passive and Assertive Secularism: Historical Conditions, Ideological Struggles, and State Policies toward Religion" *World Politics* 59 (July 2007): 568–594. See also the article by the same author "Reinterpretation of Secularism in Turkey: The Case of the Justice and Development Party" in Yavuz, *The Emergence of a New Turkey*, 136–159.
10. For an analysis of the difference between secularism and laicism in the case of Turkey, see Andrew Davison, "Turkey, a 'Secular' State? The Challenge of Description," *The South Atlantic Quarterly* 102, nos. 2/3 (spring/summer, 2003): 333–350.
11. Serif Mardin, *Religion, Society, and Modernity in Turkey* (Syracuse, NY: Syracuse University Press, 2006), 135.
12. Ibid., 230.
13. Cf. Chris Houston, "The Never Ending Dance: Islamism, Kemalism and the Power of Self-institution in Turkey," *The Australian Journal of Anthropology* 17, no. 2 (2006): 161–178.
14. *International Symposium on Conservatism and Democracy*, quoted in Ozbudun and Hale, *Islamism, Democracy and Liberalism in Turkey*, 24–25.
15. Yavuz, *The Emergence of a New Turkey*, 333.
16. At the time of the writing of this chapter, the Kurdish issue entered a new phase in Turkey. After thirty-years of a bloody and costly war against the Turkish State, the Kurdish

separatist terror organization PKK's leader Abdullah Ocalan made a call on March 21st, on the day of the Nevruz, on the PKK to disarm and leave Turkey. In the moths following the disarmament call, PKK fighters have begun leaving Turkey for northern Iraq and other third countries. This is a historic moment in the modern history of the Turkish Republic. Once completed, this will be Erdogan's most important and enduring achievement as other political leaders including Turgut Ozal had tried to solve the Kurdish issue through a negotiated settlement. Resolving the Kurdish issue will open up new possibilities for Turkish domestic politics. It will also strengthen Turkey's position in the region.

17. Ibid., 333–334.
18. Ibid., 335.
19. Interview with Seref Özgencil, *The New Europe* 1, no. 2 (December 2002): 11, quoted in William Hale, "Christian Democracy and the AKP: Parallels and Contrasts," *Turkish Studies* 6, no. 2 (June 2005): 293–310, 293.
20. Nilufer Gole places the emergence of post-Islamist politics within the context of multiple modernities; see her "Snapshots of Islamic Modernities," *Daedalus* 129, no. 1 (winter 2000): 91–117. See also Robert W. Hefner, "Multiple Modernities: Christianity, Islam, and Hinduism in a Globalizing Age," *Annual Review of Anthropology* 27 (1998): 83–104.
21. For an assessment of the AK Party's economic policies, see Marcie J Patton, "The Economic Policies of Turkey's AKP Government: Rabbits from a Hat?" *The Middle East Journal* 60, no. 3 (summer 2006): 513–536.
22. Ümit Cizre, "The Anatomy of the Turkish Military's Political Autonomy," *Comparative Politics* 29, no. 2 (January 1997): 151–166.
23. For the problem of the democratic control of the military in Turkey, see Aylin Güney and Peter Karatekelioğlu, "Turkey's EU Candidacy and Civil-Military Relations: Challenges and Prospects," *Armed Forces & Society* 31, no. 3 (spring 2005): 439–462.
24. Cengiz Çandar, "Postmodern Darbe" [Postmodern Coup], *Sabah* [Istanbul], June 28, 1997.
25. Metin Heper, "The Justice and Development Party Government and the Military in Turkey," *Turkish Studies* 6, no. 2 (June 2005): 215–231.
26. For the political context of civilian-military relations in Turkey, see Umit Cizre, "Problems of Democratic Governance of Civil-Military Relations in Turkey and the European Union Enlargement Zone," *European Journal of Political Research* 43 (2004): 107–125.
27. For the constitutional debate and legal amendments under AK Party, see Ergun Özbudun and Ömer F. Gençkaya, *Democratization and the Politics of Constitution-Making in Turkey* (Budapest: Central European University Press, 2009).
28. For the Turkish perceptions of the West as a cultural, religious, and political entity, see Ibrahim Kalin, Bekir Berat Özipek, and Kudret Bülbül, *Türkiye'de Toplumun Batı Algısı: Din, Kültür, Siyaset* [The Perception of the West in Turkish Society: Religion, Culture, Politics] (Ankara: SETA Yayınları, 2008). For a summary of this study in English, see the same authors, "A Fragmented Vision: Perceptions of the West in Turkish Society," co-authored with Kudret Bulbul and Bekir Berat Ozipek, *Insight Turkey* 10, no. 1 (2008): 129–147.
29. See, for instance, Robert Kagan, *Dangerous Nation: America's Foreign Policy from Its Earliest Days to the Dawn of the Twentieth Century* (New York: Vintage, 2007), where the author argues that US foreign policy has always been expansionist and interventionist.
30. See, for instance, Alice Amsden's *The Rise of "The Rest": Challenges to the West from Late-Industrializing Economies* (Oxford: Oxford University Press, 2003).
31. Cf. Ibrahim Kalin, "US-Turkish Relations under Obama: Promise, Challenge and Opportunity in the 21st Century," *The Journal of Balkan and Near East Studies* 12, no. 1 (2010): 93–108.

32. For more on "strategic depth" in English, see Alexander Murinson, "The Strategic Depth Doctrine in Turkish Foreign Policy," *Middle Eastern Studies* 42, no. 6 (November 2006): 945–964. See also Ahmet Davutoğlu, "Turkey's Foreign Policy Vision: An Assessment of 2007," *Insight Turkey* 10, no. 1 (January–March 2008): 77–96.
33. Davutoğlu, "Turkey's Foreign Policy Vision," 79–83.
34. For an assesment of Turkish foreign policy from a new geopolitical point of view, see Ibrahim Kalin, "Turkish Foreign Policy: Framework, Values and Mechanisms," *International Journal* LXVII, no. 1 (winter 2011–2012): 7–21.
35. See, for instance, the essays by Bilgin and Elis, Beng, Altunisik, and Altinay in the special soft power issue of *Insight Turkey* 10, no. 2 (April–June 2008) on Turkey's soft power. For the Arab interest in new Turkey, see Ibrahim Kalin, "Debating Turkey in the Middle East: The Dawn of a New Geopolitical Imagination," *Insight Turkey* 11, no. 1 (winter 2009): 83–96. See also my "Soft Power and Public Diplomacy in Turkey," *Perceptions* XVI, no. 3 (Autumn 2011): 5–23.
36. Cf. Elie Podeh, "'The Final Fall of the Ottoman Empire': Arab Discourse over Turkey's Accession to the European Union," *Turkish Studies* 8, no. 3 (September 2007): 317–328.
37. Abdullah Gül, "Turkey's Role in a Changing Middle East Environment," *Mediterranean Quarterly* (winter 2004): 4.

CHAPTER 29

SUDAN: THE INSECURITY OF POWER AND THE REVENGE OF THE STATE

ABDELWAHAB EL-AFFENDI[1]

In one of the rare reports recording Prophet Muhammad's sense of humor, it is mentioned that an elderly lady once approached him with a request to pray for her to enter paradise. "Mother of so-and-so" the Prophet replied, "no old woman ever enters paradise." The woman turned away in tears, but the Prophet immediately sent someone to tell her that what he meant was that she would not be an old woman in paradise, since all those admitted become youthful again (al-Albani 1996, 1221–1222).

The same can be said about Islamic movements (and for that matter, Communist movements, armies, etc.): an Islamic movement does not take power *as an Islamic movement*. This is especially so when it takes power by force. When a movement (or an organization) takes power by force, it becomes its first victim. In a coup, when a group of (usually middle-ranking) officers takes power in the name of the military, the first thing to go is the military's discipline and hierarchy. The putschists would have to create an alternative mechanism to control the army "from outside." This is usually a kind of intelligence apparatus, a "conspiratorial" clique for whom the army becomes the main threat.

The same process happened in communist revolutions and coups, where a group of party bosses usually conspired to dominate and "purge" all those who stood in their way—in the name of the revolution, of course. Communist rule had thus invariably ended up as one-man rule backed up by the security-intelligence apparatus, the only mechanism to institute a proper rule of terror.

METAMORPHOSIS INTO POWER

What happened with the "National Salvation Revolution" in Sudan in June 1989 had an element of both developments: a small group of middle-ranking army officers publicly told the army (and the nation) that they had taken power in its name, but privately told Islamists that it was in fact in their name that they have assumed power.² As a result, this group had two problems instead of one: an army and a movement. The challenge of controlling these two organizations, not to mention using them to control the population at large, would determine the regime's behavior.

In theory, this was the first takeover of power by a modern Islamist movement. Following the collapse of the Turkish caliphate in 1924, only two states remained that derived legitimacy from Islamic norms: the Saudi monarchy and the Yemeni Imamate. The Moroccan and Afghan monarchies also had deep Islamic roots, but both had practically adopted secular norms of governance. When modern Islamist movements began to emerge in the 1920s shortly after the collapse of the caliphate, seeking to fill the perceived vacuum left by the disappearance of that most authoritative of Islamic institutions, none wanted to adopt any of the traditional models. For Islamists, the traditional institutions were responsible for failing both to fill the authority vacuum and to face up to the challenges of modernity. The caliphate was usually referred to as a goal, and loss of the authority of religious establishments was bemoaned; but the groups were under too much influence by modernity to accept traditional institutions at face value. It is very telling that the first major political takeover in which the Egyptian Muslim Brotherhood became involved was the 1948 abortive constitutional revolution in Yemen, a revolt against the centuries-old Imamate (Said 1995).

Even here, though, that revolt was led by traditional *'ulama'*, with the Muslim Brotherhood playing only a supporting role. Modern Islamic movements did contribute to the Islamic transformations in Iran and Afghanistan, but in both polities, they were eventually sidelined in favor of traditionalist coalitions of *'ulama'*, tribal chiefs, and/or *bazaaris*. Before and after that, some movements became junior/token partners in governments in several countries, including in Malaysia, Pakistan, Kuwait, Jordan, and Sudan itself in the 1970s and 1980s. However, Sudan was the first country where a thoroughly modern Islamic movement came to assume sole political authority in a postcaliphate state.

Crucially, however, the movement did not announce itself as such when it did. In fact following the coup of June 30, 1989, the National Salvation Revolution and its declared leader, Brigadier Omar Hasan Ahmad al-Bashir, vehemently denied any links to the Islamists. Dr. Hasan al-Turabi, leader of the National Islamic Front (NIF), and a number of his top lieutenants, were sent to jail together with other rival political leaders. For many years, the regime considered the label "NIF regime" as the most libelous accusation against it and reacted with hostility to those making it.

Turabi and other leaders explained this act of "dissimulation" by arguing that an early revelation of the true Islamic character of the regime would have led to an international onslaught, which would have stifled it at birth. The need of the regime to "disguise" itself in a nationalist garb betrayed a realization of the difficulties confronting an Islamic movement acceding to power overtly in Sudan. However, this sense of insecurity aside, the suspicion that the Sudanese Islamists may never be able to assume power as Islamists manifested itself early, in particular in the mind of Turabi. Already in the early 1960s, while still a postgraduate student in France, he lobbied unsuccessfully for the Muslim Brotherhood to be transformed into a pressure group rather than a political party (El-Affendi 1991, 63–64). This suggestion was prompted by the realization that the movement had a significant potential for success as a pressure group, but limited capability as a party. In 1955, while the Muslim Brotherhood was still a few years old, and with only a few scores of members, it had successfully pressured all major political parties into adopting the idea of an Islamic constitution.

By contrast, the performance of the group as a political party was less than impressive outside student politics.

When he assumed leadership in late 1964, Turabi immediately embarked on a policy of broadening the appeal of the movement by turning it into a "front" rather than a party. This effort was pushed further with the establishment of the NIF in 1985. In each phase, the core Islamist membership was "diluted," so to speak, by building coalitions with constituencies not traditionally supportive of Islamism. The clear implication was that this new broader membership, being not strictly "Islamist," needed to be attracted to the organization by offering something else on top of the pure Islamist message. With the establishment of the National Congress (NCP) in 1991, the organization has all but lost its Islamist specificity. In response to an outcry from a disgruntled membership, NCP members who still coveted the Islamist label were permitted to set a largely symbolic "Special Entity" (*kayan khass*; later renamed "the Islamic Movement") within the NCP.

It was in 1977, again at the instigation of Turabi, that the Muslim Brotherhood combined the realization that it was not going to accede to power in its Islamist guise with a determination to attain power within the following two decades. A general outline strategy was devised accordingly, envisaging concerted activities to expand the movement's membership tenfold within a decade, increase its influence in the state and economy, and improve its organizational capabilities by building new youth and women wings and a plethora of associated economic and civil society institutions (Turabi 1992: 71–72). Influence on the state and its bureaucracy and the accumulation of experience in running state institutions were also major objectives. A central assumption was that the Nimeiri regime would survive that long, coupled with a determination to keep it in power until the movement was ready to inherit it (Makki 1990, 161–170; El-Affendi 1991, 112; Simone 1994, 52–53; Sidahmed 1997, 191–212).

This strategy was adopted after a variety of coalition-building endeavors achieved minimal results. Turabi's preferred strategy was to fuse the Muslim Brotherhood with the two main religious-based parties (the Umma Party, based on the Ansar sect, and the Democratic Unionist Party [DUP], supported by the Khatmiyya sect), and thus form a mega-Islamic party that could dominate Sudan's democratic politics. However, the collapse of the National Front (a coalition built around this idea) amid mutual recriminations after its leader Sadiq al-Mahdi agreed to a separate "National Reconciliation" deal with Nimeiri was a blow to such hopes. Nevertheless, up until the first few months after the June 1989 coup, Turabi was still hoping for a deal with the two leaders, but they both rejected his approaches, thus steeling his determination to go down the authoritarian path (El-Affendi 1995).

It has since been argued that the shift in Turabi's stance toward democracy was due mainly to disillusionment with the operation of sectarian politics and frustration with having to play the junior partner in that game, and/or by the opportunities offered by dramatic developments such as Nimeiri's 1983 Islamization measures (Muhyiddin 2006, 20; Esposito and Voll 1996, 91–92; Sidahmed 1997, 191–193; El-Affendi 1991; Makki 1990, 75–76). Turabi's authoritarian turn was certainly remarkable, given his consistent support for democracy in his previous interventions, leading one commentator to argue that democracy occupied "a major role in al-Turabi's discourse, because of his perception that it personifies Islam's capability of readoption and readaptation of modern doctrines" (Moussalli 1999, 164; cf. El-Affendi 1991, 159–162; Al-Sulami 2003, 198–203; Ibrahim 1999).

Turabi and his supporters justified their resort to a military takeover by arguing that other actors (foreign and local) did not play according to the rules. Their argument was that the Third Democracy in Sudan had in fact collapsed in February 1989 when the army produced its famous memorandum giving the government an ultimatum to show its seriousness in either pursuing war or peace. As a result, the NIF was forced out of the coalition government. The pressure did not just come from the army, but also from foreign powers and from the southern rebel movement, another political force using violence. In addition, there was a perception that the civilian government was on the verge of collapse, and many rival groups were in a race to take over (Turabi 1992, 203; Muhyiddin 2006, 164–166; Lowrie 1993, 22; El-Affendi 1995; Simone 1994, 60–62).

The movement was also motivated by a deep sense of insecurity. Having been at the receiving end of violence from the Nimeiri regime, both at its inception and during its dying days, it did not feel it could risk another hostile military takeover. Turabi was arrested during the first few hours of Nemeiri's coup and spent about six years in jail. This has created the feeling that the movement was witnessing the "most perilous phase in its history" in those first few months in the summer of 1969 (Muhyiddin 2006, 15; Lowrie 1993, 21–22). Turabi was also in prison when Niemeiri fell, and rumors circulated about plans to execute him after a show trial. The Islamists' sense of insecurity was significantly heightened as a result of these experiences, especially as they contemplated the experience of fellow Islamists in Egypt, Iraq, Syria, and elsewhere, who suffered severe persecution.

The feeling of insecurity permeated the whole political scene. It is paradoxical, as some commentators have noted, that the unique triumph of the Sudanese people in toppling the first military regime in Sudan in October 1964 (a triumph that was miraculously duplicated in April 1985) was followed by intense "rivalry and antagonism" between rival political forces that felt threatened by each other and resorted to violence that in turn generated more violence "and locked these groups into an uphill fight for survival" (Gallab 2008, 64–65, 83). Following the dissolution of the Communist party in 1965, and the emerging consensus on an Islamic constitution, the forces of the secular left felt that they needed to take action to end the "war of political and intellectual attrition" waged against them by the Islamists (Ali 1991, 70). The violent crackdown on Islamists by the hostile regime has in turn provoked fears in the Islamist camp of a threat of "extermination" (Turabi 1992, 31–32; Ali 1991, 73).

This sense of insecurity, especially as it intensified with the outbreak of the civil war, played a crucial role in influencing the decision on the coup, and also in mobilizing support for it among some of the more reluctant supporters. However, it has to be noted that in spite of Turabi's theoretical emphasis on democracy, he has never ruled out the use of force to achieve the transition to an Islamic political order (El-Affendi 1991, 60–62; Turabi 1992, 249–254). By the late 1970s, the default plan was that the movement could build sufficient popular support and social influence so as to be the most powerful political party and the automatic successor to the Nimeiri regime. The movement was taken aback by the speed with which the regime collapsed and the leadership was thrown completely off balance and appeared paralyzed during that period, especially since Turabi and a number of other key leaders were in prison when it all happened. The idea of mounting a coup was seriously considered at the time, but in the end it proved unnecessary (Makki 1990, 107–108, 163–164).

The Muslim Brotherhood regained its composure fairly quickly and managed to form a new party (NIF) within weeks, and to contest the 1986 elections with remarkable success, gaining fifty-one seats in parliament and becoming the third largest party there. However, most of the seats were won in the Graduates' Constituencies or in urban areas, with little support in the countryside. More significantly, Turabi himself lost his seat in a South Khartoum constituency when all other parties united to challenge him. This bitter experience appeared to have considerably affected his earlier enthusiasm for democracy, especially since the movement, in spite of its significant electoral gains, was excluded from the coalition government that was formed in the summer of 1986. When it was finally included in 1988, mainly the two main major coalition partners (Umma and DUP) found it difficult to work together, its tenure was brief and tumultuous.

The army ultimatum of February 1989 became the final straw, leading to the collapse of that coalition government. The NIF refused to rejoin the new coalition based on an agreement concluded in November 1988 between rebel leader Col. John Garang and DUP leader Muhammad Othman al-Mirghani, stipulating the freezing of aspects of Nimeiri's Islamic laws of 1983 and the scrapping of mutual defense pacts signed with Egypt and Libya (Simone 1994, 60–62; Salih 1990, 217–218). The army memorandum not only provided the NIF leadership with the pretext to mount its coup in June, but also with a cover for the takeover. The army's move (which was surprisingly popular, given that most people shared the frustration at the inefficiency of the weak coalition government and impatience with the continuing civil war) had made the mounting of a coup that much easier, and the June coup was widely welcomed locally and internationally, as many pinned their hopes on the new change and were sympathetic to the stance taken by the army earlier that year.

Sources of Power

By then, both the Islamist movement and the political environment had experienced radical change. Abdullahi Gallab may have exaggerated somewhat in arguing that the movement had in fact turned into a corporation, with Turabi as CEO (Gallab 2008, 91–96). But the movement has certainly increased in sophistication and was able to diversify its mode of action with remarkable results. From its modest start as a student movement in 1949, it has remained a marginal actor in national politics until Hasan al-Turabi, a young law professor with a doctorate from the Sorbonne, was elected as its leader in 1964. In the 1960s, it made only modest electoral gains, but managed to dictate the political agenda. Following the Leftist May 1969 coup under Brigadier Nimeiri, the Islamists helped organize both civilian and armed opposition.

The opposition to Nimeiri provided the movement with its first breakthrough and major transformation. It was able to amass its most significant political capital through its championing of democracy and determined struggle against Nimeiri's authoritarianism. This was achieved mainly in student politics and to a lesser degree among the trade unions. During that period, its main rivals on the campus and in trade unions politics, the Communists, were discredited for supporting the regime, while the Islamists gained from identifying themselves as the steadfast leaders of the democratic opposition. A major transformation in the movement's outlook ensued, as it was forced to adopt a more liberal and pragmatic approach to ensure the widest support among the student body. Taking over the mantle of opposition to dictatorship (rather than habitual Islamist rhetoric) thus became a major source of the movement's power.

The movement's fortunes hit a low point in 1976, due to a severe crackdown following a series of failed coups. Most of its key leaders were in prison, in exile, or on the run. However, the National Reconciliation of 1977 secured the release of prisoners and the return of exiles. Some of the top leaders gained ministerial office for the first time, and the movement was able to operate in a relatively permissive atmosphere, even though it remained officially banned. In the following years, the movement also managed to thrive economically, helped in part by the introduction of Islamic banking from 1976. Its operational budget rocketed from a few tens of thousands of pounds to millions (Makki 1990, 132), and many members became CEOs or senior executives in banks and corporations, or directors of multi-million dollar international nongovernmental organizations (NGOs). It also established active youth wings and women's organizations, and expanded and strengthened its regional branches, initiating serious work in the south for the first time (Makki 1990, 113–135; Turabi 1992, 48–58, 79–81).

Of no less significance was the determined effort to infiltrate the army, the security forces, and the senior state bureaucracy. This effort, together with the organization's financial operations, had a far-reaching impact on both its character and orientation. Both the military and financial sides of the operation were by their very nature clandestine, with only a few top-level officials having full knowledge and control over them. This in turn meant that this small group had to become privileged and not fully accountable to the wider membership, leading to the creation of a powerful secret inner organization, which this author had dubbed the "super-organization" (El-Affendi 1995), since it placed itself above and outside the normal channels of accountability and communication (Turabi 1992, 87). It was this organization that decided the timing and modality of the 1989 coup (with initial approval from the relevant bodies) and proceeded to take over both the state and organization after that, with drastic consequences for both (Muhyiddin 2006, 164–166).

Other national and regional developments also had a decisive impact on the growth and conduct of the movement. In particular the decision of President Nimeiri to introduce Islamic *Shari`ah* laws in September 1983 polarized the country along sharp dividing lines. And while the introduction of Islamic laws has been the defining objective of any Islamist movements, Turabi and his colleagues were as shocked as anyone else when these laws were introduced and many regarded them as counterproductive. Nimeiri has made the decision without consultation with Turabi, who had been sacked as attorney general a few months earlier. However, after some reflection, the movement decided to use the Islamization measures as a mobilization tool to increase popular support for the "Islamic project" and undermine support for their secular rivals. To do this, they had to compromise themselves and overlook the gross human rights abuses that accompanied the implementation of those measures and even take part in those abuses. After Nimeiri's fall, they reverted to their earlier "pressure group" tactics, bringing popular pressure on the leaders of the religiously legitimized main parties who wanted to abrogate these laws. As the debate on Islamic laws became the central political debate, so the Islamists were able to occupy the center of the political stage (Makki 1990, 98–109; Esposito and Voll 2001, 140–145; Sidahmed 1997, 202, 210–221; El-Affendi 1991, 119–126).

Related to this, and no less momentous, was the reigniting of the civil war in the south after the emergence of Sudan People's Liberation Army (SPLA) in May 1983. While the eruption of the rebellion preceded both the implementation of Islamic laws (in September) and the earlier decision in June to divide the south into three provinces in violation of the

1972 Addis Ababa peace agreement, these two issues became the top of the list of rebel grievances. Significantly, the SPLA eschewed the separatist rhetoric of earlier southern rebel movements, voicing support for unity on new terms, and employing elements of Marxist rhetoric in the process (perhaps reflecting the influence of the Marxist regime in Ethiopia, where most of the SPLA support initially came from; Daly and Sikainga 1993).

As the rebellion mounted in strength, the weak and underfunded national army lost garrison after garrison, causing a sense of alarm to sweep through the country. This reached fever pitch after the rebels began to attack areas in the north, and especially after a failed coup in September 1985 was blamed on rebel sympathizers (Simone 1994, 147). The Islamists felt no qualms about exploiting, and even whipping up, feelings of insecurity among the northern Sudanese, with the result that the movement was decisively and imperceptibly shifting from an Islamist to a "northern nationalist" movement (El-Affendi 1991, 137–144; El-Affendi 1990).

It was not difficult for the movement to combine the two tendencies, since the SPLA deployed simultaneously anti-Muslim and anti-Arab rhetoric, making it easy for the Islamists to emphasize the Islamic dimension of northern Sudanese identity. However, even after taking power, the Islamist rhetoric continued to be dominated by secular themes, as when portraying the fight against the SPLA as a "defense of land and honor" (al-Ard wa al-'Ird). The connotations here were that the SPLA was an alien force threatening the country (land) and also the honor (of families and women), strong emotive themes. Even the rhetoric about Shari'ah acquired a decisively populist tone (Sidahmed 1997, 215–219).

Many analysts tended to emphasize the economic resources made available to the Islamists through Islamic banking and companies as the main factor behind the decisive breakthrough the Sudanese Islamists were able to achieve by the mid-1980s (Gallab 2008, 88–94; Sidahmed 1997, 207–210). That is only partially correct. The new economic opportunities were important, since they enabled the movement to stop membership hemorrhaging and to gain new recruits. The hype surrounding these new economic opportunities also attracted a large number of recruits. However, these opportunities were by their very nature quite limited, especially given that the control of these financial institutions remained in the hands of investors from the Gulf or from among the established Sudanese bourgeoisie. Meanwhile, the rising resentment among large sections of the population at the perceived wealth of the Islamists was much more of a political liability than the actual gains that came its way. This was especially so after Islamic banks were accused of manipulating grain prices and profiteering from the famine of 1984–1985, a very damaging allegation that critics did their best to publicize and exploit (Makki 1990, 102–106; Sidahmed 1997, 209–210). The new prosperity among the elite also provoked anger and disaffection even among the rank and file within the movement itself, in particular the "idealist" student membership, who never ceased to protest against the new "capitalism" (Muhyiddin 2006, 36–40).

The association with the Nimeiri regime was generally quite damaging on its own, in spite of the benefits the movement reaped. This was especially so given the support it built from its antiregime stance. In this regard, the reversal of the pro-democracy position by joining the Nimeiri regime after 1977 was costly in political terms, and the costs of that association continued to mount as the overall situation deteriorated. It also haunted the movement after Nimeiri's fall.

By contrast, the turmoil created by the twin revolutions of Nimeiri's Islamization and the SPLA's assertion of southern identity had a much more significant impact in shaking up

Sudanese society and undermining traditional loyalties and affiliations, creating conditions of insecurity and uncertainty that the Islamist leadership effectively exploited to its advantage. As a result, the movement changed character, becoming more analogous to ordinary secular right wing organizations than the pan-Islamic group it claimed to be. One important consequence was that the beleaguered army, hampered by low morale and grossly inadequate resources, began to regard the Islamists as its "true friend." The NIF even set up civil society organizations supportive of the war effort and organized highly publicized donations and fund-raising campaigns for this purpose. This served a dual purpose of enhancing the group's popular mobilization capabilities and causing it to pose as the "political wing" of the armed forces. This not only made infiltrating the army easier, but in fact acted as a tool of mass recruitment among disgruntled military personnel.

It can be said then that the sources of power derived only marginally from its claim to speak for Islam, even though it did use Islamic rhetoric to pressurize and embarrass the Islamically legitimized parties and deter them from scrapping the Islamic legislation passed by Nimeiri. Its rising influence came first from standing up to an unpopular autocracy, and later from association with Islamic finance, but ultimately from exploiting the insecurity caused in the north by the southern rebellion and the overall political turmoil of the 1980s.

Elements of Totalitarianism?

The growing sense of insecurity and the perceived threat to cultural identity posed by SPLA's secularist-Africanist agenda, coupled with the palpable inefficiency of the traditional parties, enabled the Islamists to finally break through into the mainstream as the most effective champions of Northern nationalism. In addition, ordinary people suffered from personal insecurity due to endemic crime (in particular burglaries and armed robberies in Greater Khartoum and outlying areas such as Darfur).

These considerations influenced the new regime's policies, with support for the war effort as its top priority. One of the draconian measures it instituted, a nightly curfew (from 11 pm to dawn) had as a side effect a drastic decline in nightly burglaries. The regime also began to implement a policy of forcibly removing the inhabitants of shantytowns to areas on the outskirts of Greater Khartoum. This policy was motivated by a perception that these refuges for the poor were both a security risk and hotbeds of crime.

Other draconian measures included dissolving all political parties and civil society associations (except religious and student organizations) and closing all independent newspapers (Article 19 1993; Lesch 1998, 113–115; Human Rights Watch 1994, 1996). The policies adopted were blamed for having "destroyed the vibrant civil society that was emerging in Sudan from 1985 to 1989" (Lesch 1996, 190). When trade unions and other groups tried to mount resistance, the crackdown was severe and brutal. Very soon opponents and observers alike began to describe the regime as totalitarian, an epithet that was justified by these draconian measures and the concerted attempts to stifle free debate and restrict political civil society activities (Gallab 2008, 103–114). Citing Mawdudi and other Islamist sources (including some Sudanese Islamist elaborations and critiques of the regime's ideology), these critics see a close link between Islamist ideology and totalitarianism, and argue that the totalitarian turn in Sudanese Islamism was far from coincidental (Gallab 2008, 99–107).

The idea that Islamism does contain a totalitarian inclination (affirmed explicitly by Mawdudi and implicitly by many others) has been the subject of discussion for some time (El-Affendi 2008; Whine 2001). One could also find support for similar inclinations in Turabi from his affirmation of his principle of "unitarianism," which opposes not only separation of religion from daily affairs, but also any differentiation within society. The whole of life should be subsumed under religion, while the whole community must be united (Lowrie 1993, 13–14). However, at the theoretical level at least, this view can be countered by Turabi's own assertion that the state in Islam must be limited (Lowrie 1993, 23–26).

The Sudanese regime did indeed make a determined effort in its early stages to restrict, control, and redirect all forms of social activity. However, its efforts were a nonstarter, due first to the unique structure of Sudanese society itself: multicultural and ethnically and regionally diverse, it was difficult to subjugate it to centralized control. This was even more so given the limited resources at the disposal of the Sudanese state at the time and the fact that it was already locked in a fierce civil war that left large areas of the country outside its control. The state's weakness was exacerbated by its international and regional isolation, as both armed and civil opposition found active regional and international support. The worsening economic situation made the regime even more unpopular and strengthened opposition further. In fact, even the underlying Islamic orientation of the regime hampered its efforts to undermine the opposition, since it provoked "rival claims that embedded themselves in Islam." Thus far from being "an empowering force for the Sudanese regime, the Islamists and their political system," Islam "turned out to be a constraining element for their state project" (Gallab 2008, 132–133). This problem was compounded by the regime's decision to camouflage its Islamic identity, and related adoption of a 'lenient' implementation" of its own Islamic laws encoded in the 1991 Criminal Act, an approach critics found puzzling from a movement that had made so much fuss about the uncompromising implementation of Islamic laws (Sidahmed 1997, 220). Thus in spite of the frequent adoption of Islamic rhetoric, including the invocation of jihad in defense of the regime and its Islamic project (Sidahmed 2002, 83–96; Gallab 2008, 114–128; Mahmoud 2007), the regime had more generally adopted a rather pragmatic line, subordinating *Shari'ah* and Islamic norms to the expediency of power politics, to the extent that it has been accused of appearing to "have alienated itself by itself from [its] very religious ideal" (Sidahmed 1997, 225–226).

The regime itself has continued to evolve. During its first year, it adopted very harsh repressive and economically restrictive policies, while avoiding any explicit Islamist claims. But starting from its second year, it began to adopt a fully fledged economic liberalization policy. Later, it began to gradually open up the political system. By 1998, it adopted a new constitution (following a partial peace agreement in 1997 with a number of rebel factions from the south), permitting a limited multiparty system and more media freedoms. Following a split in 1999 in which the regime's strong man, Hasan Turabi, was stripped of his powers, the regime opened up some more (Gallab 2008; Esposito and Voll 2001, 140–145).

In 2005, the Comprehensive Peace Agreement (CPA) ended the war in the south and led to new constitutional changes accommodating the demands of non-Muslims within a "one Sudan, two systems" schema,[3] permitting the implementation of *Shari'ah* in the north and a secular system in the south. If it had worked and if the south had not opted for separation, then the resulting system might have come to resemble Malaysia's consociational democracy, but with a less privileged position for Islam and Muslims.

These shifts in policy have led some observers to argue that the regime had in fact lived through two phases: a totalitarian "first Islamic republic" until the fall of Turabi in 1999, followed by a "second republic," which was merely authoritarian (Gallab 2008). Some commentators have already started speaking of a "post-Islamist" order in Sudan, using a term coined by Asef Bayat to describe the radical shift in some Islamist circles (mainly, but not exclusively, in Iran) toward a more liberal, even secularizing, reinterpretation of Islamism (Bayat 2005, 2007).[4]

However, the ongoing crisis in Darfur, which erupted just as peace in the south was approaching, continues to cast a dark shadow over the political process. Some observers saw a direct link between the Darfur crisis and the split within the regime (Gallab 2008, 155–161), a view espoused by the regime that accuses Turabi and his supporters of having fomented the rebellion in Darfur (Hoile 2005, 15–24). The regime's policies have certainly contributed to the deterioration of the situation there by sidelining an important section of its Darfurian Islamists backers who later joined various rebel factions. But that was not the main cause of the conflict that has displaced millions and caused tens of thousands of deaths, not to say bringing about the first criminal indictment of a sitting president as the International Criminal Court charged President al-Bashir with war crimes in 2009. A number of complex and interconnected factors, including the political mismanagement of multiple crises in that region, are responsible for the catastrophe (El-Affendi 2009; Cf. Mamdani 2009). The charges of totalitarianism pale in contrast to the serious allegations of genocide, the first to be leveled against a Muslim government since the World War I allegations against Turkey with regards to Armenians.

Conclusion

As the first assumption of power by modern Islamist group, the military takeover of June 1989 in Sudan has produced many valuable lessons about the complexity of contemporary Muslim politics. In spite of Sudan's unique status of having been shaped by the millenarian Mahdist revolution of late nineteenth century, causing its politics to be dominated by religious figures and movements, the phenomenal rise of Islamism had been influenced more by extrareligious factors. The Islamists gained in popularity by defending democracy in the early 1970s, pioneering Islamic finance in the mid-1970s, and championing northern Sudanese nationalism in the 1980s. But their fight was as much with traditional religious and social forces as it was with their secularist rivals. Three radical revolutions, the left-wing takeover in May 1969 under Nimeiri, the latter's sudden foray into Islamization, and the southern rebellion in the 1980s weakened both rival camps: the traditionalists were disoriented and exposed, while the secularists were discredited and decimated by infighting. The ambitious objectives of the southern rebels heightened the sense of insecurity among Sudanese northerners, making them more receptive to the hardline rhetoric adopted by the Islamists.

But for these very reasons, the takeover was not Islamist in the strictest sense of the term, and not only because the coup leaders hid their true colors and insisted that they were mere nationalists. The leaders of the movement had realized long before that that in order to seize and retain power in a multireligious and diverse country like Sudan (and under the prevailing international order), they needed to water down Islamic objectives and adopt a more pragmatic (some may say Machiavellian) approach. This tendency was accentuated by the exigencies of maintaining power under challenging circumstances, and was decisively ensconced after the 1999 split where the two rival factions both deployed Islamist rhetoric, thus greatly devaluing its impact and utility.

More importantly, however, this episode brings into focus the limits of modern Islamist activism. As the later experiences in Turkey and Iraq have shown, Sudan was not the only instance where Islamists had to shed their "skin," so to speak, before they could accede to power. Turabi had pushed the Islamist project to its very limit, and had revealed the limitations of modern Islamic reformism (El-Affendi 2006, 154–155). And although he has since engaged in some limited self-criticism and reaffirmed in a recent book the centrality of democracy to any Islamic order (Turabi 2003), his credibility has taken quite a serious blow due to his association with authoritarian practices during his period in power.

This said, however, Turabi's main sin may not be an aspiration to set up a totalitarian state, but to subject the state to a power outside it. Both due to his own belief in the priority of society over the state and to his personal status (since he was forced due to the movement's dissimulation to remain outside the state) he had striven to empower structures he had set up outside the state and subject the state to his personal authority. This had led to many embarrassing episodes, as when decisions taken by the state at the highest level had to be reversed when he did not like them. The struggle between the shadowy "movement" and the state reached a decisive moment when Turabi's second in command, Ali Osman Taha, became first vice-president. As a result, an influential section in the movement decided to side with the state against the movement. Turabi's resistance was brutally crushed. It was the "revenge of the state" against those who thought they could bypass it.

Notes

1. The author is a fellow in the Global Uncertainties Programme, funded jointly by the Economic and Social Research Council (ESRC) and the Arts and Humanities Research Council (AHRC), and would like to express his gratitude for the support of the two councils for his research.
2. In an interesting twist, it has later been revealed that the leadership's first choice to lead the coup, Brigadier Osman Hassan Ahmad, was sidelined because he refused to pledge loyalty to the movement, saying that if he were to take power in the name of the army, his loyalty would be to the army (Muhyiddin 2006, 192–193). Ahmad later resigned from the RCC over the stance on the Gulf War of 1991.
3. The idea was first proposed in Deng and Morrison 2001.
4. See the debate launched in April 2009 on the SSRC Darfur blog: http://blogs.ssrc.org/darfur/category/darfur/islamism (accessed December 9, 2009).

References

al-Albani, Nasir al-Din. 1996. *Silsilat al-Ahadith al-Sahiha*. Vol. 6. Riyadh: Maktabat al-Ma`arif.
Ali, Haydar Ibrahim. 1991. *Azmat al-Islam al-Siyassi: Al-Jabha al-Islamiyya al-Qawmiyya fi'l-Sudan Namudhjan*. Rabat: Sudanese Studies Centre.

Article 19. 1993. *Dismantling Civil Society: Suppression of Freedom of Association in Sudan*. London: Article 19, Issue 27, August 23.
Al-Sulami, Mishal Fahm. 2003. *The West and Islam: Western Liberal Democracy versus the System of Shura*. New York: Routledge Curzon.
Bayat, Asef. 2005. What Is Post-Islamism? *ISIM Review* 16: 5.
Bayat, Asef. 2007. *Making Islam Democratic Social Movements and the Post-Islamist Turn*. Stanford: Stanford University Press.
Daly, M. W., and Ahmad Alawad Sikainga, eds. 1993. *Civil War in the Sudan*. London: British Academic Press.
Deng, Francis M., and J. Stephen Morrison. 2001. *U.S. Policy to End Sudan's War*. Washington, DC: Center for Strategic and International Studies.
De Waal, Alex, ed. 2004. *Islamism and Its Enemies in the Horn of Africa*. London: Hurst and Company.
El-Affendi, Abdelwahab. 1990. "Discovering the South": Sudanese Dilemmas for Islam in Africa. *African Affairs* 89: 371–389.
El-Affendi, Abdelwahab. 1991. *Turabi's Revolution: Islam and Power in Sudan*. London: Grey Seal Books.
El-Affendi, Abdelwahab. 1995. *Al-Thawra wa al-Islah al-Siyasi fi al-Sudan*. London: Averroes Forum.
El-Affendi, Abdelwahab. 2006. Hassan Turabi and the Limits of Modern Islamic Reformism. In *The Blackwell Companion on Contemporary Islamic Thought*, ed. Ibrahim Abu-Rabi, 145–160. Oxford: Blackwell.
El-Affendi, Abdelwahab. 2008 [1991]. *Who Needs an Islamic State?* London: Malaysian Think Tank.
El-Affendi, Abdelwahab. 2009. *Azmat Darfur: Nazrah fi al-Judhur wa al-Hulul al-Mumkina*. Abu Dhabi: The Emirates Centre for Strategic Studies and Research.
Esposito, John L, and John O Voll. 1996. *Islam and Democracy*. Oxford: Oxford University Press.
Esposito, John L, and John O Voll. 2001. *Makers of Contemporary Islam*. Oxford: Oxford University Press.
Gallab, Abdullahi A. 2008. *The First Islamist Republic: Development and Disintegration of Islamism in the Sudan*. Aldershot: Ashgate.
Hoile, David. 2005. *Darfur in Perspective*. London: European-Sudanese Public Affairs Council.
Human Rights Watch/Africa. 1994. "In the Name of God": Repression Continues in Northern Sudan. November 1. Available at: http://www.hrw.org/sites/default/files/reports/sudan94n.pdf. Accessed May 5, 2013.
Human Rights Watch/Africa. 1996. Behind the Red Line: Political Repression in Sudan. May 1. Available at: http://www.hrw.org/en/reports/1996/05/01/behind-red-line. Accessed May 5, 2013.
Ibrahim, Abd Allah Ali. 1999. A Theology of Modernity: Hasan al-Turabi and Islamic Renewal in Sudan. *Africa Today* 46 (3/4): 195–222.
Lesch, Ann Mosley. 1996. The Destruction of Civil Society in Sudan. In *Civil Society in the Middle East*, ed. Augustus Richard Norton, 153–191. Vol. II. Leiden: E.J. Brill.
Lesch, Ann Mosley. 1998. *The Sudan: Contested National Identities*. Bloomington: Indiana University Press.
Lowrie, Arthur L., ed. 1993. *Islam, Democracy the State and the West: A Round Table with Dr. Hasan Turabi*. Tampa, FL: WISE.
Mahmoud, Mohamed. 2007. When Shari`a Governs: The Impasse of Religious Relations in Sudan. *Islam and Christian-Muslim Relations* 18: 275–286.

Makki, Hasan. 1990. *Al-Harakah al-Islamiya fi al-Sudan 1969–85*. Khartoum: Bayt al-Ma'rifa.

Mamdani, Mahmood. 2009. *Saviors and Survivors: Darfur, Politics and the War on Terror*. London: Verso.

Moussalli, Ahmad S. 1994. Hasan al-Turabi's Discourse on Democracy and Shura. *Middle Eastern Studies* 30: 52–61.

Moussalli, Ahmad S. 1999. *Moderate and Radical Islamic Fundamentalism: The Quest for Modernity, Legitimacy, and the Islamic State*. Gainesville: University Press of Florida.

Muhyiddin, Abd al-Rahim Umar. 2006. *Al-Turabi wa al-Inqadh: Sira' al-Hawiyya wa al-Hawa*. Damascus: Dar 'Ikrima.

Said, Abd al-Karim Qasim. 1995. *al-Ikhwan al-Muslimun wa'l-Haraka al-Usuliyya fi'l-Yaman*. Cairo: Maktabat Madbouli.

Salih, Kamal Osman. 1990. The Sudan, 1985–9: the Fading Democracy. *The Journal of Modern African Studies* 28(2): 199–224.

Sidahmed, Abdel Salam. 1997. *Politics and Islam in Contemporary Sudan*. London: Curzon.

Sidahmed, Abdel Salam. 2002. The Unholy War: Jihad and the Conflict in Sudan. In *Religion and Conflict in Sudan*, ed. Yusuf Fadl Hasan and Richard Gray. Nairobi: Paulines, 83–96.

Simone, Abdou Maliqalim. 1994. *In Whose image? Political Islam and Urban Practices in Sudan*. Chicago: University of Chicago Press.

Turabi, Hasan al-. 1992. *Al-Haraka al-Islamiyya: al-Tatawwur wa-al-Kasb wa-al-Manhaj* [The Islamic Movement: Its Development, Achievements and Methods]. Khartoum: The Institute of Social Research and Studies.

Turabi, Hasan al-. 2003. *Al-Siyasa wa'l-Hukm: al-Nuzum al-Sultaniyya bayn al-Usual wa Sunan al-Waqi'*. Beirut: Saqi.

Whine, Michael. 2001. Islamism and Totalitarianism: Similarities and Differences. *Totalitarian Movements and Political Religions* 2: 54–72.

CHAPTER 30

ISLAM AND THE STATE IN AFGHANISTAN

M. NAZIF SHAHRANI

Islam has been central to discourses of power and the management of social and political relations at all levels of society in modern Afghanistan. The deployment and efficacy of specific symbolic resources of Islam—that is, concepts, values, principles, ideologies, and institutional practices—by rulers and religious power elites, however, has varied through time. As Leila Ahmed (1992, 2) has pointed out: "Discourses shape and are shaped by specific moments in specific societies." In this essay, I focus on some key moments when those in power, including state and substate actors inside Afghanistan as well as international actors, have shaped discourses about Islam and power in modern Afghanistan and the effect these discourses have had in shaping subsequent events.

From Jihad in Precolonial and Colonial Times to Sacralizing the State (Pre-1919)

After the establishment of Islam as the religion of power by Arab Muslim armies in Khorasan and Mawara'unnahr, the protection, preservation, territorial expansion, and spread of Islam by any and all means, including jihad, became the most powerful motivational force of Muslim empires emanating from this region. During the final decades of the tenth century, with the rise of the Ghaznavid (975–1187) empire just south of Kabul, Islamic empires' direction of expansion jihad turned south toward the Indian subcontinent, a region rich in booty and potential converts. The centuries-long process of empire building by ambitious Central Asian men (primarily Turko-Mongols), who raised tribal *lashkars* (irregulars/militia) to invade Hindu India, came to an abrupt halt at the hands of the rising British colonial power in India and the demise of the last Muslim imperial dynasty/tribal confederacy headed by the Durrani (1747–1826) Pashtun kings.

The rising threats against Southwestern and Central Asian Muslim lands from British India in the south and tsarist Russia in the north offered the institution of jihad a new instrumental significance and efficacy. Rather than its traditional use as a motivational technique used by aspiring rulers to convince followers to conquer new lands, jihad began to be increasingly deployed during the nineteenth century by the quarreling rulers of the Kingdom of Kabul, renamed in the 1880s as the Kingdom of Afghanistan, as the ideology of choice for mobilizing the masses to defend Islam.

The efficacy of jihad for defense against European Christian colonial powers[1], was first tested successfully in the decimation of the British-Indian forces in the winter of 1841, during the First Anglo-Afghan War (1839–1842). From then on, jihad became part and parcel of anticolonial discourse both locally and regionally, ultimately effecting the fateful creation of Afghanistan as a buffer nation-state in 1880 to keep the two competing European colonial giants in the region apart[2]. Thus the narrative of the birth of the postcolonial nation-state of Afghanistan was interwoven with the discourse of jihad against the crusading *kuffari Angreez wa Rus* (English/British and Russian infidels) of the nineteenth and early twentieth centuries[3]. Grasping the mobilizing power of jihad, the British-crowned ruler, Amir Abdur Rahman Khan (1880–1901), employed it skillfully to consolidate his rule over the British-created new buffer nation-state—that is, Afghanistan. Although empowered by British India, Abdur Rahman believed Afghanistan must exist as a Muslim country and be led by a Muslim ruler, such as himself, in order to defend it by means of jihad/*ghaza* against colonialist threats (Khan 1900/1980 II:51; Kakar 1979, 177). Asta Olesen (1995, 70) suggests that by focusing on jihad the amir "defined Afghanistan as 'frontline state'" and proceeded to "sacralise...the whole juridico-economic structure of the state, making it part of a divine scheme, the order of which could not be challenged." Then, with money and weapons provided by his British-Indian patrons, he set out to consolidate his centralizing state powers, while fulfilling his assigned task of building a strong unified buffer kingdom. He dismantled traditional tribal bases of state power and legitimacy by creating a standing professional army loyal to him, as well as an administration staffed by officials appointed and paid by him.

More importantly, the amir turned to instrumental uses of Islam to boost his own legitimacy as well as to sacralize his "modern" state-building project. He claimed, much in the manner of some of the earlier Moghul emperors, to have been chosen by God as a "divine ruler" and savior of Muslims of Afghanistan. In order to impress his divine mission upon his thoroughly terrorized subjects, Amir Abdur Rahman pursued a relentless Islamization of the state by establishing *mahakimi shar'i* (shari'a courts), appointed Islamic judges (*qazis*) and standardized Islamic educational texts including Friday sermons. Distrustful of clerics and Sufi *pirs*[4], he nationalized *awaqaf* (religious endowments, the economic base of *ulama*), withheld state payments to *khanaqa murshids* (leaders of Sufi lodges), established royal madrasa to train loyal mullahs, introduced examinations for the appointment of judges and imams (prayer leaders), and appointed *muhtasibs* (Islamic supervisors of bazaars and public places) to monitor the religious knowledge and moral behavior of his Muslim subjects. The amir's intent in these measures was twofold: to confirm the conservative traditional expectation of his subjects to live by the rules of *shari'ah*, and to gain greater control over his subjects, especially the clerics and tribal chieftains. Abdur Rahman's state-building projects deployed Islam solely as a means of state power.

The "iron" amir waged jihad against the peoples of *Kafiristan* (the land of the nonbelievers) within his new kingdom and forcibly converted them to Sunni Hanafi Islam. When facing stiff resistance from the powerful chieftains of the Ghilzai Pashtun tribes in the east, he declared jihad and crushed them. To subjugate the recalcitrant non-Pashtun ethnic groups in the north and especially the powerful Shi`a Hazara *mirs* and *khans* in the central mountain regions, he obtained *fatwas* from Sunni clerics declaring them infidels and mobilized his Pashtun tribesmen to subject them by waging jihad against them and appropriated much of their pastures for the use of Pashtun mobile herders.

Upon the death of Amir Abdur Rahman, his son Amir Habibullah (ruled 1901–1919), ascended the throne peacefully, an event not to be repeated again in the modern history of Afghanistan. The instrumental uses of Islam by his father had proved effective in sacralizing the state and subordinating the clerics by co-optation into the apparatus of a unified and centralizing state. Habibullah, however, cautiously began to relax the state's heavy reliance on the discourse of jihad.

Domestically, Amir Habibullah continued his father's ambitious policies of centralization without facing any serious challenge to his rule. He assumed the title of *siraj al mellati waddin* (the lamp of nation and the faith) and like his father claimed to be the divine choice to rule over the peoples of Afghanistan. Feeling secure on the throne, Habibullah began to ease some harsher elements of his father's policies. He limited the use of torture and allowed some politically exiled families to return home from British India and the Ottoman Empire.[5] Amir Habibullah also became more conciliatory toward religious dignitaries. Indeed, his policies relied on making alliances with the *ulama* and *pirs* to insure the stability of his realm rather than on open animosity toward them. But when some clerics opposed his trip to British India in 1906 at the invitation of the British viceroy, they were summarily executed. Others who participated in an alleged plot against the amir in 1909 were also executed (Nawid 1999, 35; McChesney 1999, 17). With help and inspiration from Ottoman Turks, he opened the first modern secular schools in 1911 and permitted the publication of the newspaper *Siraj al-Akhbar,* edited by Mahmood Tarzi, a cosmopolitan intellectual recently returned from Damascus.

By the turn of the twentieth century, the discourse of Islam and jihad in Afghanistan was influenced and reinforced by the growing anticolonial jihad resistance across Asia and Africa, which had also given rise to powerful pan-Islamic reformist movements. The ideas of Jamal al-Din Afghani and his disciples to lift Muslims from their conditions of "ignorance and helplessness" through education, reform, and acquisition of modern sciences, and above all forging unity of the Muslim *ummah* to resist Western aggression and occupation, "gripped the Muslim imagination of this period" (Leila Ahmed 1992, 139). These movements, galvanized by the onset of World War I, which had engulfed the ailing Ottoman Empire, were concerned with ending the humiliating subjugation of Muslims to European colonial empires.

In Afghanistan, the call for Islamic educational reform and Muslim nationalist awakening was brought to the nascent intelligentsia at the royal court circles by the newspaper *Siraj Al-Akhbar* and its chief editor Mahmood Tarzi (see Gregorian 1967). *Siraj al-Akhbar* informed its widening circle of readers about the Muslim reformist political ideals of the Ottoman lands as well as the radical ideas of Deobandi clerics in the Indian subcontinent, which had given rise to the *Khilafat* Movement and anticolonial jihad, which set the Pashtun Frontier in British India aflame. During World War I, some `*ulama*' and nationalists supported the Ottoman caliph's call for jihad. Amir Habibullah, however, had been advised by the British, upon which he relied for financial assistance, to adhere to a policy of neutrality. Meanwhile many of his influential courtiers, including his brother Crown Prince

Nasrullah, secretly encouraged the jihad waged against Britain by the Hadda Mullah and the Akhundzada of Swat (Nawid 1999, 33–34).

The end of World War I contributed significantly to the growing ideology of national liberation and anticolonial resistance among the small circle of reform-minded elites in Afghanistan. Shortly after the end of the Great War, Amir Habibullah was assassinated during a hunting trip in eastern Afghanistan, and his third son, Amanullah, then governor of Kabul and a leading reformist, laid claim to the throne in the capital.

Nationalization of Islam (*Din wa Dawla*) and Failed Reforms of the 1920s

After initial power struggles with his uncle Crown Prince Sardar Nasrullah, Amanullah quickly secured military and political support in Kabul and assumed power as shah (1919–1929). He was admired by a small but growing urban intelligentsia and by court officials, sometimes referred to as the Young Afghans or *mashrutakhawhan* (constitutionalists), for his vehement nationalist, pan-Islamist, and modernist views. His most daring but widely expected decision after ascending the throne was the declaration of jihad against Britain to reclaim the total independence of Afghanistan. This bold move won him praise, especially from the eastern Pashtun warrior mullahs and the Sufi *pirs* along the frontiers, who eagerly joined the jihad against British India. Riding high on his newly found popularity and his alliance with the `ulama', whom he ingratiated with land grants and lofty priestly titles, Shah Amanullah offered support and encouragement for the *Khilafat* Movement in India and the anti-Bolshevik *Basmachi* fighters of Central Asia, who had taken refuge in Afghan Turkestan in the north of the country. Under pressures from British India and the USSR, however, he relented on his initial promises and gradually began to undermine the religious foundations of the state he inherited, with disastrous consequences for both his own rule and Muslims in India and especially in Bukhara (see Shahrani 2000, 2005).

Amanullah's victory in the Third Anglo-Afghan War (1919) also called the War of Independence, was won at huge costs. The recognition of the Durand Line as the frontier between independent Afghanistan and British India divided the Pashtun between the two states, resulting in disillusionment among Pashtun tribesmen. After the creation of Pakistan, disputes over the Durand Line became a festering source of political instability in Afghanistan-Pakistan relations as well as in the region generally (see Qaseem 2009). Most significantly, Amanullah's government lost considerable British financial, technical, and military aid, which made it very difficult for him to pursue his ambitious modernization programs. Shah Amanullah's ill-fated legal, constitutional, educational, and cultural reforms had lasting effects on the discourses of Islam in power long after his own abdication from the throne in 1929.

Amanullah's Islamic reformism, inspired in part by the Young Turks and later Kemal Ataturk and Reza Shah of Iran, called for a thorough *etatization* of Islam—that is, total integration and control of *din wa dowlat* (faith and state) by the monarch. Shah Amanullah and his chief political advisor Mahmood Tarzi insisted on making patriotism (love for the king and country) and modernization part of religious duties for the faithful Muslim subjects. The inculcation of these modernist "Islamic" values through modern education and media was deemed the responsibility of the modern state. Tarzi, as editor-in-chief and frequent author and publisher of *Siraj al-Akhbar*, considered neglecting the cultivation and effective application of God's greatest gift to humanity, reason (*'aqel*), as a disservice to Islam and to humanity. Hence the application of reason to Islam, in his view, distinguished *rowshanfikrs* (the enlightened Muslim thinkers) from the *ruhanis* (traditionalist religious functionaries, both *'ulama'* and *tariqat pirs*), whom he believed had held back Muslims from reclaiming their civilizational glory.

As a *rowshanfiker*, Tarzi (1290 HS [1911], 6–7) asserted, "if we assume *watan* (homeland) as a living organism (*jesm*) and *millat* or ourselves (the nation) as its flesh, skin, bone, veins, sinew and other parts of that being, then we must regard the *paadshah* (king) as the soul of that being." He concluded: "*Watan, millat* and *paadshah* are such sacred and blessed concepts that nothing and no power can separate them. [Therefore,] *if we love our watan, then it is as we love ourselves, if we love the King then it is as we have loved our very own souls*" (emphasis added; also see Gregorian 1967, 354; Shahrani 1986, 42).

To facilitate his desired reforms and social transformations, Amanullah harkened to the *shari'ah* as "the divine ordinances" and issued no fewer than seventy-six *nezamnamas* (regulations). The most important of them was the first modern constitution of the country (*Nizamnamayee Assasyee Dowlati 'Aliyaee Afghanistan*[5]) in 1923. He considered these legal documents complementary to *sharia'h* but required enlightened religious leadership to collaborate with the intelligentsia and ruling elites to implement them. To promote his Islamic patriotism and reformist agenda and to obtain the support of skeptical *'ulama'* and *pirs*, Shah Amanullah led Friday prayers in Kabul's grand mosques, delivered *khutbahs* (sermons), and assumed the title of *padari millat* (father of the nation).

The constitution of 1923 abolished slavery (Article 10); restored some civil rights to his subjects (*ra'iyat*) by rescinding forced labor (Article 22); called for an independent judiciary (Article 50 and 51); enumerated the powers of the king, subject to existing laws, together with his responsibilities to defend Islam and the nation; and, most importantly, invoked the notion of popular sovereignty (the will of the peoples of Afghanistan expressed in their presumed *bay'a*, or consent) as another basis for his legitimacy (Poulada 1973; Olesen 1995, 126). Shah Amanullah's reforms included the outlawing of *pir* and *murid* (disciple/follower) relations in the army; delegating control of education to new modern schools (for boys and girls), including a new school for the training of *qazis* (judges); assuming control of judiciary appointments; and adopting a penal code that curtailed the discretionary powers of *qazi's* in determining punishments. The constitution was to be accorded precedence (Articles 69 and 72) over the *shari'a* when these two legal codes were in conflict. Anticipating objections, King Amanulla got some *ulama* to issue a *fatwa* stating the constitution was not contrary to the *shari'ah* (Olesen 1999, 121).

The constitution nevertheless endorsed many issues that were objectionable to ultraconservative clerics and *pirs* as well to some tribal elders, such as the opening of girls' schools, interference in local marriage and wedding practices, banning polygamy and child marriage, the collection of delinquent taxes in cash only, and the imposition of new land and livestock taxes. These latter measures added to the burdens of impoverished rural subjects while increasing opportunities for official corruption, thus giving rise to the first militant opposition against Amanullah's rule in 1924. This rebellion, initiated by Pashtun tribesmen, was led by mullahs in the Province of Janubi and the adjacent region in British India. The concentration of considerable powers in the hands of the monarch, without any checks and balances, in the constitution of 1923 had also angered elements of the governing elites within the capital who were expecting a more meaningful constitutional monarchy.

Amanullah crushed the fourteen-months-long revolt and executed its leaders. However, while the war against the rebels was in progress, King Amanullah called another *loya jirgah* to review, revise, and amend all the offensive rules and regulations in the *nezamnamas* as well as the constitution. After heated discussion on women's place in society and restrictions imposed on marriages and weddings, five articles of the constitution were amended: three of them valorized Hanafi Sunni rites over others, while the other two denied equal rights to non-Muslim subjects. A historian of this period, Senzil Nawid (1999, 111) argues that by the end of the *loya jirgah* of 1925, Amanullah had capitulated to all the demands of the mullahs and had agreed to the formation of a seven-member council of 'ulama' to review and approve all future statutes.

By the mid-1920s King Amanullah had effectively squandered much of his initial domestic popularity and international credibility; his administration suffered from corruption and was in disarray (see Shahrani 1986, 48–50).[6] Disappointed and bitter, the king blamed "ignorant mullahs" for his troubles. Extended travels of the king through Europe, USSR, India, Turkey, and Iran in 1928 only deepened the growing rift between Amanullah and the religious establishment. Upon his return, Amanullah started to blame the distortion of religion and the exploitation of the masses on a conspiracy of mullahs and tribal khans. He formed a new political party, Ferqa ye Esteqlal wa Tajaddud (The Party of Freedom and Modernity), to help expunge "superstitious and heretical beliefs which do not conform with Islam but have become a part of popular belief through customs" (Nawid 1999, 144–145, 157, 223; for more details, see Shahrani 2005). Amanullah then issued decrees prohibiting traditional male headgear (caps and turbans) and instead required the use of Western-style suits in Kabul. He also banned *pir-murid* relations and restricted the activities of Deoband-trained 'ulama' in the country. All religious functionaries were required to take examinations and obtain licenses in order to work in government offices or serve as imams in the mosques. These measures predictably alienated many, including some of his ardent early supporters. A group of mullahs from the east declared the king a *kafir* (apostate) and demanded his removal from the throne. In November 1928 armed rebellion broke out in Shinwar district near the border with British India. But the warrior mullahs of the eastern Pashtun tribesmen were not the only group to rebel against the king. Tajik rebels from Kohistan and Kohdaman, just north of Kabul, also attacked the king under the banner of jihad against the "infidel king."

JIHAD AGAINST THE "INFIDEL KING" AND THE CIVIL WAR OF 1929

Upon capturing Kabul, the Tajik rebel leader forced King Amanullah to abdicate and assumed the title of Amir Habibullah. The former court religious dignitaries crowned him and bestowed upon him the appellation *khaadimi deeni rasullullah*, servant of the faith of the messenger of God (see Shahrani 1986, 49, 71–72). According to Faiz Muhammad Kateb, a partisan historian siding with the fallen king, Amir Habibullah II (Kalakani) and his group of Tajik "bandits and outlaws" were most likely reacting to pervasive social and economic oppression by government officials in their localities. Kateb suggests that religious justification for the rebellion may have been tagged on later by some opportunistic clerics from Kabul who egged Habibullah Kalakani on in order to rid themselves of Amanullah.

The new Tajik ruler championed a populist version of *shari'ah* easily understandable to the peasantry, who were deeply committed to living by Islamic law as preached and applied by their own poorly trained local mullahs. However, the credibility of claims that the rebellions were motivated against reforms repugnant to Islamic beliefs and practices is questionable, because the vast majority of peoples living in the northern, western, central, and southwestern parts of the country did not actively join the rebellion against King Amanullah.

Despite initial support from most non-Pashtun peoples of the country, the Tajik claimant to Amanullah's throne could not consolidate his power, primarily because of his ineffective, arbitrary, oppressive, and corrupt rule. More significantly, his government failed to gain recognition abroad and was unable to raise revenues, which led to serious urban economic distress. He encouraged the Basmachi (Central Asian Muslim anti-Bolshevik fighters) to resume their jihad against the USSR in the north, thus inviting Soviet opposition to his rule. Amir Habibullah Kalakani's nine-month chaotic rule and the associated civil war came to an end with the victory of King Amanullah's disgruntled general Nader Khan, a clever politician who was also Amanullah's close collateral paternal relative and his ambassador to France in the mid-1920s. With considerable financial and military aid from British India[7] and the enticement of Hazrat of Shor Bazaar to assist him, he managed to raise a tribal *lashkar* (militia) among frontier Pashtun on both sides of the border to retake Kabul and establish the last Pashtun dynasty, the Musahiban who ruled the country from 1929 to1978.

ATTEMPTED RESACRALIZATION OF STATE AND ETHNIC POLARIZATION UNDER MUSAHIBAN (1929–1978)

After capturing Kabul, a *loya jirgah* (an assembly of Pashtun tribal elders and religious dignitaries), proclaimed Field Marshal Muhammad Nader the King of Afghanistan. During his brief rule, Nader Shah (1929–1933) laid the foundation for the Musahiban dynasty and established policies and practices that shaped the course of Afghan history for the next four decades. The Musahiban dynasty ruled with few challenges, due to skillful but duplicitous domestic religious policies and practices as well as duplicity in how they presented their relationships with British India, their principal outside patron, to their subjects (see Olesen 1999, 173–176).

Nader Shah's policies were shaped by a number of factors: his own moderate modernist-nationalist orientation, the legacies of Amanullah's reform policies, the deleterious consequences of the civil war of 1929, and the exigencies of the neighboring European colonialist superpowers.

In his bid for the throne Nader Shah had relied on Pashtun tribal *lashkar* and traditional religious elites. His consolidation of power, however, was largely the result of subsidies and technical support from the British, French, and Germans, who made it possible for him to organize an army, police, and gendarme and to reestablish an effective centralized administration. He publicly attributed his success however to "the exclusive help of the Almighty God" and the "sacrifices of the peoples of Afghanistan" and flatly denied receiving any assistance from foreign powers (Gregorian 1969, 322). To legitimize his dynasty's rule and to institutionalize the concessions he had made to the frontier Pashtun tribes as well as to the traditionalist religious establishment (`ulama', ruhanis, pirs, faqirs,* and more) who supported him, he relied on one of the most important legacies of the Amanullah's era: constitutionalism.

But unlike Amanullah, who attempted to use constitutionalism as the instrument for societal transformation, Nader Shah adopted a new constitution (1931) to affirm the status quo and offer lip service to gradual reformism and modernity and to appease Amanullah's urban supporters. Article 9 of the constitution proclaimed equal rights of all subjects, Articles 27–70 established a mechanism for the formation of a bicameral parliament, which was said to be based on the Islamic principle of *shura* (consultation).[8] Articles 1–4 of his constitution established that the official religion of Afghanistan and its king as Sunni Hanafi Islam. Islam, once again in the hands of the ruler, became a means to promote centralization and greater state control. To appease the traditionalist `ulama' and especially the *ruhani*, or saintly figures, and their *murids* he also created Jami`at ul-Ulama (Society of Muslim Scholars), allegedly established to vet all government legislation, rules, and regulations for conformity with the *shari`ah*. Nader Shah ordered the first-ever printing of the Qur'an in Kabul and removed all restrictions imposed by Amanullah's regime on the role of mullahs and mawlawis in education or in government employment. As further concessions to the frontier warrior mullahs and *pirs,* the constitution also established the primacy of Sunni Hanafi *fiqh* as the sole source of *shari`ah* law, affirmed the inequality of men and women and of Sunni and Shi`a sects, and severely curtailed the rights of non-Muslim minorities in the country. Nader Shah also closed all girls' schools, appointed to the cabinet and other high government posts members of the Hazrat of Shor Bazar (Mojaddedi family), who had secured for him the support of Pashtun Ghilzai tribes, and dismantled most of King Amanullah's reforms, including abolishing more than sixty of his *nezamnamas*. The special status of the frontier Pashtun tribes was ensured through exemption from taxation and military conscription. Many rural khans and dignitaries were "elected" to or selected for the rubber-stamp bicameral parliament, giving them the satisfaction of sharing power while the police kept them in check for at least seven months of each year in Kabul.

By these constitutional and administrative means, the Musahiban family encapsulated traditional tribal and religious elites in an oligarchic structure that ran both the army and the bureaucracy. The consolidation of Musahiban power, however, was not without challenge. Nader Shah faced active opposition from pro-Amannullah forces, who especially objected to his policies of slow reform and modernization, and from disillusioned Pashtun nationalists, who objected to his duplicitous policy of friendship with British India in the face of aggressive British policy toward the frontier Pashtuns. Especially evident was anger over withholding support for the peaceful Islamic-based anticolonial movement Khudayee Khidmatgaran (Service Providers for the Sake of God), headed by Khan Abdul Ghaffar Khan, the so-called Frontier Gandhi. The Musahiban also faced armed resistance from the supporters of Habibullah Kalakani north of Kabul, from the peoples of Turkestan in northern Afghanistan, and from the southern frontier regions. Most of the incidents (assassinations, rebellions, and sabotage) were linked, correctly or not, to pro-Amanullah forces, especially the Charkhi family of the Yusufzai clan of the Ghilzai Pashtun tribe, whose supporters carried out several assassinations against the Mushiban family, including that of Nader Shah in 1933.

Nader Shah's only son, Zahir Shah (ruled 1933-1973), succeeded to the throne at age nineteen, but his two paternal uncles (Hashim Khan, prime minister 1933-1946 and Shah Mahmood, prime minister 1946-1953) and an older paternal cousin (Muhammad Daoud, prime minster1953-1963) ran the country as prime ministers before Zahir Shah could assume effective power as king in 1963. Nader Shah's assassination in 1933 was followed by a period of bloody suppression, especially by Hashim Khan, against the regime's presumed enemies. With the consolidation and routinization of Musahiban power, the physical security of the population improved, but a new pernicious sense of uncertainty, suspicion, and distrust of government settled in, especially in non-Pashtun ethnic communities in the central, north, and western regions of the country (Shahrani 1986, 53–58). Advanced Islamic training became restricted to the *madrassas* in British India, due to the loss of northern centers of Islamic learning in Bukhara and Samarkand to the Russian Bolsheviks. The efforts by the Musahiban to establish *madrasas* in some of the major cities met with very limited success as students continued to venture to the Deobandi seminaries in Muslim India and Shi`as to Mashhad and Qum in Iran (see Misbah 2008; Shirazi 2008). Modern education, initially for boys only, was revived primarily to convince the traditionalists of the compatibility of Islam with the Musahiban dynasty's policy of "limited guided modernization" and to help secure loyalty to the monarchy by creating and developing a sense of Afghan (Pashtun) nationalism among the educated youth.

By the mid-1930s, efforts to construct an Afghan national ideology revolved around the promotion of Pashtu as the official language of Afghanistan, thus "doing away with Persian," as Hashim Khan put it (Maillart 1940, 227). The Pashtu Tulana (Pashtu Academy) was created to promote Pashtu language and Pashtun culture as the font of "Afghan" national ideology. Emphasis on the Aryan origins (in vogue then among Nazis in Europe) of the majority of the peoples of Afghanistan (Pashtun, Baluch, Tajik, Nuristani, and the Pamiris) and on Pashtun culture and language were meant to justify the unity of the Pashtun across the Durand Line as the basis for the emergent notion of Afghan nationalism.

The Musahiban rulers remained ambivalent about the role of Islam in national politics but invoked it widely as a basis for national unity and preservation of national independence. Royal ambivalence toward Islam's role, combined with fear of reactions from conservative Muslim elements toward Western "isms," such as communism and unfettered capitalism, left the gradually expanding Afghan educational system devoid of any firm set of principles and shared Islamic values or ideological orientation, other than narrowly chauvinistic Pashtun-based nationalism.

The Musahiban education policy ultimately failed, whether intended or not, to prepare the schooled Afghans to effectively meet the penetration of ideological challenges, especially those of Marxism and Maoism. Their policies were relatively successful, however, in creating an alliance between the royals and the conservative traditional rural dignitaries, both religious and secular, to maintain a semblance of rural peace and order well into the 1970s. This relative center-periphery balance was further strengthened by substantial economic aid from the superpowers, making the government independent of its subjects for direct revenue collection and able to provide them with some social services. Foreign aid in military assistance also provided the government, for the first time in history, a relatively secure military base of power.

Indeed, Prime Minister Daoud (1953–1963), feeling militarily secure, launched a program of national integration and modernization by adopting a series of five-year development plans. Even though the economic and political goals of these plans were not realized, communication infrastructure was expanded into more remote areas of the country and education was made available to rural youth. His declaration of women's emancipation (unveiling) in 1959 was met by riots in the city of Kandahar, the future spiritual capital of the Taliban movement, but Daoud violently crushed them using his new mechanized armed forces. Under his rule secularism was emphasized and the Islamic part of the school curriculum was reduced considerably. Improved roads, which helped cheap manufactured goods penetrate into the periphery, induced unprecedented new needs and rural poverty.[9] The British departure from India and the creation of the new state of Pakistan offered Daoud the opportunity to dispute the validity of the Durand Line as a national border. Appealing to Pashtun nationalist sentiments on both sides of the border, he manufactured a lasting international dispute with Pakistan on the so-called Pashtunistan issue, which led to costly border closures (1961–1963) and military incidents, which culminated in his resignation as prime minister in 1963.

With the temporary departure of Prince Daoud from the political arena, Zahir Shah emerged from the shadows of his senior relatives and hesitatingly experimented (1963–1973) with *demokrasyee now* (new democracy) with a new liberal constitution in 1964. The 1964 constitution supposedly was a response to the entry of Afghan educated youth into the political arena. The New Democracy Movement, however, coincided with a thaw in the Cold War and a substantial decrease in foreign aid, a critical pillar of the political economy of Afghanistan.

Following the adoption of the new constitution and the establishment of more tolerant liberal press laws, a variety of ideologically motivated political movements, including a number of communist groups such as the pro-Soviet Khalq-Parcham Communists, began publishing papers and engaging in antigovernment agitations within the universities and high schools, especially in Kabul as well as in major provincial towns. The Jawanani Musalman (Muslim Youth) Islamist movement inspired by several Shara'iyat professors at Kabul University, who had studied at Al-Azhar University[10] and were familiar with the Egyptian Muslim Brotherhood, emerged in opposition to the communist groups. In the ensuing bloody conflict between these two competing ideological camps, who also strongly opposed the Musahiban rule, the government decided to brutally suppress the Muslim Youth movement. The Muslim Youth advocated a radical transformation of society, culture, politics, and economics, all to be achieved after capturing the power of the state. By the early 1970s these ideological, generational and rural-urban struggles consumed all institutions of the government: the military, schools, factories, and even the cabinet. Students, Marxists, and Islamists alike took their fights to the streets on a regular basis, and Zahir Shah changed prime ministers quickly to appease them, but to no avail. Slowly political discontent spiraled out of control as economic conditions worsened due to the severe drought of 1970–1971 in the region. Thus, on July 17, 1973, assisted by the Parcham faction of the Communist Party, Sardar Muhammad Daoud, the former prime minister and a royal family member, staged a bloodless palace military coup against Zahir Shah, abolished the monarchy, and declared himself president of the Republic of Afghanistan (see Roy 1990; Shahrani 1984).

Daoud, as the *rahbari inqilaab* (guide of the revolution) in his initial radio address after the coup, asserted that the new republican system was more "consistent with the true spirit of

Islam" and promised basic reforms and a "true democracy" to serve the needs of the majority (see Shahrani 1986, 62–64). Daoud's return to power was initially welcomed, except within the Muslim Youth movement and among Islamic-minded individuals, who were alarmed by his alliance with the communist Parchamis. During his five-year tenure President Daoud and his henchmen eliminated well-known nationalist politicians and launched a vicious attack in 1975 against rebellious Muslim Youth and other Islamist individuals and groups. Opposition to Daoud's regime formed not only among the Muslim Youth. Conflicting expectations about the nature of the new republican regime quickly surfaced between the young leftist military officers who executed the coup and the old time confidants of the Rahbar. During his last official visit to Moscow, President Daoud reportedly angered his host, General Secretary Leonid Brezhnev, during a heated exchange. Shortly thereafter, on April 27, 1978, the communists, his former allies, with help and guidance from the former USSR, carried out a bloody military coup, killing Daoud and many members of his immediate family and thus putting an end to nearly five decades of Musahiban rule (see Akram 2004; Osman 1388HSh). The bloody military coup staged by the Khalq-Parcham Communists (Peoples Democratic Party of Afghanistan [PDPA]) plunged the country into the abyss of decades-long proxy wars, culminating in the rise of Taliban and al-Qa`ida terrorists and the US-ISAF military intervention that followed the attacks against the United States on September 11, 2001.

Marxist Revolution, Soviet Intervention, Islamist Response, and Globalization of Jihad

The overthrow of the despised Musahiban dynasty briefly provided the PDPA with some claim of legitimacy. Their previous activities and rhetoric of identification with the "Great Russian October Revolution of 1917" and friendship with the USSR, however, quickly galvanized a growing armed opposition in many urban as well as rural parts of the country. Early uncoordinated armed attacks against the PDPA regime seemed similar to previous antigovernment jihads. Predictably, the PDPA regime also called its "defense of the gains of the Revolution" a jihad against their opponents, whom they called "imperialist lackeys" and reactionaries (Shahrani and Canfield 1984; Roy 1986).

Within months of assuming power, the two factions of the PDPA—that is, Khalq (People) and Parcham (Flag)—forced by Moscow to collaborate in executing the coup, fell upon each other in a murderous power struggle. Atrocities by the regime increased, and opposition spread across the country. Fearing the collapse of the PDPA regime, the Soviet Red Army invaded Afghanistan in December 1979 in support of the Parcham faction. But direct Soviet military intervention quickly and radically changed the conflict from a civil war into a global jihad against Afghan communists and the former USSR. Afghanistan became a new arena of "low-intensity proxy warfare" in the Cold War.

The capture of state power by the PDPA augured an unprecedented rupture between state power and Islam in Afghanistan. For the first time in historical memory, the new "revolutionary" government in Afghanistan did not assert or declare the protection of Islam (i.e., shari`a) or the defense of the faith as its primary obligation or the basis of its legitimacy. On the contrary, as a client of the USSR—an atheist Russian-dominated colonial power that had destroyed the Muslim states of Bukhara, Khiva, and Qoqand in Turkistan to the north and incorporated them into the Soviet Union—the PDPA came to be regarded by most Afghans as an enemy of Islam and Afghanistan. Therefore, popular armed jihad against PDPA regimes and their Soviet patrons was instigated in opposition to their anti-Islamic policies. The size, scale, and leadership of the armed jihad were also reflective of the altered national political dynamics and the emergence of new structural relations between the center and peripheries in Afghanistan and beyond (Roy 1990; Magnus and Naby 1998; Shahrani 2013, Shahrani and Canfield 1984).

Immediately upon assuming power, the PDPA regime rounded up thousands of suspected members of the Muslim Youth (their long-time opponents on university campuses and street demonstrations during the 1960s and 1970s) as well as members of well-known and respected *ruhani* families and countless pious individuals across the country, incarcerating and torturing them as potential enemies of the revolution. In this environment of fear and insecurity, Islamic-minded educated youth abandoned their government posts and returned home to organize and defend their own villages and valleys by taking up arms against the communist regime. As security deteriorated, large numbers of families, both urban and rural, fearing for their lives, voted with their feet, taking refuge in neighboring Pakistan and Iran. A few leaders of the Muslim Youth Movement, such as Burhanuddin Rabbani, Gulbuddin Hekmatyar, and Ahmad Shah Massoud, had been driven out of the country during the Daoud era (1973–1978) and were already living in exile in Peshawar, Pakistan. Ahmad Shah Massoud of Panjsher valley returned home to organize the resistance, and others began to organize the *muhajireen* (refugees-warriors) in support of the resistance from Peshawar and Quetta, Pakistan, or Mashhad in Iran (see Shahrani 1996).

Soviet military intervention to save the Afghan communist regime heralded major developments in Afghanistan's resistance movements. It offered the critically weakened Muslim Youth movement in the cities, who had enjoyed very little or no support among the peasantry, a new lease on political life. Lacking indigenous intellectual leadership, they relied on borrowed ideologies of Islamism from the Muslim Brotherhood and Mawdudi's Jama'at-i Islami in Pakistan. The Afghan Islamist operators were often in disagreement, revealing growing divisions along ethnolinguistic and tribal lines. Hence, like the Communist PDPA, the Muslim Youth organization also splintered and reorganized nationally and across the borders in Pakistan and Iran initially into Jamiati Islami (headed by Burhanuddin Rabbani, a Tajik from the northeastern province of Badakhshan) and Hezb-i Islami (run by Gulbuddin Hekmatyar—a *naaqilin* Pashtun from Baghlan province in the north).[11] In addition, heads of some *ruhani* families organized their own separate resistance groups. In all, seven jihadi organizations were officially recognized by Pakistan's General Zia u-Haqq and Pakistan's intelligence service, the Inter Service Intelligence Directorate (known as the ISI), and were allowed to operate out of Peshawar. All of them were Sunni and all except one, Jamiati Islami, were headed by Pashtuns or their saintly hereditary *pirs*. Simultaneously more than a dozen Shi`a groups began to operate out of Iran and central Afghanistan. These jihadi groups were divided into two camps: on the one hand, Islamist revolutionaries or "fundamentalists" aimed at capturing state power to form a vaguely defined Islamic government;

traditionalist/moderate pro-Western groups, on the other hand, simply fought to defend Islam and liberate Afghanistan and reinstate the monarchy. Such factional alignments were manifestations of the increasing politicization of sectarian, tribal, regional, and ethnolinguistic cleavages, exacerbated by the monarchy and now encouraged by multiple outside patrons, both near and far, Muslim and non-Muslim (see Roy 1990; Naby 1988; Shahrani and Canfield 1984).

Additionally, the Soviet invasion of Afghanistan offered the United States and Europeans a new opportunity to collaborate with their Muslim client states in the Gulf (United Arab Emirates and Saudi Arabia) and Egypt offered substantial covert military and economic assistance to the Afghan Mujahidin, so that they could fight their common enemy: the Soviet Union. The flow of CIA money (reportedly complemented dollar for dollar by Saudi Arabia) and weapons was managed by Pakistan's ISI. With the arrival of large financial and technical support, the Mujahidin soon lost control of their jihad to outside benefactors. Pakistan and Iran, host to more than 5 million Afghan refugees, began to impose constraints and controls on Afghan jihadi resistance groups. Outside governments, especially General Zia's Pakistan, began to speak for the Mujahiddin,[12] and the ISI decided which jihadi organizations would be given money and weapons and be allowed to operate inside Afghanistan (Coll 2004). As a result what began as a genuinely indigenous local popular jihad in Afghanistan was gradually transformed into a proxy war managed by Pakistan for their own gains. The deeply felt ordinary Afghans' discourse of jihad had been co-opted by state actors once again (this time foreign governments), just as it had been under Abdur Rahman's rule a century earlier.

The Afghan national Islamic struggle against the Communist PDPA regime and their Soviet patrons was transformed into a transnational and global jihad. Whereas jihad was initially intended to fight communism in Afghanistan, it soon expanded against any and all disbelief. The discourse of jihad predominated anti-Soviet resistance within Afghanistan as well as in Afghan *muhajirin* (Muslim refugee-warrior) camps in Pakistan and Iran. Large numbers of jihadi party publications extolled the virtues of armed jihad and the responsibility of Muslims around the globe to support the Mujahidin. Mujahiddin opened schools in refugee camps in Pakistan as well as in some liberated areas inside Afghanistan (Edwards 1993, 1995). Numerous poorly staffed madrasahs were also established for the children of Afghan *muhajirin* in the North West Frontier Province (recently renamed Khyber Pakhtunkhwa) of Pakistan, financed by individuals or groups from Saudi Arabia and other Gulf states. These madrasahs became training grounds for the Afghan resistance and incubators for the production of Taliban by the mid-1990s. Considerable US Agency for International Development funds were dedicated to writing and printing new textbooks extolling the virtues of jihad, even in books of mathematics, for the Afghan schools, both inside the country as well as in the refugee camps (see Abdulbaqi 2008; Shirazi 2008; Riley 2009).

The United States, under President Reagan, provided Afghanistan with sophisticated antiaircraft missiles and was touting Mujahidin in the international media as "holy warriors" and "freedom fighters." Muslim individuals and organizations across the globe were encouraged and invited to join the fight against the Soviets in Afghanistan. Abdullah Azzam, the well-known Jordanian-Palestinian preacher and resistance leader, took up the call by establishing an "Office of Services" (Maktab al-Khadamat) to help recruit young Muslims from the Middle East as well as from the United States and Europe for the jihad in Afghanistan. Osama Bin Laden, the rich Saudi activist, followed suit by establishing Bayt al-Ansar (House of the Helpers) in Peshawar, dedicated to assisting transnational jihadis. Both Azzam and Bin Laden later on entered Afghanistan to fight. Azzam furthermore published inspirational materials urging others to open offices in Peshawar in support of Arab fighters inside Afghanistan (Azzam 1987, 1982).[13]

Ideologically, the decade of jihad in the 1980s reaffirmed the pervasive conservative commitment to Islam among millions of Afghan refugees and the rural masses, especially in the southern Pashtun belt along the border with Pakistan. It also revived and strengthened Islamic nationalism in opposing a proven and much despised enemy, the PDPA regime and their Soviet sponsors. More significantly, resistance manifested as jihad helped some religious leaders to regain their lost power and popularity. In fragile coalitions between traditionalists and Islamists, religion provided the common glue and language of discourse for these otherwise disparate peoples and political groups. Their struggle was viewed collectively as a fight against atheism and infidels.

Horizontally structured local resistance groups based on communities of trust, loosely connected to multiple Peshawar-based jihadi centers of power and resources, exercised considerable autonomy in the environment of a failed state. These local command structures became the greatest strength of the ultimately successful anti-Soviet Afghan jihad movement. The local organizations were intensely personal, participatory, and closely knit. Trusted local clerics, in collaboration with jihadi commanders, resolved local disputes on the basis of local understanding and application of *shari`ah* and *`adat* (customary norms). They also maintained security and provided minimal public services (health, education, agriculture, etc.), often with the help of international Muslim and non-Muslim nongovernmental organizations, while defending their territory against the regime and competing jihadi parties.

At the regional and national levels these local jihadi cells were attached vertically to increasingly loose-knit, abstract, ideological and slightly hierarchical, impersonal networks with very little social density. In the heterogeneous ethnolinguistic and political environment of 1980s Afghanistan, these structures proved relatively effective during the resistance but these fragile vertical structures and their fractious leadership ultimately proved disastrous after defeating the common enemy.

The rhetoric of revolutionary Islamist Mujahidin parties had also been affected by the interests of their outside patrons as well as the changing transnational and global jihadi discourses. The most important was the emergence of "neofundamentalism" of the Salafi-Wahhabi Arab jihadi fighters in Afghanistan, characterized by anti-Shi`a sentiments and opposition to Sufism and shrine veneration, which advocated jihad against any and all forms of *kufr* (disbelief)—not just communism (Roy 1998, 1995). Prospects of assured military success triggered by the complete withdrawal of Soviet troops in 1989 made the realization of an Islamic government based on justice and equality in postcommunist Afghanistan much firmer among the peoples of Afghanistan. The expectations of Muslims worldwide who had supported the jihad in Afghanistan were also raised. After the Soviet Red Army was routed in Afghanistan and left humiliated, the USSR collapsed shortly thereafter, which brought about the fall of their puppet regime in Kabul (for details, see Roy 1990, 1995, 1998; Maley 1998; Crews and Tarzi 2008; Shahrani 2009; Shahrani and Canfield 1984).

Postjihad "Islamic Card" Games: From "Holy War" to Taliban and al-Qa`ida Terror

The Afghan jihadis triumphed against incredible military odds in its victory over the Soviet Red Army. This spectacular military victory, however, quickly turned into a tragic political failure with serious consequence for Afghanistan, the region, and the world. The reasons for this failure are complex and numerous (see Shahrani 2002). Here I will briefly touch on the following key questions: How and why did the Afghan Mujahidin lose traction among the Afghan masses so soon after their triumph? How and why did the Afghan Mujahidin and their Islamist ideology become simply an "Islamic card" to play by competing regional and distant patrons in a new "great game?" Ultimately, what have been and are the consequences of these dangerous "games" by the "friends" of Mujahidin for Islam in power and the peoples of Afghanistan, the region, and the world? I will argue that these careless and volatile postjihad Islamic card games, played by former patrons of anti-Soviet jihad in Afghanistan during the 1980s, denied any constructive role to Islam in power in Afghanistan by producing and unleashing the rampaging Taliban and al-Qa`ida terrorists not only upon the war-weary peoples of Afghanistan but also upon the international community, especially Europe and the United States.

Shortly after the fall of Dr. Najeebullah's communist regime in April 1992 at the hands of Ahmad Shah Massoud, a well-known Tajik jihadi commander, a Mujahidin transitional government of the new "Islamic Republic of Afghanistan" was cobbled together in Rawalpindi, Pakistan. But within weeks the situation in Kabul dissolved into bitter interethnic and sectarian wars encouraged and aided by outside powers (with Pakistan, Saudi Arabia, and the United States on one side and Iran, India, the Russian Federation, and China on the other). Interests of these two competing camps and their Afghan proxies (whose composition changed rapidly during the 1990s) completely overruled the interest of ordinary Muslims of Afghanistan.

Pakistan had first played the "Islamic card" using a group of Islamists who had taken refuge in Pakistan against Daoud's republican regime (1973–1978) and more blatantly against the PDPA government to undermine Pashtun nationalism in its management of Afghan jihad during the 1980s. Pakistan's ISI directorate had also favored the Pashtun Sunni Islamists groups, especially Hizbi Islami of Gulbuddin Hekmatyar. Indeed, Pakistan had groomed Hekmatyar and his party to assume power in Kabul after the fall of the communists. The reasons behind Pakistan's support for the Pashtun were fivefold: (1) to appease their own Pashtun population, who had a substantial presence in the Pakistani army and security forces while currying favor with the Afghan Pashtuns; (2) to overcome the Durand Line border dispute with Afghanistan by emphasizing Islamist ideals of Muslim brotherhood and the oft-repeated Islamist slogan of "Islam does not recognizes borders"[14]; (3) to assume the role of a "big brother" to the Pashtun-led government in Kabul in order to serve as the principal agency for Afghanistan's postwar reconstruction and development for which the Pakistanis expected to be funded lucratively by the international community; (4) to gain guaranteed free and easy transport access to the newly independent Central Asian republics for trade and investment; and (5) to gain "strategic depth" in case of a nuclear war with India (cf. Ahady 1988).

Saudi Arabia backed Pakistani policies because the Pashtun Sunni groups were deemed to be able to curb Shi`a Hazara power and Iranian influence in the country. US support aimed at denying Iran the possibility of becoming an alternative transportation corridor for Caspian Sea and Central Asian gas and oil. Therefore empowering the Pashtun in Afghanistan represented a powerful convergence of interests for Pakistan, Saudi Arabia, and the United States. To expedite the realization of their collective strategic objectives in post-communist Afghanistan, the ISI favored an outright military victory by Hizbi Islami over Najeebullah's regime following the Soviet troop withdrawal. Such a decisive military victory was not possible despite the concerted efforts by ISI and Hezbi Islami of Hekmatyar during the four years (1988–1992) following the Red Army's departure.

Commander Ahmad Shah Massoud of Jamiati Islami, a Tajik, in alliance with Rashid Dostum, an Uzbek militia leader from northern Afghanistan, fought to preempt Pakistani, Saudi, and US intentions, most likely with encouragement and support from Iran and India in April 1992. Iran also encouraged the unity of Hazara jihadi parties in creating Hizbi Wahdat (the Unity Party) under the leadership of Ali Mazari. Pakistanis and Saudis were alarmed by these developments. Fearing Iranian Shi`a influences upon the Kabul regime they prevented the inclusion of Shi`a parties in the Mujahideen transitional government that assumed power in Kabul. Although elated about keeping the Shi`a Hazaras out of the Mujahidin transitional government, all three foreign powers were unhappy about Hekmatyar being the prime minister rather than head of state. Encouraged by his foreign allies Hekmatyar began shelling Kabul from his perch in the western outskirts of the city for the next two years (1992–1994). He initiated the brutal internecine proxy wars to be fought by some utterly unbelievable factional alignments between Pashtun and non-Pashtun (Tajiks, Uzbeks, and Hazara) and Sunni and Shi`a (imamis and ismailis), which left most of Kabul in ruins (for details, see Coll 2004; Saikal 1998; Maly 1998).

In the absence of a central authority in Kabul, the country was carved out into autonomous regional entities based on ethnic-sectarian and tribal cleavages and headed by strongmen, or *shuras*.[15] Kabul was being fought over by all parties. Kandahar and the surrounding southwestern Durrani Pashtun-inhabited provinces were in utter chaos and lawless.

The rise of the Taliban in Kandahar therefore came as no surprise. Mullah Omar and his followers' ability to bring order to the region were indeed welcomed by the locals. Unhappy with Hekmatyar's support for Saddam Hussein during the Gulf War and his poor performance on the battlefield in Kabul, Pakistan grasped the utility of Mullah Omar and his Taliban movement. The Mujahideen transitional government was busy fighting proxy wars over the control of the capital and had delivered nothing of their Islamist promises to the expectant public. Their internecine warfare and mutually destructive behavior had forced the population to rely once again on their own local communities of faith and trust to protect themselves against increased violence perpetrated by the government or those aspiring for control of the state. Travel and commerce on the roads had become unsafe and traders were consistently subjected to extortion by gun-toting toll collectors. Mullah Omar and the Taliban cleared the roads in areas under their control and offered to maintain law and order by enforcing the *shari`ah*. They pledged to enforce a traditional understanding of Islam combined with elements of Pashtun male codes of honor (*pushtuwali*). Given Mullah Omar's initial popularity among the local Pashtun, his Taliban movement was quickly adopted by the government of Pakistan under Benazir Bhutto, and blessed by Saudi Arabia (Mackenzie 1998). The refinement of the Taliban's ideological message and its recruitment were handed over to the Jamiat ul-Ulama of Pakistan headed by Mowlana Sami-ul Haqq who became the Taliban movement's intellectual godfather (Rashid 2001; Marsden 1998; Shahrani 2008). Taliban fighters were recruited from Pakistani seminaries run by the Jamiat ul-Ulama of Pakistan. These seminaries, located along the border, had become a major training ground for the jihad against the USSR in the 1980s and most of their students were Afghan (Pashtun) refugees. Their ranks furthermore included units of Arab-Afghans who had joined Osama Bin Laden and Ayman al-Zawahiri and their newly formed al-Qa'ida terrorist organization. In addition, some regional and international jihadists from Kashmir, the Central Asian republics, and other Muslim lands were provided safe haven and training grounds in Taliban-controlled territories inside Afghanistan.

According to a BBC report of an interview with Benazir Bhutto on October 14, 1996, the United States and United Kingdom supplied weapons, paid for by Saudi Arabia, to the Taliban to help them overrun Kabul in September of that year, driving the Rabbani-Massoud government into the north of the country (Ahady 1998). A year later, in 1997, the Taliban, with the help of the ISI, forged an alliance with Abdul Malik, a lieutenant of General Abdur Rashid Dostum, to take Mazar-i Sharif and drive Dostum to exile. This Taliban alliance with Abdul Malik fell apart immediately after their victory, whereupon Malik's forces, in collaboration with the Hazaras, slaughtered the Taliban fighters as they tried to retreat from Mazar-i Sharif. Their initial success in capturing Mazar-i Sharif, the most important urban center in the north, however, had won the Taliban government official recognitions from Pakistan, Saudi Arabia, and the United Arab Emirates. They also received a jubilant message of congratulation from Zahir Shah, the former exiled king, for reuniting Afghanistan under the Pashtuns. From that point on the Taliban war of vengeance against the non-Pashtun in the north and center of Afghanistan (especially against Uzbeks and Hazaras) turned horrifically deadly until the end of their rule in 2001. In their rampaging attempt to conquer the northern and central areas of Afghanistan, the Taliban faced stiff resistance from the locals. Iran, India, and the Central Asian republics, as well as Russia and China, feared a Talibanization of the region and were desperately providing arms and ammunition to the newly formed Northern Alliance of the Tajiks, Uzbeks, and Hazaras to defend their territories. The many Pashtun communities across northern Afghanistan had decided to support their Taliban tribesmen from the south and served as Taliban bases and safe haven in their war to subdue the local non-Pashtun residents. This bloody war resulted in major massacres of the Hazaras by Taliban in central Afghanistan. The decimation and deportation of Uzbeks from the north was reminiscent of the era of the Iron Amir Abdur Rahman Khan in the nineteenth century (see Shahrani 2008, 2000b).

Non-Pashtun resistance was primarily fueled by an unwillingness to return to Pashtun overlordship, this time justified by the imposition of the harsh and hateful ideology of Talibanism, just as the "defense of Islam" had been used to justify Abdur Rahman's rule a century earlier. The most prominent elements of this creed were a strict interpretation of *shari'a*, imposition of *hudud* punishments, severe restriction of female education and women's rights to work, curtailing of civil liberties, policing of public morality, and banning of music, television, video tapes, and games. With the anointment of Mullah Muhammad Omar as *amir al-mu'minin* (commander of the faithful) by a large gathering of Pashtun mullahs in Kandahar, Omar became the supreme authority and his word was final on all matters.

With the Taliban reincarnating the state-sacralizing policies of Amir Abdur Rahman Khan of a century ago, Afghanistan had come full circle in instrumental uses of Islam by state power (see Roy 1998). These elements of Talibanism, as a kind of neofundamentalism, were complemented by addition of anti-Shi`a and anti-Sufi practices of the local population, as well as opposition to the West and modernity as advocated by their new international jihadist allies, the al-Qa`ida terrorist organization under bin Laden's command. The impact of the enforcement of the Taliban creed by their marauding moral police, Amri bel-Ma`ruf wa Nahi anil-Munkar (Department of Promotion of Virtues and Prevention of Vice) was oppressively felt on a daily basis, especially in Kabul and most of the northern areas they came to control. Talibanism also took its toll on Afghanistan's historical heritage: substantial parts of Kabul museums' holdings were looted and many historical monuments were destroyed, particularly the famed statues of Buddha in Bamiyan in central Afghanistan. The Taliban's rule outside the southern Pashtun areas became a reign of terror.

As Taliban control in Afghanistan increased, they robbed the opportunity for effective deployment of Islam in managing power from the peoples of Afghanistan, they allowed al-Qa`ida to expand its terrorist war against United States' interests in Saudi Arabia, Yemen, and East Africa, as well as in Europe and the United States, with a large degree of impunity. The United States and the West had been oblivious to the plight of the non-Pashtun peoples of Afghanistan under the Taliban and al-Qa`ida's reign of terror since 1996, despite repeated warnings and requests for help. It took the tragic events of September 11, 2001 to finally draw the world's attention to the terrible consequences of the Islamic card games played by the regional and international powers in Afghanistan since 1992. The United States responded on October 7, 2001 by launching a military campaign to remove the Taliban from power and launched the so-called war on terror.

US AND NORTH ATLANTIC TREATY ORGANIZATION INTERVENTION, THE RESURGENT TALIBAN, AND THE FUTURE OF ISLAMIC CARD GAMES

President George W. Bush was intent on producing a military response to the 9/11 attacks against the United States. With UN authorization and support from ISAF coalition forces and Pakistan, the United States set out to remove the Taliban from power. During the military intervention the Taliban were defeated but not destroyed. Most of them disbanded and dispersed to their villages, while their leadership along with that of al-Qa`ida was given refuge in Pakistan by their ISI protectors. Another military victory in Afghanistan had been achieved, yet the country's political future and the role of Islam in that future remained uncertain.

Following the defeat of the Taliban, President George W. Bush began talking about the US commitment to nation building and the promotion of democracy in Afghanistan, raising the hopes and expectations of the ordinary Afghans. He also stressed the fact that his war on terror was not a crusade against Islam as it targeted the terrorist extremists. The effort for rebuilding a post-Taliban Afghanistan government began in December 2001 with the Bonn Conference and Accords under the United Nations auspices. Even though representatives of different ethnic groups attended the meeting, complaints arose that the selected interim government of Afghanistan under the leadership of Hamid Karzai had been preselected by international powers. The interim government produced by the Bonn Conference was mandated to implement the Bonn Accords under the auspices of the United Nations Office of Special Representative for Afghanistan. Specifically, they were to convene Loya Jirgas (Grand Councils of Dignitaries) to elect the transitional head of state, who was in turn to create commissions for drafting and ratifying a new constitution by 2004; to hold presidential, parliamentary, and local elections; and to build Afghan security forces and bring about the disarmament and reintegration of the jihadi forces into the new Afghan National Army and Afghan National Police. With large sums of reconstruction and development funds pouring into the country, former jihadi commanders, as well as many Afghan refugees returning from Pakistan and Iran and English-speaking technocrats from the West, began to find innovative means, official and unofficial, legitimate and illegitimate, to benefit from the windfall. Improved security after the fall of Taliban also made it possible for the former Mujahidin leaders and commanders, who had appropriated considerable private and public wealth in recent years, to begin displaying and even investing their ill-gained wealth. Growing official corruption and inattention to the basic needs of Afghanistan's rural population created new space for the resurgence of Taliban among the Pashtun near the Pakistani border.

By 2006 the Taliban and al-Qa`ida had reappeared with potent Improvised Explosive Devices (IED) and suicidal attacks against the Afghan government and civilians, as well as the coalition forces. Using safe havens and training bases in Pakistan, the Taliban resurgence has gradually expanded to a much larger area of the Pashtun belt in the south and east of Afghanistan and across the border in Pakistan. Support for the Taliban remains limited to Pashtun-inhabited regions in Afghanistan and Pakistan and is motivated by a simple message: Islam must be defended against the threat of the American occupation forces, which have imposed an illegitimate corrupt and un-Islamic government in the country. US military surges during President Obama's administration, as those during his predecessor's rule, have been focused on military solutions. The United States and its coalition allies appear either unable or unwilling to address the core political and moral malaise of inappropriate governance they have established and continue to support in Afghanistan. This failure is turning the military victory of 2001 against the Taliban into yet another political failure for the peoples of Afghanistan, the region, and the world.

Conclusions

The role of Islam as the core element of Afghanistan's political culture since the 1880s has been limited to instrumental interventions by state and international powers. The institution of jihad has been most often employed by Afghans (rulers and ruled alike) for the effective mobilization of the masses against foreign occupation or intervention. Jihad has also been a favorite mobilization technique of rulers to crush their domestic opponents, both real and imagined. Those contesting power of abusive kings have also used jihad as a discursive weapon. Muslim dignitaries, whether traditionally trained `ulama' (scholars), *mashaayekh,* or *ruhanis* (Sufis mystics), or the more recently al-Azhar-trained or secularly educated Islamists, have been employed by Afghan rulers and foreign powers to serve their interests against their own peoples. The potency of the institution and rhetoric of jihad and martyrdom, as evident in the current resurgent Taliban war against the United States and coalition forces, appears to still be intact. The effective power of jihad is likely to remain strong as long as governments continue to operate without adherence to fundamental Islamic values of justice, fairness, and honesty. Jihadism will also persist as long as foreign powers, near and far, Muslim and non-Muslim, impose their will upon the peoples of Afghanistan by installing leaders who deny the right to community self-governance (see Shahrani 2009, 2003, 1998).

Claims of enforcing *shari'ah* has been another commonly used discourse by the rulers of Afghanistan. In reality, enforcement of *shari'ah* has served as a convenient instrument to extend administrative centralization through judicial courts and the educational system. Similarly, the introduction of Islamic reforms by the state has often aimed to sacralize the state and nationalize Islam in order to boost government legitimacy. Such endeavors, even when well intentioned as in the case of King Amanullah, have produced tragic results for the government as well as the ordinary peoples of Afghanistan. The promise to establish an Islamic government and push society toward modernity and progress within the framework of humane values of Islam has turned out to be nothing but empty (Roy 1994). Indeed, contrary to Qur'anic injunctions (see *Surat al-Anfaal*, 1–19) that jihadi fighters do not have any prior rights to the spoils of war, whether booty taken from the enemy or, in the case of Afghanistan, funds donated to the cause of jihad by foreign supporters, all Afghan jihadi leaders have treated all such resources as their own personal property. This has been true despite the fact that most of the sacrifices of jihad have fallen on the ordinary members of local communities.

Regardless of repeated instrumental abuses of Islam in the hands of their rulers and Afghanistan's power elites, the peoples of Afghanistan, both rural and urban, continue to invest their hopes and aspirations for better living conditions and salvation in Islam. The powerful appeal of the humanistic values of Islamic social justice, generosity, humility, compassion, and equality before God persists among the masses, despite their many disappointments. A Taliban and al-Qa'ida victory can be prevented only if the United States and its coalition partners are willing to help replace Karzai's regime by an appropriate system of governance in Afghanistan: a political system built and intent on the realization of universal democratic principles and Muslim values, and not the whim of any one person, tribe, ethnic group, or political party.

Notes

1. For a critical study of the concept of jihad and its use against European colonialism, see Peters 1979, 1977 and, for a more recent application in Afghanistan, Shahrani 1984.
2. Based on early nineteenth-century reports, the Muslim inhabitants of this area were conservatively devout but tolerant of European Christians who passed through (see Elphinstone 1839/1972). However, the use of jihad as the motivational tool of choice against European Christian colonialist powers rendered them as *kafirs* (nonbelievers, heathens) and enemies of Islam and as a threat to the freedom of Muslims among the peoples of this region. Fighting to defend Islam and Muslim territory came to be regarded as *farz* (a

religious obligation); those who fought and won became *ghazis* (victors), and those who died for the cause became *shuhada* (martyrs; see also Olesen 1995; Gregorian 1969, 118–123). This perception gradually gained greater strength and popularity, especially among the Pathan/Pushtun tribesmen on the British NWFP. These popular views toward foreign non-Muslim invaders have persisted, especially in rural areas in the country, and became virulent once again during the anti-Soviet/Communist jihad of the 1980s, culminating in the current war of the resurgent Taliban and al-Qa`ida terrorists against the United States and NATO in Afghanistan (2001–present).

3. It is important to note that the continuation of British colonial threats in the south and eastern frontiers, created by the imposition of the Durand Line (1893), induced constant uprisings, encouraged (secretly and/or openly) by the Afghan kings, led by Pashtun "Maraboutic"-type Sufi jihadists whom the British have labeled "Mad Mullah/*Faqirs*" and "firebrands of the frontier." These *pirs* or *faqirs* and their Pathan tribal devotees (*mukhlis*) became a significant feature of the Pakhtun/Pathans on both sides of the border for decades to come (see Roy 1985, 56–58; Olesen 1995, 51–53). In western and northern parts of Afghanistan, where immediate colonial threats were less pervasive, *shari`ah*-based *tariqat* organizations led by well-trained `*ulama*' as *murshids/khalifa* and their *murids* (disciples) continued without undergoing a similar process of militarization or politicization of piety (see Shahrani 1984, 149–150).

4. A number of prominent *shari`ah* `*ulama*' and *tariqat pirs* had opposed his appointment as amir by the British and had supported one of his cousins, Sardar Yaqub Khan. Upon assumption of power Amir Abdur Rahman ordered the execution of several of them and the persecution of others. He accused them of being "false leaders of religion" and the cause of the downfall of Islamic nations (Nawid 1999, 25).

5. Most notably Nader Khan, the head of the Musahiban family, who later ruled the country from 1929 to 1978 and the family of Mahmood Tarzi, who played a decisive role in shaping state policies during the 1910s and 1920s.

6. Disagreements over his policies also caused dissension within the ranks of his high officials, resulting in the departure of General Nader Khan (his minister of war) to serve as ambassador to France; Nader Khan would return in 1929 as the "Savior of the Nation" (*Najiyee Watan*) following Amanullah's abdication and the subsequent civil war.

7. The initial British financial aid in 1929 to Nader Shah was four million (40 lakhs) Indian rupees and a "certain number of Indian Rifles," according to a telegram from the viceroy to the secretary of state in London on May 15, 1935. However, Nader Shah publically denied receiving any British assistance and maintained a deceptive stance on the nature of his dealings with British India and the frontier Pashtun across the border. British support for him had a dual purpose: to help secure peace among the frontier Pashtun tribes, which was successful, and to prevent Soviet ideological and political infiltration south, which ultimately met with only limited success (for details, see Olesen 1999, 172–176).

8. Louis Dupree (1973, 464) suggests that "the 1931 Constitution of Nader Shah embodied a hodgepodge of unworkable elements. Extracted from the Turkish, Iranian, and French constitutions and the 1923 Constitution of Amanullah, plus many aspects of the Hanafi *Shari`ah* of Sunni Islam and local custom (`*adat*), several of these last [were in fact] contradictory to the *Shari`ah*." Women, he points out held, despite claims of equality in Article 7 "decidedly inferior position in Afghan society" (ibid.).

9. For an ethnographic illustration of the impact of infrastructural improvements on producing rural poverty, see Shahrani 1979, especially among the Wakhi peasants.

10. Among them was Burhanuddin Rabbani, later heading the Jami'ati Islam (Islamic Society Party), his party led in the anti-Soviet jihad of the 1980s, he became president of Afghanistan (1992–1996/2001) and was assassinated on September 23, 2011 in his home in Kabul while receiving alleged Taliban emissaries one of whom detonated a bomb hidden in his turban.
11. Hizb-i Islami splintered but kept same name as Hizbi Islami of Mowlawi Khalis. Abdurabb Rasul Sayyaf, another Kabul University teacher and a colleague of Rabbani established another competing organization called Itihadi Islami Barayee Azadi Afghanistan (Islamic Alliance for the Liberation of Afghanistan). These four regarded themselves as Islamist revolutionaries as opposed the three remaining traditional fundamentalist groups formed in Peshawar, Pakistan.
12. Ultimately during the 1988 Geneva Accords leading to Soviet troop withdrawal from Afghanistan, it was Pakistan and the United States who represented the Afghan Mujahidin.
13. By the time of the Soviet troop withdrawal in the spring of 1989, an estimated 30,000 young Arabs and scores of others from Asia, Africa and Europe, including the future founders and leaders of al-Qa'ida, had participated in the Afghanistan jihad.
14. This objective has been far from realized as reports of new armed clashes over the Durand line has resulted in President Karzai to call on the Taliban that they should 'stand with' the young Afghan soldier who was killed during the recent border fighting, 'and defend their soil.' (See Shakeela Abrahimkhil 2013).
15. Ismail Khan controlled the western, primarily Persian-speaking provinces out of Herat; the northern, primarily Uzbek-inhabited provinces were run by Rashid Dostum out of Mazar-i Sharif; the central Hazara-inhabited provinces were controlled by Hizbi Wahdat and its leader Ali Mazari; the northeastern provinces, the Panjsher valley and the Shamali plain just north of Kabul were controlled by Jama'at-i Islamiof Rabbani and Massoud; the eastern provinces, inhabited mostly by Ghilzai Pashtun tribesmen, were administered by *Shurayee Mashreqi* (Eastern Council), and Lugar, Maidan and the southwestern Pashtun provinces were under the control of Hekmatyar and his Hizbi Islami.

References

Ahmed, Leila. 1992. *Women and Gender in Islam*. New Haven & London: Yale University Press.
Maillart, Ella. 1940. "Afghanistan's Rebirth:" An Interview with H.R.H. Hashim Khan in 1937. *Journal of the Royal Central Asian Society* 27 (April, Part II): 224–228.
Abrahimkhil, Shakeela. 2013. "Karzai: Afghanistan Never Recognised the Durand Linehttp://www.tolonews.com/en/afghanistan/10381-karzai-afghanistan-never-rec ognised-the-durand-line on May 4-2013. (accessed may 6, 2013).
Shahrani, M. Nazif. 2013. Center-Periphery Relations in Afghanistan. In *Local Politics in Afghanistan: A Century of Intervention in the Social Order*. Conrad Schetter, ed. London: Hurst & Company, pp. 23–37.

CHAPTER 31

THE MUSLIM BROTHERHOOD IN EGYPT

TAREK MASOUD

INTRODUCTION

THE Society of Muslim Brothers (Jama'at al-Ikhwan al-Muslimun) has been called Egypt's "most organized," "most popular," "most active," "most influential," and "most important" opposition movement. Its stated aim is "to establish Allah's religion on Earth" in the form of an "Islamic state that implements the rulings and teachings of Islam."[1] Founded in Isma'iliya, Egypt in 1928 by an elementary schoolteacher named Hasan al-Bannā, it defies easy categorization. In a speech to movement members in 1939, al-Bannā declared:

> You are not a benevolent society, nor a political party, nor a local organization having limited purposes. Rather, you are a new soul in the heart of the nation to give it life by means of the Quran.... When asked what it is you propagate, reply that it is Islam, the message of Muhammad, the religion that contains within it government.... If you are told that you are political, answer that Islam admits no such distinction. We believe the provisions of Islam and its teachings are all inclusive, encompassing the affairs of the people in this world and the hereafter. And those who think that these teachings are concerned only with the spiritual or ritualistic aspects are mistaken in this belief because Islam is a faith and a ritual, a nation and a nationality, a religion and a state, spirit and deed, holy text and sword.[2]

The modern Muslim Brotherhood is equal parts political party, social service organization, and Islamic preaching society, and it is thought to have excelled at each of these roles.[3] The movement played a critical role in the overthrow of Egyptian president Husni Mubarak. Its political arm, the Freedom and Justice Party (Hizb al-Hurriya wa al-'Adala), captured 40 percent of the seats in the first post-Mubarak parliamentary elections, and its presidential candidate, Muhammad Mursi, won office in June 2012 against stiff competition from across the political spectrum. The Brotherhood's health care and social service provision efforts have long been rumored to rival those of the increasingly dilapidated and cash-strapped Egyptian state. And its *da'wa* activities—particularly on university campuses—have been credited with contributing to the oft-remarked-upon Islamization of Egyptian society.

The Brotherhood is not simply an Egyptian phenomenon. Almost from the outset, al-Bannā and his successors aspired to take the message of the Ikhwan globally, and today the group boasts branches in nearly every Muslim country. Many of the Muslim world's most vibrant political parties are Brotherhood parties—including the Prosperous Justice Party of Indonesia, the Pan-Malaysian Islamic Party, the Iraqi Islamic Party, Jordan's Islamic Action Front, Algeria's Movement for a Peaceful Society, Kuwait's Islamic Constitutional Movement, Yemen's Congregation for Reform, Lebanon's Islamic Group, and the Islamic Resistance Movement of the Palestinian territories (better known by its acronym, Hamas), among others. Its thinkers and writers are highly influential: from the founder al-Bannā, whose writings have been translated into several languages, including Malay and Urdu; to Sayyid Qutb, author of the magisterial Qur'anic commentary "In the Shade of the Qur'an" and the more polemical "Milestones" (often credited as the inspirational source material for violent "Islamists" from the assassins of Egyptian President Anwar Sadat to former al-Qaʿida leader Usama Bin Laden); to Muhammad al-Ghazali, the distinguished twentieth-century al-Azhar scholar and author of several classic texts on Islam and society; to Yusif al-Qaradawi, the media-savvy, Qatar-based ʿalim whose frequent appearances on the al-Jazeera program "Shariʿah and Life" (al-Shariʿawa al-Hayat) have garnered it a weekly audience of approximately 35 million people.[4]

The Brotherhood's history, influence, and geographic spread are more than sufficient to render it the object of scholarly attentions. But the fascination that the movement holds for students of the Middle East (particularly Western students of the Middle East) is rooted in more than simply an appreciation of its long history or purported popularity. The Muslim Brotherhood represents a triple challenge to observers in the West. The first is essentially political: the Muslim Brotherhood, with its stated aim of "liberating the Islamic nation in all of its parts from every non-Islamic power, aiding Muslim minorities everywhere, and working to unite Muslims until they constitute a single *ummah*," is framed as an explicit challenge to perceived Western hegemony in the Middle East.[5] The second is ideological: as a traditionalist movement with an expansive view of the proper role of religious values in shaping social, economic, and political institutions, the Brotherhood contravenes the liberal sensibilities of its scholarly observers in the West. The third is theoretical: for much of the latter half of the twentieth century, scholars argued that the political appeal of religion was waning as societies became increasingly modern and developed. The Muslim Brotherhood, with its unapologetic deployment of religious rhetoric and symbols, represents a living rejoinder to this "secularization thesis."

The nature of these challenges (political, ideological, and intellectual) that the Brotherhood poses has shaped the scholarly discourse around the movement. That literature has had three major foci: the first is on the question of the Muslim Brotherhood's "moderation." Much of the literature on the Brothers asks whether they can become "peaceful," "committed to democracy," and "rational"—in other words, whether the movement might cease defining itself in opposition to Western interests, confronting liberal sensibilities, and casting doubt upon widely accepted theories of the secularization of politics. The second focus of scholarly attention has been on the question of who joins the Muslim Brotherhood and why. This literature attempts to ascertain the political and economic dysfunctions that impel individuals to endorse so-called religious fundamentalism, with a view toward rectifying those dysfunctions. The third focuses on ascertaining the extent of the movement's political power—particularly whether its current political dominance is likely to endure.

These questions (particularly the first and third) have taken on even greater urgency with the collapse of the Mubarak regime in Egypt on February 11, 2011. Banned in 1948 and again in 1954, and prevented from establishing a political party by an Egyptian legal and constitutional framework that prohibited parties based on religion, the Brothers have for the last two years enjoyed a rare period of freedom. In April 2011, two months after Mubarak's overthrow, the Brotherhood formed the Party of Freedom and Justice, which quickly established itself as the premier political party in Egypt, winning 217 out of 508 seats in the parliamentary elections held from November 2011 to January 2012. And though the Brotherhood-led parliament was later dissolved by court order on a dubious procedural technicality, the movement more than made up for this loss by electing the leader of its political arm, a university professor named Muhammad Mursi, to the country's presidency. The Brotherhood's electoral dominance so soon after the collapse of the Mubarak regime has caused scholars to redouble their efforts to peer into the movement's soul, gauge its level of commitment to its religious agenda, and divine its future electoral fortunes. Will the new party actually work for the principles emblazoned in its name (i.e., freedom and justice), or will it be a vehicle for the promotion of a reactionary "fundamentalist" agenda and the erection of a new Iranian-style theocracy? And, as important, now that Islamists have finally seized power at the ballot box, will they enjoy continued electoral mandates? And if they lose elections, will they let go of power, or will they behave the way a former American diplomat said they would when he argued, speaking of Islamists in Algeria, that the Islamist commitment to democracy extended only to "one man, one vote, one time?"

This essay proceeds as follows. First, I describe the Muslim Brotherhood's internal organization and practices. I then explore the question of Muslim Brotherhood moderation, demonstrating points of change and consistency in the movement's ends, and in the means it deploys to achieve those ends. I conclude that the Brotherhood has had a longstanding commitment to democratic processes that begins with al-Bannā, and that the movement's brief turns to violence in the 1940s and again in the 1960s were departures from, not embodiments of, the movement's longstanding political program. I also argue that the movement has moderated its goals in response to public pressure, but that this moderation is bounded by the movement's scriptural commitments, particularly in the realm of gender relations. I then explore the Brotherhood's recent electoral victories and ask how the Brothers can be expected to fare as elections become increasingly routinized. I conclude with an agenda for further research into the Brotherhood.

The Brotherhood as Organization

As noted earlier, the Muslim Brotherhood has become synonymous with organizational effectiveness, internal discipline, and group cohesion. Indeed, journalistic and nonspecialist observers of the movement veer toward fetishizing these aspects of the Brotherhood, portraying the movement as "unbreakable," an almost unitary actor whose members are homogenized and tamed to surrender their individual preferences and behave with one mind and one purpose. This section demystifies the Muslim Brotherhood's administrative and membership structure. It first outlines the manner in which members are recruited and promoted, and then describes the movement's internal governance procedures.

Membership recruitment and promotion

The Brotherhood's storied organizational effectiveness stems in large part from a member recruitment process designed to select only the most highly skilled, committed cadres. The process is laid out by the internal regulations of the society:

> "A candidate for membership in the Society must spend at least six months under examination, and if it is demonstrated that he carries out the duties of membership and shows that he knows the purposes and means of our call, and swears to support it and respect its rules and work to achieve its aims, and the responsible parties agree to accept him as a member in the Society, then he will become a regular brother for a period of three years.
>
> "If it is demonstrated throughout the previous three years that the brother has carried out the duties of membership, then the responsible body may consider him an active brother and he gives the following oath:
>
> "'I swear to Allah the great, my commitment to the rulings of Islam, and to jihad for His sake, and to fulfilling the duties and conditions of membership in the Society of Muslim Brothers, and to obeying without question its leaders to the best of my abilities in matters pleasant and distasteful so long as they are not sinful, and I declare my allegiance with God as my guarantor.'"[6]

Once an individual has been inducted into the movement, he is integrated into its system of cells or "families" (*nizām al-usar*). The system of families was the brainchild of the Brotherhood's founder, Ḥasan al-Bannā, who instituted it in 1943 after experimenting with other organizational arrangements (Lia 1998). Each cell consists of five or six individuals—one of whom (typically the most senior) is designated as the cell's leader. The members of a cell typically live in the same vicinity, and the leader is in charge of presiding over weekly study circles, assessing and reporting on the performance of the cell's members, and directing its activities. During elections, cells (or groups of cells called *shuʿab*, or branches), undertake the work of electioneering, leafleting their neighborhoods, or arranging candidate events. Studies of clandestine cell systems like the Brotherhood's suggest that they are useful adaptations to repression—their decentralized nature makes it difficult for opponents of the movement to size it up and penetrate it (Sloan 1987, 9). But Richard Mitchell, the great chronicler of the Brotherhood's early history, finds the chief virtue of *nizām al-usar* is as a method of control:

> "The new system, the structure within which it operated, and the ideas it transmitted to its members were in fact the real basis of the power of the Society of Muslim Brothers; permitting, as it did, authority to express itself through a well-recognized, clearly defined, and tightly knit chain of command, the system became the fundamental instrument through which the leadership expressed its will." (Mitchell 1993, 198)

However, Mitchell's view of the cell system as a means of allowing the movement's leaders to command their subordinates neglects the more subtle ways in which the structure ensures compliance. Each cell is not simply a team of political activists with a finite set of tasks. Al-Bannā did not call his cells "families" by accident—it was his intention to bind men emotionally as well as organizationally. He writes, "Islam is keen to create families out of its people, to direct them to the high ideals and to strengthen their bonds and raise their brotherhood from the level of talk and abstractions to the level of deeds and actions. So take care, my brother, to be a righteous brick in this structure (Islam)." Al-Bannā (323–324) exhorts the members of each cell to do three main things:

1. Get to know each other: ... Get to know and love each other in the spirit of God, and feel the true meaning of complete Brotherhood in what is between you, and strive to ensure that nothing clouds the purity of your relationship....
2. Understand each other: ... Remain true to the program of truth, and do what God has commanded you to do, and avoid that which He has commanded you to avoid. And hold each other to a precise account on [matters of] obedience and sin. Each one of you should advise his brother whenever he sees in him any fault. And the brother should accept the advice of his brother with happiness, and should thank him for it....
3. Be responsible for each other: ... Each of you must shoulder the burden of the other, and this is the essence of faith and the kernel of brotherhood. So you should pledge yourselves to ask after and support each other, and to take the initiative to help [each other] by any available means. And see the words of God's messenger, peace be upon him: "For one among you to walk with his brother in need is better than to spend an entire month in this mosque of mine." "He who brings happiness into the home of one of the Muslims will not see from God any reward except heaven." And may God bind your hearts with His spirit, for He is the most wonderful of masters and the most wonderful of supporters. (Al-Bannā n.d., 323–324)

Al-Bannā goes on to instruct Brothers to "take care to attend all meetings, regardless of the excuse," and to "endeavor to pay dues to the family treasury." He says that the cells should use their weekly meetings to discuss personal problems faced by each Brother, to study Islamic texts (although he says "there is no place in the family for argument or challenging or raising of voices"), and to read useful books. "In order to increase the ties between the Brothers," al-Bannā offers a list of activities that the members of each family should engage in, including trips to visit "antiquities and factories," sports outings, rowing, hiking in "the mountains, deserts, or fields," bicycle tours, weekly or biweekly fasts, and praying the dawn prayer together at least once a week. Moreover, al-Bannā says, "Brothers must take care to spend the night together once a week or every two weeks" (Al-Bannā n.d., 325).

The family system generates tight bonds between members of each cell, enmeshing members in each other's lives, and in the life of the Brotherhood. As such, it is what Wellhofer (1985) called an "encapsulating organization" that immerses the member in the life of the party and insulates him or her from external pressures and competing political appeals.[7] As Wickham (2003, 16) puts it, the "integration of new recruits into the close-knit nuclei of movement networks reinforced their new Islamic commitments and weakened the hold of competing loyalties." It also enables and encourages Brothers to monitor each other's behavior. Thus, by embedding each Brother in a small group of close peers, the movement deters free riding and makes it easier to detect and punish shirking. This, in combination with the Brotherhood's selective recruitment practices, endows the movement at election times with an organizational advantage vis-à-vis parties that do not invest similar resources in member selection and group cohesion.

However, as noted earlier, we would do well not to overstate the Muslim Brotherhood's organizational strength and internal cohesion. In the end, the Brotherhood is a collective made up of human beings, and like any such collective, is not immune to fracturing. In fact, the movement has at various points in its history undergone schisms, beginning with a disagreement over al-Bannā's leadership in 1939 that saw the defection of a sizeable contingent of Brothers known as Muhammad's Youth (Lia 1997, 255). In 1996, another group of Brothers split off to form the Wasat Party (Stacher 2002). Further splits occurred in 2010, when elections to the Brotherhood's Guidance Bureau led to procedural disputes and at least one high-profile resignation. Finally, in the aftermath of the 2011 revolt against Mubarak, five members of the Muslim Brotherhood youth wing were expelled for forming their own political party, as was former Guidance Bureau member Abd al-Mun`im Abu al-Futuh, who had declared his intention to run for president in contravention of the Brotherhood's initial (and later retracted) decision not to field a candidate in the election.

These later schisms should not be surprising. During authoritarianism, the regime's tight management of the political arena meant that there were few alternative outlets for the energies of Muslim Brotherhood activists. This lack of "exit" options for individual Muslim Brotherhood activists likely worked to keep many of them in the fold. As Egypt becomes freer, individual Muslim Brotherhood activists and members will find that they have a wider array of options for the exercise of political leadership and voice. Moreover, the Muslim Brotherhood's development of a formal political arm, the Freedom and Justice Party, with its own, more transparent, membership, and funding rules, and its fundamentally *electoral* purpose, may accelerate schisms within the movement, leading to a break between those who emphasize the Brotherhood's social mission and those who attend to the reaping of votes and seats.

Governance

The pillars of the Muslim Brotherhood's system of governance are the General Guide (al-*Murshid* al-`am), the 16-member Guidance Bureau (Maktab Al-Irshad), the approximately 120-member Consultative Council (Majlis Al-*Shura*), and 31 Governorate Councils (Majlis *shura* Al-Muhafatha). This structure is also employed by branches of the Muslim Brotherhood outside Egypt, each of which is led by a "general supervisor" (*muraqib* `am). In addition, the Brotherhood has an international legislative body of at least thirty members called the General Consultative Council (Majlis Al-*Shura* Al-`Am), although its role in the governance of the Egyptian Brotherhood's affairs is minimal.

The General Guide is the Muslim Brotherhood's chief executive. According to the Brotherhood's constitution (al-Nizam al-`am), the guide, or *murshid*, is responsible for:

- "Supervising and directing all of the Society's administrative departments, monitoring those responsible for implementation, and holding them accountable for shortcomings in accordance with the Society's rules.
- "Representing the Society in all matters and speaking in its name.
- "Tasking whom it seems appropriate from among the Brothers to undertake assignments whose scope is determined by him.
- "Convening meetings of regional general supervisors when necessary."[8]

The guide must be at least forty years old, must have been an "active member" for at least fifteen years, and must "possess the requisite qualities of education (specifically knowledge of Islamic jurisprudence), practical experience, and character that qualify him to lead the Society."[9] Candidates for the position are selected by the sixteen-member Guidance Bureau after consultation with general supervisors of the Brotherhood's foreign branches, and then put to a vote of the *shura* council.

The Guidance Bureau is the Muslim Brotherhood's executive committee, responsible for running the Brotherhood's sixteen administrative departments (which include departments of political affairs, charitable activities, preaching, etc.). The members of the committee are elected by the *shura* council (from among its own members) through a secret ballot, and must represent all of Egypt's geographic regions. In addition to the sixteen elected members, the Guidance Bureau may by vote of majority appoint three additional members.[10]

The *shura* council is "the legislative authority of the Brotherhood in Egypt and is responsible for discussing and approving the general policies to be followed."[11] Each governorate is allocated a certain number of seats on the council (for example, greater Cairo gets twelve members, al-Daqahliya in the Nile Delta sends ten members, al-Sharqiya—home of Egypt's current president—gets ten members, and so on). These members are chosen by the governorate councils, from among their own membership (for example, the governorate council for al-Sharqiya, elects ten of its own members to serve as representatives on the national *shura* council). To serve as a member of either the governorate or national *shura* councils, a member must be an "active" member for at least five years, and "must have the educational and behavioral characteristics that qualify him for membership in the council."[12] In addition to the *shura* council's elected members, who number between seventy-five and ninety depending on decision of the Guidance Bureau, the bureau may also appoint twenty-five unelected members. Moreover, former members of the Guidance Bureau are considered members of the *shura* council, as long as they remain in good standing and were members of the bureau for at least two years.

The size of each governorate council is determined by the Guidance Bureau and all members are chosen by election (although the Guidance Bureau may at its discretion appoint five additional members to each governorate council). The right to vote for representatives on the governorate councils, however, extends only to the Brotherhood's "active" members in the governorate. Recall that "active" members are those who have achieved a particular level of standing within the organization, having been members in good standing for at least three years.

The Brotherhood's internal organizational characteristics are important because they bear on the two questions that animate this essay: the movement's prospects for moderation, and its likely electoral fortunes in a democratic Egypt.

The Question of Moderation

As Schwedler (2011) has pointed out, "moderation" is a multifaceted term that encompasses a variety of unrelated concepts. Scholars of Islamist moderation are generally inquiring after two things: first, the extent of change in the movement's substantive ends or goals. That is, they want to discover whether the Brotherhood might abandon (or has abandoned) its strict adherence to Islamic orthodoxy in favor of a more flexible, capacious, and liberal outlook.

The second object of inquiry is the means the movement deploys in order to achieve the ends it has chosen for itself. That is, scholars ask if the Brotherhood is committed to peaceful competition through the ballot box, or if it endorses violence.

Before proceeding, it is worth reflecting on the problems inherent in trying to divine the ideological and political commitments of organizations. When we write that "the Brotherhood believes" or "the Brotherhood is committed to," or "the Brotherhood wants," we are necessarily imposing a unity on that movement that is empirically problematic, given that dissenting voices are often heard from within it. Though the present essay employs such constructions, it is important to note at the outset that, when we ascribe certain positions to "the Brotherhood," we are actually talking about the positions of the movement's leadership at particular moments in time. Thus, humility about what that movement "believes" or "wants" is in order.

Moderation of means?

To take the latter of these questions first, suspicions about the Muslim Brotherhood's propensity toward violence (and by extension its commitment to abide by democratic processes) emerge from three sources. The first is a longstanding view of Islam (and Islamic political actors) as uniquely prone to violence (Ayoob 2004). This view, though in disfavor among academicians, retains currency in popular discussions of Islam generally and the Muslim Brotherhood in particular. A thorough refutation of it is beyond the scope of this essay, but has been undertaken by others (Armstrong 2002; Esposito 2002; Lawrence 2001). A second is the existence of alleged links between the Muslim Brotherhood and terrorist organizations such as al-Qa`ida, Islamic jihad, and the Egyptian Islamic Group. However, these connections are tenuous at best, often involving the simple fact that they have among their ranks former Muslim Brotherhood members who left the movement because it was insufficiently committed to jihad in its militaristic form. Ayman al-Zawahri, the Egyptian al-Qa`ida leader who got his start in the Brotherhood, is often cited as a "material link" between the Ikhwan and al-Qa`ida, but it is worth noting that in 1999 he penned an anti-Ikhwan volume (titled *Bitter Harvest: Sixty Years of the Muslim Brotherhood*) that condemned the organization for encouraging Muslims to stand "in voter queues before ballot boxes instead of lining them up to fight in the cause of Allah."[13]

The third source of concern over the Brotherhood's propensity for violence emerges from the fact that the movement has, at points in its history, embraced and even engaged in acts of violence. For example, in the 1940s, the Egyptian Muslim Brotherhood established a (now defunct) "special apparatus," which has been blamed for the assassination of Prime Minister Mahmud Fahmi al-Nuqrashi in 1948. However, the scholar Hasanayn Tawfiq Ibrahim has argued that the Egyptian Brotherhood's "special apparatus" was part of a political landscape in which "many political trends...had their own armed militias."[14] According to the historian Yunan Labib Rizk, both the Wafd and Young Egypt parties, inspired by the fascist shirt organizations in Germany and Italy, established paramilitary organizations—called, respectively, the Blue Shirts and the Green Shirts.[15] And though the movement has never fully acknowledged nor atoned for its role in the Nuqrashi assassination, it is worth noting that the Brothers were not alone in their use of political assassination during that particularly turbulent period of Egypt's colonial history. Anwar Sadat—who in 1970 became Egypt's president—in 1945 and 1946 participated in assassination attempts against then-Prime Minister Mustafa al-Nahhas (which failed) and pro-British Finance Minister Amin Uthman (which succeeded).[16] Thus, the Muslim Brotherhood was not unique in deploying violence in 1940s Egypt.

The Muslim Brotherhood's next flirtation with violence occurred during the regime of Gamal ʿAbd al-Nāṣir. Though the Brothers had initially supported the Free Officers coup of 1952, the movement quickly fell out of official favor, and in 1954 was accused of attempting to assassinate Nāṣir at a public rally in Alexandria. The years that followed saw the Brotherhood brutally repressed, its leaders imprisoned, executed, and exiled. One of those leaders was Sayyid Qutb, who during his prison years penned a volume, Maʿalim fi al-Tariq (usually translated as Milestones), that encouraged Muslims to wage jihad against regimes that, on account of their refusal to implement God's law, were Muslim in name only. According to Zollner (2007), Qutb became the leader of an armed, activist vanguard within the Brothers (later called the Organization of 1965), which was rounded up by Nāṣir in 1965 on charges of plotting revolution. Qutb was executed the following year, and in the season of bitter subjugation that followed, the Brotherhood's General Guide, Hasan al-Hudaybi (who had succeeded the founder, al-Bannā, upon the latter's assassination in 1949) penned a volume, Preachers Not Judges, intended to refute Qutb's call to militancy (Zollner 2007; Ashour 2009). Upon the Brothers' release from Nāṣir's prisons, the idea of advancing its political project through violence had been largely abandoned.

It is important at this point to note that the history of the Muslim Brotherhood's relationship to political violence should not be read as one of an evolution away from some violent beginning. The political assassinations of the 1940s and the Qutbian militancy of the 1960s should, instead, be understood as departures from the Brotherhood's largely nonviolent original project of social and political reform. Though narratives of the "metamorphosis" of the Muslim Brotherhood into a peaceful political movement have become commonplace, they neglect the movement's early commitment to political participation at the ballot box. In fact, it was Ḥasan al-Bannā who first decided that the Brotherhood should run for elections to Egypt's Assembly of Deputies. According to Lia (1998), this decision was made sometime in the late 1930s, although it was not until 1945 that the Brotherhood actually fielded candidates (al-Banna and the Brotherhood had come close to running in the 1942 elections, but were compelled to withdraw by the government of the time in exchange for minor policy concessions). The Brothers' reasons for entry into those early contests illustrate the extent to which the use of democratic means has long been accepted by the movement. As al-Bannā himself put it, running in elections was the natural next step in the Brotherhood's program after the movement's successful outreach in the civic arena:

> "For our message, to succeed and conquer, [requires] clear and constant communication that strikes the people's ears and reaches their hearts and souls. This, the Muslim Brotherhood believes, it has achieved in the popular realm to a degree of palpable and recognized success. What is left for them now is to take this noble message to the official realm, and the nearest path to it (the pulpit of the parliament). For it was incumbent on the Brotherhood to press with their sermons and message to this pulpit in order to raise from atop it the word of their message, and reach the ears of the representatives of the people in this limited official sphere, after it had spread and reached the people themselves in the popular public arena. And for this reason the guidance office has decided that the Muslim Brotherhood will participate in elections for the Assembly of Deputies."[17]

Thus, though al-Bannā was critical of Egyptian political parties and of the divisiveness of partisanship, this criticism did not extent to constitutional government. In a statement to Brotherhood members in 1939, he declared:

> "The truth is, Brothers, that when the inquirer looks at the principles of constitutional government, which can be summarized as the preservation of all forms of personal freedom, consultation, the derivation of all authority from the people, the responsibility of leaders in front of the masses and holding them accountable for all that they do, and the setting of limits to all authority—all of these principles appear to the inquirer as applying to the teachings of Islam and its systems and rules regarding forms of government. Therefore, the Muslim Brothers consider the constitutional system of government to the closest of the world's systems of government to Islam, and they do not call for any other system."[18]

It could be argued, then, that when today's Muslim Brothers speak of their commitment to parliamentary politics, they are not so much partaking of a newly moderate discourse as reaching into the Brotherhood's early history. In an October 2005 attempt to put to rest doubt about the Brotherhood's commitment to nonviolent political participation, `Akif declared, "We believe in and call for the peaceful alternation of power via ballot boxes within the framework of a constitutional parliamentarian republic."[19] A stronger statement is offered by Yusif al-Qaradwi (reported to have twice declined the Egyptian Muslim Brotherhood's top post), who writes:[20]

> "It is strange that some people judge democracy to be an abomination and a form of disbelief when they do not know what it is.... Democracy, which is called for by all of the world's people, on whose behalf have worked multitudes in both East and West, which the people reach after bitter struggles with tyrants in which blood was spilled and thousands—nay, millions—of lives were sacrificed as in Eastern Europe and elsewhere, and which many Islamists see as an acceptable means of curbing the excesses of dictatorship and trimming the claws of political domination which have burdened our Muslim peoples.... [Is this] an abomination or a form of disbelief, as is repeated by the superficial and the rash?"[21]

Any account of the Brotherhood's abandonment of violence or its commitment to peaceful means will likely be met with one of two rejoinders, both questioning its factual accuracy. The first, often repeated by nonspecialists, is that the Brotherhood is responsible for the assassination of Egyptian President Anwar Sadat in 1981 (see, for example, Krause 2001; Welner 2007).[22] However, there exists little evidence for this assertion. The men convicted of Sadat's assassination were all members of a violent organization known as the Islamic Group. Juergensmeyer (1995) refers to the Islamic jihad as "a radical fringe group of the Muslim Brotherhood," leaving readers with the impression that it was a faction of the Brotherhood, and not a separate organization, that carried out that deed, but the basis of that assertion is unclear. The founder of Islamic jihad, Muhammad `Abd al-Salam Faraj, is described as "a former Muslim Brotherhood member," but one "who was disillusioned by its passivity" (Zeidan 1999), suggesting that he had departed the movement in order to pursue violence.

The second rejoinder is that the Muslim Brotherhood's appetite for violence is on full display in the statements of its founder, and in its endorsement of acts of terror by Palestinians against Israeli civilians. This is a more serious claim. Hasan al-Bannā, in his epistle on jihad, argued that "the people who perfect the production of death, and know how to die the noble death, is given by God a precious life on earth and eternal bliss in the hereafter." Anticipating an argument that would be made by Sayyid Quṭb decades later, al-Bannā argued against those who declared that military jihad was somehow a "lesser" jihad, subordinate to a "greater" jihad of the perfection of personal virtue. He writes:

> "It is commonly said among many Muslims that fighting the enemy is the lesser jihad and that there is a greater jihad that is the jihad of the self. And many of them prove this with the reported saying of the prophet: 'We have returned from the lesser jihad to the greater jihad.' They said, 'What is the greater jihad?' He said: 'The jihad of the heart or the jihad of the self.' And many of them try with this to deter people from the importance of fighting and preparing for it and the intention of jihad doing what is necessary for it."

According to al-Bannā, however, there is little textual support for the idea that self-improvement is a greater jihad than fighting Islam's enemies. He says that the tradition of the prophet on which it is based is allegedly apocryphal. Instead, al-Bannā argues, jihad is to be undertaken for two reasons—first, to spread the faith, and second, to defend the lands of the faithful from invaders. In the first instance, jihad is a *fard kifāya*—an obligation that individual Muslims are relieved of if enough of their number undertake it. In the second instance, defense against encroachers, jihad is a *fard ʿayn*—incumbent on all Muslims. It is to this latter form of jihad that he devotes the greatest attention. He writes:

> "Muslims today as you know are subjugated by others and ruled by nonbelievers. Their lands have been trampled and their sanctities violated. Their enemies govern their affairs, and their faith is disrupted in their own homes, in addition to their neglect of spreading their faith. And so it is incumbent on all Muslims without exception to prepare, and to settle upon the intention of jihad and prepare for it until the opportunity arises that Allah might accomplish that which must be done."[23]

This emphasis on jihad to defend against domination clearly explains the Brotherhood's uncompromising support of the use of violence by Palestinian groups such as the Islamic Resistance Movement (Hamas). In fact, Brotherhood leaders often refer to Hamas as their movement's "military wing," and the Brotherhood's website even lists the website of Hamas' ʿIzz al-Din Qassam Brigades in its compendium of "Brotherhood websites."[24] It is thus an incontrovertible fact that the Muslim Brotherhood believes in the legitimacy of Palestinian violence against the Jewish state, even as the movement declares its own readiness to abide by the Egyptian-Israeli peace treaty. It is worth noting, however, that this support comes despite the fact that Hamas' attacks against civilians contravene the rules of jihad as articulated by al-Bannā (who argued that Islam forbade "killing women, children, and the aged, executing the wounded, assaulting monks, hermits, and the peaceful who do not fight.") The Brotherhood's refusal to condemn Hamas on these grounds is likely a function of the fact that to do so would be politically unpopular—across the Egyptian political spectrum, there is widespread support for what Egyptians see as legitimate Palestinian resistance against perceived Israeli abuses.

If the Muslim Brotherhood's endorsement of Hamas must be seen in the context of broader Arab and Egyptian opinion, al-Bannā's view of jihad as a tool for propagating Islam seems to lend credence to those who view the movement as inherently violent. Though al-Bannā declares that the rules of jihad in Islam prohibit the instigation of hostilities (p. 299), it is difficult to square this with a notion of jihad that endorses warfare to propagate the faith. In any case, in conversations with Muslim Brotherhood leaders, I was repeatedly told that the movement believes modern communication technology, which allows the easy and unprecedented transfer of ideas across peoples, has obviated the need for jihad as an instrument of *da'wa*, but I have not yet been able to collect textual evidence for this shift. Abed Kotob (1995), however, in support of this point, quotes former Brotherhood deputy guide Ahmed al-Malt, who declared, "We state the word of truth.... We summon with every available means, distant from evil, distant from offensive actions. Wisdom and good advice are our religion." Of course, these are just words, and in the absence of the outright repudiation of the founder's belief in the legitimacy of jihad to spread Islam, questions about the Muslim Brotherhood's commitment to nonviolence will continue, even if the movement continues to act in ways that are consistent with its declared belief in using only peaceful means to spread its message.

Moderation of ends?

If the Ikhwan are (domestically at least) moderate in their means, what of their ends? Have the Muslim Brothers become more tolerant and liberal over time? During the waning years of the Mubarak period, any objective review of the available evidence would force one to conclude that the Brotherhood has deprioritized the religious and moral elements of its agenda, preferring instead to focus on the reform of political institutions. One way to observe the Brotherhood's deprioritization of religion is through its activities in parliament during that time. During the authoritarian era, Muslim Brothers served in Egypt's parliament in 1976, 1979, 1984, 1987, 1995, 2000, and 2005. Springborg (2007, 8) tells us that Islamists were primarily "concern[ed] with moral issues in society," and that as a result, "in the 2000–2005 Egyptian parliament, the seventeen MB deputies devoted 80 percent of their interpellations, or questions to ministers, to matters concerning those issues, leaving a scant 20 percent for matters of economics, foreign and defense policies, and other vital governance issues." However, a closer examination of the evidence suggests otherwise. Figure 31.2 represents all interpellations issued by Brotherhood deputies from 1984 to 2005 (1990–2000 are excluded because there were no Brothers in parliament from 1990–1995 and only one from 1995–2000). A review of the data suggests that religious issues have in fact never taken up the majority of the Brotherhood's parliamentary agenda, and appear to have declined in importance during the Mubarak era. Thus, while two of the Brotherhood's five interpellations in 1984 and three of its six in 1987, dealt with religious matters, in the 2000 and 2005 parliaments religious issues were dwarfed by political ones, particularly corruption and mismanagement of public resources.[25]

We saw this reprioritization in the Brotherhood's own assessment of what it achieved in parliament. Below is a list, produced by the Brotherhood's parliamentary bloc, of the issues raised by the group's members in the legislature in 2006:

"1. The offensive drawings of the noble Prophet Muhammad, peace be upon him
"2. The ferry tragedy
"3. Avian influenza
"4. Support for judges
"5. Rejecting the emergency law

```
                    ┌─────────────────────────────────┐
                    │        Area (Mantiqa)           │
                    ├─────────────────────────────────┤
                    │      Governorate (Muhâfaza)     │
                    └─────────────────────────────────┘
```

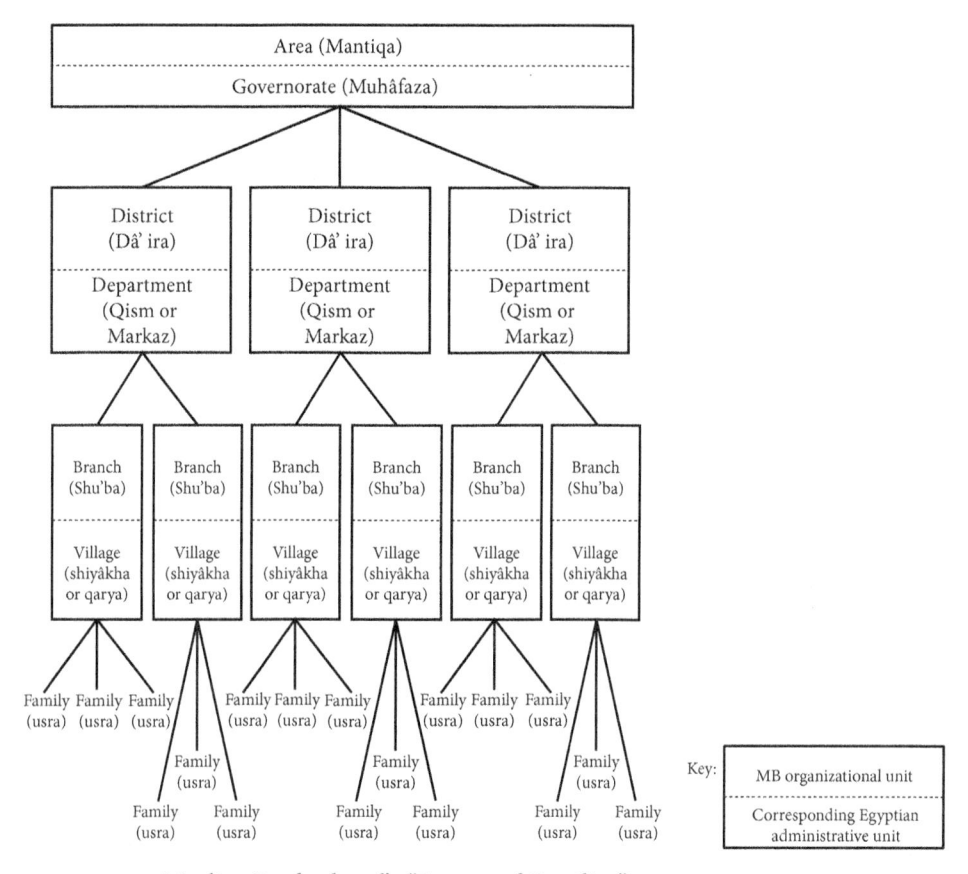

[Organizational hierarchy chart showing levels from Area/Governorate down through District/Department, Branch, Village, to Family units]

FIGURE 31.1: Muslim Brotherhood's "System of Families."

Key:
- MB organizational unit
- Corresponding Egyptian administrative unit

"6. Presidential powers
"7. Delaying of local elections
"8. Contaminated milk
"9. Exposing foreign aid fraud
"10. Withdrawal of confidence from the Minister of Justice for tampering with judicial authority
"11. Fighting neglect of industrial strongholds
" 12. Improving the level of health care and reforming health insurance
"13. Passage of the ship 'Clemenceau' [through the Suez canal] and the protection of Egypt's environment
"14. Raising the efficiency of education services and seriousness in confronting illiteracy
"15. Importation of carcinogenic pesticides
"16. Deals to purchase contaminated foodstuffs
"17. Suffering in the rail system"[26]

Though the list is topped by the Brothers' protest (along with members of the ruling party) over a Danish newspaper's satirical cartoons of the Prophet Muhammad in 2005, the bulk of the Brotherhood's time in parliament during that period appears to have been

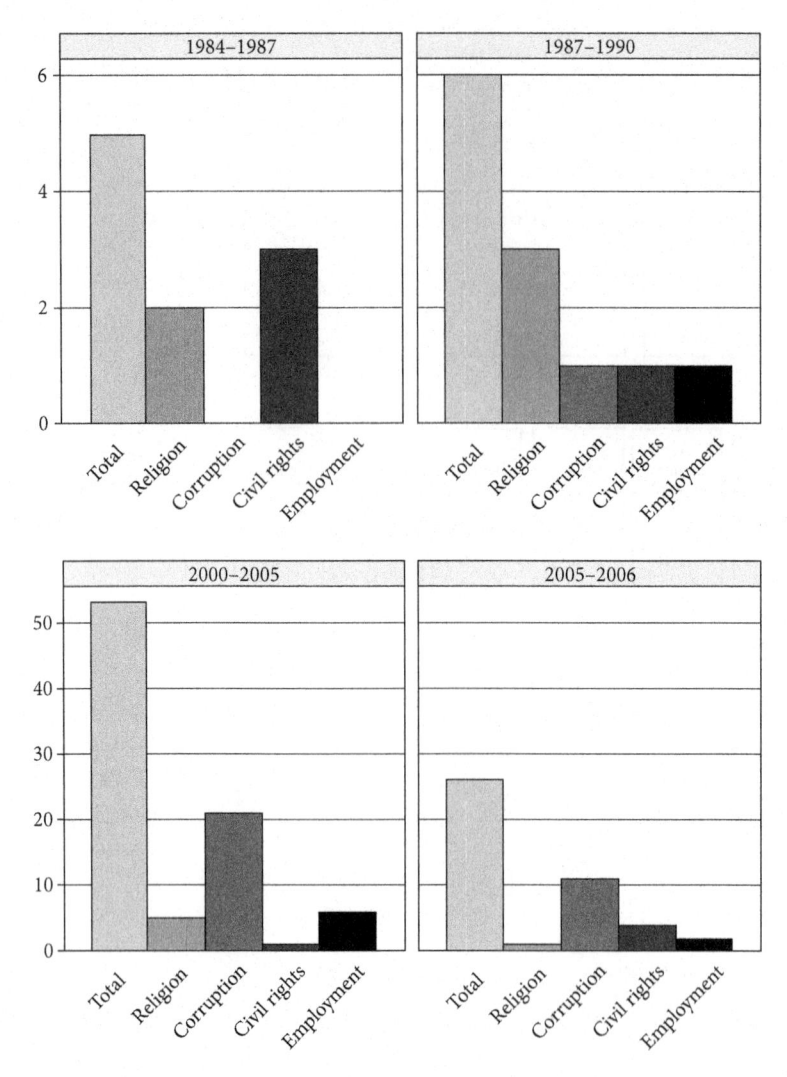

FIGURE 31.2: Interpellations by Muslim Brotherhood Deputies, by Subject Matter 1984–2006.

spent pursuing charges of government incompetence and corruption and demands for more political freedom. This should not be surprising—the dominant cleavage during the Mubarak era was not between the religious and the secular, but between the authoritarian regime and those opposed to it. During that period, the Brotherhood subordinated its religiously-conservative agenda in order to build alliances with other opposition forces who shared its goal of unseating Mubarak, but not its goal of erecting a pious polity. Some interpreted the Brother's move away from *shari`ah* during this period as more than just a tactical move. Wickham (2006) has argued that the Brothers have "back peddl[ed]...from prior calls for the strict enforcement of *Sharī`a* rule."

Similarly, Brown (2011) has argued that the Brotherhood's discourse on *shari'ah* shifted from an emphasis on letter of the *shari'ah* to an emphasis on the *maqasid* (or goals) of the *shari'ah*—an intellectual turn that reveals a willingness to experiment with nontraditional (or even Western) institutional forms and policies as long as they achieve the general aims of the *shari'ah*, which in their view are universal aims of order, public morality, and social justice.[27]

A prominent thesis posed by those who study Islamist movements is that the advent of genuine democratic competition would push groups like the Muslim Brotherhood further toward "moderation" or liberalization. However, there are two important reasons to be skeptical of such claims.. First, the Brotherhood in the post-Mubarak period faces competition not just from secularists, but also from ultra-Orthodox Salafist Islamists, who will likely force the Brotherhood to hew to a conservative line lest it lose the votes of the pious. Second, there remains a large domain of lawmaking—particularly in the realm of gender relations—that is largely settled within Sunni Muslim jurisprudence, and which religious conservatives such as the Brotherhood would be unlikely to seek to ignore or change

Competition with Salafists has in fact led the Brotherhood to backtrack on some of the limited liberalizations of its positions with respect to the *shari'ah*. For example, in 2007, the Brotherhood released a draft party platform intended to demystify the movement to potential allies among the opposition and demonstrate the Brotherhood's conformity with mainstream Egyptian opinion. The move was unsuccessful in this regard, as Brotherhood opponents seized on a section of the platform that included provisions for a council of religious scholars that would vet all laws to ensure they conformed to the *shari'ah*. Though this proposal was roundly criticized by the Brotherhood's liberal counterparts in the anti-Mubarak opposition as a move toward theocracy, it is nonetheless clear on further review that the Brothers had in mind something far short of the rule of the clerics:

> "And it is incumbent upon the legislative power to *seek the opinion* of a body of leading scholars of religion in the nation that will also be elected freely and directly from among the scholars of religion and completely and genuinely independent of the executive power in all of its technical, financial, and administrative matters.... [The body] will be assisted by committees and consultants in all scientific and worldly disciplines of assured neutrality and trustworthiness. And this applies to the President of the Republic whenever he issues a decision with the force of law during recesses of the legislative power.... *And the legislative power has, in matters where the legal decision is not a definitive one based on unchallenged textual evidence, the final decision by a majority vote against the opinion of the body. And it has the right to overrule the religious body by offering its point of view in what is sees as closer to achieving the public interest.*"[28]

What is clear here is that this religious council was envisioned as less a veto player in Egypt's institutional framework than as an advisory body that could be overruled by parliamentary majority. However, in response to public pressure, the Brotherhood backed away from that proposal, and the 2011 parliamentary elections platform of the Brotherhood's Freedom and Justice Party made no mention of it. Instead, the FJP platform declared that the Islamic state it envisions is "not a religious state governed by a class of clerics," but rather one ruled by "citizens elected according to the popular will." The new platform further stipulated that it is the courts, and not religious scholars, who are entrusted with vetting laws in a constitutional democracy:

> "*Shariah* naturally... organizes all different aspects of life for Muslims and their non-Muslim compatriots, either in the form of definitive texts—and these are few—or in the form of general guidelines and principles, the details of which are then left to [the people] for interpretation and legislation according to what is appropriate for every age and the different environments and to what achieves right and justice and the public interest. And this is the role of the legislative assemblies, with the Supreme Constitutional Court as the check on this legislation...."[29]

If this is where the Brotherhood's thinking on this issue ended, then it would constitute powerful evidence that democratic participation yields substantive moderation and liberalization. However, after the 2011 parliamentary elections brought a sizeable contingent of Salafists to the country's legislature (and, by extension, its constitutional assembly), the Brotherhood has found itself endorsing positions even more religiously conservative than the ones it laid out in 2007. For example, article 4 of the new constitution accords to al-Azhar university the advisory role envisioned for religious scholars in the 2007 document, while article 219 defines the principles of *shari'ah* in very specific terms of Islamic jurisprudence, thus marking a move away from the spirit of *shar'iah* to its actual letter.

The Brotherhood has been somewhat more consistently conservative in its view of the role of women, and this, I argue, is largely a function of the fact that gender relations are the subject of a large and largely settled body of Islamic jurisprudence, not to mention public opinion. In 1994, the Brothers issued a document titled, "The Right of Women to Vote and to Membership in Parliamentary Assemblies and to Assume Public Posts," which laid out the Brotherhood's commitment to women's political participation.[30] What is remarkable about that document—hailed at the time as a sea change in the Brothers' thought (see El-Ghobashy 2005)—is how cramped its view of women's political role was. Though the document upheld women's parliamentary participation, it did so largely on pragmatic, even contingent grounds: "Preventing the Muslim woman from participating in elections would weaken the Islamist candidates' chances of winning."[31] And while the right of women to run for and hold legislative offices is affirmed, nonetheless we are told: "We do not call for adorning [herself] or for mixing [of the sexes] and we do not call for tolerating it. The woman is commanded to adhere to her *sharī'ah* mandated dress whether she goes out to participate in elections, or to attend meetings of the assembly in which she is a member, or otherwise" (pp. 23–27) The notion of women in positions of responsibility mingling with men was troubling enough to the Brothers that they fretted about these hypothetical elected females traveling abroad without male relatives to guard their chastity, but resolved the issue by noting that the role of the parliamentarian does not require travel.[32]

Moreover, the 1994 document limited precisely what offices women could hold. For example, the Brothers withheld judgment on the right of women to hold judicial appointments, noting that the majority of religious scholars disapprove.[33] And then there was the issue of the presidency: "The public trust upon which it is agreed that women are forbidden to hold it is the grand imamate, which is analogous to the presidency of the state in our current circumstances." In the Brotherhood's 2007 party platform, they took up the issue of women and the presidency again, this time concluding: "From our point of view we see that the obligations imposed on the president of the state, who is responsible for command of the army, are among obligations that women should not be forced to undertake, because they are at odds with her nature and with her social and humanitarian roles."[34] The current party platform does not address this issue head on, but contains language encouraging "the spread of the culture of equality between the sexes, *while respecting the complementarity of [gender] roles*"—coded language for justifying differences in those roles.³⁵

Further evidence of the Brotherhood's deep conservatism on issues of gender is the movement's use of its parliamentary pulpit to fight (albeit unsuccessfully) any attempts to liberalize laws governing the personal or sexual realm, which in their view is already governed by clear religious guidance. For example, the Brothers opposed passage of the June 2008 children's rights bill, which aimed to bring Egyptian laws in line with the United Nations Convention on the Rights of the Child.³⁶ The Brothers labeled the bill a contravention of the *sharīʿah* and an "importation" that "brings punishment under the guise of mercy."³⁷ At issue were provisions criminalizing female genital cutting, raising the age of marriage to eighteen, and granting increased legal recognition to children born out of wedlock.

Though female genital mutilation has been declining in legitimacy and popularity in recent years (El-Zanaty and Way 2006), the Muslim Brotherhood's parliamentarians have defended it in parliamentary debates and in their writings. Farīd Ismāʿīl, a Brotherhood deputy from Fāqūs in al-Sharqiya, argued that the matter of circumcision should be left to the parents, in consultation with "pious, honest doctors."³⁸ Sayyid ʿAskar, a Brotherhood deputy from Tantā in al-Gharbiya and a shaykh of al-Azhar, took a more extreme view, arguing that the practice is Islamically sanctioned and brings real benefits for girls, and that "behind the attempts to criminalize [female circumcision] are Western organizations that aim to change our society's Islamic values and disfiguring its identity."³⁹ In July 2008, Kamāl Nūr al-Dīn, a Brotherhood member from al-Fayyūm, even spoke up on the floor of parliament in defense of two women doctors who were under prosecution for performing female circumcisions.⁴⁰

The Brothers also opposed provisions raising the age of marriage and making it easier to register children born outside of marriage (Egyptian law had stipulated that birth certificates must indicate the father's name). Several Muslim Brotherhood parliamentarians argued that raising the age of marriage would lead to increases in sex out of wedlock—this despite the fact that the percentage of women ages fifteen to nineteen who are married has declined, from 22 percent in 1976 to only 10 percent in 2003 (Rashad 2005, 1). Removing the requirement of listing a father on birth certificates was thought to have a similarly indecent effect. According to ʿAskar, "When the adulterous woman comes with a child and says this is my child and he has no father, she is admitting adultery, and yet there is no punishment, and this encourages adultery." Ahmad Diyāb the Brotherhood MP from Qalyūb, concurred and asked, "Shall I simply leave my daughter to come and go with her boyfriend without punishment?"⁴¹

The Brotherhood continues to make such arguments. In March 2013, the Brotherhood condemned the UN Commission on the Status of Women for its declaration entitled "End Violence Against Women." According to the Brothers, the declaration—which includes provisions raising the age of marriage, guaranteeing reproductive rights, enabling women to achieve greater autonomy within marriage—was contrary to the *sharīʿah*, and "would lead to the compete disintegration of society." The declaration, the Brotherhood declared, "would be the final step in the intellectual and cultural invasion of Muslim countries," and was "meant to undermine the family [...] and drag society to pre-Islamic ignorance."⁴²

The Brotherhood's conservatism on gender issues was also on full display in recent debates over the shape of Egypt's postrevolutionary constitution. The Muslim Brotherhood-led body charged with drafting the new charter had originally inserted language thought to limit women's rights:

"The state is committed to taking all constitutional and executive measures to ensure equality of women with men in all walks of political, cultural, economic and social life, without violation of the rules of Islamic jurisprudence. The state will provide all necessary services for mothers and children for free, and will ensure the protection of women, along with social, economic and medical care and the right to inheritance, and will ensure a balance between the woman's family responsibilities and work in society."[43]

The inclusion of this article generated intense opposition from liberal and non-Islamist quarters of Egyptian popular opinion, who argued that the inclusion of the clause "without violation of the rules of Islamic jurisprudence" rendered the state's commitment to gender equality effectively moot. However, the Islamists' compromise was not to excise the offending clause, but rather to scrap the entire article, meaning that Egypt's current post-revolutionary constitution is actually less hospitable to gender equality than the authoritarian one that preceded it.

No discussion of the Brotherhood's ideological commitments would be complete without a consideration of its stances on the role and status of religious minorities within the Egyptian polity. The Brotherhood has long hewed to the line that Coptic Christians—who make up 10 percent of the Egyptian population—bear the same rights and obligations as Muslim Egyptians. However, on deeper examination, a more complex picture emerges. The Brotherhood's 2007 party platform makes clear the limitations it envisions on the role that Christians can play in a Muslim-majority society:

"The state has fundamental religious functions, for it is responsible for protecting and defending the religion, and the Islamic state must defend the non-Muslim in his creed and worship and house of worship, and must defend Islam and protect its matters and ensure that nothing exists that contradicts the practice of Islam, in worship, proselytizing, pilgrimage to Mecca, etc. And these religious functions are vested in the president of the state or the prime minister according to the current political system. And therefore we see that the president or the prime minister, according to the current political system, bears responsibilities that are at odds with the creed of the non-Muslim, such that they render the non-Muslim exempt from having to undertake this mission, according to the Islamic *sharī'a* which does not require the non-Muslim to undertake a duty that conflicts with his beliefs."[44]

This provision generated a great deal of controversy for the Brothers when it first became public. Brown and Hamzawy (2008) have argued that it represented the views of only a faction of the Brothers, noting that prominent Muslim Brothers such as current Guidance Bureau member 'Isām al-'Aryān, former Guidance Bureau member 'Abd al-Mun'im Abū al-Futūh (who in 2011 was expelled from the movement), and former parliamentarian Gamāl Hishmat all voiced their opposition to the platform in public. But the extent to which these men's dissent represented a broad swath of opinion of the Society is not known.[45] For his part, al-'Aryān argued that the platform was correct in denying Copts the right to assume the presidency, declaring that this is no more problematic than the requirement that the president be at least forty years of age, and noting that "the Malaysian constitution reserves certain rights for Malays and certain rights for everyone else."[46] Nonetheless, this view was not reflected in the 2011 platform. In that document, the Brotherhood affirmed its belief in the right of non-Muslims to "nominate for, and assume all positions" (although the added proviso—"while preserving the society's fundamental values"—may be intended to allow the Brothers some ambiguity on this score).[47] It is worth noting that the Brotherhood's party has selected as its vice-president a Christian intellectual (who has since resigned the post). The inclusion of an article guaranteeing Christians and Jews the right to be governed by their own religious law in personal status matters may be interpreted as a move toward greater religious toleration by the Brothers, but to others it signals an attempt by the Brothers to demarcate Egyptian Muslims from non-Muslims, establishing a separate-but-equal regime that will ultimately undermine the principle of equal citizenship.

Thus, we must be cautious when assessing the level of "moderation" or substantive ideological change undertaken by the Brotherhood. Although Wickham (2006) has reported that Islamists have "soften[ed]...their positions on such sensitive issues as the civil and political rights of women and religious minorities," the record is uneven. And though the current period of openness in Egyptian politics may provide incentives for ideological evolution, it is not clear that this evolution will necessarily be in the liberal direction hypothesized by those arguing that inclusion leads to moderation. Largely conservative public opinion, well-defined scriptural limits, and competition with Salafists may all serve to limit the extent to which the Brotherhood will change its stances on these highly divisive and charged social issues.

However, the extent of ideological evolution will be determined not just by these external factors, but by internal, organizational ones. As we have seen, the Brotherhood is a hierarchical organization that attempts to attract and cultivate a committed and disciplined membership. Though the movement's leaders are elected by the membership and are presumably accountable to them, the fact that only longstanding, "active" members have the right to vote in internal elections may limit the degree to which new entrants can push the movement in new directions. The scholar Khalil al-Anani has noted that, despite their democratic appearance, the Brotherhood's exclusive governance structures serve to limit the extent to which the movement adapts to changing times.[48] However, it may equally be argued that the movement's emphasis on obedience to authority gives its top leadership greater room to maneuver—ideologically and operationally—than organizations whose leaders must hew closely to the opinions of the rank and file.

THE BROTHERHOOD IN ELECTIONS

The scholarly concern over the Muslim Brotherhood's belief in and commitment to democracy is matched only by concern over its likely fortunes under democracy. The Brotherhood's stunning success in post-Mubarak elections in Egypt seems to be the fulfillment of a longstanding prophecy. For more than a quarter century, scholars, journalists, and policymakers had declared that the Brotherhood would take power if allowed to run in free and fair elections. Fawaz Gerges declared in 2005 that "if free and open elections were held today, the Brotherhood would win a comfortable majority."[49] Likewise, an Israeli official testified in 2007 that "if free elections were held in Egypt today, the Muslim Brotherhood would win by a landslide."[50] Another analyst declared that, "the fact of the matter is, if there [were] free and fair elections throughout the Middle East, the Muslim Brotherhood would win."[51] The sociologists Davis and Robinson echoed this assessment, writing that "if truly open elections were held in Egypt today, the Muslim Brotherhood would win in a landslide." The New York Times in January 2006 informed us that Islamic opposition parties in countries like Egypt and Jordan "would probably sweep any wide-open elections."[52] The Hudson Institute's Nina Shea opined that "if an open election were held this year, few doubt that the Muslim Brotherhood would win."[53] Charles Onians (2004) quoted an unnamed Egyptian leftist activist who tells him that, "if there were free elections tomorrow, the Brotherhood would win 60 percent of the seats." Hisham Mubarak, the late Egyptian human rights activist, confided to Miller (1996 , 65) more than fifteen years ago that "if the Brotherhood ever ran in a free election, it would win overwhelmingly." More restrained was the analysis of the Jerusalem Report almost twenty years ago, which ascribed to "many observers" the belief that if the Brotherhood "ran in free elections and was given free access to the media, its supporters would take no more than 10 years to become the parliamentary majority."[54]

There was significant evidence for these predictions. The most powerful was the Muslim Brotherhood's impressive showing in Egypt's 2005 parliamentary elections, in which it won 88 out of the 444 contested seats, more than ten times the number of seats held by all other opposition parties combined. According to Hamzawy and Brown (2005), Brotherhood candidates outperformed those of the ruling National Democratic Party (al-Hizb al-Watanial-Dimuqrati) at a rate of seven to three, despite alleged electoral manipulation by regime partisans. The magnitude of the Brotherhood's victory waxes further when one considers that the group only fielded candidates for a little over a third of the parliament's seats, suggesting that if they had chosen to contest every seat they might have captured a majority of them. The Brothers also constituted the largest opposition bloc in parliament in 2000 (with seventeen seats) and 1987 (with approximately thirty-six seats).[55] And it was not just in Mubarak's parliamentary elections that the Brotherhood proved successful. The movement in the early 1980s and 1990s captured majorities on the boards of "the five most politically active syndicates, representing doctors, engineers, pharmacists, scientists, and lawyers" (Fahmy 1998), which eventually prompted the regime to freeze or otherwise restrict those syndicates.

The Brotherhood's long-running electoral dominance is ascribed to a variety of causes, of which three stand out. The first is simply that Egyptians, as Muslims, are conditioned by their religion to vote for those who promise to rule in accordance with the dictates of Islam. In this telling, the Muslim Brotherhood's desire to apply *shariah* law resonates with Egyptians on a fundamental level. There is some evidence for this position. In 2005, the World Values Survey asked Egyptians to rate, on a scale of 1 to 10, the degree to which having "religious authorities interpret the laws" forms an "essential characteristic of democracy."[56] Two-thirds of Egyptians answered the question with an 8 or above (with 47.9 percent assigning a value of 10), which suggests strongly that Egyptians believe that democracy and religion are not only compatible, but inseparable.[57]

The reverence accorded the faith, and the popular belief in the legitimacy of applying religion to politics, is something that scholars of Egypt have noted for decades. Since the late 1960s, many Egypt watchers have noted a rising religiosity in daily life. One writer has suggested that Egypt is undergoing an Islamic "revival every bit as encompassing as…the religious revival in mid-nineteenth century Christendom."[58] Scholars have found evidence for this Islamic resurgence in the increasing number of mosques,[59] the hours of religious radio and television programming,[60] and the tendency of Muslim women to don headscarves.[61] Some have dated this change to the immediate aftermath of Egypt's defeat at Israel's hands in the June 1967 War (the *naksa,* or setback, as it is called in Egypt today)—a trauma that is thought to have sent Egyptians reeling, searching for a solace to be found only in the faith. Others have attributed it to increasing urbanization: as individuals move from the security of the village to the unfamiliar territory of the city, they increasingly turn to religion to provide psychological comfort and certainty.[62]

The second potential explanation for Islamist dominance is organizational. Several scholars and writers have noted that the Muslim Brotherhood has a long history of disciplined activism, and has been able to deploy its well-honed organizational apparatus to the cause of elections with great success. As we have seen in this essay, the Brotherhood has invested in a system of membership recruitment and promotion that, at least on the margins, enhances member discipline, commitment to movement goals, and obedience to movement leaders. Others note that the Muslim Brotherhood (as well as other Islamist parties) can rely on a vast network of Islamic social institutions—such as mosques and charities—to bring them into contact with average Egyptians in a way that is not possible for secular parties that lack privileged access to these networks. A Muslim Brotherhood candidate, for example, can give a sermon in a mosque on Fridays, burnishing his reputation as a man of God and reaching thousands of voters in the process. This is something secular politicians are presumably unable to do (or at least do convincingly).

But as powerful as these arguments are, they lead us to expect that the Brotherhood should dominate all elections in Egypt, and that has not been the case. Though the Muslim Brotherhood won Egypt's presidency, even a cursory analysis of the detailed results of that election show that support for Islamists is far softer than these arguments would lead us to expect. Under Egypt's current electoral system, in order for someone to be elected president, they must win an absolute majority of votes cast. If no one manages to secure a majority, then a runoff election is held approximately three weeks later between the top two vote getters. Such an electoral system is often called a "two-round system," since such elections almost always go to runoffs. Thirteen candidates contested the 2012 presidential election's first round, including three identifiably Islamist candidates: Muhammad Mursi of the Muslim Brotherhood, an independent Islamist and scholar named Muhammad Salim al-`Awwa, and a liberal former Muslim Brotherhood leader named `Abd al-Mun`im Abu al-Futuh. Abu al-Futuh barely qualifies as an Islamist, since his campaign spent a considerable amount of time emphasizing his differences with the Brotherhood, whom he criticized for mixing religion and politics, but he is included here because he was endorsed by the Salafi Nur Party (in a tactical move designed to thwart their Muslim Brotherhood competitors).

Given everything we have read about Egyptians' innate religiosity and the Brotherhood's organizational prowess, we would have expected the Brotherhood to capture a large percentage, if not a majority of the vote. After all, as we've already seen, the Brotherhood had emerged as the leading party in parliament with more than 40 percent of the seats in that body. But this great success was not to be repeated in the initial phase of the presidential contest.[63] Instead, Muhammad Mursi of the vaunted Muslim Brotherhood only secured 25 percent of the more than 23 million votes cast. Abu al-Futuh earned only 17.5 percent, and Salim al-`Awa recorded just 1 percent of the vote. In fact, a majority of the vote went to candidates who were identifiably secular, including to Mubarak protégé and former prime minister Ahmad Shafiq (almost 24 percent of the vote), the Karama Party's Hamdin Sabahi (with 21 percent of the vote), and former foreign minister Amro Moussa (11 percent).

Though the Muslim Brotherhood's candidate eventually eked out a victory in a runoff against Ahmad Shafiq, he did so in part by calling on the support of non-Islamist voters who did not wish to see a former Mubarak-era official ascend to the presidency. Moreover, it is worth noting that voter turnout in that election was approximately 46 percent, which means that the Brotherhood candidate's eventual 52 percent of voters represents only around a quarter of eligible voters. In other words, political Islam's seemingly stunning mandate during the 2011–2012 parliamentary elections had been significantly peeled back. The presidential election demonstrated definitively that Egyptians will not automatically vote for Islamists and that there were limits to the Muslim Brotherhood's organizational magic.

Most commentators argued that the Brotherhood's modest performance in the first round of the presidential election was a function of increasing popular dissatisfaction with the movement's performance in parliament. However, no systematic data have been presented to support such a claim. Instead, it is likely that the Muslim Brotherhood won only a quarter of first round presidential votes because voters now simply knew more about the movement's competitors than they did during the parliamentary elections several months prior. Consider, for example, the presidential race's second runner up, the Karama Party's Hamdin Sabahi, who earned 23 percent of the vote. A journalist and staunch Arab nationalist, Sabahi founded the Karama party in 1996, but the party was only officially licensed after the fall of the Mubarak regime. Sabahi had served in parliament from 2000 to 2010 (representing his home district), but his party had little street presence and few members. In the 2011 parliamentary election, his party won six seats, but this was only because it ran in coalition with the Muslim Brotherhood's Freedom and Justice Party.

How was Sabahi able to go from being the head of a fringe party to come within striking distance of the eighty-four-year-old Muslim Brotherhood in the country's first free presidential election? The answer is simple: presidential elections in Egypt, as in most presidential systems, are ultimately contests between persons. Campaign organization may matter on the margins, but the extensive media coverage provided to presidential candidates can enable them to compensate for their organizational deficits with their personal attributes. The Muslim Brotherhood may be able to dominate local elections, where the movement has greater name recognition, its candidates have good reputations, and its party disburses services to voters, but these advantages diminish at the level of presidential elections, where a few favorable television interviews can make a previously little-known presidential aspirant as much a household name as the storied Muslim Brotherhood. What this suggests is that future Muslim Brotherhood electoral performance will remain highly sensitive to contextual factors, and the movement's continued dominion is by no means assured.

Conclusion

The Muslim Brotherhood is in the midst of one of the most tumultuous periods in its history. Political changes in Egypt have exerted new stress on the Brotherhood, and it is likely that they will force the movement to adapt in unprecedented and unanticipated ways. Increasingly open and competitive politics could compel the Brotherhood to liberalize further (if that will help it to capture more voters), or to retreat into conservatism in an effort to preserve the organization's identity, distinguish itself from others on the Egyptian political landscape, and better compete with more extreme Islamist parties. Splits within the movement—between liberals and conservatives, between those focused on political work and those who believe in the primacy of *da'wa*, between young and old—can be expected to remain salient, and to be joined by new ones generated by the push and pull of democratic politics. For example, though the Brothers have long decried both Western hegemony (as exercised through international institutions like the World Bank and the International Monetary Fund [IMF]) and interest-based banking (which is thought to be forbidden by the Islamic prohibition against usury), the Brotherhood in power has been engaged in intense negotiations to conclude a $4.5 billion loan from the IMF to stave off economic collapse. Future departures from ideological purity are likely, especially as the Brotherhood competes for (and wins) election to local executive offices such as governorships, mayoralties, and local councils. Moreover, as noted earlier, another potential force for change is the Muslim Brotherhood's electoral vehicle, the Freedom and Justice Party. Formally separate from the movement, and yet bound to it, the Freedom and Justice Party's need to respond to the exigencies of elections may either drive it away from the Brothers, or turn it into a force for change within the larger movement.

Regardless of what happens to the Brotherhood, the shift in Egyptian politics away from authoritarianism, and the resulting availability of information and ease of research, should enable scholars and observers of the region to begin to view the Brotherhood less as a radical, irrational organization of unknown strength and motives, and more as an ordinary political party to be studied in the same way that we study Peronists in Argentina or Green parties in Western Europe. In other words, the demystification of Egyptian politics that comes with greater openness should also lead to a demystification of the Muslim Brotherhood. Future work on that party, then, may focus less on probing the "challenges" it poses and more on what that party's experience can teach us about how parties form, behave, and change in new and developing democracies.

NOTES

1. Al-Nizam al-'Am li al-Ikhwan al-Muslimun [General Order of the Muslim Brotherhood], April 12, 1994, Section 2, Article 2.
2. Hasan al-Bannā, 1939, *Communique of the Fifth Conference*, quoted in Mitchell 1993.
3. Mona El-Ghobashy has objected to translating the Ikhwan's name as "Muslim Brotherhood," arguing forcefully that it is a "glaring but persistent mistranslation, reinforcing mystification of the Ikhwan's genesis and development." But while I agree with her that "issues of translation are more than semantic," I do not see how this one is. And in this, it seems, I am joined by the Ikhwan themselves, whose English website proudly declares itself "The Muslim Brotherhood's Official English Website." See http://www.ikhwanweb.com.
4. Bettina Graf, "IslamOnline.net: Independent, interactive, and popular," *Arab Media and Society*, January 2008.
5. Al-Nizām al-'Ām li al-Ikhwān al-Muslimīn [The General System of the Muslim Brotherhood], Section 2, Article 2.
6. Al-Nizām al-'Ām li al-Ikhwān al-Muslimīn [The General System of the Muslim Brotherhood], July 1982. Reprinted in Al-Nafīsī, 1989, pp 401–416. Emphases added.
7. Spencer E. Wellhofer, "The Electoral Effectiveness of Party Organization: Norway 1945–1977," *Scandinavian Political Studies* 8, no. 3, 1979: 171–185.

8. Al-Nizāmal-'Ām li al-Ikhwān al-Muslimīn, 1994. Article 12.
9. Al-Nizām al-'Ām li al-Ikhwān al-Muslimīn. Article 13.
10. al-La'iha al-'Amma li Jjama'at al-Ikhwan al-Muslimin [General Bylaws of the Society of Muslim Brothers]. Article 7.
11. al-La'iha al-'Amma li Jama'at al-Ikhwan al-Muslimin. Article 12.
12. al-La'iha al-'Aamma li-Jama'at al-Ikhwan al-Muslimin. Article 15.
13. Quoted in El-Ghobashy 2005.
14. Hasanayn Tawfiq Ibrahim, *Al-Nidham al-Siyasi wal-Ikhwan al-Muslimun fi Misr: Min al-Tassamuh ila al-Muwajaha 1981–1996* [The Political System and the Muslim Brotherhood in Egypt: From Tolerance to Confrontation, 1981–1996], Beirut: Dar al-Tali'ahlil-Tiba'ahwal-Nashr, 1998, p 63.
15. See Marius Deeb, *Party Politics in Egypt: The Wafd and Its Rivals 1919–1939*, London: Ithaca Press, 1979, pp 350–354; and Yunan Labib Rizk, "The Colour of Shirts," *Al-Ahram Weekly*, no. 748, June 23–29, 2005. Available at: http://weekly.ahram.org.eg/2005/748/chrncls.htm. According to Rizk, the newspaper of the Wafdist Blue Shirts was even called *al-Jihad*.
16. See Donald M. Reid, "Political Assassination in Egypt, 1910–1954," *International Journal of African Historical Studies* 15, no. 4, 1982: 625–651.
17. Quoted in Tawfiq, *Al-Wa'i, Al fikr al siyasi al mu'asir 'ind al ikhwan al muslimin* [Modern Political Thought of the Muslim Brotherhood], Maktaba al-Manar al-Islamiyya, 2001, pp 136–139.
18. Hasan al-Bannā, "Risalat al-Mu'tamar al-Khamis" [Statement to the Fifth Conference], in *Majmu'at Rasa'il al-Imam al-Shahid Hasan al-Bannā* [The Collected Letters of the Martyred Imam, Hasan al-Bannā], Maktaba al-Tawfiqiya, p 202–203.
19. http://www.ikhwanweb.com/article.php?ID=13336&SectionID=89 (accessed, June 25, 2011).
20. Owen Bowcott and Faisal al Yafai, "Scholar with a Streetwise Touch Defies Expectations and Stereotypes," *The Guardian*, Friday, July 9, 2004. Available at: http://www.guardian.co.uk/politics/2004/jul/09/religion.immigrationpolicy (accessed April 12, 2008).
21. Quoted in Mustafa Muhammad al-Tahhan, *al-Fikr al-Islami al-Mu'asir: Dirasa fi Fikr al-Ikhwan al-Muslimin* [Contemporary Islamic Thought: A Study in the Thought of the Muslim Brotherhood], Cairo: Dar al-Tawzi'awal-Nashr al-Islamiyya, 2002, p 294.
22. For examples outside of the scholarly literature, see Andrew C. McCarthy, "Fear the Muslim Brotherhood," *National Review*, January 31, 2011; Ahmed Sobhy Mansour, Testimony to Congressional Subcommittee on Terrorism, Humint, Analysis, and Counterintelligence, April 13, 2011.
23. Hasan al-Bana, "Risalat al-Jihad (Epistle on Jihad)," n.d. Available at: http://hassanalbanna.y007.com/t20-topic
24. http://www.ikhwanonline.com/new/Article.aspx?ArtID=20320&SecID=117 (accessed June 25, 2011).
25. Data on interpellations in the 1984 and 1987 parliaments are drawn from 'Awad and Tawfiq 1996. Data from 2000 to the present were collected by the author.
26. "Ādā' Nuwwāb al-Ikhwān fi al-Barlamān" [The Performance of Brotherhood Deputies in Parliament], 2006. Available at: http:www.nowabikhwan.com.
27. Nathan Brown, "Debating the Islamic Shar'a in 21st Century Egypt: Consensus and Cacophony," in Robert W. Hefner, ed. *Shari'a Politics: Islamic Law and Society in the Modern World*, Indiana University Press, 2011, pp. 94-121.

28. *Birnāmij Ḥizb al-Ikhwān al-Muslimīn: Al-Isdār al-Awwal* [Program of the Party of Muslim Brothers: First Draft], Society of Muslim Brothers, August 25, 2007. Emphasis mine.
29. *Birnāmij Ḥizb al-Hurriyawa al-`Adalah* [Program of the Freedom and Justice Party], April 2011, p 15.
30. The Society of Muslim Brothers, "Haq al-Mar'a fi al-Intikhāb wa fī `Udwiyyat al-Majālis al-Niyābiyya wa fī tawallā al-wazā'if al-`āmma" [The Rights of Women to Vote and to Membership in Parliamentary Assemblies and to Assume Public Posts], in *Al-Mar'a al-Muslimafi al-Mujtama` al-Muslim; Al-Shūrāwa Ta`adud al-Ahzāb* [The Muslim Woman in the Muslim Society; Consultation and Multipartyism], Cairo: al-Markaz al-Islāmī li al-Dirāsātwa al-Buhūth (Islamic Center for Studies and Research), March 1994.
31. Ibid., p 23.
32. Ibid., p 26.
33. Ibid., p 27.
34. Muslim Brotherhood Draft Party Platform, 2007, p 103.
35. Freedom and Justice Party Platform, 2011, p 65.
36. Gamal Essamal-Din, "Children Accorded Greater Rights," *Ahram Weekly*, no. 901, June 12–18, 2008. Available at: http://weekly.ahram.org.eg/2008/901/eg4.htm.
37. Muhammad Diā' al-Dīn, "Al-kutla tarfud qānūn al-tifl wa tasifuhu bi al-mustawrad" [The Bloc Rejects the 'Children's Law' and Describes It as Imported], The Official Website of the Muslim Brotherhood's Parliamentary Bloc, June 1, 2008. Available at: http://www.nowabikhwan.com/index.aspx?ctrl=press&ID=3b0d976f-bd45-466c-9a34-d214ff27702c.
38. FarīdIsmā`īl, "Makhātir Qanūn al-Tifl" [The Dangers of the Child Law], Website of Muslim Brotherhood Parliamentary Bloc, June 30, 2008. Available at: http://www.nowabikhwan.com/Index.aspx?ctrl=press&ID=e70fe6e1-98e7-4108-8dbf-4bb46a6820a1.
39. `Abd Allāh Shahāta, "Al-Khitān fi kitāb jadīd li `Askar" [Circumcision in a New Book by `Askar], Website of Muslim Brotherhood Parliamentary Bloc, May 24, 2008. Available at: http://www.nowabikhwan.com/Index.aspx?ctrl=press&ID=48875f85-1f16-4efa-ac03-6955a15b8a7b.
40. `Abd Allāh Shahāta, "Nūr al-Dīn yarfud mu`āqabat tabībatayn ajratan `amaliyyāt khitān" [Nūr al-Dīn Rejects the Punishment of Two Women Doctors for Performing Female Circumcisions], Website of Muslim Brotherhood Parliamentary Bloc, July 19, 2008. Available at: http://www.nowabikhwan.com/Index.aspx?ctrl=press&ID=af08b400-fcd6-494a-8e0d-d13cbd75b806.
41. Diā' al-Dīn, "Al-kutla tarfud qānūn al-tifl watasifuhu bi al-mustawrad" [The Bloc Rejects the 'Children's Law' and Describes It as Imported]. Not all objections to the law were based on narrow interpretations of the *sharī`a*. `Ilm al-dīn al-Sakhāwī, a Brotherhood MP from Basyūn in al-Gharbiyya, objected to the fact that the law only mandates maternity leave for a mother's first two births.
42. "Muslim Brotherhood Statement Denouncing UN Women Declaration for Violating Sharia Principles," March 14, 2013, available at: http://www.ikhwanweb.com/article.php?id=30731
43. http://www.egyptindependent.com/news/constitution-draft-raises-concern-about-women-s-rights.
44. Muslim Brotherhood Draft Party Platform, p 15.
45. Muhammad Bahā', "Hishmat: Madāmīnfī al-birnāmijlātu`abir `anra'y al-qawā`id" [The Program's Contents Do Not Reflect the Views of the Base], Islam Online, October 6, 2007. Available at: http://www.islamonline.net/servlet/Satellite?c=ArticleA_C&cid=1190886145593&pagename=Zone-Arabic-Daawa%2FDWALayout.

46. ʿAbd al-Munʿim Mahmūd, "ʿIsām al-ʿAryān: I'tiqālī mumārasa yawmiya li mudāhamat al-amn li nashāt al-Ikhwānwa lays lahū dalāla siwā hashāshat al-nizām" [My Detention Is a Daily Exercise in the Security's Attacks on the Brothers and Indicate Only the Regime's Fragility], *Ana Ikhwan*, October 9, 2007. Available at: http://ana-ikhwan.blogspot.com/2007/10/blog-post_09.html.
47. Freedom and Justice Party Platform, p 16.
48. Khalil al-Anani, "Old Habits Die Hard!" *Foreign Policy* (online), January 31, 2012.
49. Fawaz A. Gerges, "Making Sense of the Cartoon Controversy: From Protests to Recent Elections, Islamists Hold Sway," ABC News, February 8, 2006. Available at: http://abcnews.go.com/International/story?id=1595281&page=1.
50. Uri Dromi, "Reverberations in Egypt: Gaza Fallout," *International Herald Tribune*, June 22, 2007. Available at: http://www.iht.com/articles/2007/06/22/opinion/eddromi.php.
51. National Public Radio, June 15, 2007. Transcript available at: http://www.npr.org/templates/transcript/transcript.php?storyId=11104842.
52. James Glanz, "A Little Democracy or a Genie Unbottled," *New York Times*, January 29, 2006.
53. Nina Shea, "Freedom's Fighters: Ramy Lakah Deserves American Support," *National Review*, June 20, 2005.
54. Jeffrey Phillips, "A Holy War on the Nile," *Jerusalem Report*, June 18, 1992.
55. The movement's relatively poor performances in 1995 and 2010 were widely attributed to regime crackdowns, and saw the withdrawal of most of the Brotherhood's candidates prior to the final balloting.
56. 2005–2006 World Values Survey, Egypt. Available at: http://www.worldvaluessurvey.com.
57. I have previously cited this study in Tarek Masoud, "Liberty, Democracy, and Discord," *Washington Quarterly*, Autumn 2011.
58. Max Rodenbeck, "Is Islamism Losing Its Thunder?" *Washington Quarterly* 21, no. 2, 1998: 178.
59. Patrick D. Gaffney, *The Prophet's Pulpit: Islamic Preaching in Contemporary Egypt*, Berkeley: University of California Press, 1994, 47.
60. Lila Abu Lughod, *Local Contexts of Islamism in Popular Media*, Amsterdam: Amsterdam University Press, 2006, 11.
61. Geneive Abdo, *No God but God: Egypt and the Triumph of Islam*, New York: Oxford University Press, 2000, 149–161.
62. See Nazih N. M. Ayubi, "The Political Revival of Islam: The Case of Egypt," *International Journal of Middle East Studies* 12, no. 4, 1980: 481–499; and Olivier Roy, *The Failure of Political Islam*, Cambridge: Harvard University Press, 1994.
63. Figures for vote shares and turnout in the 2012 presidential election available at: http://en.wikipedia.org/wiki/Egyptian_presidential_election,_2012.

References

Abed, Kotob Sana, "The Accomodationists Speak: Goals and Strategies of the Muslim Brotherhood." *International Journal of Middle East Studies* 27, 1995: 321–339.
Armstrong, Karen, *Islam: A Short History*, Modern Library, 2002.
Ashour, Omar, *The De-Radicalization of Jihadists: Transforming Armed Islamist Movements*, Routledge, 2009.
Ayoob, Mohammed, "Political Islam: Image and Reality." *World Policy Journal* 21, no. 3, 2004: 1–14.

Ayoob, Mohamed, *The Many Faces of Political Islam: Religion and Politics in the Muslim World*, University of Michigan Press, 2008 .Awad, Huda Raghib, and Hasanain Tawfiq. *Al-Ikhwan al-Muslimunwa wa al-Siyasa fi Misr: Dirasa fi al-tahalufat al–intikhabiya wa al-mumarasat al- barlamaniya lil ikhwan al-muslimun fi dhil al-ta`adudiya al-siyasiya al-muqayaddah (1994–1984)* [The Muslim Brothers and Egyptian Politics: A Study of the Electoral Alliances and Parliamentary Participation of the Muslim Brothers in the Shadow of Limited Political Pluralism]. Cairo, Egypt: Kitab al-Mahrusa, 1996.

al-Banna, Hasan, *Majmu`at Rasa'il al-Imam al-Shahid Hasan al-Banna* [The Collected Letters of the Martyred Imam, Hasan al-Banna], al-Maktaba al-Tawfiqiya.

Brown, Nathan J., "Egypt: Cacophony and Consensus in the Twenty-First Century," in Robert Hefner, ed., *Shari`a Politics: Islamic Law and Society in the Modern World*, Indiana University Press, 2011, 94–120.

Davis, Nancy J., and Robert V. Robinson, "Freedom on the March? Bush's Democracy Doctrine for the Muslim World." *Contexts* 6, no. 2, 2007: 22–27.

Deeb, Marius, *Party Politics in Egypt: The Wafd and Its Rivals, 1919–39*. St Antony's Middle East Monographs. London: Ithaca Press, 1979.

El-Ghobashy, Mona, "The Metamorphosis of the Egyptian Muslim Brothers." *International Journal of Middle East Studies* 37, no. 3, 2005: 373–395.

Esposito, John, *What Everyone Needs to Know about Islam*. Oxford University Press, 2002.

Hamzawy, Amr, and Nathan J. Brown, "Can Egypt's Troubled Elections Produce a More Democratic Future?" *Policy Outlook, Carnegie Endowment of International Peace*, December, 2005.

Hamzawy, Amr, and Nathan J. Brown, "A Boon or a Bane for Democracy?" *Journal of Democracy* 19, no. 3, 2008: 49–54.

Hasanayn, Tawfiq Ibrahim. *Al-Nizam al-siyasi wa al-ikhwan al-muslimun fi misr: min al tasamuh ila al-muwajaha* [The Political Order and the Muslim Brotherhood in Egypt: From Accommodation to Confrontation]. Beirut, Lebanon: Dar al-Tali`a li al-tiba`a wa al-nashr, 1998.

Juergensmeyer, Mark, "The New Religious State." *Comparative Politics* 27, no. 4, 1995: 379–391.

Kepel, Gilles, *The Prophet and Pharaoh: Muslim Extremism in Egypt*. London: Al Saqi Books. Distributed by Zed Books, 1985.

Krause, Elliott A., "Professional Group Power in Developing Societies." *Current Sociology* 49, no. 4, July 2001: 149–175.

Lawrence, Bruce, *Shattering the Myth: Islam Beyond Violence*. Princeton: Princeton University Press, 2000.

Lia, Brynjar, *The Society of the Muslim Brothers in Egypt: The Rise of an Islamic Mass Movement, 1928–1942*. Reading, England: Ithaca Press, 1998.

Masoud, Tarek, "Islamist Parties: Are They democrats? Does It Matter?" *Journal of Democracy*, July 2008.

Masoud, Tarek, *Why Islam Wins: Electoral Ecologies and Economies of Political Islam in Contemporary Egypt*. Yale University Doctoral Dissertation, December 2008.

Miller, Judith, *God Has Ninety-Nine Names: Reporting from a Militant Middle East*. Touchstone, 1997.

Mitchell, Richard P., *The Society of the Muslim Brothers*. New York: Oxford University Press, 1993.

Onians, Charles, "Supply and Demand Democracy in Egypt." *World Policy Journal* 21, no. 2, 2004.

Rashad, Hoda, Magued Osman, and Farzaneh Roudi-Fahimi, "Marriage in the Arab World." *Population Reference Bureau*, 2005.

Reid, Donald M., "Political Assassination in Egypt, 1910–1954," *International Journal of African Historical Studies* 15, no. 4, 1982: 625–651.

Schwedler, Jillian, *Faith in Moderation: Islamist Parties in Jordan and Yemen*. Cambridge: Cambridge University Press, 2006.

Schwedler, Jillian, "Can Islamists Become Moderates?: Rethinking the Inclusion-Moderation Hypothesis." *World Politics* 63, no. 2, April 2011: 347–376.

Shahin, Emad Eldin, *Political Ascent: Contemporary Islamic Movements in North Africa*, Westview Press, 1997.

Shehata, Samer, and Joshua Stacher, "The Brotherhood Goes to Parliament." *Middle East Report* 240, 2006.

Sloan, Stephen, "Countering Terrorism in the Late 1980s and 1990s: Future Threats and Opportunities for the United States." Air University, Maxwell Air Force Base, Alabama, Report No. AU-ARI-CP-87-5, 1987.

Springborg, Robert, "Political Islam and Europe: Views from the Arab Mediterranean States and Turkey." *Center for European Policy Studies, Working document* (264), 2007.

Tahhan, Mustafa Muhammad al-, *al-Fikr al-Islami al-Mu`asir: Dirasa fi Fikr al-Ikhwan al-Muslimin* [Contemporary Islamic Thought: A Study in the Thought of the Muslim Brotherhood]. Cairo: Dar al-Tawzi`awal-Nashr al-Islamiya, 2002.

Wa`i, Tawfiq Al-, *Al-fikr al-siyasi al-mu`asir `ind al-ikhwan al-muslimin* [Modern Political Thought of the Muslim Brotherhood]. Maktabat al-Manar al-Islamiya, 2001.

Wellhofer, E. S. "The Electoral Effectiveness of Party Organization: Norway, 1945–1977," *Scandinavian Political Studies* 8, 1985: 171–185.

Welner, Michael, "Psychopathy, Media and the Psychology at the Root of Terrorism and Mass Disasters," in Wecht and Okoye, eds. *Forensic Investigation and Management of Mass Disasters*. Tuscon, AZ: Lawyers and Judges Publishing, 2007.

Wickham, Carrie Rosefsky, *Mobilizing Islam: Religion, Activism, and Political Change in Egypt*. New York: Columbia University Press, 2003.

Wickham, Carrie Rosefsky, "Democratization and Islamists: Auto- Reform." Paper presented at the annual conference of the Center for the Study of Islam and Democracy, Washington DC, May 4–5, 2006. Available at: http://www.muslimbrotherhood.co.uk.

Wickham, Carrie Rosefsky, "Changing Stripes? Islamist Parties and the Idea of Moderation." Unpublished manuscript, Emory University, 2008.

Zanatyand, Fatmael Ann Way, *Egypt Demographic and Health Survey 2005*. Cairo: Ministry of Health and Population, National Population Council, El- Zanaty and Associates, and ORC Macro, 2006.

Zeidan, Daniel, "Radical Islam in Egypt: A Comparison of Two Groups." *Middle East Review of International Affairs* 3, no. 3, September 1999.

Zollner, Barbara, *The Muslim Brotherhood: Hasan al-Hudaybi and Ideology*. London: Routledge, 2009.

＊*Islamic Movements in the Political Process*

CHAPTER 32

HAMAS IN THE PALESTINIAN TERRITORIES

BEVERLEY MILTON-EDWARDS

Hamas, the Islamic Resistance Movement (Harakat al-Muqawamah al-Islamiyyah) founded in the Palestinian territories in 1988, is generally described as a modern Islamist movement, which in its latter years has turned to terrorism to achieve its goals of establishing an Islamic state in historic Palestine. Hamas is the largest and most influential Palestinian Islamist movement. In January 2006, Hamas won the Palestinian Authority's (PA) legislative elections, defeating their secular opponents in Fatah, the largest faction of the Palestine Liberation Organization (PLO). Before 2011 it had been the only Sunni Islamist movement in the Arab world to have contested democratic elections and acceded to power. Hamas is a wing of the Muslim Brotherhood movement, which has emerged as a significant Islamist force in contemporary politics across the Middle East region. The Hamas electoral victory in 2006 played a significant part in transforming it both within the region and internationally. Since that time it has forged a strategic relation with Iran while attempting to balance its credibility with important Sunni organizations and regimes such as those in Saudi Arabia and Qatar.

In the wake of its election victory the international Quartet powers of the United States, United Nations (UN), European Union, and Russia demanded that Hamas recognize the state of Israel, end violence, and abide by previous agreements between Israel and the PLO. Hamas leaders, however, have refused to recognize the state of Israel and in this respect rejects the two-state solution formula that has been the basis of peace negotiations since 1991. Since it was elected to power, Hamas and the people of Gaza have been subject to an Israeli-led and internationally supported regime of economic sanctions because of its refusal to recognize Israel (Hovdenak 2009, 59–80). Hamas's armed wing—the Izz-al-Din al-Qassam Brigades (IQB)—has organized and carried out violent attacks, including suicide bombings and rocket attacks against Israel, both inside and over the 1967 border.

Founding

Hamas's roots lie in the Muslim Brotherhood and a local Gaza-based forerunner called al-Mujamma'. Founded by Hamas leader and spiritual guide Shaykh Ahmad Yassin in the late 1970s, with permission of the Israeli authorities, this social-reform group was a direct competitor to the PLO. Al-*Mujamma*` concentrated its activities on preaching, mosque building, and societal transformation in fierce contest with local Palestinian nationalists and leftists. Its identity was forged not in opposition to the Israeli occupation or the Zionist movement but to their Palestinian brethren (Milton-Edwards 1996, 105). The primacy of this approach was apparent in both the words and deeds of Shaykh Yassin and his followers (Mishal and Sela 2006, 23). Secularism, leftist ideologies of socialism, and communism were viewed as a threat to Muslim identity and society. Such influences were perceived as corrupting an entire generation and propelling Palestinians down a path that would lead them to all but abandon Islam in favor of Western-inspired ideologies that had failed to aid the Palestinians in their resistance against the occupier (Gunning 2007, 29; Nusse 1998).

When Hamas was established at the outbreak of the first Palestinian uprising (intifada) in December 1987 the new Islamist group initially promoted itself as a rival to the leadership of this revolt led by the PLO. From 1987 to 1993 Hamas openly competed for the hearts, mind, stones, and strike days of the Palestinians as they fought against Israel and called for an end to occupation. Hamas's identity was forged in opposition both to the PLO as the secular expression of Palestinian nationalism and to Israel as a foreign occupying force on Palestinian territory (Abu Amr 1994, 28). Hamas has traditionally opposed the PLO's claim as sole legitimate representative of the Palestinian people. It has consistently critiqued the PLO's nationalist credentials. It has frequently and violently clashed with constituent factions of the PLO, particularly the main Fatah faction in more recent years (Milton-Edwards and Farrell 2010). From 1991 on, Hamas leaders fiercely opposed the PLO's position of peace negotiations with Israel.

Hamas found support among at least a third of the Palestinian population and emerged as a threat to Israel when it formed its armed wing in 1991 and commenced attacks against Israeli soldiers and settlers in the West Bank and Gaza Strip. Hamas's hostility to Israel has been a defining feature of the movement (Reuter 2002, 101). Yet historically Israel played its part in encouraging socioreligious revivalism not only in the West Bank and Gaza Strip that gave rise to Hamas predecessors but also in the political strategy to encourage opponents to the nationalist PLO. This classic "divide and rule" device has been viciously traded as the ultimate insult against Hamas by its Palestinian opponents. It is constantly revived, reinterpreted, and adapted as a tool of political rhetoric in the contemporary domestic Palestinian narrative of antagonistic politics and enmity.

From 1993 to 2000 Hamas's violence against Israel changed in tenor and frequency. In 1994, after an Israeli settler massacred unarmed Palestinian worshippers in a mosque, Hamas ordered its first suicide missions in Israel as revenge (Sprinzak 1997). Hamas bombers targeted Israeli civilians and their actions were universally condemned as terrorism. Since 2000 and the outbreak of the second Palestinian Intifada, a variety of Palestinian armed groups, including Hamas conducted suicide bombings, the effects of which led Israel to alter its national defense doctrine in relation to the West Bank and Gaza Strip. The two most striking outcomes were the construction of the fences and barriers that now separate the Palestinian territories from Israel and the 2005 Israeli evacuation from the Gaza Strip. Hamas claimed the Israeli evacuation from Gaza as a victory—a direct outcome of their armed strategies.

Hamas has also shaped a distinctly political identity. In 2005 it made the decision to form its own political party (notwithstanding an early but aborted attempt in 1996) to contest municipal and legislative elections (Hroub 2006, 139). Here the challenge lay in conveying its religious agenda to the Palestinian electorate in both the conservative Gaza Strip and the more liberal and secular West Bank. Hamas presented itself under the slogan of "Change and Reform" and downplayed its religious credentials. The intended target of this positioning into formal electoral politics was the PLO, which by then had a reputation for corrupt and inept administration of the PA. Hamas was neither changing nor reforming its own internal hierarchy or organization but was intent on calling for further social Islamization of Palestine. It deftly avoided stating whether it was going to institute *Shari`ah* law in the Palestinian territories if elected.

IDENTITY

Hamas and its predecessor organizations have always centered their programs and activities on principles of Muslim revivalism—both individual and societal—through preaching, education, and social and welfare support initiatives. Reformism as interpreted through these principles has been tangentially coupled with processes of political radicalization transforming Hamas strategy in relation to its local Palestinian opponent, Israel, and other regional actors in the Middle East.

One outcome of this process of radicalization has been Hamas's strategies or tactics of violence and armed resistance. There is evidence of an emerging layering of identity in terms of Hamas's Islamism, violence, politics, radicalism, and reform. Hamas is also a distinctly Palestinian national Muslim movement bound to acculturated norms associated with a nationalist people engaged in an historic struggle for self-determination and independence from first a colonial power, Britain, and then an occupier, Israel. Over the decades Hamas has gone some way in reconfiguring Palestinian identity. It has succeeded in narrowing its identity to primarily Muslim and then Palestinian. In Gaza, since it succeeded in taking power, Hamas leaders have narrowed and reduced the political space. There is Islam, and anything else politically is increasingly considered *haram* (taboo). All forms of political opposition become, by Hamas definition, un-Islamic. Opponents have no comeback to such powerfully reductive religious taboos. In this respect Hamas has built what Said would refer to as an antagonistic identity that has had the power to undermine and rend asunder the Palestinian national identity project (Said 2004, 417). Secular Palestinian nationalist factions are then forced to reactive, negative rather than complementary behaviors in opposition to Hamas.

Hamas, however, is also a form of protest movement, a response to the degeneration of Palestinian discourses of empowerment through the practice of autonomy under the framework of the Oslo Accords and the institutions of control that constitute the PA. They are a response to the crisis of Arab nationalism and what Edward Said calls the "primitive resistance" arising out of "the corruption, the incompetence, and the inability to serve the needs of domestic populations by local regimes…" (Said 2004, 417). In the case of Hamas there is a duality in this "resistance" as it reconfigures local narratives both externally and internally. Outwardly, Hamas resists Israel as a foreign occupier of Palestinian land and handmaiden of US neoimperialist ambitions; inwardly, it reshapes views of the PA dominated as it was, before the elections of 2006, by a corrupt pro-Western PLO elite increasingly criticized for its failure to meet the basic needs, including human security, of the Palestinians of the West Bank, Gaza Strip, and East Jerusalem.

Hamas would counter that it has not narrowed or reduced identity but widened it in terms of Muslim appeal. But Hamas is not a pan-Islamic movement. Its pretensions to power lie within its own imagined borders of Palestine. More recently it has also had repeated and public tensions with worldwide jihadi groups such as al-Qa'ida. Indeed al-Qa'ida rebuked Hamas's decision to enter politics, arguing that armed jihad was the only path. Furthermore in August 2009 Hamas entered into armed clashes with al-Qa'ida-influenced jihadi militants based in the Gaza Strip who challenged Hamas's so-called Islamic credentials. Hamas leaders have subsequently found themselves between a rock and a hard place: one side insists that it moderates its Islamist positions in terms of political yielding to the demands of the international Quartet, and the other, radical side raises an increasingly vociferous criticism that it is not hardline or Islamic enough.

Hamas has historically been just as antagonistic to Palestinian nationalists as it has to Israel, if not more so. Its forerunners have viewed Palestinian nationalist secularists as a more pernicious danger to the success of their project than the presence and occupation of their territory by the state of Israel. The crucial issue is whether Hamas is foundationally a nationalist movement motivated by a calculation of Palestinian political and national interests or an Islamist one, driven by a wider Islamic agenda. Historically it is true that Hamas is rooted in Islam and the political movements manifest in the region associated with it. But Hamas has always confined its attacks to the territories demarcated by the state of Israel following the first Arab-Israeli war of 1948–1949 and the Palestinian territories it subsequently occupied during the war of 1967.

Hamas identifies itself in opposition to Israel, which it continues to refer to as the "Zionist entity." By doing so it denies Israel recognition as a legitimate state within the territories Hamas considers historic Palestine, as endowed in perpetuity for the Muslim people (*waqf*). Hamas has declared that its mission is to destroy the Jewish state. In the preamble to the Hamas Covenant it declares: "Israel will exist and will continue to exist until Islam will obliterate it, just as it obliterated others before it" (Hamas Covenant 1988). Hroub interprets such a call as increasingly stripped of religious import and increasingly attenuated to "the language of international law and on political...assumptions" (Hroub 2006, 38). Yet for Hamas the removal of the "Zionist entity" is a necessary condition for the realization of its ultimate goal, but not a sufficient one. Hamas's final goal is an independent state in Palestine governed in accordance with Islam. Hamas regards Israel as an aggressor and an occupier that seeks the eradication of the rights of the Palestinians to statehood. Meanwhile, Palestinian nationalist elements and factions are constructed in Hamas narratives and discourse as just as much of a threat, if not more so, in many ways, to the realization of Hamas's goal. Whereas the "Zionist entity" is a military obstacle easily displaced through the "resistance = jihad" equation, these rival Palestinian nationalist movements are competing with Hamas for the hearts, minds, and souls of Palestinians.

Resistance and Violence

Increasingly, the Hamas movement has become synonymous with the acts of violence perpetrated by its armed wing in terms of targeting Israel and its citizens. This violence is signified as ideologically and religiously motivated. Hamas violence is labeled in terms of dimensions of sacred and religious interpretations. It is also caught in the discourse of jihad as a defensive act in response to foreign rule and usurpation of Palestinian Muslims. Hamas violence then becomes more lethal and its tactics of suicide bombings willingly undertaken by Palestinian martyrdom seekers promised a heavenly reward; this is seen as a grave threat to Israeli security (Hoffman 2007). Hamas has played its own part in developing an idiom that has reconstituted Palestinian armed resistance against Israel into a religiously inspired duty or call to defense. Whether this has succeeded in truly Islamizing the Israeli-Palestinian conflict is questionable (Litvak 1998).

Hamas violence is commonly described by its opponents and designated as terrorist because many of Hamas's operations and in particular its suicide and rocket attacks have indiscriminately targeted civilians. Hamas is recognized as being the first Sunni Muslim movement to adopt such a tactic and to have it legitimated through a variety of Muslim juristic opinions (Tamimi 2007, 171). Such violence is legitimated by Hamas ideologists as a tactic in the armed resistance against a more powerful enemy and occupier of their land. It is viewed as reciprocal or retaliatory violence (Hroub 2006, 51). By categorizing Israel as an enemy and refusing to recognize it Hamas leaders have also established an absolutist argument for its violent tactics (Pape 2005, 71; Mishal and Sela 2006). Hamas violence translated as armed resistance against Israel, however, falls into the classical asymmetric dilemma of nonstate violence against a well-armed state force. The international community tends to regard such violence as terrorist and Hamas has been placed on the list of proscribed organizations by governments in Europe and the United States. Its goals, however, have been dangerously compromised by Israel's offensive and defensive measures and the turning tide of international opinion against its suicide operations. Arguments relating to proportionality or excessive force employed by Israel against Palestinian civilians simply were not enough to combat images of dead Israelis on the streets of Tel Aviv.

Even if the acceptability or legitimacy of such attacks grew among some sectors of Arab or Muslim opinion the Hamas leadership was forced to confront the issue of the role of their violence in the wake of their electoral victory in Palestinian elections in 2006 and whether such violence was translating into political gains. Transformed from the armed opposition to power holders heading the government of the PA, Hamas was in a quandary when it came to resistance and politics (Hamad 2009, 1). Hamas has faced an internal challenge and tensions between the demands of leaders in its military wing, the Izz-al-Din al-Qassam Brigades, who continue to believe that only armed attacks against Israel will lead to political concessions and the political leadership that struggles to promote Hamas the organization and Hamas the government to both internal constituencies who will vote for them in electoral contests and the international community, which treats them as an illegitimate pariah regime of fanatic fundamentalist Islamists governing the "Emirate of Gaza." Moreover, Hamas was irretrievably harmed by the United National Human Rights Council report of Israel's war against Gaza in January 2009, when it was accused of war crimes including crimes against humanity. Hamas rocket fire and associated statements by Hamas declaring that such attacks would target Israeli civilians were deemed as having the fundamental purpose of terrorism rather than legitimate resistance (UNHRC 2009, 365). The Hamas claim to legitimate resistance has been consistently undermined by its indiscriminate attacks on Israeli civilian rather than military targets. The moral saliency of such arguments and the recourse to declarations inspired by Sunni religious figures has done little to recover that legitimacy in terms of discourse on violence and resistance, politics and power.

Significantly Hamas violence and force against their Palestinian opponents is often overlooked. But this violence and recourse to force alters the nature and form of Islamic politics in the Palestinian territories. Such violence also has significant consequences in terms of nation building, plural politics, and national unity. This force has found expression through Hamas's control of the mechanisms of governance in Gaza by reconstituting the Palestinian Security Forces (PSF) and drafting in its own civil police and other armed elements (Milton-Edwards 2008, 664). It has also interfered in the independence of the judiciary and courts with respect to a variety of issues including personal status laws. Furthermore Hamas's habitual recourse to force and violence in "managing" its relationship with its political opponents—whether they be other Islamists or national secularists—is problematic in terms of wider implications for security and democracy in the Palestinian state-building project. The collapse of national unity and the near state of civil war in 2006–2007, followed by Hamas's armed takeover of PA institutions in the Gaza Strip, has compromised Hamas's claims to legitimacy both in terms of the popular constituency it relied on for electoral support as well as externally in the Arab region and beyond.

Resistance and its place in the matrix of violence have been subject to ever greater scrutiny within Hamas between its political and military leadership and in terms of Hamas's critics in relation to its strategic decisions. Strategic decisions to unilaterally ordered ceasefire in terms of suicide bomb or rocket attacks against Israel have been questioned with respect to the wider acknowledgment of the legitimate "right to resist" debate that much Palestinian contemporary discourse focuses on. Hamas hardliners and leaders of its military arm—the Izz-al-Din al-Qassam Brigades (IQB)—question the permissibility of a temporary calm (*tahdiya*) or ceasefire (*hudna*) with Israel. If the movement is dedicated to liberation by jihad there is a theological dimension to such practical strategic and political decision that Hamas has yet to reconcile (Milton-Edwards and Crooke 2004, 298). The IQB as the most prominent armed element of the Hamas movement found itself challenged by the status of the Hamas government. In the years since it played a part in the Hamas takeover of Gaza the armed wing grew in size, expertise, weaponry, and capacity. Hamas had thus developed its offensive and defensive capabilities in terms of both Israel and local armed Palestinian opponents. Before the events of December 2008 some Hamas leaders had come to believe that they were closing the gap on some kind of "balance of terror" with Israel. But they were also realistic about their limits acknowledging Israel as the stronger enemy.

In the wake of Israel's Operation Cast Lead war against Gaza (December 2008–January 2009), Hamas's military infrastructure, along with much of Gaza's civilian infrastructure, was mostly destroyed or degraded. Hamas had not even been able to score symbolic guerrilla-style victories similar to those of its Islamist compatriots in Hizballah against Israel in the Lebanon war of 2006. Almost a year later Hamas's political leadership announced a new unilateral truce with Israel but its military leadership publicly complained that such a move undermined the resistance option.

In sum, Hamas resistance alone cannot succeed in the goal that the movement has set itself. Nevertheless Hamas violence has altered the dynamics of the Israeli-Palestinian conflict. Israel, in response to Hamas's suicide bombing campaigns, returned to a national security doctrine that polarized peoples and established physical, political, and psychological distance that has become increasingly insurmountable. Israel has learned also that a military option alone will not topple Hamas from power.

Peace

Hamas is portrayed as a radical antipeace movement. In this respect it is perceived as a classical spoiler. Not only has Hamas opposed peace deals concluded between Israel and other Arab actors including the PLO and Arab states such as Egypt and Jordan but it is ideologically motivated to also derail peace and pursue conflict settlement only through a victory achieved through armed resistance/jihad. In much of the literature on conflict resolution and debates about the transition from terrorism to peace Hamas is portrayed as an exception to a comparative transition made by other armed groups, such as the African National Congress (ANC), or PIRA. Hamas was and remains the original "spoiler" of the Palestinian-Israeli conflict in the twenty-first century (Stedman 2003, 104). As "spoilers" Hamas has perceived the Oslo process as inimical to its goals and has been willing to employ violence strategically to undermine it (Milton-Edwards 1996). Hamas's tactics have thus played a part in polarizing the Israeli-Palestinian conflict, disrupting efforts to negotiate a form of peace.

Thus Hamas remains characterized—in terms of peace through negotiations—as marginal, held responsible for derailing peace and organizing terror attacks against Israel and undermining the efforts of pro-negotiation Palestinian leaders like President Mahmoud Abbas. In many respects Hamas—despite the legitimacy of electoral support—has been unable or unwilling to break from such characterization. In this instance Hamas has much in common with other armed elements excluded from peace processes in intractable conflicts across the globe. They are outside spoilers viewing peace (compromise with Israel) as a threat (Zahar 2003, 118).

Hamas has eschewed Western diplomatic initiatives and negotiated solutions to the Israeli-Palestinian conflict as a plot and condemned the role of Arab organizations in supporting such efforts (Nusse 1998, 130). Article 13 of Hamas's 1988 charter declares that peaceful solutions and international conferences will not, according to their ideological viewpoint, serve Muslim interests. Instead Hamas declares that only jihad can bring peace and serve Muslim rights (Hamas 1988). Hamas rejected the peacemaking efforts of the international community that gave rise to the Madrid process and the Oslo process and the Declaration of Principles signed between Israel and the PLO in September 1993. It rejected these on the grounds that such accords did not serve the historic rights of the Palestinian Muslim people. For Hamas the emphasis lies on the long-term goal of liberating all of historic Palestine through the means of jihad. It has struggled with interim initiatives and its position on them (Hroub 2000, 60). It is contended that such a struggle is apparent between different wings or stands of thought within the movement (Gunning 2007, 237).

Hamas was not alone in condemning the Oslo process in terms of a just solution to Palestinian rights but it did suffer in terms of popularity when the PA was initially established in 1993–1994, and peace talks with Israel commenced. Hamas joined the Palestinian Rejectionist camp opposed to the accords. Concurrently Hamas's popularity rose when the peace process foundered and an intriguing equation has since emerged in diplomatic terms that works according to the formula that progress in the peace process with Israel equals Palestinian support for Hamas opponents in the PLO. Peace process setbacks and collapse equal growing support for Hamas. It can be argued that Hamas too began to believe in this formula as demonstrated through its attempts throughout the mid- to late 1990s to derail the peace process through its suicide bombing campaigns against Israel (Shlaim 2006, 252). Rising popularity for Hamas, however, had as much to do with the increasing taint of corruption and maladministration within the Fatah-controlled PA. The majority of Palestinians have clung to the hope of peace and progress in the peace negotiations with Israel and have eschewed Hamas's spoiler approach.

Hamas was particularly challenged (and continues to be so) by the Saudi-sponsored Arab peace initiative of 2002 (revived in 2007), which offered the state of Israel normalization with Arab states in the Middle East if it agreed to withdraw from the occupied territories and settlement of the refugee issue based on UN Resolution 194. Regarded as the best hope for conflict settlement to date, Hamas responded to its announcement in 2002 by launching one of its deadliest suicide bomb attacks on Israelis attending a Passover meal. When the peace plan was revived in 2007 Hamas refused, once again, to endorse the plan because of the condition of recognition of Israel. Hamas leaders have largely remained intransigent and refused to yield on the recognition issue. Hamas remains ideologically opposed to current proposals based on the Oslo Accords, Roadmap, Clinton Parameters, and Annapolis and still refuses to budge on the issue of Israel's right to exist unless the occupation is terminated and the offer of statehood within the 1967 borders is on the table. The absence of any option for Hamas but to remain marginalized from the political process and conflict resolution through serious engagement with Palestinian partners implies a resort to previous type. This means that the strategy of hardliners such as one of Hamas's founders and leaders Dr. Mahmoud Zahar and others has prevailed. Such a strategy was reflected in the reversion to Hamas threats of violence against Israel and pro-negotiation Palestinians, who are denounced as "bearers of the yellow flags." Discovering alternate peace proposals beyond either the rhetoric and slogans of "jihad to victory" or a 10–20 year *hudna* (formal ceasefire) option has clearly challenged the movement throughout its existence and would require a form of yielding and compromise only possible if it were part of instead of excluded from serious sustained peace-building efforts.

Control

In June 2007 following six days of intra-Palestinian armed violence and clashes Hamas effectively ousted Fatah partisans and official PSF from their command positions in the Gaza Strip. Hamas thus assumed control of government functions throughout the region. President Abbas declared the Hamas move an illegal coup, and appointed his own emergency government headed by former World Bank official Salam Fayyad in the West Bank. Palestinian governance was split in two. From this point Hamas the movement and Hamas the government in the Gaza Strip also began to reflect internal tensions apparent within the movement's leadership over strategy and direction. This was important because, despite the self-deprecation of Hamas leaders, it was clear that the rank and file supporters considered their "strong leadership" one of their most appealing features. Hamas's discipline among the majority of its rank and file has also been widely recognized. Communicating a clear direction and strategy thus became an enormous challenge for Hamas because it was now burdened in unprecedented ways. While there were leaders in Hamas who still favored negotiation with Israel and a long-term *hudna,* they were finding it harder to make their case.

It became clear that a variety of fissures were thus apparent within the House of Hamas. While such fissures are yet to assume the character of dynastic power struggles common to Fatah they are important nonetheless. Real differences of opinion within the movement have opened up over the following issues: dialogue with Fatah; power-sharing with Fatah; strategy on the crossings and borders from the Gaza Strip; governance and security in the Gaza Strip; Hamas power and direction in the West Bank; popular mobilization; truce and "calm"; relations with the Arab world, including with Syria and Egypt in the wake of the Arab Spring; and armed resistance tactics.

In public Hamas's leaders vehemently deny the existence of divisions but in private some moderate leaders of Hamas admitted that there are differences and that they have been highlighted by the waxing and waning of certain key personalities and certain geographic centers of influence. The Hamas leadership in the West Bank, for example, made overtures to the PA leadership there—joining President Abbas for Friday prayers in the Muqat`a after Gaza leaders intimated they would pray there next year as its rulers. The public airing of an epistle from a major Hamas leader that called Hamas's takeover and rule of Gaza a trap and a grave strategic mistake also undermined the leadership. Hardline opinions then appeared to prevail, with the armed wing of Hamas prepared to go on war footing again and vowing to treat as treason any agreement with Israel that gave up Palestinian land, and to retake Jerusalem's holy sites. The divergence among Hamas leaders was thought to be the key explanation behind the rocket attacks on Israel. Hamas leadership failed to reach consensus on this element of the resistance because of infighting and tensions between figures like Ahmad Yousef, Ismail Haniyeh, and Mahmoud Zahar.

Since 2007 Hamas has tried to engender regional support in a fierce contest with President Abbas and the Fatah movement. At times it may have appeared that Hamas had scored some victories over Fatah but in sum the jury is still out as regional power balances are reordered in the wake of the Arab Spring. Not once has a single Arab state or group of states come down decisively on Hamas's side to declare support for it in terms of the demands of the Quartet, opposing the sanctions/boycott regime, Arab League peace efforts, the Annapolis conference, or the declaration of the illegitimacy of the Hamas government after June 2007. Hamas has now lost a staunch ally in Syria and hence has also departed from the Resistance Axis. It gained some support from Qatar and a post-Mubarak governed Egypt. By December 2008, the Hamas movement, aided by a popular mandate on the one hand and Tehran on the other, had thus emerged as the singular most well-armed and organized element of the Muslim Brotherhood in the Middle East region. Hamas had not only succeeded in defeating its enemies at the ballot box but also through its command of a rapidly expanding armed infrastructure. Its comprehension of strategic advantage in an asymmetric war with Israel and its allies had the potential for major regional repercussions. It had succeeded in consolidating its rule in Gaza making the option of ousting them from power through force of arms or the ballot box increasingly unlikely for their opponents (Milton-Edwards 2008). Despite the international boycott and Israeli siege of Gaza, Hamas had strengthened its links with Iran and Syria, increased its armed capacity, and presided over a society in Gaza that was becoming progressively less secular in outlook (Milton-Edwards and Farrell 2010).

As a constituent element of the Muslim Brotherhood movement (Ikhwan al-Muslimeen) it enjoyed a newfound influence and importance. More specifically, the Hamas leadership demonstrated to its opponents that peacemaking on the wider Palestinian-Israeli and Arab-Israeli track was no longer possible without them. This meant that Hamas had achieved certain strategic goals in terms of not only the Palestinian state project but regional politics as well.

For Hamas's opponents and enemies there were a limited number of options open to them as they examined the movement, its status, and future prospects. By 2013, and in the wake of the Israeli war against Gaza, some of those options became obsolete or unworkable and others because of the Arab Spring had to be included with a revised perspective and expectations. Military and strategic objectives and political and economic pressures were recalibrated as Israel, its allies in the United States, the European Union, the Palestinian nationalist leadership of the PLO, and the PA government of Salam Fayyad assessed their chances of undermining or defeating Hamas in order that their vision of the Palestinian future could better be achieved.

Hamas's future is assured. One way or another it remains, despite setbacks and attempts by its enemies to undermine and obliterate support for it, a populist national Muslim movement among Palestinians. The implications of this divination for Hamas's Palestinian opponents and for the government of Israel and the leadership of surrounding and regional Arab and other states are sizeable when tied to the current dynamic of regional politics and the Arab Spring and international interventions.

References

Abu Amr, Z. 1994. *Islamic Fundamentalism in the West Bank and Gaza*. Bloomington: Indiana University Press.
Gunning, J. 2007. *Hamas in Politics, democracy, Religion and Violence*. London: Hurst and Company.
Hamad, G. 2009. On Resistance and Politics, *Crises magazine*. Available at: http://www.crisesmagazine.org/index.php/May-25-June-1/palestinian-factions-and-the-gap-between-resistance-and-politics.html, accessed October 9, 2009.
Hamas. 1988. Covenant of the Islamic Resistance Movement. Available at: http://avalon.law.yale.edu/20th_century/hamas.asp, accessed October 12, 2009.
Hoffman, B. 2007. The Logic of Suicide Terrorism. *Rand Report*. Washington: RAND.
Hovdenak, A. 2009. Hamas in Transition: The Failure of Sanctions. *Democratization* 16:1: 59–80.
Hroub, K. 2000. *Hamas, Political Thought and Practice*. Washington, DC: Institute for Palestine Studies.
Hroub, K. 2006. *Hamas, a Beginners Guide*. London: Pluto Press.
Litvak, M. 1998. The Islamization of the Palestinian-Israeli Conflict: The Case of Hamas. *Middle Eastern Studies* 34:1: 148–163.
Milton-Edwards, B. 1996. *Islam and Politics in Palestine*. London: I.B. Tauris.
Milton-Edwards, B., and Crooke, A. 2004. Waving, Not Drowning: Strategic Dimensions of Ceasefires and Islamist Movements. *Security Dialogue* 35:3: 295–310.
Milton-Edwards, B. 2008. Order Without Law? An Anatomy of Hamas Security: The Executive Force (Tanfithya). *International Peacekeeping* 15:5: 663–676.
Milton-Edwards, B., and Farrell, S. 2010. *Hamas, the Islamic Resistance Movement*. Cambridge: Polity Press.
Mishal, S., and Sela, A. 2006. *The Palestinian Hamas: Vision, Violence and Coexistence*. New York: Columbia University Press.
Nusse, A. 1998. *Muslim Palestine: the Ideology of Hamas*. Amsterdam: Harwood Academic.

Pape, R. 2005. *Dying to Win: The Strategic Logic of Suicide Terrorism*. New York: Random House.
Reuter, C. 2002. *My Life Is a Weapon, a Modern History of Suicide Bombing*. Princeton: Princeton University Press.
Said, E. 2004. *Power, Politics and Culture, Interviews with Edward W. Said*. London: Bloomsbury.
Shlaim, A. 2006. The Rise and Fall of the Oslo Peace Process. In *International Relations of the Middle East*, ed. L. Fawcett. Oxford: Oxford University Press, 254–271.
Sprinzak, E. 1997. How Israel Misjudges Hamas and Its Terrorism. *Washington Post*, October 19, 1.
Stedman, J. 2003. *Peace Processes and the Challenges of Violence*. New York: Palgrave Macmillan.
Tamimi, Azzam. 2007. *Hamas: Unwritten Chapters*. London: Hurst and Company.
UNHRC. 2009. Report on the United Nations Fact-Finding Mission on the Gaza Conflict. Available at: http://www2.ohchr.org/english/bodies/hrcouncil/docs/12session/A-HRC-12-48.pdf, accessed October 9, 2009.
Zahar, M. 2003. Reframing the Spoiler Debate in Peace Processes. In *Contemporary Peacemaking*, ed. John Darby and Robert MacGinty. New York: Palgrave Macmillan, 159–178.

CHAPTER 33

HIZBULLAH IN LEBANON

BASSEL F. SALLOUKH AND SHOGHIG MIKAELIAN

No organization better symbolized the rise of Islamist politics in the 1980s than Lebanon's Hizbullah. Labeled a terrorist organization by its detractors, Hizbullah has metamorphosed into one of Lebanon's most institutionalized political parties, boasting an impressive organizational, military, and security structure, a sophisticated social welfare network, and a powerful support base among the country's Shi`a constituency and beyond. It has also demonstrated unexpected levels of political, ideological, and military agility. It accommodated itself incrementally to Lebanese nationalism despite the party's subscription to the *wilayat al-faqih* (guardianship of the jurisconsult) doctrine and its original call for the founding of an Islamic state in Lebanon; it opted to participate in Lebanon's confessional and clientelistic political system although it had considered it an unjust one and called for its overhaul and declared a religious ban on any kind of dealings with state institutions; and, finally, it steadily developed its military doctrines and capabilities from a resistance movement to a form of hybrid warfare combining elements of classical military doctrine and guerrilla warfare aimed at deterring a future Israeli attack against Lebanon.

Since the assassination of former Prime Minister Rafiq al-Hariri on February 14, 2005, the consequent withdrawal of Syrian military forces from Lebanon on April 26, 2005, and, more recently, the uprisings in a number of Arab states, but especially Syria, Hizbullah has found itself in the eye of an overlapping domestic and regional storm. This has triggered intense debate on the party's nature, loyalties, and intentions, underscoring the necessity of a critical reflection on its origins and doctrine, as well as its domestic and regional roles. This essay debates these themes, comparing and contrasting Hizbullah's past and present manifestations, and traces its doctrinal, political, and military metamorphoses. It examines how the party has reconciled its adherence to the doctrine of *wilayat al-faqih* with claims that it is a Lebanese movement with a Lebanese identity; how it has accommodated itself to the political scene in post-Ta'if and post-Syria Lebanon; and how it has juggled the overlapping domestic and regional struggles that present it with both opportunities as well as significant threats.

The Origins of Hizbullah

A set of overlapping variables created the socioeconomic, political, and ideological conditions for Hizbullah's emergence (Hamzeh 2004, 6–26; Alagha 2006, 19–35; Saad-Ghorayeb 2002, 7–15; Azani 2009, 47–62). Hizbullah's debut on to the Lebanese political scene in 1984, when a number of small but disparate Islamist Shi`a groups coalesced together, was part and parcel of the protracted rise of the Shi`a community in Lebanon. Hitherto a marginalized community, denied its proper place in the making of the history of those areas later stitched together to form independent Lebanon (Hemadé 2008), and excluded from meaningful political power and representation, the political mobilization of the Shi`a in Lebanon commenced in earnest in the 1960s. Under the leadership of the charismatic and indefatigable Imam Musa al-Sadr, Shi`a political consciousness was transformed from a fatalistic and quietist to an activist, revolutionary one (Ajami 1986; Halawi 1992; Traboulsi 2007, 177–180). A legacy of economic deprivation and political disenfranchisement created the socioeconomic underpinnings for the radical, mass Shi`a politics of the 1980s (Nasr 1985). Moreover the political mobilization caused by modernization processes gave rise to cracks in the feudal and clientelistic structures of authority among the Shi`a, undermining the power of the traditional elite, the *zu`ama*, thus providing radical parties and activist clerics the opportunity to attract young Shi`as—whether on the peripheries of the country or refugees living on the margins of Beirut—to the new ideologies they offered (Norton 1988). This process was exacerbated by Israel's multiple invasions of Lebanon, which created a displaced but politically mobilized Shi`a constituency.

Transnational Shi`a networks and ideologies also played a role in Hizbullah's emergence. Well before the demonstration effect of the Islamic revolution in Iran in 1978–1979 was felt in Lebanon, the holy city of Najaf in Iraq served as a focal point for Shi`a religious students. The religious seminaries in Najaf were undergoing a process of radicalization of Shi`a thought under the leadership of firebrand clerics such as Ayatollah Muhammad Baqer al-Sadr and Ayatollah Khomeini. Young Shi`a students flocked to Najaf for their religious training. For example, when Hassan Nasrallah traveled to Najaf to study under Baqer al-Sadr he became Abbas al-Musawi's protégé.[1] New ideas traveled from the religious seminaries of Najaf to Lebanon via the hundreds of Lebanese Shi`a who, after their expulsion to Lebanon by the Ba`athist Iraqi regime, established the Lebanese counterpart of the Iraqi Da`wah party (Mallat 1988; Saad-Ghorayeb 2002, 13; Ranstorp 1997, 26–27). This Najafi connection, but especially the Najafi experience of many members of the Hizbullah leadership, played a formative role in the party's ideological platform and organizational structure (Ranstorp 1997, 27).

Roschanack Shaery-Eisenlohr (2007) also contends that the contest between two antishah transnational Shi`a networks played an important role in Hizbullah's later emergence. This competition over the religious leadership (*marja`iya*) of the Shi`a community in Lebanon between, on the one hand, Musa al-Sadr and his allies in the antishah Iranian opposition, namely Mostafa Chamran, and, on the other hand, the anti-Sadr group consisting of Khomeini's inner circle composed of Mohammad Montazeri, Jalal al-Din Farsi, and Ali-Akbar Mohtashami, created a fissure within Lebanon's Shi`a community expressed in terms of fidelity to the Palestinians in Lebanon and the Palestinian cause (Shaery-Eisenlohr 2007, 277–279). Sadr, who followed the religious authorities of Najaf and resisted the subordination of Lebanon's Shi`a to Khomeini's authority, saw no contradiction between supporting the Palestinian cause and improving Shi`a political and social conditions in Lebanon. The anti-Sadr group accused its Iranian opponents, Sadr, and his Amal[2] Movement of being anti-Palestinian and nonrevolutionary in their accommodation of the Lebanese confessional system. This transnational cleavage had a profound effect on Shi`a politics in Lebanon after the success of the revolution in Iran, paving the way for Hizbullah's emergence. The centrality of the Palestinian cause in this contest also shaped Hizbullah's future discourse and ideology.

Israel's 1982 invasion of Lebanon was a direct catalyst for Hizbullah's birth. The decision by Amal's leader Nabih Berri to participate, alongside Bashir Gemayel, Israel's Maronite ally and leader of the anti-Palestinian Lebanese Forces, in a National Salvation Committee formed in the wake of the invasion, provoking a schism within the movement. Consequently several key members led by Hussein al-Musawi broke away from Amal and established Islamic Amal (Amal al-Islamiya). This split reflected the aforementioned contest over control of Lebanon's Shi`a community and the respective groups' stances toward the Lebanese political system. Amal's rejection of Khomeini's doctrine of *wilayat al-faqih* accounted for Iran's overt support to Islamic Amal and, subsequently, Hizbullah, as an alternative to Amal's leadership of the Shi`a community and a precursor for the establishment of an alternative *marja`iya* than Najaf's (Shaery-Eiselohr 2008, 108; Abisaab 2009).

Shi`a intrasectarian competition, the security situation in South Lebanon, and a bludgeoned Syria provided the Iranian leadership—keen to export its revolutionary model and enhance its position in the region and the Islamic world—the opportunity to gain a foothold in Lebanon. An earlier proposition in 1980 by the anti-Sadr group in Tehran to send Iranian troops to South Lebanon to fend off Israeli attacks had been rejected by Amal and Chamran (Shaery-Eisenlohr 2007, 279–280). This time, however, with Mohtashami serving as ambassador in Syria, and as part of an Iranian-Syrian military agreement, plus Syria's determination to sabotage attempts by some groups, such as Amal, to improve their relations with the United States, some 1,000 Iranian Revolutionary Guards troops were deployed in June 1982 in Ba'albak via Syria to provide military training and religious indoctrination to an ever-growing group of Amal defectors who espoused the concept of *wilayat al-faqih* (Blanford 2011; Deeb 1988, 697; Norton 1990, 125, 132; Lutfi 2008; Sabra 2009a).[3] The mission of the Revolutionary Guards troops dispatched to Lebanon, according to one of its commanders, was to "propagate the idea that Israel is defeatable" (Shaery-Eiselohr 2008, 110), a motto that would become a regular feature of Hizbullah's discourse on the Arab-Israeli conflict.

The first group of trainees that formed the nucleus of Hizbullah were 180 volunteers—including then twenty-two-year-old Hassan Nasrallah—mostly affiliated with the religious seminary (*al-hawza al-diniya*) formed by Sayyed Abbas al-Musawi, Shaykh Subhi al-Tufaili, and Shaykh Muhammad Yezbek in the village of al-Nabi Sheet in the Eastern Beqa` (Sabra 2009a). To this pioneer group gravitated members of the Lebanese branch of the Da`wah Party, Islamic Amal, the Islamic Revolutionary Committees (al-Lijan al-Thawriya al-Islamiya), the Muslim Youth (al-Shabab al-Muslem), and the Lebanese Union of Muslim Students (al-Ittihad al-Lunbani lil-Talaba al-Muslemin). Two principles were emphasized in the training camps set up by the Revolutionary Guards in the Beqa`: unwavering resistance to Israel and loyalty to the doctrine of *wilayat al-faqih* (Ibid.). Abbas al-Musawi, later elected second secretary-general of Hizbullah, argued that it was necessary to pledge allegiance to the *waliy al-faqih* given that the Lebanese Shi`a lacked what he referred to as an "aware leader" who could confront Israel's actions in Lebanon (Shaery-Eisenlohr 2008, 113). Mohtashami liaised between Tehran and the Musawi-Tufaili-Yezbek cell, after which Musawi traveled to meet Khomeini in Qum, who blessed the creation of the new party. This original group remained shrouded with secrecy and known only by the label Shura Lubnan (Consultative [Council of] Lebanon), until Sayyed Ibrahim Amin al-Sayyed made public the new name of the organization, Hizbullah, in an interview in the Lebanese weekly *al-Shira`* in August 1984 (Sabra 2009a).

BETWEEN *WILAYAT AL-FAQIH* AND THE LEBANESE CONFESSIONAL SYSTEM

No other party's loyalty to Lebanon has been questioned in post-Ta'if and especially post-Syria Lebanon as much as Hizbullah's. Moreover, Western representations of Hizbullah have been mostly negative (Kramer 1987; Ranstorp 1997). Policymakers and academics alike have made extensive use of the "terrorist" label to refer to the party, and since the terrorist attacks of 9/11 several Western governments have placed Hizbullah on terror lists on account of its actual and/or supposed activities in the 1980s and 1990s, its alleged connections to al-Qa`ida (Stern 2003), and its real or imagined global agendas. These accusations serve to essentialize the party as a terrorist group akin to al-Qa`ida and a proxy for the Syrian and Iranian regimes and their geopolitical objectives. Essentialization, in turn, serves to justify state-endorsed violence and mobilizes support for state policies against Hizbullah (Bhatia 2005, 12–15; Harb and Leenders 2005, 174).

Hizbullah's detractors tend to rely primarily, although not solely, on the party's first communiqué, dated February 16, 1985, a document titled "Open Letter to the Downtrodden in Lebanon and the World" (Alagha 2006, 223–238). Though more a manifesto (Hamzeh 2004, 27) than an ideological statement, and largely outdated a mere seven years after its release owing to domestic and regional developments and Hizbullah's own radical transformations, the themes outlined in the letter (Norton 1999, 11–16) and the vitriolic statements it contained are often presented as an accurate representation of Hizbullah's position on a host of issues. This was exacerbated by Hizbullah's failure for the next twenty-five years to release a new and updated document explicating its vision of the world and Lebanon. Consequently, domestic suspicions surrounding Hizbullah's loyalty to Lebanon and its agenda for Lebanon's future have been based largely on its championing of the idea of an Islamic state in its Open Letter, its firm refusal to disavow it, and its leaders' subscription to the doctrine of *wilayat al-faqih*. What, then, is the role of the *wilayat al-faqih* doctrine in Hizbullah's political thought, and how has Hizbullah reconciled it with its Lebanese identity? The clearest answers to these questions have been presented by the deputy secretary-general of Hizbullah, Shaykh Na`im Qassem, in his book on Hizbullah.

According to Qassem, the *wilaya* is "necessary for the preservation and application of Islam, for it is not possible to deal with the large Muslim project via personal initiatives or deeds separated from one another" (2002, 70). Qassem goes on to note that the boundaries specified by *wali al-faqih* take into account the "subjective conditions and particularities of each group or country" (Ibid., 76). Hizbullah's conduct is thus situated within the "orientations and regulations drawn by *wali al-faqih*," while day-to-day political work, social and educational activities, and the struggle against Israel in all its details are the prerogatives of the party's leadership, which is elected by party members according to internal regulations (Ibid.). These powers reflect, according to Qassem, substantial independence in operational performance, entailing no daily follow-up by *wali al-faqih*. Indeed, resort to the *wali* is only necessary when the leadership of the party faces important decisions that could impact performance, such as the decision to participate in the 1992 parliamentary elections in Lebanon (Qassem 2002, 267–273; Saad-Ghorayeb 2002, 67–68; Norton 2007, 100). Qassem is also careful to point out that adherence to the *wilayat al-faqih* doctrine does not limit Hizbullah's circle of domestic activities or the cultivation of various relationships—including regional and international ones (2002, 76–77). Hizbullah's position between the Lebanese state and the *faqih* is described as one that harmonizes the Islamic method with Lebanese citizenship (Ibid., 77).

Qassem's exposition of the *wilayat al-faqih* doctrine is an oblique way to counter the charge that Hizbullah's religious-political ties to Iran render it a proxy serving Tehran's geopolitical interests, and that by accepting the authority of the *faqih* (jurist), Ayatollah Khomeini then Ayatollah Ali Khamenei, Hizbullah has relinquished its operational and decision-making autonomy. The seemingly appealing picture portrayed by Qassem notwithstanding, the overlapping of "pan-Islamic interests"—as defined by the *faqih*—with Lebanese interests, does not resolve the fundamental problem of conflicting *national* interests. After all, one of the main jurisdictions of the *faqih* is decisions pertaining to war and peace, a prerogative that, when combined with Hizbullah's weapons arsenal, infringes on Lebanon's sovereignty, strips the Lebanese Armed Forces (LAF) of its monopoly over legitimate violence, and renders Lebanon an advanced battlefield for Iran's geopolitical conflicts. Nor does Hizbullah's argument that its weapons arsenal is an asset that Lebanon can ill afford to relinquish short of a comprehensive regional settlement pass muster with many sections of Lebanese society—namely, the Sunnis, the Druze, and at least half the Christians—who charge that the party's coercive capabilities serve to ensure the Shi`a a greater share in the balance of sectarian power in post-Syria Lebanon (Salloukh 2009a).

How much is Hizbullah wedded to the doctrine of *wilayat al-faqih* and to the directives of the *faqih* on both ideological and operational issues remains a matter of speculation, however. Nizar Hamzeh is categorical on this issue, contending that the doctrine "is the nerve center of Hizbullah's combined political and religious functions" (2004, 35). On the other hand Amal Saad-Ghorayeb argues that "the *Faqih* only initiates directives on matters that concern the entire *umma*.... But in matters specific to particular states... he awaits a request for his intervention before delivering any rulings" (2002, 68), which suggests that Hizbullah enjoys a wide margin of independent decision making on national issues. Similarly, Shaery-Eisenlohr opines that although it is "junior in position compared to the" *faqih*, Hizbullah "exercises its agency," and Khamenei's rulings are "a product of dialogue" with the party (2008, 209). Nicholas Blanford states that "Iran has a clear understanding of Hezbollah's domestic realities and grants [Hizbullah's secretary-general Sayyed Hassan] Nasrallah autonomy in matters related to Lebanese policy" (2011, 482). Adam Shatz also suggests that "Hizbollah [sic] has long ceased to be an Iranian-controlled militia," and that "Khamenei has never overruled Nasrallah" (2004). Some have even suggested that a number of high-ranking members within Hizbullah, especially the group originally identified with the Lebanese branch of the Da`wa Party, follow Grand Ayatollah Ali al-Sistani's *marja`iya* rather than Khamenei's (Sabra 2009b). Yet other Lebanese observers suggest that although Hizbullah enjoys substantial decision-making autonomy on matters Lebanese, it defers to Tehran on geopolitical issues, especially those pertaining to the Arab-Israeli conflict and the prerequisites of the Iranian-Syrian alliance.[4]

In tandem with its adherence to the *wilayat al-faqih* doctrine and its pan-Islamic religious overtones, Hizbullah has embraced two other nationalisms that have increasingly shaped its leaders' discourse and the party's symbols: Arab and Lebanese nationalism. In Hizbullah's worldview, the Palestinian cause is not only an Islamic cause but also an Arab one. Nasrallah's speeches regularly address Arab concerns, especially the importance of Arab solidarity in confronting Israeli and US designs in the region, but also the responsibility of Arab regimes in helping the Palestinians survive on their land and confront Israel. In the same vein, eager to allay suspicions of loyalty to Iran and its close political, financial, and military ties with Tehran, Hizbullah has fully embraced and even accentuated its Lebanese identity since 1992, when, in addition to its historic decision to participate in parliamentary elections, it reached out to other segments of Lebanese society to build a broader support base (Norton 1999, 34). Even the party's slogan on its flag was altered from the antisystemic *al-Thawra al-Islamiya fi Lubnan* (the Islamic Revolution in Lebanon) to the more accommodating *al-Muqawama al-Islamiya fi Lubnan* (the Islamic Resistance in Lebanon), thus underscoring the party's national allegiances and integration into the Lebanese political system (al-Amin 2009). Similarly, Israel's withdrawal from Lebanon in 2000 and the "divine victory" (*al-nasr al-ilahi*) of 2006 have been portrayed as victories for all Lebanese rather than for the Shi`a sect alone. On the morrow of the 2006 war Hizbullah deployed an array of locutions and visual symbols to reinvent itself as a Lebanese party. Propaganda video clips on the party's *al-Manar* television station make increasing use of Lebanese flags alongside Hizbullah's.

Perhaps the best testaments to Hizbullah's self-reinvention is the fundamental difference between the 1985 Open Letter and its second and much anticipated political manifesto released on November 30, 2009 titled *Al-Wathiqa al-Siyasiya li-Hizbullah* (Hizbullah's Political Document, henceforth *Wathiqa*; Hizbullah 2009). While the Open Letter advocated perpetual militancy within the rigid oppressor/oppressed binary, the *Wathiqa* offers a more nuanced view of the world, the region, and Lebanon, and of Hizbullah's position within each of these systems. Moreover, and unlike the Open Letter, the *Wathiqa* makes no mention of Hizbullah's aspirations to establish an Islamic state in Lebanon.

The *Wathiqa* underscores the centrality of the Palestinian issue in Hizbullah's ideology and worldview, labeling it "the central [and] primary and most important [issue] for Arabs and Muslims" (Ibid., 21). It declares its categorical and nonnegotiable rejection of any settlement or normalization with, and recognition of, Israel and emphasizes the right of return of all Palestinian refugees to their original homes (Ibid., 29–30). This aligns Hizbullah with Iran's geopolitical choices and places the party at odds with the pro-United States, so-called moderate Arab states. Moreover, the *Wathiqa* discusses relations with Iran from the perspective of the latter's support to the Palestinian issue, calling for closer cooperation among Muslim states.

Borrowing from the ideological lexicon of the Left and the anti-globalization movement, the *Wathiqa* describes Hizbullah's resistance as a consequence of US and Israeli hegemonic desires over the region. It describes Israel as a permanent and existential threat to Lebanon due to its aggressive, colonialist, and expansionist nature. Similarly, the United States is derided not only for its imperial abrasiveness and unconditional support for Israel but also for its support of Arab authoritarian regimes and its role in sowing sectarian sedition in the region. It is also accused of deploying the terrorist label as a pretext for spreading its hegemony by criminalizing entire peoples. In a tone reminiscent of the Open Letter, the *Wathiqa* declares that "American terrorism is the root of all terrorism in the world" (Ibid., 8), offering recipes for countering US and Israeli policies. At the center of this counterhegemonic discourse is popular, armed resistance—embodied by Hizbullah's own model—and its pivotal role in deterring the enemy.

Embracing Lebanese identity in no uncertain terms, the crucial section on Lebanon opens with the declaration that "Lebanon is our homeland and the homeland of our fathers and grandfathers, and it is the homeland of our children and grandchildren and all future generations." The *Wathiqa* rejects "any kind of unconcealed or camouflaged divisions [*taqsim*] or federalism," and calls for the establishment of a "strong," "impenetrable," "independent," and "indivisible" Lebanon. However, this Lebanon can only emerge if it has "a just, capable, and strong state" and "a political system that truly represents the will of the people and its aspirations for justice, freedom, security, stability, felicity, and dignity" (Ibid., 12).

Although the *Wathiqa* celebrates Lebanon's religious pluralism, political confessionalism is identified as the fundamental defect of the Lebanese political system and a hindrance to any meaningful reform; it also impedes the establishment of a "correct democracy" (Ibid., 15) where the elected majority rules and the elected minority assumes the opposition. Given the structural defects of the confessional system, and Christian sensitivities toward deconfessionalism, it then follows that consociational democracy is the most practical interim solution because it is "the true embodiment of the spirit of the Constitution and the essence of the pact of national coexistence" (Ibid.). Of course, Hizbullah subscribes to a particular interpretation of Lebanon's consociational democracy. On this post-Doha Agreement[5] view, the main sectarian communities enjoy veto power in the process of government formation and in cabinet decision making in accordance with the preamble of the constitution[6] but at the expense of the voting mechanisms stipulated in article 65 of the constitution.[7] Needless to say, this constitutional interpretation clashes with that of Hizbullah's political opponents, who deny the political system's consociational provisions (Salloukh 2009a; Traboulsi 2009).

Be that as it may, Hizbullah's consociational interpretation of the confessional system anticipates the open-ended mission of the party's military wing (*muqawama*) in deterring any future Israeli aggression. The *Wathiqa* describes the linear trajectory of the party's armed wing "from a liberation force to a confrontational and balance [of power] force and then to a deterrence and defensive force" (2009, 4). On one view, this is Hizbullah's way of describing its metamorphoses from being an ideological-political-security apparatus created by the Iranian regime during the revolution's export phase, to a national liberation movement against the Israeli occupation of South Lebanon in the 1990s, to its role as an elite commando unit in the Iranian-US confrontation after Israel's withdrawal from Lebanon in 2000, to finally mutating into a deterrence force against Israel after the military successes of the 2006 war (al-Zayn 2009; Blanford 2011, 305). This deterrence role extends beyond Lebanon, however, serving Iran's geopolitical confrontation with the United States and, in the preuprising period, Syria's strategy to liberate the occupied Golan Heights.

Janus-Faced Hizbullah: Managing Domestic and External Challenges

For an organization born with a mission to resist Israel, Hizbullah's integration into Lebanese politics has been a gradual and sometimes challenging process. Hamzeh dates the party's shift from the militant mode of the 1980s to its "gradualist pragmatism" phase to 1989 (2004, 108–110). This was a result of the victory of the pragmatists over the militants in two overlapping transnational contests: the first pitting Ali-Akbar Hashimi Rafsanjani's group against the militants led by Mohtashami and Shaykh Hasan Kharoubi in Iran, and the second inside Hizbullah's clerical leadership pitting the pragmatic camp led by Abbas al-Musawi and Nasrallah against the militant camp gathered around Tufaili and Hussein al-Musawi. The pragmatist camp, representing the majority of the party's rank and file, favored a gradual route toward establishing an Islamic order in Lebanon, to the objections of the militants who argued for a strategy based on radical and perpetual militancy (Ibid., 110; Abisaab 2009, 232).

Hizbullah's integration into the Lebanese political arena has hitherto passed through three distinct phases (Bayram 2009). The first, and most controversial, phase opens in 1982 with the party's founding. Hizbullah is accused of having carried out a number of terrorist attacks during this phase, under the guise of different organizations and labels, namely Islamic jihad (Hamzeh 2004, 85–86).[8] This militant phase ends with the victory of the pragmatist camp in 1989, though its practical manifestation was only felt with the leadership change from Tufaili to Abbas al-Musawi in May 1991, and the subsequent decision to contest the 1992 parliamentary elections.

During the second phase (1992–2005) Hizbullah accommodated itself to Syria's almost total control of Lebanon after October 1990. The party overlooked the massacre perpetrated on February 24, 1987 by Syrian troops against Hizbullah members in the Fathalla barracks (AbuKhalil 1990, 15), shelved aside its earlier rejection of the Ta'if Accord (Norton 1990, 135), and accepted the postwar division of roles imposed by Damascus on the Shi`a community, by which Hizbullah was granted monopoly over the armed resistance against Israel (Traboulsi 2007, 230), while Berri's Amal Movement controlled the Shi`a share of Lebanon's confessional and neopatrimonial political system (Harb 2007, 13). Indeed, Hizbullah demonstrated a surprising degree of political accommodation during this phase, entering into counterintuitive cross-ideological and cross-sectarian electoral alliances (Hamzeh 1993; Hamzeh 2004, 112–135; Salloukh 2006).

It was also during this second phase that Hizbullah cemented its relation to its followers by developing a complex corporatist institutional structure penetrating Shi`a communities in the south, the Ba`albak-Hermel region in the Beqa`, and Beirut's southern suburbs (Hamzeh 2004, 44–79; Harik 2004, 81–94). This was achieved through an intricate web of institutions and units, mapped out in Table 33.1, providing support in various spheres, ranging from the reconstruction of houses destroyed in multiple wars with Israel, the provision of financial support and social services to the families of injured and "martyred" Hizbullah fighters, and the provision of health and educational services to the public, to the production of nonmaterial symbolic capital targeted at the party's constituency. Marketed by Hizbullah's ideologues as a part of the decision to integrate into the very confessional system they had vehemently

Table 33.1 The Major Organizations and Units Comprising Hizbullah's Institutional Infrastructure, by Sphere of Activity.

Organization/Unit	Sphere
Jihad al-Bina' (Holy Struggle for Construction)	Reconstruction
Mu'assasat al-Shahid (Martyrs Foundation)	Financial support and social services
Mu'assasat al-Jarha (Foundation for the Wounded)	Financial support and social services
Jam'iyat al-Imdad al-Khayriya al-Islamiya (Islamic Charitable Imdad Association)	Charity (financial support, education, and other services)
Madares al-Imdad (Al-Imdad Schools)	Education
Al-Hay'a al-Sahiya al-Islamiya (The Islamic Health Unit)	Health services (hospitals, health centers, dispensaries, dental clinics, etc.)
Al-Ta`bi'a al-Tarbawiya (The Educational Mobilization Unit)	Educational services, educational financial support, and youth mobilization
Madares al-Mahdi (Al-Mahdi Schools)	Education
Madares al-Mustafa (Al-Mustafa Schools)	Education
Al-Manar Television	Media
Al-Nour Radio Station	Media
Al-Intiqad (previously *al-`Ahd*) Weekly Paper	Media
Al-Markaz al-Istishari lil-Dirasaat wal-Tawthiq (The Consultative Center for Studies and Documentation)	Research

Source: Various Hizbullah organizations' websites.

rejected (Qassem 2002, 112), this corporatist structure amounted to a veritable shadow state, and served as an agent of political recruitment, indoctrination, control, and integrated mobilization of the Shi`a community (Hamzeh 2004; Le Thomas 2010). It is financed by funds funneled to Hizbullah from Iran, especially Iranian religious endowments (*bonyads*), plus the party's own charities and businesses (Blanford 2009). While no concrete data are available on the amount of Iranian funding the party receives each year, US government estimates have placed it in the range of $100–200 million a year (Slavin 2008, 9).

In addition to its successful resistance record, Hizbullah's elaborate institutional network has enabled it to win over the loyalty of a substantial section of the Shi`a community (Harik 2004). However, Iranian support has exposed the party to charges that it is a mere tool of Tehran's geopolitical interests and that Hizbullah has created an alien, post-revolutionary Iran-styled Shi`a Islamic society in Lebanon (Sharara 1996). Undoubtedly, Iranian support for Hizbullah has been instrumental in sustaining the holistic network of institutions charged with producing and disseminating the norms and symbols mobilizing the party's followers and producing the "resistance society" (*mujtama` al-muqawama*; Qassem 2008) that serves to consolidate the foundations of a desired "Islamic sphere" (*al-hala al-islamiya*; Qassem 2002, 16), thus guaranteeing Hizbullah a high level of communal hegemony (Harb and Leenders 2005). This has introduced some new norms and everyday practices that may appear unfamiliar to earlier generations of Lebanese Shi`as (Qasir

2010). However, as Harb and Leenders suggest, the new society Hizbullah has sought to organize is a consequence of the party's efforts "to reconcile its Islamist agenda with a form of Lebanese nationalism" (2005, 178–179) grounded in national contexts and negotiated through local institutions, providing Hizbullah a substantial level of embeddedness and legitimacy within the Shi`a community. Nor should transnational networks serve to obfuscate the emergence of new nationalisms and modern but religious local identities (Deeb 2006). Shaery-Eisenlohr demonstrates persuasively how, because they are context sensitive and "reconfigured in articulation with local sociopolitical and economic realities and interests" (2008, 10), Hizbullah's and other Lebanese Shi`a actors' transnational relations with Iran "have helped articulate new Shi`ite-centered Lebanese national narratives" (Ibid., 2). In turn, these polyphonic Shi`a narratives of the Lebanese nation challenge the dominant Maronite and Sunni imaginaries of Lebanese nationalism and their concomitant balance of sectarian power relations.

The third phase of Hizbullah's domestic integration commenced with Hariri's assassination in 2005 and Syria's subsequent withdrawal from Lebanon. Hizbullah's immediate reaction to the domestic sea changes unleashed by Hariri's assassination was to resolve to participate directly in government affairs, joining Prime Minister Fu'ad al-Siniora's cabinet of July 19, 2005, and signaling its determination to represent, alongside Berri, Shi`a political interests in state institutions. Nasrallah was now occupied with the nimble footwork of Lebanese politics, and the party found itself in the throes of an overlapping domestic and regional contest over post-Syria Lebanon (Salloukh 2009a; Wiegand 2009).

Although presented as a political contest between multisectarian political blocs—the March 14 alliance and the March 8 opposition—over different visions of Lebanon's domestic and foreign politics, this was a crude sectarian power struggle over who rules the post-Syria Lebanese state. It overlapped with a wider regional geopolitical contest pitting Iran and Syria against the United States and its allies among the so-called moderate Arab states, namely, Saudi Arabia, Egypt, Jordan, and the United Arab Emirates. For the next four years Hizbullah felt besieged by forces that sought to contain or paralyze its political and military capabilities either via an external military confrontation such as the 2006 war, the international justice of the United Nations (UN) Special Tribunal for Lebanon investigating Hariri's assassination, or the incrementally aggressive policies of the Saniora government, backed by its international allies and protected by the threat of a Sunni-Shi`a sectarian civil war, Hizbullah's worst nightmare. The violent takeover of West Beirut on the morrow of the Saniora government's May 5, 2008 decision to consider Hizbullah's clandestine telecommunications network illegal and replace a pro-Hizbullah airport security chief was a response to these concentric juggernauts. The promulgation of the Doha Agreement on May 21, 2008 ended the political stalemate in the country and announced Hizbullah's definitive integration into and acceptance of the Lebanese confessional political system. As mentioned, this hinged on two provisos, however, recognizing the system's consociational nature and accepting the open-ended, deterrence function of Hizbullah's weapons arsenal (Bayram 2009; al-Zayn 2009). Syria's descent to civil war reanimated Lebanon's overlapping contests and placed Hizbullah in a difficult position. Hizbullah's open support of Bashar al-Assad's regime—as the latter attempts to crush what started as a genuine democratic uprising but mutated into an all-out geopolitical struggle for Syria—undermined the party's transnational appeal and its credentials as an Islamist organization resisting injustice and oppression. At a time of a growing sectarianization of the region, and with Hizbullah condemning the Bahraini Sunni regime's violent clampdown against the kingdom's Shi`a majority, the party finds itself accused of supporting a minority `Alawi regime suppressing the demands of Syria's Sunni majority. This has exacerbated sectarian tensions in Lebanon and, consequently, jeopardized Hizbullah's immediate security environment.

Hizbullah's hybrid political-military and domestic-regional nature (ICG 2003) has meant that the aforementioned domestic phases have approximate external parallels. On the morrow of Israel's 1982 invasion of Lebanon Hizbullah gradually emerged as the dominant resistance to the occupation. Hizbullah suicide attacks against Israeli forces in South Lebanon exposed Israel's vulnerability to a new method of resistance far deadlier than those deployed in the past, and just as importantly, more difficult to foil. This dilemma was not restricted to suicide bombings; it became the main feature of Israel's decades-long struggle against Hizbullah's armed activities, with catastrophic consequences for broad segments of the Lebanese population, who often became the target of deliberate attacks aimed at forcing Hizbullah to halt its activities. Notwithstanding the indiscriminate violence against civilian targets and the Iron Fist policy that was adopted by Israel in response to Hizbullah's resistance activities, this period was marked by an increasing pace of attacks against both the Israeli Defense Forces (IDF) and its proxy militia, the South Lebanon Army (SLA). Although they were typically small scale and did not exact large numbers of casualties, their combined effect was the steady demoralization of the IDF and SLA (Blanford 2011; Zisser 2006, 87).

Syria's control over Lebanon after 1990 raised the dangerous prospect of disarmament to which the party responded in 1991 with a political and public relations campaign that elicited an official recognition of its resistance role and sanctioned its weapons arsenal (Azani 2009, 91, 150–151). However, this campaign would not have succeeded absent the pivotal role Hizbullah's resistance was playing in Syria's own geopolitical interests. Thus, while contributing to the objective of liberating occupied Lebanese territories, Hizbullah's activities in the period stretching from 1993 and 2000 were intricately linked to Syria's geopolitical strategy vis-à-vis Israel and the peace process (Salloukh 2005).

On May 24, 2000, with the last Israeli tanks rolling out of Lebanon, Hizbullah's eighteen-year struggle for the liberation of South Lebanon appeared to have ended. Hailed by Hizbullah as an unprecedented victory in the Arab-Israeli conflict, the withdrawal nevertheless presented the party with significant challenges. It stripped it of its raison d'être, namely resisting Israel's occupation. In effect, Hizbullah became what the International Crisis Group aptly labeled "a rebel without a cause" (2003). Hizbullah argued that the total liberation of Lebanon had not been achieved due to the continued presence of Israeli forces in the Sheb`a Farms, a thin strip of land that Israel and the UN consider to be part of the Golan Heights, but considered by Syria and Lebanon to be part of Lebanon. These justifications failed to convince many Lebanese, who viewed Hizbullah's weapons arsenal as deployed at the service of Syria's regional interests and, increasingly, Iran's, geopolitical ambitions (Salloukh 2005).

The Israeli withdrawal from Lebanon in May 2000 and Bashar al-Assad's assumption of power shortly thereafter heralded a new phase for Hizbullah with Syria. It transformed this relationship from one in which Syria exerted tremendous leverage over the party to one in which the two interacted as rough equals and cooperated in pursuit of their mutual interests (Blanford 2011, 312). This newly established partnership experienced and weathered its first test in 2004 with the passage of UN Security Council Resolution 1559, followed by Hariri's assassination, subjecting Syria to enormous popular and international pressure to withdraw its forces from Lebanon. The mounting pressures on both Hizbullah and Syria, especially after 2005, fortified rather than weakened the close partnership between the two. Indeed, Damascus outsourced its Lebanon policy to Hizbullah (Salloukh 2009b). Equally important, and in tandem with this radical makeover in the Hizbullah-Syria relationship, Hizbullah became embroiled in the US-Iranian geopolitical confrontation in the region. Since 2005 Hizbullah has firmly entrenched one foot in Lebanon and has gained a political and military foothold in the geopolitical struggles over the region, juggling intricately, but often dangerously, domestic and regional threats, interests, opportunities, and relations.

Hizbullah's July–August 2006 war against Israel demonstrated the extent of the professionalization of Hizbullah's fighting force and the party's painstaking efforts since 2000 at preparing, on all levels, for a future confrontation with Israel (Blanford 2011; Harel and Issacharoff 2008). Resistance tactics were supplanted with a new doctrine in tune with new geopolitical and technological realities. This new doctrine presented a form of hybrid warfare that blended Hizbullah's unique "brand" of disciplined irregular warfare with an impressive conventional arsenal (Hoffman 2009, 37). Hizbullah's new military doctrine is unique in a number of ways. The weapons at the disposal of Hizbullah fighters differ greatly from those available to other guerrilla forces; the updated arsenal, which remained largely unanticipated by Hizbullah's enemies until and even throughout the July–August 2006 war, provided it with important strategic and tactical gains compared to the pre-2000 period. Moreover, Hizbullah's highly disciplined, motivated, and well-trained fighting units—a hybrid of guerrillas and regular troops—functioned in a semiautonomous capacity, enjoying a large degree of freedom in operational decisions while remaining in constant touch with senior commanders through a secret communications network (Ibid.). Hizbullah's ability to survive the July–August 2006 war and emerge from its ruins with declarations of a "divine victory" gave its weapons a new lease on life, although not one that went unchallenged. From then on, it added to the Sheb`a Farms pretext the argument that its long experience in fighting Israel and its proven record of defeating it, first in 2000 and again in 2006, combined with the underdeveloped capabilities of the LAF and Lebanon's inability to withstand future Israeli aggressions, meant that the country could ill afford to disarm Hizbullah. Unexpectedly "the rebel," to quote Reinoud Leenders, had "regained his cause" (2006).

Mutual deterrence, or the "balance of terror," between Hizbullah and Israel has rendered intelligence activities all the more attractive as an alternative form and arena of warfare. The assassination in Damascus of Hizbullah's military mastermind Imad Mughniyé on February 12, 2008 and Hizbullah's clear but open-ended vow for revenge are part and parcel of the new struggle between Israel and Hizbullah. The Israeli spy networks uncovered in Lebanon since the 2006 war—some of which operated inside Beirut's southern suburbs, Hizbullah's security backyard—are also reflective of this ongoing intelligence warfare (Bayram 2010). The increasingly cohesive relationship between Hizbullah and Iran, and the additional deterrence and danger it brings to Hizbullah, are bound to fuel further this intelligence warfare, although one that does not preclude another armed conflagration.

Conclusion

Hizbullah's conditional acceptance of the Lebanese confessional system is in many ways a return to the reformist principles Musa al-Sadr advocated in the late 1960s and 1970s. The party whose Iranian ideologues had rejected Sadr's accommodation of Lebanese nationalism and the country's confessional system now finds itself the guardian of Shi`a sectarian rights within this system. But this has not come at the expense of Hizbullah's ideological affiliation with Iran, or its weapons arsenal and geopolitical alliances. The party has found a new calling for its weapons, namely the deterrence of a potential future Israeli attack against Lebanon or Hizbullah's regional allies. This open-ended national and geopolitical military vocation elicits the opposition of a substantial sector of Lebanese society, including many Shi`as, as well as Hizbullah's regional and international opponents. Whether or not Hizbullah's weapons arsenal can deter such an attack remains to be proven. The party's military involvement in Syria risks exposing it to a potential confrontation on three simultaneous fronts – against Israel in the south of the country, Salafi-jihadi groups in Syria, and domestic groups in Lebanon. In the meantime, the party is preparing assiduously for "the next war" against Israel (Saab and Blanford 2011) while hoping that it will not transpire.

Notes

1. See the special report on Nasrallah in *al-Diyar*, March 19, 2010.
2. Acronym for *Afwaj al-Muqawama al-Lubnaniya*, the Lebanese Resistance Brigades.
3. Mohtashami recounts that after the 1982 Israeli invasion of Lebanon Khomeini decided to halt the airlifting of Revolutionary Guards and Basij troops to Syria and Lebanon because they were bound to face logistical difficulties, and instead resolved to "train Shi`a youth in Lebanon, and this is how Hizbullah was born" (Lutfi 2008).
4. Salloukh interviews with Lebanese political analysts, Beirut, January 2010.
5. The Doha Agreement was signed in Doha, Qatar on May 21, 2008. It put an end to Hizbullah's military takeover of Beirut and settled the three-year-long political crisis in the country. It called for the election of a compromise candidate, then army commander Michel Suleiman, president, and the formation of a national unity government, one in which the opposition possessed veto power (Salloukh 2009a, 145–146).
6. The preamble of the Ta'if Accord reads: "Illegitimate is the authority that negates the covenant of mutual coexistence" (Salloukh 2009a, 148).
7. According to article 65 of the constitution, decisions in the cabinet are made in a consensual manner. If a consensus proves elusive then decisions are taken by a majority vote. Important topics, however, require a difficult two-thirds vote to pass in the cabinet.
8. The attacks attributed to Hizbullah are the April 1983 bombing of the US Embassy in Beirut, the October 1983 bombing of the Marine Barracks, the 1985 hijacking of a TWA flight, and the kidnappings of a number of foreigners. Shatz contends that although Islamic Jihad claimed responsibility for these attacks, the group "shared many of the same leaders as Hezbollah," giving rise to US allegations that it was merely a cover for Hizbullah's shadowy military wing (2004). Hizbullah is also charged with the March 17, 1992 bombing of the Israeli Embassy and the July 18, 1994 bombing of a Jewish community center in Buenos Aires, both in retaliation to Israel's assassination of Abbas al-Musawi on February 16, 1992. Upon Musawi's assassination the party elected Hassan Nasrallah as its third secretary general.

References

Abisaab, Rula Jurdi. 2009. Lebanese Shi`ites and the Marja`iyya: Polemic in the Late Twentieth Century. *British Journal of Middle Eastern Studies* 36, no. 2: 215–239.

AbuKhalil, As`ad. 1990. Syria and the Shiites: Al-Asad's Policy in Lebanon. *Third World Quarterly* 12, no. 2: 1–20.

Ajami, Fouad. 1986. *The Vanished Imam: Musa al-Sadr and the Shia of Lebanon*. Ithaca: Cornell University Press.

Alagha, Joseph Elie. 2006. *The Shifts in Hizbullah's Ideology: Religious Ideology, Political Ideology, and Political Program*. Amsterdam: Amsterdam University Press.

al-Amin, Ibrahim. 2009. Wathiqat Hizbullah: Tarakum `Aqdayn min al-Mumarasa [Hizbullah's Document: The Accumulation of Two Decades of Practice]. *al-Akhbar*, December 1: 3.

Azani, Eitan. 2009. *Hezbollah: The Story of the Party of God*. New York: Palgrave Macmillan.

Bayram, Ibrahim. 2009. Hizbullah fi Sana [Hizbullah in a Year]. *al-Nahar*, December 31: 4.

Bayram, Ibrahim. 2010. Al-Harb al-Amniya al-Makhfiya Bayna Isra'il wal-Muqawama: Nazrat Hizballah Ila al-Ab`ad wal-Ahdaf wa-Ayna al-Masrah? [The Hidden Security War Between Israel and the Resistance: Hizbullah's Outlook on the Dimensions and Objectives, and Where Is the Stage?] *al-Nahar*, February 18: 13.

Bhatia, Michael V. 2005. Fighting Words: Naming Terrorists, Bandits, Rebels and Other Violent Actors. *Third World Quarterly* 26, no. 1: 5–22.

Blanford, Nicholas. 2009. Will Iran's Political Turmoil Shake Hezbollah? *Christian Science Monitor*, July 20: 6.

Blanford, Nicholas. 2011. *Warriors of God: Inside Hezbollah's Thirty-Year Struggle Against Israel*. New York: Random House.

Deeb, Lara. 2006. *An Enchanted Modern: Gender and Public Piety in Shi`i Lebanon*. Princeton: Princeton University Press.

Deeb, Marius. 1988. Shia Movements in Lebanon: Their formation, ideology, social basis, and links with Iran and Syria. *Third World Quarterly* 10, no. 2: 683–698.

Halawi, Majed. 1992. *A Lebanon Defied: Musa al-Sadr and the Shi`a Community*. Boulder: Westview Press.

Hamzeh, A. Nizar. 1993. Lebanon's Hizbullah: From Islamic Revolution to Parliamentary Accommodation. *Third World Quarterly* 14, no. 2: 321–337.

Hamzeh, A. Nizar. 2004. *In The Path of Hizbullah*. Syracuse: Syracuse University Press.

Harb, Mona, and Reinoud Leenders. 2005. Know Thy Enemy: Hizbullah, "Terrorism" and the Politics of Perception. *Third World Quarterly* 26, no. 1: 173–197.

Harb, Mona. 2007. Deconstructing Hizballah and Its Suburb. *Middle East Report* 242 (spring): 12–17.

Harel, Amos, and Avi Issacharoff. 2008. *34 Days: Israel, Hezbollah, and the War in Lebanon*. New York: Palgrave Macmillan.

Harik, Judith Palmer. 2004. *Hezbollah: The Changing Face of Terrorism*. London: I.B. Tauris.

Hemadé, Sa'doun. 2008. *Tarikh al-Shi`a fi Lubnan* [The History of the Shi`a in Lebanon]. 2 vols. Beirut: Dar al-Khayal.

Hizbullah. 2009. *Al-Wathiqa al-Siyasiya li-Hizbullah* [Hizbullah's Political Document]. Beirut.

Hoffman, Frank G. 2009. Hybrid Warfare and Challenges. *Joint Forces Quarterly* 52 (First Quarter), http://www.ndu.edu/inss/Press/jfq_pages/editions/i52/9.pdf (accessed January 2010).

International Crisis Group. 2003. Hizbollah: Rebel without A Cause? July 30, http://www.crisisgroup.org/home/getfile.cfm?id=507&tid=1828&l=1 (accessed July 2003).

Kramer, Martin. 1987. *The Moral Logic of Hizbullah*. Tel Aviv University: The Shiloah Institute.

Le Thomas, Catherine. 2010. Socialization Agencies and Party Dynamics: Functions and Uses of Hizballah Schools in Lebanon. In *Returning to Political Parties? Partisan Logic and Political Transformations in the Arab World*, ed. Myriam Catusse and Karam Karam, 217–249. Beirut: Lebanese Center for Policy Studies.

Leenders, Reinoud. 2006. How the Rebel Regained His Cause: Hizbullah & the Sixth Arab-Israeli War. *MIT Electronic Journal of Middle East Studies* 6 (summer): 38–56.

Lutfi, Manal. 2008. Akhtari : Hizbullah wa Hamas wa-l-Jihad Abna' Shar'iyun lil-Thawra al-Iraniya [Akhtari: Hizbullah and Hamas and the Jihad Are the Legitimate Children of the Iranian Revolution]. *Al-Sharq al-Awsat*, May 14, http://www.asharqalawsat.com/print. asp?did=470671 (accessed May 16, 2008).

Mallat, Chibli. 1988. *Aspects of Shi'i Thought from the South of Lebanon*. Oxford: Centre for Lebanese Studies.

Nasr, Salim. 1985. Roots of the Shi'i Movement. *MERIP Reports* 133: 10–16.

Norton, Augustus Richard. 1988. *Amal and the Shi'a: Struggle for the Soul of Lebanon*. Austin: University of Texas Press.

Norton, Augustus Richard. 1990. Lebanon: The Internal Conflict and the Iranian Connection. In *The Iranian Revolution: Its Global Impact*, ed. John L. Esposito, 116–137. Miami: Florida International University Press.

Norton, Augustus Richard. 1999. *Hizballah of Lebanon: Extremist Ideals vs. Mundane Politics*. New York: Council on Foreign Relations.

Norton, Augustus Richard. 2007. *Hezbollah: A Short History*. Princeton: Princeton University Press.

Qasir, Qassem. 2010. Hakatha Yahdur al-Imam al-Mahdi fi-l-Dahiya [This Is How the Imam Mahdi Appears in Beirut's Southern Suburb]. *al-Nahar*, March 24: 9.

Qassem, Na'im. 2002. *Hizbullah: al-Manhaj. al-Tajriba. al-Mustaqbal* [Hizbullah: The Method. The Experience. The Future]. Beirut: Dar al-Hadi.

Qassem, Na'im. 2008. *Mujtama' al-Muqawama: Iradat al-Shahada wa Sina'at al-Intisar* [Society of the Resistance: The Will for Martyrdom and the Making of Victory]. Beirut: Ma'had al-Ma'aref al-Hikmiya.

Ranstorp, Magnus. 1997. *HizbAllah in Lebanon: The Politics of the Western Hostage Crisis*. New York: St. Martin's Press.

Saab, Bilal Y., and Nicholas Blanford. 2011. The Next War: How Another Conflict between Hizballah and Israel Could Look and How Both Sides Are Preparing for It. Analysis Paper 24. Washington: The Saban Center at Brookings.

Saad-Ghorayeb, Amal. 2002. *Hizbullah: Politics and Religion*. London: Pluto Press.

Sabra, Hasan. 2009a. Hizb al-Da'wa Sharik Nasrallah fi Hizbullah [Hizb al-Da'wa Is Nasrallah's Partner in Hizbullah]. *al-Shira'*, no. 1412 (October 17, 2009), http://alshiraa.com/details. php?id=1653 (accessed October 28, 2009).

Sabra, Hasan. 2009b. Marakez Quwa Dakhel Hizbullah li-'Azel Nasrallah ? [Centers of Power inside Hizbullah to Isolate Nasrallah?] *al-Shira'*, no. 1413. October 23, 2009, http://alshiraa. com/details.php?id=1715 (accessed October 28, 2009).

Salloukh, Bassel F. 2005. Syria and Lebanon: A Brotherhood Transformed. *Middle East Report* 236: 14–21.

Salloukh, Bassel F. 2006. The Limits of Electoral Engineering in Divided Societies: Elections in Postwar Lebanon. *Canadian Journal of Political Science* 39, no. 3: 635–655.

Salloukh, Bassel F. 2009a. Democracy in Lebanon: The Primacy of the Sectarian System. In *The Struggle for Democracy in the Middle East*, ed. Nathan Brown and Emad El-Din Shahin, 134–150. London: Routledge Press.

Salloukh, Bassel F. 2009b. Demystifying Syrian Foreign Policy under Bashar. In *Demystifying Syria*, ed. Fred Lawson, 159–179. London: Saqi Books.

Shaery-Eisenlohr, Roschanack. 2007. Postrevolutionary Iran and Shi`i Lebanon: Contested Histories of Shi`i Transnationalism. *International Journal of Middle East Studies* 39, no. 2: 271–289.

Shaery-Eisenlohr, Roschanack. 2008. *Shi`ite Lebanon: Transnational Religion and the Making of National Identities*. New York: Columbia University Press.

Sharara, Waddah. 1996. *Dawlat "Hizbullah": Lubnan Mujtama`an Islamiyan* [Hizbullah's State: Lebanon as an Islamic Society]. Beirut: Dar al-Nahar lil-Nashr.

Shatz, Adam. 2004. In Search of Hezbollah. *The New York Review of Books* 51, no. 7 (April 29), http://www.nybooks.com/articles/17060 (accessed November 2009).

Slavin, Barbara. 2008. *Mullahs, Money, and Militias: How Iran Exerts Its influence in the Middle East*. United States Institute of Peace Special Report 206 (June), http://www.usip.org/files/resources/sr206.pdf (accessed January 2010).

Stern, Jessica. 2003. The Protean Enemy. *Foreign Affairs* 82, no. 4 (July–August): 27–40.

Traboulsi, Fawwaz. 2007. *A History of Modern Lebanon*. London: Pluto Press.

Traboulsi, Fawwaz. 2009. Wathiqat "Hizbullah": Hal "al-Nizam" min al-Iman? [Hizbullah's Document: Is the System a Branch of Belief?] *al-Safir*, December 2: 1 & 6.

Wiegand, Krista E. 2009. Reformation of a Terrorist Group: Hezbollah as a Lebanese Political Party. *Studies in Conflict & Terrorism* 32, no. 8: 669–680.

al-Zayn, Jihad. 2009. Qira'a la Munaqasha li-"Hizbullah" Muwathiqan [Interpreting, Not Deliberating, Hizbullah as Documenter]. *al-Nahar*, December 3: 9.

Zisser, Eyal. 2006. Hizballah and Israel: Strategic Threat on the Northern Border. *Israel Affairs* 12, no. 1 (January): 86–106.

CHAPTER 34

ISLAMIC MOVEMENTS IN ALGERIA, MOROCCO, AND TUNISIA

MICHAEL J. WILLIS

THE states of the central Maghreb—Algeria, Tunisia, and Morocco—represent some of the most prominent and important case studies of Islamic movements' involvement in political processes. Islamic movements began to compete in elections in the late 1980s, rapidly emerging as the largest opposition force in all three states and ultimately dominating elections. In 1991 the Islamic Salvation Front, or FIS (Front Islamique du Salut), came close to winning a comprehensive majority in the National Assembly in Algeria. In Tunisia and Morocco, Islamic parties emerged as the largest forces in national parliaments elected in the autumn of 2011 and thus entered government for the first time as dominant parties in ruling coalitions.

Islamic movements did not play a direct formal role in the political processes of the three states in the immediate aftermath of their achievement of independence from French colonial control in the 1950s and 1960s. Organizations inspired by the *Salafiya* reform movement of the late nineteenth and early twentieth centuries had played a significant role in the nationalist movements of all three countries but had been effectively subsumed within the main nationalist organizations during the struggles for independence. Independent Islamic associations only began to appear again at the very end of the 1960s and were mostly small and apolitical. The closed nature of the political systems in the region in that period, with Algeria and Tunisia under single-party rule and the Moroccan monarchy having suspended the kingdom's constitution and parliament in 1965, meant that there were few avenues for political participation even for those Islamic organizations interested in involving themselves in formal politics. The regimes in all three states did, however, tolerate and even gently encourage the growth of these groups, particularly on the university campuses, in the early 1970s as counterbalances to the bigger perceived threat of the political Left.

Islamic movements grew steadily across the region throughout the 1970s as the appeal of the groups spread out from the initial core of figures who had been primarily concerned about the perceived secularist drift of the states in the 1960s to encompass a wider section of the population. This was particularly the case for those who had become increasingly disillusioned by the continued exclusion of the ordinary population from political decision making in the states, especially when social and economic conditions began to deteriorate as stagnant economies failed to keep pace with the rapid population growth experienced in the decades that followed independence.

As social and economic and ultimately political pressures mounted in the three states, the ruling elites were progressively persuaded of the need to open up their tightly controlled political systems to other groups, at least symbolically, to relieve some of these pressures that from the late 1970s had begun to find their expression in sporadic but often serious outbreaks of social unrest and protest. Islamic movements took advantage of these developments in all three states to try to participate in formal political processes.

The Venture into Electoral Politics: Tunisia and Algeria

The decision in 1981 by Tunisia's aging president, Habib Bourguiba, to allow the legalization of political parties other than his ruling PSD (Parti Socialiste Destourien) led the country's main and hitherto clandestine Islamic movement—the Islamic Group (al-Jama`a al-Islamiya)—to organize a press conference in June of that year to announce its intention to form a legal political party—the Islamic Tendency Movement (Harakat al-Ittijah al-Islami) usually referred to by its French acronym: MTI (Mouvement de la Tendance Islamique). The regime, however, only allowed the legalization of small, tame, and unthreatening parties and the proposed new party was not only refused legalization by the Tunisian authorities but had its leaders arrested and imprisoned for having formed an illegal organization, spread false news, and defamed the president (Shahin 1997, 85–87). A second and more promising opening occurred at the end of the decade when Bourguiba's successor, Zine al-`Abidin Ben `Ali, released the imprisoned MTI leadership, met with the movement's leadership, and invited the movement to join other opposition forces to discussions for the creation in 1988 of a national pact with the regime to establish a more genuinely pluralistic party political system.

The following year, in 1989, the Algerian regime also decided to open up the Algerian political system to forces beyond the ruling FLN (Front de Libération Nationale) with a new constitution introduced in February that allowed for the formation of "organizations of a political character" following an unprecedented and extended period of serious social unrest the previous October. In response to this development, the leaders of Algeria's much more ideologically and organizationally diverse Islamic movement met to discuss the formation of an Islamic political party. No unanimity was achieved on the question but a number of key figures were persuaded and formally created a political party—the FIS—in March 1989. Those senior figures that declined to join the party were motivated by a combination of ideological and personal considerations but, perhaps most importantly, a concern that the opening could prove—like that in Tunisia in 1981—to be a trap for the Islamic movement (Willis 1997, 115–118). Although there had been much greater agreement among the founders of the MTI in Tunisia to enter politics, the decision had similarly not been unanimous and several factions of the movement left it in the run-up to and following the decision to establish the MTI. Those that joined the MTI and the FIS were, though, convinced that the formation of a political party and participation in elections would serve the ends of the movement.

The decision to form a political party was not, however, a guarantee of entry into the political process since every political party had to apply for legal recognition from the state. The Law on Political Parties in both Tunisia and Algeria appeared to exclude the possibility of the legalization of Islamist political parties. In Algeria "sectarian practice" and parties based on "an exclusively confessional basis" were ruled out while in Tunisia, the law stated that "no party is entitled to make reference, either in its principles, its objectives, its action or its program, to religion, to language, to race or to region" (Willis 1997, 119; Hermassi 1991, 199). In Tunisia, the MTI tried to adapt to these provisions and formally changed its name to the al-Nahdah (Renaissance) Party in 1989. By contrast, the FIS made no changes to its program or its title and received formal recognition as a legal party in September 1989. The Algerian president, Chadli Benjedid, was able to justify the seeming exception given to the FIS by emphasizing that the FIS was not "exclusively" confessional. In reality, the party's recognition was due more to political rather than legal factors. In the few short months since its formation the FIS had grown rapidly in terms of popular support and there were concerns within the Algerian regime that a refusal to grant recognition to the party would lead to renewed social unrest, particularly given the popularity the new party seemed to be attracting among the poor urban youth, who had been at the forefront of the protests and demonstrations of October 1988. President Chadli and his allies also hoped that a legalized FIS would serve as a counterbalance to the FLN, which had come to be dominated by enemies to the president and his program of economic reform that he had begun to introduce earlier in the decade (Willis 1997, 118–121; Roberts 1994).

The political openings in both Tunisia and Algeria led to the countries' first real multiparty elections in which the al-Nahdah Party and the FIS made significant impacts. In Tunisia, the al-Nahdah Party had still not received official recognition as a legal political party by the time of the national legislative elections of April 1989. Initially indicating that it would not vigorously contest the election in order not to create problems, al-Nahdah, under pressure from its base, ran members as independent candidates who performed very well—finishing second to the ruling party, outpolling all the other opposition parties, and recording impressive shares of the vote in many of Tunisia's main cities (Hermassi 1991, 200–201). In Algeria the performance of the FIS was even more impressive, with the party totally dominating regional (*wilaya*) and commune elections in June 1990, receiving well over half of the votes cast, and winning control of the majority of councils at both levels.

The strength of their electoral performances fully positioned the two Islamist parties as the most direct challengers to the existing political orders in Tunisia and Algeria. It was a situation that led to the eventual exclusion and repression of both parties. In the case of al-Nahdah, relations with the Ben Ali regime declined steadily from 1989, culminating in the official break-up and repression of the party and, indeed, the wider Islamist movement in 1991. In Algeria the authorities moved to combat the FIS by introducing changes to the electoral law and by gerrymandering electoral districts in advance of the national legislative elections. When the party organized street protests against the changes in May 1991, the authorities broke up the protests and arrested and imprisoned the senior leaders of the party. President Chadli resisted calls to ban the party outright out of the conviction that it had been sufficiently hobbled by the new electoral law, the imprisonment of its leaders, and increased competition from other political parties (Willis 1997, 171–186). In spite of these handicaps, the FIS decided to still contest the national legislative elections that were eventually held in December 1991. Defying expectations, the party dominated the elections, winning 47 percent of the vote and nearly winning an outright majority of seats in the first round of voting. Alarmed by the prospect of a FIS majority in the National Assembly, senior figures from within the country's elite and military deposed President Chadli in an effective palace coup in early January, cancelled the second round of voting, and annulled the results of the first round. A few weeks later the FIS was formally dissolved and outlawed by the government.

ELECTORAL POLITICS: THE MOROCCAN EXPERIENCE

The dramas that Algeria and Tunisia experienced regarding the participation of Islamists in formal political processes in the late 1980s and early 1990s were noticeably absent in Morocco during this period. The official discourse of the Moroccan state attributed this to the religious status and dimension of the Moroccan monarch as a descendant of the Prophet Muhammad and "commander of the faithful" (*amir al-mu'minin*), which undercut the primary Islamist accusation of the secularization of the state. Although this factor played its part, the existence of a slightly more pluralistic political landscape in Morocco that allowed the existence of opposition parties had also prevented the sort of buildup of popular protest and pressure that had been witnessed in Algeria and Tunisia and that had led to the emergence of mass opposition movements such as the FIS and MTI/al-Nahdah (Willis 2007, 152–153). Islamist sentiment had, nevertheless, grown in Morocco during the 1980s and witnessing events unfolding elsewhere in the Maghreb, Morocco's King Hassan moved to mitigate any threat that might have been posed, by seeking to co-opt the kingdom's main Islamist movements into formal participation in the political process on the royal palace's terms. From early 1990, approaches were made via the Minister for Religious Affairs to the two largest Islamist movements: Justice and Spirituality (al-Adl wal Ihsan) and the Islamic Group (al-Jama'a al-Islamiya). Although overtures to Justice and Spirituality ultimately foundered on the group's refusal to recognize the religious authority of the monarchy in return for being allowed to form a political party, more progress was made with the Islamic Group, which accepted the palace's conditions. Refusing the group's request to form their own political party, the authorities permitted it to join a small and largely moribund existing party—the Mouvement Populaire Démocratique Constitutionnel (MPDC)—in 1996 and put up a limited number of candidates in the national legislative elections of November 1997. The party won a small number of seats (nine) and in October 1998 changed the name of the party to the Party of Justice and Development (PJD), reflecting the effective takeover of the existing party by the organization, which itself had renamed itself the Unity and Reform (At-Tawhid wa al-Islah) movement (Willis 1999).

The PJD grew significantly thereafter and at the next set of national legislative elections in September 2002 more than quadrupled its representation in the Chamber of Deputies to become the third largest party in the chamber and the largest opposition party. Significantly the party had, as in 1997, only put up a limited number of candidates. Although publicly attributing this to the relative youth and inexperience of the party, the party's leaders privately acknowledged that it was limiting its ambitions as part of a deliberate strategy aimed at reducing fears of an Islamist electoral victory and in this way avoided the repression experienced by al-Nahdah and the FIS after their strong electoral performances. As one senior member of the party remarked in 2002, "The Algerian scenario is the fear of all Moroccans" (Willis 2004). The PJD continued to grow, attracting more votes than any other party in the legislative elections of 2007 and was only prevented from becoming the largest presence in the Chamber of Deputies by blatant gerrymandering of the electoral districts by the Moroccan authorities (Willis 2008). The PJD accepted this as the price of maintaining its place in the formal political system. In this way the monarchy appeared to have succeeded in its original objective of co-opting and removing the threat of at least a part of the Islamist movement.

Co-option and Competition

The co-option of the Islamist opposition also became an objective of the regime in Algeria in the 1990s in its effort to undermine support for the armed insurrection it faced following the exclusion of the FIS from the political process in 1992. Two small Islamist parties that had had a marginal influence during the FIS's dominance of the electoral landscape were allowed to continue to operate after 1992 in the hope that they would absorb the mass support enjoyed by the FIS in its legal lifetime. Formed by senior Islamist figures that had declined to join the FIS on its creation in 1989, the Movement for an Islamic Society (Harakat al-Mujtama` al-Islami—often referred to as HAMAS) and the al-Nahdah Movement (not to be confused with its Tunisian namesake) were felt by the Algerian authorities to eschew the radicalism and populism of the FIS. Both were, however, obliged to operate in the much more tightly controlled and manipulated political landscape that the Algerian regime crafted in the latter part of the 1990s. HAMAS proved fundamentally co-operative, agreeing to change its name to the Movement for a *Peaceful* Society (Harakat Mujtama` al-Slim) and accepting to join the governing coalition where it was rewarded with a series of minor ministerial portfolios. Al-Nahdah proved less compliant, continuing to criticize the military-dominated regime and calling for the relegalization of the FIS and its readmission to the formal political process. As a consequence, the authorities sponsored an internal coup against the leadership of the party under Abdallah Djaballah, who left with the majority of the party's members to found a new party, Islah, in 1999. Islah split itself in 2009 following Djaballah's refusal to participate in the presidential elections of that year, which he saw as worthless given the closed nature of the political system.

Despite the presence of often substantial numbers of deputies from Islamist parties in the elected institutions of the Algerian state, their significance and influence were limited as real power remained in the hands of the senior figures in the country's military and increasingly from 1999 the president, Abdelaziz Bouteflika. The Movement for a Peaceful Society's participation in the parliamentary coalition rendered it little real influence, and elections became increasingly manipulated and less and less credible during the 2000s. In 2009 the party formally split in two as a result of differences on strategy between the two most senior figures in the party and against a background of mounting accusations of corruption against the party's ministers in the governing coalition.

In this way the experiences of Morocco and Algeria began to converge in the opening decade of the twenty-first century as the co-option of Islamist parties into formal political processes and institutions with limited political influence appeared to succeed in disarming their organizational challenge to the established political order. At the same time, this process failed to co-opt the electoral constituencies of the parties, as increasingly low turnout rates in elections indicated. The exact nature of this electoral constituency is worth considering. Few thoroughgoing studies of the Islamist parties' support bases have been done but certain general trends were apparent, not least through observing the often admittedly flawed election data produced in the three countries. The first observation is that support for al-Nahdah, the FIS, and the PJD had been predominantly—even overwhelmingly—urban in make-up. Election results showed that all three parties performed strongest in large cities while concomitantly doing less well in more rural areas of the country (Hermassi 1991, 200–201; Willis 1997, 230; Willis 2004, 67). Which particular sections of the urban population were more inclined to vote for Islamist parties was more difficult to divine, but the fact that the parties generally received fairly even support across urban areas suggested that the parties enjoyed support across class and income groups, thus undermining the common assumption that it was the poor and underprivileged that were the bedrock of support for the Maghrebi Islamist parties.

Where this lost constituency turned to after the 1990s is uncertain. Part of it turned to Islamist organizations outside of the formal political system. In the case of Algeria, many Algerians remained committed to the FIS as both a party and a movement long after it had been formally dissolved in 1992. In Morocco, the Justice and Spirituality movement enjoyed significant popular support for its oppositional stance and claimed credit for the low turnout in elections through its calls to boycott them. In Tunisia, where no attempt was made by the regime to co-opt or even allow Islamist parties, the al-Nahdah Party remained a significant political force, particularly from exile after it was formally broken up by the authorities in 1991. In the case of the FIS, however, repression, exile, and the simple passage of time gradually weakened the memory, following, and influence of the party, making it largely irrelevant to events inside Algeria by the latter part of the 2000s. Justice and Spirituality in Morocco, although continually harassed by the Moroccan authorities, never suffered the systematic repression experienced by FIS and al-Nahdah and thus felt able to benefit from the co-option of the PJD. Many in the movement worried, though, that they risked marginalization if they continued to stay out of formal political processes (Willis 2007, 167).

There were concerns that part of the electoral constituency of the Islamist parties had also been lost to far more extremist Islamist groups, particularly those advocating the use of violence. The evidence for this is limited. While there were cases of individual former members of Islamist political parties joining extremist groups, there does not appear to have been a large-scale defection to these groups not least because of the very small membership of such organizations. In the case of Algeria in the 1990s there appeared to be a clear movement of support from the FIS to the armed groups, but even there the membership of the armed groups—numbering at its height several thousand—was nowhere near the 3 million voters that the FIS had attracted in the election of December 1991.

LINKS TO VIOLENCE

The issue of the link between the Islamist political parties and violence and extremism has been a constant theme of Islamist political participation in political processes in the Maghreb. In both Tunisia and Algeria the regimes justified the exclusion and repression of al-Nahdah in 1991 and the FIS in 1992 by claiming that both had resorted to violence to achieve their aims. In Tunisia, the authorities claimed that al-Nahdah was secretly plotting the overthrow of the regime, pointing to an attack on an office of the ruling party by al-Nahdah militants and, more substantively, the discovery of an arms cache as evidence (Hamdi 1998, 71–72). In Algeria, the authorities used protests and outbreaks of violence that occurred in the aftermath of the cancellation of the elections as formal justification for the dissolution of the party (Willis 1997, 256).

The substance of the claims that the parties had resorted to violence varied. In Tunisia, the attack on the ruling party's office (in which a security guard died) was probably correctly portrayed by Nahda's leadership as a mistake by young party members who had left the guard tied up in the building that they then set on fire. The claim of a fully fledged armed plot was more difficult to substantiate. Members of the MTI had set up a clandestine "Security Group" in the 1980s, whose motives were unclear but varied between protection for the movement during the periods of repression under Bourguiba and plans for an armed takeover of the state. It appears that certain of them had even planned to effect a coup d'etat against Bourguiba on November 8, 1987 but had been deliberately forestalled by Ben Ali moving himself to depose the aging president the day before (Hamdi 1998, 57–62). To what extent this group represented the leadership of the MTI is similarly unclear. The fact that the majority of the senior leaders of the movement spent most of the 1980s in prison meant that the Security Group became increasingly autonomous from the political leadership and although most were convicted of involvement in the alleged plots of the early 1990s, evidence of their involvement was in reality fairly scant (Shahin 1997, 102–103). In Algeria, acts of violence had been carried out by members of the FIS in the early weeks of 1992, but these had been in response to the cancellation of the elections and were disavowed by the FIS's leadership, which continued to appeal for restraint from the party's supporters right up until the final dissolution of the party and their own arrests (Willis 1997, 252–254).

In this way the leaderships of both al-Nahdah and the FIS were largely innocent of the charges of violence lodged against them by the governments. There was, however, the perception that both parties were part of a wider Islamist movement, elements of which were quite prepared to use violence. These links also became a major debating point in discussions about the involvement of Islamist political parties in formal political processes in all three Maghreb states. In Tunisia's case, extremist groups had carried out bomb attacks on tourist hotels in Sousse and Monastir in the summer of 1987, but attempts by the authorities to link the MTI leadership to these attacks had, however, failed. In the case of Algeria, the links were much stronger. Members of an armed Islamist group that had operated in the country in the 1980s joined the FIS on its creation together with individuals who had fought as volunteers in the war in Afghanistan against the Soviet Union. Although only a minority of the broad coalition of Islamists that made up the FIS, these elements were responsible for incidents of violence during the party's short legal lifetime (Willis 1997, 143–144, 205–207, 227–229). By the latter part of 1991 most of these elements either had been arrested by the

Algerian authorities or had been formally purged from the party. It was these elements that rose to prominence again when violence began to mount following the decision to cancel the election and formally ban the FIS in 1992. For them and for a section of the FIS's support base, these developments effectively closed the option of formal participation in the Algerian political system to achieve their objectives and necessitated armed struggle against the state. For some groups still closely allied to the FIS, armed struggle had the specific objective of forcing the regime to relegalize the FIS and restart elections. For more extreme elements, many of whom had always viewed the electoral and participationist option as illegitimate, the violent overthrow of the regime became the only acceptable option.

Attempts were also made in Morocco to exclude Islamist parties from formal political processes because of their alleged links to violence. In the wake of suicide bombings carried out in Casablanca in May 2003 efforts were made to link the PJD with the attacks. Unable to establish a direct link between the party and the group found to be responsible for the bombings, critics of the PJD argued instead that the party had helped create the conditions for the attacks on the Western and Jewish targets chosen by the bombers through the anti-Western and anti-Israeli rhetoric it had used, particularly in its newspapers. Certain voices within the regime and some of the political parties argued that the PJD should therefore be banned. After an intense internal debate the Moroccan authorities decided against banning the party not least out of fear that it could strengthen support for extremist groups in much the same way that the dissolution of the FIS had encouraged the formation of the armed groups in Algeria. The price of the PJD's survival, however, was to adopt a lower profile, put up limited numbers of candidates in local elections held later that year, and tone down its rhetoric (Willis 2007, 162–163).

The debate over the Islamist parties' links to violence and extremist Islamist groups was part of a wider debate over the broader social and political agenda of the parties. All of the parties were put under intense scrutiny regarding their position on democracy and on the rights of women and of minorities. Although this scrutiny was encouraged by the regimes who were concerned about the growth in popularity of the Islamists, they also reflected more genuine concerns from foreign, particularly Western, governments and, more importantly significant sections of the population in the states who were genuinely alarmed by the rise of the parties. This was particularly true for those groups that took Europe as the ideal model for the development of the Maghreb states and who saw the Islamists' agenda as one espousing the introduction of a more "Middle Eastern" model, which they viewed as not just a threat to the region's future development but also one that jeopardized existing ways of life within the region that carried in places a quite European and French imprint. Such views were prevalent in the economic and social elites of the three states but also extended to many women and some religious and ethnic minorities, who feared that the Islamists would restrict their rights should they gain political power. It was certainly true that the regimes sought to encourage and mobilize these constituencies against the Islamists particularly following the banning of al-Nahdah in Tunisia and the FIS in Algeria.

In this way the Islamist parties came under huge pressure to set out their full platform and agenda. Involvement in formal political processes meant that they were not only obliged to issue some form of platform at elections but also were regularly questioned by the domestic and foreign media. No single, common, clear ideological and policy agenda emerged through these channels, however. This is a result of the quite diverse national circumstances in which each of the parties operated. To take the main Islamist parties from the three countries: the sudden, dramatic, and relatively brief political opening of the period 1989–1992 contributed to the FIS producing only rather vague and populist statements about its program. By contrast, the PJD's much longer and calmer period of political participation led it to set out one that was increasingly full and detailed. In the case of al-Nahdah in Tunisia, the fact that the party was never formally legalized meant that while it did set out a platform it was never subject to the same media scrutiny as either the FIS or the PJD.

There were, nevertheless, certain broad concerns and stated objectives that were shared by most of the main Maghrebi Islamist parties. All retained an unease, passed down from the earliest Islamist groups formed in the 1960s, about the perceived secular drift of their societies and the concomitant marginalization of Islam from public life. In more concrete terms these concerns manifested themselves in advocacy of policies that reinforced the place of Islam and the Arabic language in education and that limited public access to gambling and alcohol. All also were unified in their expressed solidarity at the international level for pan-Islamic causes such as Chechnya, Kashmir, and, above all, Palestine. Significantly, though, and in common with other Islamist organizations and parties elsewhere, the platforms of Maghrebi Islamist parties gradually expanded out from these mainly social, cultural, and educational preoccupations to encompass broader objectives that included, most prominently, issues of social justice, corruption, and democratic accountability. The reasons for this shift were varied and range from a desire to expand an electoral base to the influence of younger members.

This led many of the parties to seek to establish links with other political parties and forces that shared these broader agendas. Following the exclusion of their parties from formal political processes in the 1990s, senior figures from both the FIS and al-Nahdah in exile established links with other opposition political parties and even signed common platforms, most notably the "Platform for a Peaceful Solution of the Algeria Crisis" in 1995. In Tunisia al-Nahdah established a dialogue with several of the country's largest critical opposition parties. In Morocco the PJD similarly sought to establish links and alliances with other parties (Willis 2000).

The Arab Spring

Islamic movements' engagement with political processes in Morocco, Tunisia, and Algeria had settled into a fairly established pattern by the end of the first decade of the twenty-first century. This saw the regimes in the three states having successfully repressed and excluded movements that they considered posed a threat to their continued dominance. In addition, those Islamic movements and parties that remained within the legal processes and systems were sufficiently hemmed in and co-opted to present no meaningful challenge. This pattern was radically shaken up by the dramatic series of popular protests that swept across the Arab world from the beginning of 2011. In common with the rest of the region, Islamic movements did not initially feature at the forefront of these protests, but became significant players in the new national political landscapes that emerged in their wake. In Tunisia, the toppling and flight of President Ben Ali on January 14 led to a spectacular resurgence for the al-Nahdah movement, which saw its leaders freed from prison and return from exile to head an organization whose structures were able to rapidly reassemble themselves despite twenty years of state repression under Ben Ali. These structures, together with legitimacy gained in the public eye through bearing the brunt of the repression of the Ben Ali regime and thus representing the clearest break with the old regime, led to the party dominating the first post-Ben Ali elections in October 2011. It won 41 percent of the seats in the new national Constituent Assembly that was tasked with drawing up a new constitution and appointing an interim government. Senior al-Nahdah members assumed ministerial positions in the new interim government, including that of prime minister, alongside members of two other non-Islamist parties that had performed relatively well in elections, and with which al-Nahdah formed a majority coalition in the Constituent Assembly.

Just four weeks after An-Nahda's electoral victory in Tunisia, legislative elections in Morocco saw the PJD win a clear plurality of the vote and similarly proceed to assume the leading position in a governing coalition with other political parties. Like al-Nahdah, the PJD appeared to have been the main beneficiary of a popular desire for change in Morocco that viewed the party as being the one most likely to effect such change. Despite these apparently parallel experiences, there were important differences between the positions the two Islamic movements found themselves in. While the Tunisian party became the leading and most powerful player in a political landscape that had been totally remade by the fall of the Ben Ali regime, its Moroccan counterpart continued to operate in a system still very much under the control of the monarchy. In contrast to Ben Ali, King Mohamed had not been overthrown by the protests that came onto the streets of the kingdom's cities, having chosen to announce major reforms to the nation's constitution to adeptly head off the protestors' demands for reform. Although the reforms ultimately introduced were much less substantial than originally promised, they were sufficient to boost support for the PJD as the party most likely to continue the dynamic of reform. The royal palace resisted the temptation to interfere with the election or to try to avoid allowing the PJD into government not least because the revised constitution now committed the king to inviting the largest party to form a government. It nevertheless made sure that the main lines of policy continued to be decided by the palace through the PJD's coalition partners and particularly the set of powerful deputy ministers it appointed to oversee the new PJD ministers. A number of the Islamic party's election promises were quietly dropped after they came into government and the party exercised a number of notable U-turns on controversial policy initiatives in the first year of office. Senior figures in the party remained convinced, however, that some influence over policy was better than none for the party. Other figures feared that the PJD was being used, as the main socialist party had when it similarly came into government in the late 1990s, as a convenient shield for the Moroccan regime to shoulder the blame for Morocco's myriad social and economic problems. Standing outside the system, the Justice and Spirituality movement that had lent its support to the kingdom's protest movement characterized the appointment of the PJD-led government as the "last card" of the Moroccan regime. By contrast, al-Nahdah's electoral victory in Tunisia presented it with real political power although this too led to it assuming responsibilities for the country's significant problems.

Legislative elections were held in Algeria in May 2012, but these notably failed to produce the sort of electoral and governmental breakthrough for the Islamist parties that had occurred in Tunisia and Morocco. This was largely because Algeria had failed to experience the emergence of the sort of mass protest movements that had arisen in most of the rest of the Arab world in 2011. The government in Algiers had been able to draw on the country's substantial revenues from oil and gas sales to dampen potential unrest through salary rises and cheap credit but, more importantly, had benefitted from a marked lack of appetite for political upheaval among the general Algerian population who had lived through the tumult and bloodshed of the 1990s. There was thus no impetus, from either the regime or the streets, to disrupt the pattern of politics that had settled in since the end of the 1990s, which consisted of largely stage-managed and increasingly meaningless elections.

Conclusion

The participation of Islamic movements in formal political processes in Algeria, Tunisia, and Morocco represents important and instructive case studies that, while displaying national particularities, also display significant commonalities. In all three states Islamic movements presented appreciable threats to the existing and longstanding political establishments that until the upheavals of 2011 were effectively countered by the regimes by varying combinations of co-option, exclusion, and repression.

The main Islamic movements in the three states also had their own characteristics shaped by the national contexts in which they emerged and operated. The fact that Tunisia witnessed the earliest and strongest emergence of a substantial Islamist movement was clearly a result of the more robustly secular direction taken by the Tunisian state under the presidency of Habib Bourguiba after independence. The more populist and militant stance and path taken by the FIS in Algeria tapped into the revolutionary traditions of the war of national liberation led by the FLN against the French. Indeed the link was explicit in the FIS's decision to call itself a "front," in the presence of veterans of the liberation struggle in the leadership of the party and in the party's stated aim to save the "lost" legacy of the original national revolution. The memory of the liberation struggle also perhaps helps explain the willingness of parts of the Algerian movement to turn to violent resistance after 1992 that contrasted sharply with the failure of the Islamic movement in Tunisia to mount a similar response when it suffered a comparable repression by the state authorities a year earlier, perhaps reflecting the more pacific and legalist traditions of modern Tunisian political history.

The fact that a sizeable Islamist movement did not emerge in Morocco until the 1990s is likely due to the presence of an existing opposition force in the shape of the nationalist and leftist opposition parties that stopped opposition channeling into a single Islamic movement as it did in Tunisia and Algeria and in Morocco's slower rate of urbanization—a phenomenon closely linked to the growth and support of Islamic movements. When it emerged, the more cautious and gradualist approach of the PJD was in line with the more conservative political culture in Morocco with its wariness of revolutionary ideas and rapid change.

The emergence of governments led by Islamist parties in Tunisia and Morocco in the closing weeks of 2011 ushered in a new era for the participation of Islamic movements in political processes in the region. Confined for so long to political opposition both outside as well as within official political structures, al-Nahdah, and the PJD finally had some opportunity to put into practice policies and ideas that had hitherto only existed in the movements' literature and rhetoric. This opportunity promised to provide an important insight into whether

Islamic movements were able to produce a notably different or new form of politics and society in their countries.

References

Hamdi, M. E. 1998. *The Politicization of Islam: A Case Study of Tunisia*. Boulder: Westview.

Hermassi, E. 1991. The Islamicist Movement and November 7. In *Tunisia: The Political Economy of Reform*, ed. I. W. Zartman. Boulder: Lynne Rienner: 193–204.

Roberts, H. 1994. From Radical Mission to Equivocal Ambition: the Expansion and Manipulation of Algerian Islamism, 1979–1992. In *Accounting for Fundamentalisms: The Dynamic Character of Movements*, ed. M. E. Marty and R. S. Appleby. The Fundamentalism Project. Chicago: University of Chicago Press: 428–489.

Roberts, H. 2003. *The Battlefield: Algeria 1988–2002. Studies in a Broken Polity*.London: Verso.

Shahin, E. E. 1997. *Political Ascent: Contemporary Islamic Movements in North Africa*. Boulder: Westview.

Tamimi, A. S. 2001. *Rachid Ghannouchi: A Democrat within Islamism*. Oxford: Oxford University Press.

Willis, M. 1997. *The Islamist Challenge in Algeria: A Political History*. New York: New York University Press.

Willis, M. 1999. Between Alternance and the Makhzen: At-Tawhid wa Al-Islah's Entry into Moroccan Politics. *The Journal of North African Studies* 4(3): 45–80.

Willis, M. 2000. Islamism in Algeria: The Politics of Inclusion and Exclusion. In *The Arab-African and Islamic Worlds: Interdisciplinary Studies*, ed. R. K. Lacey and R. M. Coury. New York: Peter Lang: 71–94.

Willis, M. 2004. Morocco's Islamists and the Legislative Elections of 2002: The Strange Case of the Party That Did Not Want to Win. *Mediterranean Politics* 9(1): 53–81.

Willis, M. 2007. Justice and Development or Justice and Spirituality?: The Challenge of Morocco's Nonviolent Islamist Movements. In *The Maghrib in the New Century: Identity, Religion and Politics*, ed., B. Maddy-Weitzman and D. Zisenwine. Gainesville: University of Florida Press: 150–174.

Willis, M. 2008. Islamism, Democratization and Disillusionment: Morocco's Legislative Elections of 2007. King Mohammed VI Fellowship in Moroccan and Mediterranean Studies Research paper No.1. Available at: http://www.sant.ox.ac.uk/mec/morocco/Islamism-Democratisation-Disillusionment.pdf. Accessed December 4, 2009.

Willis, M. 2012. *Politics and Power in the Maghreb. Algeria, Tunisia and Morocco from Independence to the Arab Spring*. New York: Columbia University Press.

Zeghal, M. 2008. *Islamism in Morocco: Religion, Authoritarianism and Electoral Politics*. Princeton: Markus Wiener.

CHAPTER 35

THE ISLAMIC ACTION FRONT IN JORDAN

SHADI HAMID

The Islamic Action Front (IAF)—the political arm of Jordan's Muslim Brotherhood—was established in 1992 at the height of the country's once-promising democratic "experiment." Since then, it has struggled to respond and adapt to an increasingly authoritarian political environment. It has, however, remained, by a wide margin, the largest and best-organized political party in Jordan. Among the region's Islamist parties, the IAF stands out for a number of reasons, including its commitment to "loyal opposition." Even in the worst of times, including the crackdown of 2005–2007, the party went out of its way to declare its allegiance to the monarchy. The "Jordanian Spring" has seen a further deterioration in regime-opposition relations, with the IAF, for the first time, flirting with pointed criticisms of the king and warning that the situation may be reaching a point of no return.

The IAF will tread cautiously, just as it always has. Protests in Jordan have brought to the fore growing tensions between indigenous Jordanians and those of Palestinian origin. The IAF, with its strong Palestinian make-up, faces the challenge of transcending such divisions and navigating a political arena in a country where the regime itself, for the first time since the early 1970s, finds itself under existential threat.

FROM THE MUSLIM BROTHERHOOD TO THE ISLAMIC ACTION FRONT

The IAF's parent movement, the Jordanian Muslim Brotherhood, was formed in 1945 in a markedly different context, one in which it found itself allied with the conservative Hashemite monarchy. Interestingly, the organization's headquarters were inaugurated under the patronage of King Abdullah, the first—and one of the only—times the formation of a Brotherhood branch has been blessed by an Arab regime (Abdul Kazem 1997, 15).

Unique among its neighbors, the Brotherhood enjoyed a cooperative, sometimes even close, relationship with the Jordanian monarchy through the 1980s. With the rise of the Left in the 1950s, the Brotherhood sided with the regime, lending its support to the coup that unseated the socialist prime minister Sulayman al-Nabulsi in 1957. In its formative period, the Brotherhood remained primarily a social and religious movement with a relative disinterest in direct political action. With a handful of deputies in parliament, the Brotherhood withheld confidence from successive governments in the 1960s and 1970s, almost always over what it saw as the failure to uphold *Shari'ah* law. Beyond this, it lacked a well-defined political agenda. Drawing on Jordanian government and intelligence documents, Amnon Cohen notes that "among the prime targets of the [Brotherhood's] criticism were moral laxity (the consumption of alcohol, the importing of dancers and other forms of entertainment, and the deterioration of the school curricula by laying too much stress on Western values)" (Amnon 1982, 148).

The Brotherhood was content to coexist with the monarchy and register opposition to specific policies while avoiding anything that might be construed as a challenge to the foundations of the political order. It was rewarded with a relative degree of freedom to set up a wide-ranging infrastructure of social services and begin the slow work of building a mass membership organization. It gained control of educational policy, with prominent Brotherhood leader Ishaq Farhan's 1970 appointment as minister of education marking one of the Arab world's first instances of Islamist participation in government.

This convenient exchange of interests began to fray in the late 1970s, when, like much of the region, Jordan was swept by a popular upsurge in religiosity. This cultural sea change was helped along by the infusion of economic assistance from oil-rich Gulf nations and remittances from Jordanian expatriates, which, together, would come to account for nearly half of Jordan's gross national product (Satloff 1986, 7). A new Islamist fervor grew in intensity, and the Brotherhood found itself in a position to benefit.

The Brotherhood performed unexpectedly well in 1984's parliamentary by-elections, winning two out of the three seats it contested and swept the elections for the University of Jordan's student union. The group soon set its sights on the landmark 1989 elections, which marked the beginning of Jordan's much-heralded democratic "experiment." The Brotherhood won nearly 85 percent of the seats it contested, ending up with twenty-two seats in a parliament of eighty, while independent Islamists won another twelve seats. For the first time, the electoral side of the Brotherhood's diverse activities became a central focus for the organization.

Meanwhile, the regime was preparing to formally lift martial law and legalize political parties. Anticipating these changes, the Brotherhood raised the idea of forming an Islamist party soon after the 1989 elections, with Brotherhood leaders beginning preparations in the middle of 1990 (al-Kilani 1994, 98). After more than two years of planning, the IAF was inaugurated in December 1992. The decision to form a party was not without dissenters. A faction that came to be known as the "hawks" (*suqoor*), led by Mohammed Abu Faris and Hammam Said, opposed the idea, fearing the party would come to overshadow the movement. Ironically, both would later take on leading roles in the IAF.

Upon its founding, Ishaq Farhan commented that the IAF is not "a religious party nor a sectarian or regional one; rather it is an Islamic party that brings together citizens for political action from an Islamic perspective" (al-Kilani 1994, 99). However, the IAF's bylaws, or *al-nizam al-asasi*, did not diverge significantly from that of the Brotherhood, with a continued emphasis on the centrality of Islamic law. The preamble lays out the party's rationale: "In recognition of the urgency of standing firm in the face of the civilizational threat against the ummah—a threat that represents a dangerous phase in the ongoing colonial enterprise—[there is a need to] protect our civilization... and to strive to lead this ummah with God's law" (al-Assasi 1992, 1).[1]

The IAF was originally intended as a broad front for all Islamists. Early on, however, many independent Islamists resigned after performing below expectations in internal elections for the Shura Council (Majlis al-Shura) and Executive Bureau (al-Maktab al-Tanfidhi). Most leadership positions went to Brotherhood members. Although the IAF is technically distinct from the Brotherhood administratively and financially, the Brotherhood has exerted strong influence over its direction due to overlapping memberships and leaderships.

The party entered the scene at the peak of democratization, but the regime soon turned against it. The events of 1993 can be viewed as a turning point for both sides. King Hussein unilaterally enacted the so-called one-person, one-vote electoral law (*sawt al-wahid*), whose primary objective was to limit Islamist power at the polls.[2] With talk of a peace settlement with Israel, the king needed a pliant parliament in order to guarantee ratification. Renate Dieterich calls the legislation "a decision which set in motion a rollback of the whole democratic process" (Dietrich 2002, 134). Before 1993, Islamists were capable of winning a majority. In the 1989 parliamentary elections, they came close, winning thirty-four out of eighty seats.[3] Under the new provisions, such an outcome became extremely difficult, if not impossible. Remarkably, at its most gerrymandered, pro-government regions were represented by one parliamentarian per 5,700 constituents, while pro-IAF areas were represented by as little as one parliamentarian per 52,000 people.[4] The changes threw the IAF into disarray, provoking a heated internal debate over whether to sit out the elections. Eventually, after the king issued a public call for the IAF to participate, 87 of 101 Shura Council members voted in favor of participation. In addition to using the legislative process to oppose the treaty, the Brotherhood, according to Ibrahim Gharaibeh, "wished to avoid confronting the authorities to the point of *kasr al-'adhm* (breaking of bones)" (Gharaibeh 1997, 129). A violent crackdown was something Jordan's Islamic movement feared in light of events in Algeria, where the Islamic Salvation Front was destroyed by the regime when it became too powerful.

Some within the movement felt the Brotherhood and IAF had capitulated to the government. According to Ziad Abu Ghanimeh, a Brotherhood leader who resigned from the group, "There were secret meetings with the [government], and we soon learned that there was a trend toward entering the elections... the agreement being that they would enter the elections and receive 16 seats, and the government would have a say on who the names were. In other words, they would choose who they wanted.... There was a deal."[5]

The IAF's 1993 electoral program was a sign of things to come—it was a longer, more detailed document than the Brotherhood's 1989 iteration and included an expanded discussion of the importance of promoting political freedoms and human rights (although still not going so far as to used the word "democracy"). Jihad Abu Eis, formerly a journalist with the Islamist weekly *Al-Sabeel*, notes the Brotherhood's historical reticence to use democratic terminology: "In the past, Islamists saw this term as a concession to the West and worried it would lead to the same consequences as in the West, such as moral decay."[6] This reticence was being eroded.

The IAF contested 35 out of 110 seats; in a significant drop in its representation, it won only 16. With an overwhelmingly pro-regime parliament, the government was able to easily ratify the 1994 peace treaty with Israel, an event that foreshadowed the subsequent deterioration of relations between Islamists and the monarchy.

The IAF's Prioritization of Democracy

Jordan's Islamists found themselves the primary target of the regime's post-1993 de-democratization. In a March 1995 letter to Prime Minister Abd al-Salam al-Majali, the IAF laid out four areas of concern: the growing number of politically motivated arrests, government interference in student union elections, the prevention of preachers from delivering sermons, and a return to the rhetoric and policies of martial law (Letter to Prime Minister 1995).

After yet another contentious internal debate, the Brotherhood and IAF chose to boycott the 1997 elections. Reflecting the Islamic movement's growing prioritization of democracy, the boycott statement argues that the three "pillars" of democracy—freedom of expression, free elections, and political party pluralism—had been destroyed by the government (Limadha 1997). This fear of democracy's collapse is cited as the reason for taking drastic action: "[We] believe that the decision to boycott the 1997 parliamentary elections is necessary to establish democracy and protect the homeland." Moreover, the boycott represents "an attempt to put a stop to the deterioration of democracy and to protect what remains and restore what was usurped." Ibrahim Gharaibeh, still a Brotherhood member at the time, explains that the boycott was "a way to put pressure [on the regime], a means of political participation, and a method to improve the conditions of the political game."[7] The decision does not appear to have hinged at all on religious concerns or Islamic law, which were not mentioned in the boycott document.

It was a decision that many in the IAF would come to regret. Lacking a platform in parliament, Islamists were increasingly marginalized over the next years—a period that included the dissolution of parliament in 2001 and two years of King Abdullah's rule by fiat.[8] After 1997, "the government's siege on the Brotherhood only got worse," says Nael Masalha, a prominent Brotherhood figure.[9] In the lead-up to the 2003 polls, the Brotherhood and IAF overwhelmingly came out in support of reentering the parliamentary process. For the first time in nearly ten years, the IAF began to prepare a new electoral platform. Much had changed in the span of the previous decade, and, not surprisingly, so too did the party's program.

The 2003 program begins on a different note than the 1993 version. The introduction, subtitled "Why We Participate in Parliamentary Elections," states that "the IAF party considers its presence in parliament as one of the political means to the realization of the sentiment 'Islam is the solution' and a means of building the nation's strength" (Na'am wa 2003, 5). Explaining the significance of using the longtime Brotherhood slogan, the party pledges to "facilitate a climate that helps to realize the objectives of the people in freedom, shura, and democracy, and protecting the rights of the people on the basis that they are the source of authority."

Increasingly, the IAF turned its attention to the priority of constitutional and political reform. The party's 2005 "reform initiative" represents the most comprehensive and far-reaching expression of its pro-democracy focus. Nathan Brown calls it "a document so full of liberal and democratic ideas and language that a leader of a secular opposition party was forced to confess that it differed little from the programs of other parties" (Brown 2006, 9).

The initiative was released just as the regime was intensifying its crackdown on Islamist activists, targeting Jordan's emboldened professional associations. With a weak party system—the IAF has long Jordan's only party with a nationwide, grassroots presence—the associations had grown in importance, becoming a center of opposition to the regime's staunchly pro-U.S. foreign policy. Not surprisingly, the most prominent of them—the lawyers and engineers' syndicates—were led by Brotherhood and IAF members. With King Abdullah putting Jordan even more firmly within the U.S. orbit, the regime had little patience left for the associations' high-profile activities against normalization with Israel. In March 2005, for instance, Prime Minister Faisal al-Fayez's government presented a draft law on professional associations to parliament; the law would authorize the Audit Bureau to monitor each association's funds to ensure they were being spent only on internal activities. If there was ever any doubt over the government's intentions, Minister of Interior Samir Habashneh explained that the law aimed to eliminate the "prevalent influence of one current"—meaning Islamists—within the associations (*Jordan Times a* 2005; Hamid 2005).

From 2005 to 2007, the confrontation between Islamists and the regime reached its peak. Jordan saw the coordinated bombing of three Amman hotels in November 2005, one of the worst terrorist attacks in the country's history. More than sixty died in the blasts. The attack came just one month after the release of the IAF's reform initiative, which was quickly forgotten as a result. As Freedom House reports, "Abdullah replaced his security advisers, dissolved the Senate, and appointed a new prime minister, Marouf al-Bakhit, along with a new cabinet.... Political reform was stalled with the renewed focus on security" (*Country Report Jordan* 2007). Antiterrorism legislation was rushed through, limiting judicial review and expanding the power of military courts.

ISLAMISTS AND THE ZARQAWI AFFAIR

In June 2006, Abu Musab al-Zarqawi, leader of al-Qa`ida in Iraq and mastermind of the Amman bombings, was killed by an American airstrike. Zarqawi hailed from a prominent East Bank tribe in Zarqa, the second-largest city in Jordan. Four IAF parliamentarians attended his wake and paid condolences to the family. One of them, Mohamed Abu Faris, called Zarqawi a "martyr" on an Al-Jazeera television program. The four were charged with "fueling national discord and inciting sectarianism," despite the fact that eleven non-Islamist members of parliament (MPs) also attended the wake (*Jordan Times b* 2006). The arrest of such prominent Islamists was unprecedented. Rank-and-file members had often been detained for short periods; IAF leaders, though, and especially those with parliamentary immunity, faced harassment and other restrictions on their activities but rarely prison time.

A month after the Zarqawi affair, the government moved decisively against the Islamic Center Society (ICS), the Brotherhood's charity arm, with prosecutors alleging financial violations (*Jordan Times c* 2006). The following week, the ICS board was dissolved and a new one appointed in its place. This, too, signaled a new escalation. It was the first time the regime had ever taken serious action against the Brotherhood's social service activities, long one of the "red lines" in the relationship between Islamists and the regime.

A number of meetings were held between government and Brotherhood officials with the hope of avoiding further escalation. For their part, the Brotherhood and the IAF issued a joint statement, in which they condemned all forms of extremism, stated that no group has a monopoly in defining the principles of the nation, and highlighted their support for ideological and political pluralism. The statement was released on the same day that the public prosecutor announced it was pursuing legal action against the ICS (Brown 2006, 20). These "clarifications" were controversial within the IAF not necessarily for their content, but for their deference to the regime. Their conciliatory tone did not appear to have worked, as the regime continued criminal proceedings against three of the four IAF MPs who attended Zarqawi's wake. Fifteen Brotherhood Shura Council members tendered their resignations in protest of the organization's unwillingness to take a stronger stand against the government (*Jordan Times d* 2006).

THE IAF AND THE JORDANIAN SPRING

The Arab Spring reached Jordan on January 14, 2011, when leftists and tribal leaders emboldened by the Tunisian uprising protested against Prime Minister Samir al-Rifaʿi's government. Protesters complained of high taxation, rising prices, and the lack of jobs. Jordan's Islamists—including the IAF, which had just boycotted the country's November 2010 parliamentary elections—quickly joined the protests. Despite the removal of al-Rifaʿi and various conciliatory gestures from the state, demonstrations persisted; during one stretch from January through April, protests were held on twelve successive Fridays (although their size was usually limited to a few thousand). Eventually, amid promises from the king to pursue democratizing reforms, protests subsided.

After the enactment of a new, widely criticized electoral law, however, Jordan's protest movement regained its vitality, with the Brotherhood and IAF at its forefront. On October 5, 2012, a day after the king dissolved the Jordanian parliament and called for elections, Jordan witnessed its largest protests since the onset of the Arab Spring. A Brotherhood-led coalition of opposition parties rallied at least 15,000 protesters in Amman to demand democratic reform, an end to corruption, and a new electoral law (al-Khalidi 2012). The Brotherhood called for the 2013 parliamentary elections to be delayed and for an immediate move to negotiating table with King Abdullah himself (al-Samadi 2012). The regime, however, went ahead with elections in January 2013. For the second straight time, the IAF boycotted.

THE IAF: POSITIONS AND POLICIES

From its inception, the IAF has had little chance to demonstrate the practical application of its evolving ideas on governance. I have already alluded to the party's public embrace of democratic tenets—including alternation of power, popular sovereignty, separation of powers, and judicial independence—and the diminishing focus on *Shariʿah* law. It is also worth considering here the IAF's orientation on economics, education, foreign affairs, and the role of women, as well as its relations with secular and liberal parties.

Economic policy

Like other Islamist parties, the IAF has not been known to emphasize economic issues, aside from vague (though often effective) calls to root out corruption and stand for social justice. In the past, the IAF advocated limiting or abolishing the practice of usury, but this is no longer featured in their programs. The IAF's economic program includes appeals for a more active government role in fighting poverty and combating unemployment. It also calls for reducing the trade deficit, protecting national industry, and seeking alternative energy sources. On labor rights, the IAF supports the right of workers to unionize in both private and public industry and advocates full healthcare coverage for workers (*Na'am al-Islam* 2007, 26). There is, however, relatively little in the way of specifics on how to realize these goals. The IAF's failure to prioritize economic issues is, in part, a function of the party's predominantly professional, middle-class composition.

The party generally displays a greater interest in international economic concerns, as these tend to intersect with its foreign policy message. For example, it calls for "a national plan to gradually free Jordan from the World Bank and International Monetary Fund" (*Na'am al-Islam* 2007, 25) and urges the "monitoring of foreign investment and resisting its control over the national economy" (*Na'am al-Islam* 2007, 22).

Education policy

Along with political reform, education policy has been a major domestic concern of the IAF. This fits into the Muslim Brotherhood's bottom-up approach to Islamization, to be achieved by inculcating religious values in a new generation of Jordanians. Along these lines, the IAF states its interest in "the building of the distinctive Islamic personality" (*Ru'yat al-Haraka* 2005, 43). The Brotherhood and IAF have long advocated a prohibition on the mixing of sexes in educational institutions, as it "threatens the moral values of the individual and society" (*Na'am wa* 2003, 11).

Policy prescriptions are primarily concerned with grounding the educational curriculum in an Islamic methodology, while at the same time calling for modernization of educational methods by encouraging critical inquiry, putting an end to rote memorization, and nurturing leadership qualities among students (*Na'am al-Islam* 2007, 13). The IAF calls for raising teacher salaries, devoting more resources to fighting illiteracy, and emphasizing Arabic language skills.

The IAF views education as one of the key battlegrounds in the confrontation with Israel—in its view the "number one issue facing Arabs and Muslims." Its 1993 electoral platform calls for education policy to be redirected to "wage war against educational normalization with the Jewish enemy." Increasingly suspicious of the regime's pro-West alignment, the Brotherhood warns against "importing foreign experts due to the danger of their influence [on the country's educational system]."[10] The IAF's 2005 reform initiative tied educational policy more closely to its broader vision of societal reform, noting that the educational system should promote the values of "justice, tolerance, freedom, and respect for the other" (*Ru'yat al-Haraka* 2005, 44).

The IAF puts many of these ideas intro practice through the Brotherhood's extensive network of kindergartens and primary and secondary schools. For a time, the Brotherhood was also at the helm of Zarqa Private University, including under the leadership of the IAF's Ishaq Farhan, who received his doctorate in education from Columbia University.

Role of women

Where the Muslim Brotherhood's first electoral program in 1989 included only one sentence explicitly mentioning women's concerns, subsequent platforms have included entire sections addressing the role of women. The IAF's 2007 program, for example, calls for "promoting societal awareness of a woman's legal rights," including "her right to work, to education, and to choose a husband" (*Na'am al-Islam* 2007, 12).

The IAF has gradually become more supportive of female political participation. There were no women in the founding Shura Council of the IAF. By 2002, there were six. In 2003, the party ran its first-ever woman candidate for parliament, Hayat al-Meseimi. But while women have played a growing role in the party, they remain underrepresented at the leadership level. No women, for instance, have been elected to the party's Executive Bureau. Women's participation is largely channeled through the Women's Sector (*al-qita' al-nisa'i*), whose primary concern is to "increase membership of women within the IAF" (Clark 2003, 301).

The IAF has been attacked for opposing two of King Abdullah's signature initiatives: the abolition of reduced sentences for "honor crimes" and the granting of *khul'a*, which allows Muslim women to extract themselves from a marriage without demonstrating cause. It is worth noting, however, that Islamist leaders did not frame their positions in explicitly religious terms—the IAF is on the record condemning honor crimes—but as part of a broader opposition to Western cultural influence and the erosion of the family unit.

Foreign policy

The IAF, and Jordan's Islamic movement more generally, has demonstrated a more pronounced interest in foreign policy than many of its counterparts. This is particularly true with respect to the Israeli-Palestinian conflict. This focus can be attributed to Jordan's proximity to the West Bank and Jerusalem, but also to the fact that the majority of Jordanians are of Palestinian origin. Palestinians face discrimination in political life but are well represented in the leadership of both the Brotherhood and the IAF. Until Hamas was forced out of Jordan in 1999, the group—effectively the Palestinian Muslim Brotherhood—shared an office with the Jordanian Brotherhood in the latter's headquarters in Amman's Islamic Hospital.

Not surprisingly, the pro-West orientation of the Jordanian monarchy has been a key determinant of Islamist relations with the regime. A critical point of departure was King Hussein's signing of the peace agreement with Israel in 1994, which permanently altered his relationship with the Islamist opposition. (The treaty was ratified by parliament in a fifty-five to twenty-three vote, with all sixteen IAF deputies voting against.)

Where other Islamist parties have had strong anti-Israel stances while signaling openness to a peace settlement, the IAF's public positions have neither wavered nor evolved. In its 2007 electoral platform, the IAF affirms that "no one has the right to give up any part of Palestinian land," which, for the party, includes Israel proper. "Our conflict with the occupier," the program explains, "is a theological and civilizational one that will not end with a peace treaty. It is a conflict of existence and not one of borders" (*Na'am al-Islam* 2007, 30).

Behind the headlines, the Israel question has been a contentious one within the organization, pitting "doves" (*hama'im*) against "hawks" (*suqoor*). In the 2000s, a growing tendency within the IAF, known as the "fourth trend" (*al-tayyar al rabi'*), or "Hamasists," emerged as a force in the party's sometimes vigorous internal maneuvering. Doves, who tend to be indigenous Jordanians, have advocated a greater focus on domestic affairs and a "Jordan-first" approach to foreign policy. Seen as regime loyalists, they have generally worked to distance the IAF from Hamas. Meanwhile, hawks as well as the so-called fourth trend, the most prominent of whom are of Palestinian origin, prioritize the conflict with Israel and advocate closer ties with Hamas.

Since 1993, the IAF has been invited to join the government several times, but has refused on the grounds that it cannot be part of a cabinet that has relations with Israel. Two prominent doves, Abdullah al-Akaileh and Bassam al-Emoush, left the IAF in the 1990s largely over the question of executive branch participation. While continuing to oppose the peace treaty, they, and others, believed that the Islamic movement should adopt a more pragmatic approach by opposing "normalization" rather than the peace treaty itself.

Relations with secular parties

Despite the democratic opening of 1989, Jillian Schwedler notes that in the eleventh parliament (1989–1993) "Islamist deputies...shunned cooperation with [other] parties" (Schwedler 2006, 109). There had been a degree of coordination on foreign policy concerns, such as the Gulf War, but relatively little on domestic political reform. This began to change in 1993, with one of the first major instances of Islamist coordination with secular parties—a joint press conference opposing the new electoral law—coming in response to the regime's most concerted effort yet to limit opposition influence.

In 1994, the IAF, along with twelve mostly leftist and nationalist parties, formed the Higher Committee for the Coordination of National Opposition Parties (HCCNOP).[11] Unlike many other cross-ideological coalitions in the Arab world, the HCCNOP stood the test of time. An active coalition that meets as often as every week, it has had a set of regular, agreed-upon internal procedures, with leadership rotating every three months between the parties (Clark 2006, 547). During each rotation, the chairing party sets the agenda and represents the coalition in the press. This means that, despite the fact the IAF is larger than all the other parties combined, it would formally lead the coalition only a small fraction of the time.

That said, due to the weakness of the other parties and the IAF's dominance, the HCCNOP's ultimate significance has been open to question. In her study of the coalition, Janine Clark finds that cooperation is "limited to the coordination of activities over which the IAF sees eye to eye with other parties" (Clark 2006, 540). While there may be little ideological give-and-take, the HCCNOP has been successful as a mechanism to pool resources and amplify impact on issues of mutual concern. As Ishaq Farhan explains, the coalition's objective is to "crystallize points of agreement."[12]

Organizational Structure

The Brotherhood had long been hampered by an ad hoc decision-making process. Certain leaders—usually those with close relations to the regime—would meet with the king and other senior officials and then present whatever was agreed upon as a fait accompli. This was how the IAF, for instance, entered the 1993 elections, with Brotherhood Overseer-General Abd al-Rahman Khalifa and King Hussein agreeing on the terms of participation. The unilateral decision by Khalifa predetermined the subsequent Shura Council vote within the IAF.

With government pressure on the organization increasing and internal debates more contentious, the need for a set of binding, regularized procedures became more critical. Over time, the institutionalization of internal democratic practices effectively mediated what might otherwise have been crippling divisions.

Nathan Brown has argued that the IAF "may be the most democratic party in the region in terms of its internal operations" (Brown 2006, 3). This claim is worth exploring more closely. The IAF has three main decision-making bodies: the Executive Bureau, the Shura Council, and the internal court, which loosely mirror the three branches of government—the executive, the legislature, and the judiciary.

The 120-member Shura Council is effectively the party's legislative branch, setting policy and making major decisions, including whether to participate in elections. The nine-member Executive Bureau is tasked with the execution of policy and day-to-day management within the guidelines set by the Shura Council. The party's internal court, about which relatively little has been written, interprets the organization's bylaws as embodied by the *al-nizam al-assasi*. It also deals with the controversial matter of suspension of membership or expulsion. The internal court operates with considerable autonomy, to the extent that it has launched proceedings against some of the IAF's most senior figures, including Zaki Bani Irsheid, who, as secretary-general, was the IAF's top official through May 2009. Bani Irsheid was "charged" with undermining his own party's candidates in the 2007 parliamentary elections, due to his disagreement over the Shura Council's decision to contest the polls. In this particular example, we can see how each "branch" of the IAF operated independently and, at times, at cross-purposes with the others.

The IAF also developed a fourth, irregular source of internal decision making—*al-istifta al-'am*, or the general referendum. The results of this process, while not necessarily binding, tend to be respected by the organization's leadership. The general referendum allows every member of the IAF to register his opinion on major issues facing the party. The process is usually initiated by the Executive Bureau, as it did in the lead-up to the 1997 elections, when the referendum returned a pro-boycott result, with 66 percent voting against participation.[13]

THE IAF AT A CROSSROADS

The 2007 elections, arguably the most fraudulent in Jordan's history, marked the culmination of regime efforts to marginalize the Islamic movement. On the day of the country's June municipal elections, the IAF formally withdrew its candidates in protest of government interference. The journalist Ayman al-Safadi warned that the country was entering an "era of broken bones" (al-Safadi 2007). Recognizing the risk of such a confrontation, the IAF did its part to ease tensions ahead of the November parliamentary elections. In order to assure the government it was interested in "participation, not domination" (*al-musharika wa laysa al-mughalaba*), the party ran only twenty-two candidates, its lowest number ever. IAF doves, who had a majority in the Executive Bureau, reached an understanding with Prime Minister Marouf al-Bakhit in which they agreed to contest a reduced number of seats and avoid running explicitly pro-Hamas and antigovernment candidates.[14] In exchange, the Brotherhood received assurances the elections would be free and fair. But they were not: less than 10 out of 110 seats went to the opposition, with the IAF winning only 6.

For many Islamists, the results of the 2007 polls called into question the utility of participating in elections that were seemingly always stacked against them. Despite embracing key democratic precepts and modernizing its election platform, the IAF found itself victim to unprecedented electoral manipulation and mounting legal restrictions. Moderation, it appeared, was being punished.

Hawks in both the Muslim Brotherhood and the IAF used the result to attack the doves' handling of the elections, leading to unprecedented internal tensions that spilled into public view. The Brotherhood's Shura Council was dissolved and early elections were called. In a surprise result, the fiery preacher Hammam Said defeated the dovish Salem Falahat for the post of overseer-general in a close twenty-three to twenty-two vote, marking the first time a Palestinian had ever been elected head of the Jordanian Brotherhood. Within the IAF, meanwhile, internal negotiations continued over a number of controversies, including Zaki Bani Irsheid's pending trial by the IAF internal court. Despite such tensions, the Brotherhood and the IAF managed to avoid any mass defections or splits, thanks in part to its successful institutionalization of procedures for resolving internal disagreements.

With the tide rising in favor of the hawks, many commentators warned of the Islamic movement's impending radicalization. After Said's election in 2008, Matthew Levitt and David Schenker suggested that the Brotherhood "can no longer be considered 'loyal' to the kingdom" (Levitt and Schenker 2008). However, once elected, Said toned down the abrasive rhetoric, emphasized domestic issues, and reached out to the government. As Abd al-Majid Thneibat, former head of the Brotherhood, explained, "there are a set of given political principles [that the organization operates by] which no Overseer-General is able to change."[15] Indeed, the region's Islamist parties and the IAF in particular have depended on strong, durable institutions rather than strong individual personalities—in contrast with many of their secular counterparts.

The party's cautious, deliberative approach has historically served it well, but, in a time of regional upheaval, it has come under growing pressure to take advantage of a restless public and an increasingly unpopular king. In the wake of the Arab Spring, the Brotherhood escalated its pressure on the government by coupling its announced boycott of the 2013 elections with mass protests in the capitol. But, while the Brotherhood and IAF have adopted a more confident, confrontational stance, they continue to tread carefully on sensitive issues surrounding the king and his family. IAF Secretary-General Hamza Mansour has affirmed that the Brotherhood remains committed to systemic reform "under the ceiling of the monarchy" Mansour 2012).

Others like Zaki Bani Irsheid have been more keen to push the accepted limits. Protests on November 16, 2012—which the Brotherhood, among many others, had called for—saw unprecedented calls for the fall of the Jordanian regime. Bani Irsheid, in his role as deputy leader of the Brotherhood, openly sympathized with the calls. "Those who are calling for the fall of the regime are increasing," he said. "This cannot and should not be ignored" (AFP 2012). In other statements, Bani Irsheid specifically pointed to the king's role: "Every day the King delays intervention to reverse the resolution that ignited this, things become more complicated. The street may take the country's governance to the point of no return" (Al-Najjar 2012).

The sharpness of the rhetoric is new, but the tensions are not. For years, particularly since the turn to repression of the 1990s, Jordan's Islamists have found themselves pledging allegiance to the same political system that had insisted on marginalizing them. It is a delicate, difficult dance, and one that may not be sustainable. If it ever does come to the "point of no return," to use the words of Bani Irsheid, the IAF—like its counterparts in Egypt and Tunisia—will find itself in a strong position to fill the inevitable power vacuum.

Notes

1. All translations my own unless otherwise noted.
2. The law enforced the use of the single nontransferable vote (SNTV), an exceedingly rare voting system that particularly disadvantages organized political parties. It is used on the national level by only two other countries in the world, Afghanistan and the Republic of Vanuatu (see "Assessment of the Electoral Framework: The Hashemite Kingdom of Jordan," Democracy Reporting International and New Jordan Research Center [Berlin, Germany: Democracy Reporting International, 2007, p 16). In Libya's July 2012 elections, 80 of the General National Congress's 200 members were elected using SNTV.
3. This is the total number of both Muslim Brotherhood and independent Islamist members of parliament.
4. See "Assessment of the Electoral Framework: The Hashemite Kingdom of Jordan," p 19.
5. Interview with Ziad Abu Ghanimeh, Amman, May 28, 2005.
6. Interview by author with Jihad Abu Eis, Amman, May 27, 2005.
7. Interview by author with Ibrahim Gharaibeh, Amman, June 2, 2005.
8. For more on King Abdullah's approach to reform, see Shadi Hamid, "Jordan: The Myth of the Democratizing Monarchy," in eds. Nathan Brown and Emad Shahin, *The Struggle Over Democracy in the Middle East* (New York: Routledge, 2009).
9. Interview with author, Nael Masalha, April 20, 2005.
10. *Na'am, Al-Islam Hoa al-Hal: Al-Barnamaj al-Intakhabi li-Murashahi Hizb al-Jabha al-'Amal al-Islami, 1993–1997*, p 12.
11. The other parties include the Jordanian Communist Party and two Ba'athist parties.
12. Interview by author with Ishaq Farhan, Zarqa, Jordan, May 16, 2005.
13. Interview with Bassam al-Emoush, Zarqa, May 29, 2005.
14. This issue is contested by IAF leaders and has been a source of great controversy within the organization. Some officials whom I interviewed vigorously denied the existence of any "deal" between the government and the IAF. However, there is ample evidence that there was at least an understanding, although it is unclear how explicit it was or to what extent it was the initiative of individual leaders acting without official authorization from the party. However, several senior IAF leaders and former members confirmed the existence of such an "understanding," while others suggested there was some degree of "coordination."
15. Interview by author with Abdel Majid Thneibat, Amman, August 27, 2008.

References

Abdul Kazem, Ali. 1997. "The Muslim Brotherhood: The Historic Background and the Ideological Origins," in *The Islamic Movement in Jordan*, ed. Jillian Schwedler (Amman: Al-Urdun Al-Jadid Research Center).
Agence France Presse. 2012. "Thousands of Angry Jordanians Call for King to Go." November 16. http://english.ahram.org.eg/News/58316.aspx.

Brown, Nathan J. 2006. *Jordan and Its Islamic Movement*. The Carnegie Endowment, Washington, DC, November.
Buck, Tobias. 2012. "Jordan's Opposition Groups Stage Protest." *The Financial Times*. FT.com. October 5. http://www.ft.com/intl/cms/s/0/fe0ad976-0f09-11e2-9895-00144feabdc0.html-#axzz2C6OaaxKU. Accessed November 13, 2012.
Clark, Janine Astrid, and Jillian Schwedler. 2003. Who Opened the Window? Women's Activism in Islamist Parties. *Comparative Politics* 35, April.
Clark, Janine A. 2006. The Conditions of Islamist Moderation: Unpacking Cross-Ideological Cooperation in Jordan. *International Journal of Middle East Studies* 38, November.
Cohen, Amnon. 1982. *Political Parties in the West Bank under the Jordanian Regime, 1949–1967*. Ithaca, NY: Cornell University Press.
al-Emoush, Bassam. 2008. Letter to Prime Minister. IAF Parliamentary Bloc, March 25, 1995. Reproduced in *Mahatat fi Tarikh al-Ikhwan al-Muslimin* [Stations in the History of the Muslim Brotherhood]. Amman: Academics for Publishing and Distribution.
"Freedom in the World—Jordan." 2007. Freedom House. http://www.freedomhouse.org/modules/mod_call_dsp_country-fiw.cfm?year=2007&country=7203.
Dietrich, Renate. 2002. The Weakness of the Rule Is the Strength of the Rule. In *Jordan in Transition: 1990–2000*, ed. George Joffe. New York: Palgrave.
Gharaibeh, Ibrahim. 1997. *Jama`a al-Ikhwan al-Muslimin fi al-Urdun, 1946–1996* [The Society of Muslim Brothers in Jordan]. Amman: Al-Urdun Al-Jadid Research Center.
Hamid, Shadi. 2005. Jordan: Democracy at a Dead End. *Arab Reform Bulletin*. Carnegie Endowment, May.
Hamzeh, Alia Shukri, and Rakan Saaideh. 2005. "Government Refers Unions' Draft Law to House." *Jordan Times a*, March 7.
Hussein, Mohammad ben. 2006. "Human Rights Activists Criticize Arrest of IAF Deputies." *Jordan Times b*, June 17.
Hussein, Mohammad ben. 2006. "Islamist Shura Council Rejects Members' Resignations." *Jordan Times d*, July 23.
"Islamic Charity Referred to Public Prosecutor." 2006. *Jordan Times*, July 6.
al-Khalidi, Suleiman. 2012. "In Biggest Protest: Jordan Islamists Demand Change." Reuters, October 5, 2012. http://www.reuters.com/article/2012/10/05/us-jordan-protests-idUSBRE8940ZF20121005.
al-Kilani, Musa. 1994. *Al-Harakat al-Islamiya fi al-Urdun wa Falastin* [Islamic Movements in Jordan and Palestine]. Amman: Dar al-Bashir.
Levitt, Matthew, and David Schenker. 2008. Amman Warms to Hamas. Washington Institute for Near East Policy, August 28. http://www.washingtoninstitute.org/templateC05.php?CID=2925.
al-Najjar, Muhammad. 2012. "*Hal yatahawwal al-Urdun nahwa 'Isqat al-Nidham'?*" [Is Jordan Turning towards the "Fall of the Regime"?]. *Al Jazeera*. AlJazeera.net, November 12. http://www.aljazeera.net/light/f6451603-4dff-4ca1-9c10-122741d17432/d85e4ebc-513e-48e9-8 09f-2a194000ad60. Accessed November 18, 2012.
al-Nizam al-Assasi. 1992. Islamic Action Front, Amman.
al-Safadi, Ayman. 2007. "*Marhalat Kasr al-`Idham*" [Era of Broken Bones]. *Al-Ghad*, August 5.
al-Samadi, Tamer. 2012. "'*Ikhwan' al-Urdun yatlubun ta'jeel al-intikhabat wa liqa' al-Malak wa ahzab mu`arada ta`tazam al-musharaka wufq tafahhumat ma` al-dawla*" [Jordan's Brotherhood Demands Elections' Postponement and a Meeting with King; Opposition Parties Intend to Participate According to Understandings with State]. *Al-Hayat*. Alhayat.com, October 22. http://alhayat.com/Details/446654. Accessed November 13, 2012.

Satloff, Robert. 1986. *Troubles on the East Bank: Challenges to the Domestic Stability of Jordan*. New York: Praeger.

Schwedler, Jillian. 2006. *Faith in Moderation: Islamist Parties in Jordan and Yemen*. Cambridge, UK: Cambridge University Press.

Na`am, Al-Islam Hoa al-Hal: Al-Barnamaj al-Intakhabi li-Murashahi Hizb al-Jabha al-`Amal al-Islami, 1993–1997 [Yes, Islam Is the Solution: The Electoral Program of the Islamic Action Front Candidates]. Amman. October 1993.

1997. *Limadha Yuqati` al-Ikwhan al-Muslimun al-Intakhabat al-Niyabiya li-`Am 1997, Hadha Bayanun li-al Nas* [Why Is the Muslim Brotherhood Boycotting the Parliamentary Elections in 1997? A Statement to the People]. Amman. July 13.

2003. *Na`am wa ila al-abad al-Islam huwa al-hal: Al-Barnamaj al-Intakhabi li-Murashahi Hizb Jabhta al-`Amal al-Islami, 2003–2007* [Yes and Forever, Islam Is the Solution: The Electoral Program of the Islamic Action Front Candidates].

2005. *Ru'iat al-Haraka al-Islamiya li al-Islah fi al-Urdun* [Perspective of the Islamic Movement toward Reform in Jordan]. The Islamic Action Front and the Muslim Brotherhood.

2007. *Na`am, al-Islam huwa al-hal: Al Al-Barnamaj al-Intakhabi li-Murashahi Hizb al-Jabhat al-Amal al-Islami, 2007–2011* [Yes, Islam Is the Solution: The Electoral Program of the Islamic Action Front Candidates]. October.

2012. "*Mansour: Al-hal fi al-tawafuq 'ala qanoon intikhab wa jadwalat baqi al-matalib*" [Mansour: The Solution Lies in Agreement on Election Law and Scheduling Other Demands]. October 8 http://www.ikhwanjo.com/#3%2011709. Accessed November 13, 2012.

2011. "Rallies for Reform Held in Jordan." *Al Jazeera*. Aljazeera.com, February 4. http://www.aljazeera.com/news/middleeast/2011/02/201124141624836763.html. Accessed November 13, 2012.

CHAPTER 36

NAHDLATUL ULAMA IN INDONESIA

ANDRÉE FEILLARD

THE last decade represented a major shift for Indonesia's largest Islamic organization, the Nahdlatul Ulama (NU, the Renaissance of *'Ulamā'*): it acquired a national political role in 1999 with the election of its chairman Abdurrahman Wahid as president of the Republic of Indonesia, and an international one after 9/11 when all parties sought the help of this mass organization, maybe the largest in the world, as it boasts some 40 million sympathizers.[1]

But the year 2001 was not such a good year after all for the NU: President Abdurrahman Wahid's impeachment in July was a major setback, indeed an affront. Memories of the painful defeat faded in the new geopolitical urgency when, two months later, the 9/11 tragedy offered a new beginning with the United States, its allies, and Middle Eastern countries, suddenly multiplying visits at its headquarters, rivaling for its support.

Born in 1926 in a time of strong reformist zeal as an association of *'Ulamā'* and traders defending both traditionalist religious practices (the Shafi'i school of law, the saints cult, and Sufi brotherhoods) and their economic interests, the NU was one of the few Islamic organizations to have weathered the turbulent decades of the twentieth century almost unhurt. Traditionalist in its rituals, the NU did show a capacity to adapt to modernity, opening its Islamic boarding schools (*pesantren* in Java) to general subjects from the 1920s on, following the model of the Islamic schools of the Reformist Muhammadiyah, Indonesia's second largest Islamic organization until today. During World War II, Japan's occupation served to promote Islamic organizations to a national role, politicizing the *kiai* (*'Ulamā'* in Java); later, the anticolonial struggle (1945–1949) brought them in close contact to secular nationalist groups and the military. And in the 1950s, the newly independent republic offered them the opportunity to enter parliament and governments.[2] As a political party able to capture 18 percent of the electorate, the NU survived thanks to subtle strategies of conciliation often with secular nationalists, which earned it being branded opportunists by modern-educated Muslim reformists. The post-1965 Soeharto period was one of frustration for Islamic organizations in general, as hopes of a role in rebuilding anticommunist Indonesia were dashed, a role viewed as legitimate for the NU after its very active contribution both to the bloody anticommunist repression and to the constitutional rise to the presidency of General Soeharto.

One can imagine that this first decade of democracy in the twenty-first century has been upsetting, full of hopes and fears for the old guard of '*Ulamā*' closely watching a new world coming, with the third and fourth NU generations being increasingly in charge. This essay will look at the impact on this old institution of the young democracy that converged with a wave of violent Islamist radicalism. A decade of democracy has opened unexpected opportunities for the NU, which had survived a whole century as a marginal partner in a political world dominated by secular authoritarian governments.

These opportunities have carried their own costs and benefits. The increased international role of the '*Ulamā*' highlights NU's ambivalence, at times denying any radical Islamist responsibility but also playing an active moderating role. Second, on the national scene, the Wahid presidency showed that liberal Islam had to bow not only to old status quo forces but also to Islamist conservatives, who have found some support within the traditionalist organization itself. Wahid's impeachment brought into the open latent tensions, triggering a new assertiveness of conservatives trying to reclaim the organization's leadership. This in turn freed the young liberal generation to look for their own political expression in new Islamist or in ostensibly secular parties. I argue that, despite the relative discredit from a chaotic political role under the Wahid presidency, young traditionalist scholars remain central as assistants to secular democrats in search of an efficient discourse to counter Islamist influence. But for the '*Ulamā*', ten years after 1998, nostalgia at the comfortable position of the late 1980s goes with a recognition that there is no way back. How best to defend the NU's interests and those of its individual members is now a more complex question with many answers.

The Impact of 9/11 and the Bali Bombings: From Denial to Mediation

The year before 9/11 may have been one of the most painful for millions of NU sympathizers who saw the demise of their charismatic chief, elected by a coalition of Islamic parties, ousted by that same coalition less than two years later (October 1999–July 2001). Major issues had been at stake, but foreign affairs played a crucial role as his proposal to restore commercial ties with Israel was the first of many highly divisive issues. Wahid, popularly known as Gus Dur, had earlier been the first Muslim Indonesian public figure to visit Israel to witness the signing of a peace agreement with Jordan in 1994.

The 9/11 events and more so the Afghanistan war, presented in a rather anti-US light by the Indonesian media, converged with a mood of disillusionment at Wahid's impeachment in July 2001 to nurture an anti-Western stance that had become unusual for the old "moderate" organization.

In September 2001, secular Megawati Soekarnoputri had just been elected president of Indonesia with the voices of the conservative Muslim politicians who had rejected her only two years before. She became the first foreign head of state to meet President George W. Bush after the World Trade Center attacks during a trip to the United States planned before 9/11.

Never before had the geopolitical order become such a subject of preoccupation for NU politicians: the first reaction was one of denial of any link between 9/11 and radical violent Islamism. Conspiracy theories blaming either the Mossad or American neoconservatives were highly popular in 'Ulamā' circles, the older generation preferring the first, the left-leaning young activists the second. In the educated *pesantren* elite, some muttered comparisons with Hiroshima. Strong anti-Semitism popped up in private conversations, at times in public speeches.

All of a sudden, this Java-based rural mass organization became the focus of foreign attention. Hasyim Muzadi, Wahid's replacement as NU chairman, received visit after visit of ambassadors from both Western and Middle Eastern countries. Invitations to foreign countries poured in. As one NU executive commented with satisfaction in the internal magazine *Aula*, 'Ulamā', who had painfully earned a few rupiah leading *tahlilan* prayers for the deceased were now suddenly offered world tours. Western countries started to respond to NU's quest for programs of human resources development, whereas so far they came from Middle Eastern countries such as Egypt, Sudan, Syria, Libya, Yemen, and Saudi Arabia. The United States, the United Kingdom, and Australia were particularly active in launching invitations. Several tours were organized for *pesantren* leaders in the United Kingdom.[3]

In the wake of the war in Iraq, Hasyim Muzadi went to the Vatican with religious leaders from all faiths on a tour organized by the foreign ministry, in order to demonstrate that all faiths oppose war and to counter the "war against Islam" theory. He also visited Iran where he was charmed by Ahmadinejad. Hasyim often adopted a rather anti-Western and certainly antiliberal position, but he has also been active in efforts to ease interreligious tensions.

The NU started playing a new diplomatic role. In 2003, it hosted the first International Conference of Islamic Scholars (ICIS), aimed among other things at "fostering respect and understanding between Muslims and non-Muslims" (Bush 2009, 195). ICIS was later institutionalized as a biennial event organized under the sponsorship of the Indonesian Ministry of Foreign Affairs. At its thirty-second congress, the NU innovated by inviting foreign Islamic scholars for a one-day session on international issues, confirming the international dimension added by Hasyim Muzadi in the past ten years.[4] This foreign exposure continued with diplomatic trips in conflict areas. Hasyim Muzadi was invited by Bangkok several times to mediate with the southern Thaï insurgents. He went to Libya to meet with Mu'ammar al-Qadhafi. Later, Abdurrahman Wahid himself tried to mediate in Kuala Lumpur between the government and Anwar Ibrahim. Although observers do not attribute much success to these initiatives, in general the traditionalist organization was seen as a stabilizing factor, especially so in the domestic scene.

The first Bali bombings (202 dead in October 2002) and the Maluku interreligious conflict (up to 8000 dead, 1999–2002) had indeed made NU's expected moderating role crucial. Radical Islamist violence, long denied, had become reality at home. Megawati's conservative Vice-President Hamzah Haz, a NU politician, openly showed his support for Abu Bakar Ba'asyir, then accused of ties with the Jemaah Islamiyah group, involved in the Bali bombings. But the NU headquarters, while remaining courteous to the radicals who sought its help, kept a safe distance from the group, as it had mostly done during the Darul Islam rebellion of the 1950s. It proudly repeated that "no terrorist came from NU Islamic boarding schools."

No other issue has highlighted NU's ambivalence toward the West more than international Islamic radicalism, but this stance was also linked to a highly conflictual domestic context.

The Wahid Presidency: A Spiral of Failure

After thirty-two years of authoritarian regime under Soeharto, the NU had become a central player in the new democracy because of its representativeness as a mass organization that could escape years of control touching political parties. The NU had been increasingly influential as a lobby in the 1980s and in the 1990s, courted by all political forces after its decision to "withdraw from politics" in 1984—phrased as "a return to the spirit of 1926," but de facto a withdrawal of its exclusive support to the sole Islamic political party PPP (Party of Unity and Development).

After the 1984 withdrawal, although cadres were not allowed to hold formal positions simultaneously in NU and political parties, Wahid repeatedly called on activists to join all political parties, which they did mostly in favor of the government party Golkar and for a minority in favor of the very secular PDI (later PDI-P, Democratic Party-Struggle), led by former President Soekarno's daughter Megawati. In 1991, Abdurrahman Wahid went further, creating a Forum Demokrasi opposing the new Association of Indonesian Muslim Intellectuals (ICMI), which Soeharto had co-opted after the army grew more critical of his nepotism and corruption. But unwilling to risk jeopardizing improving relations with the regime, no major 'Ulamā' joined the Forum Demokrasi.

Soon after Soeharto's fall in 1998, the liberalization of political life (forty-eight political parties in 1999, instead of three during Soeharto) presented the dilemma of whether NU should create its own political party. The 'Ulamā's attraction to politics has varied over time depending on the persons in charge, but the NU itself was created by an 'Ulamā' politician, Wahab Hasbullah. To defend the traditionalist dogma against reformist Muslims, and in search of subsidies for Islamic boarding schools and other infrastructures, the control of the Ministry of Religious Affairs had been a key objective since independence. Other executive positions were also coveted for patronage purposes, be it for subsidies or tenders needed by the clientele. Finally, access to parliament made sure that no laws would pass that were not in accordance with traditionalist Islamic rules and values. Politics was thus always considered a necessity, but its modalities were debatable. Moreover, 'Ulamā' involved in politics were of two kinds: for many it was for the interests of the *umat*, also understood as NU members or sympathizers, for others self-interest prevailed. Increasingly so, liberal NU intellectuals complain, *kiais* entered the political arena simply for their living, becoming less dedicated to society and more dependent on power holders (Interview K. H. Husein Muhammad, May 27, 2010).

After Wahid created the PKB (Party of National Awakening) in 1998, debates were muted on whether it should become an official vehicle for the *kiais*' organization (Bush 2009, 161–164). The new party would clearly benefit from NU's infrastructure, connections, and grass roots networks built up long ago. Reentry into politics accelerated considerably when the NU chairman decided to be a candidate for the presidency of the republic. Wahid did so against the advice of the most senior *kiais*, afraid that a failure would have dramatic effects on the whole organization (Feillard 2002, 121–122). As noted by Martin van Bruinessen, while the young generation of socially committed activists was anxious about patronage politics, the local-level leadership seemed happy at the potential benefits the presidency would have. The gap between the two seemed enormous (Bruinessen 2002, 22).

With Wahid's election as president of Indonesia in October 1999, the question arose of whether the NU (with its party, the PKB) would become a support structure for Wahid himself, which it did, abandoning its role as an autonomous counterbalance to the state (Bush 2009, 170).

But this turned out to be a tricky exercise. Defending the president became embarrassing for both PKB and NU, as Wahid's policies earned him new enemies every day. After raising Islamist ire with the proposal to open trade relations with Israel, Wahid proposed to lift the 1966 ban on communism. Later, he turned against the military close to the old status quo forces, provoking reactions from some military elements who used Islamist militia to fan ethnic and religious violence in the Moluccas (Kingsbury and Fernandes 2005, 25; Noorhaidi 2002, 148). Increasingly, Wahid, who was nearly blind, concentrated on holding to power in a purely defensive attitude (Mietzner 2001, 43). But his missteps and misstatements played into the opposition's hands. He was accused of corruption and incompetence. A siege mentality followed the 1999 euphoria.

Wahid loyalists, feeling unfairness and powerlessness, reacted at times with violence, leading to a tug of war between some NU Banser paramilitaries and the media accused of bias in favor of reformist/modernist Islam. From November 2000, demonstrations of force by the Banser paramilitaries and acts of intimidation multiplied against the modern-educated reformists. Between February and July 2001, according to a Muhammadiyah publication, political violence touched five universities, twelve schools, five clinics, four mosques, and nine representative offices linked to the Muhammadiyah, as well as at least eighteen houses of the organization's local leaders (Sophiaan et al. 2002, 23). Preceding his ouster, Wahid himself reacted with verbal attacks on nongovernmental organizations (NGOs) and the press, "a tool of foreign interests," in a blatant reversal of the long lasting reciprocal close relationship with NGOs (Bush 2009, 174).[5]

Fiqh experts were consulted on whether this insubordination to the president could legitimately be fought as *bughot* (insurgents against a legitimate ruler). '*Ulamā*' agreed that demonstrations and other actions against the legitimate ruler were acceptable only "if the president is prov`en to have violated the constitution, which itself is not in contradiction with the *Shari`a*," and "if these efforts do not create a worse state of affairs (*mafsadah*, cause of evil)" (Feillard 2002, 131). This decision in favor of *bughot*, in defense of Wahid, was however not signed by NU's supreme leader (*rois aam*) Sahal Mahfudh.

An extraordinary session of the Consultative Assembly (MPR) impeached Wahid on July 23, 2001, with almost no street protests. NU's executive chairman Hasyim Muzadi himself, increasingly critical of Wahid's policies, was instrumental in preventing street violence, creating a split between the two men that was to last a long time. To calm Wahid loyalists, Megawati chose a NU person as vice-president, Hamzah Haz, a conservative politician—just as Wahid had chosen her as vice-president in 1999 to avoid reactions from her fierce loyalists, often the Javanese less pious lower class (van Bruinessen 2002; Feillard 2002; Bush 2009). The enormous expectations put on Wahid's presidency were reduced to nothing. For his own followers, disappointment peaked at his last moment effort to disband the Consultative Assembly.

This painful and shameful moment for Wahid and the whole NU became the starting point of a multitude of political divisions, which impacted deeply on this mass organization that had enjoyed undeniable respect under Wahid's leadership for the past two decades. A feeling of "unfair" treatment and humiliation was widely shared in NU, leaving indelible scars (van Bruinessen 2002, 38; Feillard 2002, 137).

The consequences of this impeachment were numerous. The following splits definitely weakened PKB's quasimonopoly on the Nahdlatul Ulama constituency, which went to other political parties and to a lesser extent to new political parties created by NU cadres. Within the PKB itself a split in 2005 crippled the party for months, and in 2007 it finally escaped Wahid's control into the hands of his own nephew, Muhaimin Iskandar. Within only ten years, the PKB had lost half of its electorate (from less than 12 percent in 1999 to 4.9 percent in 2009, with 5.1 million votes). In East Java, its stronghold, a province of 37 million, PKB had been number one in 2004 with over 30 percent of the vote, but in 2009 it fell behind two so-called secular nationalist parties, President Susilo's Partai Demokrat and Megawati's PDI-P. Indeed, the PKB's loss of so many votes was due to not only spontaneous voters disaffection, but also the result of Wahid's own campaigning in favor of Gerindra, the new party of General Prabowo, Soeharto's former son-in-law—much to the concern of Wahid's liberal friends. In 2009 it seemed that NU's own standing was now dropping. Its leaders became less courted for the presidential elections: while in 2004 all but one of the five presidential candidates were accompanied by one traditionalist partner, in 2009 only one man boasted special ties to the organization, that is, former Vice-President Yusuf Kalla who only obtained 18 percent of the vote, as against 60 percent for incumbent President Susilo Bambang Yudhoyono.

However this sharp drop of votes should not be viewed as a total failure, as both the NU and the PKB have remained key players and potential partners for politicians in search of religious credentials. This is especially so at the local level and in traditionalist strongholds. The near election of a PPP cadre and NU activist, Mrs. Kofifah Indar Parawansa, as governor of Indonesia's most populous province, East Java, in 2008 is a case in point (the elected governor had one of Wahid's nephews as vice-governor). At the district level, NU cadres do remain in demand. For example, in the district of Kendal (Central Java), all NU cadres had been adopted by one or another political party in the 2009 elections (Dimyati Rois, December 9, 2008). The son of *Kiai* Dimyati Rois, an influential `alim, was easily elected as member of the national parliament in 2009 with about 60,000 votes, coming much ahead of the second candidate from Golkar, a national figure, Siswono, who reached a mere 17,000 votes.

Voters may be less tied to brokers coming in the name of `Ulamā' (Ufen 2008, 36), but direct family ties continue to play a role, especially when they activate religious networks and structures such as those of former students, *majelis ta`lim* (religious gatherings) and NU-affiliated organizations of women (Muslimat), younger women (Fatayat, IPPNU), younger men (IPNU), or students (PMII). Thus, Nafisah, the wife of Nahdlatul Ulamas' supreme leader, *rois aam* Sahal Mahfudh, was elected to the regions representative Council (DPD) in 2004 partly thanks to the Association of NU women, the Muslimat.

All in all, politics had brought some evident benefits: access to government positions and spoils that strengthened NU's structural networks of schools and clinics. But the costs were also high as money politics, factionalism, and intraparty authoritarianism were damaging the image of PKB, as it did for all political parties (Ufen 2008, 24).[6]

Political participation was not only a risky affair as a result of the discredit politicians easily suffered for mismanagement or corruption, but worse, the `Ulamā' soon discovered they had another good ideological reason to stay on the political scene as democracy had ended up promoting a brand of Islam that they had opposed from the very creation of their association in 1926.

When Democracy Promotes a New Islam

The new Muslim Brotherhood-inspired Prosperous Justice Party (PKS, formerly Party of Justice, or PK) presented an increasingly serious challenge to political parties. The Muhammadiyah in particular, linked to PAN (Party of National Mandate), reacted as early as 2006 with a decree appealing to its members "to liberate themselves from PKS' objectives." For the PKB also, PKS' challenge was starting to be taken seriously, as was the Hizbut Tahrir Indonesia (HTI), most visible and active in East Java, especially in Surabaya, a NU stronghold. It was not merely a question of losing adherents and voters but also assets like mosques or schools that, both NU and Muhammadiyah claimed, PKS and HTI were silently taking over.

In 1999, the PK was a tiny party with only 1.3 percent of the vote, but a clever rebranding with less stress on *Shari'ah* and more on corruption fighting gained the new PKS a rise to 7.3 percent in 2004, enough to become the preferred ally of elected President Susilo Bambang Yudhoyono. PKS chairman Hidayat Nur Wahid was picked up as head of the state's supreme body, the Consultative Assembly (MPR). In opinion polls, he now surpassed in popularity NU's own star, Abdurrahman Wahid.

This ascension became a matter of worry after 2004 when the *kiais* realized the PKS could court the traditionalist constituency itself. So far, there had been sympathy among some Javanese *kiais* for these young *dakwah* activists who were not only seen as models of piety but also models of activism (Feillard 2008). Their progression on the nonreligious campuses of the scripturalist *dakwah* movement, also called *usroh* and later *tarbiyah*, small groups modeled after the Egyptian Muslim Brotherhood, had somehow escaped their attention in the 1980s, maybe because it was also a time when campuses of State Institutes of Islamic Studies (IAIN) were on the contrary the center of a movement advocating "contextualization." But in nonreligious universities, the *dakwah* activists had progressively marginalized the old "modernist" association of Muslim Students HMI Himpunan Mahasiswa Islam, The Association of Muslim Students

closer to the progressive Renewal (*Pembaharuan*) Movement (Latif 2008, 369–383). After Soeharto's fall in 1998, the *tarbiyah/usroh* clandestine movement became a powerful student association (KAMMI, Indonesian Muslim Student Action Union) and a political party soon after, the PK, the Party of Justice.

At the provincial level, "*ulamā*", and politicians worried when the 2004 elections showed that PKS results had become increasingly close to those of the PKB. In urbanized areas, such as Semarang and the northeast of Yogyakarta for example, the young *dakwah* party was stronger than the '*Ulamā*' party. The new electoral system of 2003 had contributed to favoring smaller or middle-sized parties, including the PKS.[7]

As was the case for the Muhammadiyah, the NU now took the measure of the new phenomenon. PKS flags were seen in the remotest villages of Java, where the PKS itself had no representative. More alarming was the all-encompassing discourse presented by the new party, which made possible a shift of votes in its favor: it claimed to be acceptable by all, "by the NU, the Muhammadiyah, Persis, Al Irsyad, al Khairat, al Washliyah, Mathlaul Anwar, Majelis Tafsir Quran and others," a very exhaustive list of major Islamic organizations. Then the '*Ulamā*' complained that, in a bid to make inroads into the traditionalist constituency, the party had started accepting as *khilaf* (an acceptable point of disagreement) rituals rejected by reformists as innovations (*bidah*), such as prayers for the deceased (*tahlilan*) and reading sessions of the Yasin verses (*Yasinan*). Moreover PKS cadres were allowed to pray the traditionalist or the reformist way.[8] The boundaries between traditionalist and reformist constituencies were suddenly blurred: whereas Muhammadiyah's PAN party, faithful to the reformist dogma and sensitive to *bidah* transgressions, would never reach traditionalist voters, now the PKS could.

The *dakwah* party also tried a rapprochement with NU local leaders, in search of coalition partners. Nothing unusual here, as PKS tactical alliances did take place with other parties as well, including the very secular PDI-P and the minor Christian PDS (Partai Damai Sejahtera, Prosperous Peace Party). They occurred also with the PKB in Central Java for local executive elections (*pilkada*) in Demak and Pekalongan.

The '*Ulamā*' may have been overly worried about the young *dakwah* activists, who seem to hold the traditionalist constituency as one of the most difficult to absorb, whereas other parties such as Golkar, PPP, and PAN are qualified as soft (*empuk*; Feillard 2008, 227). Whatever the case, the PKS recognized that "marginalized NU" people were willing to join: among their seven MPs in the provincial Parliament of Central Java, four had a NU background.

The NU was divided about just how fragile it now was. The *kiais* living in East Java, its stronghold, tended to be more confident than those of Central Java. There major *kiais* privately accused the PKS of *takiyah* (dissimulation, hiding one's true opinions and beliefs) for presenting a democratic image. To face this competition, some proposed to revive old evening sessions of *Lailatul Ijtima*, religious sessions used in the 1950s to promote political messages (Feillard 2008, 223–224). Others expressed their powerlessness and helplessness at the size of the phenomenon of new Islamic groups' deployment.

Fear of the PKS was probably excessive as it was only very partly responsible for PKB's loss of some 5 million votes over ten years that went mostly to the Islamic PPP, but also to Golkar and to President Susilo's Partai Demokrat, the two reputedly "secular" parties. They indeed had made intensive efforts to court the larger constituency of self-consciously devout Muslims. Partai Demokrat insisted it was "religious" besides being "nationalist." But some of the PKS predictions were right. PKS indeed became Indonesia's largest Islamic political party in 2009, although with a smaller share of the vote than predicted (7.8 percent and not the 20 percent announced). The NU that ranked first among Islamic political parties since the Masyumi ban of 1960 had lost the position it was holding for forty-nine years.

Ideological Tensions

For some time after Soeharto's fall, Wahid was able to impose his liberal line. When he decided to create the PKB as an "open" party accepting non-Muslims, many *kiais* and politicians had difficulties to accept the innovation, but they were given no real choice. Moderation became the rule. In 2000, the NU (and the Muhammadiyah) opposed a move by Islamist parties to further Islamize the Republic's constitution. Liberals were also happy with Wahid's decision as president of Indonesia to suppress a 1967 decree that restricted the practice of Confucianism, which was added to the officially recognized religions, Islam, Protestantism, Catholicism, Hinduism, and Buddhism. But it soon appeared that Wahid had his hands tied by his alliance with Islamist parties. His liberal disciples regretted that he agreed to give Aceh a right to Shari'ah implementation, derived from the decentralization laws, and which resulted in the creation of a religious police (*wilayatul hisbah*) controlling among others that women do wear the veil and that men and women keep proper distance (*khalwat*). They also regretted his acceptance of local Shari'ah by-laws in some other regencies, which included making veiling mandatory for civil servants (thirteen of sixty by-laws listed touched veiling; Arskal Salim 2008, 11–13), forbidding shops to open during Friday prayers, banning women to go out at night without a *mahram*. These policies were, so some loyalists regretted, "the opposite of what Wahid had been fighting for, total religious freedom without any state intervention" (Rumadi 2002, 145–146).

Although Shari'ah by-laws passed by local administrations were present in NU-dominated areas such as East Java (mostly morality actions against drinking, gambling, prostitution), they were in fact not necessarily initiated by Islamic parties but also by reputedly "secular" parties such as Golkar, mainly part of electoral strategies. Divergences of views within the Islamic mass organization became evident on the question of Islamic law, highlighted during parliamentary debates on the Antipornography Law in 2006 and 2008. The 2006 draft law had produced an outcry among the intelligentsia, artists and women activists, as its vague wording endangered artistic and intellectual production: writings, poetry, films, photos, paintings deemed to "exploit the attraction" of a sensual part of the body, of erotic dancing, or even a kiss would be banned.

Wahid's PKB joined the democratic PDI-P to counter the draft. The three Islamist parties (PKS, PPP [Partai Persatuan Pembangunan, United Development Party], and PBB [Partai Bulan Bintang, Crescent Star Party]), argued in favor of the law. One major argument was that "the majority agrees" (numerically Muslims make up 88 percent of the population), an old argument popping up again since 2000, whereas the antilaw activists responded, among others, that the 1945 national consensus wanted all citizens to be equal before the law, the non-Muslim minorities becoming an argument against Shari'ah implementation. Finally, a revised draft was voted by parliament in November 2008, still countered by liberals who complained of a too vague wording again: it spoke of banning what gave an "impression of nudity" and appealed on civil society to cooperate in eradicating pornography, thus potentially legitimating moral order Islamist militia active since the early 2000s. This time the law had the support of the PKB, which was no longer under Wahid's leadership since 2007. It has been so far very rarely applied, as non-Muslim regions such as Hindu Bali filed a judicial review but the debate highlighted a generational rift within the NU: the association of senior women Muslimat praised the law, some younger Fatayat cadres did not.

The PDI-P was finally alone (with a small Christian party, the PDS) in opposition to the law, attracting the sympathy of Muslim liberals. This coincided with a time when, paradoxically, the PDI-P started to Islamize its own image, following the example of other "secular" parties such as Golkar and the Partai Demokrat. All were intent on not letting Islamic symbols benefit merely Islamic parties. The appeal of Soekarnoist nationalism had proven to be no longer enough in 2004, when the PDI-P lost over 16 percent of its voters in five years (from 35 percent 1999 it fell to 18 percent). The nationalist party, ranking first in 1955, had realized that its electorate of mostly "nominal" Javanese Muslims had definitely become more pious.[9]

Taking stock of this evolution, the secular PDI-P innovated before the 2009 elections, creating an official body to enhance its Islamic image and channel Islamic support, the BAMUSI (Baitul Muslimin Indonesia). A well-known NU *kiai* was later appointed at one of its heads, Said Aqil Siraj, a Saudi graduate, while many of BAMUSI's Java local representatives were NU activists. Furthermore, the PDI-P co-opted a new brand of MP candidates, clever and religious (*agamis*), including some *pesantren*-trained Muslim intellectuals of high caliber such as Zuhairi Misrawi, an Al-Azhar graduate active in the liberal NGO P3M (Perhimpunan Pengembangan pesantren dan Masyarakat/Society for Islamic boarding schools and Community Development). These candidates differed from earlier PDI-P candidates with Islamic credentials, who were picked up for their family links, but enjoyed no real reputation as Islamic scholars.

How far PDI-P was able to attract voters from outside its constituency is uncertain. What is clear is that the new political freedom acquired since 1984 (PPP withdrawal) and 1998 (democratic transition) as well as the ideological debates arising out of demands for more *Shari'ah* pressed Muslim activists to take position. While conservative Islamist NU cadres like Tamsil Linrung in Sulawesi went to the moderately Islamist PKS, liberal or pluralist activists like Zuhairi Misrawi in Madura chose the secular PDI-P. He and others are still rare pioneers but they may open the way for politicians of a new brand, *pesantren*-trained activists politically representing pluralism or secularism. Later, NU's young liberal star, Ulil Abshar Abdalla joined the Partai Demokrat. This development is still in an embryonic stage, but it reinforces the de-alignment of Indonesian politics theory exposed by Ufen (2008).

Certainly, these ideological debates gave a new impetus to Muslim scholars who had been for three decades at the center of the Renewal Movement (Pembaharuan), a movement that had made Indonesia, in the words of Michael Feener, "arguably the world's most vibrant center of contemporary Islamic thought" (Feener 2007, 225). Debates about the *Shari'ah* had become concrete issues, thus attracting attention outside the religious expert's sphere.

THE PLURALIST HERITAGE IN THE SERVICE OF DEMOCRACY

The post-1998 era brought many NU cadres into PKB politics but young university students also found new jobs in the NGOs multiplying in the new Reformasi era (Bruinessen and Wajidi 2006, 231). The gap between them and NU's politicized Banser paramilitia widened. The authority of the traditional elite, the *kiais* and their children, the so-called Gus started to be questioned by both the young NU generation and by the radical reformists who accused NU loyalists of deifying the *kiais*. The internal split appeared clearly at the 2004 NU congress, which turned down Wahid's designated nominee for the organization's chairmanship, Masdar Mas'udi, a pioneer intellectual involved in social justice and human rights advocacy.

NU conservatives were reasserting their authority, which was strengthened by their presence in the National Council of 'Ulamā' (MUI), a semiofficial *fatwa*-making body whose power had increased in the post-Soeharto period mainly because additional tasks such as the "halalization" of products and Islamic finance had given it new authority in mostly weak governments (Feener 2007). A point of rupture was reached between the ultraconservatives and the "moderates" in July 2005 when the MUI issued an eleven-point fatwa against "liberalism" (meaning liberal, progressive Islam), pluralism, secularism, shamanism, and the Ahmadiyah sect. 'Ulamā' from the NU were key figures in the *fatwa* commission. Within the Nahdlatul Ulama itself, the growing rift between the *kiais* and Gus Dur could only strengthen the conservative current's resolve to let free their reservations about him, despite his almost untouchable position as the grandchild of the revered NU founder, Hasyim Asy'ari.

The centers of the Renewal Movement, the State Institutes of Islamic Studies (IAIN, UIN), where the teaching of the classical Islamic sciences was opened to historical and contextualizing methodologies since the 1970s, became the target of intense competition (Azra et al. 2007, 185–191; Latif 2008, 383–395). In 2001, they developed a new civics curriculum to provide more effective education on democratic institutions, political participation, and civic values (Bush 2009, 195). In 2003, the law faculty was, however, renamed Fakultas Syariah dan Qanun, working no longer only on the development of *fiqh*, but of positive law as well (Feener 2007, 219). In 2005, radical Islamists directed their sharp critique against the Islamic state universities accused of being the breeding ground for "apostasy."[10] The young liberals, Ulil Abshar Abdalla and Moqsith Ghazali, both from JIL (Liberal Islamic Network) accepted facing their censors courageously in a tense debate. This debate was certainly witness to the radicals' audacious assertiveness but also to the remarkable capacity Indonesian extreme polarities have had to address each other, a development observed by Michael Feener (2007, 221).

In parallel to the relative decline of liberal influence within the NU's leadership, democracy has promoted *fiqh* experts who have been increasingly solicited to give informed answers to new questions. Polygamy, for example, has been increasingly popular in Islamist circles and raised intensive discussions. Veiling has become an issue again with the adoption of local *Shari'ah* by-laws imposing it in some schools or administrations. In 2011, East Java, some NU *'ulamā'* have endorsed a governor's ban on Ahmadiyya, and are pressing for a ban on (minor) Shiite groups.

Since the 2000s, sectarian violence affecting interreligious relations have created a new urgency. In response, some *fiqh* experts and liberal intellectuals have proposed daring solutions spread in the form of books.[11] A young scholar, Mun'im Sirry, edited a volume titled *Fiqih Lintas Agama* (Interreligious Fiqh) with a clear pluralist orientation, provoking the ire of Islamists. In *Fiqh Perempuan* (The Fiqh of Women), *Kiai* Husein Muhammad revolutionizes *fiqh* on veiling, marital rape, and female circumcision by highlighting the variety of views among medieval and modern Muslim jurists, arguing they reflect social realities that should also be considered today. Established *pesantren* textbooks also undergo critical study. The *'Uqud al-Lujjayn* (The Couple's Contract) of Muhammad Nawawi of Banten (West Java) has been sharply criticized for its gender biases by *pesantren*-trained scholars who questioned the soundness of the *hadith* cited by this reputed *'Ulamā'*. The most controversial issues are those on interreligious relations.

These attempts "to move forward in the engaged study of Islam through works of epistemological critiques (*kritik nalar*) in order to open up new areas for critical social thought" have been called *"post-traditionalisme"* (Feener 2007, 193). But this movement is not unique to the traditionalists as the modernists have themselves had their own revitalization of Islamic intellectualism. Interestingly, facing conservative Islamists, they have sometimes both joined forces in favor of contextualized interpretations of Islam. So as to enhance their religious legitimacy when Muhammadiyah intellectuals issued a book advocating religious tolerance in 2001 (*Tafsir Tematik al-Quran tentang Hubungan Sosial Antarumat Beragama/ Qur'anic Thematic Tafsir on Interfaith Relations*), they presented a graduate from the well-known NU *pesantren* Tambakberas in Jombang, Chamim Ilyas, as one of the *Tafsir*'s contributors.[12] Such close collaboration in "contextualization" between traditionalist and reformist institutions would have been unthinkable before.

The impact of intellectuals and NGO work may not be that visible all the time but, as Bruinessen and Wajidi argue, they have created a "counter-elite within the NU constituency," socially engaged men and women (Bruinessen and Wajidi 2006, 243). And this elite has found wide acceptance among the better-educated *pesantren* graduates. This activism has translated into the emergence of a new kind of *kiai* and women activists who have proven a real commitment to the interests of the common people rather than the entrepreneurial class and the local power holders (Bruinessen and Wajidi 2006). More recently, NU-affiliated NGOs have again focused on community empowerment, this time through a monitoring of local government budgets and pro-poor advocacy with local government officials (Bush 2009, 198). For Robin Bush, this intellectual movement survived the political turmoil and finally had "a life of its own" (Bush 2009, 196). She adds that, unfortunately, efforts by Western governments to reach out to the Muslim world have impacted badly on "moderate" Muslim NGOs, discredited as agents of the West, something ironic given that "the civil society discourse was indigenous and pre-dated the current dichotomy between 'Western' and 'Islamic' values" (Bush 2009, 197).

Concluding Remarks

More than a decade into the democracy (Reformasi), the old question of how best to defend the NU's interests is relevant again. But, unlike the late 1970s when politicians were accused by the *'Ulamā'* of behaving like "rats," the answers are today as varied as the local contexts. The feeling of having been hijacked by something stronger than them is often expressed among the *'Ulamā'*, leading some to argue in favor of "a return to the original spirit" of the mass organization in 1926, meaning taking more distance from politics, such as in the 1980s when it commanded more respect. This was the motto of many candidates for NU's leadership at its thirty-second congress in March 2010, including the winner, Said Aqil Siraj, who made a simple election campaign arguing for a return to the Islamic boarding school ("*Kembali ke pesantren*"). Siraj was applauded when he promised he would not accept a post of vice-president of Indonesia, while the campaign against Hasyim Muzadi was mainly that he had been "too political."

But what such a proposal of a "return to Islamic boarding schools" might mean remains vague: should the NU have no political party of its own? No NU cadres as members of parliament or in executive jobs? All this sounds unlikely. NU sympathizers have already been freed to vote for any party; should they be retied? In fact, they may be freed at the national level, but they often keep tied at the local level as the NU has been an aggregate of many local authorities, the *kiais*, unlike the Muhammadiyah.

Opinions vary on the way to seek influence without too much damage. Eighty-three-year-old *Kiai* Muchith Muzadi, the brother of Hasyim and one of the "political withdrawal" architects, complained that Nahdlatul Ulama's neutrality had been abused by all parties, that politicians have scrambled to co-opt NU cadres and *'Ulamā'*, but with little benefit for the NU itself. For him, it will take twenty to thirty years for the organization to recover its past strength (Interview December 8, 2008). Central Java NU chairman

Muhammad Adnan is realistic that NU's vote will no longer be contained in one single party, and the question remains of how to make elected MPs give priority to the Nahdlatul Ulama rather than to their party's interests (Interview December 6, 2008). But the influential rural *Kiai* Dimyati Rois, whose son was just elected member of parliament, is happy on the contrary of what he sees everywhere as the "victory" of Nahdlatul Ulama: all now practice Islam the traditionalist way, and the NU is "acknowledged to be the world's largest Islamic organization" (Interview December 9, 2008).

Internecine strife may have however damaged the image of this century-old organization. In 2001, only 24.5 percent "almost always trusted" (*hampir selalu percaya*) religious leaders, according to one opinion poll, a figure which went up to 41 percent in 2007 (under the secular government of Susilo), but trust in political parties was low (8 percent) in 2007.[13] After all, the freedom given to activists in 1984 to choose any political party without restriction may have allowed the NU to escape the unlucky fate of its political party, the PKB. In September 2012, NU's national conference showed it intended to remain a source of moral and political inspiration for Indonesian society, calling for the death sentence as punishment for corruptors and proposing the end of direct elections for local leaders as a means to fight money politics. Some commentators were quick to call it "pure rhetoric," or to regret NU's "simplistic" proposals to face real problems (*Kompas*, September 17, 2012).

On the positive side, it should be noted that the educational scene is significantly more stable than the political. The education provided in most Islamic schools, and all the more in *madrasah* associated with NU and likeminded traditionalists on the outer islands, remain impressively open and forward looking on matters of curriculum and educational worldview (Hefner 2009, 28, 55–105). Polls do show that commitment to *Shariʿah* is almost as strong as that to democracy, but, Hefner points out, there is a strong resolve among Muslim educators and the public to resolve this tension peacefully, and this still distinguishes Indonesia and NU from traditionalists and educators in most other parts of the Muslim world.

However, with Abdurrahman Wahid's death December 30, 2009, liberal Muslims have been orphaned: although they are autonomous, the question remains to whom they will run for protection when facing fundamentalist zeal if the state keeps short of showing a strict defense of freedom of speech. The thirty-second NU congress showed liberals are already facing a more daring conservative current within their own traditionalist organization: in theological debating commissions, recommendations were made in favor of female circumcision against NU's younger women Fatayat organization (accused of being agents of the Western funding agencies), and in favor of secret marriages (*kawin sirri*), rejected by NU feminists as a way to escape limits put by state laws on polygamy. At the end of the congress, the younger *Kiai* Husein Muhammad commented: "We have entered a conservative era. With Wahid's death, we have suffered a great loss" (*Kita kehilangan besar*; Interview March 29, 2010).[14] One major breakthrough at the congress was, however, the decision to open NU representations at a lower administrative level, thus multiplying NU offices (*anak ranting*). This is supposed to democratize the organization and lessen central control, but skeptics argue that the combination of the *kiais*' strong power locally and weak management will remain a handicap.

Like others before, Susilo Bambang Yudhoyono's government believes in a partnership with traditionalist Islam, including in new roles. In 2009, the very secular Ministry of Education during Soeharto days, after having been in the hands of the Reformist

Muhammadiyah for ten years, was handed over to a cadre of the NU, former rector of the prestigious Technology Institute (ITS) of Surabaya. Traditionalist Islam's help might become increasingly precious as the government faces increased opposition. This clearly occurred in the Bank Century affair, which embarrassed the government of President Susilo, abandoned by his own allies (the Islamic parties coalition that included the PKS) but supported by NU's PKB.

Liberals hoped that Hasyim's replacement as NU chief executive by Said Aqil Siraj (Prof. Dr.), a Saudi graduate with Shi`a sympathies, and brewed by Abdurrahman Wahid in the 1990s, might restrengthen the "moderate" line. But Siraj has had to keep a tight line between the two as he himself lacks Gus Dur's exceptional charisma, audacity, and legitimacy, while he has to cement a now more divided NU.[15] Despite his cautiousness, Said Aqil Siraj has maintained NU's voice as a key element in the government's drive against violent Islamist radicalism.

Notes

1. The figure is an estimation based on electoral results in 1955 and 1971, when the NU obtained each time about 18 percent of the vote. That figure has decreased in the past decade, as the political system has been liberalized, and NU voters are spreading their vote among several parties. According to a recent survey cited in Mulani and Liddle (2004), slightly over 40 percent of Indonesians identify more or less with the NU and 17 percent do so strongly. If we are to measure NU's strength from the number of Islamic boarding schools associated with it, then of the 14,556 *pesantren* registered at the ministry of religions in 2004 (as against 6,321 in 1991), about 9,000 are said by *Kiai* Aziz Masyhuri of the Association of Indonesian Islamic boarding schools to be affiliated with the NU (Interview, November 2004, Boyolali).
2. The NU held sway over the Ministry of Religious Affairs, with 102,000 employees in 1967, giving it a client network of huge dimensions.
3. The British Council invited twelve major *pesantren* directors from Java in 2003, at the Markfield Institute of Higher Education, followed by fifty other *pesantren* NU representatives sent to Leeds University in 2005 and 2006 (*Laporan Program Rintisan Latihan Manajemen Pengasuh Pondok Pesantren ke Inggris*, September 14–October 18, 2003, PBNU, British Council, British Embassy). Ironically, these trips may have contributed to widening the gap between conservatives and liberals (as explained below), as some of the courses were openly antiliberal. Among others, they heard Dr. Farid Elshayyal on Orientalism.
4. Personal observations at the NU Congress, Makassar, Sulawesi, March 22–28, 2010.
5. Wahid had earlier disappointed NGO activists by adapting his discourse to circumstances when, facing Megawati's bid for president, this active supporter of women rights had said she was unacceptable to the (Muslim) "majority" as a woman. In April 2000, Wahid had banned the live television broadcasting of a session of the parliament (Bush 2009, 174).
6. Transparency International Indonesia ranked the Indonesian Parliament and political parties first in their 2004 corruption index before any government offices (*Jakarta Post*, December 10, 2004, in Ufen 2008, 27).
7. In Central Java, all PKS seats in 2004 were "cheap" seats, given to smaller parties not reaching the required number of voters in a specified district (for details, see Feillard 2008, 225–226).

8. Some *"ulamā'* I met in Central Java accused the PKS of having gone as far as accepting the pre-Islamic ritual of *ruwetan*, a kind of exorcism, clearly *bidah* for any orthodox *"ulamā'*. Worse, the *'"ulamā'* claimed, PKS would even have tried to court the least Islamized Javanese or *abangan* by tolerating the *togel*, a very popular lottery.
9. In 2008 its cadres cited an opinion poll showing that 73 percent of their voters now did their daily prayers. Opinion polls show indeed a high number of swing voters (47 percent according to the LSI, 73 percent according to the PKS; Ufen 2008).
10. *Ada Pemurtadan di IAIN* [There Is Apostasy in the IAIN] by Hartono Ahmad Jaiz, 2005, was discussed at the IAIN in an extremely tense atmosphere (personal observations in Ciputat, April 16, 2005).
11. Social justice is widely debated among *pesantren*-based Muslim scholars. Zuhairi Misrawi advocates an approach based upon a "humanist vision of Islam," compared to *fundamentalisme* that combines literalist understanding of the textual tradition with the political ideologization of religious symbols.
12. Majelis Tarjih dan Pengembangan Pemikiran Islam PP Muhammadiyah, *Tafsir Tematik al-Quran tentang Hubungan Sosial Antarumat Beragama*, Pustaka SM, Yogyakarta, 2000, pp XXIV–220.
13. Surveys by Pusat Pengkajian Islam dan Masyarakat, PPIM, UIN Jakarta, Islam dan Kebangsaan, Temuan Survey Nasional, 2001, 2007.
14. In debates, liberal arguments were at times well presented, but the end result was determined by the presiding *'ulamā'*, some of whom belonged to the conservative camp. Among others, *Kiai* Husein complained of *kiais'* refusal to take into account empirical facts. As he explained, some time ago, he and other *kiais* had invited three medical doctors to testify on the side effects of female circumcision, but the *'ulamā'* were not receptive and said they would only trust NU medical doctors.
15. The executive board set up after the thirty-second congress has already been challenged as it included as vice-executive chairman a soon-to-retire official from the Intelligence Agency (BIN), As'ad Said Ali, who happens to be a NU activist close to the supreme NU leadership. But liberals are happy that the board also includes three young progressives, in the midst of otherwise conservative *kiais*. *Kiai* Sahal Mahfudh was reelected at the head of the Syuriah, the supreme body, a respected scholar who has kept a very low profile.

References

Arskal Salim, 2008. Perda Berbasis Agama dan Perlindungan Konstitusional Penegakan HAM. *Jurnal Perempuan* 60, September, 7–38, Jakarta.

Azra, Azyumardi, Afrianty Dina, and W. Robert Hefner. 2007. Pesantren and Madrasa: Muslim Schools and National Ideals in Indonesia. In *Schooling Islam. The Culture and Politics of Modern Muslim Education*, ed. Robert W. Hefner and Muhammad Qasim Zaman, 172–198. Princeton: Princeton University Press.

Barton, Greg. 2002. *Gus Dur: The Authorized Biography of Abdurrahman Wahid*. Jakarta: Equinox Publishing.

Bruinessen, Martin van. 2002. Back to Situbondo? Nahdlatul Ulama Attitudes towards Abdurrahman Wahid's Presidency and His Fall. In *Indonesia in Search of Transition*, eds. Henk Schulte Nordholt and Irwan Abdullah, 15–46. Yogyakarta: Pustaka Pelajar.

Bruinessen, Martin van, and Wajidi Farid. 2006. *Syu'un ijtima'iyah* and the *kiai rakyat*: Traditionalist Islam, Civil Society and Social Concerns. In *Indonesian Transitions*, ed. Henk Schulte Nordholt, 205–248. Yogyakarta: Pustaka Pelajar.

Bush, Robin. 2009. *Nahdlatul Ulama and the Struggle for Power within Islam and Politics in Indonesia*. Singapore: ISEAS.

Effendi, Djohan. 2008. *A Renewal without Breaking Tradition: The Emergence of a New Discourse in Indonesia's Nahdlatul Ulama during the Abdurrahman Wahid Era*. Yogyakarta: Interfidei.

Feener, Michael. 2007. *Muslim Legal Thought in Modern Indonesia*. Cambridge: Cambridge University Press.

Feillard, Andrée. 2002. Indonesian Traditionalist Islam's Troubled Experience with Democracy (1999–2001). *Archipel* 64: 117–144.

Feillard, Andrée. 2008. Islamisme et démocratie en Indonésie, quand la tradition se rapproche de la cause des femmes. *Archipel* 75: 199–230.

Hefner, Robert W. 2009. *Making Modern Muslims, the Politics of Islamic Education in Southeast Asia*.Honolulu: University of Hawai'i Press.

Hosen, Nadirsyah. 2004. Nahdlatul Ulama and Collective Ijtihad. *New Zealand Journal of Asian Studies* 6, 1: 5–26.

Kingsbury, Damien and Fernandes, Clinton. 2005. Terrorism in Archipelagic Southeast Asia. In *Violence in Between: Conflict and Security in Archipelagic Southeast Asia*, ed. Damien Kingsbury, 9–52. Singapore: Monash Asia Institute, Clayton, ISEAS.

Laffan, Michael F. 2005. The *Fatwa* Debated? Shura in One Indonesian Context. *Islamic Law and Society* 12, 1: 93–121.

Latif, Yudi. 2008. *Indonesian Muslim Intelligentsia and Power*. Singapore: Institute of Southeast Asian Studies.

Mietzner, Marcus. 2001. Abdurrahman's Indonesia: Political Conflict and Institutional Crisis. In *Indonesia Today: Challenges of History*, ed. Grayson Lloyd and Shannon L. Smith, 29–44. Singapore: Research School of Pacific and Asian Studies/Institute of Southeast Asian Studies.

Mujani, Saiful, and R. William Liddle. 2004. Indonesia's Approaching Elections; Politics, Islam and Public Opinion. *Journal of Democracy* 15: 109–123.

Noorhaidi, Hasan. 2002. Between Faith and Politics: The Rise of the Laskar Jihad in the Era of Transition in Indonesia. *Indonesia* 73: 145–169.

Rumadi. 2002. Dinamika Keagamaan dalam Pemerintahan Gus Dur. In *Neraca Gus Dur di Panggung Kekuasaan*, ed. Khamami Zada, 119–154. Jakarta: Lakpesdam.

Sophiaan, Ainur R., Faaisol Taslean, and Nadjib Hamid. 2002. *Muhammadiyah korban Kekerasan Politik*. Surabaya: Muhammadiyah Office Report.

Turmudi, Endang, ed. 2003. *Nahdlatul Ulama: Ideology, Politics, and the Formation of Khaira Ummah*. Jakarta: LP. Ma'arif NU.

Ufen, Andreas. 2008. From *Aliran* to Dealignment: Political Parties in Post-Suharto Indonesia. *South East Asia Research* 16, 1: 5–41.

CHAPTER 37

JAMA`AT-I ISLAMI IN PAKISTAN

KAMRAN BOKHARI

INTRODUCTION

PAKISTAN is engaged in an intense struggle with religious extremism and militancy—a situation that has raised international concerns about its future viability as a nation-state. The country's religiopolitical landscape has always been very diverse and ultraconservative in outlook but in recent decades there has been greater expansion, fragmentation, and radicalization of this Islamist topography. Further complicating this picture is the post-September 11 situation in which Pakistan has become the de facto global hub of the al-Qa`ida-led transnational jihadist movement—a development that is having a profound impact on indigenous Islamist groups—both violent and nonviolent ones.

In these circumstances, it is all the more important to try to obtain a sense of the direction in which Pakistani Islamism is headed. An analysis of the nearly seven-decade experience of Pakistan's main Islamist movement, Jama`at-i-Islami (JI), can provide valuable insights in this regard. JI's trajectory, its complex interaction with the state, society, secular political forces, and competing Islamist and other religious groups, can be instructive not just in terms of the future prospects of the group itself but also the future Islamist trend in the country and even beyond.

Like the Muslim Brotherhood (MB) in the Arab world, JI in South Asia (particularly in Pakistan) is a political movement, which seeks to establish an Islamic state via democratic means. That said, JI's Islamism is much more conservative and radical than that of the MB. It is for this reason; its ideas have never found broad appeal among the Pakistani masses limiting its constituency to a largely urban-based religiously conservative class but with a secular education.

Despite the fact that its size and appeal has remained limited, JI is the country's premier Islamist movement (as well as Pakistan's most organized political party), whose ideology, while not having a mass appeal, has played an influential role in the historical and gradual Islamization of the Pakistani state and (to a lesser degree) society. The fact that, unlike its rivals—Jama`at Ulama-i-Islam (JUI), Jama`at Ulama-i-Pakistan (JUP), and so on, JI has a—more or less—national presence along with its largely nonsectarian character that has allowed it to create a sphere of influence among a cross-section of the urban educated middle classes. Understanding JI is also important because it has been at the center of all major upheavals in the country while treading along a constitutional path.

Genesis, Opposition to Muslim Separatism, and the Creation of Pakistan

JI was conceived in a specific political context in British India in 1941 as a religiopolitical movement. For JI's founder and principal theoretician, Sayyid Abul Ala Mawdudi, the agenda of the Indian National Congress, as a secular movement that would empower the country's Hindu majority, was obviously unacceptable. Mawdudi, however, was equally opposed to Congress' main rival, the All India Muslim League (AIML), even though it was demanding a separate homeland for Muslims in a post-British India.

AIML was problematic for Mawdudi for a number of reasons. First, the JI founder opposed nationalism as an un-Islamic idea. Second, AIML was led by a secular Westernized elite, which he felt was incapable of fulfilling the role of a vanguard that could realize a state based on Islam. Mawdudi, like many of his counterparts around the world, felt that the Muslim political resurgence was not possible without Islamic intellectual revival, and the AIML's call for Pakistan would not lead to the desired outcome.

What is interesting here is that JI did not come into being in an environment devoid of Muslim religious movements. On the contrary, Jama`at Ulama-i-Hind (JUH), the largest national-level association of Deobandi theologians and jurists had been in existence for over twenty-two years. Likewise, the historical rivals of the Deobandis, the Barelvis, had a vibrant movement—spawned by the writings of Ahmed Reza Khan Barelvi—active since the late nineteenth century. Additionally, the apolitical socioreligious movement, Tablighi Jama`at, an offshoot of the Deobandi movement founded by Maulana Muhammad Ilyas al-Kandhalvi, preceded JI by fifteen years.

JI, however, was founded not just as a rejection of the secular outlook that the Indian Muslim elite subscribed to but also as a rejection of the prevailing state of religious scholarship and activism among the Muslims of the South Asian subcontinent. From Mawdudi's point of view, the Western-educated Muslim elite was not capable of leading the Muslim masses toward a renaissance in keeping with their religious principles. At the same time, he believed that the traditional religious leaders were incapable of providing religious guidance let alone political leadership. JI was thus intended to be a movement, which sought to provide intellectual leadership to the Muslims of British India that was modern but not secular and religious but not traditional in the sense that was being offered by the `ulama' class. It was envisioned by its founders to be a group rejecting both the secular and religious trends of the time.

In this regard, JI was distinct from its religious competitors in that it was not a group composed of mullahs. Mawdudi, whose ideas remain the core of the Sunni Islamist ideology of JI, was not an `alim in that he had not been recognized by the Ulama`ulama' as having been qualified from any of the seminaries of the established schools of thought, Deobandi, Barelvi (the two rival sects dividing the predominantly Hanafi-Sunni Muslims of prepartition India), or even the Ahl-e-Hadith. While JI had its eyes set on projecting itself as an alternative to the AIML and did not consider itself in competition with the Ulama ʿulama' class, it quickly ran into problems on both ends.

The strong opposition from the ʿulama' meant it had to struggle hard to establish its credentials as a legitimate religious movement. On the other front, its opposition to the demand for (a separate Muslim nation-state) Pakistan, which had become quite popular with the masses, not only prevented JI from making much headway; the stance would continue to haunt it for decades. Pakistan eventually came into existence forcing JI to profoundly alter course.

Constitutionalism, Islamic Republic, and Civil War

JI was still struggling to find its bearing when Pakistan was established in 1947. Thus far the relatively nascent movement was trying to find its space between secular Muslim separatists and the Ulama ʿulama'-driven religious movements in a country ruled by British colonialists and where Muslims were a weak minority. With the establishment of Pakistan, JI now had to deal with a country whose raison d'être was Islam and one whose creation it had opposed.

Before the partition, Islam was to a large degree a unifying force in ethnocommunal terms but afterward it became a hotly contested subject. But even before its inception, there was immense debate as to whether Pakistan would be an "Islamic" state in which the politicolegal system would be based on the Shariʿah or a secular state intended to safeguard the material interests of the South Asian Muslims from the perceived threat from the Hindu majority. This debate intensified even further after the creation of the country in the contentious efforts to craft a constitution. Here is where JI found an opening, which it could not only try and use to shed its past as an opponent of the idea of Pakistan, but could also position itself as a national political force because it had an advantage over both the Muslim League and the mullah-dominated religiopolitical parties.

The Muslim League was caught in the web that it had itself spun to rally Muslim masses to the idea of Pakistan as an entity based on religion. The ambiguity surrounding the nature of the republic further complicated matters. As it is, the Muslim League was ill equipped intellectually and was not able to compete on religious matters as they pertained to politics. Moreover, with the early death of Mohammed Ali Jinnah, the founder of Pakistan, and the assassination of his deputy and first prime minister of Pakistan, Liaquat Ali Khan, the League began to disintegrate not too long after Pakistan's founding.

The mullah-led political forces such as JUI were nowhere near as articulate as was JI, which was armed with a modern discourse on Islam enunciated by Mawdudi who sought to promote Islam as an ideology rivaling capitalism and communism. In contrast, the madrasah-educated Ulama ʿulama' were steeped in tradition and could not partake in the national debate as effectively as JI could. Thus, JI was quickly able to assume a dominant voice in the constitutional debates and began to aggressively push for a constitution based on Islam.

Maududi's lectures on state radio, his writings, and JI's national campaign played a key role in shaping the Objectives Resolution in 1949 approved by the Constituent Assembly, which was the critical document that further exacerbated the controversy over the role of Islam in the Pakistani state. JI also played a key role in allying with other religious forces in the anti-Ahmadiyah movement during the early 1950s. Not only did this movement and JI's role in it solidify the place of religion in politics, but it also placed the state on the defensive insofar as its commitment to Islam was concerned.

The net result of the efforts led by JI was that the country's first constitution in 1956 declared Pakistan an Islamic republic whose laws would not contravene Islam. According to the new charter, the state needed to adopt measures that would enable the Muslim majority citizenry to lead their individual and collective lives according to the precepts outlined in the Qur'an and Sunnah. It further mandated that there would be no legislation that contradicted Islamic laws, all existing laws would be brought into conformity with Islam, and parliament would decide whether a certain law ran counter to Islamic principles or not. The constitution called for the establishment of a state body engaging in Islamic research and instruction to ensure the construction of an Islamic civil society.

Clearly, these stipulations were vague and subject to interpretation where the religious forces, especially JI, held a monopoly over religious discourse. In other words, what was "Islamic" and what was not fell in the purview of the religious sector. Even JI, which was the first Islamist force in South Asia, created as a modern religious response to Western secular political thought, was still intellectually struggling to offer much beyond the cutting and pasting of medieval *fiqh* onto a contemporary template.

JI along with the other religious forces, while having heavily influenced the constitutional process, were unsuccessful in getting the state to operationalize the "Islamic" provisions. In fact, the state, which was dominated by secular civil bureaucratic, military, and political forces, resisted any such moves. Despite its success in shaping the constitutional process, JI was not in any position to force the hand of the state and for a number of reasons.

The first had to do with the structural realities of the Pakistani state. Despite the fact that the 1956 constitution envisioned a democratic polity, the path toward electoral politics was derailed very early on. The first president of the country (a retired two-star general turned civil servant), Iskander Mirza, dismissed four consecutive prime ministers over the course of the next two years and then eventually abrogated the nascent constitution and imposed martial law in October 1958. Three weeks later, then military chief, General Ayub Khan, who had been made chief martial law administrator by President Mirza, ousted the latter and assumed power himself, marking the beginning of military rule.

The country's first military regime sought to impose a secular order and was less tolerant of Islamism, especially JI. As a result the government of now Field Marshall Ayub Khan cracked down hard against JI, banning the group, shutting down its facilities, arresting its leaders, including Mawdudi himself. It was during this period that JI aligned itself with secular parties to campaign against military rule, which can be considered as the first time JI began to make significant moves toward the amalgamation of Islam and democracy.

Maududi, as early as February 1957, had stressed that since there was a constitutional and democratic system in place in the country, it would be un-Islamic for JI to adopt any extraconstitutional means of effecting political change, and thus the establishment of an Islamic state could only be brought about via electoral politics. But it was not until it came face to face with the realities of living under the Ayub Khan military regime that the struggle for democracy became an integral part of its goal to establish its envisioned Islamic state in Pakistan.

For the first decade or so after independence, JI was largely focused on trying to steer Pakistan from being a secular Muslim nation-state toward an Islamic polity via the constitutional debates and by aligning itself with various religious forces. Constitutional and democratic politics were important insofar as making sure that the foundations of the new state were not secular and instead in synch with religion. The new era in the form of the Ayub regime prompted JI to join hands with nonreligious forces in a struggle to restore democracy.

Thus, JI joined the antigovernment faction of the Muslim League, the ethnonationalist Awami League, and the Marxist National Awami Party to form the Combined Opposition Parties alliance. JI's willingness to embrace political pragmatism was mirrored in its backing of the candidacy of Fatimah Jinnah (the sister and close confidant of Pakistan's founder, Mohammed Ali Jinnah) in the 1965 presidential election. JI's support of Jinnah's candidacy was extraordinary on a number of levels.

First, it showed that the Islamist movement, which by then for all intents and purposes, had become a political party, was ready to play by the rules of the constitution, even if it was crafted by a military regime, and which was quite diluted in terms of Islam when compared to the 1956 constitution. Second, it was willing to back the candidacy of a female candidate despite its view that women could not be heads of state in an Islamic order. Third, JI backed an individual who hailed from a heterodox sect (Shi`a Ismaili Khoja) and was very secular in her ways.

JI clearly wanted to be seen as part of the political mainstream and Mawdudi was stressing that the only way in which JI could expand its influence in society was through public outreach. JI was hoping that the ouster of the Ayub regime would lead to elections, which in turn would lead to democratic order. The expectation was that a democratic environment would be conducive for JI to expand itself at the grassroots level and also engage in its *da`wah* activities.

After a four-year struggle the opposition movement forced President Ayub Khan to resign from office and hand over power to then army chief, General Yahya Khan, whose military regime organized the country's first national-level parliamentary elections in 1970. JI won only 4 seats out of some 150 candidates it fielded as the conservative vote was divided among JI, JUI, JUP, and three different factions of the Muslim League. But JI's poor performance can also be attributed to the fact that it had only been a decade or so that the party had begun focusing on electoral politics; its public appeal was limited because of its strict requirements for membership; and because JI (along with its Islamist competitors) have never been successful at translating social conservatism and religiosity into votes.

But in those days, the 1960s, a much larger geopolitical issue was steering the country toward yet another partition. Pakistan consisted of two wings—east and west—separated by over a thousand miles of Indian territory. Very early on West Pakistan assumed a dominant position and East Pakistan, dominated by ethnic Bengalis, was marginalized.

East Pakistan with a larger population was allocated 162 parliamentary seats while West Pakistan had 138. The Bengali ethnic party, Awami League, with an agenda for sweeping autonomy for both wings, bagged 160 seats in the east while the newly formed Pakistan People's Party (PPP), won 81 seats (all in West Pakistan). The results of the election meant that the eastern wing of the country was on its way to undermining the dominance of the West Pakistani elite, which was unacceptable to the military regime and to the PPP, especially given the Awami League's separatist agenda. The political struggle quickly turned into a civil war, which in late 1971 turned into the third Indo-Pakistani war after New Delhi intervened militarily on the side of the Bengali separatists. JI participated in the war by forming Islamist militias known as al-Badr and al-Shams, which fought alongside the Pakistan army against East Pakistani separatists. JI's participation in the 1971 war underscored a critical metamorphosis of the party.

In a short span of less than three decades, it had evolved from a party that opposed the creation of Pakistan to taking up arms to defend its territorial integrity. It had accepted Pakistani nationalism but was opposed to Bengali separatism given its ethno-sub-nationalistic, secular, and socialist nature. Another key point to note is that it aligned with the secular military establishment, while at the same time it continued to oppose the state on ideological grounds.

The decision to form the al-Shams and al-Badr paramilitary units and side with the Pakistani army in its efforts to use force to quell the Bengali rebellion in East Pakistan further undermined JI's standing. It was accused of having participated in the mass killings of Bengalis during the 1971 war. While Pakistan's army had long been employing irregulars (including religiously motivated militia forces) in its fighting with India for control over Kashmir, this was the first time that JI cooperated with the army.

In fact, JI's decision to form paramilitary organizations in East Pakistan was in sharp contrast to its stance in the 1948 war (during which the Kashmir region was de facto divided between India and Pakistan) in which Mawdudi opposed the idea of nonstate actors declaring jihad, arguing that declaration of war was a state prerogative. JI's position was that either Pakistan formally declares war against India or abides by the terms of a cease-fire. In the case of East Pakistan, however, JI supported the idea that nonstate actors were legitimate instruments of war, and thus marked JI's first experience with armed struggle.

The al-Shams and al-Badr paramilitary units were composed of a JI cadre based in East Pakistan who fought fellow Muslims rebelling against the state. Given that the popular sentiment supported independence from Pakistan, JI's actions would tarnish its standing in Bangladesh, the state that emerged after the secession of East Pakistan similar to the case when Pakistan was carved out of British India.

Just as JI accepted Pakistan in 1947 (while leaving behind a counterpart organization in India), JI in East Pakistan eventually accepted the reality of the establishment of the state of Bangladesh and has since been working as a counterpart entity to the main JI organization in Pakistan. JI Bangladesh has not been able to make much headway in the country because of its history as having collaborated with the Pakistani army in the efforts to suppress Bengali nationalism. In recent months the JI of Bangladesh has been the under a great deal of pressure as at least two of its senior leaders have been sentenced to death in tribunals examining their alleged role in large-scale killings, rape, and arson, and as a result the country has seen a growing Islamist-secular polarization..

MILITARY DICTATORSHIPS, DEMOCRACY, AND ISLAMIZATION

Where JI's participation in the war to prevent the secession of East Pakistan damaged its standing in Bangladesh, it did not allow the party to enhance its standing in what now remained of Pakistan (the Western half) either. JI had to contend with the rise of the PPP to power when its leader Zulfikar Ali Bhutto became president after General Yahya Khan resigned the post in the wake of public pressure and that from within the army itself, following the defeat in the 1971 war. Bhutto's party was quite popular given that it was the largest party in the country (following the secession of East Pakistan).

The disastrous defeat in the 1971 war coupled with Bhutto's rise to power brought a very quick end to the alignment between JI and the state, thrusting the relationship back toward antagonism. That said, in the early years, JI was more focused on making sure that the moves toward the crafting of the 1973 constitution did not override the gains it had made in terms of the Islamic provisions it was able to have included in the 1956 charter. Unlike in the past, JI was able to make use of the fact that Bhutto sought a national consensus on the new constitution.

Thus, JI (in league with other religious and right-wing forces) was far more successful in that the 1973 charter specifically stated that Islam was the state religion. The teachings of the Qur'an and Sunnah in the form of Islamic studies were declared compulsory. A Council of Islamic Ideology was furthermore mandated to shape legislation in compliance with religious precepts. Moreover, the new constitution defined who is a Muslim. One year later this led to the second amendment to the constitution, which declared the heterodox Ahmadiyah sect as a non-Muslim communal group.

Meanwhile, JI had entered a new phase in that its founder due to ill health stepped down as party chief. Mawdudi's close lieutenant, Mian Tufail Muhammad, succeeded him as amir of the movement in 1972. Muhammad did not even come close to possessing the intellectual and leadership skills that Mawdudi had and as a result contributed to the stagnation of JI even though the political environment in the country had become considerably conducive for JI to operate more freely.

It was also at this point in its history that JI swung back to emphasizing Islam over democracy and there were two seemingly paradoxical factors informing this shift.

First, the establishment of a civilian government and the founding of a consensual constitution to a considerable extent alleviated the fears that JI had during the Ayub martial law. In other words, the goal of a constitutional democratic order, which Mawdudi saw as a prerequisite to enabling the establishment of an "Islamic" state, had been largely achieved. Having achieved a democratic political order, JI thus began focusing on how to Islamize the Pakistani state.

Second, the PPP sought to shape Pakistan into a secular/socialist republic and that too via democratic politics—an arena where JI was not in a position to compete. Not only was the PPP very popular but it also had the advantage in that it held the lion's share of seats in the legislature that was left over after East Pakistan seceded 81 of the 138 allocated to West Pakistan (which was the entire country by then), while the strength of all the other parties in parliament was in the single digits. This situation allowed the PPP to not only form the first post-Bangladesh government but also lead the efforts toward the formulation of the first constitution drafted by an elected parliament.

The ruling party's popularity, Bhutto's own towering figure, and the weakness of the military-intelligence establishment thus allowed the PPP the opportunity to try and establish a single-party state. Even though it ushered in an era of democratic politics, the PPP government had become quite autocratic and was increasingly engaged in repression of political opponents. To a great degree it was due to the ethnotribal uprising in

Baluchistan that the Bhutto government sought to put down through a massive army operation. Additionally, however, Bhutto dismissed the provincial governments in North-West Frontier Province (since 2009 referred to as Khyber-Pakhtunkhwa) and Baluchistan dominated by opposition parties.

Growing opposition among secular political forces against the Bhutto government was a boon for JI, which was yet again busy aligning with religious and right-wing forces in the form of Nizam-i-Mustafa Tehrik (Movement for the System of Muhammad). Eventually, JI would play a pivotal role in the formation of the Pakistan National Alliance (PNA)—an anti-PPP coalition of nine different parties of secular, left-wing, and religious, right-wing, persuasions. The PNA contested the 1977 elections, the first one to be held in accordance with the 1973 constitution, but won only 36 seats while the PPP garnered 155—an outcome that the opposition condemned as the result of foul play on the part of the government.

The PNA took to the streets demanding fresh elections, which very quickly forced the government to open talks with the opposition as a means of finding a resolution to the crisis. JI's key role in the post-poll PNA agitation is underscored by the fact that a key deputy amir of the Islamist party, Ghafoor Ahmed, was part of the three-man negotiating team that held parleys with the government team led by Bhutto himself. The talks were still in play when the army led by its chief, General Mohammed Zia-ul-Haq, mounted a coup and imposed the third martial on the country on July 5, 1977.

Zia's move to get rid of the Bhutto government and the military dictator's strong Islamist leanings led to another shift in JI's modus operandi where it supported the military regime, especially since it pushed for the implementation of an Islamic system on the country. Having seen during the Bhutto era how secular parties had an edge in the democratic process, JI decided that supporting the military regime of General Zia would help the party advance toward its goal of rendering Pakistan an Islamic state.

In addition to the fact that Zia was ideologically an Islamist, the general needed to legitimize his military rule and continue to postpone fresh elections, which he pledged to hold within ninety days of the imposition of martial law. That a critical mass within the public had been fired up by the anti-Bhutto Nizam-i-Mustafa movement made it clear to Zia that Islamization of the state would help him consolidate power. Furthermore, he had help from JI, which joined the cabinet.

Within a year, however, the JI cabinet members resigned their seats after it had become clear that Zia's commitment to the goal of Islamic state was not on par with that of the party. Although it had left the government, JI did not come out in opposition to the military regime and thus steered clear of the Movement for the Restoration of Democracy that had been established in the early 1980s and was led by the PPP and included most of the country's secular and left-leaning forces as well as the Islamist JUI. Not joining the anti-Zia political movement tarnished the image of JI in terms of its democratic credentials even though the relationship between JI and the Zia regime was a complex one.

By the 1980s, JI's student wing, Islami Jama'at-i-Talaba (IJT), had emerged as a powerful force on campuses. Zia saw student organizations, especially IJT, as a threat and when the student group swept union elections in early 1984, the Zia regime banned student organizations and unions, which led to IJT waging a nine-month long nationwide campaign against the military government. The mother party, JI, however was not in favor of the movement in great part due to Zia's close personal relationship with JI chief given that both hailed from the same Arain *biradari*.

Perhaps the most important factor shaping JI's close relationship with the Zia regime was the Soviet military intervention in neighboring Afghanistan. The Zia regime needed to mobilize both national- and international-level religious forces to counter the Soviet threat and JI played a key role on both levels. In fact, JI was at the center of a transnational network of state and nonstate actors that included the United States, Pakistan, Saudi Arabia, Afghan Islamist insurgent groups, and volunteers from all across the Arab/Muslim world.

It had close links to many of the Afghan insurgent groups in the seven-party alliance of Afghan Islamist insurgent groups, but particularly Hizbi-i-Islami of Gulbadeen Hekmatyaar, which was also the favorite of the Zia government. The war in Afghanistan during the 1980s created the circumstances in which Islamist movements of the Middle East came into prolonged direct contact with those of South Asia. JI thus had its first exposure to transnational jihadism with the movement not only playing the role of facilitator in the international effort to defeat Soviet forces and its Marxist allies on both sides of the Durand Line, its cadre, especially those from its student wing, IJT, fought alongside the Afghan insurgents.

When the Afghan war began, JI was already torn in terms of how to go about working toward its original goal of establishing an Islamic state in Pakistan—take advantage of Zia's Islamization initiative and/or oppose the regime because in the long run it would be an obstacle to establishing an Islamic state in keeping with the party's ideals. Zia's Islamization drive was empowering the religious right, which in many ways was helpful for JI. The military leader did not share, however, JI's vision of an Islamic polity. Furthermore, Zia's appropriation of JI's agenda was also making it difficult for the Islamist party to expand its social support—not to mention the damage to its image for aligning with the military regime.

The Afghan Islamist insurgency against the Marxist regime and Soviet troops backing it further complicated matters given that now JI was caught between the need to simultaneously maintain an already ambiguous policy toward the state insofar as domestic agenda was concerned and support its foreign policy toward Afghanistan. The lack of democracy at home and jihad next door led to a certain radicalization of the movement, which could be seen in the gun battles its student wing, IJT, was involved in with rival student groups affiliated with secular parties across the nation's campuses in the mid- to late 1980s.

The Zia regime's domestic policy of Islamization created a dilemma for JI in that the state had appropriated the agenda of the party. On top of that the Afghan jihad created the circumstances where JI was even less distinguishable from the state. Then the decision to remain separate from the PPP-led Movement for Restoration of Democracy further tarnished JI's image as a supporter of the military dictatorship. But perhaps the most significant development was the need to balance between supporting fellow Islamists in Afghanistan in their armed struggle toward the establishment of an "Islamic" polity and adhering to its constitutional approach and that too under a martial law regime. JI was trying to justify armed struggle as a means of establishing an "Islamic" state in Afghanistan while at the same time insisting that in Pakistan the means to the same goal was via electoral politics at a time when the military regime was not allowing free and fair elections.

As the 1980s wore on JI's influence in the Zia regime increasingly began to wane—because Zia had cultivated several other social and political forces particularly a revived Pakistan Muslim League to support his regime and did not really need JI in addition to the hit to its standing among the public. It was fortunate to win ten national and thirteen provincial seats in the 1985 partyless elections held by the military government. Two years later JI elected a new leader in Qazi Hussain Ahmed, who while maintaining the ideological position of the party tried to steer it toward populist politics but with little success.

Toward the final days of the Zia regime, JI was increasingly becoming anti-Zia—to the point that its leadership was considering alignment with the PPP then led by former Pakistani Prime Minister Benazir Bhutto. Zia's death in the mysterious plane crash in August 1988 prevented the alignment from actually taking place. The PPP emerged as the major benefactor of the death of Zia, and JI joined an alliance of right of center anti-PPP parties called Islami Jamhoori Ittihad (IJI), which was led by the Pakistan Muslim League and engineered by the country's military-intelligence establishment.

JI, as a component of the IJI, competed in the elections of 1988, winning only eight seats in the national assembly and thirteen in the provincial assemblies; in the elections of 1990, its tally of seats stood at eight and twenty. In the 1993 elections JI contested as part of the Pakistan Islamic Front, winning only three seats to the national assembly and six to provincial assemblies and it boycotted the 1997 polls. Thus, during the eleven-year period of civilian rule (1988–1999), JI experienced further decline.

SEPTEMBER 11 AND THE MUSHARRAFIAN ERA

The coming to power of Pakistan's fourth military ruler, General Pervez Musharraf, in a 1999 coup initially did not change JI's decline. The September 11 attacks and Islamabad's move to align with Washington in the war against radical Islamism, especially the invasion of neighboring Afghanistan, provided JI with the opportunity to stage a comeback onto the national scene. In addition to the international situation there was also the effort by the Musharraf government to undo the Islamization of Zia with his own brand of secularism that he referred to as "enlightened moderation."

As a result, JI joined forces with five other religiopolitical parties—Jama`at Ulama-i-Islam-F, JUP, Jama`at Ulama-i-Islam-S, Jama`at Ahl-i-Hadith, and Pakistan Islami Tehrik (a Shi`a party)—to form the Mutahiddah Majlis-i-Amal (MMA), an alliance of religiopolitical parties, representing the various Pakistani religious schools of thought. While JI maintained its identity as a distinct political party, it conducted most of its political activities under the banner of the MMA.

The MMA was able to take advantage of the anti-American sentiment within Pakistan (especially its Pashtun majority areas) in the aftermath of the ouster of the Taliban regime in neighboring Afghanistan and make unprecedented electoral gains by winning some sixty seats in the national parliament. Additionally, the MMA swept the provincial legislative vote in the North-West Frontier Province (NWFP) to form a government there and won enough seats in the legislature in Baluchistan province to form a local coalition government with the pro-Musharraf Pakistan Muslim League faction. Another critical reason for unprecedented performance in the 2002 elections was the move by the Musharraf regime to engage in electoral and constitutional engineering in order to contain the country's two main political parties from gaining too many seats while facilitating the electoral rise of the MMA. Musharraf also leveraged the MMA in its dealings with the United States in the war against jihadism.

JI along with the JUI-F were the main driving forces behind the MMA with JI being the smaller of the two groups. While the JUI-F accounts for the lion's share of the seats controlled by the MMA, JI provided the alliance with its organizational structure. Moreover, JI chief Qazi Hussain Ahmed also served as the president of the MMA. The MMA in 2003 supported Musharraf in his bid to gain a much needed vote of confidence from parliament and on the issue of the seventeenth amendment in 2003 that allowed the military ruler to gain indemnity for the 1999 coup and all the changes he had effected to the Pakistani political system since.

Shortly thereafter the alliance increasingly assumed an anti-Musharraf position especially with regards to Islamabad's support for Washington in the war on terror. This issue has also created tensions between JI and JUI where the former emerged as the more hardline group while the more rural-based JUI has opted for a more pragmatic approach. Part of the radical agenda of the JI can be attributed to the hawkish attitude of its leader Ahmed. The tensions between the two groups ultimately led to the breakup of the alliance with JI going back to its status as an individual party.

JI in major ways participated in the legal-judicial movement that kicked off in the wake of Musharraf's 2007 decision to fire Supreme Court Chief Justice Iftikhar Muhammad Chaudhry. It was, however, unable to take advantage of the large civil society unrest and expand its influence. Its decision to boycott the last elections in 2008 contributed to its increased marginalization as a political force and the vote translated into a major defeat for both pro-Musharraf and Islamist forces (MMA minus JI). The election of Syed Munawar Hassan, a former left-wing student activist turned Islamist hardliner, as its fourth amir in 2009 has further led to its isolation from the political mainstream.

Conclusion

During its seventy-year history, JI has had a complex trajectory in pursuit of its goal of establishing an "Islamic" state via democracy while dealing with the fact that Pakistan has been ruled by the country's military for more than half of its existence. Like many other Islamist movements it has not been able to ideologically move beyond the precepts laid down by its founder. While not intended to be a group of mullahs it has ended up being no different other than the fact that its leadership and cadre are educated in secular curriculums.

Because the religious landscape was divided along sectarian lines (Barelvi, Deobandi, Shi`a, and Ahl-i-Hadith) Mawdudi was very careful in trying not to have JI be relegated as just another sect. The majority of Pakistanis who adhere to the Barelvi sect ultimately lumped JI as another face of Wahhabism along with Deobandis and the Ahl-i-Hadith. Thus despite trying to remain above the sectarian fray, JI could not succeed in positioning itself as a nonsectarian force. In fact, over the years, Deobandism managed to expand its influence, but JI could not.

Owing to its commitment to the democratic process, JI could be considered as a relatively moderate Islamist movement. However, its agenda has all along remained radical, which has prevented it from broadening its popular appeal. Additionally, its calls for an Islamic revolution have conflicted with its stated commitment to constitutional politics.

The party's structure and demand for ideological discipline from its membership has prevented JI from gaining a mass following. A key factor contributing to this is the emphasis on quality of members as opposed to quantity. Put differently, JI has suffered from a vanguard dilemma, which has had a limiting effect on how much it competes with mainstream parties (PPP and PML-N) and the rival Islamist, JUI-F.

A key aspect to note here is that JI has been far more of a religiously conservative entity than its counterpart in the Arab world, the MB. The MB, especially in the wake of the 2011 Arab unrest, seems to be trying to follow the path of Turkey's post-Islamist ruling Justice and Development Party, whereas JI is moving in the opposite direction. The Turkish party opted for political pragmatism and has shed its Islamist ideological past. Much of it has to do with the fact that JI was always far more conservative than Arab Islamist movements, but it is also because Pakistan as a country has over the years seen the growth of radical and extremist impulses. We see the Egyptian MB move toward the formation of a political party as separate from the wider movement, but JI continues to shun such an approach.

JI faces a great deal of competition from a wide range of forces that includes the proliferation of *masajids, madaris*, and *Ulama 'ulama'* associations; rival Islamist groups; sectarian outfits; and most importantly militant groups, especially the Pakistani Taliban rebels aligned with al-Qa'ida and the successor entities to groups cultivated by Islamabad during the 1980s and 1990s as instruments of foreign policy vis-à-vis India and Afghanistan. The U.S. invasion of Afghanistan, which had the unintended consequence of not just al-Qa'ida's relocation to Pakistan but also the spillover of Talibanization, further increased the competition for JI.

Ironically, JI's stint in power under the MMA banner (2002–2007) when the religious alliance ran the government in the northwestern Khyber-Pakhtunkhwa province facilitated the rise of competition in the form of the Pakistani Taliban movement. The JI/MMA provincial government turned a blind eye to the activities of the Taliban, allowing them to gain power in the tribal areas as well as the province. It is no coincidence that the main Pakistani Taliban rebel grouping, the Tehrik-i-Taliban Pakistan, was founded a month after the end of the five-year term of the MMA government.

There is emerging evidence that many of JI's youth cadre, especially those from its more hawkish student wing, IJT, in recent years have become disgruntled with JI's approach and have joined al-Qa'ida. By some accounts, JI dissidents form a significant group of al-Qa'ida's presence in Pakistan. Ex-IJT members have to a great degree been responsible for the Pakistanization of al-Qa'ida.

Struggling for relevance in age of jihadism, the state of the JI can be gauged from comparing its status with that of its Arab counterpart, the MB. The MB, owing to its historically pragmatic approach has democratically won the presidency in Egypt whereas JI in the aftermath of the May 11, 2013 elections is trying to become a junior partner in the provincial government in Khyber-Pakhtunkhwa where cricketer-turned-politician Imran Khan's party won the largest number of seats and JI bagged 7—behind its traditional Islamist rival JUI

At a time when the country's has moved to the political right, JI is thus caught between rival Islamist and right-of-center mainstream parties and Taliban rebels. This growing competition has forced JI to assume a more radical posture in order to remain competitive and has maintained an ambiguous stance toward extremism and terrorism that has engulfed the country in the past four years. JI was never able to supplant the traditional religious sectors of society and now it is drowning in an atmosphere of intensifying intra-Islamist contention dominating by violent Islamists. It is unlikely that JI will be able to reverse the trend where it is a dissipating force lost in an increasingly fragmenting Islamist bayou dominated by militant actors who are taking advantage of the weakening of the Pakistani state.

References

Abbott, Freeland. "The Jamaat-i-Islami of Pakistan." *Middle East Journal* 11.1 (Winter 1957): 37–51. Lahore, 2004.
Adams, Charles J. "The Ideology of Mawlana Mawdudi." In *South Asian Politics and Religion*, edited by Donald E. Smith, 371–397. Princeton, 1966.
Adams, Charles J. "Mawdudi and the Islamic State." In *Voices of Resurgent Islam*, edited by John L. Esposito, 99–133. New York, 1983.
Ahmad, Abdul-Ghafūr. *Phir Mārshal Lā Ā-Giyā* [Then Came the Martial Law]. Lahore, 1988.
Ahmad, Mumtaz. "Islamic Fundamentalism in South Asia: The Jamaat-i-Islami and the Tablighi Jamaat." In *Fundamentalisms Observed*, edited by Martin E. Marty and R. Scott Appleby 457–530. Chicago, 1991.
Ahmad, Sayed Riaz. *Islam & Modern Political Institutions in Pakistan: A Study of Mawlana Maududi*.
Binder, Leonard. *Religion and Politics in Pakistan*. Berkeley, 1961.
Hasan, Masudul. *Sayyid Abul A'ala Maududi and His Thought*. 2 vols. Lahore, 1984.
Kennedy, Charles H. "Islamization and Legal Reform in Pakistan, 1979–89." *Pacific Affairs* 63.1 (Spring 1990): 62–77.
Maududi, Syed Abul Aala. *Islamic Way of Life*. Riyadh, XXXX.
Maududi, Syed Abul Aala. *Islam Ka Nazriya-e-Siyasi*. Lahore, 1971.
Maududi, Syed Abul Aala. *Masala-e-Qaumiyat*. Lahore, 1986.
Maududi, Syed Abul Aala. *Islami Nizam Aur Maghrabi Ladeeni Jamhooriyat*. Lahore, 1986.
Maududi, Syed Abul Aala. *Islami Hukumat Kis Tarah Qaim Hoti Hai?* Lahore, 1987.
Maududi, Syed Abul Aala. *Siyasat Eik Deeni Taqaza*. Lahore, 1986.
Maududi, Syed Abul Aala. *Tehrik Aur Karkun*. Lahore, 1998.
Maududi, Syed Abul Aala. *Khilafat Aur Mulukiyat*. Lahore, 1998.
Maududi, Syed Abul Aala. *Islami Riyasat*. Lahore, 2000.
Maududi, Syed Abul Aala. *Sunnat Ki Aini Hesiyat*. Lahore, 2000.
Munīr, Muhammad. *From Jinnah to Zia*. Lahore, 1979.
Nasr, Seyyed Vali Reza. "Islamic Opposition to the Islamic State: The Jamā'at-i, Islāmī, 1977–1988." *International Journal of Middle East Studies* 24.4 (November 1992): 261–283.
Nasr, Seyyed Vali Reza. "Students, Islam, and Politics: Islāmī Jami'at-i Ṭalaba in Pakistan." *Middle East Journal* 46.1 (Winter 1992): 59–76.
Nasr, Seyyed Vali Reza. *The Vanguard of the Islamic Revolution: The Jama'at-i Islami of Pakistan*. Berkeley, 1994.
Nasr, Seyyed Vali Reza. *Mawdudi and the Making of Islamic Revivalism*. New York, 1996.

CHAPTER 38

ISLAMIC MOVEMENTS IN MALAYSIA

FRED R. VON DER MEHDEN

A SIGNIFICANT trend in postindependence Malaysia has been the expanding role of the national government in defining and administering Islamic issues. This has taken place in an environment of increasing politicization of Islam and the rise of Islamic consciousness. The focus of this essay will be on the goals and policies of the major actor in this movement, the United Malay National Organization (UMNO). A Malay-Muslim party, it has been the dominant partner in the ruling multiethnic coalition (originally called the Alliance and now the Barisan Nasional or National Front) that has ruled Malaysia since independence. UMNO's power is evidenced by the fact that every prime minister, deputy prime minister, and home minister has been from UMNO. In the face of the significant resurgence of Islam that has taken place in Malaysia in the past forty years, UMNO has developed several goals. It has sought to maintain its Malay-Muslim constituency, ensure that religious issues do not endanger the delicate balance of ethnic-religious groups in Malaysia and, in the process, contain organizations and individuals with religious and political views contrary to government policy.

This essay will survey factors that have influenced the federal government's move toward policies of greater Islamization and control over Islamic affairs. These elements include intra-Malay-Muslim politics, the rise of nongovernmental Islamic and student organizations, and the perceived dangers of radical Islam. It will then analyze efforts employed by the national government to control this process, including coercion, co-optation, and the development of new religious institutions to legitimate UMNO as the protector of Islam and Malays.

In attempting to achieve these goals, UMNO has faced several impediments.

There is a strong co-identity between Malay ethnicity and Islam and the Malaysian constitution stresses the special place of the Malays and Islam. UMNO has needed to balance this protected role of the Malay-Muslim against the necessity of maintaining a coalition that includes members of the country's Chinese, Indian, and other non-Malay communities. Within UMNO itself, the leadership has needed to placate members with a long held commitment to a greater role for Islam in society and the state. From the very beginning of UMNO there have been parliamentary backbenchers and members of UMNO branches with more conservative views than the leadership.

The constitution also provides a federal framework with only limited powers given to the states, except for in the administration of Islam, which is defined as the prerogative of the states. In the nine Malaysian states with sultans, they are constitutionally in charge of the management of Islamic religious affairs in their state. The Council of Rulers, composed of the sultans, plays that role at the national level. The Islamic court system that was institutionalized during the colonial era is fragmented in laws and punishment due to federal divisions. Each state has its own religious regulations and penalties and there are further divisions of jurisdictions within states. Although there has been increased involvement in religious issues by the center, state powers in the religious realm remain important. If a state and the federal government are ruled by the same party it is easier to ensure that federal policies will be implemented. Even in these states, Islamic courts have ruled counter to federal government desires. Where the opposition administers a state it is more possible, in certain circumstances, to impede policies promulgated by those in power at the center.

One caveat must be underscored. Although the Barisan has a multiethnic and religious membership, decisions on Islam are made by UMNO and its representatives. It falls upon UMNO to define Islamic goals and policies. Although non-Malay partners in the coalition may object to some of the Islamic polices and rhetoric forwarded by UMNO leadership, their influence in these matters continues to be marginalized.

Intra-Malay-Muslim Competition

A significant factor that drives Malay-Muslim politics and policies has been the often complex competition between Malaysia's two major Malay-Muslim political parties, UMNO and the Parti Islam Se-Malaysia (Islamic Party of Malaysia [PAS]). Until recent years, PAS has presented itself as a purely Malay-Islamic party. Both UMNO and PAS have sought to be seen as the chief defender of Islam and Malay rights and frequently UMNO's Islamic policies have been influenced by efforts to counter PAS rhetoric and actions. Malaysia has never had mass nongovernment Islamic organizations such as the Muhammadiyah and Nahdlatul *Ulama* in Indonesia. Thus, much of the debate on Islamic issues at the national, local, and state levels has been between these two parties plus the input of smaller, but significant nongovernmental groups.

Both PAS and UMNO have displayed changing priorities and rhetoric over the years with regard to Malay-Islamic issues. In the early years after independence, the party that later became PAS rejected the alliance with non-Malay-Muslim parties, called for limits on non-Malay citizenship, and declared its support for an Islamic state. UMNO leadership was and continues to be criticized for not paying sufficient attention to Malay interests and not fulfilling the needs and desires of the Islamic community. Although PAS rhetoric reiterated these criticisms in one fashion or another in the following decades, its position has not always been clear and consistent. PAS has formed electoral alliances with non-Malay parties, presented differing agendas over time, and now accepts non-Malays into the party.

At least in rhetoric, UMNO has articulated different emphases over time regarding ethnicity and religion. UMNO has consistently declared itself to be the chief defender of both

Malay and Muslim rights, but has displayed changing priorities over time. In the years following independence, UMNO national leaders were relatively muted with regard to tying government policies to religion or ethnicity. This changed after the intercommunal riots of 1969. The major economic program in the following decades was the New Economic Plan (NEP), which sought to redress the economic imbalance in society by aiding the *bumiputra* (Sons of the Soil, primarily Malays). The NEP initially was promulgated without reference to religion, but later the government attempted to give it Islamic legitimacy, mainly in reaction to attacks from PAS and nongovernmental Islamic organizations on both secular and religious grounds. Critics argued that the NEP was corrupt and aided only the elites and called for an Islamic solution to redress social and economic inequalities.

This ethnic emphasis can be contrasted by the rhetoric of Prime Minister Mohammad Mahathir, who governed Malaysia for over two decades after 1981. Known for his efforts to expand the role of government in Islam, he questioned the efficacy of special rights for Malays and the success of the NEP in achieving its goals. He sought to employ Islam within the endemic ethnic rivalry of the country as a means of developing a more modern Malay-Muslim. He has underscored the necessity for Malay-Muslims to modernize in order to compete with non-Malays and protect their religion and to project to the world a model of a modern, moderate, and progressive version of Islam.

PAS not only presents UMNO with an electoral confrontation, but also challenges its legitimacy. PAS has defined Islam in a more traditional manner and has supported the implementation of this view through a variety of laws seeking to restrict un-Islamic practices and attempting to legislate a more Shari`ah-based agenda. Holding at least one state during most of the postindependence era, there have been frequent tensions between PAS-controlled states and the federal government over interpretations of the role of Islam in society and governance. A classic example of PAS-UMNO differences over how to interpret Islamic jurisdiction has been PAS efforts to establish *hudud* laws (strict interpretation of Shari`ah law with severe punishment for transgressors) in states under its control. This has been part of the PAS argument that a legitimate Islamic government should implement the entire Shari`ah. This was condemned as being inimical to the Malaysian model of a modern tolerant society, although UMNO found it difficult to openly counter it. The primacy of federal authority over the states and the inability to gain the requisite number of parliamentary votes for a constitutional amendment doomed PAS efforts to implement *hudud* laws in states under its control.

Tensions between the two parties have been intensified by concepts such as *kafir-mengafir* (accusations of being an infidel) as supporters of one party have accused the other of not being true Muslims. These charges have been made against particular religious schools, *ulama,* and teachers, and party membership and leadership. The depth of their differences between the two parties was highlighted by a statement of the PAS commissioner for the state of Terengganu, who condemned UMNO and the ruling coalition for retaining the colonial-generated infidel constitution, declared that actions against UMNO were jihad and that those dying in the conflict would be martyrs, and stated that condoning separation of religion and politics showed the perpetrator to be an enemy of Islam.

For its part, the government has sought to demonize PAS and has accused it and other organizations of being tied to "extremist" principles. PAS has been variously defined as radical or extremist, antimodernization, and antidemocratic. The agenda of PAS has been termed un-Islamic and opposed to government efforts to develop a more tolerant Islam.

Ironically, parts of PAS programs have positively resonated among many UMNO members suspicious of non-Muslims and who have supported some of the more radical elements of the PAS agenda. Since 9/11 efforts have been made to link PAS to violent "terrorist" groups such as Southeast Asia's most prominent regional extremist organization, Jemaah Islamiyah (Islamic Organization).

PAS has thus been a threat to UMNO in particular because it has competed for votes in the name of Malay rights and Islamic ideals and programs. It has challenged the call of UMNO leadership for a more modern, moderate, and progressive Islam with interpretations of Islam that resonated with more conservative Muslims, particularly in rural areas. While PAS has displayed mixed electoral results and declared moribund more than once, it has been resilient. This has led UMNO and the ruling coalition to attempt to develop means of limiting PAS influence.

Dakwah and Student Movements

The second challenge to the Barisan and UMNO goals and policies came from the rise of new Islamic associations in the 1970s. There were few significant national Islamic organizations other than political parties in the years prior to the 1970s. In the first generation after independence in 1957, UMNO leaders did not heavily emphasize religion, giving greater attention to economic development. However, they continued to declare themselves as the defenders of Malay and Islamic rights. There were efforts to reinforce UMNO's Islamic character, as evidenced by the large number of mosques built by the government and support for Islamic education in schools. In part this more secular agenda of this earlier generation of UMNO leaders was due to the personal perspectives of party leadership and in larger part due to the fact that UMNO was the chief party in a multiethnic and multireligious coalition. Maintaining the cooperation of other parties in the coalition limited UMNO leaders at the national level from articulating a more vigorous Islamic agenda. Thus, Tengku Abdul Rahman, the country's first prime minister, stated his opposition to employing "narrow nationalism and the Koran in order to win a few seats," and famously declared that "unless we are prepared to drown every non-Malay, we can never think of an Islamic administration." The cooperative spirit of the national leadership toward non-Malay-Muslims was not always apparent at the local party level, and it was often said that a prospective national leader would aggressively emphasize his or her Malay and Islamic credentials until rising to national leadership when that stance tended to be muted. This took place at a time when the federal government did not actively challenge state religious prerogatives.

The 1970s were important in the movement toward greater federal involvement in Islamic affairs. In large part, this was a reaction to events of the time that appeared to pose a threat to the Malaysian Muslim political and religious establishment. The 1970s was a decade during which a host of foreign events strengthened Islamic consciousness in Malaysia. These included the Soviet occupation and war in Afghanistan, the continuing Arab-Israeli dispute, and the Iranian Revolution. The decade also was the era of the implementation of the NEP and its Malay orientation and the rise of the Islamic resurgence in Malaysia. Among many manifestations of the increase in Islamic consciousness was the growth of nongovernmental religious and student organizations. Many of them were antiestablishment and highly critical of UMNO and government policies regarding Malays and Muslims. Reinforcing UMNO's disquiet was the close relationship of some of these organizations with PAS, which itself became more consciously Islamic at this time. Thus, the 1970s became a decade of the proliferation of nongovernmental Islamic associations and the beginning of new government efforts to contain their activities. At its core were *dakwah* (or *da'wah,* meaning "the call" or "summons") groups that emphasized the need for greater understanding and renewal of their faith among Muslims. There were also *dakwah* groups that sought to convert non-Muslims to Islam.

By the end of the decade there were half a dozen major *dakwah* organizations and dozens of smaller groups. Most *dakwah* associations were nongovernmental. Their agendas varied from the Islamic Da'wah Foundation founded in the 1970s with its mission to coordinate *dakwah* groups to more ephemeral groups. Many of the latter articulated radical agendas, an extreme example being the Army of Allah, accused of the desecration of Hindu temples. Across the political and religious spectrum, *dakwah* groups have differed in size, mission, interpretation of the role of Islam, and relationship to the government or its opposition.

Two *dakwah* groups that were seen as more serious threats to the government's control of Islamic affairs were Darul Arqam (Muslim Converts Association) and the Angkatan Belia Islam Malaysia (Islamic Youth Movement of Malaysia, or ABIM). Each presented a different danger to the establishment. Darul Arqam was a Sufi-influenced organization with religious views that were defined by religious and secular authorities as "deviant" from the true teachings of Islam. However, it also developed educational, welfare, and commercial activities that were presented as models of how Islam should be implemented in comparison with establishment programs. Darul Arqam was very successful in the economic sphere and developed a considerable loyal membership. In the 1970s and 1980s it attempted to become a major alternative model to that of UMNO. It was ultimately banned in 1994 for reasons that were debated at the time. The government accused it of religious deviancy and planning to employ violence while others have explained its banning based upon on other reasons, including the possibility of Darul Arqam becoming a political challenger to UMNO interests and the doctrines of the religious establishment.

ABIM has been widely analyzed in the literature and will not be described in detail here. Rather, this section will concentrate on why ABIM was negatively viewed by the political and religious establishment and was a factor promoting government efforts to control Islamic groups. Worrying those in authority was the sheer size of ABIM, combined with its charismatic leadership, critical views of Malaysia's political, economic, and religious establishment, and contacts with PAS and external Islamic groups. Although it had less than 200 members when formed in 1972, it quickly grew to become the country's largest student organization with approximately 35,000 to 40,000 followers. At the time, ABIM had a national presence with branches throughout the country, but the perceived primary danger it presented was its strength in Malaysian universities. Prior to the NEP, most university students were non-Malay, but the NEP led to a major increase in the number of Malays that came into the tertiary education system. Many came from rural areas and small towns and initially were unaccustomed to requirements of institutions of higher learning. In this alien and often urban environment they frequently reacted negatively to what they saw as an un-Islamic environment. To these must be added students and faculty who had been educated in the West or the Middle East. Abroad they came in contact with radical ideas from activists such as Sayyid Qutb, Hassan al-Banna, and Mawlana Mawdudi. This made for a potent mixture that UMNO and the conservative Islamic establishment perceived as a growing threat.

ABIM was led by an articulate and charismatic individual, Anwar Ibrahim, who called for reform in the social, political, and religious system within Islamic values. While many ABIM members were more conservative than Anwar Ibrahim, he supported working within Malaysia's multiethnic society and did not seek to mirror Middle Eastern models. He defined Islam more in terms of social justice, not the Islam of the more conservative "*Shari`ah* Muslims." There was support for an Islamic state within ABIM, but details remained unclear. Its strong social justice platform often put it at odds with those in authority as the leadership of ABIM charged the government and UMNO with corruption and not caring for the Malay people. It also criticized the numerous government means of controlling the opposition, such as the Internal Security Act (ISA).

Adding to UMNO discomfort was the early relationship between ABIM and PAS. It is alleged that ABIM gave its support to PAS in the 1978 elections, although ABIM was not as conservative in its views of Islam. PAS sought an alliance with ABIM, but was unsuccessful due in part to differences between the more radical PAS policies and more cautious ABIM views. Members of both organizations have interacted politically and there have been desertions from one organization to another. ABIM was also suspect because of contacts of ABIM leadership with the Iranian Revolution, although Anwar Ibrahim did not see Iran as a model for Malaysia. After Anwar Ibrahim was co-opted by Prime Minister Mohamad Mahathir and joined the government, ABIM's impact diminished.

In addition to nongovernment *dakwah* associations, there were government-sponsored organizations that sought to counter undesirable *dakwah* activities and statements critical of religious and secular authority. An early example of a government-aided institution was the establishment of the Pertubuhan Kebajakan Islam Se-Malaysia, or PERKIM (All-Muslim Welfare Organization) and similar institutions in Sabah and Sarawak. It was funded by the government along with Middle Eastern donors. Its chief function was to convert non-Muslims to Islam. Converts were frequently presented on television to discuss their conversion. However, PERKIM has also been a means of coordinating "acceptable" *dakwah* organizations.

A final group critical of UMNO's policies related to Islam is to be found within elements of the *ulama*. These religious leaders historically have been extremely influential at the state and local levels. The *ulama* have been seen as both useful partners and opponents to UMNO goals. From the inauguration of what is now PAS, both parties have sought to align *ulama* with their respective causes. *Ulama* have been financially aided by both parties and given sermons criticizing the other party, and there have been frequent reports of *ulamas* boycotted by those supporting their political opponents. The government has attempted to co-opt and control them by forming state and national institutions including state religious councils and the National Fatwa Council. This has been difficult to accomplish in states not held by the Barisan. In National Front-administered states the government can use its appointive powers to shape institutions such as state mufti and religious councils. It has also been possible to employ national legislation, such as the ISA, to detain *ulama* considered deviant in their religious views or accused of being involved in violence. Those preaching at private mosques have remained relatively free of federal control, although preachers at government mosques must obtain a license. The major *ulama* organization has historically been tied to PAS. It should be noted that there have been UMNO leaders with negative views of the *ulama*, considering them to be ill trained. Mahathir was particularly critical, stating that the decline of Islam resulted from their rejection of secular knowledge.

Radical Violent Groups

The danger of violence has long been a government explanation for the need to curb criticism. The reality is that no other country, except for the city-state of Singapore and the small north Borneo Sultanate of Brunei Darussalam, has had fewer fatalities from political or religious violence in the past half century. Even the 1969 riots that led to the large number of deaths (one to two thousand, depending upon the source), pales in comparison with casualties from separatist movements in Burma (Myanmar), Thailand, and the Philippines or the Indo-China War and hundreds of thousands killed in the aftermath of an attempted coup in Indonesia in 1965. Since the official end of the "emergency" in 1960, violent religiously driven events have been few and the death toll comparatively small. In 1980 a group of exiled Chams attacked a police station in the name of cleansing the country of evil and establishing an Islamic state. In the incident eight members of the sect were killed. No domestic Islamic groups were involved. In 2000 a group that followed a deviationist leader sought to overthrow the regime and establish an Islamic state. Arms were stolen from the military and attacks launched against un-Islamic targets. In the end, there were three deaths aside from the execution of several leaders. Nineteen were eventually tried under the ISA. The one violent event with domestic political implications that led to significant fatalities was the "Memali Incident" in 1985. At that time, government forces clashed with villagers led by a strong PAS stalwart who was accused of teaching "deviant" Islam. Eighteen villagers and police were reported killed. This deadly confrontation led to accusations and counteraccusations from PAS and UMNO. It can be argued that the limited nature of religious violence in Malaysia makes any such act more dramatic and aberrant to the country's more tolerant expression of Islam. Events of this nature reinforce the government rationale for its control policies.

Since the mid-1980s most Islamic radical organizations espousing violence have been small and unable to maintain organizational continuity. Information about their activities and specific threat to the secular and religious establishment has often been poorly defined. Organizations targeted by the government after 2000 show the limited nature of the danger posed. The so-called Jihad Gang consisting of only nine men who reportedly carried out actions including armed robbery and attacks on police and politicians. More widely publicized by the government was the Kumpulan Militan Malaysia, or KMM (Malaysian Militant Group) formed in 1995 and first revealed in 2001.

There has been considerable debate regarding KMM activities and membership and there are those who discount government statements on this shadowy group. Of ten individuals initially held by the government under the ISA, eight were reportedly PAS members. It was also supposedly linked to regional "terrorism."

There is no question that planning by mostly non-Malaysians for international radical violence has taken place in Malaysia, including a meeting in Kuala Lumpur of international extremists at which 9/11 and the attack on the USS Cole in Yemen were discussed. There is also evidence of interaction between small cells of Malaysian Islamic radicals and international extremist groups such as al-Qa'ida and Jeemah Islamiyah. However, the exact relationship between them remains murky.

These events and organizations, along with the dangers posed by 9/11 and its aftermath, were used by the government to legitimize its efforts to contain unacceptable interpretations of Islam and to control possible seditious action. The Mahathir government largely succeeded in isolating violent Islamic radicals. The events of 9/11 and possible threats from extremism were also employed, with limited success, to underscore criticisms of PAS for encouraging radical Islam. The alleged involvement of PAS in the Memali incident and KMM was reinforced by the intensity of PAS critical comments of Western foreign policy.

Methods of Control

To meet these perceived threats to its power and to communal peace, the federal government has employed a variety of tools. These have included coercion, the formation of counterorganizations to reinforce limits to the political and religious opposition, and efforts to define itself as the legitimate protector of Islam. Many of its legal powers were initially not directed toward religious-oriented activities. Rather, its arsenal of powers was first primarily promulgated to meet the needs of the "emergency," the conflict against domestic communist insurgency that had lasted from 1948 to 1960 and efforts to diminish ethnic conflict after the 1969 riots. Over time, many of these acts were amended to meet newer perceived threats.

The legislation seen by many critics of the government as the most serious challenge to their rights was the ISA. Formulated in 1960 as a continuation of a colonial regulation to control the communist insurgency, it allows the government to hold a person for sixty days without trail, after which detention can be renewed every two years. As amended in 1989, there can be no judicial review of decisions by the government on the implementation of the ISA. Since its inception it has been employed against a wide range of organizations and individuals, including a significant number from the Islamic opposition. Among those targeted under the ISA have been Anwar Ibrahim and many of his ABIM followers for organizing peasant demonstrations as well as leaders and members of numerous *dakwah* organizations, the most publicized being Darul Arqam. PAS members have long been targets of the ISA and those held in preventative detention have included elected officials, major voices in the party, and past and present members.

The ISA has been used as a means of controlling critics in the name of eliminating "deviancy," defined as interpretations contrary to acceptable Islam. Deviancy is defined by the government and punishment can include long-term detention. Scholars, members of *dakwah* organizations, and others have been arrested in the name of eliminating religious "deviancy." Accusations of deviancy have been made by religious spokesmen and groups, state religious courts, and the federal government. Sufi, Ahmadiyah, and Shi'a interpretations of Islam have come under the suspicion of deviancy and their members detained and organizations restricted or banned. The Shi'i has been denounced for fragmenting Malaysia's religious community and there was worry that there would be negative fallout from the Iranian Revolution among opposition groups. Contacts between PAS and ABIM with the new Iranian regime furthered government opposition to Shi'a influence. It should be noted that the impact of Wahabbi interpretations have been under close scrutiny, given the number of radical groups in the region who have ties to Wahabbi beliefs. This has been somewhat more delicate, given Malaysia's close ties to the Wahabbi Kingdom of Saudi Arabia.

Other legislation that has been employed to contain the religious opposition includes the Societies Act of 1960 as amended, the Universities and University Colleges Act, and the Printing Presses and Publicity Act of 1984. The Societies Act required associations of more than seven members to register with the government and agree to uphold constitutional principles. A society can be rejected or asked to represent the request with recommended changes. Once registered, the association can be deregistered and the home minister has the right to search the premises of an association. The act was employed to control the rise of *dakwah* and student groups that expressed deviant or radical agendas.

The government sought to control the increasing number of student and faculty critics on Malaysian campuses. In response to demonstrations during the 1969 riots and their aftermath, the Universities and University Colleges Act was promulgated. It was then used against *dakwah* groups with ABIM becoming a major target of the act. Neither student groups nor faculty can make public political statements supporting or opposing a political party or trade union, and student organization events require the respective vice-chancellor's approval. A significant number of students have been detained under this legislation. For a period, these restrictions on student groups expedited the rise of off-campus *dakwah* associations with fewer government controls. Recent student efforts to soften the act have, as yet, not been successful.

Legislation that can also be employed to limit criticism is the Police Act of 1967 and the Printing Presses and Publication Act of 1984. The former puts limitations on the right to assembly by requiring prior permission for almost all public meetings. The latter mirrors a colonial regulation to deal with the "emergency." It necessitates annual permission for a license for newspapers and other publications. Opposition party papers can only be distributed to its own members. When combined with a virtual blackout of opposition criticism on national television, both religious and secular opponents have a very limited ability to present their views in public. Serious inroads on this control have recently come from the internet and various critical blogs. However, the government is equipped with powerful tools to control dissident individuals and groups, including the ISA, the Societies Act, the Police Act, the Presses and Publication Act, and other legislation.

CO-OPTATION AND LEGITIMIZATION

UMNO sought to establish new Islamic institutions that generally had two purposes, to legitimize UMNO as the real protector of Islam in Malaysia with concrete results to prove it and to further its long-term efforts to define Islam in "acceptable" ways. Among primarily symbolic actions have been the annual Koranic Reading Contest held in Merdeka Stadium with large prize money for the winners and the celebration of National *Dakwah* Month begun in 1979. There were also the establishments of institutions that were initially thought to be symbolic, but became considerably more successful than envisioned. Thus, when the First Islamic Bank was established in 1883, UMNO leaders put in largely token amounts, although there was substantial government input. Many inside and outside of the Barisan did not consider that it would play a significant role in Malaysia's economy. However, by

2006 it and conventional banks offering banking within *Shari`ah* principles accounted for 8.2 percent of the assets of the total banking system of Malaysia.

At the inauguration of the International Islamic University (IIU), there were similar low expectations and which was replaced in 2012 some viewed it as primarily symbolic. It was opened in 1983 with the support of the government of Malaysia and a number of other Muslim states. It began in cramped housing at the old Teachers College with a student body of 153 and only two faculties, law and economics. However, within a decade the student body rose to over 3,000 undergraduates and 400 postgraduates taking classes in a dozen disciplines. The campus was moved to large modern facilities and now has approximately 20,000 students and thirteen faculties. As an international university it has students from over forty countries. The university meets several needs. It provides the first university system within an Islamic context within the religious framework espoused by the government. It also reinforces domestic and international Islamic legitimacy of the government and shows a concrete example of its commitment. In addition to the IIU, the Islamic Teachers' College was established in 1980 and the Islamic Medical Center in 1983.

At the federal level the most important actor in determining the boundaries of Islam in Malaysia has been the Jabatan Kemajuan Islam Malaysia, or JAKIM (Department of Islamic Development in Malaysia). It defines deviancy and monitors organizations, publications, and public statements in order to judge their Islamic legitimacy. JAKIM has rehabilitation centers where religious deviants are expected to learn acceptable Islamic principles. It also is expected to coordinate *dakwah* groups and has monitored Wahabbi, Shi`a, and other possible disruptive beliefs. In addition to identifying halal products, the department has been active in aiding the government in formulation policy positions on family law and "indecency." There are limits to its powers. It does not have the ability to detain or fine targeted individuals or groups and Malaysia's federal system can further limit its effectiveness in states held by the opposition. However, JAKIM's positions can be implemented through other government-run legislation and institutions.

There have been a series of government-sponsored activities and new organizations formed to frame the role of Islam in education. One factor behind these policies was the desire to control the content of what was being taught in schools about Islam and to by-pass educational programs in PAS-governed states. From the 1961 Education Act until the mid-1970s, teaching Islam in public schools passed from the states to the federal government. Later, Islamic knowledge became a requirement for Muslim entrance into teacher's colleges and in 1979 it became a required examination subject for Muslim students for the Malaysian Higher School Certificate (SPM). *Ulama* within the Department of Islamic Development in Malaysia formulated the curricula of these courses. Some critics at the time argued that this penalized Muslim students who needed to do well in another subject (although non-Malay must take moral values). In 1974 religious textbooks were chosen by federal authorities. In the aftermath of 9/11 and the emphasis on the control of "terrorist" groups the government turned to containing private religious schools that were allegedly perpetuating radical beliefs and activities. As a result, a large number of schools tied to PAS had to transfer to becoming national schools.

Other institutions formed to underscore the government's commitment to Islam have been the Institut Kefahaman Islam Malaysia, or IKIM (Malaysian Institute of Islamic Understanding), the Majlis Kebangsaan Halehwal Islam Malaysia (Malaysian National Islamic Research Centre), the Pusat Penyelidekan Islam Malaysia (National Council for Islamic Affairs), the Islamic Missionary and Training Institute, the Islamic Dakwah Foundation, and a wide range of other national advisory groups, including those concentrating upon education and the advancement of *Shari'ah* law. The most notable of these has been IKIM. It was founded in 1992 to be an intellectual channel for the UMNO interpretation of Islam, although it also is a vehicle for interaction with other faiths. It became a means of fostering Mahathir's modern moderate Islamic and economic system. It publishes extensively on Islamic subjects, has its own radio station, and maintains contacts within the international Islamic community.

Perhaps the most striking example of co-optation, aside from the recruitment of Anwar Ibrahim, relates to the Islamic state issue. Under the constitution, Islam is the state religion, but PAS and numerous other Islamic groups and individuals have long called for an Islamic state, based upon the *Shari'ah*. The exact dimensions of that state were not spelled out by PAS until Mahathir announced in 2001 that Malaysia was already an Islamic state. The basis of this statement was the Islamization process that had taken place primarily during his administration. He asserted that Malaysia had met the requirements of an Islamic state. This was in contradiction to many previous statements by Mahathir that the country was not and could not be an Islamic state. His depiction of Malaysia as an Islamic state also was contrary to the general supposition that such a state required that it be ruled by *Shari'ah* law. Mahathir's declaration sharpened the divide between UMNO and its Muslim opposition and the non-Malay electorate. His interpretation of the Islamic state issue elicited negative reactions from non-Muslim parties both within and outside of the Barisan. It underscored the extent to which the emphasis of early UMNO upon the primary need to maintain harmony had eroded, although Mahathir emphasized his long held position that Islamic-related policies would not be allowed to adversely affect non-Muslims. In reality the Islamization issue has cost the Barisan votes from the non-Muslim electorate.

PAS has often found its Islamic agenda co-opted by this process of Islamization. It has attempted to meet this challenge in several ways. It has sought to reinforce PAS-controlled Islamic institutions within states it administers. It regularly criticizes UMNO religious policies as not going far enough or un-Islamic. On the religious state issue, it denies that Malaysia is an Islamic state and presented a detailed exposition on its interpretation of how such a state should be defined. At the same time, PAS has attempted to portray itself as more flexible and prepared to move beyond its traditional Malay-Muslim platforms. In recent national elections PAS combined its tradition of protector of Islam with a more secular platform. It found electoral success in attacking UMNO as corrupt, pro-capitalist, and not committed to aiding the poor and called for reform and a democratic system.

Conclusions

In the years immediately after independence, the general consensus within the government was that it was essential to maintain peace and harmony among the Malay-Muslim and non-Malay communities. Even the "emergency" that still existed during this period was also communal, given the high percentage of Chinese in the communist insurgency. However, there continued to be opposition to this precept within the Malay-Muslim community. Within UMNO itself, many members were at odds with party leadership over its more secular and intercommunal agenda. These simmering tensions came to the forefront with the so-called racial riots of 1969. In its efforts to maintain stability after the 1969 violence, the Malaysian government built upon colonial policies of control to provide the foundation of efforts to contain ethnic and religious opposition in the years that followed.

The national legal and legislative control mechanisms that followed were not only important as a means of controlling divisive or critical organizations and individuals. They also could be employed by the national government to circumvent efforts by the opposition to define the Islamic framework in states it controlled. Powerful tools to ensure interpretations of Islam amenable to the government included acts such as the ISA, the Societies Bill, and those dealing with the press's and universities' freedom of expression. When these were married to the declared right of the federal government to define "un-Islamic deviancy," the capacity to frame how Islam was to be defined was further strengthened. Mahathir's co-optation strategy and the development of new Islamic institutions at the national level helped to further erode the traditional domination of the states over Islamic affairs. As a result, religious organizations with interpretations of Islam inimical to the national vision have been weakened. This arsenal of acts has certainly been part of the explanation for the relatively low level of ethnoreligious violence as compared to most other Southeast Asian countries.

The movement of power from the periphery to the center in Malaysia is not unusual in modern polities. Almost all contemporary federal systems have witnessed an increasing role of national governments and a concomitant weakening of state or provincial authority. The role of Malaysia's federal government in Islamic affairs is significantly different than it was fifty years ago. Yet, the very existence of a working federal system and the ability of the opposition to win at the state level has been a serious impediment to UMNO's efforts to enforce its own interpretation of the meaning and role of Islam. At the state and local levels, federal authorities continue to face impediments to their efforts to control the activities of religious critics. Nor has PAS cracked under government pressure and efforts to define it as extremist and opposed to the modern and moderate version of Islam espoused by UMNO leadership. The 1998 elections showed that PAS has again redefined itself by emphasizing issues such as social justice and joining with other non-Islamic-centered parties to confront UMNO and the Barisan. In sum, differences regarding the interpretation and implementation of Islam will continue to play a significant role in Malaysia's future.

References

Anwar, Zainah. 1987. *Islamic Revivalism in Malaysia: Dakwah Among Students*. Petaling Jaya: Peladunk.
Chandra, Muzzafar. 1987. *Islamic Resurgence in Malaysia*. Petaling Jaya: Penerbit Fajar Bakti.
Croissant, Aurel, Martin, Beate, and Kneip, Sascha, eds. 2006. *The Politics of Death: Political Violence in Southeast Asia*. Berlin: Lit.
Liow, Joseph. 2009. New York: Oxford University Press.
Martinez, Patricia. 2001. "The Islamic State or the State or State of Islam in Malaysia." *Contemporary Southeast Asia* 23, 3: 474–503.
Means, Gordon. 1991. *Malaysian Politics: The Second Generation*. Singapore: Oxford University Press.

Means, Gordon. 2009. *Political Islam in Southeast Asia*. Boulder: Lynne Reinner Publishers.
Milne, R. S., and Mauzy, Diane. 1999. *Malaysian Politics under Mahathir*. London: Routledge.
Mutalib, Hussin. 1990. *Islam and Ethnicity in Malay Politics*. Singapore: Oxford University Press.
Nagata, Judith. 1984. *The Reflowering of Malaysian Islam: Modern Religious Radicals and Their Roots*. Vancouver: University of British Columbia Press.
Nasr, Syyed Vali Reza. 2001. *Islamic Leviathan: Islam and the Making of State Power*. New York: Oxford University Press.
Weiss, Meredith. 2006. *Protest and Possibilities: Civil Society and Coalitions for Change in Malaysia*. Stanford: Stanford University Press.

Jihadi Political Islam

CHAPTER 39

AL-JAMA`A AL-ISLAMIYA AND THE AL-JIHAD GROUP IN EGYPT

NAEL SHAMA

INTRODUCTION

THIS essay looks into modern militant Islamic groups in Egypt. Looking into the history and development of modern jihadist groups in Egypt, in particular al-Jama`a al-Islamiya and the al-Jihad Group, derives its importance from the fact that the groups provide a compelling example of how violent social groups can be encouraged to moderate their ideologies and practices through communication, dialogue, and reeducation. Despite many attempts at deradicalization in various Muslim-majority countries, the Egyptian deradicalization experience has been a real success story. It has therefore attracted wide scholarly interest. Omar Ashour's essential study on the historical development of al-Jama`a al-Islamiya concluded that the group "has shown a remarkable ability to change on both the behavioral and the ideological levels" (Ashour 2007: 624). Subsequently, other important studies confirmed this conclusion. Gunaratna and Bin Ali, for example, point out that Egypt's counter-radicalization program "is the first and the most extensive of any Arab country" (2009: 289). Blaydes and Rubin concur, underlining the fact that compared to al-Jama`a al-Islamiya, "no other religious terrorist group of this size to this date has offered a program of religious re-interpretation on the scale of the experience in Egypt" (2008: 462).

This essay discusses the genesis of Egypt's largest militant groups, al-Jama`ah Al-Islamiya (hereafter al-Jama`a) and the Islamic Jihad Group (hereafter al-Jihad), their conflict with the state at the height of the radicalization phase, and the ideological underpinnings of both the radicalization and the deradicalization phases.

The Islamic revival in Egypt was born out of the national distress that followed the military defeat against Israel in 1967, and was advanced by the tacit backing of Sadat's Egypt of Islamists, which aimed at undermining the leftist and Nasserist opposition. The socioeconomic difficulties of the 1970s provided a perfect milieu for the radicalization of the disenfranchised young Muslim activists, who were discontented about the status quo and adamant at changing it. In the radical phase, radical Islamists perceived their government as "atheist" and used violence to change the prevailing political order, but an exhausting and blood-spattered two-decade battle with the state put an end to their ill-advised mission.

The different factors that explain the deradicalization process that started in the late 1990s are surveyed in this essay. The decline of popular support resulting from the bloody conflict against the state, the long periods spent by Islamists in jail that prompted them to revise their ideologies, the heavy cost of the state's repression, and the realization of the failure of the use of force against the state all contributed to the shunning of violence and the gradual reintegration into society.

Origins and Development

Egypt in the early 1970s was ripe for major transformations in politics and society. In 1970, President Gamal Abdel-Nasser, whose charismatic authority dominated Egypt's political space in the 1950s and 1960s, died. A few years earlier, his political program, premised on socialism and pan-Arabism, was dealt a severe blow following Egypt's humiliating defeat against Israel in the Six Day War. Nasser's successor, Anwar Sadat, quickly changed the state's political structure, its socioeconomic outlook, and its pattern of international alliances. After years of experimentation with socialist ideas, the open-door economic policy (*infitah*) ushered in the age of capitalism, and a controlled form of political pluralism replaced Nasser's single-party system, the Arab Socialist Union. In addition, the two-decade alliance with the Soviet Union was terminated and replaced with increased dependence on the United States, which in a few years paved the way for peace with Israel, Egypt's former nemesis. Domestically, the nascent, largely unplanned, economic opening policy and an uncontrollable population boom gave rise to an economic crisis characterized by growing unemployment rates, skyrocketing inflation, rampant corruption, and a growing gap between the haves and the have-nots. Massive migration from rural areas to big cities, most notably Cairo, led to overcrowding and strained the country's ailing infrastructure and its public services.

It is within these turbulent times that modern Islamic movements rose to prominence on university campuses, particularly in Cairo, Alexandria, and Assiut, attracting increased membership and sympathy among students through offering a wide range of social services, such as organized lectures, trips, textbooks at discounted rates, and attempts to improve the conditions of student housing. This Islamic movement, then still a large and divided entity composed of several multi-ideological groups with no well-defined hierarchy or chain of command and without a common political blueprint, took advantage of Sadat's tacit approval of Islamists, which aimed at undermining the well-organized and vociferous Nasserist and leftist opposition. The backing of authorities, coupled with the well-planned and assiduous work of Islamists, enabled the Islamic movement to control the student unions by 1976–1977. But the short honeymoon between the state and Islamists soon ended following Sadat's electric-shock Mideast diplomacy, which started with his visit to Jerusalem in 1977, and culminated in the signing of the Egyptian-Israeli peace treaty in 1979. Islamists were furious about peace with Israel, worried about the rapid Westernization of Egyptian society, and alarmed at the socioeconomic pitfalls of the *infitah* policy, and their opposition to Sadat and his policies were vocally expressed in their widely read publications.

Confrontation ensued, and in 1979 all student unions in Egyptian universities were officially banned, depriving the Islamic movement of the organization that gave legal cover and funding to its myriad activities. Although many of its members remained committed to da'wa (proselytizing), others opted for militant underground action.

The first symptoms of Islamic revival in Egypt had in fact emerged following the 1967 War. The public shock at the unanticipated results of the war, in which three Arab armies were defeated in just six days, whereas Israel expanded to three times its prewar size, raised one soul-searching question: "Why were we so badly defeated?" Several answers emerged out of the postwar trauma: that Egyptians did not embrace socialism wholeheartedly, that Egyptians abandoned scientific knowledge in an age of science and technology, and most importantly that Egyptians were not religious enough. Proponents of the religious explanation attributed the most devastating event in Egypt's modern history to the lack of piety; "We left God, so God left us," they assured their fellow countrymen. The primacy of this interpretation led to the demise of the secular/nationalist formula espoused by Nasser and the birth of the "religionization" of the Arab-Israeli conflict, which was mostly evident by the heavy use of religious terminology during the 1973 War (Ayubi 1980: 489–490).

By the early 1970s, a conspicuous increase in Islamic consciousness permeated almost every aspect of Egyptian society. The proliferation of Islamic literature, an increase in the percentage of men growing beards and women wearing the *hijab* (veil), the spread of Qur'an-reading circles, and the mushrooming of vast networks of Islamic associations, banks, hospitals, and schools signaled an increase in the involvement of Islam in the country's social and culture life. In this milieu, Islam thrived, its symbols became en vogue, and sheikhs turned into celebrities. Unsurprisingly, state officials flirted with Islamic ideals as a means of legitimizing unpopular state policies. Indeed, to cope with, and take advantage of, this powerful "Islamization from below" wave, the Egyptian state embarked on a similarly powerful "Islamization from above" initiative. The state reasoned that the Islamic groups' idiosyncratic reading of religious texts should be challenged, and that a "proper" alternative interpretation of religious instructions should be presented to the general public. Under both Sadat and Mubarak, and in tandem with the growing threat of radical Islamic groups, the state increasingly relied on the efforts of the official religious establishment. Between 1970 and 1985, for instance, the publications of Al-Azhar University, the 1,000-year-old center of Sunni Islamic learning, increased fourfold, and the student intake of state-sponsored religious institutions more than tripled (Hafez 1997: 304–305). In a similar vein, President Sadat flirted with Islam to augment his fragile rule and legitimize his sudden restructuring of policy and ideology. He emphasized that Muhammad was his first name, labeled himself the "pious president," and filled his speeches with references to the Qur'an and heavy usage of Islamic symbols. In addition, he amended the constitution in 1980 so that it explicitly stipulated that the principles of *shari'ah* (Islamic law) constituted "the primary source of legislation."

The post-1967 Islamic revival was both the cause and effect of the rise and growth of the Islamic groups in the 1970s. Working from their strong bases in public universities, al-Jama'a played a profound role in the Islamization of society through preaching Islamic values and norms, calling for the wearing of the *hijab* among the female student population, establishing prayer rooms in university buildings, segregating sexes in classrooms, and banning parties and musical concerts on campuses. The message of al-Jama'a resonated powerfully with the Egyptian public. In a display of their newly acquired influence, the mass Eid prayers organized by al-Jama'a in stadiums or large squares in 1976 attracted more than 50,000 in Cairo and around 40,000 in Alexandria (Abu El-Fotouh 2010: 50–51).

The proliferation of *ahli* (private) mosques, particularly in poverty-ridden slum areas, facilitated the spread of revolutionary Islamic ideas and values among the frustrated Muslim youth, who aspired to change the miserable realities that they experienced day and night in their underdeveloped socioeconomic environment. The number of these privately run mosques was estimated at 20,000 when Sadat took over in 1970, but they had more than doubled by Sadat's death in 1981 (Hafez 1997: 307). Because political liberties were curtailed and little dissent was tolerated, these mosques, over which the Ministry of Religious Endowments had little control, became the only institution where open discussions over politics and religion could freely take place.

The confrontation between Sadat's regime and Islamic groups put its members at a crucial crossroad: while some continued their peaceful *da'wa* to Islam despite the routine security crackdowns, or joined the relatively moderate Muslim Brotherhood (MB), others decided to carry arms against the state. It was at this juncture that the militant al-Jama'a was born. Other militant organizations emerged at the same time, most notably al-Jihad, which was made up of two clusters of Islamic groups, one in Cairo led by Muhammad Abdel-Salam Faraj and another in Assiut led by Karam Zudi. Members of al-Jama'a were implicated in the assassinations of President Anwar Sadat in 1981 (in collaboration with al-jihad) and the speaker of Egyptian parliament Rif'at Al-Mahgoub in 1990, in addition to a number of failed assassination attempts against top officials and intellectuals. The group also targeted secular intellectuals, police officers, Coptic Christians, tourist venues, and places of entertainment, which resulted in a sweeping wave of violence that sent shockwaves through Egyptian society in the 1980s and 1990s. The two-decade conflict between the state and militant Islamists, considered by some analysts to be on the scale of a "mini civil war," resulted in the death of over 1,200 people in the period between 1992 and 1996 alone. It is estimated that 90–95 percent of the violence in the 1980s and 1990s was perpetrated by al-Jama'a (Blaydes and Rubin 2008: 467; Goerzig and Al-Hashimi 2007: 2).

There was a perceptible regional influence in the rise of al-Jama'a. All the top leaders implicated in Sadat's assassination came from Al-Sa'id (Upper Egypt), and Sa'idis also constituted a majority among the lower ranks. For instance, of the 280 conspirators accused, 183 came from Upper Egypt, and 73 lived in the Cairo neighborhoods that were inhabited primarily by southern (Upper Egyptian) migrants (Fandy 1994: 607–608). The stronghold of al-Jama'a was in Upper Egypt's main cities, such as Assiut, Sohag, and Qena, distant from the tight control of the central state in the capital city of Cairo. This particular sociopolitical setting had a profound influence on the ideology of al-Jama'a, which, according to Fandi, was influenced by Sa'idi grievances against the injustice and neglect of the north, peculiar Sa'idi traditions, and Islam (Ibid.: 622). The issues of poverty and underdevelopment, prevailing in the south due to the neglect of successive Cairo-based central governments, appear prominently in the pronouncements of al-Jama'a (Ibid.: 610).

The fusion of young age, modest social background, and high education in a milieu characterized by sharp economic and social tensions turned into a blast against the existing political order. A study conducted on members of al-Jihad demonstrated that among the 280 members tried following Sadat's murder, 43.9 percent were students, 14.6 percent were workers, and 12.5 percent were professionals. The same study showed that 70 percent of these members were in the 21–30 age range (Hafez 1997: 306–307). Many of them were recent migrants from the countryside to big cities, thus they were cut off from the traditional networks of societal support they had enjoyed in their hometowns. Their high career expectations and desire to achieve social mobility were dashed by the enormous economic and social difficulties of city life. To these disenfranchised youth, joining jihadist groups was driven by the pursuit of a comforting identity and the deep-rooted need to feel a sense of achievement.

Although al-Jama'a and al-Jihad joined forces in a major military operation—the first successful assassination attempt of an Egyptian leader in decades—the two groups split while in prison shortly thereafter due to disagreements on leadership, ideology, and tactics. First, whereas the historical leadership of al-Jama'a unanimously chose professor of Islamic jurisprudence Shaykh Omar Abd Al-Rahman as their leader, the leading figures of al-Jihad rejected that choice on the grounds of his blindness, a deficiency that in their opinion inhibited his ability to run an organization of a military nature. The second disagreement was rooted in each group's understanding of the theological concept of *al-uzr bil-jahl* (excuse due to ignorance), which upholds that violating Islamic laws could be exempted from punishment if the violating person was ignorant about these laws. Al-Jihad leaders insisted that ignorance would not be a valid excuse, if the violating party did not exert "enough effort" to learn or understand Islamic laws. According to this interpretation, leaders of secular Islamic regimes, and the security officers who serve these regimes, are legitimate targets of violence, their ignorance of Islamic rules notwithstanding. Third, the leaders of al-Jama'a emphasized overt *da'wa* to Islam in mosques, universities, and all domains of public life. On the other hand, al-Jihad, a small, secret, and disciplined group, cared less about its spiritual influence in society and favored instead clandestine military actions, including the overthrow of the regime through a coup that, its leaders believed, would be followed by wide popular support (Ashour 2007: 607–608).

The influence of al-Jihad in Egypt waned significantly following the arrest of a large number of its members in 1981. The release of many of its cadres in the late 1980s and early 1990s did not revive the group domestically, as many of these members headed to Pakistan and Afghanistan to escape the crackdown of Egyptian authorities and to fight the Soviet occupation of Afghanistan. Their ties to Egypt since then have been very loose, and it is widely believed that al-Jihad has not carried out any attacks in Egypt since the early 1990s. In exile, al-Jihad, under the leadership of Ayman Al-Zawahiry, joined forces with Bin Laden's al-Qa'ida, constituting what became known as "Qaedat al-Jihad" (the Base of Jihad). After the local demise of al-jihad, al-Jama'a remained the only large Islamic group that is committed to the use of violent means against the Egyptian government.

Ideology

At a very general level, members of al-Jama'a and al-Jihad belong to the Salafi creed. The Sunni-based school of *Salafism*, derived from the Arabic noun *salaf* (predecessors), believes that true Islam is to be found in the teachings and understanding of religious texts provided in words and deeds by the first three generations of Islam, namely, the *sahabah* (the companions of the Prophet), *al-tabi'un* (the followers), and *tabi al-tabi'un* (those after the followers). Dogmatic and puritanical, there is little room for change and innovation in *Salafism*.

Based on scriptural evidence, *Salafism* believes that any kind of innovation (or *bid'ah*, in their own terminology), be it celebrating the birth of Prophet Muhammad, commemorating the death of a saint, or applying the tenets of democracy, is unacceptable to God and dangerous to the Islamic faith. The principle of *ijtihad* (independent juristic reasoning), prevalent in many other Islamic schools of thought, is in most cases prohibited by *Salafism*.

The centrality of the notion of *jihad* (holy war) in militant Islamist thought is self-evident. The core idea behind the militant acts of al-Jama'a and al-Jihad against the Egyptian government was the belief that Muslim governments are duty bound to implement the *shar'ia*. Accordingly, the secular governments in Muslim-majority states that were not fully committed to the unqualified implementation of *shar'ia* were considered illegitimate, in fact ungodly. They were perceived as "atheist states," against which jihad became a religious duty for all true believers. It is crucial, here, to point out that the notion of jihad in Arabic covers a broad semantic spectrum, and is not limited to the practice of going into military battle. In fact, Muslims' "spiritual jihad" against committing sins and all sorts of wrongdoings is of supreme importance in the teachings of Islam. In addition, jihad cannot be only practiced with the sword as it is often assumed; jihad can be performed through preaching or by providing financial support. However, Egyptian militants adopted a peculiar interpretation of jihad, which emphasized the use of force as the primary means to change the corrupt reality. The contemporary literature on these militants therefore describes them as "salafi-jihadis."

As the discourse of al-Jama'a and al-Jihad clearly demonstrates, the use of force was not only condoned but also favored. Inherent admiration of crude force, and the profound role it should play in politics, can be easily sensed from the early writings of these revolutionary Islamists. For example, Tal'at Fu'ad Qasim, a founding member of the *majlis al-shura* (governing council) of al-Jama'a and a former al-Jama'a spokesman, opined that "the only way to express yourself in this world is through force, the only language that is understood" (Qasim et al. 1996: 41).

The peculiar understanding of jihad adopted by al-Jama'a and al-Jihad finds its roots in a booklet written by the engineer-turned-preacher Muhammad Abdel-Salam Faraj titled *Al-Farida Al-Ghaiba* (The Neglected Duty). In this pamphlet, Faraj argues that the duty of jihad in modern times is neglected, even denied by some Muslims, and that this main pillar of Islam has to be revived since it is the only method to set up a true Islamic state. It is, therefore, the duty of all believers to engage in jihad against the rulers of Egypt who are apostates, and who take unbelievers as their close allies. Because they shirked the duty of jihad, Faraj denied the approaches of both the MB, who sought to change the political system from within through peaceful means, and the *al-Takfir wa al-Hijra* (Excommunication and Migration) group,[1] who favored migration from the infidel society until its members became strong enough to take part in jihad.

Both al-Jama'a and al-Jihad rejected democracy and prohibited the formation of, or the participation in, political parties. They argued that democracy in its very essence substitutes the will of God with the will of the masses, and that it is the antithesis of Islam's concept of *hakimiyya*, the acceptance that the right of judgment and legislation belongs only to God (Mustafa 1992: 172–173).

Although the MB shared with al-Jama'a and al-Jihad the ultimate goal of dethroning secular Muslim governments and instituting in their place Islamic states that rule according to *shar'ia*, they differed over the tactics used to achieve this goal. After two decades of repression under Nasser, the MB shunned violence in the 1970s, and has since then opted for working *within* existing social and political structures in the hope of producing deep change in politics and society over the long run. Much younger in age and devoid of the rich, five-decade historical experience of the MB, the new jihadists of the 1970s were impatient, fond of quick change, and against any kind of compromise with the state. Thus their actions carried a great deal of impulsiveness and naiveté. They rejected the MB's pragmatism, and its "soft" approach to the "atheist" regime and society, and accused it of relinquishing the cause of jihad. According to Abdel-Moneim Abu El-Fotouh, a pioneering founder of al-Jama`a at Cairo University who joined the MB in the late 1970s before al-Jama`a turned to violence:

> Salafist and Jihadist tendencies coloured the way we viewed the Brotherhood. Viewed through our revolutionary lens, the Brotherhood did not seem at the time to be close to our vision.... Perhaps, had we not joined the Brotherhood, my generation would have turned into Ayman El-Zawahris and Bin Ladens. The wing of the Islamic group which took up arms against the state was precisely the group that did not join the ranks of the Brotherhood. (Abdel-Latif 2005)

The new Islamists' antistate (and antisociety) animus was influenced by the writings of the leading Islamic theologian Sayed Qutb (1906–1966), who argued that Muslim society lived in a state of *jahiliya* (pre-Islamic ignorance), and that anything non-Islamic is necessarily evil. The solution, according to Qutb, was to use preaching and jihad in chorus to establish a true Muslim community. Interestingly, the MB, of whom Qutb was a leading member in the 1950s and 1960s, distanced itself from his ideas, adopting a moderate and centrist approach in Islamist thought, whereas the *Salafi-jihadi* creed is still inspired by Qutb's ideas and program of action. As Lynch notes, Qutb "is both the key link and point of divergence between the mainstream MB and its more radical cousins" (Lynch 2010: 469).

DERADICALIZATION AND AFTER

In a surprising move, the incarcerated leadership of al-Jama`a declared in July 1997 a unilateral, unconditional, and immediate cease-fire with the Egyptian state and its institutions. With the exception of the Luxor massacre (which took place a few months later due to the lack of communication between the jailed leadership and fugitive members), the al-Jama`a has not undertaken any violent actions against the state or society since this declaration. The cease-fire was followed with thorough ideological revisions that produced far-reaching consequences; it is estimated that 20,000 to 30,000 jihadi Islamists, most of them belonging to al-Jama`a, have since repented (Tammam 2008).

The deradicalization process of al-Jama`a went, generally speaking, through four consecutive stages. The first stage was marked by deliberations among a number of the jailed leaders of al-Jama`a about the need to change course, as well as the public announcement of renouncing violence and accepting co-existence. The second stage focused on backing up this behavioral transformation with ideological evidence, through the production of new theological literature on the meaning of jihad, its scope, and its limitations. The third stage involved the efforts to convince the middle-ranking leaders and the grassroots of the new policy and its ideological foundations. In the fourth stage, the new changes in ideology and behavior were addressed to the Egyptian public and the Muslim world (Ashour 2007: 612).

Many mediation efforts between Islamic militants and the Egyptian state took place prior to the cease-fire declaration; all failed.[2] They included several attempts made by scholars of Al-Azhar University, the establishment in 1993 of a "mediation committee" (made up of prominent religious scholars) with the backing of Muhammad Abdel-Halim Moussa, Egypt's interior minister, and other attempts sponsored by intellectuals or members of the ruling National Democratic Party (Al-Batran 2011: 162–168; Al-Zayat 2005: 273–274). These mediation attempts came closer to political negotiations than to religious revisions of ideology, and this is precisely why they failed. In these negotiations, the state was not willing to offer concessions to the "terrorists" who had jeopardized its security and legitimacy, and the militants were still oblivious to the implications of the acute divergence in power capabilities between them and the state, and hence were still optimistic of the long-term outcome of the conflict.

The road to deradicalization was long and bumpy. The cease-fire initiative and the ideological transformations that followed it were initially rejected by some of the exiled al-Jama`a leaders (most notably Rifa`i Taha, then leader of the Shura Council abroad) on the grounds that they could not be taken seriously, since they were taken under duress. Long negotiations between the historical leadership and those living abroad followed and an agreement on the renunciation of violence was only reached in 1999. The ideological reversal was also met with distrust and suspicion by Egyptian authorities. It was only when it became clear that the leaders of al-Jama`a were sincere about their interest in revising the theoretical basis of their violent activities that the Egyptian authorities became deeply involved in the deradicalization program. That involvement proved to be crucial. In fact, it could be argued that the success of the program could not have been realized without the state's active cooperation and support. Egyptian authorities provided jailed Islamists with key theological books and religious texts to which they had no previous access. The vast majority of these Islamists had received no formal religious education, their knowledge about doctrinal matters was strikingly limited, and hence the effort was essentially to educate—not just reeducate—these members. In addition, the state facilitated direct communication between the top leaders, who steered the doctrinal revisions, and middle- and low-ranking members, who had to be convinced of the new ideas if the initiative was to succeed. In 2002, the historical leaders of al-Jama`a (e.g., Karam Zuhdi, Nagih Ibrahim, and Osama Hafez) toured more than a few of Egypt's major prisons in Egypt to meet with their followers and sympathizers, and present to them the underpinnings of their new ideology in depth. Long debates and discussions followed, and many questions were asked throughout the process, but the effort eventually succeeded in persuading thousands of the new ideology. In a display of goodwill, thousands of repentant prisoners were released and efforts were made to improve living conditions in prisons after the success of the ideological turnabout.

It could be argued that the ideological revisions constitute the cornerstone in this revolutionary shift in the history of al-Jama`a; without them, the change would have been reduced to a narrow, temporary conversion of tactics, not a profound alteration of key beliefs. The principle ideologues of al-Jama`a produced in 2002 a multivolume work, titled *Tashih al-Mafahim* (Correcting Concepts), which explained the reasons behind the cease-fire initiative and delved into what had gone wrong in the group's jihad against the Egyptian state. The book was soon followed by other studies that dealt with numerous issues, ranging from a theological rebuttal of the ideology of al-Qa'ida and the statements of its leaders, and a critique of the "clash of civilizations" theory, to an apology to the victims of past terrorist attacks.

In the footsteps of al-Jama'a, al-Jihad dejustified the use of violence through the works of its chief ideologue, Dr. Sayed Imam Al-Sherif (alias Dr. Fadl), commander of al-Jihad from 1987 to 1993, who had joined ranks with al-Qa'ida in the 1990s before being extradited to Egypt in 2004. In 2007, Al-Sherif authored a book titled *Rationalizing Jihadi Actions in Egypt and the World*, in which he revised his old ideas and explained the main beliefs of his new manifesto. In the new understanding, he explained that the lives of Muslims and foreign visitors to Muslim countries must be preserved, that jihad is not the duty of individual Muslims, that jihad against the rulers of Muslim countries is both prohibited and counterproductive for the Islamic nation (*ummah*), and that there is a great difference between raising awareness about *sharia'h* and imposing *fatwas* (Islamic decrees).

Many reasons can be cited as possible causes of the ideological transformation. First, the decline of popular support, particularly after the Luxor massacre, may have strengthened the inclination toward the revision of long-held ideologies and practices. Although a large segment of Egypt's society initially sympathized with the cause of Islamic militants either out of affiliation with the Islamic approach to solving the nation's woes or out of contempt for a government they perceived as illegitimate and corrupt, this segment did not sympathize with the violent means employed by Islamists to make change. In the battle for the hearts and minds of Egyptians, the state-sponsored media and the official religious establishment spared no effort to highlight the bloodshed and economic devastation resulting from the terrorist attacks undertaken by al-Jama'a and al-Jihad. The extensive media coverage, for example, of the death of a schoolgirl during the failed attempted murder of former Prime Minister Atef Sedki in 1993 drew wide condemnations and incited anger against the bloody methods of al-Jama'a. As a result, many al-Jama'a leaders felt concerned that their operational tactics had estranged the public and stained the image of Islam in society (Gunaratna and Bin Ali 2009: 288).

Second, the ideological revisions cannot be separated from the milieu from which they first emerged, namely, prisons and detention centers. Prison life in Mubarak's Egypt, where isolation is mixed with maltreatment and harsh living conditions, left a significant impact on prisoners. The solitude away from normal life gave ample time for thinking about what had gone wrong, and how their past strategy should be reformed. Moreover, discussions and debates among inmates exposed them to new ideas and perspectives on the pillars of their ideology. As Montasser Al-Zayat, notable lawyer of Islamic groups, noted:

> In the beginning, they [members of al-Jama'a] had only one opinion and idea and refused to accept other opinions. In prison, they were exposed to other ideas and teachings and began accepting different opinions. It had to do with knowledge and experience. After 20 years, they matured, read, and understood the book properly. (Quoted in Goerzig and Al-Hashimi 2007: 12)

Third, state repression is undoubtedly one of the key reasons behind the ideological revisions of al-Jama'a and al-Jihad. In its bitter fight against militant Islamists during the 1980s and 1990s, the state resorted to various techniques of repression to root out the danger of Islamic militants: mass detentions, extrajudicial arrests (including what many perceived to be a shoot-to-kill policy), torture, military tribunals, and executions. The state's iron-fisted measures may have induced militant Islamists to rethink their strategies and seek reconciliation. Suffice it to say that in 1994 alone, an average of five people were killed and fifty arrested each day,[3] and three insurgents hanged every month (Heikal 1995: 28). Also, prior to the deradicalization phase, the total number of Islamist detainees reached 30,000 (Ashour 2007: 612).

Fourth, after years of violent confrontation came the bitter realization of the failure of the use of force to change the political system, particularly against a forceful, ferocious adversary who had used all measures at its disposal to undermine the radical Islamic movement. A basic cost/benefit approach clearly revealed that the losses incurred in the ongoing battle against the state far outweighed the benefits accomplished. In the words of one of al-Jama`a leaders, Ali Muhammad Al-Sharif:

> Today, many young Muslims have risen up against their Muslim country and institutions, on the pretext that this is jihad. As a result, young Muslims have caused enormous catastrophes, and the nation has been weakened. The young people fought for the sake of da`wa, and da`wa was prevented; they fought for the sake of a minority detained in the prisons, and the number of detainees grew.... They should have realized that as long as the outcome of the fighting was bad, this fighting could not be called religiously correct. It is a kind of fighting that is forbidden by the religion. (Quoted in Gunartna and Bin Ali 2009: 285)

In the new literature, the leaders of al-Jama`a emphasized that the perpetuation of the conflict is not in anyone's interest; it is a zero-sum game for all parties involved, and for the welfare of Egypt and the image of Islam:

> It is obvious that in the fight between Islamic groups and the police, neither one can benefit. The state also cannot benefit from the lasting violence. However, the biggest benefactor in the struggle within Egypt are the enemies of Egypt and Islam. They are the ones who will make political and financial gains at the expense of Egyptian people's blood. (Quoted in Georzig and Al-Hashimi 2007: 13)

The concern over the negative repercussions of the conflict, and the conviction that its perpetuation is in nobody's interest, led many former jihadists to conclude that antagonizing the state became religiously forbidden. For example, senior al-Jama`a leader Safwat Abdel-Ghani explained that:

> The fighting which occurred split of [sic] the umma (the Islamic nation) and harmed the interests of society and did not realize [any] benefit for the people. Consequently, it became an action without meaning and legally forbidden since it lead [sic] to greater detriment. (Quoted in Blaydes and Rubin 2008: 473)

In brief, "change" is the key word to understanding the history of radical Islamists in Egypt. They were initially driven by the need to change reality, but when they realized they were unable to produce that change, they sought to change themselves and their beliefs and actions.

The new arguments articulated by the ideologues of al-Jama`a and al-Jihad departed significantly from their earlier theoretical production. First, according to the new understanding, a ruler can still be tolerated and not judged as an apostate, even if he refrains from applying *sharia`h*. The yardstick used to measure the infidelity of Muslim rulers is no longer their rejection of the unconditional *application* of *sharia`h*, but their *recognition* that manmade laws are superior to the rulings of Allah. As Karam Zuhdi explains, "Even if the ruler does not apply a law or laws from the Islamic *shari'ah*, he is not considered an infidel as long as he does not hold a position that his man-made rulings are better than the rulings of Allah" (Quoted in Gunartna and Bin Ali 2009: 284). In addition, al-Jama'a leaders argued that the true knowledge of Islam lies in the hands of '*ulama*' (religious scholars), and thus the decision over who is, and who is not, an apostate should be left to their discretion. As a result of this ideological revolution, some of the leaders of al-Jama'a went as far as publicly admitting regret for their involvement in the assassination of President Sadat in 1981. Second, in their new understanding of jihad, the use of force is to be used only against external enemies in the case of war. It is not permissible to fight civilians—Muslim or non-Muslim—unless they have initiated violence. The true jihad, al-Jama'a now articulated, is "not only the violence. It is also the time of prayer. It is about making friends, supporting family, and contributing to the welfare of the society" (Goerzig and Al-Hashimi 2007: 14).

The sudden proliferation of new political parties in Egypt following the demise of Mubarak's regime in early 2011 encouraged these former jihadists to take a further step away from their violent past, by forming political parties that will accept the rules of the democratic state, and indulge totally in party politics. Even before the end of Mubarak's era, al-Jama'a had, through its active presence on the internet, paid attention to social issues hitherto unaddressed in its discourse, such as education and unemployment, and engaged in intellectual discussions on timely debates, ranging from the role of the Coptic diaspora in Egyptian politics to secularism and the rising tide of the "new preachers" in the public domain (Tammam 2008). These tendencies have reinforced the integration of al-Jama'a into the fabric of Egyptian politics and its departure from its former pro-violence stances. Nevertheless, integration into society has not, for many members, been fully achieved. Many former jihadists have faced enormous difficulties following their release after many years in jail. Without a decent educational background or work experience, and stigmatized and ostracized by society, many were unable to make ends meet. Overcoming the challenge of reintegration into society is absolutely paramount if the success of the deradicalization scheme is to be maintained. To achieve this, efforts at rehabilitating former jihadists require the complete support of the government as well as civil society organizations.

Conclusion

Since their violent activities are justified by sacred and fixed religious teachings, the views and behavior of violent religious groups are generally assumed to be impervious to change. Empirical evidence from the Egyptian case, however, suggests otherwise. In fact, the experience of modern Islamic movements in Egypt has been characterized by one recurring pattern, where extremism and offense have been followed by moderation and revision of both ideology and tactics. The MB, Egypt's mainstream Islamic movement, used violent acts to achieve political ends in the period from the 1940s to the 1960s but eschewed violence in the 1970s. From the 1980s onward, the MB has opted for active, peaceful participation in the political process, eyeing membership of parliamentary and municipal councils and professional guilds. The same applies to al-Jama'a and al-Jihad, whose deradicalization programs since the late 1990s have produced the same results. Indeed, several former al-Jama'a members, including Tarek al-Zumur and Safwat Abdel-Ghani, established the Al-Binna' wa al-Tanmiya (Building and Development) Party in June 2011. The party participated in the first post-Mubarak parliamentary elections (held from November 2011 to January 2012) as part of the Islamic Alliance, and won thirteen seats, most of them in Upper Egypt governorates. The party supported the moderate Islamist candidate Abdel-Moneim Abu El-Fotouh in the first round of the presidential elections (held in May–June 2012), and Mohamed Morsi, the MB's candidate, in the runoff election that pitted him against General Ahmed Shafik, Mubarak's last prime minister. In the same vein, several political parties (e.g., Al-Salama wa al-Tanmiya [Safety and Development] and the Democratic Jihad) have been established by different factions of al-Jihad, but none of these parties had been legally recognized until the time of writing.

The experience of al-Jama'a and al-Jihad groups proves that counterterrorism strategies must not rely on the sword alone. It is possible through dialogue and communication to encourage terrorists to delegitimize the use of violence and participate, freely and peacefully, in party politics. Our belief in the possibility of this outcome will be consolidated when we remember that change is not only possible, but is in fact inevitable, provided that its prerequisites are met. As the Greek philosopher Heraclitus intelligently phrased it 2,500 years ago, "Nothing endures but change."

Notes

1. The al-Takfir wa al-Hijra group, also known as Jama'at al-Muslimin (Society of Muslims), is a radical Islamic group that emerged in the 1970s under the leadership of Shukri Mustafa. The group was responsible for the kidnap and murder of the Minister of Religious Endowments Muhammad Hussein Al-Dhahabi in 1977.
2. Omar Ashour estimated that at least fourteen attempts had taken place to mediate between the state and al-Jama'a to put an end to violence (Ashour 2007: 614).
3. Other estimates indicate that at the peak of confrontations between the state and Islamic militants, "one Egyptian a day was dying in the war against the Islamists" (The Retreat from Fundamentalism, *The Economist*, April 29, 1999).

References

Abdel-Latif, Omayma. 2005. Abdel-Moneim Abul-Futuh: A Different Kind of Syndicalism. *Al-Ahram Weekly* 743. http://weekly.ahram.org.eg/2005/743/profile.htm (accessed May 9, 2011).

Al-Batran, Hamdy. 2011. *Ta'amulat fi 'unf wa tawbat al-jama'at al-islamiya* [Reflections on the Violence and Repentance of Islamic Groups]. Cairo: Dar al-'Ayn li al-Nashr.

Al-Zayat, Montasser. 2005. *Al-Jama'at al-islamiya: ru'iya min al-dakhil* [Islamic Groups: An Insider View]. Cairo: Dar Misr al-Mahrusa.

Ashour, Omar. 2007. Lions Tamed? An Inquiry into the Causes of De-Radicalization of Armed Islamist Movements: The Case of the Egyptian Islamic Group. *The Middle East Journal* 61: 596–625.

Ayubi, Nazih. 1980. The Political Revival of Islam: The Case of Egypt. *International Journal of Middle Eastern Studies* 12: 481–499.

Blaydes, Lisa, and Lawrence Rubin. 2008. Ideological Reorientation and Counterterrorism: Confronting Militant Islam in Egypt. *Terrorism and Political Violence* 20: 461–479.

Fandy, Mamoun. 1994. Egypt's Islamic Group: Regional Revenge? *The Middle East Journal* 48: 607–625.

Goerzig, Carolin, and Khaled Al-Hashimi. 2007. Change through Debate—Egypt's Counterterrorism Strategy towards the Gamaa Islamia. Paper presented at the sixth Pan-European Conference on International Relations, September 12–15, in Turin, Italy.

Gunaratna, Rohan, and Mohamed Bin Ali. 2009. De-Radicalization Initiatives in Egypt: A Preliminary Insight. *Studies in Conflict and Terrorism* 32: 277–291.

Hafez, M. H. 1997. Explaining the Origins of Islamic Resurgence: Islamic Revivalism in Egypt and Indonesia. *The Journal of Social, Political and Economic Studies* 22: 295–324.

Heikal, Mohamed Hassanein. 1995. *1995: Egypt's Gate to the Twenty First Century*. Cairo: Dar El-Shorouk.

Lynch, Marc. 2010. Islam Divided between Salafi-Jihad and the Ikhwan. *Studies in Conflict & Terrorism* 33: 467–487.

Mustafa, Hala. 1992. *Al-islam al-siyassi fi misr: min harakat al-islah ila gama`at al-`unf* [Political Islam in Egypt: From Reform Movements to Violence Groups]. Cairo: Al-Ahram Center for Political and Strategic Studies.

Peters, Rudolph. 1986. The Political Relevance of the Doctrine of Jihad in Sadat's Egypt. In *National and International Politics in the Middle East: Essays in Honour of Elie Kedourie*, ed. Edward Ingram, 252–271. London: Frank Cass.

Qasim, Tal`at Fu'ad, Hisham Mubarak, Souhail Shadoud, and Steve Tamari. 1996. What Does the Gama`a Islamiyya Want? An Interview with Tal`at Fu'ad Qasim. *Middle East Report* 198: 40–46.

Tammam, Hussam. 2008. Repentant Jihadists and the Changing Face of Islamism. *Arab Reform Bulletin*. http://carnegieendowment.org/arb/?fa=show&article=21945 (accessed May 9, 2011).

Tammam, Hussam. 2010. *Abdel-Moneim Abu El-Fotouh: shahid `ala tarikh al-haraka al-islamiya fi misr, 1970–1984* [Abdel-Moneim Abu El-Fotouh: A Witness on the History of the Islamic Movement in Egypt, 1970–1984]. Cairo: Dar El-Shorouk.

CHAPTER 40

JIHADISTS IN IRAQ

DAVID ROMANO

JIHAD AND JIHADISTS

THE concept of jihad in Islam can refer to an inner struggle to remain true to the faith and lead an exemplary life (*jihad al-akbar*, or "the greater jihad"). The term also refers to the more commonly known undertaking of a specific kind of warfare in Islam. A jihad is a collective duty of Muslims when declared by proper Muslim religious authorities and conducted in the interests (generally interpreted as defensive) of the Muslim community, and can only be waged against non-Muslims. In practice, of course, many Muslim political leaders and movements over the years have tried to invoke a jihad by means and in circumstances that deviate significantly from these standards. Iranian and Iraqi leaders often referred to their 1980–1988 war against each other as a jihad, for instance, and even occasionally used the term in their respective counterinsurgency campaigns against Kurdish rebels.

For the purposes of the discussion here, however, a jihadist is an individual or political movement that primarily focuses its attention, discourse, and activities on the conduct of a violent, uncompromising campaign that they term a "jihad" (whether or not most other members of the Muslim community, including the community's preeminent religious authorities, would agree with the jihad appellation). Individuals or movements that occasionally brandish the term in a limited context, but do not seem to center both their identity and political discourse on a jihad, are thus not viewed as jihadists. Violent Sunni groups espousing an intolerant, militant interpretation of Islam, such as al-Qaʿida, its affiliates, and various national branches of the Islamic Jihad organization, represent the most well-known jihadists. A Shiite movement such as Hizbullah in Lebanon, which especially in its early days did define itself and focus its activities almost solely around a jihad of pushing Israeli forces out of Lebanon, appears qualitatively different than the jihadi groups discussed here, however. Daniel Kimmage discusses the difference in a commentary titled "Al-Qaeda Addresses the Jihad-Versus-Resistance Conflict" (2006). Comparing the discourse of al-Qaʿida and Hizbullah leaders, Kimmage states:

The statements by al-Zawahiri and Nasrallah highlight rival discourses—that of jihad, a global project to remake the world; and that of resistance, a regional project against a specific enemy. Jihad attracts adherents through the sweep and ambition of its aims, yet remains beholden to its violent means and narrow, exclusionary vision, as demonstrated by the sectarian carnage in Iraq. Resistance offers greater inclusion and flexibility, yet seems capable of displaying those qualities only during the conflict with an external enemy, as demonstrated by the contentious domestic political experiences of both Hizbullah and various Palestinian factions.

In Iraq, the major Shiite armed groups—the Badr Brigades and Moqtada al-Sadr's Mahdi Army—appear solely concerned with their local Iraqi context, amenable to political compromises with other groups, active in other realms besides armed struggle, and not prone to a discourse overflowing with jihadist language. Like Hizbullah of Lebanon, most observers would not refer to them as "jihadist."

Unambiguous criteria for labeling a group jihadi remain elusive, however, particularly because Islamist groups are not monolithic entities. Their ideologies, strategies, and identities frequently evolve and change as well. Hence, limiting the jihadi appellation to armed Islamist groups advocating a global jihad, rather than a struggle limited to the confines of their own state boundaries ("the near enemy"), seems unsatisfactory. Many of the Islamist insurgent groups in Iraq who reject al-Qaʿida's global agenda nevertheless refer to themselves as "jihadi."[1] Additionally, just as al-Qaʿida became adept at inserting itself into the local conflicts of various Muslim groups, local jihadists can easily morph into a more global jihadi orientation under the right circumstances. The discussion here therefore applies the somewhat vague, imperfect definition of jihadist mentioned above: an individual or political movement that primarily focuses its attention, discourse, and activities on the conduct of a violent, uncompromising campaign that they term a jihad.

Pre-2003 Iraq—Authoritarian Controls

In the Iraqi context, a limited number of jihadi groups existed before 2003. Saddam Hussein's government maintained strong authoritarian rule over the country (with the exception of the Kurdish Autonomous Region, to be examined shortly), and worked assiduously to suppress both Islamist and non-Islamist dissent to the regime. Although Shiite Iraqi opposition movements such as *al-Daʿwa* (founded in 1957) and SCIRI (the Supreme Council for the Islamic Revolution in Iraq, founded in 1982) occasionally referred to their struggle against Saddam's regime as a jihad, they did not call themselves jihadists and only targeted high Iraqi regime officials, rather than Sunnis in general. The discourse of jihad thus seemed to play a much less important role for these Shiite movements than a more commonplace rhetoric of opposing an authoritarian, iniquitous ruler.

Among the Sunni Arab population of Iraq, no noteworthy jihadi groups existed before the 2003 invasion. The Iraqi Muslim Brotherhood, which alternated between periods of nonviolent strategies and occasional coup plots,[2] was effectively suppressed after 1971—including possible extremist jihadi splinter movements that emerged from other national branches of the Brotherhood in places like Egypt and Jordan. Pre-2003 Iraqi governments always came from the Sunni Arab minority in any case, offering this group a greater and disproportionate allotment of resources and hence a reduced incentive to revolt.

While Iraqi Kurdish opposition groups mounted a steady series of revolts since the British creation of Iraq in the 1920s, their opposition took an overwhelmingly secular, Kurdish nationalist tone rather than an Islamist one. Successive regimes in Baghdad actually tended to brandish more Islamist rhetoric countering Kurdish revolts than the Kurds employed in their opposition—naming government military campaigns after *suras* in the Qur'an (the *Anfal* campaigns of 1987–1988), or forming special units tasked with the pacification of Kurdistan with names such as *Fursan Salah al-Dīn* (the "Knights of Salladin," the Muslim general famous for his campaigns against the non-Muslim crusaders—implying that Kurdish rebels were also enemies of Islam).[3] Additionally, the religious pluralism of Iraqi Kurdistan, with its population of Christians, Jews (until the 1950s), Sunnis, Shiites, Yezidis, Ahl-al-Haq, Sarlus, Shakak, and a plethora of Sufi orders, seemed to initially discourage the creation of Islamist groups in the area. Such religious pluralism led many Kurds and scholars to declare Iraqi Kurdistan infertile ground for conservative political Islam (Shourush 2002: 136).

Nonetheless, a number of small Kurdish jihadist groups eventually emerged in Iraqi Kurdistan by the 1990s. Most of the Kurdish jihadist organizations emerged as splinter movements from more moderate Kurdish Islamist groups, which enjoyed increasing popularity in the 1990s. Four different factors may provide some explanation for the heightened popularity of Kurdish Islamism in general, including the jihadi groups: (1) Saddam's attempt to undercut Kurdish nationalists by supporting and using nascent Islamists, including violent jihadists; (2) neighboring Iran's influence in Iraqi Kurdistan, particularly since it became autonomous in 1991; (3) the widespread despair in Kurdistan in the wake of the chemical attacks on Halabja and ethnic cleansing pursued by Baghdad, both of which Kurdish nationalist and leftist parties proved powerless to stop; and (4) links with a generalized, global Islamist movement, particularly after the retreat of the Soviet Union from Afghanistan.

The Islamic Movement of Kurdistan (IMK) was founded sometime around 1986–1988, toward the end of the Iran-Iraq war. The Iranian government played an important role in the organization's creation, financing, and protection, seeking to create an Islamist force in Iraq and an ally against the Ba`athists in Baghdad.

Although the IMK generally claimed to uphold a moderate Islamist agenda and a willingness to participate in the institutionalized political process of Iraqi Kurdistan, it also displayed jihadi tendencies at times. Some sources state that the IMK had Egyptian members from the Egyptian Islamic jihad organization.[4] Additionally, Egyptian Islamist Sayid Qutb's books were translated into Kurdish and influenced the IMK into adopting a somewhat jihadist outlook.[5] Many of the IMK's most important members consisted of Islamist Kurds returning from the war against the Soviets in Afghanistan, which increased pressure within the organization to adopt jihadist tactics. Many of these returning Afghan veterans later broke off from the IMK to found more violent Islamist groups (discussed below).

The IMK first established itself in the forbidding eastern corner of the Kurdish Autonomous Zone:

> The Howraman area that for centuries has been a centre of religious activity and home to both Sunni Islam and various Sufi sects was especially hospitable. The Howraman region hugs the border with Iran south of Suleimaniyeh; its district centre is the sizeable town of Halabja. The

region is largely self-contained, separated from the rest of Kurdistan by towering mountains to the south and east, and the large Sirwan reservoir, also known as Darbandikhan Lake, to the north and west. Only one paved road connects Halabja with Suleimaniyeh. (ICG 2003: 2)

Following the withdrawal of Saddam's forces from the region in late 1991, the IMK acted as part of the Kurdistan Front amalgamation of various secular, communist, nationalist, and Islamist Kurdish organizations, and ran in the 1992 Kurdish elections. It only garnered around 5 percent of the popular vote, however, after which the group focused on consolidating its power in the mountainous Halabja region where it enjoyed the most popularity (Ibid.). It fielded around 500 armed fighters.

In the summer of 1994, fighting broke out between the two main parties of the Kurdistan Regional Government (KRG), the Kurdistan Democratic Party (KDP), and Patriotic Union of Kurdistan (PUK). During the next four years of armed civil conflict, the KDP and PUK tried to use the IMK and other newer Kurdish Islamist groups (discussed below) against each other. The increasing power vacuum as the KDP and PUK fought each other to a standstill, along with continuing Iranian support, allowed the IMK to thrive. Under strong Iranian pressure, the PUK in 1996 withdrew from the Halabja-Howraman area (including villages along the Iranian border such as Biyara, Tawala, Khormal, Gool, Panjwin, Sargat, and Said Sadiq) and effectively ceded it to the IMK. Although the IMK intermittently participated in the PUK-administered part of the KRG, the two groups also frequently clashed with each other. Each time the PUK appeared ready and able to destroy the IMK, Iran intervened and brokered an agreement.[6] The IMK alternated between bellicose jihadist rhetoric and conciliatory statements about the organization's peaceful approach and willingness to function within the political system—either a reflection of divisions and tensions within the IMK or simple opportunism. At times when the IMK decided to pursue a more moderate nonjihadi line (mainly 1997–1998 and after 2001), several splinter groups broke off from it to found more radical jihadi movements.

These primarily Kurdish jihadi splinter groups, led by both Kurdish and non-Iraqi Arab veterans of the Afghan war against the Soviets, included Kurdish Hamas, the Second Soran Force, Mullah Krekar's Reformist Group, and Ali Bapir's Islamic Group.[7] Together with another small jihadi organization that emerged in the Erbil region of Iraqi Kurdistan in 2000, Tawhid, these groups promoted a militant Salafi interpretation of Islam and advocated a violent jihad locally as well as in support of fellow jihadists in Afghanistan, Chechnya, Bosnia, and other possible fronts. In Kurdistan, Hamas and Tawhid militants in particular staged attacks on bookstores, clubs, beauty salons, and tourist areas. They threw acid at women who did not dress "modestly" and assassinated or attempted to assassinate prominent Kurdish officials of the KDP and PUK (ICG 2003: 4). In September of 2001, Tawheed, Hamas, and the Second Soran Force united to become Jund al-Islam, which went on to incorporate Mullah Krekar's "Reformist Group" in December 2001 and change its name to Ansar al-Islam. At the September 2001 meeting to unify these jihadi groups,

> ...three Afghan-trained Arabs witnessed the agreement: Abu Abdul Rahman, who serves as bin Ladin's representative for the supervision of unity and media in Kurdistan; Abu Wa'il, an expert and instructor in sabotage; and Abu Dardaa', an instructor in terrorism and assassination.... Upon the signing, the three transferred to Jund al-Islam a $300 000 grant supplied by bin Laden. In total, the report claimed that 60 of the approximately 400 fighters in Jund al-Islam received training in Afghanistan.[8]

The coming together of these Islamist groups purportedly occurred at least in part with the urging of Osama Bin Laden, who wanted a stronger, unified jihad in northern Iraq. Mullah Krekar, one of Ansar al-Islam's leaders, lived in Pakistan in the 1980s and studied Islamic jurisprudence under the Abdullah Azzam, Osama Bin Laden's mentor (Rangwala 2002). Ansar al-Islam's roughly 800 fighters included Palestinians, Iranians, Jordanians, Afghans, and Arabs from various countries, according to a PUK agent who lived in the area they controlled.[9] Both foreign fighters joining the group and supplies arrived via Iran (the territory controlled by Ansar al-Islam and Ali Bapir's Islamic Group straddle the border of Iran and Iraqi Kurdistan), indicating that Iranian authorities either supported these Sunni jihadist groups before 2003 or at least turned a blind eye toward their activities. Colin Powell referred to the group in his February 2003 speech at the United Nations as part of American efforts to make the case for an invasion of Iraq.

Whatever the other merits or problems of Operation Iraqi Freedom, in March of 2003 a joint U.S. Special Forces and PUK series of operations dislodged Ansar al-Islam from its territory along the Iranian border, killing and capturing many of the militants. Although a large number of Ansar militants fled into Iran just before and during the U.S.-PUK attack on their territory, the attack crippled the group.[10] Simultaneously, KRG and American forces disarmed the IMK's militia and that of Ali Bapir's Islamic Group (Ali Bapir was himself arrested and incarcerated for a time). Critically for the KRG, direct U.S. support in 2003 forestalled the kind of Iranian intervention that used to prevent the elimination of militant Kurdish Islamist movements. This allowed KRG security forces to eject jihadist groups from Iraqi Kurdistan in 2003. In late 2003 and 2004, steady arrests of remaining jihadists in the Kurdish region of Iraq occurred, while some remnants of Ansar al-Islam migrated southward and found common cause with emerging jihadist networks in the Arab parts of Iraq. Between March 2003 and 2010, jihadists were only able to conduct around a dozen terrorist bombings and attacks in the Kurdish region. The worst of these were simultaneous bombings of KDP and PUK offices in February 2004, which killed over 100 people, including several leaders of both parties. Responsibility for these bombings was claimed by Ansar al-Sunna, however, a new non-Kurdish jihadist group that probably incorporated some ex-Ansar al-Islam militants and emerged in September 2003 in the Sunni Triangle of Iraq.

Post-2003 Iraq—A New Cause Célèbre for Sunni Jihadists

Given the widespread and growing phenomena of Islamist opposition in the Arab world after the 1970s, there was a high likelihood of such movements emerging in Iraq as soon as Ba'athist authoritarian controls relaxed (as the discussion above showed, Islamist movements sprang up in Iraqi Kurdistan precisely when the region became autonomous and suffered from a vacuum in political authority). If some elements of such an Islamist political awakening took on a jihadist coloring, this too would parallel developments in neighboring states. Further preparing the ground for such a development, Saddam Hussein after the 1980–1988 Iran-Iraq war increasingly moved to Islamicize his regime's image—adding the phrase "God is great" to the Iraqi flag (1991), referring to Islam more frequently in public, and pushing back some of the gains toward equality that Iraqi women achieved under

Ba'athism (Brown 2006, 51–70). By 2003 religion thus already occupied a more prominent place for a new generation of Iraqis that grew up under Western imposed sanctions, isolated from much of the world.

The 2003 U.S. invasion of Iraq removed Ba'athist authoritarian controls over the country and failed to replace Saddam's regime with timely or effective alternate political and security authorities. The situation in Iraq immediately preceding the invasion and the political vacuum created by the 2003 occupation thus combined with widespread Muslim perceptions of a Western imperialist venture targeting Islam to create a kind of "perfect storm" for jihadist agitators. Although a significant proportion of the Muslim world could view the North Atlantic Treaty Organization (NATO) invasion of Afghanistan as a somewhat more justifiable response to the 9/11 attacks, the subsequent addition of Iraq to the U.S. roster of targets elicited widespread Muslim anger. Al-Qa'ida, the preeminent global jihadist network, found itself seriously weakened due to the Afghanistan campaign. With the invasion of Iraq, however, new vigor was added to the movement as more volunteers and donors became willing to support a defensive jihad there. The new front in Iraq attracted Sunni Muslims from neighboring countries and as far off as north Africa and Europe. While most Iraqis, particularly Shiites and Kurds, welcomed the removal of Saddam, the subsequent problem-ridden occupation of Paul Bremmer's Coalition Provisional Authority (CPA) stoked increasing resentment.[11] As the occupation of Iraq appeared to set itself up for a long tenure and Paul Bremmer's autocratic style of governing rankled more and more Iraqis, insurgent groups began to appear. Iraqis reacted most negatively toward what they perceived as the humiliations of an open-ended occupation that failed to deliver speedy reconstruction and services. Arab Sunnis, the group least supportive of Saddam's removal to begin with, formed by far the most important part of the insurgency.

Two central policies of the CPA contributed significantly to the vigor of the jihadist movement in Iraq between 2003 and 2007: de-Ba'athification (Paul Bremer's "Executive Order Number One") and the disbanding of the Iraqi Army ("Executive Order Number Two"). De-Ba'athification was pursued too broadly, pushing some 85,000 Iraqi civil servants (including teachers, engineers, and doctors) into unemployment and compromising the new government's ability to run Iraq (Art and Waltz 2009: 297; Usher 2008). Many of these Iraqis had joined the Ba'ath party as a simple prerequisite to career advancement under Saddam, rather than out of political conviction. In the 1950s, 1960s and 1970s, Iraqi civil servants had also become accustomed to coups that changed their government but still expected them to come to work and run the day-to-day affairs of the country. With Executive Order Number One, they suddenly and for the first time found themselves with no future, while Iraqis in general witnessed education services, garbage collection, electricity, and other services grind to a halt. The jihadi message under such circumstances claimed that the United States simply did not want Iraq to function normally; if the Americans were not intent on destroying Iraq, surely the most powerful country in the world could provide Iraqis with garbage collection and electricity? The CPA's proclivity for awarding rebuilding contracts to well-placed American firms rather than Iraqi companies only added to the unemployment and perception of exploitation.[12]

The disbanding of the Iraqi Army likewise pushed some 400,000 trained fighters into pensionless unemployment overnight, with no provisions made for their demobilization and reintegration into society.[13] Although some officials claimed the Iraqi Army had already disintegrated during the invasion of Iraq, the large majority of Iraqi soldiers could have been reorganized and put to use in short order (Ferguson 2007). These army units could have been decisive in preventing the lawlessness and looting that occurred in the first few weeks after the fall of Saddam's government. They could have been used to maintain and guard weapon depots, government facilities, and border crossings or just paid their regular salary in return for good behavior and staying in their barracks. Instead, many of these unemployed army veterans became insurgents, whether of the jihadi, nationalist, or opportunist variety. According to Toby Dodge,

> The security vacuum that came to dominate Iraq did a great deal to undermine the initial impression of US omnipotence and helped turn criminal violence and looting into an organized and politically motivated insurgency. The initial goodwill that greeted the liberation of Baghdad quickly turned into popular disenchantment with the occupation's failure to establish order, and into increased nationalist resentment of it. To this extent the insurgency has fed off the mistakes of the occupation, utilizing the anger and alienation felt among sections of society. (2006: 214–215)

In this way, ex-Ba'athists, former soldiers, common criminals, and many average nationalist Iraqis (mostly Sunni Arabs) came to form a multifaceted coalition intent on fighting foreign occupiers, their local allies, and the new Shiite and Kurdish authorities in the country. Foreign jihadists entering Iraq were able to insert themselves into this mixed Iraqi nationalist insurgency, recruit adherents, solicit funds (including from some neighboring states),[14] mount brazen attacks, sabotage reconstruction projects, and destabilize the new Iraqi government in general.

The Jihadists

The plethora of jihadist groups that emerged in Iraq after the toppling of Saddam's government had mostly Iraqi members. Extremely secretive, these groups were often quite small, they sometimes had overlapping memberships and frequently changed names or announced the formation of a new organization. The occupation of Iraq had the early effect of serving as a ready recruiting tool for radical Islamists, creating many more jihadi movements than one would expect after the dismantling of the Ba'athist government. Many criminal groups also posed as nationalist or religious insurgents, taking advantage of the security vacuum to kidnap foreigners or wealthy Iraqis and demand high ransoms for their release. Foreign jihadists only accounted for a small minority of insurgents in Iraq—no more than two thousand at any one time, or about one in ten Iraqi insurgents (Grier 2006). The U.S. Pentagon estimated in 2007 that "approximately 90 percent of suicide bombers in Iraq are foreign fighters," however, coming mainly through Syria at a rate of fifty to eighty suicide bombers per month (U.S. Department of Defense, "Measuring Stability and Security in Iraq," September 2007: 7). As with the Kurdish jihadist groups discussed earlier, several of the Sunnī Arab jihadist leaders were veterans of Afghanistan and/or other jihadi fronts such as Bosnia and Chechnya.

The Memorial Institute for the Prevention of Terrorism (MIPT) listed in 2008 (the last year data was collected by them) a dizzying number of Sunnī and suspected Sunnī armed

Islamist groups in Iraq. Combined with a profile of jihadi groups from the al-Haq Islamic news website and interpreted by Jamestown Foundation analyst Abdul Hameed Bakier (2008), the following list emerges:

- Within the umbrella of the Mujahideen Shura Council, six groups: the al-Ahwal Brigades, AQI (formerly Tawhid and *Jihad*), the Islamic Jihad Brigades, Jaish al-Taifa al-Mansoura, the Ansar al-Tawhid Brigades, and the al-Ghuraba Brigades.
- Groups allied with the Mujahideen Shura Council in a larger front called the "Islamic State of Iraq" (Bakier 2008) included Jama'at Jund al-Sahaba, Saraya Fursan al-Tawhid, Saraya Milat Ibrahim, the Kurdistan Brigades (referred to as "Jihad Pegah" in the MIPT data set), and Ansar al-Tawhid wa al-Sunna Brigades.
- An additional three organizations that the MIPT classified as tied to AQI included the Brigades of Imam al-Hassan al-Basri, Saraya al-Ghadhab al-Islami (Brigades of Islamic Rage), and the Saad bin Abi Waqas Brigades.
- Within the Political Council for Iraqi Resistance front, the Islamic Army in Iraq, the Mujahideen Army, Ansar al-Sunna, Jaysh al-Fatiheen, Iraqi Hamas, and the Islamic Front for Iraqi Resistance.
- Within the "Jihad and Change Front": the 1920 Revolutionary Brigades, the al-Rashidin Army, the Army of Muslims in Iraq (listed by Bakier as "Jaysh al-Muslimin fi'l 'Iraq"), the Islamic Movement of Iraqi Mujahideen, Saraya Jund al-Rahman, Saraya al-Da'wa wa'l-Ribat, the al-Tamkeen Brigades, and the Muhammad al-Fatah Brigades.
- Within a somewhat residual front of many of the smallest groups: Jaysh al-Naqshabandi, Jaysh al-Sahaba, Jaysh al-Morabitin, Jaysh Hamza, Jaysh al-Risala, Jaysh Ibn al-Waleed, the United Mujahideen Leadership, the al-Tahrir Brigades, Jaysh Tahrir al-Iraq, Saraya al-Shohada, Jaysh al-Sabirin, the Jihad ala Ard al-Rafidayn Brigades, Jaysh al-Faris, Saraya al-Jihad fi'l Basra, Saraya al-Fallujah, the Popular National Front for the Liberation of Iraq, Saraya altaf al-Husseinia Revolution, Saraya Tahrir al-Janub, Jaysh Hanein, Saraya Diyala for Jihad and Tahrir, and Saraya al-Majd for Liberation of Iraq.
- Bakier (2008) states, "There are over twenty-five more small and mostly unknown groups mentioned in al-Haq's study that have not been mentioned in the media, nor have they been known to perpetrate significant attacks on U.S. or Iraqi forces." Many of these groups, such as the "Holders of the Black Banners" and "Usd Allah" (Lions of God) appear in the MPIT list of armed groups in Iraq, but with only a single known attack and little additional information.

It bears repeating that (1) the large majority of these Sunnī jihadist groups appear to have been small operations, sometimes no more than a dozen people; (2) jihadists frequently announced a "new" group's existence in order to appear more numerous; (3) criminal groups in the kidnap and extortion market often attempted to appear more formidable (or legitimate) by posing as insurgent groups with a political agenda; and (4) many of these groups appear to have had a short lifespan, mounting a single or a handful of attacks and then falling off the radar.

From the list above, the most significant jihadi groups that emerged after 2003 were al-Qa'ida in Iraq ([AQI], which in turn directed the front known as the Islamic State of

Iraq), Ansar al-Sunna, the Islamic Army in Iraq, the 1920 Revolutionary Brigades, and the Islamic Front for Iraqi Resistance (JAAMI). AQI, Ansar al-Sunna, and smaller groups allied with them accounted for most of the foreign jihadists who went to Iraq, and were mostly responsible for the devastating campaign of suicide bombings across the country. AQI's founder, Abu Musab Zarqawi, was a Jordanian Sunni Arab veteran of the Afghan war against the Soviets and ran a jihadist training camp in Afghanistan before the 2001 9/11 attacks. He fled Afghanistan when NATO forces invaded, relocating to Iraq while Saddam Hussein's regime still ruled the country. When Coalition Forces led by the United States invaded Iraq, he founded a jihadist group called "Monotheism and Jihad" (Tawhid and Jihad). Zarqawi quickly became known for his brutal tactics, including beheading hostages and mass casualty bombings of Iraqi Shiite civilians. His group's most famous attacks included:

> ...the bombing of the Jordanian Embassy in Baghdad in August 2003; the bombing of UN headquarters in Baghdad on August 19, 2003; the Najaf bombings on August 29, 2003, that killed Shiite leader Muhammad Baqir al-Hakim; the bombing of the Italian military headquarters in al-Nasiria on October 12, 2003; the Amman hotel bombing of November 9, 2005; and the September, 2007 assassination of the head of al-Anbar's Awakening council, Shaykh Abdul Sattar Abu Risha. AQM also kidnapped and killed American Nicholas Berg, four Egyptian diplomats, one Algerian diplomat and two local staff from the Moroccan Embassy in Baghdad. (Bakier 2008)

Added to this list should be numerous bombings over the years that targeted and killed thousands of especially Shiite civilians on pilgrimages, in pet markets in Baghdad, at religious festivals, and other venues. In October 2004 Zarqawi turned his long-time association with al-Qa`ida into a formal relationship, renaming his organization "the al-Qaeda Organization in the Land of the Two Rivers" (commonly known as al-Qa`ida in Iraq). AQI's goal was to establish an Islamic caliphate in Iraq, after which the caliphate would be expanded to encompass other states in the region. Its strategy involved (1) targeting Coalition Forces and anyone involved in the occupation of Iraq so as to eventually force them out; (2) destabilizing the nascent Iraqi government, which was dominated by Shiites and Kurds, so as to prevent the new Iraqi state from functioning; (3) cajoling or more often coercing other Sunni groups, including jihadis, into submitting to AQI's leadership; and (4) targeting Shiites so as to foment a civil war in Iraq, which would push the fearful Sunni Arabs (only some 20 percent of Iraq's population compared to roughly 60 percent Shiite Arabs and 20 percent Kurds) into AQI's orbit and leave occupying forces caught in the middle and anxious to leave Iraq.[15] AQI's indiscriminate targeting of Muslim civilians (even Shiites) attracted criticism from al-Qa`ida leaders in Afghanistan and even from Zarqawi's mentor, Sheikh Abu Muhammad al-Maqdisi, but Zarqawi continued the disgusting tactics (Byman and Pollack 2008: 61). Zarqawi was finally killed by Coalition Forces in June 2006. Those who took over the leadership of AQI continued his basic strategy, although they seemed to avoid the grisly videotaped beheading of hostages favored in 2004 and 2005.

Ansar al-Sunna cooperated with AQI for a time and pursued many of the same tactics, specializing in suicide bombings at large gatherings (they did not share AQI's affinity for Shiite civilian targets, however). Ansar al-Sunna jihadists, a great many of them non-Iraqi and some of them likely Kurdish veterans of Ansar al-Islam, made Palestinian Hamas style videos before their missions, explaining the reasons for their sacrifice and the demands of the jihad. The organization took responsibility for hundreds of attacks between 2003 and

2010, the most famous of which was the above mentioned February 2004 attack on offices of the KDP and PUK, which killed 109 people, including several top KDP leaders.

The Islamic Army in Iraq, the 1920 Revolutionary Brigades, and the Islamic Front for Iraqi Resistance (JAAMI) between them accounted for many more insurgents and many more attacks in Iraq, but these incidents tended to be the "less newsworthy" small arms fire and improvised explosive devices that targeted Coalition Forces. They also occasionally took foreign hostages and deployed suicide bombers against military targets, something that did make headlines. All three groups lacked the sizeable number of foreign jihadis of AQI and Ansar al-Sunna, being made up mostly of Iraqi Arab Sunni tribesmen, townspeople, resurfacing Muslim Brothers, peasants, and former Iraqi soldiers. The Iraqi nationalist component of these groups' ideology (Iraqi nationalism seen through a Sunni Arab lens, that is) appeared at least as strong as their Islamism.

The MIPT listed only a few Iraqi Shiite (or probably Shiite, based on limited information) armed groups in Iraq in its 2008 Terrorism Knowledge Base (TKB) data set: Moqtada al-Sadr's Mahdi Army, the Karbala Brigades, and Abu al-Abbas, the Imam Hussein Brigades, the Divine Wrath Brigades, the Movement of Islamic Action of Iraq, and the Jihadist Martyrs Brigades in Iraq.[16] It is not clear why the Badr Brigade militia of the Islamic Supreme Council of Iraq (ISCI) does not appear in the list, as it was the largest Shiite armed group in Iraq, followed by the Mahdi Army. Neither the Badr Brigades nor the Mahdi Army are considered jihadist by the criteria discussed above, however. Of the other six groups, four of them (the Karbala Brigades, Abu al-Abbas, the Movement of Islamic Action of Iraq, and the Jihadist Martyrs Brigades in Iraq) appear to have conducted only a single operation in their entire history (a rocket attack, a kidnaping, a bombing, and a kidnaping, respectively). Of the other two, the Divine Wrath Brigades conducted a few explosives attacks and kidnaped a high-ranking Iraqi government official (Ibid.). The Imam Hussein Brigades mounted more serious and deadly attacks against the Iraqi government and American, British, Indian, Italian, and Romanian targets in Iraq, but little is known of the group apart from its name (which refers to one of the most revered figures of Shiite Muslims). The fact that the group released its claims of responsibility via the same website used by Sunni Islamist insurgents in Iraq, including AQI, confuses the issue somewhat, however. In any case, the two significant armed Shiite groups in post-2003 Iraq, the Badr Brigades and the Mahdi Army, did not merit the moniker of "jihadist," although the Mahdi Army in particular often proved quite ready and willing to engage with Sunni rivals or attack Coalition Forces.

In Search of Iraqi Stability

By 2005–2006, the jihadist-led insurgency and violence between Sunni Arabs and Shiites (particularly those of the Mahdi Army), threatened to overwhelm Iraq. Stabilizing the country began to look like an impossible task for the U.S.-led occupation and nascent Iraqi government. Three principal factors brought Iraq back from the brink, at least for a time: (1) the drawing down of Moqtada al-Sadr's Mahdi Army through a combination political incorporation and United States-government of Iraq coercive force; (2) a temporary surge in American troops that helped bring Baghdad, Anbar Province, and other areas under control; and most importantly (3) AQI's heavy handedness and brutality, which alienated even

Iraqi Sunnis, including the tribes of Anbar province and jihadist groups such as the 1920 Revolutionary Brigades, the Islamic Army in Iraq, the JAAMI, and Ansar al-Sunna.

AQI's habit of attacking anyone who refused to follow its lead, including fellow Sunni jihadis and Sunni Arab tribesmen, alienated many. The presence of many foreign jihadis in AQI ranks rankled many Iraqis' nationalist sentiments, especially as AQI killed huge numbers of Iraqi civilians in an endless parade of grisly bombings or imposed a harsh, totalitarian, and puritanical brand of Islamic law in towns and villages it came to control for a time. At the same time that these AQI mistakes coalesced into increasing Iraqi enmity for the group, a revised counterinsurgency strategy under U.S. General David Petraeus reached out to Sunni Arabs in 2006. Offering local security autonomy and generous financial and military assistance to Arab Sunni tribes willing to change sides and assist in the campaign against AQI, American commanders began organizing tribes (including many that once sided with the jihadists) into "Awakening Councils," also known as "Concerned Local Citizens," "Sons of Iraq" and "the Anbar Awakening" (McGary 2009, 43–59). These groups increasingly cooperated with Coalition Forces, providing essential intelligence and fighting alongside their former American enemies against AQI jihadists. As the Sunni Arab tribes began to turn the tide against AQI, increasing numbers of Iraqi nationalist jihadists—those from the Islamic Army in Iraq, the 1920 Revolutionary Brigades (whose leader was killed by AQI), and the Islamic Front for Iraqi Resistance (JAAMI) effectively ceased being jihadists and joined the Awakening movements and Coalition Forces to fight AQI. Although disagreements within these groups led to some splinter movements breaking off and siding with AQI, the overall dynamic led to a pacification of Anbar province and a severe weakening of AQI and the jihadist cause in Iraq. Simultaneously, Sunni Arab political groups such as the Iraqi Islamic Party (a descendant of the Iraqi Muslim Brotherhood) increasingly demonstrated that engagement with the Iraqi political system, especially via participation in elections, offered a viable strategy to have Sunni Arab voices heard.[17]

By 2010 levels of violence in Iraq had declined considerably, although it was still too early to write the epitaph for the jihadist campaign or the post-2003 instability in the country.[18]

For long-term stability in Iraq, much will depend on a complex array of factors, including the Shiite-led government in Baghdad's willingness to share power with Arab Sunnis and Kurds. If the Iraqi experience leaves an association in much of the public's minds equating jihadis with the most grisly of AQI's campaign of terror, not to mention an unsuccessful insurgency, al-Qa`ida, and its allies will have suffered a serious blow.

Notes

1. The 1920 Revolutionary Brigades/Islamic Resistance Movement in Iraq, for instance, seeks to establish an Islamic caliphate in Iraq and claims to reject the targeting of civilians. On one of the jihadi websites, however, the group writes, "We don't claim to be the only jihadi group, but ask all our members to obey the leadership" (cited in Bakier 2008). The 1920 Revolutionary Brigades, along with the Islamic Army in Iraq, are considered relatively moderate Islamist insurgents focused only on Iraq (at least for the moment). They have fought al-Qa`ida in Iraq on several occasions. Nonetheless, Abdul Hameed Bakier writes, "Regardless of discord with some jihadi groups and internal fighting with al-Qa`ida, al-Jaysh al-Islami [the Islamic Army] declares it has

no animosity with any jihadi group, but rather endeavors to unite with them under a single leadership" (Ibid.).
2. Muslim Brotherhood military coup and violent takeover attempts were discovered and thwarted in 1954 (the "Islamic Liberation Army" movement), 1961 (the "Islamic Military Organization within Iraq"), and 1971 (the "Muslim Brotherhood Secret Group")—Author's interview with Niazi Said Ali, director of the Institute for Training Specialists and PUK intelligence official in charge of monitoring Islamist groups, March 11, 2004, Qalachwalan, Iraq.
3. Portions of the following discussion on pre-2003 Kurdish jihadi groups are adapted from Romano, 2007.
4. Author's interview with Jamal Hussein, Omeid Qaradaghi, Bahman Tahir, Ali Mustafa, and Kara Fathi, former Islamists now working at the Bureau of Democratic Organizations (Suleimaniya), February 1, 2004.
5. Author's interview with Jamal Hussein, Omeid Qaradaghi, Bahman Tahir, Ali Mustafa, and Kara Fathi, former Islamists now working at the Bureau of Democratic Organizations (Suleimaniya), February 1, 2004.
6. Author's interview with Fareid Assasad, president of the Institute for Strategic Studies (Suleimaniya), February 22, 2004.
7. Iraqi Kurdish opinions on Ali Bapir's Islamic Group remain divided, with some seeing the movement as jihadist but more strategic about hiding its nature until it grows stronger, and others viewing the group as more moderate. Also, this discussion omits some of the smallest groups and temporary names of other groups (such as Jund al-Islam, which became Ansar al-Islam when Mullah Krekar's "Reformist Group" joined it). For more on this, see Romano 2007.
8. For more on the purported al-Qa'ida link, see Jonathan Schanzer, *Al-Qaeda's Armies* (New York: Specialist Press International, 2004), Chapter Six ("Northern Iraq").
9. Author's interview with Shaho Ali Aziz, chief of PUK in Biyara and former PUK spy against Ansar, December 19, 2003.
10. Author's interview with Taleb Kader Rahman and three other Biyara villagers, December 19, 2003, Biyara.
11. A CNN/USA Today Gallup Nationwide Poll of Iraq taken in 2004 asked Iraqis, "Thinking about any hardships you might have suffered since the US, Britain invasion, do you personally think that ousting Saddam Hussein was worth it or not?" Sixty-one percent replied, "Yes, it was worth it." The same poll, however, as well as an Oxford Research International Ltd. "National Survey of Iraq" (February 2004), show less favorable Iraqi views of the Coalition Provisional Authority and the occupation of the country.
12. In November of 2003, the author saw Iraqi engineers (among others) protesting by the Green Zone in Baghdad. They held signs that read, "We built this country—we can rebuild it! Award us contracts."
13. For an overview of this policy and its impact, including interviews with many top ORHA and CPA officials who were stunned by the decision to completely disband the Iraqi Army without provisions for demobilization, see Charles Ferguson's documentary, *No End in Sight* (2007).
14. According to both U.S. Army and Kurdish intelligence sources interviewed by the author in 2003 and 2004, Syrian agents paid individual Iraqis anywhere between $50 and $250 per attack on coalition troops (interviews conducted in Suleimaniya, Kirkuk, and Erbil). For an overview of the issue, see Tanter 2009.

15. A letter from Zarqawi to the al-Qa`ida leadership in Afghanistan outlining this strategy was intercepted in 2004. In the letter, Zarqawi devotes more space to expressing his loathing of Shiites than he does condemning Coalition Forces. The text of the letter is available on GlobalSecurity.org's website: http://www.globalsecurity.org/wmd/library/news/iraq/2004/02/040212-al-zarqawi.htm.
16. The MIPT TKB data set is now held by START, the National Consortium for the Study of Terrorism and Responses to Terrorism at the University of Maryland. It is available at http://www.start.umd.edu/start/data/.
17. The Iraqi Islamic Party's willingness to engage in the new Iraqi political system attracted the AQI to attack it since 2003.
18. For time line graphs that demonstrate the significant decline in violence, see the quarterly reports available from the United States Department of Defense, "Measuring Stability and Security in Iraq," available at http://www.defense.gov/home/features/iraq_reports/index.html.

References

Art, Robert J., and Kenneth Neil Waltz. 2009. *The Use of Force*. Boulder: Rowman & Littlefield.
Bakier, Abdul Hameed. 2008. Iraq's Islamic Mujahideen Profiled by jihadi Websites: Parts One and Two. *Terrorism Focus* 5(December 3): 41.
Byman, Daniel L., and Kenneth Pollack. 2008. Iraq's Long-Term Impact on jihadist Terrorism. *The Annals of the American Academy of Political and Social Science* 618: 55–68.
Brown, Lucy, and David Romano. 2006. Women in Post-Saddam Iraq: One Step forward or Two Steps Back? *NWSA Journal* 18: 51–70.
CNN/USA Today Gallup. *Nationwide Poll of Iraq*, 2004.
Dodge, Toby. 2006. War and Resistance in Iraq: From Regime Change to Collapsed State. In *The Iraq War: Causes and Consequences*, ed. Rick Fawn and Raymond Hinnebusch, 211–224. Boulder: Lynne Rienner Publishers.
Ferguson, Charles. 2007. *No End in Sight: The American Occupation of Iraq* (documentary film).
Grier, Peter. 2006. Iraq Draws Foreign jihadists, but Not in Droves. *Christian Science Monitor*, October 3. Available at http://www.csmonitor.com/2006/1003/p03s03-woiq.html (accessed January 31, 2010).
International Crisis Group. 2003. *Radical Islam in Iraqi Kurdistan: The Mouse That Roared?* February 7. Available at http://www.crisisgroup.org/~/media/Files/Middle%20East%20North%20Africa/Iraq%20Syria%20Lebanon/Iraq/B004%20Radical%20Islam%20In%20Iraqi%20Kurdistan%20The%20Mouse%20That%20Roared.pdf (accessed January 31, 2010).
Kimmage, Daniel. 2006. Al-Qaeda Addresses the jihad-Versus-Resistance Conflict. Radio Free Europe/Radio Liberty. July 31, By Country: Iraq. Available at http://www.rferl.org/content/article/1070232.html (accessed January 23, 2010).
McGary, John A. 2009. The Anbar Awakening: An Alliance of Incentives. *The Washington Quarterly* 32, 1(January): 43–59.
Memorial Institute for the Prevention of Terrorism. 2008. Terrorism Knowledge Base (TKB) "Terrorism Organization Profiles" (TOP). Available at http://www.start.umd.edu/start/data/ (accessed December 10, 2008).
Oxford Research International Ltd. 2004. *National Survey of Iraq*, February.
Rangwala, Glen. 2002. Iraq's Major Political Groupings. Iraq Watch, October 1. Available at http://www.iraqwatch.org/perspectives/rangwala-100102.htm (accessed July 20, 2005).

Romano, David. 2007. An Outline of Kurdish Islamist Groups in Iraq. *Jamestown Occasional Papers Series*, September 17, 1–20.

Rubin, Michael. 2001. The Islamist Threat from Iraqi Kurdistan. *Middle East Intelligence Bulletin*, December. Available at http://www.meforum.org/meib/articles/0112_ir1.htm (accessed May 6, 2013)

Rubin, Michael. 2004. Ansar al-Sunna: Iraq's New Terrorist Threat. *Middle East Intelligence Bulletin*, May. Available at http://www.meforum.org/meib/articles/0405_iraq1.htm (accessed May, 2013)

Schanzer, Jonathan. 2004. *Al-Qaeda's Armies*. New York: Specialist Press International.

Shourush, Sami. 2002. The Religious Composition of the Kurdish Society: Sufi Orders, Sects and Religions. In *Ayatollahs, Sufis and Ideologues: State, Religion and Social Movements in Iraq*, ed. Faleh Absul-Jabar, 115–139. London: Saqi Books.

Tanter, Raymond, and Stephen Kersting. 2009. Syria's Role in the Iraq Insurgency. *In Focus*, Spring. Available at http://www.jewishpolicycenter.org/827/syrias-role-in-the-iraq-insurgency (accessed May 6, 2013)

United States Department of Defense. Measuring Stability and Security in Iraq. *Quarterly Reports*. Available at http://www.defense.gov/home/features/iraq_reports/index.html (accessed January 29, 2010).

Usher, Sebastian. 2008. Baathist Mistake Corrected Amid Concern. *BBC News, Middle East*, January 12. Available at http://news.bbc.co.uk/2/hi/middle_east/7185276.stm (accessed January 31, 2010).

CHAPTER 41

AL-QAIDA AND ITS AFFILIATES

JASON BURKE

AL-QAIDA

EVEN a decade after the attacks of September 11 2001 and nearly a quarter of a century since it was founded as a group and conceptualized as a mode of action in the Pakistani frontier city of Peshawar, little consensus exists on exactly what "al-Qaida" is. Even before the 9-11 attacks, specialists, law enforcement agents, and counterterrorist officials were at odds over the nature of al-Qaida, even over its name. Considerable differences could be observed between the analyses of various American intelligence agencies, such as the Federal Bureau of Investigation (FBI) and the Central Intelligence Agency, and between dominant American analyses and those most prevalent in much of Europe, for example. The debate has remained highly politicized and ideological ever since, with broad divisions emerging between those who favor a conception of al-Qaida as a relatively organized, hierarchical group with definable lines of command and responsibility and a significant ability to initiate, commission, and execute terrorist strikes over a significant portion of the world—essentially a top-down organizational model—and those who emphasize other elements, describing "al-Qaida" as a phenomenon rather than a group, underlining its decentralized structure, its complex and dynamic ideological appeal, and the variety of relations between any leadership elements and the militants and militant groups it comprises (Hoffman 2008, 24–40). Describing it as the ultimate networked, or "bottom-up," group and drawing heavily on academic work on social movements in some cases or on social networking in others, some have gone as far as to question whether "al-Qaida" as broadly understood in popular discourse and debate exists at all (Sageman 2008). Over recent years the analysis of al-Qaida by intelligence services as varied as those of the United States, Britain, Saudi Arabia, Israel, and Pakistan has evolved significantly. So has that in academic circles and in the media. Yet despite an immense amount of research, the availability of a huge body of trial evidence, an enormous quantity of material obtained through the interrogation or interview of militants, and the accumulated statements of key individuals such as Osama bin Laden and Ayman al-Zawahiri as well as a host of other lesser known but equally significant figures, the debate is far from over.

This uncertainty reflects the essential nature of the subject. Trying to compress a dynamic and changing phenomenon into one single definition or matching it with one single label is hard. There are several "al-Qaidas" that all exist simultaneously. These range from a relatively traditional leadership group as outlined by some scholars to the much broader social movement seen by others. This article will briefly explore these various "al-Qaidas" and show how over time they have interacted all while continually evolving in response to both exogenous and endogenous factors.

Four main phases in the history of the al-Qaida phenomenon can be distinguished. The first lasted from the creation of the group known as al-Qaida in August 1988 through to the return of many of its founder members to Afghanistan in 1996. The second lasted from that date until the war of the autumn of 2001 that saw the deposition of the Taliban regime in Afghanistan, the flight of the al-Qaida leadership, the dispersal of most of its key human assets, and the destruction of much of its infrastructure. Third witnessed the spread of al-Qaida's ideology and methodology. The fourth, starting around 2004, continues today.

In each of the first three phases a different element of the phenomenon that is al-Qaida was dominant. In the earliest, it is the core leadership, the *al-qaida al-sulbah*, or "vanguard of the strong," envisaged by Abdallah Azzam, the primary ideologue of the international militants who came to support, aid, and occasionally fight alongside Afghan resistance factions battling the Soviets and their local auxiliaries during the 1980s (Azzam 1988). Azzam, whose concept of the vanguard drew heavily on the thinking of Sayyid Qutb, was a key influence on the founders of al-Qaida though tensions had developed between the older leader and men such as bin Laden and al-Zawahiri before Azzam's assassination in 1989 (Springer et al. 2009, 132).

In the second phase, from 1996 to 2001, it is the broad web of different "affiliated groups" and of volunteers that the leadership was able to knit together around the physical "base" (a common meaning of the Arabic word *al-qai`da*) that they had successfully established in Afghanistan that together constitute the most significant element of the phenomenon of al-Qaida. This base and the "network of networks" connected to it were to prove critical in the preparation of the 1998 attacks on the American embassies in East Africa, the 2000 attack on the US navy warship the USS Cole in Yemen, and finally the 9-11 attacks themselves. The networks were also to prove critical to the evolution of al-Qaida in its broadest sense later.

Phase three saw the al-Qaida ideology and methodology dominant. Again, the Arabic word *al-Qaida* can be translated as "a maxim or a rule" (Burke 2004, 102). In court in 2001, FBI agents said that when they asked one junior member of the teams that had taken part in the 1998 East Africa attacks what al-Qaida was, the response was that it was "a formula system" (*USA v. Bin Laden* 2001). With the leadership on the run, its operatives and volunteers scattered, and its infrastructure destroyed in the 2001 war, it was this sense of al-Qaida as an ideology that became temporarily the most important in the years that immediately followed. The leadership was less obvious during this phase, having become "virtual," restricted to intermittent video or web appearances, and with their practical ability to incite, commission, or execute operations greatly reduced. The base had gone. The networked affiliates were under great pressure. The spread of the ideology, however, benefited greatly from a climate of heightened political consciousness and radicalization as a result of the wars in Afghanistan and then in Iraq along with a wide variety of other events, measures, and statements associated with the "Global War on Terror" announced by American President George W. Bush in the aftermath of the 9-11 attacks.

The fourth phase starts in around 2004—though precise periodization is both difficult and undesirable given the dynamic nature of the phenomenon. Various key developments mark this period: the partial reconstitution of an infrastructure in the tribal areas of Pakistan, the radicalization of a significant number of young Muslims in the West, and the consequent emergence of new hybrid types of the relationship that distant cells and individuals may have with the al-Qaida leadership and a new "network of networks" emerging in terms of links between the hardcore leadership and groups such as "al-Qaida in the Maghreb" or the Pakistani Taliban. In this phase, from around 2004, all the various elements outlined above—the "hardcore" leadership element, the "base," the "network of networks," the affiliates, and the ideology of al-Qaida—are very present. There are signs that a fifth and new phase may be in the process of becoming identifiable, in part defined by the growing backlash against violent extremism now identifiable among Islamic communities worldwide. This is explored further at the end of this article following a final survey examining what al-Qaida constitutes today. To start with, however, the first three phases of al-Qaida are explored in more detail.

The Vanguard. 1988 to 1996

Al-Qaida as a group was founded in 1988 in a series of meetings. Described by its fifteen founder members as an "organized military faction"—its total strength probably did not exceed several dozen—its aim was to weld together the disparate and disunited international extremists who had fought together against the Soviets to form a force that could be turned against repressive "apostate" regimes across the Islamic world. Simultaneously, the group aimed to radicalize and mobilize the masses of the Muslim world who, deceived by their rulers and the tame state media, had failed hitherto to recognize their true duties and interests with the goal of provoking a general uprising of the *ummah* to usher in a new era of social justice. Anti-Western sentiment, though present, was a relatively minor theme (*Illinois v. Enaam Arnout*). These tasks, however, proved more difficult than bin Laden, the Saudi-born leader of the group, had envisaged. Like most of the militants, bin Laden returned home as the Soviets withdrew from Afghanistan and the war there descended into an anarchic civil conflict. Disappointed by the lack of sympathy for his views and the rejection of his proposal to raise an army of *mujahideen* to protect the kingdom against Saddam Hussein, he became a fierce critic of the house of al-Saud and was forced into exile in Sudan in 1991, where he was joined by Ayman al-Zawahiri, the head of the Egyptian Islamic jihad group and another veteran of the campaign against the Soviets. Khartoum at the time resembled the Peshawar of a few years before, as the Sudanese government had welcomed a range of radical Islamic groups over previous years. Bin Laden, however, was not a significant figure among them at the time, and few other Islamic militants had heard of al-Qaida. The defining feature of the groups present in Khartoum was their lack of any common goal or methodology. Though their rhetoric was sometimes international, their focus in reality remained largely national (Wright 2008, 163,175, 197; Burke 2004, 143–157).

The original project of al-Qaida made little progress. Bin Laden was distracted by schemes in support of the Sudanese government. His attempts to build contacts among militants fighting in the Yemen, Chechnya, and the Balkans were broadly unsuccessful though some relationships were established in Somalia, where individuals associated with al-Qaida played a marginal role in the fighting in 1993 that saw significant American casualties. A media committee set up in London achieved little. Algerian groups angrily rejected bin Laden's proffered help, even threatening violence. The check to their ambitions led the al-Qaida leadership to begin theorizing their campaign differently, with a greater emphasis on attacking America that was seen as the key prop of local regimes. In 1996, bin Laden was expelled from Khartoum and accepted an invitation of protection from three warlords in the east of Afghanistan (Burke 2004, 157; Wright 2008; Mekhennet et al. 2008).

THE BASE. 1996 TO 2001

Several immediate problems confronted bin Laden and the score or so associates who arrived with him at the airstrip of Jalalabad, the eastern Afghan city in May 1996. The most immediate was their own security. A second was the advance of the Taliban toward the east of Afghanistan, where they had settled. Contrary to what is consistently reported, Bin Laden and his associates were not invited back to Afghanistan by the Taliban but by their opponents and consequently knew little about the movement that had swept across much of the country over the previous two years and had had no contact with its leaders. A third problem was that, not only did bin Laden and those with him have only a very limited infrastructure at their own disposal, but also many other militant groups were already established in Afghanistan with a large system of camps and guesthouses.

Over the next five years not only did bin Laden and al-Zawahiri, who joined him in Afghanistan, resolve these challenges but they were able to construct a slightly chaotic but nonetheless functioning organization that harnessed and channeled the energy generated by many of the broader trends within Islamic militancy in the mid-1990s. By the end of the decade, they had amassed sufficient resources in terms of recruits, leadership elements, expertise, and money to conceive and execute audacious attacks on US interests in East Africa, on an American warship off the Yemen, and eventually on the American mainland itself. This was coupled with a critical and deeply controversial shift in strategy from targeting the "near enemy" in the Middle East to the "far enemy" of the West and predominantly America that was revealed at a 1998 press conference that announced the formation of the "World Islamic Front against Zionists and Crusaders."

This progress toward their goals was achieved by various measures. Bin Laden had succeeded in building an unstable but increasingly close relationship with the Taliban leadership that ensured security and the status of primus inter pares among the various Arab, central Asian, and Pakistani groups in Afghanistan at the time. Though the closeness of bin Laden to Mullah Mohammed Omar, the Taliban leader, can be exaggerated—there were frequent rows between the two men, particularly over bin Laden's media appearances—Omar nonetheless angrily refused successive demands from America or Saudi Arabia that he expel his guest. Alongside their efforts to build a strong relationship with the Taliban, the al-Qaida leadership increased its efforts to reach out to other groups around the world, essentially offering access to al-Qaida's resources in return for a varying degree of organizational linkage and, in some cases, little more than nominal allegiance. Often groups initiated the contact, sending emissaries to al-Qaida seeking assistance with their own local ambitions. On other occasions, it was the al-Qaida leadership who reached out to various entities and individuals engaged in radical Islamic militancy around the world. A network of relationships stretching from Morocco to Singapore was thus established.

This success was reinforced by a sophisticated media campaign that played on the successes in East Africa to attract recruits. Al-Qaida's internationalism gave it a significant advantage in the rude competition among extremist groups at the time, many of whom were still limited to a more parochial vision and agenda. Thus, by 2000 not only had al-Qaida successfully appropriated much of the extremist infrastructure in Afghanistan, acquiring "the base" it had previously lacked, but it also had successfully become the key node at the center of an array of different and interlocking networks with an increasingly high profile throughout the Islamic world and beyond. Al-Qaida had also succeeded in attracting many of the most significant thinkers or operatives active in global militancy at the time. One was Khaled Sheikh Mohammed, the originator of the 9-11 plan. Others, however, such as the strategist Mustafa Setmarian Nasar, better known as Abu Musab al-Suri, kept their distance, and it is important to remember, however, that deep divisions remained within al-Qaida leadership elements about bin Laden's chosen strategy of striking the "far enemy" and of attacking on American soil. Since 1998 if not before there had been broad and often bitter argument within militant circles in Afghanistan, in the Middle East, and among activists in Europe and elsewhere over tactical, strategic, and religious and ethical questions—such as the advisability and justification of striking "civilian" targets. Many, often citing the example of the conflict in Algeria, worried about the effectiveness of indiscriminate targeting on public opinion (9-11 Report 2004, 250–252; Springer 2008, 25–28).

AL-QAIDA IN THE WORLD. 2001 TO 2004

In the immediate aftermath of the September 11 attacks, analysts, journalists, and governments scrambled to impose a variety of different interpretations of what al-Qaida was. Many contributions to this process were highly questionable. A variety of states—Russia, Uzbekistan, Algeria, China, the Philippines, and others—announced that long-standing insurgencies or extremist activity within their own borders were in fact fomented by bin Laden's al-Qaida. This had two advantages for them, simultaneously disguising the responsibility of their own incompetence, taste for brutal repression, and/or corruption for the violence while potentially releasing significant diplomatic and material aid from Washington. Other states—such as India—immediately instrumentalized the new focus on bin Laden in old conflicts such as that with Pakistan over Kashmir.

The situation naturally was much more complicated. Al-Qaida had lost its infrastructure, its reserves of volunteers, and a significant number of key players in the war of 2001. Mohammed Atef, the group's Egyptian-born military commander known as Abu Hafs, had been killed by a missile fired from an American unmanned drone, one of the first uses of the technology (Dawoud 2001). In the flight from Afghanistan, the leadership, already riven by internal dissent as discussed above, split definitively with many of those who had disagreed with bin Laden's decision to strike the American homeland, heading to Iran rather than to Pakistan, where their erstwhile leader and al-Zawahiri swiftly found a haven (9-11 Report 2004, 251; Harmony Project 2007).

Yet though the base had disappeared, the "network of networks" had not. Over the next two years, a series of bomb attacks on Western targets in Turkey, Kenya, Indonesia, and the Maghreb were carried out by small groups indirectly linked to the al-Qaida "hardcore." Many involved militants who had fled Afghanistan in 2001 and had then returned to their own or third countries. Others involved key individuals, such as Riduan Isamuddin in Indonesia, who had acted as go-betweens linking networks of militants with few previous international connections to the al-Qaida leadership prior to 9-11 and were thus able to galvanize local groups into action in the aftermath of the 2001 war. Some, such as attacks in Morocco in 2002 or in Saudi Arabia where a wave of violence shook Westerners and the ruling royal family a year later, involved both returning veterans of the Afghan training camps and new local recruits. The ease with which such returnees were able to draw in individuals who had had no previous involvement with violent militancy was striking.

This was because not only were the networked groups still active but the third element of al-Qaida, the ideology, was thriving too. The 9-11 attacks and the reaction had broadcast bin Laden's name and message across the world. His "single narrative" of an Islamic world, weakened by a lack of faith within and threatened by an aggressive West set on its subordination and division, gained traction in substantial segments of many populations within the Islamic world. The invasion of Iraq in 2003 reinforced this trend, facilitating "top-down" recruitment by existing militants and increasing the flow upward of individuals attracted by "al-Qaida-ism." In 2004 and 2005, the result of this was particularly evident in Europe, where between 16 and 20 million Muslims live, when Madrid and London saw bomb attacks on mass transport systems that caused 252 deaths and injured thousands. The Madrid attack trial testimony has now revealed was only linked tangentially to the al-Qaida leadership and was largely the work of a group of relatively recent Moroccan immigrants. Though some connections between senior militants involved in al-Qaida and some individuals involved in the Madrid attack did exist, these reveal the essentially associative nature of modern Islamic militant activism not a structured command and control system (Atran 2008; Pargeter 2008, 115–139). The London attacks, however, signified a slightly different relationship between local cells that had formed autonomously and the al-Qaida central leadership, which will be discussed further below. This dominance of the ideology and its primary role in the development of autonomous cells—so-called freelancers or "home-grown terrorists"—was theorized at the time by a variety of militant thinkers linked to al-Qaida. Most prominent among them was Mustafa bin Abd al-Qadir Setmarian Nasar (b. 1958), known as Abu Musab al-Suri, who argued that, far from being on the offensive as bin Laden and al-Zawahiri thought, the global Islamic militant movement was on the defensive in the face of extremely powerful opposed forces. The answer, he said, was "nazim la tanzim," or "system, not organization" (Lia 2006). This distilled previous developments in al-Qaida strategic thinking, further emphasizing the idea that the role of militant leaders was to be "inciter-in-chief" rather than simply to organize and execute attacks (Scheuer 2005). Al-Suri spent many years studying the failure of radical movements in his native land, Egypt, Algeria, and elsewhere and concluded that "sectional, secret, and pyramidal organizations" had failed. Only "open fronts" of semiconventional warfare or a radically decentralized model had any chance of success. The former would only follow the latter and al-Suri argued that "resistance must become a strategic phenomenon, along the lines of the Palestinian Intifada, [in] all corners of the Islamic world." Al-Suri was far from the only militant thinker who wanted such a shift. In 2006 Egyptian strategist and activist Muhammed Khalil al-Hakaymah published a book titled *How to Kill Alone* stressing the need for radical decentralization. As the author and many others recognized, however, not only did this approach sacrifice a level of competence and thus capacity for the enhanced resilience to counterterrorist efforts that it brought, but it also risked indiscriminate attacks on targets that would not be seen as legitimate by Muslim populations and a consequent loss of the crucial public support (Springer et al. 2009; Kepel 2008, 137–140).

A final key development during this period was the involvement of al-Qaida in Iraq, which is discussed more deeply elsewhere in this publication. Jihadist militants had been present in the north of Iraq—though not in the areas controlled by Saddam Hussein—for some years before 9-11. A microcosm of the split between mainstream Islamists and extremist "jihadists" had been seen toward the end of the 1990s in the small world of Kurdish radicalism. In 2000 and 2001, bin Laden had responded to requests for assistance from individuals based within Iraqi Kurdistan and had established links with several of these relatively small radical groups (Burke 2004, 222–227). However bin Laden was unable to exploit this relationship in the aftermath of 9-11 and it was an independent Jordanian-born militant activist, Ahmed Fadeel al-Nazal al-Khalayleh, better known as Abu Musab al-Zarqawi (b. 1966), who, having evacuated the rudimentary training camp he had set up in the west of Afghanistan as the Taliban regime had collapsed, had made his way to northern Iraq. Al-Zarqawi was thus ideally situated to exploit the new situation and the volunteers from overseas that the 2003 invasion brought. While similar groups suffered in Saudi Arabia and the Far East, al-Zarqawi was able to establish working relations with local Iraqi Sunni tribes and to former Ba'ath party resistance elements. He was also successful in welding at least some of the existing radical Islamic militant networks into a chaotic and fragmented web of cells and groups nominally loyal to him and, after a public pledge of allegiance in October 2004, to al-Qaida too. However, relations with local tribes and communities in Iraq would deteriorate very rapidly and al-Zarqawi would be killed in June 2006 after a series of rows over strategy with bin Laden and al-Zawahiri. The networks he had tenuously drawn together would fragment still further after his death.

AL-QAIDA. 2005 TO THE PRESENT DAY

What, then, is al-Qaida today? Once again, the phenomenon of al-Qaida has evolved substantially since 2005. Six main factors have determined its development and will be examined in the pages below: the reconstitution of an "al-Qaida hardcore" with some kind of infrastructure in Pakistan, the conflicts in Afghanistan and the growing insurgency in Pakistan, the continuing radicalization of a significant if small number of European Muslims, the failure of the al-Qaida project of fomenting and federating violence legitimized by a radical Islamic discourse in Iraq and its relative success in some other locations, emerging or continued Islamic militant activity entirely independent of al-Qaida in places such as Indonesia, and finally the growing rejection of the al-Qaida ideology and "brand" across much of the Islamic world.

First, there is the reconstitution of some semblance of an infrastructure of training camps, safe houses for leadership elements, and accommodation for volunteers in the Federally Administered Tribal Areas of Pakistan (FATA). This is where bin Laden and al-Zawhiri are believed to be hiding and where, since around 2004, a scattered but nonetheless functioning system of small-scale often temporary training camps and accommodation for volunteers has existed. There is even a media production outfit, al-Sahab, that produces relatively sophisticated videos at regular intervals that are then uploaded onto the internet or passed to TV companies, notably al-Jazeera, for broadcast (*Al-Sahab* 2007). Since the summer of 2008, the al-Qaida leadership in FATA has suffered from a series of controversial attacks from unmanned drones that have killed a number of senior and middle-ranking operatives, albeit at the cost of significant civilian casualties (*Newsweek* 2006).

The second key factor in determining the current shape and evolution of al-Qaida and its affiliates is the cross-border conflict involving the Afghan and the Pakistani Taliban and a variety of other groups networked with them. This is a complex and fragmented picture, but in broad terms on one side of the border, the Afghan Taliban is fighting a forty-plus member coalition of international troops and their local allies and auxiliaries. On the other side of the border a complex and shifting coalition of groups that together call themselves the Pakistani Taliban are fighting Islamabad's military forces, which themselves receive support from the United States. This ongoing double-sided conflict is one of the main reasons that the al-Qaida leadership still has something resembling a safe haven. However, the relationship of the al-Qaida leadership with the disparate elements of both Afghan and Pakistani Taliban is typically complex. Though often deploying the language of international Islamic radicalism, both the Afghan and the Pakistani Taliban remain relatively local in their focus. Links between the Afghan Taliban and the al-Qaida leadership remain personal rather than organizational. The same is the case with the Pakistani Taliban. Though some international militants have advised senior members of the Pakistani Taliban on tactics and techniques, such as the excavation of tunnels and the construction of other fortifications discovered during fighting in November 2008 in the agency of Bajaur, and have even cooperated on specific operations, the Pakistani Taliban are in no way an al-Qaida affiliate, remaining very much rooted in the social, tribal, and economic context of the North West Frontier Province and the FATA as well as in the area's insurrectional history. Two other main groupings in the region—the network of Jalaluddin Haqqani, the ageing cleric, former mujahideen commander, and current Afghan Taliban senior figure, and the militants of central Asian origin associated with Tahir Yuldashev—have formidable military capacity but little desire to involve themselves in projects beyond their immediate strategic environment and are entirely independent of al-Qaida's leadership (Gul 2009; Ali 2009).

The third major development shaping the al-Qaida phenomenon currently is the continuing radicalization of small but nonetheless significant numbers of Western European Muslims, including some converts, who then travel to the FATA seeking training, strategic advice, and logistic assistance. The 2005 bombings in London as well as at least three subsequent plots in the United Kingdom and several in Germany have featured such individuals who, radicalized in their home countries, subsequently traveled to Pakistan, where they were sometimes inducted by al-Qaida. British intelligence estimates the number of British volunteers as around thirty each year, some of whom cross the frontier to fight against coalition forces in Afghanistan. Others return home (author interview 2008). The local Pakistani groups such as Jaish-e-Mohammed or Lashkar-e-Tayyaba, some of which still maintain fundraising and logistic networks in the United Kingdom, often act as intermediaries for British volunteers; almost all are young British-Pakistani males from the relatively deprived areas of northern England, where large Pakistani communities have grown up (Tankel 2009). These groups provide a first point of contact on arrival in Pakistan and may act as a conduit, as it is suspected happened in the case of bombers involved in the London attacks of July 7, 2005, to al-Qaida figures (House of Commons Report 2006). The German connection is via a breakaway group of Uzbek militants who have peeled away from Yuldashev's fighters and have provided training to volunteers arriving from Europe. There are also volunteers from a wide range of other nations and backgrounds, ranging from American-born converts to central Asian, southwest Chinese Uighur or Far Eastern aspirant militants, though their numbers remain small (Kaiser 2007; Kaiser, Rosenbach and Stark 2007). It is also worth noting that accounts differ as to the reception such volunteers receive in the FATA. One group of Belgian returning recruits told interrogators that they had been only cursorily trained, had been badly cared for, and had been forced to pay large sums for rent and equipment. Others have spoken of a sophisticated and impressive system dealing with arrivals from overseas (Vinas 2009). It is also worth noting that, as with volunteers who traveled to Afghanistan in the late 1990s, most such individuals seek not to perpetrate attacks in their own homelands but to fight alongside the Taliban. Such strikes are suggested to them by senior al-Qaida leadership figures while they are in Pakistan.

A fourth development is the failure of the al-Qaida project in Iraq, where a combination of military pressure, the revulsion of local populations, and the rejection by local Sunni tribes had effectively ended the attempt to turn the Tigris and Euphrates valley into a new theater of jihad by around 2007. Though the hopes of the al-Qaida leadership were disappointed there, campaigns in parts of the Maghreb, the Sahel, and Yemen have met with relatively more success. After many years of trying, al-Zawahiri and bin Laden finally brought the remnants of the Algerian militant groups from the 1990s under their umbrella. In September 2006, the Groupe Salafiste pour la Prédication et le Combat (GSPC) announced it had allied itself with al-Qaida and then, in early 2007, announced the formation of al-Qaida in the Maghreb (AQIM), a theoretical fusion of Algerian, Moroccan, and other groups whose aim was to prosecute a campaign of violence against Western interests, particularly former colonial occupiers such as France, and to establish a "pure" Islamic state in their various homelands (Philips and Evans 2007, 296; Tawil 2009). Though boosted since 2003 by young Algerians who had fought in Iraq, AQIM remained short of men and resources. Nonetheless it managed several spectacular and successful attacks in Algeria ranging from bombings of key government and international buildings to ambushes of security personnel. For the first time in Algerian militancy, these strikes involved coordinated suicide bombings. These attacks have taken place alongside several hundred smaller incidents in which local civil defense forces are often targeted. Some of the renewed violence in Algeria has spilled over into the Sahel, where countries such as Mali and Mauritania have also seen an upsurge of militancy with kidnaps of foreigners and regular firefights with local security forces though the exact mix of religiously inspired violence, local politics, tribal conflict, and criminality remain difficult to ascertain with any certainty.

In Pakistan too, the al-Qaida leadership has had some success in creating new "affiliates" or at least in building bonds that did not exist a decade ago. There, local groups once exclusively committed to sectarian violence within Pakistan or to irregular *fedayeen*-style attacks in Kashmir have become significantly more international in their outlook and have grown closer to al-Qaida as they have done so. The murder of Daniel Pearl, a Jewish American journalist, in Karachi in 2001 was one of the earliest indications of this trend. Subsequently this process appears to have accelerated with ad hoc cooperation between Pakistani groups formerly devoted to purely sectarian or regional agendas and the al-Qaida hardcore evident in attacks such as that in Lahore in March 2009 against the Sri Lankan cricket team. One factor in this has been the general broadening of the appeal of bin Laden's original call for a global, rather than a local, campaign of violence. Another factor has been Pakistan's new role as a key ally of the United States in the American campaign against radical Islam. It is important not to exaggerate this logic, however. The attacks in Mumbai in late 2008 had little to do with al-Qaida and everything to do with the specific regional and local context at the time.

A fifth important trend has been the return of purely autonomous actions by a variety of groups or networks. In Indonesia, a breakaway group from the Jemmah Islamiya organization continued to mount spectacular bomb attacks against Western interests. However, there is little evidence of a link between them and the al-Qaida leadership elements. Court trials of militants in Indonesia reveal a process of grassroots activism and low-level radicalization that has no link with the reconstituted hardcore leadership in FATA and serves as a useful reminder that al-Qaida has only ever exploited existing conflicts that often have long histories and deep roots in multiple social, economic, political, and cultural factors that long predate the arrival of bin Laden et al. on the international militant scene. Whether or not such activities constitute an element of "al-Qaida" takes us back to the definitional problems explored in early pages of this article (International Crisis Group 2009). Indonesia is a perfect example of the final and crucial development since 2005 that has been in the view taken generally of al-Qaida and related violent extremism in much of the Islamic world. Al-Qaida had been founded in part to coordinate efforts to mobilize and radicalize the supposed "Islamic masses." In a book he published at the end of 2001, Zawahiri spoke of how *mujahideen* should above all avoid "dying in silence" and railed against the "huge gap in understanding between the jihad movement and the people" (Al Quds Al Arabi 2002). Al-Qaida's strategy was one of "propaganda by deed," familiar to any student of terrorism over the last two centuries. Though it is clearly still too early to say, the strategy appears not to have achieved its primary goal of sparking a generalized uprising among Muslims from Morocco to Malaysia and it is beginning to look in fact as if the opposite has been achieved. In almost every country directly experiencing radical Islamic violence, support for bin Laden and al-Qaida, often at relatively high levels in the immediate aftermath of 9-11, the war in Afghanistan, and particularly the conflict in Iraq, has collapsed. In Indonesia in 2002 (before the first bombing in Bali in October of that year), 26 percent of people believed that suicide bombing with civilian targets was justified in the defense of Islam. In 2009 the total was 7 percent. In Pakistan, a robust level of support for such actions, 41 percent in 2004, dropped sharply when bombs started exploding in local cities, reaching just 5 percent by 2009. In Jordan, the evidence is even stronger. In early 2005, levels were at 57 percent. After bombers sent by Abu Musab al-Zarqawi killed sixty in three hotels in Amman, including a large number of wedding guests, support halved and by 2009, was just 12 percent. Support for bin Laden himself has tracked this trend, going from 59 percent in Indonesia in 2003 and 52 percent in Pakistan in 2005 to 25 percent and 18 percent, respectively, in 2009 (Pew Global Attitudes Survey 2009, 83–86).

This has naturally posed significant challenges to the al-Qaida leadership with a variety of senior figures, including at least one founding member, publicly declaring that not only is the strategy of bin Laden wrong but repudiating violence too. Senior militants in Egypt, Libya, and Algeria have renounced their previous allies (Wright 2008). The senior al-Qaida leadership has struggled to find an adequate response to this. An unprecedented internet question and answer session with al-Zawahiri in December 2007 and January 2008 saw the al-Qaida leader testily rebutting a series of questions about the strategy he and his associates had pursued and rejecting repeated criticism of the targeting of "innocents" it implied (Janes Terrorism and Insurgency News 2008).

As scholar Olivier Roy has noted, al-Qaida and the associated contemporary radical Islamic militancy is a generational phenomenon (Roy, author interview 2005; Roy 2004). Al-Qaida has now existed for more than twenty years. Though further spectacular and bloody attacks are possible, indeed likely, it seems unlikely that the original aims of the founders of the group will be fulfilled. One reason for this may well be that, rather than offering a response to globalization, al-Qaida in fact simply represented an alternative form of globalization and has thus provoked a similar response from local communities deeply uneasy with ideas, individuals, and modes of action that, for them, appear foreign and lacking in authenticity. Most of those groups achieving relative success a decade after the September 11 attacks—the Pakistani and Afghan Taliban, al-Qaida in the Maghreb, *al-Shahab* in Somalia—have a strong local flavor. Interestingly, Indonesia's Jemaa Islamiyya, heavily involved in violence in 2002, has renounced such tactics on the basis that, though there is a global threat to Islam that may justify "resistance" elsewhere, there is none locally. Again, this shift is rooted in the recognition that there is little tolerance for armed struggle among the Indonesian people.

Taken together, these trends are likely to profoundly weaken al-Qaida and its affiliates in coming years and this essential weakness will define the next phase of development of the leadership, the network of networks, and the ideology. The key question now is whether this apparent weakness is temporary—perhaps simply cyclical—or more permanent. The above words should have made abundantly clear that the development and growth of al-Qaida has been far from linear. Whatever the answer, there is every probability that, however much genuine threat it poses, the phenomenon of al-Qaida will continue to evolve and will continue to exert a considerable influence on the international scene for many decades to come.

Author Interviews

Author interviews with Libyan militants in Sudan at the time.
Witness statement of Vinas Bryant, December 7, 2008, author collection.
Author interviews with United Kingdom, Pakistani intelligence officials, London, Riyadh, Islamabad, Kabul, 2008–2009, and United States.
Author interview with British intelligence official, Islamabad, 2008.
Author interview with Olivier Roy, Paris, December 2005.

REFERENCES

Ali, Imtiaz. 2009. A Profile of Baitullah Mehsud. *Foreign Policy*, July 9. Available at http://www.foreignpolicy.com/articles/2009/07/09/pakistans_bin_laden (accessed July 31, 2009).

As-Sahab: al-Qaida's Video Production Unit. 2007. Shaun Waterman, UPI, Washington, September 20.

Atran, Scott. 2008. Who Becomes a Terrorist Today. *Perspectives on Terrorism* 11, no. 5. Available at http://www.terrorismanalysts.com/pt/index.php/pot/article/view/35/html (accessed July 31, 2009).

Azzam, Abdullah Azzam. 1988. Al-Qaida al-Sulba. *Jihad Magazine* 41. April.

Belgian Federal Police. Interrogation Testimonies of Hisham Beyayo and Walid Othmani. November 2008. Brussels, Belgium.

Burke, Jason. 2004. *Al-Qaeda: The True Story of Radical Islam*. Delhi: Penguin.

Dawoud, Khaled. 2001. Obituary of Mohammed Atef, Khaled Dawoud. *The Guardian*, November 19. Available at http://www.guardian.co.uk/news/2001/nov/19/guardianobituaries.afghanistan (accessed July 31, 2010).

Gebauer, Matthias. 2008. "Bavarian Taliban Video": The Smiling Suicide Bomber. *Der Spiegel*, March 27. Available at http://www.spiegel.de/international/world/bavarian-taliban-video-the-smiling-suicide-bomber-a-543768.html (accessed July 31, 2009).

Gul, Imtiaz. 2009. *The Al-Qaida Connection—Taliban Terror in Tribal Areas*. Delhi: Penguin, Viking.

Harmony Project, Cracks in the Foundation: Leadership Schisms in al-Qa'ida from 1989–2006. 2007. Combating Terrorism Center, West Point, NY. Available at http://ctc.usma.edu/harmony/harmony_menu.asp (accessed July 9, 2009).

Hoffman, Bruce. 2008. The Myth of Grass Roots Terrorism. *Foreign Affairs*, May–June. 87, No. 3 (p. 133)

Illinois v. Enaam Arnaout. Accounts of the Foundation of al-Qaida Draw on Documents from US District Court, April 2002.

Intelligence and Security Committee. *A Report of the Official Account of the Bombings in London on July 7, 2005*. 2006. House of Commons, May 11.

International Crisis Group. *Indonesia: Radicalisation of the "Palembang Group."* 2009. International Crisis Group. Asia Briefing, 92. May 20.

International Crisis Group. *Indonesia: The Hotel Bombings*. 2009. International Crisis Group. Asian Briefing, 94. July 24.

Janes Terrorism and Insurgency News. 2008. *Zawahiri Answers Back*. May 2. Available at http://www.janes.com/regional_news/europe/security/terrorism/jtsm/jtsm080502_1_n.shtml (accessed June 20, 2010).

Kaiser, Simon, Marcel Rosenbach, and Holger Stark. 2007. Operation Alberich, How the CIA Helped Germany Foil Terror Plot. *Der Spiegel*, October 9. Available at http://www.spiegel.de/international/germany/operation-alberich-how-the-cia-helped-germany-foil-terror-plot-a-504837.html (accessed July 31, 2009).

Kepel, Gilles. 2008. *Terreur et Martyre*. Paris: Flammarion.

Knights under the Banner of the Prophet. 2002. *Al Quds al Arabi Newspaper*, December.

Lia, Brynjar. 2006. *The al-Qaida Strategist Abu Musab al Suri: A Profile*. Presentation to Oslo Militære Samfund seminar. Oslo, Norway, March.

Mekhennet, Souad, Michael Moss, et al. 2008. Ragtag Insurgency Gains a Lifeline from Al Qaida. *New York Times*, July 1, 2008. Available at http://www.nytimes.com/2008/07/01/world/africa/01algeria.html?pagewanted=all&_r=0 (accessed July 31, 2009).

National Commission on Terrorist Attacks upon the United States. The 9-11 Report: The National Commission on Terrorist Attacks on the United States. 2004. W.W. Norton & Co., July 22.

Operation Crevice trial transcripts, prosecution evidence. 2006. London.

Pargeter, Alison. 2008. *The New Frontiers of Jihad*. London: I.B. Tauris.

Pew Charitable Trusts, Pew Global Research Centre. 2007. *Global Attitudes Towards Islamic Extremism and Terrorism*. August 29. Washington, DC.

Pew Charitable Trusts, Pew Research Centre. 2008. *Global Public Opinion in the Bush Years (2001–2008)*. December 18. Washington, DC.

Philips, John, and Martin Evans. 2007. *Algeria: Anger of the Dispossessed*. London: Yale University Press.

Reidel, Bruce. 2007. Al-Qaida Strikes Back. *Foreign Affairs* 86, no. 3(May–June): 24–40.

Roy, Oliver. 2004. *Globalised Islam*. London: C Hurst & Co Publishers Ltd.

Sageman, Mark. 2008. *Leaderless Jihad: Terror Networks in the Twenty-First Century*. Philadelphia: University of Pennsylvania Press.

Scheuer, Michael. 2005. Coalition Warfare: How bin Laden Uses the World Islamic Front against Crusaders and Jews. *Jamestown Foundation Terrorism Focus* 2, 7.

Springer, Devin R., James L. Regens, and David N. Edger. 2009. *Islamic Radicalism and Global Jihad*. Washington, DC: Georgetown University Press.

Tankel, Stephen. 2009. *Lashkar-e-Taiba, From 9-11 to Mumbai*. London: King's College, London University.

Tawil, Camille. 2009. New Strategies in al-Qaida's Battle for Algeria. *Jamestown Terrorism Monitor*, July. Available at http://www.jamestown.org/single/?no_cache=1&tx_ttnews[swords]=8fd5893941d69d0be3f378576261ae3e&tx_ttnews[any_of_the_words]=PKK&tx_ttnews[pointer]=5&tx_ttnews[tt_news]=35325&tx_ttnews[backPid]=7&cHash=c3b8177b38#.UdlE9FMkjJw (accessed August 31, 2009).

USA v. Usama bin Laden. 2001. New York Southern District Court, Direct Examination of Agent Perkins, March 19, 2001. Available at www.cryptome.org (accessed August 2009).

Vinas, Bryant Neal. 2009. Audition by FBI, March.

Wright, Lawrence. 2008. The Rebellion Within. *New Yorker*, June. Available at http://www.newyorker.com/reporting/2008/06/02/080602fa_fact_wright (accessed August 31, 2009).

Index

Abacha, Sani, 387
Abbas, Mahmoud, 511, 512, 513
Abdalla, Ulil Abshar, 567, 568
Abdel-Ghani, Safwat, 612, 614
Abdi, Abbas, 241
'Abduh, Muhammad, 27, 31, 32–34, 36–37, 130, 162, 220
Abdullah, King of Jordan, 544, 547, 548, 549, 551
Abdullah, King of Saudi Arabia, 297
Abdullah, Salih bin, 214
Abdullahi, Khalifa, 204
Abdur Rahman Khan, Amir of Afghanistan, 454–55, 473n4
Abou El Fadl, Khaled, 3–20
Abrahamian, Ervand, 182
Abu al-Abbas, 625
Abu al-Futuh, Abd al-Mun 'im, 480, 495, 609, 614
Abu Bakr mosque, 315
Abu Dharr al-Ghifari, 169, 251–52
Abu Sayyaf Group, 350
'adah, 9, 11
al-'adalah al-ijtima'iyyah, 163
Adams, John Quincy, 264
'Adl wa al-Ihsan, al-, 119, 359–60, 364–65, 366, 371, 535
Adnan, Muhammad, 570
adultery. *See zina*
Afaq, 361
Affendi, Abdelwahab El-, 3, 73
Afghan Arabs, 316–17
Afghani, Jamal al-Din al-, 27, 31–32, 36–37, 220, 292, 455
Afghanistan, 453–72
 and Bin Laden, 633
 and the Chechen War, 316
 and Durand Line, 473n3, 474n14
 and Islamic democracy, 84
 and Islamic nationalism, 456–58
 and jihadists, 453–56, 474n13
 and Marxist revolution, 463–66
 and Musahiban dynasty, 459–63
 and post-jihad political failures, 467–70
 and post-Taliban rebuilding, 470–71
 precolonial and colonial periods, 453–56
 and radical militant Islamist agenda, 295, 296
 and the Soviet Union, 538
 Taliban in, 637
 and the United States, 83, 242, 273, 314, 559, 585
 veteran fighters from, 210, 316, 618, 619, 622, 624
Africa. *See* Maghreb; North Africa; sub-Saharan Africa; *specific countries*
African Americans, 265, 267, 272
Agha, Hadji Hadji, 312
ahkam al-Qur'an, 9–10
ahl al-bayt (Prophet's family), 10
Ahl al-Sunna wa al-'Jamâ'a, 365
Ahmad, Irfan, 3, 324–39
Ahmad, Khurshid, 146
Ahmad, Mirza Ghulam, 150
Ahmad, Osman Hassan, 450n2
Ahmadinejad, Mahmoud, 191, 198n84, 241, 242, 401, 402, 404, 406, 560
Ahmadi sect, 150
Ahmadiyah, 346–47
Ahmad Khan, Sayyid, 29, 31
Ahmed, Ghafoor, 581
Ahmed, Leila, 453
Ahmed, Qazi Hussain, 331, 584
al-Ahrâm, 47, 48
Ajami, Fouad, 75, 77
al-Akaileh, Abdullah, 552
Akdogan, Yalcin, 428–29
Akhavi, Shahrough, 3, 159–68, 169–79
Akif, Mehmet, 31
'Akif, Muhammad Mahdi, 101, 484

AK Party. *See* Justice and Development Party (AKP)
Al al-Shaykh family, 411
Al-Arian, Abdullah A., 263–77
Alash Orda, 309, 312
Alawi, Ahmad al-, 372
Albani, Nassir al-Din al-, 213. *See also* Muslim Brotherhood
Albania, 282, 390n6
alcohol prohibition, 18, 45, 49, 228
Algeria, 532–42
  and al-Banna's ideology, 131
  and Arab Spring, 540–42
  constitution, 304n1
  and co-option of Islamist parties, 536–37
  elections in, 532
  electoral politics in, 533–35
  and grassroots Islam, 362–64
  independence, 52n4
  and Islamic statehood, 356
  and Islam in Europe, 286, 287
  and Islam in North Africa, 353
  and lobbying Islamic agenda, 302
  militant groups in, 638
  and Modernist-Salafiya movement, 37
  and the Movement for a Peaceful Society (HAMS), 476
  and nationalism, 353, 354–55
  and partisan Islamist agenda, 299
  and political Islam, 63
  and "post-Islamism," 367–68, 369, 370, 374–75
  and radical militant Islamist agenda, 296, 297
  and secularism, 82
  and socialist revolution, 356–61
  and Sufi resurgence, 371, 372, 373
  and terrorist groups, 388
  and violence, 538–40
Algiers Charter, 356
Algiers Faculté, 357
Ali, As'ad Said, 572n15
'Ali, Husayn b., 173
Ali, Muhammad, 263
Aliev, Haci Ali Akram, 315
Aliev, Heidar, 313, 314
Aliev, Ilham, 313
Allah, Shah Wali, 28, 29, 30

'Allal al-Fasi, Muhammad, 354
Alliance of Civilizations Initiative, 434
All India Muslim League (AIML), 575, 576
All-Muslim Welfare Organization (PERKIM), 592
almsgiving, 223, 224
Al-'Utaybi, 415
Alwani, Taha Jabir al-, 303
Amal Movement, 523
American Enterprise Institute, 408
American Muslim Alliance (AMA), 268
American Muslim Civic Leadership Institute (AMCLI), 275
American Muslim Council (AMC), 268
American Muslim Political Coordination Council (AMPCC), 271
American Muslims for Palestine (AMP), 275
American Muslim Taskforce on Civil Rights and Elections (AMT), 274
Aminzadeh, Mohsen, 242
amir almu'minin (Commander of the Faithful), 359–60
Amman, Jordan, 639
Amnizade, R. R., 91
analytic philosophy, 248
Anand, Javed, 325
Andijan revolt, 314
Angkatan Belia Islam Malaysia (ABIM), 63, 64, 591–92, 595
Anglo-American secularism, 79–80
Anglo-Muhammadan Courts (India), 20
Animal Rights Party, 283
animism, 341
Ansar, 301
Ansar al-Sunna, 620, 624
Ansari, Hamid al-, 226–27
anticolonial movements, 144–45
anti-Semitism, 53n8
anti-Westernism, 37–38
apolitical Muslimhood agenda, 290–92
apostasy, 18, 149–50, 165, 205, 294, 317, 347, 458, 568, 608, 612–13, 632
Appeal to All Laboring Muslims of Russia and the East, 309
'*aql* (reason), 9, 11, 31, 33–34
'Aqqad, 'Abbas al-, 159–60
al-Aqsa Mosque, 60
Arab Feminist Union, 113

Arabism, 212
Arab-Israeli conflict (1967), 605
Arab-Israel War (1948), 141, 508
Arab nationalism, 35, 59, 61, 213, 496, 507, 521. *See also* pan-Arabism
Arab Socialist Union, 604
Arab Spring
   and Algeria, 363
   and apolitical Muslimhood agenda, 292
   and democracy, 1, 68
   and gender issues, 112
   and Hamas, 513
   impact in the Maghreb, 352, 540–42
   and Islamic democracy, 83
   and Islamic politics in the Middle East, 289
   in Jordan, 544, 549
   and the Muslim Brotherhood, 554
   and partisan Islamist agenda, 299–300
   and political Islam, 65
   and "post-Islamism," 367, 369
   and radical militant Islamist agenda, 297
   and *shari`ah*, 22–24
`Arafat, A., 93
Arat, Yesim, 117
`Arif, `Abd al-Salam, 161
Arinc, Bulent, 425
Aristotelian philosophy, 162
Arjomand, Said Amir, 255
Armed Islamic Groups (GIA), 362
armed resistance agenda, 298–99
Armenia, 434
Arqam, Darul, 594
al-'Aryan, 'Isam, 492
Asad, Muhammad, 165
asbab al-nuzul (occasions of revelation), 10
ash 'ariyah doctrine, 215
Asia, 120, 122n7. *See also* Central Asia; South Asia; Southeast Asia
'Askar, Sayyid, 491
Asrar-e Hezar Saleh (Hakamizadeh), 194n7
Assad, Bashar al-, 293, 525
assembly-based democracy, 69–70
Assembly of the Experts, 189, 190, 300
Association for the Study of the Middle East and Africa (ASMEA), 75
Association for the Unity and Progress of Islam (AMUPI), 382

Association of Algerian Muslim `Ulama' (AUMA), 37, 354, 357
Association of Indonesian Muslim Intellectuals (ICMI), 561
Asy'ari, Hasyim, 568
Ataturk, Mustafa Kemal, 132, 433, 456
Atef, Mohammed, 634
Athenian democracy, 70
Al-Tawhid wa al-Islah (Unity and Reform) movement, 535
Aushev, Bashir, 318–19
authoritarianism, 3
   and al-Banna's ideology, 135
   and global communications, 420
   and Iran, 191
   and Iraq, 617
   and Islamic democracy, 74, 76–77, 84
   and Islamic law, 21
   and Khomeini, 193
   and the Muslim Brotherhood, 488
   and political economy of Islamism, 93, 94, 98, 105
   and political Islam, 63
   secular authoritarianism in Central Asia, 310–11, 313–15, 320
   and sub-Saharan Africa, 382
   and Sudan, 442, 449
authority, legal, 16
autocrats, 292–94
Awami League (AL), 324, 333, 334, 335n2, 578–79
`Awdah, Abdel Qadir, 214
'Awwa, Muhammad Salim al-, 219, 225, 303, 495
Ayubi, Nazih, 92
Ayub Khan, Muhammad, 577, 578
Azam, Ghulam, 332–33
Azerbaijan, 308, 309, 312, 313, 314–15, 320n1
Al-Azhar, 222–24, 293–94, 462, 490, 605, 610
Azhar, Shaykh al-, 223
Azzam, Abdullah, 465–66, 620, 631

Ba'asyir, Abu Bakar, 560
Ba'ath party, 621
Babangida, Ibrahim, 387
Badawi, Abdullah, 64, 344, 346
Badis, Abd al-Hamid b., 37
Badran, Margot, 2, 112–23

Badr Brigades, 617, 625
Bahrain, 291, 299
Bahy, Muhammad al-, 223
Baitul Muslimin Indonesia (BAMUSI), 566–67
al-Bakhit, Marouf, 548, 553–54
Bakier, Abdul Hameed, 623, 626n1
Baladi, al-Fadhil Al-, 214
Al-Balagh Cultural Society, 226
Bali bombings (2002), 560
The Balkans, 282
Balkhi, 'Abdullah ibn 'Umar al-, 170
Banchoff, Thomas, 285
Bangladesh, 324–26, 327, 330–34, 335n9
Bangladesh Nationalist Party (BNP), 333
bangsa moro, 349
Bani Irsheid, Zaki, 553, 554
Bani Sadr, Abu al-Hasan, 196n41, 249
banking, Islamic, 146, 208
Banna, Gamal al-, 65
Banna, Hasan al-, 65, 129–41
  background, 129–31
  and democracy and *shura*, 136–40
  and Ghannushi's ideology, 213, 214
  and Islam and politics, 134–36
  and *jihad*, 485–86
  and the Muslim Brotherhood, 475, 476, 478–79, 480
  and political violence, 483–85
  and Qaradawi's ideology, 222
  and Qutb's ideology, 165
  and *shari'ah* and the Islamic state, 131–34
  and stereotypes of Islam, 334
  and student movements, 591–92
Bapir, Ali, 619, 620
Baqer al-Sadr, Muhammad, 517
Barelvi, Ahmed Reza Khan, 575
Barison Nasional (National Front), 344–45
Barlas, Asma, 120
Barnier, Michel, 227
Baroso, Jose Manuel, 279
Basaev, Shamil, 308, 317, 318
Al-Bashir, 212
Bashir, Isam al-Din al-, 301, 303
Bashir, Omar Hasan al-, 62, 606, 441, 449
Basmachi revolt, 310, 456, 459
Bayat, Asef, 82, 84, 93, 193–94, 369, 370, 449
Bayt al-Ansar (House of the Helpers), 466

Bazargan, Mehdi, 186, 196n41
Bazzaz, Abd al-Rahman al-, 59
Beeman, William O., 3, 399–408
Behdad, S., 100
Beheshti, Mohammad, 171, 238
Belgium, 281, 284, 285, 287
Ben Ali, Zine El Abidine, 217–18, 220, 293, 353, 361, 366–67, 369, 373, 533–34, 540–41
Ben Badis, Abd al-Hamid, 354
Bengali nationalism, 332, 348
Bengalis, 578–79
Benin, 381, 387
Benjedid, Chadli, 362, 534–35
Benkirane, Abdelilah, 366
Bennabi, Malik, 213, 214, 217, 220
Berg, Nicholas, 624
Berman, Paul, 324
Berque, Jacques, 170, 171
Berri, Nabih, 518, 523, 525
Beslan school siege, 319
"Beware the Enemies of Islam," 104
Bhutto, Benazir, 469, 583
Bhutto, Zulfikar Ali, 60, 330, 580–81
Bihi, 'Abdallah Bayn, 225
Bin Ali, Mohamed, 603
Bin Baz, Abdulaziz, 416, 417, 419
Binder, Leonard, 161
Bin Laden, Osama
  coordinating of Islamist groups, 620
  establishment of al-Qaeda, 469
  and Islamic politics in South Asia, 334, 466
  and Kurdish radicalism, 636
  and militant Salafism, 27
  and al-Qaeda, 631, 632–33
  statements by, on al-Qaida, 630
  support for, 639–40
  and Taliban, 633
  and training in Afghanistan, 619
  and Turabi's ideology, 210
Bin-Nafisa, S., 93
Al-Binna' wa al-Tanmiya (Building and Development) Party (Egypt), 614
Bishri, Tariq al-, 219, 227
Bitter Harvest (Zawahiri), 482
Black Nationalism, 263, 265–66
Black Widows, 319

Blanford, Nicholas, 520
Bokhari, Kamran, 4, 574–86
Boko Haram movement, 388
Bolkestein, Frits, 279
Bolsheviks, 309
Bosnia, 269, 283
Bossi, Umberto, 284
Botswana, 390n6
Boumediene, Houari, 357, 358, 362
Bourguiba, Habib, 63, 212, 215–17, 293, 360–62, 366, 372, 533
Bouteflika, Abdelaziz, 363, 536
Bremmer, Paul, 621
Brezhnev, Leonid, 463
Briscoe, Phil, 324
British common law, 8
British National Party (BNP), 281
Brooks, David, 399
Brown, Carl, 352
Brown, Nathan J., 489, 492, 494, 547, 553
Bruinessen, Martin van, 561
Brumberg, Daniel, 186, 188
Brunei, 340, 351n1
Brussels, Belgium, 285
Buddhism, 349
Bukhara, 307, 311
Bulaç, Ali, 65
Burke, Jason, 4, 630–40
Burkina Faso, 381, 387
Burma-Myanmar, 340, 348–49
Buroujerdi, Mohamad Hossein, 182–83, 194n11
Bush, George H. W., 268
Bush, George W., 271–72, 399, 470, 559, 632
Bush, Robin, 569
Buti, Shaykh Sa'id Ramadan al-, 213

caliphate, 35, 58, 74, 132–33, 210, 289, 373
Canal Zone, 161
Cantori, Luis, 219
capitalism, 59, 79, 160, 176, 229
Carson, Andre, 274
Casanova, José, 79
Catholic Church, 79, 83, 285, 350
Caucasus, 307, 308, 320n1
Cavanaugh, William, 52n6, 53n9
censorship, 324

Center for Protection of Religious Freedoms, 315
Center for the Dialogue of Civilizations, 242
Center for the Propagation of Islamic Verities, 169
Central Asia, 307–20
    and the Chechen War, 316–17
    and Dagestan, 317–20
    and extent of Russian control, 320n1
    Islam's vitality in, 307–8
    and the North Caucasus conflict, 316
    and outside influences, 311–12
    Russian/Soviet rule, 308–10
    and secular authoritarianism, 313–15
    and Soviet antireligious policies, 310–11
    and Soviet collapse, 312
Central Office of the Honorable Leader's Representative in the Universities, 253
Centre for Social Cohesion, 324
Centre of Arab Unity Studies, 218
Césaire, Aimé, 175
Chad, 381
Chamber of Deputies (Jordan), 103
Chamran, Mostafa, 517
charity, 207, 223, 364. *See also zakat*
Charkhi family, 460–61
Chaudhry, Iftikhar Muhammad, 584
Chechen Red Army, 309
Chechen War, 308, 314, 316–17, 321n17
Chechnya, 316–17, 320n1
Cherribi, Sam, 3, 278–88
Christian Democrats, 287
Christians and Christianity
    in Egypt, 492–93
    Erdogan on universal values, 429
    and Islamic democracy, 83
    and Justice and Development Party (AK Party), 429–30
    and the Muslim Brotherhood, 492–93
    as religious minority, 290
    and Soroush's ideology, 256
citizenship, 22, 44, 73, 74, 290
civil contract *('aqd)*, 72
Civilized Alternative Party, 365
civil law, 8
civil liberties, 243, 255, 427, 428
civil marriage, 46–49

civil rights, 84, 265, 267–72, 269–72, 274–75, 287
civil society
  and Ghannushi's ideology, 219
  and Iran, 191
  and Islamic democracy, 82
  and Khomeini's ideology, 191
  and Morocco, 359–60
  and Soroush's ideology, 255
  and sub-Saharan Africa, 384, 385–86
  and Turabi's ideology, 207–8, 209
Clark, Janine, 93, 552
"clash of civilizations" thesis, 74–75, 268, 434, 611
class conflict, 172–73, 175
clientalist politics, 105
Clinton, Bill, 269, 270, 271
Coalition of Builders of Islamic Iran, 406, 407
Coalition Provisional Authority in Iraq (CPA), 399, 621
codification of law, 20
Cold War, 59, 210, 268, 307, 382, 383, 389
collective reasoning, 134–35, 226
colonialism
  British, 161
  decolonization, 231, 282
  and Islamic democracy, 74, 77, 81
  and Islamic reformism, 50–51
  and Islam in Europe, 280
  and Khomeini, 185
  and Mawdudi's ideology, 144–45
  and North African nationalism, 353–55
  and North America, 264
  and Qaradawi's ideology, 231
  and secularism, 81
  and *shari'ah*, 7, 19–20
  and Shari'ati's ideology, 176
  and sub-Saharan Africa, 380, 390n4, 390n5
  See also imperialism
Columbus, Christopher, 263–64
Combined Opposition Parties, 332, 578
common law, 8, 14
communication technologies, 419, 420
communism, 59, 145, 177, 361
Congregation for Reform (Yemen), 476
consensus, 35
conservatism, 35, 181, 187, 357, 368
Conservative Democracy (Akdogan), 428–29

Constituent Assembly, 329–30
Constitutional and Democratic Popular Movement (MPCD), 376n6
constitutions and constitutionalism
  and Chechnya, 316
  and Islamic democracy, 72–73
  and Islamic rule, 304n1
  and Islam in Southeast Asia, 346
  and Kenya, 386
  and Khomeini, 182–83, 186, 189, 191
  and Morocco, 365
  and Pakistan, 327
  and ruling Islamic agenda, 300
  and Southeast Asia, 343
consultation. *See shura*
Consultative Center for Studies and Documentation (Al-Markaz al-Istishari lil-Dirasaat wal-Tawthiq), *524*
Coptic Christians, 46–49, 51, 290
Corbin, Henry, 258n2
Council for Good Government (CGG), 269
Council of 'Ulama', 359
Council on American-Islamic Relations (CAIR), 268, 273
Court of Justice of the European Communities (ECJ), 279
Crimean Tatars, 309
criminal law, 45, 48–49. *See also shari'ah*
Crone, Patricia, 75
crusades, 80, 280
cultural assimilation, 226
cultural openness, 243
Cultural Revolution (Iran), 249–50, 251
Cultural Revolution Council (CRC), 249

Dagestan, 312, 317–20, 320n1
Dahl, Robert, 70
dakwah groups, 591–92, 595
Daneshjouan e Khatt e Emam, 239
Danish People's Party (DPP), 284
Daoud, Muhammad, 461, 462–63, 467
Dar al-'Ulum, 159
Dardri, Yusuf al-, 297
Darqawi order, 372
Darul Arqam (Muslim Converts Association), 591
Darul Islam, 57, 346, 560
Dati, Rachida, 287

Datta, Sreeradha, 335n2
Davis, Nancy J., 103, 493
Davutoglu, Ahmet, 435
da'wah (religious call), 37, 163, 164, 302, 617
Da'wah Party (Lebanon), 518, 520
dawla. *See din* and *dawla*
Daylami, 'Abd Al-Wahhab Al-, 303
decolonization, 231, 282
Delong-Bas, Natana J., 3, 411–21
Delors, Jacques, 279
democracy and democratization, 68–84
  in Afghanistan, 462, 463, 470
  and al-Banna's ideology, 136–40
  and al-Jama'a al-Islamiya (Islamic Group), 608
  and Anglo-American secularism, 79–80
  and the Arab Spring, 1
  defining democracy, 70
  and Ghannushi's ideology, 216, 219–20
  and grassroots Islam, 362
  and "guided democracy," 343
  and Islamic Action Front, 547–48
  and the Islamic establishment, 74–75, 75–76
  and Islamic Jihad Group (al-Jihad Group), 608
  and Islam in Europe, 287
  and Islam in South Asia, 325, 329
  and Islam in Southeast Asia, 343
  Islam's history with, 72–74
  and Khatami's ideology, 240, 244
  and Khomeini, 191, 193
  and Mawdudi's ideology, 148, 152, 334–35
  and Modernist-Salafiya movement, 35
  and the Muslim Brotherhood, 140, 477, 490, 493
  and Muslim experience with secularism, 81–83
  and Muslim religious toleration, 80–81
  and Pakistan, 577–78, 580
  points of contention on, 76–78
  and political economy of Islamism, 90, 105
  and political Islam, 62
  and Qaradawi, 23
  and Qaradawi's ideology, 230–31
  religion's history with, 70–72
  and religion-state relations, 78–79
  and secular authoritarianism in Central Asia, 313
  and *shari'ah*, 23–24
  and *shura*, 136–40
  and sub-Saharan Africa, 383–88
  and Sudan, 442, 444
  trends in the Islamic world, 68–70
  and Turabi's ideology, 206–7
  and Turkey, 426–27
Democracy in America (Tocqueville), 71
Democratic Action Committee, 332
Democratic Constitutional Rally (RCD), 366
Democratic Party-Struggle (PDI, later PDI-P), 561, 566–67
Democratic Republic of Congo, 379
demographic trends, 314, 380
Deobandis, 147
Department of Islamic Development, 343–44, 596
deradicalization, 296–97, 603–4, 609–13
dervishes, 292
Desert Storm, 294
despotism, 23, 82
Destourian Socialist Party, 366
development, 349, 364
De Waal, Alex, 208
Al-Dhahabi, Muhammad Hussein, 614n1
dhimmis, 149
dialectic process, 172–73
Diallo, Ayuba Suleiman, 264
Diamond, Larry, 399
dictatorships, 82
dietary restrictions, 228
Dieterich, Renate, 546
Din, Kamal Nur, al-, 491
din and *dawla*, 57–58, 59–60, 61–65, 66, 374, 456–58
Divine Will, 11, 12, 13, 18, 257
Divine Wrath Brigades, 625
divorce, 286
Djaballah, Abdallah, 536
Djerejian, Edward, 77
Djibouti, 304n1
Dodge, Toby, 622
Doha Agreement (2008), 525, 528n5
Dole, Bob, 270
Dostum, Abdur Rashid, 469

"dual containment," 187–88
Dudaev, Dzhokar, 316–17
Dukkali, Abu Shu'ayb b. Abd al-Rahman al-, 37
Dupree, Louis, 473n8
Durkheim, Émile, 92
Dyab, Ahmad, 491
Dzhabarov, P. I., 312

East Africa, 382
Eastern Europe, 282–82, 285
East Pakistan, 331–32
economic conditions
   and the Algerian revolution, 358
   and Chechen conflict, 319, 320
   and Ghannushi's ideology, 214
   and Islam in Central Asia, 314–15
   and Islam in Southeast Asia, 349
   and political economy of Islamism, 94–97
   unemployment, 314–15, 319
ecumenicalism, 255–56, 303–4
Edip, Halide, 326
Edolat Party, 312, 313
education
   in Afghanistan, 455, 456, 457, 460, 461, 469
   and Arabization in North Africa, 375n5
   and gender issues, 113, 208, 222, 419
   and Islamic Action Front, 550
   and Modernist-Salafiya movement, 31, 33
   and Mujahiddin-sponsored schools, 465
   and North American immigration, 266–67
   in Pakistan, 331
   and reformism of Khatami, 238
   in Saudi Arabia, 416, 418, 419, 420, 421
   and Soviet antireligious policies, 307
   and sub-Saharan Africa, 381–82
   and Wahhabism, 419
   and Western culture, 20
   See also students and student groups
Educational Mobilization Unit (Al-Ta`bi'a al-Tarbawiya), *524*
effendiyya, 204
Egypt, 603–14
   and Afghan Mujahiddin, 465
   and apolitical Muslimhood agenda, 291, 292
   and Arabization in North Africa, 375–76n5
   and Arab Spring, 513
   and Banna, 131, 484
   Christian population of, 492–93
   constitution, 304n1
   and Coptic Christians, 46–49, 51
   deradicatlization in, 603, 604, 609–13
   elections in, 477, 493–96, 500n55
   and Erdogan, 426
   and gender issues, 113, 120, 123n23
   and immigration to North America, 266
   independence, 52n4
   and Islamic democracy, 77
   and Islamic feminism, 120
   and Islam in Europe, 287
   Luxor massacre (1997), 609, 611
   militant groups in, 603–14
   and Modernist-Salafiya movement, 31, 32–34
   mosques in, 606
   and Nuqrashi assassination, 482
   parliament of, 486–88, 490
   and partisan Islamist agenda, 299, 300
   and political economy of Islamism, 89, 92, 93, 98–100, 104–5
   and political parties, 139–40, 352, 613
   and postrevolution elections, 22, 24
   presidency of, 490
   prison life in, 611
   and privatization, 101
   and Qutb's ideology, 166
   and radical Islamists, 296, 297, 603–4
   and redistribution, 103–4
   religious revival in, 494, 603–4, 605–6
   Revolution of 1952, 222
   Revolution of 2011, 3, 23, 224
   role of ideology in, 607–9
   and secularism, 54n31, 82
   and *shari`ah*, 488–92, 494
   and the Six Day War, 494–95, 603–4, 605
   socioeconomic setting of, 606
   state repression of militants, 611–12
   and statist secularelligious agenda, 293–94
   and sub-Saharan Islamism, 389
   and Sudanese politics, 204
   and Sufi resurgence, 373
   women in, 490–93
   See also Muslim Brotherhood
Egyptian Feminist Union, 116
Eickelman, Dale, 76

Elcibey, Abul Fazl, 313
electronic networking, 226–27
Ellison, Keith, 274
Elshtain, Jean Bethke, 71
Emoush, Bassam al-, 552
Enayat, Hamid, 73, 181
The End of History and the Last Man (Fukuyama), 42
England, 8. *See also* United Kingdom
Enlightenment, 71, 174, 208
Ennahda, 217–18, 220, 363
Enneifer, Ahmida, 213, 214
epistemology, 246, 250–54, 257–58
equality and egalitarianism
 and democratization of *shura,* 139
 and French *laïcité,* 50, 293, 334, 382, 385
 and gender issues, 119–20, 121, 216
 and modern nation-states, 44
 and Qutb's ideology, 161
 and Shari`ati's ideology, 172
 and Soroush's ideology, 255
 See also women and gender issues
Eraslan, Sibel, 117
Erbakan, Necmettin, 425, 432
Erdogan, Recep Tayyip, 82, 424, 425, 426, 428, 429–30, 434–35, 438n16
Eritrea, 381, 389
Ershad, Hussain, 333
Esposito, John L., 1, 75, 219
Ethiopia, 381, 384, 389–90, 390n5
ethnicity
 and Chechen conflict, 319
 ethnic cleansing, 282, 310
 and Islam in Europe, 278
 and Islam in Southeast Asia, 348–49
Etoile Nord-Africaine, 354
Ettela'at, 195n12
Europe
 and Afghanistan, 465
 European Charter of Human Rights, 286
 Islam and politics in, 278–87
 and Modernist-Salafiya movement, 34
 and Muslim politicians, 280–82
 and responses to religious pluralism, 285–86
 and secularism, 81

 and single-issue parties, 283–84
 See also Eastern Europe; *specific countries*
European Council for Fatwa and Research (ECFR), 226
European Union (EU)
 growth of, 278
 and Hamas, 505, 514
 and Islam in Europe, 279, 281–82, 287
 and responses to religious pluralism, 285
 and Turkey, 279, 423, 425, 432–33, 434, 435
existential philosophy, 172
Expansion of the Prophetic Experience (Soroush), 255–56
Expediency Council, 196–97n55

Fadaiyan-e Islam, 194n11
failed states, 383, 388–90
Faith-Based and Community Initiative, 272
Falahat, Salem, 554
The Fall and Rise of the Islamic State (Feldman), 81
family law, 8, 48, 49, 119, 224, 385
Fanon, Frantz, 172, 175, 178n2
faqih, 180, 182, 252, 400–401, 409. See also velayat-e faqih; wilayat al-faqih
Farabi, Abu Nasr al-, 237, 307
Faraj, Muhammad 'Abd al-Salam, 484, 606, 608
Farbeh-tar az eideolozhi (Soroush), 251
Farhan, Ishaq, al-, 545, 550, 552
Al-Farida Al-Ghaiba (Faraj), 608
Faris, Mohammed Abu, 545, 548
Farooque, Mujtaba, 328
far right politics, 280–81, 287
Farsi, Jalal al-Din, 517
fascism, 145
Fatah movement, 513
Fatima, daughter of the Prophet, 10, 178n1
Fatima Al Zahra Shi`a mosque, 315
Fattah, Moataz A., 289–306
fatwas
 contrasted with *hukm,* 15
 and Egyptian Islamism, 611
 and Islamic politics in Afghanistan, 455
 and Islamic politics in Southeast Asia, 348, 567
 and Islamic politics in the Middle East, 293–94

fatwas (*Cont.*)
  and Islam in North America, 272
  and Khomeini's ideology, 189
  and Qaradawi's ideology, 224, 226, 227, 231
  and Soroush's ideology, 252
  and statist secularreligious agenda, 293
Fawzan, Salih al-, 233n44, 415
Fayez, Faisal al-, 548
Faysal, King of Saudi Arabia, 60
Fayyad, Salam, 512, 514
Faza'il-i Balkh (Balkhi), 170
Federally Administered Tribal Areas of Pakistan (FATA), 637, 638
Feener, Michael, 567, 568
Feillard, Andrée, 4, 558–71
Feldman, Noah, 76, 81
female genital mutilation, 491, 570, 572n14
feminism, 37, 113–14, 116, 119–21, 122n7
Ferguson, Charles, 627n13
Ferqa ye Esteqlal wa Tajaddud (Party of Freedom and Modernity), 458
Feyziyeh Madreseh, 181, 183
Fiamma Tricolore, 281
Fifth Republic (France), 184
Fighting Islamic Group, 297
al-Fikr al-Jadid (magazine), 160
finality of Islam, 252–53
fiqh
  contrasted with *shari'ah*, 12–16, 52n2
  "*fiqhi* positivism," 253
  fiqh madhabs, 289
  and gender issues, 115, 118–19
  and Khomeini's ideology, 193
  and renewal of Islamic jurisprudence, 228–29, 231
  and Shi'i Islam, 258n2
  and Soroush's ideology, 251
Fiqh al-Zakat (Qaradawi), 224
fitra, 11, 33, 134
Five Principles (Pantjasila), 59
"flying imams" case, 274
folk Islam, 311
foreign policy, 74, 80, 83, 269
forfeiture, 44–45, 47–48, 51–52, 54n32
Fortuyn, Pim, 283, 284
Forum Demokrasi, 561
Foundation for the Wounded (Mu'assasat al-Jarha), 524

Fox, Jonathan, 71–72
France
  and anti-Semitism, 53n8
  and civil law, 8
  and EU membership of Turkey, 433, 434
  and European colonialism, 280, 354
  Fifth Republic, 184
  French existentialism, 173
  French Revolution, 241
  and Ghannushi's ideology, 213
  headscarf controversy, 226
  and Islam in Europe, 281, 284, 286, 287
  and *laïcité*, 50, 293, 334, 382, 385
  and responses to religious pluralism, 285
  and rise of the nation-state, 44
  and secularism, 325
  and sub-Saharan Africa, 381, 382, 385, 390n4
Freedom and Justice Party, 99, 105, 475, 477, 480, 489, 497
Freedom House, 69
freedom of expression, 286
freedom of religion, 424, 426, 427, 428, 431
Freedom Party (FPO), 281
Freedom Party (PVV), 281
free trade, 99, 100, 101
French Revolution, 241
Front de Libération Nationale (FLN), 533, 542
Front Islamique du Salut (FIS). *See* Islamic Salvation Front (FIS)
Front National, 281, 284
Frunze, Mikhail, 309
Fukuyama, Francis, 42, 68
Fuller, Graham, 84
fundamentalism, Islamic, 89, 184, 205, 334–35
fuqaha (Islamic jurists), 22, 72, 118, 180, 182

Gaddafi, Muammar. *See* Qaddafi, Muammar
Gallab, Abdullahi, 444
Gandhi, Indira, 328
Gandhi, Mohandas, 326, 327
Ganguly, Sumit, 325, 335n2
Garang, John, 444
Garaudy, Roger, 217
Gayushov, Altoy, 315
Gaza Strip, 117, 298, 505, 506–10, 512–14
Ghazwat, 308
Gazgireeve, Aza, 318

Gellner, Ernest, 75, 219
Gemayel, Bashir, 518
General Union of Tunisian Workers (UGTT), 361
Gerges, Fawaz, 493
German People's Union (DVU), 284
Germany, 284, 285, 433, 434, 638
Ghaddafi, Mu'ammar al-. *See* Qaddafi, Muammar
Ghamari-Tabrizi, Behrooz, 3, 246–59
Ghamidi, Javed Ahmed, 146, 152, 331
Ghana, 387
Ghanimeh, Ziad Abu, 546
Ghannoushim, 325
Ghannushi, Rashid al-, 3, 63, 65, 129, 212–20, 227, 361, 373
Gharaibeh, Ibrahim, 546, 547
Gharbzadegi (Al-e Ahmad), 185
Ghazali, Abu Hamid al-, 29, 217
Ghazali, Moqsith, 568
Ghazali, Muhammad al-, 58, 134, 214, 222, 476
Ghazali, Zainab al-, 116
Ghuzlan, Mahmud, 101
glasnost, 312
globalization
  and communications, 420
  global Islamic groups, 295
  and Islam in South Asia, 326
  and Pakistan, 331
  and political economy of Islamism, 99
  and political Islam, 64–65
  and al-Qaeda, 640
  and Turabi's ideology, 205
Gnosticism, 247, 255, 258n2
Golan Heights, 522
Golden Age of the Islamic Renaissance, 247
Golpayegani, Safi, 315
Gorbachev, Mikhail, 316
Gordon, Michael R., 399
Gore, Al, 271–72
Gorus, Milli, 425
Gospels, 49
Gräf, Bettina, 3, 222–36
Gramsci, Antonio, 176
Grand Mosque of Mecca, 416
grassroots Islam, 361–62, 362–64, 369
Great Britain
  and Afghanistan, 454–56, 473n3, 473n7
  and colonial India, 453–54
  and European colonialism, 280
  and First Anglo-Afghan War, 454
  and Hamas, 507
  and Islam in Europe, 281, 284–85
  and legal legacy, 20
  and Third Anglo-Afghan War, 456
Great Occultation, 185
Greece, 280, 284, 285, 434
Green Alliance, 363
Green Movement, 120, 192, 193, 242
Groupe Salafiste pour la Prédication et le Combat (GSPC), 638
Guardian Council, 73, 187–88, 197n71, 239, 240, 244n6
guest workers, 280, 286
Guevara, Che, 175
guided democracy, 343
Gul, Abdullah, 425, 426, 435–36
Gulf War, 210, 268
Gullen movement, 314
Gunaratna, Rohan, 603
Gurvitch, Georges, 170, 172
Gus Dur. *See* Wahid, Abdurrahman (Gus Dur)

Habannaka, Shaykh, 213
Habashneh, Samir, 548
Habermas, Jürgen, 255
Hadad-Adel, Gholam-Ali, 406
Haddad, al-Tahir al-, 220
hadith
  and Islamic politics in South Asia, 326
  and Islamic politics in Southeast Asia, 568
  and Mawdudi's ideology, 153n12
  and Modernist-Salafiya movement, 30–31
  and Pakistani politics, 330
  and Qaradawi's ideology, 223
  and redistribution, 102
  and Saudi gender politics, 418
  and schools of Islamic jurisprudence, 10
  and Soroush's ideology, 251, 257, 264
  and Sufi scholarship, 29
  and Turabi's ideology, 206
Hadj, Messali, 354
Haeri, Abd al Karim, 181, 182

Haider, Jorg, 284
Hajari, Maryam Hasan al-, 226–27
Hajjarian, Said, 241, 242
Hakamizadeh, 194n7
Hakaymah, Muhammed Khalil al-, 636
hakimiyya, 137, 139, 140–41, 147, 150–51, 152
hakimiyyat Allah, 163
Halevy, Efraim, 227
Hallaj, Mansur al-, 173–74
Hamas, 505–14
   and Algeria, 536
   and armed resistance agenda, 298–99
   divisions within, 513
   founding of, 505–7
   future of, 514
   and gender issues, 117
   identity of, 506, 507–8
   influence of, 505
   and Iran, 407
   in Iraq, 619
   Izz al-Din al-Qassam Brigades (IQB) of, 505, 509, 510
   and jihad, 508, 509, 510, 511, 512
   and Jordan, 551
   and Kurdish region, 619
   and the Muslim Brotherhood, 476, 485, 505
   and peace, 511–12
   and PLO, 506
   and political economy of Islamism, 92
   and radical militant Islamist agenda, 295
   resistance and violence associated with, 508–10
   suicide missions of, 506, 509, 510, 512
   terrorist designation of, 506, 509, 511
   and Turabi's ideology, 210
Hamid, Shadi, 4, 544–55
Hamzawy, Amr, 492, 494
Hamzeh, Nizar, 520
Hanafi, Hasan, 59
Hanafi school of jurisprudence, 17, 28, 45, 311, 454, 473, 575
Hanbali school of jurisprudence, 29, 45, 223
Hanifa, Abu, 54n27
Haniyeh, Ismail, 513
Hanoun, Louisa, 302
Haqq, Mowlana Sami-ul, 469
Haqqani, Jalaluddin, 637
Harakat al-Jihad, 356

Harakat al-Nahdah, 217, 363
Harakat Mujtama' al-Silm, 363
Harashi, Sulayman Ibn Salih al-, 233n44
Harb, Mona, 525
Hariri, Rafiq al-, 516, 525, 527
Hasan, Zoya, 325
Hasbullah, Wahab, 561
Hashemi, Nader, 2, 68–88
Hashemite Monarchy (Jordan), 4
Hashmi, Taj, 335n2
Hasina, Sheikha, 324, 333
Hassan, Syed Munawar, 584
Hassan II, King of Morocco, 359, 362, 364, 535
Al-Hay'a al-Sahiya al-Islamiya (The Islamic Health Unit), 524
Haz, Hamzah, 560, 562
head coverings, 65, 226, 409n10, 424, 426, 428, 494
Hechter, M. C., 89
Hefner, W. Robert, 570
Hekmatyar, Gulbuddin, 464, 467, 468, 582
Hellenic Front, 284
Hermassi, Elbaki, 360
hermeneutics, 9–10, 11, 184, 246, 247, 255–56, 257–58
Hezb-i Islami, 464
Hezbollah. *See* Hizbullah
hezbollahi mob groups, 248, 249
Hidden Imam doctrine, 178n1, 184
High Administrative Court (Egypt), 46, 47–48, 51
High Council of Cultural Revolution, 238
Higher Committee for the Coordination of National Opposition Parities (HCCNOP), 552
High State Council, 362
hijab, 114–16, 605. *See also* head coverings
Hindus, 326–27, 341
hisba, 295, 296
Hishmat, 'Abd al-Mun'im Gamal, 492
historical determinism, 172
Hizb al-Tahrir al-Islami (Islamic Liberation Party), 213, 295, 314, 373
Hizbi Islami, 467, 468, 474n11, 582
Hizbullah, 516–28
   Al-Wathiqa al-Siyaiya li-Hizbullah manifesto, 521–22
   armed forces and military doctrine of, 527

institutional infrastructure of, 523–25
integration into Lebanese politics of, 523
and Iran, 520, 525, 527
and Islamic politics in the Middle East, 298
and Israel, 518–19, 521–22, 523, 526–27
and jihad, 523, 528n8, 616
"Open Letter" document of, 519, 521
origins of, 517–19, 528n3
and political economy of Islamic politics, 92, 93
and reformism in Iran, 407
splits and schisms in, 518
suicide missions of, 526
and Syria, 518, 523, 525–27
terrorist designation of, 516, 519, 528n8
and Turabi's ideology, 210
wilayat al-faqih doctrine of, 516, 518–21
Hizb ul Takfir, 314
Hizbut Tahrir Indonesia (HTI), 564
Hobbes, Thomas, 53n9
Holy Struggle for Construction, *524*
homogenization of Islam, 251
honor crimes, 317, 551
Hoogland, Eric, 409n7, 409n10
Horn of Africa, 379, 381, 388, 389
Hosseini, Ziba Mir-, 114
Houidek, Mesbah, 357
Houthis, 297
How to Kill Alone (Hakaymah), 636
Hudaybi, Hasan al-, 165, 483
hudud law, 14, 18–19, 22, 301, 346
Hujjat Allah al-Balighah (God's Conclusive Argument) (Allah), 29
hukumat-i ilahiyah (divine government), 147–48, 149, 151
human rights, 50, 78, 82, 140, 189, 208, 243, 314. *See also* women and gender issues
Hungary, 281
Hunter, Shireen, 3, 307–23
Huntington, Samuel, 53n10, 74–75, 241–42, 268, 434
huquq al-'ibad (rights of humans), 17
huquq Allah (rights of God), 17
al-Hurriyat al-'Amma fi al-Dawla al-Islamiya (Ghannushi), 217, 218
Husayn, Imam, 173, 175
Husayniyyah-yi Irshad, 177

Husri, Sati' Al-, 213
Hussein, King of Jordan, 60, 546, 553
Hussein, Saddam, 294, 408, 417, 468, 617, 618, 620, 627n11
Huwaidi, Fahmi, 219
hybrid legal systems, 20

'ibadat, 16
Ibn 'Abd al-Wahhab, Muhammad. *See* Wahhab, Muhammad b. Abd al-
Ibn 'Arabi, 247
Ibn 'Ashur, 217
Ibn Hazm, 217
Ibn Ibrahim Al al-Shaykh, Muhammad, 416
Ibn Rushd, 162, 217
Ibn Saud, Abdulaziz ibn Muhammad, 412
Ibn Saud, Abdullah, 415, 417, 420
Ibn Saud, Fahd, 417
Ibn Saud, Faisal, 416
Ibn Saud, Muhammad (d. 1765), 411
Ibn Sina, Abu Ali (Avicenna), 247, 251–52, 307
Ibn Taymiyyah
  and al-Banna's ideology, 132, 141
  and development of Wahhabism, 29
  and Ghannushi's ideology, 217
  and Islamic reformism, 45
  and Mawdudi's ideology, 149
  and Modernist-Salafiya movement, 36
  and stereotypes of Islam, 334
  and violent Wahhabism, 412–13
Ibrahim, Anwar, 63, 64, 82, 560, 592, 594
Ibrahim, Hasanayn Tawfiq, 482
Ibrahimi, Ahmed Taleb, 357
Ibrahimi, Bachir, 357
Ibrahimoghlu, Ilgar, 315
ibtila', 205
idealism, 253
Idel-Ural Republic, 309
identity politics
  and gender issues, 113
  and Islam in Europe, 279
  and Islam in Southeast Asia, 340–41
  and political economy of Islamism, 99
  See also ethnicity; women and gender issues
Idris, King of Libya, 355
ijma', 9–11, 72, 206, 228, 252

ijtihad
    and Muhammad ʿAbduh, 33
    and complexity of Middle East Islam, 90
    and democracy, 72
    and gender issues, 113
    and Khomeini, 181, 193
    and misconceptions of Islam, 15–16, 20–21
    and Modernist-Salafiya movement, 29, 35
    myth of closure, 20–21
    and reformism, 28
    and Shariʿati's ideology, 175
    and Shiʿi jurisprudence, 9
    and Soroush's ideology, 247
    and Turabi's ideology, 205
Ikhwan, 213, 215, 482. *See also* Muslim Brotherhood
illiteracy, 95–97, *96*
Illuminationism, 247
Ilyas, Chamim, 568–69
Ilyas, Mawlana Muhammad, 213
Ilyas, Qasim Rasool, 328
Imam Hussein Brigades, 625
Al-Imdad Schools (*Madares al-Imdad*), *524*
immigrants and immigration
    guest workers in Europe, 280
    and Islamic feminism, 122n7
    and Islam in Europe, 283–84, 285–86
    and Islam in North America, 265
    and Islam in Southeast Asia, 349
    and nostalgia for homelands, 286–87
imperialism
    and Islamic democracy, 81
    and Islamic statehood, 56
    and Khomeini, 189
    and Khomeini's ideology, 184
    and misconceptions of Islam, 21–22
    and nationalism, 56
    and secularism, 81
    and Shariʿati's ideology, 176
    See also colonialism
indeterminacy, 257
India
    British India, 453, 459, 473n7, 575
    and decolonization, 282
    and Indo-Pakistani war, 579, 580
    and Islamic politics in South Asia, 324–26, 326–27, 330–31, 332, 334–35, 453
    and Islam in Europe, 286, 287

    and Mawdudi, 144
    and Modernist-Salafiya movement, 31
    Mumbai attacks (2008), 639
    and transformation of Jamaʿat-e Islami, 328–29
Indian National Congress, 144, 326
individualism, 173
Indonesia, 558–71
    corruption in, 563, 571n6
    and decolonization, 282
    and democracy, 390n6
    and European colonialism, 280
    and identity politics, 340–41
    and Islamic democracy, 69
    and Islamic nationalism, 59
    and Islamic political issues, 345–48
    and Islamic politics in Southeast Asia, 340
    and majority Muslim populations, 342–44
    militant groups in, 639–40
    and political economy of Islamism, 105
    and political parties, 344–45
    and the Prosperous Justice Party (PKS), 476, 564–65
    and secularism, 82
    and *shariʿah*, 24, 566–67, 568, 570
    and terrorist attacks of 9/11, 559–60
    and Wahid presidency, 561–63
    women in, 566
Indori, Rafi Ahmad, 331
Inglehart, Ronald, 286
Ingushetia, 318–19
Ingush Regiment, 318
inheritance laws, 8, 228, 230
Inner City Muslim Action Network (Iman), 275
Inns of Court, 15
Institut Kefahaman Islam Malaysia (IKIM), 596, 597
instrumentalization of Islam, 231
intercession, divine, 29–30
interest prohibition, 49, 105, 228
Internal Security Act (ISA), 592
International Conference of Islamic Scholars (ICIS), 560
International Crimes Tribunal (ICJ), 333
International Islamic University (IIU), 596
International Monetary Fund (IMF), 99–100, 367, 550

international relations, 175–76
International Union for Muslim Scholars (IUMS), 225–26, 303
Internet, 420
Inter Service Intelligence (ISI), 325
Al-Intiqad (previously *al-'Ahd*) Weekly Paper, *524*
Iqbal, Muhammad, 29, 31, 213, 220
Iqtidar, Humeira, 331
Iran
    and Afghanistan, 464, 465, 468
    armed forces of, 518
    and Azerbaijan, 314
    and constitutionalism, 73
    and democracy, 73
    elections in, 405–6
    and gender issues, 115, 116, 118
    and globalization, 64
    governmental structures, 401–5
    and Hamas, 505, 513
    and Hizbullah, 520, 525, 527
    and Iran-Iraq War, 186–87, 189, 406
    and Iraqi Kurdistan, 618
    and Islamic democracy, 77
    and Islamic feminism, 120
    and legacy of Khomeinism, 190–92
    and Malaysian Islamic groups, 594
    nuclear capability of, 434
    and political economy of Islamism, 105
    and privatization, 100
    and radical militant Islamist agenda, 295
    and reformism, 407–8
    and religious minorities, 290
    and resistance movements, 176
    and ruling Islamic agenda, 300–301
    and secularism, 82
    theocracy and legitimacy, 400–401
    and Turkey, 434
    and the United States, 522, 525, 624
    Western misconceptions of, 399–400
    women of, 409n10
    See also Iranian Revolution
Iranian Revolution, 57, 249–50, 311–12
    and Algeria, 358
    and end of Cold War, 210
    and Ghannushi's ideology, 215–16
    and Islam in Southeast Asia, 342
    and Mawdudi's ideology, 148
    and political Islam, 61
    and "post-Islamism," 368
    and Shari'ati's ideology, 175
    and sub-Saharan Africa, 383
    and Tunisia, 215–16
Iranian Student Confederation, 169
Iran-Iraq War, 186–87, 189, 406
Iraq
    and armed resistance agenda, 298
    Coalition Provisional Authority in Iraq (CPA), 399
    constitution, 304n1
    disbanding of army, 621–22
    Hamas in, 619
    independence, 52n4
    and Iranian foreign policy, 242
    and Iran-Iraq War, 186–87, 189, 406
    Iraqi Islamic Party, 476
    and Islamic democracy, 77, 83, 84
    jihadists in, 616–26
    and Khomeini, 185
    Kurdish region of, 618–20, 636
    Muslim Brotherhood in, 617
    Najaf, 517
    and radical militant Islamist agenda, 296, 297
    and secularism, 82
    suicide bombers in, 622, 624
    US invasion of, 434, 621
    women in, 619, 620–21
Iraqi Islamic Party, 476
Ireland, 280
Isamuddin, Riduan, 635
Islah Party, 98, 117, 367, 370, 536
Islam, Ansar al-, 619, 620
Islam, the Human Being, and Marxism (Shari'ati), 177
Islam and the Secular State (Na'im), 50
Islamic Action Front (IAF), 544–55
    and democracy, 547–48
    economic policy of, 549–50
    education policy of, 550
    establishment of, 544, 545
    foreign policy of, 551–52
    and Islamic politics in the Middle East, 299
    and Israel, 546
    and Jordanian Spring, 549
    and the Muslim Brotherhood, 476, 544–46

Islamic Action Front (IAF) (*Cont.*)
  organizational structure of, 552–53
  and political economy of Islamic politics, 89, 92, 99, 102
  and redistribution, 103
  and secular parties, 552
  and *shari'ah*, 545, 549
  on status of women, 551
  and Zarqawi, 548–49
Islamic Alliance for the Liberation of Afghanistan, 474n11
Islamic Amal (Amal al-Islamiya), 518
Islamic Army in Iraq, 625
Islamic Association of Niger (AIN), 382
Islamic Awakening, 224, 225
The Islamic Awakening between Rejection and Extremism (Qaradawi), 224
Islamic Center Society (ICS) of the Muslim Brotherhood, 548
Islamic Centrist Party, 92
Islamic Charitable Imdad Association (Jam'iyat al-Imdad al-Khayriya al-Islamiya), 524
Islamic Constitution, 57
Islamic Constitutional Movement (Kuwait), 476
Islamic Consultative Assembly (Majiles), 243–44
Islamic Courts Union (ICU), 389
Islamic Da'wah Foundation, 591, 597
Islamic feminism, 119–21, 122n7
Islamic Front for Iraqi Resistance (JAAMI), 625, 626
Islamic Group, 482, 535. *See also* al-Jama'a al-Islamiya
Islamic Group (Lebanon), 476
Islamic Group of Ali Bapir, 619, 620, 627n7
Islamic Health Unit (Al-Hay'a al-Sahiya al-Islamiya), 524
Islami Chhatra Shibir (ICS), 325
Islamic Jihad Group, 210, 296, 603–14
Islamic Missionary and Training Institute, 597
Islamic Movement of Kurdistan (IMK), 618, 619
Islamic Movement of Uzbekistan (IMU), 313–14
Islamic Party (Great Britain), 284–85
Islamic Party of Azerbaijan (IPA), 315
Islamic Party of Malaysia (PAS), 588, 591, 592–93, 594, 596, 597, 598
Islamic Progressive Party, 35
Islamic Rebirth Party, 312, 313
Islamic Republican Party, 186, 196n52
Islamic Republic of Ichkeria, 317
Islamic Republic of Iran, 185. *See also* Iran
Islamic Republic Party, 249
Islamic Resistance Movement in Iraq, 626n1
Islamic Revolutionary Committees (al-Lijan al-Thawriya al-Islamiya), 518
Islamic Salvation Army (AIS), 297
Islamic Salvation Front (FIS), 63, 295, 297, 357, 362, 532–40, 542, 546
Islamic Society of North America (ISNA), 267, 268, 274
Islamic statehood
  and al-Banna's ideology, 131–34
  and Algeria, 356–57
  and Islam in North Africa, 355
  and Islam in Southeast Asia, 345
  and Khomeini, 188
  and Libya, 356
  and Mawdudi's ideology, 147–49
  and neo-Salafism, 375n1
Islamic Student Association, 237, 250–51
Islamic Tendency Movement. *See* Mouvement de la Tendence Islamique (MTI)
Islamic Thought Seminar, 214
"Islamic World's Democracy Deficit" (Freedom House), 69
Islamic Youth League of Malaysia (ABIM), 343
Islamic Youth Movement of Malaysia (ABIM), 591–92, 595
Islami Jama'at-i-Talaba (IJT), 581, 582, 585
Islami Jamhoori Ittihad (IJI), 583
Islamism. *See specific groups and movements*
Islamistische Partij (Belgium), 284
Islamist Party of Justice and Development (PJD), 363, 364, 370, 374, 375, 376n7
Islami Tehrik, 583
Islamitische Partij Deutschland, 285
Islamization process, 21–22, 302
"Islamology," 171
IslamOnline.net, 226
Islamophobia, 274
al-Islam wa al-Dimuqratiya (Bennabi), 217

al-Islam wa al-Nasraniya (`Abduh), 33
Islom Lashkeri, 313
Isma'il, Farid, 491
Israel
   Arabû Israeli conflict (1967), 605
   armed forces of, 526
   and ecumenical Islamic agenda, 304
   and Hamas, 505–14
   and Hizbullah, 518–19, 521–22, 523, 526–27
   and Islamic Action Front, 546
   Israeli-Palestinian conflict, 551–52
   and Lebanon, 516–23, 526–27
   Operation Cast Lead, 510
   and Palestine conflict, 83, 84
   and Qaradawi's ideology, 229
   and Qutb's ideology, 160
   and religious minorities, 290
   and Saudi-sponsored Arab peace initiative of 2002, 512
   and the Six Day War, 166, 494–95, 603–4, 605
   and suicide bombings, 506, 509, 510, 512, 526
   and Turkey, 434
   and violence associated with Muslim Brotherhood, 484–85
istihsan, 11
Istiqlal party, 359
istishab, 9
Italy, 281, 284
Itihad party, 139–40
Ittifaq al Muslimin, 309
Izala movement, 383
Izz-ad-Din al-Qassam Brigades (IQB), 505, 509, 510
'Izzat, Hiba Ra'uf, 116, 227

Jabatan Kemajuan Islam Malaysia (JAKIM), 596
al-Jabha al-Islamiya li al-Inqadh, 362
jabr-i tarikh (historical determinism), 172
Jackson, Sherman A., 2, 42–55
Jad, Islah, 117
Jadid movement, 309
jahiliyyah, 149, 166
Jaish-e-Mohammed, 637–38
al-Jama'a al-Islamiya
   and assassination of Sadat, 606–7
   cease-fire of, 609–10
   and democracy, 608
   and deradicatlization, 609–13
   emergence of, 606
   ideology of, 607–9, 610–11
   and Islamic politics in North Africa, 365
   and Islamic politics in the Middle East, 296
   and jihad, 608–9, 613
   and Moroccan elections, 535
   and religious revival in Egypt, 605
   and *shari`ah,* 608
   and socioeconomics of Egypt, 606
al-Jama`a al-Libiya al-Islamiya al-Muqatila, 356
al-Jama`a al-Salafi ya li al-Da`wa wa al-Qital, 362
Jama`at Ahl-i-Hadith, 583
al-Jama`at al-Islamiya al-Musallaha, 362
Jama'at al-Muslimin (Society of Muslims), 614n1
Jamâ`at al-Sirat al-Mustaqîm, 365
Jama`at Ansar al-Sunnah, 297
Jama`at-i Islami (JI), 214, 216, 574–86
   and the Chechen conflict, 319
   and constitutional politics, 576–79
   described, 574–75
   and Mawdudi, 144, 146, 147, 151–52
   and military dictatorships, 579–83
   and nationalism, 57
   and North American immigration, 266
   origin and purpose of, 575–76
   and the political center, 429
   and September 11 terrorist attacks, 583–84
   and the Soviet-Afghan War, 312, 464, 474
Jama'at of the Central Asian Mujahedin, 314
Jama'at Ulama-i-Hind (JUH), 575
Jama'at Ulama-i-Islam (JUI), 574, 576, 578
Jama`at Ulama-i-Islam-F, 583, 584, 585
Jama`at Ulama-i-Islam-S, 583
Jama'at Ulama-i-Pakistan (JUP), 574, 578, 583
Jamai, Aboubakr, 366
Jama`t Izalat al Bid`a wa Iqamat as Sunna, 383
Jamiati Islami, 464, 468
Jami'at ul-Ulama (Society of Muslim Scholars), 460, 469
Jamiatul-Ulema-e-Hind, 326

Jam'iyat al-Imdad al-Khayriya al-Islamiya, *524*
Japanese Americans, 285
Jasmine Revolution, 373
Al Jazeera, 226, 227, 420, 637
Jefferson, Thomas, 264
Jemaah Islamiyah group, 341, 346, 560, 590, 594, 639–40
Jeyshullah (Army of God), 315
Jibril, Mahmoud, 373–74
Jihad al-Bina, *524*
jihad and jihadists
   and Abdulaziz bin Muhammad, 412
   and Afghanistan, 453–56, 471–72
   Afghan jihadi groups, 464–66, 467
   al-Banna on purpose of, 485
   attraction of, 415
   and authoritarian controls, 617–20
   definition of, 616
   and deradicalization, 613
   and Egypt, 603–14
   and Hamas, 508, 509, 510, 511, 512
   and Hizbullah, 523, 528n8, 616
   integration of jihadists into society, 613
   in Iraq, 616–26
   and Mawdudi's ideology, 147–48
   as mobilization technique, 454, 471–72, 472n2
   and the Muslim Brotherhood, 482, 484–85
   and nationalism, 57
   and Pakistan, 574
   and political Islam, 3, 4
   and al-Qaeda, 616
   and Qutb, 163, 165, 618
   and radical militant Islamist agenda, 295–97
   recruitment of Muslim youths for, 465–66
   and Salafism, 365
   and Somalia, 389–90
   and sub-Saharan Africa, 389
   and tsarist Russia, 453
   and Tunisian development, 360
   and Turabi's ideology, 209, 210–11
   and Wahhabism, 412, 413, 414–15, 420
   al-Zawahiri on, 639
   See also specific organizations
Jihad Gang, 593
al-Jihad Group. *See* Islamic Jihad Group
Jihadi-Salafism, 38
Jihadist Martyrs Brigades in Iraq, 625
Jinnah, Fatimah, 152, 330, 578
Jinnah, Mohammed Ali, 576
jizyah, 149
Jobbik, 281
Johnson, Lyndon, 266
Jordan, 544–55
   and al-Banna's ideology, 131
   and apolitical Muslimhood agenda, 291
   constitution, 304n1
   economy of, 549–50
   elections and electoral law in, 545–47, 549, 553–54, 555n2
   and Hamas, 551
   and Israeli-Palestinian conflict, 551–52
   Jordanian Spring, 544, 549
   and the Muslim Brotherhood, 476
   and partisan Islamist agenda, 299
   and political economy of Islamic politics, 92
   and political economy of Islamism, 89, 93, 100, 104–5
   and "post-Islamism," 368
   and privatization, 101, 102
   and radical militant Islamist agenda, 296
   and redistribution, 103
   religiosity in, 545
   and *shari'ah*, 545, 549
   terrorist attacks in, 548
   women in, 551
   See also Islamic Action Front (IAF)
Judaism, 83, 256, 429
judicial reforms, 360
Juergensmeyer, Mark, 325, 484
jumud, 34
Jund al-Islam, 619
June War, 163
Juppé, Alain, 281
jurisprudence. *See fiqh*
justice, 23, 139, 172. *See also shari'ah*
Justice and Construction Party, 370, 373
Justice and Development Party (AKP), 423–37
   and center-periphery political relations, 427–28
   coup attempts against, 432
   and EU membership, 423, 432–33
   and foreign policy, 433–36

and freedom of religion, 424, 426, 427, 428, 431
and Islamic democracy, 77
and Islamic politics in North Africa, 370
and Islamic politics in the Middle East, 295
and Islamic statehood, 64, 65
and judicial reforms, 431, 432
and militant secularism, 426–27
and partisan Islamist agenda, 299–300
performance of, 430–31
and the political center, 428–30
and political economy of Islamic politics, 89, 102
political ideology of, 425–26
and privatization, 102
reformist agenda of, 423–24, 436
Justice and Benevolence Party, 535
"just war" theory, 147–48

Kabardino-Balkaria, 319
Kabir, Bhuian Md Monoar, 335n2
Kabul University, 462
Kadets, 309
Kadhi courts, 386
Kadivar, Mohsen, 191, 241
Kadyrov, Ahkmed, 317
Kadyrov, Ramazan, 317
kafir, 146, 149
kafirs (nonbelievers, heathens), 472n2
Kalin, Ibrahim, 3, 423–37
Kalla, Yusuf, 563
Kandhalvi, Maulana Muhammad Ilyas al-, 575
Karama Party (Egypt) (*See* Dignity Party), 495, 496
Karbala Brigades, 625
Karimov, Islam, 313
Karlekar, Hiranmay, 325
Karzai, Hamid, 471, 472, 474n14
Kasavyurt agreement, 317
Kashani, Seyyed Abolqasem, 194n11
Kashf al-Asrar (Khomeini), 182, 183
Kashmir, 330
Kasravi, Ahmad, 194n7
Kassim, Mouloud, 357
Kateb, Faiz Muhammad, 458–59
Kawakibi, Abd al-Rahman al-, 220
Kayhan-e Farhangi, 250–51

al-kaynunah al-rabbaniya (divine immanence), 163, 164
Kazakh people, 309
Kazakhstan, 312, 313, 314
Kazim, Safinaz, 116
Keane, John, 69
Kedourie, Elie, 74
Kemal, Seyyid Ahmad, 31
Kenya, 381, 386
Kepel, Gilles, 92, 296, 370
Kerlos IV, pope, 46
Kerry, John, 273
Keyhan, 238
Khadija (wife of Prophet Muhammad), 419
Khalid, Khalid Muhammad, 58
Khalifa, Abd al-Rahman, 553
Khalili, Ahmad al-, 225
Khamenei, Ali, 186, 188, 190, 192, 198n85, 253, 401–2, 404, 407, 520–21
Khan, Amanullah, 456, 457–59, 460
Khan, Ayyub, 60, 330, 332
Khan, Habibullah, Amir of Afghanistan, 455–56
Khan, Hashim, 461
Khan, Imran, 585
Khan, Khan Abdul Ghaffar, 460
Khan, Liaqat, 332, 576
Khan, Nasrullah, 456
Khan, Suheil, 272
Khan, Wahiduddin, 152
Khan, Yahya, 332
Khan, Zahir, 461, 462
Khatami, Mohammad, 237–44
  background, 237
  distinctive discourse of, 243–44
  and globalization, 64
  and Iranian elections, 405–6
  and Iranian governmental structures, 402, 404–5
  and the Iranian reform movement, 238–42
  and the Iranian Revolution, 238
  and Khomeini's ideology, 191
  legacy of, 242–43
  and political Islam, 64
  and Soroush's ideology, 254
Khatami, Mohammad Reza, 242
Khatami, Rouhollah, 237

Khatmiyyah tariqa, 204, 301
Khawarj, 166
Khayyat, Haytham Al-, 303
khilafat, 147, 148
Khomeini, Ahmad, 237
Khomeini, Mostafa, 195n33
Khomeini, Ruhollah
 and al-Banna, 129
 background, 180–81
 and constitutionalism, 182–83
 death, 251
 exile, 183
 and Ghannushi's ideology, 216
 and Gnosticism, 258n2
 and Hizbullah, 517–18, 519, 520, 528n3
 and Iranian governmental structures, 402
 key quotes, 180
 and Khatami, 238
 legacy of, 190–92
 and Mawdudi's ideology, 148
 and political Islam, 61
 and "post-Islamism," 368
 and privatization, 100
 and revolutionary sentiment, 184–85
 and Sharia'ati's ideology, 171, 177
 and Soroush's ideology, 247–48
 and theocracy in Iran, 401
 and *vali-ye faqih* concept, 186–87, 187–90
Khwarazmi, Muhammad Ibn Musa al-, 307
Kimmage, Daniel, 616–17
King Abdullah University for Science and Technology (KAUST), 421
Kirghizstan, 313–14
Kirkpatrick, Jean, 68
Kitab al Asrar (Sadra), 192
Kitab al-Tawhid, 29
Kiyan, 251
Kjaersgaard, Pia, 284
kofar, 293
Kok, Wim, 282–83
Kommando Jihad, 346
kopvoddentax, 281
Kosovo, 282
Krekar, Mullah, 619, 620
Kriegel, Blandine, 325
Kufah, 11
kufr (disbelief), 137, 139, 147, 466

Kumpulan Militan Malaysia (KMM), 593, 594
Künkler, Mirjam, 390n6
Kurdistan Democratic Party (KDP), 619, 625
Kurdistan Regional Government (KRG), 619, 620
kutub al-raqa'iq (moralistic pamphlets), 19
Kuwait, 118, 417
 and apolitical Muslimhood agenda, 291, 292
 constitution, 304n1
 Islamic Constitutional Movement, 476
 and partisan Islamist agenda, 299
Kyarov, Anatoly, 319

Laitin, D. D., 91
Larbaoui, Omar, 357
Lashkar-e-Tayyaba, 637–38
Laskar Jihad, 346
Lauzière, Henry, 36
law, 50. *See also shari'ah*
The Lawful and the Prohibited in Islam (Qaradawi), 223, 224
Layachi, Azzedine, 3, 352–78
Layth, Abu, 297
Lazard, Gilbert, 170
Lebanon, 516–28
 armed forces of, 520, 526
 and armed resistance agenda, 298
 economic deprivation in, 517
 Islamic Group, 476
 and Islam in Europe, 287
 and Israel, 516–23, 526–27
 jihad and jihadists in, 616
 nationalism in, 521
 and political economy of Islamism, 92, 93
 and "post-Islamism," 368
 and religious minorities, 290
 sovereignty of, 520
 and statist secularreligious agenda, 293
 and Syria, 526–27
 and UN Special Tribunal for Lebanon, 525
 See also Hizbullah
Leenders, Reinoud, 525, 527
legal authority, 17–18. *See also shari'ah*
legal centralism, 43
legal monism, 43–51, 54n32
legal pluralism, 46

Lenin, Vladimir Ilyich, 309
Leninism, 176
Le Party des Musulman de France, 284
Le Pen, Jean-Marie, 284
A Letter Concerning Toleration (Locke), 79–80
Leviathan, 53n9
Levitt, Matthew, 554
Lewis, Bernard, 68, 74, 77, 78, 268
liberal democracy, 70, 151, 252, 383–88
liberalism, 76, 77–78, 119
liberation, personal, 173–74
liberation movements, 248, 299
liberation theology, 247
Liberia, 390n5
Libya
  and apolitical Muslimhood agenda, 291
  constitution, 304n1
  and democracy, 390n7
  independence, 52n4
  and Islamic statehood, 355–56
  and Islam in North Africa, 353
  and nationalism, 60, 354
  and partisan Islamist agenda, 299–300
  and "post-Islamism," 367, 368, 369, 370, 374
  and postrevolution elections, 22, 24
  and radical militant Islamist agenda, 296, 297
  and Sufi resurgence, 373–74
  and terrorist groups, 389
Liddle, R. William, 571n1
The Life and Death of Democracy (Keane), 69
Ligachev, Yegor, 316
Lijst Pim Fortuyn (LPF), 283, 284
Lilla, Mark, 79
Lim, H., 100
linguistics, 15
Linrung, Tamsil, 567
literacy, 95–97, 96
Livingstone, Ken, 227
lobbying Islamic agenda, 302–3
local Islamic groups, 295
Locke, John, 72, 79–80
logic, 162. *See also* reason and rationality
London bombings, 230, 285, 635, 637
Luxor massacre (1997), 609, 611

Ma'alim fi al-Tariq (Qutb), 483
Macarius III, pope, 46

Madagascar, 379
Madani, Abbasi, 63, 357
Madani, Muhammad ibn Khalifa al-, 372
Madaniya order, 372
Madares al-Mahdi (Al-Mahdi Schools), 524
Madares al-Mustafa (Al-Mustafa Schools), 524
madhhab (school of law), 14–16, 29, 34
madrasas, 461, 465
Madrid bombings, 285, 635
Maghreb, 352–54, 361–62, 367, 369–70, 375, 388–89, 532–43, 638
Mahathir, Mohammad, 63–64, 343–46, 589, 592–94, 597–98
Mahdavi, Mjotaba, 3, 180–99
Mahdi, Muhammad Ahmad al-, 28, 204, 400
Mahdi, Sadiq al-, 62, 442
Mahdi Army of Moqtada al-Sadr, 617, 625
Al-Mahdi Schools (Madares al- Mahdi), 524
Mahdism, 204
Mahfudh, Sahal, 562, 563, 572n15
Mahmood, Shah, 461
Mahsouli, Sadeq, 198n84
Majali, Abd al-Salam al-, 547
Majelis Mujahidin Indonesia (MMI), 346
Majelis Ulama Indonesia (MUI), 346, 348
majils, 187–88, 193, 329
Majlis Kebangsaan Halehwal Islam Malaysia, 596
majoritarian rule, 23
Malaviya, Madanmohan, 326
Malaysia, 63, 340, 587–98
  constitution of, 587
  and co-optation strategy, 595–97
  ethnic emphasis in, 587
  and federal methods of control, 594–95, 597–98
  and globalization, 64
  and identity politics, 340–41
  Intra-Malay-Muslim Competition, 588–90
  and Islamic feminism, 120
  and Islamic political issues, 345–48
  and majority Muslim populations, 342–44
  Malay constitution, 587–88
  Pan-Malaysian Islamic Party, 476
  and political economy of Islamism, 105
  and political parties, 344–45
  and radical violent movements, 593–94

Malaysia (*Cont.*)
  and *shari`ah*, 24
  and student movements, 590–93
  and United Malay National Organization (UMNO), 587–93
Malaysian Institute of Islamic Understanding (IKIM), 596, 597
Malaysian Militant Group (KMM), 593, 594
Mali, 385, 389, 390n6
Malik, Abdul, 469
Maliki, Nouri al-, 297, 383
Maliki school of jurisprudence, 28, 45, 215, 379
Malt, Ahmed al-, 486
Manai, Ahmed, 213
al-Manar, 34, 35
al-Manar al-Jadid, 230
Al-Manar Television, 524
Mansour, Hamza, 554
Maqdisi, Abu Muhammad al-, 624
Mardin, Serif, 427
marja-e-taqlid, 400
marriage, 46–49, 228, 491
martyrdom, 23, 161, 229
Martyrs Foundation (Mu'assasat al-Shahid), 524
Marv, 307
Marxism, 75, 107n38, 172–73, 175–77, 191, 246–50, 257, 291, 326
Masalha, Nael, 547
Mashariqi thought, 216
Mashur, Mustafa, 224
"Masked Dogmatism" (Soroush), 258n3
Maskhadov, Aslan, 318
maslahah (consideration of public interest), 34
Masoud, Tarek, 2, 3, 89–111, 475–97
Massignon, Christian, 170
Massignon, Louis, 170
mass media, 226–27, 231
Massoud, Ahmad Shah, 464, 467, 468
materialism, 136, 208–9
Mauritania, 381, 382
Mauritius, 390n6
Mawardi, al-, 132, 141
Mawdudi, Sayyid Abu al-`Ala, 3, 48–49, 140, 144–53, 213, 575, 576–77, 578, 584, 591–92
  and al-Banna, 129, 140
  background, 144–45, 326
  founding of Jama`at-e Islami, 324
  and Ghannushi's ideology, 214, 216
  and Islam as a way of life, 145–47
  and Islamic politics in Sudan, 447
  and the Islamic state, 147–49
  and Islam in South Asia, 324–25, 329, 331
  and Pakistani politics, 332
  and Qutb's ideology, 163, 164
  and role of non Muslims, 149–50
  and stereotypes of Islam, 334
  and western modernity, 150–51
May 23 Movement, 239
Mazari, Ali, 468
Mecca, Saudi Arabia, 416
media, 226–27, 231, 284, 420, 448, 456–57, 595
Medina, Saudi Arabia, 11
Medvedev, Dmitry, 318
Mehden, Fred R. von der, 3, 4, 340–51, 587–98
Mehdi, Mohammad T., 267
Mejelle, 20
Melville, Herman, 264
Memali Incident (1985), 593, 594
Memorial Institute for the Prevention of Terrorism (MIPT), 622–23
Meseimi, Hayat al-, 551
Messiri, Abd al-Wahhab al-, 219
metaphilosophy, 247
metaphysics, 258n2. *See also* Sufism
Middle East, 289–304
  and apolitical Muslimhood agenda, 290–92
  and armed resistance agenda, 298–99
  complexity of Islam in, 289–90
  and decolonization, 282
  and democracy, 69
  and ecumenical Islamic agenda, 303–4
  and lobbying Islamic agenda, 302–3
  and Modernist-Salafiya movement, 36
  and partisan Islamist agenda, 299–300
  peace in, 435–36
  and radical militant Islamist agenda, 294–98
  and ruling Islamic agenda, 300–302
  and statist secularreligious agenda, 292–94
  and Turkey, 435–36
  See also specific countries

Middle East Peace Process, 269
migrant workers, 160
Mikaelian, Shoghig, 4, 516–28
Milestones (Qutb), 165, 483
militancy, 229
Militant Clerics' Socieity, 405
Militant-Salafism, 27, 38
military rulers. *See specific leaders and countries*
Miller, Judith, 494
Milosevic, Slobodan, 282
Milton-Edwards, Beverley, 3–4, 505–14
al-minhaj al-islami (Islamic way), 163, 164
Ministry of Religious Affairs (Tunisia), 360
Mir Arab Madrassa, 311
Mirghani, Mohammed Osman al-, 204
Mirza, Iskander, 577
Misrawi, Zuhairi, 567, 572n11
Mitchell, Richard, 478
Mixed Courts (Egypt), 20
modernity and modernization
    and Afghanistan, 456, 461, 462, 472
    and Algeria, 358
    and democracy, 68, 71
    and gender issues, 119
    and the Iranian Revolution, 186
    and Islamic democracy, 74, 78
    and Islamic nationalism, 60
    and Khatami's ideology, 244
    and Mawdudi, 145, 326
    and Modernist-Salafiya movement, 27–38
    and Nahdlatul Ulama, 558
    and political Islam, 61
    and Qaradawi, 222, 231
    and radical nationalism, 59
    and secularism, 81–82
    and *shari`ah*, 7, 19–22
    and Tunisia, 360–62
    and Turabi's ideology, 204–5
    and Turkey, 427, 429, 431, 433
    and Western influence, 150–51
Mohamad V, King of Morocco, 58, 359
Mohamad VI, King of Morocco, 364, 365, 371, 541
Mohammed, Khaled Sheikh, 634
Mohtashami, Ali-Akbar, 517, 523, 528n3
Mo`in, Mostafa, 242

Mojahedin of the Islamic Revolution Organization, 196n52
monarchism, 182, 184, 185
Mongol invasions, 80
monopoly powers, 50
Montazeri, Hossein-Ali, 189, 198n85
Montazeri, Mohammad, 237, 517
Moore, Barrington, 191
Moorish Science Temple, 265
moral law, 33–34
Mourou, Abd al-Fattah, 214, 218
Morocco
    and apolitical Muslimhood agenda, 291
    and Arab Spring, 540, 541
    constitution, 304n1
    and co-option of Islamist parties, 537
    elections in, 532, 535–36
    emergence of Islamist movement in, 542
    and grassroots Islam, 362
    independence, 52n4
    and Islamic feminism, 120
    and Islamic politics in North Africa, 359–60, 364–66
    and Islamic statehood, 356
    and Islam in Europe, 286, 287
    and Islam in North Africa, 353
    and Modernist-Salafiya movement, 37
    and nationalism, 60, 353, 354
    and political economy of Islamism, 105
    and political Islam, 65
    and "post-Islamism," 367–68, 369, 370, 374–75
    and religious minorities, 290
    and religious political parties, 352
    and Sufi resurgence, 371, 373, 374
    and violence, 539, 540
Moro Islamic Liberation Front (MILF), 350
Moro National Liberation Front (MNLF), 350
Morsi, Mohammed, 65, 92, 99–100, 614
Mosaddeq, Mohammed, 182–83, 195n12
Mossad, 227
Motahhari, Morteza, 247–48, 252
Mousavi, Mir Hossein, 82, 187, 238, 242, 406
Moussa, Amro, 495
Moussa, Muhammad Abdel-Halim, 610
Moussalli, Ahmad, 3, 129–43
Mouvement de la Tendence Islamique (MTI), 63, 216–17, 361, 533, 534, 538

Mouvement Populaire Démocratique Consitutionnel (MPDC), 535
Movement for a Peaceful Society (Algeria), 476, 536
Movement for Restoration of Democracy, 582
Movement for Unity and Jihad in West Africa (MUJWA), 389
Movement of Islamic Action of Iraq, 625
Movement of Society for Peace (MSP), 299, 363, 367
Movement of Society of Peace and Islah, 370
Mozambique, 379, 384
muʿamalat, 16, 19
Muʾassasat al-Jarha (Foundation for the Wounded), 524
Muʾassasat al-Shahid (Martyrs Foundation), 524
Mubarak, Hosni, 94, 95, 211, 224, 299, 475, 477, 480, 486
Mudawwana, 119
Mughal Empire, 144
Mughni, Haya al-, 118
Mughniyé, Imad, 527
muhajirin (Muslim refugee-warrior), 464, 465
Muhammad, Elijah, 265
Muhammad, Husein, 568, 570
Muhammad, Mian Tufail, 580
Muhammad, Prophet, 8, 10, 18, 32, 57, 334, 440
Muhammad, Warith Deen, 267, 269
Muhammadiyah, 345
Muhammad's Youth, 480
Muhawarat al-muslih wa al-muqallid (Rida), 34
mujaddid, 28
Mujaddidi Naqshbandiya, 29
mujahadin, 210, 312, 465, 467, 468, 474n12
Mujaheddin-e Khalq, 408
al-Mujahid (el-Moujahed), 175
Mujani, Saiful, 571n1
Mujiburrahman, Sheikh, 332, 333
mujtahid, 28, 175, 400, 409n4
al-Mujtamaʿ al-Tunisi: Tahlil Hadari (Ghannushi), 217
mukus, 8
Mumbai attacks (2008), 639
munasaha, 297

Muqarabat fi al-ʿAlmaniyya wa al-Mujtamaʿ al-Madani (Ghannushi), 219
Mursi, Muhammad, 475, 477, 495
Musaddiq, Muhammad, 169
Musahiban dynasty, 459, 460–63, 473n5
Musavi, Mir-Hossein. *See* Mousavi, Mir Hossein
Musawi, Hussein al-, 518
Musawi, Sayyed Abbas al-, 517–19, 523
Musharraf, Pervez, 331, 583
Muslim (magazine), 326
Muslim American Society (MAS), 268–69
Muslim Brotherhood, 475–97
 and Afghani youth, 462
 and al-Banna, 130–31, 131–32, 134, 140
 and apolitical Muslimhood agenda, 291
 and Arabization in North Africa, 375–76n5
 and Arab Spring, 554
 and the caliphate, 132–33
 charity arm of, 548
 described, 475–77
 and education, 550
 and elections, 106n5, 493–96, 500n55
 founding of, 475
 and gender issues, 116, 120–21, 208
 and Ghannushi's ideology, 217
 governance of, 480–81
 and Hamas, 505
 and immigration to North America, 266
 and Iraq, 617
 and Islamic democracy, 73, 77
 and Islamic reformism, 48
 and Islam in North Africa, 356
 and Islamist-Salafism, 27, 37
 and Jordan, 544–46, 547–49
 and Morocco, 364
 and Muslim Youth, 464
 and nationalism, 56
 organizational strength of, 475
 organizational structure of, 477–81
 and partisan Islamist agenda, 299
 political arm of (Freedom and Justice Party), 475
 and political economy of Islamism, 89, 90, 91, 92, 94, 95, 98–100, 105
 and political Islam, 62–63, 65
 and political moderation, 481–93
 and "post-Islamism," 370

priorities of, 585
and privatization, 101, 102
and Qaradawi, 222, 223, 224, 225
and Qutb, 160, 165
recruitment, 478–80
and redistribution, 103–4
and religious revival, 606
and ruling Islamic agenda, 301
scope and roles of, 475
and the Soviet-Afghan War, 312
and Sudan, 443
tensions within, 496–97
and Turabi, 206–7, 208
and violence, 608–9, 613
and Yemen, 441–42
and *zakat*, 107n38
Muslim commonwealth, 209
Muslim law, 8–9. *See also shari`ah*
Muslim League, 144, 327, 576, 578, 582
Muslimov, S., 311
Muslim Politics (Eickelman and Piscatori), 76
Muslim Public Affairs Council (MPAC), 268
Muslim Public Service Network (MPSN), 275
Muslim Sisters, 116
Muslim Spiritual Boards, 311
Muslim Students Association (MSA), 266–67
Muslim Women's Society, 116
Muslim Youth (al-Shabab al-Muslem), 518
Muslim Youth (Jawanani Musalman), 462, 463, 464
Mustafa, Shukri, 614n1
Al-Mustafa Schools (Madares al-Mustafa), 524
Mutahhari, Murtada, 174
Mutahiddah Majlis-i-Amal (MMA), 583–84, 585
Mu'tazilis, 33–34
Muttaheda Majlis-e-Amal (MMA), 331
Muzadi, Hasyim, 560, 562, 569
Muzadi, Muchith, 569
Myanmar. *See* Burma-Myanmar
mysticism, 181, 255, 292. *See also* Sufism
Mzali, Mohamed, 216

Nabulsi, Sulayman al-, 545
Nachtwey, J., 93
Nader Khan, Muhammad, 459–61, 473n5, 473n6
Nadwi, Abu al-Hasan al-, 213

Nadwi, Abullais Islahi, 328
Naguib, Muhammad, 160
Nahdah Party, 63, 105, 361, 367, 370, 373, 534, 536–38, 540–42
Nahdlatul Ulama (NU), 558–71
  and Bali bombings (2002), 560
  and competing parties, 564–65
  establishment of, 558
  identification of Indonesians with, 571n1
  ideological tensions in, 565–67
  and Islamic politics in Southeast Asia, 344, 345
  and modernity, 558
  and pluralism, 567–69
  and *shari`ah*, 566–67
  and terrorist attacks of 9/11, 559–60
  and Wahid presidency, 561–63
Nahhas, Mustafa al-, 483
Na`im, Abdullahi an-, 50, 51, 65, 113
Na'ini, Mohammad, 400
Najaf, Iran, 183, 195n33
Najeebullah, Mohammad, 467, 468
Najib, Tun Razak, 346
Nalchik uprising, 319
Namangani, Jumma, 313, 314
Napoleonic Code (1804), 20
Nasar, Mustafa bin Abd al-Qadir Setmarian (Abu Musab al-Suri), 634, 635–36
naskh (abrogation), 10
Nasr, Vali, 82, 153n2
Nasrallah, Hassan, 518, 523, 525, 528, 617
Nasser, Gamal Abdel
  and al-Banna, 131
  and Algerian revolution, 358
  and Ghannushi's ideology, 212–13
  imprisonment of Islamists, 101
  and the Muslim Brotherhood, 483
  and Qaradawi's ideology, 222–23
  and Qutb's ideology, 160, 165
  secular/nationalist emphasis of, 604, 605
  and statist secularreligious agenda, 293–94
National Alliance, 284
National Assembly, 331
National Association of the Zawyas, 372
National Awami Party, 578
National Coalition to Protect Political Freedom (NCPPF), 270
National Congress (NCP) in Sudan, 442

National Congress of the Chechen People, 317
National Council of 'Ulama' (MUI), 567
National Council on Islamic Affairs, 267
National Covenant (Egypt), 58
National Democratic Party (Egypt), 494, 610
National Democratic Party (NPD), 284
National Democratic Rally (RND), 363, 376n6
National Democrats (Sweden), 281
National Forces Alliance, 373–74
National Front (France), 281
National Front for the Salvation of Libya, 373
National Front Party, 373
National Islamic Front (NIF), 3, 62, 206, 299, 441–42, 443, 447
nationalism
   in Afghanistan, 455, 456, 461
   and al-Banna's ideology, 134
   Arab nationalism, 521
   and Hamas, 507
   and the Iranian Revolution, 186
   and Islamic democracy, 79
   and Islamic radicalism, 58–61
   and Islamic statehood, 56
   and Islam in Central Asia, 311, 312
   and Islam in Europe, 281
   and Islam in North Africa, 353–55
   and Islam in Southeast Asia, 340
   in Lebanon, 521
   in Malaysia, 590
   and Modernist-Salafiya movement, 38
   nation-states, 42–52, 43–44, 50–51, 50–52, 79, 231
   in Pakistan, 579
   and political Islam, 56–58, 65
   and Qutb's ideology, 159–60
   and sub-Saharan Africa, 381–82
   See also Islamic statehood
National Liberation Front (FLN), 63, 356, 362, 363
National Origins Act, 265
National Outlook Movement of Turkey, 425
National Salvation Party, 117
National Salvation Revolution in Sudan, 440–41
National Unionist Party (NUP), 204
National Union of Popular Forces (UNFP), 359
Nation of Islam, 265, 267

natural law, 33
Navab Safavi, Mojtaba, 194n11
Nawawi, Muhammad, 568
Nawid, Senzil, 458
Nazarbaev, Nursultan, 313
The Neglected Duty (Faraj), 608
neoconservatism, 191–92
Neo-Destour Party, 354
neofundamentalism, 466, 470
neoliberalism, 1, 191, 227
neo-Salafism, 367, 372, 375n1
Netanyahu, Benjamin, 227
Netherlands, 280–87
Netherlands Institute for War Documentation (NIOD), 282–83
New Religious Pluralism (Banchoff), 285
New World Order, 219
New York Times, 270, 274, 399, 493–94
nifaz-i Shari'ah, 147
Niger, 384, 385
Nigeria, 118, 387
Nimeiri, Gaafar, 206, 442–46, 449
1920 Revolutionary Brigades, 625, 626n1
nizam-i mustafa, 147
Nizam-i-Mustafa Tehrik (Movement for the System of Muhammad), 581
nizam-i zindagi, 145
Nomani, Manzur, 326
nongovernmental organizations (NGOs), 207, 219, 233n32
non-Muslims, 149–50, 224, 290. *See also* pluralism, religious
nonviolent Islamic groups, 295
Nord, Liga, 281
Norris, Pippa, 286
North Africa, 352–75
   and decolonization, 282
   and grassroots Islam, 361–62
   and Islam in Europe, 281, 284
   and Modernist-Salafiya movement, 36–37
   and "post-Islamism," 367–74
   and the Sanusiya movement, 30
   See also specific countries
North American Islamic Trust (NAIT), 267
North American Muslims, 263–76
   background of, 263–65
   and civil rights activism, 267–72
   and impact of September 11 attacks, 272–75

and Islamic feminism, 123n18
modern Islamic community, 266–67
prospects for, 275–76
and westernizing influence, 59
North Atlantic Treaty Organization (NATO), 282, 295, 434, 621
North Caucasus, 308, 316
Northern League, 284
Northern Nigeria, 388
North Ossetia, 319
North-West Frontier Province (NWFP), 559
Nouri, Ali Akbar Nategh, 239
Nouri, Fazlollah, 182
Al-Nour Radio Station, 524
Numayri, Ja'far, 62
Nuqrashi, Mahmud Fahmi al-, 482
Nuri, Ali Akbar Nateq, 254
Nuri, Fazlollah, 400
Nur Party, 92, 105
Nursi, Said, 314
Nyerere, Julius, 386

Obama, Barack, 274–75, 399, 434, 471
Objectives Resolution, 329–30
Ocalan, Abdullah, 438n16
oil resources, 240
Oklahoma City bombing, 269
Olesen, Asta, 454
oligarchy, 198n84
Omar, Mohammed, 468–69, 633
Onians, Charles, 494
Organization of 1965, 483
Organization of the Islamic Conference (OIC), 60, 210, 274–75, 342, 387
Organization of the People's Mujahedin, 249
Orthodox Egyptian Coptic Church, 46–49, 51
Oslo peace process, 507, 511, 512
Osman, Fathi Muhammad, 215
Osman, Omar, 266
Ottoman Empire, 30, 31, 36, 144, 210, 265, 281, 327
Ozal, Turgut, 425, 429, 438n16

Pahlavi, Reza (son of deposed shah), 408
Pahlavi dynasty, 181
Pakistan, 574–86
  and Afghan jihadi groups, 464, 465
  and Bangladesh, 331–33, 335

  constitutionalism and civil war, 576–79
  constitution of, 152
  creation of, 575–76
  drone strikes in, 637
  Federally Administered Tribal Areas of, 637, 638
  and gender issues, 118
  and immigration to North America, 266
  independence, 52n4
  Inter Service Intelligence Directorate (ISI), 464, 465, 467, 469
  and Islamic politics in South Asia, 324, 325–26, 328
  and Islamic statehood, 60
  and Islam in Europe, 286, 287
  and Mawdudi, 144, 146, 152–53, 327
  military dictatorship, 579–83
  and minority rights, 149
  and Mujahiidin, 465, 474n12
  and non-Muslim minorities, 149–50
  and Omar's Taliban movement, 468–69
  Peshawar, 464, 466, 474n11, 630
  and political Islam, 62
  and al-Qaeda, 638–39
  and radical militant Islamist agenda, 295
  religious education in, 214
  and secular authoritarianism in Central Asia, 314
  and September 11 terrorist attacks, 583–84
  and the Soviet-Afghan War, 312
  suicide bombers in, 639
  support for the Pashtun, 467–68
  Taliban in, 637
  and transformation of Jama'at-e Islami, 329–31
  tribal areas, 637, 638
Pakistan Democratic Movement, 332
Pakistan National Alliance (PNA), 581
Pakistan People's Party (PPP), 60, 332, 578, 580–81, 582
Palestine and Palestinians, 92, 229, 484–85, 505–14
Palestine Liberation Organization (PLO), 210, 505, 506, 507–8, 511, 514
Palestinian Authority (PA), 505, 507, 513, 514
Palestinian Security Forces (PSF), 510
pan-Arabism, 212–13, 356, 604. See also Arab nationalism

pancasila, 342–43, 344
Pan-Malaysian Islamic Party, 476
Parawansa, Kofifah Indar, 563
parliamentary systems, 152, 313, 343
Parti Islam Se-Malaysia (PAS), 57, 63–64, 345–47, 588–90, 591–93, 594, 596–97, 598
Partij voor de Vrijheid, 281
partisanship, 139–40, 299–300
Party of Freedom (PVV), 283
Party of Islam, 312, 315
Party of Justice (PK), 564
Party of Justice and Development (PJD), 89, 535–37, 539–40, 541, 542
Party of National Awakening (PKB), 561, 562, 563, 566
Party of Unity and Development (PPP), 561
Pasha, Ahmad Taymur, 130
Pasha, Isma`il Sidqi, 140
Pasha, Muhammad Ali, 32
Pashtu language, 461
Pashtun tribes, 454–60, 467, 469, 471
Pashtu Tulana (Pashtu Academy), 461
patriarchal ideology, 112–16, 118–21, 123n23
Patriot Act, 273
Patriotic Union of Kurdistan (PUK), 619
Pearl, Daniel, 639
People of the Book, 47, 49
Peoples Democratic Party of Afghanistan, 463–64, 465, 466, 467
People's Mojahedin Organization, 189
Pepinsky, T., 103
perestroika, 312, 315
Permanent Committee of Ifta', 419
Perry, E. J., 91
Personal Status Regime, 49, 216, 220
Pertubuhan Kebajakan Islam Se-Malaysia (PERKIM), 592
Petraeus, David, 626
Philippines, 340, 348–49, 350
philosophy, 162, 181, 289
pilgrimage, 37
Pipes, Daniel, 75
piracy, 389–90
Piscatori, James, 76
Platonic philosophy, 162
pluralism, religious
  and apolitical Muslimhood agenda, 290
  and complexity of Middle East Islam, 90
  and ecumenical Islamic agenda, 303
  and Indonesia, 567–69
  and Iraqi Kurdistan, 618
  and Islamic democracy, 80
  and Islam in Europe, 278, 285–86
  and Islam in Southeast Asia, 345, 346
  and Khomeini's ideology, 192
  and the Muslim Brotherhood, 140
  and Qaradawi's ideology, 224, 230–31
  and Saudi Arabia, 413
  and Soroush's ideology, 254, 255–56, 257
  and Turkey, 426
Poe, Edgar Allan, 264
Poland, 281
political economy, 2, 89–105
  and economic platforms of Islamist parties, 97–100
  and institutional support for Islamism, 94–97
  and privatization, 100–102
  and redistribution, 102–4
  and socioeconomic supports for Islamism, 90–93
political Islam
  and al-Banna's ideology, 133
  defined, 1, 375n1
  and globalization, 64–65
  impact in the Maghreb, 352–53
  and Qutb's ideology, 159
  in South Asia, 324–26, 326–27, 327–33, 333–35
  and the state, 56–66
  and sub-Saharan Africa, 388–90
  and Sufi resurgence, 370–74
political parties
  and apolitical Muslimhood agenda, 292
  and Islam in Europe, 287
  and Islam in Southeast Asia, 344–45
  and Mawdudi's ideology, 148
  platforms of, 97–100
  and political economy of Islamism, 97–100
  See also specific party names
political rights, 118
"Politics as a Vocation" (Weber), 243
polyarchy, 70
polytheism, 29, 137
Popper, Karl, 248

Popular Arabic and Islamic Conference (PAIC), 210
populism, 21, 183, 184, 192, 330
positive law, 228
positivism, 253
post-Cold War era, 83
postcolonial era, 81–82, 353, 380–83
post-Islamism, 353, 367–74
postpositivism, 248
poverty, 92, 94, 95–97, 104–5, 107n38, 319, 349
Powell, Colin, 620
Preachers Not Judges (Hudaybi), 483
precedents, 14
predestination, 257
premodern Muslim states, 44–45
privatization, 100–102, 105
Prodi, Romano, 279
progressivism, 60
property rights, 100
proselytism, 210, 226–27
Prosperous Justice Party (PKS), 476, 564–65
Protestantism, 43, 79, 285
Pruzan-Jorgensen, Julie E., 119
purification, 192
Puritanical-Salafism, 27, 37–38
Pusat Penyelidekan Islam Malaysia, 596–97
Pushkin, Alexander, 320n6

Qaddafi, Muammar, 227, 294, 353, 355–56, 369, 372–74, 389, 390n7, 560
qadhf (defamation), 18
Qadianis, 150
Qadi justice, 7, 9
Qadiriya order, 30
al-Qaeda (al-Qa'ida), 630–40
 and Afghanistan jihad, 474n13, 621
 and al-Jama'a, 611
 base membership of, 633–34, 635
 and Bin Laden, 631, 632–33
 declining support for, 639–40
 establishment of, 469, 632
 expansion of, 470
 four main phases of, 631–32
 goals of, 632
 and Hamas, 508
 ideology of, 632, 635, 636
 infrastructure of, 637
 in Iraq, 4
 and Islamic Jihad Group (al-Jihad Group), 607
 and Islamic politics in Central Asia, 314
 and Islamic politics in North Africa, 367
 and Islamic politics in the Middle East, 295–96
 and Islam in North Africa, 363
 and jihad, 616
 in the Maghreb, 297, 388–89, 638
 and Malaysian Islamic radicals, 594
 and Mawdudi's ideology, 149, 152
 media production of, 637
 and the Muslim Brotherhood, 482
 network of, 630, 631, 632, 634, 636
 origins of, 463, 467
 and Pakistan, 574, 585, 638–39
 present state of, 636–40
 al-Qa'ida in Iraq (AQI), 623–26
 resurgence of, 471
 and secular authoritarianism in Central Asia, 313
 and Taliban, 637
 and terrorist attacks of 9/11, 470
 vanguard of, 632
 Western European recruits for, 637–38
 and Zarqawi, 548–49, 624, 628n15
Qaedat al-Jihad (the Base of Jihad), 607
Qajar dynasty, 181
Qaradawi, Yusuf al-, 222–32
 background, 222
 and democracy and pluralism, 230–31
 and ecumenical Islamic agenda, 303
 and electronic networking, 226–27
 and gender issues, 230
 and Ghannushi, 214
 and legal authority, 49
 and moderation, 229
 and the Muslim Brotherhood, 476, 484
 and North American immigration, 266
 on punishment for adultery, 54n27
 and renewal of Islamic jurisprudence, 228–29
 support for revolutions, 23
 on use of violence, 229–30
Al-Qaradawi Center for Islamic Moderation and Renewal, 226
Qaradawi.net, 226
al-Qarafi, 217

Qasim, Tal'at Fu'ad, 608
Qassem, Shaykh Na'im, 519–20
Qatar, 223, 231, 304n1, 413, 513
Qatar Foundation, 226, 233n32
Qayyim, Ibn al-, 29, 45
qisas, 19
al-Qiyam al-Islamiya, 357, 358
qiyas, 9, 10–11
Qom, Iran, 195n12
quietism, 183–84, 193, 194n11
Qur'an
  and al-Banna's ideology, 131
  and the caliphate, 133
  and democracy, 72
  and democratization of *shura*, 139–40
  and ecumenical Islamic agenda, 303
  and equality, 138–39
  and gender issues, 113, 114
  and Ghannushi's ideology, 214
  and *hudud* penalties, 18
  and Islamic feminism, 120
  and Mawdudi's ideology, 144, 145, 148
  and Modernist-Salafiya movement, 27, 29, 35–36
  on non-Muslim minorities, 149, 150
  and oaths of office, 264
  and Pakistani politics, 330
  and People of the Book, 47
  and political economy of Islamism, 105
  Pushkin on, 320n6
  and Qaradawi's ideology, 222
  and Qutb's ideology, 164
  and redistribution, 102
  and schools of Islamic jurisprudence, 9–10
  and *shari'ah*, 10, 11
  and social justice, 135
  and Soroush's ideology, 252, 256
  and state rule over religion, 187
  and Turabi's ideology, 205, 206
Qur'anic Preservation Society (QPS), 214
Qutb, Muhammad, 213
Qutb, Sayyid, 159–67
  and al-Banna, 129, 140
  and Algerian revolution, 358
  and Azzam, 631
  background, 159–61
  and Egyptian Islamism, 609
  and Ghannushi's ideology, 213, 214, 215, 216
  and Iraqi jihadists, 618
  and Islamic reformism, 49
  and the Islamic state, 131
  and Islamic statehood, 56
  and Islam in South Asia, 324
  and Mawdudi's ideology, 149
  and the Muslim Brotherhood, 476, 483, 485
  and political Islam, 61
  and privatization, 100
  and social thought, 161–66
  and stereotypes of Islam, 334
  and student movements, 591–92

Rabbani, Burhanuddin, 464, 474n10
racism, 53n8, 160
radical Islamism, 56, 58–61, 292, 294–98, 320, 325, 341
Rafsanjani, Ali Akbar Hashemi, 82, 191, 238, 241, 245n8, 245n16, 403–4, 523
Rahim, Abdu, 331–32
Rahimi, Mohammad Reza, 198n84
Rahman, Abu Abdul, 619
Rahman, Omar Abd al-, 607
Rahman, Tengku Abdul, 590
Rahnema, Ali, 171
Rain Foundation, 242
Ramadan, 223
Ramadan, Tariq, 227
al-Rashidun, 10
Rassemblement Constitutionel Démocratique (RCD), 218
Rastakhiz Party, 185
Rationalizing Jihadi Actions in Egypt and the World (Al-Sherif), 611
Rawls, John, 255
Raysuni, Ahmad al-, 227, 303
Razak, Abdul Tun, 343
Raziq, Ali Abd al-, 57–58
Reagan, Ronald, 465
reason and rationality, 11, 32, 162, 215, 247, 256, 258n2, 457
Refah Party, 117
reformism, 42–52
  and Ghannushi, 220

and *ijtihad,* 28
of Islamic jurisprudence, 228–29
and Islamic nationalism, 60
and Khatami, 238–42
and Modernist-Salafiya movement, 27, 30–31, 35
and nation-states, 50–52
and "post-Islamism," 368
and Qaradawi, 222, 227–28
and Shari'ati, 169
and Soroush, 250
and Sufi resurgence, 371
Reformist Group of Krekar, 619
refugees, 318
regional Islamic groups, 295
Renaissance and Virtue Party (PRV), 365
Renaissance Movement Party, 89
renewal, 28, 30–31. *See also* revivalism; Salafist movement
Renewal Movement (Pembaharuan), 567, 568
republicanism, 186, 193
Republican Party (US), 68
Republican Party in Turkey, 428
Republic of North Ossetia, 319
The Restless Universe, 247–48
revelation, 10, 31, 33
revivalism, 27–38, 252. *See also* Salafist movement
Revolutionary Command Council (RCC), 160
Revolutionary Guard (Iran), 191, 193, 197n71, 217, 248
revolutionary Islam, 59–60, 257
Reza Shah Pahlavi, Shah of Iran, 169, 177, 182, 185, 195n12, 456–57
Rida, Muhammad Rashid, 27, 34–36, 37, 130, 220
ridda (apostasy), 18
Rifa'i, Samir al-, 549
Rights of Non-Muslims in Islamic State (Mawdudi), 48–49
Rizk, Yunan Labib, 482
Robinson, Robert V., 103, 379, 493
Rois, Kiai Dimyati, 563
Romano, David, 4, 616–26
Rousseau, Jean Jacques, 71

rowshanfikrs (enlightened Muslim thinkers), 457
Roy, Olivier, 370, 640
Rubin, Michel, 399
ruhanis (traditionalist religious functionaries), 457
ruling Islamic agenda, 300–302
Rumi, 255
Rushdie, Salman, 189, 324
Russia, 307, 453, 505. *See also* Soviet Union
Russo-Iranian Wars, 320n1
Rwanda, 379
Saad-Ghorayeb, Amal, 520
Sabahi, Hamdin, 495, 496
Sadat, Anwar
  assassination attempts made by, 482–83
  assassination of, 165, 484, 606–7, 613
  and emergence of Islamic movements, 604
  identification with Islam of, 605
  and Islamic politics in the Middle East, 294, 296
  and the Muslim Brotherhood, 101, 476, 484
  and number of mosques in Egypt, 606
  and Qaradawi's ideology, 223
  and the Six Day War, 166
Sadeghi, Zohreh, 237
Sadr, Baqir As-, 217
Sadr, Muqtada al-, 399, 617, 625
Sadr, Musa al-, 237, 517–18, 528
Sadra, Mulla, 192, 247–48, 258n2
Sadri, Ahmad, 237–45
Sadri, Mahmoud, 3, 237–45
Saeed, Abdullah, 2, 27–38
Saeed, Hafiz Mohammad, 331
Safadi, Ayman al-, 553
Safarov, Polad, 315
Safire, William, 399
Sahel, 379, 388, 638
Sahnoun, Ahmed, 357
sahwah shaykhs, 417
Said, Edward, 507
Said, Hammam, 545, 554
Sa'id, Jawat, 213
saint veneration, 29–30, 371
Sait, S., 100
salaf, 35–36
Salafi Nur Party, 495

Salafist Group for Preaching and Combat (GSPC), 388
Salafist movement, 27–38
   and apolitical Muslimhood agenda, 290, 292
   defined, 375n2
   and ecumenical Islamic agenda, 304
   and Egyptian Islamism, 607–9
   and Ghannushi's ideology, 215
   and Islam in Central Asia, 314–15, 318, 319
   and Islam in North Africa, 354–55, 532
   and Islam in Southeast Asia, 341–42
   and Morocco, 359–60, 364–65
   neo-Salafism, 367
   and "post-Islamism," 368
   and Qaradawi's ideology, 231, 233n44
   and radical militant Islamist agenda, 295
   and Soroush's ideology, 251
   and statist seculareligious agenda, 294
   and Sufi resurgence, 371, 372
Salih, Muhammad, 313
Salih, Shaykh Adib al-, 213
Salloukh, Bassel F., 4, 516–28
Sanhuri, 'Abd ar-Razzaq as-, 228
Sanusi, Muhammad b. Ali al-, 28, 29, 30
Sanusiyya Sufism, 30, 60, 354, 355–56, 367
sariqa (alcohol prohibition), 18, 45, 49, 228
Sarkozy, Nicolas, 281
Sartre, Jean Paul, 170, 172
Satanic Verses (Rushdie), 189
satellite television, 420
Saud, Abd al-Aziz b. al-, 35
Saudi Arabia, 411–21
   and apolitical Muslimhood agenda, 292
   and development of Wahhabism, 411–12
   and gender issues, 65, 116, 417–19, 421
   and globalization, 420
   and Hamas, 512
   and Islam in Southeast Asia, 341–42
   and Malaysia, 595
   and Omar's Taliban movement, 469
   and Pakistan, 468
   peace initative of 2002, 512
   and radical militant Islamist agenda, 296, 297
   and reformism, 421
   regional influence of, 341–42
   and religious authority in, 300, 411–12, 414–15
   and religious minorities, 290
   social influence of Wahhabism, 415–17
   and the Soviet-Afghan War, 312, 465
   and sub-Saharan Africa, 383
   and Wahhabi violence, 412–13
Sayyaf, Abdurabb Rasul, 474n11
Sayyed, Sayyed Ibrahim Amin al-, 519
sazandegi, 191
Scandinavia, 280
Schacht, Joseph, 11
Schenker, David, 554
Scheve, K., 103
Schwedler, Jillian, 481, 552
science
   and Mawdudi, 326
   and Modernist-Salafiya movement, 31, 32, 33
scientific revolution, 79
scientific socialism, 248
   and subjectivity of religion, 255–56
second Chechen War, 317–18
second Intifada, 229, 231
Second Soran Force, 619
second wave feminism, 113–14
secret evidence, 269–72
Secret Evidence Repeal Act, 272
sectarianism, 204
secularism
   and Afghanistan, 462
   and al-Banna's ideology, 141
   and apolitical Muslimhood agenda, 290
   and authoritarianism in Central Asia, 310–11, 313–15
   conflated with atheism, 608
   and Egypt, 54n31
   and French *laïcité*, 50, 293, 334, 382, 385
   and gender issues, 113, 117–18
   and Ghannushi's ideology, 219
   and Iran, 400–401, 404
   and the Iranian Revolution, 186
   and Islamic democracy, 74–75, 78–80, 81–83
   and Islamic reformism, 51
   and Islamic statehood, 58, 59
   and Islam in Europe, 281, 287
   and Islam in South Asia, 326–27

and Khomeini, 182, 193
militant secularism, 426–27
and Modernist-Salafiya movement, 36, 37–38
and nation states, 50–52
and partisan Islamist agenda, 300
and political Islam, 65
and Qaradawi's ideology, 229, 231
seculareligious agenda, 292–94
and Turabi's ideology, 204, 205
and Turkey, 424, 426–27, 429, 431–32
and Western modernity, 150–51
Sedki, Atef, 611
segregation, 116, 151
Senegal, 382–83, 385, 390n6
"Senoussism," 60
separation of religion and state (SRAS), 71–72, 80, 290
September 11 terrorist attacks
  and Bin Laden, 635
  impact on North American Muslims, 272–75
  and Islamic democracy, 68, 83
  and Islam in Europe, 283, 285
  and Islam in South Asia, 325
  and Malaysia, 593, 594
  and Mawdudi's ideology, 152
  and Nahdlatul Ulama, 558, 559–60
  and origins of terrorist organizations, 463
  and Pakistan, 583
  and Qaradawi, 230
  and Saudi politics, 413, 416, 417
  and scholarship on political Islam, 2
  and stereotypes of Islam, 334
  US response to, 470
  and violent Wahhabism, 413
sexual liberation, 286
Shabazz, El-Hajj Malik El-, 265, 266
Shabestari, Mojtahed, 191
Shaddili i, Sidi Abu al-Hassan al-, 372
Shadhliya order, 30, 372
Shaery-Eisenlohr, Roschanack, 517, 520, 525
Shafik, Ahmed, 495, 614
Shafi school of jurisprudence, 45, 379
Shafrawi, Ibrahim `Abduh al-, 233n44
Shahin, Emad El-Din, 1
Shahrani, M. Nazif, 3, 453–72
Shaltut, Mahmud, 223

Shama, Nael, 4, 603–14
Shanoudah III, pope, 46–48, 51
Shapirov, Aslanbek, 309
Shari`a and Life, 226
shari`ah
  and Afghanistan, 454, 457, 459, 460, 469, 472
  and al-Banna, 131–34, 134–35, 138, 141
  and Algeria, 362
  and al-Jama'a al-Islamiya, 608
  and the Arab Spring, 22–24
  and Central Asia, 309, 317, 318
  and complexity of Middle East Islam, 289–90
  and democracy, 73
  and Egypt, 488–92, 494
  and *fiqh*, 12–16, 52n2
  and grassroots Islam, 362
  and Indonesia, 566–67, 568, 570
  and infidelity of Muslim rulers, 612–13
  and Iranian governmental structures, 403
  and the Islamic Action Front (IAF), 545, 549
  and Islamic Jihad Group (al-Jihad Group), 608
  Islamic law *vs.* Muslim law, 8–9
  and Jordan, 545, 549
  and Khomeini, 180–82, 184–85, 193
  and legal monism, 48
  and Malaysia, 589, 597
  and modernity, 19–22
  and the Muslim Brotherhood, 488–92, 494
  and Nahdlatul Ulama (NU), 566–67
  and the nation-state, 54n32
  nature and purpose of, 11–12
  and North Africa, 356
  and Pakistan, 576
  and partisan Islamist agenda, 300
  and political Islam, 61, 63
  and Qutb, 159, 161, 166
  and reformism, 42–52
  rights of God and humans, 17–19
  sacred and profane in, 16–17
  and Soroush, 253, 256
  sources of, 9–11
  and Southeast Asia, 341–43, 346
  and statist seculareligious agenda, 293–94
  and sub-Saharan Africa, 387–88

shari`ah (Cont.)
   and Sudan, 445, 446, 448
   and systemic view of Islam, 146
   and Tunisia, 360
   and Turabi, 205–8
Shari`ati, Ali, 3, 169–77
   background, 169–72
   death of, 177
   and individual responsibility, 173
   and international relations, 175–76
   and liberation, 173–74
   and Shi'i exceptionalism, 172–73
   and Soroush's ideology, 247, 248, 251, 252
   and ulama's role, 174–75
Shari`ati, Muhammad Taqi, 169
Sharif, Ali Muhammad al-, 612
Sharif, Sayyid Imam al- (Dr. Fadl), 297
Shatz, Adam, 520, 528n8
Shawkani, Muhammad b. Ali al-, 28
Shea, Nina, 494
Sherif, Sayed Imam al-, 611
Shi'a Islam
   and apolitical Muslimhood agenda, 290
   and complexity of Middle East Islam, 289
   and ecumenical Islamic agenda, 303–4
   formal clergy of, 409n4
   in Iran, 400
   and Islam in Central Asia, 315
   and Islam in Southeast Asia, 346
   and Khomeini, 183–84, 184–85
   marja-e-taqlid of, 400
   and Najaf in Iraq, 517
   and ruling Islamic agenda, 300
   and secularism, 82
   and "Seyed" designation, 237
   and *shari`ah*, 9, 460
   and Shari`ati's ideology, 169, 170
   and Soroush, 247
   and sub-Saharan Africa, 390n3
   Sunni Islam compared to, 400
Shihab, 37
Shirazi, Naser Makarem, 254
shirk (associationism), 29, 137, 412
shura
   and al-Banna's ideology, 136–40, 141
   and democracy, 72, 136–40
   and Islam in South Asia, 328, 329
   and Pakistani politics, 330

   and political Islam, 62
   and Qutb's ideology, 163
   and Soroush's ideology, 252
   and Turabi's ideology, 206
Siba`i, Mustafa al-, 213
Siddiqui, Niloufer, 3, 144–55
Sierra Leone, 381
"simple" Islam, 38
Singapore, 340
single-issue parties, 283–84
Siniora, Fu'ad al-, 525
Siraj, Said Aqil, 567, 569, 571
Siraj al-Akhbar (Afghanistan newspaper), 455, 457
Sirhindi, Ahmad, 29
Sirry, Mun'im, 568
Sister Clara Muhammad Schools, 267
Six Day War, 166, 225, 494–95, 603–5
slavery, 84, 264
social activism, 169, 291, 302–3
social contract, 74, 132
socialism
   and Algeria, 356–61
   and Islamic nationalism, 60
   and Islam in North Africa, 356
   and Pakistan, 330
   and political Islam, 61
   and Qaradawi's ideology, 229
Socialist Labor Front, 92
social justice
   and al-Banna's ideology, 135
   and gender issues, 112–13, 114
   and Indian politics, 328–29
   and political economy of Islamism, 99
   and political Islam, 65
   and Qutb's ideology, 161, 163
   and redistribution, 104
   and Shari`ati's ideology, 170, 172, 174–75, 176
   and Soroush's ideology, 248
Social Justice in Islam, 160
social services, 93, 298
social theory, 172
Society for Islamic Culture, 140
Society for Removal of Innovation and Reestablishment of the Sunna, 383
Society for Struggle against Communism in Turkey, 312

Society of Combatant Clerics, 196n52
socioeconomic supports for Islamism, 90–93
Socrates, 70
Soekarnoputri, Megawati, 559, 560–63, 571n5
Soltani, Abdelatif, 357
Somalia, 298, 304n1, 383, 389–90
Son of the Village and the Kuttab (Qaradawi), 225
Sora, 'Abd al-Rahman Ibrahima, 264
Soroush, Abdolkarim, 246–58
  background, 246–47
  and critique of Islamist truth claims, 250–54
  and critique of Marxism, 246–50
  and determinist doctrine, 257
  and hermeneutics and religious pluralism, 255–56
  intellectual influence of, 257–58
  and Khatami's ideology, 240–41
  and Khomeini's ideology, 191
  and reason and religion, 256–57
South Africa, 120, 387
South Asia, 324–35
  framework for analyzing Islam in, 324–26
  and ideology of Jama`at-e Islami, 326–27
  and transformation of Jama`at-e Islami, 327–33
  See also specific countries
South Caucasus, 308, 309
Southeast Asia, 340–51
  key factors in, 340–42
  and Muslim majority states, 340, 342–48
  and Muslim minority states, 340, 348–50
  See also specific countries
South Sudan, 390n2
sovereignty issues
  and al-Banna's ideology, 134, 138
  and democracy, 71, 73
  and Islamic nationalism, 60
  and Khatami, 243–44
  and Khomeini, 180, 184, 196n37
  and legal monism, 48
  and Mawdudi, 147, 148, 327
  and monopoly of power, 50
  and the nation-state, 46–49
  and North Caucasus, 316
  and Pakistan, 329–30, 331
  premodern Muslim states, 45

  and Qutb's ideology, 164
  and rise of the nation-state, 43–44
  and Shari`ati's ideology, 175
  See also hakimiyya
Soviet-Aghan War, 311
Soviet Union
  and Afghanistan, 463–64, 465–66, 467, 538
  collapse of, 282, 312
  and end of Cold War, 210
  and Islam in Central Asia, 307
Spain, 263–64, 279–80, 290, 349–50
Spinoza, Baruch, 72
spirituality, 30. *See also* Sufism
Spiritual Journeys (Sadra), 258n2
Springborg, Robert, 486
Srebrenica, 282–83
Sri Lanka, 639
Stalin, Joseph, 308–11
Stalinism, 177, 248–49
Stasavage, D., 103
State Institutes of Islamic Studies (IAIN, UIN), 568
State Security Court, 217
statist secularreligious agenda, 292–94
Stepan, Alfred, 71
stereotypes of Islam, 333–34
The Stillborn God (Lilla), 79
Straight Paths (Soroush), 255
Strategic Depth: Turkey's International Position (Davutoglu), 435
students and student groups, 591, 595, 604–5. *See also* education
sub-Saharan Africa, 379–90
  background of Islam in, 379–80
  and political liberalization, 383–88
  and postcolonial states, 380–83
  and weakened states, 388–90
  See also specific countries
Sudan, 440–50
  and Egyptian Islamism, 211
  and gender issues, 116, 118
  and Ghannushi's ideology, 216
  independence, 52n4
  and the Iranian Revolution, 215
  and Islamic democracy, 77
  and Islamic politics in sub-Saharan Africa, 381

Sudan (*Cont.*)
   liberation of the arts, 209
   and limits of Islamist activism, 449–50
   and the "National Salvation Revolution" in (1989), 440–44
   and partisan Islamist agenda, 299
   partition of, 390n2
   and political Islam, 62, 63
   and resistance movements, 176
   and ruling Islamic agenda, 300, 301
   and *shari`ah*, 382
   sources of political power, 444–47
   and sub-Saharan Islamism, 389
   and Sufism, 176
   and totalitarian elements, 447–49
   and Turabi's ideology, 203–5, 205–11
Sudan People's Liberation Army (SPLA), 445–46
Suez Canal, 130, 161
suffrage issues, 118
Sufism
   and al-Banna, 130
   and apolitical Muslimhood agenda, 290, 292
   attacks on, 376n8
   and complexity of Middle East Islam, 289
   and Ghannushi's ideology, 213, 215
   and Islamic politics in Afghanistan, 456
   and Islam in Central Asia, 318, 319
   and Islam in North Africa, 354
   and Modernist-Salafiya movement, 29–30
   and Morocco, 365, 366
   and post-Islamism, 367–74, 370
   and Sanusiyya movement, 30, 60, 354, 355–56, 367
   and Shari`ati's ideology, 176
   and statist secularreligious agenda, 294
   and sub-Saharan Africa, 379–80, 383, 384
   and Turabi's ideology, 204
Suharto (Soeharto), 342–43, 344, 345, 558, 561, 570
Suhrawardi, Shahab al-Din, 247
suicide attacks. *See* terrorism and violence
Sukarno, 59, 342–43, 344, 345
Sulayman, Sultan, 371
Suleiman, Michel, 528n5
Suleimanov, Gamet, 315
Sullivan, D. J., 93

Sultan-Galiev, Mirsaid, 309
sunnah
   and al-Banna's ideology, 131
   and Mawdudi, 145
   and Modernist-Salafiya movement, 27, 29, 35–36
   and non-Muslim minorities, 150
   and reformism, 28
   and *shari`ah*, 9–10
   and social justice, 135
   and state rule over religion, 187
Sunni Islam
   in Afghanistan, 460
   and American Muslims, 267
   and apolitical Muslimhood agenda, 290
   in Iran, 400
   and Islam in Central Asia, 314
   and jihad, 616
   legal "schools" of, 400
   persecution of the Shi`a, 178n1
   and *shari`ah*, 9, 10
   Shi`a Islam compared to, 400
   and sub-Saharan Africa, 379
   and Wahhabism, 412
   See also Salafist movement
Supreme Council for the Islamic Revolution in Iraq (SCIRI), 617
Supreme Council of Kenyan Muslims (SUPKEM), 382, 386
Supreme Council of Tanzanian Muslims (BAKWATA), 382, 387
Suri, Abu Musab al-, 634, 635–36
Susilo Bambang Yudhoyono, 563–65, 570–71
Suweilam, Samir Abdullah Al (Emir Khattab), 316, 318
Swaan, Abram de, 281
Swahili coast, 379
Sweden, 280, 281
syncretism, 341, 379–80
Syria
   civil war in, 525
   and Golan Heights, 522
   and Hamas, 513
   and Hizbullah, 518, 523, 525–27
   independence, 52n4
   and Lebanon, 523, 526–27
   and "post-Islamism," 368
   and radical militant Islamist agenda, 295

and secularism, 82
and statist secularreligious agenda, 293
suicide bombers from, 622
and Turkey, 434
and the United States, 525
Syrian Muslim Brotherhood, 300
systemic view of Islam, 133–34, 135, 141, 145–47, 152, 159

Tabataba'i, Allameh, 258n2
Al-Ta`bi'a al-Tarbawiya (The Educational Mobilization Unit), 524
Tablighi Jama`at, 62–63, 213–14, 292, 575
al-Tabra'a, 297
Taha, Ali Osman, 450
Tahfim al-Qur'an (Mawdudi), 147
Tahtawi, Rifa`a Rafi` al-, 220
Ta'if Accord, 528n6
al-tajammu` al-haraki al-`udwi, 163
tajdid, 209
Tajik Civil War, 320n8
Tajikistan, 312, 313, 314, 320n8
Tajik rebels, 458–59
Tajzadeh, Mostafa, 242
al-takaful al-ijtima`i, 163
Takeyh, Ray, 356
takfir, 295, 296, 412–13, 415, 417
Takfirchilar, 314
Takfir wa al-Hijra group, 614n1
taklif (legal obligation or duty), 10, 13
talfiq, 35
Talib, `Ali b. Abi, 169, 173, 177–78n1
Taliban
    in Afghanistan, 637
    and Bin Laden, 633
    and the Chechen War, 317
    control of Afghanistan, 469–70
    ideological message of, 469
    and Karzai, 474n14
    and Mawdudi's ideology, 149
    and Mujahiddin-sponsored schools, 465
    in Pakistan, 585, 637
    and al-Qaeda, 637
    and radical militant Islamist agenda, 295, 296
    recruitment of fighters, 469
    resurgence of, 471, 472
    rise of, 463, 467, 469

    and secular authoritarianism in Central Asia, 313, 314
    and United States, 469, 470
    Western assistance to, 469
Taliqani, Mahmud, 171
Tamimi, Azzam, 3, 212–21
Tanzania, 381, 386–87, 388
Taoufiq, Ahmed, 371
taqlid, 9, 15, 21, 28, 29, 31, 34
tarahil, 160
tarjih, 12
Tarjuman al-Qur'an, 144
Tarrow, S. G., 91
Tarzi, Mahmood, 455, 456, 457, 473n5
Tashih al-Mafahim (Correcting Concepts), 610
Tashkent Soviet, 309
Taskhiri, Muhammad `Ali al-, 225, 303–4
Tatarstan, 316
al-tawfi q bayn al-madhahib, 16
tawhid (unity of God), 29–30, 139–40, 163, 176, 206, 252, 411, 413
taxes, 8, 103–4, 149. *See also zakat*
Taylor, Charles, 80
Tayyib, Shaykh al-Azhar Ahmad al-, 23
ta'zir punishments, 19
Tehran, Iran, 402, 405
Tehrik-i-Taliban Pakistan, 585
television, 226–27, 291, 420
territory, defense of Muslim controlled, 472n2
terrorism and violence
    African embassy bombings, 315, 388, 631
    Amman, Jordan bombings, 639
    Bali bombings, 560
    in Bangladesh, 335n2
    Beslan school siege, 319
    Casablanca bombings, 365
    and counterterrorism strategies, 614
    in Dagestan, 317–18
    declining support for, 365–66, 639
    and failed states, 388–90
    of Hamas, 506, 509, 510, 512
    of Hizbullah, 526
    in Iraq, 622, 624
    and Islamist parties of Maghreb states, 537–39
    Israel suicide attacks, 506, 509, 510, 512, 526
    London bombings, 230, 285, 635, 637

terrorism and violence (*Cont.*)
  Luxor massacre, 609, 611
  Madrid bombings, 285, 635
  in Morocco, 365–66
  Mumbai attacks, 639
  and the Muslim Brotherhood, 477, 482–86, 608–9, 613
  Oklahoma City bombing, 269
  and Pakistan, 593–94
  and Qaradawi's ideology, 229–30, 231
  South Asia, 325
  Southeast Asia, 350
  Sri Lankan cricket team attack, 639
  and support for al-Qaida, 639
  from Syria, 622
  USS *Cole* attack, 593, 631
  and Wahhabism, 412–13
  See also September 11 terrorist attacks; *specific groups and individuals*
Terrorism Knowledge Base (TKB), 625
Tessler, Mark, 93
Thailand, 348–49, 350
Thani, Shaykh Khalifa b. Hamad Al, 223
theocracy, 184
theodemocracy, 148, 334
Thneibat, Abd al-Majid, 554
Tidjani, Hachemi, 357
Tijaniya order, 30
Tilly, Charles, 187
Tocqueville, Alexis de, 71
Togan, Zaki Validi, 309
toleration, religious, 80–81, 364. *See also* pluralism, religious
Torah, 49
totalitarianism, 76–77, 249–50, 257, 447–49, 450
tribal affiliations, 8, 301, 637, 638
Trouillot, Michel-Rolph, 325
Tuareg people, 389
Tudeh Party, 182
Tufaili, Subhi al-, 518
Tunisia, 532–42
  and al-Banna's ideology, 131
  and apolitical Muslimhood agenda, 291
  and Arab Spring, 540–42
  constitution, 304n1
  and co-option of Islamist parties, 536–37
  electoral politics in, 532, 533–35
  and gender issues, 120, 123n23
  and Ghannushi's ideology, 213
  and grassroots Islam, 362, 366–67
  independence, 52n4
  and Islamic politics in North Africa, 353, 360–62
  and Islamic statehood, 356
  and Islam in Europe, 286, 287
  and liberal democracy, 215
  and nationalism, 353, 354–55
  and partisan Islamist agenda, 300
  and political economy of Islamism, 89, 105
  and political Islam, 65
  and "post-Islamism," 368, 369, 370, 374–75
  and postrevolution elections, 22, 24
  and religious political parties, 352
  and secularism, 82
  and statist secularreligious agenda, 293
  and Sufi resurgence, 371, 372–73
  and violence, 538–40
Tunisian Renaissance Party, 300
Tunsi, Khayr al-Din al-, 214, 220
Turabi, 'Abdallah al-, 203–4
Turabi, Hamad al-, 204
Turabi, Hassan al-, 203–11
  and al-Banna, 129
  background, 203–5
  and Ghannushi's ideology, 215
  ideology, 205–11
  and Islamic politics in Sudan, 441–44, 445, 448–49, 450
  and Islamic politics in the Middle East, 301
  and Islamic statehood, 62, 63
  and North American immigration, 266
Turkestan, 309
Turkestan Red Army, 309
Turkey, 423–37
  and apolitical Muslimhood agenda, 291
  and center-periphery relations, 427–28
  and "conservative democracy," 425–26
  and democracy, 390n6
  and the European Union, 279, 423, 425, 432–33, 434, 435
  and foreign policy, 433–36
  and gender issues, 117
  and good governance, 430–31
  and Islamic democracy, 68, 77, 83
  and Islamic feminism, 120

and Islam in Central Asia, 314
and Islam in Europe, 281–82, 284, 286
and judicial reforms, 431–33
and Kurdish issue, 437n16
and militant secularism, 426–27
and partisan Islamist agenda, 300
and political economy of Islamism, 89, 105
and political Islam, 64, 65
and privatization, 102
and redefinition of political center, 428–30
and rise of AK Party, 423–24
and secularism, 82
and the Soviet-Afghan War, 312
and statist secularreligious agenda, 293
See also Justice and Development Party (AKP)
Turkmenistan, 320n1
Twelver Shi'ites, 177–78n1, 184, 314, 400

'Udah, Salman Al-, 303
Ufen, Andreas, 567
Uganda, 381
Ugodov, Movladi, 318
'ulama'
  and apolitical Muslimhood agenda, 292
  and complexity of Middle East Islam, 289–90
  and ecumenical Islamic agenda, 303
  and Islam in North Africa, 355, 356
  and Khomeini, 181, 182, 186, 193
  and Mawdudi's ideology, 152–53
  and Modernist-Salafiya movement, 34, 37
  and Qutb's ideology, 164, 166
  and radical militant Islamist agenda, 297
  and ruling Islamic agenda, 300
  and Shari'ati's ideology, 174–75
  and Soroush's ideology, 253
  and statist secularreligious agenda, 294
  and Sufi resurgence, 371
ummah
  and al-Banna's ideology, 133, 139–40, 141
  and ecumenical Islamic agenda, 303, 304
  and globalization, 64
  and Islamic nationalism, 60–61
  and Islamic statehood, 56
  and political Islam, 65
  and radical militant Islamist agenda, 296

and Turabi's ideology, 206
and Western modernity, 150
Ummah Party, 204
Umma Party, 92
Umra Hajj pilgrimage, 313
unemployment, 314–15, 319
Union of Socialist Forces (USFP), 376n7
Union of Young Muslims, 312
United Arab Emirates, 304n1, 465
United Development Party (PPP), 344
United Kingdom, 286, 287, 469, 637–38
United Malay National Organization (UMNO), 4, 344–46, 587–93, 595, 597–98
United National Human Rights Council, 509
United Nations (UN), 208, 241, 491, 505, 525
United Nations Development Program (UNDP), 69
United States
  and Afghanistan, 465–66, 471, 472
  and anti-American sentiment, 559, 583
  citizenship model, 290
  drone technology of, 634, 637
  and Hamas, 505, 514
  intelligence agencies of, 630
  and Iran, 183, 407, 408, 522, 525
  and Iraq, 434
  and Islamic armed resistance agenda, 298–99
  and Islamic politics in Afghanistan, 468
  and nuclear-armed nations, 407
  and post-imperial America, 433
  and radical militant Islamist agenda, 296
  and secularism, 50
  and Syria, 525
  terrorist attacks of 9/11, 413, 416, 417
  and Turkey, 434
  and weapons supplied to Taliban, 469
Unity and Reform movement, 535
Universal Declaration of Human Rights, 70
urbanization, 92
'urf, 9
Urshuma, Mansur, 308
US Agency for International Development, 465
US Congress, 264, 274
US House of Representatives, 270
USS *Cole* attack, 593, 631
US Senate, 269

usury, 228
Uthman, Amin, 483
Uzbekistan, 312, 313
Uzbek militants, 638
al-'uzr bil-jahl (excuse due to ignorance), 607

Van Gogh, Theo, 285
veiling. *See* head coverings
velayat-e faqih, 180, 184–93, 195n22, 196n37, 197n71, 198n85, 401
Velayat-e-Faqih ("Regency of the Jurisprudent"), 401
Velayati, Ali Akbar, 253–54
Villalón, Leonardo A., 3, 379–93
violence. *See* terrorism and violence
Virtue Party of Turkey, 425
Vlaams Belang, 284
Voll, John O., 2, 56–67, 75, 219
Voridis, Makis, 284
voting and voter turnout
  in Egypt, 496
  in Indonesia, 563
  in Iran, 402, 405
  in Saudi Arabia, 419
  voting rights, 118, 183
  of women, 419

Wafd Party, 139, 160, 482
Wahhab, Muhammad b. Abd al-, 27, 29–30, 301, 411–13, 418–19
Wahhabism, 411–21
  and apolitical Muslimhood agenda, 292
  conversion emphasis of, 412
  and counterrevolutionary arguments, 23
  and impact of the global communications era, 420
  influence of, in Saudi society, 415–17
  and Islam in Central Asia, 319
  and Islam in Southeast Asia, 341–42
  jihad in, 412, 413, 414–15, 420
  lack of tolerance in, 413
  in Malaysia, 594–95
  and Modernist-Salafiya movement, 35, 37
  and Morocco, 364–65
  nature and development of, 411–12
  and Puritanical-Salafism, 27
  and Qaradawi's ideology, 223
  and reform, 421

  and ruling Islamic agenda, 301
  and Soroush's ideology, 251
  and Sufi resurgence, 372
  and *takfir* ideology, 412–13, 417
  and violence, 412–13
  voice of authority in, 414–15
  and women, 416, 417–19, 421
Wahid, Abdurrahman (Gus Dur), 343, 558–63, 565–68, 570–71, 571n5
Wa'il, Abu, 619
Walloon National Front, 281
al-waqi'iyyah (praxis), 163
War on Terror, 273, 331
war powers, 43–44
Wars of Religion, 43, 52n4, 79, 80
wasatiyya, 224, 229, 231, 303
Wasatiyya Center, 226
Wasat Party, 480
Washington Post, 270, 325
Al-Wathiqa al-Siyaiya li-Hizbullah manifesto, 521–22
Wathiqat al-Azhar, 23–24
weak states, 53n10
Webb, Alexander Russell, 264–65
Weber, Max, 243
websites, 226
"Wednesday night circle," 250
Weiss, Leopold, 165
Welborne, B., 103
Welfare Party of India (WPI), 328, 329
Welfare Party (Refah Partisi) of Turkey, 426
welfare state, 329
Wellhofer, Spencer E., 479
West Africa, 381, 388
West Bank, 506–8, 512–13
Western culture
  and democracy, 76
  and Ghannushi, 212
  and imperialism, 184
  and Islamic democracy, 78–79, 83
  and Islamic statehood, 56
  law, 21
  and Mawdudi, 144, 148, 326
  and Modernist-Salafiya movement, 31, 32, 33
  and modernity, 150–51
  science, 32
  and secularism, 82
  and *shari'ah*, 20

and Tunisia, 360
and Turabi's ideology, 206
Western Europe, 59
Westphalian international system, 209
White, Joshua T., 3, 144–55
White Revolution (Iran), 60, 183
Wickham, Carrie Rosefsky, 479, 488, 493
wilayat al-faqih, 516, 518–19, 519–22. *See also* velayat-e faqih
Willis, Michael J., 4, 532–43
Winter, Filip de, 284
women and gender issues, 112–21
  and Afghanistan, 457, 458, 460, 462, 469
  and democracy, 69
  education of, 419
  and Egypt, 490–93, 605
  female genital mutilation, 37, 491, 570
  and feminism, 37, 113–14, 116, 119–21, 122n7
  gender justice, 118–19
  gender segregation, 419
  and Ghannushi, 216, 217
  and head coverings, 65, 226, 409n10, 424, 426, 428, 494
  and the *hijab,* 115–16
  and "honor crimes," 551
  and Indian politics, 328–29
  and Indonesia, 566
  and Iran, 402, 407, 409n10
  and Iraq, 619, 620–21
  and Islamic Action Front, 551
  and the Islamic activism, 116–17
  and Islamic militancy, 314
  and Islamic political movements, 114–19
  and Islamic reformism, 50
  and Khomeini, 183
  and Mawdudi, 151
  and Modernist-Salafiya movement, 27, 38n2
  and the Muslim Brotherhood, 477, 490–93
  and New Islamism, 120–21
  and Pakistan, 578
  and political Islam, 65
  and the private sphere, 116
  and Qaradawi, 222, 224, 230
  and Saudi Arabia, 416, 417–19, 421
  and secularism, 117–18
  and Soroush, 255
  and sub-Saharan Africa, 384–85, 387

  and Sudan, 442, 445
  and Tunisia, 360
  and Turabi, 208
  and Turkey, 424
  and Wahhabism, 416, 417–19, 421
  and Western modernity, 151
  women suffrage, 118, 183
Women's Action Department, 117
Woodward, Peter, 3, 203–11
Worker's Party (Algeria), 302
World Bank, 367, 550
World Christian Database, 292
World Economic Forum, 242
World Forum for Proximity of Islamic Schools of Thought, 303
World Values Survey, 494
World War I, 72, 144
World War II
  and al-Banna, 140
  and Iran, 187
  and Islamic statehood, 56
  and Islam in Central Asia, 311
  and Islam in Europe, 285
  and *Khatmiyya* movement, 204
  and the Muslim Brotherhood, 140–41
  and nationalism, 56–58
  and political Islam, 65

X, Malcolm, 265

Yanderbaev, Zelimkhan, 317
Yassin, Abdeslam, 359, 371, 373
Yassin, Ahmad, 505–6
Yassine, Nadia, 119
Yazdi, Mesbah, 254
Yazid, Mustafa Abu al-, 297
Yeltsin, Boris, 316
Yemen
  abortive constitutional revolution in (1948), 441
  Congregation for Reform, 476
  and gender issues, 117–18
  and partisan Islamist agenda, 299, 300
  and political economy of Islamism, 93, 98–99
  and al-Qaeda, 638
  and radical militant Islamist agenda, 296, 297

Yemen (*Cont.*)
  and secularism, 82
  and USS Cole incident, 593, 631
Yemeni Congregation for Reform, 299
Yevkurov, Yunus Bek, 318
Yevloyev, Magomad, 318
Yezbek, Muhammad, 518
Yoldash, Tahir, 313
Young Egypt, 482
Yousef, Ahmad, 513
youth
  of Afghanistan, 461, 462, 464
  and gender issues, 121
  and gender issues in Islam, 112
  and grassroots Islam, 362
  of Iran, 402, 407–8
  and Islam in Central Asia, 314
  and Islam in Europe, 286
  and student movements, 590–93
  of Sudan, 442, 445
Yugoslavia, 269, 282, 283
Yuldashev, Tahir, 637

Zade, Zia Yusuf, 312
Zahar, Mahmoud, 512, 513

zakat, 101, 102–3, 107n38, 223, 224
al-Zamakhshari, 217
Zanzibar, 386
Zapatero, José Luis Rodríguez, 434
Zarqawi, Abu Musab al-, 548–49, 624, 628n15, 636
Zawahiri, Ayman al-, 27, 297, 469, 482, 607, 617, 630–33, 636, 639
Zayat, Montasser al-, 611
Zaydi Shi`a community, 297
Zia, Khaleda, 333
Zia-ul-Haq, Mohammed, 62, 312, 330, 464, 581–83
Ziaurrahman, 333
Zimmis, 48
zina, 18, 45, 46, 49, 54n27, 118–19, 387
Zionism, 160
Zaytouna Mosque-University, 360
Zollner, Barbara, 483
Zoroastianism, 45
Zudi, Karam, 606
Zuhayli, Shaykh Wahba al-, 213
Zuhdi, Karam, 613
Zumur, Tarek al-, 614
Zyazikov, Murat, 318

CPSIA information can be obtained
at www.ICGtesting.com
Printed in the USA
BVOW11s0356250716

456330BV00003B/5/P

9 780190 631938